ISHERWOOD: A LIFE REVEALED

ISHERWOOD

a life revealed

PETER PARKER

Random House New York

LIBRARY OF CONGRESS CATALOGING-IN-PUBLICATION DATA
Parker, Peter
Isherwood : a life revealed / Peter Parker.
p. cm
Originally published: London : Picador, 2004.
Includes bibliographical references and index.
ISBN 1-4000-6249-7 (acid-free paper)
1. Isherwood, Christopher, 1904– 2. Isherwood, Christopher, 1904—Friends and associates.
3. Authors, English—20th centruy—Biography. 4. Gay men—Great Britain—Biography.
5. British—California—Biography. 6. British—Germany—Biography. I. Title.
PR6017.S5Z79 2004
823'.912—dc22
[B]   2004053185

246897531

FIRST U.S. EDITION

Book design by Casey Hampton

for R.P.W.

CONTENTS

ACKNOWLEDGMENTS

More than thirty years ago a fellow schoolboy, Nick Barnes, suggested I might enjoy a book called *Mr Norris Changes Trains*. He had no idea where this would lead, but my first thanks go to him, wherever he is. Since then I have accumulated a very large number of debts all around the world.

Don Bachardy entrusted me with the task of writing this book, gave me unrestricted access to a vast wealth of material, sent me photocopies of vital papers, had me to stay in Santa Monica, smoothed my path to people I needed to interview, answered innumerable questions both in person and by letter, and never asked querulously how the book was progressing even when it must have been evident that it wasn't. He courageously signed away any right of approval of the text, and although he felt unable to give the book his endorsement when he finally read it, I remain enormously grateful to him.

I have worked principally from photocopies of the original typescripts and manuscripts of Isherwood's 1939–1983 diaries, which are officially sealed until January 1, 2030, but Katherine Bucknell's immaculately edited *Diaries, Volume One: 1939–1960* and *Lost Years: A Memoir, 1945–1951* have remained at my elbow throughout. Kate and I have been exchanging opinions and ideas for well over a decade and, although we may not always have agreed, this book has benefited immeasurably from her knowledge of, and enthusiasm for, everything to do with Isherwood. I have also been lucky enough to receive help and encouragement from other writers working in the same field, notably Edward Mendelson, Nicholas Jenkins, John Sutherland, Richard Davenport-Hines, Selina Hastings, Miranda Carter, Adrian Wright and the late Martin Taylor. Two earlier biographies of Isherwood, by Brian Finney and Jonathan Fryer, have proved extremely helpful. Jonathan Fryer also gave me some of his notes, drew my attention to George Lassalle's disobliging account of Isherwood on St. Nicholas, and lent me his extensive correspondence with Bill Caskey.

Isherwood's oldest friend, Edward Upward, has been enthusiastic about the project from the very start and provided me with a great deal of information that no one else could have supplied. The late Sir Stephen Spender gave me every assistance, including access to papers officially closed to public scrutiny. Lady Spender has continued to provide me with documents and information and has proved as generous as her husband with her time and help. Humphrey Spender's remarkable memory and reckless candor have enlivened many pages, and he also allowed me to reproduce some of his wonderful photographs. In Paris the late Ghisa Drouin (Gisa Soleweitschick) recalled her time in Berlin with Isherwood and firmly pointed out the differences between herself and "Natalia Landauer." I owe the account of Jean Ross's life largely to her sister Billee Hughes, and her daughter, the late Sarah Cockburn. The late Lincoln Kirstein provided numerous insights into his close but troubled relationship with Isherwood and handed over his entire collection of letters from Isherwood as a gift. I owe a special debt to the late Jim Charlton, to the late Jack Hewit, and to "Vernon," who requested that I should retain the pseudonym bestowed on him by Isherwood but wrote me numerous long and detailed letters. A few other names have been changed in this book to spare blushes.

Various other people have provided particular help. Geoffrey Elborn had the imagination and generosity to lend me a computer after my own had been stolen, and provided me with assorted snippets of information. John Byrne pointed me in the direction of letters and papers and even provided me with photocopies; Shaun Whiteside translated German letters and texts for me; and Virginia Spencer Carr asked the late Paul Bowles questions on my behalf. On several trips to New York, Larry Ashmead lent me his Manhattan apartment in exchange for some very light cat-sitting duties. Don and the late Carol Shields were generous and stimulating hosts in Berkeley, and Carol's characteristically acute insights into the hazards and limitations of biography remain with me constantly. As a non-driver, I am very grateful to Lucy Bucknell, who ferried me round various Isherwood sites in California, and to Ashley Russell, without whom I would never have got to Freshwater Bay (nor gained insights into some aspects of Isherwood's character). Long conversations with Casey Hammond brought several ideas about Isherwood into much sharper focus. Sissy von Westphalen brought me to Berlin to take part in her SFB television film *"Cabaret" - Zeit*. She and Peter Sohn were perfect hosts and I would like to thank the whole cast and crew of the film, in particular the co-director, Karen Reisz, and Jonathan Katz, who supplied an unsettling ghost of Isherwood for me to trail around the city. Thanks, too, to Ursula Miller at Nollendorfstrasse 17, and Konstanza Prinzessin Löwenstein. Paul Bailey recalled his several meetings with Isherwood and introduced me to Niladri Chatterjee, who has not only kept me up to the mark for many years on Isherwood and other matters but also persuaded me to follow in my subject's reluctant footsteps to Calcutta. My thanks go to him and his hugely hospitable family: his parents, Kshitish Ranjan Chatterjee and Manju Chatterjee, and his sister, Irani Chatterjee. Thanks also to Tapan and Sobha Chattopadhyay, who arranged for me to visit the Ramarkrishna Mission Institute of Culture.

The papers that now make up the Christopher Isherwood Collection at the Huntington Library were still in private hands when I consulted them, but I subsequently visited the library for a final and productive trawl. I would like to thank Sue Hodson and all the staff at the Huntington for the assistance they have given me since they acquired the collection, not least in cataloguing the papers and compiling the incalculably useful Isherwood Finding Aid. Among the many archivists and librarians who have gone out of their way to be friendly and helpful, I would especially like to record my gratitude to Sally Brown and Chris Fletcher at the British Library; Steve Crook at the Berg Collection, the New York Public Library; and Cathy Henderson at the Harry Ransom Humanities Research Center, University of Texas at Austin. I also thank librarians, archivists and curators, past and present, at the following institutions: Tom Staley, Tara Wenger, Sue Murphy, John Kirkpatrick, Pat Fox and all the pages at HRHRC; Nancy Burrows, Alison Dinicola, Gayle Richardson, Carolyn Powell, Robert Ritchie, Anne Marr and Mona Noureldin at the Huntington; Lori Curtis (Head of Special Collections and Archives, McFarlin Library), Sid Huttner, Milissa Burkart, Jennifer Carlson and Walt Mauer at the University of Tulsa; Vincent Giroux and staff at the Beinecke Library, Yale University; Susan S. Snyder, Bonnie Hardwick and staff at the Bancroft Library, University of California at Berkeley; Patrick Lawlor, Jean W. Ashton and staff at the Butler Library, Columbia University, New York; Philip Reed and Nicholas Clark at the Britten-Pears Library; Michael Bott and staff at the University of Reading Library; Michael Meredith at Eton College Library; Tony Byrne, Melanie Bowram, Nicola-Jane Levy, Liz Winter and Alexander Leiffheidt at Corpus Christi College, Cambridge; Pauline McCausland and Trevor Gibbs at St. Edmund's School, Hindhead; James Codd and Sue Knowles at the BBC Written Archives Centre; Manfred Baumgardt at the Bibliothek und Archiv of the Schwules Museum, Berlin; J. Kevin O'Brien of the U.S. Department of Justice; Robin Gibson and Helen Trumpeteler at the National Portrait Gallery; Hilary Tanner at the British Film Institute; The Old Reptonian Society; The Old Sedberghian Club; the London Library; and the British Library.

A large number of individuals have provided me with material, information, assistance, encouragement and hospitality: Gilbert Adair, Jon Andersson, John Andrewes, Ian and Ann Angus, Adam Bager, Robin Baird-Smith, Julian Barnes, James Berg, Richard Beswick, Biggles, Mark Bostridge, Peter Bower (Wyberslegh Hall), Alan and Edna Bradley, John H. Bradley, David Bradshaw, Thomas Bradshaw-Isherwood, the late Neville Braybrooke, Michael Brett, Isabel Broad, the late May Buckingham, Sam Burford, Suzanna Burford, Ken Butler, the late Paul Cadmus, Joachim Campe, Humphrey Carpenter, the late Gabriel Carritt, Anne Chisolm, the late Alan Clodd, Berwick Coates, Joel Conarroe, Michael and Margaret Crick, John Cruft, the late Kiki Cruft, Timothy d'Arch Smith, Michael Davie, the late Michael De-la-Noy, Paul Delany, Michael di Capua, Jane Dorrell, Margaret Drabble, John Drummond, Maureen Duffy, Lindsay Duguid, Gregory Evans, Duncan Fallowell, Mary Fedden, Jack Fontan, Chris Freeman, Peter Funnell, P. N. Furbank, Jonathan Galassi, Tony Garrett, David Goudge, Derek Granger, Edward Greene, Elspeth Griffiths (Sedbergh School), Valerie Grove, Thom Gunn, Rod Hall, the late Bill Harris, Linda Hart, Christopher Hawtree, Alison Hennegan, Rachel Hewitt, Patrick Higgins, C.A.R. Hills, Tim Hilton, Philip Hoare, David Hockney, Merlin Holland, John Holmstrom, Michael Holroyd, the late Evelyn Hooker, Glen Horowitz, Miles Huddleston, Kay Jackson and Claudean Schulz (The Wild Flower Inn at Austin), Daniel Jewel, Hubert Kennedy, Francis King, Jeremy Kingston, Richard Lamb, Gavin Lambert, Marie-

Jaqueline Lancaster, David Leavitt, David Leddick, Hermione Lee, Jeremy Lewis, Marco Livingstone, Marguerite Littman, Sarah Long and Joe Hunter, Julian Machin, Anne Maier, Fowke Mangeot, Gordon Marsden, Armistead Maupin, David McLaughlin, the late Robert Medley, Jeffrey Meyers, David Miller, Anita Money, Elizabeth Monkhouse, Pamela Monkhouse, A.V.E.P. Montagu, Kitty Morris, Anthea Morton-Saner (Curtis Brown), Brian Oatley, Patrick O'Connor, José Roberto O'Shea, Anthony Page, Norman Page, Jan Piggott, David Plante, John Plowright (Repton School), Jane Pritchard (Rambert Dance Company), Patrick Quinn, George Ramsden, Michael Ratcliffe, John Ridley, Ronald Riggs, the late Wendy Rintoul, Elaine Robson-Scott, Dame Miriam Rothschild, Don and Paula Sanders, Tony Scotland, Ivan Seery, Nigel Semmens, Peyton Skipwith, Colin Spencer, Nikos Stangos, Graeme T. Steel, Peter Steele, the late Tania Stern, Charlotte Stewart, Jim Stroud, Stephen Stuart-Smith, the late Robert Tewdwr Moss, Richard Thompson, Ian Thomson, Jeremy Trafford, Jeremy Trevathan, Raleigh Trevelyan, Ray Unger, Peter Vansittart, the late Swami Vidyatmananda, Gilly Vincent, the late Tom Wakefield, Keith Walker, Craig Westwood, Ian Whitcomb, Edmund White, James P. White, Donald Windham, the late Patrick Woodcock, Michael and Pat York, Sebastian Yorke and Theo Zinn. I hope that anyone who has been accidentally overlooked will put this down to inattention rather than ingratitude.

I would like to thank all those who gave me permission to quote from their own letters, diaries and other unpublished papers, in particular Edward Upward, Humphrey Spender, the late Stephen Spender, Donald Windham, Jeremy Kingston, the late Jim Charlton and the late Paul Cadmus.

Other unpublished and copyright material is quoted by kind permission of the following: Julian Barnes and the Special Collections at Boston University (Dodie Smith and Alec Beesley); Georges Borschardt and HRHRC (Tennessee Williams); The Trustees of the Britten-Pears Foundation (Benjamin Britten); Katherine Bucknell (John Layard memoir, courtesy James Greene); Suzanna Burford (Roger Burford); Jane Dorrell and the McFarlin Library, University of Tulsa (Amiya Sandwich); the T. S. Eliot Estate, Faber and Faber, and King's College Library, Cambridge (T. S. Eliot); Angela Ellis and King's College Library, Cambridge (Ashley Dukes); Duff Hart-Davis and Durham University (William Plomer); David Higham Associates (Graham Greene); Miles Huddleston, Charles Osborne and the Manuscripts Division, Department of Rare Books and Special Collections, Princeton University Library (John Lehmann); Nicholas Jenkins (Lincoln Kirstein); Edward Mendelson (W. H. Auden, including "Who is that funny-looking young man"); Pamela Monkhouse (Patrick Monkhouse); Roland Philipps (Beatrix Lehmann); Lady Spender (Stephen Spender); Simon Stern (James Stern); Swami Veetamohananda of the Centre Védantique Ramakrichna, Gretz (Swami Vidyatmananda); and Peter Viertel (Berthold Viertel).

Quotations from W. H. Auden's Berlin Journal of 1929, notebook of 1964–1965 and his letters to Stephen Spender, Naomi Mitchison, Olive Mangeot, John Auden and Mina Curtiss are reproduced by kind permission of the Berg Collection of English American Literature, the New York Public Library (Astor, Lenox and Tilden Foundation). Material from its James Stern and Edward Upward collections is used by kind permission of the British Library. Papers from the Curtis Brown and Random

House Archives are quoted by kind permission of Curtis Brown Ltd., Random House, Inc., and the Butler Library, Columbia University. Quotations from material in its Stephen Spender papers are quoted by kind permission of the Bancroft Library, University of California at Berkeley.

In spite of our best efforts, it has not always been possible to trace copyright holders, and the publishers would be pleased to hear from any who have proved elusive or been overlooked.

For negotiating the passage of this project from vague idea to finished product I would like to thank Bruce Hunter of David Higham Associates in London and Emma Sweeney and the late Claire Smith of Harold Ober Associates in New York. Over the years the book has had numerous editors, most of whom have (perhaps wisely) moved jobs since its inception. I am particularly indebted to Roland Philipps and Will Schwalbe, who signed it up in the first place. In the U.K., Peter Straus and particularly George Morley embodied the virtues of patience without, as it were, benefiting from its supposed rewards. Maria Rejt at Picador has proved an exemplary publisher, remaining unfazed by the assorted problems that assailed the book at a point when we all thought it could be safely put to bed. She has remained loyal, supportive and remarkably good-humored, as did her assistant Adelaide Docx. It was my good fortune to have the meticulous and sympathetic Helen Campbell to copyedit the text, and the unflappable Liz Davis as managing editor. Christine Shuttleworth not only provided an exhaustive index but also corrected some schoolboy howlers in my renderings of German words. At Morrow/HarperCollins in the United States, Dan Menaker was a marvelously engaged and enthusiastic editor, full of sound advice, not all of which I took. The book eventually followed him to Random House, where I thank Will Murphy and Stephanie Higgs. I would also like to record my gratitude to the late and much missed Robert Jones, and to thank Don Fehr for his continuing interest in the book long after it became clear he was not going to be its publisher.

I owe a particular debt of gratitude, as always, to my mother and my late father—and special thanks which need no explanation go to Thomas Blaikie, Georgina Hammick, and the late Diana Petre. Of the many people who have endured vicariously the writing of this biography, no one endured more or endured it more stoically than Christopher Potter. He also subjected several versions of the text to his severe but invaluable editorial eye, and provided moral and financial support throughout. Without him, none of this—nor indeed anything else—would be possible.

It seems appropriate to dedicate a book that is so much concerned with old and enduring friendships to someone I have known longer than either of us cares to calculate. I met Richard Walker at school and he has been part of my life ever since. This book is for him.

Peter Parker
London E3
December 2003

part one

ENGLAND MADE ME

ONE

I N THE FIRST DAYS OF 1986, CHRISTOPHER ISHERWOOD LAY DYING
at his home in Southern California. He had not said much for several weeks, and
he was drifting in and out of consciousness. He occasionally cried out for his
mother or for his old nanny. Traveling forward into the unknown, he was also traveling backward through loops of memory, across thousands of miles, to where he
started out on the long journey that was about to end. The world, and Isherwood's circumstances, had changed almost beyond recognition since 1904, but despite adopting many roles over the years, despite shedding both names and nationality,
Isherwood had always known that the past was inescapable. It lay in hiding, as it always had, ready to leap out and reclaim him.

Isherwood's relationship with the past was complicated. He respected—or
feared—it enough to give the word a capital initial, more often than not, when he
wrote it down, a tribute he also accorded his mother. For Isherwood "the Past" and
"my Mother" were almost the same thing. This was partly because his mother had a
characteristically English reverence for anything that happened in earlier times, in
particular before the First World War. She also had a genuine and well-informed interest in old buildings, paintings and furniture, but this antiquarianism struck her son
as having more to do with psychology than scholarship. For Kathleen Isherwood, the
past represented a place to which she could escape, the place where she had been
most happy; for Christopher Isherwood, the past was a treacherous bog into which
you would be sucked down and suffocated. He once said that by going to live in
America, he was "separating himself from Mother and Motherland at one stroke."
Much of his life, and the many journeys he made, can be seen as a series of attempts
to put as great a distance as he could between himself and the person he imagined his
family and society wanted him to be.

Before emigrating to America in 1939, Isherwood tried to settle his account with
the past. Like Robert Graves before him, he waved goodbye to all that in a fictionalized autobiography. *Lions and Shadows* opens with an account of the author in the

Sixth Form of his unnamed public school. Years later, Isherwood complained that what he disliked about conventional autobiographies was that "the author says (in effect) 'before I tell you about me I shall tell you about them' and so the parents are forever separated from the child who is doing the telling—when, actually, the opposite is true, the parents are now only alive within the child and as a part of him." In fact, Isherwood's mother was very much alive when he published *Lions and Shadows,* but she is ruthlessly excised from the narrative, as is his younger brother, and his father, who was killed in the First World War. The book contains several vague references to "my family," but the reader has no idea of its individual components. In order to scratch his parents and brother from the record, Isherwood also had to avoid much mention of his childhood. It is as if he wished to present himself as arriving in the world fully formed, having already attained the age of reason.

This attempt at parthenogenesis is characteristic of Isherwood's approach to public self-presentation. More even than most writers, Isherwood liked to imagine himself his own creation, and he was quite prepared to rewrite history in order to improve on the facts for aesthetic or personal reasons. He did so with every appearance of candor, for he was a consummate actor both on the page and in person. His boyish appearance, which persisted well into middle age, and his clear blue eyes were not only seductive but suggested a frankness and openness of character. He possessed a great deal of charm, which he often used strategically but which also became at times something he switched on almost without noticing. His writing frequently beguiles— and even misleads—the reader in much the same way.

Isherwood's distrust of the past did not of course prevent him from making use of it in his work. Few writers have relied as much upon their own lives as Isherwood did in order to write books. Almost everything he wrote, even his occasional book reviewing, contains an autobiographical strand. Toward the end of his career, having exhausted the possibilities of using his own life to generate fiction, Isherwood turned to more or less "straight" autobiography, although in both *Kathleen and Frank* and *Christopher and His Kind,* he referred to his younger self in the third person, as if writing about a separate character whose connection with the narrator was at best tenuous. After toying in novels with fictional characters called "William Bradshaw" (his own middle names) and "Christopher Isherwood," who are to all intents and purposes self-portraits, he ends up writing books that supposedly present his life undisguised and unadorned. On the opening page of *Christopher and His Kind,* he refers—rather as if it had very little to do with him—to "a book called *Lions and Shadows,* published in 1938, which describes Christopher Isherwood's life between the ages of seventeen and twenty-four." In that book, he continues: "The Author conceals important facts about himself. He over-dramatizes many episodes and gives his characters fictitious names." Having dispensed with this rival chronicler of his life, Isherwood states: "The book I am now going to write will be as frank and factual as I can make it, especially as far as I myself am concerned." Once again, the reader is led into believing that everything that follows is "true," but in this book, as in the books about his parents and his guru—as indeed in *Lions and Shadows*—facts are concealed, episodes are over-dramatized and real people are given fictitious names. There were perfectly honorable, non-literary reasons for some of this, largely to do with protecting people's identity or privacy, but Isherwood was still intent on molding his life, finding patterns and, increasingly, proselytizing.

I sherwood's tardy interest in family history was largely solipsistic. His antecedents were interesting insofar as Christopher Isherwood was the end result. His approach to them was archaeological rather than strictly genealogical, discovering his family within himself. Consequently, generations of respectable forebears are ignored and only those whose characters seemed in some way to have contributed to Isherwood's own personal mythology make their appearances in *Kathleen and Frank*. How far these characters are full and true portraits of historical figures is open to doubt. When Isherwood began work on the book, his brother Richard suggested that he was inclined to focus on those aspects of their father that made him seem most like the sort of man Isherwood wanted him to be. Thereafter Isherwood had to be on guard against a tendency to remake his father in his own image. He also needed to reconcile the woman who emerges from the diaries she kept throughout her long life with the Mother he had created, or at any rate "over-dramatized," in order to represent everything he wanted to reject. Isherwood's notions about his parents were evident in the title he originally gave *Kathleen and Frank,* a title bestowed on the work even before it was in progress, before he had done any research at all: *Hero-Father, Demon-Mother.*

I sherwood's family background was important not only because he made use of it in his fiction but also because it gave him something tangible against which to rebel. Of the writers who came to be associated with the 1930s, Christopher William Bradshaw-Isherwood was socially by far the grandest. W. H. Auden, Edward Upward, C. Day-Lewis, Louis MacNeice and Stephen Spender had all been born into the British bourgeoisie, the sons of doctors, clergymen and journalists. Isherwood's father may have been a professional soldier, but he came from a family of landed gentry which had a "seat" in Cheshire and was able to trace its origins back into the sixteenth century. "The landowning classes" against whom writers of the Left spent much of their time inveighing were incarnated in almost cartoon fashion by Isherwood's own grandfather, John Henry Bradshaw-Isherwood, Justice of the Peace and squire of Marple. It was Kathleen Isherwood's almost mystical reverence for Marple Hall and the traditions it represented, rather than a passion for social equality, that made the young Isherwood want to see the place reduced to rubble. For Isherwood the political was always, from the very outset, personal.

The landed gentry is a section of upper-middle-class English society whose lineage is elaborately set out between the red covers of a stout volume popularly known as *Burke*. The weight of the past, about which Isherwood so often complained, was not in fact as heavy for his family as for others recorded in this book. In the 1952 edition of *Burke's Landed Gentry,* Isherwood's ancestors come under the heading "Bradshaw-Isherwood of Marple," but are listed alphabetically under "I" for plain Isherwood, as if there were some doubt as to the authenticity of this double-barreled name. Indeed, it is the Bradshaws who are traceable back beyond the sixteenth century, not the Isherwoods. The Bradshaws may have been gentry, but they did not become landed until 1606 when a certain Henry Bradshawe, who had lived as a tenant at Marple Hall and Wyberslegh Hall in Cheshire, bought both properties from his landlord. The Isherwoods did not enter the picture for another 170 or so years, when Henry's great-great-granddaughter Mary married *en secondes noces* Nathaniel Isherwood of Bolton-le-Moors in neighboring Lancashire. Nathaniel Isherwood was certainly *not* gentry, coming as he did from a prosperous family of felt manufacturers and therefore "in trade." It was Mary and Nathaniel's second son, Thomas, who assumed the name Bradshawe-Isherwood upon becoming head of the family when his elder brother died, and this name persisted until the twentieth century, by which time the redundant final "e" of "Bradshawe" had been quietly dropped.

It did not suit Isherwood's purposes to describe himself as coming from the landed gentry. In *Lions and Shadows* he writes of himself at the age of sixteen: "I was an upper-middle-class Puritan, cautious, a bit stingy, with a stake in the land." The particular bit of land in which Isherwood had a stake was Marple Hall, although this information is strategically omitted from the book. In fact Marple Hall was to play a vital role in Isherwood's life, not only as somewhere he spent much of his childhood, but also as the symbol of everything about England he wanted to escape. A large estate on the Cheshire-Derbyshire border, Marple Hall consisted of an Elizabethan mansion and some twenty farms. Built of local sandstone in 1658, but incorporating the remains of an earlier timber-framed dwelling, the house itself was more imposing than beautiful. The most striking thing about it was its setting, for as one approached it along a drive through parkland, it seemed set in a hollow. At the back of the house, however, there was a terrace, beyond which the ground fell away sharply to the River Goyt, so that from the other side of the water it seemed to stand on an impressive sandstone bluff. The Hall had been enlarged toward the end of the eighteenth century: one half of the house had the original seventeenth-century pointed gables and long, mullioned windows, while the other had Dutch gables and tall sashes. The entrance porch, with simple Ionic columns topped by a wooden balustrade, was placed at the point where Elizabethan met Queen Anne, and any discrepancy in architectural style was disguised beneath the ivy that swarmed over the façade. A somewhat romantic and inaccurate picture of the house was to be found in John Leigh's *Lays and Legends of Cheshire:*

> *High on a craggy steep there stands,*
> *Near Marple's fertile vale,*
> *An ancient ivy-covered house*
> *That overlooks the dale.*
>
> *And lofty woods of elm and oak*
> *That ancient house enclose,*
> *And on those walls a neighbouring yew*
> *Its sombre shadow throws.*
>
> *A many gabled house it is*
> *With antique turrets crowned*

And many a quaint device, designed
In carvings rude is found.

The turrets in fact belonged to the stable-block, a highly decorative building which had an ornate, squat, step-gabled clock tower set over the entrance to the cobbled yard.

The interior of the Hall was rather more harmonious than the exterior, with dark, color-washed walls hung with Elizabethan and Jacobean family portraits, and plain white plaster ceilings. Most of the furnishings were very much of the period and of good quality without being particularly distinguished—just the sort of thing one might expect in the home of a north-of-England squire. There were, however, a couple of very well preserved early-eighteenth-century tapestries depicting classical subjects, which came from the Gobelin factory and were signed by de la Croix and de Blond, *tapissiers royaux* to Louis XIV. The low-ceilinged hall, with its flagstone floor, was something of a showpiece, with the obligatory array of weaponry, complete suits of armor, stags' heads and stained glass, hooded porters' chairs, a longcase clock, and Jacobean chests upon which stood Chinese vases and pewter trenchers. A fine oak staircase, with elaborate urns on the newel posts and a tapestry-hung half-landing, rose out of the hall to the first floor. The dining room was furnished with heavy oak chairs of the seventeenth century, typical of the region, and there was a handsome library with glass-fronted bookcases, paneling and a fireplace, all in the Gothic revival style. The drawing room had Gothic windows and contained a highly decorative pink marble fireplace, its mantelpiece supported by caryatids, brought back from his travels in Italy by Isherwood's Uncle Henry. Also on the ground floor were the paneled Oak Parlour and, at the back of the house, a conservatory.

For visitors, who paid a shilling to be shown round the house, the most historically interesting room was the Bradshaw Room, dominated by a large four-poster bed. Round the top of the tester ran a motto: "A MAN WITHOUT MERCY OF MERCY SHALL MISS BUT HE SHALL HAVE MERCY THAT MERCYFULL IS." It was in this bed, contemplating this homily, that John Bradshawe, the family's most distinguished, or notorious, forebear, supposedly slept. Lord President of the High Court of Justice, "Bradshawe the Regicide" presided over the trial of Charles I, pronounced the verdict, refused to allow the condemned man to speak, and put his florid but firm signature on the monarch's death warrant. Bradshawe's great-niece, Mary, eventually inherited the Marple Hall estate, and it was she who married Nathaniel Isherwood the felt-maker. Mary's son, also Nathaniel, married a local heiress, Elizabeth Brabins of nearby Brabins (or Brabyns) Hall, who was always known as Moll and was to feature alarmingly in the lives of Christopher Isherwood and his brother Richard. The younger Nathaniel died without issue and it was his parents' second son, the philoprogenitive Thomas, who continued the family line, marrying twice and fathering seventeen children. His heir, John, was Isherwood's great-great-grandfather.

Although his father, Frank, was merely a second son, Isherwood was from birth heir to the estate, since Frank's older brother, Henry, had shown no inclination to marry. By the rules of primogeniture, which governed and caused so much ill-feeling among the British landed classes, Marple Hall would pass first to Henry, then to Frank, who would in turn pass it down to his son, Christopher, who would in turn hand it on to his son, and so *ad infinitum*. Profligacy, inertia, death, sex and a touch of madness eventually destroyed this tidy plan, and today the estate is dispersed and the Hall itself demolished. Everything the radical young Isherwood wished upon his inheritance came to pass with almost apocalyptic thoroughness.

On August 26, 1904, the day Christopher Isherwood was born, the future looked assured. At the christening, his mother recorded in her diary, "Mr. Isherwood said I had done my duty and done it well!! To which I quite agreed." This touch of asperity is characteristic of Kathleen and of her relations with her in-laws, whom she respected more for what they represented than for who they actually were. Kathleen Machell-Smith was born in Bury St Edmunds on October 7, 1868. Her father, Frederick, was a wine merchant in the town, co-proprietor of Messrs. Machell-Smith and Oliver in Cornhill. Her mother had been a Miss Emily Smythies Greene, the eldest child of the first marriage of Edward Greene of Nether Hall, chairman of the famous brewing dynasty Greene King and Sons. It was this professional interest in drink that brought Frederick and the Greenes together and thus led to his marriage. The Greenes were a great deal more distinguished and interesting than the Machell-Smiths: Emily's brother, Kathleen's beloved Uncle Walter, was a Justice of the Peace, a Master of Foxhounds, Deputy Lieutenant and High Sheriff of the county, and a Member of Parliament, eventually rewarded with a baronetcy in 1900; one sister married T. C. Fry, successively headmaster of Berkhamsted and Dean of Lincoln; a nephew, handsome young Raymond Greene, was elected to Parliament in 1895 as the Conservative Member for the Chesterton Division of Cambridge and remained there until 1906; another branch of the closely knit family boasted Sir Graham Greene, who was Permanent Secretary of the Admiralty throughout much of the First World War, and his nephew and namesake, whose career as a writer paralleled Isherwood's. Throughout her life Kathleen kept in touch with hordes of relations from her mother's family, but almost none from her father's.

As in the case of the Bradshaw-Isherwoods, there was some doubt as to the authenticity of the hyphen linking Machell and Smith. At their respective christenings both of Isherwood's parents were given their supplementary family names: Francis Edward Bradshaw and Kathleen Machell. Frederick's father had indeed been plain Mr. Smith, his mother a Miss Machell. (Frederick's family were originally called Talbock, and no one seemed to know why they exchanged this unusual name for the commonplace one of Smith.) Frederick had run away to sea at the age of seventeen, partly in protest at his father's second marriage, and spent some time in Australia in the mounted police, surviving a shipwreck during his voyage back to England a few years later. This early hardship and uneasy relations with his family appear to have permanently soured his character, although he must have had something apart from good looks to attract Emily, who was nine years his junior. In spite of Frederick's cantankerous nature, which deteriorated still further with age, the marriage was a success, resulting in an only and much-loved child. By the time Frederick died, however, his behavior was such that he had managed to alienate both his wife and daughter, and it was this which may have drawn Emily and Kathleen into an unusually close relationship of the sort more common when a daughter remains unmarried.

There was a time when it looked as if spinsterhood would be Kathleen's lot. An early romance, which began at the age of fourteen when she met a young Etonian at a dance, came to nothing—though the jottings Kathleen made in her diary seven years later, when the young man announced his engagement to someone else, suggest that she had entertained genuine hopes. A move to London must have increased Kathleen's chances of attracting a husband, more particularly one with a faint prospect of coming up to her parents' exacting standards. The family had been obliged to leave a house in chilly Suffolk for a rather more cozy mansion block in Kensington's Gloucester Road because of Emily's health. Quite what was wrong with Emily is unclear; one suspects not very much. However, throughout her life she frequently used her "delicate" constitution in order to get her own way. Her grandson described her (with a certain sneaking admiration) as "a great psychosomatic virtuoso," and—rather in the manner of a medium producing ectoplasm—she was able to come down with any number of disgustingly authentic swellings and infections when she felt she was in any danger of being thwarted. Kathleen never once doubted her mother's frail health, and at times her diary, with its anguished accounts of poor dear Mama's latest illness, reads like a pharmacopoeia.

Kathleen was an accomplished and attractive young woman, who enjoyed the social life of her Greene relations. She was often invited to balls and house parties at Nether Hall and kept a large scrapbook of clippings from the local newspapers recording these events. Where journalists have been inattentive, she has edited the copy, crossing out the names of those who had failed to attend and in one instance adding "Miss Machell-Smith" to the list of guests. She also enjoyed somewhat sedate fancy-dress parties at public venues such as the Manchester Assembly Rooms, where in February 1891 she appeared as "Crown Derby China." Little is known of her education, though at the age of twenty-seven she took courses at the Chelsea Centre of the London Society for the Extension of University Teaching and was awarded two certificates by the Universities Joint Board in English Architecture and Eastern and Western Architecture. For the latter she gained a distinction, the only candidate to do so.

It is probable that her early schooling had been at the hands of governesses: there was certainly something rather unfinished about her. She was a compulsive and extremely fluent diarist and correspondent, covering page after page with her elegant, flowing handwriting. As with many women of her class at this period, she was more expressive than literate, her letters and diaries heavily scored with underlinings and scattered with clusters of exclamation marks. Her spelling was fairly good, but her punctuation was erratic, sentences running into each other, broken up by the occasional comma and a great many dashes. Even when she finally drew up momentarily at a full stop, she often rushed ahead into a new sentence without troubling to mark its start with a capital letter. She never mastered the distinction between the plural and possessive forms of nouns, so that a "friends" house often lacked an apostrophe, while a litter of "kitten's" gained one. Her letters and journals show someone who was in many ways conventional: she was a devout Christian, had a proper respect for royalty, and believed that people should know and keep to their place in the social hierarchy. But she was also very observant, and was amused by much of what she saw, noting down the foibles of friends and relations with a dry, understated wit. This was something she shared with both her sons. In spite of being in thrall to two difficult parents (her sense of duty overlaid with genuine devotion), she was an independent spirit, unafraid of offering her own views, and sticking to them. Isherwood characterized her as stubborn, but what he really meant by this was that she would not alter her standards and opinions to suit him.

Among Kathleen's accomplishments was the co-authoring of a book which had been published to polite notices in the summer of 1895. The author of *Our Rambles in Old London* is given as E. S. Machell-Smith, but Kathleen was darling Mama's companion on the excursions (she is occasionally mentioned as "K.") and she no doubt contributed to the text. She certainly provided the sketches of St. George's Inn at Southwark, Charles Lamb's house in Islington and the Staple Inn at Holborn, as well as a map of old Southwark, marking the site of the Globe and other Elizabethan places of entertainment. The book is one of those charming, slim volumes of topography for which Augustus Hare had started a vogue in the last quarter of the nineteenth century. Conversational in tone, self-consciously amateur, graced by references to the classics of English literature, such books tended to lack the bracing dash of vinegar with which Hare himself seasoned his descriptive tours of London and other cities. *Our Rambles* is no exception, though it is lively enough and full of neo-Dickensian portraits of London types.

Kathleen would always retain a taste for such excursions, becoming something of an expert on London's architecture and history, and she kept detailed diaries about her travels in England and abroad. These outings no doubt represented a measure of independence, since Frederick did everything in his power to keep Kathleen on a short leash. This may have been partly out of spite, since he had been very reluctant to leave the hunting and shooting life he conducted in Suffolk for the rather aimless social round of London. His income still derived from the wine business, and he remained—perhaps appropriately—chairman of the Stowmarket Explosives Co., but in London he was obliged to fill the empty hours by becoming a committee man. He took his duties as chairman of the Alliance Dairy Co. seriously, bicycling round their various premises, and devoted a great deal of his time to the local Conservative Association. Another abortive romance was conducted by Kathleen with someone the Machell-Smiths dubbed "The Child," though it seems the relationship was broken off by Kathleen herself rather than by parental interference. It was while this relationship was in its protracted death throes that Kathleen went to visit Maud Greenway, a friend of long standing who had married into the army and lived in the garrison town of Colchester in Essex. It was here, in July 1895, that she met Frank Bradshaw-Isherwood.

Nine months younger than Kathleen, Frank was born at Marple Hall on July 1, 1869. His upbringing, in a large house, surrounded by brothers and sisters, had been very different from Kathleen's. As well as his elder brother, the handsome and homosexual Henry (born in 1868), he had three younger siblings: Mary, who was always known as "Moey" (1871); John, who was always known as "Jack" (1876); and Esther (1878). As so often happened in such families, the eldest son stood to inherit the estate, while the younger children were obliged to fend for themselves, although they received some income from the family and would eventually be provided for in their father's will. A sensitive and artistic young man, whose watercolor paintings displayed genuine talent rather than mere amateur charm, Frank seems an unlikely recruit to the British army. It was, however, traditional for the second son in such families to follow a military career, with subsequent sons entering the Church or the law. Jack chose the latter profession, spending much of his life working—not very happily—among wills and probate at Somerset House in London. "He sat in a large room with lots of other people at an uncomfortable desk," one relative remembered, "with piles of scruffy looking files and nothing apparently to do after dealing with one but to get on with the next." His real passion was for music and his closest friend was the composer Cyril Scott, with whom he had been at school, and with whom he shared a flat in London, enjoying a bachelor life until he married in his forties. Interestingly, in view of his nephew's later involvement with Eastern religion, Jack practiced yoga and embraced faddish diets. Esther—undoubtedly the beauty of the family, but perhaps its most conventional member—married a clergyman. Moey, who had left-wing views, mixed with the local mill-girls and played golf, suffered poor health and remained a spinster. She had a small career as an author of "improving" children's books, many of which were published by the Society for the Promotion of Christian Knowledge, and in later life she ran an antique shop with a German woman companion, who had originally been her nurse.

When Frank first met Kathleen, he was a lieutenant in the York and Lancaster Regiment, which he had joined in 1892 after graduating from Sandhurst. He was not, however, a conventional career soldier. Before attending the military academy, he had been to school at Cheltenham College and university at Clare College, Cambridge, so his education had been broad. He was widely read, played the piano well, composed songs, and was keenly interested in art and architecture. A cousin who was a subaltern in Frank's regiment later told Isherwood: "Your father was a conscientious officer but I doubt whether his heart was really in soldiering. My mother always said that he hoped on attaining the approximate seniority to be appointed Commandant of Kneller Hall at Twickenham, the Army School of Music, as the summit of his career, and no doubt she got that from your Mother. He always wanted things done properly, and if they were not there was no doubt that he was displeased, but his displeasure was never noisily or violently or sarcastically expressed." Although Frank's character had a distinctly feline quality, he was in most ways an old-fashioned masculine figure, keen on drill and keeping fit. He had no interest in team games, but was naturally athletic and took part in regimental cross-country runs. A full but well-kempt moustache gave him a military air when he was in uniform, but combined with his sensitive features to suggest a bohemian streak when he was in civilian clothes and a straw boater standing before an easel.

There is no evidence that Frank had enjoyed any affairs before meeting Kathleen, but he did have at least one close female friend. Ethel Colburn Mayne was a writer a few years his senior whom he had met when his regiment was stationed in Ireland in the early 1890s. The daughter of an Irish Resident Magistrate, she was shortly to move to London where she began contributing stories to *The Yellow Book* under the pseudonym Frances E. Huntly. She would later make a considerable literary reputation for herself, not only as a writer of Jamesian novels and short stories but also as a translator from French and German, and as a biographer of Byron and his family.

Frank always referred to her with exaggerated gallantry as "Venus," and during his courtship would occasionally arouse Kathleen's jealousy by alluding to Mayne, with whom he in fact conducted a platonic friendship, mostly by letters.

In many ways Frank and Kathleen were ideally suited, but their relationship would always be companionable rather than passionate, and they did not appear to strike sparks off each other when they first met. Indeed, they did not see each other again until some eight months later, when in February 1896 Kathleen paid another visit to Colchester. "Mr. Isherwood of the York and Lancaster came to dine and sang after," Kathleen wrote in her diary. "Liked him very much, he is so fond of pictures and architecture, and actually declared he enjoyed an afternoon at Westminster Abbey far more than Westminster Aquarium!!" Frank's preference for Westminster Abbey, as an emblem of the past and a repository of British history, over the somewhat vulgar Royal Aquarium (an entertainments complex housing a variety theater as well as exotic fish), clearly scored high with the co-author of *Our Rambles*.

Frank may have had a sympathetic appreciation of old London, but he was merely one of several partners with whom Kathleen danced when, two days later, she attended a sergeants' dance at the drill hall. Her next sight of him, seven weeks later, was in drag, "splendid as Sister Anne" in a burlesque organized by Maud Greenway. Frank often played female roles in amateur theatricals, his luxuriant moustache presumably adding to the comedy of the proceedings. Although Kathleen went bicycling and sketching with Frank (apparently unchaperoned) when she visited Colchester again that August, there was little sense of a burgeoning romance. Frank appeared in further theatricals the following February ("Mr. Isherwood as Sarah the general servant was simply killing"), but it is clear that Kathleen was an amused observer rather than an eager participant when she went backstage and noted "a good deal of lovemaking being practised among the ladies and gentlemen of the chorus." More to her taste was an outing to the National Gallery with Frank the following week, chaperoned by Mama, at which she discovered that he was not only well informed about painting but liked much the same pictures as she did.

At the beginning of 1898 Maud Greenway's family, the Sykeses, gave this dilatory courtship a shove by inviting both Kathleen and Frank to their house in Cheshire. There were outings to a ball, a pantomime and Manchester's Whitworth Art Gallery, and on January 11 Frank took Kathleen to see Marple Hall. While the royalist and romantic Kathleen may have had equivocal feelings about Frank's most famous ancestor (in later years she would often attend the yearly service held at Whitehall in the Martyr King's memory), Marple Hall appealed to both her sense of history and her interest in architecture. "It is an awfully picturesque approach and a most fascinating old place," she wrote in her diary after her first visit. "I like the drawing room so much with the bow window looking over the terrace and hills beyond, and the room itself full of old china, pictures, tapestry and old furniture. The whole house is very rambling and fascinating." It would be some time, however, before Marple Hall acquired a central place in her life.

Shortly after this visit, Frank went on an extended trip to the Continent, accompanied by his sister Moey. He and Kathleen did not meet for over a year, but in July 1899 Frank was invited to spend some time with Kathleen and her mother in Oxford. It was perfect summer weather and Frank, like so many before and since, found the university city conducive to romance. Just over a fortnight later, while they were both in Cheshire, he invited Kathleen to accompany him on a drive to Chorley Hall, during which he proposed to her. She wrote in her diary that Frank's proposal was "utterly unexpected," which suggests she considered him a friend rather than a suitor. Although looking much younger than her age, Kathleen was now approaching her thirty-first birthday and may already have resigned herself to spinsterhood. A fortnight later, they both visited the Greenways, who had now moved to Hexham in Northumberland, and it was during this brief holiday that Kathleen gave Frank her answer. It was to Emily rather than Frederick that Frank wrote "the momentous letter" about his intentions toward their daughter. He was probably aware that his financial standing would give Frederick an excuse to raise objections to the marriage. Emily would be a vital ally in any future battle, and it made good tactical sense to win her over by taking her into their confidence. It was also arranged for Kathleen to meet Frank's mother, upon whom she made a very favorable impression.

Before the two families exchanged fire, however, a rather more pressing war had broken out in South Africa, and Frank's regiment was put under mobilization orders. Mrs. Isherwood invited Kathleen to stay with her at the Station Hotel in York, so that the young couple could meet before Frank set sail for the Cape. "Mama very unhappy over it and Papa most disapproving," Kathleen wrote in her diary. "So had to give it up, though can see no reason for not going, myself. Felt cross and virtuous."

Cross and virtuous Kathleen may very well have felt, but she was also being rather naïve. The proposed visit seems to have been the first her father had heard of her serious involvement with Frank. He was no doubt affronted that both his wife and Mrs. Isherwood had not only known about it for some time but had already lined up on the side of the young people. Furthermore, a railway hotel lacked respectability as a place for a couple to meet, even when properly chaperoned. Frederick may also have been genuinely concerned for his daughter's welfare: an impecunious young man who was about to sail halfway round the world to fight in a war was hardly an ideal fiancé.

There is one further aspect to Frederick's opposition to a match between Kathleen and Frank, an opposition which became more entrenched as time passed. Although Frederick was undoubtedly an upright Christian gentleman, his income was derived from his wine merchant's business—a rather superior trade, but trade nonetheless. The Isherwoods' income derived from land, and this placed them on a significantly higher rung of the social ladder. It may well be that Frederick, who had been obliged to give up his life as a country gentleman, resented the easy squire's existence enjoyed by Frank's father. However precarious Frank's financial position may have been, his family background was certainly more distinguished than that of Kathleen. At a period where a great deal was made of the most subtle social distinctions, Frederick must have been aware that he was at something of a disadvantage and immediately determined that the Isherwoods were not going to be allowed to dictate terms simply because they owned a large slice of east Cheshire. This would explain not only Frederick's opposition to the match but also the high-handed manner in which he communicated with the Isherwoods.

Frank eventually met Frederick when he came down to London on a night's leave. Frederick would later claim that Frank gave him an undertaking that no engagement would be announced, or even understood, without further consultation. There were to be no more meetings before Frank sailed in mid-December 1899.

During the next seven months, Frank wrote to Kathleen regularly. He saw a great deal of action, survived some fierce battles, and then contracted typhoid, suffering the aftereffects throughout his life. (Isherwood recalled the alarming sight through a half-open door of his father on the lavatory, his face contorted in pain from stomach cramps.) In July 1900 Frank was sent back to England on a hospital ship. His return, so keenly anticipated, was somewhat muted. Given their equivocal status as a couple, Frank spent much of his time with his own family and Kathleen felt rather neglected. Emily, vying for attention, developed the unusual ailment of "throat-gout." Frederick seemed disinclined to alter his position, blandly pretending that nothing was going on between his daughter and young Isherwood, thus earning himself a nickname: "The Ignorer."

Frank's attempts to negotiate with Frederick merely served to harden the latter's opposition to the match. Obliged to come up with some concrete objections, Frederick opened up on two fronts. The first was that he thought Frank had behaved dishonorably in continuing to correspond with Kathleen as if they were engaged after he had given assurances that he would not do so. This no doubt made Frederick feel a lot better, but his behavior had been so unreasonable that no one could honestly blame Frank for not keeping his word. More seriously, he demanded certain assurances about Frank's financial prospects. Much of this was sheer bluff, since Kathleen was of an age where she did not need her father's consent to marry—although she would dearly have liked his blessing, as Frederick very well knew. Frederick would probably have made similar objections to any man who wanted to take away his daughter, but questions of honor and finance had to be taken seriously. He refused to meet Frank, preferring to communicate by unpleasantly terse letters.

The Isherwoods, meanwhile, did their best to accommodate Frederick's demands, which were a marriage settlement, somewhere for the couple to live, and a reasonable income. What Frank could offer was a settlement of £200 a year, the loan of Wyberslegh Hall, which remained part of the Marple estate, an income of £300 a year plus allowances, savings of £400, and £65 out of public funds for his service in the war. Wyberslegh Hall, reputed to have been the birthplace of Bradshawe the Regicide, was a substantial manor house, originally built in the fifteenth century, situated on high ground about three miles from Marple Hall above the small village of High Lane. A tenant farmer now occupied the back part of the house, which opened onto a yard and agricultural buildings, while the more gracious front of the house was sublet on short leases. This front part was in need of extensive repairs and alterations, not least to make it properly self-contained. The Isherwoods said they would undertake this expensive work by way of a wedding gift to Frank and his bride, but this offer failed to satisfy Frederick, who wanted an assurance that the couple would receive rent from the house (some £50 a year) should they move, thus ensuring that they would have funds to live elsewhere.

John Isherwood had only a life interest in the estate, and this meant that any provisions for the future had to be approved by his successor, Henry, who took his duties as heir very lightly indeed and seemed disinclined to help. Henry spent much of his time abroad, mostly in Italy, where he whiled away his time in the company of young men. Although Kathleen almost certainly knew nothing of Henry's foreign diversions, she disliked and disapproved of him. For one thing, he had converted to Roman Catholicism, and had even briefly entered a monastery. Kathleen had an ingrained prejudice against Catholics, which was not unusual for the time and was to some extent shared by the Isherwoods. "A pretty state of affairs—Henry worshipping the Virgin Mary!" John had exclaimed when his son was received into the Church by one of its most distinguished divines, Cardinal Vaughan of Westminster. The most disagreeable thing about Henry, however, was his complacency, emphasized by his drawling upper-class voice in which the final "g" of such words as huntin', shootin', fishin' and amusin' was fashionably dropped. It would have seemed "monstrously unfair" (to use one of Kathleen's favorite expressions) that Henry led such a life of ease, while Frank had spent his formative years in the army, had risked his life for his country in the Boer War, and was now prevented from marrying because his older brother would not guarantee him sufficient funds. Frank was unwilling to push Henry too far, and this led to his quarreling with Kathleen, as Frederick no doubt intended it should.

Before Frank returned to South Africa, in February 1901, he had gone for an interview with a colonel in the Volunteers. If he was to marry, he did not want to spend his time in dreary garrison towns, and was seeking the post of adjutant to the 4th Battalion of the Cheshire Regiment, which was conveniently based in Stockport, the nearest large town to Wyberslegh. By the time he returned to England in May 1902, he had been promoted to captain and his appointment as adjutant had been confirmed.

In the summer of 1901, Kathleen's father had undergone an operation on his bladder, probably to remove some sort of constriction or blockage. His convalescence was long and disheartening, and he was to spend much of his time in and out of nursing homes and undergoing further surgical treatment. The wound from the incision appears not to have healed properly and, for the rest of Frederick's life, was subject to reinfection. This must have been painful, debilitating and humiliating, and it certainly did nothing to improve the old man's temper. Cheering progress in his condition was invariably followed by depressing relapses, and Frederick vented much of his frustration upon Frank.

The battle, however, was almost over. Henry finally agreed that Frank, or his widow and children, should have Wyberslegh, or receive the £50 a year rent if they moved, until the deaths of Kathleen's parents. In the event of Frank's death, the marriage settlement of £200 a year would be paid to Kathleen and their children. His conditions met, Frederick was obliged to bow to the inevitable, though he did so with astonishingly ill grace.

Frank and Kathleen were married from Nether Hall on March 17, 1903. After much sulking and grumbling, Frederick finally consented to attend his daughter's wedding and was at the church to give her away. (Kathleen later claimed that he gave in only because she had threatened to enlist her uncle, Sir Walter Greene, in his place.) The couple spent a brief honeymoon in Cambridge, where they were joined by Kathleen's mother, before traveling to High Lane in order to take possession of Wyberslegh Hall.

Although Kathleen spent less than seven years of her married life at Wyberslegh, in subsequent wanderings the house would always be the place she thought of as her spiritual home. She even claimed that she had "seen" the house before, as if in a dream. It was the oldest house she ever inhabited, and the most beautiful. It stood on a ridge in a narrow lane, and was reached by a small garden gate, which opened onto a path through rhododendrons leading to the front door. The garden was modest in size, but beyond it were open fields, and from its commanding position one could see for miles across the Cheshire Plain. Directly beneath, Stockport was spreading out, its old center marked by the thin, dark spire of St. George's, where someone had written the word "traitor" opposite Bradshawe the Regicide's name in the parish records. Isherwood described this view as "a wilderness of houses, of endless suburbs opening into each other," an "industrial wilderness" of "great, tall smoke-stacks, the factory chimneys, pouring out great manes of black smoke across the sky." The house itself seemed quite small from the outside, with two projecting bays on either side topped by stepped gables known locally as crowsteps. The central block also had crenellations which gave the house the air of a toy fort. The front door, with its lion's-head knocker, opened into a hall, from which a curved staircase led to the upper story. On the ground floor were a parlor, a drawing room and a dining room, with a kitchen area (a later addition) in the rear. On the top floor were two large bedrooms, one in each bay, separated by a corridor running along the front of the house, off which were spare rooms, a linen room, a bathroom and a lavatory. At the end of the corridor, above the kitchen, was modest accommodation for servants, and a back staircase led directly down into their domestic domain. The kitchen door, set in the red-brick Victorian extension, opened onto the farmyard, thus clearly defining the spheres of gentry, employees and tenants. In some ways the farm had the better outlook, across a completely unspoiled landscape to a romantic North Country ridge, Cobden Edge, and Derbyshire's wild Peak District beyond. This view could, however, be appreciated from the main house's upstairs back windows. Keenly mythologizing, Isherwood claimed that the contrasting scenes visible from the house, "England's green and pleasant land" on one side and "dark satanic mills" on the other, "were very, very much part of my early life." They provided "two views of life—and a reminder that both existed," which was quite a lot to absorb for a child who spent only his first three and a half years there.

While Kathleen's affection for Wyberslegh was bound up with the joy of being newly married, her feelings about Marple Hall owed more to the importance she attached to history. Here was a genuine ancestral home, occupied by the same family for many generations and handed down the line to the present day. Kathleen's sense of the past had much to do with her notion of historical continuity, and this had been provided by the Bradshaw-Isherwoods. She was also someone who appreciated fine objects, and she put together a portfolio of photographs, sketches and watercolors—by herself and Frank—depicting the Hall and cataloguing its contents. It seems likely that this portfolio was a by-product of the family history Kathleen compiled between about 1906 and 1918 for her first son. By this time, Kathleen's position in the family had altered considerably.

TWO

A FTER A PROTRACTED AND PAINFUL LABOR LASTING ALMOST eighteen hours, Kathleen gave birth to Christopher Isherwood at 11:45 p.m. on Friday, August 26, 1904. He was the first of John and Elizabeth Isherwood's grandchildren, and had missed sharing his birthday with his grandfather by a mere fifteen minutes. Kathleen was someone who took note of any sort of anniversary and set great store by propitious or coincidental dates, a superstition Isherwood himself was to share. She managed to convince herself, and everyone else, that Christopher's "real" birthday was August 27, on the grounds that he had "only a quarter of an hour's existence on the 26th and that was only from the merciful intervention of the doctors!" In other words, had nature been allowed to take its painful course, the birth would undoubtedly have taken place the following day. Even after John Isherwood's death, Kathleen continued to celebrate Christopher's birthday a day late, and it was not until he emigrated to America in 1939 that she acknowledged August 26 as the proper date. Isherwood himself, who had a great deal more in common with his mother than he ever cared to admit, subsequently claimed that he "later welcomed the change, because of the rhyme: Friday's child is full of woe, Saturday's child has far to go. For the 27th had been a Saturday, and who wants to be full of woe? Christopher began very early to dream of travel." If true, this would be neat, but the usual version of the anonymous rhyme proclaims that "Friday's child is loving and giving, Saturday's child works hard for his living" (woe and travel belonging to Wednesday and Thursday respectively).

Prompted partly by maternal pride, but also by a sense of historical destiny, Kathleen began compiling a manuscript book, illustrated with decorative borders, drawings and photographs, tracing the early years of her son. What she designated "The Babys Progress" (without the apostrophe) was recorded in great detail, from the cutting of his first tooth in April 1905 to the publication of his first novel in May 1928. Physical details were observed and noted: "COLOUR OF HAIR fair & soft and very little of it—! COLOUR OF EYES greyish, but inclined to hazel, & a decided brown patch in the right eye—at nine months old, the hazel look entirely disappeared, & became a clear grey-blue, with still a small light brown patch in the right one—!" Christopher's development was carefully monitored: height, weight, chest and circumference of head. "That our sons may grow up as the young plants," Kathleen wrote optimistically at the head of the height chart, quoting Psalm CXLIV. By the time she came to record his weight, however, it must have become apparent that her young plant was not going to shoot up very tall, and so she turned to Ben Jonson:

> It is not growing like a tree
> In bulk, doth make Man better be;
> In small proportions we just beauties see;
>   And in short measures life may perfect be.

Isherwood eventually grew to be a mere five feet eight, and was somewhat disproportionate, with a large head, and legs too short for the length of his torso.

The baby was christened on September 27 in Disley, the neighboring village to High Lane, at St. Mary's church, a Victorian building distinguished by an unusual and attractive cupola. Considering the dynastic importance of this occasion, the ceremony was very sparsely attended: Kathleen and Frank, the baby's nurse, John and Elizabeth Isherwood and Emily Machell-Smith. Frederick had entirely dissociated himself from his grandson's birth: "I hear [. . .] Mrs. Isherwood and child are doing well. It must be a relief to you," he wrote sourly to his wife—and he boycotted the christening. As godparents, Frank and Kathleen had chosen Colonel Alexander Kearsey, one of Frank's fellow officers with whom he had served in South Africa; Kathleen's favorite first cousin, Agatha Greene; and Henry Isherwood. Although all of them were to prove conscientious in later years, none of them attended the service. The appointment of Henry was tactical rather than heartfelt. Kathleen was evidently willing to put her son's future prospects before her personal feelings—though not to the point of choosing "Henry" as one of the child's names. "Christopher" was almost certainly chosen because Kathleen liked the name, although she managed to dredge up a Machell great-uncle called Christopher in order to justify her choice. "William" is a name that occurs frequently on the Bradshaw family tree and was also the name of Frank's friend William Bradshaw (no relation), who was killed during the Boer War. During his infancy, Isherwood was often called "William" and referred to in Kathleen's diary as "C.W." Frank persisted in occasionally referring to his son as "William" up until 1914. Isherwood was also christened Bradshaw, though Kathleen insisted upon treating this as a family name and joining it to "Isherwood" by a hyphen; even his initials were often rendered "C.W.B-I." A bookplate almost certainly designed by Kathleen, which depicted the front of Wyberslegh Hall flanked by two trees, rendered him as "C.W.B-Isherwood."

Most of the family had been christened in Marple or at St. George's, Stockport. Marple Old Church, an attractive Georgian building where the Isherwood family pews had their own fireplace, was no longer in use since it could not accommodate the burgeoning local population. Christopher was the first member of the family to have been christened at Disley since 1655, and the church was probably chosen because it was the local one for Wyberslegh Hall. "C.W. protested slightly, as is required of all orthodox babies, and behaved very well—" Kathleen wrote in her diary, "and the day ranks amongst the days of great Events."

The nurse had been hired to attend Kathleen only during her confinement and it now became necessary to find a proper nanny. There seems never to have been any suggestion that an old Isherwood nanny should be brought out of retirement to oversee the new generation, as is customary among the upper classes. Perhaps there wasn't one. Kathleen appears once again to have asserted her independence, since the young woman she eventually employed was not local but came from Kathleen's home town of Bury St Edmunds. To Kathleen, the thirty-year-old Annie Avis would always be "Nurse," even long after her duties in the nursery had ended. To Isherwood, she was beloved "Nanny," his friend, confidante and protector. In her turn Nanny clearly adored her young charge—a circumstance of which he was to take full advantage. The portrait of her he provided many years later in *Kathleen and Frank* is lively but not entirely believable. It certainly bears little relation to the recollections of his brother, Richard, who spent far more time in her charge than Isherwood ever did. It is the natural privilege of the firstborn to be the favorite, particularly when he is seen as the young heir. "Master Christopher" knew precisely how to handle Nanny and exploit her affection for him.

The mutual devotion of Nanny and her charge could be very trying for everyone else. Particularly to be dreaded was Nanny's brief yearly holiday: "Nurse went off a little before 9," Kathleen recorded in July 1906. "She and C both in tears—the latter howled . . . However we got through the day better than might have been expected . . . He retired to bed very swollen about the eyes soon after six and had a good night, tired out." Nanny's return could be equally traumatic: "Poor C quite overwhelmed, did not recognize her at first in her holiday attire and felt it was too much to have another nurse imposed on him!—simply yelled. But when he became calmer, seemed very pleased to have her back."

Although Kathleen was a doting mother, circumstances frequently parted her from her son. In the custom of the time, she and Frank would pay visits to friends or take trips abroad unencumbered by their child. Furthermore, Frank's career in the military made for a somewhat peripatetic life, involving prolonged and frequent domestic upheaval as new postings came through and new accommodation had to be found. What was less usual, and particular to Kathleen, was her relationship with her mother, who lived up to the pet name she gave to herself: "Baby Mama." She continued to make huge demands on her daughter's time, and Frank must have been very patient to put up with Kathleen's regular absences to dance attendance on the old woman.

By the time Christopher was born, Grandfather Frederick's health was failing badly. The lowering atmosphere of the sickroom told upon Emily—who relished only her own illnesses—and in June 1905 she entrusted Frederick to the care of her sister Julia at Berkhamsted (where Julia's husband, Charles Fry, was headmaster), and joined Kathleen, Christopher and Nanny at Penmaenmawr, a small seaside town in Colwyn Bay, North Wales, where they would often spend summer holidays. After ten days she received what Kathleen described as a "very worrying and aggravating" letter from Julia, summoning her back to take charge of her husband, who was not expected to live many months. Kathleen suspected that Aunt Julia had simply found the burden of nursing too time-consuming. "She also suggests that M ought to do everything she can 'to make his last days happy' which I call exceedingly imperti-nent," Kathleen reported furiously in her diary. The entire family was obliged to leave Penmaenmawr, "C.W. taking farewell of several admirers on the station"—a scene that would be echoed frequently in Isherwood's adult years. Frederick's condi-tion seemed little worse, but at the end of October Kathleen returned from a month's holiday with Frank in Spain to find her father in terminal decline, and he died on No-vember 19.

Even after death, Frederick exerted a malign power. At one point during Kathleen and Frank's long courtship, he had cut his daughter out of his will in favor of some cousins. Although, toward the end, he stated his intention to change the will back again, he never did so, which meant that the money he left to Emily for her lifetime would not now go to Kathleen on her mother's death. Attempts to negotiate with the cousins were unsuccessful. "They are evidently aware they are behaving badly," Kathleen wrote, "and one thing is, it would have been hateful to have it returned in any other spirit than as my right and I need not have anything further to do with them now. They were so good as to say they might 'reconsider the matter if I am left badly provided for'—Thank heaven I needn't descend to that!" Emily, meanwhile, left Cranley Mansions, the home she had shared with Frederick in Gloucester Road, for a smaller flat at the top of a house at 14 Buckingham Street, just off the Strand, and for the next few years this was Kathleen's London base.

Kathleen's home, however, remained Wyberslegh. There were regular visits to Marple Hall, where Christopher was frequently photographed with his Isherwood grandparents, most particularly on the "joint" birthday. Even decked out in the lacy frocks and bonnets of Edwardian childhood summers, he strikes a confident figure. As he grew, his clothes (many of them made by Nanny) became more masculine in cut, but none the less extravagant. An astonishing costume he wore at the age of three consisted of a white frock coat with a vast astrakhan collar and deep cuffs, white socks and pumps, and an astrakhan hat with a cockade. It might have been made for a Ruritanian princeling in some long-forgotten operetta. Kathleen noted that he took "a great interest in his clothes, and insists on looking at himself in the glass when he has anything new on." At the age of twenty-two months, this miniature dandy "very loudly protested he didn't like 'them darty [i.e. dirty] shoes' " when Kathleen brought him some brown shoes instead of white ones.

By the time he was two, Christopher had become quite articulate, and could "string together quite long sentences saying each word very carefully and distinctly," Kathleen recorded. "His vocabulary very varied and large, can say little verses of four lines and knows the ending to each line of every nursery rhyme he possesses." Isherwood suspected that Kathleen had underlined the observation about his vocab-ulary many years later, when he had become a writer. She had also underlined the ob-servation: "Will look at books for hours and likes being read to," and added: "All through his childhood he never seemed at a loss for words and was generally rather happy in his choice of words to best express his meaning." This may have been writ-ten after the event, but it is almost certainly true. Kathleen encouraged his interest in books and writing from an early age.

One of the key writers of Isherwood's childhood was Beatrix Potter. He almost literally grew up with Potter's series of *Tales,* which started publication two years before he was born and continued at a steady rate throughout his childhood. The creatures in Potter's stories may talk and wear pinafores and poke-bonnets, but they remain true to their (not always admirable) animal natures. Potter recounts their adventures with a dry and sometimes savage humor and illustrated the books with exquisite watercolors depicting a countryside—in fact, largely the Lake District—which would have seemed very familiar to a child growing up in the north of England. Isherwood felt that the old house in which Mr. Samuel Whiskers and his wife Anna Maria (a pair of rats) kidnap the unfortunate Tom Kitten and attempt to turn him into a roly-poly pudding bore a strong resemblance to Marple Hall, with its nooks, crannies, dark passageways, shadowy corners and sinister scufflings behind the wainscoting. Potter was a sophisticated writer, who once told her publisher when he objected to the use of "conversed": "children like a fine word occasionally." In *The Tale of the Flopsy Bunnies* (1909), lettuces are described as "soporific," and reading these stories no doubt contributed to Isherwood's rapidly growing vocabulary.

He also enjoyed the fairy stories of Hans Christian Andersen and, later on, W. Harrison Ainsworth's *The Tower of London* (1840), a colorful account of the imprisonment and death of Lady Jane Grey which introduced generations of English children to English history, and the works of Charles Dickens, of which *Oliver Twist* was his favorite. Isherwood discovered most of these books, along with the works of John Buchan and Sir Walter Scott, in the company of his mother, who enjoyed reading as a companionable occupation: as soon as Christopher was old enough, mother and son took turns reading books aloud to each other.

For the first seven years of his life Isherwood was an only child, subject to the privileges and privations of this position. As with most children, his friends were found among the offspring of his parents' acquaintances, and that meant the children of "gentlemen." One of the Isherwoods' neighbors recalled that Disley was "a bit feudal." Most of the inhabitants were the tenants of Lord Newton of Lyme Hall, but there were also a number of "gentlemen's residences." The gentlemen played the villagers in local cricket matches, but did not mix socially. One family the Isherwoods got to know well were the Monkhouses, who lived at Meadow Bank, a house on a ridge above the village. Allan Monkhouse was a journalist on the *Manchester Guardian,* where he had started out as a cotton correspondent, subsequently becoming theater critic and literary editor. He also wrote several novels, and was the first professional writer Isherwood ever met. His first wife had died shortly after their marriage, but at the age of forty he married a woman almost half his age, who was an accomplished musician and painter. Allan Monkhouse's unmarried sister, Florence, who was a professional artist, also lived in the village, and these were just the sort of cultured people Kathleen and Frank liked. Allan and Dorothy Monkhouse had four children: the eldest, Patrick (Paddy), was born five months before Christopher, and was followed by Rachel two years later, then Johnny in 1908 and Elizabeth in 1912.

Paddy and Rachel attended Christmas tea parties at Wyberslegh, along with three children named Coyne, the sons of the gardener at Marple. It is a curious aspect of the British class system that, in the countryside at any rate, children were allowed to cross the social divide. While it was perfectly acceptable for Christopher to play with the gardener's children, and even invite them to tea, it would have been inconceivable for the two sets of parents to have mixed socially. Few other friends are mentioned in Kathleen's diaries at this period, perhaps partly because Christopher was inclined to misbehave. "Mrs. Singleton's little girl came to tea with Christopher," Kathleen noted shortly after Christmas 1906. "I grieve to say he slapped her." None of these children appear in Isherwood's early literary production, *The History of My Friends,* begun around 1912. By this time, the Isherwoods had long since moved from Wyberslegh, and the unsettled nature of their lives must have meant that childhood friendships were difficult to maintain. Marple Hall remained a base, however, and the Monkhouses would continue to figure in Isherwood's life. In particular, Isherwood maintained a close friendship with Paddy, who was a regular correspondent during their years at school and university, and became his confidant for a while.

As a small child, Christopher got on better with adults, flirting outrageously with his parents' friends and neighbors. "Miss Monkhouse to tea and C.W. made up to her tremendously, put his head on one side and made such eyes!" In a rather more restrained fashion, this is what Isherwood continued to do throughout his life, making almost anyone he encountered imagine that they were his special, favored friend. Indulgent grandparents did little to curb his excesses, and Grandpa Isherwood delightedly reported that on a train journey he had paid to upgrade a third-class railway ticket to first class "because Christopher didn't like travelling in an ordinary carriage with no carpet."

Grandpa and Granny Isherwood were by this time a rather frail old couple. John had suffered a stroke in his forties, which left him slightly disabled. His mouth was lopsided and he was inclined to dribble. His management of the Marple Hall estate was extremely lax, and its steep decline really began with him. ("Considering Father, it's remarkable we're not all congenital idiots," Jack exclaimed in exasperation one day after trying to sort out the family finances.) Idle and extravagant, John was a rather remote figure, who liked best driving around Marple village, very much the country squire. Isherwood later claimed that the local people were respectful to his grandfather's face, but despised him behind his back, regarding him as "an obsolete masquerader in a moth-eaten pageant." This is almost certainly untrue. As Richard Isherwood observed: "Marple was too stagnant and unprogressive for that." In any case, Squire Isherwood was an amiable figure, chiefly interested in cricket, which he would travel to Manchester to watch. Over the years he grew increasingly vague: he often left his fly-buttons open and once managed to set fire to his newspaper in the Members' Enclosure at Old Trafford. In spite of this, if one can judge public opinion by the local press, the Isherwoods were treated with positively fawning respect and the *Cheshire Herald* kept its readers well informed about the family's life. For example, during the First World War, when Mrs. Isherwood's brother, Captain John Luce RN, of the *Glasgow,* sank a German cruiser, the newspaper announced: "We have again the pleasurable opportunity of offering congratulations to the revered family at Marple Hall for the glorious part another member of the family has played in the war."

If anything, Elizabeth Isherwood was even further removed from everyday life than her husband. She had poor health and in photographs presents a tiny, wizened figure. Isherwood remembered her as a wraithlike presence wandering around the house muttering to herself. She nevertheless continued to perform public duties as the squire's wife, events Kathleen dutifully but not altogether respectfully recorded in her diary. On one occasion Kathleen accompanied her parents-in-law "up to the Technical School by the Canal where a presentation of a stamped leather hand-bag was to be made by Mrs Isherwood (from her & members of the Nursery Committee) to the secretary Mrs Beeley who is retiring and leaving Marple. Mrs Isherwood did it very graciously & sweetly, the more wonderful that she had no idea which was Mrs Beeley, or why she was having a present, & had forgotten the whole proceeding's before we were home."

Kathleen may have mocked her in-laws, but she still believed in what they represented, and as Christopher's second birthday approached she started compiling a "History of Marple Hall," handwritten and illustrated with her own sketches. A single page of this document survives, and it concerns one of the legends about the Hall's inhabitants. Like many ancient houses in Britain, Marple was supposed to be haunted. Naturally enough, one of Marple's ghosts was connected with the family's dark history, and was said to walk the upstairs corridor past the room where Judge Bradshawe was supposed to have slept. Like all self-respecting ghosts, it was headless and was celebrated in an old lay. Another ghost was supposed to take the form of Esther Bradshawe, the only daughter of the judge's brother Henry. According to the legend, Esther's soldier lover had been drowned in the Mere Pool, after which she went mad and spent the rest of her life—and indeed her afterlife—wandering disconsolately beside the river playing a lute. The discovery of a cavalier helmet and pair of spurs when the Pool was drained early in the nineteenth century appeared to authenticate this story, but in fact Henry Bradshawe had two daughters, neither of whom was named Esther.

Marple Hall did however lay claim to one restless spirit whose existence was vouched for by both Isherwood and his brother. This was Nathaniel Isherwood's wife, Moll of Brabyns, whose portrait hung on the front staircase at Marple Hall. Nathaniel had died within a year of their marriage, and since he and Moll had no children, the estate passed to his younger brother. Moll was obliged to leave her new home and move back to her father's house, Brabyns Hall. Although she subsequently remarried, she was so disgruntled to be ousted from Marple that her spirit was to be seen wandering round the Hall, apparently looking for her wedding ring. This last detail was probably no more than a bit of embroidery and came about because in her portrait Moll wears no wedding band—though the painting presumably predated her brief marriage. Moll was also believed to have a particular dislike of children, all of whom she regarded as potential usurpers.

Although this story sounds as fanciful as the one about "Esther Bradshawe," Moll's ghost had been observed by two of Isherwood's great-great-aunts while they were in their teens. The servants all fervently believed in Moll's ghost, claiming that strange noises were heard whenever her portrait was taken down from its commanding position during the annual spring cleaning. In the summer of 1907, Kathleen had difficulty persuading the maids to remove the painting to the drawing room so that she could make a pencil sketch of it, an action that apparently resulted in more inexplicable noises. A month or so later, Christopher and Nanny went to spend a week at Marple while Kathleen and Frank were on a sketching holiday in Oxford. During their first night in the old nursery at the top of the house, Christopher woke up Nanny to tell her that a "muzzy old woman" was sitting at the end of his bed. He did not seem frightened, but complained: "I don't like her, Nanny, no I don't." Nanny could see nothing, but she was certain that Christopher was not imagining things, and claimed that she "felt conscious of a third presence in the room," and heard peculiar noises. The same thing happened every night during their visit, with Christopher supplying details of the figure's appearance, and describing its movements as it left the room by the window or door. The fact that he was not frightened may explain why he and Nanny did not move out of the nursery to sleep in another room.

Kathleen recorded these events, as told to her by Nanny, in her diary, without saying whether or not she believed in the ghost; she noted, however, that "Frank thinks there is no doubt Christopher saw her." In Isherwood's own account, written in the late 1960s, he relies entirely upon Kathleen's diary to tell this story and states that he "is now inclined to believe that he did see *something*," which suggests that he did not actually remember the experience. It is perfectly possible that "an imaginative precocious child," as Isherwood described himself, could have concocted this story from what he knew of the legends surrounding Moll. He spent a great deal of time in the company of the Marple Hall housemaids while they went about their duties, and would no doubt have heard about the recent "disturbances" after Moll's portrait had been moved.

In later years Isherwood lived in other houses that were "haunted": not ancient family seats, but a New York apartment and a small house in Santa Monica, where a "ghost" was seen not by him but by one of his houseguests. His mother was thought by others to be psychic, though Kathleen herself was inclined to dismiss the idea. And then there are the genuinely mysterious events which took place at Marple a few months after the "appearance" of Moll. Toward the end of October 1907, Kathleen and Frank took a month's holiday in Spain and once again Nanny and Christopher went to stay at Marple. In spite of their previous experience, they were placed in the nursery. What happened on the night of October 29 remains inexplicable.

Christopher had been put to bed in his high-sided cot, as usual, with a night-light burning, and Nanny had gone downstairs to the servants' hall to have her supper, having first asked one of the maids to listen out in case the child woke up and cried. This maid came downstairs shortly after Nanny had finished her supper and reported that all was quiet in the nursery. Just then a strange noise was heard on the terrace outside the servants' hall—"a sort of shuffling and deep sighing." Almost immediately Christopher's voice was heard calling for Nanny, who went to the door leading to an anteroom, where she found her charge standing barefoot in his nightshirt. He wasn't in the least bit cold or alarmed and said that he was ready to go back to bed. When asked how he came to be standing outside the servants' hall, he replied that his father had taken him out of bed and carried him downstairs. Nanny took the little boy back up to the nursery, where she discovered that the main light was on and the door jammed shut. Frightened now, they made their way downstairs again, meeting Grandpa Isherwood on his way up. When they told him what had happened, he went in search of Jack, who was staying at the Hall and was discovered in the drawing room playing the piano to his mother. Jack went up to the nursery and managed to force open the door. He discovered that a chair had been wedged between the door and a chest of drawers. The sides of the cot had been let down. He searched two large cupboards in the room but found nothing.

It would have been impossible to have rearranged the furniture from outside the room, and the only means of escape from the inside was through the windows, which were mullioned. Even had an adult managed to squeeze through the narrow windows, he or she would have had to climb down the side of the house, a precarious descent with only ivy for support. The intruder would also have had to gain a nervous three-year-old's trust or complicity, and got back up to the top floor of the house, moved the furniture and escaped through the window in a very short time indeed. Everyone thought that some sort of supernatural agency had been involved. Jack suggested that

> whatever it was that carried Christopher down, put on a semblance of Frank in order that the child might not be frightened, and that his guardian angel, if such it was, had removed him from the room because there was some influence in it harmful to him . . . and that the episode of the door, and the lights and the cot were done to enhance the fact and to insure notice being taken of it.

In recalling events, Nanny said that when she had opened the door to the servants' hall and found Christopher standing there, she was aware of something just behind him which immediately disappeared. She also thought she may have seen a shadow moving against the light in the nursery when she went up to return Christopher to bed, but both these claims were sufficiently vague to suggest an element of auto-suggestion, or elaboration after the facts.

Isherwood could never explain what had happened, and had no recollection whatever of his adventure. A hoax would have been physically impossible. It would also have been pointless. He adds, however, that "It was Kathleen who chose, without any evidence, to connect Moll of Brabyns with October 29—perhaps because she felt an instinctive need to give meaning to the apparently meaningless."

There may have been another explanation for dragging Moll into the story in view of this ancestor's dislike of usurping children. Shortly before she went on her trip to Spain, Kathleen, who would one day, she supposed, live at Marple Hall when Frank or Christopher inherited it from Henry, found herself in a position similar to Moll's. To everyone's astonishment, Henry announced that he had become engaged. The luckless bride was Muriel Bagshawe, an heiress whose properties would bring in £5,000 per annum. As well as being wealthy, Muriel lived in Knightsbridge, "opposite the barracks and very central," as Kathleen noted after visiting her. This would prove very convenient for Henry, who liked to avail himself of the sexual services traditionally offered by the guardsmen who were stationed there. The couple, who would by Royal Licence assume the preposterous triple-barreled surname of Bradshaw-

Isherwood-Bagshawe, had met some time before, and may even have entered upon an understanding, but the announcement of their impending marriage took everyone by surprise.

The implications of this union were of course deeply disturbing. If Henry and Muriel had a son, then Marple Hall and its entire estate would pass not to Christopher but to his new cousin. Henry's sexual preference may have been for soldiers and young Italians, but this did not necessarily preclude more orthodox couplings for dynastic purposes. Like Moll's before her, Kathleen's dreams of living at Marple seemed to be under threat. Worse still, she was suddenly faced with the prospect of leaving Wyberslegh Hall. Frank, who had been bicycling every day to and from Stockport to carry out his duties as adjutant of the 4th Volunteer Battalion of the Cheshire Regiment, was ordered to rejoin his regiment at York. Kathleen, who never saw herself as an army wife, was very keen that Frank should leave the force altogether and get a job as a constable. To secure a proper pension, however, Frank needed to remain in the army until his fifteen years' service was up. An application to join the Devon Constabulary was rejected, which meant Frank was doomed to return to the regular army when his appointment as adjutant came to an end. He and Kathleen had to resign themselves to leaving Wyberslegh and finding new accommodations near the barracks.

On February 29, 1908, in heavy snow, the family left Wyberslegh Hall for "The Cottage" in Strenshall, a village just outside York. Nothing about the new house pleased Kathleen, and she spent much of her time complaining to her diary about it, comparing it with beloved Wyberslegh. It was not only the house that she hated: the whole village, its surrounding landscape and the climate all depressed her. "Eight weeks have gone since we came here," she recorded toward the end of April. "It feels like eight months." She described the village as "a most deadly little hole" and complained of the smell of a nearby tannery.

Fortunately, this posting was temporary and after eight months the Isherwoods moved to the garrison town of Aldershot on the Hampshire-Surrey border. This meant yet another upheaval, but anything was preferable to staying at Strenshall, particularly since their new house, Frimley Lodge, soon looked "so nice and homelike and oldfashioned, quite unlike a soldier's house!!" It was not, however, Wyberslegh, and any hope of returning there, even in the distant future, had received yet another setback. Frank and Kathleen discovered that Henry and Muriel's marriage settlement allowed for the Marple Hall estate to pass to a daughter as well as a son. The explanation offered for this change of plan was that Muriel's own property could descend through a male or female line and so it had become necessary to bring Henry's side of the family in line with this. Henry promised that in the event of his producing an heir, they would "make it up to Christopher if he required it and opportunity was given us."

Family holidays were spent—with or without Mama—usually at Penmaenmawr or at Ventnor on the Isle of Wight, and there were regular visits to Marple, where Kathleen was careful not to take walks in the vicinity of the newly tenanted Wyberslegh. Whenever possible, she and Frank escaped on sketching holidays or to London and the theaters, not that she always enjoyed the plays they saw, as her tart assessment of Masefield's verse drama, *The Tragedy of Nan,* shows: "Lilah McCarthy very good but a dismal play in which she murders her lover one's only regret being she did not murder the aunt as well—all in Devonshire dialect." All too often, carefully planned excursions were ruined by unexpected army orders. Kathleen was furious when Frank's Derby Leave was canceled at the last moment, thus preventing a sketching excursion to Winchester. "You can never make a single plan in the Army without having it upset," she complained, "and never can be sure of anything—indeed that is the only thing you can be sure of." Worse still, in February 1910 came "the astounding and most unwelcome news" that the regiment was "to move to Woking for a year" in the autumn. After inspecting some "most depressing villas" beside the railway line, she declared Woking a "detestable jerry built hole." In the event, the regiment stayed where it was, and so it was in Frimley Lodge that Frank and Kathleen's second child was born.

Kathleen's second pregnancy was almost certainly unplanned. She was now forty-two, and so the risk of things going wrong had increased considerably since the birth of her first child. Although she barely mentions her pregnancy in her diaries, it is evident that it was not easy. Some six weeks after conception she complained that she had felt "very seedy" all month "& quite sick of it, & being so depressed." The first explicit reference to her condition comes in June 1911 when she went to see the doctor. "From various tappings, and soundings, he concludes all is as it should be and the inmate indubitably alive . . . said medicines should be able to prevent the much greater nervousness I feel this time." She decided that "the gloom of a gloomy Sunday in Frimley is unspeakable!" and so in July accompanied her mother to Littlehampton for a fortnight. The South Coast town turned out to be "the ugliest seaside I have been to since I married!," and further despondency was caused by the announcement that the regiment was moving to Limerick in Ireland at precisely the time Kathleen's baby was due. Frank applied for leave in order to delay the move to Ireland until after the baby's birth, but this was refused. He had been gazetted as major in May and his commanding officer insisted that he needed someone of that rank to help him settle the regiment into its new barracks. Frank felt that the only option left to him was to resign from the regiment. The army, however, refused to accept his resignation unless he agreed to serve in the part-time militia for a further five years. This would have made it almost impossible for him to do a full-time civilian job and support his family, and he eventually decided that he would have to remain in the army and go to Ireland. In the event, the posting was delayed until the end of November.

Having resigned herself to bearing another child, Kathleen hoped that she might have a daughter. The first week of September was the hottest on record and she was extremely uncomfortable, but finally, on Sunday, October 1, at 1:15 a.m. she gave birth to a boy. "Rather a disappointment that it was not the longed-for daughter," Kathleen noted, "however Frank prefers sons." Kathleen may often have complained about life, but she usually came round to accepting things she could do nothing about. Although the baby was rather spotty, he had his father's "innocent" pale blue eyes, and within days Kathleen was writing: "I begin to think how much nicer a son is than a daughter, who would probably have been very modern and not what I like!" Richard Graham Bradshaw-Isherwood turned out to be not at all modern in his manner or outlook, and in many ways he would fill the role in his mother's life traditionally more suited to that of a daughter.

Unsurprisingly, Christopher, who was happily accustomed to being an only child, had somewhat equivocal feelings about his new brother. "Poor C rather hurt in his mind thinking R was receiving more attention than himself," Kathleen noted shortly after Richard's birth. He asserted his independence by coming home from school unaccompanied, getting "as far as top of hill where Nurse met him rather to his disgust." Christopher's education had begun informally three years earlier at Strenshall, when Kathleen provided rudimentary lessons in the alphabet and counting. By the time he was almost five he had written his first letter, in block capitals and addressed to Nanny. Frank helped him compile a daily nursery newspaper, largely made up of comic strips, called *The Toy-Drawer Times,* and began teaching him French and PE. Drill classes alongside several other little boys were continued at Frimley by a regimental sergeant, and the following May his general education was entrusted to a Mr. Penrose, who was able to report at the end of the first term that "Christopher's natural abilities are excellent, and his marks would have been far higher if his conduct had always equalled his aptitude for learning. He is a good boy, but does not like discipline, and lost many marks by talking at the wrong time. Figures seem to be his weak point; but, with application, he could learn anything." He nevertheless came top of the class, which consisted of five boys.

After Frank's duties at the barracks ended in the late afternoon, he spent time with Christopher, writing illustrated adaptations of the adventure and science-fiction stories of such writers as A. Conan Doyle, A. G. Henty, Alexandre Dumas and H. G. Wells on the backs of the duplicate copies of army papers. For his seventh birthday, Christopher was given a toy theater with elaborate cardboard backdrops and cut-out characters, and the productions he mounted were advertised by posters pinned to the nursery door. Frank showed him how to imitate lightning by blowing resin through a tube into the flame of a candle standing in the wings. Like most children of the period, Christopher had Charles Lamb's *Tales from Shakespeare* read to him, and several of the plays he put on were versions of Shakespearean tragedy reduced to their melodramatic essentials. His version of *Macbeth,* for example, consisted of Duncan's murder, Banquo's ghost and the sleepwalking scene, and lasted all of fifteen minutes. His priggish decision to bowdlerize Lady Macbeth's famous cry to "Out, spot!" made Frank laugh, whereupon Christopher lost his temper and stopped the performance.

Another theatrical performance involved Christopher dressing up as a woman, rather as Frank had done in regimental plays. Christopher, however, was deadly serious, and his play *La Lettre* owed a debt to Sarah Bernhardt, whom he could not have seen but had probably heard about since his Granny Emmy, as Emily was known, was a great fan. Dressed in some of Kathleen's clothes, he made his entrance clutching a letter, opened it, exclaimed, "*Il est mort!,*" and fell to the ground in a dead faint. He once embarrassed Frank by performing the play, unannounced, when the Isherwoods had visitors. Thereafter it was banned.

The relationship between father and son remained close, however, and Christopher trailed around the house after Frank, watching him shave and do his calisthenics. Isherwood later claimed that watching his father exercise in nothing but a pair of underpants was a distinctly erotic experience, but this sounds like a later gloss rather than an actual memory. Frank seems always to have made time for his elder son, and clearly enjoyed his company. Later on, Christopher was given a Box Brownie camera by his Isherwood grandparents, and Frank helped him to take and develop his own snapshots.

Meanwhile, Kathleen was also encouraging Christopher to write, and at around this time, when Christopher was six or seven, he started compiling *The History of My Friends,* "a tiny book, made of cut-down pieces of notepaper fastened together with a pin." It was in fact written by Kathleen, supposedly at Christopher's dictation, but one suspects that, as with several of Isherwood's earliest literary productions, Kathleen's contribution went beyond mere stenography. Some of the *History* sounds authentically childlike, but it also contains some decidedly adult turns of phrase. Of Arthur Forbes, whom Isherwood met when he was five, he writes: "When we went for a walk we generally had fights, because he used to find all sorts of grublets and sticks that I wanted. He routled in the dirt, and always saw them first and then we used to fight when the Nannies weren't looking. Sometimes we played quite nicely and calmly but occasionally we fought. I am afraid the fighting consisted in snatching and tears. . . ." Christopher may have had an advanced vocabulary for his age and been able always to find the right words "to best express his meaning," as Kathleen claimed, but that last observation sounds suspiciously like her own. That said, the young Isherwood developed a talent for literary mimicry, and, brought up principally among adults, he often sounded older than his years.

At the beginning of November 1911 Frank rejoined his regiment in Limerick. Kathleen packed up the Frimley house, then went with the children to Marple Hall for Christmas. On New Year's Day 1912 she joined Frank in Ireland and set about house-hunting. Roden House turned out to be even better than Frimley Lodge, a quaint, cottagey dwelling inhabited until recently by elderly spinster sisters. "There was something very romantic too and unobvious about it all," Kathleen wrote, "and so unlike the regular soldiering house," but the social life was not much of an improvement on that at Frimley. Jack Reid, the son of Frank's cousin, Madgie Reid, was a subaltern in the regiment and recalled that the Isherwoods "pretty much kept themselves to themselves. They were a devoted couple, they had their books and their sketching and their plans for foreign holidays, and [Frank] had his music, and I don't think that either the Regiment or the local society provided much congenial company."

They were shortly joined by Nanny and the two boys. Isherwood said that when his father's regiment marched to church parade every Sunday the Irish, resentful of this army of occupation, would take pot-shots at them from rooftops and that boys in the street would yell "Dirty Protestant!" at him as he passed. It was his first intimation of what it was like to be an outsider, the member of an unpopular minority. His education continued at Miss Mercer's High School for Girls, which despite its name also taught a handful of boys. Isherwood left no record of his experiences at this overwhelmingly female establishment, but Kathleen reported that he soon settled in and seemed to enjoy it, coming top of the class at the end of his first term. The inattention and talkativeness complained about by Mr. Penrose were no longer evident, and in October of that year, Miss Mercer wrote a fulsome letter to Kathleen, which was bound into "The Babys Progress":

> Your boy is a most satisfactory pupil in every way, decidedly clever and original, as well as being attentive. He is so straightforward and reliable that I often think he would make an ideal clergyman. He seems very happy in School, and has a very keen sense of anything amusing, which is a great boon to anyone of his earnest temperament.

The following April, Isherwood was transferred to a small private day school for boys run by a Miss Burns. "We made the change on account of the 'male society,' " Kathleen noted, but nevertheless sent him to dancing classes, which he did not enjoy.

An even bigger change took place in May the following year, when Christopher started as a boarder at St. Edmund's in Hindhead, Surrey, a preparatory school run by Cyril Morgan Brown, whose formidable mother was one of Frank's great-aunts. Kathleen had paid a family visit to the school back in 1909. "Thought the arrangements nice," she noted, "but not favourably impressed with the Morgan Brown manner's . . . !" Indeed, St. Edmund's had not been the obvious or only choice for Christopher, and Kathleen and Frank had inspected several other schools. None of these can have made any sort of impression, since St. Edmund's was chosen even though Isherwood's parents had considerable reservations about it. "Horrified at lunch to see several of the boys playing with their forks and spoons and balancing balls," Kathleen noted after looking the place over. "No one said anything. Still it felt kindly. Cyril Brown rather dreamy." Cyril Morgan Brown may have struck adults as a shambling, ineffectual figure, dressed always in a Norfolk jacket (replaced only when threadbare), but he still carried with him traces of a more impressive past, and was able to strike fear into his pupils. Isherwood recalled that he was "powerfully built, with broad stooping shoulders and a striding, ricketty walk. [. . .] He was extremely flat-footed and strikingly handsome. His grey hair was still wavy and thick. He had a drooping white moustache and bushy eyebrows which he could draw down into a most terrifying frown. He had cold bright rather inhuman eyes, like an old Viking Chief."

St. Edmund's had been founded in Hunstanton on the Norfolk coast in 1874 by Cyril's father, an indigent curate recently down from Oxford. By the early years of the century it had outgrown its original premises, and in September 1907, with Cyril now acting as headmaster, the school moved to an unlovely house called Blencathra, situated on high ground in a densely wooded area of Surrey. The house had been rented out for some time, and the Morgan Browns were shown round it by its last tenant, George Bernard Shaw. While some parents preferred to keep their sons in the bracing atmosphere of coastal Norfolk, and so found new schools for them in the area, twenty-seven pupils moved to Hindhead, which was conveniently situated within an hour's train journey from London. By 1914 the school was thriving and the number of pupils had risen to around seventy.

Although Cyril Morgan Brown's parents had retired, the school was still very much a family business. It was generally put about that Cyril's wife was dead, but she had in fact suffered some sort of breakdown early in their marriage and was incarcerated in an institution. Consequently, Cyril ran the school with his sister, Monica, and his daughter, Rosamira, usually referred to by the boys as "Miss Mona" and "Miss Rosa." Mona, Isherwood recalled, "was weatherbeaten in the English way, with a brown leathery skin. Her way of talking to the boys was dry, good-humoured and on the whole friendly." Rosa was attractive, "well-built, full of energy and fun, with beautiful rich thick hair, which she twisted up on top of her head but on which, it was rumoured, she could sit." Another of Cyril's sisters, "Miss Dora," acted as matron. Morgan Brown was known as "Mr. Cyril" to his face and "Ciddy" behind his back.

The customary preliminaries for a small boy embarking on a boarding-school education were put in motion. The estate carpenter at Marple Hall was commissioned to construct a wooden playbox, in which the young master would keep toys and other personal effects, and Christopher was taken to a studio to be photographed in his new "Etons," the standard school uniform of the period. At the end of April, Kathleen and Christopher returned to England and went to stay with Granny Emmy in Buckingham Street, where they enjoyed "a little London season together": visits to Madame Tussaud's, Regent's Park Zoo, the Natural History Museum, Westminster Abbey, Maskelyne and Devant's Mysteries in Regent Street and aerobatics at Hendon.

The house in which Emily lived had numerous historical associations to interest the author of *Our Rambles*. It was built on the site of an earlier house which had been occupied by, among others, Samuel Pepys, Robert Harley, Earl of Oxford, and the painters William Etty and Clarkson Stanfield. It stood at the bottom of the street overlooking the Victoria Embankment Gardens and the York Watergate, a solid, rusticated structure built to the designs of Inigo Jones for George Villiers, Duke of Buckingham, who could alight from his barge on the Thames and step up to York House, long since demolished. Granny Emmy's flat was on the fourth floor and was reached by a circular staircase rising up under a glass dome. The house attracted a number of interesting tenants, including, in the flat opposite Emily's, Oscar Wilde's younger son, Vyvyan Holland. The American artist Joseph Pennell was another neighbor and became a friend of Emily, giving her several of his etchings, including one of the Panama Canal. Looking back on his many visits to Buckingham Street, Isherwood made it part of his personal mythology. "The combination of this Panama Canal picture, the presence of the river leading down to the sea, and of Charing Cross Station leading to Dover and the Continent, made Granny Emmy's flat, for Christopher, a sort of magic gateway to travel," he wrote.

Emily certainly fitted in with her surroundings. At this period she was an imposing, distinctly theatrical figure. "Granny Emmy knew how to create an atmosphere of mystery," Isherwood recalled. "The couch on which she lay was protected by various screens, so you only reached her by degrees. And the flat was full of strange pungent smells; the smell of pot-pourri, certain homeopathic medicines, and the odour of her furs." She modeled herself on her stage heroine, Sarah Bernhardt. "Emily didn't really look like her, but she somehow managed to convey the Bernhardt aura. She wore a reddish wig and spoke French wherever possible. And she adored the theatre." This was a passion she shared with Christopher, and it was to the theater that they went on the last night of his stay, to see Granville Barker's production of *A Midsummer Night's Dream*.

To Christopher at that age the theatre was chiefly and literally a magic show— more magic than the magicians, Maskelyne and Devant. He seems to have been

enchanted by the lights and the colours, and the sounds of the actors' voices re-
sounding and dominating the audience. The supreme excitement of this magic lay
in one's exposure to it; it was right there in the same room, and yet it was utterly
other. In this sense, it was almost like having a vision. Magic, the conjuror's art,
on the other hand was not at all magical, it seems, to Christopher; he was very
well aware that the tricks were tricks, and what appealed to him, I suppose, was
the charade of the mystification, and its application to himself. He didn't see himself acting in Shakespeare but he did certainly see himself conjuring and very
soon after this he began studying card-tricks, reading Hoffman's books on Modern Magic, More Magic, etc. and actually buying conjuring apparatus from a shop
called Goldstone's just off Leicester Square.

Meanwhile, there was St. Edmund's to be faced. Kathleen escorted her son to
Waterloo, the platforms of which were thronged with small boys in uniform. There
she handed him over to Cyril Morgan Brown, who was looking, she thought, "very
incapable and dazed." "Nurse felt parting with him, I know, very much," Kathleen
had written, but when she saw her son standing alone, a stranger among the other
boys, she felt this wrench keenly herself. She may have recalled Christopher's unhappy experiences at dancing classes in Ireland. "If only he would learn the art of
self-defence," she had written at the time, "it worries me so to think of what he will
do at school." Now that the moment had arrived, both mother and child attempted not
to show each other up in front of the more seasoned pupils. "It was all we could do,
both of us, to put a good face on it," Kathleen wrote, "but he just managed to keep
back the tears. It was a truly dreadful moment to me, seeing him go off so small and
inexperienced into the unknown." This was something Kathleen felt every time her
son set off on the travels that characterized his life.

Like all parents who send their young children away to school, Kathleen spent the
next few days worrying how Christopher was faring. Pupils wrote letters every
Sunday, and so she had to wait three anxious days for news. When it came, it was
in the form of "a rather pathetic little letter though very restrained." She also received a letter from Mona Morgan Brown, which was rather more reassuring. Addressing Kathleen formally as "Dear Mrs Bradshaw Isherwood," Mona wrote that
Christopher "seems a very jolly little chap and one feels very friendlily disposed
towards him, over and above the fact that he is a relation." The fact that he was a
relation, albeit a distant one, did not in fact incline Cyril to feel particularly
friendly. Part of the problem was Kathleen's low opinion of the Morgan Browns. "I
think, if you can bear it, you should ask them to call you Kathleen," Frank wrote
from Limerick after Kathleen had forwarded Mona's letter. "They are people who
think a good deal of it and Mona at any rate is really very nice. I like Cyril too, myself." This was not an easy thing to ask of Kathleen, who regarded all school-teachers
as glorified servants: she customarily referred to Morgan Brown as "Little Cyril."

Christopher arrived at St. Edmund's to find a telegram—"YOUR FATHER'S BLESS-
ING GOOD LUCK FRANK"—as well as a letter "to welcome you at school." A few days
later Christopher received another letter:

My Dear Boy,

I was very glad to see your letter, and to find that you were 'fairly happy' at school. I think that is as much as you can expect for the first few days at any rate and when you get to know everyone better I expect you will find them very nice. I rather feel for you about the cricket. I always found it very dull. However it is a fine healthy game and you will have to play it as Doctor Candy said so. I advise you to try, and get as good at it as you can, and that will make it more interesting. Football is much better fun though I never really liked that till I was about forty, and too old to play much. Are you going to send me some photos of the flying to develop? Capt. Burdett is going to the flying school next week and hopes to get into the Flying Corps. With much love as always your affectionate Father.

Frank remains a somewhat shadowy figure in Isherwood's life, but in these few lines he comes startlingly and movingly alive. Few boys plunged into the frighteningly unfamiliar world of boarding school can have received so affectionate and understanding a letter from a father.

In 1932, Isherwood wrote his "Memoirs" of St. Edmund's, which he rechristened "Pine House." "Facing Page One of the Prospectus," he wrote, "is a photograph of the School from the South, an aggressive gabled building in the early Edwardian style, about the size of a private hotel. The brick work is varied here and there with sham frontings of criss-cross timber and stucco. In the foreground is a plantation of dwarf conifers, such as are almost always to be seen in the grounds of better-class lunatic asylums." The aggression is in fact all Isherwood's, since by the time he wrote this, he was in full revolt against the establishment and the Past. The description remains, however, more or less accurate. The house had been substantially altered when it was turned into a school, with the addition of new wings on either side, containing classrooms and dormitories, and a small red-brick chapel built on to the front. While the principal rooms of the school were still recognizably those of a private house, the boys' domain resembled servants' quarters, with many small rooms off dark corridors. Since it was popularly believed that too much light was bad for growing children, no dormitory faced south, and the warren of interconnecting passages was made additionally gloomy by unadorned, shoulder-high panelling varnished to a treacly brown. Bathrooms and the large changing rooms were cheerlessly institutional, tiled in white and dark blue. The dining room was perhaps the most attractive room, its vaguely Arts and Crafts architecture emphasized by inspiring frescoes of British heroes (Raleigh, Chaucer, the Black Prince), saints (Augustine, Michael, George and, of course, Edmund) and allegorical figures (Faith, Hope and Charity) painted in a style some way after Burne-Jones. A large black-and-white reproduction of G. F. Watt's *Sir Galahad* also hung in the hall, which was presided over at meal-times by Ciddy, whose chair was carefully positioned beneath the fresco of St. Edmund.

Isherwood claimed that he fell foul of Cyril Morgan Brown (rechristened "W. N. Price-Jones" in the "Memoirs") at breakfast on his first morning at school. Spreading a slice of bread with butter and marmalade, he became aware that everyone was watching him, most of them "grinning, with expressions of furtive, malicious pleasure." Looking down the table, he saw Ciddy glaring at him.

'Are you deaf?'

'I'm sorry, sir.'

'I said: Are you deaf?'

'Yes, sir . . . I mean, No, sir.'

This raised a titter among the audience. But Mr Price-Jones' eyebrows only drew down more forbiddingly. He rose to his feet, and, to my great alarm, came lumbering over to where I sat.

'I didn't think you'd be that particular kind of a pig,' he said.

And now, for the first time, I realized what I had done to offend. Reaching his arms over my shoulders, Mr Price-Jones picked up the bread and the knife from my plate and methodically scraped off the marmalade. This he proceeded to re-store to the marmalade dish. I remember that he had long sensitive powerful hands with little scruffs of grey hair on the backs of his fingers.

'Don't let me see you doing that again,' he said. 'You're not in the pig-sty any more now.'

With this he strode back to his chair. The boys made a few jokes and then for-got me. They were used to scenes of this kind. Breakfast was resumed. I went on mechanically eating my bread and butter, blushing furiously, trying to keep back the tears of home-sickness, misery and rage. I wanted to tell Mr Price-Jones that at Home I had *always,* all my life, been allowed to eat marmalade with butter. No-body had ever so much as suggested that this was wrong, or indeed that any moral issue was involved. And Mr Price-Jones had insulted my home. Had called it a pig-sty. I wanted to tell him that he was a liar, but I didn't.

Had such a scene occurred, it would indeed have been humiliating, but it seems highly unlikely that Ciddy, even if he reprimanded Isherwood, would publicly and gratu-itously insult his own relations. Furthermore, we know from Mona's letter that Christo-pher sat beside her at the dining table that morning, and that she was obliged to encourage him to clean his plate. These "Memoirs" are an early example of Isherwood embroidering for effect what is being offered to the reader as candid autobiography.

In *Kathleen and Frank,* Isherwood described himself at the age of ten as "a tire-less chatterer, a physical coward who lacked team spirit, a bright scholar who soon got bored and lazy, a terrible showoff." Small wonder that the Morgan Browns found it easy not to show their young cousin undue favoritism. Kathleen was inclined to think they erred too far in the opposite direction, but one could hardly blame them. Christopher could be a trying child.

A photograph taken about this period shows a large-headed excitable little boy with a feminine rather chinless profile and wiry light brown hair sticking up on the crown with a bristle like a shaving-brush. Although I had spent the first seven years of my life as an only son, I was not solitary in my habits. I had already been to three kindergartens and made many friends of my own age. This is not to say however that I was not what is called 'spoiled'. I liked the sound of my own voice, asked too many questions and must needs argue every point on which my elders saw fit to correct me. I had also, I am told, an irritating way of using precociously grown-up words and turns of speech.

Shortly after the beginning of his first term, Rosa asked him what he had done with his cricket shirt, to which he piped in reply: "I haven't the remotest idea." To his great surprise, this superior, young-heir manner earned him a ringing slap across the face.

In later life Isherwood recalled little of these early schooldays. "The images which have remained in the memory," he wrote fifty years later,

> are not in themselves terrible or rigorous: they are of boot-lockers, wooden desks, lists on boards, name-tags in clothes—yes, the name pre-eminently; the name which makes you in a sense nameless, less individual rather than more so: Bradshaw-Isherwood, C.W. in its place on some alphabetical list; the cold daily, hourly reminder that you are not the unique, the loved, the household's darling, but just one among many. I suppose that this loss of identity is really much of the painfulness which lies at the bottom of what is miscalled Homesickness; it is not Home that one cries for but one's home-self.

During that first term, Bradshaw-Isherwood, C. W., distinguished himself both in the classroom and on the playing fields. He passed the half-term examinations with honors, carried off the Divinity Prize, and on Sports Day won a silver cup for the quarter-mile handicap—largely because he had mistakenly been given a 100-yard start on account of his size. Isherwood's diminutive figure scorched round the track, maintaining his lead over the rest of the field and being cheered on from the sidelines. Ciddy was not amused. Isherwood later decided that running was the only sport that interested him because he was already "becoming, in the human jungle, one of those animals who live by escape."

Kathleen came to collect Christopher from school at the end of term on July 29. He "looked very well and seemed much the same," she reported, "not grown but very untidy! Ink on his coat and a dirty collar!" Two days later they returned to Limerick, where fears about an Irish rebellion had been suddenly dispelled by a much greater threat. Austria had declared war on Serbia and it had become apparent that such an emergency might easily spread far beyond the Balkans. The regiment, which had been in camp near Fermoy, had been ordered back to barracks. Frank met his wife and son at the dock and said that he was expecting the order for mobilization at any moment. "It seems so appalling, one can't take it in," Kathleen wrote in her diary. "I never thought of Irish troops [that is, British troops stationed in Ireland] being called upon." But called upon they were on August 4, 1914, the first day of what came to be known, with some justification, as the Great War.

Isherwood retained a clear memory of his father announcing that the mobilization order had come. "It presents itself in the form of a picture; a very faded one, but perfectly clear," he wrote in 1967. "Indeed, it also contains the only remaining memory-record of the sound of Frank's voice; it sounds controlled, calm but full of tension." Unlike many English families on that Bank Holiday weekend, the Isherwoods were immediately affected by the war, and within ten days Frank had sailed for England, where he was to undergo training at Cambridge. Ten days after that, Kathleen, Nanny and the children left Ireland for Marple Hall, where Nanny and Richard would be based for most of the war. On September 7 the order to embark came through and Kathleen traveled to Cambridge with another officer's wife to make their farewells. "It makes it so different leaving someone behind who really cares for you," Frank wrote from Southampton the following day. "Think of me at night and perhaps you will be able to realize whether I am all right or not." On September 14 Kathleen went back to Limerick to close up Roden House.

By this time, Christopher had returned to St. Edmund's for his second term, and moved up a class. If he was anxious about his father, he did not show it. It is quite likely that, as yet untouched by the war, the boys of St. Edmund's were more thrilled than worried by it. Private education at the period did much to promote warfare as a noble and exciting undertaking, and casualties were talked of in terms of "glorious sacrifice." At this stage of the war a great deal of glamour still attached to a man in uniform, and when Frank heard that he was to have some leave he suggested to Kathleen that they should visit Christopher at St. Edmund's: "He might like to exhibit a Father who comes hot from the Front." Meanwhile, he wrote to Christopher on the latter's tenth birthday: "I am so glad to hear that you have been so nice and kind and good to your Mother. You must try to do all you can for her while I am away. It is a dreadful time for her and you can do more to make it bearable than anyone else . . . So always consider her . . . Excuse this 'Pi jaw.' I haven't treated you to many, have I?" Indeed, this is the only surviving letter from Frank to his son that remotely resembles a sermon. It was one that would have considerable repercussions.

Richard's reaction to his father's sudden departure is more difficult to assess. He was not yet three when Frank marched away, and would retain very little memory of him. Christopher's fears that he would cease to be the center of attention after Richard was born had proved unfounded. "I am afraid [Richard] will always have to play second fiddle to Christopher at Marple at any rate," Frank wrote from the Front. "But I don't think he is the sort which will much mind." For Richard there was no choice, whether he minded or not, and this sense that he would always be second-best—and not only at Marple—seems to have been inculcated from his earliest years. If there was ever a book recording Baby Richard's Progress, it has not survived, and there would be few enough triumphs to report in it. Kathleen and Frank were probably as conscientious as most parents of the period, but there is no doubt which of their children they favored. Frank's attitude toward his younger son is clear from the many disparaging references in the letters he wrote Kathleen from the Front. "Mama seems to be enjoying Richard's society," he wrote when Richard was visiting Marple Hall, "I hope she is. He is rather trying to the nerves!" Sent a snapshot of Richard, he replied: "I don't think much of Richard's photo—He looks little better than an idiot in it." When Christopher returned to St. Edmund's for the new term, and Kathleen went to stay at Buckingham Street, Frank wrote: "You will hardly I am afraid be able to have Richard in London with you, in any case he could not be such a comfort and companion as our eldest son!" While Christopher was commended as a "wit," Frank found "Richard's efforts at conversation . . . almost as pathetic as some of the attempts at conversation" he heard at the Front.

The contrast between the references to Richard and those to Christopher could hardly be more marked, and cannot entirely be explained by the obvious differences between a three-year-old and a ten-year-old. Even Christopher's failings were viewed sympathetically: "I am very sorry Christopher was feeling unwilling to go back to school. I am afraid little boys bore him as much as big ones do me." This favoritism may have communicated itself to Richard, who had already developed a "violent temperament," and it seems likely that the seeds of the psychological problems that were to beset him throughout his life were sown during his early childhood.

Richard was certainly a difficult child—fractious, destructive and frequently hysterical—but whether this was a result of his parents' attitude to him, or vice versa, is hard to judge. "I am sorry Richard is pettish and disagreeable," Frank wrote in November 1914. "Tell him from me that soldiers (and their sons) are never like that and ready to put up with any disappointments. He is quite old enough to be impressed by that, and not old enough to know how untrue it is." Richard had every reason to be pettish and disagreeable at this period. The previous month, he had endured a terrifying encounter with yet another Marple Hall ghost. He and Nanny had been put in the nursery where Christopher had previously suffered disturbed nights. Kathleen arrived at Marple to find great excitement over Richard's claim that he had seen Moll of Brabyns. She took Richard aside and gently questioned him. "I asked him if the old woman had said anything to him, and he said, 'she says "you muft go away" and she come and look at me in bed, and I say "I don't want to go away" and she say "Oh, but you muft" ' (he still talks indistinctly). He repeated this several times but did not appear frightened. He also said that she sits in the corner by the chest of drawers and has a pussycat with her and a sash on." It is curious that Kathleen was not alerted by the anomalous detail of the cat in this account. In the portrait of Moll her companion was a small dog, and this is the sort of slip that a three-year-old might make when he was not telling the truth. Years later Richard confessed that the apparition had in fact taken the unusual form of a dressmaker's dummy, with a large screw protruding from its neck instead of a head. He did not suppose that anyone would have believed this and so, prompted by the servants, he said that he had seen the "muzzy old woman" that Christopher had at the same age. In time he came to believe that the apparition was in fact Moll of Brabyns: "She probably took the form of a dress-stand to me because she thought it would scare me off more effectively. I had a morbid fear of seeing dress stands in shop windows."[1] Richard may not have struck Kathleen as frightened, but he was a naturally nervous child, terrified of thunder for example, and this experience undoubtedly further undermined what little self-confidence he had.

I n March 1915, shortly after Frank had visited St. Edmund's while on leave, Christopher developed measles, as did several other pupils. Frank advised Kathleen against visiting her son, since she had not had the disease herself, but both parents became anxious when Christopher's temperature started to rise. "Purden [a fellow officer] says that a temperature of 104° or 105° for measles is very high and as all the Brown patients have been like that, he thinks their thermometer is probably

---

1. Psychic phenomena continued to affect the Old Nursery. A woman who came to look after Grandpa Isherwood during his final illness several years after Richard's experience stayed in the room and complained that "she sometimes when doing her hair in front of the mirror used to see a reflection of something or someone moving about, and once something hit her on the arm, but she couldn't see anything."

wrong. He says they very often are unreliable unless tested properly." It would hardly have surprised Kathleen to discover that the Morgan Browns had a faulty thermometer, but Christopher's condition deteriorated alarmingly, and "black measles" were diagnosed. Kathleen anxiously recorded the progress of her son's illness in the memoranda section of her diary. On March 16 she wrote, "the general condition of the boys pointed to some general affection of the blood & specialist & bacteriologist came down." "Septic pneumonia" was diagnosed, and Christopher's temperature continued to fluctuate. Defying Frank's instructions, Kathleen visited St. Edmund's on March 20 and "found C. with head bandaged for ear ache & shade over his eyes which have been bad . . . & in rather a tearful state." Gradually Christopher's temperature got back to normal, and at the end of the month he was collected by a family friend in a "closed motor" and driven to Portsmouth, where Kathleen met him to travel on to Ventnor, where he was to convalesce.

Frank wondered whether this enforced absence from school might provide an opportunity for removing Christopher from St. Edmund's permanently. "I don't much agree with the Dr about boarding schools," he wrote on April 9, "as I think most boys, Richard for instance, are much better at them, but in Christopher's case I shouldn't object at all to sending him as a day boy if it were possible. The whole point of sending him to school was to flatten him out, so to speak, and make him like the other boys, and when all is said and done I don't know that this is at all desirable or necessary, and I for one would much rather have him as he is." Any decision about Christopher's future, however, was rapidly overtaken by events.

On April 27 Frank, who had been gazetted a lieutenant-colonel in February after being mentioned in dispatches, was ordered to Ypres to command the 1st Battalion. "You mustn't be anxious as the fighting up there seems virtually over," Frank wrote to Kathleen. In this he was gravely mistaken, and he soon found himself in trenches under heavy shellfire and gas attacks. The battalion came out of the line on May 7, but was ordered to return the following day and attempt to retake some trenches lost during the night. That evening, at eight o'clock, an attack was launched. Like a great many such actions, it was ill-prepared and mounted against absurd odds. Frank plunged into the bloody chaos of battle and simply vanished.

Meanwhile, Christopher was no longer infectious and he and Kathleen were joined at Ventnor by Nanny and Richard. Christopher then began to experience severe pains in his legs, and this was diagnosed as rheumatic fever. At the end of the holiday the family was due to return to Marple Hall, but Nanny was causing difficulties: "La Bonne est très desagreablés apropos de Marple," Kathleen noted in her diary in the mixture of English and approximate French she used to write about servant problems. "Dit qu'elle est si worried there, elle n'aime pas rester there pour long-temps. Si inconsiderate maintenant que jai na pas un maison—un semaine at the pit mouth would do her discontent beaucoup de bien." Nanny's "mauvais humeurs" notwithstanding, on May 11 Kathleen and Christopher traveled to Marple, where it was planned that Christopher should continue his convalescence. The following day Kathleen received a telegram reporting that Frank had been wounded.

What actually happened to Frank remains a mystery, one compounded by numerous conflicting reports of the action during the night of May 8 and 9. On May 13

Kathleen traveled to London to see if she could get any further information. She hoped to find members of the regiment who had been wounded in the attack and invalided home. "Meanwhile, Marple people are manifesting keen anxiety," the local paper reported, "and on Thursday morning, as the Squire drove through the village, people came out to inquire for tidings."

As the days passed and there was no further news of Frank, the War Office's assurance that he "could not possibly be missing" began to look unduly optimistic. At second or third hand Kathleen received contradictory reports from various hospitals of men who had seen Frank being wounded by shrapnel in the arm, or the leg, having his wounds bound on the spot, or being taken to a dressing-station. Kathleen trudged round the hospitals in an increasingly desperate quest for some concrete information. On June 3 the inquiries made by the War Office resulted in a wire to say that Frank was officially missing—"a fact which has been obvious for some time," as Kathleen commented in her diary. On June 19 news came from a Scottish hospital from a soldier who claimed to have seen Frank killed by a shell, but this witness was not considered altogether reliable. Finally, on June 24, seven long weeks after Kathleen first heard that Frank had been wounded, she received a letter from the Red Cross: "We very much regret to say that according to the Geneva list of June 12th received here on the 23rd inst., it is intimated that a disc was found on a dead soldier close to Frezenberg early in May with the following inscription on it:—Isherwood. F.E.B. Y & L Regiment, Siche 5. C of E. We greatly fear this disc may have belonged to Col. Isherwood." Kathleen must have been expecting this, but the blow when it finally came was devastating. When she reproduced this letter in her diary, she made only one comment: "—and so passes hope and life."

This was not quite true: at the beginning of July, the day after Frank's birthday (which brought "heaps of dreadful letters"), Henry Isherwood suggested placing an announcement in the papers, but Kathleen was "against doing so at present." A week later, however, she received a letter from the War Office stating their belief, based upon reports and the discovery of the identity disc, that Frank was dead, and asking whether she was "prepared to accept this information." Kathleen was, and on July 11 sent her blue serge coat and skirt to be dyed black. Frank's death was announced in the papers on September 8.

Among the many letters of condolence Kathleen received was one from her aunt, Julia Fry, written from Lincoln, where her husband was now Dean. "You have your darling boys to live for," she wrote:

'Of all the dearest bonds we prove,
Thou countest sons' and mothers' love
Most sacred, most Thine own'

You will teach them the deepest love for such a Father & in that work you will feel you four are still one family although divided by that narrow line.

This was a notion Kathleen would take to heart—with catastrophic results for all concerned.

THREE

W HAT IMMEDIATE IMPACT THE DEATH OF FRANK HAD UPON HIS eleven-year-old son is unclear. Isherwood left no account of his feelings at the time, or what he remembered of them, though these can readily be imagined. Although there is no evidence that Isherwood was re-creating an actual experience, it is possible that he drew upon memories of this period in his second novel, *The Memorial,* in which Eric Vernon receives news of his father's death in action during his first, unhappy year at public school. "Eric was very, very sorry to hear that his father had been killed. The news added poignantly to his sense of desolation in the midst of the great school. . . . For a week, Eric was almost intolerably unhappy, for a week only just less so, for a week still very miserable. Then he knew he could bear it. It was no better, but he was stronger." By the end of term Eric is naturally pleased and excited at the prospect of the school holidays, unaware of what the atmosphere at home will be like.

> He was sent up to his mother in her room, as if to an invalid. He had come in, a little sobered, apprehensive, after knocking—utterly unprepared for the awful shock he was to receive. For a moment, he hardly recognized Lily. She was hideous with grief. Her eyes swollen into slits, her mouth heavy and pouting, her face blotched and sallow. He hung back, scared. The smile shrank from his lips. She gave a kind of hoarse cry. He rushed into her arms. That was agony. He knew then that everything he'd imagined he'd suffered at school was nothing, mere selfishness, triviality. She reopened the wound and tore it ten times wider. And now it would have made no difference to Eric if ten fathers had been killed. It was only for her that he felt. Father was dead. But she was alive and suffering like this under his very eyes. He could do absolutely nothing.

As with Eric, what affected Christopher and Richard most was not so much the loss of their father as the effect this loss had on their mother. Unlike many of the tragic figures swathed in black who thronged London, Kathleen was not a young woman. Widows in their twenties and thirties could, after coming to terms with their loss, contemplate the possibility of marrying again; Kathleen, though she looked much younger, was forty-seven. From the moment the woman from Barker's department store came to fit her for her mourning clothes, her principal identity was that of a war widow, and although she did her best to attend to her two children, the emotional center of her life for many years would be her dead husband. Her natural propensity to regard the past as a *paradis perdu* was given added force by the fact that twelve years of happily married life had come to so brutal an end.

By dying in the war, Frank also underwent an instant metamorphosis from fond parent to distant icon. Well-meaning adults began to hold him up as a hero worthy of emulation: the man whom Isherwood was able to amuse with his conjuring tricks and his jokes suddenly became a god who had to be placated by decorous behavior. The effect of this was to distance Isherwood from the man who had really been his father: "the Frank who had told stories and done drawings for him and taught him the magic of make-believe"; the Frank who had written those touching, sympathetic and unpatronizing letters when he started at St. Edmund's; the Frank who wrote: "I don't think it matters very much what Christopher learns as long as he remains himself and keeps his individuality and develops on his own lines." It was not until he was in his mid-sixties that Isherwood rediscovered this man and grew once more to love him. For Richard, this process never took place. Too young to have any physical memory of Frank, he grew up the orphan of a Hero-Father, and this mythical figure was used to rebuke and terrorize him. "I did so hate being everlastingly told about him when I was young," Richard recalled. "Everyone kept saying how perfect he was, such a hero, and so good at everything. He was always held up as someone you could never hope to be worthy of, and whenever I did anything wrong I was told I was a disgrace to him. I used to have nightmares that he was coming back to live with us! And then I was horrified, and I wanted to run away from home and hide somewhere before he arrived. I used to simply loathe him!"

Had Frank died in England, as the result of an accident or illness, things would have been very different. Even when the bodies of soldiers were recovered, they were never brought back to England for burial. There were no funerals to act as a focus for grief, and in the case of those who were missing but presumed dead, there was not even a grave in a military cemetery to visit. Worse still, there was always the faint hope, which for the duration of the war never quite died, that Frank was still alive, perhaps a prisoner somewhere. It was just about possible that in the chaos and violence of battle he could have lost his identity tag. The conflicting stories about his fate—that he had been placed, wounded, in a ditch; that he had been loaded onto an ambulance, which according to one report had been hit by a shell; that he had been seen either dead or dying, covered in blood from wounds in the head and chest—cruelly prolonged both hope and dread.

Kathleen's diaries suggest that while she had accepted the War Office's conclusion that Frank was no longer alive, she still needed positive proof of his death. The sort of confirmation provided by a Mrs. Cook, whom she had known in Limerick, was not particularly helpful, but, in view of the experiences her children had undergone at Marple, it certainly gave her pause. Shortly after Frank's death had been announced, Kathleen received a letter from Mrs. Cook. As Kathleen told her sister-in-law Moey, Mrs. Cook

> said she felt she __must__ write, because she had got a powerful message for me from Frank—she said she always felt he had a message to give her—and that it came through by means of an Ouija board (whatever that may be?). It came through thus: 'Dear friends—I'm delighted you remember . . . many times I think of you & the happy days in Limerick.' Then she asked the question, why did I always feel you were alive when I touched the letters you wrote? (He had written to her about things sent out to him.) 'Because we had sympathy about many things & I am more alive than ever I was on earth.' 'Would you like your wife to know?' 'She does not believe—please ask Charlie Bellairs, he can help me.' 'What is your difficulty?' 'Both children are calling for me and I try to calm them—but my wife does miss me and [I] cannot come to let her know my presence. Tell her not to sorrow. I am waiting and watching for her—all is well—peace be with you.' A second message came through again. Again Charlie Bellairs (?) was referred to & again a message asking her to tell me, that he lived for me, & the children. I have not as yet mentioned the letter to __anyone__—I received it about a month ago. I couldn't feel it was really Frank, and yet I __can't__ dismiss it without feeling there is __something__. The woman, & a friend of hers equally psychic touched the board & on the same occasion other messages came through, all from soldiers connected with the neighbourhood. I do not know how the name of Charlie Bellairs can have come up?

Charles Bellairs, the husband of Frank's great-aunt Anna (and an uncle of Cyril Morgan Brown), was long since dead, so it is unsurprising that Kathleen was puzzled to hear him mentioned in this context. She subsequently read *Raymond,* Sir Oliver Lodge's controversial account of his communications, via a medium, with his son, who had been killed in action. "Not I thought very inspiring," she commented. "That he still _is_, one believes without these [i.e. séances]—& I enormously dislike the 'controls' who are supposed to bring the messages through & speak through the medium, there is something so vulgar & common about them especially one called Feda." She nevertheless took an interest in the experiences of her psychic friend, Jem Barlow, who with a Miss Somerville was conducting similar experiments at the same time and had been "in communication with Miss Martin who passed over a year ago." A few years earlier, at a séance attended by both Kathleen and Frank, Miss Barlow had supposedly conjured up the spirit of Frank's great-grandfather, who had warned them against Henry.

From day to day Kathleen had to maintain a capable façade for the sake of the children, but in the small pages of her diary she lamented her loss. She was occasionally distracted from grief by a number of practical considerations, the first of which was to find somewhere to live. Richard and Nanny were more or less permanently installed at Marple Hall, while Christopher had sufficiently recuperated from his rheumatic fever by September to be able to return to St. Edmund's (under the doctor's supervision) for the autumn term. A week before this, Grandpa Isherwood had offered Wyberslegh Hall to his daughter-in-law, the tenant having conveniently died. Kathleen felt unable to accept, since Wyberslegh held too many memories for her and she could not imagine living there without Frank. She also had her mother to consider. Emily's health would not stand the cold and damp of Cheshire and she would have hated to leave London and its theaters. Kathleen consequently spent much of 1915 shuttling between Marple and London, also spending time with Uncle Walter at Nether Hall and Uncle Charlie and Aunt Julia at the Deanery, Lincoln. Everywhere she went seemed to bring back memories of earlier visits when she had been accompanied by Frank. "The misery & the loneliness grow worse & worse," she wrote in August.

Christopher returned to St. Edmund's the son of a war hero. In this he was not alone, and other little boys had black armbands stitched to their jackets: the isolation or pariah status endured by children at boarding schools when a parent died during peace-time was thus grimly mitigated. At least Isherwood had received news of his father's death at home, in the company of his mother. Less fortunate pupils were taken out of classrooms to have the news broken to them by a member of staff. Isherwood recalled that the principal reaction of pupils to such a death would be curiosity: "Did you blub much?" boys eagerly asked the bereaved. While fellow pupils instinctively knew how to behave, confining their condolences to a brief "Bad luck, Isherwood!" the Morgan Browns kept going on about their dead cousin as an ideal for his son to emulate.

Meanwhile, food supplies were running low (butter had long since been replaced by a disgusting substance derived from coconuts), and in July 1917 the school suffered "a plague of indigestion or internal upset" caused by the "Standard War Bread." "Perhaps it made Cyril Brown write that irritable report saying C's conduct was quite satisfactory in a rather colourless way, adding that he didn't think about anything but his own comfort," Kathleen commented crossly in her diary. Christopher himself started to keep a diary in 1917. It was almost certainly given to him by his mother, as it is identical to the ones she kept herself throughout her life. Measuring approximately five inches by three inches, the books contained a page for every day with twenty lines on which to record events. They were prefaced with a memorandum, in which Kathleen jotted down such information as the names and addresses of reliable dressmakers and window-cleaners, and Christopher noted fielding positions for cricket, the wives of Henry VIII, and—prophetically—"The well-known publisher (Methuen)." For Christopher, this 1917 diary inaugurated a lifelong habit of chronicling his days, and in this too he followed the example of his mother. The first of Kathleen's diaries to survive dates from 1883, when she was fourteen, though she did not start to keep a diary regularly until seven years later, after which she scarcely missed recording a single day until the penultimate year of her life.

Like most schoolboy diaries, Isherwood's provides one with facts rather than insights. The eternal round of lessons, chapel, walks, "progressive games," concerts, lectures (usually on the war) and ragging was much the same as that endured by any boy at prep school, reflected all too accurately in the entry for February 12: "Work in morning walk in afternoon. In choir. More work. Nothing special." Occasionally, however, one finds something of significance: "Unwell, kept in with Tudor and Crowther-Smith, looking at James's cigarette cards." Here we find the germ of one of Isherwood's best-known stories, "Gems of Belgian Architecture," which incidentally provides a lively account of St. Edmund's during the war. Like all schools, St. Edmund's was subject to "crazes," a hobby or activity that captured the collective imagination of the pupils. It might be marbles, postage stamps or war games, but in this case it was the collecting of the small pictorial cards given away free with packets of cigarettes. The idea was to collect a complete set of the cards, one from each packet, and paste them into elaborate albums provided by the cigarette manufacturers. Because duplicates were inevitable, collectors devised elaborate systems of swapping and barter.

The title of Isherwood's story refers to a series of cigarette cards that actually existed, and must have had a special poignancy at this period, when the most famous gem of Belgian architecture was the shell-battered Cloth Hall at Ypres. Some cards were harder to find than others and the story perfectly describes the fevered activity, plotting, ruses and actual theft involved in making up sets. To some extent the cards were incidental: they provided a focus for personal politics within the school whereby some boys were naturally popular, while others needed to curry favor; where through some quirk of character or recognized achievement (usually on the playing fields) certain pupils emerged as leaders and surrounded themselves with loyal gangs, while others were content to follow, hoping to catch a little reflected glory. Some boys worked the system to their best advantage, changing sides as the wind changed and indulging in a little espionage. These crazes showed boys at their most primitive and tribal.

Just as in Isherwood's story, the boys of St. Edmund's visited an encampment of Canadian soldiers on a nearby common in order to beg cards to make up complete sets. It was also on this common that the punishment of "gorse-bushing" took place on the last Sunday of term. This day was known as "Pay Day," when pupils took advantage of being given a free run of the grounds to settle feuds and scores. As in the story, miscreants were thrown by their schoolfellows into the prickly clumps of furze that grew in abundance on the sandy soil. The gorse-bushing of Dwight in "Gems of Belgian Architecture" is based upon the punishment meted out to a boy called Parker, who was considered "sidey," attracting undue attention to himself. Isherwood might well have been in danger of showing "side," but he was also pragmatic, and had taken heed from Parker's painful comeuppance. "I never much liked the Grounds," he recalled. "Even during my last term I was rather afraid of going out into them alone. Even on a bright summer morning they seemed curiously sinister and still. The red school buildings were hidden from the rifle range by a thick belt of pine trees; and if you went further, across the drive, deep into the gorse, you might imagine yourself to be miles from any human dwelling." This area was inhabited by vipers, hunted by gangs of senior boys with their trouser-legs tied at the ankle and armed with sticks. Isherwood did not join in these enthusiastic culls (which often resulted in the deaths of harmless grass snakes along with the vipers), since he shared his mother's morbid fear of snakes. His favorite of the Sherlock Holmes stories was "The Speckled Band," which gave him an authentic thrill of horror every time he read it.

Although he was later to characterize himself as a "mouse-faced, enigmatic, de-mure little [boy], with bright uneasy eyes," he seems to have been a conventional enough child. His passion for theater and conjuring might seem to prefigure his later career as a writer, but they are in no way unusual hobbies for a twelve-year-old schoolboy. A genuinely unconventional boy now entered his life, however. The son of a doctor, Wystan Hugh Auden had followed his older brother, John, to St. Edmund's. John had acquired the nickname of Dodo, and so, with schoolboy logic, Wystan was dubbed Dodo Minor. While physically Auden shared some of the extinct bird's clumsiness, his mind was anything but dead. "He was precociously clever, un-tidy, lazy and, with the masters, inclined to be insolent," Isherwood recalled.

His ambition was to be a mining engineer; and his playbox was full of thick sci-entific books on geology and metals and machines, borrowed from his father's li-brary . . . [Auden] had discovered, very early in life, the key to the bookcase which contained anatomical manuals with coloured German plates. To several of us, including myself, he confided the first naughty stupendous breath-taking hints about the facts of sex. I remember him chiefly for his naughtiness, his insolence, his smirking tantalising air of knowing disreputable and exciting secrets. With his hinted forbidden knowledge and stock of mispronounced scientific words, por-tentously uttered, he enjoyed among us, his semi-savage credulous schoolfellows, the status of a kind of witch-doctor.

Auden was to hold a similar position among his fellows as the century progressed, the self-appointed leader of his literary generation. He achieved this partly through his high intelligence, partly through an air, derived both from this and from his con-stant processing of arcane knowledge, of natural authority, and partly through sheer bossiness. A grubby, unprepossessing little boy, with a dead white complexion, untidy tow-colored hair, blunt-fingered, ink-stained hands and an habitual, myopic scowl, Auden did not seem a natural leader. This negligence of his person probably con-tributed to his authority rather than detracting from it, however. People rightly sup-posed that his mind was on more important matters than clean collars and neat cuffs.

Despite his sophistication, Auden was some two and a half years younger than Isherwood, and did not arrive at St. Edmund's until the autumn term of 1915. The first mention of him in Isherwood's diary occurs on Sunday, February 25, 1917: "Chapel in morning. Did not go out, but wrote letter. Concert after dinner, I played 'The Merry Peasant.' Then walked with Auden ii. Reading." He may have got to know Auden ii better toward the end of that term, since they both came down with German measles and, along with several other boys, were obliged to remain at school for the first few days of the Easter holidays. In telegraphic form, the diary gives the outline of Christopher's days, but never pauses for reflection or explanation, so that one gets no sense of his relationships with any of his fellow pupils, except by totting up the number of times certain boys are mentioned. Auden does not stand out, unlike Scott, the son of a factory owner who lived in Stockport and often came over to Marple Hall to shoot sparrows with Christopher, or Abrahall and Russell-Roberts, both of whom are featured in *The History of My Friends*.

Isherwood made good progress at St. Edmund's, taking music and carpentry lessons alongside more academic subjects. He was taught piano by a Miss Bertha Lowe, who was somewhat deaf and used a primitive hearing aid consisting of an earplug attached to a metal cup by a tube. (Unkind boys would occasionally drop gravel into this cup while Miss Lowe's attention was directed elsewhere.) At the end of the autumn term in 1917 he arrived at Marple laden with several prizes: for English, for the Holiday Competition (won for an illustrated diary of a tour of the West Country undertaken with Kathleen), and for a limerick. He even won the Star Prize for good conduct.

It now fell to Kathleen to choose a public school for her son. There seems to have been no suggestion that he should follow his father to Cheltenham, but in June 1918 he went to Charterhouse to sit for a scholarship—"not that Cyril thought he had any <u>chance</u> of gaining one," Kathleen noted. To her great satisfaction, however, Christopher did well enough to be excused taking the Common Entrance examination. Unfortunately, the school was oversubscribed and neither a letter from the Dean of Lincoln nor Kathleen's own interview with a housemaster there ("a very kind little man") could secure Christopher the firm promise of a place. Oddly enough, Kathleen seems not to have considered Berkhamsted, where in 1910 her cousin Charles Greene had taken over the headmastership from Uncle Charlie Fry. Christopher's cousin and future fellow novelist, Graham Greene, was due to move from the Junior to the Senior School there in the autumn term. Perhaps Kathleen felt that Christopher had had enough of being taught by relatives. She did, however, consider (and in some cases visit) a number of other schools, including Radley, Bradfield, Shrewsbury, Wellington and Sherborne. Uncle Charlie himself proved "quite unilluminating . . . & talks of the importance of <u>internal tone</u>, but as he does not know it, at any of the schools I have seen, <u>how am</u> I to find out for myself?" He suggested Gresham's in Norfolk, where Christopher would once again have been a fellow pupil of W. H. Auden, "but not only is it miles away, but it has not the name or traditions of Charterhouse which is what seems to count." Numerous friends and relations were consulted and Christopher spent part of the summer holidays in 1918 composing a poem on the subject, which Kathleen copied into a book to be presented to Grandpa Isherwood on his birthday. "Choosing a School" describes the difficulties experienced by a Mrs. Brown and quite accurately reflects the dilemma Kathleen found herself in, with advice coming at her from all sides. It is quite a sophisticated poem, and it remains unclear how much of it (and its erratic punctuation) is Isherwood's and how much his mother's.

For nearly a month she wrestled hard
With printed prospectus's, by the yard
She said 'School-Hunting I can abide
No longer, I'll get my friends to decide.'

That afternoon at half-past-four,
Her friends came knocking at the door.
Mrs Fitz-Hogge, and Lady Boffin
(Who suffered from terrible fits of coughing)

Mrs Jones, Miss Snagge and Mrs Baker
(Who had huge bills from her dress-maker)

Then Mrs Brown, in the middle of tea
Announced to the general company
'I've decided, as is the general rule
To send my boy to a Public School.'

'Rugby, of course' says Mrs Jones
'Rugby has always the best of tones!'
'Rugby, indeed!' says Miss Snagge with heat
'But you will find Repton hard to beat!'
'Thats perfect rubbish!' says Mrs Fitz-Hogge
'Harrow has always been top-dog'
'Remember you're speaking to a Lady!'
'I consider Harrow distinctly shady!'

But Mrs Baker immediately said
'Far the best school is Berkhamsted.
People may talk of Eton and Radley
But at both of those places they feed them so badly!
As for the rest, well my brother-in-law
Told me—but I'd better not say any more!'

But Lady Boffin with purple cheek
Cries out, 'Be quiet, I demand to speak'
'You observe that I'm perfectly calm and cool!
Now I will tell you the only school!'
But alas! the illustrious Lady Boffin
Was seized with a terrible fit of coughing.

At last, when of this occupation she tired
She cried 'Fetch a doctor' and promptly expired

The funeral was over, six months had passed
Since Lady Boffin had breathed her last.
And Mrs Brown who had given a wreath
Was deep in thought on Hampstead Heath.

All the schools were full up! She had tried every one
All they said was—'We haven't a place for your son!'
So at last she engaged a Mr Sniggers
Supposed to be wonderfully good at figures
Who taught such a little and charged such a lot
That she dismissed him upon the spot!

And now, as I see you're beginning to doze
I'll draw this very long tale to its close!

Kathleen did not in fact have to resort to a private tutor, and it was the poem's Dickensianly named Miss Snagge who provided the best solution. Christopher himself had been taken to look over Repton and "had much liked the look of" it. Among its advantages was that Jack Isherwood was an Old Boy, it was in Derbyshire, within reasonable reach of Marple, and Christopher's St. Edmund's friend Michael Scott was a pupil there. Although she had been warned about Repton's "moral tone" by some people who had had first-hand experience there as matrons, Kathleen decided to pay the school another visit in November.

She arrived to discover that the Armistice had been declared, and this must have seemed a very good omen. She then journeyed on to London, but, although she was relieved that the fighting was over, she could not wholeheartedly join in the capital's celebrations. "The end has been accomplished, Germany is crushed, & the Lives have not been given in vain," she wrote in her diary. "Right has triumphed at last . . . but one does not feel in tune with the mad rejoicing of these horrible young women waving flag's & the squeals & whistling & shouting & the jostling crowds. We have won but we have paid the Price . . . Had a headache all day."

Christopher sat the Common Entrance for Repton and received the results in early December. In spite of his fears that he would be let down by his mathematics (always a weak point), he came third out of eighteen: "Cyril's comment is 'quite good!' " Apart from a last school report, it would be Ciddy's final, grudging judgment upon his inimical young cousin. On January 17, 1919, Christopher entered the Hall, his uncle Jack's old house at Repton.

Founded in the middle of the sixteenth century, Repton had endured a checkered early history, but like many of the older foundations, it had undergone a renaissance in the mid-nineteenth century when it became established as one of the leading public schools in the country. It had a reputation for sports, nurturing the talents of a number of world-class cricketers, and for appointing several distinguished ecclesiastics as headmaster, three of whom in succession went on to be Archbishops of Canterbury. In 1919 the headmaster was the Rev. Geoffrey Fisher, who had held this post since the beginning of the war. At the time of his appointment he was only twenty-seven, and Kathleen, who referred to him always as "little Fisher," commented: "I assume he must be clever to have got such a post." He was, and was considered a remarkable headmaster.

"I had arrived at my public school thoroughly sick of masters and mistresses, having been emotionally messed about by them at my preparatory school, where the war years had given full licence for every sort of dishonest cant about loyalty, selfishness, patriotism, playing the game and dishonouring the dead," Isherwood wrote from the vantage point of the late 1930s. "Now I wanted to be left alone." This is the authentic voice of his generation, but it is unlikely to have been what he really felt at the age of fourteen. He was placed in the top form of the lower school among boys who were on average a year older than he, and certainly seems to have applied himself, bringing back a good report at the end of his first term. "Has worked very well indeed all through," his form master wrote. "He is thoroughly painstaking and his English essay is most promising." Kathleen noted in "The Babys Progress" that "At fourteen Christopher's taste's almost entirely literary & he is very fond of poetry." He compiled a fifty-page commonplace book of poetry while at Repton in his clear, well-formed hand, containing works by such authors as Tennyson, Browning, Kipling, Chesterton, Belloc, Yeats, Stevenson, Drinkwater, Masefield, Hardy, de la Mare—and a couple of his schoolboy contemporaries. He frequently mentions the books, poems and plays he was reading in letters home to his mother: *Moonfleet, Silas Marner, The Dynasts, The Maid of France, Sea Life in Nelson's Time, The Queen's Quair,* most of which suggest an interest in British history. The book with which he identified most strongly, however, was *Wuthering Heights.* He had been brought up in a wild countryside very similar to that of Emily Brontë's novel, and claimed that the moorland visible from Wyberslegh stretched away to the northeast almost without urban interruption all the way to Haworth. Reading the book, he always felt himself back in the landscape of his early childhood and recalled the way Wyberslegh Hall was frequently battered by strong winds, making it resemble Wuthering Heights, the isolated house with which, by happy coincidence, it shared its initials. The Brontës were virtually regarded as "local" authors and Isherwood almost certainly learned about them at a young age. Among his aunt Moey's publications was *The Brontë Birthday Record,* "containing Extracts for Every Day in the Year from the Works of The Sisters Brontë," and Kathleen went to lectures on the sisters. For Isherwood, however, *Wuthering Heights* and its author became a cult. "The idea of the sternness of the moors, the bitterness of death and the finality of parting are something peculiarly suited to the tastes of a very young man, who hasn't yet experienced any of them," he acknowledged.

The experience of looking after her sickly parents made Kathleen inclined to fuss over her children's health, and she meticulously recorded every cough or sniffle in her diaries, as indeed Isherwood would do as an adult: the seeds of his hypochondria were undoubtedly sown in his childhood. It was a period when parents believed that all children, unless brutishly robust, needed "building up," usually by means of variously revolting tonics. Doctors were frequently summoned to Marple to inspect the children and advise upon courses of exercise or treatment. While Christopher would cause only the most anxious parent fears on behalf of his health, Richard was frequently unwell. "He looks so pink & white & so quickly changes colour & seems so limp & tired, & his little tummy distended," Kathleen confided to her diary in February 1918. A local doctor put the six-year-old child on a diet of Bovril and jelly and "advised above all plenty of air, regular hours—no eating between meals—regular ways—rest after lunch, no pushing as regards lessons, or ever any cramming to get scholarships but interests such as telescope & young society, drilling (inclined to be knock-kneed) massage if legs ache." It is probable that Richard's mysterious illnesses and weaknesses had some psychological cause, and the picture that gradually emerges from Kathleen's diaries is of a seriously disturbed child.

Richard continued to spend most of his time at Marple in Nanny's charge, although Kathleen visited often and the whole family always took a long summer holiday together. Kathleen complained that "there is a good deal about 'preferring his poor old Nannie,' <u>obviously put in his head</u>! as is the inclination to be jealous of Christopher & the fancy that Mummie isnt so nice to him & belongs to Bubbie [Richard's pet name for his brother]." A pretty child, with a great mass of curls, Richard occasionally behaved "like the little angel that he always looks but which alas he is far from being," as Kathleen put it. More often, he was inclined to sulk or throw tantrums, working himself up into an hysterical state, "tears & laughter never very far apart." He also developed a passion for railways and spent much of his time playing with toy trains, drawing engines and signals, or persuading Nanny or Kathleen to take him for walks along embankments or over bridges where he could watch real locomotives. This would seem a perfectly ordinary hobby for a small boy, but there was something monomaniacal and obsessive in Richard's interest. "R talked incessantly about trains & stations & places," Kathleen recorded after a walk in the country, "—wish so he had less limited interests—the beauties of nature are quite wasted on him." To some extent she indulged him, making him an elaborate railway guide to Fairyland, complete with a carefully worked-out timetable for trains from Browneytown to Clangettypop and an explanation of the fares, paid in bobbins. For his eighth birthday he demanded and received *Bradshaw's Railway Guide*—not exactly light reading for a child. He barely saw any other children, and when Kathleen was not at Marple he spent most of his time in the company of the servants or his frail and *distrait* grandparents, who were not overfond of children, even their own.

Richard's apparent devotion to Nanny was not reciprocated. There was never any doubt at all which of her two charges was her favorite, and she evidently found Richard's company a strain. It was always said that whereas Christopher took after his mother's side of the family, Richard was a true Isherwood; in particular he resembled his uncle Henry.

I was always being told by M[um] and Nannie how very like I was to Henry and how selfish he was, so utterly different from Frank. Nannie was fiendish about this, but for all that I think she rather admired H., snobbishly, for his grand manner—unlike Mum who had the lowest opinion of him. She said soothingly to me 'Never mind, so long as you don't grow up like him.' But I felt that I was doomed completely already for being so like him in appearance. I had begun reading 'Mrs Markham's History of England', and had come upon John of Gaunt and Charles the second and various other royal personages having 'natural children', and I said to M. anxiously, 'Mum, I'm not a natural child of Uncle Henry's, am I? I thought you and my father might have adopted me off him?', to which M. replied with a shudder and severely 'Don't even suggest such a thing, Richard.'

Richard also greatly disliked the nickname Christopher and Kathleen had bestowed on him: Flabjury. The origins of this name are not known, but it doesn't sound altogether affectionate. "It used to bother me terribly," Richard recalled. "I felt that I was some horrible elf." Intentionally or not, the "flab" element of the name suggested a lack of physical or moral backbone, and among the many fears to which Richard was subject was one of cows, frequently encountered during country walks. Nanny would tell him that his father would be ashamed of such cowardice and that if he were alive he would beat him. (In fact, Frank shared his son's fear of cattle.)

Richard's continuing devotion to Nanny was an early manifestation of a distinct (and distinctly erotic) streak of masochism in his character. Deprived of friends his own age, he was drawn to older boys such as Michael Scott, whom Isherwood continued to see during holidays spent at Marple, sometimes staying the night at the family house nearby. "I remember dimly what a violent 'crush' I had on him," Richard wrote toward the end of his life, "and thought him the handsomest most attractive big boy I had ever seen, and that I was always running after him to attract his notice— How he *must* have loathed the sight of me (although he never showed it), his nice friend's loathsome little brother—and so I was loathsome." Isherwood teased Richard by telling him that the Scotts would kidnap him and that his only means of escape would be through the cellar, round which Mr. Scott was rumored to chase his sons when drunk. Far from being alarmed, Richard remembered, "the prospect thrilled me to the core of *possibly* sharing a room and perhaps a bed too with your friend, and I felt I would willingly clean his boots, etc., etc."

It is possible that Richard's avowed preference for Nanny over Kathleen was a bid for his mother's attention. In later years Richard recognized that he had been extremely jealous of Frank. It would be all too easy to diagnose Richard as suffering from an Oedipus complex, but a simpler view of things was that Frank represented a very real rival for Kathleen's attention. Kathleen was still keenly mourning her husband, and while Christopher had been old enough to remember his father, and understand and share something of her loss, Richard simply knew that the attention his mother would normally have paid him was being diverted elsewhere. This deprivation was exacerbated by the fact that, for practical reasons, he was separated from his mother for much of this formative period of his life. Kathleen felt very guilty that, with Mama in London and Christopher in Hindhead, she didn't spend as much time with Richard as she ought. In the backs of her diaries she would tot up the exact number of days she had spent in his company during the year—157 in 1918, 163 in 1919—as if trying to reassure herself that she was a responsible mother. In the early years of the century, most upper-middle-class children saw less of their parents than their nannies, but they did at least live in the same house. For much of the time Kathleen was literally beyond reach.

Kathleen hoped that school would have a "sedative" effect on Richard. With this in mind, she decided to send him to the junior school at Berkhamsted in October 1919. Reluctant to let him board, she planned to rent a house in the town, where Nanny and Richard could live, and where she would spend what time she could spare from her mother and other calls upon her days and energy. Meanwhile, the three of them took lodgings there, paying frequent visits to the numerous Greene cousins who had colonized the town. On his first day at school, Richard was entrusted to the care of the headmaster, Mr. Frost, and returned for lunch "very excited & happy & rather incoherent as to the mornings events . . . apparently they had heard about birds & about Queen Ethelburga, & they had done some writing & some spelling." ("The Lives of the Queens of England" was another of Richard's burgeoning obsessions— "a violent hobby of mine in those days," as he later put it.) On the second day, Richard came out at midday "all excitability & on wires," but was pacified after being taken by Nanny to look at trains. Thereafter, the chief difficulty was getting Richard through the school gates. He was an unusually apprehensive child whose fears were rarely allayed by experience. Many mornings began badly: "R. had a very unhappy day, starting with irritability & tear's & flying into uncontrolled temper simply stamping & shaking & screaming, in a way which makes me very unhappy . . . the attacks come on like sudden shower's with bright intervals of sunshine & happiness between." Kathleen discussed her son's progress with his headmaster, who was concerned that Richard failed to join in with the other boys' games, but "seemed to think [he] was gradually falling into the ways quite nicely, as long as things went smoothly as they had begun, & 'there were no accidents.' He saw of course how terribly nervous & highly strung he was, & oddly enough had cut out of the D.M. [*Daily Mail*] an article on nervous children & their treatment, the same as I had! it agreeing so entirely with his great idea to take no notice, & behave as if there was nothing unusual about them or the things they did." Behaving as if there was nothing unusual about her sons or the things they did was to be Kathleen's method of dealing with them throughout her long life.

While Richard's experiences of his new school could hardly be described as an unqualified success ("he . . . now seems to have got school too much on his brain, though mercifully there is not much longer now," Kathleen wrote in keen anticipation of the Christmas holidays), Christopher was thriving at Repton. He was confirmed in November 1919 and, said his report, was "doing well in all ways." He even enjoyed the Officers' Training Corps and spent part of the Easter holiday in 1920 in camp near Aldershot, from which he paid a visit to the family's old house Frimley Lodge. He had begun to assert his independence and, rather than taking the train with the rest of the family, traveled that summer to Penmaenmawr on his bicycle, a journey of more than ninety miles that took two days. In December he passed his certificate exam with credit in history, English, Greek, Latin, divinity and even in mathematics, for which he had required extra coaching.

At the beginning of 1921, although still nominally in the Upper Fifth, he became a history specialist and was able to give up all other subjects apart from Latin, divinity and French—"a boon & a blessing," as he described it to his mother. Classes were held in an historic and civilized room in the old Priory, recently restored in memory of those who had died in the war. There was oak panelling, a beamed ceiling, tall bookcases and a huge open fireplace; boys sat around tables in comfortably upholstered chairs. When not being taught, sixth-formers were allowed to work during timetabled free periods in the equally relaxed atmosphere of the library. Becoming a history specialist also brought Isherwood into contact with two people who would have a great influence upon him, one a master, the other a fellow pupil.

Graham Burrell Smith, who taught history, had been one of Fisher's first and best appointments. It is significant that *Lions and Shadows,* which is subtitled "An Education in the Twenties," should start with a description of G. B. Smith as "Mr Holmes": "a short, stout, middle-aged man with reddish hair just beginning to get thin on the crown." Physically unimpressive, the forty-year-old Smith was nevertheless a charismatic figure who had learned the art of capturing and holding the attention of his pupils, rather in the manner of an expert angler playing trout. As Isherwood acknowledged, there were some among the pupils who got away, but Isherwood himself swallowed the bait and was hooked. Not that Smith made an immediate impression: a paper he delivered to the Literary Society on "Poetry and Politics of the Nineteenth Century" was described by Isherwood as "rather boring" but "mercifully short." At the age of sixteen and a half, and perhaps influenced by Kathleen, Isherwood was a severe and somewhat patronizing critic of those employed to teach him: "Unfortunately, he had too obviously 'got up' the subject to make it really interesting," he informed his mother. Smith was not someone who dished out praise to his pupils and it is possible that Isherwood was piqued to have essays handed back with "There are some sane things in it" and other laconic remarks scribbled at the bottom. A later pupil, W. B. Gallie, remembered Smith's "unusual combination of approachability and shrewd, sometimes critical, common sense. He would always listen carefully and think over what we said to him; he usually gave boys the benefit of the doubt when their motives were questionable; but he would point out weaknesses or inconsistencies in any suggestion or complaint with a devastating pungency." He was unconventional and inclined to be mildly subversive, encouraging pupils to form their own opinions, even when these did not fit in with the prevailing ethos of the school. "As a teacher of history S[mith] was a profound liberalizing influence," Gallie continued.

> Very soon boys were talking of his 'bomb-shells', though an apter metaphor would have been 'prickings'—of almost any kind of pretentiousness and humbug, particularly nationalistic humbug [. . .] The lesson would go forward, intensely interesting if never inspiring, until suddenly—the bomb would drop: something awful about, say, the Protestant persecution of scientific thought, or the rise of British parliamentary institutions, or Nelson's relations with the British admiralty, or the late nineteenth-century scramble for colonies. But as a teacher of history S[mith] was something more than an exorciser of Protestant or British prejudices: he taught us to see the complexity of every morally important political issue.

By the end of the year, Isherwood looked to Smith for advice on all matters and had fallen wholly under his influence.

The other person to have a profound and even more subversive influence upon Isherwood was Edward Upward. Just under a year older than Isherwood, the short and darkly handsome Upward was in a different house and so the two boys had not met before now. The impact was instant and lasted throughout their lives. "Never in my life have I been so strongly and immediately attracted to any personality, before or since," Isherwood wrote in 1938. "Everything about him appealed to me. He was a natural anarchist, a born romantic revolutionary." It is doubtful whether any notions of revolution, romantic or otherwise, had entered Isherwood's head before he met Upward. Although he was never a particularly biddable child, Isherwood did not learn true rebellion until now; in the nursery he had been merely despotic. He later described going to St. Edmund's as "perhaps the most valuable single experience of my life," adding: "But it could only teach non-conformism." This was written very much after the event and he had until now remained a conventional boy, willingly accepting the values of his upbringing and education. The letters he wrote to his mother show him as a mature and responsible youth, who had taken on his father's role, insofar as that was possible for a sixteen-year-old. Although he addressed Kathleen as "My darling Mummie" and signed himself "Ever your very loving son Christopher XXXXXX," he wrote to her on terms of near-equality, and gave her frequent and firm advice about such matters as Richard's education. The remarks he passed on Repton and his relatives could be mildly satirical, but this merely echoed Kathleen, whose own views (notwithstanding the occasional amused cocking of an eyebrow) remained impregnably conservative. It did not occur to Christopher to question the standards and beliefs of his background. He would later reinvent his father as an "Anti-Heroic Hero," a key figure in his personal mythology, but the evidence suggests that at this period in his life he saw Frank as everyone else did, without irony, as someone who had died for his country and whose self-sacrifice, although tragic, had been unequivocally noble. Those who lost members of their families in the war often consoled themselves with this notion; the (rare) alternative was bitterness and anger and a revolt against the whole idea of the war. Isherwood was no Sassoon, however, and two poems he wrote while at St. Edmund's demonstrate that he had swallowed the school's prevailing ethos without blinking. "A Lay of Modern Germany" is modeled on Macaulay's *Lays of Ancient Rome*, a popular volume in classrooms ever since it was first published in 1842. Isherwood's version is partly written in a "German" accent: "Then how can man die petter / Than facing fearful odds / And gassing vell dese English swine / Who tink that they are gods." This was written about a year after Frank's death and was followed by a parody of Lewis Carroll's "Father William" (itself a parody of Robert Southey).

> 'You are old, Father William,' the Crown Prince said,
> 'And your hair has become very white,
> And yet you incessantly can't go to bed,
> Do you think at your age it is right?'
>
> 'In my youth,' Kaiser William replied to his son,
> 'I slept every night without pain,
> But now that I think of the crimes that we've done
> I never shall slumber again.'

Both poems are skillful but entirely conventional, echoing (perhaps significantly) Kathleen's frequent outbursts against the German nation in her diaries. There is no sense in these poems of personal animosity toward a country that had deprived the young author of his father. All the energy of the poem has gone into its prosody, and wartime issues of *Punch* contain similarly clever but impersonal propagandist parodies.

Upward changed all that. He provided, Isherwood said, "the kind of education you can only get from people of your own age." Upward had been brought up in Romford, Essex, where his father was a general practitioner and although there was a strain of nonconformism in his parents' generation, his background was as conventional as Isherwood's. Unlike Isherwood, however, he had refused to be confirmed, and did not take the Officers' Training Corps the least bit seriously. The atmosphere at Repton may have been less feverish than it had been during the war, but the corps was still pursued with appropriately martial solemnity by the authorities. Upward regarded the whole thing as an irrelevancy. In this he was not alone, and he recalled that slacking and larking were commonplace at the summer camps where several schools got together: "Eton behaved themselves in the most disgraceful manner. We used to have concerts in a big tent, and before it started they'd be singing all kinds of lewd songs, and they were always the most slovenly on parade." The Repton corps was overseen by a master called Snape who would instruct miscreants to "Salute the flag as if you meant it!" but was generally disregarded. Upward had recently arrived at the conclusion that he was not as useless as people had been telling him ever since prep school. "The trouble was that I was 'incomp' as a fag and I was therefore thought to be 'incomp' at everything else." Experience soon showed him that this was not the case and that his elders were not necessarily his betters.

Mocking the OTC could not have come easily to someone whose father had been killed in the war, but gradually Isherwood came to recognize that the sort of reverence people claimed to feel for Frank was a way of keeping him in line. He had been placed "under an obligation to be worthy of Frank, his Hero-Father, at all times and in all ways," he recalled.

> Cyril and Rosa [Morgan Brown] were the first to make him aware of this obligation. Later there were many more who tried to do so: people he actually met, and disembodied voices from pulpits, newspapers, books. He began to think of them collectively as The Others.
>
> It was easy for these impressive adults to make a suggestible little boy feel guilty. Yet he soon started to react against his guilt. Timidly and secretly at first, but with passion, with a rage against The Others which possessed him to the marrow of his bones, he rejected their Hero-Father. Such a rejection leads to a much larger one. By denying your duty toward the Hero-Father, you deny the authority of the Flag, the Old School Tie, the Unknown Soldier, The Land That Bore You and the God of Battles. Christopher's realization that he had done this—and that he must tell The Others he had done it—came to him only by degrees and not until he was nearly grown up.

He and Upward began to create an entire category of people who represented "the other side" and who earned their sneers and condemnation.

It is possible that had it not been for Upward, Isherwood might have pursued the sort of career his mother had in mind for him, that of an academic or a librarian. Another crucial element in his nascent rebellion, however, was the growing recognition that he was homosexual, a circumstance which would place him firmly and forever at odds with the majority. It has been suggested, by Upward among others, that Isherwood "chose" to become homosexual as an act of rebellion against his mother, his class and society in general. Having embraced the gay liberation movement of the 1970s, Isherwood himself was inclined to peddle this myth. An episode with a woman in the 1920s demonstrated that he was "capable" of heterosexual intercourse and therefore, the argument went, it followed that he had a choice in the matter of his sexual orientation. This runs counter to all the evidence about his youthful development, and everything else about his life suggests that he would never have made a very convincing full-time heterosexual. In later life he would ask young men who came to see him whether they "fell in love with" (rather than merely had sex with) men or women. He recognized that the distinction was important. Isherwood's one documented heterosexual experience was unaccompanied by any emotional involvement and had been in the nature of an experiment, the seizing (as he would often do) of an opportunity to learn something about himself.

According to Upward, "everyone was homosexual, up to a point, at Repton." That point was sexual expression, and most boys contented themselves with romantic friendships. Some pupils, of course, did become sexually involved with each other, and those who were caught were summarily expelled. And not only pupils: Upward's own housemaster was obliged to leave when the prefects complained to the headmaster about "certain practices." Isherwood attracted several admirers, and was later to court junior boys assiduously, but he was probably too idealistic and puritanical to go any further. Upward does not believe that Isherwood had any sort of sexual experience until he went to university. Isherwood's "innocence" may be gauged by the way he wrote to his mother about these friendships. A boy called Knights appropriated proofs of some studio photographs of Isherwood, which Kathleen had sent him. "Knights was very tiresome about the photo, which he declares he will keep until he gets a proper one!" he reported in February 1921. He was later obliged to send for six more copies, "as they seem to be somewhat in demand." The exchange of photographs was commonplace in schools at this period and did not necessarily suggest infatuation, but one senses here a certain flirtatious urgency. Kathleen appears to have met Knights and approved of him, even though his father was "a wretched suburban business man," as Isherwood put it; she was less keen on a boy called Hardwick. "You will be relieved to hear that Hardwick was not 'one of the lucky prizewinners,' as Richard would say!" he reassured her when describing the distribution of photographs. He nevertheless continued to be friends with the boy, occasionally teasing his mother about this: "My relations with [Hardwick] remain unchanged," he wrote during the summer term of 1921. "We play tennis quite a lot together, as I am getting rather tired of convention; & people soon give up talking!"

The "proper" photographs so much in demand were almost certainly reproductions of one taken in April 1921 by Eric Falk, a boy in Isherwood's house who, like Upward, would remain a lifelong friend. This photograph would provide an enduring image of the young Isherwood when it was used as a frontispiece for *Lions and Shadows*. Dressed and posed casually, Isherwood looks at the camera with relaxed self-assurance. He wears a flannel suit, the jacket of which is buttoned over a knitted waistcoat; his tie is neatly knotted, but the shirt has a soft pointed collar, held fashionably tight by a pin. His hands are thrust negligently into his trouser pockets. The hair is neatly brushed and parted just left of center, and although his face has yet to attain its mature leanness, which would emphasize his prominent, bony nose, this is recognizably the same young man who appears in publicity photographs during the 1930s. This image marks the beginning of a lifelong awareness of and interest in the kind of person he was, the sort of figure he presented to the world. At the age of sixteen and a half, Christopher Isherwood had discovered his principal subject.

In March 1921 Elizabeth Isherwood, who had been growing increasingly feeble, died. Kathleen decided not to attend the funeral, and Christopher, as the heir to Marple, went in her place. "That evening I was taken into Grannie's room," he told Kathleen in a detailed letter about the funeral. "She was lying in her coffin just like one of those ivory or marble figures you see on old tombs—looking very unreal & expressionless—but without at all giving you the impression that you were looking at a dead body. All the variations that make a person had gone—as Aunt Esther said." The following afternoon the cortège made its way to Marple Old Church, where Elizabeth was to join her husband's ancestors in the family vault. As befitted his status, Isherwood accompanied his grandfather in the first of the carriages following the hearse. The committal was held on the steps of the vault. "There was a tremendous wind blowing & crowds of people standing round, which rather vulgarized the ceremony," Isherwood told his mother (no doubt echoing her own prejudices). "But the really touching moment was when poor Grandad, on going away, made a little bow to the vault, as if saying goodbye."

The summer term saw Isherwood's first appearance in print as a writer of fiction. "The Hang-Yü Mysteries" ("By S*x R*hm*r") was published in *The Phœnix,* an optimistically titled Repton magazine which ran to only one issue. As the joke authorship ascription signals, this 800-word story (like Isherwood's St. Edmund's poems) was an exercise in parody. Sax Rohmer was the popular author of *Dr. Fu Manchu* (1913), a thriller about an evil Oriental criminal which spawned a whole series devoured by generations of schoolboys—and by Grandpa Isherwood, whose taste in reading remained unsophisticated. Like much pulp fiction, Rohmer's addictive prose, made up in equal parts of cliché and the comic-grotesque, is ripe for parody, and parody is often a feature of literary apprenticeship. What is remarkable about "The Hang-Yü Mysteries" is not so much its accuracy—it is a *reductio ad absurdum* of Rohmer's work—as the aplomb with which the sixteen-year-old Isherwood pulls it off. It is early evidence of what he later dismissed as a "fatal facility for pastiche," but it also bears witness to a genuine literary flair, as in the apt inventiveness of the simile in his scene-setting: "The stars blazed down evilly through semi-opaque whorls of river-fog, foul and clinging as a market girl's yashmak." Isherwood's taste for the macabre and sinister, derived from childhood readings of Dickens and Ainsworth, was encouraged by Upward, whose adolescent poetry tended to be Gothic in atmosphere and expression. The combination of these influences was to become part of the two young writers' shared imaginative landscape and was to color their early literary collaborations.

Another important influence on Isherwood's early literary endeavors was the school story, a vogue for which had swept the country in the years before the First World War and still continued, hardly abated, in its wake. When the following summer Isherwood started to write a novel, he temporarily abandoned the thriller genre for something closer to his own experience. In this he was encouraged by the example of Hector Wintle, a fellow pupil who spent much of his time in the library writing a novel of school life, the results of which he bravely showed to his loftily unimpressed peers. Isherwood and his friends pounced with uncharitable delight on "the spelling mistakes, *doubles entendres* and marvels of grammar" that littered the manuscript of "Donald Stanton," but in his own quiet, imperturbable way, Wintle was achieving something an aspirant writer such as Isherwood rather envied. As the mathematics master who discovered Wintle misusing school time to scribble away at his fiction recognized, this industry was "very creditable indeed," and so Isherwood embarked upon a similar project. The forty-five manuscript pages that survive of this enterprise lack a title, but a prefatory page is boldly inscribed:

PART ONE
CHAPTER I
'TWO DAYS'

The archetype of the school story is Thomas Hughes's *Tom Brown's Schooldays* (1857), and Isherwood's fragment opens in traditional style with the young protagonist, Dick Tresham, looking forward to his second term at Rugtonstead—a conflation, presumably, of Paddy Monkhouse's Rugby, Isherwood's own Repton and (misspelled) his brother's Berkhamsted. Lying in bed the morning before he sets off for the new term, Dick reads Hughes's classic, admiring the wicked, bullying Flashman but mildly nauseated by "little Arthur," the delicate and defenseless junior Tom adopts as a protégé. This is an early hint that Dick Tresham is not a self-portrait, and as the story develops, a gap widens between the protagonist and the narrator. In its delineation of the divisions between the games-players and the scholarly types, its portraits of the typical schoolboy, Dick, and the prefect-poet Traynor ("tall and aesthetic with rather sad grey eyes"), its glancing references to "beastliness" ("He had to leave, in the middle of his last term. Wretched business, but they couldn't keep him of course . . ."), this fragment is very much in the traditional mold. Isherwood had read Alec Waugh's scandalous assault upon public-school values, *The Loom of Youth* (1915), in December 1921 and dismissed it as "most awful trash," and his own work in this field is more in line with the anodyne works of Hugh Walpole and Ian Hay.

In September 1921 Kathleen at last found a house in which to settle with her family, including Mama, who had been advised by her doctors to leave her sumptuous eyrie in Buckingham Street because the stairs were putting too much strain on her heart. Emily was now eighty-one and would need even more cosseting than usual to keep ill-health at bay. Number 36 St. Mary Abbot's Terrace, just off Kensington High Street to the southwest of Holland Park, was demolished in the 1930s and the site filled by a large block of flats, but in 1921 the street was part of an enclave of houses much favored by artists. Although the Buckingham Street flat had been used as Kathleen's London base, it was not in any way a family home; one advantage of the new house was that Richard, who was now ten, could once again live with his mother. He left Berkhamsted at the end of the winter term and was enrolled at Norland Place School in neighboring Addison Road. Isherwood was very excited at the prospect of a new house, but was concerned that his mother might not be asking the agents all the right questions. "Is the telephone lease included in the rent?" he asked anxiously, "as I believe they are <u>ruinous</u> and you had better be careful what you let yourself in for." Any pleasure Kathleen may have had at the prospect of a new home was spoiled by her mother, who now proved very reluctant to leave her own house for one she perversely regarded as her daughter's, even though her own name was on the lease. She sulked and complained and went down with several recondite illnesses, but was eventually removed to Kensington along with the rest of the family.

While this domestic upheaval was taking place, Isherwood traveled to Cambridge with Edward Upward in order to take a scholarship examination. Kathleen had always imagined Christopher at Oxford, possibly because Oxford had happy associations for her of sketching holidays with Frank. G. B. Smith, however, had been at Cambridge, and wanted his protégé to follow in his footsteps. "He gives several reasons for this," Isherwood told his mother:

> He knows all the strings at Cambridge, none at Oxford.
> Cambridge goes in for pure History as a study. Oxford caters for politicians & lawyers.
> He said that Corpus Christi would be the best college. <u>Not</u> because he was there, but because:
> > It is now extremely go-ahead
> > It is full of Reptonians
> Smyth has been offered, if he does well, the post of <u>sub college librarian</u>, he would then pass on to the British Museum & finally return as <u>chief librarian</u>.[1] Mr G. B. Smith said that he could almost certainly get me a similar post, if I did well. In which case I should be set up for life. I hope you will agree with all this, which seems to me the path of destiny!?

Kathleen was not going to give up her romantic notion of Christopher among the honey-colored stone of Oxford without a struggle, and Isherwood was obliged to persuade her in a letter that, with its forceful underlinings, almost parodied her own: "I quite feel for you in your preference of Oxford surroundings, but <u>emphatically</u> think that it would be a great mistake to go against Mr G. B. Smith, whose influence & knowledge of the ropes would be <u>well worth</u> having. Mr G. B. Smith <u>quite</u> sees the undesirability of going off this year, even if I <u>did</u> get a scholarship. Hence the special arrangement with the Corpus Christi people that any scholarship I might get would be held over to next year &, <u>if I did better</u>, <u>increased</u>." Kathleen's letters have been lost, but Isherwood's replies make it clear that she took some persuading to relinquish the dream of Oxford. Eventually a compromise was reached: "After some consultation with Mr Fisher it was decided that I had better try my luck at Corpus <u>this</u> year—but, if this is an entire failure, to hold Oxford in view for <u>next</u>." The real lure, however, was that Upward planned to go to Corpus.

Isherwood crammed hard for the scholarship, without much optimism about his prospects. "Even though there is hardly any chance of my getting anything this year,

---

1. Charles H. E. Smyth, a contemporary—and butt—of Upward and Isherwood, in fact became a clergyman and religious historian. Isherwood portrays him as "Browne" in *Lions and Shadows*.

it will be interesting to see how I do," he wrote—though this may have been a placatory white lie. In the event he did better than anyone expected, winning a £40 exhibition. This, in effect, settled the argument about Oxford and Cambridge.

At Christmas the family went to Marple Hall as usual, but the remainder of the school holiday was spent at St. Mary Abbot's Terrace. Isherwood's return to Repton for the new term seemed to Kathleen "like the departure of a sun-beam," all the more so since Richard was proving characteristically unenthusiastic about his new school and took to his bed after three unhappy days there. He remained at home for a fortnight before making his second attempt. Almost immediately, he went down with a persistent cough which kept him once more at home. The school decided that he could not return until completely cured, which meant that he would miss the greater part of his first term. More worrying than his physical health, however, was his mental state. Kathleen had an interview with his teacher, who "thought his case very unusual but not one to despair over, & said it seemed to her (as so many have said) that he had had some great shock or fright he was so easily startled & frightened." Although Kathleen does not mention it, she must have had in mind Richard's encounter with the Marple Hall ghost. Later that year Richard went through another bad phase, to which memories of the Marple Hall ghost certainly contributed. "Poor R very restless in the night," Kathleen wrote in her diary. "So worried by disturbed ideas that he must say out loud the reprimands (most mild) he had had at school, worried over his wickedness over Moll of Brabyns that she might come to London, of the horror of having once been shut in the old Nursery a most cruel thing to do, with a temperament like his." It is not clear from this who it was that shut Richard in the haunted nursery, but it was almost certainly Nanny. Even if it wasn't, he was supposed to be in her charge and she was therefore responsible for his welfare. Part of the reason that Richard felt he was wicked was that Nanny was always telling him so. She continued to use Frank to instill fear into the hapless boy. He once "had a vision of Frank as a furious-looking lion watching me from the throne of God and itching to pounce on me." This is not merely rhetorical: on top of all his other difficulties, Richard was gradually developing a religious mania which largely manifested itself in a belief that he was incapable of doing good and that he was destined for eternal damnation. A sense of sin must have been instilled at an early age, and almost certainly by Nanny. Kathleen herself was capable of insensitivity: this latest nervous *crise* occurred at the time she and Richard were reading Bunyan's *Pilgrim's Progress* together—hardly the most reassuring bedtime story for a timid ten-year-old. No wonder Richard, constantly harried about his own naughtiness, grew fearful of the fires of hell. Kathleen thought that swimming lessons might help to make him more independent, but he proved panicky about water. She also had high hopes of one of his fellow pupils, who lived in the same street. "Do hope that Richard may make friends with him, as he is an only child too," she noted—a slip that says much about how she viewed her younger son.

The February of 1922 was very cold in Derbyshire, with thick ice forming on ponds, allowing Christopher his first experience of skating. In the absence of ice, Isherwood would become a fanatical roller-skater, spending hours when in London at the local rink in nearby Olympia. Much of the action of his early, unpublished novel, *Lions and Shadows,* is set at "The Velodrome," where young people hurtled around the wooden rink in a thunder of wheels. Edward Upward had left Repton to spend some time abroad learning French before taking his place at Corpus Christi in the autumn. The two boys corresponded, but few letters survive from this period. Upward's influence in absentia seems to have been concentrated on Isherwood's development as a poet, one whose work was making regular appearances in the *Reptonian* under the obscure nom de plume of "Cacoëthes." This word, which has come to mean a mania for something harmful, derives from the Latin for a malignant disease, which is itself derived from the Greek word for an evil disposition, and one might have expected someone who chose this pseudonym to indulge in some Thersites-like ranting. "The Unresting," which appeared in the school magazine in February, was judged by Upward "damned good," but it is a conventional and high-flown love sonnet. Isherwood sent it in draft to his mother, remarking: "If I ever take up with a young woman I shall tell her that all these poems were written to her!" The poet describes himself as "torn between vision and desire," which may have had more to do with one of his schoolfellows than with any young woman. "Although I could not pick out one phrase (except perhaps 'some prize of the *mad hour*') which seems distinctly Rupert Brookean," Upward wrote perceptively, "yet I feel that there is Rupert Brooke behind it all." His extended criticism of this poem marked the beginning of a lifelong commentary conducted by these two writers about each other's work. Although a history specialist, Isherwood was becoming more and more attracted to literature, as he explained to his mother:

> I have been reading various books on social reform for Mr G. B. Smith, whose one idea seems to be to create a frenzy of enthusiasm—and hence, I suppose, invective. But after all—it is no use explaining to him that my real enthusiasms are all literary. History is what I earn my living by! And the more I read these violent books he gives me, the more I feel how unpractical and prejudiced they are—and how much better Shelley or Browning or Rupert Brooke expressed the same ideas. So you see—History can only give one nasty clear-headed emptiness (as Mr G.B.S. himself practically admits), while Literature gives you—well, everything. But I don't think that having no illusions about the value of History upsets my work really—so you needn't be in the least exercised about it.

During Isherwood's final summer term, G. B. Smith invited him to join himself and a small group of boys on an Alpine walking tour along the Swiss-French border. Since, apart from Isherwood, all of those taking part—Upward, Geoffrey Kingsford (who appears in *Lions and Shadows* as "Queensford") and Smyth—had already left Repton, it would seem that this trip was a private enterprise, undertaken by the teacher without the school's involvement. The cost would be £30, Isherwood told his mother, "& Mr G.B. Smith will undertake to pay all extras—and arrange everything, including passports etc." He recognized that Kathleen might need some persuading. "I quite realize, darling, that this is rather a selfish scheme. It would take a large chunk out of our time together—as I shouldn't be back until Sept. 2nd—or thereabouts." He nevertheless used Smith as a lever: "He seems to think it will be <u>extremely</u> helpful to me from the point of view of knowledge, language and experience—which, of course, it <u>will</u>."

That G. B. Smith invited Isherwood to join an already planned tour suggests a growing intimacy between him and his pupil. One of Smith's later pupils, who also knew Isherwood, assumed that there was a special quality to this relationship beyond that of master and pupil. Though there was never any suggestion of impropriety, it seems almost certain that in the best traditions of English private education Smith was homosexual. He certainly had favorites among his pupils, and the tone of those letters he wrote to Isherwood that survive have a curiously unpedagogic, almost flirtatious tone. There is no evidence that Isherwood ever discussed sexual matters with Smith or even showed him his early attempts at fiction, all of which had distinct homoerotic overtones. Isherwood later described Smith's manner as "cold and friendly," which suggests that Smith remained aware of the gulf that divided him from even his most cherished pupils, and was even more aware of the dangers of crossing it.

In between writing poetry and planning his holiday, Isherwood was clearly finding time to do some work, and was presented with prizes for history, literature and the English essay. He also won his Form Prize at the end of term. His letters to his mother grow increasingly bumptious during this period, perhaps because he felt he had (with the assistance of G. B. Smith) begun to assert his independence. The tone is teasing though affectionate, especially when referring to his friends. "I enclose some of Hardwick's photos," he wrote in May. "There were no good ones of me. Please don't be shocked at the rather gross picture of H. in pyjamas. He had his other things on underneath." Kathleen had been obliged to accept her son's friendship with Hardwick, who had accompanied Christopher on a five-day bicycling tour during the Easter holidays. "Fisher said the other day—but perhaps I oughtn't to tell you!" he wrote about his new friend George Fisher (no relation to the headmaster). Kathleen's curiosity was evidently piqued, for in his next letter Christopher wrote: "I don't believe <u>Richard</u> wants to know in the least what Fisher said about you. I am surprised and grieved that you take any interest! However, since you must have it, he said you were one of the few people whom he'd care to have as a mother! There!"

After attending OTC Camp, Isherwood came up to London to buy clothes for his holiday. Kathleen was introduced to G. B. Smith, whom she recognized as a formidable adversary: "a <u>very</u> determined little man with keen appraising eyes—I <u>think</u> kindly, but am sure obstinate!" Armed with new flannel trousers and a sports jacket, and Mothersill (a well-known preventative for seasickness), Isherwood set off on his first European tour, sailing with Smith and Kingsford from Southampton to Le Havre, then traveling to Paris by train, collecting Upward at Rouen. They spent a day in the capital sightseeing before taking a sleeper train to Aix-les-Bains, proceeding from there to Annecy. During a trip round Lac d'Annecy on a steamer, Upward announced that he had discovered a new hero in Baudelaire, and that evening Isherwood dashed around the bookshops in search of a copy of *Les Fleurs du Mal*. The following day the party went by steam tram to Thônes, walking up from there to spend the night at Col des Aravis, before setting off the following morning for Flumet, where they caught a charabanc for Chamonix.

In *Lions and Shadows* Isherwood claims that he and Upward had made a pact to remain loftily dismissive of Alpine scenery, "consigning mountains to the great rubbish-heap of objects and ideas admired by our adversaries, 'the other side,' and therefore condemned." Although he loved the scenery, Smith encouraged his two charges in their ostentatious refusal to conform. Isherwood portrays Smith as a sort of conjurer, presenting the more spectacular of the sights to his group as a series of special effects; it was an example Isherwood himself took to heart, and his description of the holiday in *Lions and Shadows* is artfully presented, bearing out his prefatory "Note to the Reader," in which he admits that he has "used a novelist's license in describing my incidents and drawing my characters." A characteristic passage is his description of his first sight of Mont Blanc, which had been obscured by mist on their arrival at Col des Aravis.

> Next morning the sunshine woke us early. Chalmers [i.e. Upward], with whom I shared a room, was the first out of bed; yawning, stretching himself, he hobbled over to the window, started back in mock horror: 'Good God! It's arrived!'
> Mont Blanc confronted us, dazzling, immense, cut sharp out of the blue sky; more preposterous than the most baroque wedding cake, more convincing than the best photograph. It fairly took my breath away. It made me want to laugh.
> 'I don't believe it!'
> 'Neither do I!'

This, of course, is how it *should* have happened, but the truth was rather less dramatic. "It was misty when we arrived," Isherwood told his mother, "but, going down, we had the most gorgeous view of the Mont Blanc Range." The version in *Lions and Shadows* may not be factually accurate, but it presents a very vivid impression of the teenage Isherwood and Upward and the flavor of their friendship. It is also an example of Isherwood's concern with truth rather than facts, something that would be a feature of all his writing. To reveal the essence of a person or a situation, it was often necessary to alter details or even invent them. This was in fact part of the writer's art.

Isherwood returned to Repton for his final term in September, taking up an appointment as literary editor of the school magazine. He may also have been taking another look at his school novel, because he embarked on a second draft immediately after the end of term. Isherwood later named E. F. Benson as a model, and this author's sentimental, hugely popular but covertly erotic *David Blaize* (1916) was to influence Isherwood in a more particular way than he was prepared to admit in *Lions and Shadows*. In Benson's novel, the "hopelessly seraphic face" of the eponymous hero attracts the attention of an older boy called Maddox. Isherwood's very own David Blaize arrived in the shape of a boy with the appropriate name of Austen Darling, who became one of his fags at the beginning of the term. "There are a great many changes in the House since last term," Isherwood told Kathleen in his first letter home. "Almost everybody has left [. . .]. Everyone you meet is a new boy, and they are of all sizes and sorts." It was Darling's size and sort that particularly appealed to Isherwood. "My fags, Darling and Berry, are most amusing. Especially Darling. He is, I think, Canadian, and climbs about all over the place putting up pictures and so on. He is only about 3 feet high." Short himself, Isherwood would always be attracted to those even smaller and slighter—and younger—than himself. They brought out his protective, as well as his romantic, sympathies, and in many of his subsequent relationships he would adopt the role of an older brother, or even a father. Darling was four years younger than Isherwood, which would seem very little in the adult world, but the gulf between a fourteen-year-old and an eighteen-year-old in an English public school was enormous, and the only officially sanctioned relationship would be strictly hierarchical, that of master and servant.

Isherwood's enchantment with Darling was such that he could not resist mentioning the boy at every opportunity in letters home. "The fags continue very amusing," he told Kathleen the following week. "The other morning I heard a kind of far-away chanting going on somewhere overhead. It sounded like angels. I looked up and saw Darling standing over me singing to himself through his teeth." It remains a matter of speculation whether or not Darling (who was killed in action during the Second World War) recognized the effect he was having upon his besotted fagmaster. In order to spend extra time with Darling, Isherwood recruited him to be a secretarial assistant on the *Reptonian*. In *Lions and Shadows,* Isherwood recalls that he once caned Darling, for losing a pair of football boots. "I don't suppose I hurt him much; next day, of course, the whole thing was elaborately turned into a joke. Nevertheless, a certain confidence had been broken between us, we shared a sense of humiliation like an indecent secret; our relations could never be quite the same again." This was untrue, and Upward recalled that Isherwood caned Darling partly in order to test his potential for sexual sadism and admitted he found the experience distinctly erotic.

Thinly disguised, Darling made frequent appearances in Isherwood's earliest attempts at fiction. In the second draft of the school novel already mentioned, Darling is clearly the model for the naughty but angelic-looking fag Wirwick, who has "a heavenly smile." As late as 1927, Darling would make an appearance in an unfinished school novel, "The Winter Term," aptly subtitled "a romance." When a housemaster is injured in a road accident, the somewhat priggish and remote Head of House, Charles Symondson, is obliged to take on extra responsibilities. His determination to improve the "tone" of the House in the wake of a sexual scandal the previous term is compromised by his obsession with his fag, Loring, who had himself been implicated in the goings-on. Charles is forever finding jobs for Loring in order to ensure the boy spends time with him in his study, just as Isherwood recruited Darling to the *Reptonian.* Isherwood eventually completed only six chapters of this novel, but in 1947 came across the manuscript and made a note of how he had intended the plot to resolve itself. "Late one night. Charles finds Loring & Nicholas [his best friend] together in Nick's study. He assumes they are having an affair, is utterly disgusted, furiously jealous and goes out, deciding to say nothing about it, because he feels the moral weakness of his own position. He is so upset that he gets flu and retires to the sickroom for several days." At the end of term, "he snubs Loring, who tries to say Goodbye to him. Then, when it is too late, in a taxi driving down to the station, Nicholas, with great embarrassment, confesses to Charles that he *had* made a pass at Loring when Charles surprised them together, but that Loring had refused—saying that the only person he felt that way about was Charles himself, and that Charles didn't seem to want it." This is almost certainly wishful thinking rather than an accurate record of the relationship of Isherwood and Darling, between whom there appears to have been no estrangement, whatever Isherwood might have claimed in *Lions and Shadows*. But it almost certainly reflects the nature of Isherwood's guilty but romantically exciting passion for his junior. Adolescent boys would continue to be the principal emotional focus of Isherwood's life for many years.

In December Isherwood, accompanied by a fellow pupil named J. R. Chalmers,[2] went up to Cambridge to take a scholarship examination in the hope of upgrading his exhibition. Kathleen can hardly have been reassured by reports of how certain Old Reptonians were getting on at the university. "The other day I heard from Upward, who doesn't seem to care for Cambridge," Isherwood blithely reported in November. "I can't think why they sent him there. Orpen threw squibs [fireworks] about the street on November 5th and got arrested! His trial came off on Friday. Mr G.B.S. thinks he will probably be sent down."[3] Kathleen would have been even more alarmed if she had seen the letter from Upward her son had mentioned.

> Yes, Cambridge is damnable—as you anticipated—but in a rather different way. My God, if Repton was unmitigated Hell then Cambridge is insidious Hell!! Everything is so 'nice', comfortable and perfect up here; one imagines at first that there is nothing to be desired [. . .] Nevertheless, mind you get a scholarship in history and come up here. I shall die or go about with women of the *town* or something, unless I find somebody in the college with some proper blood in his veins. Smyth assures me confidently that there is none such. I believe it. For God's sake arrive! Have no fears about intellectual conversations, they aren't very rampant. I shall take to drink.

Just before the end of term Isherwood learned that his exhibition had been converted into an £80 scholarship. "I congratulate him very heartily," Fisher wrote. "To get top scholarship is very good. His career here has been thoroughly to his credit and greatly to our benefit. He has been useful in many ways and I am very attached to him. Floreat Florebit." Isherwood was now ready to enter the wider world.

---

2. Isherwood borrowed this boy's surname as a pseudonym for Upward in *Lions and Shadows*. This literary disguise was subsequently used by both Stephen Spender and Upward himself.

3. Christopher Orpen was a notably reckless figure whose character and antics Isherwood drew upon for the character of Maurice Scriven in *The Memorial*.

FOUR

FTER SPENDING CHRISTMAS AT MARPLE AS USUAL, ISHERWOOD
returned to Kensington where he began assembling what Kathleen called "his
grown-up trousseau": a blue serge suit and greatcoat and other clothes. He also
started receiving pocket money of £2 a month "for buses & odds & ends." As was customary, it was decided that he should spend part of the nine months between leaving
Repton and taking up his place at university traveling and learning a foreign language.
G. B. Smith had advised him to spend some time in Germany, "as that is the language
which I especially need." Quite why Isherwood needed to speak German remains a
mystery, but may have had something to do with his plans to become a librarian,
where a third language (apart from English and French, in which he had received a
grounding at school) might prove useful. Germany was unlikely to have appealed
much to Kathleen, and in the event Isherwood ended up in France. Kathleen went to
inspect the register of suitable families at the famous scholastic agency Gabbitas and
Thring, then wrote to Edward Upward's father for advice about Rouen. In February
Isherwood started without much enthusiasm a course of eighteen French lessons at the
Hugo School in Earl's Court. He spent most of his free time at the cinema and the
roller-skating rink, often in the company of friends such as Hector Wintle.

Although Isherwood remained a keen theatergoer, his real passion was a more
modern one for the movies. This started when he was living in Limerick, where he
frequently visited the small local cinema, which in those pre-war days was something of a novelty. He avidly followed all the detective and cowboy serials that were
the basic staple of early film, and it was here, he later claimed, that his interest in the
outward appearances of people, blown up to a vast size on the screen, was first stim-
ulated. "I was a born film fan," he wrote.

[Upward] was inclined to laugh at my indiscriminate appetite for anything and
everything shown on a screen. He pointed out, quite truly, that as soon as I was inside a cinema I seemed to lose all critical sense; if we went together, I was per-

petually on the defensive, excusing the film's absurdities, eagerly praising its slightest merits. [. . .] The cinema puts people under a microscope: you can stare at them, you can examine them as though they were insects. True, the behaviour you see on the screen isn't natural behaviour; it is acting, and often very bad acting, too. But the acting has always a certain relation to ordinary life; and, after a short while, to an *habitué* like myself, it is as little of an annoyance as Elizabethan handwriting is to the expert in old documents. Viewed from this standpoint, the stupidest film may be full of astonishing revelations about the tempo and dynamics of everyday life; you see how actions look in relation to each other; how much space they occupy and how much time.

This, clearly, is theorizing after the event, but it is undoubtedly true that films would be very influential on Isherwood's writing. For the moment, however, movie-going was a pleasure to be indulged. It could also be something of a guilty pleasure. Cinema is a more voyeuristic art form than the theater, largely because the actors are not actually present. Without a live actor to return, and even seem to respond to the viewer's gaze, reciprocation becomes a matter of fantasy, which can be indulged at a safe distance and in the darkness of the auditorium. Isherwood's devouring gaze had recently become focused upon the diminutive figure of Jackie Coogan, the American child star who had achieved worldwide fame in 1921 in the title role of Charlie Chaplin's *The Kid*. Coogan's next major role was the title one in a silent version of *Oliver Twist*, a film Isherwood saw at least eight times in February and March, following the film from cinema to cinema across London. Kathleen, Richard, Nanny and Hector Wintle were all dragged along to admire the liquid-eyed moppet ("a delightful little boy though not in the least one's idea of Oliver Twist" in Kathleen's judgment), and Isherwood somehow managed to acquire some publicity stills from the film, photographs he kept all his life. That summer he began to make a cinema scrapbook, clipping text and photographs from such magazines as *Photoplay* and pasting them into an album, along with his own one-line comments on films he had seen, arranged alphabetically by title. He kept this up for some fifteen months. The book contains more photographs of Coogan than of any other actor, and Isherwood seems to have seen all the films the little star made in 1922 and 1923: *Trouble:* "Adequate Coogan, but mannerisms are creeping in. Oh, this pathos!"; *Daddy:* "The beginning of the fatal attempt to make Coogan consciously pathetic. Still, Coogan."

Richard's education, meanwhile, continued to be disrupted. He had outgrown Norland Place and been enrolled at Wilkinson's, a superior establishment in Notting Hill Gate. "Richard in very low spirits," Kathleen recorded. "It was quite a Charles and Mary Lamb walk down Addison Road & seeing him off there in the bus." Any hopes that he would settle were rapidly dispelled. After a promising start, he started "going to pieces." In order to relieve his mother, Isherwood occasionally took turns escorting the reluctant and tearful pupil to the bus stop: "It is most harrowing, these scenes," Kathleen wrote, "& reduces me utterly." In the absence of a firm paternal hand, Kathleen relied upon her elder son to instill some form of discipline in Richard, who began skipping gym and football and then lying about it. Kathleen ascribed this dishonesty to fear, but Isherwood eventually ran out of excuses for his brother and, "after long threatening to do so," administered a caning. In retrospect he described this as a "grotesque and horrible incident [. . .] even worse because it was done in self-righteousness." In any case, it seemed to have had no effect, and a few days later Richard arrived home in the evening "looking very miserable. The idea of football had been too much for him, & the fear that he would disgrace himself over it, so without saying anything he had slipped away before lunch & had been wandering about in the street ever since afraid to return home. He had eaten no breakfast had had no lunch & was in a state of collapse." He rapidly developed a temperature and the doctor prescribed rest and a "nerve tonic." Kathleen went to see the father and son who ran the school and found them unexpectedly sympathetic. It was agreed that Richard would be excused from games for the rest of term. He was now eleven, and although the Wilkinsons thought him "backward," they attributed this to his record of inter-rupted schooling and thought that he was doing reasonably well. Having managed to escape school for a week, Richard was now determined never to return. "How much should he be forced to face things?" Kathleen wondered. "Surely the more he shirks the more difficult things are?" Richard worried that his fellow pupils would know that he had run away, but it was decided he must return to the school. Christopher was de-puted to take him all the way there, but it was a foggy morning and Richard managed to give his brother the slip. A search party was launched, and Nanny eventually found the frightened boy sitting in the churchyard near his old school.

There seemed little point in forcing Richard to go back to Wilkinson's and so Kathleen, on the advice of her doctor, took him to see a "child specialist." Richard was given a thorough examination and pronounced to be perfectly well physically. The specialist advised finding a small school of perhaps a dozen or twenty pupils, preferably with sea air. He thought it better for Richard to board than to undergo the daily trauma of leaving his home to attend a local school. Kathleen eventually found an establishment called Northwood House at Herne Bay on the north Kent coast.

Given the strained atmosphere at home, it must have been with feelings of relief that Isherwood left Kensington in April to travel to Rouen, where he lodged with a Professor Morel at Le Vert Logis off the Boulevard Saint Hilaire. "The Pro-fessor, a charming old man, makes me work like the devil," Isherwood told Eric Falk, who was staying in Grenoble. Other pupils included a boy from Siam "of a horrible, rich brown, such as characterizes Madame's most lethal efforts at interpreting choco-late shape," and a Glaswegian youth called Stewart, on whom Isherwood developed a crush. Stewart was the owner of a Triumph motorcycle, and he and Isherwood spent much of their free time speeding through the surrounding countryside. A medallion of Isherwood's name-saint, St. Christopher, was attached to the bike's headlamp and seemed auspicious for the developing relationship, but this talisman did not prevent several minor accidents. These merely added to the excitement: "You can imagine how this Romance, with a little spice of danger added, tickled my very jaded pallet [*sic*]. I pounced upon it. We now go out every evening almost; so much so that I miss it dreadfully when we don't." Even so, Isherwood was obliged to admit that Stewart was not his *beau idéal*. He "has too long a jaw and he doesn't shave as often as he might, but—I am too old a stager to be deceived as to my feelings. I think he belongs to the most interesting category of all—the Ugly Keennesses."

Despite the arcane attractions of Stewart, and the more remote ones of Jackie Coogan, Darling was still very much Number One Boy. Shortly before setting off for France, Isherwood had met him off the Repton train and spent a day with him. "The flame still burns brightly before Darling's altar," he told Upward. "There is no really pure love like the passion for a child." Now, however, Darling's unreliability as a correspondent caused his admirer some anxiety. "Apropos des coeurs, splendid and otherwise, Gott Strafe Darling," he exclaimed to Falk in pseudo-Gothic script. "He has *never* written. I was, I believe, a sincere friend when we parted at Charing + — however that may be, I am now madly keen on him. Isn't it wicked? I wonder whether I have annoyed him, or whether some serpent has interfered. Bear witness, oh Falk, that I swear to smash such an one, though it be mine own familiar friend." His "keenness" on Darling was increased by the realization that Stewart, who had unromantically contracted German measles, was not really his type: "Only a glamour cast by idleness enveloped him. I still like him very much indeed, without having an idea or wish in common." They nevertheless continued to take motorbike rides together, exchanging hearty exclamations about the machine's performance.

Although he was away from home, and in wicked France, Isherwood remained sexually inexperienced, though one would hardly guess so from the tone he adopted in letters to Falk. He portrayed himself as a debauched, world-weary *roué*. "I am keen on the three tarts in Rouen," he announced. "One is in the nearest bike shop, the second mends roads and the third I saw in a cinema. The French type of male beauty is sentimentally effeminate, lending itself to open-necked collars and sailor-suits." Though still a devoted "Cooganite," he reported that "There is also a superb French film star, to judge by his portraits. His name is Jean Forest and he should shortly appear at Grenoble in 'Crainquebille.' Go and see it." Another dark beauty, the nine-year-old Forest took a Coogan-like role as a *gamin des rues* in this, his first film, adapted from a story by Anatole France. That Isherwood should judge him a superb star without actually having seen him act says much about the nature of his interest. Falk was also instructed to report back on any "tarts" he may have seen in the town.

Isherwood's fantasies and frustrations found release in writing, and he told Falk that although he had burned a work called "One Man's God," he had completed two short stories. "Abandoning all concealment," he had conceived one of them as "a yarn for Homos," written to amuse his friends. "The Wrong God" was about

> a gent called Fryne—a real 'character', like Sherlock Holmes; the complete hunter of Boys, the subtle and patient Nimrod of London. [. . .] Fryne meets a man who insists on taking him to see the films of Billy Brighteyes, the Wonder Kid. The result is idolatry of the said Billy for six weeks, until Fryne's friend leaves for India; and Fryne, too late, discovers that he was keen on *him* all the time and only enjoyed the films because of *his* presence. All this is set forth in 6000 words of sloppy flippancy; but a good plot will out, and the ensemble is not so bad as its parts.

Although fantastic, the story incorporated elements from Isherwood's own life and surroundings: the fixation upon a child star is evidently autobiographical, and the story contained episodes set at a roller-skating rink, while Fryne's room in Golgotha

Crescent was based upon Hector Wintle's room at his parents' house in Oxford Gardens, West London.

Deciding to entrust his "honour and reputation to a 25 centime stamp and the French postal system," Isherwood sent the story, marked "STRICTLY PRIVATE" and secreted within some magazines, to Falk for his comments. Although entreated to make allowances for the story's hurried composition and lack of polish, Falk appears to have been a merciless critic. "I appreciate your frankness about it and also, as far as can be expected of an author, your taste," Isherwood wrote back. "Pornographic stories are, at best, an impasse; and a little timely cold water on my head will, no doubt, prevent me from further loitering there." He was pleased that Falk had at least appreciated the "opening descriptions," which he would salvage and incorporate in a novel he was planning.

By now Isherwood was greatly looking forward to returning to England, particularly since he had been invited to Repton by G. B. Smith, who had been appointed school librarian and needed help in his project of completely reorganizing the books. "You shall have a perfect effusion from Repton, where I anticipate an emotional crisis of the first order," Isherwood warned Falk. "Emotional crises, next to having my hair shampooed, are my pet luxury. It is glorious to suffer. [. . .] Alas, I have no Past, no Present, no Future. Life is a shapeless grey jelly, of which I have eaten too much. Oh for Repton and its news! I shall never be beaten again, unless I get horsewhipped by an infuriated father." Although much of this is sheer adolescent posing, written for effect and to entertain a friend, it nevertheless contains a core of truth. These letters show Isherwood trying out what would become his principal literary method: coloratura decorations of autobiographical themes. With practice, he would learn to embellish rather than merely exaggerate, and do so with sufficient grace and conviction to make his readers unsure where fiction takes over from fact.

His pose certainly impressed Paddy Monkhouse, who later that year celebrated Isherwood's erotic interest in young boys in a scurrilous poem titled "A merry tragicall *Lover's Complaint* by *Christopher B.*" These witty verses contain references to Darling and Jean Forest before galloping to a fantastical and obscene conclusion:

When first I started roving
This country of the blind,
And set myself to loving
The chosen of mankind,
My early vision rested
On stately seventeen,
And schoolboys were invested
With evanescent sheen.

But soon those emblems tragic—
Broken voice and shaven chin—
Had blown away the magic
And let the cynic in.
So I left his whiskers curling,
Took leave (with many a sigh),

Fixed on a fourteen-yearling
*   And let the world go by.*

I spent a month or two in
*   Attempting to be fond:*
But we tottered into ruin—
*   He couldn't correspond.*
My spiritual famine
*   Was relieved (thank God again)*
By a little Breton gamin
*   Who was very nearly ten.*

And now I am in heaven
*   (At least, I greatly thrive)*
With an infant son of Devon
*   Who has only topped his five.*
And before the year is over
*   (What a year for broken troths!)*
I shall be the ardent lover
*   Of a baby in long clothes.*

I shall then pursue the spectre
*   Of a little embryo:*
Wed a woman, and respect her
*   (Nature has decreed it so)*
And the while with heat and hasting
*   Her consent is to be won*
I shall only be foretasting
*   Of my unbegotten son.*

In Christopher's absence, Richard's educational problems had come to a head. Although destined for Herne Bay, Richard had asked that he might be allowed to give Wilkinson's another chance. Kathleen reluctantly agreed, but on the eve of the new term Richard was "in a despairing state of mind bordering on hysteria—begging to be allowed to throw himself from the window or be sent to prison, or away to boarding school—anything rather than go back." He woke at six the following morning "miserable & hysterical," but nevertheless set off for Notting Hill, accompanied by Nanny. As they were crossing Holland Park Avenue, he ran away, shouting that he would never return to the school. Nanny set off in pursuit, but lost him almost immediately. She spent the rest of the day searching the area fruitlessly and when he failed to turn up at home for tea, Kathleen went to the police station to report him missing. She was told to call again with a description if he had not returned by nine. He had not, but late in the evening Kathleen received a telephone call from Richard's former landlady in Berkhamsted, Mrs. Cass, to say that he had been with her but had then set off for the station; she was just checking to see that he had got back home. After the

Greenes had been alerted, Richard finally returned to Mrs. Cass's, where he was put to bed. He returned to London the following afternoon, "very tearful & repentant & rather frightened." His passion for railways had served him well the previous day: after bolting from Nanny, he had walked all the way to Harrow, some eight miles, where he bought a train ticket with the money he had been given for the school magazine.

The Wilkinsons suggested that Richard might stay with them for a trial week, so that he would not have to face the daily ordeal of leaving home. Shortly after he had been deposited with them, they phoned to say that he had run away. About an hour later, Richard appeared on his mother's doorstep. It is hardly surprising that by now Kathleen felt "quite worn out." She went to consult Jack Isherwood, who suggested issuing an ultimatum: Richard must choose between Wilkinson's, Herne Bay or Berkhamsted. This was put to Richard and resulted, as might have been predicted, in "storms of tears." "I feel as if the situation was beyond me," Kathleen wrote, "& am quite unable to judge what would be best for him. It is clear he can't go on doing nothing." By now even the kindly Wilkinsons were running out of patience. They suggested that unless he returned to their school within the next two days, Kathleen should send him away to Herne Bay. This deadline was extended and Richard set off to Wilkinson's alone, but immediately he saw some of the other boys, he knew he couldn't face them and returned home. Kathleen started packing his trunk for Northwood House.

The day of Richard's departure was, Kathleen wrote, "one of the most <u>utterley miserable</u> days I have ever spent." Richard awoke at five, determined to escape to the Wilkinsons to ask for one more chance. Kathleen locked the front and back doors, then had to lock the garden gate after Richard had attempted to climb out of the schoolroom window. "He ran up and down like a distracted hunted animal declaring it would kill him to go away & crying & imploring—it was <u>simply agony</u>." The headmaster of Northwood House, Mr. Wells, arrived with his brother in order to conduct the distraught pupil to the station. Richard made two unsuccessful bids to escape this formidable escort—one at Victoria Station, the other upon arrival at Herne Bay—but that evening Mr. Wells telephoned to say that he was sure the boy would settle within a couple of days. This view was confirmed by Christopher, who wrote from Rouen to assure his mother that she had done the right thing and tell her that the third day at a new school "was generally the crisis of misery." Although she received no news the following day, Kathleen resisted telephoning the school. By the next day her patience was tried in the extreme. Young Mr. Wilkinson was sent for and agreed to telephone Wells. "The Brute might be more open with him," Kathleen felt, but Wilkinson could gather nothing definite, while the late post brought an unhappy letter from Richard pleading to be removed from the school. The following day Kathleen received a letter "of a semi-facetious order" from Wells, who she felt had "a lot to learn if he hopes to placate parents."

Richard weathered a mild case of mumps and eventually seemed to settle in, though he was "not at <u>all</u> resigned to being so far from London." Evidently realizing that Kathleen was determined he should stay at boarding school, Richard told his grandmother about one of the masters who visited the dormitory after lights-out to kiss his favorite pupils good night. Richard—who, inevitably, was not one of the favorites—wasn't worried by the teacher's behavior, but he hoped that Emily would be sufficiently shocked to insist that Kathleen remove her son from such an environment. Emily merely exclaimed, "Horrible hateful man!" and said no more about it. "She wasn't in the least interested," Richard recalled. "She was a conscientious grandmother, or tried to be, but she disliked children in any case and I think resented my filial claims on M."

Richard returned to St. Mary Abbot's Terrace for the summer holidays at the end of July. Although he looked well and had a healthy tan, he had developed an alarming twitch which affected his right arm and leg. "The jerking up of the right shoulder as if in self defence & the furtive look accompanying it seem to come on in fits," Kathleen noted. These spasms, Mr. Wells blandly informed Kathleen, had started on Richard's first day at Northwood House—"as if being paralysed with fright had caused a nervous affection [sic]," Kathleen added. A doctor who had successfully treated one of Richard's cousins was consulted: he recommended a largely vegetarian diet, plenty of fresh air away from London, and a course of massage and "Swedish exercises."

At the beginning of July, with unmixed feelings of relief, Isherwood left Rouen. He arrived home a published author, since his poem "Mapperley Plains" had recently appeared in the annual volume of *Public School Verse.* He had written the poem the previous year after returning from an OTC field day, and it describes the poet marching along in a group, dreaming of Mapperley Plains. He had remembered this evocative name from a competition organized by the school, where postcards were attached to toy balloons before releasing them in the air. The postcards carried a request that whoever found the balloon should send the card back to Repton; the card that came from furthest afield would be considered the winner. One card was returned from Mapperley Plains. Isherwood later discovered that, far from being "so strange and fair," as the poem states, Mapperley Plains is a suburb of Nottingham, in the heart of the industrial Midlands. The poem, which consists of three stanzas and is skilled, though conventional in thought and expression, had been subjected to a long and stern appraisal by Upward, after which it had been substantially revised. It appeared in *Public School Verse* in the company of "a bevy of homosexual sonnets by frenzied Hunters [like Fryne] who have not yet recovered from Brooke, referring to the belovèd as 'Splendid-Hearted,' etc." The poem also brought Isherwood his first review: in the *Bookman* Katherine Tynan wrote: "Not often does one find the Natural magic, but it is in C. W. B. Isherwood's 'Mapperley Plains' [. . .] There is the authentic touch."

The first thing Isherwood did upon his return to England was catch up on all the new films, scribbling his comments about them in his tiny handwriting in his scrapbook and recommending them to such correspondents as Falk and Monkhouse. He also embarked upon a novel he had titled "Lions and Shadows"—"simply an emotional and romantic phrase which pleased me, without my consciously knowing why, because of its private reference to something buried deep within me, something which made me feel excited and obscurely ashamed." The title was borrowed from a line in *Fiery Particles,* a recently published volume of short stories (based upon his experiences in the war) by C. E. Montague, a now largely forgotten English drama critic and journalist: "arrant lovers of living, mighty hunters of lions and shadows. . . ." Isherwood may well have come across this writer through Allan Monkhouse, who was a colleague of Montague on the *Manchester Guardian* and a collaborator with him and others on a collection of dramatic criticism entitled *The Manchester Stage* (1900). Montague was also a reasonably fashionable writer for the immediate post-war generation, his view of the war summed up by the title of his 1922 novel: *Disenchantment*. But, as Isherwood confessed, "Lions and Shadows" was simply a phrase that appealed to him and had nothing to do with Montague's actual book. Or indeed his own, which was to occupy him, on and off, for the next eighteen months, and was not finally abandoned for several years.

While the rest of the family were on holiday in Devon, Isherwood joined Edward Upward at Repton, where they spent a weekend in the library with G. B. Smith. The teacher had continued to take a pedagogic interest in his former pupil's future, advising him against attempting to persuade Corpus to let him change courses. It seems that Isherwood had decided that a future writer would be better off studying English literature rather than history, but if so had not informed his mother of the fact. Unfortunately for him, Smith very much took Kathleen's line and told Isherwood, "I don't regard pure literature seaworthy without ballast, you butterfly, you cobweb, you skimmer of other people's cookery." He went on: "But I declaim in vain. I should never convince you of the need for breadth, of the value of drudgery, of the necessity of getting into the minds of men constituted differently from yourself, of the vital importance of your doing for once in a way something that you don't like." He advised Isherwood to do history for a year and then see if he might change courses.[1] Isherwood appears to have ignored this advice and did in fact approach the College Tutor, William Spens, with a request to study English, even if this meant abandoning his scholarship. Spens would not be moved.

The relationship between Smith and Isherwood had subtly altered now that they were no longer master and pupil, and Smith was inclined to let down his guard, addressing his correspondent as "My Dear Benjie." He frequently attempted to get Isherwood to join him on foreign holidays and wrote highly indiscreet letters about the staff and boys at Repton, telling him for example: "Four masters going at the end of term—guess who. Two voluntarily, two not, but good work anyhow; could do with some new blood." The tone of these letters is distinctly teasing, and one wonders quite how innocent Smith's observation was that Darling was (academically) "hot stuff."

After helping Smith, Isherwood and Upward traveled on to Marple Hall. There the library proved rather more interesting, since Uncle Henry had been adding to it. In his own way Henry was something of a scholar, though one of somewhat specialized interests. He had been translatin'—"in Literal English," as he put it—the *Hermaphroditus* of Antony Panormita. He owned the 1824 Coburg edition of Panormita's works, "the best edition," according to H. S. Ashbee's celebrated bibli-

---

1. In *Lions and Shadows* Isherwood conjures up a scene in which he is given this advice after a boozy lunch on his last day at Repton. In fact, the lines Isherwood gives Mr. Holmes to speak are copied from a letter written by Smith several months later.

ography, *Index Librorum Prohibitorum*—though Henry's copy lacked plates. With or without its twenty-one engravings, this was a rare book, since, as Ashbee noted in 1877, "the German police are now destroying every copy they can lay hands on." Panormita was a writer of the Italian Renaissance, born in Palermo in 1394 and dying in 1471. The *Hermaphroditus* collected together a number of Latin and Greek erotic texts, and Henry evidently spent many a happy hour cloistered in the library at Marple, lexicons at his elbow, making his English version not only of poems and epigrams, but also of the "ample notes," which Ashbee recorded "have been pronounced more scandalous than the text." While working on the "Figurarum Veneris Ennumeratio," he started illustrating the ninety methods of sexual intercourse with inept drawings of stick figures.

Henry's translation, in small notebooks, was no doubt kept in a locked drawer, but Upward and Isherwood came across a copy of Havelock Ellis's sexological writings, which they read aloud to each other with great interest. Since Ellis's *Studies in the Psychology of Sex* was not available in an English edition until 1935, Henry's copy must have been smuggled back from one of his trips to the Continent. Henry took a prurient interest in the two young men, evidently imagining—or hoping—that they were conducting a homosexual relationship. They spent several days at Marple, and one evening, after Henry had retired, got drunk "in a scientific way," jotting down notes at intervals recording how they felt as the alcohol altered their consciousness.

B ack in London Jackie Coogan's new film, *Circus Boy,* had opened; Isherwood saw it several times. "Perhaps Jackie Coogan's best picture. At any rate, the one in which he seems most at home," he noted in his scrapbook. As the new term started at Repton, he went to the station to see pupils off on the school train. His own first term at Cambridge was due to start on October 12, and Kathleen set about sorting and packing clothes, cutlery and other items Christopher would need. Two days before term started, she accompanied Christopher to Corpus Christi and helped him settle into his rooms, F3, which were on the same staircase as Upward's, on the first floor, next to the porter's lodge, overlooking the new court. She opened an account for Christopher at Lloyd's Bank in Trinity Street, and bought more furniture for his rooms while he attended Spens's welcoming address for freshmen.

Isherwood's tutor was Kenneth Pickthorn, who came highly recommended by Upward. "Pickthorn is the only man I like," he had written during his second term at Corpus: "he is one of us! He appreciates the sinister irony of life, and having realized that I do also he is well disposed." G. B. Smith also approved of Pickthorn. "I wouldn't have you miss a single one of the home truths you will get from Pickthorn," he had written, when counseling Isherwood to stick to the original plan of studying history. "You will wriggle & shed several skins & will be quite a respectable animal at the end of it." In *Lions and Shadows* Pickthorn appears under the botanical pseudonym of "Mr Gorse." "Pale and fair-haired, his handsome, aggressively intelligent face was like the edge of a very sharp tool. He was still under thirty; and his violent abruptness made him seem younger, less sure of himself, than the smooth-voiced sophisticated undergraduates of the post-war generation, who accepted his lurid comments on their work with polite unruffled mock humility and ever so slightly raised eyebrows."[2] Isherwood gives a brilliantly dramatized account of his first tutorial with Pickthorn, in which he was obliged to read aloud an essay entitled "Better England free than England sober." If, as seems likely, Pickthorn suggested this provocative subject, it says much for his methods of teaching, and one can see why Upward and Isherwood thought he was "one of us." Still fresh from the triumphs of Repton, Isherwood rose to his new tutor's challenge. The essay survives, carefully preserved among Isherwood's papers, and although he makes mockery of it in *Lions and Shadows* it is a remarkable piece of work. The tone, certainly, borders on the insolent, but then this is what one might expect of a sharp nineteen-year-old, given the challenge of the commission: if Isherwood is showing off, it is at his tutor's invitation. Furthermore, it is the showing off of an aspirant writer, stretching his wings a little and testing the air.

The sale and consumption of alcohol was a topical issue in 1923. British licensing laws, which regulated and restricted the opening hours of public houses, were a relatively recent introduction, brought in during the First World War under the draconian umbrella of the Defence of the Realm Act, or "DORA," as it was satirically known, this acronym summoning up the image of a prim and puritanical aunt-figure. Like millions of Englishmen ever since, until the licensing laws were changed in the 1990s, Isherwood held up Continental Europe as a paragon of civilized attitudes toward social drinking. Having been there himself, Isherwood was able to refer to France with worldly authority: "In France, where a man may drink at any hour at which the proprietor cares to serve him, the number of drunkards appears to be, if anything, less than in England. The feeling of leisure which Café-life fosters seems to induce restraint. Insobriety is often the result of undue haste." Insobriety was to be a recurring feature of Isherwood's life, but more significant than these reflections are the opening paragraphs of the essay, in which Isherwood outlines a relationship between the state and the individual, between "the Others" and people such as himself.

> If the State has ceased to be a tyrant and become a father, its powers are patriarchal. Not only does it thwart crime, suppress public nuisance and quell public disturbance, but it strives, in measure, to enforce upon the individual such abstract precepts of morality and philosophy as are generally accepted by its members. It is this No-man's-land of compulsory Ethics which will, almost certainly, be the battleground of the Future.
>
> The demands of the State in this sphere are often just; sometimes they rest, indirectly, upon the Public welfare; occasionally they have no more solid basis than conventional prejudice. The State has been essentially pessimistic in its legislation, it has anticipated the worst, and consequently, since there is a sort of autosuggestion in these matters, has encountered it. To realise the truth of this, we have only to reflect how much our Censorship has done to promote interest in French Literature and Drama, a field of aesthetic enjoyment where every prospect

---

2. Isherwood may also have given Pickthorn the pseudonym "Gorse" because his brusque remarks on the work of his more bumptious pupils were the scholarly equivalent of a St. Edmund's "gorse-bushing."

pleases and only the reader is vile. But apart from the harm done by such drastic measures, the wound they inflict upon individual liberty is far deeper. That Blasphemy should be punished like Sedition, that Homo-sexualism should be treated as Rape, that Opium-taking should be stamped out like a disease—these things and many other offend the feelings even when the Reason approves them. For all of us, however 'public spirited' or otherwise bigoted we may be, cling secretly and passionately to Man's inalienable right to damnation.

Here is someone who has read his Baudelaire, but beneath the decadent posturing is a genuine concern for something which would preoccupy Isherwood throughout his life: the freedom of the individual to pursue his personal life without the interference of the State.

Isherwood claimed that he was chastened by Pickthorn's reaction to this essay, but not sufficiently so to buckle down to any real work. Organized distractions included the Gravediggers, a College play-reading society, the name of which may have been its principal attraction. Isherwood joined during his first term and eventually became the club's secretary, a job for which his small but immaculate handwriting recommended him. His passion, however, remained films, and he spent much of his time at the cinema. He joined the University Film Society, which at the end of his first term visited studios in Shepherd's Bush in London to watch the shooting of a costume drama. One of the founders of the film society was Roger Burford, who was supposedly studying English at Caius College but was more usually to be found making amateur movies and writing film reviews for an undergraduate magazine. Isherwood invited Burford, who was a year his junior, to his rooms for tea and macaroons, and the two young men immediately struck up a friendship. "He had straw-coloured hair, horn-rimmed spectacles, a receding chin and a mild, diffident, attractive voice," Isherwood wrote in *Lions and Shadows,* where Burford appears as "Roger East." George Pearson of BWP Ltd., a film production company, had given a lecture at the film society, and both Isherwood and Burford wondered whether they might find a career in movies.

The social world of the University did not hold much appeal for Isherwood, and the main point of going to Corpus had always been to spend more time in the company of Edward Upward. Upward had arrived at Cambridge "in exceedingly decadent mood and spent an awful lot of time playing poker and drinking." He had joined a club called the Young Visiters (after Daisy Ashford's novel, which had been published in 1919). "The less posh of the two Corpus drinking clubs," the Young Visiters was open to undergraduates who were "public school, intelligent and good-looking," which made Upward a natural candidate for election. At the same time, he realized that their world was not his, and he later coined the term "Poshocracy" to describe the University's social elite.

Isherwood's arrival transformed Upward's Cambridge world, not only in the conventional sense but also in an almost mystical one. The two young men began to conjure from the city's dark, narrow and fog-bound winter streets another world altogether, and from this would create a fictional realm that laid the foundations of their literary careers. They attended lectures and wrote essays, but had by now determined to be writers, and much of their time was spent in extracurricular reading and writing. Although they mixed with their fellow undergraduates, maintaining links with those with whom they had been at Repton, such as Smyth and Orpen, they gradually withdrew into a life of the imagination.

Many of Isherwood's friendships took the form of a conspiracy, and none was more conspiratorial than his friendship with Upward. Throughout his life, but particularly in the wake of the new sexual liberation of the 1960s and 1970s, Isherwood drew up battle lines across the sexual divide, glaring balefully across the chasm that separated him from the heterosexual majority. Most of Isherwood's closest friends were homosexual, and such alliances drew strength from the knowledge that Christopher and his kind were beyond society's—and, for much of his life, the law's—pale. Upward was different: although he suffered some traditional stirrings of the heart over junior boys at Repton, he was by nature entirely heterosexual. Oddly enough, this strengthened the bond between himself and Isherwood. He approved of Isherwood's homosexuality as an act of rebellion against society and his background, and probably emboldened Isherwood to see homosexuality as the choice of heroes rather than as a quirk of nature. Each was able to encourage the other in his sexual pursuits, and there were never any of the sort of complications that might have arisen over sexual rivalry.

Upward was more sexually advanced than Isherwood and had already enjoyed romances with young women. "At that time you couldn't contact women from Newnham or Girton," he recalled. "You only saw them at lectures. So you picked up shop girls, mainly. My first experience of kissing was with a shop girl at the cinema." This momentous occasion was described in a letter to Isherwood, the heightened language of which was characteristic of their correspondence at this period, and a feature of their literary collaborations.

> In desperation and in distrust of the filmy scaffolding of the universe I have fallen away to the walks of mist and the byeways [sic] of vice. I met her (Milly) one moonlit Sunday evening, and since then we have conversed in dark places, and I have tasted her lips, and felt the smooth contour of undulating surfaces. This is no vainglorious exaggeration; it is the naked truth. I looked for experience, and now that I have had it I find that it is no fuller nor warmer than imagination. When I felt her, it seemed to me that I had done the thing a thousand times before; such a poor shadow is sensation.

Even at Corpus, which Upward had encouragingly described as "a hot-bed of homo-sexualism," Isherwood had only two sexual encounters, one of them with Christopher Jacobs, the son of W. W. Jacobs, author of "The Monkey's Paw." He was not without admirers, however. One of his doting contemporaries, A. D. Francis, who drunkenly told him during a commemoration dinner that his eyes resembled periwinkles, was kicked down the stairs for his pains. Apparently undaunted, Francis continued to pursue Isherwood by letter. All he wanted to do was to help. "Get out of your head that I want anything out of you," he wrote in July 1924. "I will not weary you with metaphors or emphasize in what a very small boat we are together, navigating fearfully." Isherwood, clearly, did not at all see himself in the same boat, and in December attempted to give the importunate Francis the brush-off. "Thank you for saying the worst," Francis wrote, "of course one knew it all the time. But such is my idiocy, I think most people's idiocy, that they can only take a definite statement. But a certainty one takes like the other beastly things in the world. It is the doubts, which are awful." If Francis had intended to prick Isherwood's conscience, he was to be disappointed. Five days later he telephoned Isherwood, who hung up without speaking. Francis finally wrote a letter in which he allowed himself "the rare luxury of being really angry": "Your attitude is frankly bloody," he complained.

> I do not know of any squalid reptile, which would not be capable of more generosity. I have given what I can, and I have not demanded much [. . .] I have paid you that rare compliment of liking you for yourself. Not for any quality or attainment, but for the most insane, and yet the most satisfactory reason, because you are yourself. I do claim therefore to some show of friendship on your part; it is so mean and ungenerous of you, so cowardly. It is not likely that you will ever see me again after a few months. Why be hiding always behind this accursed safety curtain.
>
> Let me be candid and say anyhow, what I feel about you. It is just that in you I feel I can find expression for parts of myself, which I cannot in anybody else. Some parts of myself I can find in all sorts of people. The whole of myself a complete sympathy I have never found yet, except in my mother, and her I lost long ago. So I need you rather badly and when you are mean and beastly, I feel very bitterly.

Isherwood was unmoved, and Francis eventually gave up. "It is always said to be a dreadful mistake to write letters," Francis noted, and indeed these seemed to have caused Isherwood more amusement than compassion. Five years later he came across them again and delightedly sent them to Upward. "Here they are. Perhaps the most sacred and beautiful things, next to De Profundis, in the English tongue. Poor Davy—if he could see the ruins of his darling, now."

Much of Isherwood's sexuality was channeled into the imaginary world he and Upward had begun to create. This was a world which ran parallel to the real one, and it owed its genesis to a walk the two young men took one evening along Silver Street, which runs down from Trumpington Street, past Queen's College, toward the River Cam. Turning in to a small alley, they were confronted by "a strange-looking, rusty-hinged little old door in a high blank wall." "It's the doorway into the Other Town," Upward remarked, and in their imaginations they passed through it into a secret realm, made up at first from stray phrases which caught their fancy, and borrowings from favorite books, but eventually acquiring a genuine fictional solidity. If this door ever existed, it has long since disappeared. Ever since he read Beatrix Potter's *The Tale of Samuel Whiskers,* Isherwood had "a feeling that just by opening some little door, by getting through some nook or cranny, you will find yourself in another world altogether," and here it was. In order to stoke their fantasies, he and Upward took to walking round Cambridge after dark, searching for further "evidence" of the Other Town. They described themselves as "psychic tourists discovering a metaphysical University town." A street sign marking Garret Hostel Bridge provided Upward with the notion of the "Rats' Hostel," a term which encompassed what Isherwood called "the special brand of medieval surrealism which we had made our own."

"I remember an evening of violent excitement in which we gave to this whole atmosphere that surrounded us the title of the Rats' Hostel," Upward wrote, and there was a febrile quality to their lives as they allowed their imaginations to race and dream up new aspects of their fantasy world. One of the key figures in this constantly evolving realm was the Watcher in Spanish: "A presence representing our combined personalities. A bogey to whom we appealed, or whom we tried to deceive. The sneering umpire of our lives. Bred from Guy Fawkes and Poe's Raven." They pretended that there was some sort of conspiracy afoot in Cambridge and began to find sinister undertones in the most ordinary exchanges with shopkeepers and College servants. Walks would be enlivened when one or other of them would point out the secret import of some perfectly normal activity they might encounter. They also enlisted their favorite writers—notably Wilfred Owen, Katherine Mansfield and Emily Brontë—in the cause. They made a cult of these authors, referring to them familiarly as Wilfred, Kathy and Emmy, partly in mock-tribute to the minor poet Robert Nichols, who had given a lecture at Repton in which he referred to Wordsworth as "Wordy." For no very obvious reason, these writers "seemed in some way specially connected with our idea of the Rats' Hostel. We talked about them as if they were personal friends, wondered what they would have said on certain occasions, how they would have behaved, what advice they would have given us. One thing we never for a moment doubted: that they would have loathed Cambridge and all its works."

It is significant that it was Upward who was credited with the leap of imagination which brought this whole nebulous world alive, for although it was a game for two players which owed its energy to the way in which each of them bounced ideas off the other, the reference points owed a great deal to the charnel-house atmosphere of Upward's poetry. The Other Town could not have existed without Isherwood, but Upward's was the more creative imagination, as became clear when the two of them began to write stories based upon the fantastic world they increasingly inhabited. Isherwood was a brilliant pasticheur, and could write very funny dialogue, whereas Upward had a highly sophisticated and atmospheric prose style, full of striking, dreamlike images. The stories were written entirely for their own amusement and were not intended for publication, or even for any eyes other than their own. The actual writing was not a collaboration: each sat in his own room to write a story which was then passed to the other to be read. "We capped each other's fantastic inventions," Isherwood recalled, "drawing, for the furniture of our private fairy-story world, on memories of *Alice in Wonderland,* Beatrix Potter and Grimm, and on the imagery of Sir Thomas Browne, Poe and the ballads. We examined, with new interest, the three Dürer engravings in [Upward's] room. *Melancolia* specially excited us." Two characters emerged from these stories as narrators, a pair of pornographers called Edward Hynd and Christopher Starn, who were the authors' alter egos. The Hynd and Starn stories waxed in length and grossness: Isherwood's "The Horror in the Tower," written in the style of Conan Doyle, was about a coprophagous aristocrat, and Upward's "The Little Hotel" featured a brothel for necrophiles, while titles such as "The Loathly Succubus" and "The Leviathan of the Urinals" give fair warning of their content. The stories were rarely finished: "Most of our fragments come to an end when we have supplied sufficient hints to make plain to each other, though not perhaps to the general reader, how the action will develop," they stated.

They once made the mistake of showing their efforts to Smyth, who, as a future don and clergyman, was an odd choice. Unsurprisingly, Smyth was thoroughly disgusted, and he was subsequently absorbed into the stories as "Laily," "an ideal, imaginary don, the representative of all his kind, [. . .] our special enemy and butt." The name was taken from an ancient ballad, which referred to the laily (or loathsome) worm, and in a characteristic interchange between the fictional and real world it was thereafter bestowed upon the unfortunate Smyth. Isherwood's description of the fictional Laily in *Lions and Shadows* is very similar to descriptions of Smyth in Upward's letters: "He was the typical swotter, the book-worm, the academic pot-hunter; but, at the same time, being eager to succeed with and be accepted by the Poshocracy, he was careful to pretend an enthusiasm for athletics and team spirit."

The Other Town gradually evolved into a village they called Mortmere, combining the French word for death with the archaic word for a lake, familiar to Isherwood from the Mere Pool after which Marple had been named. The village was situated on the Atlantic coast, as is clear from the map of the area drawn by Upward on which such landmarks as Hainwort Fields, Belstreet Down, the Wormwood Hills and the River Stool are clearly marked. What became a saga of interrelated stories opened with a description of Mortmere Rectory, where the incumbent was the Reverend Casmir Welken. Although he appeared perfectly normal on the surface, Welken suffered nightly visitations from his dead wife in the form of a succubus as punishment for "moral offences with a choirboy" called Boy Radnor. Apparently unrepentant, Welken coerced Radnor to assist him in an experiment to manufacture angels in the belfry: "and thus his original offence, introduced into this ritual, becomes itself a mechanical and even distasteful duty." Other characters swiftly followed. Harold Wrygrave was Welken's curate and taught at Frisbald College, a local public school for boys. The headmaster there was Gustave Shreeve, who was involved in a longrunning rivalry with Wherry (the architect responsible for Mortmere's terrible railway accident) for the affections of Anthony Belmare, the ravishing young son of the local landowner, Henry Belmare. Mr. Belmare's sister was an artist, devoted to her savage tom-cat and responsible for the frescoes in the village hall. Ronald Gunball was a former sportsman and a "grotesque liar" in the permanent grip of *delirium tremens,* usually to be found accompanied by his dog, Griever. He contracted Suffolk Ulcers and was healed by the local GP, Dr. Mears, by the application of "a species of inland seaweed only to be found in the crypt of Mortmere church." This famous cure was known as the Mortmere Miracle, but Gunball subsequently contracted Londonderry Mange, and died "in an obscure seaside town." Mears was also a psychologist, busily engaged in attempting to classify people into two categories, Dragoons and Dorys, further subdivided into such types as Puss-Dragoons, Repellers, Pouters and Throstles. (His work was probably inspired by Isherwood and Upward's recent perusal of Havelock Ellis, who categorized people into sexual types.) The Skull and Trumpet Inn, where every night the drinkers turned into animals, was run by Sergeant Claptree, and there were several other minor characters, including the local whore, Alison Kemp, and Gaspard Farfox, a private detective and conjurer. Reynard Moxon was drafted in from Upward's "The Little Hotel," where he had "borrowed" Egyptian mummies from the local museum for the sexual delectation of his clients. Nocturnal in his habits, Moxon owned a pet snake, which he disguised as a baby and wheeled around in a pram. He was, the authors confessed, "the embodiment of our conception of the appearance and habits of Mr T. S. Eliot."

When, during the summer term of 1924, Upward was obliged to do some work for his Tripos, he and Isherwood saw rather less of each other. Without Upward's constant stimulus, and in the strong summer light, Mortmere began to fade a little, and so Isherwood pursued more orthodox literary ambitions. He was still working on his novel, "Lions and Shadows," and was also writing short stories, all of which drew upon his experiences at Repton. Three of these survive, two of which were published in the *Oxford Outlook,* of which his friend Paddy Monkhouse had become editor. These stories exist in manuscript, written in Isherwood's tiny, neat handwriting, with barely an erasure. The first of them, "The Old Game," is the most ambitious, but would have been the most difficult to publish, since it describes a homosexual seduction. In Mortmere, Isherwood could allow his sexual fantasies about schoolboys free rein, with every sort of activity described in lurid detail. "The Old Game," however, is a far more sober and serious piece.

Dated "February 22–25th '24," it is written, appropriately enough, in a lined school exercise book. The young protagonist, Charles, arrives in Devon in order to be coached in Greek by a clergyman for the Oxford University entrance exam. As he unpacks his bags, a photograph of a young boy in cricketing flannels falls out of his Bible. "Charles looked at it for a moment—then 'Damn you!' he said, and tearing the pasteboard into several pieces tossed them into the grate behind its painted, paper fan." At church the following day, he notices a father and son, the latter about sixteen, attractive but weak-looking. He learns that the boy, Jack Foster, for some reason is not at school, although it is term-time. The following week the Vicar decides to get up a tennis party. Jack is invited, but his father brusquely declines on his behalf. When Charles subsequently meets Jack in the local village, the younger boy reluctantly confesses that he was obliged to leave his school after a sexual scandal.

> Our house, when I first came, was beastly right through. There weren't a dozen people in it who were decent. You can guess what sort of chance I had! Why, the first time, I didn't know what was happening . . . Everyone did it. Nobody cared or said anything. It was an open joke. People went about boasting of it. And the ones that had been horrible the night before laughed and smiled at you in the passage the next morning as though nothing had ever happened. God knows I don't set up to be moral, but it was filthy. And I knew it . . .

After such a confession, Jack assumes Charles will not want to have anything to do with him. His only consolation is that he was "not such a beast as the older ones are, who get hold of younger boys and spoil all their decency before they are old enough to stop them." Charles, having been just such an older one at his own school, is not in the least shocked by Jack's tale, and later attempts to seduce him. Jack is reluctant, fearing that this will spoil the friendship that has been developing between them in the absence of his father, who has been called away on urgent business. Just as Charles is about to get his own way ("If you must—"), they are interrupted by the unexpected appearance of the Vicar's daughter. They make an assignation the following afternoon to go boating, and Charles finally gets his way midstream:

> Jack cast a glance of appeal at Charles; but already his face was softening. There was a kind of furtive pleasure in his smile:
> 'Oh, all right,' he said, at last; and added, with a bitter, tired little laugh: 'Only don't go and upset the boat.'

The language in which the boys discuss homosexuality in terms of corruption and "beastliness" is taken directly from *David Blaize,* but Charles's remorseless seduction of the unwilling Jack shows a rather more modern sensibility. There is a tension in the story between "decency" and cynicism, and this probably reflects Isherwood's own feelings about sex. It is worth remembering that for all his sophisticated talk with friends about "tarts" and his stories for Upward about bizarre sexual practices, Isherwood's actual sexual experience was small—particularly when you compare his time at University with that of such people as Evelyn Waugh and Brian Howard, who were enjoying considerable homosexual success at Oxford during the same period. Isherwood's continuing obsession with the world of school and his romantic fixation upon younger boys kept him emotionally in the Sixth Form for some time to come.

It is no coincidence that at the beginning of January 1924, the month before he wrote "The Old Game," Isherwood had invited Darling to stay with him in London, and took him to the theater, the cinema, a circus and the skating rink. By now Darling was rising sixteen, about the same age as Jack in the story. Isherwood appears to have been trying to establish his relationship with Darling on a more equal footing, though the disparity in their ages was still sufficient to keep them in the roles of mentor and acolyte. It is doubtful whether Isherwood was as scheming as Charles, but one suspects that he was sorely tempted while he had Darling under his roof in Kensington. He was also interested in "a Westminster boy," who was providing him with "awfully good copy," he told Upward. "Am plotting to arouse him with the Hymn to Truth[3] and the Old Game."

The other two stories Isherwood wrote at this period, "The Hero" (dated March 26) and "Two Brothers" (dated March 30) are also essentially public-school tales. The former describes the friendship between two junior boys: Wayne is unprepossessing with an exaggerated inferiority complex, Thompson is an attractive sporting hero. When Wayne rescues Thompson from drowning, he is publicly commended. He

> saw the timbers of the hall sway before his eyes in a shudder of intoxicating pride, voices sounded triumphantly in his ears, hands seized his own; and as the school surged out under the cold night and the stars, Gerald Wayne knew himself to be a hero.
> But, strangely enough, next term, Thompson went about with Sleath.

Thus the traditional happy ending of the school story is subverted.

---

3. "The Hymn to Truth" was one of Upward's poems. "Rouse nursing earth from sloth with bawdy cries," the poet commands; "Crown our frail loves with a venereal stain." It is, however, rather too high-flown to have been employed with much success as an aphrodisiac.

"Two Brothers" is a sententious and overwrought piece, in which the narrator is attempting to write a letter of condolence to a contemporary whose twin brother has been killed in a motoring accident. He recalls how these sporting twins had been taken up at university by someone called (rather obviously) Tansy-Rogers, "who asked me to tea to meet his 'mascots.' I went, in a spirit of curiosity, and found Billy and Bob, two discomfited, tame giants, sitting in the midst of a semi-circle of spectators [. . .] Tansy-Rogers came up to me, swaying from the hips, and murmured in my ear: 'Aren't they *divine*?' It was simply revolting." This suggests that Isherwood was still very uneasy about homosexuality, or at any rate did not want to be associated with pansy aesthetes.

At first Isherwood thought this story "immortal," but he soon realized it was "tosh." The most interesting thing about it, apart from what it tells us about Isherwood's own homosexual desires, is that it may reflect some of his feelings about his own mother's bereavement. The epigraph, used here with savage irony, is just the sort of phrase Kathleen might have copied into the front of one of her diaries: "Remembrance and the faithful thought." Upward recalled that it was at Cambridge that Isherwood really began to turn against his mother and everything she stood for: her refusal to leave the past behind, her almost sacred devotion to her dead hero-husband, her snobbish cult of the family and her selfish ambitions for her son. "The teenage Christopher respected this cult at first," Isherwood later acknowledged, "then it began to anger him. He became jealous of the past, because that was when Kathleen had been really happy, she said. Nothing he or Richard could ever do would compensate her for its loss. Christopher decided that this cult of the past was a form of sulking. He turned against it." In doing so, he would work himself up into a frenzy of loathing, although this may have been partly for Upward's benefit. He recalled how Upward, "rubbing his hands together in gleeful ecstacies of hate," would comment on the more or less innocent antics of the Poshocracy. Kathleen now became the subject of unholy glee. "Just think of her!" Isherwood would exclaim. "Sitting in front of a fire in Kensington, warming her cunt!" Further fun was had at the expense of Christianity now that Upward had encouraged Isherwood to reject the faith in which they had both been brought up. They habitually referred to Christ as "Beaver" because the Savior was usually depicted with a beard, and casual and inventive blasphemy became a regular feature of the correspondence. Expletives such as "Lofty Jesus" and "Christ's arse" pepper their letters, and one of Upward's was decorated with a crucifix captioned "Ridicule pendu."

Isherwood also entered a phase of ferocious philistine iconoclasm. It was not that long since he had enjoyed giving the guided tour of Marple Hall to visitors, accompanying or standing in for his grandfather. He now declared that the Hall should be torn down, its contents tossed onto a pyre, and that the ancient buildings of Cambridge should also be razed. A reverence for the past had led to his being forced to study history rather than English literature. "In approaching his subject, the historian must relinquish all the weaknesses of human sentimentality," he wrote in a parodic letter, supposedly written on his deathbed by Starn (transformed for these purposes from a pornographer into an academic) and addressed to a godson.

He must learn to distinguish facts from causes, text from interpretation, real from theoretical. The absolute, the existent is all that matters to him. He must not gaze upon Truth with the myopic eyes of Poetry. Art is the clog, the impediment—the shell which he tosses aside having extracted from it the pearl of reality. It does not concern him that Man's passions and desires have from time to time interrupted the imposing banality of the Cycle—his business is with the ever-accumulating mass of facts, which must be employed to build up the skeletons of the Actual, unhampered by any shred of natural impulse.

Entrusting his scholarly papers to the godson, Starn hopes they will be recognized as

the work of a serious devotee of the Historical Method. If there is in them any departure from the strict path of narrative or accepted tradition, if there is anywhere a hint of originality, or a lapse into fanciful or metaphorical expression, be lenient to the memory of the author, remembering that his was but human clay, subject to the natural frailties of idealism, imagination and ambition.

It was precisely these qualities that Isherwood felt Cambridge was stifling in him.

Isherwood would later characterize Kathleen's hopes for his future as snobbish and constricting, but it is easy to see why she would be keen to see her son settled in a secure track though school and university to a proper job. The fearful example of Uncle Henry—the idle, extravagant and dilettante heir to the estate—was constantly before her, and if Richard's disrupted education continued, the prospects for his future did not look very happy. Kathleen was no doubt aware of her Christopher's discontent, but evidently had no idea of the depth of his feelings, or of the particular animosity he had begun to feel for her. No letters from Isherwood to his mother survive from this period, but there seems little doubt that when he was actually with Kathleen during the University vacations, he was both kind and civil to her, accompanying her to the theater, concerts and exhibitions, and even visiting relatives. Kathleen's own diaries, which in subsequent years give a vivid impression of the unhappiness she endured over the behavior of her elder son, leave no record of any open discord at this time.

Alienated from his mother, Isherwood attempted to co-opt his father as an ally. Since Frank was dead, and therefore unable to answer back, Isherwood could recreate him as he saw fit. He decided that Frank had in fact been an "Anti-Heroic Hero," a figure he set up in opposition to the "Hero-Father" invented by family, teachers and other in authority. Isherwood later acknowledged sardonically:

Nothing had to be invented. Christopher had only to select certain of Frank's characteristics, doings and sayings (which meant censoring the rest) and make a person out of them, giving it Frank's body and voice.

The Anti-Heroic Hero always appears in uniform, because this is his disguise; he isn't really a soldier. He is an artist who has renounced his painting, music and writing in order to dedicate his life to an antimilitary masquerade. He lives this masquerade right through, day by day to the end, and crowns his performance by actually getting himself killed in battle. By thus fooling everybody (except Christopher) into believing he is the Hero-Father, he demonstrates the absurdity of the military mystique and its solemn cult of War and Death.

[. . .]

There was a report, which Christopher accepted because he wanted to believe it, that Frank was last seen signalling directions to his men with a short swagger cane as he led them into action. Christopher made this symbolic: The Anti-Heroic Hero mocks the loud Wagnerian Hero-Death by flourishing a stick like a baton at it, as if conducting an opera.

Isherwood may have reacted against the whole received idea of the First World War, but as someone who had made his own cult of the distinctly homoerotic poetry of Wilfred Owen, he was bound to acknowledge that the trenches held a morbid and compulsive fascination for him.

Like most of my generation, I was obsessed by a complex of terrors and longings connected with the idea 'War'. 'War', in this purely neurotic sense, meant The Test. The test of your courage, of your maturity, of your sexual prowess: 'Are you really a Man?' Subconsciously, I believe, I longed to be subjected to this test; but I also dreaded failure. I dreaded failure so much—indeed, I was so certain that I *should* fail—that, consciously, I denied my longing to be tested, altogether. I denied my all-consuming morbid interest in the idea of 'war'. The War, I said, was obscene, not even thrilling, a nuisance, a bore.

Although Isherwood's particular obsession with this idea may have been neurotic, it was not unusual. Boys who were at preparatory and public schools during the First World War were constantly being reminded of the sacrifices being made on the fields of battle by their elders and (it was always implied) betters. Old Boys, fresh from training schools, returned in uniform and spoke of the great adventure that lay ahead. The names of the fallen were read out at chapel, where prayers were offered up for victory over the enemy. Boys who failed to show sufficient sporting prowess were told that slackers would not be wanted in the trenches. Dodged tackles were equated with cowardice in the face of the enemy. The classical notion that those whom the gods loved die young and *Dulce et decorum est pro patria mori* were drummed into pupils in the classroom. War invaded every aspect of school life. No wonder small boys spent so much time needlessly worrying that when it became their turn to go to war they would be unable to live up to the examples so constantly thrust before them. Isherwood's own feelings of inadequacy were exacerbated by constant reference to his dead hero-father, whom he had no hope of emulating. Even after the immediate danger had passed, and the survivors had limped home, those just too young to have fought were left with the nagging question unanswered of how they would have fared.

It was his notion of "The Test" that led Isherwood to buy himself an AJS motorbike, a machine that could be used to assess his courage. Riding a motorbike was hardly the same thing as going over the top in the war, but it was, as Isherwood remembered from his time in Rouen, a thrilling and dangerous occupation. Having bought the bike for £55, he was obliged to use it, but he no longer had Stewart to cling to and was wholly responsible for this powerful piece of machinery. "How I loathed and enjoyed those rides!" he recalled. Indeed, he was so nervous about his own personal safety and the impression he was making, that he walked the bike to a relatively quiet street before mounting it. "I thus began to fail the Test almost before it had begun." He would practice on a long straight road in the country, nerving himself to maintain high speeds. On one occasion, having thoroughly frightened himself after the bike wobbled alarmingly as he accelerated, he dismounted and wheeled it all the way back into town, "bending every few yards to peer and frown at the engine, so that passers-by should think it was out of order."

Another rather more important test Isherwood failed concerned the Poshocracy. He had been invited to various social gatherings organized by this elite at Corpus and found, rather to his shame, that he enjoyed them. "I could talk their language, I could make jokes, I could strike the right note—and if the Watcher appeared, well, he was merely an addition to my audience. Later, of course, in the sobering atmosphere of [Upward's] room, I mimicked and sneered, hypocritically describing my sayings and doings as a spy's ruse in the midst of the enemy camp." On one occasion, however, Isherwood's loyalties were tested and found sadly wanting. Having failed to recruit Upward, the Poshocracy decided to take its revenge. Returning one evening to his rooms, accompanied by Isherwood, Upward was visited by a group of young men, whom he attempted to entertain by offering them drinks. He then noticed that one of the undergraduates had taken a pat of butter from a cupboard and was cutting it up for his friends, who started flicking bits up at the ceiling. Everyone was fairly drunk and it all seemed reasonably harmless, if messy, fun. Then Upward began to suspect that worse was to come and that in fact the Poshocracy, who were now rummaging through cupboards and examining various objects, planned to vandalize his room. He hit back, by throwing butter at the young men, and gradually things got out of hand. Upward berated his unwelcome guests, who then started to leave. Suddenly, Upward realized that Isherwood was leaving with them. "Why hadn't he come to my aid?" Upward later wrote in a fictionalized account of this episode.

> He can't have been so drunk as to be totally unaware of what the Poshocrats had been up to. Why hadn't he made at least some gesture against them, however ineffectual, given some sign that he was on my side, not on theirs? He had just sat there, neutral. Or worse than neutral, an accomplice by default. My anger at his disloyalty steadily rose as I stood alone in my room after they had all gone [. . .] it seemed to me that the whole of the imaginative world we'd been constructing and living in together was fraudulent. I sat down at my table and wrote him a letter in which I broke with him forever.

The letter was never sent, Upward having realized the following morning that drink was largely to blame for Isherwood's behavior. Although Upward regarded it as a serious betrayal, he would not allow it to destroy so intricate and involved a friendship.

When Spens had given Isherwood permission to buy the motorbike, he had warned: "Don't let it keep you from your work for the Mays." Although Isherwood spent most of his time at Cambridge writing fiction, he managed to pass these important examinations. The College had expected him to get a first, but Isherwood himself was relieved to have got an upper second, since, he assured Kathleen, he knew he had done badly and had felt ill on the day of the exam. His feelings about his academic work were relieved in a heavily ironic squib he wrote that summer in the guise of his Mortmere alter ego, Christopher Starn, "A Letter Written to the Tutor of Corpus after a Year's Historical Study."

Dear Sir,

At the end of this, my first academic year, I feel that it would be unmannerly in me not to acquaint you, in some sort, with the progress of my studies and their benefits conferred upon myself.

For I cannot, in honour, permit myself to forget how great a part has been played by you, sir, in the direction and discipline of my youthful and intemperate zeal into channels whose superior advantages were, at the time of matriculation, unapparent to my unexperienced eye; and I must, therefore, ever be deeply sensible of the effects of a timely obedience to your maturer judgement, these effects being, in my prejudiced estimation, apparent to the most indifferent observer.

Firstly, among them, I must mention that vain and chimerical aspiration toward the pursuit of letters which had troubled my adolescence. That ardour, that boyish fantasy, has, I rejoice to say, entirely deserted me. As mariner to his haven after storm, I have found myself becalmed from the billows of an intemperate youth, and can look back from the safe haven of study, upon all those commotions, with the mild satirical gaze of riper experience.

And so on. As with much of Isherwood's earliest writing, this is a very skillful parody, in this case mimicking the sort of letters that appear in the Victorian novel.

Isherwood never gave Cambridge much credit for his education. "Upward educated me," he insisted. "We educated each other," Upward countered. "Our most startling discovery was Shakespeare, whose fame we had assumed to be one of the many frauds our elders had tried to impose on us. I discovered him when I read Bradley on *Hamlet,* and then the play itself, during my third and last year. Christopher was disgusted at what he regarded as 'insincerity' on my part, but after reading Bradley and *Hamlet* he too was convinced." Isherwood also credited Upward with introducing him to Proust. When not reading such books as George Moore's *Esther Waters* aloud to each other, or working on Mortmere, Isherwood and Upward busily wrote their diaries. They had been inspired to do so by W.N.P. Barbellion, the pseudonymous author of *The Journal of a Disappointed Man.* Described by H. G. Wells in his introduction to the *Journal* as "an intensely egotistical young naturalist," Barbellion (who was in fact named Bruce Frederick Cummings) had suffered from disseminated sclerosis, a progressive disease of the spine, and died in 1919 at the age of thirty-one. The final two entries in the *Journal,* dated October 1917, consist of one word each: "Miserable" and "Self-disgust." This may indeed have been what Barbellion felt—he certainly had good reason to—but there was a certain amount of play-acting about it. A note stating that Barbellion had died two months after writing the last entry was in fact put there by Barbellion himself, who survived another two years. His brother, A. J. Cummings, said that the many letters he continued to receive from readers of the *Journal* long after its original publication in 1919 "almost without exception come from people under thirty": "The young, as one might expect, have understood him better than the old because they could spontaneously share his thoughts and moods and ardent emotions." Isherwood and Upward certainly felt this, and Barbellion joined Wilfred, Kathy and Emmy in that pantheon of doomed young writers. In choosing Barbellion's diaries as a model for his own, Isherwood acknowledged:

> My chief difficulty was that, unlike Barbellion, I wasn't dying of an obscure kind of paralysis—though, in reading some of my more desperate entries, you would hardly suspect it: 'Too miserable to write any more . . .' 'All the same symptoms . . .' 'This is the end . . .' By these outbursts, I meant, as a rule, simply that I was bored (a perfectly legitimate complaint, too often and too easily sneered at by elders, in the young), or that I couldn't get on with *Lions and Shadows.*

He did, however, learn a valuable literary lesson from Barbellion. A. J. Cummings objected to Wells's characterization of his brother, pointing out that "Barbellion was intensely interested in himself, but he was also intensely interested in other people [. . .] He had an *objective* interest in himself. He regarded himself, quite naturally, as he regarded the creatures he dissected in the laboratory, as a specimen to be examined and classified; and he did his work with the detailed skill and truthful approach of a scientific investigator." This is the sort of objectivity Isherwood himself would attempt to emulate later in his career.

Meanwhile, old John Isherwood had died on May 9, 1924. "Felt very grieved," Kathleen wrote. "He has been such a kind friend to us & it means an end to Marple as a home where one always received a welcome." She had no illusions that Henry would be as hospitable: indeed, she was not even invited to the funeral, and was informed of its date too late to send flowers. Isherwood rode up to Marple from Cambridge on the AJS, this journey probably representing the bike's only long and useful excursion in all the time he had it. A few days later, Kathleen was very pleased to be invited to visit Marple Hall. "Very affable letter from Henry willing to meet me at Stockport, & asking which room I should like," she recorded with some surprise. The visit went well and Kathleen packed up some boxes of books to take back to London, a legacy for Christopher. Henry announced that he would probably let the Hall for a while and take a flat in London.

Later that year, another link with the past was broken when Kathleen's mother died at the age of eighty-three. By the winter, Emily appeared to be in a slow but steady decline. She rallied sufficiently to accompany her daughter to the Gauguin exhibition at the Leicester Galleries, but was having great difficulty in sleeping. Her pulse remained strong, but at the beginning of November she developed pneumonia. On Monday, November 10, the doctor suggested that Christopher should be summoned from Cambridge, but Emily died that night. "The sense of loss and of not being able to speak to her & tell her things is indescribable," Kathleen wrote in her diary. "I feel how little she realized how deeply my life is bound up in her's . . . I might have been so much more loving to her . . . & now it is too late. If one only felt sure she could understand and forgive." It seems unlikely that Emily could have died unaware of her daughter's tireless devotion, and the notion that Kathleen could have done more than she did is absurd. Emily was not an easy woman and had demanded more of Kathleen than was her right. In response, Kathleen had shown exemplary patience throughout. Her self-lacerating outburst may have been prompted by feelings of guilt; although she never says so, her grief must have been mixed with a certain sense of relief, a feeling she would have found hard to acknowledge. Christopher came up from Cambridge and the funeral was held a few days later at Golders Green Crematorium. Her ashes were scattered there, not at Brompton Cemetery, where her husband had lain, unvisited and unregarded, since 1905. Kathleen and Christopher decided to remedy this and laid wreaths on Frederick's neglected grave.

Prompted by her mother's death, Kathleen rather tactlessly told Richard that she needed to make sure that her own affairs were in order in case she, too, should be "called on a long journey." "I said that I wanted to go too," Richard remembered,

> it seemed infinitely preferable to having to go back to school—to which M. replied '*No* Richard, you must go on and work out your salvation.' She added 'Of course I shall be there to help you', which was sorry comfort. I had a horror of dying at school and being interred in the nearby village churchyard and begged M. when she used to visit me at school to make sure I was buried in the Brompton Cemetery in the same grave as Frederick, and M. saying 'Don't worry, the school people won't want to be bothered with your funeral. I'll see to it. You could come up on the train in the guard's van.'

The headmaster was now concerned about Richard's tonsils and "the possibility of their arresting his development." Whatever Kathleen made of this unorthodox view, she was obliged to accept Mr. Wells's opinion that Richard was "backward & mentally young for his age preferring the company of those 2 or 3 years younger than himself." Richard was also physically backward: he was thirteen, but his testicles had not yet descended properly. The poor boy was frequently hauled up before doctors to be prodded and probed, prescribed elixirs and dietary regimes to get him up to size, given lessons in boxing, gymnastics and swimming; but no one appeared to know what was really wrong with him.

Another factor in Richard's life that increased his sense of inferiority was that he had become obsessed by his older brother. During their childhood, Christopher had done his best to entertain Richard in the school holidays they spent together at Marple Hall, gamely dressing up as the Fairy King for his little brother's amusement. As Christopher grew up, however, Richard had been left behind and was well aware of the gulf that had opened up between them, putting it down to what he called "purbity." Isherwood scarcely seemed aware of his brother, except when called upon to discipline him; Richard, on the other hand, began to look up to Christopher with the sort of romantic devotion a boy at school might have for his fag-master. "I worshipped your combined manly youth and good looks—just *perfect,*" Richard confessed in his late fifties—and possibly after rather a lot to drink. "But I imagined if I told you so you would regard me with a 'healthy' contempt." Isherwood was so busy mooning over other boys that he failed to notice that he had himself become the subject of a distinctly erotic obsession. Richard recalled a visit to Cambridge and being taken punting on the Backs: "You laid your hand on my bare head, to steady yourself, and the feel of your hand sent a most enjoyable thrill through me, and I longed for you to do it again and wished that I had the courage to ask you to. I felt that in return I would most willingly wait on you hand and foot. But I suppose that if you had known how I felt you would have recoiled with combined contempt and revulsion!" This masochistic devotion would continue for several years. When Richard was about fourteen or fifteen, he and Christopher got into a heated argument. "I forget what the bone of contention was—and it doesn't matter. We both got very worked up, you warned me to 'shut up' and at last, as I wouldn't, you slapped my face: it gave me such a thrill of enjoyment that I longed to ask you to do it again, *and* again & again." These recollections may seem the nostalgic fantasies of a man with too much spare time on his hands, but there seems no reason to doubt their truth. As Isherwood wrote when discussing Richard's account of the Marple Hall ghost: "The relations between Richard and Christopher as adults had never been complicated by pretences or concealments. Christopher would have said without hesitation that he couldn't imagine Richard ever telling him a lie." Although Richard grew out of this incestuous phase, he remained devoted to his brother, whom he continued to regard as in every way superior to himself.

Isherwood himself was now in his second year at Cambridge, but he was no nearer choosing a career to follow when he graduated, and his future was beginning to look as unsettled as Richard's. After his very first term there he had confided to Kathleen that being at university was not helping him toward any clear decisions. Kathleen still dreamed of his becoming a don, but acknowledged that life at Cambridge "does not seem to attract him. It is disappointing but useless to give it up without anything definite to take up." He still wanted to be a writer, but the eminently practical Kathleen was unwilling to encourage him in so precarious a profession, particularly after she read *A Taste of Honey,* a highly precocious novel by Eric Maschwitz, with whom Christopher had been at Repton. "A truly remarkable book for any one of his age," she noted. "Very sexual & somehow particularly horrid for a boy to have written [. . .] I don't think either the heroine or the hero are the least real & their behaviour is inexcusable!—but it is well written." Isherwood was three years Maschwitz's junior, but he had nearly completed his own novel, "Lions and Shadows." In December he met the Repton train in London, as usual, and whisked Darling off to lunch and the theater. Perhaps emotionally and imaginatively recharged by this encounter, and by further visits to the rink, he was able to work on the book during the vacation, finishing it on January 7, 1925.

"Lions and Shadows" occupied "four thick typescript files," only one of which (the last, containing 145 pages) survives.[4] Isherwood gives a brief account of the book in *Lions and Shadows,* quoting what appear to be the opening three paragraphs. He dismisses the novel as mere pastiche: "I churned it out, as smooth as butter—arch, pretty, competent, quaint." Judging by the pages that survive, this is a reasonably fair assessment, but the novel's plot is even more embarrassing than Isherwood was prepared to admit.

---

4. This lay for some time in the McFarlin Library at the University of Tulsa, Oklahoma, mistakenly catalogued as part of the typescript of Isherwood's later autobiography, *Lions and Shadows.* It came with a collection of Richard Isherwood's papers, many of which had been destroyed, and it is possible that a similar fate befell the other three files.

He relates that the protagonist, Leonard Merrows, is prevented from attending Rugtonstead by illness, and is therefore obsessed by the whole idea of public school—as indeed was his creator. This theme would hardly sustain a long narrative, and what Isherwood suppresses from his later account of the novel is the plot concerning Leonard's relationships with Betty Desleigh, a childhood friend who lives in a beautiful house on the Sussex Downs, and with Charles Franklyn, an older youth who picks him up at a skating rink.

Using Isherwood's own account of it and the fragment that remains, it is possible to provide a partial reconstruction of this lost novel. Leonard Merrows is born in a large house in Ireland, but is educated at an English preparatory school, St. Yniol's. At some point in his life, he has mislaid his parents, and in the extant portion of the novel, set in 1921 and 1922, he is living with his bachelor uncle, Major George Cushant (late of the Indian Army), who shares a house in London with an unmarried sister, Edith. Leonard admires and is fond of his uncle, but Aunt Edith seems unable to communicate any feeling whatsoever. At St. Yniol's, he has had an important friendship with a boy called Alan Dayling, who calls him "Bunny." A bout of rheumatic fever has left Leonard with a weak heart (as it had Hector Wintle) and thus prevented him from accompanying Dayling to Rugtonstead. Instead he is tutored at home. Leonard seems to have no friends in London and envies the schoolboys and army cadets who arrive in pairs at the Empire Velodrome, a roller-skating rink he has taken to frequenting. The remaining fragment opens (mid-sentence) with Leonard, who is aged fourteen and a half, taking his first turn on the floor of the rink. He soon becomes an accomplished skater, and it is this that first attracts the attention of Charles Franklyn, the eighteen-year-old son of a Manchester businessman, who is attempting to make his way in literary journalism in London. Charles sings to himself as he skates:

> He was singing the tune of Auld Lang Syne, but the words were not those of the song. Presently, Leonard heard them quite distinctly:
>
> > '... *Their uniforms were spick and span,*
> > *And they wore their Sunday suits,*
> > *But we knew the work they had been at*
> > *By the quicklime on their boots.*'

The reader will recognize, even if Leonard doesn't, that the words are from Oscar Wilde's *The Ballad of Reading Gaol*, and this is the first hint we get of Charles's particular interest in a boy some four years his junior. After Leonard has deliberately shown off, Charles invites him to tea and the two youths strike up a friendship.

> There was no doubt that [Leonard's] new friend was able to exert a curious influence over him. In Franklyn's company, he was altogether a different person. He spoke a great deal, laughed more than was his wont, displayed an unsuspected capacity for making silly jokes and generally fell in with the inconsequent humour of his companion. Charles was, in fact, drawing Leonard 'out of himself'. When

the two were together, Leonard's whole bearing changed. His face was flushed, his eyes sparkled, his gestures were full of animation.

Not everyone approves of the burgeoning friendship. "I don't know what it is, Leonard, and I don't want to be unjust, but I must say I don't exactly cotton on to this new friend of yours," says Uncle George. "May be my fancy. But it seems to me he's one of these flibberty-gibberty kind of customers. Perhaps he's all right. But I don't know. Not the fellow I'd've chosen myself when I was your age." Certainly, Charles's whimsical fantasies about Leonard's "fairy-tale" background are a little suspect, as is his mantelpiece crowded with photographs of boys of various ages. Charles reveals that he is planning to write a novel titled "Lions and Shadows." "And do I come into the book?" Leonard asks. "I daresay I may make some casual reference to you," replies Charles, smiling. After Leonard leaves, Charles puts on a record of "I'm Always Chasing Rainbows."

Shortly afterward, the magazine Charles is working for collapses and he is forced to work in his father's firm in Manchester. After a year, he returns and picks up his friendship with Leonard once again. Leonard has encountered Dayling in London and has been upset by how much he has changed and coarsened. Charles explains that this is what can happen to people who have been to public school and treats Leonard to a long disquisition on the subject of schools and the relationships there between study-holders and fags. He has now decided to set "Lions and Shadows" partly at a skating rink. It is to be about an Austrian Jew who falls in love with a female instructor there and becomes an expert skater in order to win her: "The hero is a person who is always getting what he wants and then finding that it isn't what he wants, after all. It's a very old idea, but I'm going to treat it in a new way." The plot sounds fantastic, and Leonard thinks he is being teased.

Leonard is subsequently invited to stay with Betty Desleigh and her father at Windeshall. Betty too has changed and is "no longer the little girl who had shared the strange, unspoken secrets, the magic which had invested his other visits to Windeshall [. . .] Betty was a human being, a real person—like himself." Recognizing this development does not help Leonard accommodate it.

> He had been embarrassed and irritated when Charles had called him a fairy, an elf-child, but wasn't there, after all, something unnatural about himself? Something queer? Why was he so cold, so unmoved by all the passion which others seemed to feel? Why couldn't he fall in with Betty's mood and flirt—yes, *flirt* with her. That was what she wanted. The thing the nursemaids did in the park on Sunday afternoons. The thing that every butcher's boy in Kensington knew about. This silliness called love which, Charles assured him, he didn't like because he hadn't tried it. Well, here was his chance—

Even ignoring the unfortunate and surely unconscious double entendres, most readers will by this point have some idea why Leonard is unable to fall in with Betty's mood. Ashamed of his behavior, which has left Betty in tears on the Downs, and having had a symbolic encounter with a horribly dead rabbit ("Poor Bunny!"), he tries to make it up with her, and on the final night of his visit the two young people indulge in some passionate, though not terribly convincing, kissing in the garden.

Leonard returns to London in order to prepare for an extended trip to France. This marks the end of a phase in his life, since Uncle George has married and Leonard is to live with Aunt Edith in a cottage outside Guildford on his return from Caen. He spends his last evening with Charles, who suspects they will never meet again and disappears into the London night murmuring:

> Strangely our love began and ended thus—
> Met in a Rink and parted on a 'bus.

Sitting on that bus, Leonard looks back over the Past and now feels free to face the Future. He has one last glimpse of an advertisement for Vitanov tonic in the form of a large sword, which Charles had pointed out to him on an earlier journey through Piccadilly, and sails out of the novel toward his own new life: "On the hill-crest, the traffic flashed and sparkled. The great houses rose up, black, funereal. Something made him turn and look back, and there, far behind him, above the thronging street, stood the sky-sign—a fiery sword over the Eden he had lost."[5]

It is evident from what remains of it that "Lions and Shadows" was an accomplished piece of work, even if it was largely pastiche. Isherwood himself noted the influence of Hugh Walpole, Compton Mackenzie and E. F. Benson, but there may have been an even less admissible model. In 1920, at the age of twenty-two, Beverly Nichols, who later became a well-known popular journalist, particularly in women's magazines, published his first novel. *Prelude* was a romantic—not to say soppy—tale of a boy's experiences at school and in the trenches and was just the sort of novel that Isherwood would have greedily but guiltily read at this period. Some of Isherwood's scene-painting in "Lions and Shadows" bears the stamp of Nichols's overwrought prose, the sort of writing he and Upward designated "quisb." This invented word, the origins of which have been forgotten, was used to describe anything that was toe-curlingly embarrassing:

> 'Hark!' said Betty. 'The cuckoo!'
> And Leonard, listening, heard, deep in the woods below, the divided call, that suggests, more instantly than any words, the mystery that lurks in noontide heat, in green summer shadows, in the murmur of the bee—the call, ironical and far-off, which mocks at Nature's unfolding pageantry, at the transient loveliness she parades, seeming to ask 'Whither?' and 'Where?'

This almost reads like a deliberate parody of Nichols at his most lushly rural, but there is nothing here to suggest that Isherwood, if not convincingly engaged with his

---

5. It is possible that Isherwood got the idea for this sign from his brother. In an undated fragment of a short story by Richard called "The Sign," the protagonist recalls that on the bus returning him to his hated prep school he passed a pub and looked back to see the word "COURAGE" (a brand of beer) shining out in neon lettering.

subject matter, is nevertheless anything other than serious. Even less heartfelt are his descriptions of the relationship between Leonard and Betty:

> Betty bit her lip, and tears of anger stood in her eyes. And now Leonard realized for the first time the manner in which she had changed. He could no longer put things right with a naïve apology, as he would have done four years ago. He had hurt something fragile. He was a blunderer. He despised himself.

Fueled by frequent cups of coffee, Isherwood once spent a whole night reading the entire novel aloud to Upward, who interrupted to jeer at any particularly overripe passage. In mitigation, Isherwood explained that the novel was really all about The Test, which had been reduced somewhat in scope. Instead of facing war, a boy had to face school, and in the novel Leonard worries about how he might have fared at Rugtonstead had he not been prevented by illness from going there. Isherwood later acknowledged that this substitution of Rugtonstead for the trenches did not really carry much conviction. The truth was that Isherwood was even more obsessed by school than he was by The Test. It was not until the end of the decade, when he started work on *The Memorial*, that he would be able to write about the First World War.

"Lions and Shadows" is what Isherwood thought a novel ought to be, a fascinating apprentice work, which tells us not only about Isherwood's craft but also his life and psychology. The novel contains many verbal echoes that a more mature artist would have removed. For example, Betty's original surname (altered by hand in the extant typescript) is "Disleigh," which, with the fact that her father is a writer, connects her with the Monkhouse family, who lived in Disley. It is possible that Betty was suggested by Rachel Monkhouse, whom Isherwood had described as "the only girl I have even been sincerely friends with," but whose friendship had gradually evolved on her part into a quite serious and unwelcome crush. "Alan Dayling" is an obvious echo of "Austen Darling," but this may be a guarded tribute to the beloved rather than anything more significant. The missing portions of the novel presumably contained a description of Dayling's friendship with Leonard, but in any case the two boys are contemporaries. The relationship between Isherwood and Darling is more accurately reflected in that between Charles and Leonard, whose disparity in age matches that of the author and his former fag. Leonard's diminutive stature, which he shares with both Isherwood and Darling, is mentioned, and the discussion about fags and study-holders evidently draws upon Isherwood's own experiences. Charles represents Isherwood the aspirant writer and sophisticate, the Isherwood who reads Rupert Brooke and Baudelaire (as Charles does) and writes airily to his friends about "tarts." When he parts from Leonard for the last time, Charles asks:

> 'You know that novel of mine?'
> 'Yes,' said Leonard, ' "Lions and Shadows"?'
> 'I'm going to write it quite soon now. Only it will be entirely different. It'll be all about you.'
> 'About me?'
> 'Yes. I see it as plain as daylight . . . It'll be about your life—from the time you were brought away from Ireland to the present day.'

In other words, it will be the novel we are reading, Christopher Isherwood's "Lions and Shadows."

Isherwood was drawing upon his own life, as he would always do, when writing this novel. St. Yniol's—a "large house of dark red weatherbeaten brick, surrounded by pinewoods"—is recognizably St. Edmund's. Aunt Edith's obsession with the Past, symbolized by her room full of photographs, is clearly borrowed from Kathleen. "The Past has power," the photographs tell her. "Live in it. Never mind the Present. The Present fades, but the Past is always there." Charles's determination to be a writer in the face of cautious family opposition reflects Isherwood's disagreements with Kathleen about his future. "I wouldn't stand in your way, whatever you cared to take up, if you could do well at it," Charles's father says. "But this writing business— of course I don't understand much about Art myself, but it doesn't seem to me that it's going to *get* you anywhere."

This was certainly one of Kathleen's concerns. At the beginning of February she had received "a very depressed" letter from him, in which he said he was "finding Cambridge more than usually unpleasant and [was] overcome with lethargy & not working." "If only he would pull himself together," Kathleen commented, "for he is clever enough." If Isherwood did pull himself together, then it was not to concentrate upon his studies, but to embark almost immediately upon a new novel, "Christopher Garland," all trace of which has disappeared. He gives a brief outline of the book in *Lions and Shadows:*

> A young man's first year after leaving school. The action takes place in London, Sussex and Cambridge. Roughly speaking, it is to show how the young man is, through a series of experiences and incidents, gradually committed to art—to the art which he had, at first, not taken very seriously.
>
> The story opens with the arrival of the young man after his last term at school; goes on to his first great period of inspiration, while staying in Sussex. Then comes Cambridge, with its terrible stupefying effect on the brain and spirit. In the vacation, the young man, cut off from his friends by his perceptions but not yet fully initiate, drifts into a dismal struggle with the personality of the aunt with whom he lives. A love affair with a friend's fiancée brings him to himself and, with its renunciation, he enters upon a period, if not of peace, at least of courage and assurance for the future.

Judging by this outline, "Christopher Garland" was, like "Lions and Shadows," less interesting as a work of literature than for what it told the reader about the author's state of mind. As Isherwood later commented, the book was about "Isherwood the Artist," about his dedication to the art of fiction. There was some wishful thinking here, since he was currently more likely to end up as a schoolteacher than a full-time writer. But as Upward recalled: "What mattered more than anything else to us at Cambridge was Art—not just our art but also the art of those writers, musicians and painters we most admired." Isherwood himself stated: "Edward Upward helped me create the image of myself as The Writer." Upward, he felt, believed in suffering: "I longed to suffer." A favorite quotation was Wordsworth's lines inspired by the death of that "marvellous boy" Thomas Chatterton: "We Poets in our youth begin in gladness; / But thereof come in the end despondency and madness." This sense of what it was to be an "Artist" (almost always with a capital initial) was to persist for some time.

The fact that Isherwood read "Christopher Garland" aloud to his mother is significant: was it intended as a barely coded appeal, a way of telling her that he was genuinely serious about becoming a writer? His ambitions received a blow in March when he gave "Lions and Shadows" to Ethel Colburn Mayne to read. Mayne had kept in touch with the Isherwoods after Frank's death and by the 1920s was living in London, toward the far end of the Holland Road on the westernmost fringes of Kensington. She had by now published several novels and volumes of short stories, had translated a volume of Dostoyevsky's letters and produced *Enchanters of Men* (1909), a book about femmes fatales, running from Diane de Poitiers to Adah Menken, the much-married American circus equestrienne who rather late in life became Swinburne's "Dolores." This last book, and her subsequent work on Byron and his family, were proof that Mayne was unconventional and unshockable. Isherwood described her as a "wise and understanding lady [...] whose delicacy of perception had become fortified by a robust and sometimes quite unladylike Irish wit." She held forthright, not to say radical, opinions, thoroughly disapproving, for example, of the Boer War, even though her beloved Frank was a participant. (She once told Isherwood: "At least you can be thankful Frank wasn't killed in *that* war—as bad as having your father shot while he was robbing a house.") Her verdict on "Lions and Shadows" is not recorded, but it was clearly less positive than Isherwood had hoped. "I longed to hear all about it," Kathleen wrote, "but [Christopher] came back depressed, I know how much it has meant to him." Isherwood had confided instead in Edward Upward, who responded by pronouncing an obscene doggerel curse upon Miss Mayne, calling for her to be crushed by a train and gang-raped by Zulus. Kathleen noted that Christopher seemed "very bored & tired & depressed. I am afraid for one thing the novel has been a disappointment—everything seems so different to what it used [to be]—he is so much less happy & so listless—& I do not know how to make things any better."

Back at Cambridge, Isherwood realized that he had little hope of making up the ground he had lost the previous year and that he was bound to do badly in the Tripos examination in June. Since there was no chance of his getting a first, and he was too proud to attempt to scrape a second, he decided to fail altogether: and, encouraged by Upward, he decided to fail in style. It was important to demonstrate to the authorities that he had the intellectual capacity to pass the examinations if he chose, and to this end he wrote answers that were at once clever, insolent and academically suicidal. Some essays he wrote in concealed verse (including a sonnet on the Restoration), others in the facetious style of *Punch*. Rather than answer one "rather unfortunately worded" question, he subjected it to lethal textual analysis. Very pleased with himself, he copied out all his answers to show to Upward, and walked out of the examination hall and away from any prospect of an academic future. The following day, he wrote to tell his mother that there was no hope of his having passed the examination. "It was a blow, & felt quite stunned," Kathleen confessed. "I suppose I had never believed really in his failing."

On June 11 Isherwood packed up his room and left Cambridge. The following day he went to see a Mr. Taylor of Stoll Films, arranging an interview for later in the month. Encouraged by George Pearson's lecture to the film society, Isherwood and Roger Burford had decided to look for jobs as screenwriters in the movie industry. Five days later a wire came from Cambridge, summoning Isherwood to an interview with the Tutor. "After a good deal of abuse Spens ended by wishing him good luck," Kathleen reported, characteristically taking her son's side, even though he deserved everything Spens threw at him. Not unnaturally, Spens felt betrayed by someone who had come to the College on a top scholarship. He nevertheless allowed Isherwood to withdraw his name from the College books, a civilized alternative to being sent down. "Years afterwards," Isherwood wrote in *Lions and Shadows,* "someone told me that Mr. Holmes [i.e. G. B. Smith] had got possession, by intrigue or theft, of my Tripos papers; and kept them, ever since, in a locked drawer. I hope this is true. It would be just like him." Smith may have been doting, but he wasn't as doting as all that. As Isherwood knew perfectly well, Smith did in fact have the papers, "sent to me by Bill Spens in an attempt to justify his action," he told his former pupil. "As if it needed any justification!" At the time, Smith was rather less amused, as Isherwood was well aware. "I am never furious or contemptuous," he told his errant protégé in July. "I never regret the past or remember it except to take precautions for the future. What matters is what people are & are going to be, not what they have or have not done. So it will be open to us to discuss the future & not the past." In subsequent letters he addresses Isherwood as "Sweet lad" and "Dear heart," so presumably he forgave him.

Isherwood may have been a little shamed by his interview with Spens and by Smith's reprimand, but he was unrepentant. Apart from anything else, he was having his short story "The Hero" published that month in the *Oxford Outlook.* Since he had been at Cambridge, the story was published anonymously and so he did not have the pleasure of seeing his name in print; but it was a start. At the end of the month, he set off for the Isle of Wight, where he was to spend three weeks at Freshwater Bay at the western end of the island. He stayed with a Miss Johnstone at a boarding-house called Marine Villa, a pretty building with a veranda, on which Isherwood liked to work, with the sea, framed by ilex, glittering in the near distance. He was shortly joined by Upward, and the two young men spent much of their time writing. Among other things they produced a poem of twenty-five stanzas entitled "The Recessional from Cambridge." In *Lions and Shadows,* Isherwood recalls that when he was being interviewed by Mr. Spens, he was at a loss to say anything: "How could I talk to this perfect stranger about Mortmere and Hynd and Starn and the Dürers and Laily and the willows by Garret Hostel Bridge?" "The Recessional" depicts the triumphant departure from Cambridge of both Hynd and Starn (Upward and Isherwood), accompanied by an entire Mortmere cavalcade. The loss, it is suggested, is Cambridge's, and the city will be a duller place without them all.

> Yes, tutor, before ever you have heard
>   The tapping of the maid who brings you tea
>   Your letters and hot water, we shall be

In Mortmere, once again. Before you have stirred,
    Before the sperm-stains on the sheets can harden
    We shall be having breakfast in the Rectory Garden.

Oh farewell, tutor; prosper in your ways
    Accept apologies for our desertion
    We never meant to cast the least aspersion
Upon your system. It is beyond praise.
    Only just now we do not need an emetic
    Nor wish to undergo a local anaesthetic.

Yes, sir, we know the ingratitude is appalling
    We know the nature of our indiscretion
    We know that when one chooses a profession—
Pardon a moment, but our friends are calling—
    Yes, yes . . . Quite true . . . Well, so long . . . Best of luck.
    May you, throughout your life, ne'er lack a friend or fuck.

FIVE

I T WAS ALL VERY WELL BLOWING A CHEERFULLY OBSCENE (AND
metrically lame) raspberry at Cambridge, but now that Isherwood and Upward
had arrived at Mortmere, what were they to do? The call of Mortmere certainly
interrupted any consideration of a profession, but decisions about their future could
not be postponed indefinitely. For the moment, however, they were on holiday, and
long summer days free from the burden of study (never a particularly heavy one)
stretched ahead of them.

Mortmere would continue to exert a terrible fascination over both writers; in particular, Upward would find it very hard to strike out in the direction of a fiction less
fantastic and personally allusive, more firmly anchored in the real world and accessible to a wide audience. Both writers were pursuing individual projects alongside the
Mortmere saga. While Isherwood continued to toy with ideas derived from his own
experiences at school and university, Upward tried to write a realistic satire set in a
golf club, based on his observations of his parents' social life in Essex. By now Mortmere had generated a great deal of material, some of which seemed to have potential
for development. The problem lay in adapting and sufficiently bowdlerizing the stories to make a coherent and publishable narrative. Throughout the autumn, Isherwood and Upward would meet most weekends to work on this project. When
separated they wrote to each other regularly, and these letters—scatological, blas-
phemous, largely incomprehensible, and in Upward's case often in verse—were an
integral part of the mad world they had created. They also exchanged views about
books they were reading, recommending or damning writers—from T. S. Eliot to
Margaret Kennedy—with all the authority and self-assurance of the young.

On August 26, Isherwood had what his mother called his "real but unofficial"
twenty-first birthday. To celebrate, he took Nanny and Richard for a drive in Richmond Park in his recently acquired second-hand Renault. He had bought the car earlier that month with his Post Office savings, and it had cost him £105. New, it would
have cost £1,100, but it was an outdated model. A large olive-green vehicle, "with

great brass headlamps, a gate-change gear and black leather upholstery like a cab," it could carry seven people and reach a maximum speed of forty miles per hour when traveling downhill. The garage owner had been giving Isherwood driving lessons, but this was the first time the novice had ventured out unchaperoned. Although Isherwood neglects to mention the fact in *Lions and Shadows,* Kathleen reimbursed him for this extravagant purchase, giving him the money as a birthday present. It was a welcome gift, since the previous week he had returned from his interview with the Stoll Studios without any prospect of a job. According to Roger Burford, who accompanied him to the film studios, a former aircraft factory in Cricklewood, Isherwood blew his chances when Sir Oswald Stoll gestured to several shelves of popular novels and said, "You will have to read all these books." "Why?" Isherwood replied. They subsequently wrote to George Pearson, who told them that he wished there were more opportunities for public-school and Oxbridge-educated men in the film industry, but at present there simply weren't enough jobs to go round. He suggested they both find other employment and try again the following spring.

Uncle Henry failed even to send his nephew a birthday card, but the following month he summoned Christopher to lunch. The purpose of this meeting was to suggest that now Christopher had attained his majority he was old enough as the eventual heir to decide what to do with Marple Hall. Henry had not lived there since his father's death, and had no intention of ever doing so. He was far happier living in London, and had taken a flat in South Eaton Place, Belgravia, again within walking distance of a guards' barracks. Over lunch he suggested that they should sell Marple Hall and presented Christopher with papers to sign. Although she knew of Henry's intentions, Kathleen was nevertheless devastated when Christopher returned home and told her what had happened. There is little doubt that Isherwood took a particular pleasure in being the bearer of news he knew would upset her. Here was one piece of her beloved Past he could personally consign to the dustbin. Kathleen naturally blamed Henry, but she had also lost patience with her son. "How anyone could be so taken in, & do anything so unspeakably foolish as to sign papers is more than I can understand or forgive," she wrote, "but the Christopher of old is dead." In the event, Henry decided to keep Marple and install a caretaker.

The following day marked another stage in Isherwood's disengagement from his mother, when he took up a new job. Eric Falk had recently returned from a holiday in France with the family of the violinist André Mangeot, with whom he had become friends. During the holiday, Mangeot's younger son, Sylvain, had fallen off his bicycle and cut his knee very badly on the pedal. Back in London, the eleven-year-old boy was confined to the family home at 21 Cresswell Place just off the Old Brompton Road while his wound healed. Falk suggested that Sylvain might enjoy a spin in Richmond Park in Isherwood's new car, possibly recognizing that Isherwood himself would not be averse to the company of an attractive and intelligent schoolboy. When the two young men returned Sylvain to Cresswell Place, they were invited to stay to tea. In the course of conversation, it emerged that André Mangeot was looking for a secretary—particularly one who could read French and had a large motorcar at his disposal. He and Isherwood immediately warmed to each other, and by the time the tea things were cleared had struck a deal whereby Isherwood would take the job on a month's trial.

Born in Paris in 1883, André Mangeot was a highly gifted violinist, who had studied at the Paris Conservatoire, then come to England as a young man to play in the Queen's Hall Orchestra and at Covent Garden. He became a naturalized British subject and in 1919 founded the International String Quartet, with Boris Pecker on second violin, Harry Berly on the viola and John Barbirolli on cello. The quartet was soon established as one of Europe's leading chamber music groups, and Mangeot became renowned for fostering young British talent, among both players and composers. He had, for example, recognized that Barbirolli was an unusually gifted student and had plucked him out of the Royal Academy of Music for his quartet, and he would later give the first performance of the nineteen-year-old Benjamin Britten's *Phantasy Quartet*. He was also a fine teacher, who had a particular sympathy for talented young women, several of whom fell in love with him. As well as playing and teaching, and touring with the quartet on the Continent, he founded the Westminster Music Society and ran a series of monthly subscription concerts at the St. John's Institute in Tufton Street. His wife, Olive, acted as the Society's secretary.

"Dark and elegant, a cigarette between her sharply-coloured lips," Olive Mangeot seemed to Isherwood "rather my idea of a Russian woman out of a Tchekhov story." Eighteen months younger than her husband, she was in fact English, the daughter of Frank Reed Fowke, Assistant Secretary of the Board of Education. Her own education had been undertaken by governesses, and she remained an erratic speller (always adding a "u" to "gift" for example), but she had been brought up in a highly cultured home. Her father was a distinguished watercolorist and knew a great many artists, and her mother, Isabella, was the daughter of Sir Henry Cole, the well-known industrial designer who became the first director of the Victoria and Albert Museum. Family holidays were spent on the Normandy coast, where Fowke would pass the day sketching on the beach, and it was while he was thus occupied at Wimereux one year that he was approached by André Mangeot, who was holidaying back in his native France. The two men got into conversation and Fowke invited the personable young Frenchman to his hotel in order to meet his wife and daughters. Isabella was alarmed by Mangeot's bohemian appearance and declared, "I'm not having that long-haired youth meet my daughters"; but Fowke insisted and within a week Mangeot had won over the entire family. He proposed to Olive and the couple were married in 1910.

The following year, Olive gave birth to their first son, who was christened Fowke after his grandfather. Mangeot had wanted to call him Jean, after a favorite brother killed in the war, but Olive insisted he should have what she somewhat eccentrically described as an English name, which she soon discovered nobody knew how to pronounce. (It rhymes with "joke.") Just over a year and a half later, a second son was born and christened Sylvain Edouard André. Olive had taken instruction and learned a great deal about the Roman Catholic Church, but she never actually converted. The children were brought up in the faith, but were not otherwise much disciplined by their parents, who thought it better to present rational arguments as to why Fowke and Sylvain should or should not do certain things rather than actually ordering or forbidding anything. They were, however, kept in line by the fifth member of the household, Hilda Hawes, a buxom countrywoman with fat red cheeks and a very down-to-earth manner. She had come to the family as a teenager to be cook and housekeeper and, apart from a brief excursion to marry a man who shortly afterward ran away to join the Indian Army, she remained with them for the rest of her life. She stood for no nonsense from anyone and was no respecter of persons. "She was very tough on us as boys," Fowke Mangeot recalled, "but she adored us." And she was ferociously protective of the family, particularly if anyone had the temerity to criticize any of its members. Isherwood was, quite rightly, rather frightened of her.

In the early days the family rarely had much money, partly because André was naturally generous and inclined to spend concert fees that ought to have gone into the housekeeping on taking people out to dinner. Despite financial worries, the Mangeots kept more or less open house at Cresswell Place, a plain, flat-fronted double mews cottage. Most of the downstairs was taken up by a large music room, but there were also two garages, one of which was later converted into a study. The dining room and kitchen were upstairs, along with three bedrooms, one of which the boys shared, another of which, rather inconveniently reached through the bathroom, was occupied by Hilda. There was no office, and so the large amounts of paperwork connected with the quartet—correspondence with concert-hall managers, festival organizers, music societies, hotels and boarding-houses, record companies and the BBC—tended to infiltrate the living quarters, frequently getting lost among concert programs and the domestic detritus of a young and energetic family. "This is how real human people lived," Isherwood thought, as his

> eyes wandered over the comfortable untidiness of the large room; the music stacked on the grand piano; the pencil, pipe, orange and block of resin beside the keyboard; the violin on the chair next to the tennis-racket; the fishing-rods in the corner; the photographs with scrawled inscriptions; the Japanese prints on the whitewashed brick walls; the Breton cupboard crammed with music-stands, pictures, books, clothes. People living together, busy, friendly, intent upon their work, had created the atmosphere in this house: nothing was planned, forced, formal, consciously quaint. Mentally, I compared it with my own, with [Wintle's] home: it was difficult to realize, even, that we were all inhabiting the same city. This was another world.

It was a world to which Isherwood longed to belong, representing "the New Life," which he contrasted with "the Old Life" embodied by Kathleen in St. Mary Abbot's Terrace. Until now, he had merely despised Kathleen's life and values, but the Mangeots provided him with a positive, alternative. This was a theme Isherwood began to explore in his writing, and Cresswell Place would be depicted with almost photographic accuracy in *The Memorial,* where it became the London home of Mary Scriven, a character closely based on Olive Mangeot.[1]

---

1. Compare the description of Cresswell Place just quoted with the one of the Scrivens' house: "with stacks of paper everywhere, the Breton armoire, the Steineln poster on the wall, the bed, the dressing-table, the shelf of yellow paper-bound books, the gay chessboard curtains at the windows. Rather like the inside of a caravan. At night you went to bed on the camouflaged divan surrounded by the day's débris—letters, newspapers, press cuttings, other people's musical instruments, tennis rackets, and usually a little dirty crockery or a few beer glasses which had escaped notice in the wash-up after a picnic meal."

Isherwood now began commuting between these two contrasting worlds. He reported to work each day shortly after breakfast, having walked south through Earls Court from St. Mary Abbot's Terrace, and remained at Cresswell Place until lunchtime. The first morning was spent beginning the daunting task of catching up on a vast backlog of correspondence, most of which had been thrust unsorted into a suitcase. Mangeot dictated in French, which Isherwood—profiting at last from the dreary months he spent under Professor Morel's tutelage in Rouen—took down and then translated into English. This relatively simple task was complicated by Mangeot's habit of reading through Isherwood's version, then making further alterations, all of which had to be incorporated in a new fair copy. Although he had yet to receive any sort of salary, Isherwood seemed happy to perform duties beyond the usual scope of secretary, and one Sunday, after he had been employed for just over a week, he obligingly drove the Mangeots to Hythe in Kent in order to visit Sylvain, who had returned to his prep school there.

In early October Kathleen got her first glimpse of M. and Mme Mangeot, when she accompanied Hector Wintle to a performance of Pirandello's *And That's the Truth* at the Lyric Theatre. "I thought they both looked nice," she reported, "but wished I could have got a better view." The Mangeots may have *looked* nice, but Kathleen was worried that they appeared to be exploiting their enthusiastic new secretary, who had bought a portable typewriter with some birthday money, the better to carry out his duties. Furthermore, there was still no sign of his being paid. Isherwood nevertheless seemed keen to do whatever the Mangeots wanted, even at weekends, and even when he had a nasty cold. Kathleen was particularly suspicious of Olive, who later in the month telephoned to ask whether Christopher could drive her once more to Hythe, since Sylvain had injured his knee again. "It must be very useful to have a secretary who can motor one about," Kathleen commented sharply in her diary. By this time, Mangeot had finally broached the subject of a salary, which was calculated upon available funds. Isherwood would be paid £1 a week, plus 10 percent of the takings from concerts, which could raise the sum to as much as £6 a week. The job itself remained not very clearly defined. As well as dealing with correspondence (now neatly typed on printed stationery, which listed the members of the Music Society Quartet—as it was currently known—and "Secretary: C. B. Isherwood"), Isherwood attended concerts, checking tickets at the door, spent evenings at Cresswell Place listening to broadcasts on the radio, and drove the quartet to and from musical engagements. Kathleen complained that she saw very little of him: when he wasn't with the Mangeots, he was writing behind the closed door of his room, or out at the cinema or theater with friends, notably George Fisher, the Repton contemporary who had so admired Kathleen.

O n December 16, Fisher's younger brother, Stanley, who was at Oxford, came to tea at St. Mary Abbot's Terrace. With him he brought a fellow undergraduate from Christ Church, W. H. Auden, who was spending part of the Christmas holidays with him. Like many prep-school friendships, the one between Auden and Isherwood had not survived their departures to different public schools. Auden had grown larger but no tidier, and, despite his fashionable but rumpled suit and an ostentatiously brandished pipe, he was recognizably the scruffy schoolboy Isherwood had last seen seven years previously, almost to the day. At first he seemed standoffish, more interested in exploring Isherwood's bookshelves than in joining in the conversation. He nevertheless stayed behind after Fisher had left and soon he and Isherwood began to recall their time at St. Edmund's and discuss the various characters they had known there, Auden doing very funny impersonations of Cyril Morgan Brown and others. It is likely that Auden would have explained that he was at Fisher's house rather than his own home in Birmingham because relations with his mother had become strained, and (being Auden) he may well have explained why: his loss of faith and his homosexuality. (Auden's "attitude to sex, in its simplicity and utter lack of inhibition, fairly took my breath away," Isherwood remembered.) Family discord and sexual unorthodoxy would have forged an immediate bond between the two young men, and a further one was the discovery that they were both attempting to write. Auden offered to send Isherwood some of his poems. Isherwood recalled that at St. Edmund's Auden had displayed "no literary interests whatever," and so his expectations were not high when a few days later a large envelope arrived in the post. To his surprise, the poems it contained—although imitative of Thomas Hardy and Edward Thomas— were extremely competent.

Auden, in characteristically magisterial fashion, kept very few letters, and not a single one from Isherwood has survived. Isherwood, on the other hand, shared his mother's obsession with documenting life, and kept large files of correspondence, which eventually included a substantial number of Auden's letters. Equally magisterially, Auden rarely bothered to date his letters, so keeping track of the developing friendship between the two young men is difficult. It is evident, however, that Isherwood responded encouragingly to the poems he had been sent, and consequently received more. An undated letter addressed "My dear Beesh" and signed "Dodo" may well be the first letter Isherwood ever received from Auden, a response to his comments on the first batch of poems he had been sent. "Dodo" is what Isherwood would have called Auden at school, and "Beesh" was Auden's version of "Bish," a contracted form of "Bisherwood," itself derived from "C. W. B.-Isherwood," which is how Isherwood was styled at St. Edmund's. (Isherwood later credited Auden with the knowledge that *biche* is the French slang word for "lesbian.") "A thousand thanks for your embarrassing praise and stimulating criticism," Auden wrote in a stylish but barely legible scrawl. "Re the list of 3rd rate, I disagree only about Farglow, 'There is so much' and Friendship, all of which I like! probably however you are quite right. I quite agree about the abandonment in certain cases, and shall cut them where possible."

Because Auden became the leading figure of his literary generation, it has always been assumed and frequently asserted that Isherwood followed in his wake. Isherwood's seniority, however, was (and remained) an important factor in their relationship. The two-and-a-half-year age difference might have counted for little had they not first become friends at prep school, where such things mattered greatly. Auden was now an undergraduate at the end of his first term, whereas Isherwood was in the adult world, earning a living and mixing with real artists such as André Mangeot and his quartet. Isherwood himself later wrote that throughout the 1920s and 1930s, "I still saw Auden, to some degree, as the small boy, three years my junior whom I had known at my first boarding-school." This may explain why Auden was prepared to take notice of Isherwood's criticisms of his work, criticism for which Isherwood was

not otherwise particularly qualified. As a practitioner of poetry, Isherwood was neither very experienced nor very distinguished, despite Katherine Tynan's public com-
mendation of "Mapperley Plains." Stephen Spender, writing in 1979 about the
relationship between the two young men, noted:

> There is an element of the arbitrary, on Auden's side, about even his closest rela-
> tionships. An example of arbitrariness is his choice of Isherwood as the judge
> who would decide finally for him what were the good and what the bad lines in
> his poetry. An intelligent choice, of course, because it set up Isherwood's intuitive
> judgement against A[uden]'s intellect but at the same time, however good a judge,
> Isherwood must have been fallible; to set him up as infallible was to give him a
> fixed place in Auden's constellation of his friends. One might say this was not al-
> together fair to Isherwood. . . .

Auden could, however, trust Isherwood to be frank and firm in his comments. He
also recognized that Isherwood enjoyed this role, liking nothing more than to exercise his will and get his own way. "Don't you love to boss just everybody, everybody," Auden exclaimed in a poem, "To make us all dance to your tune." Isherwood
had needed to exercise his will in his battles with his mother and by now this had become almost a reflex action. It was as if he expected to be thwarted as a matter of
course and so rarely relaxed his vigilance. Spender noted that Isherwood's

> round shining eyes had a steadiness which seemed to come from the strain of ef-
> fort, as though their feat of balancing themselves in Christopher's face at the same
> time balanced the whole world which they saw. They were the eyes of someone
> who, when he is a passenger in an aeroplane, thinks that the machine is kept in the
> air by an act of his will, and that unless he continues to look steadily in front of
> him it will fall instantly to the ground. These eyes were under sharp-angled eye-
> brows which added to the impression of his being a strained school leader.

It was an impressive performance, but a performance all the same. As Spender observed, "He was well aware of these effects."

There are no further references to Auden in Kathleen's diaries until April 1926, but
toward the end of January Isherwood spent a night in Oxford and almost certainly visited his old school-friend. In any case, they were by now in regular correspondence, as
Auden bombarded Isherwood with poems and ideas. Like Isherwood himself, Auden
was an attentive apprentice in the workshops of his literary elders, but whereas Isherwood's writing was influenced by a somewhat narrow pantheon of English middlebrow
authors, Auden's reflected his eclectic taste in reading. He borrowed styles and ideas
from wherever he could find them, incorporating them in his work. This magpie tendency did not always make for clarity, but it did make Auden's poetry seem impressive.
Even at their most difficult to understand, the poems always had authority. Isherwood
later came up with his own theory about the complexity of Auden's early poetry:

> When Auden was younger, he was very lazy. He hated polishing and making cor-
> rections. If I didn't like a poem, he threw it away and wrote another. If I liked one

line, he would keep it and work it into a new poem. In this way, whole poems
were constructed which were simply anthologies of my favourite lines, entirely
regardless of grammar or sense. This is the simple explanation of much of
Auden's celebrated obscurity.

Although there may be some truth in this, it is an exaggeration, rather as Isherwood's
portrait of "Hugh Weston" in *Lions and Shadows* (published during the same period
as these comments) is a caricature of Auden. Given Isherwood's seniority, he felt able
to view the poet as a "brilliant teenager" in need of guidance.

Another young person who wanted Isherwood's advice about poetry was Sylvain
Mangeot. Shortly before he returned to school in January, Sylvain bought some
expensive paper and began drawing cartoons of animals on them. He also tried his
hand at some rhymes, but displeased with these, and having a captive writer at hand,
asked whether Isherwood could provide new verses to accompany his paintings.
Scribbling furiously to keep up with Sylvain's impressive rate of production, Isherwood contributed twenty-nine poems, describing (among other creatures) a giraffe, a
hippo, an elephant, an ostrich, a whale, a ballet-dancing hare, Farmer Stoat, Admiral
Duck, the Weasel King and a very odd and slightly drunk-looking pink-and-black
rabbit. The whole project was finished in less than a week, bound up and presented
to Olive and André. The title page read, in Sylvain's neat hand:

PEOPLE ONE
OUGHT TO KNOW
BY
C.W.B.-ISHERWOOD
AND
S.E. MANGEOT.
1ST & ONLY EDITION.

This was followed by a limitation page:

THIS EDITION IS LIMITED
TO ONE COPY, NUMBERED AND
SIGNED BY THE AUTHORS; OF WHICH
THIS IS NUMBER 1.

Author and artist both added their signatures, Sylvain's more adult and sophisticated
than Isherwood's. It was dedicated "TO URSULA" and inscribed "To Mother and Daddy
from Sylvain and Christopher, January 1926."[2] Presumably Olive was delighted with
this collaboration between the nice young secretary and her son. Kathleen borrowed
the book and made her own careful facsimile, tracing Sylvain's original drawings.

---

2. Ursula Macdonald was the daughter of a family friend who lived with the Mangeots while studying the cello at the Royal College of Music.

Sylvain's pictures are extremely characterful and colorful, while Isherwood's verses fit into a long tradition of English nonsense poetry. The only obvious literary borrowing is the rhyming of the words "Alice" and "Buckingham Palace" in "Snail," clearly lifted from A. A. Milne's famous poem in *When We Were Very Young*. (Isherwood gave Kathleen a copy of this book on January 16.) The doggerel verses were never intended for publication, but the poem about "The common cormorant (or shag)" gained popular currency after being included in *The Poet's Tongue* (1935), an anthology for schools co-edited by Auden and an eccentric headmaster called John Garrett. Typically, Auden reproduced the poem from memory and so not entirely accurately (incidentally improving the scansion). It was frequently republished in this version, and without the author being identified, until 1966, when Isherwood included the original version in *Exhumations*.

Several of the poems in *People One Ought to Know* (which was itself eventually published in 1982) contain private jokes: Horsey, who "in his youth loved footer," is André; the snail who complains of being constantly called from his rest by the telephone, though characterized as male, is Olive; Siegfried the seal, who is so proud of his new blazer, is Fowke (whose name is similar to the French for seal: *phoque*); Sylvain himself is the cadging badger, who asks the poet for his car ("This was going rather far") and drops "clumsy hints" about forthcoming birthdays.

As Kathleen noted sourly in her diary, Isherwood often remained at Cresswell Place for lunch, and spent his evenings with the Mangeots, either dining with them or accompanying them to concerts or the theater. "At first, I could hardly believe in my astounding good luck," he recalled. "That I should be allowed to come to this house every day; to have a part, however insignificant, in the life of the [Mangeot] family, seemed too wonderful to be true." A romantic account of his relationship with the Mangeots would provide one of the most delightful episodes in *Lions and Shadows*, but it was one calculated to offend his mother, who is all but excised from the book. "I had long since fallen in love with the entire family," he wrote. "My attitude towards them became violently possessive. I was jealous of their friends. Looking enviously through old photograph albums of past holidays and concert tours, I hated to think of all the years of their company I had missed." All the years, in other words, he had wasted in the company of his own family.

At forty, Olive was just old enough to be Isherwood's mother, but at the same time seemed his contemporary, unlike Kathleen, who—for all her trips to the theater to see such modernists as Pirandello—remained spiritually a Victorian. Olive was the sort of mother "Isherwood the Artist" felt he ought to have had, a truly sympathetic and open person in whom he could genuinely confide. She was, Isherwood observed, "one of the most placid people I have ever known. She had a genius for making herself comfortable: if there were five minutes to spare before a concert, she would sink, with a sigh of pleasure, into the nearest chair, and, if possible, put her feet up [. . .] In that agitated household, with its continual coming and going, its flurry and excitement, she radiated ease and calm—and contrived, nevertheless, to get through as much work as any two of us put together." This image of Olive precisely matches that of Mary Scriven in *The Memorial*, a character who also shares Olive's genial tolerance, her inability to spell, and her fondness for mock-Cockney expressions. Isherwood started out by following Hilda's lead and addressing Olive as "Madame" (André was "The

Governor"), but he later invented a nickname for her: "Mop." No one can now remember the origins of this name, but it stuck, and even her family occasionally used it. Letters to "Dear Madame" from "your affectionate secretary" were later addressed to "Darling Mop" and signed "your loving eldest, Christopher"—an indication of how far Isherwood saw himself a part of this unusual family. Olive herself soon became very attached to Isherwood and they developed a relationship independent of André. She was no doubt flattered and amused to be adopted as an honorary mother. In *The Memorial,* Mary Scriven, looking at the younger generation, thinks: "yes, they are all my children."

Fowke, whom Isherwood unkindly described as "livelier, less intelligent, more English" than his brother, was undoubtedly the more stolid child and more conventional personality. At the age of seven he announced that he would become a chartered accountant, partly because he had seen the splendor in which a family friend, Nicholas Waterhouse (of the famous Price Waterhouse accountancy firm), lived in Chelsea and had compared this with his parents' financially precarious existence. Having decided that at least one member of the family should earn a proper wage, he would leave Westminster School at sixteen to become an articled clerk in Waterhouse's office. Isherwood described the aptly named Sylvain, a pale, dark-haired, sharp-featured, faun-like child, as "riper and more self-possessed than his age." Sylvain was also academically bright, and would later join Fowke at Westminster as a King's Scholar, a boy who appeared out of the ordinary, "a real star," even to his contemporaries. Within the family, Fowke and Sylvain were sometimes known as "Foxer" and "Tiggy," both names apparently derived from Beatrix Potter. Isherwood must have been entranced to discover that the two boys had been brought up on Potter's books and delighted in acting out scenes from the stories. Both boys found the new secretary fun to be with, but it was Sylvain who developed the closer relationship.

Quite what form that relationship took is difficult now to judge, but it seems likely that it was colored by hero-worship on one side and a sort of romantic paternalism on the other. No letters about the Mangeots survive to those correspondents such as Eric Falk and Paddy Monkhouse in whom Isherwood once confided his passions for young boys, but it is perhaps significant that Isherwood's friendship with Darling faded at around the same time that he got to know Sylvain. Darling was still at school, but Isherwood no longer met the Repton train at the beginning of the school holidays. Isherwood was certainly still keen on young boys, telling Roger Burford, who was teaching Greek at a prep school, "I had better not come to Wootton Court, for your charges' sake." Burford must have jokingly suggested that he and Isherwood should set up a prep school themselves, for Isherwood continued: "No, no, my boy—no schoolmastering for me. I have the soul of a Hayley Morris.[3] Our school would certainly be run on startling lines—too startling, perhaps."

Something of Isherwood's feelings about Sylvain and his family may be gleaned from the new novel Isherwood had started writing. "The Summer at the House" was, he said, "inspired, vaguely, by my vision of the life of the [Mangeot] family." It opens

---

3. The defendant in a highly publicized rape case of the period.

in a welter of self-consciously fine writing with the arrival of Eric Mynors,[4] a young tutor, at a country railway station. ("Rain was drifting down through the air, so finely that he could scarcely feel it upon his skin. Yet, through its touch, he had, it seemed, perception of the sombre quietness of that countryside, of the black spear-topped firs above the railway cutting, of the small hollow valley and of the rain-cold hills." And so on.) Eric is met by his pupil, a seventeen-year-old youth called Robin Saunier, the son of an Anglo-French marriage. M. Saunier, a French watercolorist, is dead, and the household consists of Robin's English mother and her niece, Claire, a young woman roughly Eric's age. Like Isherwood at the Mangeots', Eric feels instantly at home: "A cold secret shudder of happiness woke in his heart and passed irresistibly over his whole body." After dinner that first night, during which the excitable Robin talks a great deal, the two women retire to bed, leaving Eric alone at the table with his pupil.

> 'I'm so sorry,' Robin said, when they were alone together, moving his chair close to Eric's. 'Have I really been tiring you? If you like, I won't say another word until you've finished.'
> He was very charming, with his serious grey eyes and quick sensitive smile. Already, in this first pang of response to the boy's charm, Eric seemed to feel the power of its whole spell upon him; and it was with the mild sarcasm which instinctively he had adopted against it as his only weapon, that he replied:
> 'Oh, I'm not nearly tired enough, yet. Go on talking; you'll give me an appetite for bed.'

Robin's flirtatiously challenging behavior is enough to give anyone an appetite for bed, but Eric appears to be drawn rather more conventionally to Claire. Perhaps sensing this, Robin produces another sort of weapon, a revolver, and in a highly melodramatic scene, after he has been teased about the gun by his mother, discharges it during a struggle with Eric, who is attempting to disarm him. Eric explains to the alarmed Mme Saunier that the gun went off accidentally when he was inspecting it. Eric's chief reaction to the incident, once the shock has worn off, is that he dreads Robin's apologies and pleas for forgiveness. They agree to say no more about it and, although Robin evidently has difficulty in controlling his temper on occasions, normal relations between pupil and tutor are restored. If indeed their relationship could be so described:

> [Robin's] other emotional displays were as violent; their impulse often as obscure.
> 'Eric,' he asked suddenly, after one of them, 'you don't *mind* being kissed, do you?'
> 'Why should I?' said Eric laughing.

---

4. The unusual surname was borrowed from Isherwood's Cambridge contemporary, a mathematics scholar named Humphrey Mynors, who stayed on at Corpus Christi to become Assistant Tutor and during the war served as the Secretary of the Bank of England. Although Isherwood knew Mynors reasonably well (they were both members of The Gravediggers), it remains unclear why he should use this name for an autobiographical character.

Small boys might well kiss their tutors, but Robin is supposed to be seventeen, and any tutor less obtuse than Eric might think such behavior rather peculiar.

The emotional and sexual muddle Eric appears to be in is partly caused by his relations with the women of the house. In the course of his conversations with the suspiciously androgynous Claire, Eric learns that she had trained as a pianist but failed to become a professional, a circumstance that has embittered her. She rather frightens him: "She had a certain hard cold jewel-like radiance which shone weirdly through her boy's features. Eric was conscious of it, was awed by it, as by the consciousness of an invisible presence." He is even more awed by Mme Saunier, who says that she wants to be friends with Eric.

'Why, of course . . .' said Eric smiling, 'what else should we be?'

'Ah,' she shook her head, 'it's difficult. More difficult than you may think, you young people . . .'

She was beautiful as she said this. Her beauty, which before had wrought no more than a vague confusion of his senses, became for him, at that moment, articulate. In her dark lucid eyes he seemed to see all that she was, all that she had been. She was a woman. She had suffered pain, had known sorrow. One day, she would be old. He felt his whole being humbled before her knowledge and her sad beauty.

Given such passages, it is hardly surprising that Isherwood had not dared show this work-in-progress to Edward Upward, and he abandoned the novel after writing six chapters. The rest of the book, Isherwood explained in a self-mocking afterword, would have been "developed along the best neo-Russian gradients," full of "*genre* incidents." Eric and Robin go riding up in the hills, where Robin falls off his horse and sprains his ankle. In the confusion, the horses gallop away, and the two young men are obliged to spend the night in a deserted "Wuthering Heights" sort of farmhouse, which is reputed to be haunted. There is a great storm, during which lightning sets fire to an outbuilding. "And Robin, need we add, clings around Eric's neck." When they return the following morning, it becomes clear to the reader (though not to Eric) that Mme Saunier had been more concerned for the safety of Eric than she had been for that of her son.

Then another incident. A picture Eric comes across stowed away in a box-room. Obviously Auguste Saunier's masterpiece. It is of a harlot. He can't think why they don't have the thing downstairs, and only realises later that it represents Madame Saunier herself. So he comes to realise that Auguste must have loathed her. And what an awful life she must have had. He has conceived a sort of worship for Madame Saunier, but is *not* in love with her. Henceforward, the reader's eyes are opened, and they see, in *her* treatment of *him,* hopeless attempts to awaken love. All fail. [. . .]

So poor old Mme S., quite desperate, at last consents to be engaged to Colonel Woodford, her lifelong admirer, who'd loved her even before Auguste's day. Tension follows. She is miserable. Everyone is jumpy. Mme S. goes about haggard, and once Eric catches her playing with Robin's revolver. Then, just before the wedding, there's a frightful storm, and Madame Saunier goes out into the dark to visit Colonel Woodford and takes the short cut and lets herself fall over the quarry cliff. She is brought in and dies, definitely saying that she loves Eric. Colonel Woodford goes back home and grimly gets into bed and dies. Eric lies ill for weeks.

Much later he has a final interview with Claire. She is still ironic, disgusted etc etc, but has very very kindly said she'll marry Gerald [a local farmer with whom she's been conducting an on-and-off affair], whom she doesn't love now, in order that they shall both be unhappy ever afterwards.

And then, a last pretty close-up, with Eric saying goodbye to Robin; and Robin (who's been left cash) suddenly breaking out: Can't I come with you, Eric? I'll be your servant, anything. And Eric turns with eyes blurred with tears of joy, and

Well, goodbye, chicks.
Ever your loving Uncle,
Sir E. F. Fyodr Benson Turgenev Newboltovich

Although Isherwood is sending himself up rotten here, nothing in the surviving chapters makes one think that this outline is anything other than genuine.

"The Summer at the House" is obviously not a straightforward attempt to translate Isherwood's involvement with the Mangeot family into fiction; Eric's relations with Mme Saunier and her son could be seen as a sort of fantasy projection of Isherwood's relations with Olive and Sylvain. And it was not all fantasy. Olive knew that her husband had been having affairs with some of his pupils and evidently felt that his persistent infidelities freed her to pursue her own extramarital relationships. Although perfectly well aware of Isherwood's sexuality, she once made an unsuccessful pass at him in the Cresswell Place house. Fortunately, both she and Isherwood were sensible enough to laugh off this faux pas and remain on the best of terms.

At the end of March, Isherwood traveled to Carbis Bay in Cornwall, where, in sight of the lighthouse Virginia Woolf would shortly make famous, Edward Upward had an uncongenial job as a private tutor to an adolescent brother and sister, whom he taught in a summer-house at the bottom of the garden. The boy was sixteen, but Upward warned Isherwood: "I doubt whether he would be to your taste. He has dark hair and vagueness. But you would be charmed perhaps by other points—such as a lack of all public school smears and presence of thick wrists." He subsequently had a dream in which the boy said of Isherwood, "Yes, he got well on top of me." Upward told Isherwood: "It is plain that what interests and impresses him is not that he has given way to you against his will, but that your methods are so brilliantly convincing." Teaching occupied only the mornings and Upward had been whiling away his free hours trying to write, and composing highly literary letters to Isherwood, in which the unremarkable town of St. Ives was transformed by his almost visionary gifts into another Mortmere. This was a sort of limbering-up for *The Market Town,* a Mortmere novel he was planning based upon his observations. He had hit upon the notion of making Mortmere into a fantasy projection of the narrator, an amalgam of Hynd and Starn called Hearn.

The two young men had decided to spend an Easter break in the Scilly Isles, an easy journey by ferry from Penzance, and Isherwood had brought along the manuscript of "The Summer at the House" in the hope that Upward's company—or perhaps a glimpse of his male pupil—would stimulate him to continue writing it. Upward, however, had made a major literary discovery, which would alter the course of Isherwood's writing, setting him upon more fruitful paths and eventually establishing his reputation. He had been reading E. M. Forster's *Howards End,* originally published in 1910, and had developed from this novel the concept of "tea-tabling." As Upward explained eagerly to his friend:

> Forster's the only one who understands what the modern novel ought to be ... Our frightful mistake was that we believed in tragedy: the point is, tragedy's quite impossible nowadays ... We ought to aim at being essentially comic writers ... The whole of Forster's technique is based on the tea-table: instead of trying to screw all his scenes up to the highest possible pitch, he tones them down until they sound like mothers'-meeting gossip ... In fact, there's actually *less* emphasis laid on the big scenes than on the unimportant ones: that's what's so utterly terrific. It's the completely new kind of accentuation—like a person talking a different language. ...

This notion struck Isherwood with the force of a revelation, and he knew almost at once that there was no point in continuing with the luridly melodramatic "The Summer at the House." This saved him the embarrassment of showing the manuscript to Upward, from whom he expected no mercy. ("My latest novel is at the bottom of Hugh Town Harbour," he told Roger Burford.) Inspired by his surroundings on St. Mary's, the largest of the Scilly Isles, he mapped out the plot of an entirely new novel, discussing it in detail with Upward. His vision of "The New Life" with "The Wonderful Family," represented by the Mangeots, was temporarily abandoned in favor of a confrontation with "The Old Life" he had endured with his mother. Always eager to make use of new experience, he decided that the novel should be set in the Scilly Isles, in the very hotel in Hugh Town in which he and Upward were staying. The principal characters would be two young men, one of whom (standing in for "Isherwood the Artist") wants to be a painter but has been obliged by his family to work as a clerk, the other a medical student called Mew who is an amalgam of Upward and Hector Wintle. Romantic interest would be provided by a fourteen-year-old girl (almost certainly suggested by Upward's pupil, who was of a similar age and had begun to interest her tutor), who attracts both the Upward-Wintle character and a representative of the Poshocracy called Worth, who is partly derived from Charles Wilcox in *Howards End.* It is possible that Isherwood also based Worth on Paddy Monkhouse, who had a distinct strain of Oxbridge heartiness in his character. Isherwood recalled Paddy once looking in a mirror at the age of seventeen and declaring: "No one could call me handsome, but I think I might be described as brutally impressive." The girl dies in a climbing accident, for which Worth is blamed by Mew. Back in London, the rivalry between the two suitors continues, though the object of their interest is now the Isherwood figure's sister. Worth naturally wins, his sort of brutal impressiveness being just the thing to earn the approval of the young woman's mother. Not content with getting the sister, he also attempts to exert fatherly authority over the Isherwood figure, who runs away. Believing (quite rightly) that Mew has been an undermining influence on the artist, Worth goes to the student's rooms to remonstrate. In the course of an argument, Mew strikes Worth dead with a poker, thus reversing the famous scene in *Howards End* where the philistine Charles kills the bookish Leonard Bast. While the plot was in its way as melodramatic as that of "The Summer at the House," the narrative would be casual and ironic, the climactic scene played, Upward suggested, "as almost pure farce." The novel would have the arty title *Seascape with Figures*.

Isherwood returned to London with one chapter of the novel already started, but was interrupted by the General Strike, which took place in May. For all his much-vaunted rebelliousness, Isherwood did not take this opportunity to fire a few shots in what rapidly came to take on the aspect of a class war. Young men from the Varsities immediately volunteered to fill the places vacated by striking workers, or became "special constables" who exercised their temporary powers in keeping the country running. Unlike Kathleen, who roundly declared "But *of course* I take sides!" and was thoroughly rejuvenated by this national crisis, "looking fresher and more alive than she'd looked for years," Isherwood was paralyzed into uncomfortable neutrality. Naturally, he did not wish to side with the Poshocracy, who regarded their own participation in the strike as a "tremendous upper-middle-class lark," but neither did he want to take the part of the Mangeots' Hilda, who gloated over the brutal treatment handed out to blacklegs. Friends such as Wintle and Falk were helping to keep the Underground system and the docks working, while Auden, for no very clear reason, joined the other side, inexpertly driving a car for the Trades Union Congress. Upward was perhaps the only person who might have helped Isherwood decide where his allegiances ought to be, but he was back in Cornwall, unreachable because the strike had disrupted the postal service. For the first time in his life Isherwood had to make a political decision.

He tried to persuade himself that as an intellectual he should remain aloof, part of "some mystical Third Estate, isolated above the battle." Eventually, after several weeks of dithering, he returned to principles: what could he do that would most upset his mother? At Chelsea Town Hall he volunteered for the least popular job on offer, happy in the knowledge that while other parents could boast in Kensington drawing rooms that their sons were driving trams or directing traffic, Kathleen could hardly admit that her beloved Christopher had volunteered to work on a sewage farm. In the event, it had taken Isherwood so long to proffer his services that the strike was over before he had a chance to get his artist's hands dirty. This, at any rate, was the version of events Isherwood would present to the world in his autobiography. In fact, on May 10, he put his name down "on special reserve" for work on the Underground or in a canteen. Not for the first or last time when a crisis was averted, he would feel a curious mixture of relief and shame. Isherwood likened this episode to the triumph of the Poshocracy in Upward's rooms, when in the course of "a jolly sham fight with pats of butter" he had betrayed his friend and sided with the enemy.

Isherwood was in fact the least political member of his particular generation. His primary loyalty would always be to the individual. Although he lined up with the Left in the class war, he fought his own personal battle from within these sheltering ranks.

Antagonism toward his mother and (as he saw it) all she stood for would always be a more important motivating force in both his life and his art than any more idealistically political sympathies. What mattered to him was life and how one engaged with it. Kathleen's adherence to an increasingly distant and increasingly mythologized Past seemed to him essentially life-denying. In order to embrace life, and the future, he needed to get away from her, and he had begun looking for rooms of his own. He received an annual allowance of £150 from Kathleen, and paid nothing toward his board and lodging at St. Mary Abbot's Terrace. The price of freedom was considerable: the first digs he inspected, in Vincent Square near Victoria, provided a bedroom and sitting room and breakfast only for £1 6s. a week, which he could not afford unless he found a full-time and better-paid job than the one he had with the Mangeots. Unfortunately, he had no qualifications, not even a pass degree. What he needed was something reasonably well paid and not too demanding, which would leave him with enough free time to write. "Parents on the look-out for a private tutor were not too particular, I was told. I put down my name on the books of the scholastic agents, Messrs. Gabbitas and Thring."

Having done this, he reasonably supposed he might take another working holiday, this time back at Freshwater Bay. In July he booked once more into Marine Villa, welcomed back by Miss Johnstone and accompanied by W. H. Auden, who had adopted a large black felt hat for the occasion—an appropriate article of clothing, he insisted, for a poet. Despite his determination to defy convention, Isherwood maintained a certain sense of propriety, and this was offended by Auden's ostentatious headgear. The two young men were stared at in the streets, and young people went so far as to snigger openly, but when Isherwood protested, Auden airily asserted that "Laughter is the first sign of sexual attraction."

There was, of course, a great deal of laughter in Auden's relationship with Isherwood, and it is probable that it was during this holiday that they became lovers. A poem Isherwood wrote at the time states that at Marine Villa "fumbling begins / In the room with the view." They certainly consolidated their friendship at Freshwater, a friendship that was to be both personally and professionally crucial in both their lives. Introducing a sexual dimension would have been one way of doing this. In *Christopher and His Kind,* Isherwood mentions with studied casualness that by January 1937 he and Auden "had been going to bed together, unromantically but with much pleasure, for the past ten years, whenever an opportunity offered itself," but he later dated their sexual relationship as lasting from 1926 to 1938. "They couldn't think of themselves as lovers," Isherwood wrote of himself and Auden, but it is evident that Auden did. For him it was far more than a matter of simple convenience. When Isherwood was asked about the relationship by Humphrey Carpenter, who was writing a biography of Auden, he replied, "No, I do *not* think that Auden was in love with me—at least not as I understand the word, romantically." This, as he knew perfectly well, was untrue. Indeed, only a few years before he answered Carpenter's question, recalling another lover, Isherwood had written: "I think Auden identified with Jack a little. For he too had been in love with Christopher." Since by this time Auden was dead, the only person Isherwood could have been protecting when lying to Carpenter was himself, and it is possible that he still felt some guilt about having failed to reciprocate Auden's deeper feelings. Auden's sole reference to his long-standing affair with Isherwood was characteristically elliptical. In 1947 he made a list of what his biographer Edward Mendelson calls "the great emotional milestones of his life," providing a date, a name and his own age at the time. "These names commemorate the sexual loves that had the greatest effect on his work and life," Mendelson comments; "infatuations and mere sexual friendships are omitted." The list is very short, consisting of five entries, the second of which is: "1926 Christopher 19." Auden became nineteen in February 1926.

Isherwood insisted that his relationship with Auden "was rooted in schoolboy memories and the mood of its sexuality was adolescent," and claimed that he and Auden "were conscious of this and it embarrassed them slightly—that is to say, the sophisticated adult friends were embarrassed by the schoolboy sex partners." He also told Carpenter that "The value of the sexmaking [with Auden] was that it kept an adolescent quality in our relationship alive—almost as if we could go back together into the past whenever we were so inclined." Isherwood may have deprecated his mother's absorption in the Past, but did not always apply the same strictures to himself. The past represented by the classroom, or more accurately by the dormitory, was somewhere Isherwood was very happy to revisit. An important factor in his relationship with Auden was that they were both, as Auden delicately put it, among those "who find their emotional interests in their juniors." And not only emotional. Sexually, too, both Isherwood and Auden were drawn to adolescents or even younger boys, and would remain so throughout the 1920s and 1930s. Richard Isherwood remembered that his brother had for some reason been spending time with an elderly woman who lived in Reading and had a homosexual husband. "And there was a young boy called *George* who you were interested in, you showed me some snapshots of him and I remember being struck by his keenly expressive eyes, wasn't his father the rich old lady's chauffeur? and the mother and aunt servants in the house? but George looked about 12 or 13?" Isherwood had also become interested in Paddy Monkhouse's fifteen-year-old brother, Johnny, who was making a name for himself on the playing fields at Rugby. Paddy took Isherwood to Lord's to watch this sporting prodigy play cricket, and Isherwood was instantly smitten by the attractive, long-legged boy, with his mop of fair hair that had earned him the family nickname of "Mr. Honeypot." The next person on Auden's list of "sexual loves," the next "emotional milestone," would be Michael Yates, a thirteen-year-old schoolboy.

Richard Isherwood himself seems to have caught Auden's attention. He had appeared as Antonio in a Northwood School production of *The Merchant of Venice* and been photographed in Elizabethan costume. Kathleen dated the photograph December 17, 1925, so it seems likely that Auden wrote "The Photograph of a Boy in Costume" sometime during the following year.

In hose and doublet and great ruff you stand,
  Resting one hand
Upon your hip, and through the arch of the door
Looking, as I have never seen you look before;

Stately and proud and wise,
  With sombre eyes

As of one prematurely schooled
In all that life has ruled,

Showing to me, in face as in posed arm,
*   A phantom's calm,*
As if indeed you were
A shadow from those far days, haunting here.

It is possible that Auden had been influenced by the work of clergyman-poets such as the Rev. E. E. Bradford, author of *Passing the Love of Women* and *The Romance of Youth*. In the company of his Oxford contemporary John Betjeman, who shared this interest, he would later make pilgrimages to attend services where Bradford and the Rev. S. E. Cottam (author of *Cameos of Boyhood*) were officiating. Auden would have met Richard on visits to St. Mary Abbot's Terrace, and this poem suggests that he knew a good deal about him. In his Elizabethan garb, Richard might well be representing one of his ancestors or indeed a ghost haunting Marple Hall, as the last stanza suggests.

Professionally, since Auden was a poet and Isherwood a novelist, there was no serious rivalry, and each felt free to borrow from the other. Isherwood had already introduced Auden to Upward and the world of Mortmere, which was to prove influential in Auden's work of this period. It seems likely that it was during this holiday that Isherwood wrote one of his most accomplished Mortmere stories, "The Javanese Sapphires." The story contains a reference to the paddle-steamer that plied between Portsmouth and the Isle of Wight, and its opening, with Gunball talking loudly and embarrassingly to the narrator on a bus, recalls Auden's antics. The story was written not only for Upward but also for Sylvain Mangeot, which perhaps explains its success as a complete narrative. As its title hints, "The Javanese Sapphires" is one of Isherwood's cod Sherlock Holmes tales and it was evidently influenced by "The Tale of the Speckled Band." It is not only one of the few completed Mortmere stories to survive but also the most satisfactory of them, with a fantastical but coherent plot in which Reynard Moxon, assisted by a large black python, becomes a jewel thief.

Isherwood also wrote a poem during this holiday. Appropriately titled "Souvenir de Vacances," it was taken away by Auden and published the following year in *Oxford Poetry*, which he was editing with Cecil Day-Lewis. Since Isherwood had no connections whatsoever with Oxford, the poem appeared anonymously. Like "The Javanese Sapphires," it is a skillful parody—this time of T. S. Eliot, under whose literary spell Auden had fallen after reading *The Waste Land* in the spring of 1926. "The earliest symptoms of Eliot-influence were most alarming," Isherwood recalled. "Like a patient who has received an over-powerful inoculation, Auden developed a severe attack of allusions, jargonitis and private jokes." Isherwood's own effort is prefaced by an arcane quotation from T. S. Eliot's critical work *The Sacred Wood* (1920): "— Precisely. And they are that which they know."

That day the steak was bad, he came. We found
The cormorant shot last year for a spy.

My friend the author in a Lisbon hat
Was ordered from a pub for quoting Tourneur;
Read to us, after lunch, Professor Stinkbomb
On the Greek Games. Wilde would have been appalled.

The Great Bear points the wrong way to the Pole.
The tide snores on the shale; the downs are chill
Under a cracked moon. At Marine Villa
The lamp gulps mucous blackness; fumbling begins
In the room with the view. Only her spaniel
Shuffles upon the stairs, hunting for cheese.

I took your MS. up into the box-room.
It shows much promise. Thirteen sticky years
Tumbled out of a trunk. Dead as these snaps,
Letters, or notes scribbled on graph-paper
Are. For Imago was a dactyl then,
And Phantasy rhymed with some other word.

Even if one recognizes some of the landmarks of Isherwood's imaginative landscape in these lines (spies, Sylvain's cormorant, Auden's hat, Marine Villa, promising manuscripts), it is nevertheless hard to get one's bearings. Perhaps the poem should be recognized as a private joke made public, which has no other meaning than to tease Auden.

More important, Isherwood had also managed to do some work on "Seascape with Figures" before he returned to London on July 20, four days earlier than originally planned, because André Mangeot was ill and Olive was having difficulty coping with his correspondence. Edward Upward came up from Cornwall to stay the night at St. Mary Abbot's Terrace, where he sat in the garden reading Isherwood's new manuscript. "He thought it very good," Kathleen reported, "much the best thing [Christopher] has done—I am so glad—(C. thinks so much of his opinion)." The two young men had decided to take a continental holiday in August, and after much debate—Scotland, Spain (where the Mangeots would be holidaying), Ireland and Norway were all considered—they decided upon a mock-nostalgic journey round the Haute Savoie, last seen five years before in the company of G. B. Smith. They stopped off in Paris to buy a book for Mangeot (possibly a copy of James Joyce's *Ulysses,* the first unlimited English edition of which, banned in England, had been published in the French capital in 1922), then traveled to Annecy, where beds were scarce because of a *fête* and they were obliged to book into the royal suite in the town's best hotel. Upward suggested they abandon the trip and return to England, but owing to some misunderstanding with porters they ended up on a train into the mountains heading for the Col des Aravis. The only separate rooms to be had were in an "annexe," which turned out to be a cowshed. "So we preferred to share a double bed, only it wasn't and we kept bumping into each other and swearing all night," Isherwood told Olive. The arrival of "eleven car-loads of trippers" and the sight of a joint of ham smothered with flies made them decide to walk down to Flumet, where a Frenchwoman "took a fancy to

Edward and kept mixing our salad for us." They subsequently made their way by foot, train and hay-wain to the Hôtel des Voyageurs at Bourg Saint-Maurice. It was here, Isherwood reported, that Upward said that he had had enough and so set back for England: "But I wouldn't go, because I want to have some more adventures." These adventures centered on a boy Isherwood had glimpsed, and he in fact abandoned Upward in pursuit of this quarry. An edited version of these events was given to his real and adopted mothers. "I have met a schoolmaster from Hazelmere," he told Olive. "He has got two boys with him—16 and 13—who he is taking for a trip. They are very bored, and we spend a lot of time together being jolly." Quite how far this jollity went is unclear, but it is likely that there was no more to it than the sort of fantasies Isherwood's fellow Reptonian Denton Welch would write about.

Isherwood told Olive to "give my best to the Governor and tell him that I really will try to be more serious in the Autumn because by then I will be twenty-two." This suggests that until Gabbitas and Thring came up with something more remunerative, Isherwood intended to continue to work as secretary to the quartet. It is also the first hint we have that Isherwood's relations with the Mangeots were showing signs of strain. Fowke felt that during 1926 his father gradually began to resent the amount of time Isherwood was spending in Olive's company. He knew perfectly well that Isherwood was homosexual, but he nevertheless began to be rather jealous. Perhaps he had some inkling that Olive's feelings for Isherwood were not as innocently maternal as he had previously supposed. He may also have wondered whether it was a good thing that this willing employee was spending so much time with Sylvain, the son with whom André himself had a particularly strong bond. He might have thought the relationship not altogether healthy, but it is more likely that he was slightly jealous, as he was of Isherwood's friendship with Olive. Furthermore, Mangeot had begun to suspect that Isherwood was basically "*frivole,*" as he put it. "He thought that Christopher didn't pull his weight in life, that he was a scamp who was prepared to live where and how he could."

Isherwood nevertheless continued to spend a great deal of time with the family, introducing them to friends such as Upward and Auden. The latter was a great favorite and became involved in all manner of escapades, particularly around Guy Fawkes Night, which was also Sylvain's birthday. On one occasion they had to beat a hasty retreat on Wimbledon Common after Auden had disregarded a policeman's instructions that he was to let off no more fireworks. As soon as the constable strode off into the fog, Auden lit the last rocket, which shot into the air with a banshee scream. As a police whistle sounded there was a crash of breaking glass and the party stumbled off in search of the Renault to make their getaway. Such was the excitement, and Isherwood's driving, that one member of the party was sick as they passed through Putney. On another occasion Auden stuck a miniature rocket in his hatband, from which it shot into the air, leaving a smoking hole in the phlegmatic poet's trilby. Even Auden's habitual untidiness was regarded with amused indulgence at Cresswell Place, where he sometimes stayed the night. "Ooh, you *dirty* boy!" Hilda would exclaim as she collected the clothes he had discarded and took them away to wash. Upward was a rather more crucial influence upon the household, for he was becoming increasingly interested in left-wing politics, and his friendship with Olive eventually led to her becoming an avowedly communist member of the Chelsea Labour Party.

I sherwood may have enjoyed jolly times with the Mangeots, but he was also undergoing a genuine crisis in the late summer and autumn of 1926. He describes this in highly colored and highly amusing terms in his autobiography *Lions and Shadows,* where he characterizes himself as a posturing adolescent, frequently making grand but empty gestures, such as running away to Wales with the first volume of *A la recherche du temps perdu* but returning to London after four days, or buying a Browning automatic pistol and writing his will, then consulting Hector Wintle about the best place to aim when committing suicide. He depicts his friends and family looking on with detached amusement, as if he were capering upon a stage in a particularly ludicrous melodrama. It is one of the book's best comic set pieces, but seems to bear little relation to what really happened.

The diaries he kept at the time were later destroyed, but Kathleen's survive, and it is clear from these that Isherwood was passing through a very difficult period indeed. There were long and painful conversations with his mother, who had at last resigned herself to his leaving the family home. "I shall miss his company," she wrote in early September, "but I see that it is inevitable that he should want to go, & of course one is bound to get more lonely as the years go on & it is natural he should want to be on his own I suppose, & feel more independent & of course it isn't as it used to be . . ." Kathleen continued to regard the Mangeots as a bad influence: their return from a summer holiday in France seemed to have "created fresh unrest," she noted toward the end of the month, by which time Isherwood had received a discouraging report from Gabbitas and Thring and seemed no nearer actually finding somewhere else to live.

To make matters worse, Richard was undergoing yet another educational crisis. Kathleen had long since lost all patience with Mr. Wells at Northwood House, and it was in any case time for Richard to move on. He was clearly unfit for the rigors of an English public school, and so Kathleen had sent him to a clergyman in Rye who specialized in teaching backward boys. He lived there with the tutor and another disturbed boy "suffering from the same sort of dreads as himself." For a while all seemed to go well, but by the summer term he had become "more nervy," and when Kathleen came to see him he was seized by a panic attack during the night. This seems to have been connected with the room in which he was staying, and the tutor told Kathleen he thought Richard "<u>must</u> have had a shock or fright some time— perhaps when he was quite small." This is precisely what Richard's teacher at Norland Place had thought, but once again, if Kathleen made the connection between Richard's disturbances and his experiences at Marple Hall, she does not say so. By the autumn it had become clear that the Rye experiment was a failure, and Kathleen had to look once again for a new school. Meanwhile, she engaged the services of a tutor in London, whom Richard would visit daily. Unfortunately he turned out to be "absolutely like Cyril Morgan Brown and about as old." In despair, she decided to consult a "specialist" in Harley Street. This decision may have been prompted by the Charles Greenes, who in the summer of 1921 placed Kathleen's sixteen-year-old nephew Graham in the care of a psychoanalyst named Kenneth Richmond, with successful results. Like Richard, Greene had been extremely unhappy at school, where he had been bullied to such an extent that he ran away. Richard was now fifteen, though he appeared much younger, and the prospect of his settling at any school at such a late stage was looking increasingly remote.

If Kathleen imagined that the psychiatrist she consulted was going to reassure her, then she was in for a bad shock. "To see Crichton Miller," she reported, "who took down every sort of detail with patience & care & was extremely pessimistic & left one with the impression that the sooner one disappeared off the face of the earth the better for everyone—& that there was nothing whatever to be done—possibly if one went a way for a year it might be better for the unfortunate victim who had so suffered at my hands . . . and with all he was so attractive & convincing . . . felt reduced to the very depths." A couple of days later, Richard himself went to see Crichton Miller, followed by Christopher, possibly at the psychiatrist's request. During her interviews with the doctor Kathleen presumably mentioned the difficulties she was having with her other son, who had already made plans to separate himself from her.

In the event, Richard went to Hastingleigh on the Kentish North Downs to an establishment run by a couple named Scrymson-Nichol. Kathleen put him on a train at Charing Cross on the morning of October 21, but at four in the afternoon received a wire from Mr. Nichol to say that his pupil had not yet arrived. Inquiries were made and a railway guard said he had seen a boy get out of the train at London Bridge station. Further frantic telephone calls produced no results, but at six in the evening, Richard arrived back at St. Mary Abbot's Terrace, having walked all the way from London Bridge, a distance of some seven miles, and having eaten nothing since breakfast. The following day, Kathleen took Richard to the school in his uncle Jack's car. The Nichols put one of their bedrooms at Kathleen's disposal for the first night, and seemed altogether sympathetic. Indeed, Richard settled in quite well, and astonished the Nichols with his knowledge of history and dates.

I sherwood finished "Seascape with Figures" on October 20 and took it to an agency to be typed. When it came back he gave it to Kathleen to read. "I don't like the tone as well as 'Lions & Shadows,' " she confessed, "much more sexual & vindictive but it is very interesting & a clever study of a family we know! the end too is good." The vindictiveness of the novel was principally apparent in its portrait of the protagonist's mother, and it is unsurprising that Kathleen did not much care for the book's tone. What is surprising, and admirable, is that she could see beyond the brutal caricature of herself and her values and recognize the novel's qualities.

Isherwood also showed the manuscript to Ethel Mayne, who suggested that the little girl's fatal accident should be deleted, but was sufficiently encouraging for Isherwood to submit the novel to two publishers during the autumn. Both rejected it. Isherwood decided to put the book aside and think about his next project. He intended to write a novel about the post-war generation. He had great ambitions for this book and, more important, he had a title: *The North-West Passage*. The novel would not, of course, have anything directly to do with Amundsen's perilous journey from the Atlantic to the Pacific round the northern coast of America, but the idea was similar. Isherwood intended once more to deal with The Test and the different ways of approaching it. Two types of hero developed in his mind: "The Truly Strong Man" and "The Truly Weak Man." It was the latter, "the neurotic hero," who interested him.

'The truly strong man', calm, balanced, aware of his strength, sits drinking quietly in the bar; it is not necessary for him to try to prove to himself that he is not
afraid, by joining the Foreign Legion, seeking out the most dangerous wild animals in the remotest tropical jungles, leaving his comfortable home in a snowstorm to climb the impossible glacier. In other words, the Test exists only for the
Truly Weak Man; no matter whether he passes it or whether he fails, he cannot
alter his essential nature. The Truly Strong Man travels straight across the broad
America of normal life, taking always the direct, reasonable route. But 'America'
is just what the truly weak man, the neurotic hero, dreads. And so, with immense
daring, with an infinitely greater expenditure of nervous energy, money, time,
physical and mental resources, he prefers to attempt the huge northern circuit, the
laborious, terrible north-west passage, avoiding life; and his end, if he does not
turn back, is to be lost forever in the blizzard and the ice.

This was all very well as a grand concept, but Isherwood did not as yet have any idea
how to construct a plot and assemble a cast of characters that could illustrate it.

Meanwhile, he was at last making progress with his scheme to get away from his
mother. "Owing to this outbreak of infant paralasys," Kathleen reported, "several
schools are closing down & boys are needing temporary tutors." In November, Isherwood went "to see some Jews in Holland Park," as Kathleen put it, and was offered the
job of tutoring their eleven-year-old son until Christmas. Isherwood did not find his
pupil particularly congenial, complaining to Kathleen after two weeks that the boy
"seemed more stupid & inattentive & uninterested than ever." Although he did not
enjoy the work, it earned him sufficient money to look once more for his own rooms.
He had told Kathleen that he could no longer endure the house, and in particular the
cooking, which was undertaken by an inept woman called Elizabeth, who stayed with
the Isherwoods for years and did their teeth and digestion no good at all. Happily,
Roger Burford was getting married and vacating his bed-sitting-room at 26 Redcliffe
Road, just off Fulham Road on the borders of Chelsea and South Kensington.

Isherwood had kept in touch with his old Cambridge friend, who had also started
writing fiction. An early effort had been subjected to a long and somewhat patronizing critique by Isherwood. "There is much that I admire in it," he told Burford
grandly. "Your competence, chiefly, in conducting the plot and making it reasonable
and sane. And your characters are all good, which is the more surprising because I
think your dialogue is weak." Isherwood did have the grace to concede that he was
not, perhaps, the ideal reader of a "study of post-war sexual relations" between men
and women. "How can I criticize a book like yours when I am an atheistical homo-
sexualist with an obsession about Death?" he concluded, signing his letter "Lovingly,
Bisherwood." Burford nevertheless destroyed the book and started on a crime novel
instead. He had also consulted Isherwood about his personal life. Having spent two
terms at Leicester School of Art, he had started producing paintings and had met a
fellow artist named Stella Wilkinson. It seems that Stella was involved with another
man at the time, and was worried that she might still hanker after him if she married
Burford. "Your romantic dilemma is altogether outside my experience or compre-
hension," Isherwood told Burford, but the couple overcame their doubts and started
living together, much to the dismay of Burford's conventional parents. Isherwood

thoroughly approved not only of the fact that Burford was "living in sin" but of Stella herself. An attractively gamine figure with bobbed hair, she was a highly accomplished artist. To her chagrin, she sold fewer canvases than Roger, whose skills were more decorative than bold. Stella mostly painted huge and fleshy female nudes, sometimes alone, sometimes in intimate pairs and groups. Isherwood called her "Star," sometimes "My darling Star," and she was probably the first woman of his own age he counted as a real friend—perhaps because she seemed very much one of the boys.

The Burfords were not due to move out of Redcliffe Road until the New Year. Determined not to endure another Christmas with Kathleen, Isherwood told her that she should go away, leaving him in peace in the Kensington house. Kathleen would also be denied the company of Richard, since it was felt that he would be much better left undisturbed down in Kent. Kathleen noted the irony that "the one who can, doesn't want to live at home, & R who wants to cant." "With a sinking heart," she booked into the Landsdowne Grove Hotel in Bath, where she would spend the holiday with an old friend from Limerick days. At least this was a happier prospect than spending Christmas with some cousins, surrounded by their children: "I feel I simply couldnt face a young Christmas party away from my own two." Kathleen nevertheless still managed to sympathize with her son. "I do feel so sorry for C. & understand how he is torn," she wrote, "but it is so difficult to talk about & I cant put it into words."

The Burfords got married at the local register office on January 8, 1927. The only witnesses were Isherwood and an art student with the glorious name of Rhubarb Lucas. After the extremely casual service, the bride and groom and their two guests retired to the Burfords' new flat for a wedding breakfast of custard and cake washed down with Chianti. Isherwood gave the Burfords a rocking horse as a wedding present, painted silver and white and immediately christened "Fart." His friends had not moved very far: their new home was just on the other side of the Fulham Road from Redcliffe Road, where Isherwood was now installed. Kathleen described the street as containing "quiet looking houses that had seen better day's but many of them quite freshly painted & cared for." The rent was £1 a week for the room and another pound for food, and the lease was indefinite. An additional bonus was that the house was only a couple of streets away from the Mangeots in Cresswell Place. Like the protagonist in his new novel, Isherwood was "very fond of his comforts," and although he now thought of himself as leading an independent life apart from his mother, he visited St. Mary Abbot's Terrace several times a week, for lunch, tea or dinner. Even so, Kathleen complained that she felt lonely and unwanted, "as if everything nice was ended." She decided to move into her son's old room, which she had redecorated, and cleaned out the little room next door for Richard to sleep in when he returned from exile in Kent for the Easter holidays.

Isherwood's tutoring job came to an end with the beginning of the new school term. Fortunately, his employers put him on to "another little Jew at Hampstead," an eight-year-old named Ian Scott-Kilvert. Kathleen reported that during his first day in Hampstead Christopher had "had rather a trying time with the Mother, Mrs Lang." Ian's mother had three children from her first marriage—Derek, Ian and Pam—but had recently remarried. Derek was away at boarding school and Pam, too young for lessons, was still in the charge of a nanny. Mrs. Lang could indeed be trying, if one can trust the sketches her employee made describing life in the large, overheated house. Several details of the house and its occupants were later incorporated in *Lions and Shadows,* where Ian appears as "Graham." In the sketches Mrs. Lang is reincarnated as Mrs. Hope-Jones, who makes a highly theatrical entrance when visiting the nursery, which a bored tutor called Charles is obliged to share with the nanny, Miss Forster:

'Ah, *there* you all are! Didn't *anybody* hear me? I've been calling and calling. The bathroom door is standing *wide* open! I could feel the draught downstairs in my bedroom. I suppose I must go round this house from morning till night shutting my own doors?'

Mrs Hope-Jones was wearing pink silk pyjamas and a kimono. Her pink slippers were edged with swansdown. A tiny dishevelled figure with enormous shadowed eyes under a mop of reddish brown, almost flame-coloured hair. Charles had been suspicious, at their first meeting, of the hair. But, as far as his inexpert judgement went, the colour was natural. At any rate, if it wasn't, it was well done.

He supposed, vaguely, that she was a jewess. In her voice, in her gestures, in her tastes there was a definitely exotic flavouring. As for her complexion, well, it might have been anything—originally. The faint wild-rose flush on Mrs Hope-Jones' cheeks reminded Charles of a sunset painting in oils executed by his landlady's brother. The flesh of her neck and hands was a rather unpleasant goosey white. In evening dress, her arms and shoulders looked indecently naked, like a little slug.

She must have run upstairs. She was quite breathless. She broke off on a faint gasp. Her wide-open eyes, child-like in their pathos, searched their faces, fixed with tragic horror on something she saw over Graham's shoulder.

'Miss *Forster*! Do you know what this *cost*? And here it is lying *trampled* on the ground!'

Miss Forster's lips slightly moved. Mrs Hope-Jones had whipped up Betty's silk scarf from the carpet and was holding it aloft like a trapped snake.

This uncharitable portrait is clearly exaggerated for effect, but one senses Isherwood's British distaste for what he perceived as a sort of oriental exoticism. This is something that persisted throughout his life, and in the 1970s he would recall Mrs. Lang as "vulgar as shit and maybe even a Jewess," which says much about his attitudes.

Mrs. Lang had every reason to play the tragedienne, since shortly after Isherwood started working for her she discovered that her new husband was homosexual. Her original suspicions had been confirmed when she hired a private detective, who presented her with damning evidence. She apparently told Isherwood about this and advised him, "Oh, Mr Isherwood, beware of men!" Though he found Mrs. Lang tiresome, Isherwood became interested in his pupil, who was a clever but nervous child, always fidgeting but evidently taking in everything his tutor taught him. Ian was an attractive boy, about the same age as Jackie Coogan at the peak of his career, but Isherwood's interest seems to have been entirely innocent.

In his new digs Isherwood was doing a great deal of writing. Perhaps in an attempt to get Repton out of his system, he started writing "The Winter Term," the school novel in which Darling played so prominent a part, but the six chapters he managed to complete, though competent, seemed to mark a step backward in his development as a writer. A great deal more interesting was his short story "Gems of Belgian Architecture," inspired by his renewed friendship with Auden. Auden had become very interested in Icelandic sagas and he and Isherwood had noticed that there was a striking resemblance between the atmosphere of these ancient stories and that of a modern English preparatory school. The influence of both the sagas and the school would mark much of their collaborative work, as well as their own individual poems and fiction, notably Auden's *The Orators* and Isherwood's story.

While Isherwood's earlier public-school fictions were formulaic and might have been written by any middlebrow novelist of the period, "Gems of Belgian Architecture" is a truly original work, in which Isherwood rose to a challenge from Upward, who had asked in a letter: "Can a prep school story be written which wouldn't sound like *Chums*?" "Gems" certainly bore no relation to the sort of tale to be found in that popular boys' magazine. The story draws on Isherwood's memories of St. Edmund's and falls into two halves. The first takes place during the war and describes the maneuvers by which rival groups of schoolboys attempt to collect a complete set of the eponymous cigarette cards. It ends with the unexplained disappearance of a set. The second half takes place a few years later when several of the characters, now at public schools or universities, return to take part in an end-of-term rugby match and solve the mystery of the vanishing cards. Isherwood later wrote that he was inspired by meeting at university an old schoolfellow he had always disliked. This "charming, amusing, highly sophisticated young man" bore no resemblance whatever to the schoolboy he had once been. "I planned to show a group of characters who had not only changed individually in the process of growing up but have evolved historically, as it were, from the tenth to the twentieth century. Dwight, Griffin and the rest of them can revisit the school where their old saga-life is being lived, by another generation; but they themselves can make no contact with it. They have become anachronisms. . . . All this might have been marvellous if I had had the art to show it."

This is unnecessarily modest, though it explains why Isherwood chose not to publish the story until 1966, where it became one of the "exhibits" in *Exhumations*, his volume of "bits and pieces" that was presented to readers as a sort of indirect, fragmentary autobiography. "Gems" plunges straight into the enclosed schoolboy world, which it evokes more through reported speech than by description, making bold use of prep-school slang. It is narrated by someone who is part of this world and talks like a schoolboy but does not exist as a character within the story. It may be hard for anyone not conversant with schoolboy lore and language to follow easily what is going on, and to that extent it is comparable with other works of modernist literature. Isherwood himself thought that many readers would "end up baffled" and felt it necessary to explain the plot in a prefatory note when he finally published the story. It is in fact a tour de force and much the most sophisticated and accomplished thing he had written by this time, rivaled only by "Seascape with Figures," which he was rewriting at the same period. Isherwood remains totally in control of his material and the story not only re-creates life at a school with absolute conviction but also answers the demands of narrative coherence. It is a notable, and a notably literary, contribution to the genre of the school story.

The job with the Langs lasted until the beginning of May 1927, after which Isherwood decided to go to Freshwater Bay until the end of July, booking as usual into Marine Villa. This was another working holiday, the chief purpose of which was to finish the new draft of "Seascape with Figures" and to learn German. In June Kathleen, who was concerned about Miss Johnstone's catering, came to the Isle of Wight to spend a week with her son. This island had many literary and historical associations of the sort Kathleen was always keen to explore. She and Christopher went for walks along the cliffs together, visited Carisbrooke Castle, Alum Bay and Osborne House (which Kathleen found "very period," a term of high approbation), and altogether had a pleasant few days together. Even so, when Kathleen returned to London, she did so with a feeling that her son's attentiveness had been dutiful and that he would have much preferred her not to have come at all. "The wall seems to grow higher," she wrote, "and why in addition this undercurrent of grievance?"

It seems that part of Isherwood's grievance was to do with Kathleen's concern for his future. Although she took a great deal of interest in his writing, and genuinely wanted him to succeed, she did not consider being a novelist a career. Tutoring was merely a stop-gap measure, and there did not appear to be anything beyond it. Kathleen's sympathy must at times have been trying, and it would have been difficult for anyone to write in a house with his mother popping in and out and asking how things were going, particularly if he suspected that she regarded his work as a glorified hobby. Although Kathleen's diaries often refer to Isherwood's spending whole mornings or afternoons in his room writing, it would appear that he made real progress only when away from the house, either on the Isle of Wight or in his digs.

It was in Marine Villa that Isherwood finally completed "Seascape with Figures," to which he had now given an even worse title, "An Artist to His Circle." Kathleen read the new version in September. "Very well written," she conceded, though she went on to comment: "the setting depressing & none of the characters in any way lovable! but the story is well told despite its lack of beauty." ("Beauty" was just the sort of word, when used by his mother of a book, that would drive Isherwood to paroxysms of disgust, suggesting to him pastel shades and vague but lofty spiritual values.) Isherwood had sensibly discarded the character of the young girl who died in melodramatic circumstances in the Scilly Isles, and had altered the ending so that the student merely has an inconclusive fight with the Poshocrat (interrupted by his landlady) rather than killing him. The story is far more focused on the artist-clerk's struggle to escape from his mother and her uninspiring ambitions for him. The "grievance" that Kathleen wondered over is apparent in the novel, and it is possible that Isherwood's hostile attitude toward his mother was fueled by the fact that he was re-creating their relationship in fiction. As would happen throughout Isherwood's career, life and art fed into each other, the boundaries blurring.

While the novel is not strictly autobiographical in its plotting, it is clearly drawn from life in detail and atmosphere. Isherwood described it as the "story of a trivial but furious battle which the combatants fight out passionately and dirtily to the finish, using whatever weapons come to their hands." The principal battle is between a widow called Mrs. Lindsay and her son, Philip, who wants to pursue a career as an artist. When he throws up his job as a city clerk, Mrs. Lindsay is furious.

'So what do you mean to do?'

'You know quite well. I want to have a chance of painting and writing.'

'Painting and writing!' She shied like a little pony at the words. 'How are you to live?'

'I suppose I can sell my work.'

'You've been doing a lot while you were away, of course?'

'Of course,' he lied.

Her question, as in older, earlier quarrels, had seemed telepathic. She regarded him for a moment, searchingly. But next she asked:

'Whatever made you do it?'

'Because I loathed the office. I told you so over and over again.'

This is how talk ends, carefully made plans, arguments discussed night after night. I do want to make Mother admit that I'm right; and really it's difficult to see how any reasonable adult could conceivably. There *can* be nothing for her to say. Now here he was, answering like a half-scared insolent schoolboy.

The exchange ends with Mrs. Lindsay, after some "easily" shed tears, leaving the room "with a small gesture of irritation that seemed a mere comma in their argument; inconclusive, leaving nearly everything still to be said." Thus, one imagines, did many of the author's own quarrels with his mother end, without either side conceding defeat.

When a final attempt to escape his mother's clutches results in a recurrence of childhood rheumatic fever, Philip is obliged to return to the family home. "Philip's got his own 'studio' now," Mrs. Lindsay tells visitors. "It used to be the box-room." He is having some success with his paintings, she says, a couple of which had been sold at a local charity bazaar. He has also won second prize in a newspaper poetry competition, the submission having been made without his knowledge by Mrs. Lindsay's companion, Miss Durrant. Philip is reduced once more to a mere dabbler, a talented amateur.

As if the whole scenario of the novel were not hurtful enough, Isherwood inserted a number of digs which would mean little to the general reader and were aimed specifically at Kathleen. The house in Bellingham Gardens shares the same number as the one in St. Mary Abbot's Terrace, 36, and is in the same area of North Kensington, an area described as being on the edge of a slum district and in the vicinity of both a gasworks and a brothel. Recently repainted white, it is in "pretentious contrast with its dingy neighbour houses," but once inside the visitor is overwhelmed with the nauseating smells of bad cooking and drains. Kathleen's concern for her son's future and her worries over bills and other domestic problems are heartlessly pilloried, as is her devotion to the memory of her dead husband and her preoccupation with the Past. Her taste is mocked, as is her painting when the view from a window is gratuitously described as "delicately pencilled, luminous, insipid, resembling a watercolour by an elderly gentlewoman."

It is this animus, of course, that gives the book its ferocious and compelling vigor. The "ecstasies of hate" Isherwood experienced at Cambridge have been channeled to make art, as they would be in much of his other work, which is frequently energized by antipathy. Mrs. Lindsay may win the battle, but her victory is pyrrhic: as the

Harley Street specialist warned Kathleen, mothers destroy their children, and Mrs. Lindsay also ruins her daughter's life. This was Isherwood's message to his mother, and in case Kathleen had missed the point, shortly after she read the book, he accompanied her to a play called *The Silver Cord*. The play told the story of a mother with two sons, one married, the other engaged. "The Mother nearly succeeds in separating both couples by the selfishness of her love & keeping the sons tied to her side," Kathleen noted. "An exaggerated example amusing & boring & saddening but up to a point interesting—it seems the best thing a Mother can do is cease to exist when her sons are grown up. . . ."

N ow that the novel was finished, Isherwood was advised by Upward to change the title. After toying with several unpromising alternatives—"The Old Life," "The Family of the Artist"—Isherwood decided on *All the Conspirators,* a phrase which came to him from a distant memory of Shakespeare's *Julius Caesar:* "All the conspirators save only he / Did that they did in envy of great Caesar. . . ." He acknowledged that "the life of Julius Caesar couldn't by any conceivable stretch of ingenuity be related to the squabbles of a middle-class family in North Kensington," but then this was hardly the point. Like "Lions and Shadows," it "sounded grand." As a phrase, isolated from its context, it also had some relevance to the plot of the novel, in which the conspiracies of the old and the young, of the conventional and the bohemian, are ranged against each other.

That autumn the novel was once more sent round publishers, but without success. Worse still, Isherwood's landlady in Redcliffe Road had run into financial difficulties. She leased the house herself, subletting it to tenants, and had got hopelessly behind with the rent. Eventually, the bailiffs arrived and started loading her furniture into a van. Isherwood sent for the Burfords, and Roger managed to cash a cheque to pay off her debt. The bailiffs may have been stopped, but it was clear that the landlady could no longer afford a whole house, so she decided to give it up and move into a flat. Isherwood had in fact become dissatisfied with his rooms and had already given notice, but now he had to leave sooner than he intended, and at the beginning of November he moved back into his mother's house. Gabbitas and Thring seemed unable to find more work for him and it may have been this sense of defeat that led him to decide to train as a doctor. This unlikely course seems to have been selected almost arbitrarily. In *Lions and Shadows* he states that the idea was first put into his head by a young veteran of the First World War named Lester, with whom he had become friendly at Freshwater. Isherwood listened enthralled as Lester regaled him with graphic accounts of his experiences at the Front. Here was someone who had faced The Test and passed with honor. From Isherwood's account it seems clear that Lester was suffering the aftereffects of war trauma, but he was flattered when the unstable young man told him he would make a good doctor. A more reliable adviser was Hector Wintle, whose discouraging murmurs came from experience, but Upward held up the example of Chekhov and became quite excited at the prospect of his friend gathering copy from hospital wards, deathbeds and dissecting rooms. And so the matter was settled. It was in fact too late to apply for the new academic year, which meant that Isherwood had plenty of time in which to write another novel first—and to change his mind. The Test could be delayed a while yet.

Meanwhile, in the middle of November he took a temporary job as tutor to the son of one of Kathleen's friends, Marjorie Ross. The job would be almost full time and would bring in thirty-six shillings a week. His pupil had the unusual name of Hercules, but was always known as Herky. Isherwood was clearly drawn to the boy and, as with Fowke and Sylvain Mangeot, would maintain a friendship with him after the job came to an end in mid-December.

The New Year brought with it some very welcome news. On January 5, 1928, Isherwood learned that Jonathan Cape had accepted *All the Conspirators* for publication. He did not bother to inform his mother, who heard the news only when Roger Burford blurted it out. One advantage of Cape as a publisher was that he wanted only a few minor alterations to the manuscript. Phillpots, who had also shown interest, wanted Isherwood to alter the ending, and he had refused to do this. Cape would pay £30 on publication in May and a further royalty on any copies sold after the first three thousand.

Relations between Kathleen and her son continued to deteriorate. Kathleen complained that when she returned from a brief holiday, she received "the most chilly of welcomes" from Christopher, who "didn't even trouble to get up" to greet her and pointedly went out to dinner that night. A couple of weeks later, however, they went together to view a new house in Pembroke Gardens. Kathleen had been looking at several houses in this street, which was on the south side of Kensington High Street in a quiet little backwater, away from the traffic that shook the foundations of St. Mary Abbot's Terrace. Number 19 was smaller than Kathleen's present house, but it had three reception rooms and seven bedrooms. While Kathleen decided whether or not to take the lease, Christopher impatiently declared that he could not write in the present house and had decided to go up to Cheshire, where Rachel Monkhouse had found rooms for him at Disley Hall Farm. The farmhouse was on high ground, looking across to the Monkhouses' home, Meadow Bank, on a facing hill. Christopher and Rachel could wave to each other out of their bedroom windows, a circumstance that interested her more than it did him. His accommodation consisted of a huge beamed sitting room, containing a piano, a harmonium and an oven, and a large bedroom. The Monkhouses provided a nearby supply of books, and of hot water should he require baths.

One reason Isherwood wanted to live at Disley was that he was already working on a new novel, part of which was set in the area and drew upon the life of his grandparents. *The North-West Passage* had been abandoned, and instead Isherwood decided once more to attempt to write about what he called "The Old Life" (represented by Kathleen and Marple Hall) and "The New Life" (represented by the Mangeots and their young bohemian friends). Upward recalled Isherwood at St. Mary Abbot's Terrace "striding about his room in the excitement of working out the plot, while every now and then I interjected my suggestions just as I had done when he'd been planning *Seascape with Figures* during our holiday in the Scilly Isles. I shall never forget his trick of crooking a forefinger and briefly biting it whenever an especially promising idea came to him." Isherwood now made copious notes about the themes, characters and structure of the novel, which as yet had no title, but which would eventually evolve to become *The Memorial.* He headed these "preliminary ideas about my novel," which run to twelve closely written pages, with a quotation from

Henry James's story "The Beldonald Holbein"—"The whole thing was to be the death of one or the other of them, but they never spoke of it at tea"—but the principal literary influence was once again E. M. Forster. In dealing with what he called " 'The House' motif," Isherwood intended a youthful riposte to such literary elders as John Galsworthy, whose family sagas centered on the symbolic significance of an ancient family home. From the outset it is clear that Isherwood intended to use Marple Hall and his mother's exaggerated respect for the feudal life it supposedly represented as a theme of the book. In these early notes the family who live at the Hall are called Vernon, just as they are in the published novel, and this is the name of the family that built Marple Hall. The Squire is named John, just as Isherwood's grandfather had been, and at his death he leaves the estate in similar financial disarray. Isherwood wondered whether the Hall might be bought by a parvenu mill-owner who would in effect succeed John as Squire, "wealth-respect succeeding birth-respect" for the local people. "And then," Isherwood concluded, "if I show that the Vernons had, several hundred years ago, risen from the ranks of wealth and gradually earned birth-respect *through* wealth-respect, the cycle will be complete." This history, of course, is borrowed from the original Bradshawe-Isherwood union when the wealthy parvenu feltmaker Nathaniel Isherwood married into the established, landed Bradshawe family in the mid-eighteenth century.

In both character and circumstances Squire Vernon's daughter-in-law, Lily, widowed in the war and subject to "a romantic grief," would be closely modeled on Kathleen. "Lily is a 'lady' to the last. But under the surface she has to have secret romantic stimuli—religious or erotic," Isherwood wrote.

> The important blague about the Hall is that outside people try to fasten it on to the Vernons' backs as 'The House'. Lily particularly does this—because she comes from the South, & because of her temperament [. . .] I should like to make Lily sympathetic by her sheer naiveté, under the Kensington exterior [. . .] Lily's husband. Professional soldier. Dead. Their romance the epitome of love in the Old Life [. . .] Lily must have a military admirer, whom she turns down because, [being] so romantic, she is utterly divorced from life and couldn't face a marriage [. . .] She is faintly amazed and sorrowful that she has forfeited [her son] Eric's love. I think he lives in the house and is very nice to her. Earlier, he had been violent.[. . .] We are shown how Lily's grief is something utterly selfish, since it bars Eric from her. We are given Eric's life at the Hall and how he has come to regard [his aunt] Mary's ménage as The Wonderful Family.

Mary is Lily's sister-in-law and would be based partly on Olive Mangeot.

An intriguing thread of the story concerns Lily's old school-friend Miss Prendegast, who would come to live with her at one point in the proposed narrative: "Miss P. should be a comic Lesbian who plays a lot of Bridge and manages the flat. She tries to emotionalise her relation with Lily, but Lily isn't having any. The discovery that Lily, behind all her romantic ninnery, is hard as bricks." The inspiration for Miss Prendegast was almost certainly Maimie Tristram, a woman whose attachment to Kathleen was something of an embarrassment. Maimie was ten years younger than Kathleen and it is not known where or how the two women met, but they were neighbors in Cheshire at the time of Kathleen's marriage. In old age Richard became somewhat obsessed by Maimie, who had long since died. Although she married and had a son, Leonard, Maimie may well have been "lesbean," as Richard insisted. His evidence for this was his own memories and a handful of what he described as "spicey" letters from Maimie to Kathleen, which Isherwood declined to quote in *Kathleen and Frank,* chiefly because Leonard was still alive. Those that survive (in Richard's transcription) date from the early years of Kathleen's married life.

Maimie whimsically saw herself as a fairy-vassal to Queen Kathleen. "How extraordinary it is to think that only this time last year I was not in love—nor in any year but this is my twenty-seventh romantic year," she wrote in the summer of 1904. (Presumably Mr. Tristram did not occupy any prominent place in his wife's emotional life.) "O I'm sure my love for you is quite as wonderful and Romantic as the love I read of in books. I wonder . . . Are you glad I love you so—and o Queen do you love me a little? Do you give your little maid a *special* kind of love all her own—however little?" There appears to have been some sort of crisis in the relationship shortly after this, perhaps because with a new baby Kathleen had better things to do than pander to her admirer's demanding fantasies. She mentions a visit from a "very overwrought" Maimie toward the end of September, and although the breach appears to have healed, Maimie continued to be "exacting." She was also capable of furious and unreasonable jealousy, and could become very upset when denied full regal attention. In January 1906 Kathleen wrote in her diary, in one of the few entries that give any hint of the nature of this relationship: "Letter from Maimie to say that everything is over between us (I was so friendly to the Bury's at the Carver's dance). After all I think that our friendship must have been more misery than happiness to her." A few days later, Maimie came to call, "all in black," and on February 14 Kathleen recorded that she received no valentine cards. The break was not clean, however, and the friendship appears to have continued, though on a less passionate note. Having had two husbands, Maimie eventually settled down with a Mrs. Seeley.

Isherwood's note about Lily and Miss Prendegast suggests that he was aware of this curious episode in his mother's life and was quite prepared to add to her embarrassment by incorporating it in a novel. In the end he discarded Miss Prendegast, perhaps preferring to concentrate on the central male character he had already decided to make "a sublimated homosexual."

After five weeks at Disley, Isherwood returned to London, to discover that he had been invited to Germany by one of Kathleen's cousins. The younger son of Aunt Julia, who had recently died, Basil Fry was the British vice-consul in Bremen. Sixteen years Kathleen's junior, he was now forty-four, a rather stiff bachelor in whom any sense of humor had long since been ousted by an exaggerated sense of his own dignity. He saw himself as a man of deep culture and learning, and larded his conversation with quotations in Latin and Greek. He was, in fact, precisely the sort of donnish figure Isherwood detested on principle. When Fry invited his young cousin to stay in Germany, however, Isherwood readily accepted. Apart from anything else, it would give him the opportunity to brush up his German, which he had had little opportunity to use since he had started learning it the previous summer. He may also have thought, quite rightly, that Fry would provide him with good Mortmerish copy.

Meanwhile, Isherwood went in pursuit of other experiences with a friend of the Mangeots named Bill de Lichtenberg (the "Bill Scott" of *Lions and Shadows*). Like Stella Burford, de Lichtenberg was a painter and a true bohemian. It is likely that Isherwood had de Lichtenberg's modernist, almost abstract landscapes in mind when describing the sort of paintings Philip Lindsay was attempting in *All the Conspirators*. Very gregarious, de Lichtenberg had great energy, often expended on parties or on driving his smart French saloon car extremely fast over long distances. Isherwood would return from these excursions in the small hours, causing Kathleen a great deal of anxiety. On one occasion, subsequently made famous in Auden's poem "Missing," de Lichtenberg drove Isherwood all through the night, arriving in Edinburgh in time for lunch the following day. This was merely the first leg in a drunken spree in which they toured Scotland, ending up at Cape Wrath. Kathleen was somewhat surprised to receive a postcard from Inverness, since she had understood that the two young men had set off for Wales. Over the next few days further cards and wires followed asking for all post and a set of clean clothes to be sent to addresses in Scottish towns along the route. In all, Isherwood and de Lichtenberg spent almost three weeks away before breezing in for breakfast having driven all the way from Bettyhill on the far northern coast of Scotland. Such excursions recalled Isherwood's daring motorbike rides with Stewart in the countryside around Rouen, and carried with them that same feeling of escape. But, as he gloomily acknowledged, "sooner or later, you will come to a halt; sooner or later, that dreary governess, that gloomy male nurse will catch you up; will arrive, on the slow train, to fetch you back to your nursery prison of minor obligations, duties, habits, ties."

He could no more escape from his life than Philip Lindsay could, and he returned to do some holiday tutoring at the Langs', killing time before he sailed to Bremen. He and Upward had arranged to spend a week at Freshwater Bay, and it was while he was there that the advance copies of *All the Conspirators* arrived. Upward took a photo of the proud author, posing very self-consciously with a copy of the book under one arm on the veranda of Marine Villa, where much of it had been written. The book was, appropriately, dedicated to Upward, and Isherwood added an inscription describing it as "*ce livre peu digne de son esprit subtil et dédaigneux.*" He returned to London for its publication, which took place on May 18. "The rain fell in heavy torrents," he wrote in his diary. "Day of my triumph. There were no flags in the streets." His mother was herself now in Scotland on holiday and so he enjoyed a celebratory dinner with the Mangeots at Cresswell Place, followed by a trip to the theater with Fowke, Rachel Monkhouse (who was studying singing with André Mangeot) and a young woman named Ruth Riley, who would shortly become engaged to de Lichtenberg. Afterward he returned to Cresswell Place where he, André and Olive "drank to its success, at midnight, in beer."

The inclusion of Rachel Monkhouse in these festivities is surprising, since she and Isherwood had endured some sort of scene a few days earlier. The relevant page is missing from Isherwood's diary, which opens: "me with wistful, half-reproachful sex. I must never see her alone again." That this refers to Rachel is confirmed by further remarks about her in this fragmentary diary. At the play, Isherwood recorded, he "talked chiefly to Ruth and was aware of Rachel's reproachful pathos. The most mawkish girl I have ever met." It seems that while he was staying at Disley his comradely friendliness toward Rachel had been misinterpreted by her. It must have been particularly galling for Isherwood to be so ardently admired, not as he would have liked by young Johnny Monkhouse but by the boy's sister, and his reaction to the unfortunate Rachel was proportionally hostile.

Luckily, he was able to escape to Germany, and the following morning, carrying a suitcase packed for him by Nanny, he reported to the United Shipping Company's office in Fenchurch Street. He was conducted by a clerk to the docks, where he found the *Hero*, "a small dirty steamer the colour of Gregory powders," swarming with men loading crates into the holds. He was introduced to the captain, a man called Cooper, who cheerily predicted that his young passenger would suffer from seasickness, but in the privacy of his tiny cabin, no bigger than a large cupboard, Isherwood surreptitiously took a dose of Mothersill. As the rain began to fall, the boat set off through a series of locks and out onto the river. A high tea of soused mackerel awaited him in the saloon, where he ate to the accompaniment of a terrific thunderstorm. Going back on deck, he saw the cranes and gantries that lined the river gradually give way to fields as the boat chugged along the estuary toward the open sea.

Still groggy from a third dose of Mothersill, Isherwood emerged on deck the following morning into bright daylight. The boat was rolling steadily, but he was able to enjoy a good breakfast with tea "strong as brass." After inspecting the engine-room, he took up a position aft and read Samuel Butler's *The Way of All Flesh*, waited on by a Welsh cabin-boy. "Conrad lied," he wrote in his diary. "This boat is as comfortable as a Southampton liner." That night he awoke at midnight to see the lights of Germany, and in the early hours of the morning they moored at Blumenthal on the Weser estuary, where the cargo of wool bales was unloaded. Captain Cooper told an unimpressed Isherwood that hundreds of young women were employed to clean the wool in conditions so hot that they worked stripped to the waist. The *Hero* then set off further down the Weser to dock at Bremen, where Isherwood was met by an official and led to the consular office. Here Basil Fry awaited him, fulfilling every Mortmere expectation, as Isherwood happily reported to Edward Upward. "My cousin is a prig, a fool and a neuter," he wrote. "Hatefully tall. His Oxford titter." In his diary he recorded his first impressions: "Very tall, gawky, small-headed, with moustache, weak lips, dyspeptic's nose and huge Edwardian collars." Fry may have been unprepossessing, but Isherwood's first glimpse of Germany was rather more alluring. "We drove through the vine-grown suburbs. Dense lilac. The clean houses with fronts of embossed stucco. Gay trams. Boulevards. Past a Laocoon fountain, the vomiting python pleasantly drenching the shoulders of the statue under hot sunlight." Other pleasant sights caught his eye, and he wrote prophetically: "My vision of Germany is utterly the boys' country. In their absurd ingle's coloured lace-up shirts, socks and braided yachting-forage caps. All on bicycles."[5]

---

5. "Ingle" was one of the many archaic words employed by Isherwood and Upward in their private language: first recorded in the late sixteenth century, it means "catamite" and had been obsolete since 1878.

Uncle Charlie Fry awaited his great-nephew at Basil's rooms in Elassestrasse and Isherwood spared the distinguished old man nothing in recording his impressions of him.

I hate his benevolently authoritative white beard and his clergyman's grief at the loss of his wife. Describing some expedition of the past, he said: 'Yes, Basil was there and Charlie [his elder son] and—' dropping his voice—'dear Mrs Fry.' An old school pupil, now consul at Hamburg, was there. He told Uncle Charlie that he looked just the same as twenty years before. The old man's senile pleasure. His vitality is loathsome. So was Basil's filial heartiness. 'My dear old father.' They all disregarded me utterly. The house is pleasant, with ugly, airy, high rooms, appallingly bad paintings, white sliding doors. A pair of skis in the corner and an oil portrait of Basil in consular uniform. The old Dean's beastly, because sneaking and proprietary, pride in his sons. 'The cheese here is the best I know.' (It was very inferior camembert.) Fussing because Basil hadn't put down all his qualifications—such as Oxford M.A.—in the 'Foreign Office Bible'.

Cruel as this is—after all, the Frys' only crime was to be old and rather stuffy—it is skillfully done.

That evening Basil hosted a consular dinner at a restaurant, for which Isherwood was obliged to borrow the vice-consul's tails. The evening was dull and not much enlivened by Basil's speeches ("He speaks French fluently but exactly as though it were English," his young cousin noted). A great deal was drunk, however, and this appears to have emboldened a South American diplomat to attempt some sort of seduction of Isherwood, who characterized him as "a requiem shark bugger." Wittily addressing Isherwood as "Little Fry," the man poured him a full tumbler of liqueur brandy— "clearly an exciter," or aphrodisiac. Basil attempted unsuccessfully to prevent Isherwood from drinking this, but intervened more forcibly when the diplomat attempted to lure Isherwood to "some sort of brothel." All this, of course, made marvelous copy, and was assiduously written up in a diary for future use.

The following morning Isherwood was horrified to discover that Fry expected him to take a cold bath, assuring him that it would do him good. Fry did his best to entertain his guest, assigning a Czech office boy named Rudolf to escort him to the picture gallery (which turned out to be closed) and introducing him to "a spotty young man" called Forgan, who had recently left school and was in Bremen to learn German. "We failed to interest each other," Isherwood complained, although he was evidently pleased to be introduced to Forgan's "very sleek handsome French friend," with whom he played ping-pong. His brief holiday ended disastrously when Fry took him, Forgan and the Uruguayan consul, "a wizened little man of seventy" who spoke only French, on a weekend boating trip. Things got off to a bad start on the first evening, when Fry took a wrong turning in the Wesen and ended up at a tiny village rather than Elsfleth, where he had intended to spend the night in comfort. They returned to the main river as darkness fell, but they had left the map in the car. Then the boat's engine ran out of fuel and they were obliged to hoist the sail. It was a calm night and they did not reach their destination until after midnight. Fry spent half an hour in the cold and dark ineptly attempting to moor the boat. The hotel turned out to be full. Fry and the consul were offered beds in a neighboring house, but Isherwood and Forgan had to spend the night in the tiny cabin aboard the yacht. "It will be an experience for you," Fry told his cousin.

Isherwood slept in his clothes and awoke feeling frowsy, but his first view of Elsfleth in the bright morning sun restored his spirits. "All the boats were crowned with sprays of aspen," he wrote. "Schoolboys had plucked sprigs of it and fixed them on the handlebars of their bikes." Even this failed to prevent him from sulking, however, and when Fry made him carry the rucksack, he deliberately dragged it along bumping against the curbstones. It was another calm day and they had to use the boat's motor to get them to Oldenburg. Fry had decided that Forgan was rather more responsive than Isherwood and so ostentatiously conferred with him about the route and the running of the boat. Isherwood sat on deck in the blazing sun reading Edgar Wallace, which made him dizzy, but he cheered up considerably when the engine broke down. "Boys watched the engineer trying to make the motor go," he wrote. "They wear belts and braces and striped cotton shirts. Long stockings within shorts." All attempts to get the engine to start failed and at five in the evening they decided to hoist sail in a vain attempt to catch a breath of wind. They were eventually forced to take a tow from a pleasure steamer crowded with trippers. Isherwood looked on at Fry's discomfiture with quiet enjoyment, and spent some time observing one of the male holidaymakers flirting quite openly with a schoolboy on the launch.

At Oldenburg Fry knew the manager of the best hotel and so secured comfortable rooms. Isherwood spent the following morning exploring the town with the consul while the motor was being repaired. Shortly before lunch they set off for home, and all went well until they were back in the Wesen.

> Basil, messing and fussing with the sails, sent the mainsail crutch overboard. He cursed us for not catching it. Forgan slewed the boat round, and the piece of wood to which the motor was clamped broke off. The motor nearly went too. We had to sail back to Lesum. Hours and hours. Every other boat in the river passed us. The banks were crowded with bathers and people listening to bands.

Fry's ignominy was complete.

Back in Elassestrasse, Fry tried to restore cordial relations by discussing literature with his bookish young cousin, but did not get off to a good start with his observation that "Keats was a clean-hearted lad." Evidence of Fry's own clean heart was provided by one of his own poems, written in youth, which he read aloud to Isherwood. "Some quisby romantic attachment to a foreign girl that wasn't followed up. His attitude to his work is always that he has now lost the knack. Like a juggling trick." He evidently regarded writing as something any reasonably intelligent young man might pursue, just so long as it remained a hobby. "I'm really a man of action," he declared. "I don't care about books. I expect to get all there is out of a book and then throw it away. I never want to read it again."

The last morning of the holiday dawned bleakly. "I dreamt that Orpen had become very tall. Sylvain will be like that too, I thought. Woke in utter misery." Learning that the *Hero* would not be ready to sail until later, Isherwood spent the morning with Rudolf visiting a particularly Mortmerish exhibition of mummified corpses.

Back on board, Captain Cooper told Isherwood of his own visit to this macabre show. He had been intrigued by one of the female corpses: "I thought to myself: I'd like to see how things have panned out down there. She was wearing a pair of black drawers. So I said to my brother: Just watch old Tirpitz [i.e. the German guard]. And I lifted them up. And there was nothing at all. The rats must have got her." This sort of conversation was commonplace on board the ship, and the following day, as they headed toward open water, Isherwood listened to the second mate and second engineer swapping stories about horrible accidents. The captain gave him a pornographic novel translated from the French to read: "He was pleased because I got through it in an hour." On the morning of June 1, the *Hero* entered the Thames, and Isherwood, his diary bulging with copy, was back at St. Mary Abbot's Terrace in time for lunch.

During Isherwood's absence Kathleen had beaten down the owners of 19 Pembroke Gardens, taken a seventeen-year lease for £1,500, and was now ready to move in. Number 19 was a handsome semi-detached, flat-fronted, four-story house, one of several that lined the street. Steps led up to a front door on the ground floor, another set leading down behind railings to a semi-basement, which contained a kitchen and, opening out into the garden, a small sitting room. The front room of the house had a projecting bay window, and there were three front windows in the first and second floors, the top ones prettily arched. There was plenty of room for everyone: Kathleen, Christopher, Richard, Nanny and Elizabeth the cook. Not that Elizabeth was pleased with her new quarters: she "grumbled incessantly" that the kitchen was too dark, though it is doubtful that even floodlighting would have done anything to improve her cuisine. "How strange that a week ago we were at St Mary's," Kathleen wrote on her first Sunday in the new house; "this seems so much more homely & loveable . . . indeed nice as [the old house] was there are no associations of happiness with it . . . rather the reverse."

Once they were settled in, Isherwood went to see Auden in Oxford and had a "terrific" dinner, including champagne. There was not in fact a great deal to celebrate, since most of the reviews of *All the Conspirators* had been "bad or mediocre," several of them patronizingly referring to the twenty-three-year-old author's "extreme youth." *Punch* could not decide whether the book had been written by an author with his tongue firmly in his cheek or whether Isherwood was "badly troubled with that kind of portentous solemnity which so often accompanies the mental growing pains of the very young." Only the critic of the *Manchester Guardian* treated the novel with the respect it deserved, praising both the author's technique and psychological acuity.

> In it the play of five characters upon each other is realized with a subtlety that often approaches divination. In the process, too, each character is fully defined, in itself a rare achievement to-day, when most of our moralists content themselves with painting one or, at the most, two protagonists against a background of stage properties. Technically, too, Mr Isherwood's counterpoint is very interesting. It is at the same time brilliantly controlled and pointed and consistently suggestive. One of his characters, looking back on an argument, finds it 'inconclusive, leaving nearly everything still to be said'. And much of the dialogue leaves this impression upon us. So much is held in reserve, and yet so much of significance is

suggested that we share the excitement of explorers hot upon the scent of some great discovery.

Even so, the book failed to sell more than three hundred copies and was heavily remaindered.

It was almost certainly during this visit that Isherwood and Auden were photographed together by Eric Bramall, apparently at the suggestion of Stanley Fisher. No one seems to know why these photographs were taken. They look like publicity shots, but were posed long before the subjects became literary collaborators. In one photograph, Auden and Isherwood sit side by side, facing each other. The pose is carefully casual, but Auden looks a great deal more relaxed than Isherwood does: he holds a cigarette negligently in his right hand, while Isherwood's arms are rather awkwardly folded. In their light-colored suits and ties, their cowlicks falling to left (Isherwood) and right (Auden), they appear to mirror each other. Two other photographs in the series also appear to predict the way in which the professional and personal lives of these two young men would be entwined. In one photograph, Auden is sitting on a chair, in half-profile, reading a book—probably a copy of *All the Conspirators*. Isherwood stands behind him, apparently reading over his shoulder. In another the positions are reversed: Isherwood reads, Auden stands behind. Although it is Isherwood who rests one hand on Auden's shoulder (Auden merely holds the back of Isherwood's chair), there is something about the photographs that suggests that Auden, once again looking more at ease, was more involved in their affair than Isherwood was.

In his magisterial way, Auden had already decided that Isherwood was to be the novelist of the future, and no amount of poor reviews was going to make him change his mind. His proselytizing was such that one young undergraduate he had befriended was genuinely shocked by Isherwood's bad press. "It is curious," Stephen Spender wrote, "that before I knew Isherwood and before I had read a word by him, I had been so convinced by his legend, that I read these reviews with an indignation which makes me still recall them better than I can reviews of my own books." Spender had come up to University College in 1927, originally to read history. He subsequently changed his mind and was now studying politics, philosophy and economics, although he spent most of his time reading literature. Born into a distinguished liberal family in 1909, he was the third son of the journalist Harold Spender; his mother was Jewish, of German-Danish descent, and had died when Stephen was twelve. Determined to be a poet, Spender had arrived at Oxford charged with youthful egotism. "I was incapable of being interested in my fellow undergraduates just for themselves," he admitted. "I wanted them to be interested in me and in what interested me—in that order." Disappointed that the undergraduates at University College "cared only for games, drinking and girls," the naïve and romantic youth took his revenge on them "by becoming self-consciously their opposite. I became affected, wore a red tie, cultivated friends outside the college, was unpatriotic, declared myself a pacifist and a Socialist, a genius." One of those he cultivated was Gabriel Carritt, the son of one of his philosophy tutors. Carritt was an extremely handsome young man, who had come up to Oxford at the same time as Spender and was at Christ Church. He had been educated at Sedbergh, where Isherwood's old history teacher

G. B. Smith was now headmaster, and had distinguished himself both in the class-room and on the playing fields. Although resolutely heterosexual, he had been courted by Auden, who had developed a crush on him. In spite of the frustrations in-evitable in so lopsided a relationship, the two remained close friends, and through Auden, Carritt met a number of other distinguished undergraduates, including Rex Warner and Richard Crossman. Carritt would talk of these people to Spender, who naturally longed to be introduced into such an elite. In the event, it was another un-dergraduate, Archie Campbell, who arranged for Spender to meet Auden at a lunch party. Auden's manner was as aloof and discouraging as it had been toward Isher-wood when they met as adults, but although there was an inauspicious difference of opinion over the merits of a contemporary poet, Auden suggested that Spender might like to drop in at his room in Christ Church.

Spender did so and was subjected to a lecture on the nature of poetry, an art in which it became clear Auden saw himself shortly becoming pre-eminent. "A group of emergent artists existed in his mind," Spender recalled, "like a cabinet in the mind of a party leader." If Auden himself was to be his generation's Poet (his status con-firmed by the capital initial), then an old school-friend named Robert Medley was to be the Painter and Isherwood would be the Novelist. Auden asked if Spender ever wrote poems, and was astonished when the young man replied that he wrote four a day. Auden sternly remarked that for his own part he wrote one poem every three weeks, which made Spender decide immediately to cut his production rate to match that of his new Master. Thereafter, Spender would show Auden what he had written, earning the occasional terse mark of approval. Auden soon accepted Spender as a member of his select group of friends, perhaps recognizing in the excitable young man a willing, not to say abject, disciple. Spender had no hope of becoming *the* Poet, that position having already been taken, but Auden conceded that Spender might become *a* poet. In fact, Spender had other talents, and showed Auden a story he had written about an obsessive relationship he had pursued with an English boy he had met at a Swiss pension shortly before coming up to Oxford. Auden was so im-pressed by this narrative that he proclaimed that Spender should abandon poetry and concentrate upon autobiographical prose. He quite rightly discerned that the story was just the sort of thing that would interest Isherwood and so showed it to him. Auden fur-ther decided that these two masters of autobiographical narrative should meet.

"He burst in upon us," Isherwood recalled, "blushing, sniggering loudly, contriv-ing to trip over the edge of the carpet—an immensely tall, shambling boy of nineteen, with a great scarlet poppy-face, wild frizzy hair, and eyes the violent colour of blue-bells." Spender was precisely what one might have expected from his story: "The hero was so absorbingly interested in himself, in his own sensations and in everybody who came into contact with him that you couldn't help sharing his interest. In fact, the experience was so vivid as to be quite painful. You blushed for him, you squirmed at his every faux-pas; you wanted, simultaneously, to kick and protect and shake him." Isherwood recalled that "In an instant, without introductions, we were all laughing and talking at the top of our voices," but Spender's recollections were rather different, and probably more accurate. He claimed that when he arrived in Auden's room, the two friends were going through one of Auden's poems, Isherwood offering stern criticism. When they had finished, Isherwood made "a quite formal little speech saying he had read [Spender's] manuscript, and that he regarded it as one of the most striking things he had read by a young writer for a long time, and so on." This certainly sounds like Isherwood in pedagogic mode when faced with yet another "brilliant teenager." It was not so much Spender's literary technique that interested him—the story's "grammar was awful, its dialogue stilted and its style naive"—as his egotism. In his own work Isherwood too was aiming to involve readers in his own character and feelings and in the people he met. Indeed, this would be the blueprint for his career as a writer. In Spender he found someone who was, and would remain, a kindred spirit, and they became friends almost at once.

Spender's family lived in Hampstead and he and Isherwood met several times during the summer vacation. Spender was occupied by not very expertly printing a small edition ("About 45 copies," as the limitation page put it) of Auden's poetry on a hand-press. The small pamphlet contained twenty poems, was bound in a burnt-orange paper wrapper and was dedicated "TO CHRISTOPHER ISHERWOOD." Each copy was numbered, and Auden gave his mentor No. 2, having at first made a number of corrections in black ink, not only of Spender's misprints but also incorporating his own second thoughts, notably about punctuation. He inscribed it "To Christopher with love from the Author. 'Dura virum nutrix.' " The Latin tag, which means "the harsh nurse of men," was presumably a reference to Isherwood's literary midwifery. It was a just tribute.

In June Isherwood returned to Freshwater Bay for a week, where he most likely expanded his diary entries about Basil Fry and Bremen into a semi-fictional narrative. (The handwriting of this fragment suggests that it was written during this period.) He returned to endure "a long talk [. . .] about things generally" with his mother, who found him "priggish and rather insufferable!" On Monday, June 25, Isherwood went along to register his name as a medical student at the Westminster Hospital, thus supposedly setting his course for the next few years.

In August he had another holiday at Marine Villa, where he was joined by both Upward and Hector Wintle. Isherwood and Upward resumed their experiment with "automatic writing," first attempted at Marple Hall five years earlier, fueled by the contents of Uncle Henry's cellar. This time they cleared their minds, took up a pen and wrote whatever came into their heads. The results were predictably extravagant, and Upward later recalled that, far from exercising no control over their thought processes, the two young men vied to make their efforts "as extraordinary as possible." Wintle characteristically took the experiment very seriously, with unexciting results. The holiday came to an abrupt end when, after Upward and Wintle had left, Miss Johnstone had a stroke and died. Fortunately, she had realized that she was ill and had summoned her sister, so Isherwood did not have the unpleasant experience of dealing with his stricken landlady or coping with matters after her death.

Meanwhile he was seeing a great deal of his friends, notably André and Olive Mangeot, Auden (with whom he went to Stamford Bridge to watch dirt-track racing) and Upward, but also young boys such as Sylvain and Herky Ross (both fourteen), whom he took on day-trips to Brighton and Southend. Kathleen, not perhaps fully aware of the nature of Isherwood's interest, was particularly annoyed by this. "I do think it is very selfish the way he utterly ignores Richard & never suggests taking him anywhere though he spends hours messing round with that younger Mangeot boy, & Herky Ross." The days when Kathleen could confer with Christopher about Richard's difficulties were long over. Although he professed himself "very horrified at [Richard's] lack of any ideas or interest in his future," he tended to keep himself "politely aloof" from his brother's troubles. "He might do so much if only he would," Kathleen complained, "but he refuses to so much as express any opinion on the best course." While Isherwood had been in Bremen, Richard had once again run away from school. The excuse this time was a fellow pupil whom he found intolerable. The Nichols had been obliged to motor up to London in order to retrieve their serially absconding pupil, who went back with them, leaving Kathleen, as so often before, "thoroughly worn out by a most unhappy day." Richard had now been entered for exams with the London Matriculation Board, but shortly before he was due to take them Mr. Nichol unexpectedly and inconveniently dropped dead. Richard subsequently decided that he did not want to sit the exams, which he felt he had no hope of passing, and proposed getting a job doing parish work in Stepney. One of his masochistic fantasies had been inspired by a newspaper report of a court case brought by the parents of a boy who had been caught rifling a young clergyman's desk. The clergyman had taken down the boy's trousers and underpants and spanked him, and was served with a writ for assault. "I must say I envied the boy because the clergyman looked such a strikingly handsome young man!" Richard recalled. "And if I had been the boy I would have begged him to do it again—although the boy claimed that his behind was black and blue." Throughout Richard's youth, religion and punishment were always associated in his mind, and it may have been in pursuit of chastisement or salvation that he suggested this job in Stepney.

Another alternative was for him to take a shorthand and typing course. Kathleen received advice and offers of help from all quarters, notably the Greenes and Uncle Charlie Fry, and felt that Richard ought to be made to sit the exams. She set about interviewing a motley assortment of private tutors, and eventually engaged a Mrs. Wood, who was optimistic of Richard's chances of passing his exams if he took them in the summer. "She spoke very nicely of him," Kathleen acknowledged, "but I do wish she was a man." Although nearly seventeen, Richard seemed much younger and was still treated by both his mother and brother as a small, troublesome boy.

Isherwood found himself in a similar situation to Richard's when at the beginning of October he reluctantly enrolled as a medical student at King's College London. "It was like starting school all over again," he recalled, "not as the prize scholar, the scholarship candidate, but as the backward, overgrown boy who finds himself left behind in the infants' class." Like one of the undergraduates he had seen at Cambridge who were continuing their education after war service, Isherwood found himself a veteran of life among boys fresh out of school. "Amidst those pink unfinished faces I felt like a man of forty," he wrote. "Nor was it any good my trying to imagine myself their superior on account of my advanced years; in the one essential subject I knew far less than they did. At school, I had done little or no science, my mathematics were disgraceful, chemistry I had never even touched." He was at a complete loss in the world of Bunsen burners and periodic tables, of micrometer screw-gauges and

Boyle's Law, of cotyledons and osmosis. He conscientiously filled notebooks labeled "Physics" and "Practical Zoology," but his heart wasn't in it and he soon found himself falling hopelessly behind in his studies. It was with a great sense of relief and release that he hurried home each day after the lectures were over to work on his new novel, which had by now come into focus and acquired a title: *The Memorial.* By mid-December a first draft had been completed, but he was "very dissatisfied" with it and blamed its failure on his having only evenings free to work on it.

Shortly before Christmas Auden returned to England from Berlin, where he had been living since August. He had been staying as the paying guest of a family in Wansee, a lakeside colony of middle-class villas to the southwest of the city, with the Grünewald to the north and the Potsdamer Forest to the south. Picturesque as this was, Auden was more interested in the working-class Hallesches Tor district, where *Strassenjungen,* or street-boys, hung around in dingy bars and were prepared to go to bed with anyone who paid them. Auden was also full of new ideas about psychology, which he had encountered through John Layard, an English anthropologist he had met in Berlin.

Layard, who was born in 1891, had read medieval and modern languages at King's College Cambridge and then accompanied W.H.R. Rivers to Malekula in the New Hebrides to carry out anthropological fieldwork there in 1914 and 1915. Rivers subsequently worked as a psychologist at Craiglockhart Hospital near Edinburgh, treating victims of shell-shock, among them Siegfried Sassoon, but Layard's return to England was less fruitful. He felt that he had been a complete failure in every aspect of his life and that this was partly the result of being "at the tail-end of a good family which for generations had been going downhill and was now petering out into insanity." He suffered a catastrophic nervous collapse, which led to "emotional paralysis with symptoms of extreme physical exhaustion." Obliged to spend most of his time in bed, he was nevertheless unable to sleep without drugs of one sort or another. He was eventually referred to the American psychologist Homer Lane, who almost certainly saved his life. Lane explained that there was no such thing as "bad blood" in the physiological sense, but that "false thinking" might become so firmly rooted within a family that it would result in psychological problems. Lane promulgated the Doctrine of Original Virtue, believing that "human nature is innately good; the unconscious processes are in no way immoral." He preached that the only sin was that of "disobedience to the inner law of our own nature." Repression led to neurosis, which would manifest itself in criminal activity or disease. Psychological and physical health could only be achieved by being true to oneself.

Unfortunately, Lane died in 1925, before Layard's course was complete. Using money he had earned by working at the Cambridge Museum of Ethnology, where he was employed to arrange material from the Malekula trip, he traveled to Vienna to undergo analysis with Wilhelm Stekel, but this had not been a success. He felt Stekel was unjustly accusing him of resistance. In 1926 he went to Berlin in search of an analyst who would complete Lane's good work, and it was there, in August 1928, that he met Auden, who had been given his name by a mutual acquaintance. Layard, who was bisexual, was immediately struck by Auden's appearance. "His face was absolutely smooth and angelic," he recalled "—the kind of face that turns out to be really 'wicked' [. . .] I fell for him like a ninepin." They talked into the small hours and Layard suggested Auden stay the night, which meant sharing a bed. Auden agreed, but rejected Layard's advances, explaining that he was involved with a boy called Pieps. He offered to take Layard to a bar where he could meet *Strassenjungen*. Layard was entirely inexperienced, and like Isherwood before him, astonished by Auden's blasé attitude toward sex. The idea of paying for sex outraged all his notions, but he overcame his scruples and accompanied Auden to the Cosy Corner, a scruffy little café in Zossenerstrasse, where he met a boy named Heine with whom he embarked upon a relationship which consumed all his time and energy.

Through Layard, Auden was rapidly becoming a disciple of Homer Lane, and he communicated this enthusiasm to Isherwood, for whom the psychologist's theories had an immediate appeal. In particular, Lane's idea that repression was often caused by family and upbringing must have struck a chord. In Mortmerish mood, Isherwood would declare that he too was at "the tail-end of a good family which for generations had been going downhill and was now petering out into insanity": the almost gaga Grandpa Isherwood, a cousin and her husband who had both ended up in an asylum after a violent domestic disturbance, and even Richard, providing evidence of this. Lane had told Layard that his paralysis had been caused by his being made to conform during childhood: "You never were allowed as a child to walk to please yourself," he had explained. "You must have been prevented from enjoying your own powers as a child, and, when they had broken your spirit, they then 'taught' you to walk and act the way they wanted you to. If you walk now, you'll only be obeying them. That's why you can't. Your independent spirit is too strong. It will not let you walk while you are subservient to notions that are not yours." Isherwood may well have recalled the way Cyril Morgan Brown and others had attempted to bully him into conformity, and have considered once more his mother's notion of what sort of life he should be leading. He had been sufficiently indulged not to suffer any sort of paralysis, either of the body or the spirit, but he may have ascribed the difficulties he was having with his writing to Kathleen's disapproval of his choice of career. In Berlin, it seemed, he could not only discover more about Lane's theories from John Layard, but he would find an arena in which to be true to his own nature—in particular, his sexual nature, which he would be able to explore in the company of compliant *Strassenjungen*.

This realization effectively put an end to Isherwood's misguided scheme to become a doctor, and a few days after Christmas he told Kathleen that he intended to abandon the course at King's College. "He thinks the college is interfering with his writing—& the work of both suffers in consequence," she reported despondently. "I suppose it was inevitable, but I had so hoped it would not have come so soon, he had seemed so much happier going off to regular work—to have the time & yet not the inclination, must be far more nerve racking than to feel if one had the time one could write. He does not seem to be one of the fortunate people who can combine their writing with other work. it is disappointing."

They agreed that he should return for one more term, since the fees had been paid in advance. With the prospect of liberation before him, Isherwood marked time. "I visited the medical school nearly every day," he recalled, "much as one drops into a club." He spent much more time drinking with Robert Moody, a fellow student who had been at Oxford with Auden and became a close friend. Kathleen may have hoped that, once back at King's College, Isherwood would eventually settle down, but he was now determined to join Auden in Berlin. On Thursday, March 14, 1929, he took the boat train to Dover and boarded the ferry to Ostende.

SIX

THE TRAIN THAT PULLED IN TO THE FRIEDRICHSTRASSE BAHNHOF on March 15, 1929, carried Isherwood into the city with which his name would always be associated. This first trip to Berlin lasted less than a week, however, and was in the nature of a scouting expedition. "To Christopher, Berlin meant Boys," Isherwood later declared, but this is something of an oversimplification. He had undoubtedly been enticed to the city by Auden's accounts of the comparative sexual freedom to be found there and by the prospect of meeting John Layard, but Berlin meant a great deal more than that. He must have recognized that he could hardly have chosen a city with more hateful associations for Kathleen, who could never forgive Germany for the war in which her husband had died. If Kathleen herself regarded her son's trip as some sort of betrayal, she did not confide as much in her diary, her only comment being that he returned "after an interesting time." Quite how interesting she could not have guessed.

Isherwood almost certainly stayed with Auden, who had moved to rooms in Kreuzberg, a working-class area in the southeast of the city. Fürbringerstrasse 8 was similar to thousands of houses in Berlin, where the front door opens into a passage leading to one or more gloomy courtyards containing a large number of flats. Like most of the houses in the street, the frontage was shabby and unadorned, although elaborate moldings on some of its neighbors suggested a more elegant past. The street conveniently bisected Zossenerstrasse, where the Cosy Corner stood at Number 7. Auden immediately introduced Isherwood into this exciting new world. Stepping through the leather curtain that hung across the doorway of the café, Isherwood entered a new domain, one unimaginably far removed from the Kensington drawing rooms he had left behind him in London, and he picked up a boy named Paul on his first visit. It was here, too, that Isherwood was introduced to John Layard, with whom he excitedly discussed the theories of Homer Lane. By now Auden had grown a little disenchanted with Layard, feeling perhaps that he had rather outgrown him. Layard's worship of Lane and his openness about himself sometimes made him seem naïve or even sentimental. Auden had talked up Layard to such a degree when he had visited Isherwood the previous Christmas that he now became nervous about introducing them. When Layard got on to his pet notion that Lane operated through "love," Auden started to squirm. "I was ashamed in front of Christopher," he admitted in the diary he began to keep in the wake of Isherwood's visit, "though on other occasions I agree with a great deal of what [Layard] says. But what we think we believe varies with our company." In spite of his superior knowledge and experience of the world, significantly enlarged by seven months in Berlin, Auden still regarded Isherwood as an older brother who might turn out to be less easily impressed by one's latest enthusiasms. He need not have worried: Isherwood fell under Layard's spell and embraced Homer Lane's theories with such enthusiasm that Stephen Spender was under the impression that it was Isherwood rather than Auden who was the true evangelist.

Another significant landmark in Auden's guided tour of Berlin was the splendidly named and equally splendidly appointed Institut für Sexualwissenschaft. Founded in 1919 by the pioneering sexologist Dr. Magnus Hirschfeld, the Institute for Sexual Science stood on the corner of In Den Zelten and Beethovenstrasse on the northwestern edge of the Tiergarten, Berlin's vast 630-acre central park. It was housed in an imposing mansion, which had been built for the violinist Joachim, and had last been inhabited by Count Hatzfeld, Germany's former ambassador in France. Although it had been a scientific institute since Hirschfeld acquired it, the building retained much of its original opulence. The public rooms still suggested the residence of an ambassador rather than a clinic or hospital. "No cold walls, no linoleum on the floor, no uncomfortable chairs and no smell of disinfectants," a journalist reported in 1922. "This is a private house: carpets, pictures on the walls, and nowhere a plate saying 'No entrance.' And it is full of life everywhere, with patients, doctors and other people who work there. There are also very quiet rooms. Dr. Hirschfeld led me into a very beautiful and spacious one with three large windows toward the Tiergarten. It is furnished in Biedermeier style: a long sofa, tables, chairs—all very comfortable. I saw several large vitrines with collections of glassware and porcelain." It was also hung with portraits of distinguished patrons and personalities who had supported Hirschfeld and his work, and these jostled somewhat incongruously for wall space with photographs of transvestites before and after receiving treatment at the Institute—treatment that was intended not to "cure" them but to make them at ease with themselves.

Born in 1868, the son of a distinguished Jewish doctor, Hirschfeld had started out as a naturopath, but was always attracted to the fringes of medicine and in particular to sexual psychology. In 1896 he produced a pamphlet on the subject of homosexuality entitled *Sappho und Socrates*. This was inspired by the case of one of his patients, a young man who had committed suicide on the eve of his marriage because he was homosexual. The patient had left a letter for Hirschfeld, urging him to use his unhappy story to draw the public's attention to the plight of men unable to come to terms with their sexuality. Homosexual himself, Hirschfeld was inspired to make his life's work the explanation of sexual psychology to the general public. *Sappho und Socrates* was published under a nom de plume, but before long Hirschfeld's own name became synonymous with "the homosexual question." Many of Hirschfeld's theories about sexual orientation now seem primitive, but the important message he tried to get across was that homosexuality was not a disease, still less a crime, and ought to be accepted as part of the wide spectrum of human sexual responses.

In 1897 Hirschfeld had set up the Wissenschaftlich-humanitären Komitee, or Scientific-Humanitarian Committee, with the specific aim of repealing Paragraph 175 of the Reichsstrafgesetzbuch, which outlawed homosexuality in Germany. The Committee drafted a petition to submit to the Reichstag, but this was rejected. They subsequently made a second petition and collected some 6,000 signatures from among the great and the good: politicians, members of the judiciary, doctors and scientists (including Krafft-Ebing and Einstein), artists such as George Grosz and Käthe Kollwitz, and writers such as Wedekind, Rilke, Hesse, Stefan Zweig and Heinrich Mann. (Mann's equally distinguished—and predominantly homosexual—brother Thomas signed, then withdrew his signature.) Once again, the petition was rejected, but Hirschfeld felt that he had enough support to continue the battle and meanwhile educate public opinion. In 1899 he produced the first of his "Jahrbücher für sexuelle Zwischenstufen," annual publications devoted to writings on what he called "sexual intermediaries." Contributors included scientists, criminologists, doctors, ethnologists, and almost anyone who had a view on the subject—even if that view did not match Hirschfeld's own. Hirschfeld was also publishing numerous books, among them *Der Urnische Mensch* ("Urning People," 1903), in which he set out his belief that homosexuality was a natural condition that people were born with ("Urning" being the word he coined for homosexuality); *Die Homosexualität des Mannes und des Weibes* (1914), a vast tome describing the biology and sociology of homosexuality, drawing upon the case histories of some 10,000 men and women; and *Sexualpathologie* (three volumes, 1916–1920), written principally for doctors and medical students.

The Institute acted not only as a clinic and research center but also as a place of public education. There was a large library of some thirty thousand books and an archive which consisted of transvestite and fetishist effects and photographs of sexual "types" and famous homosexuals such as Oscar Wilde and Frederick the Great. Some 4,000 people visited the Institute during its first year, and many more attended the numerous lectures that were given by Hirschfeld and others on all aspects of sexuality. In 1921 Hirschfeld acquired a neighboring building at In Den Zelten 9A, which had a large hall on the ground floor where he held lectures and public discussions. Three years later Hirschfeld handed the Institute over to the government—an indication of how seriously his work was taken—but continued to run it as director. Auden was grandly disapproving of the museum, describing it as "pornography for science. A eunuch's pleasure," but for Isherwood it exerted a great, if nervous, fascination. Hirschfeld's idea of categorizing people according to the various shadings of their sexuality can have seemed scarcely less bizarre than the work of Mortmere's Dr. Mears, with his "Puss-Dragoons," "Imperials," "Repellers," "Poupees," "Throstles," and so on. At the same time, Isherwood was forced to acknowledge many of the exhibits in Dr. Hirschfeld's freak-show as his own sexual kin. Homosexuality, he now knew, was not some private peccadillo he had in common with Auden and a few other friends, but something that was scientifically recognized and shared by all manner of people.

Berlin may have meant Boys but, despite Hirschfeld's efforts, homosexuality remained illegal in Germany as it did in England. One would hardly have guessed this from the large number of clubs and bars operating in the city. Almost a quarter of Curt Moreck's *Führer durch das "lasterhafte" Berlin* ("Guide to 'Immoral' Berlin"), published in 1931, is devoted to homosexual, lesbian and transvestite bars. Beautifully produced, with illustrations by leading artists such as Christian Schad, Paul Kamm, George Grosz and Jeanne Mammen, Moreck's book was undoubtedly part of what Isherwood described as Berlin's "commercial 'line,' " written for gawping visitors. There was a brisk trade in guidebooks to the city with such enticing titles as *Berlin: Was Nicht im Baedeker Steht* ("What's Not in Baedeker"), promising all sorts of debauchery. Even those who disapproved of such things did their bit to increase Berlin's lurid reputation. In his admiring 1931 book, *Hitler,* Wyndham Lewis's aghast description of the famous Eldorado bar in Motzstrasse probably encouraged as many people to rush there as to avoid it. Lewis understood that Berlin boasted 160 bars where "every variety of Perversion is properly and adequately represented," making it the undisputed "Haupstadt of Vice." While it is true that a number of these bars were, as Isherwood rather snootily complained, "dens of pseudo-vice catering to heterosexual tourists," where "screaming boys in drag and monocled Eton-cropped girls in dinner-jackets play-acted the high jinks of Sodom and Gomorrah," a large percentage of them were genuinely what Moreck described as "*Stammlokale des mannmännlichen Eros*" catering for "the tribe." Indeed, although subject to occasional purges and clamp-downs, Berlin had a long-standing reputation as the homosexual capital of Europe.

Not everyone was impressed. Visiting Berlin a couple of years before Isherwood, the English aesthete Brian Howard was dismayed by what he found at the optimistically named Adonis-Diele in Kreuzberg's Alexandrinenstrasse: "the dirtiest, ugliest crew I ever laid eyes on. Two beastly little boys of 14 who kept kissing one another, and the worst pianist in the world." The Cosy Corner, where he managed to pick up a boy, was "little better." "My young gentleman was the only one in the least possible," he wrote of the café's clientèle, but "he spoilt it all by trying to get twice as much money out of me afterwards as he should have done."

Even so, such things were far easier to arrange in Germany than in Britain, where any homosexual activity had to be pursued in secret. Moreck would have had a thin time of it writing a similar book about London. An important difference between the two countries was that in Germany economic necessity had made people flout the law, and uncertainty over the country's future had created an atmosphere of *carpe diem.* The authorities seemed inclined to turn a blind eye to the thriving homosexual subculture of Berlin, but since the denizens of bars such as the Cosy Corner were often involved in petty crime, these establishments were subject to raids by "*die Grüner,*" as the police were known because of their green uniforms. On one occasion, Auden, Isherwood and Layard were sitting in the Cosy Corner when the proprietor gave out a general warning that the *Grüner* were on their way. They were in pursuit of three boys who had absconded from a reformatory. The three Englishmen were persuaded to lend the boys their overcoats, and in this hastily improvised disguise the youths walked calmly out of the bar to safety, returning the coats to their rightful owners in Alexanderplatz after the danger had passed. Isherwood must have relished this opportunity to outwit the Others.

It was at the Cosy Corner that Isherwood met a young Czech named Berthold Szczesny. Among his friends Szczesny was known as "Bubi," which Isherwood translated as "Baby." It could indeed have been a corruption of the German word *Baby,* but may also have been derived from *Bub,* the German word for "boy" or "lad"—thus making Bubi emblematic of all Isherwood desired of Berlin—or *Bube,* "rogue." Any or all of these would have been appropriate, as Szczesny was a pretty, smooth-skinned, blue-eyed, blond-haired and demanding young man, who was frequently in trouble with the police. Isherwood fell for him at once.

Although Bubi differed from those youths upon whom Isherwood had previously concentrated his affections—Darling, Sylvain Mangeot and Johnny Monkhouse—in that he was sexually available, he nevertheless retained a romantic aura for his admirer. The romance, in this case, was less that of *David Blaize* than of *La Dame aux Camélias.* What could be more suitable for Isherwood the Artist than to fall in love with a courtesan? Bubi was "the most obliging of companions," but he was basically heterosexual and tended to spend the money he extracted from Isherwood on liaisons with female prostitutes. Isherwood tried hard to play down the commercial aspect of their relationship and this led to rows. *"Du bist kein Puppenjunge,"* he would insist. *"Du bist mein Freund"*: "You're not a rent-boy. You're my friend."[1] Auden, whose own dealings with *Pupenjungen* made him take a somewhat cynical view of Isherwood's "romance," was less sure. Among the films they saw during Isherwood's visit was *Die Büchse der Pandora,* G. W. Pabst's adaptation of Wedekind's "Lulu" plays, which had been released that year. Auden told his friend that he thought the film most appropriate, since it graphically demonstrated the dangers of falling in love with a whore. Isherwood nevertheless went through agonies of jealousy when Bubi failed to turn up for appointments.

Part of Bubi's appeal was his foreignness, the fact that he spoke no English, but this was also a complication in the relationship, since Isherwood's German remained rudimentary. Auden commented on this in "This Loved One," a poem he wrote about Isherwood's relationship with Bubi. In the second stanza, he observes:

Face that the sun
Is supple on
May stir but here
Is no new year;
This gratitude for gifts is less
Than the old loss;
Touching is shaking hands
On mortgaged lands;

---

1. The correct word for rent-boy was *Pupenjunge,* or "fart-boy"; *"Puppenjunge,"* or "doll-boy," was a necessary euphemism coined by the author J. H. Mackay for the title of his 1926 novel about a young male prostitute. (Mackay uses the correct spelling in the actual text.)

And smiling of
This gracious greeting
'Good day, good luck'
Is no real meeting

Isherwood might see springlike stirrings in his lover's expression, but "here / Is no new year," Auden warns. Bubi himself, though sexually compliant, is no more attainable than any of Isherwood's previous crushes: his affection is as evanescent as the sunshine, which promises more than it can sustain in March, a month during which northern European weather is notoriously unsettled. Their physical intimacy, "touching," is a mere business gesture, just as their conversation—restricted by the lack of a mutual language to the "gracious" but empty salutations of the tourist's phrase-book ("Good day, good luck"), accompanied by a great deal of defensive "smiling"—is "no real meeting" of personalities. Indeed, Isherwood was obliged to get Auden to coach him in simple phrases so that he could explain his feelings to his errant lover: *"Du weisst schon was gestern mit mir los was. Ich bin eifersüchtig weil Du einen anderen Freund hast"* ("You know very well what the matter was with me yesterday: I'm jealous because you have another friend"). Not that this helped a great deal: "Christopher appears to have trotted this out alright," Auden noted, "but couldn't understand the answer."

Judging by Auden's journal, Isherwood's visit had been unsettling. "Pimping for someone on whom one has a transference creates the most [contrary?] feelings," he wrote. "Transference" is a Freudian term meaning the redirecting of feelings toward a substitute person; it usually occurs during therapy and it is not altogether clear what Auden (who was well read in Freud) meant by this. Perhaps he was trying to account for—and play down—his feelings about Isherwood and the jealousy he was evidently experiencing. When Isherwood went off with the boy on his first night in Berlin, Auden wrote: "I got drunk, partly as a counterblast to the knowledge that C did not want Paul particularly." And a later discussion of this episode left Auden feeling "beastly." "The fact is, when you're with Bubi you don't believe you ever had Paul," Auden complained. And when Isherwood went out with Bubi, Auden felt "unhappy." Things were not much better when Auden accompanied the pair.

> Chiefly I remember Christopher and Bubi playing ping-pong. The sense of bare flesh, the blue sky through the glass and the general sexy atmosphere made one feel like a participator in a fertility rite. At coffee, 'Kann er mich gut leiden?' ['Does he fancy me?'] On Charlottenburg station, 'Mensch, er ist ganz verrückt nach dir' ['Man, he's wild about you'] All went well till after lunch. [. . .] In the pine-wood I felt the third baboon[2] and a public-school one. Sunday walks to be back in time for chapel. In the train all was gloom recovering a little after tea and later in bed.

---

2. "The Third Baboon" was a term invented by Isherwood after browsing in the work of Havelock Ellis, where the author quotes a naturalist describing a male baboon masturbating while watching two others copulating.

The style of Auden's journal is almost as elliptical as his poetry, but it seems clear that going to bed with Isherwood cheered Auden up after a fairly dismal day. In the next journal entry, however, Auden complained: "Christopher seemed so babyish in his struggle with his note book and his sulks." "We shook hands meaningly as we parted," he reported after Isherwood had returned to London.

Although this first trip to Berlin was brief, Isherwood came to see it as "one of the decisive events of my life." It not only introduced him to a city that he would make his own and provide him with material for two of his best-known books, it also inaugurated a long period of travel in which he was looking for a place he could feel both free and at home. He arrived back in England with his wrist encircled by a cheap bracelet he had been given by Bubi. This was not only a tangible reminder of the erotic and romantic possibilities offered by Berlin but also an emblem of Isherwood's emancipation. Far from being shocked by this piece of jewelry as Isherwood had hoped she would be, Kathleen was "only vaguely puzzled that he should care to wear anything so common."

Isherwood was determined to return to Berlin as soon as possible, but was committed to accompany Olive and Sylvain Mangeot on three weeks' holiday to the south of France, a few miles from the Riviera, where (as Richard later put it) "the man-thirsty Rachel [Monkhouse] was gadding about with André." Rachel's younger sister, Elizabeth, doubts that an affair was taking place, as does Fowke Mangeot, but the Isherwoods maintained that the Monkhouse family had been hoodwinked by the forty-six-year-old musician and his twenty-three-year-old pupil, and "didn't even smell a rat" when Mangeot went to stay at Meadow Bank. As Richard sarcastically put it, "they thought that he took a fatherly interest in her." What is not in doubt is that Olive was beginning to tire of her husband's relationships with his female students and that the Mangeots' marriage was gradually unraveling.

On the morning of their departure, Isherwood woke up with a temperature, feeling distinctly unwell, but he insisted that he was up to the journey. This holiday was to produce something of a crisis in the relationship between Isherwood, Olive and Sylvain, a crisis of which Richard claimed to have received some sort of psychic warning. On the day the party left, Richard was alone in his bedroom at Pembroke Gardens when he thought he heard Christopher—at that moment speeding southward across France on a train—call out. Richard was convinced that his brother had been involved in an accident and spent the next couple of days dreading a telegram. In fact the travelers arrived safely at their destination, and although Isherwood had developed flu, he gradually recuperated in the sun. Olive was no sooner through with nursing her "loving eldest" back to health than Sylvain went down with rheumatic fever. It was altogether a less restful three weeks than had been planned. Auden, having heard of their troubles, jotted down his own version of events in the diary he kept in Berlin:

> Till he was 16 C[hristopher] was devoted to his mother. Now to force women to be his mother he is a bugger so that he can tell them about it, but he finds he can't. O[live] is the nearest he can get. But O[live]'s children are growing up, and she is estranged from her husband. She toys [?] with both son and lover and falls in love with him. C[hristopher] wanting a wife too, falls in love with S[ylvain], O[live]'s

youngest son. S[ylvain] has a transference on C[hristopher], [illeg] and wants him to be an elder brother, not a husband. When S[ylvain] is no longer attractive, he feels C[hristopher]'s failing interest, and gets rheumatic fever. In the night calls to C[hristopher] to bring him the pot, as he says he can't get out of bed. C[hristopher] pretends not to hear, as S[ylvain] gets up.

This Freudian interpretation, written when Auden was firmly under the spell of Homer Lane, is presumably based on what Isherwood told him about the holiday and therefore cannot be discounted. Although suspicious of Auden's motives, Fowke Mangeot conceded that there were "elements of truth" in this analysis. Isherwood's dream in Bremen the previous May that Sylvain would grow tall, a dream from which he woke "in utter misery," suggests that there may indeed have been some waning of interest on his part as the boy, now fifteen, grew up. In the wake of his sexually fulfilling experiences in Berlin, a romantic attachment to Sylvain may have lost some of its appeal. Auden's analysis also bears a striking resemblance to the relationships between the tutor, his employer and her son in "The Summer at the House," the abandoned novel Isherwood described as being "inspired, vaguely, by my vision of the life of" the Mangeots. If Auden had read this manuscript, he might well have confused life and (for want of a better word) art, but it seems unlikely that Isherwood would have shown it to him.

I sherwood returned from his French trip in a very restless and discontented mood, eager to get back to Berlin as soon as possible. He had a long, confrontational discussion with his mother, "explaining to [her] how little if anything we have in common—deploring my lack of broadness of view on sexual subjects or the charity & kindness with which it should be regarded—also my incapacity of seeing beauty in the ugly things in life." Kathleen was upset, but not impressed: "I on my side deplore the way he deceives himself . . . !" she wrote. Once again, Isherwood seemed to expect his mother to have the liberal outlook of Olive Mangeot, but this was unrealistic. Kathleen was seventeen years older than her rival and had been brought up in wholly conventional circles, and entirely in the Victorian era. By the time the old Queen died and the twentieth century dawned, Kathleen was already thirty-two, and she was now sixty. She was also continually haunted by the image of Uncle Henry, a warning of what Christopher might become. Another instance of Henry's irresponsibility presented itself a week or so after this painful conversation, when Christopher announced over dinner that he had arranged with his uncle and the family solicitor to sell off all the furniture at Marple Hall. This was the furniture that Kathleen had spent much of her time sketching and cataloguing, and Isherwood, who seemed very pleased with himself when he made the announcement, no doubt knew how much the decision would upset her. "It seems like losing an old friend who one perhaps seldom sees but whose existence is a pleasure & support," Kathleen lamented.

An attempt by Kathleen to mend bridges by suggesting a few days together in Freshwater Bay was summarily rebuffed ("Idiotic of me," she conceded), and further divisions were highlighted by the General Election on May 30: Kathleen and Nanny voted Conservative; Christopher and Elizabeth voted Liberal. Indeed, given almost any subject, Christopher and Kathleen could be guaranteed to disagree. "Christopher used to say that if Kathleen and he had landed on an alien planet where there were two political parties about which they knew nothing, the Uggs and the Oggs, she would have instantly chosen one of them and he the other, simply by reacting to the sound of their names." Where once they had derived pleasure from reading the classic novels aloud to each other, they now argued about the merits of contemporary fiction. For example, Isherwood admired the novels of Ivy Compton-Burnett, and Kathleen evidently felt she knew why: she noted that the characters in *Brothers and Sisters,* which she read that summer, all talked "in the half cynical, semi clever & 'critical of their elders' fashion." Isherwood later claimed that Kathleen used to enrage him by using the word "soothing" of a book as a term of approbation. It is quite possible that Kathleen did this partly to goad her son, for although she hankered continually after a romantic past, she always made a genuine effort to keep up with new plays and books, even when she didn't in the end much care for them.

Isherwood went to Freshwater alone, in order to work on *The Memorial,* then on July 2 joined Auden and Layard at Rothehütte in the Harz Mountains where they were holidaying with one of Auden's German boys, Otto Küsel. At Isherwood's request, Auden had invited Berthold Szczesny to join them, but on the appointed day Bubi failed to arrive. Isherwood determined to travel to Berlin in search of his missing lover. Fearing that Isherwood, whose German was still fragmentary despite weeks spent studying a home tutorial book, would be lost in Berlin without him, Auden gave him the name of Francis Turville-Petre, an English archaeologist who knew his way round the city's clubs and dives. Their inquiries elicited the information that the law had once again caught up with Bubi and that, wanted by the police, he had gone on the run. Isherwood was obliged to return to Rothehütte alone, shortly followed by the police, who had heard that a young Englishman had been inquiring after their man. While he was answering questions and having his papers checked, a letter arrived from Bubi, who was hiding out in Holland, a country he was not legally entitled to enter. He intended to sail for South America as a deck-hand and asked whether Isherwood could possibly send him some money. Enchanted that Bubi was fulfilling the role of romantic outlaw in which he had been cast, Isherwood immediately wired Kathleen for £5 and determined to make his way to Amsterdam. Auden agreed to accompany him, even though (or perhaps because) Otto had been taken into custody by the police, who had discovered that the youth had absconded from a reformatory.

It did not take long for Isherwood and Auden to find Bubi, whom they bumped into outside the post office where he had gone in order to see if there were any letters for him. It was an emotional reunion, and one Bubi dragged out for all it was worth, managing to extract another £5 from Isherwood, who again had to send to England for it. Having seen Bubi on his way, the two young Englishmen spent a day touring the canals of the city. In the visitors' book they were asked to sign at the end of the tour, Auden wrote two lines from a poem by Ilya Ehrenburg:

Read about us and marvel!
You did not live in our time—be sorry!

This cheeky appropriation of Ehrenburg had more to do with the personal mythology Auden and Isherwood were creating than with any sentiments about political revolution. The nearest either of them had got to solidarity with the workers was sleeping with them, and this was usually on a quid pro quo basis, either by direct payment or gifts. The challenge was, however, a prophetic one, for it is likely that it was at Rothe-hütte that Auden asked Isherwood to help him with a play he was writing, thus inaugurating a fruitful and enduring literary partnership.

The play, appropriately enough, was to be called "The Reformatory," probably inspired by Otto's stories of his life (he and Bubi were to be the play's dedicatees). It was in part a response to Peter Martin Lampel's play *Revolte in Erziehungshaus,* which attacked social and sexual repression and had caused a stir when it was premiered in Berlin earlier that year, when Auden had seen it. It is also notable that Homer Lane had run reform schools for boys in both England and America, and that Gabriel Carritt was considering a career in dealing with juvenile delinquency (he subsequently won a scholarship to Columbia University in New York to study the subject). Parts of a portentously titled "Preliminary Statement" the two authors jotted down at around this time, which seems to relate to this play, are clearly influenced by Lane: "Symptoms are an attempt at cure," "Cancer is the individual's version of the moral tragedy of society," and so on. Auden had probably started work on the play in the spring of 1929, possibly during Isherwood's visit to Berlin that March. His first reference to the play was in his journal on April 15, and five days later he noted: "A Play is poetry of action. The dialogue should be corresponding[ly] a simplification. E.g. Hrotswitha. The Prep School atmosphere. That is what I want." And with Isherwood, his contemporary at St. Edmund's and author of "Gems of Belgian Architecture," that was what he would get.

At this period Auden habitually referred to "The Reformatory" as "my play" and it is not known precisely when he asked Isherwood to become his collaborator; but it seems likely that Isherwood was there, if only as a sounding board, from the play's inception. Collaboration would be important for both authors, not only with each other, but with later partners. One of its attractions, particularly for Isherwood, was that collaboration was a form of conspiracy. This is the form it had taken with his first literary partner, Edward Upward. During Isherwood's visit to Berlin, Auden had written in his journal (apropos of two *Strassenjungen* whose behavior he had been observing), "That is what friendship is. Fellow conspiracy." Many years later, in another journal kept while in Berlin, Auden (perhaps reminded by the city of his earliest collaboration) wrote: "The marriage of true minds. Between two collaborators, whatever their sex, age, or appearance, there is always an erotic bond. Queers, to whom normal marriage and parenthood are forbidden, are fools if they do not deliberately look for tasks which require collaboration, and the right person with whom to collaborate." There is no doubt that in Isherwood he had found the right person. Quite apart from the fact that Isherwood's experience as a writer of narrative would prove useful in constructing a coherent plot, for Auden there would always be the sheer pleasure of working alongside someone he loved. "In my own case," his diary continued, "collaboration has brought me greater erotic joy—as distinct from sexual pleasure—than any sexual relation I have had." The prep-school atmosphere seems to have prevailed not only in the finished play (retitled *The Enemies of a Bishop*) but during the periods Auden and Isherwood spent together swapping ideas and working out a plot.

The Enemies of a Bishop was completed, typed and corrected, and submitted, without success, to Jonathan Cape. Its rejection is hardly surprising, since it is clearly an apprentice work, a trial run for later collaborations. Indeed, Auden reused material in a subsequent play, *The Chase* (1934), which also contains a subplot about a reformatory, which in turn was cannibalized for *The Dog Beneath the Skin,* the first of the Auden/Isherwood plays to reach the stage. Subtitled "Die When I Say When" and described on the title page as "A Morality in Four Acts," *The Enemies of a Bishop* is a Mortmerish farrago, in which some rather fine poems (including "This Loved One") mercifully interrupt—though without discernible relevance—a great deal of appalling dialogue, notably the authors' approximation of "Cockney," used by the reformatory boys: "We'll 'ave ter git a disguise, like, when we're aht. I reckon we can pinch some duds at the stytion. Luvverly night, ain't it? I don't think." Even if it had had more dramatic merit, the play would have been unperformable in the 1920s owing to its cheerful depiction of the white slave trade, lesbianism, homosexual prostitution, flagellation and transvestism, its use of such words as "arse," an exchange in "eggy-peggy" language about a female character's "tegight cegunt," and the general atmosphere of schoolboy depravity. As might be expected, it contains a number of in-jokes and private references.

The Enemies of a Bishop anticipated Auden and Isherwood's later collaborations, in which verse and prose form a rather better amalgam. It is unclear how the work was divided between the two authors, and although it is safe to assume that the poetry is Auden's (though possibly still at this stage "edited" by Isherwood), it is likely that the dialogue was a genuine collaboration, arising out of discussions such as the one that produced Isherwood and Upward's "Introductory Dialogue" to Mortmere and indeed the "Preliminary Statement." Much of the actual writing was done when the two authors were apart, and they probably worked on the play separately, then got together to edit and collate the material. That this working method did not always make for coherence may be judged by *Enemies,* which lacks the discipline of later collaborations.

Looking "very tired" and "heavily out of pocket," Isherwood arrived back in Kensington on July 19, bringing Auden with him for lunch and a bath. They had come all the way by boat to Gravesend, and were greeted with one of Elizabeth's least enticing offerings: a pie made from meat which was "off." Isherwood's holiday had proved more expensive than he had planned, and with no prospect of profitable work in view he was obliged to sell a gold watch and chain for £13. He did, however, find another tutoring job in Bettyhill, in the far north of Scotland, a place he had visited on his excursion with Bill de Lichtenberg. On the morning of his departure he had another long talk with his mother. "It seems like a vicious circle," Kathleen wrote; "if one difficulty is surmounted another appears so that any happier solution seems impossible but the fault is considered to be entirely mine." By now Isherwood had decided that his immediate future lay in Berlin, and he had no intention of settling to any sort of permanent job in the U.K. It was merely a matter of marking time.

Isherwood's new pupil was a boy named Wallace Lanigan, whose mother ran a hotel in Bettyhill. Not much is known about this job, except that it was not very taxing and ended with Isherwood's dismissal. "The wind roars from Iceland and there's nothing to do," Isherwood complained to Roger Burford. "I'm supposed to be look-ing after the kid of the proprietress here, but he'd rather climb the roof or play pitch and toss with the chauffeur." For Isherwood himself, the job had some significance in that he went to bed with his employer (who was either a widow or divorced) and thus, at the age of nearly twenty-five, had what he referred to as his "first—and last—com-plete sex experience with a woman." (If there were incomplete ones, he did not record them.) He later explained that both he and Mrs. Lanigan had been drunk, but that he had found sex with her both interesting and enjoyable. He was narcissistically aroused by the fact that she found him attractive and even flattered when she told him the following day that she could tell that he was experienced. He felt that Bubi was responsible for his growth in sexual self-confidence, but decided that this heterosex-ual experiment need not be repeated.

> Do I now want to go to bed with more women and girls? Of course not, as long as I can have boys. Why do I prefer boys? Because of their shape and their voices and their smell and the way they move. And boys can be romantic. I can put them into my myth and fall in love with them. Girls can be absolutely beautiful but never romantic. In fact, their utter lack of romance is what I find most likeable about them. They're so sensible.

Isherwood's myth of himself was not fully formed in 1929, and this deliberately provocative analysis was written almost half a century later, by which time he had be-come a figurehead of the Gay Liberation movement and spent much of his time en-couraging the troops. He goes on to play devil's advocate:

> Couldn't you get yourself excited by the shape of girls, too—if you worked hard at it? Perhaps. And couldn't you invent another myth—to put girls into? Why the hell should I? Well, it would be a lot more convenient if you did. Then you wouldn't have all these problems. Society would accept you. You wouldn't be out of step with nearly everybody else.
>
> It was at this point in his self-examination that Christopher would become suddenly, blindly furious. Damn Nearly Everybody. Girls are what the State and the Church and the Law and the Press and the Medical profession endorse, and command me to desire. My mother endorses them, too. She is silently, brutishly willing me to get married and breed grandchildren for her. Her will is the will of Nearly Everybody, and in their will is my death. My will is to live according to my nature, and to find a place where I can be what I am . . . But I'll admit this—even if my nature were like theirs, I should still have to fight them, in one way or another. If boys didn't exist, I should have to invent them.

This is exhilarating rhetoric, but it is the rhetoric of the 1970s, not the 1920s. Although anyone who is homosexual in what Isherwood later, and with characteristic exaggera-tion, called "a heterosexual dictatorship" might feel alienated from that society, there is no evidence whatsoever that Isherwood felt particularly stigmatized, nor indeed that his mother was willing him, brutishly or otherwise, to marry and produce children at this period. Kathleen's sexual attitudes may have struck Isherwood as illiberal and antiquated, but the principal cause of his resentment toward her was not that she would not accept his sexuality but that she would not accept his choice of career.

The reason for Isherwood being sacked as a tutor after less than a month is not known, but relations between him and his employer must have been rather awkward in the wake of their one-night stand. Stephen Spender had a dim recollection about Isherwood falling in love with his pupil, which would provide another reason for dismissal. There is no mention of Wallace Lanigan in any surviving papers, although there are three photographs of him in one of Isherwood's albums (two with Isherwood and one with Mrs. Lanigan). If Isherwood did indeed fall in love with Wallace, then sleeping with the boy's mother might have had a hidden and alarmingly Freudian motive. Psychologically, it would also connect Isherwood's relationship with the Lanigans to his relationship with Sylvain and Olive Mangeot—and to "The Summer at the House."

Isherwood's unexpected return to London caused considerable upset at Pembroke Gardens, since Kathleen and Richard were about to travel to Italy for a few weeks' holiday and Nanny was also going on "a grand tour" (visiting Algiers of all places). Arrangements had been made for the house to be looked after by Emily, the housemaid, but she said quite firmly that "if C. was home she would rather not undertake it." Perhaps like Kathleen she found his manner offensively arrogant and may have recalled a recent bout of illness during which he pettishly dismissed the doctor. As Kathleen observed then, "he is amazingly childish and unreasonable sometimes, & takes himself so very seriously! which is curious in a person who is not at all lacking in a sense of humour." Nanny, always keen to stir things up, informed Kathleen that the real reason for Emily's change of mind was that with Christopher there she would not be able to use the house to entertain her men friends. Fortunately Emily eventually agreed to stay, on the clear understanding that she did not have to tidy up after Isherwood and that he made his own breakfast.

Isherwood was now steeling himself to embark on a third draft of *The Memorial*. He had already worked out a structure for the book, in which there was a complicated time line and the action was seen from the viewpoint of several interrelated characters. "Technically, this novel is written like a detective story," he had noted among his "preliminary ideas," "—the façade of the characters' lives in 1928 is first presented (corresponding to the given 'situation' after the murder before the detective arrives. These people's lives are, so to speak, the 'murder.') Then—moving back in time to 1919, and moving forward to, say, 1923—we elucidate the significance of the 1928 section." Having thought a little further about the plot, however, and about the ages of his characters, he decided to alter the dates, and the novel is divided into four books. It opens in 1928 with contrasting portraits of the two principal female characters, Lily Vernon and Mary Scriven, who are sisters-in-law. Like their originals—Kathleen and Olive Mangeot—they represent the Old Life and the New Life, the theme that Isherwood had been pursuing doggedly but unsuccessfully in earlier and incomplete fictions. Lily believes in the social order embodied by the Hall, where her husband's family have lived for centuries; Mary is a bohemian who lives in cultured disarray and accepts social fluidity. The first section of the novel ends with the botched suicide attempt in Berlin of Edward Blake, a homosexual friend of Lily's dead war-hero husband, Richard. This remarkably vivid scene, perhaps the most powerful in the novel, was very closely based on the recent suicide attempt of John Layard. After "betraying" Auden by sleeping with one of his German boyfriends, Layard had placed a revolver in his mouth and pulled the trigger. The bullet had somehow failed to do any serious damage as it passed through the roof of his mouth, up his nasal passage and into the front of his skull, where it became lodged. Isherwood's description of the shooting and its consequences is almost identical to Layard's own account of his misadventure, right down to the hallucinations and sensations Layard experienced as he came round and realized he had not in fact killed himself. Edward Blake and Richard Vernon are the novel's representatives of the Truly Weak Man and the Truly Strong Man.

The second book goes back to the day in 1920 when the war memorial of the title is being unveiled. The characters of Lily and Mary are once again pointedly and amusingly contrasted, while Lily's awkward, seventeen-year-old son, Eric, undergoes agonies of guilt because he would far rather be spending the day with his cousins. The third book travels forward to 1925 and is set mostly at Cambridge, where Eric and his popular and reckless cousin Maurice are both undergraduates. The fourth book takes a final glimpse at the characters in 1929, by which time the New Life has triumphed over the Old Life. The Hall has been sold off to the Ramsbothams, a local family of mill-owners (based on Isherwood's childhood friends the Scotts), and Mary's daughter Anne is to marry one of the sons.

Isherwood had submitted the second draft to Upward, telling him that he was unsatisfied with it. Upward replied bluntly: "Totally rewrite chapters 2, 3, & 4 of Book II. They illuminate nothing except the technical machinery." He described one of the characters as "lacerating false," thought that Mary Scriven "utterly fails to communicate," and claimed that the first chapter contained "two of the most remarkable quisbs of our time." He did, however, praise the first and third books. "I'll reread it a third time and let you know how everything I've written here fails to describe my impressions," he concluded. "But it's far better than you said. Buggered by Book II. I was extremely angry." It was in the nature of their friendship that Upward and Isherwood could be brutally frank about each other's writing, but Isherwood was distracted from the suggested rewriting by a small job that came his way through Auden that autumn.

Auden had himself taken a tutoring job on his return to England from Berlin. His employer ran a small publishing house, the Blackamore Press, and Auden secured Isherwood a commission to translate Baudelaire's *Journaux intimes*. Isherwood was now rather more interested in German than in French, but Baudelaire had been something of a hero ever since Upward discovered *Les Fleurs du Mal* in 1922. In any case, he needed some income, and so he set to, producing a translation that was not altogether accurate, but is highly readable and has been reprinted several times, in both Britain and America. "I discovered that I could understand about three words of it," Isherwood told Roger Burford, "and what was my relief when I met T. S. Eliot, who is writing the preface, and found that he understood about four." It was first published in 1930 in an elegant limited edition of four hundred copies, fifty of them signed by Eliot, who in fact knew rather more than four words of French and was not at all amused when the reviews pointed out that the text contained a number of errors.

Isherwood described the *Intimate Journals* as "an assortment of wonderful fragments, cryptic memoranda, literary notes, quotations, rough drafts of prose poems, explosions of political anger and personal spleen." In form, they were not unlike the aphoristic salmagundi of Auden and Isherwood's "Preliminary Statement," and may well have influenced the two young writers as they drew up their manifesto. Isherwood undoubtedly identified with Baudelaire, particularly at this unsettled period of his life. "Baudelaire was one of the first writers of 'the poetry of departure,' " he later noted. "His longing for escape—from the nineteenth century and himself—fastened nostalgically upon ships. 'When,' he imagines them asking, 'shall we set sail for happiness?' " He also observed that Baudelaire "experienced mingled feelings of love, exasperation, pity, rebellion and hatred" for his mother, which was certainly something with which Isherwood could identify.

B y the autumn of 1929 Isherwood was himself longing to escape and set sail for happiness. The important thing was to get away from Kathleen and Kensington, and the most pleasing prospect remained Berlin. Packing two suitcases and a rucksack, he bought a single ticket and on November 29 set off once more for Germany. "[He] may be away some months," Kathleen wrote, ". . . how lonely it seems . . . I used to think long ago of our travelling together . . . [. . .] I do hope it will be a success . . ."

It was certainly not a success at first. Isherwood had booked into the Pension Kosmann at Tauentzienstrasse 4, just off the Wittenbergplatz and opposite the Kaufhaus des Westens, one of the city's large department stores, but this proved too expensive. He also discovered that, even after the hours he'd spent poring over *German in Three Months Without a Master,* he was unable to ask for a stamp at the post office—or even find the post office. Fortunately he discovered that there was a small inexpensive room to let on the opposite side of the Tiergarten in the building next door to the Hirschfeld institute, in an apartment owned by Hirschfeld's sister and already partly occupied by Francis Turville-Petre. In Den Zelten was a broad, elegant street, taking its name from the canvas awnings (*Zelten*) of outdoor restaurants, beneath which, after promenading in the park during the summer months, people took refreshment and rest. Hirschfeld himself had his consulting room, received visitors and gave parties in stately rooms in the Institute's central block, which was fronted by railings and a garden and looked out over the junction of Beethovenstrasse and In Den Zelten. This was flanked by two equally grand wings stretching along each of these streets. The Institute's official address was In Den Zelten 10, but its entrance was at Beethovenstrasse 3.

Isherwood's room was small and dark and overlooked a courtyard rather than the Tiergarten, but it was a suitably Baudelairean setting for Isherwood the Artist to work on his book. Unfortunately, he had omitted to pack the manuscript and had to send to England for it. Isherwood may have wanted to get away from his mother, but she still had her uses, and Kathleen made the first of many journeys to the post office, embarking upon a new unpaid job as his agent.

Lunch could be taken in the dining room of the Institute among the staff and patients. The advantage of this, Isherwood told Kathleen, was that he would be in the company of people who spoke only German and he would therefore gradually absorb the language. Kathleen describes the Institute as "a clinic," and it may be that Isherwood did not tell her its precise nature. What chiefly mattered to her was that Christopher was living in a good neighborhood, one she thought of as the equivalent of London's Regent's Park.

Turville-Petre failed to recognize Isherwood when he paid his initial visit, mistaking him for a youth he had slept with the previous night. "Do forgive me, lovey," the archaeologist said when Isherwood had identified himself, "—my mind's a total blank before I've had lunch." His mind was often pretty much a blank at other hours of the day, most of which he spent drinking. He was merely marking time, waiting to complete a course of treatment at the Institute to cure his syphilis, before setting off on another dig. Turville-Petre was a supporter as well as a patient of Hirschfeld, listed among those who founded the World League for Sexual Reform, and attending a congress in 1928. He also gave the occasional lecture at the Institute on such subjects as "sexual ethnography," but when Isherwood knew him he spent a considerable portion of the day in bed, either alone convalescing, or with some boy or other he had picked up. Tall, slender and dolichocephalic, he was a familiar figure in the bars of Berlin, and among the *Strassenjungen* he was known as "Der Franni," a name anglicized by English friends to "Fronny."

Three years Isherwood's senior, Francis Adrian Joseph Turville-Petre had been born into a distinguished Roman Catholic family. He joined the British School of Archaeology in Jerusalem, and in May 1925 made a major archaeological discovery in a small cave called the Mugharet-el-Emireh at Tabghar, just to the north of Tiberias. He found parts of the skull of a Neanderthal similar in type to those previously undiscovered outside Europe. The "Galilee Skull," as the fragments became known, proved that humanoids had lived in Palestine much earlier than had previously been supposed. Sir Arthur Keith, a leading expert on fossilized human remains, predicted that the discovery "would always rank among the important events of pre-history," while Professor John Garstang, head of the School, used his clever student's example to encourage other young men to choose archaeology as a profession.

The excavation at Tabghar proved to be the zenith of Fronny's work, however, resulting in his only book, an account of the dig entitled *Researches in Prehistoric Galilee,* published in 1927. Thereafter he seems to have fallen foul of the British School, and his promising career came to an abrupt end. Garstang recalled that when Turville-Petre first visited Palestine "he disappeared for weeks at a time, but always emerged with notes and specimens and keener than ever." This strain of independence appears to have been less appreciated once Turville-Petre had joined the School, where it began to be looked upon as rather too maverick. His determination to go his own way meant that despite his wide knowledge and gifts, his career was often blocked by those in authority. His reputation for drinking and carrying on liaisons with Arab boys did little to commend him to archaeological circles and it seems possible he was banned from several sites.

N ow that Isherwood was virtually living at the Institute, he got to know Magnus Hirschfeld, whose pioneering work in the field of human sexuality would have a direct impact on his life. Hirschfeld lived with his much younger lover, Karl Giese, who also acted as the Institute's secretary. Such was the disparity in their ages that the relationship between Hirschfeld and Giese seemed more like that of father and son than of lovers. Indeed, Giese usually addressed Hirschfeld as "Papa." By the time Isherwood met them, they had been together for about a decade and would remain partners until Hirschfeld's death in 1935. A photograph of them, arm in arm, shows the contrast between the stocky, professorially unkempt older man, with his heavy moustache and his academic's spectacles and bow-tie, and the tall, handsome younger man, with his neat dark hair, his immaculate leather gloves and his rather dashing neck-scarf. Giese may have looked like the tough but suave hero of a 1930s film, but his manner was markedly effeminate, as can be seen in a photograph of him giving a lecture in the Institute's Ernst Haekel Saal, where his tall figure droops sinuously before a blackboard. Isherwood depicted him off duty in his "cosy little nest" of a sitting room in the Institute: "In repose, Karl's long handsome face was melancholy. But soon he would be giggling and rolling his eyes. Touching the back of his head with his fingertips, as if patting bobbed curls, he would strike an It-Girl pose."

Giese had appeared in *Anders als die Andern* ("Different from the Others"), a startlingly advanced film about homosexuality made in 1919. This was no underground project, but a mainstream film with a distinguished cast led by Conrad Veidt and featuring the famous cabaret dancer Anita Berber, typecast as a predatory vamp. Veidt plays the role of Paul Körner, a successful concert violinist whose career is threatened because he is homosexual. Two women fall in love with him, one played by Berber (who was herself married to a homosexual), but Paul is more interested in the Berber character's brother, Kurt. Paul is eventually driven to suicide by a blackmailer, and Kurt decides to join him in death but is dissuaded by a doctor, played by Hirschfeld, who entreats him instead to fight for reforms that will prevent further tragedies. As well as appearing in the film, Hirschfeld collaborated with the director, Richard Oswald, on the script and was credited with "medical guidance" on the project. Giese appeared as the young Paul. He was a good physical match for Veidt, but made a somewhat overgrown schoolboy, his knobbly knees and bulging calves bursting out of his sailor-suit. The mixture of melodrama and propaganda, based on a real case, not unnaturally proved controversial, and the film was banned in several places; but it was also regarded as genuinely educational, and a private screening, introduced by Hirschfeld, was held at the Institute for government ministers. The film opened in May 1919 and ran for just over a year before the authorities banned it.[3]

Isherwood preferred Giese to Hirschfeld, but grew to admire the campaigning doctor. The other people he got to know well at the Institute were Günter Maeder and Erwin Hansen. Maeder was an old school-friend of Giese and acted as "second secretary," which involved him taking on "everything which the first secretary did not want to do." One job was to accompany Hirschfeld on nightly walks in the Tiergarten to observe male prostitutes plying their trade. He also gave lectures, helped with consultations and typed the manuscripts Hirschfeld wrote in the small hours, which was the only time the Herr Sanitätsrat could spare from his other duties. Hansen's role at the Institute remains unclear. A former gymnastics instructor in the German army, he

---

3. No complete print of the film now exists, but a fragment with inter-titles in cyrillic script (perhaps a version specially edited for the Soviet Union) survives.

had damaged the nerves of one arm in a fight and retired to run the Adonis-Diele, the homosexual bar which so disappointed Brian Howard. He was a staunch supporter of the German Communist Party, the KPD, and with his good arm occasionally took a whip to Giese, whose masochistic desires Hirschfeld could understand psychologically but remained unwilling to satisfy personally.

For Christmas 1929 Giese gave Isherwood an inscribed copy of *Der Puppenjunge*. This proselytizing novel about the relationship between a young man and a teenage rent-boy was first published in 1926. The story itself is melodramatic and mawkish, but its setting, among Berlin's *Strassenjungen* and the streets and bars in which they worked, is wholly authentic, as the subtitle indicates: *"Die Geschichte einer namenlosen Lieben aus der Friedrichstrasse."*[4] The author's name was given as "Sagitta," which was a pseudonym of John Henry Mackay, a writer well known for his books on philosophy and anarchism. Mackay was born in Greenock in 1864, but spent almost all his life in Germany, where he was brought as a baby by his German mother after the early death of his Scottish father. He wrote novels, poetry, biography and assorted other works of nonfiction. His principal cause, apart from anarchism and egoism (he wrote a biography of the egoist philosopher Max Stirner), was pederasty. His own sexual partners tended to fall into the age range of fourteen to seventeen, and as "Sagitta" he wrote several books defending sexual relationships between men and teenage boys.

The eponymous *Puppenjunge* of Mackay's novel is Gunther Nielsen, a boy of about fifteen or sixteen from a rural village who runs away to Berlin. He is inspired by the example of another village boy who had returned from Berlin transformed into an elegant and well-off sophisticate, full of tales of the easy money to be made in the capital.[5] Quite how this money is to be made is not explained. Arriving in Berlin, Gunther heads for the Kaiser-Galerie, commonly known as "the Passage," a busy arcade running between Unter den Linden and Behrenstrasse. He notices a number of youths hanging around in groups, but has no idea what they are doing, or what the men who eye him up and down want from him. He soon learns and is introduced to prostitution.

The story follows the separate adventures of Gunther and a twenty-year-old named Hermann, who had glimpsed the boy once, then lost him in the crowd. Although Gunther's life on the streets and in the famous bars of the city is described in great detail, it is Hermann's longing for a boy to love that is the real subject of the book. He naïvely believes that he can "rescue" Gunther from his sordid existence, and when the boy disappears Hermann plunges after him into the homosexual underworld in order to discover his whereabouts.

---

4. "A story of nameless love in the Friedrichstrasse," *"namenlosen Lieben"* having the same connotations as Wilde's "love that dare not speak its name."

5. Auden borrowed this scene for his poem "Which of you waking early." The action is transposed to England, but the image is taken directly from Mackay's novel:

> As a boy lately come up from country to town
> Returns for the day to his village in expensive shoes,
> Standing scornful in a ring of old companions
> Amazes them with new expressions, with strange hints . . .

When *Der Puppenjunge* was translated into English in 1985, Isherwood provided the American publisher with a puff: "I have always loved this book dearly—despite and even because of its occasional sentimental absurdities. It gives a picture of the Berlin sexual underworld early in this century which I know, from my own experience, to be authentic." Mackay's novel struck an immediate chord with Isherwood, who was also looking for the ideal young partner, a boy he could sentimentalize as Hermann had Gunther. Having discarded his customary schoolmaster's outfit of tweed jacket and gray flannels for a more proletarian roll-necked sweater and bell-bottoms, he spent much of his time in the bars and clubs. There were a great many to choose from—between sixty-five and eighty, according to various city guides, ranging from rough-and-ready dives such as the Cosy Corner and the Adonis-Diele to the positively luxurious Alexander-Palast in Landsbergstrasse, with its huge ballroom in which couples danced to a Big Band. Some of these bars catered for a particular clientèle, in others all sorts of homosexual types mingled: elderly, carefully dressed and powdered *Tanten* or "aunties"; teenage *Strassenjungen,* dressed to look as young as possible, often in knee-revealing shorts or sailor suits; exquisitely made-up youths with oiled Eton crops (*Bubikopfen*) aping the mannerisms of their favorite film stars; tough, working-class *Metzgers* or butcher-boys, few of whom had ever been on the business side of a meat counter. Although these bars were scattered throughout the city, the best-known ones tended to be in the east, transvestite and lesbian bars being more widespread in the West End.

Most of these venues operated solely at night. During the day, Isherwood got on with his writing, dutifully sitting in local cafés most days, working on *The Memorial* and watching the world go by. As in London, he regularly went to the cinema, and since the German film industry was the most active in Europe, there was plenty to see, including several films that became classics. *Der Blaue Engel, Die Drei-groschenoper, Mädchen in Uniform, Kameradschaft* and *M* all received their premieres while Isherwood was in Berlin. Isherwood could afford this sort of *flâneur* existence because he received a quarterly allowance from his uncle Henry in exchange for letters about life among the *Pupenjungen.* As heir to the estate, it was natural that Isherwood should receive some income from it, but there was also a sexual bond between Isherwood and his uncle, and they enjoyed drunken dinners together swapping anecdotes about their adventures with Gunthers and guardsmen. At the end of such evenings, Isherwood claimed, "I would get a kiss from him which was rather too warm and searching for any nephew, even one's favourite." In February 1930, however, Henry's allowance failed to arrive. Communications between In Den Zelten and Pembroke Gardens failed to produce any money and so on February 19 Isherwood returned to London to sort things out. On arrival he was obliged to spend a day in bed, having contracted a throat infection. Auden diagnosed this malady as "liar's quinsy," but in fact Isherwood was about to tell his mother some home truths.

I sherwood's determination to live what seemed to his mother the feckless life of a literary man, encouraged and materially supported by her irresponsible brother-in-law, had led to Kathleen's transferring her attention to her younger son, about whose future she began to entertain unrealistic hopes. In spite of every indication of immaturity and instability, Richard, she felt, might follow some more secure career than that of a novelist. Her plans had received a severe setback the previous December when Richard's bid to matriculate at St. John's College Oxford had been unsuccessful. He had in fact "failed in all three subjects." This was not altogether surprising, since the latest in a long and unsatisfactory line of "specialists" declared that Richard was undoubtedly backward, showing a "want of dependability and initiative," and was "certainly two years behind"—more like fifteen than seventeen. The specialist believed that Richard's problems were caused by a parathyroid deficiency. The parathyroid gland produces a hormone which controls levels of calcium in the blood, but if insufficient secretions are produced a condition known as tetany can result. In tetany an abnormal increase in nerve and muscle activity leads to spasms in the arms and legs. It is quite possible that Richard suffered from parathyroid deficiency—he certainly suffered from twitches of one sort or another—but it seems more likely that his backwardness and nervousness were of psychological rather than physiological origins. He was nevertheless put on a course of supplements and told to return to the doctor in two months.

It had been suggested that Richard could always re-sit the exams, but he decided that he did not want to undergo more cramming, would never cope with life at Oxford even if he got there, and would far rather abandon any further education in favor of a job. Experience had taught Kathleen that Richard was very easily discouraged and so she attempted to persuade him of the benefits of completing his studies. Richard, however, could be quite as stubborn as his mother, who complained that he "cant or wont see that unless he finishes his education he is of no use." Whatever anyone else thought, Richard had decided that he was no longer a child to be ordered about. He had taken to visiting Tower Hill, where members of the public stood on soap-boxes and made speeches to anyone who would listen. It may have been here that he met a curate based in Shadwell, a depressed area in the East End of London just north of the docks. This meeting revived the idea Richard had entertained the previous year of doing parish work in Stepney, and he became the curate's part-time secretary. The work was irregular, however, and Richard never seemed to know from one day to the next whether he would be needed. Kathleen thought this "sketchy way of going on" highly unsatisfactory and made inquiries about enrolling him at a college in Chelsea where he could acquire typing and bookkeeping skills. When she returned from the college, she found Richard at home. He announced that he had managed to persuade a man with a business just off the Commercial Road to give him a week's trial as a clerk of some kind. She was, she confessed, "Amazed at the enterprise."

Richard's enterprise was even greater than Kathleen imagined. Fearful that his mother was still determined to send him back to the tutor who was cramming him for the Oxford entrance examination, he had in fact invented the job, even providing a name and address for his imaginary employer and producing a pay packet. According to Isherwood, when Kathleen discovered Richard's deception she was furious, exclaiming: "If your father was alive you wouldn't dare behave like this!" "The two of them were victims of a classic situation," Isherwood observed, "forced to become enemies against their will. Christopher must surely have understood this, and known that it was his duty to play the affectionate peacemaker and help them work out a new way of living with each other. But, instead, he sided with Richard against Kathleen." Isherwood recalled that he "revenged himself on the tired tearful woman for all the humiliations he had endured at the hands of others"—though quite what these humiliations were he neglects to explain. He told her "coldly and aggressively" about his sexual exploits in Berlin, and "made his acts of homosexual love sound like acts of defiance, directed against Kathleen." Shortly afterward, he says, he returned to Germany, "having told Kathleen that he could never live in her house again."

Isherwood's reaction seems extreme in the circumstances, but then the circumstances were not quite as Isherwood describes them. The event that precipitated his furious return to Berlin was far more disturbing than an invented job, and it ended up with Richard in the dock at the law courts. He had, as Kathleen delicately put it, "got into difficulties." These difficulties involved a young woman who had accused Richard of exposing himself. She had reported him to the police and he was taken into custody. Kathleen had been telephoned by a representative of Pierron and Morley, solicitors who practiced opposite the West London police court, and she and Christopher went at once to the firm's office, where the gravity of the charge was explained to them. "Disliked Mr Morley very much," she wrote in her diary, "but it was obvious R. needed a solicitor ... We went into Court & bail given. Poor R ... it seems to me simply monstrous that such offences (& in this case unwitting I am sure) could possibly be a case of prison. The magistrate suggested it should be kept as quiet as possible, (as if it was necessary to say that!!)." Bail was granted and after Kathleen had handed over £10 Richard was released.

The effect of keeping up appearances and of hoping that no one would find out what was going on must have placed an enormous strain on Kathleen. The following day, apart from going to consult her GP, she did not venture out of doors. The Monday after, Isherwood went with Richard to the solicitor's office, returning shortly before lunch—"and then," wrote Kathleen, "all my dreams of a happier state of things were dispelled." It seems likely that the two brothers had spent part of the morning discussing what had happened, and that what Richard said of his life had encouraged Isherwood to attack his mother. Isherwood felt entirely justified in blaming Kathleen for everything, partly thanks to his recent introduction to the work of Georg Groddeck, a psychologist who had treated John Layard the previous year. Auden had taken up Groddeck's theories with great enthusiasm, combining them with those of Homer Lane, D. H. Lawrence and Layard himself. He incorporated some of Groddeck's ideas in his poetry and lectured Isherwood on the psychologist's theories about psychosomatic illness. What particularly appealed to Isherwood was Groddeck's diagnosis that (as Isherwood himself somewhat reductively put it) "Everything was sex, and it was all the parent's fault." This was something Isherwood was very happy to tell his mother. Some idea of the force of his assault may be gathered from the broken sentences in which Kathleen reported it: "to inspire such bitter hatred & to have ruined two lives, to have failed every time one's help was needed ... to feel ones death was the only reparation, ... 'even to go to the ends of the earth, would not suffice & would death really kill the bond? ... no words to describe the bitterness of it ... Did not go out till after tea & then with R to the type writing place opposite the polytechnic [in Chelsea]—but what is the good of anything, all one touches seems to bring unhappiness ... to be the wrong thing. & hatred in place of love ..."

The following day Isherwood went to spend two nights in Birmingham with Auden, returning to London in order to accompany Richard to court on March 28.

Kathleen passed an anxious morning, but at 12:30 Isherwood telephoned to tell her that the case had been dismissed "& without any stipulation." The defense seems to have been that Richard had been caught short and been observed urinating, exposing himself unintentionally to the woman who reported him. He had been coached by the solicitor and evidently made a better impression than the young woman, who "looked hardly more than 14 [. . .] and got rather confused." When the magistrate dismissed the case, someone in the court shouted out that Richard had only got off because he was a toff, and that had he been a workingman he would have been found guilty. It is possible that Richard was indeed guilty as charged. He later wrote that the case "arose indirectly through poor M.'s conscientiously meant opposition to me not going back to the tutor," which suggests that he may well have exposed himself in some sort of wild bid to escape this fate. As he wrote in the same letter, "My affairs did seem to have reached rather a desperate pass and I felt that I just couldn't carry on as M. wanted me to."

Any relief Kathleen felt about the verdict was overshadowed by "a great deal of futile conversation all leading nowhere" back at Pembroke Gardens. Looking back across almost half a century, Isherwood felt that Kathleen had not been shocked by his accounts of his sex life, because she did not really believe in homosexuality: "How could there be real sex without women?" As far as he was concerned, Kathleen regarded his homosexual activity with the same lack of seriousness as she did his writing: they were what young men did before coming to their emotional and financial senses and assuming the twin mantles of responsibility and respectability. "She was," he recalled, "obstinate, wilfully stupid and maddeningly pathetic." She was, in other words, a character of his own devising: Mrs. Lindsay in *All the Conspirators.*

Kathleen merely noted in her diary: "We talked most of the afternoon—largely on Sex." Whether or not Richard's sexuality was discussed is not known, but in the wake of the court case this seems likely. Richard too was homosexual, though if Kathleen was not prepared to take seriously the actively pursued sexual life of her mature older son, then she was unlikely to regard any manifestation of Richard's desires as anything other than a passing phase, perhaps only to be expected of a backward teenager.

Isherwood had escaped from Kathleen by abandoning his studies at King's College and going to live abroad, but no such solution offered itself to Richard, who was still a minor. In revolt against the values embraced by his mother, Isherwood found it easy to blame her for all the ills that befell his brother. "He accused her of having tried to wreck his life and of being now determined to wreck Richard's. She had tried to turn Christopher into a Cambridge don, he said, to gratify her selfish daydreams of the kind of son she wanted him to be. And since he had foiled her, by getting himself thrown out of college, she was trying to turn Richard into an Oxford don against his will." The prospect of turning Richard into anything at all was remote at this period. In retrospect Richard felt that Kathleen "must have been deeply if secretly relieved when I had done with schools and tutors and she no longer had to think about my education. True, I wasn't earning anything but it must have been a great deal cheaper having me at home than having to pay other people to feed me." This may have been true up to a point, but Kathleen was desperately anxious about what would become of this son who seemed disinclined to think about any sort of settled or productive future for himself. "It seems a great effort to make up his mind to do anything now," she complained. He seemed "more than ever disinclined to meet anyone he knows," refusing, for example, to take tea with a family friend, with whom he had previously been on very cordial terms. All he appeared to want to do was keep up his scrapbooks and spend most of each day at Tower Hill. "It seems the most hopelessly unsatisfactory life and utterly aimless."

Isherwood invited John Layard to meet Richard, presumably thinking that his brother's physical and psychological health would improve if he were allowed to be true to his own nature. He states in *Christopher and His Kind* that Layard talked to Kathleen "with his usual bluntness," that he "impressed her favourably," and that "she agreed meekly that she had made many mistakes." This does not sound in the least like Kathleen, who was in fact out when Layard came to call and only saw him "for a few minutes" on her return. Her only comment on him in her diary is: "He was a good deal older than I expected & very striking and unusual." Richard continued to see Layard occasionally and on an informal basis for several weeks, usually taking tea with him and the scoutmaster with whom he was living, but his problems seem to have persisted.

The two brothers were brought much closer together by this episode, which marked the beginning of their relationship as adults, "after years of being 'miles apart,'" as Richard put it. "You seemed a semi-remote person from 1926–30," he told Isherwood many years later, "someone of whose aspirations and tastes and views I had little or no knowledge." An example of this innocence was when he suggested to his mother that a girl they had met at a party might make Christopher "a nice bride." Kathleen contemptuously replied: "Don't be a fool, Richard!" To an elder brother, Richard's tantrums as a child had merely seemed tiresome, but this new rebelliousness, though hysterical and unfocused, evidently struck a chord with Isherwood, who began treating Richard more as an equal and an ally. According to Upward, Isherwood "felt that he would like to have put Richard out of his mother's power," that most of his brother's problems would be solved if he were allowed some freedom and independence. The two brothers began taking tea together in Christopher's room rather than joining Kathleen and Nanny downstairs. "Richard was often rash and childish in his dealings with the outside world," Isherwood wrote, "but the eyes with which he observed it were searching and mature and his comments were as candid as Layard's. Christopher realized, with surprise and pleasure, that he had a brother to whom he could tell absolutely anything about himself without shame." One result of this, of course, was that Kathleen, instead of getting her elder son's support, as she had in the past, was subjected to complaints and lectures: "C. very unhappy . . . full of hatred & resentments . . . & it seems hopeless his ever living at home again."[6]

---

6. Isherwood's motive for suppressing the real cause of this decisive argument with his mother was honorable. He was very protective of Richard, who was still living when *Christopher and His Kind* was published, and did not feel that this ancient court case should be made public. Richard had no such qualms: "You mustn't think of omitting my police court case, over the young woman, if it has *any* bearing on the book," he entreated his brother, "or hesitate to say that I was responsible for that sad rift between you and M., I shan't be annoyed."

Uncle Henry had been in touch and, according to Kathleen, "did the heavy uncle in grand style." Isherwood could not recall precisely what Henry had said, but speculated that he may have suggested that his nephew "settle down in London and get a job." Once again Isherwood seems to be blending fact and fiction, and this sounds more like Arthur Langbridge, the family friend who acts in loco parentis to Philip Lindsay in *All the Conspirators,* than it does Henry Isherwood. If Henry had really wanted Isherwood to remain in London then he could have stopped his allowance, but he enjoyed his nephew's tales of *lasterhafte* Berlin far too much to do that. Although he never did pay the quarter's money he owed, he sent £15 won at the casino in Monte Carlo as an advance on the next quarter. Neither this advance nor its source suggests that Henry was attempting to influence the course of his nephew's life into more respectable and profitable channels.

On Thursday, May 8, 1930, Isherwood set off back to Berlin, spending £4 10s. of Henry's winnings on a second-class one-way ticket. Any chance of a last-minute reconciliation between mother and son was foiled by Olive Mangeot, who came to sit with Isherwood while he packed. ("She must be very thick skinned!" Kathleen commented.) It was the fifteenth anniversary of Frank's death, and this must have added to Kathleen's misery: "As [Christopher] does not wish to ever come back to live here again . . . it is the end . . . and feeling as he does about the house & its occupants, it is hopeless to attempt it . . . everything seems to have become more & more difficult & unhappy & he begged that I would refuse to have him again, even if he suggested coming." Having lost her husband, she had now lost one of her sons, and the other was likely to follow, since he seemed to be "proving an apt pupil to C's ideas." She and Nanny set about clearing Christopher's bedroom, arranging his clothes and books in cupboards "so that all his things are all tidy and ready when he wants to take them away."

I sherwood had kept on his room at In Den Zelten, but was now alone there since Fronny, apparently cured of syphilis, had departed for the East where he was hoping to resume his archaeological career. Isherwood had been back in Berlin for a couple of weeks when he met a teenager named Walter Wolff, who had been born in a part of eastern Germany which had been handed over to Poland under the terms of the Treaty of Versailles. Rather than take on Polish citizenship, Walter's family had moved to Berlin, where they lived at Simeonstrasse 4 in Hallesches Tor, a slum area slightly to the north of where Isherwood had stayed with Auden on his first visit to the city. Isherwood described Walter, whom he portrayed in *Goodbye to Berlin* as Otto Nowak, as "rather like Star." Walter certainly had Stella Burford's gamine appeal. He was an attractive youth with a broad grin and fair hair which he brushed back from his forehead, but which tended to fall forward into a cowlick over his left eye. He was around sixteen or seventeen and looked it, in spite of his attempts to appear more mature by adopting for the colder months a trench-coat and a trilby hat worn at a rakish angle. Very much aware of his charms, he was an incorrigible narcissist, a fact which somehow made him seem even more desirable to Isherwood. Like Bubi, he was principally heterosexual, but he enjoyed sex wherever he found it and was easily aroused by Isherwood's physical infatuation with him. Indeed, Isherwood was so excited by Walter that he expected everyone else to share his passion.

As Isherwood admitted, "Although [Walter's] attractiveness was very much a matter of taste—he certainly wasn't conventionally handsome—Christopher always felt proud to be seen with him in public. When they went to their favourite cabaret, which was also a restaurant, Christopher would keep looking away from the stage to see if people at the other tables were admiring [Walter]." Isherwood described Walter as absurdly self-dramatizing, but alluring even in his absurdity, a young man whose sense of humor usually prevented him from taking himself as seriously as he might have wished.

Walter spoke no English, but by now Isherwood's German had improved sufficiently for this to be no longer the barrier it had been with Bubi. Indeed, he now had enough command of the language to supplement his small allowance by offering English lessons. Since Walter soon became a drain on Isherwood's meager resources, any extra money was very welcome, and Isherwood started collecting a number of pupils whom he tutored on an individual basis. A routine developed whereby he would write in the mornings and teach in the afternoons. The necessity of supporting Walter meant that even with this extra income Isherwood was obliged to live frugally, dining in the cheapest restaurants on horsemeat and offal. Although such financial strictures were necessary, they also suited Isherwood's conception of himself as the struggling writer, a role he played all the more convincingly because in Stephen Spender he had a captive and impressionable audience.

Spender was in what turned out to be his final year at Oxford, which he would eventually leave without taking a degree. The previous summer he had followed Auden and Isherwood's lead and spent a holiday in Germany. He recalled walking in Hyde Park one summer evening in 1929, listening to a diatribe from Isherwood against Oxbridge and all it stood for, the middle-class world and its worn-out values. "He spoke of Germany as the country where all the obstructions and complexities of this life were cut through." At the time, Isherwood was basing this observation on (at best) a week in Berlin and a fortnight in the Harz Mountains, but this did not diminish its impact on Spender, who decided there and then to leave Oxford and embark upon a new life devoted to writing. The first step in this journey took him to Hamburg, where he began keeping a journal. It opened with the solemn declaration: "Now I shall begin to live." He stated his resolution "To do absolutely none of the work set for me by my Oxford tutor," a figure who had been very thoroughly usurped by Isherwood. The lessons offered by Isherwood would be in living and writing.

Spender was always inclined to exaggerate his naivety, his indecisiveness and his willing subservience to others, and in the worldly, stubborn and domineering Isherwood he found an ideal counterpart. "We walked round the Serpentine," he recalled of that fateful evening, "and it was as though Christopher were making circles round my world. The weak centre of this was that I did not do what I wanted and I did not ask what I needed." Isherwood—who had managed to abandon not only his studies at Cambridge but also those at King's College—was quite prepared to tell him, and it seems certain that his influence on Spender's university career was as decisive as Upward's influence had been on his own. Above all, Spender wanted to belong to the charmed circle of talented young men who spoke of each other with a mixture of deference and mockery. "Christopher spoke of 'the Gang,' who were also 'the Elect,' " Spender recalled. "I felt a sense of privilege, for however weak I might be, I knew that he did consider me as one of them. With this talk about the Gang, there went a whole vocabulary, strangely Salvationist, and of course not 'serious' except in so far as all such special languages are a real bond between people." At this stage in their relationship Isherwood manipulated his eager disciple like a popular schoolboy dealing with an adoring junior, encouraging him to consider himself part of the Gang but giving frequent reminders of the lowly position he occupied in it. Undeterred by this treatment, Spender declared: "After my work, all I live for is my friends."

Spender had already started sending Isherwood his poems, and now showed him the draft of a novel he had written entitled "Escape." Given such an opportunity, Isherwood could not resist playing tutor, adopting a tone which might easily be mistaken for that of one of those dons he so despised. "You asked me to be candid about it," he wrote in his tiny, precise hand.

Nothing would induce me to be so unless I thought, as I always have and still do, that you have real talent. But, frankly, if you'd asked my advice about sending this book to a publisher's, I should have said: Don't.

When I read parts of it—the Swiss scene, the visit to the cousin's, the walking tour—they seemed to be good. And they are good. The last section is, I think, complete trash. I mean the part following Charles's father's death.

But what I really complain of is the book as a whole. It simply hasn't come off. It is so violent, so hectic, so queer, so utterly seen from within—that at the end of it one feels that Charles is a madman, with a madman's indifference to reality and a madman's terrific but shallow and quite meaningless passions. You are not a madman. The failure of Charles as a character is therefore not a failure in your sanity but in your art. Your other characters are nearly all convincing. Donald, Ainger and Marston are all brilliantly conveyed, I think. Michael and Helen are scarcely less good. There is the stuff here, all right; but you've tortured it into this strange crude frame. I can suggest no alterations. If Cape's don't like it—and if they do, I think the loss will be yours—I should put the M.S. on one side for a year. Then your increased sophistication, your wider aesthetic experience and your sense of humour will help you to reconstruct it. Write something else meanwhile. Something which you stand absolutely outside of. Yes, even if it's imitative, boring, trivial. You must develop consciousness in your art. At present there is none. You are right down in the scrum with your characters, not up in the grandstand, as you ought to be. You must see round things more. I think, as a matter of fact, that most of the novel, as subject-matter, is too near to you. You haven't digested it. You describe scenes but you are unable to suggest to the reader what their significance is. The earliest part of the book is by far the most digested, the most consciously 'told' and 'seen'. This is no mere accident. You are farthest away from it.

I'm afraid you may not take this quite in the spirit in which it was written. Never mind. I'd rather, for once, be honest than pleasant. Perhaps in time you'll come to agree with what I've said. When I was two years older than you are, a woman whom I took as my literary judge [i.e. E. C. Mayne] told me that the novel I'd just been three years writing was complete tripe. I shot neither her nor myself, and have lived to have tea with her many times since.

Thank you so much for my time at Oxford. This letter is the best return I can make for your kindness. Don't just ignore it or decide that I have some sinister motive in writing it. There really is none.

> My best respects—
> Christopher.

Fortunately, Spender took this lecture in good part and replied that he was not in the least offended and would not allow Cape to publish the book even if they wanted to.

Quite apart from showing Isherwood's character, and illustrating his relationship with Spender, the letter also gives an insight into Isherwood's approach to his own writing: the need to "develop consciousness" as a writer, to stand aloof from one's characters, looking at them and their actions from the outside and seeing things in the round, with objectivity. The writer needs to allow his raw material to mature before he uses it, and he must ensure that it is used to some purpose, not merely as a record. Facts and observations need to be shaped and ordered to turn them into art. The trick, of course, was to make all this seem artless.

In July, Isherwood received a visit from W. H. Auden, who was now working at a private school in Scotland. He brought with him a proof copy of his first commercially published volume of *Poems,* which (like the 1928 pamphlet) was dedicated "TO CHRISTOPHER ISHERWOOD." Auden inscribed it:

> *Gewidmet Christophe, is Das Buch*
> *Obwhol Der Ciddy ist gestorben:*
> *Wir beide kommen endlich durch*
> *Obwohl Die Puppens sind verdorben.*
> Wystan Auden
> Berlin Juli 11th, 1930

"This book is dedicated to Christopher although Ciddy is dead: We'll both make it in the end, although the rent boys are morally ruined." The printed dedication was less explicit, but hardly less sly. Ostensibly it was a plea to honor the living rather than the dead, but the sexual connotations were clear:

> *Let us honour if we can*
> *The vertical man*
> *Though we value none*
> *But the horizontal one.*

Auden's visit was followed toward the end of August by one from Edward Upward, whom Isherwood conducted round the sights of Berlin, including a "buggers' ball" and the Hirschfeld institute, where Upward was propositioned by Karl Giese. On his return to England, Upward was summoned to Pembroke Gardens to give Kathleen an account of her dear Christopher's life in Berlin. The only communication she had received since Isherwood's return to Germany had been a picture postcard sent from Hamburg in August, although Isherwood was now in regular correspondence with Richard. She can hardly have been very reassured by Upward's account. "I went to see Mater yesterday," he reported back to Isherwood, "and sat in your transmogrified room. I have betrayed everything, but very diplomatically. My only blunder was letting her know that you were paying for Walter. I was properly trapped. And I'm far from sure that I managed to convince her that buggery isn't unnatural. However I insisted that you were more terrific than ever in England."

Upward's visit undoubtedly sharpened Isherwood's awareness of what was going on in the city outside the *Nachtlokale*. To the heterosexual Upward, who was becoming increasingly drawn to communism, Berlin meant Politics rather than Boys. Unlike Isherwood, he did not have an allowance and was obliged to take work wherever he could find it. The principal attraction of teaching in private schools was that it provided him with long holidays, during which he could get down to some concentrated writing. Several of the schools that had employed him seemed alarmingly reminiscent of Mortmere's Frisbald College, and while these provided him with ample copy for both his fiction and his letters to Isherwood, Upward would have been only too happy to give up schoolmastering had he been able to afford it. He reluctantly took a job at Scarborough, consoling himself that he should "at least be able to poison a few of the boys against Christ and their country." It was during this period that he wrote one of his finest short stories, "Sunday," in which he successfully combined the visionary qualities of his Mortmere writings with left-wing politics. It takes the form of a brief interior monologue which ends with the narrator deciding to commit himself to Marxism by attending a political meeting. Upward himself was not yet ready to take this step, and it would be another year before he even made real contact with the British Communist Party. Like "The Colleagues," a story he had written the previous year, "Sunday" is a statement of intent, which ends: "It will take time. But it is the only hope. He will at least have made a start." This was rather more than Isherwood had done, even though he was living in the most politically volatile city in Europe.

Berlin was the very heart of the Weimar Republic, which had been founded in 1919 in the wake of Germany's disastrous defeat in the First World War. The country had been declared a republic even before the Armistice had been signed, and Kaiser Wilhelm II had been forced to abdicate on November 9, 1918. Any hope that this change of constitution would herald a more just world was rapidly dashed by the punitive terms of the Treaty of Versailles, terms which led to economic chaos, political unrest and, eventually, the rise of Nazism. It was wholly appropriate that the Kaiser had been obliged to bow to pressure from Berlin, a city he had always mistrusted because of its revolutionary tendencies, not only in politics (it had given birth to a socialist workers' party as early as 1875) but also in culture. The capital of Prussia, a state associated in the popular imagination with an aristocratic and military conservatism, Berlin was also a center of dissidence, where the left-wing working class and the intellectual avant-garde challenged the social status quo.

The economic depression caused by the war and exacerbated by the peace further undermined the stability of the city. By 1923 inflation was completely out of control, with the mark becoming impossible any longer to pin against the dollar. The pre-war exchange rate had been 4.1 marks to the U.S. dollar; by November 1923 it stood (if that is the word) at 4,200,000,000,000,000 marks to the dollar. Foreign loans led to a little more stability the following year, and in 1925 Paul von Beneckendorff und von

Hindenburg, the seventy-eight-year-old retired general who had been responsible for Germany's military strategy in the war, was persuaded to stand for election and became the new Reichspräsident. Hindenburg had no political experience, but was someone the country could respect—not so much the father of his people, perhaps, as the grandfather. Furthermore, he was an old-fashioned conservative, a man who exuded Junker authority, a quality wholeheartedly welcomed by those who feared the rise of the Left. As a former general, and one who would have preferred to fight on rather than surrender in 1918, he was likely to approve of his country's plans for rearmament.

Hitler took full advantage of the economic crisis in Germany, finding support among the growing numbers of the unemployed and others disillusioned with their leaders. The Nazi Party was officially banned in Berlin in 1927, but under the leadership of the defiant, rabble-rousing Joseph Goebbels, whom Hitler had appointed the city's *Gauleiter,* it simply went underground, regrouping under the guise of various sporting clubs and other associations. The Nazis could offer those without occupation or hope a sense of belonging and purpose, and while the Party did not have a great deal of success at elections during this period, its membership grew rapidly, from 17,000 in 1926 to around a million by the autumn of 1930. To the strains of *"Die Fahne hoch,"* an anthem with words composed by Horst Wessel, a local leader of the Sturm-Abteilung, or SA, who had been elevated to the status of "martyr" after being shot dead in a brawl with a fellow pimp, brown-shirted members of Hitler's stormtroopers marched about the streets, spoiling for a fight and adding to the city's growing atmosphere of menace. Further attempts to stop this sort of behavior by banning Nazi badges and uniforms proved wholly ineffective. In the September elections the Nazis won a staggering 107 seats in the Reichstag, putting them in second place after the Social Democrats.

At Cambridge, Isherwood and Upward were too deeply involved in their own world to take much notice of what was going on outside it. "We weren't political and never read newspapers," Upward remembered. "We thought all politicians were scoundrels and self seekers." Any political convictions they had manifested themselves negatively, in reaction to the complacent conservatism of their parents. "My father was *Daily Mail* and *The Times,*" Upward recalled, "and my mother too was definitely Conservative, though some of her ideas were not Conservative." The same might be said of Kathleen Isherwood, though Isherwood persisted in regarding her as a case study in nostalgic, reactionary Toryism, a patronizing and unthinking representative of an outmoded ruling class. Upward, however, had gone beyond personal animus and was developing into a mature, and somewhat austere, political thinker. What he saw on the streets of Berlin, with the Nazis gaining in power and popularity, increased his sense that communism was "the best hope of freeing the world from conflict." As Isherwood put it, "Here was the seething brew of history in the making—a brew which would test the truth of all the political theories, just as actual cooking tests the cookery books. The Berlin brew seethed with unemployment, malnutrition, stock market panic, hatred of the Versailles Treaty and other potent ingredients."

This brew meant rather different things to the two young men. Although, when he witnessed communists and Nazis brawling on the pavements, Isherwood was clear which side he was on, he was perhaps more excited than alarmed by such manifestations of political instability. He was, after all, a writer, and there was no doubt that life in Berlin provided him with very good copy. On the first page of the fictionalized "Berlin Diary" he wrote about the autumn of 1930, he stated: "I am a camera with its shutter open, quite passive, recording, not thinking."[7] Although exaggerated for literary effect, this famous sentence not only described his working methods as a writer quite accurately but also made clear his policy of non-involvement. His *real* diary, the one he wrote almost daily but subsequently destroyed, would have shown that he was in fact very much involved in Berlin life, but he saw his public role as a writer to provide an accurate record of a city and a society perched on the edge of an abyss. Here indeed was history in the making, not the dead history that dulled his senses at Cambridge, nor the enveloping quilt of the Past in which his mother lay cocooned in Kensington, but people and events that were changing the world.

Isherwood's political allegiances in 1930 were less a reaction to the Nazis than the result of his own experience among working-class Berliners, and the influence of Upward as his "political mentor." He was particularly reassured by Upward's reply to his inquiry about communism and homosexuality. "As far as I know Lenin said nothing about buggery," Upward wrote. "Perhaps there wasn't any in Russia." This sounds suspiciously Party line, but Upward himself certainly didn't regard homosexuality as a decadent bourgeois vice. "The position of buggery in a communist state will depend largely on the number of buggers who are communists," he wrote, evidently hoping for a new recruit. "In any case persecution of buggers is anti-Leninist." Isherwood later admitted that he "found no difficulty in responding to Communism romantically, as a brotherhood of man," but he knew that he would never share Upward's growing commitment. "He began to regard Edward as a conventionally pious Catholic might regard a friend who had made up his mind to become a priest."

The romance of communism was increased for Isherwood when, at the beginning of October, he moved in with Walter Wolff's family in Simeonstrasse, where they had a cramped flat on the top floor of a tenement building. It had only one small bedroom, which Walter shared with his elder brother. The rest of the family slept in the living room in two double beds, jammed in with chairs and the table at which they ate their meals. In one bed Walter's father contentedly snored away the nights after a hard day's work with a furniture removals firm; the other was shared by Walter's mother and his younger sister, a child of twelve. Grateful for the small rent her son's friend would bring into the house, Frau Wolff volunteered once more to share her husband's bed. Walter's twenty-year-old brother was obliged to surrender his single bed to Isherwood and sleep with his little sister. Since, as Frau Wolff was well aware, Walter and Isherwood were involved in a sexual relationship, this arrangement was espe-

---

7. Upward had brought Isherwood's camera with him to Berlin, and this may well have prompted the image. It is also worth noting that one of Isherwood and Upward's literary cult figures, Katherine Mansfield, used a similar image when describing the process of writing. "I have not been able to think that I should not have made such observations as I have made of people, however cruel they may seem," she said in a magazine interview in 1924. "After all, I did observe those things and I had to set them down. I've been a camera. But that's just the point. I've been a selective camera, and it has been my attitude that has determined the selection."

cially hard on her other son, who unsurprisingly rejected the friendly overtures of this unwelcome English cuckoo in the tiny family nest.

"Slumming," as Isherwood acknowledged, "seemed a thrilling adventure," and the crowded and unsanitary conditions of the Simeonstrasse flat, with its oppressively hot kitchen stove at which Frau Wolff cooked lung hash, its single lavatory down a flight of stairs and shared with three other households, and only a kitchen sink to wash in, undoubtedly provided him with an *echt* working-class Berlin experience. The flat had in fact been condemned by the authorities, and its atmosphere can have done little for the health of Frau Wolff, who was suffering from tuberculosis. She nevertheless appeared cheerful and evidently considered it an honor that an English gentleman should be living under her leaking roof. Isherwood got on well with all the family except Walter's dour brother, but to Kathleen the setup sounded very unsatisfactory: "A family of five living in three rooms & the Mother threatened with consumption which makes me feel <u>very</u> anxious not only that but the whole arrangement seems unhealthy & how can he possibly write in such an atmosphere . . . and he pays them 25/- a week."

Isherwood now entered what Spender, who visited Berlin that autumn, described as his "most heroic period of poverty." He was not only living in a slum, but was also "sacrificing everything to buying new suits for Walter." Isherwood felt that Spender, who was recalling this period many years later, was being satirical, but his admiring, impressionable friend was entirely serious. "In the early stages of our friendship," Spender recalled, "I was drawn to him by the adventurousness of his life. His renunciation of England, his poverty, his friendship, his independence, his work, all struck me as heroic." This was, of course, precisely what Isherwood intended.

Spender had announced that he would be visiting Berlin "to see a girl whom I hope perhaps to marry," and suggested that Isherwood might like to meet her. Isherwood replied that he would be "honoured and interested to meet the girl," but would be unlikely to do so immediately. "The truth is, I'm very apathetic here," he wrote. "I let myself be carried along on a current of boys, cinemas, elopements to the country, interviews with police, writing my novel." As so often when writing to friends in England, Isherwood was playing at being the world-weary Englishman abroad, spicing this with Mortmerish hints about the authorities in order to keep his audience hooked. It is possible, given his involvement with the *Pupenjungen,* that he did have encounters with the police, but if so they were insufficiently serious or memorable for him to recall them in *Christopher and His Kind.* "It is all so pleasant, and I have utterly lost any sense of strangeness in being abroad," Isherwood assured his correspondent. "I feel at home. I even don't particularly care when I see England again. I only wish sometimes that certain people were out here. And when I read in my diary about my life at home and all the squabbling and fury and silliness, it's like people on the moon." Spender fell for this line, recalling: "I corresponded with him in the spirit of writing letters to a Polar explorer. I thought of him in the centre of the northern European plain, gripped in icy cold, across the stormy and black channel. His letters were of a besieged person, facing creditors, the elements, and the breakdown of a civilization, surrounded by a little loyal crew." Isherwood not only wanted to impress Spender but to flatter him, and it is clear that the recipient of this letter should imagine himself among the "certain people" whose presence would gladden the writer.

In the event, it seems Isherwood did not meet Spender's young woman until Spender himself arrived in Berlin that autumn. Gisa Soleweitschick had been sixteen years old when Spender met her while on a skiing holiday in Switzerland in 1928. The daughter of a Lithuanian banker, she had spent her early childhood in Moscow, but when the Revolution started in 1917 the family had been forced to leave Russia at one hour's notice, abandoning all their possessions. They joined Gisa's grandparents back in Lithuania, where her father was made Director of the National Lithuanian Bank, a job which allowed him quickly to recoup his losses. He decided to settle his family in Berlin, visiting them whenever he could, which was not often. His wife, who had been a successful portrait painter, admired by Monet whom she had got to know in Paris, gave up her work in order to look after her daughter and two older sons. They arrived in Berlin when inflation was rampant and when Lithuanian currency could buy a great deal, and they lived in a large, handsome apartment in Konstanzerstrasse in the fashionable area of Wilmersdorf. Gisa's elder brother was a lawyer, the younger a talented jazz musician who was making a career for himself with Ufa (Universal Film AG), Germany's largest motion-picture company.

Spender's suggestion that he might marry Gisa can hardly have been entirely serious. In the same letter in which he had announced this intention, he also told Isherwood that although he had "stopped being in love" with a fellow undergraduate who was the subject of several poems, "I still catch my breath when he comes into the room." By the time he reached Berlin, any further idea about marrying Gisa seemed to have been dropped. In any case, Gisa was entirely uninterested in young men at this time, partly because she had been obliged to fend off the advances of her younger brother's bumptious Ufa friends.

I sherwood's romantic slumming in Hallesches Tor came to an abrupt end after a month or so, when Frau Wolff had to be removed to a sanatorium. Isherwood was quite relieved to leave the flat, since he and Walter were enduring one of their periodic fallings-out. He moved a few streets east to the equally run-down district of Kottbuser Tor, where he took a room at Admiralstrasse 38. Although the area was seedy, Admiralstrasse ran from the chaotic Kottbusser Platz, a junction of several streets dominated by the station of the overhead railway, down to the Admiral Brücke, a bridge crossing a canal lined by trees and more prosperous-looking dwellings. A possible legacy of Simeonstrasse was that Isherwood was no sooner settled in than he suffered an outbreak of carbuncles on his back, stomach and legs. He was laid up for several weeks, attended by a doctor who Kathleen thought sounded incompetent. While he was convalescing, Kathleen arranged for his bank to extend his credit for another six months, and this meant that in December he was able to move to Schöneberg, a rather better area of the city, taking a room at Nollendorfstrasse 17 as a tenant of Frl. Meta Thurau.

Nollendorfstrasse was the right side of the railway tracks and, although dowdy, was distinctly middle-class and within easy reach of the fashionable shops in the West End. With its once grand houses now subdivided into flats, its crumbling cornices caked in soot, its plaster mermaids barely able to support its balconies, and its grubby windows rattled by the trains of the elevated railway in Nollendorf-Platz, it was an area that had seen better times. The same might be said of Isherwood's new

landlady, who seemed to embody the decline suffered by the city in the wake of the
First World War. Obliged to rent out rooms to a variety of financially unreliable and
morally dubious tenants, Frl. Thurau took a philosophical view of life, and seemed
resigned to sleeping on a divan in the living room, while barmen, streetwalkers and
writers entertained their guests in the bedrooms. Her apartment occupied the top two
floors of the five-story building, built around 1905, and was reached up a wide staircase cast into perpetual gloom by the stained-glass windows on the landings. The
largest central rooms retained something of their former elegance with high, elaborately molded and paneled ceilings, some of them painted with birds, swags and
gamboling putti. They each had several sets of double doors leading to the smaller
rooms off them and were dominated by huge "gorgeously coloured" ceramic stoves.
Thurau was in her mid-fifties. Heavy-bosomed, with a sharp nose and twinkling eyes,
she reminded Isherwood of Beatrix Potter's hedgehog-laundress Mrs. Tiggy-Winkle
as she went about her daily business of tidying up the flat. She evidently regarded
Isherwood as a cut above her usual run of lodgers and she treated him with great indulgence, addressing him as "Herr Issyvoo," a nickname that came to represent his
Berlin persona.

SEVEN

BY CHRISTMAS 1930 ISHERWOOD HAD FINISHED A THIRD DRAFT OF *The Memorial*. He sent the manuscript back to London with Auden, who had been in Berlin on a brief visit. Auden and Spender, who was arranging for the manuscript to be typed and sent to Jonathan Cape, visited Kathleen to give her a report on Isherwood's life in Berlin, now that he appeared to have settled permanently in the city. Spender made a favorable impression on Kathleen, partly because he told her that he thought *The Memorial* a masterpiece. She described him as "an attractive young man," but evidently thought his poetically unkempt hair needed some attention. Thereafter, whenever Richard was looking particularly disheveled, Kathleen would say to him: "Richard darling, I wish you'd tidy your hair, it looks *so* Stephenish." A copy of the novel was given to Upward, who evidently thought Isherwood's revisions had been successful. "I have read the Memorial through twice and shall have to read it through at least another three times before I know exactly how terrific it is," he pronounced. "All delays, destructions, boys, pangs, debauches, are now totally justified." With some exaggeration he declared that the novel "would survive through sheer amazement of copy—even if the architecture weren't, as it is, greater than all [Henry] James. All that remains is to rewrite War and Peace. What makes your book so terrific is that there's no whiff of immature experiment about it. It's as startling as the Gospel might have been to Emperor Constantine. No other work will be accepted after the Bolshevism of England."

Having sorted out Isherwood's literary affairs in London, Stephen Spender joined the great author in Berlin at the beginning of 1931, taking a room at the Pension Gramatke in Motzstrasse, on the corner of Viktoria-Luise-Platz. This was a few minutes' walk away from Nollendorfstrasse, and the two young writers spent a great deal of time in each other's company. Isherwood was also introduced to Spender's younger brother, Humphrey. Born a year after Stephen, Humphrey was a student at the Architectural Association in London. One day, he had walked into the kitchen of the family house "looking particularly pale, anxious and depressed" and been told by Stephen: "I know what's wrong with you, Humphrey: you need a trip to Berlin." Humphrey was well aware of the sexual implications of this remark, but he was also anxious to visit Berlin to look at the modern architecture for which the city had become famous, notably Fritz Hoeger's imposing brick Kirche am Hohen-zollernplatz and Erich Mendelsohn's rhythmical concrete Shellhaus. He undertook several architectural tours of Berlin and Potsdam in Isherwood's company and soon began to consider himself a close friend. "He was liable to laugh at and be amused by and interested in exactly the same kind of dotty situations that I was," Humphrey recalled. "The image I have of him, which is aural as well as visual, is of him observing things in his dry voice: sardonic, objective, disinterested." Isherwood, six years Humphrey's senior, found him "a charming, easygoing, friendly young man." He soon learned that Humphrey spoke far better German than he (or indeed Stephen) did and was both impressed and shamed when Humphrey asked him why he never used the subjunctive mood. Since Isherwood had learned German with the principal intention of chatting up boys, the subjunctive had not seemed essential, but he now set to learn it with a will.

Although studying to be an architect, Humphrey was also very interested in photography. He had learned a great deal at an early age while working as a "darkroom slave" to his eldest brother, Michael, a scientist with a specialized interest in photographing railways. Both he and Stephen owned sophisticated cameras and had become particularly keen on photographing people; Stephen had even thought of taking lessons in portrait photography while in Berlin, but complained that his room was too dark to use as a studio. He began using his camera as a sort of visual diary, recording his life and that of his friends, and Humphrey followed suit.

Isherwood, meanwhile, with *The Memorial* safely out of the way, was devoting more of his time to his own diary, in which he recorded daily life in Berlin and the activities of people he met there. These diaries, he hoped, would provide the raw material for an epic novel he was planning to write. He once said that one of the things he wanted to convey in his books was "the experience of meeting certain kinds of people, the experience of the encounter," and his greatest strength as a writer would always lie in the creation of characters who come instantly alive off the page. As *The Memorial* amply demonstrated, he was quite capable of dealing with a complicated narrative structure, and several of his books have ingenious and compelling plots; but he would make his name as a writer whose characters seemed to have a vitality that carried them beyond the final pages of a novel. Although most of these characters were drawn from life, they were also his own creations. "You cut corners, you invent, you simplify," he explained; "you heighten certain lights and deepen certain shadows, as you might in a portrait." Stephen Spender recalled that at Nollendorfstrasse Isherwood was "surrounded by the models for his creations, like one of those portraits of a writer by a bad painter, in which the writer is depicted meditating in his chair whilst the characters of his novels radiate round him under a glowing cloud of dirty varnish, not unlike the mote-laden lighting of Fräulein Thurau's apartment." Frl. Thurau herself was so much like a caricature of the *gemütlich* Berlin landlady that she became the least exaggerated of the portraits in the books Isherwood wrote about the city, but a visitor to the apartment might also bump into the originals of Fritz Wendel, Mr. Norris and Sally Bowles.

Fritz Wendel, whom Isherwood depicted as a romantic heterosexual philanderer, was based on a young Hungarian businessman known as Franz von Ullmann, who worked for a publishing company. Like Fritz, he spent a great deal of time boasting about his conquests, although in Ullmann's case the quarry was male. "He has a kind but lascivious & self-indulgent heart and knows six languages none of which he can speak with even approximate correctness," Spender wrote. "He is fond of tawny lads; is a Jew; is a baron; is not really called von Ullmann at all, but I forget what; wears a necklace; & is selfish, gay & friendly." For his part, Isherwood always found Ullmann a tonic: "such a bottle of Eno's Salts—always on the fizz."

It was at Ullmann's apartment that Isherwood and Spender first met a young Englishwoman named Jean Ross, who achieved unwelcome immortality in the character of Sally Bowles. An aspiring actress, Ross had come to Berlin with a girlfriend in search of work. She had not had much success, but decided to stay on in the city even though she spoke no German and had no obvious means of support. She found work in cabaret, chiefly because there was a demand for people who could sing in English. Singing in tune mattered less, which was just as well. Ross always claimed that Isherwood "grossly underrated" her singing abilities, but her family agreed that this was one aspect of Sally Bowles that Isherwood got absolutely right. In the world of cabaret, putting across a song was more important than strict musicality. Gravel-voiced Claire Waldoff was hugely popular, while Marlene Dietrich, who tended to slip between octaves in the trickier parts of Friedrich Holländer's songs, was nevertheless plucked from a revue called *Zwei Kravatten* to achieve worldwide fame as the cabaret singer Lola Lola in *Der Blaue Engel*. Like Dietrich's, Ross's singing voice was fashionably low-pitched, though Isherwood thought that this was less natural than a kind of general impersonation of the sort of voice people favored at the time. No one seems to knows which clubs Ross worked in, but Sally Bowles sings in the Lady Windermere, which Isherwood located "just off the Tauntzienstrasse," a short walk from Nollendorfstrasse. This was in fact an area dominated by lesbian bars, although cabaret venues had sprung up all over the city.

According to Spender, at that first meeting in Ullmann's apartment Ross dominated the conversation, describing men with whom she had slept. Spender was rather shocked and, playing up to this, Ross delved into her handbag and brought out a diaphragm, which she waved in the faces of the startled young men. When they left, Isherwood asked Spender what he had made of Jean. "I think she's absolutely repulsive," he replied priggishly. Isherwood disagreed. "I think she's really a little girl," he said. "Next time I see her I'm going to throw a cushion at her."

Many of the more outrageous anecdotes Isherwood used in his portrait of Sally Bowles were taken from Ross's unusual life. Born in Alexandria in 1911, she was the daughter of a cotton classifier at the Bank of Egypt, who had originally gone to Egypt from his native Liverpool as an employee of Carvers, an import-export firm. He became reasonably wealthy, consolidating his finances and his standing in the world by marrying well into what his daughter called "yeoman stock." In fact, Jean's mother was highly cultivated and would have studied architecture had she not met her future husband. Jean was the eldest of four children. In the early 1920s, she was sent to an expensive and superior girls' boarding-school near Leatherhead, which she loathed. Her parents remained in Egypt and the children traveled by boat to and from England, which gave them early a sense of independence.

Jean was academically bright, and by the time she was sixteen she had done all the coursework required for the Sixth Form. She was told that she would nevertheless have to remain at the hated school for a final year and occupy her time doing the same work all over again. In order to get herself expelled, she told another pupil that she was pregnant. This got back to the headmistress, who called Jean in to her study to ask whether this terrible confession was true. Jean remembered standing by the fireplace, feeling the cold marble under her hand while she debated "for the longest thirty seconds of my life" whether to tell the truth, which would have condemned her to remaining at the school, or lie and suffer the consequences. She assured the headmistress that she was pregnant and was instantly banished to the sanatorium so that she could not "contaminate" other pupils. An aunt was summoned from Cheshire to take her away, and to this woman, who asked, "Are you still like the Virgin Mary?," Jean confessed that she had invented the pregnancy. She was summarily expelled and dispatched by her embarrassed parents to a Swiss finishing school.

When Jean's maternal grandfather died, he left money in trust for the "maintenance and education" of his grandchildren, and this gave her a small allowance— "enough to get by on," though she often complained about the trustees. She went to the Royal Academy of Dramatic Arts for a year, but became very disillusioned by the quality of the teaching there. She nevertheless won the prize for French acting, which entitled her to take the lead role in a play of her choice. She chose Racine's *Phèdre*, scandalizing her teacher, who said that no one could play the part without experience of life—and in any case, Jean was "destined to be a comedienne." Following this advice, she went to audition for a role in *Why Sailors Leave Home,* a "quota quickie" comedy, directed by the erstwhile husband of the popular Lancashire singer Gracie Fields. The flimsy plot hung upon the supposedly hilarious notion of a Cockney put in charge of a sheikh's harem. Jean, who had a dark complexion and was able to speak some Arabic, appeared as a slave girl, improvising lines which fortunately nobody understood. (She claimed that when the film reached Alexandria, the family servants reported back to their appalled employers the things Miss Jean had been saying on screen at the local cinema.) It was at this point that she heard a rumor that there was work for young actresses in Germany, and so came to Berlin. As well as singing, she modeled clothes for fashion magazines and continued to pursue a career as an actress, appearing as Anitra in Max Reinhardt's production of *Peer Gynt.* At one period she shared lodgings with a German morphine addict named Erika, who was the mistress of Richard Crossman, the future cabinet minister. Since Crossman spoke no German and Erika spoke no English, Jean was obliged to translate Crossman's letters, and would later say that after this she could never take him seriously as a politician.

Isherwood was fascinated by these stories and cultivated his acquaintance with this remarkable young woman, part of whose attraction was that she appeared to represent "the whole idea of militant bohemia." This, as far as Isherwood was concerned, made them soul-mates. Their relationship had a great deal of "the prep-school atmosphere" about it, and if Ross was not precisely one of the boys, her independence and her air of the would-be *demi-mondaine* made her a forceful, though unthreatening, equal. Isherwood said of Sally Bowles that she "is not an obvious tart. She is a little girl who has listened to what the grown-ups had said about tarts, and who was trying to copy those things." The same might have been said of Ross. Part of Isherwood and Ross's mutual attraction was that each of them was playing a role—that of promising young novelist and promising young actress, sexually sophisticated free spirits in wicked Berlin—and each of them needed an audience. In a curious way they believed in each other.

Sally Bowles's first name was probably suggested by a Berlin acquaintance of Isherwood's named Sally Coole, who was the model for the tough journalist Helen Pratt in *Mr Norris Changes Trains*.[1] The surname was borrowed from the twenty-year-old American composer Paul Bowles, who had come to Berlin to study with Aaron Copland. Bowles carried with him letters of introduction to both Isherwood and Spender, and for a period the three men, along with Copland and sometimes Jean Ross, met every day at 1:30 p.m. for lunch at the Café des Westens on Kurfürstendamm, where that rather more regretful visitor to Berlin, Rupert Brooke, wrote his famously nostalgic poem "The Old Vicarage, Grantchester." Bowles much preferred Isherwood to Spender, finding the latter rather too self-consciously a poet. "I soon found that Isherwood with Spender was a very different person from Isherwood by himself," Bowles recalled. "Together they were overwhelmingly British, two members of a secret society constantly making references to esoteric data not available to outsiders [. . .] At all our meetings I felt that I was being treated with good-humoured condescension. They accepted Aaron, but they did not accept me because they considered me too young and inexperienced or perhaps merely uninteresting." Isherwood did in fact find Bowles interesting: not for his music, an art Isherwood never much appreciated, but for his youthful good looks, which was something he always did.

Another person who provided Isherwood with plenty to write about in his diary was Gerald Hamilton, the man he was to immortalize as Mr. Arthur Norris.[2] It is not known precisely how Isherwood and Hamilton got to know each other during the winter of 1930–31. Sometimes Hamilton said that he was a tenant of Frl. Thurau, at other times he said that he was merely a frequent visitor to the apartment. It seems almost certain, however, that at this period he was living in flat in Derfflingerstrasse, just to the east of Lützow-Platz. On another occasion Hamilton claimed that he first met Isherwood at the Berlin lodgings of Aleister Crowley, but elsewhere he stated that they were already friends when they decided to call on the Great Beast, having visited a gallery where some of his pictures were on show. Hamilton was Crowley's lodger for about six months, and this may have included Christmas 1931, when he

---

1. Isherwood never knew whether Coole read the book or recognized herself in it. He admitted that he had portrayed her in a "revolting aspect" but that he continued to have "the warmest feelings towards her and intended no spite."
2. For no discernible reason, Gerald Hamilton's fictional alter ego was given the name of the art master at Repton.

and Isherwood attended Crowley's festive party. Jean Ross recalled one occasion when a visit she and Isherwood were paying Crowley was interrupted by bailiffs who started removing the furniture, a scene Isherwood appropriated for *Mr Norris Changes Trains.*

Hamilton was working in Berlin as a sales representative for *The Times,* a job that he would eventually lose because of his involvement in left-wing politics. Throughout his long and disgraceful life he was devoted to many causes, but the principal one always remained himself. He was incapable of recognizing, let alone telling, the truth, and any account of his life must be approached with caution. He eventually wrote three autobiographies, none of which can be relied upon. He claimed to be the grandson of Lord Ernest Hamilton, a "brother of the seventh Marquess and first Duke of Abercorn," but both name and lineage were assumed. He was in fact the son of Francis Souter, a middle-class Scottish businessman, who apparently bought a partnership in Holliday, Wise & Co., a leading firm of dealers in china. According to Hamilton, his forebears had lived in Northern Ireland since the seventeenth century on an estate given to them by James I. In fact, Mr. Souter's official address was not "The White House, County Tyrone," but Egerton Crescent, London SW. He and his wife, who Hamilton claimed was a niece of Lord Galway, were living in Shanghai when Gerald was born on November 1, 1890. Mrs. Souter died within a year of her only child's birth, and Gerald liked to boast that he was "suckled on Chinese breasts." He was sent back to England in the charge of two Chinese amahs to live with his maternal grandparents, and began his education at Lambrook, a prep school near Bracknell in Berkshire. "I remember my parents' surprise when they received my first report," Hamilton wrote in one of his autobiographies (apparently forgetting that by this time his mother was supposed to have died some years earlier), "and the headmaster's comments were limited to the words: 'Shows unusual intelligence for his age, but unfortunately is such a greedy boy.' " In January 1905 he started at Rugby, where he was entered on the school register as Gerald Frank Hamilton Souter. It was later noted: "There is (and this is quite unusual in the Register) no record of any subsequent career."

Unusual, perhaps, but not altogether surprising, for little in what Hamilton described with ironic understatement as "this interval of mild adventure called life" would redound to the credit of his old school. When he left Rugby in January 1908, his father offered him the choice between going to university and traveling round the world. Naturally, Hamilton took the latter option, and was to spend much of his life wandering the globe, either on more or less secret missions of one sort or another or in an attempt to evade the law and his many creditors. He continued to live on an allowance from his father, but failed to settle down to any sort of job, and further infuriated his parent by converting to Roman Catholicism as a result of being nursed back to health from a near-fatal bout of dysentery by an aristocratic nun ("a sister of the then Lord Denbigh"). Summoned back from his travels to London, he had a final interview with his father, who agreed to his continuing to receive a small allowance, which was augmented by an indulgent aunt. He then "set off again in search of new emotions and experiences," taking in Italy, Germany, Austria and Russia. He claimed that two of his father's sisters had been brought up at the court of Hesse-Darmstadt and had kept in touch with their former companion, Princess Alexandra of Hesse, who had subsequently become the Russian Tsarina, and so young Gerald was invited to Tsarkoe Seloe to meet the rest of the doomed Imperial family. He also met Rasputin, whom he much admired. Quite how the sisters of a Scottish merchant came to be part of a German court is unclear: it may have been one of Hamilton's inventions. According to his memoirs, he had an entrée into almost every court in Europe, and he eventually wrote a book entitled *Blood Royal* about his encounters with the relics of moribund or officially defunct monarchies.

By 1913 Hamilton's father felt that he had supported his son long enough and discontinued the allowance. Informed by a lawyer that in an emergency he could raise money from his parents' marriage settlement, Hamilton embarked upon a life in which indigence and extravagance were held in precarious balance. In the event of his father's death, he stood to inherit his mother's "not inconsiderable fortune," but meanwhile he was obliged to raise money from insurance companies and moneylenders, using his forthcoming legacy as security. Or so he stated in one of his memoirs. Elsewhere, he claimed that he came into his mother's money when he reached his majority, which would have been in 1911. His father asked what he intended to do with his inheritance. "I propose to squander it," Hamilton replied, and got through £38,000 in three years. Having lost his faith, but not his taste for the grander and more glamorous trappings and personalities of the Church, he was temporarily reconverted to Roman Catholicism. He claimed that this ceremony took place not in a church but at the Palace Music Hall, which he was visiting with Father Martindale, S.J. During Basil Hallam's rendition of "Oh Hades! The Ladies!" Hamilton made his confession from behind a theater program and was granted absolution, this indicated by the Jesuit's "opening his watch."

His wavering Catholicism and supposed family connections with County Tyrone led Hamilton to espouse the cause of Irish nationalism, and he claimed a close friendship with Sir Roger Casement. Shortly after the outbreak of the First World War, he set off for Rome to seek a private audience with the Pope. Italy was still a neutral country and Hamilton implored the pontiff to exert his influence to keep it that way and to stop the war altogether. He then went on to Spain, where, "claiming as an Irishman the privileges of a neutral," he frequented the embassies of both the Allied and Central Powers. While in Madrid, he received letters from Casement summoning him to Berlin, "as he had matters of extreme importance to discuss with me." He wrote to Casement in code, informing the great patriot of his "most resolute and unwavering intention to dissuade him, as far as it lay in my power, from any undertaking likely to cause loss of life in Ireland, or to compromise the chances of Irish liberty at the Peace Conference which would conclude the war." He returned to London, where he was arrested and questioned at Scotland Yard. Unable to find any evidence against Hamilton, the Commissioner of Police "had recourse to a very unfair expedient, preferring a charge against me under the Criminal Law Amendment Act of 1888." This, as Hamilton omits to explain, was the same law under which Oscar Wilde had been tried and sentenced to two years' hard labor. That Hamilton shared Wilde's sexual tastes was evident from *Desert Dreamers,* a novel about an Englishman's love for his young Arab guide, which he published under the pseudonym of "Patrick Weston" in 1914. It is probable that his arrest for "gross indecency" was entirely justified under the law and had nothing at all to do with his political activities.

Refused bail, Hamilton spent a short period in Brixton prison on remand, but was released on bail on Christmas Eve 1915. Hamilton forgets to tell us what happened when the case came to court, if it ever did.

His freedom did not last long, since he was shortly rearrested and returned to Brixton as a "military lodger," pending charges for high treason. He was vilified by Horatio Bottomley, whose rabble-rousing magazine *John Bull* ran a headline "Hang Hamilton!," a slogan that Hamilton said "was repeated on posters throughout the country." The authorities resisted this widespread demonstration of popular sentiment and Hamilton eventually appeared before a military tribunal, after which he was "detained during His Majesty's pleasure, and, at any rate until the conclusion of the hostilities, under Clause 14B of the Defence of the Realm Act." This was a law under which resident aliens and others whom the government viewed with suspicion were interned during the war. Casement was less fortunate and was executed for high treason in August 1916. Hamilton was eventually released under certain restrictions on Christmas Eve 1918.

After leaving prison, Hamilton divided his time between charitable works and political and criminal intrigues, including one to restore King Constantine to the Greek throne and another to obtain French residency for the former Egyptian Khedive, Abbas Himli. Visiting Germany in 1919, he was appalled by the conditions under which people were living as a result of the blockade, which had continued after the war. He worked for the Fight the Famine Council and for the Save the Children Fund, and was once more to be found in private conclave at the Vatican enlisting the support of a deeply appreciative Pope, who ordered that on Holy Innocents' Day a collection should be taken in Catholic churches throughout the world and donated to the SCF. "The reason I showed such unwonted energy and enthusiasm in this matter is that I have always regarded children as a peculiarly sacred trust," Hamilton later declared.

This image of a saintly ambassador of good will, draped, as he put it, in "the mantle of charity," does not bear close inspection. In 1920 Hamilton embarked on a five-year affair with an eighteen-year-old cocaine addict and former soldier named Georg Skrzydlewski. "He looked like Adonis and was utterly wicked," Hamilton recalled in old age, and introduced his friend and protector to some of the most louche dives Berlin had to offer. Hamilton found himself sitting at tables in dingy basement clubs and cafés with prostitutes, rent boys, pimps, drug pushers and cat burglars. He was fascinated by these lives led on the frayed margins of society, and as a former jailbird regarded them with a certain amount of fellow feeling. It was probably here that he discovered and indulged his masochistic tendencies: Isherwood reported after one of Hamilton's sexual encounters that "from the cracking of whips one might have imagined oneself in the Argentine." Hamilton set up Skrzydlewski in a flat in Frankfurt, but the young man would disappear for days at a time, causing his protector a great deal of delicious anguish.

During this period, Hamilton was himself disappearing to conduct various deals in neighboring European countries, the most notorious of which was "the Case of the Pearl Necklace." This incredibly complex affair involved the exiled Prince Aziz Hassan of Egypt, the gambling-obsessed Baron de Tilleghem, one jeweler in Nice called Perelli and another in Milan called Gatti. Suffice it to say that Hamilton devised an extremely elaborate plot in order to help the baron out of some financial difficulties and, loudly protesting his innocence, was arrested, tried and convicted of swindling. Having served little more than a year in an Italian prison, he managed to secure his release after an appeal. He was subsequently expelled from Italy. "Whatever the reasons may have been, no opportunity whatever was afforded me of defending myself," Hamilton complained, "and I left at a moment's notice for the Swiss frontier, abandoning even, in my hurried flight, my trunks and pictures." Fortunately, his aunt had died and left him "her entire fortune," very sensibly "in the shape of a Trust Fund, the income of which I could enjoy without being allowed to tamper with the capital." He traveled to Frankfurt, where he embarked upon a career as a broadcaster. Unable easily to purchase *The Times* in Frankfurt, he wrote a letter of complaint to Printing House Square, and when told that the newspaper was intending to appoint a sales manager for the whole of Germany, he at once applied for the job, and got it. "This serves to show with what ease anybody can to-day obtain a responsible position, no matter what his past life might have been," Hamilton recalled piously. "I was able to provide the usual references; I did not have to tell a single lie, and I found myself suddenly launched into this most respectable and responsible post. The ease with which I obtained it is only another illustration of the vast scale of hypocrisy upon which the standards of our civilization really depend."

It was fortunate for Hamilton that this was the case, for both his highly public record and his extraordinary appearance were against him. Indeed, it would be hard to imagine anyone who looked less respectable and responsible. He once wrote that at the age of eight, when he was sent to his prep school, "my long hair, my delicate complexion and my general appearance of being a second little Lord Fauntleroy must have worked as a distinct provocation to my companions." At the age of forty, when Isherwood first met him, the long hair had long since gone, replaced by wigs made up of hairs individually set into a net stretched over fish-skin. Despite their expense, these wigs were attached somewhat precariously to Hamilton's pate and fooled no one. Their purchase on his head must have been further compromised by the fact (if it was a fact) that beneath them was affixed a small chamois leather pouch in which he carried two small capsules of potassium cyanide, obtained from "a friendly chemist" in Kiel and to be used if ever he got into a really tight corner. His appearance without a wig was even more alarming, the bald dome emphasizing the heaviness of his jowls. He had deep-set eyes, a bulbous nose and a fleshy, loose-lipped mouth. In contrast to his heavy build, he had almost obscenely delicate hands, which he kept immaculately manicured, as if to dispel rumors that in financial and other matters they were usually far from clean. He dressed very neatly and formally, and his manners were almost parodically Edwardian. He had about him an unnerving and faintly repulsive combination of the gross and the fastidious, so that his carefully cultivated air of gentlemanly probity was fatally undermined by an indelible aura of shiftiness and unreliability.

Isherwood may well have been attracted to Hamilton, as he was to Jean Ross, by the impression that his new friend was playing a part. However, whereas Ross was an innocent with pretensions to wickedness, Hamilton was a genuinely wicked person who protested his innocence. His volumes of memoirs are preposterous exercises in self-exculpation, and it seems likely that this process was already at work when he met Isherwood, who recalled that Hamilton was able to talk about his nefarious past "without showing any genuine indignation and without exactly defending himself. He was well aware of his own double standard and he couldn't help giggling in the midst of his solemn sincerities." Such is the artful blend of fact and fiction in the books Isherwood wrote about Berlin that it is difficult to differentiate between his characters and their models. Ross came to resent being known as "the real Sally Bowles," but Hamilton enjoyed boasting that he was the model for Mr. Norris, typically exploiting the connection while unconvincingly insisting that certain aspects of the character were pure invention. "It seems to me that Christopher 'recognized' Gerald Hamilton as Arthur Norris, his character-to-be, almost as soon as he set eyes on him," Isherwood wrote in 1976. Some people felt that in "recognizing" Mr. Norris, Isherwood failed to see Mr. Hamilton for what he was. Stephen Spender insisted that Hamilton, far from being an amiable rogue, was genuinely evil, that in one case he had blackmailed a young man who was driven to suicide. Isherwood never quite acknowledged this aspect of Hamilton's character, though he eventually characterized him as "an icy cynic," whose misdeeds were "tiresome rather than amusing." By this time, however, Arthur Norris was a distant memory, superseded by the elderly and demanding original, who had long since served his purpose in Isherwood's life.

Another Berlin character gradually evolving in Isherwood's mind was Natalia Landauer, an earnest young Jewish woman who was partly modeled on Gisa Soleweitschick, with whom he and Spender were now spending a great deal of time. Every week they came to the Soleweitschicks' Konstanzerstrasse apartment for Sunday lunch, after which Gisa's mother would send them on their way, their pockets stuffed with fruit and other food. Gisa was studying the history of art and was extremely well read for someone so young, quite capable of discussing the merits of Tolstoy or Dostoyevsky with older professional writers such as Isherwood and Spender. In the evenings they went to the cinema or—with rather less enthusiasm on Isherwood's part—concerts. These cultural excursions would be followed by a walk in the Tiergarten, where the arts would be discussed. Spender observed the struggle of wills going on between his two friends, "with Gisa standing for Art and the things of the spirit, Christopher for human relationships and for war against all self-conscious aesthetic and intellectual pretensions." Gisa was not someone to be patronized, however, and when Isherwood failed to appreciate some piece of music to which she had forced him to listen, she would rebuke him. "I said to him very often: 'You are a fool!' " she recalled. Another of her favorite remarks when Isherwood failed to respond to her enthusiasms was: "Then I'm sorry. I can't help you"—a saying Isherwood stored away for Natalia Landauer to use. "I came home afterwards," Gisa recalled, "and told my mother: 'You know, these two young men will be very famous. They are so intelligent.' I was entranced, you know, because the friends of my brothers were—pfui!—*nothing*, interested only in girls." Gisa's mother had instantly recognized that the two Englishmen were not in the least interested in girls, which is why she allowed her young daughter to go out with them unchaperoned, sometimes not returning until the small hours. Gisa, innocent in all sexual matters despite her intellectual precocity and sophistication, was puzzled but relieved that she did not have to fight off her new friends' advances, attributing this to fine English manners.

There was a definite sense of "Oriental untouchability" about Gisa, which Isherwood—used to the more relaxed company of Jean Ross—found odd. Indeed, the women were such a contrast that, although they never met in real life, Isherwood could not resist bringing them together in fiction, in *Goodbye to Berlin*. He later acknowledged that Gisa "was an altogether warmer and emotionally more responsive person than Natalia," but that he was "driven into the position, for purely technical reasons, of making Natalia an opposite of Sally Bowles." Natalia Landauer may be largely based on Gisa, but her physical appearance, family background and connections were borrowed from a school-friend of Gisa's named Annie Joël. Over sixty years later, Gisa would go through *Goodbye to Berlin,* saying, "Yes, that's me, and, well, that is possible—but not that. No. That's Annie Joël." Annie's father was a director of Wertheim's, the large department store on Leipzigerstrasse, one of the ladder of streets running parallel to Unter den Linden. Wertheim's was the first of Berlin's famous *Warenhäuser,* covering some 22,350 square yards at the western end of the street, close to the Tiergarten. It was an opulent palace of commerce, built around a glass-roofed central court and with an imposing façade of granite columns decorated with ironwork. Like most of the department stores, Wertheim's was founded and owned by a Jewish family. It was this connection that inspired Isherwood to make Natalia the cousin of Bernhard Landauer in his novel.

Bernhard was based on Wilfrid Israel, whose family had founded what they regarded as *"Das Kaufhaus in Centrum"* in the old eastern center of the city. Although is was dominated by the "Rote Rathaus"—the city's "new" town hall, built in the 1860s to a supposedly Renaissance plan but resembling nothing so much as a biscuit factory—the historic area around the Alexanderplatz was no longer the center of Berlin in any real meaning of the term. The family firm, N. Israel, was founded by and named after Wilfrid's great-grandfather in 1815, and initially sold linen, but by the turn of the century it had become a large department store, with some claim to be the oldest in the city. It stood opposite the town hall, manufacturing and supplying goods to generations of Berliners. The business was inherited by Wilfrid's father, Berthold, in 1893, shortly before he married his first cousin, Amy Solomon. The daughter of a successful businessman, Amy had been born in England, where her grandfather was Chief Rabbi, and so the marriage took place in London. By this time, the Israels were established in a fashionable area of Berlin on the southern edge of the Tiergarten, but the Anglophile Amy, who paid frequent visits to her family, arranged to be in England when her son was born in 1899.

A high level of culture apart, the Israel household was run on English lines and the children educated at home by a British governess. It was a very formal upbringing, but not in the least philistine, and by the time he was old enough to attend the Mommsen *Gymnasium,* Wilfrid had undertaken a grand tour of Italy and intended to become an artist. His studies were interrupted by the First World War, although he had no intention of fighting, having (under the guidance of Albert Einsten and the editor Maximillian Harden) become a pacifist. Rather than allowing Wilfrid to attend a military tribunal, his family arranged for him to be declared medically unfit, which he probably was, since he suffered from poor health throughout his life. He joined a welfare organization that distributed food and clothing to offset the severe privations

Germany was suffering on the home front. This was funded by the Society of Friends in Britain and the International Red Cross, and the work continued after the war ended, encountering considerable official opposition in England. Wilfrid subsequently worked to forge links between pacifist organizations in England and Germany and much of his life would be dedicated to international cooperation in the face of rising militarism. He also became an advocate of Zionism.

In 1921 he joined the family firm and, after a period of training in business, became N. Israel's general manager, but he continued to travel, sending back reports to the Deutsche Liga für Volkerbund, an internationalist organization. He lobbied for help to be sent to Soviet Russia, which was in the grip of famine, working with Fridjof Nansen, the Norwegian explorer whom the Red Cross had appointed High Commissioner for Russian Relief. He traveled to India, where he became deeply influenced by Gandhi's policy of passive resistance and noted strong parallels between Eastern and Western culture. All these ideas he brought back to Germany, where (since he clearly had no aptitude for business) his father appointed him head of personnel, responsible for the welfare of N. Israel's two thousand employees. He instituted a business school in which students learned about every aspect of the company from production to the sales floor, and used some of his own personal wealth to fund various humanitarian and internationalist projects. He also financed the Hebrew National Theatre, a touring company, and promoted contemporary art, although his own tastes ran to older work.

By the time Isherwood met him, Israel had left the family home and was living alone in a small flat in Bendlerstrasse, which ran south from the Tiergarten and was a short walk from Nollendorfstrasse. He spent most weekends at the large villa his family had built in 1918 at Wannsee, half an hour's drive from Berlin. The Bendlerstrasse flat was on the top floor and had been double-glazed, which gave it a curiously muffled atmosphere and suggested that the occupant required protecting against the outside world. The décor was understated, showing off to advantage the fine objects—oriental sculptures and paintings from the Italian Renaissance—that Israel collected. Tall, handsome, dapper and reserved, Israel struck Isherwood as a rather remote and enigmatic figure, devoted to culture and not very interested in his work for the family firm. Although Isherwood was one of the very few people Israel admitted to his sanctum, the friendship between the two men was uneasy.

Isherwood distrusted "culture-worshippers," as he called them, affecting to believe that such people merely pretended to like standing in front of paintings or attending concerts. Culture-worshipers, he asserted, were essentially anti-life, finding in a detached appreciation of the arts a substitute for a proper engagement with the messy business of living. This view clearly derived from his observations of Kathleen, who he felt had retreated from the world after Frank's death, going on decorous architectural expeditions in which the distressing present could be momentarily dispelled by frequent immersions in the past. Isherwood was, of course, far more cultured than he liked to pretend, but it is perhaps significant that he preferred the contemporary cinema, a populist art form, to more intellectually demanding cultural outings. Although the Theater am Nollendorf-Platz was the leading radical theater, run by the famous Erwin Piscator, Isherwood seems to have spent far more time at the Mozart-Saal, a misleadingly named cinema housed in the same building, lapping up anything that was on offer, from radical Expressionist masterpieces to the most undemanding escapist pap. His general attitude to the arts, however, was that time spent trailing round a picture gallery could be more profitably used trawling the bars.

In *Goodbye to Berlin,* Bernhard says, "I am afraid that I am a quite unnecessarily complicated piece of mechanism"—which, as Isherwood later acknowledged, suggested that "he thinks 'Isherwood' quite unnecessarily crude." For his part, Isherwood found Israel altogether too refined, even going so far as to describe Bernhard's *profile* as "over-civilized." The principal difficulty in the relationship, however, was that Isherwood felt that Israel disapproved of him. "He is kind. But he condemns me in his heart," Isherwood told Spender. In retrospect, Isherwood thought that this may have been because Israel, who was very discreetly homosexual, "condemned Christopher for his aggressive frankness about his own sex life." Israel needed to be discreet, since homosexuality was entirely unacceptable in the sort of *haut bourgeois* Jewish society he inhabited: his father's brother had felt obliged to commit suicide after being accused of making homosexual overtures to a former soldier, even though he protested his innocence. It is more likely, however, that Israel, if he condemned Isherwood at all, condemned him as a frivol. Israel's active involvement in international affairs certainly made Isherwood's political commitment seem dilettante. He appears to have discussed politics with Spender in more depth than he ever did with Isherwood, telling him, for instance, that if the Nazis came to power, Jews "should close their businesses and get out into the streets, remaining there, as a protest, and refusing to go home even if the Storm Troopers fired on them." He believed that this would be the only way to "arouse the conscience of the world." It is possible (he is vague on this point) that Isherwood did not learn of Israel's internationalist work until much later. Israel probably had to be as discreet about his political work as he was about his sexuality, and, suspecting that Isherwood was not really very interested in it, did not talk about it a great deal. This would explain why in *Goodbye to Berlin* Bernhard Landauer is portrayed as a passive fatalist rather than someone who was quite as aware as anyone else of what the rise of Nazism meant for Germany and its Jews, and was quietly but determinedly trying to do something about it.

I n March 1931 Isherwood traveled to London in order to consult the literary agent Spencer Curtis Brown. There had been no word as yet from Jonathan Cape about *The Memorial,* and Isherwood had begun to suspect that the book might be turned down. During the ten-day visit, he stayed at Pembroke Gardens even though he had begged his mother ten months earlier never again to let him into the house. Perhaps because Isherwood had put a geographical distance between himself and Kathleen there had been some thawing in his relationship with her. "Christopher had made peace with Kathleen by default," Isherwood recalled in *Christopher and His Kind.* "She was a passive fortress and he had stopped attacking her. What was the use? She was impregnable anyway. They had exchanged a few letters, in which their differences were never referred to." In fact, Kathleen had begun receiving regular letters from Berlin again, and also continued to obtain news of Christopher from those of his friends who had visited him there. While Upward, Auden and Spender gave suitably enthusiastic and no doubt edited accounts of Isherwood's circumstances, a young man named Edward Pollock was less reassuring. Pollock had been stranded in Europe without a passport or money the previous year, and Isherwood had helped him out. The picture Pollock painted of Isherwood's life in Germany had left Kathleen "very sad about C. and the influence at work," she wrote in her diary, clearly referring to Walter Wolff. She added that Pollock thought Isherwood "*really* wants to come back to England," which sounds like wishful thinking on her part.

On his first night at Pembroke Gardens Isherwood stayed up talking with his mother until one a.m. "It was almost as it used to be long ago," she felt. It wasn't, of course, nor ever would be again. Within two days of his arrival Kathleen feared that "the state of things is worse than ever [. . .] he is restless and not happy . . . & absorbed in Walter who is more a cause of misery than happiness . . . and we do not count, at least I do not even exist . . . !" Isherwood was indeed much preoccupied with his unreliable lover. "I dream of Walter every night and wake in baths of sweat," he wrote to Spender. A few days later he wrote again, "Nothing but one letter from Walter and no mention of money, so haven't sent any. I feel a sort of absurd terror he'll simply melt into air before I return"—just as the boy in *Der Puppenjunge* did. Spender, however, allayed these fears with a wire: "All well Walter."

On March 14 Isherwood received a letter from Cape rejecting *The Memorial*. "I realize that there is a risk in letting you go," the publisher wrote, "as you may make a connection elsewhere which will endure [. . .] It certainly should be published and it will in my opinion achieve a *succès d'estime*." This was clearly not the sort of *succès* that Cape, who had lost money on *All the Conspirators*, was seeking. The letter was a model of its kind: disappointing but not entirely disheartening. Curtis Brown suggested sending the typescript to Leonard and Virginia Woolf at the Hogarth Press. Isherwood escaped to Scarborough to discuss the rejection with Edward Upward.

On the day of his return to Berlin, Isherwood received a wire from André Mangeot demanding to see him. Olive had finally divorced her husband in January, citing one of his pupils, the twenty-two-year-old violinist Anne McNaghten, as co-respondent. She and Fowke had moved to a house at 32 Gunter Grove, a street running between Fulham Road and King's Road, where she rented rooms, and at this period leased a studio to Bill de Lichtenberg, where he worked and held exhibitions. André and Sylvain remained at Cresswell Place. The boys were nineteen and seventeen respectively and there was no question as to which parent each would live with. Fowke always felt closer to Olive and believed that his father had a special affinity with Sylvain. In any case, they both saw a great deal of both parents, since the divorce, though painful, was not acrimonious. Fowke, who recalled that in his father's life "there were endless other girlies—they were all over the place," felt that in the end his mother simply thought: "Bugger it! Enough is enough." André, however, was a reluctant divorcé. "My mother bore it and bore it and bore it," Fowke remembered. "But when she made up her mind, that was it. Finished. My father could *never* understand how Olive could divorce him." Mangeot decided that Isherwood was to blame for the collapse of the marriage and that he may even have encouraged Olive to sue for divorce. Many years later, Dodie Smith, who had become a close friend of Isherwood in America during the Second World War, was introduced to Mangeot. Recognizing the name, she asked whether he was the M. Mangeot who had once employed Christopher Isherwood. Mangeot replied "in the saddest of French voices,

'Oh, yes, I knew him—to my great sorrow. He broke up my life!' " Mangeot went on to tell Smith that Isherwood "had turned his wife and his quartet against him. He went into no details—there was no time." Fowke felt that there was some truth in this allegation:

> He certainly alienated my mother. Up to the time of Isherwood's arrival, whatever else happened, my parents were very close to each other and wanted to do things with each other, holidays and so on. So I think [my father] had some justification there. The quartet is slightly less likely—though I don't think Christopher was *entirely* innocent. I think he probably stirred the pot a bit with Boris Pecker, who was the second violin and was rather jealous of not alternating as first violin with my father. There is no doubt that as far as my father was concerned Isherwood betrayed the confidence and trust he'd placed in him.

It is possible that Mangeot, having finally overstepped the mark with his wife, was simply looking around for someone else to blame. He may have held Isherwood responsible for putting temptation in his way, in the shape of Rachel Monkhouse. It is also possible that Olive found the strength to separate from her husband after Isherwood had introduced her to a circle of young intellectuals, some of whom (including Edward Upward and Gabriel Carritt) she happily took to her bed. This was always managed discreetly, but if André had found out, he would have known that it was Isherwood who had acted as go-between.

Isherwood decided to ignore Mangeot's summons and spent his last day in London having lunch with Olive and visiting John Layard, who was languishing in a nursing home having suffered a collapse after the recent death of his mother. He returned to Pembroke Gardens for an early dinner before going with Eric Falk to Liverpool Street Station to catch the 8:15 p.m. train. While he was on his way to the station Mangeot rang Pembroke Gardens again, where Kathleen loyally informed him that the train did not leave until 8:30. By the time Mangeot reached the station, Isherwood was safely on his way to the Continent, although he jokingly told Spender that the irate musician might still come after him "with a revolver and wipe out his injuries in blood."

Accompanying Isherwood was Archie Campbell, the young man who had introduced Spender to Auden at Oxford. Campbell was now a law tutor at the university. Extremely learned and very intense, he also had "the filthiest mind imaginable," according to Spender. He kept a diary, originally in French, then in Gaelic—presumably to prevent francophone snoopers from reading what he'd written. He was homosexual, but terrified of acting upon his impulses in England and consequently sex-starved and neurotic.

In Berlin he introduced Isherwood to a wealthy American named John Blomshield. Although married, Blomshield was entirely homosexual and had the sort of unlimited funds that enabled him to enjoy the city in a way Isherwood never could. He was also generous, and decided that Isherwood, Spender and Jean Ross should be given a taste of the high life. "He altered our lives for about a week," Spender recalled—a week Isherwood re-created in *Goodbye to Berlin,* where Blomshield in-spired the character of Clive, the rich young man who takes up, treats and then un-ceremoniously dumps Chris and Sally.

As well as planning his epic novel about Berlin, Isherwood was working on an autobiography, and it would be some time before he decided which of his experi-ences would be fictionalized in the novel and which would be reserved for the non-fiction work. Throughout his career, Isherwood shifted material around between projects in this way, mining his copious diaries for episodes which would be incor-porated into the draft of a book, then dropped to be picked up again, sometimes decades later. At this stage, for example, he intended to include an account of his stay in Bremen with Basil Fry in the autobiography: in the event, he discarded it and it did not resurface until 1962 when it formed the first part of his episodic autobiographical novel, *Down There on a Visit.*

Meanwhile, his "characters" obligingly continued to provide him with useful copy. He and Jean Ross had become fast friends after Ross came to live in the Nol-lendorfstrasse flat, probably at the end of 1930. She continued to have various affairs, usually with people in the theater or the film industry. One of these was a tall blond Jewish musician named Götz von Eick, with whom she fell in love. An overheated Tennessee Williams, who met von Eick in the 1940s, described him wearing "very sheer silky trousers and a pale green shirt unbuttoned to reveal his pale gold chest"; he was, Williams declared, *"excruciatingly* beautiful" and "the most exciting man I have ever looked at." In the summer of 1931 Ross became pregnant by von Eick, and had to have an illegal and unskillfully performed abortion, during which she nearly died, because the doctor left a swab inside her. Like his fictional counterpart, Klaus Linke in *Goodbye to Berlin,* von Eick shortly left Germany, not to work in the British film industry, but for Hollywood, where he changed his name to Peter van Eyck. His "Aryan" looks led to his having a successful career playing Nazi villains in several films, including *The Moon Is Down, Five Graves to Cairo* and *Desert Fox.*

Other lodgers at Frl. Thurau's increasingly ramshackle apartment included the girlfriend of a chemist, who brought home samples of "very posh Paris scent" for everyone to try out, and who had "a disease of the throat which no doctor can cure or even name." She occupied the room opposite Isherwood's. In the attic room above the bathroom was a young woman who worked in a fruit shop and had the clap, which she passed on to the "young man of no fixed occupation" (in fact a car thief) who occupied the other back bedroom. Isherwood claimed that he was "the only whole member of the household. Every morning, when I wake, I feel myself cau-tiously all over to make sure I haven't got any of their complaints." Frl. Thurau seems to have accepted the antics of her paying guests with good grace, though one of Jean Ross's lovers left the bedclothes in such a state that he was banished from the house.

It was probably shortly after his return to Berlin that Isherwood met the mysteri-ous Rudolph or Rolf Katz, an influential figure in his life, but one about whom he was uncharacteristically reticent. There is no mention of Katz in *Christopher and His Kind,* although in his travel book, *The Condor and the Cows,* Isherwood describes meeting this friend from his past in Buenos Aires in the 1940s, and in *Down There on a Visit* Katz appears, without introduction or explanation, as "Dr Fisch." Quite how the two men met is unclear, but it is likely that it was through sex rather than politics. Jewish, homosexual and an active member of the German Communist Party, the KPD, since 1921, Katz was everything the rising Nazi Party most abhorred. He was by training an economist, had worked as a correspondent for *Imprecor,* a journal of international communism, and was, Isherwood later recalled, "one of the very few people I have ever met who has really read, studied and digested Marx." Stout and physically unprepossessing, Katz nevertheless had undoubted presence. Isherwood was awed by his intelligence and his grasp of any given political situation. Meeting him again in Argentina in 1948, he wrote:

> It was so exactly like the old days in his flat out in the Berlin suburbs that, at moments, I felt quite young again—a woolly-minded boy asking naive questions and being answered by the great face of the oracle opposite, the soft, powerful, pipe-smoking figure in the comfortable chair. Set in pale fleshy cheeks, Rolf's dark blue eyes, small well-formed nose and firm mouth have the beauty of intellectual honesty. He is the truly cogitative man. My ignorance and mental clumsiness amuse him, as always. He smiles indulgently. Gripping his pipe between white even teeth, he begins to speak in his rapid indistinct German, with strange bubbling sounds: 'No, Christopher—please excuse me if I say this—but again your question is incorrectly formulated—If we are to come to a basic understanding of this problem, it will be necessary to examine not only its economic and quasi-economic, but also its social-political aspects—and, in order to do this, we must not lose sight of the fact that—' The voice goes on and on. I listen very carefully, knowing by experience that, sooner or later, Rolf will say something quite simple and definite, something I can understand.

Katz lived on the Reichs-Strasse, to the west of the city on the borders of the Grünewald. Spender often took a train to Grünewald with Isherwood and walked among the trees and lakes there, talking, but he never met Katz. "Christopher always had these very *powerful* kind of friendships with people I never met," he recalled. "He used to talk about Katz. He'd have dinner with him and Katz would tell him everything about the situation. He was one of those people who knew everything that was going to happen." Indeed, Katz was probably the most politically involved person Isherwood knew in Berlin, and was undoubtedly the person from whom Isherwood learned most about current German politics. It is probable that the character simply identified as "D." in the final section of *Goodbye to Berlin* (a diary of the 1932–33 winter) is Katz. The narrator is surprised to meet him in the Russian tea-shop on Kleist-Strasse, imagining that Germany would have become too dangerous for him. "But the situation is so interesting here . . ." D. explains calmly, before introducing the alarmed "Isherwood" loudly and a little ironically to his companion as "a confirmed anti-fascist." D. slips across the border to Holland two months later, just as Katz fled Germany for France in early 1933 after Hitler had accused the communists of burning down the Reichstag and started arresting the Party leaders. The last mention of a meeting with Katz in Berlin in Isherwood's 1933 appointments diary is for February 14, a fortnight before the fire. But he was not to disappear from Isherwood's life altogether.

I sherwood spent part of the summer of 1931 at Sellin on Insel Rügen. Lying in the Baltic Sea just off the coast of Pomerania, some 120 miles north of Berlin, Rügen was a popular destination for German holidaymakers. Sellin was a beautifully sheltered seaside resort, built in a pine forest on an inland bay on the southeastern side of the island. Isherwood, Spender and Walter booked into the Pension Idyll, where they were joined by Auden, who had come over from England to spend part of the school holidays with his friends. It was during this holiday that Spender took a photograph of himself, Auden and Isherwood that has been frequently reproduced and which he later described—in a letter to Isherwood and therefore not altogether seriously—as "the most famous photograph in the history of the world, of US THREE." It was taken with what he called "a masturbatory camera designed for narcissists"—in other words, a fairly sophisticated piece of equipment with a delayed-shutter mechanism. "Stephen, in the middle, has his arms around Wystan and Christopher and an expression on his face which suggests an off-duty Jesus relaxing with 'these little ones,' " Isherwood commented; "Christopher, compared with the others, is such a very little one that he looks as if he is standing in a hole." It may not be the most famous photograph in the world, but it is one that has considerable iconographical significance. It has become an enduring image of three young men who (in Evelyn Waugh's disgruntled phrase) "ganged up and captured the decade."

In retrospect, the Pension's name came to seem ironic, since Isherwood and Walter spent much of their time quarreling. Walter found plenty of female playmates among the bronzed *Mädchen* at Sellin, and this made Isherwood extremely jealous. Isherwood would turn much of this unhappiness to good account in "On Ruegen Island," the third section of *Goodbye to Berlin,* where he becomes the observer and recorder of a similar relationship between Peter Wilkinson and Otto Nowak. The previous winter, Isherwood had decided that Spender's presence had been beneficial for his relationship with Walter, but the Sellin holiday was so unsatisfactory that he was now inclined to blame his friend.

In mid-July he and Walter returned to Berlin, where he took a temporary room at Kleist-Strasse 9, just to the west of Frl. Thurau's establishment, on a main road which connected Wittenberg-Platz and Nollendorf-Platz. The final blow for his holiday was that he had cut his foot on a piece of tin while bathing in the sea and ended up with a poisoned toe, which continued to bother him for several weeks. Spender departed for Salzburg, but almost immediately wanted to get back to Berlin. Isherwood was not encouraging. "I have a very nice but expensive room here," he wrote. "I think I could find you something cheaper two doors away. I think it is better we don't all live right on top of each other, don't you? I believe that was partly the trouble at Rügen. Anyhow I'm resolved not to live with Walter again for a long time. Because these last days, when he's been in to see me for quite short periods, have been absolutely wonderful—as though I'd met and fallen in love with a quite different boy." Re-reading this letter forty years later, Isherwood noted: "This is the first indication that Stephen has been getting on Christopher's nerves. Christopher only mentions [Walter] because he is embarrassed to have to admit that he doesn't want Stephen living in the same apartment with him." While Isherwood needed an audience when things were going well with Walter, he did not much care to have a close friend such as Spender witnessing his jealousy and humiliation when the young man was misbehaving. He particularly didn't want one with a camera. One of the many photographs Spender took of Isherwood and Walter shows all too clearly the tension between them: Walter, bare-chested, his hair flopping down in bangs, strums a guitar, oblivious of Isherwood, who—grim-faced, the veins standing out on his rigidly folded arms—sits behind him, looking very unhappy indeed. Despite Isherwood's protestations of enthusiasm for Spender's return to Berlin, the recipient could hardly ignore the letter's overall lack of genuine warmth.

Isherwood clearly felt that his "pupil" had overstepped the mark and needed putting in his place. When Spender wrote a few weeks later to say that his friend the German academic Ernst Robert Curtius had criticized the new novel he was working on (later published as *The Temple*), Isherwood replied firmly: "What does Curtius know about Form? *I* tell you it is a good, well-constructed piece of work. Isn't that enough for you?" In case Spender had not taken the hint contained in his last letter, Isherwood (having painted a sorrowful picture of himself confined to the house by his toe and enduring "murderously hot" weather) urged him not to come to Berlin. "It would be a quite needless sacrifice on your part—your obvious course being to proceed to London via Bonn and not waste any more money." Isherwood unwisely added that he was expecting Edward Upward in Berlin in mid-August. The opportunity of meeting this hitherto unglimpsed writer, so often mentioned by both Auden and Isherwood, was not to be passed up. Spender ignored Isherwood's hints and took the Berlin route back to London, booking into Jean Ross's room in Nollendorfstrasse while she was away for a fortnight. "I'm very glad you're coming," Isherwood wrote once it became clear that Spender was not to be dissuaded, "though not quite sure if it's wise considering your finances. However."

It would have been difficult for Isherwood to be too unwelcoming, since Spender was now acting as an auxiliary literary agent. It had been at Spender's suggestion that Isherwood had employed David Higham at Curtis Brown to act as official agent for *The Memorial,* but Higham was not having a great deal of success: after Cape's rejection, the book had been turned down by three other publishers. For some time Spender had been recommending the novel to John Lehmann, who had recently been appointed manager at the Hogarth Press. Spender met Lehmann, who was two years his senior, through the latter's sister Rosamond, a great beauty who had enjoyed an enormous success with her first novel, *Dusty Answer.* Partly autobiographical, the novel described the scholarly and sentimental education of a young woman and was very bold in its depiction of male and female homosexuality. Lehmann herself was heterosexual, and already on her second marriage (to the communist painter Wogan Philipps), but her brother was homosexual, and one of her sisters, the actress and writer Beatrix Lehmann, was bisexual. Spender was very struck by Rosamond, as were most men who met her, and it was partly to deflect his growing devotion that she decided to attempt to set him up with John, who was an aspiring poet. In December 1930 she introduced the two young men at the Lehmann family home on the Thames at Bourne End in Berkshire and sent them off on a walk along the tow-path, hoping that in such an idyllic setting they would fall instantly in love. Like all the Lehmanns, John was very good-looking, but in a rather severe way, with prematurely gray hair, a straight nose and cold blue eyes. He was a great deal keener on the idea of an affair than Spender, who recognized at once that Rosamond's brother was not his type. They did, however, have many interests and enthusiasms in common. Lehmann subsequently invited Spender to lunch, after which he said, "Don't you think it would be *splendid* if we went to bed together?" Spender was almost tempted, chiefly because he was thinking how much amusement this proposal and its acceptance would give Isherwood. He could not, however, overcome his aversion to Lehmann's "steely will, his body like a scabbard enclosing his determination."

Lehmann and Spender nevertheless became friends, although their relationship was frequently disturbed by rows of one sort or another. Spender was canny enough to realize that in his new job Lehmann could be a useful ally. Adopting an Isherwood-like air of effortless superiority, he told Lehmann:

> There are four or so friends who work together, although they are not all known to each other. They are W. H. Auden, Christopher Isherwood, Edward Upward and I. I only know Christopher and Wystan Auden of the other three, but I believe that Edward Upward, whom I do not know, has had a great influence on Christopher. Auden travelled to Germany, and that is how Christopher and then I came here. Whatever one of us does in writing or travelling or taking jobs, it is a kind of exploration which may be followed up by the other two or three. Of Christopher and Wystan I feel that what makes me value their friendship more than that of all my friends, is that they are interested only in moral problems.

This was not strictly accurate, and Spender's attempt to elaborate is heavily scored out. "I can't really explain more than that," he continued. "The point of the work we do is to explain what we mean. Of Christopher Isherwood I can only say that he has been for a long time and still is a hero to me. But I think that anything I say further is likely to put you off and make you think that we are all prigs." Lehmann was not in the least put off, and saw the opportunity to become publisher in chief to this group of young men who looked set to take over the literary world. His principal preoccupation at the time was an anthology of contemporary poetry to be called *New Signatures,* edited by the poet and mountaineer Michael Roberts. Since the anthology was to introduce the new generation of young poets to the reading public, Lehmann was keen that the signatures of Spender and his friends should be included. Spender had to explain to a disappointed Lehmann that Isherwood did not write poetry. Perhaps Lehmann would be interested in Isherwood's novel?

Lehmann was, partly because Spender had talked so much about Isherwood and had astutely puffed *The Memorial* as "an extremely important work for our generation." The publisher of *New Signatures* could hardly resist such bait and found the novel just as Spender had described it. It had, Lehmann felt, "an exact feeling for the deeper moods of our generation with its delayed war-shock and conviction of the futility of the old pattern of social life and convention." He passed the typescript to the Woolfs with a strong recommendation they should publish it. Of an older, pre-war generation, the Woolfs decided they would like to read the young author's previous novel before deciding on this one. "I'm afraid that'll be its death-blow," Isherwood responded gloomily when he heard the news. Spender must have been a little concerned too, since he had previously described *All the Conspirators* unenticingly to

Lehmann as "rather smart and young-mannish." By September, however, he was back in London and was able to telephone Kathleen to tell her that the Hogarth Press had accepted *The Memorial* for publication.

This news came just in time. Isherwood was, as usual, chronically short of money, often obliged to rely on small loans or handouts from Spender and Upward, and his mother was about to exercise some parental authority, perhaps threatening to cut off his allowance, which she felt he was squandering on Walter. She even appeared to blame Walter for her son's poisoned toe, exclaiming in her diary, "That hateful Berlin and all it contains."[3] Upon hearing of the publisher's decision, Isherwood wrote to Upward: "Phew, that was a close one. Mater's hand was on the pen, in fact she'd already begun a pretty nasty letter inside there last week when the telephone bell rang and Stephen blurted out the news of the reprieve. Richard was sent out to the grocer's for purple rockets and Nanny hurriedly rummaged out Christmas festoons from the cellar." Publication was scheduled for the following February.

I sherwood had now returned to the large, welcoming bosom of Frl. Thurau in Nollendorfstrasse. He had intended to visit London in October but he had just got a new tutoring job for which he had to spend every morning going for walks with an eleven-year-old German boy. The boy, he explained to Richard, had "spent the last two years in New York and speaks perfect American. I am to stop him saying Yes Sir, oh Boy, Yep and Lookit. It is a quite impossible job. In fact I am beginning to talk with an American accent myself." He had also been offered a job with Gerald Hamilton's Anglo-American News Agency. This particular enterprise of Hamilton's goes unmentioned in his autobiographies and perhaps never got off the ground. Isherwood thought it "look[ed] like being a pretty good hive of Bolshevik crooks." Perhaps inspired by the recent troubles experienced by Jean Ross, and having presumably set aside his Catholic scruples, Hamilton was also involved at this period with a campaign for the legalization of abortion. "So deep was my feeling on this subject," he recalled, "that I spoke about it at a mass meeting at the Sportspalast in Berlin, to an enthusiastic audience of 12,000." His passion was not apparently shared by his employers at Printing House Square and he was relieved of his duties as sales manager for *The Times*. This led to a certain amount of financial embarrassment and he spent even more of his time evading creditors and fending off the bailiffs. *The Times* had also grown increasingly concerned about Hamilton's political affiliations. "It is true that I was in touch with the leading German Communists," Hamilton confessed, and claimed the friendship of Willi Münzenberg, "the notorious Communist, who presides in Berlin on behalf of Moscow over the doings of the League Against Imperialism and the Friends of Soviet Russia," as British intelligence described him. Münzenberg ran a number of front organizations from Berlin under the umbrella of the workers' relief organization the Internationale Arbeiterhilfe or IAH, for whom Isherwood subsequently did some work as a translator. This work may have come through Hamilton, whose relationship with the communist leader is guyed by Isher-

---

3. This outburst may also have had something to do with the date on which it was made, August 4, 1931, the seventeenth anniversary of the outbreak of the First World War.

wood in *Mr Norris Changes Trains,* in which the character of Ludwig Bayer was clearly suggested by Münzenberg. Isherwood's other link with Münzenberg was Rolf Katz, a rather more committed and reliable associate in the KPD, who had at one point provided a temporary job for Walter Wolff.[4]

Another committed anti-fascist with whom Isherwood became friends in the autumn of 1931 was Klaus Mann, the eldest son of the great German novelist Thomas Mann. The Mann family presented a model of bourgeois respectability, but was in fact riven by sexual and psychological irregularity. Thomas Mann had married Katia Pringsheim, an attractive and cultured woman from a wealthy Jewish background, in 1905, and they had six children, of whom the two eldest, Erika and Klaus, had been born in 1905 and 1906 respectively. Both Erika and Klaus were predominantly homosexual, as was their father, who had married Katia virtually on the rebound from a four-year relationship with a painter named Paul Ehrenberg. His marriage notwithstanding, Thomas Mann continued to regard his relationship with Ehrenberg as the "central emotional experience" of his life. Unable to commit himself to an adult homosexual relationship, Mann spent his life becoming romantically obsessed with a succession of boys and youths: most famously Wladyslaw Moes, the ten-year-old who inspired the character of Tadzio in Mann's novella *Death in Venice;* most worryingly the thirteen-year-old Klaus, whom he had surprised one evening romping naked around his bedroom. "Strong impression of his developing, magnificent body," the doting father noted in his diary. "Strong emotion." A whole pattern of incest and sexual ambiguity is to be discerned in the Mann's family history, stemming from the likelihood that Thomas was more attracted to his wife's twin brother than he was to Katia herself. Katia and her brother did look very alike, but not as much as Erika and Klaus did. Although separated by a year, Erika and Klaus pretended to be quasi-identical twins: an extraordinary photograph taken of them in their twenties depicts a sleek couple inhabiting some realm where the borders of kinship and gender have been irrevocably blurred. Nor was it merely a matter of appearance: at the age of seventeen Klaus quixotically proposed marriage to the playwright Frank Wedekind's daughter Pamela, who had previously been Erika's lover. This was Klaus's only recorded bid for heterosexuality, but in 1925 Pamela Wedekind found herself the

---

4. Münzenberg was also an associate of the Hon. Ivor Montagu, the younger son of the Liberal peer Lord Swaythling. One of Münzenberg's schemes, inspired by Lenin's recognition of the cinema as the most valuable of art forms for the purposes of propaganda, was the distribution in Europe of Soviet films. The British government had attempted to ban the distribution and exhibition of such films: in 1926, to take one famous example, Sergei Eisenstein's *Battleship Potemkin* was refused a certificate by the British Board of Film Censors. One way round such bans was for private individuals to import the films and show them in club conditions. Such activities were carefully monitored by the security services, and one of the organizations on which they kept a file was the Cambridge Film Society, of which Montagu (an undergraduate at King's College) had been director in 1924, when Isherwood was a member. No minutes or other documentation concerning the Society appear to have been preserved. The MI5 file exists in the Public Records Office, but this belongs to the later 1920s, at which period Montagu still maintained links with the University and was having his letters regularly intercepted by the authorities.

dedicatee of her former suitor's *Der Fromme Tanz* ("The Pious Dance"), a novel set in the sexually ambiguous world of Weimar Berlin.

Defying the huge shadow cast by his father (and indeed by his uncle, Heinrich Mann), Klaus Mann was determined to become a writer, and at the age of eighteen had a volume of short stories published. That same year, 1925, he appeared in Hamburg, along with Erika, Pamela Wedekind and a well-known homosexual actor named Gustaf Gründgens, in his own play, *Anja and Esther.* Thomas Mann did not attend the play, his interest in his son having waned with Klaus's adolescence, but it attracted a great deal of publicity because it starred the "children of famous poets," as the newspapers put it. The following year Erika married Gründgens, though the marriage did not last long and they were divorced in 1929. Brother and sister had spent 1927 and 1928 traveling round the world, but back in Germany became increasingly involved in left-wing politics. When Isherwood met him, the unstable Klaus had been experimenting with drugs, and he soon became addicted to them. Isherwood recalled that Mann was

> anxious to say *precisely* what he means. He takes all conversation earnestly, no matter if the topic is light or serious, but always with ease and flexibility. He never lectures you. He listens, answers, discusses. His great charm lay in this openness, this eager, unaffected approach. His quiet, intimate laughter enlivened even the gloomiest subjects. For Klaus never had to pretend to be serious, to pull a long face, like a hypocrite in church. He *was* serious. He minded deeply, he cared passionately, about the tragedies and the great issues of the time—and he took it for granted that *you* cared, too.

Isherwood undoubtedly did care, although he was inclined to treat Germany's political instability as if it were another episode in the Mortmere saga, joking about his duties as a bomb-maker, decorating his letters with the hammer and sickle and signing them "Rote Front." His association with Mann and Katz, however, and the ever-deepening crisis added to the sense that Berlin was entering what Spender dubbed the "*Weimardämmerung.*" Isherwood's letters home became a good deal less larky. "How is England?" Isherwood asked Spender in October. "Germany is pretty bloody. This Revolution-Next-Week atmosphere has stopped being quite such a joke and somehow the feeling that nothing catastrophic really will happen only makes it worse. I think everybody everywhere is being ground down slowly by an enormous tool. I feel myself getting smaller and smaller."

Isherwood was also approaching a *Walterdämmerung.* When Spender expressed concern that his planned return to Berlin in November for an extended period might not be welcome, Isherwood replied: "I'm frightfully glad you're coming and of course it's the most utter nonsense your thinking you 'spoil' my relationship with Walter, quite apart from the fact that nowadays there's precious little relationship at all to spoil." A disparity in feeling and commitment would be inevitable in any relationship between an upper-middle-class English intellectual in his late twenties and a teenage, working-class Berliner, but Isherwood was still sufficiently romantic to believe that such barriers could be overcome. There was a long and noble history in Germany of *Blutbruderschaft,* where youths swore eternal brotherhood, symbolized by the mingling of their blood. One of Berlin's best-known homosexual magazines, founded in 1919 and still available at this period, was titled *Die Freundschaft*. While artists such as Otto Schoff were producing explicit erotic etchings of boys in action, there was a rather less sub rosa but none the less suspect trade in homophilic art. K. Oechsler's celebrated *Nach dem Picknick,* for example, painted in 1930, shows two rugged young men with angelic faces lying against each other among some ferns, enjoying a post-prandial—or possibly post-coital—rest.

Isherwood later claimed that he "couldn't relax sexually with a member of his own class or nation"—although this had never stopped him from enjoying sex with Auden "whenever the opportunity afforded itself." Spender, too, wondered whether it was really possible to have an affair with a social and intellectual equal. "I am sure that if one could pull off such a relationship it would be terrific," he told John Lehmann. "But is it possible?" Spender had become involved with a youth he had met in Berlin during the summer. Georg was the son of Russian émigrés, and "not a bit literary." "I know too that relationships like mine with Georg are very much substitutes," Spender admitted. "I could never face the electric shocks and the pain of having an 'affair' with someone who was my 'intellectual equal.' When I meet someone who is absolutely different from me and never touched by the realization of problems that are my world and whole life, I am able to accept something gratefully from him. But I think the intellectual world is a world of universals, and a person who lives in that world needs contacts with someone outside it, with the individual." Spender's suggestion that such relationships were a form of escapism into a world apparently untouched by the serious concerns of the intellectual is both lofty and naïve. The "problems" that beset Spender no doubt seemed, and were, serious, but there is a failure here to recognize that the lives of impoverished young working-class men, eking out an existence as sexual partners to romantic foreigners, were plagued by rather more concrete difficulties. These young men may have adopted a jaunty air as they loitered in the lamplit streets, whistling "up at the lighted windows of warm rooms where the beds are already turned down for the night," but they cannot have been as carefree as they sometimes appeared.

For their English lovers, the cost of maintaining such a relationship was considerable. In Berlin, Spender was living on 350 marks (about £25) a month, of which 60 marks were paid to Georg. Sixty marks was also what Spender paid per month in rent, and a further 120 marks went on everyday expenses, including food. As Spender noted, after allowing "something more for extras," including it seems the occasional handout of extra money to the "extravagant" Georg, he was left with a little money each month, but not enough to pay off his overdraft. Isherwood's income would have been distributed in a similar way.

These financial arrangements were not, of course, really satisfactory, but it was better than paying rent-boys ten marks a time, which Spender remembered as the going rate. Nevertheless, the constant specter of payment, either directly or in kind, put a considerable strain on a relationship. It was not a question of exploitation exactly, since each partner was both victim and beneficiary of the setup. The Englishmen may have been taking advantage of the boys' lack of means, but then the Germans were perfectly willing partners, and seem genuinely to have enjoyed the sexual dimension of such relationships, even when they really preferred girls. Furthermore, the boys were quite shameless about taking advantage of the affection and the protective instincts they inspired in their benefactors. "All boys are sharks," Isherwood acknowledged. "It is only a question how well or gracefully they cadge." Any attempt to bring the boys into line by withholding money would be doomed to failure because they would simply return to the streets or find another benefactor. Despite the Englishmen's apparent social and financial advantages, the power in such relationships generally resided with the boys.

When things were going well and the sun was shining, Isherwood did not really begrudge Walter the money. But increasingly things were going badly. Oddly, although utterly faithless, Walter was capable of jealousy—or at any rate was concerned in case Isherwood found someone else upon whom to squander his marks. Isherwood was in fact involved with several other young men, including Karl-Heinz Müller, who had acted as cicerone and model to the English artist Glyn Philpot when he visited Berlin in the autumn of 1931. Karl-Heinz was a regular feature in Isherwood's Berlin life, but there were other, more transient encounters. On one occasion, Isherwood arrived home with a youth he had picked up while drunk. Unfortunately for him, Walter was lying in wait. "You can picture the scene which followed," he told Spender. Isherwood was accustomed (though not reconciled) to Walter's affairs with women, but when Walter betrayed him with another man—"a tout from S. America who promised to take him to Paris"—Isherwood felt that he had endured enough and did his best to break off the relationship. Walter, however, proved tenacious.

Consequently, Isherwood remained short of money. Matters were made even worse when in September 1931 the British government abandoned the gold standard. This resulted in a devaluation of the pound against foreign currencies, and Isherwood's allowance no longer covered his expenses. "For God's sake try and scrounge some reviewing or something for us before you leave London," he urged Spender, "as things are looking pretty black here." He could not afford many scruples, and although he described the contents of the first issue of *Action,* the New Party's magazine, as "the rankest John Bull stuff," he wrote to its editor, Harold Nicolson, offering him the occasional "Berlin Letter" and asking whether he might review books. The New Party had been founded earlier in the year by Oswald Mosley, and was swiftly (and presciently) anathematized by the communist *Daily Worker* as "fascist." "They're the dirtiest lot of scum in England," Edward Upward warned Isherwood, "but provided they pay you properly and don't require you to make statements about the communists I suppose no harm will be done. Whatever happens write nothing about politics—otherwise we shall never be able to meet again." As this letter shows, Upward was by now thoroughly committed to communism and was regularly attending the Party's committee rooms in Bethnal Green in the East End of London. "Don't believe a word you hear about the communists," he wrote. "It's quite untrue that they falsify the news. All bourgeois news is false, consciously or unconsciously. Naturally police spies and alarmed dabblers in communism don't or won't understand this [. . .] All this talk about communist extremism is trash." Aware this lecture was becoming rather wild, he added: "I'm ill or I shouldn't be writing like this. Stephen alarmed me. But for Mortmere's sake don't commit yourself."

On his return to Berlin, Spender settled into rooms in Kleist-Strasse and was once again almost constantly in Isherwood's company. When Upward announced that he had joined the Communist Party, the two friends were astonished and impressed. "Communism to us was an extremist, almost unnatural cause," Spender recalled, "and we found it hard to believe that any of our friends could be communists. However, [Upward's] action deepened our interest in Berlin politics. We discussed them with our friends, went to political meetings, read the newspapers and a good deal of political literature attentively. Whenever we could, we went to see those Russian films which were shown often in Berlin at this period: *Earth, The General Line, The Mother, Potemkin, Ten Days That Shook the World, The Way into Life*, etc."—all of them presumably distributed by Willi Münzenberg in the hope of rallying the proletariat to the communist cause. "We used to go on long journeys to little cinemas in the outer suburbs of Berlin, and there among the grimy tenements we saw images of the New Life of the workers building with machine tools and tractors their socially just new world under the shadows of baroque statues reflected in ruffled waters of Leningrad, or against waving, shadow-pencilled plains of corn." Isherwood was probably more interested in the means than the end, revolution and street-battles making rather better copy than a socially just new world. He later described the first book he wrote about 1930s Berlin, *Mr Norris Changes Trains*, as "a heartless fairy-story about a real city in which human beings were suffering the miseries of political violence and near starvation," and he castigated "the young foreigner who passed gaily through these scenes of desolation, misinterpreting them to suit his childish fantasy" as a "monster." In fact the narrator's insouciant objectivity was what gave the Berlin books their immediacy and their "truth." This was after all a city in which appalling things were shrugged off or regarded as a price worth paying for the improvements political change would supposedly bring.

In January 1932, at Spender's prompting, Isherwood wrote to his new publisher, John Lehmann, to tell him about his literary projects. "At present I'm writing an autobiographical book, not a novel, about my education—preparatory school, public school and University. After this is finished I shall start a book about Berlin, which will probably be a novel written in diary-form and semi-political. Then I have another autobiographical book in mind. And possibly a travel book. So you see, I have no lack of raw material! It is only a question of time and energy." It is not known what the last two books were: it is possible that Isherwood, who had in fact done very little traveling outside Germany, was bluffing. In the meantime he wondered whether he might contribute to the "Hogarth Letters" series. The Press had invited a number of authors to write pamphlets "in letter form and anything between 4,000 and 10,000 words [. . .] to any one, dead or alive, real or imaginary, on any subject," as Leonard Woolf explained to E. M. Forster. Most writers chose imaginary or emblematic correspondents (Virginia Woolf's *Letter to a Young Poet* and Hugh Walpole's *Letter to a Young Novelist,* and so on), and Isherwood suggested he might write a *Letter to an Enemy.* "The 'Enemy,' " he explained, "is a sort of embodiment of everything I detest—and has, I hasten to add, absolutely nothing to do with Mr Wyndham Lewis." "The moods, the pleasures and preoccupations of the early 'thirties are so far away now that they seem beyond recapture," Lehmann recalled in 1957; "but as I turn again the pages of the little booklets of the Hogarth Letters, it appears to me that they preserve, like a row of jam jars on the larder shelf, the essence and the flavour of the time." Unfortunately, there was no Isherwood to take down from the shelf since he never wrote his Letter.

He was, however, working on his book about school and university, producing a brief but detailed account of St. Edmund's. Lehmann was keener on the Berlin project, but as Isherwood explained, "I don't feel nearly ready to write it yet. I should probably have to get away from Berlin first. Whereas the other book is all in my head already." By March, however, he appeared to be concentrating on his Berlin novel again and told Lehmann he hoped to have it finished by the autumn—unless he decided to scrap it altogether. "I'm afraid it's rather difficult to send you bits of it," he told the eager publisher, "as it is written entirely in the form of a diary, without any break in the narrative. It will have lots of characters and be full of 'news' about Berlin. I think the climax will be during these elections [of March 1932, when the Nazis gained in power and Hindenburg failed to get an overall majority]. Frank journalism, in fact." The book's working title was "In the Winter."

Meanwhile, *The Memorial* was published by the Hogarth Press on February 17, 1932. Isherwood had agreed to indicate the time line and to expunge the phrase "he can lick his arse," and Lehmann had commissioned a very beautiful but wholly uncommercial dust-jacket, depicting the masklike faces of a woman and a boy flanking a bare tree, from the painter John Banting, a friend of Humphrey Spender. "E. M. Forster is said to like *The Memorial* and to be writing an article boosting it," Isherwood told Upward with studied casualness. Forster read and admired the novel, but did not give it the public endorsement it needed, and although it received some respectful reviews, few recognized what an accomplished novel it was, and sales were poor. "They are actually £1 more than I'd reckoned!" Isherwood told Lehmann when the figures came through. "As long as one or two good critics like my work I am really quite satisfied. I am only sorry that I haven't been a financial success because I know that the Hogarth Press has lost money on me."

As well as being the sort of novel that enhances a young writer's reputation, *The Memorial* served a second, more private purpose. It was another carefully mounted assault upon the character and values of Kathleen Bradshaw-Isherwood, one even more offensive and hurtful than *All the Conspirators*. The novel was dedicated "To My Father," which may have been appropriate given the book's central image of a war memorial, but not everyone agreed that it was a fitting tribute to a dead hero. Uncle Jack's son, Thomas, recalled that for some considerable time after the novel was published the young author was considered persona non grata in the family.

This is hardly surprising. Although clearly a work of fiction, the novel borrowed a great deal from life, with little attempt at disguise. The use of the name "Vernon" for the principal family did not spare the Bradshaw-Isherwoods' blushes among their Cheshire neighbors, who would have been perfectly aware that Marple Hall was built by the Vernon family. Furthermore, the Hall is quite clearly based on Marple in many of its architectural details and its setting. The village of Chapel Bridge is recognizably Marple, and Gatesley, where the Scrivens live in a house based on the Monkhouses' Meadow Bank, is Disley. There are references to such local features as Cobden Edge and Kinder Scout and to local families named Cooper (the Wyberslegh tenants) and Townend (tenants of one of the other estate farms). Caretakers are brought in to look after the empty Hall, just as they were by Uncle Henry, and they are called Compstall, the name of a hamlet just to the northwest of Marple. The vulgar, mill-owning Mr. Ramsbotham is based on the father of Isherwood's childhood friend Michael Scott. Names ending in "-botham" (properly pronounced "-bottom," though such variations as "beau-tham" have been adopted by the genteel) are common in Cheshire and Lancashire and had long been a staple of music-hall jokes, but it is likely that Isherwood chose the name as a deliberate dig at the long-serving family solicitor, Herbert Sidebotham.

The cruelest portrait in the book, however, was that of Kathleen in the character of Lily Vernon. In later life Isherwood described Lily and Major Charlesworth, the elderly admirer who accompanies her on genteel archaeological outings, as "offensively dull substitutes for Kathleen and Frank," but this is not entirely accurate. Although, as Kathleen noted when she first met him, Frank was "fond of pictures and architecture," Charlesworth (whose name was borrowed from one of Kathleen's friends) is less like Isherwood's father than Kathleen's cousin Raymond Smythies, who frequently accompanied her on outings similar to those described in the novel. Frank is much more apparent in the novel as Richard Vernon, the dead "hero-father," a constant source of reproach to his son. Lily, however, resembles Kathleen in thought, word and deed. She will not let go of the past, which she regards with a snobbish romanticism. The world she still believes in passionately, where everyone has their place, is represented by her gaga father-in-law, a comic-grotesque figure whose appearances in the village are treated with absurd but nevertheless genuine deference. Even this is not quite enough for her. When the local poor emerge from their cottages to thank Mrs. Vernon for giving them parcels, Lily wishes that "they would have curtsied as she'd seen the villagers do in a village in Suffolk where she sometimes went to stay [and which was the county of Kathleen's birth]. It was the only thing she criticized about Chapel Bridge—the people seemed so very off-hand. The bows were little more than nods." Her dismay upon discovering that the names on the memorial are undifferentiated by rank is Kathleen's. Like Kathleen, Lily paints accomplished watercolors. Major Charlesworth's view of her sanctity parodies Kathleen's status as a "Holy Widow," but it is clear in several small touches that such women are destructive, even murderous. When dining with Eric, we are told, Lily "had placed the tablespoon and fork further apart, brushing the tumbler with her silk sleeve, making it faintly ring. A sailor was almost instantaneously drowned." Although Eric's ungainliness, unruly hair, self-disgust, religious fervor and repressed hero-worship all suggest Richard Isherwood, his preference for the Scriven household over his own, his hatred of the Past and desire to destroy large portions of Cambridge obviously belong to Isherwood himself.

Re-reading the book, Upward still thought it masterly but now expressed some reservations. Most of these were technical, and he thought the novel contained too many hints that only the initiated would understand, but he was also concerned about Isherwood's handling of homosexuality in the novel. Although Isherwood had drawn extensively on his own experiences in Berlin when depicting the life of Edward Blake, Upward thought the book "might have been written by someone who knew nothing at all about buggery [. . .] I starved for a scene in which [Edward] would have some fairly violent emotional exchange with a boy—as for example the scene when Walter locked you out of your room. Anything—as long as it showed even remotely what buggery is really like. But I suppose that wouldn't have been allowed by Hogarth." This was undoubtedly true, as Isherwood knew, since Spender had been having great difficulty finding anyone willing to take the risk of publishing his novel *The Temple,* which had an explicitly homosexual theme. As it was, one reviewer felt that *The Memorial* "contained a disproportionately large number of homosexual characters."

With its bold and complex structure, its confident handling of the non-chronological narrative and the large cast of fully realized characters of all ages and backgrounds, *The Memorial* is a remarkably assured novel. Unlike Isherwood's later novels, which tend to be more directly autobiographical, it creates an autonomous fictional world. Auden and Spender were unstinting in their praise, the former declaring that "If it isn't at once recognized as a masterpiece, I give up hope of any taste in this country." Auden was of course somewhat partisan, but *The Memorial* remains one of Isherwood's best, and least regarded, books.

In April Isherwood accepted an invitation to spend a couple of months with Francis Turville-Petre, who had returned to Germany and had rented a lakeside house in Mohrin, a village on the Polish-German border some sixty-five kilometers to the northeast of the capital. Fronny was living with a youth named Werner, had persuaded Erwin Hansen to act as his cook-housekeeper, and hired a sixteen-year-old Berliner named Heinz Neddermeyer to help around the house. Heinz was a semi-orphan, an only child whose mother had died young and who, although in contact with his father, lived with his elderly grandmother in a basement flat in Frankfurter Allee in the eastern part of the city. Unlike the flashy, narcissistic, self-assured Walter, with his rowdily affectionate family, he seemed alluringly vulnerable. What he wanted, Isherwood decided, was an elder brother.

Heinz was not conventionally attractive. He had a virtually bridgeless nose, the result of a childhood fight, which emphasized the fullness of his lips, and these features, along with his "round head and close-curling hair," Isherwood thought, "gave him a somewhat negroid appearance." He nicknamed him "Nigger Boy." In fact (the damaged nose apart), this look was not that unusual in Berlin and could more properly be described as Slavic. Heinz also had large, trusting brown eyes, and it was probably this as much as anything that made him so attractive to Isherwood, who was almost exactly twice his age. He was less bright and worldly than Walter, but also less devious and exploitative. Isherwood realized that he "had found someone emotionally innocent, entirely vulnerable and uncritical, whom he could protect and cherish as his very own." In other words, he had found the person for whom he had been looking in all his relationships with adolescents. He may not have recognized this immediately. He later wrote that he "wasn't yet aware that he was letting himself in for a relationship which would be far more serious than any he had had in his life." Indeed, he was still involved with Walter and with several other young men, including Karl-Heinz Müller.

Mohrin was a very small community and since there was very little to do there it was an ideal place to get down to some work. Without the distractions of the Berlin bars and such friends as Jean Ross and Gerald Hamilton, without the constant worry about Walter, and with Erwin Hansen to cook and clean, Isherwood was making real progress with his various projects at the Villa Pressmann, or "Männer Haus," as he punningly christened it. This joke seemed rather less funny when they received a visit from the local police, after a disgruntled shopkeeper wrote a letter "denouncing us as buggers." Fortunately, Hansen was able to sort things out, but this incident gave them all an unpleasant shock.

Isherwood later claimed that Fronny "soon got tired of Mohrin and began going off to Berlin for long weekends, taking Erwin with him." Fronny might well have been bored, but another reason for his spending time in Berlin was that he and Isherwood had frequent rows about their respective lovers. There was an inherent difficulty in the whole setup at Villa Pressmann and in the relationships the Englishmen were having with their German lovers. While Werner had been invited to the villa as a guest, Heinz had initially been recruited as a servant. For Fronny the fact that Isherwood and Heinz were now lovers presented problems of etiquette and he insisted that Isherwood should pay half Heinz's wages. Isherwood agreed to this, but disliked the fact that Fronny continued to treat Heinz as a hired hand. One evening he returned from a visit to see Katz in Berlin to find that Fronny had got drunk and been rude to Heinz, who had promptly given notice. "I persuaded him to stay, of course," he told Spender. "However, two can play at that game. I have started being poisonous to Werner." Isherwood's campaign against the unfortunate Werner merely made matters worse. "I was so unpleasant to Werner that Fronny took him away with him to Berlin on Sunday night," Isherwood confessed. "Erwin went with them and is to return this evening. I have had two idyllic days with Heinz, who takes it as a matter of course that he shall do all the housework and cooking while I write my novel. Yesterday I worked the whole day except between 2.0 and 4.0 P.M. when, at Heinz's suggestion, we went to bed. Why aren't all boys like this?"

Isherwood's ideal boy was expected to look after him and keep out of his way while he worked, then join him eagerly in bed. Unlike the disruptive and distracting Walter, Heinz was pliable and cooperative, actually enjoying the work—or so Isherwood decided. "No lover, however literary, could have shared Christopher's work with him," he recalled. "But Heinz did the next best thing; while Christopher wrote, Heinz collaborated with him indirectly by sweeping the floors, tidying up the garden, cooking the meals."[5] He and Heinz "were absurdly like the most ordinary happily married heterosexual couple," Isherwood declared, and it is undoubtedly true that in the 1930s the majority of men would have expected their wives to fulfill a role similar to that of Heinz in Isherwood's well-ordered life. However, such notions are surprising coming from someone purportedly in revolt against the standards and attitudes of his own upper-middle-class background.

Among the visitors to the Villa Pressmann was Spender, who had recently moved to a room at Lützow-Platz 10, and planned to bring Georg with him. Isherwood recalled that he had "tried hard to discourage" Spender from visiting, "but Stephen had seemed unconscious of Christopher's attitude." In fact Spender was painfully con-

---

5. Not that Heinz's cooking was always a success. "Heinz cooked a Schnitzel here last night," Isherwood told Spender on one occasion. "God knows what he did to it. He made it smell exactly like an Airdale [sic] dog."

scious of Isherwood's attitude, particularly since he had assumed he would be spending the whole of April at the villa. "For some reason they are obviously very anxious I shouldn't come, which rather annoyed me at first," he told Lehmann, "but now I feel pleased about it, as I am planning an independent life which is always a good thing." A fortnight later, Spender was still trying to convince himself of this: "I have thoroughly made up my mind that it is all for the best," he declared bravely. It is possible he also said something to Kathleen, whom he occasionally telephoned or visited with news of Isherwood. According to Richard, Kathleen suspected (quite wrongly) that Spender was in love with her son and thought that Christopher was "rather hard on him."

Isherwood ascribed his unfriendliness to the effect he feared the camera-wielding Spender would have on his burgeoning love affair with Heinz. "Clicking that camera, Stephen seemed to mock and expose you, even while he flattered you with his piercing curiosity. Jealously, almost superstitiously, Christopher feared that Stephen would somehow alter his image in Heinz's eyes and make Heinz unable to go on loving him." Isherwood knew all about flattering people with a piercing curiosity and it may be that he was also worried that Spender was proving too apt a disciple. He attempted to use the prospect of other guests to put off Spender. "*Two* great waddling flap-cunted pouter-bubbed whores are coming for Whitsun," he warned. "They'll eat up our food and fuck with our boys and poison all the fish in the lake. Don't blame me if Georg returns with Siph." Spender ignored this letter and in the event the visit went well. "It is awfully nice and tremendous fun," he reported back to Lehmann. "They do everything themselves, cooking, cleaning the house—everything. That's really how I would like to live most of all."

Spender was determined to engineer a meeting between Isherwood and Lehmann, whom he had invited to Insel Rügen for a week. This plan was foiled by the German post, and by the time Isherwood learned that Lehmann was going to be passing through Berlin on his way back to London it was too late to organize a rendezvous. In July Isherwood and Heinz joined Spender at Sellin, booking into the Pension Seeadler, which stood in a meadow alongside a church. Spender continued to remain at the ill-fated Pension Idyll "in spite of and because of the arrival of several dozen schoolboys from Berlin," Isherwood told Lehmann. The two friends used towels to signal to each other from upstairs windows, rather as Isherwood had done in Disley with Rachel Monkhouse. After "holding out for a fortnight," Spender relinquished the schoolboys and, along with his brother Humphrey, took rooms in the Seeadler, which was run by Christian evangelicals, and was suitably ascetic. "We have Bibel Stunden at all hours of the day," Spender complained. "They don't give us enough to eat, at least they didn't until we made them give us 6 meals a day instead of 3 for about a fortnight, and what we do eat is imbibed on chairs in the passage. The coffee is made from petroleum. Otherwise the place is quite nice."

They would escape this atmosphere by going for walks inland or sunning themselves on the beach. As Isherwood described in "On Ruegen Island," holidaymakers built low sand bulwarks to give themselves a modicum of privacy, and constructed elaborate sandcastles decorated with miniature pennants, many of them bearing the swastika. Despite this grim portent, the holiday was carefree, much of it—such as the occasion when Isherwood buried Heinz up to his neck in the sand—recorded on camera by Humphrey.

The Sellin party was joined by Wilfrid Israel and a new friend, William Robson-Scott, who had been introduced to Isherwood by a mutual acquaintance working as a Berlin correspondent for the *Manchester Guardian*. Three years older than Isherwood, Robson-Scott was a lecturer in English at Berlin University. He had the appearance of an English schoolmaster, with round horn-rimmed spectacles and hair which Isherwood described as "short and vigorous, like grass clinging to the edge of a cliff." Although he later married very happily, he was at this time homosexual and, according to Isherwood, occasionally paid boys to beat him. It may have been this streak of masochism which led Isherwood to use some of his mannerisms for the character of Peter Wilkinson in *Goodbye to Berlin,* who suffers a great deal of psychological torment in his relationship with Otto Nowak—as, of course, Isherwood did in his relationship with Walter. For his part, Robson-Scott thought Isherwood "a very *precise* sort of man. If you went anywhere with him you saw him watching like a very intelligent bird, picking up everything that there was to be seen and assimilated."

"There was something toughly resilient in William's make-up," Isherwood recalled. "He could bend before storms without breaking." He had learned to do this during his traumatic childhood. His mother died when he was ten, and the following year his elder brother died in a freak accident while shooting crows in the family garden. (William had discovered the body.) His other brother enlisted in 1914 and almost immediately succumbed to influenza. Having suffered three deaths in the family before he was fifteen, Robson-Scott had become deeply apprehensive about life, believing that if one loved somebody the natural consequence of this would be their death. He underwent therapy, becoming a patient of Freud's principal British disciple, Ernest Jones. A gifted linguist, he taught himself Dutch while working as a publisher in London, and subsequently was appointed as a lecturer at Birkbeck College. He decided, however, that there was very little Dutch literature worth reading, and so taught himself German and translated Freud's *The Future of Illusion*. He came to Berlin partly to continue his analysis, and almost immediately found himself a job at the University. His entanglements with various boys provided Isherwood with much sympathetic amusement and Isherwood dedicated *Lions and Shadows* to him.

It was almost certainly after they returned to Berlin at the end of July that Humphrey Spender took the famous photograph of Isherwood standing at the window of a Berlin apartment, a photograph that fixed Isherwood in his Berlin persona and might almost have been an illustration of the opening lines of *Goodbye to Berlin:*

> From my window, the deep solemn massive street. Cellar-shops where the lamps burn all day, under the shadow of top-heavy balconied façades, dirty plaster frontages embossed with scroll-work and heraldic devices. The whole district is like this: street leading into street of houses like shabby monumental safes crammed with the tarnished valuables and second-hand furniture of a bankrupt middle class.
>
> I am a camera with its shutter open, quite passive, recording, not thinking. Recording the man shaving at the window opposite and the woman in the kimono washing her hair. Some day, all this will have to be developed, carefully printed, fixed.

In fact the window in which Isherwood is standing, often wrongly identified, was in Stephen Spender's room, overlooking Lützow-Platz, a wintry photograph of which, also taken by Humphrey Spender, was used on the dust-jacket of the first edition of *Goodbye to Berlin*. Isherwood appears to be looking out of the window, his left arm raised casually, his hand resting on the glass. The photograph was in fact carefully staged. A discussion of the cowlick that Isherwood shared with Hitler led to the suggestion that Isherwood should raise his arm in a parody of the Nazi salute, although Nazis saluted with the right arm.

Such salutes had become even more widespread after the election on July 30, when the Nazis gained a majority in the Reichstag. The government had been driven out of office, the President of the Police arrested, and martial law declared in Berlin. Isherwood nevertheless determined to stay on in the city, but on August 4 he returned to London to spend two months at Pembroke Gardens. Given Kathleen's feelings about Walter, Isherwood did not mention Heinz to her. Upward assured Isherwood that Kathleen almost certainly would have taken her dear Christopher's new boyfriend in her stride. "It's quite astonishing how you have educated that woman," he told Isherwood. "I foresee a time when, like the son who was sent to Australia for stealing, you will be able to do nothing wrong." Isherwood spent his time in London working on his epic novel and catching up with old friends. He saw a good deal of Hector Wintle, who had just published a novel, *Edgar Prothero,* which he had dedicated to Isherwood, and was about to depart for China as a ship's doctor. Isherwood also saw Jean Ross, who had recently left Berlin and was living at the Pembridge Gardens Hotel in Notting Hill, and Olive Mangeot, who now spent much of her time standing on street corners peddling copies of the *Daily Worker.*

It was during this trip that Isherwood finally got to meet John Lehmann at the Hogarth Press. He was slightly wary of his new publisher, but nevertheless soon started signing letters to him with "Best love." The two young men had more in common than they would care to admit, including a certain coldness behind their blue eyes and a habit of lecturing their friends on literary matters. This made for a complicated relationship, which remained cordial but was never entirely secure. Like most authors, Isherwood was aware that it was necessary to treat publishers with caution. The principal difference between the two men, however, was that Lehmann had absolutely no sense of humor, least of all about himself. As it was, he shortly left the Hogarth Press in order to follow in the footsteps of his new friends, living abroad and devoting himself to writing, specifically to poetry. This was an unwise decision, since his real talent was as an editor, and his own writing—his poetry in particular—was very poor indeed. He saw himself as a d'Artagnan to the Athos, Porthos and Aramis of Auden, Spender and Isherwood, but he simply lacked the style.

Isherwood also met people with whom he could relax and enter close friendships unsullied by commerce. Spender introduced him to William Plomer, who in turn introduced him to E. M. Forster, the writer who had probably had more influence on him than any other. As often happened with Forster, his friendship with Plomer had started with a disinterested fan letter, which he had written in July 1929 after reading a story in Plomer's first collection, *I Speak of Africa*. The two men met later that year at a party hosted by the Woolfs, who were Plomer's publishers. By this time the twenty-five-year-old Plomer, who had been born and spent much of his early life in

South Africa, had settled in England, where he became part of a distinct homosexual-literary coterie, which included Forster and his close friend and confidant, J. R. Ackerley. Unlike the reckless Ackerley, who worked in the BBC Talks Department and was to become the long-serving literary editor of the Corporation's magazine *The Listener* in 1935, Plomer was a discreet man, although almost equally energetic in his pursuit of sexual encounters among the capital's complaisant working classes. A solid and soberly dressed figure with owlish spectacles (a legacy of Rugby's appalling wartime diet, he claimed), Plomer had the reassuring air of a GP on call; but he also had an anarchic and macabre sense of humor which erupted in such ballads as "The Dorking Thigh" and his novel *The Case Is Altered*. (The latter was based on the violent murder of Plomer's landlady, fragments of whom he had been obliged to pick off the soft furnishings.) His first novel, *Turbott Wolfe,* was a bold study of miscegenation, published in 1926 to excellent reviews in England but cries of outrage in South Africa. It was followed in 1931 by *Sado*, a reasonably discreet but nevertheless undisguised account of a relationship between an Englishman and a young Japanese, a relationship based upon his own affair with a student while he was teaching in Tokyo in the late 1920s. Spender had sent the novel to Isherwood, who had grandly judged it "awfully good of its kind." In fact Isherwood became a great admirer of Plomer as well as a good friend and the grateful recipient of his amusing letters and absurd picture postcards, written in a beautiful calligraphic hand, often in violet ink. Plomer enjoyed receiving letters in Isherwood's "very small, regular, and evidently imperturbable handwriting," which was in marked contrast to his own. He described him as "a letter writer of exceptional brilliance." This was undoubtedly true of this period, when Isherwood saw himself as a reporter sending lively dispatches back to England from the Berlin front. "The latest is that there'll probably be a Coup d'Etat here," he wrote that October.

> Papen will light Schleicher's cigar with the constitution and the Reichstag will be turned into a drill-hall for little Nazi patriots.[6] Poor old Germany, she's not much of an Etat to coup. There was the usual goose-stepping parade on Hindenburg's birthday, and a most pathetic talkie of Hindenburg, propped up with billiard-cues and held together with string, stumbling through an Address to the People which he could hardly read, although it was painted in half-inch letters, because, as national Hero, he isn't allowed to wear spectacles. The Address was the usual dope—an appeal to all capitalist parties to stop fighting each other and unite to smash the Labour Movement. Or, in other words, to 'forget mere political differences and present a resolute front to the enemies of the Fatherland'.

No wonder Plomer declared that "In the early Thirties I would sooner have a report on Germany from Christopher Isherwood than from Sir Neville Henderson."[7] Others

---

6. Franz von Papen had been elected Chancellor in June; General Kurt von Schleicher, the ruthless head of the German army, was serving as Minister of Defense in von Papen's cabinet and would succeed him as Chancellor in December.

7. Henderson was a distinguished career diplomat who later became British ambassador to Germany.

agreed. Harold Nicolson had failed to secure a regular "Berlin Letter" from Isherwood but had commissioned him to write an article for *Action* on "The Youth Movement in Germany," and the following year Ackerley would unsuccessfully attempt to recruit him to report on the May Day celebrations in Berlin for the BBC, recommending him to the Corporation as "an intelligent and serious-minded young man."

Plomer described Isherwood at this period as: "Compactly built, with his commanding nose, Hitlerian lock of fair hair falling over one bright eye, and the other looking equally bright under a bristly eyebrow already inclined to beetle, an expression of amusement in a photo-finish with an expression of amazement as he came to the conclusion of a story and almost choking with delight at the climax." In spite of stern declarations of political commitment, and occasional youthful priggishness, Isherwood's circle rarely confused seriousness with solemnity, as their letters amply demonstrate. Even the increasingly doctrinaire Upward, who remained by far the most politically committed of the group, continued to regale Isherwood with hilariously scabrous and surrealist accounts of his life. "When [Isherwood] appeared in person," Plomer recalled, "his conversation continued in exactly the same tone as his letters. 'Amazing' was one of his favourite words, and his capacity to be amazed by the behaviour of the human species, so recklessly displayed everywhere, made him a most entertaining talker."

Forster was a rather more daunting prospect than the genial Plomer. While Plomer was a mere eight months older than Isherwood, Forster was of Kathleen and Frank's generation, born in 1879, and had for many years been one of the leading novelists of the time. When he had heard that Forster had read and admired *The Memorial,* Isherwood announced: "My literary career is over—I don't give a damn for the Nobel Prize or the Order of Merit—*I've been praised by Forster!*" Now that he was going to be introduced to the great man over lunch, he was rather nervous, but disguised his apprehension with a joke, telling Spender: "I shall spend the entire morning making-up." The lunch took place in Forster's flat at 26 Brunswick Square in Bloomsbury, and Isherwood at once fell under Forster's spell. "Christopher made a good disciple," he recalled; "like most arrogant people, he loved to bow down unconditionally from time to time. No doubt he gazed at Forster with devoted eyes and set himself to entertain him with tales of Berlin and the boy world, judiciously spiced with expressions of social concern—for he must have been aware from the start that he had to deal with a moralist."

Forster became one of the first and most important guru figures in Isherwood's life. The phrase Isherwood used about him was one he would use about his own father: an "anti-heroic hero." Just as Isherwood was to some extent looking for the younger brother in his relationships with teenagers, he was often looking for a father, or at any rate a father figure, in his relationships with older friends. Forster was quite literally old enough to be Isherwood's father, but at the same time youthful and sympathetic enough in his opinions and outlook to be his friend, and he became a benign counterpart to that other substitute father, Rolf Katz, who was a somewhat stern parent, forever delivering lectures. Forster was subsequently invited to tea on a day when Kathleen and Richard were safely out of the way on one of their archaeological expeditions.

"Dear Isherwood—we do drop 'Mr,' don't we?" Forster's first surviving letter to Isherwood opened. He was thanking Isherwood for sending him *All the Conspira-*

tors. "I don't like it as much as 'The Memorial,' " Forster wrote, "but that is not the point, and there are things in it that I like very much." Forster did not say what these were, but he must have recognized that the novel was in some ways a tribute to his own work, and this would have pleased him. No one much minds being told that someone prefers their second book to their first. "I didn't send you my novel so much because I thought it had any particular merit," Isherwood replied, "as because I once refused to show it to you, and this seemed to me afterwards silly." That "once" suggests a rapidly developing friendship, though the two men cannot have seen much of each other since Isherwood would be in London only another two weeks.

Isherwood was obliged to sort out two important relationships during his visit. The first was with André Mangeot, with whom he needed to come to some sort of accommodation. One reason for pacifying Mangeot may have been that Isherwood intended to describe his life at Cresswell Place in the autobiographical book he was still hoping to write. The meeting must have gone well, since Isherwood lunched with Mangeot the day before he returned to Berlin. Thereafter, however, the two men seem to have had almost nothing to do with each other.

The other matter was even more awkward. As Isherwood later acknowledged, part of the pleasure of being in London was that he was considered "the self-exiled mysterious 'Man from Berlin.' " This was not a role he wanted Stephen Spender to usurp. He was also concerned about maintaining some sort of copyright on the material he had been assiduously collecting in the city for his various literary projects. Since he and Spender spent so much time in each other's company and knew many of the same people, who was to say which of them had "literary rights" in, say, Jean Ross or Gerald Hamilton? Although principally a poet, Spender continued to write short stories, often autobiographical, and Isherwood did not want to be scooped. Spender recalled that the actual quarrel took place publicly at a party given by William Plomer and his partner Anthony Butts.

> Christopher showed so clearly his irritation with me that I decided I must lead a life which was far more independent of his. So the next day I called at his mother's house in Kensington, where he was staying. I explained that I had noticed I was getting on his nerves, and that when we returned to Berlin we should see nothing, or very little, of each other. He said he was quite unaware of any strain, and that of course we should meet, exactly as before. I went away not at all relieved, because I thought he was refusing, more out of pride than friendship, to face a situation which he himself had made obvious. Moreover, he had expressed his views in the accents of ironic correctitude with which Auden, [Upward] and he could sometimes be insulting. Next day I received a letter from him saying that if I returned to Berlin he would not do so, that my life was poison to him, that I lived on publicity, that I was intolerably indiscreet, etc.

Spender was so upset by the letter that he burned it, and instead of returning to Berlin he spent the winter in Barcelona. Spender undoubtedly was, and remained, indiscreet— it was one of the things that made him such good company—but Isherwood's letter was a bluff. It is inconceivable he would not have returned to Berlin, regardless of Spender's plans, and he evidently hoped that if he barked loud enough his former disciple would take fright. Spender did, later admitting to Isherwood that he had been "very 'erschuttert' [shaken] by our row." "It is not exactly that I want to be with you or see you very much," he explained (adding in the margin: "I hope you will understand what I mean by this. I mean I don't want to repeat our former experiment").

> But you are the one person who *could* always understand me whether we are together or not, if you are willing to try. Or, rather, in a curious way, Freeman [the 'Marston' of Spender's early love poems] is another, because he is the only other person who has seen me at my best & worst & yet trusts me completely. Of course, whatever happens, I shall go on living just in the same way, & I shall go on with my work, but if I felt you had abandoned the irritating, continual effort to love me & forgive me I would be very disappointed: in fact much more than that. You & Freeman are the people I most like. For Freeman everything is simple & there is no conflict. With you it is different, but in spite of everything you are always fighting & there is something very clear in my picture of you.

Once Spender had been frightened off, Isherwood was happy to resume normal relations. "He needed Stephen's friendship as much as Stephen needed his," he recalled. "Christopher tended to make friends with his moral superiors. It was only with Stephen that he had faults in common—which was relaxing and created a special kind of intimacy, when it didn't provoke competition." It was an intimacy which endured, although there were frequent occasions over the years when the two men annoyed each other.

Spender felt that this brief spat significantly altered their relationship. "It made me break with my habit of dependence on Christopher," he wrote. "Christopher was at fault, perhaps, in not simply accepting my offer that we should agree to see less of one another. But I had been seriously at fault long before this, and doubtless my attempt to manipulate a change in our relationship, after my prolonged and deceptive docility, was irritating." Both accounts of the quarrel were written long afterward and both, in their feline way, give a vivid sense of this lifelong friendship.

Isherwood also got some useful work done during his stay in London, making use of Richard's secretarial skills by dictating episodes from his novel to him. Quite why he chose this method of composition is not known. As he acknowledged, "It is immeasurably more embarrassing for a writer to invent crudely in someone else's presence than to confide to him the most shameful personal revelations." Lehmann, however, noted that Isherwood had the knack of working out a complex story and being able to carry it in his head before writing it down, and in later years Isherwood often dictated work, either to a stenographer or to a tape recorder. It may also have been that, since he was working on material concerning Jean Ross and the Wolffs, gradually transforming them respectively into the loquacious Sally Bowles and the rowdy Nowaks, he needed to test the dialogue by saying it aloud, before an audience. The story he produced about Sally Bowles in particular has large sections of pure dialogue. Richard was not typing this material, merely writing it out longhand, and although his handwriting was clear, it resembled that of a child, the large rounded letters printed rather than joined up, and the paper was often decorated with inky blots. He was now twenty-one, but his handwriting remained childlike throughout his life. Isherwood's hand also resembled that of a schoolboy, but an older and rather more sophisticated one. It was meticulously neat, rarely disfigured by crossings-out or other alterations, and although tiny nearly always perfectly legible. Isherwood once said that in the 1920s his small writing was an indication of self-hatred, but it persisted through much happier times when he was far more at ease with himself and the world. It is nevertheless true that the unusual handwriting of both brothers suggested something about their personalities: Isherwood's that primness and steely will Auden recognized, the person who treated Spender with "ironic correctitude"; Richard's a man trapped by circumstances in his childhood. It is possible that Isherwood found his own handwriting a strain on his eyesight: one of his trips during the London visit was to an optician to be fitted with new spectacles, which he was careful to remove before being photographed. Whatever the reason, dictating to Richard, which he continued to do during the 1930s, was, he said, "a supreme act of intimacy." By the time he was ready to return to Berlin at the end of September, he had finished a draft.

As well as helping his brother, Richard was also writing his own fiction. Only fragments of stories survive, none of them dated, and since Richard's handwriting never altered throughout his life any more than his interests did, it is impossible to guess when these were written. He certainly produced something at this period that was of sufficient merit to be submitted to the Hogarth Press, where it was read by Virginia Woolf herself. "She said she was glad to see it," William Plomer told Isherwood, "but found it rather 'like knitting.'" For some reason Plomer had been delegated to return the manuscript to the author, but confessed, "I can't remember his Christian name, nor, apparently, can anybody else. He is universally known as 'Christopher's brother' & although people seem to remember every detail about him they have no idea what he is called." This, of course, was part of the problem. Richard had been doing very little in the two and a half years since he refused to continue his education. Any notion that he might find some sort of employment or constructive occupation seems to have been abandoned. He occasionally went to Wyberslegh to help on the farm, but this was more in the nature of a holiday than a job. Apart from that, he carried out small errands—shopping, returning library books—for his mother's friends and accompanied Kathleen to museums, exhibitions, the cinema and theater (usually at matinées). He pursued the sort of aimless life an unmarried daughter might have done in the Victorian era, and indeed hardly seemed to belong to the modern world at all.

Isherwood continued to work on his novel back in Nollendorfstrasse, tutored assorted pupils, and, showing perfect political evenhandedness, earned some money translating a report on the work of the IAH for Münzenberg's secretary and writing his article for *Action*. He was in fact considering joining the IAH: "It's the next nearest thing to being a communist," he told Spender. Conversations in London with Upward and the persistent bullying in Berlin of Rolf Katz (who was glumly predicting that there would soon be a military dictatorship in Berlin under von Schleicher) may have put this notion briefly into his head. He almost began to believe that he might be on the winning side since in the November elections (the fifth held that year) the Nazi vote fell by some two million, losing them thirty-four seats in the Reichstag, whereas the Communist Party made considerable gains. Isherwood's gleeful announcement that Berlin was "bright pillar-box red" may have been strictly true, but elsewhere in Germany the Nazis continued to hold sway.

Some of Isherwood's friends still found him politically muddled and naïve. Katz had been "horrified" when Isherwood remarked, "I should have understood Marx if I had met Marx." The observation was, Isherwood insisted "very self-revealing, and not nearly so arrogant as [Katz] thought it sounded." It was evidence of Upward's conviction that Isherwood could only grasp abstract ideas by meeting and talking to those who formulated them. "Katz gave me another terrific ticking-off the other day for not being a properly educated revolutionary writer," he complained to Spender. "He is very right and very wrong. I wish I didn't realize so clearly that these lectures are his particular way of sadistically psycho-buggering me." Isherwood still saw his function as a writer less to analyze politics than to observe their effect on human lives, something brought horribly alive when he witnessed the actions of some Nazis who were returning from a rally at the Sport-Palast through Bülowstrasse, an area that was staunchly communist.

> Suddenly about seven of them who were walking just in front of us attacked a youth of seventeen and drove him into a doorway, stabbing him with the spikes on the ends of their rolled banners. It was all over in a quarter of a minute and the Nazis had run off. The youth was such a clot of blood that we couldn't see how badly he was hurt, but I think one of the spikes had gone into his eye. Some men who were passing put him into a taxi. Six policemen were standing about twenty yards away, but they carefully didn't see anything.

This description comes from a letter to Spender. Isherwood re-created it in the final section of *Goodbye to Berlin,* and the skill with which he did so shows that the book was not, as he affected to believe while writing it, merely "frank journalism":

> All at once, the three SA men came face to face with a youth of seventeen or eighteen, dressed in civilian clothes, who was hurrying along in the opposite direction. I heard one of the Nazis shout: 'That's him!' and immediately all three of them flung themselves upon the young man. He uttered a scream, and tried to dodge, but they were too quick for him. In a moment they had jostled him into the shadow of a house entrance, and were standing over him, kicking him and stabbing at him with the sharp metal points of their banners. All this happened with such incredible speed that I could hardly believe my eyes—already, the three SA men had left their victim, and were barging their way through the crowd; they made for the stairs which led up to the station of the Overhead Railway.
>
> Another passer-by and myself were the first to reach the doorway where the young man was lying. He lay huddled crookedly in the corner, like an abandoned sack. As they picked him up, I got a sickening glimpse of his face—his left eye

was poked half out, and blood poured from the wound. He wasn't dead. Somebody volunteered to take him to the hospital in a taxi.

The violence is all the more shocking because of the detached, unsensational tone Isherwood adopts, and this was a literary strategy that he used very expertly throughout *Goodbye to Berlin*.

Isherwood's letters to Plomer and Spender may not have had the sober tone and political acumen of Sir Neville Henderson's reports, but they vividly conveyed the atmosphere of a city plunging into ever-increasing anarchy. Accounts of strikes and riots are interspersed with the saga of his landlady's genital boils ("They keep arriving just as if they'd made an appointment with each other," she complained), Gerald Hamilton's attendance at the wedding of the Crown Prince of Sweden's eldest son to Princess Sybilla of Coburg, Karl-Heinz Müller's nasty dose of clap, and such neighbors as "an exceedingly fat American named Mr Williams," who, "when the weather is fine, [. . .] stands in front of his door and snaps up boys like a toad catching flies."

He was able to observe Mr. Williams regularly because in November he moved into the large front room at Nollendorfstrasse. "It is lighter for the Winter months," he explained to Spender, "and, for some reason, easier to heat. Frl. Thurau is very reproachful because I insist on turning out all her potted plants. The moist stink when the oven is alight is probably as near as I shall get to a tropical forest." Isherwood's landlady consoled herself with a new lodger, "a Norwegian film actor, with incredibly beautiful blonde hair." "He plays a card game called Black Peter with Frl. Thurau and the two whores. The loser has some kind of indecent picture—a cunt or penis or bubs—drawn on his cheek or forehead with an eyebrow pencil. By the end of the evening they are all as black as niggers." Once again, Isherwood struck the heroic pose when writing to Spender: "I get uglier and more shrivelled every day. My hair is scurfy and drops out, my teeth are bad, my breath smells. However, I do see that it is absolutely necessary for me to stay on here at present. The last part of my novel requires a lot of research to document it."

Isherwood was clearly not quite as unappetizing as he claimed, and although he was seeing Heinz a couple of times a week, he continued to have sex with other boys, including the feckless Walter, who had been sacked by Katz for bad timekeeping and had got someone pregnant. He evidently asked Isherwood for money toward an abortion, but this was not something Isherwood felt morally bound to fund. He was, however, prepared to pay for services rendered: "Walter called for me at Katz's flat yesterday morning before eight A.M.," he told Spender. "The weather was glorious. We undressed in a wood and fucked. It cost twenty marks." Shortly afterward he appealed to Wilfrid Israel to find Walter some work as an errand-boy to a publisher and told Walter that he could no longer give him an allowance. Thereafter he saw a great deal less of him, but was not altogether happy when Walter found "a rich cosmopolitan actor with a car" to take care of him. After "a number of bogus reconciliations," which Isherwood soon realized "were only dictated by the state of Walter's finances," Isherwood finally broke off relations altogether.

Among the other young men Isherwood took to his bed was Stephen Spender's friend Georg. "I have a ridiculous and shameful confession to make to you," he told Spender. "I hope it will merely make you laugh."

He arrived at tea-time one afternoon, quite unexpectedly. There seemed to be no doubt whatever in his mind as to why I'd asked him. After tea he lay down on the couch and began to undress. I was first surprised and then amused and then interested. We neither of us enjoyed it in the least. Afterwards I said that I didn't want to insult him but it was possible he'd accept a trifling token of esteem. And Georg said that of course in ordinary circumstances he wouldn't dream of taking money from me, but it *did* so happen that he *was* in temporary difficulties. Afterwards I caught nine large living crabs.

There is one suspicious discrepancy in this account: Georg's arrival, Isherwood writes, was "quite unexpected," and yet in the next sentence he says that he had asked Georg to tea. Whatever the case, Spender was amused by the incident, which was fortunate, since he and Isherwood had only just patched up their quarrel. Isherwood had taken a considerable risk in making this confession, particularly since he was replying to a letter in which Spender explained that his forthcoming volume of *Poems* would not, after all, carry a dedication to Isherwood. He added that Isherwood should not think of dedicating any book to him. "Of course I quite understand about the dedication," Isherwood replied, adopting the aloof, rather formal tone he always did when saving face. "In fact, I'd half thought of writing and suggesting it to you myself. As for not dedicating anything to you—well, I shall ask you to reconsider that one day."[8] He did, however, apologize for his behavior: "I am an entirely impossible character; unstable, ill-natured, petty and selfish. I don't say this in a mealy-mouthed way. I have the virtues of my defects. But I can't imagine that I ever could or should be able to live intimately with an equal for long. In future I hope I shan't attempt it. I'm too old to change myself."

When Isherwood received his undedicated copy of *Poems,* he told Spender, "I feel nearly as pleased with the book as if I'd written it myself—and kept taking it out of the shelf and turning over the pages. [. . .] I still stick to my favourites: The Port. Children who were rough. Oh young men. After they have tired. And above all the Pylons. The Pylons is the best thing in the book, I think. At any rate, it is the best bit of work technically and is also very exciting." Isherwood may not have written the book himself, but he had made a significant contribution to it, not least by altering the final line of what became one of Spender's most famous poems, "The Truly Great." Spender had originally written "And left the air signed with their vivid honour," but Isherwood suggested that the "vivid" should be moved to qualify "air." Whether or not he was aware of it, Isherwood was playing Sassoon to Spender's Owen, and there is something in the two young men's relationship which recalls the friendship of the two earlier writers.

There were times when Isherwood found having Berlin to himself, as it were, rather lonely. His relationship with Heinz seemed set to last and certainly seemed more stable than the one with Walter. "In the old days I was obsessed with

---

8. The second edition of Spender's *Poems* carried the curious dedication "*Inscribed* To CHRISTOPHER ISHERWOOD." None of Isherwood's books is dedicated to Spender.

the idea of a Hochfrequenz! Höchste Lebensgefahr! relationship, which gave off ten-foot sparks and electrocuted everyone in the neighbourhood," he told Spender.[9] "Now I see there's something to be said for decency and a little mutual consideration and pleasantness. Thanks to Heinz." For all his virtues, however, Heinz could not provide the sort of intellectual companionship—or, with his slender grasp of English, the sort of audience—that Isherwood needed. Isherwood was therefore delighted when John Lehmann's sister Beatrix arrived in the city. Like Jean Ross before her, she came in the forlorn hope of finding work with Ufa as an actress. Beatrix had looked forward to dining with Isherwood on her first day in the city, but he couldn't make this. Instead, she "went to his slum for tea," a description of Nollendorfstrasse that would have mortally offended Frl. Thurau. "And *was* I glad to see him!" she told her sister Rosamond. She found him "sympathetic and amused" when she told him of the difficulties in her personal life. Unlike Rosamond, "Peggy" Lehmann was no great beauty, but she was certainly striking in appearance. Fiercely left-wing, funny, a gifted actress and mimic, and an admirer of his writing, she represented for Isherwood "woman in an acceptable form," as Spender put it. Isherwood himself thought he and Peggy were "much alike in temperament, a natural elder sister and elder brother," which was indeed the only relationship with a woman Isherwood wanted. They shared a sense of humor and brought out the best in each other. That first day they "made dates for future cheap fun," and thereafter met regularly. "I see a lot of Christopher and like him more and more," she told Rosamond. "He is just a spot tragic I think. And undeveloped in a way that doesn't disgust but only makes one's heart ache. He and I and a peculiar, be-wigged, Edwardian, Oscar-Wildeish person called Gerald Hamilton (ask John) lunch together in a filthy pension most days. Three giant courses for one mark! It's all very funny and slightly nightmare." She also met Wilfrid Israel, whom she described as "aristocratic and more beautiful than anything I've ever seen." She rather shared Isherwood's view of him as tantalizingly mysterious and almost impossibly refined. "Quite certainly homo, but nobody really knows anything about him," she told Rosamond. "He took me out the other evening and I felt dirty-fingered and clumsy. He is so princely and exquisite. But it gave me a deeper insight into the Jewish character than ever before."

Despairing of making any money by acting, Beatrix thought that she might take another look at a novel she had written, hoping that she would be inspired by Isherwood's company and example. She became his closest woman friend, but she was due to return to England at the beginning of 1933, and this added to Isherwood's sense of gloom. Gisa Soleweitschick had also left Berlin to continue her studies in Paris, and Christmas was particularly dispiriting. "On Christmas Eve I got stupidly drunk with Sikes [unidentified] and felt like death afterwards," he confessed to Spender. "Since then I've had flu. On Sylvester [i.e. New Year's Eve] I didn't get drunk and sat in the Kleist feeling sad. I have been seeing far too much of the dielen [bars] lately—always a bad symptom. The last few weeks have been full of sloth and sore throats and cutting a wisdom tooth. The weather clammy and ghastly." To add to

---

9. Signs stating "*Hochfrequenz! Höchste Lebensgefahr!*" were attached to electrical installations in German warning of high voltage and extreme danger.

his miseries, Uncle Henry was late with his allowance. "I fuss around the town, scratching up money like a hen," he compained to Spender. He was cheered a little by a ten-day visit from Auden, "who enjoyed himself very much, a different one every night." John Lehmann visited Berlin in February, but became embroiled in so many romances with street-boys that he did not see as much of Isherwood as he had intended. What he did see, he did not altogether like:

> His childish vindictiveness, his constant need to assert the belief in his own 'power'. His rapid hostility and intolerance, his malice. But then there's his feminine side, seen in his writings, his sex. And what's attractive, his fondness for just easy contacts, silly intimate jokes, absurd stories, anything with a tang of salaciousness or rebelliousness in it. His façade of hardness, with the underlying sentimentality, and the comic contrast of his smallness—as he sits on a sofa with a gleam on his face, he looks quite charmingly ridiculous [. . .] Notice also (suddenly seen in the Bank) his weak chin contrasting with his autocratic nose and intelligent forehead. His jealous unwillingness to let me see or come to know his other friends. (Or is that my imagination?)

Isherwood may have become more involved with the political life of the city, but toward the end of January 1933 he was complaining somewhat unpresciently to Spender that the situation in Germany seemed "very dull." "I expect there's a great deal going on behind the scenes, but one is not aware of it. Papen visits Hindenburg, Hitler visits Papen, Hitler and Papen visit Schleicher, Hugenberg visits Hindenberg and finds him out.[10] And so forth. There is no longer the slightly exhilarating awareness of crisis in the gestures of beggars and tram-conductors." He made a resolution to end six weeks of idleness and start work on his novel the very next day. "The Two Months Plan will be inaugurated with special celebrations. The shock troops attack at ten. Stalin has ordered that at least five hundred words must be written by lunchtime. In the afternoon there will be a monster demonstration against the Emotional Life." This appears to be the first time that Isherwood used military imagery to describe his writing methods, but it is a metaphor that he would return to again and again throughout his life. He saw writing as a battle, often mounted against almost insuperable opposing forces. There would be feints and retreats, but the only thing to do, experience taught him, was to keep on fighting.

The struggle seemed less daunting when he received practical encouragement from editors. Invited by Michael Roberts to contribute to *New Country,* an anthology of "Prose and Poetry by the authors of *New Signatures,*" Isherwood had sent his account of life with the Wolffs in Simeonstrasse, which he intended to incorporate in his epic Berlin novel. "It seems so idiotic to be dressed up in a sky-blue uniform as Youth knock, knock, knocking at the door," he complained to Plomer. "And when Roberts writes about wishing to represent the 'new spirit in literature, politics and education,' I just feel frankly scared. What *is* the new spirit? How could I manage to in-

---

10. Alfred Hugenberg, financier and chairman of the German Nationalist Party, who lent support to Hitler.

ject some of it into a description of a sanitorium [sic] for consumptive paupers?" Roberts evidently shared Isherwood's doubts about the story and rejected it, but accepted "An Evening at the Bay," an episode from the autobiography Isherwood was writing in tandem with his German epic. The story describes a visit by Hector Wintle to Freshwater Bay, when Isherwood and Upward were staying there in 1928. Written largely in dialogue, and set in the hotel bar where the three friends spent many evenings, it describes Upward and Isherwood encouraging Wintle to pick up a girl. Although quite bold in its depiction of courtship ("He'll get a bit of geography, with luck. She's only a teaser," someone remarks as Wintle sets off in pursuit of the girl), it may have seemed a safer bet to Roberts than the obliquely homosexual Wolff episode. Roberts may also have sensed that the latter was, as Isherwood later told John Lehmann, partly written as a riposte to the sort of story that romanticized the working classes. Since Roberts's anthology was intended as a forum for the best in committed left-wing writing, Isherwood's ironic, dissenting voice would hardly be appropriate. "An Evening at the Bay," however, was a well-observed slice of "ordinary life" in which Isherwood faithfully recorded the language of his predominantly working-class characters.

Whatever the case, Isherwood had now become a landmark in the "New Country" being mapped out back in England, alongside Upward, whose protagonist dedicates himself to the cause at the end of the short story "Sunday," Spender writing on "Poetry and the Revolution," Auden (who never actually joined the Communist Party) rallying the workers in the poem "A Communist to Others," C. Day-Lewis addressing a "Letter to a Young Revolutionary," and Charles Madge appealing "to the Intelligentsia." "I think, and the writers of this book obviously agree, that there is only one way of life for us," Roberts wrote optimistically; "to renounce the [capitalist] system now and to live by fighting against it." There was nothing very obvious in "An Evening at the Bay" to suggest Isherwood's determination to overthrow capitalism, but this was the first occasion on which his name became publicly linked with those of the writers who would come to represent the 1930s, in particular Auden and Spender.

By the time *New Country* appeared, large political changes had taken place in Germany. On January 30 Adolf Hitler was appointed Chancellor, even though he had threatened to take drastic measures to remove dissidents and undesirables (chiefly socialists and Jews) from public office as soon as he took charge. Hindenburg, who had long opposed taking Hitler into the government, was gradually won over, assured that the "Austrian corporal" could be kept under control if the cabinet was carefully selected. Such assurances were invalidated when the new Chancellor instantly demanded another election. "All words fail," Isherwood commented of the news that "Charlie Chaplin" was to join "Father Christmas" (the elderly Hugenberg, who was largely responsible for delivering this late *Weinachtsgeschenk* to the German people) in the cabinet. "Adolf, with his rectangular black moustache, has come to stay, and brought all his friends," Isherwood informed Plomer. "Nazis are to be enrolled as 'auxiliary police,' which means that one must now not only be murdered but that it is illegal to offer any resistance." Any hope that Hitler might be contained went up in flames with the Reichstag on February 27. The arson was carried out by Nazi stormtroopers but was blamed on the communists, thus giving Hitler the excuse to bring in draconian measures to limit the powers and freedom of those who opposed him. Restrictions were put on the press, freedom of speech and the right of assembly. Having failed to achieve an overall majority for his party in the election of March 5, Hitler demanded and got an Enabling Act, which gave him the unlimited powers of a dictator.

One of the first things the Nazis did was to close down the tiny Anti-War Museum, founded in 1925 by the writer Ernst Friedrich and partly sponsored by Wilfrid Israel. Members of the SA smashed up the museum and took away numerous papers, including some of Israel's letters. Israel himself was arrested, questioned, and released. Then, on March 30, another squad of stormtroopers arrived at the family store to demand that all Jewish employees should be sacked on the spot. Israel refused, and was told he would be taken into custody, along with his brother, who also worked for the company, and the firm's financial director. When Israel asked on whose authority they were being arrested, an over-excited SA man aimed a gun at his head and was only prevented from pulling the trigger by his commander. Even when held at a detention center, Israel refused to comply, but was released several hours later thanks to the intervention of a Nazi member of his own staff. Two days later came the official anti-Jewish boycott and N. Israel was picketed, very politely, according to Isherwood, who had gone to see what was happening. By way of protest, Isherwood entered the store and made a token purchase. Coming out again, he recognized that one of the stormtroopers standing at the entrance was a boy he had known at the Cosy Corner.

The anti-Jewish measures did not affect Isherwood directly, but the Nazis were also keen to eradicate any forms of "decadence" from Germany. On March 4 it had been announced that the Polizeipräsident had with immediate effect closed down a large number of bars and dance-halls, including the Kleist-Kasino, where Isherwood had spent such an unsatisfactory New Year's Eve. The Hirschfeld institute was raided later that month by the Gestapo, who were principally interested in finding out whether any documents in the archives related to members of the Nazi Party. It seems possible that Hitler was already aware of "corrupt" elements in the SA, which was commanded by the indiscreetly homosexual Ernst Roehm. Hirschfeld, realizing the threat not only to the Institute but also to his personal safety, had gone into exile, leaving Karl Giese in charge. Giese was under no illusions about the Nazis and had already begun removing important documents and artifacts from the archive and taking them abroad.

Isherwood recognized that he could not remain in Berlin much longer and on April 5, the day measures were brought in to ban Jews from the teaching professions and the Civil Service, he arrived back in London, bringing with him many of his possessions. He stayed in England until the end of the month, seeing friends and family, including William Robson-Scott, who was also making preparations to leave Berlin, and Gerald Hamilton, who had already fled after being interviewed by the political police. The latter, Kathleen noted, had "had an extremely adventurous life."

Although Isherwood had failed to persuade E. M. Forster to visit Berlin, the two writers had maintained a correspondence, and had become sufficiently intimate for Forster to show Isherwood the manuscript of *Maurice,* the novel he had written just before the First World War and dedicated "to a Happier Year." Maurice is a conventional young man from the suburbs who, after being rejected by a fellow undergraduate at Cambridge called Clive Durham with whom he had enjoyed a passionate but chaste affair, finds sexual fulfillment in the arms of a gamekeeper, Alec Scudder. Maurice imagines a future with Scudder, but the divisions of class threaten to destroy their burgeoning affair. Eventually each is persuaded of the other's good intentions, but Scudder is due to emigrate to South America. Forster had originally supplied a happy epilogue, set some years later, in which Scudder has returned from abroad and the two men are discovered living together as woodcutters in an arcadian greenwood. On the advice of friends, who found it both unconvincing and absurd, he deleted it, and the version that Isherwood read ends with Maurice seeing Scudder off at Southampton, then turning "his face towards England, in brave blur of exalted emotion."

Compared with Isherwood's experiences in the dives of Berlin, Forster's account of homosexual dalliance in Edwardian England must have seemed rather tame. Isherwood was nevertheless deeply touched to have been entrusted with the unpublished manuscript, and although he thought *Maurice* artistically "inferior" to Forster's other novels, it seemed to him "superior because of its purer passion, its franker declaration of its author's faith." On April 18 Forster came to tea at Pembroke Gardens to hear the reaction of the new generation to his period romance. He was concerned that the story might seem terribly dated. "Why *shouldn't* it date?" Isherwood replied. There followed a scene which, in Isherwood's recollection, had as much symbolic as personal significance:

> My memory sees them sitting together, facing each other. Christopher sits gazing at this master of their art, the great prophet of their tribe, who declares that there can be real love, love without limits or excuse, between two men. Here he is, humble in his greatness, unsure of his own genius. Christopher stammers some words of praise and devotion, his eyes brimming with tears. And Forster—amused and touched, but more touched than amused—leans forward and kisses him on the cheek.

If this scene were the subject of a genre painting, it might be called "Handing On the Baton." Forster, his career as a novelist over because he felt "weariness of the only subject that I both can and may treat—the love of men for women & vice versa," gives his blessing to a younger, bolder generation of writers who will be able to write frankly about homosexuality.

Isherwood was doing just that in his Berlin epic, and during his time in London spent most mornings dictating the latest draft to Richard. While he was writing of the city, news reached him that three English teachers had been arrested there. He also received a letter from Frl. Thurau to say that the police had been making inquiries about him. The seriousness of the situation in Berlin was also brought home to Isherwood when he received an unexpected visit from his first Berlin boyfriend, Berthold Szczesny, an older and more responsible character than the Bubi whom Isherwood had known in 1929. He was still flouting the law, but in a good cause: smuggling Jewish refugees into England on a Dutch cargo ship.

Whatever the risks, Isherwood had no choice but to return to Berlin, which he did on April 30. He was unsure about his future, but by now convinced that he would have to leave Germany sooner rather than later, taking Heinz with him. In his correspondence with Forster there is mention of a trip to Manchuria, but the details of this have been lost. There was also a suggestion that Isherwood and Heinz might go to Brazil, but in the end they decided to take up Francis Turville-Petre's invitation to join him on the Greek island of St. Nicholas, which he was currently excavating. Erwin Hansen was going to the island to take up his duties once more as Fronny's cook-housekeeper, and Isherwood and Heinz could travel with him. Isherwood appealed to his mother for money to cover the inevitable expenses of the move and she sent him £75.

Quite why Fronny issued the invitation is unclear. He and Isherwood had, after all, lived together in an atmosphere of considerable tension in Mohrin. Perhaps Fronny felt the need of some intellectual company. Any qualms Isherwood might have had were overcome partly because the prospect of a sunny Greek isle would have seemed particularly enticing after the dismal winter he had just endured in Berlin. It was also becoming clearer by the day that he would shortly have to leave the city. The Hirschfeld institute had been closed down and ransacked by physical education students from the Hochschule für Leibesübungen during the first week of May. Assorted records, including the card index of the World League for Sexual Reform, had been stolen with the intention that they would provide the Nazis with useful lists of subversive degenerates who could be rounded up and expelled or imprisoned. On May 10 a large number of books, pamphlets and other material looted from the Institute's library and archive were heaped up in the Opernplatz, along with works by other "undesirable" writers removed from the city's libraries, and set alight. The bronze bust of Hirschfeld, which had been presented to him on his sixtieth birthday, was impaled on a pole and carried through the streets to be tossed on the pyre, which blazed in the middle of a square which had considerable symbolic significance, bounded on one side by the University and on the other by the Opera House. Isherwood and Robson-Scott mingled with the cheering crowds and watched jubilant young SA thugs unload trucks full of books and hurl them into the consuming flames. Isherwood cried "Shame!"—"but not," he later admitted, "very loudly."

In the early hours of May 13 Isherwood sat down for the last time at his desk in Nollendorfstrasse and prepared to say goodbye to Berlin. Conscious of striking the right, heroic note of the sort friends such as Spender would expect, he wrote:

It is a quarter past midnight, and I have just finished packing. In eight hours I am going to leave Berlin, perhaps for ever. The papers say there has been an earthquake in Greece. I am not exactly tired, I feel only as if I were convalescent from a severe illness. For days I have worried, worried whether H[einz] would get his passport, whether E[rwin] would be arrested, whether they will remember to call us in the hotel in Belgrade to catch the Athens train. I have already made the whole journey several times in my head, composed funny post cards to all my friends. And now the day which seemed too good, too bad to be true, the day when I should leave Germany, has arrived, and I only know about the Future that, however often and however variously I have imagined it to myself, the reality will be quite different.

Isherwood later felt embarrassed by the pose he struck here, particularly in the "last long pompously false sentence." It was, however, a significant moment in his life. He was leaving behind him a city in which he had come to maturity and one which had provided him with material for several books. He was also abandoning the place he had come to regard as home. "The real appeal of living there," he later said, "was that I now became a permanent foreigner." There was no going back, and Fronny's island was only a temporary stopping point. It was not only his own future that seemed uncertain, but also that of his lover. In Berlin he could have parted from Heinz whenever he liked, but he could hardly abandon him outside Germany. By taking Heinz to Greece, removing him from his home and family, he was making himself responsible for someone else's life, taking on a commitment which had no obvious end.

EIGHT

A T SIX O'CLOCK ON THE MORNING OF MAY 13, 1933, ISHERWOOD SET
off with Heinz for the Anhalterbahnhof, where they were joined by Hansen,
who was very drunk. He greeted his traveling companions with the clench-
fisted salute of the *Rote Front,* and then this curiously assorted trio boarded the train
for Prague.

"We are all here, and it seems, of course, quite unreal," Isherwood wrote from the
Imperial Hotel in the Czech capital later that day. "The hotel is big, middling good,
of the 'station' type. The chambermaids sing all day, very beautifully, like actresses
in light opera." The manager told Hansen that the hotel was full of people who were
fleeing Germany. They spent the following morning sightseeing before catching an
afternoon train to Vienna, arriving in the Austrian capital at half past eight in the
evening with nowhere to stay because Hansen had failed to confirm his plans with
some people who had offered to put them up. They booked into a small hotel, where
Heinz awoke the next day with a bad cold. Despite this inauspicious introduction to
the city, Isherwood declared: "I should like to live here. Everywhere are bulging
baroque churches, classical fountains. And the people are so pleasant. One man,
whom we asked the way to the Alderstrasse, accompanied us there, lecturing on the
buildings we passed." Hansen had now managed to contact his hosts, Jewish doctors
named Furst. After spending the afternoon at the Prater, where they rode on the big
wheel and the miniature railway, Isherwood and Heinz joined Hansen at the Fursts'
for dinner. "They talked and talked and talked, keeping us waiting for supper," Isherwood grumbled. "I get bored with E[rwin] when he starts being the heroic exile. We
all know that Nazis are behaving like swine, but why such a *fuss*? Fussing is for Jews,
émigrés, not for communists. It doesn't become the beaten soldiers in battle to fuss.
If they didn't want to be beaten, why did they start fighting[?]" It is possible that in
Hansen's heroic posturing, Isherwood was embarrassed to glimpse something of the
figure he tended to present to his friends in England. As an active communist, Hansen

was in quite as much danger from the Nazis as the Jews were. However, as he suggested in his portrayal of Wilfrid Israel as Bernhard Landauer, Isherwood tended to regard Jews as constitutionally passive, almost as if they were somehow colluding in their persecution.

Two days later they boarded a train for Athens. "Soldiers with fixed bayonets along the line. Rain, heavy and cold. As it got dark the empty train rushed through the deserted country, guarded by solitary armed men, towards the frontier." They arrived in Athens at noon the following day, and were met by Francis Turville-Petre, who was accompanied by an Armenian boy named Tasso. "Hullo, lovey," Fronny greeted them. "I never thought you'd come." "He has syphilis again," Isherwood noted. "He lives in a cellar flat, with a hybrid canary. We sat for hours in a café while it rained in torrents." Braving the appalling weather, they made an excursion to see some ruins, and had dinner in a German restaurant. "Tomorrow the island. It is said to be swarming with snakes."

The following morning they set off in an overloaded car containing five passengers, four suitcases, a tin of benzine, some blankets purchased by Fronny from the thieves' market, Isherwood's portable typewriter, the canary, and a flea-ridden dog called Jo-Jo who was sick over Isherwood's trousers. The vertiginous road wound through the mountains in "a succession of fearful curves," and the last thirty kilometers to Chalia, a coastal village near Chalkis, was a dirt track, only just navigable. When they reached the beach there was no sign of the private boat that was supposed to meet them. St. Nicholas was so close to the mainland that it was possible to attract the attention of the island's inhabitants by shouting, but there was no response. Since there seemed little prospect of the boat's arriving, the party went to Chalkis and booked into "the imposingly fronted but tumbledown Hotel Palirria," which was in the process of being rebuilt. "At supper there was nothing which Heinz and I could satisfactorily eat. To bed early."

The following morning Fronny's chauffeur, Mitso, piloted the boat ashore and at noon the party set off for the island, where they were greeted by "a very beautiful dark-eyed boy," half-Turkish, named Nikko, whom Fronny was paying to have cured of syphilis. St. Nicholas was owned communally by the 319 inhabitants of Chalia, but had been leased to Fronny for ten years at £3 per annum. It was beautifully situated, lying in the narrow strait between Euboea and mainland Greece, so that one looked across the blue water to mountains on every side, rearing up out of olive groves and standing out against a vast sweep of sky. The island itself was about a kilometer long, much of it densely wooded, and with a small hill at one end. Fronny had colonized only a small portion of it, including a tumulus promisingly littered with pot-sherds. The only buildings were a small church, which was used once or twice a year, and a roofless hut, which Hansen set about making into a kitchen. There were plans to build a house, but so far the only accommodation was some crude huts which Nikko and Mitso had started making out of branches. All water had to be transported to St. Nicholas from the mainland in benzine cans and, Isherwood complained, "tastes accordingly." "Every arrangement depends on it not raining," he noted ominously.

On the first night Hansen, Nikko and Mitso slept outside, while Tasso bedded down in the boat. Fronny graciously offered Isherwood and Heinz the only bed in the hut and settled down beside them on a mattress on the ground. "It was a very fine night and the stars shone," Isherwood wrote in his diary. "Tasso sang in his boat, and the three lanterns made three little worlds of light in the utter darkness of the island." This romantic impression of life on the island would not last long. Isherwood had been inclined to boast of the frugal accommodation he had chosen in Berlin, but even the Wolffs' overcrowded apartment must have seemed luxurious compared with the arrangements on St. Nicholas. The following morning, in intense heat, he and Heinz were set to work digging a latrine, while Fronny conferred with the builders. Although Hansen and Heinz got on well with Fronny's boys, Isherwood was already developing an antipathy to Tasso. "Tasso is Jewish, flashy, lazy and energetic by fits, a very good cook. He wears a beret, a black shirt and mechanic's overalls with a flower by his ear." He had allowed the little fingernail on his left hand to grow very long, something the admiring Fronny told Isherwood was fashionable, but which must have made manual work awkward. He had a streak of wanton, childlike cruelty. On one occasion he captured an owl and, having tied it by one leg to the hut, threatened to poke its eye out. Fortunately the others released it before he could do any harm. Worst of all was his voice, "a plangent sing-song voice which goes right through ones bones." Isherwood was also finding Hansen's drunken conversation boring, and he decided to ask for a hut of his own situated as far as possible from the other inhabitants.

Food was brought from the mainland but a certain amount of self-sufficiency was encouraged. There were fishing expeditions, during which Nikko laid a line baited with two hundred hooks, and night-time excursions to spear octopuses. The masons hired to build proper accommodation shot rabbits with a gun "probably first used for freeing Greece by Lord Byron." Fronny set a good example by spending an afternoon gathering snails, which Hansen boiled up with tomatoes, producing a soup which Heinz refused to eat. "Erwin lectured him on daintiness. H. boiled himself two eggs and ate them gloomily on the shore."

"At the moment I feel a bit depressed," Isherwood admitted on his third evening on the island. "I even begin to feel that I may not stay here long. I hate having to keep everything in suitcases." Forced to abandon Berlin, which may have been politically unstable but had seemed like home, Isherwood now faced the prospect of an unsettled period in his life. Heinz had changed everything, and their stay on St. Nicholas would put their relationship to the test. It was one thing to carry on an affair within the sexual *demi-monde* of a large city such as Berlin, where replacement lovers could be found "with suspicious ease," as Isherwood put it, but quite another to do so on the move. "*Wir haben Wanderblut,*" Heinz decided, but however romantic it must have seemed to set off on their travels with no particular destination in mind, this sense of freedom was compromised by the need to have one's papers in order, particularly given the uncertain future of the whole of Europe. Before the First World War it would have been possible to live a wandering life without rules and restrictions, but the introduction of passports, although supposedly allowing citizens to visit other countries without let or hindrance, severely curtailed free passage. Most important, Isherwood had chosen Heinz out of all the boys on offer, taken him from Berlin, and invested a great deal in their future together. If this relationship foundered, what would be left?

———

Work soon began on Isherwood and Heinz's hut, situated aloofly from the others on the slope of the hill, and a table for Isherwood to write at was brought over from the mainland. So far there had been little time to do much apart from keeping up his diary and his correspondence. Everyone was expected to endure a certain amount of discomfort and hardship, but no one endured more, or with more patience, than Fronny himself. "He never stops working at something or planning something from morning to night," Isherwood wrote with grudging admiration.

> F. is the last to go to bed at night and the first to get up in the morning. He is always suggesting to Erwin that we shall eat some impossibly nasty and cheap kind of food. Erwin puts this down to stinginess, and so it partly is, but it is also largely because F. can put up with practically anything, and so doesn't see why others shouldn't too. He is very patient with me but obviously pained at my dislike of brackish water, food cooked in train oil and high fish and resinated wine.

In an attempt to introduce basic food hygiene, Fronny issued instructions that refuse should be placed in a tin, rather than left lying around: hitherto squadrons of flies rose off the food "with a hum like an aeroplane" whenever anyone entered the kitchen. "Never let me forget, lulled into self-approbation by these Boy Scout hardships, that this trip is a mere dilettante's summer vacation," Isherwood wrote after a dinner of octopus and rice. "I ran away from the Front Line when I left Berlin. Now I am taking part in an OTC sham fight which no possible mishap can dignify. My only excuse to the Court Martial is that I finish my novel." This was easier said than done, and Isherwood's attempts to get down to work were disturbed by the winds, which came suddenly upon the island and blew his papers everywhere, and by the builders who insisted that he demonstrate the workings of his typewriter, which they imagined to be some sort of musical instrument. The antics of the boys, and Fronny's furious but short-lived altercations with his staff, were a further distraction. There were occasional visits to Athens, where Isherwood and Heinz went shopping and sightseeing and luxuriated in a few nights' comfort in cheap hotels. It was in Athens that they decided to seal their relationship with tokens of commitment: "The rings. Finally we went out and bought them, spending too much money." Since it was clearly going to be some time before their hut was ready, they also bought a bell-tent, which although not reliably waterproof added to their sense of being cozily apart from the others.

Among visitors to the island was an Englishman named MacGregor, who turned up in the first week of June. MacGregor had been sent out to Singapore at the age of sixteen and soon afterward contracted cerebral malaria. He then started to drink heavily, and seems to have led a peripatetic life. He was very British in appearance and manner, wearing shorts and a rowing vest, and once making a special trip to Chalia in the vain hope of finding a barber who could give him a shave. Although he had traveled extensively, he had no aptitude for languages, believing that all the English had to do to make themselves understood abroad was to talk slowly and very loudly. He was conventionally right-wing, and accused Isherwood of being "a filthy communist." "He is boyishly rude," Isherwood complained, "and this I find boring." His idea of friendly banter was to say things like "If you don't mind my saying so, I think your hat's awful," and "What an ugly name Heinz is—it reminds me of baked beans." His arrival on the island was celebrated by everyone getting very drunk on the emergency supply of cognac which had been bought in order to revive anyone bitten by snakes, and this set a pattern for many evenings. "He only seems sympathetic when one remembers how badly he has had malaria or realizes that he is like a dog with a sore foot, snapping at everyone," Isherwood confessed. "His inane good looks and over-heavy chin. His hike in Albania and the Peleponnese—alone. No wonder." These notes on MacGregor's character and conduct would prove useful when Isherwood came to write *Down There on a Visit,* in which the young man is portrayed as Geoffrey.

The combination of heat and alcohol, the uncertain quality of the food, and the almost continual noise of the masons' singing and hammering and the builders' explosives all contributed to the fact that for much of the time Isherwood felt distinctly unwell, suffering headaches and bouts of queasiness. "Reading the Diary of a Flagellant," he wrote on July 14. "I am homesick for the old Berlin. The Berlin of the old Passage, the Eldorado, the massage saloons. Red plush. Upholstered vice. Steifel mädchen, transvestites, the bookshops in the Friederichstraße. The Cosy Corner. The Zelten Balls. Revolte in Erziehungshaus. Freud. Schableth and die Freundin. Felt ill all day. Sores on my feet from old mosquito and flea bites. Very stiff. Baking calm." This baking calm seemed to enfold Isherwood, who spent much of his time sunbathing and reading American thrillers when he should have been getting on with his novel. He was furious when Mitso reported him to Fronny for idling in the sun rather than doing anything constructive.

"I can't bring myself to write a line," he admitted. "I just idle and sweat and long for a drink. Heinz is my one support. He makes everything tolerable." When Heinz wasn't being a support, and went off with the boys, Isherwood became tormented by suspicion and jealousy. Like an anxious working parent with a bored child, he did not want Heinz to linger by his desk, where he was a distraction, but he wanted to keep him in view, not liking him to wander too far. This provoked outbursts of bad temper and sulking.

There was a time when Isherwood was touched by what he saw as they approached St. Nicholas across the water:

> Looking at the huts of branches and the two tents, with the hens rooting and the ducks quacking, the smoke going up from the plank roof of the kitchen, one thinks: People live there. It is a little world. And the figures of Tasso in his overalls, Erwin shuffling out pontifical in his dressing gown, assume a dignity, an air of romance which invests the earliest pioneers.

This air of romance was dispelled when he reached the island, however:

> Everything was in disorder. No tea. No eggs. One of the chickens dead. Work on the house held up through lack of asbestos. Nothing washed up. Our tent blown

open, two of the pegs torn out, our straw hats blown about a hundred yards and stuck under bushes. All the bushes festooned with toilet paper. I was very angry and yelled at Tasso, who was offended and complained to F.

That night a large carton of cigarettes went missing. "It is no use pretending to myself that I don't think the Greeks are dagoes—the swine of the earth," Isherwood decided. "(When Petro first washed up, he used to wipe the dirty dishes with a cloth which had been round Tasso's head—not wash them at all.) [. . .] I have to keep making little assertions of my will against the heat. I have just cleared the lamp, fetched water, filled my fountain pen, sorted our clothes. Otherwise I should lie down on the bed and feel very unhappy."

The only thing that could make this existence bearable was writing. "Today I have written," he recorded the day after this outburst. "Why not always? Ah, what joy, what holy peace. No more annoyance with the Greeks, with the island, with anything. And what is to prevent me writing *something* every day from now on until I die?" He knew perfectly well: "Chiefly vague apprehension of a journey, a visit to the doctor, a European War. A bad slothful start to the day. Meals late. Having lost my temper. Lack of continuity. Loneliness. I like best to work when people are near. Preferably H. The first few actions of the day are enormously important. They decide who is going to be master. Especially making the bed. Routine and discipline."

The loneliness Isherwood was experiencing was a loneliness for his friends. Heinz may have been good company, but he was limited company. He spoke almost no English and had not enjoyed the sort of education that Isherwood had, nor did he share Isherwood's intellectual interests. Isherwood's relationship with Fronny, though perfectly cordial, was not altogether easy, besides which Fronny had projects on hand that demanded all his attention. Although he could hardly bring himself to admit it, Isherwood sorely missed the sort of company and conversation Spender, Auden or Upward would have provided.

Any advance he made in his work seemed always to be followed by days of illness and inertia. "I have pains after every meal, shit blood, feel as weak as a cat," he reported in early July. Alarmed by these symptoms, he went to Chalkis in search of medical advice. Inquiries at the ironmonger's produced a doctor who examined him on a broken sofa behind the chemist's shop and diagnosed inflammation of the intestine. The dietary regime on St. Nicholas was enough to inflame anyone's intestines, even someone who had made a virtue of eating the poorest sort of food in Berlin, but colitis can also be caused by stress. Isherwood was now forced to acknowledge that he was "potentially jealous of everybody on the island—of everybody to whom H. makes himself in the slightest degree agreeable." This access of jealousy also meant that there was a decisive and unwelcome shift in the balance of the relationship. Heinz was supposed to be the younger brother, the person Isherwood could look after. Isherwood decided that in order to retain this dominance he would have to behave in a more generous and trusting manner. "My general behaviour to H. is often dishonourable," he admitted. "I am always catching him by girls' school prefect manoeuvres—putting him on his honour, making him feel he has behaved badly, and so forth. I am very adroit at this. I ask him to do something for me (out of pure laziness) and then, when he begins to argue, rise with a slight sigh and do it myself—thus letting him think: After all, I needn't really have refused. It is so subtly rotten, so dishonest." This would have to stop, as would his needling over Heinz's friendships with the boys.

> The discovery of my jealousy would put a weapon into his hands which dislike would soon teach him how best to wield. I wonder if he dislikes me already, finds my demands upon his time boring and wearisome. At times, perhaps. And if I am jealous here, what shall I be in a big city where there will be men and women who will really want to take him away from me?
>
> There is only one protection, one hope for me. Let me strive and struggle for a certain calm, a certain balance. Let me have courage. Never, never admit one's weakness to one's dearest friend. The only happiness, or indeed sanity, is in a core of detachment. A vital proud core of utter utter indifference, so that one goes one's way. In all humility. But alone.[1]

Throughout his life, Isherwood would make similar vows in his diaries: work harder, conquer idleness, stop wasting time on working up resentments, treat people better. They often remained statements of intent rather than implemented plans of action, but at least he understood that recognizing and acknowledging faults of character was not the same thing as mending them.

A core of detachment may have been necessary for Isherwood the Artist, but he discovered through Heinz that in human relations it could never be more than a pose, a mask held in place by sheer willpower. As Auden and others had observed, Isherwood's will was extremely strong. Although his attachment to Heinz was genuine, another reason the relationship *had* to work was pride. Stephen Spender recalled that Isherwood always needed to believe that his friends thought as much of his lovers as he did, and would imagine without any evidence whatsoever that they envied him in his affairs. He needed people to find his lovers attractive, and generally believed that they did. This was not, of course, always the case, but Isherwood's belief in the universal appeal of this or that boy persisted. This partly explains why he mistrusted Heinz's friendships with the island's boys: as with Walter, Heinz was so self-evidently desirable that everyone must be out to seduce him.

Isherwood's vow to behave better was not carried through and his diary records day after day spoiled by pointless wrangling. "Our extraordinary cruelty," he noted of his relationship with Heinz. "We discussed how life on the island had ruined our characters." They sometimes patched up their quarrels by taking day excursions to Euboea or the mainland, away from the tensions of St Nicholas, but the real difficulty about leaving the island permanently was that they had nowhere to go. By now Isherwood was having serious quarrels with Fronny, one over Petro, a boy covered in sores and rumored to be suffering from both syphilis *and* gonorrhea, who nevertheless continued to work in the kitchen. Isherwood said that he and Heinz would do the washing up, but foolishly added that of course they would pay less rent. "F. de-

---

1. This somewhat melodramatic passage was silently edited (and considerably toned down) by Isherwood when he came to quote it in *Christopher and His Kind*.

murred. You can stay as my guest, he sent a message by Erwin, but you can't pay less." If, as Isherwood later claimed, this invitation excluded Heinz, he did not mention this in the diary, nor his fury at Fronny's persistence in treating Heinz "as a servant who was living with the gentlefolk, under false pretences." A week later, however, he reported that Fronny had "burst out again against H," so some resentment must have been simmering.

In between moaning about the heat and his health ("I wish I was dead," he declared on July 26), Isherwood managed to finish another section of his Berlin novel by the end of the month, and on August 1 he and Heinz traveled to Athens to have their permits renewed. "I have conquered the heat," he announced ten days later. "The mountains and the idiot-blue sea are no longer emanations of Cosmic Hate, but just mountains and sea. All day I have not been idle. I have made the beds, written, read, swum." All was not as well as it seemed, however. "Heinz has not been near me. Now he has gone out in the boat with Costa and the gay little flea-like fisher boy, Clianthis, to lay down nets. He will not be back for several hours. I looked crossly at him as I went by, and now I am sorry I did this, because I must control myself absolutely, always, and not fawn and whine. Utter indifference. Not cold. Friendly. Always ready to meet the advance. Never making it. This is possible if I work."

He also recorded that "a skinny Anglo-Greek who was educated in England arrived to stay." This was George Lassalle, who was later to achieve fame as a cookery writer. Lassalle had met Fronny at a luncheon club in Athens, and was subsequently invited to visit the island. Fronny warned him that there were two other people staying, refugees from Berlin. "They're a bit fussy as guests but you won't see much of them. They keep themselves to themselves. In fact they're beginning to bore me." Fronny mentioned that one of his troublesome guests was Christopher Isherwood: "He's written a book people think is promising. And there's his little German friend, of course. If you don't mind, I won't introduce you straight off when we land. Isherwood's sure to want to complain about something. But they'll probably be having their siesta. With any luck, we can slip by." Lassalle claims that he heard "the querulous sound of voices in dispute" from the bell-tent. "Pay no attention to them," Fronny advised. "They're at it day and night. They're both out of the same Berlin gutter, you understand." This account, written many years later, is at odds with Isherwood's contemporary diary in which he recorded that Heinz had not been near him all day. It is possible that Lassalle was recalling a later occasion, since over the next couple of days relations between Isherwood and Heinz deteriorated alarmingly. Isherwood felt that he had "probably got into the position of being the sink down which [Heinz's] bile and bad moods drain off. We all have such a sink, or sinks, but I don't want to be it. I must seriously face the idea of leaving him." Heinz managed to get in first, however, and announced the following day that he intended to return to Berlin. Isherwood asked him to postpone his decision until he had thought about it more.

> After lunch I talked to him again, and shed tears, and finally he said: Well, all right, I'll stay with you, but we'll go to Paris at once.
> And so it's been left. Since then we haven't spoken to each other. My own feelings and his are both in such a muddle that it's better not. He is quite aston-

ishingly muddle-headed, a confusion of resentments. I suppose we shall have to part, but it shan't be till I want to.

Not a stroke of work done, of course.

Nearly thirty, and as silly as ever.

The following day he resolved to "be patient and let myself be snubbed, and begin the infinitely slow labour of repairing the damage. Not that I believe it can be repaired. But I must leave him, as I left W[alter], in my own time." His determination to be the one to decide if and when the relationship should end seems ruthless, but to be left by Heinz, in whom he had invested so much, and whose qualities he had frequently praised to his friends, would have been a terrible blow to Isherwood's pride. He must also have felt that having failed with Heinz he would fail in any relationship: "It seems as if my sex-life might be over, now, for good."

Although things had looked a little better in the morning, when Isherwood and Heinz went rowing together, by evening the situation was as bad as ever. While Heinz, with the help of two pocket dictionaries, chatted with the builders, Isherwood sat in his tent, scribbling away in his diary.

> I am eaten up with jealousy and devoured by boredom. The truth is, I don't know how to establish any kind of contact with this boy. I wonder if I have ever had any, or if it's all been lust and self-deception from the very beginning. Now the fruity voice of Jan Kiepura [from the gramophone] is demanding, for the hundredth time, what so schön sein, wie Deine Liebe? [what is as beautiful as your love?] Calm. It will all pass. You will be happier again than this. And more unhappy.
>
> Oh Friend, you whom I dream about in the dark nights, you whose face I try to see behind the faces of these boys—will you ever come to me? The one who understands, the one who never says that he understands. Or am I not worthy of you? Be near me tonight in my little tent.

This invocation may be self-dramatizing, even self-pitying, but it was undoubtedly sincere.

Toward the end of August Isherwood was obliged to acknowledge: "I'm in a dead period. Tired of Heinz, tired of myself. No work. To get away, away from here. Away away away away. Away." They did get away for the weekend of Isherwood's birthday, which they spent in Athens "very pleasantly, chiefly in bed," but they knew that they would have to return to St. Nicholas: "we can't afford not to." Since Isherwood was managing to do little work there was no immediate prospect of any earnings from his writing. The income from teaching had of course come to an end when he left Berlin, and so he was living off Uncle Henry's allowance. His godmother Aggie Trevor had died in July, leaving him £300, but he had not yet received this legacy. Meanwhile, he was trapped on the island and in an unsatisfactory relationship. A pattern had emerged in their rows: "It was so simple, like draughts. I moved. H. moved. I moved. Until H. had preposterously demanded that I should buy him a boat. No, of course I won't. You won't? No. Then I shall go to Berlin. I shrugged my shoulders."

This argument appears to have brought things to a head and on the evening of September 6 they finally left the island and went by early train to Athens the following morning, intending to go their separate ways. Isherwood had hoped to cash a cheque with one of Fronny's friends, but the man wasn't in town. This meant there was only enough money to buy Heinz's ticket to Berlin. When they got to the travel agent, however, all the sleeping-berths had been booked. "After lunch H. said: If you give me 6,000 [drachmas], I'll stay with you. I said: Certainly not. I'm not going to buy you." Eventually Heinz agreed to come with him on the steamer to Marseilles, after which Isherwood intended to travel to London via Paris. This did not mean that relations between them had improved much. "Well, we've got a fine little sulk attack on here," Isherwood reported the following day. "H. went out yesterday evening for a walk by himself and refused to have any dinner. And this morning he's sitting about with a face like death and won't speak. I shall have to get rid of him as soon as I'm in Paris."

Although Isherwood does not record it in his diary, he had a final, humiliating encounter with Fronny, who as a farewell gesture had treated him and Heinz to lunch at Costi's, the most expensive restaurant in Athens. George Lassalle had also been invited. "Do help me out," Fronny begged him. "I've simply nothing to say to those two pathetic characters, and if there isn't someone there that Christopher doesn't know, there's bound to be a quarrel. I'm sure that, in front of a stranger, Christopher will be very careful to be on his best behaviour. He talks well . . . about himself, of course." Lassalle was not entirely a stranger. He claimed that he spent only one night on the island and did not meet Isherwood and Heinz there, but his memory must have been at fault, since Isherwood mentions him on several occasions in the diary, and even describes him as "entertaining." That the feeling was not mutual is evident from Lassalle's sour portrait of Isherwood in his memoirs. The food and wine were both excellent, Lassalle remembered:

> But if I had expected to learn anything of Isherwood's conversational powers, I was disappointed, as German was the only language in which the master would deign to speak.
>
> This I felt to be a deliberate snub, as did Francis, who said, 'Can we talk in English? George doesn't speak any German.'
>
> 'I don't see why,' said Isherwood. 'There are three of us who do. So we're in the majority.'
>
> We finished our meal in a mutually resentful silence. Francis immediately called for the bill, wrote a cheque for the amount due, and got up. As I rose from the table with him, he said loudly, 'What a despicable little runt you are, Isherwood', and we walked out of Costi's without farewells being exchanged. I felt rather inclined to share Francis's verdict, especially when, twenty-nine years later, I read in Isherwood's *Down There on a Visit* his malicious travesty of his former benefactor.

Lassalle's memory may have been faulty, but it seems inconceivable that he would have invented this scene. Isherwood may well have chosen not to record so unpleasant an end to a friendship in his diary, and in any case he was more preoccupied with the immediate problem of his relationship with Heinz. He possibly felt that he and Fronny would patch things up again, just as they had after Mohrin. Indeed, they seem to have done so, since they met once more, in Egypt in 1938, four years before Fronny's syphilis finally caught up with him and killed him. This last memory of Fronny in Athens must have faded, since Isherwood retained an affectionate interest in his erstwhile friend. The portrait of Fronny—who was in any case never Isherwood's "benefactor"—as Ambrose in *Down There on a Visit,* far from being "a malicious travesty," is written with a certain amount of admiration and affection.

It was presumably for Heinz's benefit that Isherwood insisted that German be spoken at this unhappy lunch, but this consideration seems to have had little effect on Heinz's black mood. He and Isherwood boarded the *Andros* on September 9 and made the long, picturesque sea voyage to France. "Slowly, my smashed nerves are recovering," Isherwood wrote, "tuning themselves to the steady heart-throb of the ship. But so far I can't shit."

They got to Marseilles in the early morning of September 13 and spent the day there, during which they had their hats stolen in "the whore's alley," before boarding a filthy third-class train for Paris. They arrived the following morning and went directly to Meudon, a southwestern suburb of the city, to stay with Rolf Katz, who was living there temporarily after leaving Berlin. They spent a fortnight in Paris, during which they evidently settled their differences, for when he got to London on September 30, Isherwood was accompanied by the young German.

Their arrival at Pembroke Gardens had been delayed because customs officials at Newhaven had queried Heinz's papers. Kathleen had been obliged to issue a hasty written invitation in order to assure the authorities that Heinz had somewhere to stay in England, as a result of which he was granted a visitor's permit for two weeks. "He understands very little English," Kathleen wrote of this unexpected guest, "& can speak it even less, but seemed to have nice manners, sitting quite patiently while C told us all about his time on the island, etc." Isherwood was keen to introduce Heinz to his friends and spent the first day of their visit with Olive Mangeot and Stephen Spender. Over the next few days Heinz had lunch with Hector Wintle and his fiancée, tea with William Plomer and Humphrey Spender, saw Beatrix Lehmann in a play, went on a motoring trip to Windsor with Eric Falk, attended the Ballets Russes and a boxing match, helped Stephen Spender decorate his new flat, and drove down to spend a weekend at the Downs School, near Malvern, where Auden was having a great success teaching small boys. (Isherwood suggested that Auden's next volume of poems should be called "The Passions of a Pedagogue.") It was while they were with Auden that they learned that Germany had left the League of Nations. Isherwood returned to Pembroke Gardens "very depressed," Kathleen reported. It was not merely the international crisis that depressed Isherwood: the following day Heinz had to return to Berlin.

Isherwood felt that Kathleen treated Heinz with condescension—although he admitted that Heinz himself seemed unaware of this and thought her kind. It was unrealistic of Isherwood to expect his mother to welcome Heinz naturally and unreservedly. She had been brought up in social isolation from working-class people, who functioned chiefly in her world as servants or as the beneficiaries of charitable works. There was also the question of Heinz's nationality: his parents' generation was the one that started the war in which her husband had been killed. Worse still,

Isherwood had not been straight with her about his friendship with the boy. Having told her that they had met only recently, in France, he subsequently revealed in conversation—"with a carelessness which was part of his aggression towards her," he later decided—that Heinz had been with him in Greece. Isherwood may have wanted Kathleen to acknowledge Heinz's importance in his life, but never gave her the chance. Even if he had, he could hardly have expected his mother to be overjoyed. No doubt Heinz made a better impression than Walter would have, but experience had taught Kathleen that any working-class foreigner Christopher befriended would complicate his life and prove a drain on his emotional and financial resources. In this, as in much else, she was quite right.

Isherwood's plans were vague, but they still included Heinz. The first priority was to get him a *Sichtvermark,* or visa, so that he could leave Germany, but this would take some time. Meanwhile, Isherwood had to get on with his Berlin novel, and he acquired a congenial young typist in the shape of Herky Ross, who started coming to the house regularly, but left after three weeks in order to undergo an operation on his knee. By this time, Isherwood had found a job through Jean Ross which was to occupy him for several months.

Isherwood had introduced Ross to Olive Mangeot, and the two women had become close friends. They were both actively involved in left-wing politics, and the bond between them strengthened when Ross moved into Gunter Grove as a lodger. She was currently involved in a relationship with the journalist Claud Cockburn, whom she had met earlier in the year at the Café Royal. Cockburn had been in Berlin at the same time as Ross, and friends had tried to introduce them, but Ross had resisted the invitation. The first thing Cockburn did when they finally met was to ask Ross to cash a cheque for him. The following morning, he phoned to ask her not to attempt to pay the cheque into her account because it would bounce. Undeterred by this portent of unreliability, or by the fact that Cockburn had already been married to an American woman whom he left when she became pregnant, Ross—in true Sally Bowles style—decided that she was in love.

Ross had achieved some success as an actress in the theater, but she was now working in a different capacity in the film industry, where there were opportunities for bilingual scriptwriters and go-betweens for the newly exiled German directors and their British co-workers. She had got to know the Austrian film director Berthold Viertel, who was in England working on a screen adaptation of Ernst Lothar's novel *Kleine Freundin* ("Little Friend") for Gaumont-British, the leading film production company in the country at that period. The sentimental and melodramatic story involved a young girl attempting suicide in order to prevent her parents from divorcing. Viertel had been working with Margaret Kennedy, whose *The Constant Nymph* had been published in 1924 and become the decade's best-selling novel. Kennedy must have seemed an ideal choice as a collaborator, since *The Constant Nymph* also dealt with parents and children and had been very successfully adapted by the author for both the stage and the cinema. In the event, however, Viertel did not find Kennedy *sympathische* and was happy to release her when she had an unexpected chance to produce one of her own plays on stage. Viertel needed to find a writer in a hurry and so Ross suggested Isherwood, hoping to recommend him by lending the director a copy of *The Memorial*. Viertel liked the book and also liked the author when he met him on November 18. Two days later Isherwood went to Gaumont's headquarters at Shepherd's Bush to meet the studio bosses over lunch, and as a result he was offered the job, at £20 a week. According to the proposed schedule, this would earn Isherwood £100; he asked for £150 and eventually settled for £125, half on signing the contract, half on delivery. Jean Ross, who asked for half of Isherwood's first week's salary as a commission, came round with a copy of Kennedy's script the following afternoon and spent two days discussing it, no doubt delighted to give her friend the benefit of her experience in the profession.

"Mr Isherwood," Viertel greeted his collaborator, "we are like two men who meet in a brothel. It is impossible that we should feel shame before each other." Isherwood, however, was more excited than ashamed. On the face of it, the project was not particularly appealing, but he was fulfilling an early dream by working in the movies. What this meant at first was long daily meetings with Viertel in his "horrible, expensive little Knightsbridge flat, reeking of tobacco, buttered toast and white paint." Together they "plodded through endless weeks of writing, rewriting, black coffee, chain-smoking and cuts. Viertel suffered agonies. Once started, his cynicism vanished: it was impossible for him to give less than his heart's blood: our little girl's fate involved the stars in their courses. 'Here we are,' he cried, 'breaking our heads off, fighting for truth.' "

Viertel had been born into a prosperous Jewish family in Vienna in 1885, and at the age of sixteen had some of his poems published in *Die Fackel* ("The Flame"), one of the city's leading radical journals. Poetry remained Viertel's principal love, but he had also worked in the theater and as a journalist and had aspirations as a novelist. His burgeoning career as a stage director was interrupted by the First World War, in which he served in the infantry on the Eastern Front. He met his second wife, Salka, toward the end of 1916, while on leave in Vienna. The daughter of a Jewish lawyer, Salka Steuermann had been born in 1889 in Sambor, a garrison town in Galicia, which was then part of Poland, though under Austrian rule. Her real first name was Salome, a choice her parents might have regretted when she announced in early childhood that she wanted to make her career upon the stage. Although she was burdened with a Polish accent, and was not conventionally attractive, Salka managed to get taken on by the director of the Vienna Burgtheater, and subsequently joined Max Reinhardt's company in Berlin. By the time she was introduced to Viertel, she was enjoying a successful career on the stage. They married in 1916 and produced three sons in quick succession.

Viertel had made several films during the early 1920s, principally for financial reasons, and was taken up by the director F. W. Murnau, who had made his reputation with the expressionist vampire movie *Nosferatu*. When Murnau went to Hollywood, he managed to get Viertel a three-year contract with the Fox Studio there. In 1928 the entire Viertel family went to California, where they settled at the edge of the Pacific in Santa Monica. Glad as he was of the work, Viertel found the projects to which he was assigned irrelevant and uninteresting. He made eight films, not only for Fox but also for Warner Bros. and Paramount, but after four years he returned to Europe in search of more rewarding work, leaving his family behind. Appalled by what he saw in Germany, he went to England in search of a job. By the time Isherwood met him, Viertel was in his late forties and diabetes and enforced exile had taken their toll.

The slender figure Salka had first met had broadened and become rather shambling; the "strong, attractive face dominated by a broad forehead, thick eyebrows and dark, compelling eyes" had become a "brilliant Jewish death's-head."

Although Viertel and Isherwood took *Little Friend* seriously, its essential triviality was emphasized by the fact that it was written and filmed against the backdrop of the worsening crisis in Europe. In Leipzig the Nazis were conducting a show trial of communists accused of burning down the Reichstag building on the night of February 27. Viertel and Isherwood followed the trial avidly while working on their script, and Viertel would spend part of the day discussing articles and letters he intended to send to the press. Further political debate would take place over lunch, which they took at the Kensington Palace Hotel at a table within sight of the Gaumont-British executives who always ate there. Viertel thought that their appearance there would intimidate these men. "The animals must see their tamer," he said.

When not discussing politics, Viertel talked about women, how they were "necessary for him—their perfume, their aura." He described his numerous affairs, starting with a young Frenchwoman he'd met in Vienna when he was nineteen. She had "black fuzzy hair like an Abyssinian, and was very passionate," he told Isherwood. "A woman like that, when she is awakened, when she gets the man she wants—she is amazing, amazing. You have no idea. Sensuality is a whole separate world. What we see on the outside, what comes up to the surface—it's nothing. It's like a mine. You can explore vast regions, going deeper and deeper." Just how little idea Isherwood had shortly became apparent to Viertel. The only heterosexual mine Isherwood had explored had been that of Mrs. Lanigan back in 1929. "You are a typical mother's boy, I think," Viertel told him. "You are very repressed sexually. But you must not be. The right woman will change that."

Viertel tended to see things in cinematic terms. Describing the end of his affair with the Frenchwoman, he said, "And she is going down the street, quite without a word and the tears pouring down her face—like a beaten army." In his spare time he was dictating a novel to his assistant, Käthe, who was acting as stenographer for the script. The novel was called *Amalia, or The Hell of Chastity,* and described the sex life of a middle-aged woman. There was also a political element to the book, in which Viertel compared post-war Germany with the homosexual "vampire" and mass murderer Fritz Haarmann, who killed at least twenty-eight youths in Hanover by biting their throats, then dismembered their bodies, selling the joints as meat on the black market.

In between these distractions, Isherwood and Viertel somehow managed to write their script, and Isherwood went home at 2:30 a.m. on December 22, 1933, relieved that they had completed it. The following day, however, he went round to Viertel's flat to find his collaborator in despair after "a night of agony" during which he had decided that the script was no good. It had become clear that Viertel would need Isherwood's assistance for far longer than the originally contracted five weeks, and in mid-December Isherwood had agreed to stay on right through the shooting of the film. He would officially be designated dialogue director, although his principal role was as a go-between when Viertel and the executives got into disputes. The prospect of working in a studio and being present on set excited Isherwood, but it meant that he would have to postpone his plan to join Heinz in Berlin. He was missing Heinz terribly and was fearful that if their separation were extended much further it might become permanent. "What a year," he exclaimed when summing up 1933 in his diary. He recalled scenes from his last months in Berlin, all of them leading to the moment when Heinz's father gave his son permission to go to Greece:

> H coming over to congratulate me on my birthday and H watching them load the steamer at Piraeus and H walking with me up the hill at Meudon in search of the aerodrome and H at dinner [at Pembroke Gardens] being polite and H waving from the departing train. And then three months of work. Dull. Featureless. I hope with some result.
>
> The usual new year's resolutions: Conservation of Energy. Courage. Calm.
>
> And may he come back. Just this once. I ask nothing else.

Not all that work had been on the *Little Friend* script. Isherwood had also made some progress with his Berlin novel. He had observed the city closely and studied its denizens, and he had all the material he needed stored up in the volumes of his diaries. His task now was to find some way of using these riches in a single narrative. One of his difficulties was that the characters all appeared to have a life of their own and each of them seemed quite capable of running away with any plot Isherwood devised. So far, he had written a number of individual character sketches, and he had come up with a title for the book: *The Lost*. This, he admitted, sounded rather better in German: the longer, more drawn-out "*Die Verlorenen*" had an appropriately despairing timbre. Even so, "The Lost" could be used to describe most of the characters he intended including in the book:

> It meant 'those who have lost their own way'—that Mass of Germans who were now being herded blindly into the future by their Nazi shepherds. It meant 'the doomed'—those who, like Bernhard Landauer, were already marked down as Hitler's victims. And, in a lighter, ironic sense it meant 'those who respectable Society regards as moral outcasts'—Sally Bowles the 'lost' girl, Otto Nowak the 'lost' boy and Mr Norris who has committed the unpardonable crime of having been found out.

On December 17, possibly prompted by the knowledge that his work for the studio was to be extended, he wrote a "Reconsideration" of the novel, trying to sort out where he had got to and where he was heading. He had reduced the number of principal characters to three: Bernhard Landauer, Arthur Norris and Isherwood's alter ego, Paul. Also appearing would be Sally Bowles and her lover Klaus, possibly Natalia Landauer, and two young Germans, Otto (based largely on Walter Wolff) and Lothar. The action was to be confined to the winter of 1932–33, and was to open with Norris visiting "some personage (deposed royalty?)" in a hotel in Holland, Switzerland or Belgium. "Forms still observed. Suite. In rather low water. Possibly Arthur wishes to negotiate loan? First words: 'The weather seems to be clearing now, your Majesty?' " These notes suggest that the activities of Mr. Norris were to be played out in ironic counterpoint to the gathering crisis in Berlin, where the political weather was doing anything but clear. Norris would continue his life impervious to all this, maintaining his links with a world that had already vanished.

Norris would then travel to Berlin and meet the novel's other main characters. Isherwood made an important decision about how he was to tell his story: "We follow [Norris] with the camera eye, objectively. We have none of his thoughts—only see what he sees, hear what he hears." This would further assist Isherwood in his portrayal of someone as slippery as Norris: "There should be many false directions here— Assumed names. Obvious contradictions, etc. etc.—to arouse the reader's curiosity." The first sequence would end in a bar, "the opposite pole" to where it started, and it is here that Norris meets Paul by appointment. "The sequence ends with Arthur's words: 'Dear me, I *have* had a day!'" This exclamation is characteristic of Gerald Hamilton's habit of ironic understatement. One of his favorite expressions, much repeated, was: "Well, well, we live in stirring times; tea-stirring times!"

This was all very well, but Isherwood was still unsure precisely what the book was to be about. "It is vital to the success of the whole presentation that 'Love' is clearly shown for what it is—one of the chief preoccupations of The Lost," he decided on December 23. "The link which binds all the chief characters is that, in some way or other, each one of them is conscious of the mental, economic and ideological bankruptcy of the world in which they live." But he could not decide on the relationships of the characters to each other—or even on their sexual orientation. "I don't think Bernhard need be homosexual," he felt at one point. "He could be attracted to Sally, while realizing what she was. And perhaps the week-end he does finally spend with her would be the last straw of his self-disgust." Two days later, he noted: "relationship between Bernhard and Klaus is important. Perhaps sublimated love for K. Thus his interest in the abortion and in Sally."

The political affiliations of the characters also troubled him. "There's no real reason why Otto and Lothar shouldn't be fused," he decided. "Is Otto credible as a communist? No. But as a street-rowdy calling himself a communist? Yes." But a couple of days later he was "bothered by the idea of making Otto a communist. Do we after all need Lothar?" As he would do throughout his career, Isherwood jotted down notes about work in progress, which were in effect conversations with himself. On Christmas Day he wrote:

> Three things are working out through the book:
> The story of Arthur's career and final downfall.
> The story of Paul's relations with the Party, Otto and his own mother.
> The story of Bernhard's relations with Sally and Klaus.
> And all this must echo and re-echo the refrain: It can't go on like this. We're the Lost. We're the Lost. Bernhard's speech in favour of Nazi government. It will destroy me—and I'm glad.

He had earlier imagined a scene in which Paul, marooned in England with witlessly chattering relatives, is suddenly desperate to speak to Otto. He telephones a bar in Berlin where a party is in progress, and a drunken youth "picks up the receiver and half as a joke, half through stupidity, holds a conversation with Paul, saying that he is Otto." Otto has in fact left the bar and gone to his death, murdered by a street-gang. "The book ends with Otto lying dead in the snow under the girders of the Overhead Railway." This scene, with its echoes of *Der Puppenjunge,* was no doubt prompted by worries over Heinz, and was rapidly discarded, along with Otto himself: "He belongs in the book of reminiscences of Berlin which I hope to write some day—not here. No, Paul's relationship is with Lothar. And Lothar is profoundly one of the Lost. He is the embodiment of the frustrated desperate working-class boy—a communist without understanding communism. He is subject to sudden attacks of Wut [rage against the hopelessness of life], tries to find in [his girlfriend] Anni what Paul tries to find in him—geltung [validity]. Hence the violence and contradictions in his attitude to Paul—his sudden revulsions of feeling. I shall cut out the Kulak household [based on the Wolffs] and make him live in a cellar. Only from now on I'll call him Otto. It suits him better." He also decided that the character of Sally Bowles was too comic and frivolous for his purposes. He would introduce a new female character, a tough, lower-middle-class, left-wing journalist called Helen who disapproves of Mr. Norris and argues with Paul. It would be Helen who tells the characters that they are "The Lost."

Before he could put any of these new ideas into practice, however, Isherwood was recalled by Viertel. He arrived early at the flat on the first day of 1934 to find his collaborator "nearly suicidal." They spent thirteen hours discussing the script, with a break for lunch at Harrods, which did little to lighten Viertel's mood. Observing the large clock in the restaurant, he intoned: "It ticks every moment. Death comes nearer. Cancer. Syphillis discovered too late. Art no good. A failure. A damn flop. Consumption. War. Poison-gas. We are dying with our heads together in the oven." Isherwood noticed that Viertel nevertheless brightened considerably when he saw an attractive waitress. The following day involved another twelve hours of work, in which they were assisted by one of Viertel's friends, a woman who was visiting England. They were at last making some progress, but Isherwood felt rather shut out by Viertel and his new collaborator, Frau G., who reduced his role to that of "a mere translator of their ideas": "I am an incompetent child with toothache, who occasionally, when he has been made to feel too inferior, sulks."

Isherwood's diary ends with this note, made on January 4. The following day, Heinz, who had finally got his exit visa, was due to arrive in England. Isherwood had rented two rooms from Olive Mangeot at Gunter Grove, presumably because it would be intolerable for all parties if the couple lived at Pembroke Gardens. Recalling the difficulties they had with the authorities when Heinz last visited England, Isherwood was apprehensive and took Auden with him to Harwich to meet the boat. Heinz was on board, bringing with him an invitation, handwritten by Kathleen at Isherwood's dictation, and, fatally, an affectionate letter Isherwood had sent him along with some cash. The letter instructed Heinz to tell the British immigration authorities that the money had come from his grandmother. Isherwood greeted Heinz and saw him into the passport office. It was here that Heinz, under questioning, produced Kathleen's letter, which confirmed the suspicions of the immigration officers. They had noticed that Heinz's passport stated that his occupation was *Hausdiener,* or domestic worker. Isherwood was summoned into the office and asked whether his mother was intending to employ the young German illegally. The officials had already guessed the true situation and were merely playing with Isherwood. As he protested at these slurs against his mother's honesty, his own letter was produced. Heinz had given it to the officials as proof that the money he carried was his. "This wasn't mere stupidity," Isherwood later commented. "It was perhaps a subconscious bitchery which develops in people who have become accustomed to do exactly what they are told." This is unjust. Heinz knew perfectly well that there was subterfuge involved in his coming to England, and the interrogation must have been frightening, especially for someone who did not speak or understand English very well. Auden, who had witnessed the entire proceedings, remarked of the customs officer: "As soon as I saw that bright-eyed little rat, I knew at once we were done for. He understood the whole situation at a glance—because he's *one of us*." Heinz was put on the next boat back to Germany.

Isherwood was obliged to pay his lover's fare back to the Continent, but he and Auden were allowed to have dinner with Heinz on board the boat before it set sail. They spent the night in a hotel, returning despondently to London by the early morning train in order for Isherwood to be at Viertel's by ten o'clock. Isherwood felt thoroughly humiliated as he tried to explain to Viertel what had happened. He could not bear the motherly sympathy of Frau G., whom he later accused of being "thick-skinned" and unwilling to acknowledge the true depths of his feeling for Heinz. He then had to return to Pembroke Gardens and the prospect of facing his mother, who had managed to find out what had happened by phoning Auden. This was just as well, since Isherwood "returned late & went straight to bed," and contrived to spend the whole of the following day (a Sunday) at Viertel's. Kathleen did eventually manage to speak to her son on the Monday, waiting up until eleven, when he finally returned from work. Isherwood told her that he would now have to join Heinz abroad as soon as the script was finished. This meant giving up the idea of working alongside Viertel while the film was being shot. Viertel was "very vexed & annoyed," Kathleen reported. "There was rather a to do."

Both Gerald Hamilton and Rolf Katz strongly advised Isherwood against traveling to Berlin, given the current political situation. They were probably aware that the Nazis were stepping up their campaign against homosexuality, which led to arrests and deportations to concentration camps, although this did not become official policy until 1937. It was eventually arranged, largely through the good offices of William Robson-Scott, that Isherwood could avoid going to Germany altogether and travel instead to Amsterdam, where Heinz would join him by train. They would then go on to Paris, always assuming that Heinz could get a French visa.

As soon as his work on the script was finished, on the evening of Saturday, January 20, Isherwood took a train to Gravesend, where he boarded a night boat to Rotterdam. He had spent the morning with Viertel, who had generously offered to keep the film job open until the following Wednesday. It was fortunate that Viertel was so keen to hold on to his collaborator, since Isherwood sent no word to England until the day after this deadline. On the Thursday afternoon Kathleen received a telephone call from Paris, where Isherwood and Heinz were staying with Rolf Katz. The French authorities had not yet granted Heinz a visa, but were due to make a decision the following day. Would Kathleen telephone Viertel, give him Isherwood's apologies, and explain the situation? Viertel was out for the evening, but when Kathleen telephoned the following morning she was relieved to find the director in an amiable and accommodating mood. Nevertheless, he would need to know by the following day whether Isherwood was prepared to be back at work on Monday to do some final polishing on the script before the actual filming started the following Thursday. Kathleen wired this information to Paris, but Isherwood telephoned in reply to say that Heinz had been refused a visa, and that he would therefore have to make some sort of plan for him. Viertel agreed that as long as Isherwood could be back by Tuesday, the job was still his. Heinz would have to stay in lodgings in Amsterdam (where Kathleen wired some money) until Isherwood had finished work on the film. Having settled Heinz with a family, and with the intention that the young German should while away the time learning English, Isherwood returned to London.

There was very little work to be done on the script, and to Isherwood's annoyance the shoot was delayed for another week while the cast was being finalized. Eventually a cast was assembled, with the fifteen-year-old Nova Pilbeam in the title role and Matheson Lang and Lydia Sherwood as her battling parents. Isherwood had tried to use his influence to get Beatrix Lehmann cast as the mother. Although he was unsuccessful, the meeting between Lehmann and Viertel had an unexpected result: they embarked on an affair.

Filming eventually started on February 21. Isherwood's duties as "dialogue director" were scarcely onerous: "During the whole of one morning," he recalled, "my only job was to say the German for knitting." Matheson Lang referred to him as "the invaluable Isherwood," but this was largely because he expected Isherwood to go through his part with him, feeding him cues whenever the actor clicked his fingers. Isherwood had plenty of time to study the craft of filmmaking, and the characters of the crew, about whom he made detailed notes. He enjoyed the camaraderie and was fascinated by the jargon, largely incomprehensible to an outsider, as when the lighting director instructed a colleague: "Hot up 74. Put in your bank. Kill that sun. We want a kidney here." He was also intrigued by the hierarchy on set, where those in the cutting room considered themselves superior to those in other departments. He got on particularly well with the film editor and with the sound recordist, who occasionally allowed him to ring the bell for silence on the set, but he could never quite be one of the boys, a group of young heterosexual men with conventional interests in cars and sports. They talked to him about their wives and girlfriends, their lust for Lydia Sherwood, their views on sex and marriage, presumably unaware that the enigmatic dialogue director was jotting everything down.

This material would prove useful when Isherwood came to write *Prater Violet,* his novel about a Viertel-like director making a British film, but he had no immediate plans to turn his experience into fiction. It was simply that he had become accustomed to recording his life. His diaries and notebooks served several purposes in the 1930s. One was therapeutic: by writing down his anxieties—about the prospect of another war in Europe, about his relationship with Heinz—he could bring them into focus and attempt to get them into perspective, even allay them to some extent. He also wrote about work in progress, sorting out problems of plot and construction. Principally, however, they were an account of the world in which he moved, of the quirks and quiddities of daily life. He was aware that out of this raw material he might be able to fashion art. His fiction was always derived from his own experiences, and he was planning at least two books of straight autobiography: the account of his education, and the "book of reminiscences of Berlin" he mentioned in his diary.

That said, in Viertel—as in Gerald Hamilton, Francis Turville-Petre, and Jean

Ross—Isherwood recognized a potential character, someone whose personality was so forceful and out of the ordinary that he seemed destined to be put into a novel. Like them, Viertel was also an outsider, a Viennese Jew in England, a committed artist in the gimcrack commercial world of the cinema. He was an altogether more respectable figure than either Hamilton or Turville-Petre, but the seriousness with which he took *Little Friend* showed a certain perverse heroism, and he could undoubtedly be monstrous. A self-proclaimed liberal, he became dictatorial behind the camera, barking out orders and keeping the actors and technicians in line. "The way you switch on this light," he admonished Lydia Sherwood in his idiosyncratic English, "makes it to such a theatrical importance that the killing of Rasputin becomes just a breakfast in comparison." If technicians ignored his instructions, Isherwood noted, Viertel "remarked that this only showed the necessity of socialism. 'In Russia they would all be shot.' " Even so, Viertel was generally liked by the crew—perhaps because his rages were no more than to be expected from an excitable foreigner and were difficult to take altogether seriously, particularly when they were undermined by his uncertain use of English idiom. When a carpenter built a sham door, not realizing that one of the actors had to open it, Viertel stormed off the set, shouting: "You are all like stubborn monkeys!" A few seconds later, he came back to amend this: "No—not monkeys! Donkeys!"

Isherwood delighted in this aspect of Viertel's character, finding that at the studio their old relationship of master and slave underwent a change and that they were "thrown even more closely together, as allies against the Others." The Others included the studio bosses, whom Viertel and Isherwood treated with no more respect than was politic. Viertel particularly resented the man who was assigned as associate producer on the film, Robert Stevenson.[2] Isherwood was later to compare Stevenson with a "smiling young renaissance cardinal," but Viertel was more dismissive. "They have given me this ugly dwarf to sit on my back," he complained. "They" were the British executives, chief of whom was Michael Balcon, whose older brother, Shan, gave Isherwood a lesson in the subtleties of racism. The Balcons were Sephardic Jews from Spain, whose name derived from the fact that their house was sufficiently grand to have a balcony. They were an aristocratic race, he explained, and should not be confused with the likes of Viertel, an Eastern European Ashkenazim. Balcon regarded the Ashkenazim as "so-called Jews," disreputable mongrels whose manners and behavior reflected badly on "real Jews" such as himself.

Isherwood thoroughly enjoyed life at the studio: seeing Conrad Veidt at work, or sitting in the local pub with such legendary figures as Robert Flaherty.[3] He also delighted in his new role of someone "in films," and eagerly showed such friends as Forster round the set. It rapidly became apparent, however, that the filming was going

---

2. Stevenson had been a contemporary of Isherwood at Cambridge, though they did not know each other then. He had been a scriptwriter and later went to Hollywood where Isherwood worked with him on a propaganda film in 1940. He subsequently directed a large number of highly successful films for the Disney studio, including *Mary Poppins*.

3. The American-born Flaherty was a former explorer who became a pioneering documentary maker, notable for such films as *Nanook of the North,* about a family of Inuits, and *Moana,* which was set in the South Seas. He was at this time working rather closer to home on *Man of Arran.*

to take much longer than expected. This might mean more money for Isherwood, but it would also delay his reunion with Heinz. He offered to pay John Lehmann to travel to Amsterdam to find out if all was well, but Lehmann was unable to get away. Isherwood's mounting anxiety about Heinz was no doubt the reason behind his telling Kathleen that he was so "dissatisfied with the film & the dialogue, as adapted" that he hoped the studio would refuse to pay him beyond the stipulated five weeks. In the event, he left before the film had finished shooting (a fact skillfully glossed over in *Christopher and His Kind*), and at the end of March went to Amsterdam to rescue his friend. Viertel seems to have taken the defection of his collaborator philosophically, but did not reply to Isherwood's "kind good-bye letter." "Why did I not write to you at all?" he asked later in the year. "That's a mystery of my heart. Not that I was angry with you because you left me alone in the middle of our work. Perhaps I had a feeling that the whole thing, including myself[,] was merely a finished or completed episode in your life. You had escaped and I didn't want to persue [*sic*] you into your Noa-Noa-Paradise."

The "Paradise" to which Isherwood escaped with Heinz was Gran Canaria—not, as he had romantically hoped, Tahiti, since the French authorities there had demanded "the most complicated formalities." The prospect of Las Palmas, he told Forster, was "not very thrilling, but it ought to be warm and nice, and all the really interesting places are so expensive." One of the books Isherwood had with him was *A Passage to India*. "I hadn't read it for ten years, nearly," he told the author, "and I see now how it has influenced everything I feel about novel-writing." Isherwood, like Joe Ackerley, answered Forster's need for "someone of another generation to speed me up and divert me from the *pottering* kindness which is naturally required by my life." Friendship with Forster, though always enlivened by a great deal of fun, was a serious business. He interested himself in all aspects of his younger friends' lives, and was always ready to offer advice without waiting to be asked. He was also prepared to be interventionist when he felt the occasion demanded it, and those who disliked him thought him meddlesome. "Character is the thing I care about," he told Isherwood, "both in myself and others." As Forster waited for what he called "the coming smash," he was increasingly putting his faith in personal relationships. "I don't think any one could possess social nerves today, unless he was a fool or a communist," he had written to Isherwood in February, "and I am too intelligent to be the first, and too old to be the second. All that I can do is work out a private ethic which, in the outbreak of a war, might be helpful to me. The individual is more than ever the goods." Isherwood's relationship with Heinz, which defied the generally accepted and potentially warring divisions of class and nationality, must have seemed a cause for optimism. It recalled the discarded epilogue to *Maurice,* where "two men can defy the world" and find an emblematic "greenwood" in which they can pursue their lives without the interference of Church and State. "I feel as if you were with us on this trip," Isherwood wrote as the S.S. *Zeelandia* steamed toward the Canaries.

Now that Isherwood had cast off from England once again, and thrown in his lot with Heinz, he was committed to wandering the world until he found somewhere they could both settle, unharried by immigration checks and customs officials.

A sense of impermanence was acknowledged when Isherwood gave his address as c/o the Banco Hispano Americano in Las Palmas, rather than the Towers Strand Hotel, where he and Heinz booked into a rooftop annex, the only accommodation available there. The management was apologetic, but Isherwood and Heinz enjoyed living apart from the hotel's other guests, many of whom were German tourists who spent their time at a club or playing golf. From their eyrie they could see across the bay to the extinct volcano on Tenerife, and in 1934 Las Palmas, though part of Spain, still seemed exotic, "an African town," surrounded by banana groves through which brightly colored canaries flew, as common as sparrows in England. Furthermore, Isherwood told Forster, whom he hoped to entice to the island, there were no snakes and no customs office.

The shadow of an impending European war fell across this Eden, and the knowledge that he had once again run away haunted Isherwood. He could always claim, quite rightly, that he was morally obliged to take responsibility for Heinz, but he nevertheless worried about what his friends in England would think of him. "Olive showed me your letter in which you said something about being silently judged," Upward wrote. "Of course, that's all trash, because—though Marx may not have said it— each of us helps the revolution best by using his own weapons. And your best weapon is obviously writing." This was generous and reassuring, but by late May Isherwood's weapon seemed very blunt indeed, and he was forced to acknowledge that *The Lost* had reached an impasse. "The original scheme broke down because of Paul and Helen [the journalist]. Paul may have been legitimate as a character, but I'm weary of his tragedy. Its day is over. It is too late to make a fuss about anyone's relation to his mother. As for Helen, her 'conversion' to communism stinks. I know nothing about it." Abandoning this draft, he tried to write what he described as "a chatty memoir of my Berlin life," but found that it "involved so much posing that I gave it up in disgust."

> So we come back to the possibility of writing a novel about Norris alone, as he seems to be the only workable character. What would be the nature of this novel?
>
> I think it must be in the first person. The narrator being myself. There are great difficulties in this method, but worse difficulties still in trying to give the whole of Mr Norris's character in the third person. I think that a discursive, frankly artificial, objective, rather Conradesque style could be evolved for conveying Mr Norris's background. His youth, pampered childhood, overextravagance, etc.

The style Isherwood was aiming at was suggested by the Conrad of *The Secret Agent*, a masterpiece of irony and objectivity set among the incompetent revolutionaries in late-Victorian London.

The idea of extricating Norris from the tangled skein of *The Lost* brought immediate results. Isherwood and Heinz left Las Palmas for Tenerife on June 6 and two days later settled into the Pavillion Troika in Orotava, "a little tea-house" kept by a homosexual couple, one English, the other German-American. Every day Isherwood sat in the tropical garden, bashing out the novel on his portable Corona, and a little over two months later, the book was finished. "It is a kind of glorified shocker; not unlike the productions of my cousin Graham Greene," he told Lehmann. To Forster, who had just become president of the recently founded National Council for Civil Liberties, he described the novel as "less a blow for anyone's freedom than a home-made jam-pot grenade flung rather wildly at Berlin." Equally wild was Isherwood's decision to entrust the only typescript of the book to the international post, even though several magazines and a pair of spectacles he had been sent from England never arrived. "If it gets lost, I've no other copy," he told Lehmann cheerfully; "so that's that." Fortunately it arrived safely at Pembroke Gardens, where Kathleen had instructions to deliver it to Curtis Brown.

Isherwood gave the novel's narrator his own middle names, and William Bradshaw is a partial self-portrait. Unlike Isherwood, he is merely an observer of, rather than a participant in, the louche nightlife of Berlin. He describes himself as a "connoisseur of human nature," but is in fact rather naïve. Characters who would become familiar in subsequent Berlin stories are introduced, including Bradshaw's landlady, Frl. Schroeder, and the young man-about-town Fritz Wendel. The young working-class communist activist, Otto, is not the same Otto as the character in *Goodbye to Berlin,* who was closely based on Walter Wolff—although Isherwood suggests a kinship by giving him an aunt in Simeonstrasse, where Isherwood lodged with Walter's family. Other characters include Ludwig Bayer, the enigmatic communist leader, who uses the unwitting Mr. Norris to spread disinformation among the Party's enemies; Helen Pratt, a tough left-wing journalist; the prostitute Anni; and Baron Kuno von Pregnitz, a homosexual aristocrat working for the government.[4]

The great strength of the novel, however, remains Mr. Norris himself, a superb comic character, whose unreliability is established from the very outset, when Bradshaw meets him on a train. Norris is wearing a very obvious wig and is looking extremely shifty. Norris claims to be in the import-export trade, but is evasive about the exact nature of his business, and seems unduly anxious about railway and passport officials. Back in Berlin, he is full of surprises, discovered at one moment cowering in agony and ecstasy at the booted feet of a prostitute, and at another addressing a meeting of the Communist Party on "the crimes of British Imperialism in the Far East." He also has to make frequent trips abroad in order to evade his creditors and pursue business contacts and eventually involves Bradshaw and von Pregnitz in a spying plot. Unlike Bayer, who is murdered in the Spandau Barracks, von Pregnitz, who commits suicide, and Otto, who is last seen being pursued by stormtroopers, Norris is a survivor. At the end of the novel he is obliged to leave Berlin for South America, from where he sends Bradshaw a series of postcards. "Tell me, William," he asks in the novel's concluding sentence, "what have I done to deserve all this?"

Mr. Norris's exile and his anxiety about customs and immigration officials is well merited, but also reflects Isherwood and Heinz's own experiences. The novel's comedy and high spirits are constantly subverted not only by the violence and political unrest of Berlin, but also by a sense of deracination. "As you get older, William,"

---

4. Isherwood signals von Pregnitz's sexual tastes by naming him after Graf Kuno von Moltke, who was at the center of one of Germany's most infamous homosexual scandals, involving the inner circle of Kaiser Wilhelm II. Hischfeld had been involved as a professional witness at the resulting court case in 1907.

Norris observes, "you'll feel that the world gets smaller. The frontiers seem to close in, until there's scarcely room to breathe." This is indeed what Isherwood was finding and it describes exactly the circumstances in which he wrote the book, which he dedicated to Auden.

Now that the book was finished, Isherwood realized that he needed the blessing of Gerald Hamilton before going into print. Kathleen had a copy of the typescript made and sent to Paris, where Hamilton read it and affected to be deeply wounded. It required equal amounts of tact, flattery and dissimulation to persuade Hamilton of Isherwood's honorable literary intentions. "I didn't write the book with the object of insulting Gerald," Isherwood protested, "and, after some slight pain, I made him see that I didn't." He may not have wanted to insult Hamilton, but there is no doubt that he was using him. His frequent and strenuous assertions that Arthur Norris was not Gerald Hamilton were more than a little disingenuous. Indeed, he referred to Hamilton as "Mr Norris" in correspondence with Kathleen and others, and many of the details of the character's appearance and exploits are taken directly from Hamilton's life. Quite apart from the obvious physical resemblance, there are references to a background in Shanghai, an inherited fortune, a spell in prison, friendship with Frank Harris, a special coffee pot, and the authorship of a pseudonymous underground novel (*Miss Smith's Torture Chamber* standing in for *Desert Dreamers*), all of which are borrowed from Hamilton. Isherwood may have made Norris a heterosexual masochist, whereas Hamilton was a homosexual one, and provided him with a European rather than Chinese childhood, but to anyone who knew Hamilton, Mr. Norris would have been instantly recognizable. Isherwood caught his way of speaking, his mock-innocence, his shiftiness, his personal fastidiousness, his absurdity. He even gives Norris Hamilton's hoary old joke, "We live in stirring times; tea-stirring times," and his frequent excuse: "There are some incidents in my career, as you doubtless know, which are very easily capable of misinterpretation."

According to Kathleen, Hamilton's principal objection was that in the story Hamilton betrays the communists, "and he did not like to be supposed to be capable of this!" Isherwood decided to call Hamilton's bluff, telling him that since the entire plot hinged on Norris's treachery, he could not possibly alter the book, but would withdraw it if Hamilton thought it "affected his honour." Hamilton then overcame all his objections, as Isherwood had hoped he would, and gave the novel "his full & unconditional blessing." What probably made Hamilton agree to the book's being published was that the portrait, for all its mockery, is an affectionate one. Considering some of Hamilton's murkier exploits, he may well have reflected that he had got off lightly. Norris may be involved in spying and all manner of more or less illegal activities, but he comes across as a lovable rogue, naughty rather than wicked. As Forster commented: "It's marvellous [. . .] the way you've maintained standards of right and wrong and yet left Norris an endearing person. And you've made him both silly and witty, like a character in Congreve. He's awfully good."

The novel certainly found favor with the Hogarth Press. "My wife and I have read it with great pleasure," Leonard Woolf wrote. "The character of Arthur Norris is extraordinarily well done and the whole book brilliant. It did too what hardly any novels ever do, amused me intensely. I am writing to Curtis Brown and I hope we may publish it in the spring."

NINE

B Y THE SORT OF COINCIDENCE KATHLEEN TENDED TO TAKE FOR
an augury, *Little Friend* had opened on Isherwood's thirtieth birthday, August
26, 1934. She and Richard went to the matinée performance, and were so
"fearfully thrilled" at seeing Christopher's name on the credits that they stayed to
watch them the second time round. Forster wrote to say that he'd enjoyed the film so
much he saw it three times. Viertel himself was delighted, particularly when the film
opened in America and got a highly complimentary review in the *The New York
Times,* where it was hailed as "very close to being a masterpiece of its kind." The reviewer praised Viertel's restrained direction and commended the "unusually literate
script." Viertel sent Isherwood a clipping of the review, noting "You should know that
the credit of the success of 'Little Friend' which was really great in New York was
shared by you as it should have been indeed." When the film opened in London, the
Evening Standard announced that Viertel had been engaged by Gaumont-British to
film Jerome K. Jerome's *The Passing of the Third Floor Back* and that Isherwood
might be writing the screenplay. This idea came to nothing, as did another of Viertel's
plans for his reluctant collaborator. "I wanted you for the picture I am preparing now
after Tolstoi's 'The Living Corpse,' " he told Isherwood. "Stevenson and McPhail
who are both most decidedly in favour of you doubted if you would really be a good
match for Tolstoi. So I became doubtful myself, especially doubting if I should destroy your splendid isolation in order to make you unhappy by film-slavery again." It
must have been faintly galling to be considered a good match for Ernst Lothar but not
for Tolstoy, but it would in any case have been impossible for Isherwood to return to
England for any length of time unless he had been prepared to abandon Heinz.

N ow that the novel was placed with a publisher, Isherwood and Heinz embarked
on a tour of the other islands in the Canaries. They had already made some
quite strenuous expeditions, climbing the 4,350-foot Cruz de Tejeda on Gran Canaria
and the Pico de Teide on Tenerife during a brief holiday from the typewriter. These

climbs had tested Isherwood's nerve, since like his father he was frightened of heights. "Heinz wheedled me up to the top," he wrote of the Cruz de Tejeda, "from which we not only saw all the kingdoms of the world but nearly fell into the middle of them." He was quite relieved when they started the descent, but nevertheless subsequently climbed an extinct volcano on Tenerife. This was a rather more elaborate expedition, carried out in the company of a guide, two mules and a young German schoolteacher of alarmingly nationalist opinions. The two Germans seemed to enjoy each other's company, and Isherwood felt excluded. It is probably significant that the notes he made about the climb petered out after a page.

These two climbs, not particularly momentous in themselves, provided Isherwood with a great deal of literary raw material, as well as useful background for the second play he would write with Auden, *The Ascent of F6*. He wrote two stories, "A Day in Paradise" and "The Turn Round the World," almost immediately, and many years later would incorporate memories of the Canary Islands in his novel *The World in the Evening*. "A Day in Paradise" was solicited by Edward Upward for *The Ploughshare*, the official magazine of the Teachers' Anti-War Movement. It is an ironic travel sketch in which the narrator, armed with a blandly effusive guidebook, visits a tropical island. Off the tourist track he finds genuine poverty and squalor:

> Children with great dark eyes are playing in the dirt. All of them are naked and most of them have open sores on their arms and legs. The sores are disgusting if you look at them too closely; flies are crawling over them. And the stench from the little shuttered ruins of houses is most distressing. But the guide-book, that invaluable psychological prompter, rescues us from an uneasy moment. 'The life of the port,' we read, 'is extremely typical and picturesque.' So we take a snapshot of the most typical of the children (he appears to be mentally deficient), pat him, rather gingerly, on the head and give him some money.

Back home, the tourist finds that such sights are quickly blotted out by more pleasant memories, and if the occasional recollection of deprivation surfaces, "then quickly the image of the island, as the travel-bureau and the guide-book present it, will slide, like a brightly-coloured magic-lantern picture, between us and our real memories, and we shall repeat, as hundreds of others have repeated: 'Yes, indeed . . . it's a paradise on earth.' " Isherwood captures the tone of the tourist well enough, but this is fairly crude, obvious stuff and its rhetoric about "the struggle against hunger and war" being "more immediate, more universal than we dream" lacks conviction. The sketch does, however, suggest a lingering guilt about Isherwood's own months of escapism, prompted by Viertel's sharp comment about a "Noa-Noa-Paradise."

"The Turn Round the World" is an inconsequential character sketch based on two mysterious fellow passengers—a self-styled "Capitan Explorador Español" and a dapper Hungarian student—Isherwood and Heinz had met on the ferry between Las Palmas and Hierro. Isherwood had described these men briefly in his diary and in the story portrays them as professional beggars, who in their different ways feel the world owes them a living. It took two days to write and was published by Ackerley in *The Listener* in August 1935.

For Isherwood, reaching thirty was a climacteric. "It is remarkable that all the futility rhymes which E[dward Upward] and I used to invent at Cambridge ('twenty-one and nothing done; twenty-two, Life's bottom through,' etc. etc.) ended at thirty," he observed in his diary. "Perhaps they were prophetic." To Forster he wrote: "Did Villon say that, at thirty, he had drunk all his 'hontes'? Or was it thirty-three? I feel as if I still had some pretty unappetizing ones in store." He described himself to Lehmann as "Thirty years old, with a few white hairs above the ears but still wonderfully preserved, a lonely figure with a typewriter in the middle of a banana grove." He was sending himself up, of course, but a sense of his isolation is apparent in his frequent complaints that few of his friends bother to write to him and in the wistful list he provided for Lehmann of those he would invite to his birthday party if he were having one: "You, Stephen, Wystan, Edward, William [Plomer], Forster, Rosamond, Beatrix, Wogan [Phillips], Gerald, the Tonys [Lehmann and Spender's boyfriends] and Olive Mangeot." He was becoming aware that he would remain an exile for as long as he stayed with Heinz, "whose relations," he told Forster, "now more or less openly beg me to keep him out of Germany." He and Heinz were happy, he insisted, "except when we think of the Future. We hold endless conferences on where to go, what to do, when the Smash comes, but arrive nowhere. We are like two frightened rabbits."

The Canaries had served their purpose, and Isherwood could not stay in his Noa Noa Paradise forever. "As long as we stay on this island, or somewhere equally remote, life is so charming and pleasant and calm," he told Lehmann; "but nowadays a retreat seems artificial and wrong. As long as I work on a book my conscience is partially relieved, because I feel that I'm doing a job to the best of my ability and helping in my tiny way." This may be why as soon as he finished his novel he started work converting his Berlin diaries into a new book. "They ought, at least, to form an interesting set of illustrations to a serious work on Fascism," he informed Forster. "I have learnt far more about what 'educated' Nazis think since I have been here, than I ever did in Germany. Most of them are school-teachers who have never read any history." It did not seem much of a contribution compared to that of people back in England, however. "I admire passionately the people who are standing up now and telling the truth," he told Lehmann; "especially I find myself warming to [Claud] Cockburn—I get the Week regularly. Misinformed or not, he does slash out at these crooks and murderers, and he's so inexhaustibly cocky and funny; like a street-boy throwing stones at pompous windows." This was the sort of political action Isherwood found sympathetic, but he evidently felt that his own writing was the equivalent of a handful of gravel.

Isherwood and Heinz left the Canary Islands for Spain at the beginning of September and spent a few days in Morocco. It was here, as Isherwood came down the gangplank at Ceuta, that a talismanic £100 note he had been carrying with him in case of emergencies, was lifted from his pocket. He sent a cable to Kathleen, merely stating that all his money had been stolen. Kathleen, who was presumably kept in ignorance of the exact circumstances of the loss, pronounced it "most vexing for him," and immediately cabled £100 to Algeciras. In *Christopher and His Kind,* Isherwood neglects to mention that this money came from his mother's own account. Some people felt that during the 1930s Isherwood liked to give the impression that he was constantly short of money when in fact there was always a readily available source back in England if things got really difficult. The details of his income he recorded in the backs of his pocket diaries list only what he earned from his writing and teaching, and it is not clear how long Uncle Henry's allowance continued. What is evident, however, is that Kathleen spent much of her time wiring funds to her wandering son, not all of which were repaid.

After returning to Spain and visiting Granada and Madrid, Isherwood and Heinz went to Copenhagen via Amsterdam. Quite why Isherwood chose Denmark as the next stage on his journey is not known. He described Copenhagen to Forster as a "compromise"—perhaps between London and Berlin. Once there, he told Plomer that Copenhagen was "my sort of town. You can get very rich cakes and German emigrant newspapers, and there are lots of cinemas and hot baths and trams. The army spends its time lolling decadently about the railway station dressed in pantomime uniforms. And when they are building a house they put laurel wreaths on a pole and drink beer and cheer from the roof." One of his first contacts in the city was a student named Paul Kryger, who seems to have been a friend of Stephen Spender.[1] Isherwood and Heinz booked into the cheapest hotel they could find, but shortly after their arrival bumped into Spender's elder brother, Michael, and his German wife, Erika. Spender had never got on with Michael, recalling that until the age of three he always got the better of his brother in fights. "But one day, when Michael lay recumbent under my puny feet, nanny said: 'Get up, Michael, and knock Stephen down'—which Michael promptly did. And for ever after this, to the joy of nanny and all her successors, he always did." Unlike the dreamy, romantic Stephen, Michael was a scientist who espoused rationalism and valued efficiency above all else. "He took a very severe line about Stephen's lack of discipline, his 'slackness,' " their brother Humphrey recalled. "Michael's attitude to Stephen was: totally incompetent, can't put anything together, fumbling around, hopeless, hopeless. He was very intolerant and very arrogant." His manner was that of a public-school housemaster and he tended to patronize all Stephen's efforts, suggesting that anyone could write poetry if they put their mind to it and had nothing better to do with their lives. For his part, Stephen felt Michael "suffered from a kind of spiritual astigmatism." Humphrey, who had worshiped Michael until, at the age of eight, he switched his allegiance to Stephen, agreed: "He was very embarrassable, there was some kind of obstruction to natural reaction." The family was therefore very surprised when this brilliant scientist, with his hugely successful career, married Erika, who was not in the least intellectual.

Erika did, however, prove very kind to Isherwood and Heinz, arranging for them to move into a "1¾ room flat" in the modern block at Classengade 65 where she and Michael were living, dealing with agents and helping to furnish it. Isherwood did not want to spend much money on the flat since there was no guarantee that he would be allowed to remain in Denmark. Foreigners had to wait three months before applying

---

1. Isherwood asked Plomer if he remembered Kryger, "who used to be at Stephen's flat so often." By the 1990s, however, Spender could no longer remember anything about this young man.

for residency and there was no knowing whether this would be granted. Meanwhile, there was "nothing to do except call for letters at Cooks and decipher with a thumb-nail dictionary the Danish headlines in the newspapers which always mean Murder, Crisis, War," he told Stephen Spender. "Perhaps the bombs will be dropping by the time you get this letter. I am weary with funk. The typhus air-raid will be nothing to this period of waiting."

As usual, the only effective distraction was work. He started to give English lessons again, but his principal project was a new theatrical collaboration with Auden. In 1932 Auden had been approached by an old school-friend, the painter Robert Medley, whose lover, Rupert Doone, had recently founded the Group Theatre. As its name suggested, the Group Theatre was to be a cooperative venture—albeit one overseen by the domineering and neurotic Doone, a former dancer with the Ballets Russes. A draft manifesto included the stated aim: "by continually playing to-gether and by using its own producers, playwrights, painters, musicians, technicians, etc., to produce a company which will work like a well trained orchestra." Doone's balletic training can be seen in the notion that the Group should

> develop a simple way of acting that is flexible and easily adaptable to any play, whether ancient or modern [. . .] And by improvisation to bring the actor to use his own powers of invention and rid him of self-consciousness. It emphasises movement as the beginning of training and approaches it through dancing; and in the same way voice production through singing.

So far the Group had put on a production of Vanbrugh's *The Provok'd Wife* at the Everyman Theatre in Hampstead and, when it began negotiations with Auden, was installed at the Kenton Theatre, Henley-on-Thames, where *The Man Who Ate the Popomack,* a surrealist "Tragi-comedy of Love" by the poet and music critic W. J. Turner, was in rehearsal. Doone wanted Auden to write a play about Orpheus, but Auden, inspired by some medieval German poetry he had been reading, countered with the suggestion that he might write a scenario based on the *danse macabre,* and eventually produced a play entitled *The Dance of Death* in the late summer of 1933. Medley and Doone realized that Auden had written just the sort of thing they had been looking for. As Medley recalled:

> the mime/dance part [for Doone himself to play], a chorus, the unconventional structure—part medieval morality, part charade—all these features suited our purposes perfectly; and it dealt with an urgent contemporary situation [the death of capitalism] in an original and unexpected way. What is more, nobody else would touch such tendentious political doggerel; we would, and we would make a success of it.

The play was published by Faber and Faber in November 1933 and produced in a double bill with *The Deluge,* one of the Chester Mystery Plays, for two performances only in February and March 1934 at the Westminster Theatre in London. In his mem-oirs Medley stated that Isherwood had arrived at the theater accompanied by Unity Mitford, the Hitler-worshiping daughter of Lord Redesdale, in the hope that she might cause a scene. This is almost certainly untrue and there is no evidence that Isherwood knew Mitford. Auden, on the other hand, attended the play one evening in the company of John Betjeman and Mitford's sister, Diana Guinness, who shared Unity's political views and hissed loudly whenever the red flag appeared on stage.

The play's success encouraged Auden to work on a new piece, *The Chase,* which reused material from *The Fronny,* a play Auden wrote in 1930 but which was subsequently lost. *The Fronny,* as its title suggests, was partly inspired by Francis Turville-Petre, and the plot centered on the disappearance from an English village of a man called Francis Crewe. A character called Alan sets out to look for him, eventually tracing him to a city based on Berlin. Auden had shown the play to Isherwood, who had made his customary comments and suggestions, but after Faber had decided not to publish it in the same volume as his long poem *The Orators,* Auden seems to have lost confidence in it. *The Chase* recycled the idea of a missing heir and combined it with the reformatory plot of *The Enemies of a Bishop.* Auden sent it to T. S. Eliot at Faber, to Doone and Medley, and to Isherwood in the autumn of 1934. Although Doone had strong reservations, he was apparently prepared to produce the play; Isherwood's reservations, however, caused Auden to have second thoughts, and he decided to rewrite it. It was probably at this point that he invited Isherwood to collaborate on the new version.

Isherwood sketched out some "Possible scenes for play" (including one eventually written by Auden, and another, altered beyond recognition, set on Fronny's island) in his diary on November 18, and sent a detailed synopsis to Auden five days later. On December 11 he sent another letter with further suggestions, and his principal contribution to the play seems to have been the provision of a reasonably coherent plot. It might be supposed that when a poet and a novelist collaborate on a play which contained verse and prose, the division of labor would be self-evident. For Auden, however, the collaboration was not one between a poet and a novelist, but between "a realist writer like Christopher and a parabolic writer like myself." The bulk of the play, and all the poetry, was written by Auden, but Isherwood was largely responsible for four of the eleven scenes, and made important contributions to four others.

Isherwood described the play as "a sort of modern fairy tale in which a man is chosen to go out and search for the missing heir." It opens in the village of Pressan Ambo, which—like Mortmere—is at once recognizable as the sort of place in which the traditional English detective story is set but is also slightly surreal. A local man, Alan Norman, is chosen by lot to find the missing Sir Francis Crewe, his reward being a traditional one of the hand in marriage of Sir Francis's sister. He sets off on this quest accompanied by a dog, which was not intended to be realistic, but "an actor obviously inside a dog suit," as in *Peter Pan.* "After going through all kinds of adventures which are supposed to show the state of Europe and of society at that time, in various symbolic and farcical styles, it is revealed that as a matter of fact the missing heir has never left the village at all, but has simply turned himself into a dog in order to observe people."

I sherwood often attempted to lose himself in his work when he was worried, but writing a play closely bound up with contemporary politics failed to distract him from his anxiety about the European situation. "Always, in the background, the vague but increasingly prominent threat of War," he had written in his diary in May. By late November things seemed to have got even worse:

> I can't stand this any longer. I must write down what I am feeling and look at it.
>
> We are on the very edge of a European war. Perhaps it will break out today, perhaps tomorrow, perhaps in a week. I write this, and as I write of course I am hoping, superstitiously, to avert the danger by stating it. Isn't there, somewhere, a little chink of hope? Of course there is—in fact, I'm exaggerating. But things certainly look black.
>
> The last month has been a nightmare. Every day, as I go out to buy the milk, sneaking round the corner to look at the posters: Krigs fare! [Threat of War] and so on. The Danish papers take a sadistic delight in exaggerating every new alarming report. And then the waiting for the wireless news, the buying of the Times, at 6.0. The day has its little stations of torment, its temporary reprieves.
>
> Why am I in such an awful funk? Partly, of course, because I don't want to die, or worse, be horribly injured. But much more because I dread the Army itself—like going back to School again—and I dread leaving H[einz]. But, in the meanwhile, it is the waiting which is so awful. The utter helplessness. The little money I have would stop if war were declared. We should never be allowed to stay here. What would become of us? In the end, I know, I would have to return to England.
>
> What's so awful about this death by stages is that there's always a little hope, right up to the end.
>
> But I must pull myself together somehow. I must have courage. If Edward and Stephen and Olive and the others were here, it would be easier. But they aren't. There's only H. for whom I'm responsible, and who said to me this morning: You seem to have no interest for anything any more. You are making me as miserable as you are yourself—and what's the good? If War comes, it'll come. There's nothing we can do to stop it.
>
> And he's quite right.
>
> [. . .]
>
> I wish I could have a good talk to Edward. And to Forster. The knowledge that I have failed to do my duty. My place is in England with the communists. I am a deserter, and a political traitor.
>
> Whenever I buy something for the flat, I think: What's the use? We shall never use these. And my heart is like lead.

Isherwood's despondency increased when he was summoned by the Danish police for a discussion about Heinz's passport. They were "charming but extremely suspicious," Isherwood told his mother. Their suspicions had been aroused in particular by the alteration that had been made in Heinz's passport in the wake of the Harwich débâcle—it now stated that he was a language student—and they seemed convinced that Isherwood was secretly employing the young German. How could Herr Neddermeyer possibly live, they asked. Isherwood said that he gave Heinz an allowance, and attempted to make this seem above board by telling them that his mother was an old friend of Heinz's grandmother. They kept asking about Isherwood's own work and whether it was political, which puzzled him since Denmark was full of political exiles going about their business without arousing the interest of the police.

The New Year was enlivened by a three-day visit from Auden, who had flown to Copenhagen at Faber's expense on January 10 in order to collate their versions of the play, which they decided to call *Where Is Francis?* "Wystan floated down upon us from the clouds last Thursday and was caught up into heaven again this morning, at 9.30," Isherwood told Plomer. "In the interim the flat was very lively and looked like a pig-sty: Heinz cooked feverishly while we worked on the play. Wystan worked so hard that he went away this morning with violet pencil marks on his nose and ear." Isherwood spent the rest of the month typing up the play, doing some extensive rewriting as he went, all of which he outlined in a long letter to Auden. The manuscript was dispatched to England, where copies were made and distributed to Faber, Doone and others. It was Medley who suggested that the title should be changed to *The Dog Beneath the Skin*—and the play was thereafter commonly known as *Dogskin*. It was published on May 30 to mixed reviews and was scheduled to be the centerpiece of the Group Theatre's new season at the Westminster Theatre which began in the autumn.

The good news that William Morrow had bought the American rights of the Mr. Norris novel for $250 was considerably diminished by notification that if he remained in Denmark, Isherwood would have to pay Danish income tax. He considered moving on to Sweden, but discovered it was even more expensive than Denmark; Finland was cheaper, but too remote and cold. In any case, Heinz's situation was becoming more and more precarious. Compulsory military service was about to be introduced in Germany, which meant that he would be expected to return to Berlin and join up, and his passport would expire in 1938 with no hope of renewal. "I think about it all, over and over, and feel furious," Isherwood told Kathleen, "but it's no good being angry: one is simply up against the system. If you aren't extremely cunning, it destroys you. It is no good crying for sympathy."

It was at this point that Isherwood realized their only hope was to find Heinz another nationality. The fact that he had attempted to enter England illegally counted against him, but Auden asked Harold Nicolson, whom he had recently got to know, to look into the records to see how much of a bad mark this was. One idea was to travel to South Africa, where Isherwood could buy some land and a cottage in Heinz's name, which would give the German some status: Heinz "might gradually turn into a Boer and from a Boer into a Briton." Events, however, were overtaking them. "As soon as Heinz has been formally called up and has formally refused to return to that madhouse, he becomes, of course, from the Nazi point of view, a criminal," Isherwood told Kathleen. "So he must get another nationality, either by adoption or by settling in some foreign country. Adoption would probably be the easier, if one could find the right sort of people to undertake it. Failing that, some nationality which can be bought outright." It is possible that Isherwood was dropping a large hint here. What, after all, could be better than if Heinz were to become, by law, his little brother? The letter from which this extract was printed in *Christopher and His Kind* has disappeared, and so it is impossible to tell how selectively it has been quoted. What is quite evident, however, from the letters of this period that do survive is that Isherwood confided in his mother more than he would care to acknowledge

persons one has met in fiction for a long time, and absolutely real." The *London Mercury* judged it "one of the most entertaining and original English novels published this year," while the *Observer* hailed it as "an impertinent, amusing, shameless story about day and night life in Berlin at the time of the Nazi Revolution. It is, I suppose, an 'improper' book; but its impropriety is too light-hearted to give serious offence." This was undoubtedly a "selling" review, but the emphasis on the novel's amusing and lighthearted qualities continued to worry the author.

U nlike *The Memorial, Mr Norris Changes Trains* achieved sales to match its good reviews and soon went into a second edition. The book's success was gratifying, but did little to alleviate Isherwood's immediate problem, which was what to do with Heinz. He still had a forlorn hope of getting Heinz permission to enter England, where at least Isherwood himself would not have to worry about papers and passports. This would be a temporary measure, of course, but it would give Isherwood time to decide what to do next. John Lehmann, who ought to have proved more sympathetic since he had an Austrian boyfriend, suggested that Isherwood should cut his losses and send Heinz back to his family in Berlin. "I quite understand what you say about H.," Isherwood replied, "and am not so absurd as to resent it. It *is* a problem, and there will certainly be difficulties of all kinds: but as long as he doesn't want to go back I think you'll agree that it would be a pretty dirty trick to wriggle out of the whole show the minute it becomes serious. Besides, I don't want to, either." He rehearsed a similar argument with Stephen Spender, who had evidently asked Isherwood if he was committed to accepting responsibility for Heinz's future:

> About H. and conscription. I have thought the whole thing over, all ways, for weeks. But, look here, surely the fact that one is taking on responsibility isn't in itself an argument one way or the other. There would be just as much responsibility (or more) in sending him back. Suppose the war comes before he'd finished serving and suppose he was killed: who'd be responsible then? Of course, the answer to that is: you'd probably be killed too, anyhow. But it's no use talking like that . . . Again, whether H. does his service or not makes no difference at all to the problem of getting him into England . . . And, looking at it from a moral standpoint, isn't it much less defensible to go and lick their boots now when you've every intention of deserting them later? . . . My plans are to leave Europe, as soon as possible, for a country where H. can settle down and work. And, in the meanwhile, if he is called up, to do everything possible to avoid giving a direct No, employing dummy medical reports and similar devices. This all sounds rather desperate, perhaps. But I don't feel that way about it: at least, not just now. I believe, in my place, you'd do much the same.

This is the first suggestion in Isherwood's letters that he had no intention of ever returning to England on a permanent basis. His use of the word "deserting" would haunt him in the future.

A measure of his desperation was that he decided to travel to Brussels in order to consult Gerald Hamilton, who was now living there, "in the pink of health and parted forever from his wig." Isherwood later declared that "Gerald was the only person [I] knew who could get the permits Heinz needed and perhaps help him change his nationality," and that Hamilton was already "working on" acquiring a permit for Heinz to live in Belgium. Quite what this work involved is unclear, but it was almost certainly conducted on the borderline of the law. For the present, all that Hamilton required of Isherwood in return for his services was help in revising his first autobiography, *As Young as Sophocles.*

Leaving Heinz in Hamilton's charge, Isherwood spent a fortnight in London, discussing further revisions of *Dogskin* with Auden, arranging terms for its production and publication with Curtis Brown, and investigating the possibility of getting permits for himself and Heinz to emigrate to Argentina. The most fruitful outcome of this visit was a dinner with Forster at which Joe Ackerley, now *The Listener*'s literary editor, immediately recruited Isherwood as a book reviewer. The work was steady, although Isherwood became rather cavalier about deadlines, and Ackerley was later to describe him as "the most consistently brilliant" of the magazine's contributors during the 1930s. Isherwood did not want to review literary works and asked instead to be sent the autobiographies of ordinary people. This allowed him to escape from his own troubles into other people's lives. Even when he didn't have to write about them, he devoured books, as he did films, with an almost insatiable and seemingly indiscriminate appetite: *La Condition Humaine, Drei Groschen Roman, The Desire and Pursuit of the Whole, Still More Misleading Cases, The Ragged Trousered Philanthropists, Le Procès Oscar Wilde, The Destructive Element, Cleopatra, The Thin Man, Welt ohne Maske, Le Petit Roi, Limehouse Blues, The Forgotten Battalion, Police Car 17.* At this period he was reading several books a week and visiting the cinema every other day.

On May 12 Isherwood returned to Brussels, but his attempt to renew Heinz's permit failed. He was, however, able to get a three-month one for Holland, and so they went back to the pension at Emmastraat 24 in a residential suburb of Amsterdam where Heinz had lived while Isherwood was working on *Little Friend.* The house was arranged on three floors and Klaus Mann was now living there, editing a political and literary magazine he had founded called *Die Sammlung.* His sister Erika was also in town with her satirical cabaret, *Die Pfeffermühle,* which she had founded in Munich in 1933. The cabaret was ferociously anti-Nazi, and Erika was soon forced to move to Zurich. Even in Switzerland Nazi sympathizers caused so much trouble at performances that the authorities banned the show, and so it moved on again, touring other European cities. Learning that she was about to have her German citizenship revoked, Erika asked Isherwood whether he would marry her, thus instantly transforming her into a British national. Isherwood turned her down, but offered to approach Auden on her behalf. Auden immediately agreed and he and Erika were married in England on June 15. Isherwood's reasons for refusing to marry were complicated, more complicated even than he was prepared to admit in *Christopher and His Kind.* There he said he did not want to cause a major row with Kathleen, "who still obstinately hoped for grandchildren produced in wedlock, [and] would have been horrified by such a marriage of convenience." This was undoubtedly true, but Isherwood also said that he had a "rooted horror of marriage," which he regarded as "the sacrament of The Others; the supreme affirmation of their dictatorship."

Whether or not he really felt this at the time, and in such terms, is open to doubt; but it must surely have struck him as a bitter irony that he could make a homosexual woman he scarcely knew a British subject by cynically going through the motions of a legal ceremony neither of them believed in, whereas he could do nothing to change the nationality of the person with whom he was genuinely in love: Heinz.

Isherwood may not have been prepared to marry Erika, but her proposal gave him an idea for the plot of a new novel he was planning, in which the protagonist would marry a German-Jewish communist in order to provide her with British nationality. He described it to his mother as "a big novel dealing with refugees; jews and communists. I should like to include the Landauers out of my original version [i.e. *The Lost*] and also work in Viertel and the film studios and move the action about from one city to another: London. Las Palmas. Copenhagen. But this is all very vague. I expect it will boil down to another 'delightful little comedy,' with not more than half a dozen deaths." The working title of the novel was originally *Paul's Journey,* then changed to *Paul Is Alone,* and the themes were outlined in Isherwood's diary on May 22:

> The central figure: a young kleptomaniac.[2]
> His journey through Europe—Greek island, London (in film studios), Tenerife, Copenhagen.
> Greek Island—the ostriches.
> London—Jewish refugees.
> Tenerife—the secret refugees and the Nazis.
> Copenhagen—the communists.
> The figure of the young man, Paul, constantly being submerged and reappearing amidst varying groups of people. Paul represents the insanity of our times.
> The book ends with some great hysterical venture: Paul's attempted return to Germany to murder the Leader.
> Paul is half German, half English.

In retrospect Isherwood compared this novel with *The Lost,* describing it as another attempt to "pack a section of [my] past life into a plot-structure," and Paul's journey clearly mirrors Isherwood's own wanderings. Like Isherwood, Paul adopts a number of roles: "In 1, he says he's a lord. In 2, he paints himself as a romantic down-and-out. In 3, he's a film-star. In 4, he's a communist, who's had amazing escapes and done illegal work." None of this is true, but Paul "implicitly believes" the stories he tells about himself.

While planning *Paul Is Alone,* Isherwood was also working on his Berlin diaries, reviewing books for Ackerley, giving English lessons and writing the two short stories based on his experiences in the Canary Islands. After the success of

---

2. This aspect of his character may have been inspired by Edward Pollock, the young man who had given Kathleen such worrying accounts of Isherwood's life in Berlin in 1930. According to Richard, Pollock was a kleptomaniac.

Mr Norris, Isherwood was approached by numerous publishers keen to poach him from the Hogarth Press. His cousin Graham Greene had recommended the novel to E. V. Rieu, managing director of Methuen, who was extremely enthusiastic and said he would be glad if Greene would write to Isherwood on the firm's behalf. "May I make a suggestion?" Greene replied. "He lived continuously in Berlin in the years immediately preceding Hitler's success and had a great many working class contacts. If he is hopelessly tied to the Hogarth Press for his next novel, he might have very interesting material for a non-fiction book on the Berlin which Hitler took over; in fact the material of 'Mr Norris.' " Isherwood evidently felt no particular obligation to the Hogarth Press, and was happy for David Higham at Curtis Brown to enter negotiations with Methuen, who offered "£150 down for *each* of my next 3 novels—with large royalties to follow." Methuen were also prepared to offer a three-novel contract, with an advance of £300. Isherwood told Kathleen that he also had to consider the offers of other publishers. "Heinemann would advance £75 for my next book; Peter Davies would advance £100 for each of my next three novels; Cape ditto; Chapman & Hall £150 for the next three; Methuen £300! I am at present trying to find out if I can extract anything from Methuen before I have written anything at all! If so they win." In the event, Higham (who was, complained Isherwood, "getting awfully casual") left the agency to set up his own, and so Isherwood went back to being represented by Spencer Curtis Brown himself, who secured a three-novel contract, under the terms Methuen suggested, which would be implemented as soon as Isherwood became free of the Hogarth Press. A contract was duly signed on September 19, and Isherwood received a cheque for £150.

Although this advance gave Isherwood a measure of financial security, he needed as much money as possible because his future plans were so uncertain. "Ackerley has been most decent," he told Kathleen: "he says he can't send me very many books as he has such hundreds of reviewers. But he favours me grossly, all the same, and pays more than the usual rate. And now he's going round trying to canvass other editors into give me reviewing, as well." In this Ackerley was successful and Isherwood produced the occasional review for the *New Statesman.* "I've also had an offer of some translating, from Geoffrey Bles. Nothing definite, as yet. But there's quite a lot of money in it. I met him the other day in Amsterdam: rather a stupid man, but a great Norris fan!"

Meanwhile, Mr. Norris himself had been "working with the powers of darkness" in order to procure a more permanent Belgian residential permit for Heinz. Matters were not much helped by Heinz's father, who wrote to the German War Office to ask that his son might be granted extra leave to stay abroad. "If nobody had said anything, the war office would most probably have forgotten about H," Isherwood complained to his mother; "now there may well be trouble." Although this particular fear was not immediately realized, there was still the question of Heinz's residency. In order to give the authorities the impression that Heinz was financially self-sufficient, Isherwood asked Kathleen to send £30, which could be returned to her almost immediately. "You might enclose a short note: Dear Heinz, I am sending you your allowance, as usual. I hope you are well. Many Greetings." It is a measure of Kathleen's loyalty to her son that she was prepared to deceive the authorities in this way, something that would have been totally against her instinct and upbringing.

Kathleen's reward was a five-day trip to Amsterdam, which was an unexpected success. Relations between Isherwood and his mother were much happier than they had been for some time. Now that Christopher's books were being complimented by the leading critics of the day, Kathleen took great pride in him. Isherwood himself, though he would hardly admit it, must have realized how much he relied on Kathleen in financial and other matters, particularly while negotiations were going on to safeguard Heinz's future. He fulfilled his filial duties by accompanying her to various museums, galleries and other tourist sights. During one of their evening excursions he inadvertently led her into a street where scantily clad women were to be found sitting at their windows. "Kathleen behaved as though this were a street on which picturesque native craftsmen were selling their artefacts," Isherwood recalled. "She asked, in would-be appreciative tourist-tones: 'Oh, is this what they call The Red Light District?' "

Other visitors included Humphrey Spender, who had long since abandoned architecture for a career as a professional photographer, and dropped in on his way back from a hazardous journalistic assignment in Morocco in a two-seater Puss Moth airplane piloted by a drunk. "Humphrey arrived yesterday by airplane—ten minutes ahead of scheduled time, he was so impatient to see us," Isherwood told Stephen Spender, "—and when we got to the aerodrome, we found him flirting with a customs official. His baggage consists of a large green canvas sleeping bag full of shorts, and an attaché case containing his Morocco diary. It is in two versions, expurgated and unlike Revolt in the Desert and the Seven Pillars. It is most awfully good, I think. Humphrey's stories of the Red Lamp District excited us almost beyond control. In fact, Heinz had to go and have a bath." Isherwood had not lost his interest in young boys, and Humphrey remembered a long discussion about the attractions of the arms and legs of twelve-year-olds. During a trip on the canals Isherwood persuaded him to snatch a photograph of a jug-eared child of about this age, or possibly younger, who caught his fancy.

Another visitor with an interest in the young was John Lehmann, who could get as aroused as Isherwood at the sight of boys' legs. Both of them found the black corduroy shorts that formed part of the *Hitlerjugend* uniform almost unbearably exciting. Lehmann had come to Amsterdam in order to solicit material for a magazine he was hoping to launch called *New Writing*. He and Isherwood discussed the venture while sitting on the edge of a playing field on which teenage boys were taking their exercise. Isherwood declined Lehmann's request that he should join the magazine's editorial board on the grounds that he had no plans to be in England in the immediate future, although he was at the same time considering an offer (which came to nothing) to join Auden, who had recently been recruited by the film unit of the General Post Office in order to make documentaries about industrial Britain. Lehmann nevertheless felt that he could rely on Isherwood's moral support. "The reunion with C. was extraordinarily successful & happy, & I felt I could get along with him really more than any other," Lehmann wrote in his diary. "Only the S. affair was a cloud, in itself a sudden nightmare. It was only in the aeroplane returning that I suddenly asked myself why on earth C. hadn't stopped it, a question which gnawed at me, shaking again confidence in him." The "S. affair" was the argument that ensued when Isherwood showed Lehmann a story Stephen Spender was about to publish in the *London*

Mercury. "The Strange Death" featured a character fairly obviously and unflatteringly based on Lehmann, who was deeply hurt by it and presumably thought Isherwood could somehow intervene to prevent it being published. Isherwood, however, greatly admired the story, judging it the best Spender had written. Lehmann was not to be mollified, and Spender was obliged to alter the story at proof stage and write him a long letter of explanation and apology.

I n July a young German named Anton Altmann took a room at the pension in Emmastraat. Always known as Toni, Altmann was the boyfriend of the English writer and aesthete Brian Howard, who, with Harold Acton, had become an influential figure on his generation at Oxford in the mid-1920s. A great deal has been written about Howard, whose influence far outweighed his talents—though these talents were not nearly as negligible as his enemies claimed. A year younger than Isherwood, Brian Christian de Claiborne Howard was born in Surrey, although his parents were both American and his father's real surname was almost certainly Gassaway. "I may be English," Howard wrote to his beloved mother in the 1930s, "but pretty soon someone really must confide in me about my paternal grandfather . . . Heaven knows who Daddy *really* is, still less his father . . . he triumphed over me, come to think of it, quite successfully from the day I was born, in presenting me with an obviously false and pretentious name—not even adding the slight support of deed of poll." Howard nevertheless proceeded to live up to the pretensions of his name, acquiring early on a grand, high camp manner and cultivating the appearance of a dandy. Startlingly precocious, he made his literary debut as a fifteen-year-old schoolboy in the prestigious literary magazine *New Age* with a poem entitled "Balloons."

Sleek-headed, with heavy-lidded eyes, he swept into Christ Church Oxford trailing clouds of notoriety, and seemed set to conquer the world. His precocity and his ostentatious homosexuality gave him an entrée into assorted artistic circles in Europe, but he lacked the focus and discipline necessary to become a successful writer. Indeed, nothing he wrote is as memorable as Evelyn Waugh's merciless versions of him in *Put Out More Flags* and *Brideshead Revisited,* or Cyril Connolly's brilliant parody, *Where Engels Fears to Tread.* Like Isherwood, Howard spent much of the 1930s wandering round Europe in the company of his lovers, contributing reviews and articles to assorted periodicals. He met Altmann, a handsome, blond bisexual of limited education, in Munich around 1931. They spent some time in the south of France, where Toni, whose appearance normally resembled that of "a nice conventional English schoolboy, not a prefect but certainly in the Eleven," might be glimpsed sweltering in the Mediterranean sun "covered top to toe in a black leather bicycling suit, or full Tyrolean regalia."[3]

They subsequently joined the travel writer Robert Byron in Athens, enduring a visit to Fronny's island shortly before Isherwood in February 1933. Also in Athens at this time were Cyril Connolly (whom Howard had known since Eton) and his wife,

---

3. This, at any rate, was the recollection of the photographer Barbara Kerr Seymer. Humphrey Spender maintained that the cycling suit was in fact black corduroy.

one of the Group Theatre's backers. The play did not go into rehearsal until December 1935, and it finally opened at the Westminster Theatre on January 30, 1936. Auden had been obliged to do a great deal of rewriting before the play could work on stage, and various scenes, risqué material and contemporary allusions to monarchs and political leaders had been removed on the orders of the Lord Chamberlain's office, which licensed plays for production. Doone also cut a number of scenes, including the one about "Destructive Desmond," a cabaret item in which a man dressed as an inky schoolboy taunts an art expert and, goaded on by an audience of diners, destroys a Rembrandt painting. This, it need hardly be said, was one of Isherwood's contributions to the play, and although supposedly a satire on philistinism, owes much of its energy to Isherwood's detestation of culture worship. He always regretted the loss of this scene, although he eventually approved of most of the other alterations made by Auden and Doone. At the time he protested that he had not been consulted, but he knew perfectly well that the schedule did not allow for communication between London and Portugal.

The published version of the play, Isherwood had noted, provoked "universal rage and contempt," but on stage *Dogskin* proved to be "quite a fair success." One bewildered reviewer complained of a "weird evening which won the applause of as odd an audience as I have ever seen in a theatre," but the *News of the World* declared the play "not only good propaganda" but "very good entertainment—whatever your politics may be." Critics nevertheless tended to divide along party lines. The *Daily Worker,* predictably enough, praised the play's "striking assualts upon the social system," while the *Evening News* dismissed the play's politics as "pernicious nonsense." Cyril Connolly, whose review in the *New Statesman* was headed "The Muse's Day Off," was more interested in stagecraft than in politics. He felt that this "Gilbertian charade" needed a more lavish production than the one it received from Doone, which was a little unjust since the play called for some thirty actors to play over 100 parts and included numerous scene changes, which meant that the Group Theatre's resources had been stretched to the limit. *Dogskin* nevertheless proved unexpectedly popular with playgoers and its planned run of two and a half weeks was extended to six.

In retrospect Isherwood felt that "The virtue of this play, such as it is, is simply that we were completely reckless, completely irresponsible, had no idea that the play would possibly be performed, and indeed if it had been performed in its entirety at any time it would be far longer than *Hamlet,* and so we wrote in that kind of uninhibited way that you can only do once." This is a slight exaggeration, but it captures the spirit of the piece, in which cabaret songs, sketches, choruses, knockabout farce, savage satire, leftist hectoring and impenetrable private allusions all come together in a lively revue. It is rather like a very English version of Brecht and Weill's musical plays, but lacks their discipline and seriousness, and although occasionally revived (usually by students) has not maintained a place in the repertory.

Back in Portugal, Isherwood, Spender and Hyndman continued to write their joint diary. Intended for reading aloud, it gave a false impression of life at Alecrim do Norte. In fact, the experiment of living together was a failure almost from the outset. "Well, we are here," Isherwood wrote in his own diary on January 3.

And yet nothing seems settled and, in a way, beneath all the gaiety of house-keeping, the jokes about Teddy the puppy and the domestic incidents so gaily chronicled in our joint diary, my heart is heavier than ever. War seems much nearer, and we have done nothing to prepare for it. In order to get a permit to stay in Portugal at all, H. must go to the German Consulate and have his passport O.K.ed. But to do so is, of course, to run a frightful risk of being told that he must return [to Germany] to do his military service and of getting his passport confiscated. Also, in the event of supplies being cut off from England, we have no prospect of earning money here whatever.

Meanwhile, H. sulks and is silently judged by Stephen and Tony—or I sometimes imagine that they are judging him. When I feel this, I am furious with them, of course. Tony is nice enough, but he has a streak of argumentative Welsh smugness and, being only human, he enjoys himself when H. says something rude to me at dinner. H—poor devil—is merely reacting to my own gloomy moods. I am always expecting that this dull dread of the future will transform itself into a cancer in my stomach. My days are all poisoned. And I can no longer discuss things frankly with Stephen—because we are divided from each other by a secret mutual knowledge of our intentions: Stephen means to return to England if things get nasty—I don't.

Things were already getting nasty on the domestic front, but Isherwood grew too dispirited to record it, and abandoned his diary for almost two months. The mounting tensions within the house were, however, recorded by Humphrey Spender, who had come to stay in mid-January, partly in order to help him decide whether living with Stephen and Tony would be practicable. At first it seemed as though the household might settle permanently in Portugal. They went to view an old monastery which boasted fourteen large and light rooms ranged around two courtyards, the walls covered to a height of four feet with beautiful antique tiles, the ceilings coffered and painted. There was even a chapel, with a spectacular baroque altar. It was for sale at a cost of £800, but it was far larger than they needed and they decided against buying it.

This was just as well because a few days after looking over the monastery, Stephen lost his temper with Heinz, who was beating Teddy and making him yelp. "Stephen had an attack of uncontrollable anger which made him say something violent to Heinz and eventually leave the room," Humphrey noted; "when he returned, he was extremely angry and Tony rather tactlessly backed him up. Stephen then left the room again, still more angry, and a discussion with Christopher upstairs followed." Isherwood privately felt that "all this RSPCA stuff—from Stephen, at any rate: knowing H[einz] as well as he does—is the merest hypocrisy. As for Tony, he's a born prig anyway. Priggishness is written all over his primly-composed-rabbit mouth and the thick inflamed nape of his neck." On reflection, he realized that this was unjust. "I think they have honestly done their best to get on with H, who certainly can be maddening when he sulks." Isherwood believed that the row was a natural result of "the strain between Tony's Welsh bossing and Heinz's Prussian obstinacy," but seemed not to recognize the root cause of the problem. "Heinz has a violent persecution mania as far as we, and obviously most of Xtopher's friends are concerned," Humphrey observed in an astute analysis of the situation. "He imagines, not alto-

1. Marple Hall, the Cheshire seat of the Bradshaw-Isherwoods.

2. Wyberslegh Hall, where Isherwood was born. From a watercolor by Frank.

3. "Hero-Father" in mufti: Frank at his easel.

4. Kathleen and baby Christopher at Wyberslegh Hall.

5. The despot of the nursery: Isherwood kitted out by Nanny.

6. The Heir of Marple Hall: Isherwood, age five, with his beloved nanny, Annie Avis.

7. "The tail-end of a good family which for generations had been going downhill and was now petering out into insanity": Granny and Grandpa Isherwood, with Kathleen standing behind and Richard and Christopher seated in front.

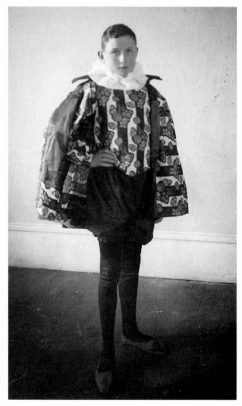

8. "The Photograph of a Boy in Costume": Richard, age fourteen, became the subject of one of W. H. Auden's early poems.

9. Christopher, in another eccentric outfit, on a seaside holiday at Pennmaenmawr.

10. Up at Corpus: Isherwood at Cambridge, 1923.

11. The Novelist with his first book: Isherwood holding an advance copy of *All the Conspirators,* taken by Edward Upward at Marine Villa, Freshwater Bay, May 1928.

12. The novel's dedicatee: Edward Upward, taken by Isherwood on the same occasion.

gether without justification, that he is very left out of things and that there is a conspiracy against him; and that Tony tries to boss him and considers him a stupid little fool (also not without justification). He is very stubborn and obstinate, and his reaction to criticism of his treatment of the animals is to continue doing whatever has been criticized, though he realizes he is in the wrong. This naturally gives rise to more criticism." Humphrey liked Heinz, but found him slow-witted and devoid of enthusiasm for anything. "This lack of enthusiasm becomes exasperating where his own particular occupations, provided for him by Xtopher, are concerned; that is, although the hens and the rabbits and the dog exist entirely with the idea that Heinz should look after them he treats the whole business as rather a bore, something which gives extra work which should be shared by everyone. So much so that he feeds and cleans them quite unmethodically and probably all wrong."

Tony was particularly apt to criticize Heinz, partly to make it clear that he was on much more of an equal footing with Spender and Isherwood than the young German ever could be. In this he was tacitly encouraged by Spender, who, Humphrey noted, "objects to the idea of Tony being taken for his 'boy' in the same way as Heinz is taken for granted by some as Christopher's boy." Indeed, it was this unspoken awareness of the difference between the relationships of Isherwood and Spender with their respective lovers that caused so much ill feeling. As Humphrey observed: "There would always be a constant rivalry between Heinz and Tony because they both feel that there are two classes represented, that of Stephen and Christopher and that of themselves, but also Tony would always feel that he is in a class superior to Heinz and Heinz would always resent (and recognize) that distinction."

Isherwood, it seems, did not recognize this distinction, or at any rate could not admit to himself that he did. "The relationship between Christopher and Heinz is complicated," Humphrey noted in his diary.

> C. makes no apparent effort to bring him into conversations, but treats him rather like a much loved dog who is expected to sit by the fire and not be a nuisance; it is therefore difficult to know exactly how much notice to take of him. [Christopher] is obviously anxious to keep any external influences from him as much as possible, for should Heinz be taken from him—by a woman for example—he would lose the decisive factor in his life, the reason for all his wanderings from country to country; the fact that Heinz is not allowed to stay in first one and then another country is the really deciding factor in Christopher's life. Without [Heinz] he would be disturbed by sex and would have no particular reason for living in any particular place. He must therefore conceal from himself all [Heinz's] faults and find little use for those who consciously or unconsciously point them out to him. He is obviously very fond of him, but I don't think in love with him; I don't think he would ever be in love with anybody.

"I suppose I wrote that partly because Christopher didn't fall in love with me," Humphrey commented more than sixty years later, not entirely seriously. He was, however, sufficiently taken with Isherwood to be in a position to wonder what being in love with him might entail. He suspected that the lover would be paid a great many compliments on his appearance and physique and would enjoy a lot of sex, but he would be unlikely to receive declamatory letters or any of the other romantic gestures commonly associated with love. Isherwood certainly found it easy to give and receive physical affection, although the fact that what gave him most erotic pleasure was to wrestle with a lover until they both became aroused suggests a lingering Puritanism. Sex usually started out in mock-innocence as a fight, even with regular sexual partners, and only gradually, almost accidentally, became erotic. It was for this reason that Magnus Hirschfeld had classified Isherwood as "infantile," by which he meant having the sexuality of a schoolboy. "At school, the boys Christopher had desired had been as scared as himself of admitting their desires," Isherwood felt. They nevertheless enjoyed "all that ass-grabbing, arm-twisting, sparring and wrestling half-naked in the changing-room"—as Isherwood continued to do long after he left school. The "innocent lust" that characterized these antics at St. Edmund's and Repton could now graduate to uninhibited sex, but the starting point remained the same. One of the principal attractions of the sort of youths Isherwood had relationships with at this period of his life was that they *were* virtually schoolboys, thus fulfilling what Isherwood later characterized as his "sexual mythology."

In suggesting that Isherwood would never be in love with anyone, Humphrey Spender also meant that he believed the demands Isherwood made in his affairs were unrealistic and that no lover could hope to fulfill them. Lovers were expected not only to be subservient but also totally in love with Isherwood: it was part of his narcissism. Humphrey thought the easygoing Heinz was very attached to Isherwood and enjoyed the sexual relationship, but was not in fact in love with him. It was necessary for Isherwood to convince himself otherwise. To a large extent he succeeded, but Humphrey decided that in reality Isherwood was less in love with Heinz than in love with the *idea* of being in love with him. He concluded that the real difference between his brother and Isherwood was that "Stephen is trying to give Tony complete independence from him whereas Christopher shields Heinz to the extent of depriving him of independence." Stephen Spender agreed. "Christopher was so protective of Heinz," he recalled. "It became terribly important to him who was served first at meals, whether Tony was served before Heinz or Heinz before Tony—that kind of thing."

Although tempers cooled after the row over Teddy, it had become evident that any plan for living together had to be abandoned. Isherwood renewed the lease of the villa for another year, while Spender and Hyndman made plans to go to Spain. Once these decisions had been made, everyone seemed to get along quite well, spending their time visiting members of the English colony, gambling unsuccessfully at the casino in Estoril, and crowding round the radio listening to news of the deepening crisis in Europe. "The situation, though not exactly worse, is going steadily bad, like a plum," Isherwood wrote on March 15. Spender and Hyndman had left the previous day, but Auden was arriving for a month to work on *The Ascent of F6,* a new play centered on a mountaineering expedition.

Auden was not an easy guest, demanding food on time, smoking incessantly, piling rugs and carpets on his bed at night:

But although I found myself glancing nervously whenever he picked up a book, fiddled with the electric-light cord or shovelled food into his mouth while reading at meals; although I was often very much annoyed by his fussing and by the mess he made—still I never for one moment was more than annoyed. I never felt opposed to him in my deepest being—as I sometimes feel opposed to almost everyone I know. We are, after all, of the same sort.

This explains why the collaboration was such a success. I can't imagine being able to work with any of my other friends. Fundamentally, Wystan and I are exceedingly polite to each other: also, our respective work on this play was fairly sharply defined [. . .] On the whole, we interfered very little with each other's work. The only scene on which we really collaborated was the last. It was understood throughout that Wystan's speciality was to be the 'woozy' and mine the 'straight' bits.

The straight bits included the play's basic plot, which Isherwood sketched out before the two authors separated to get on with their own allotted scenes.

The play describes an expedition undertaken by a young mountaineer, Michael Ransom, to climb a peak called F6, which stands in a range dividing the two colonies of British and Ostnian Sudoland. The natives of Sudoland dare not approach "the Haunted Mountain" and face its Demon, but they believe that whoever conquers it "will be lord over *both* the Sudolands, with his descendants, for a thousand years." Since the Ostnians are rumored to be mounting an expedition, it becomes vital to British interests that an Englishman be first to reach the summit. Ransom's twin brother, Sir James, works in the Colonial Office, but fails to persuade his sibling to undertake the mission. Michael wants to climb the mountain, but on his own terms and for his own reasons, not as part of some propaganda stunt. James then enlists the support of their mother, who explains to Michael that she has sacrificed herself and her feelings, concealing her love for him in an attempt to make him "truly strong." Unable to withstand this emotional appeal, Ransom agrees to attempt the ascent of F6. He is accompanied by four men: the Doctor, a sort of First World War "uncle" figure; an obsessive botanist called Lamp; a frivolous playboy called Gunn (based partly on Isherwood's Cambridge contemporary Christopher Orpen); and the serious-minded Shawcross, who hero-worships Ransom and is jealous of Gunn.

Halfway up the mountain the team visits a monastery, where they are invited to look into a crystal in which futures are foretold. The Abbot tells Ransom that the vision he had of himself saving mankind was false. He tries to persuade him to abandon the ascent and become a monk, making "the complete abnegation of the will." Ransom refuses, and the ascent continues. Lamp is swept away in an avalanche, and when Ransom chooses Gunn to accompany him to the summit, the hysterically jealous Shawcross throws himself to his death. Gunn dies in a blizzard, and Ransom is left to reach the peak alone, and it is there that he encounters the Demon, a draped figure which reveals itself as his mother.

Auden described the play as "a cross between Peer Gynt and Journey's End," but it borrows even more widely than that, with touches of Rider Haggard, J. R. Ackerley's *The Prisoners of War,* and a dash of James Hilton's popular novel *Lost Horizon.* The authors had, Isherwood admitted, already "cribbed" the scene from Ackerley's play in which the madmen pretend to be in an airplane for *Dogskin;* in *F6* they borrow its schoolboy atmosphere of rivalries and jealousies, which are more pronounced than in *Journey's End*. In particular, Shawcross's crush on Ransom is very similar to that suffered by Ackerley's protagonist, and the Doctor performs a sympathetic role similar to that of Adleby in Ackerley's play. Much of the dialogue might have come straight out of the *Boy's Own Paper*, or indeed one of Isherwood's own school stories. Isherwood's gift for pastiche also came in handy for the broadly satirical scenes involving politicians and representatives of the press, the army and the aristocracy.

Apart from the sections of the play he actually wrote, Isherwood's contribution may be discerned in many of its themes and concerns. Ransom's character and appearance ("short and blue-eyed") are partly derived from that of T. E. Lawrence, whom the authors regarded as a prime example of the neurotic hero, "The Truly Weak Man." Unlike the Truly Strong Man, who needs no challenge and will always take the most direct route, the Truly Weak Man takes the dangerous path, "and his end, if he does not turn back, is to be lost forever in the blizzard and the ice." This is precisely what happens to Ransom, who dies on top of F6. While working on *The North-West Passage,* Isherwood scribbled notes, including one which read: "People's attitudes to their own Coriolanus myth." Mrs. Ransom's appeal to her son is a conscious echo of Shakespeare's play, in which the protagonist is persuaded to a fatal course of action by his mother. Closer to home, Mrs. Ransom owes something to Kathleen, whose Volumnia-like pleading Isherwood was inclined to ignore. When Michael tells her that he has refused to climb the mountain, we hear a distinct echo of Kathleen in Mrs. Ransom's reply:

Refused it? Why? But no—I must not question
My grown-up son. You have your reasons, and I
Shall try to trust them always.

F6 itself clearly derives from the Himalayan peak K_2, which Auden's brother John (the play's dedicatee) had explored on a geological expedition, but it is possible that its name had some private significance, since it was the number of one of the rooms on Isherwood's staircase at Corpus Christi College in his first year.[1]

By the end of a month the play was complete, and Auden returned to England bearing a typescript, which he had copied for Faber by a professional typist before delivering the original to Rupert Doone. Faber were keen to see the play in print as soon as possible and proofs were ready by June. Although these were marked up by Isherwood, and the text was published in September, he and Auden subsequently regretted that they had been rushed into publication. They made substantial alterations (particularly to the final scene) for the American edition, which was published by Random House the following March. By this time, the play had been performed by the Group Theatre in a revised form.

While *F6* was going through the presses, Isherwood was trying to keep his anxiety about the future at bay by working on *Paul Is Alone*. Having made a resolution to force himself "at all costs" to finish the book, he was soon defeated by its

---

1. College records do not reveal who occupied this room in Isherwood's time.

protagonist. "Do I know Paul himself sufficiently well?" he asked. "No. My present Paul is all wrong. He isn't in the least demonic—he is only a little cissy who steals. He ought to be altogether more sullen, more stubborn, more animal. It is a mistake to make him a virgin. Van der Lubbe wasn't.[2] He must be capable of sexual vice, debauch, drug-taking, everything. Such people attempt to redeem whole lifetimes through one tonic act of violence." Isherwood could not decide what job Paul should have ("I don't know enough about waiters; but he might be a servant in a private house"), nor what social background ("Need he be of working-class origin at all?"). In all these struggles Isherwood was aware that he always needed to base his fiction on what he knew, what he had observed and understood. The less Paul stayed in focus, the more he was in danger of becoming subordinate to the more lively secondary characters, based on real people such as Francis Turville-Petre.

Upward suggested Isherwood should write the book in the first person, but this brought with it great difficulties, particularly in the final scene in which Paul makes the assassination attempt on Hitler. Isherwood also felt that Paul presented from one angle alone would prove monotonous. He then decided that his method of describing the action of the plot was wrong. "It mustn't be so newsy. It was a mistake to put in so much travel-stuff. This is a study of human relationships [. . .] Above all, I must grasp Paul firmly—from the very start." This was all very well, but: "Who and what is he?" Isherwood's notes have an increasing desperation about them, and it is clear that the real problem he was having with the novel was that he had excluded himself from it. The most memorable characters in his fiction—Mr. Norris, Sally Bowles, Ambrose—appear to be presented objectively, but they always exist in relation to the narrator: Isherwood himself or some fictional version of him. It is the interaction between Isherwood and his characters—"the experience of the encounter"—that fixes them in the reader's mind. He once told Spender that characters ceased to exist for him when he was not in the room with them, that he could not imagine what they were doing when they left his immediate presence. This is an admission which says a great deal about the place he occupied in his own work.

He had now been working on the book for over a year, producing copious notes but very little else. His last set of notes concludes with the unanswered question "How does the book end?" He was not in fact sure how the book even started, but after a month's concentrated work managed to write two chapters and begin work on a third. Then, at the end of May, "on the way down the stairs to lunch," he came to "the dazzling, irrevocable decision—not to write 'Paul is Alone' at all." He had spent most of his time writing *about* the book rather than writing it—always a bad sign. He now acknowledged this: "It is quite clear: all I'd planned was a daydream. I knew nothing about any of the characters. The whole thing must be reconstructed from the very beginning—but not here." The novel never was reconstructed, and it would be Isherwood's last attempt for some thirteen years to write a book in which the protagonist was not recognizably himself.

Once he had made the brave decision to scrap the novel, he was free to consider

---

2. Marinus van der Lubbe was the mentally unstable Dutch communist who had been tried and summarily executed for setting the Reichstag on fire.

other projects. He took another look at his proposed book of autobiographical fragments, to which he now gave the title "Scenes from an Education." Just how broadly he conceived his education was clear from the provisional list of contents he drew up, each with an allotted number of pages (between twenty and forty). His formal education seemed not to figure at all. Instead he started on the Isle of Wight with "Three Years at the Bay (Evening. Morning. Afternoon)." This would be followed by "In the Day Nursery," an account of his work as Ian Scott-Kilvert's tutor; "Medical," describing his time as a student at King's College; "Berlin Diary—Autumn 1930"; "Sally Bowles," about Jean Ross; "Pension Seeadler," set on Insel Rügen; "The Nowaks," the story describing life with the Wolffs which had just appeared in *New Writing;* "Berlin Diary—Winter 1932–33"; "On the Island," describing St. Nicholas; and "OK for Sound," set at the Gaumont-British studios.

The block caused by *Paul Is Alone* was finally lifted, and within a month he had written the "Sally Bowles" section of the new book. He drew up a new list of contents, dropping both "Pension Seeadler," which he thought did not amount to anything, and "On the Island," which refused to "compose into the sort of picture I want." He decided to replace them with "Mr Lancaster," which described his trip to Bremen with Basil Fry, and "The Landauers," which used aspects of Wilfrid Israel and Gisa Soleweitschick to describe the lives of well-to-do Jews in Berlin and how they are affected by the rise of officially sanctioned anti-semitism.

While Isherwood worked, Heinz was occupied in looking after the dwindling livestock. Some sort of "plague" affected the hens, who also succumbed to the cold and a ravening stoat. Since the cock fell victim to one or the other of these fates, it was necessary to buy fertilized eggs in the hope of hatching more chicks. The rabbit ate all but one of her babies, and the survivor suffered an eye infection. Heinz had acquired some skills in carpentry and spent much of his time building hutches and cages for the animals. He had also taken over the household accounts, opening a huge ledger every evening and noting down every escudo he and Isherwood had spent. "We live in quiet dignity, as befits country gentlemen of invisible means," Isherwood told Plomer.

This quiet dignity was brutally interrupted when the letter Isherwood had long been dreading finally arrived. On June 25 he returned from a lunch party in Estoril to find an envelope from the German consulate on the hall table. Heinz was ordered to report "some time in the near future" to be served with his call-up papers. Isherwood made an appointment with a renowned lawyer in Lisbon, who suggested that there was nothing to be done and that Heinz should bow to the inevitable and return to Germany. It was, Isherwood judged, "one of the worst days of my life": "Everything seemed to be slipping away down into a bottomless black drain. It is an awful moment when the absolute confidence of childhood—'Nanny'd never let that happen to *me*'—is shaken."

Into this atmosphere of uncertainty Kathleen made her entrance. She had been looking forward to the visit, perhaps misled by Isherwood's letters into thinking that her relationship with him had once again become as close as it used to be. It had undoubtedly improved, but Isherwood still complained in his diary:

It is amazing—even now—the barrier between us. Mostly of shyness. But, in getting older, she seems to have got heavier and harder. I'd imagined myself falling on her neck, appealing to her to forget and forgive the past, to regard H. as her son—but all that, in her presence, seems merely ridiculous. She is infinitely more broad-minded, more reasonable, than she was in the old days—I like talking to her; in fact I talk to her better and more amusingly than to anyone else; but the ice is never really broken. To H. she is pleasant, gracious, chatty. She treats him—in a perfectly nice way—like one of the servants.

The visit nevertheless went pleasantly. Kathleen wondered what Nanny would have made of the spare bed she was allotted, which "hadn't been used or aired for weeks!!!," and of the family of ducks Heinz was rearing by hand in the neighboring room, which he was also using as his carpenter's shop. "One of the usual awful crisise's has just arisen about H's passport," she told Richard, who always refused to accompany his mother on her foreign travels, "and 24 hours before I arrived, they were in one of the periodical despairs over it all—it really seems as if the only thing to do will be for H to change his nationality, which is a difficult & expensive business too—however I do hope something will be arranged as Christopher has become very attached to this place."

For Isherwood, sightseeing with Kathleen provided a welcome respite from what she described as "an atmosphere of telegraphing and long-distance telephoning." Much of the telephoning was to Gerald Hamilton, who at the beginning of July produced "fairly encouraging but necessarily expensive news" about changing Heinz's nationality. "I do trust he isn't as big a crook or as dangerous as Mme Mangeot believes him to be," Kathleen confided in her diary—as well she might, since she would have to foot the bill for these necessary expenses. Isherwood was by now in such a state that he decided that Heinz should go to stay with an English family named Norton rather than remain at the address known to the German consulate.[3] "Every time the doorbell rings we jump out of our skins," he wrote. This did not work out, however, and "for reasons which seem purely pathological"—to Isherwood, at any rate—the reluctant hosts decided after a few days that they could no longer have Heinz in the house. It seems likely that they did not want to compromise their own position as foreigners by harboring someone who was, as far as the Germans were concerned, a "*Fahnenfluchtig*," or fugitive from the flag.

Isherwood had wondered whether Kathleen would "stay on and see things through," but in the event, she left after ten days as planned. Having escorted her onto the boat to England, Isherwood went to the railway station in Lisbon to greet William Robson-Scott and his friend Rico Bixener, who were coming to stay at the villa. It was through Robson-Scott that Isherwood met the writer James Stern and his wife, Tania. Although his father belonged to a wealthy German-Jewish banking firm, Jimmy Stern had been brought up in County Meath, Ireland, the country of his aristocratic, hard-riding Anglo-Irish mother. After Eton, where he had been a close friend

---

3. The author Mary Norton was principally famous for her children's books about "The Borrowers."

both of Cyril Connolly and of Brian Howard (who had fallen hopelessly in love with him), he went briefly to Sandhurst, from which he was expelled after failing his exams. His family packed him off to Rhodesia to work on a cattle farm, and it was here that he gathered much of the material for his first volume of short stories, *The Heartless Land.* By the time the book was published in 1932, Stern was living in Paris, having worked unhappily in the family bank in Frankfurt and served as J. C. Squire's assistant on the *London Mercury.* Here he met Tania Kurella, a physical therapist of German-Polish origins, who was accompanied by her current lover, a writer called Eda Lord. Stern decided that Tania "should not be a Lesbian" any more than he should be a homosexual, which is what he had been until now. He courted her by addressing her as "Beloved Boy" and, having detached her from Lord, married her in 1935.

Isherwood and Stern were the same age and had a great deal in common. Both had struggled to become writers against the opposition of their families, and it is probable that Stern failed his Sandhurst exams deliberately, as Isherwood had his Tripos, in order to escape the sort of life that had been planned for him. Among his many literary projects, many of them unfulfilled, Stern was planning a semi-autobiographical novel set at Eton, very much the sort of book Isherwood had once tried to write. Both men fussed about their health, though Stern had more cause, having caught typhoid as a teenager, a combination of malaria and blackwater fever when he was in Africa, and psittacosis in Honolulu.

Stern's first impression of Isherwood was that he was "small and insignificant to look at. A clear open face with rather staring blue-grey eyes. Very much of the ascetic about him, and incredibly English." Indeed, for Stern's tastes, Isherwood was "a little too much like an old, decent, dutiful, worrying, English school-master." These criticisms notwithstanding, the Sterns decided that they should move into Alecrim do Norte for a few months. This was not an unqualified success, for Jimmy was undergoing some sort of nervous crisis, and spent much of his time in his room. "He hates noise and wants to be alone," Isherwood noted. "I still feel I like them both, very much indeed. Tania is so very direct and sensible, a real decent human being. And Jimmy's jumpiness is quite without venom towards the outside world. He's much too busy hating his father to have any malice left over for us. Tania will get him right in a year or two, probably." This does not sound quite as confident as Isherwood evidently intended it to, and his relationship with the Sterns, though affectionate on the surface, was to be undermined by assorted grievances over the years.

In his room Stern was daily totting up his and Tania's personal expenses—banker's habits apparently dying hard—making terse notes in his diary and writing letters to friends, something which tended to occupy a great deal of his time. He noted that Isherwood "really does less in the day than I do. Doesn't even take exercise—Yesterday only left house to telephone [. . .] The only thing that wakes him up are letters." He also noted that on some days Heinz did not utter a single word. Things had got off to a bad start the day after the Sterns had moved in. Stern had noted disapprovingly that Isherwood "gets tight on a glass of wine which doesn't suit my tastes at all." While having a celebratory lunch in Lisbon, Isherwood had rather more than a glass of wine and "was violently sick where he sat and remained sick, with T holding his head, for a good five hours." Sounding himself like an English schoolmaster, Stern commented: "I was sorry for him, as I know what sickness is, but if one can't hold one's drink one shouldn't take it."

Isherwood's immoderate drinking may have been prompted by anxiety over the outbreak of the Spanish Civil War a few days earlier. Stern recalled sitting with Isherwood being regaled with tales of Gerald Hamilton in Brussels when their laughter was interrupted by a radio bulletin, which relayed "the first news of the civil war across the border": " 'This is the beginning, only the beginning,' Christopher said, expressing my thoughts, and we glanced at one another, then away, as though to conceal our certain knowledge that at last Europe's armistice had ended. . . ."

Back in England, Kathleen set about arranging for the vast sum of £1,000 to be transferred to the account of an English lawyer in Brussels named Salinger, whom Gerald Hamilton had enlisted to procure naturalization papers for Heinz. It was not altogether clear at this point which country would prove most accommodating, but they were looking to South America. Somewhat reluctantly, Kathleen made an appointment with the foreign desk at her bank and then asked her cousin Sir Graham Greene to meet her there. Sir Graham, who was eleven years older than Kathleen, had enjoyed an illustrious career in the Admiralty, ending up Permanent Secretary from 1911 (the year he was knighted) until 1917, when he became Secretary to the Ministry of Munitions. He enjoyed a busy retirement serving on the Imperial Defence Committee. Although he may have had the connections and the clout to sort out the question of Heinz's change of nationality, he must have had distinct reservations about this foreign "friend" of his young relative. Certainly, he had proved doggedly unsympathetic when dealing with a homosexual relationship in his own immediate family. Unmarried, he lived with two of his sisters at Harston House in Cambridgeshire. Helen, the youngest of his sisters, had gone to South Africa, where she taught physical education. In the 1900s she returned to Harston, bringing with her a woman named Marie Hall, who was introduced as her "companion." Sir Graham, who suspected (quite rightly, according to one of his great-nephews) that the relationship was rather more than companionable, refused to have the woman in the house. Helen built Rose Cottage—in fact a six-bedroom house—opposite the end of the drive to the main house, and installed Marie in it. She would spend the day there, returning to Harston House after dinner to spend the night under her brother's roof, thus presumably satisfying propriety.[4] Sir Graham was immensely pompous and proper, but was liked within the family. He was Richard Isherwood's godfather, and his fondness for Kathleen was evidently such that he was able for once to lay aside his moral scruples and come to her assistance in the distinctly fishy negotiations over Heinz.

Having learned that Kathleen proposed sending Christopher £1,000, which he would then pass on to Salinger (via the notoriously unreliable Hamilton), Sir Graham and the bank official both "most emphatically" declared that the money should not be handed over until there was some sort of "guarantee or explanation or promise" of

---

4. In later years the two women moved to a prefab, in which Marie, having renamed it "Evergreene," continued to live after Helen's death.

what Salinger was actually proposing to do. They did not trust this man, about whom nobody seemed to know anything, and suggested he might double-cross the Isherwoods. Kathleen herself had come to "more and more feel there is something very shadey behind it all." Sir Graham suggested she should consult an old friend of his who had "a good deal of experience of transactions abroad," and this man agreed that it would be "perfect madness" to hand over the money to Salinger without any sort of written guarantee. Salinger was written to, but they waited in vain for any reply.

Meanwhile, Sir Graham consulted a legal adviser at the Foreign Office to find out whether a German consul in a foreign territory had the power to compel a German resident there to return to the Fatherland. The answer appeared to be that as long as Heinz's passport remained in order and that he wasn't "mixing himself up in politics," he could not be sent back to Germany. Sir Graham was also advised that naturalization papers bought in Brussels would have little validity and might even get Isherwood into trouble. Isherwood nevertheless kept sending Kathleen cables, urging her to send the money at once. These cables were in support of a letter, which finally reached Kathleen on August 10, almost a fortnight after it had been written, because the Portuguese postal service was being severely disrupted by the Civil War in neighboring Spain. The letter has vanished, but Kathleen recorded its contents in her diary:

> He begs me to send the money to Salinger, for as he says he is after all a British lawyer who works for the Embassy and that therefore it seems absurd to feel seriously suspicious, although he agrees that he had suspicions himself and only removed them by thinking out the whole business from the point of view of relative advantages to all parties concerned. He enclosed letters from Salinger (quite noncommittal) and also from Gerald Hamilton—no answer yet to the one I wrote Salinger. It is most difficult to know what steps to take with all communication taking so long to and from Portugal, and C. has not yet heard that this expensive document may involve him and Heinz and not be accepted. Salinger has told us nothing.

Isherwood himself wrote in his diary on August 9:

> My own worries are still inside me, like a dull ache in the pit of my stomach. We had another volley of telegrams this week, because M. is, not unreasonably, making difficulties about handing over the money to Salinger without guarantees. More than five weeks since this business started and still nothing settled, it seems.
>
> The news from Spain is less good. Franco has got his Moroccan reinforcements and is about to attack.

The diary breaks off here, and would not be resumed for ten months, by which time Isherwood's circumstances had altered irrevocably.

Kathleen eventually suggested that Isherwood should come to England, thus simplifying the three-way correspondence between London, Sintra and Brussels, and getting around the problem of the Portuguese post. Isherwood agreed, but meanwhile a second summons from the German consulate arrived at Alecrim do Norte. Tania Stern had boldly suggested that they should all go to the consulate and ask what would happen if Heinz disobeyed the conscription order. Isherwood decided he could not risk this, nor could he risk leaving Heinz in Portugal, and so decided to take him to Belgium and deposit him with Gerald Hamilton in Ostende before traveling on to London. Although Belgium presented some dangers, since it bordered Germany and had been the first country invaded in the previous war, it was far more accessible to England than Portugal in terms of travel (the journey from Sintra to London took a week) as well as communications.

Isherwood whiled away his time on the boat writing a long letter to the Sterns describing his fellow passengers and a conversation about the Spanish Civil War with the British consul, who boarded at Vigo. "The news this morning is depressing and alarming," he wrote, "the rebels advancing, Germany and Italy siding more and more openly with Franco, the French proletariat furious. So I again have something to worry about, which is rather a relief." There were further worries awaiting him in London. Sir Graham had discovered that Brazil was about to introduce new regulations for naturalization. He thought, however, that he might be able to enlist the help of his younger brother Edward, who knew the country well. It is not altogether clear what was being proposed, but Kathleen's diary mentions Isherwood discussing with Sir Graham "the Brussels-Equador-Brazil possibilities." Isherwood wrote to the Sterns on August 25: "Two days ago, I realized that I shan't possibly be able to return to Portugal for some time to come—certainly not before October. Things are being very complicated here and absolutely demand my presence. It is too tiresome, and I feel fearfully guilty towards you, after promising so faithfully to come back and relieve the fort. Do please forgive me and don't feel too cross."

Isherwood was acutely aware that he was leaving the Sterns in the lurch. They had intended to stay in Portugal only a few months and could not afford to rent the villa on their own. His departure meant that they would have to find somewhere else to live or move on altogether. In the same letter Isherwood confessed that even if he returned to Portugal, which he must by now have realized was unlikely, he did not want to live at Alecrim do Norte. He had evidently had some sort of quarrel with Miss Mitchell's mother, who was staying with her daughter. Stern had noted that Isherwood always treated the old woman "like a schoolboy does his housemaster's wife— as though he feared her deeply & in her presence felt guilty of some sin." Isherwood was about to incur more guilt because his hasty departure meant that he had to rely upon the Sterns to carry out a number of favors. Isherwood's old friends Roger and Stella Burford eventually took over the lease and were delegated to bring all his papers back to England, but this still left a great deal to be sorted out. "*Could* you, before you leave, pack our things—just bundle them all anyhow into all available suitcases," he asked the Sterns.

> If they don't fit, maybe you could buy a cheap new suitcase for them in Lisbon? All poultry and livestock can simply be given away—if nobody will buy it— preferably to Mrs Loweth [a neighbor], who has a poultry-run. My only desire is that old Mrs Mitchell shan't have any at all. Who will take Teddy? The servants, perhaps?

(Stern noted in his diary a few days later: "Someone, God bless him, takes Teddy away. Barking to the bitter end.") "What an awful, floppy, sponging letter," Isherwood continued.

> I feel such a worm. And I know what I'd say if anybody asked *me* to arrange all this for them. My chief hope is to play on your sympathetic natures, but somehow I can't even try to. If you just throw everything over the wall on to the rubbish-heap I shan't be much surprised.

The day after writing this letter, on his thirty-second birthday, Isherwood returned to Ostende. He was accompanied by his old medical-school friend Robert Moody, who had also made some inquiries about naturalization, and E. M. Forster, who attempted to cheer him up with a celebratory dinner party the following evening. On August 29 Kathleen arranged for the £1,000 to be transferred to a bank in Brussels where Isherwood could cash a cheque at short notice. "I have forgotten the technicalities involved," Isherwood wrote in *Christopher and His Kind* about the attempts to provide Heinz with a new nationality, "but I am fairly sure that, in Heinz's case, certain documents could only be obtained by bribery. For example, you might have to have a certificate declaring that you had been a resident of the country for a large number of years, or that you had served in the armed forces—when, in fact, you hadn't. Such certificates could of course be proved false if a hostile official chose to investigate your past, at any time in the future." Given the seriousness of the situation, and the length of time it dragged on, it is surprising that Isherwood could remember so little about it forty years later—particularly since the letters he wrote to his mother, in which he provides her with details of the negotiations, and the relevant passages in Kathleen's diaries, were at hand. Perhaps he preferred not to remember. It did not suit the scheme of that book to show Kathleen as someone who spent much of her time cooperating with her son rather than antagonizing him. As he admitted, "Christopher didn't want Kathleen to be swindled; but he felt out of place siding with her against Gerald and the lawyer. If they were lawbreakers, well, so was he."

While these letters and diaries ought to have prompted Isherwood's memory, in themselves they provide only a blurred outline of what precisely was happening. Salinger was still investigating Ecuador, but Isherwood told Kathleen that the lawyer had also "developed interesting connections with Mexico." This, he assured her, would be "absolutely legal, foolproof and above-board." In order to facilitate things, however, Salinger still required £700, which Isherwood paid into the lawyer's account at the beginning of September. At some point in Portugal, Isherwood had floated the idea with the Sterns for all four of them to go to live in Mexico. Despite the tensions that had subsequently arisen between them, this plan was still being considered. The Mexican connection appears to have been the chargé d'affaires at the legation in Brussels, who had recently been appointed to a job back in his own country. The actual papers, however, were to be issued by the Mexican consulate in Antwerp, and this could not be done until the end of November. "Salinger now guarantees that the total amount, plus his expenses, will be under a thousand," Isherwood told Kathleen toward the end of October. "He expects to return a little of it, that is to say, to us. I really and honestly think everything is as O-K as possible; always supposing something like a revolution doesn't break out in Mexico during the course of the next three weeks; and even then Salinger, who has lots of other interests in Mexico, thinks he can put things through. But we won't hilloo till we're out of the woods; and not very loud, then."

While waiting to emerge, Isherwood and Heinz settled into a pension in Brussels at 99 Rue de la Source, where they were visited by John Lehmann. Although they had maintained regular correspondence, Isherwood and Lehmann had not seen each other for fifteen months. As usually happened when they met, Lehmann suffered a sense of disillusion. Isherwood, he wrote in his diary, had "not grown less egocentric or superbly (and also at times irritatingly) conceited . . . I felt bad, thinking that after all we should drift apart, there wasn't enough harmony of idea[s] to hold us together over such long absences, our utterly different lives now . . . If it wasn't for N[ew]. W[riting]., perhaps, it occurred to me drearily, we should already be beginning to recede from one another . . . And yet he might have meant more than any." This analysis is more perceptive than Lehmann himself actually realized. His friendship with Isherwood involved a certain amount of self-deception on both sides, a refusal to acknowledge the fact that they did not really like each other as much as they professed. They confided in each other, commiserated with each other, declared their affection for each other, but the friendship was more expedient than deeply felt.

Although he could be astonishingly dense about human relationships, Lehmann nevertheless provides interesting snapshots of Isherwood during the 1930s. On this visit he noticed "C's brilliant eyes, when indulging in some fantastic burlesque joke, or describing his own projected or just written works—the most attractive and interesting thing about him. His blind spots about his close circle of friends—loyalty tipping over into obsession. . . ." The blind spot that Lehmann particularly had in mind was over Gerald Hamilton, whose friendship with Isherwood he once again tried to undermine. "I suppose it will never be forgiven me having finally told him my suspicions—but what else could I do?" Lehmann wrote in his diary after leaving Brussels. "It may—by a supremely lucky chance for him & all of us—mean his final break with the rat." Lehmann's suspicions were presumably that Hamilton had no intention of procuring papers for Heinz. Isherwood seems not to have taken notice of this warning—much less offense.

Isherwood had confessed to Lehmann that he had "never taken root, never really lived since leaving Berlin," and the wonder is that he managed to get any work done at all during this prolonged period of alarms and excursions. While he believed that work was always a therapeutic antidote to anxiety, it must have been hard to achieve any concentrated periods of writing. It is perhaps significant that the two books he had been working on, which eventually evolved into *Goodbye to Berlin* and *Lions and Shadows,* were conceived episodically, their form dictated as much by the circumstances in which they were written as by any sort of literary plan. By the beginning of December, he had completed two chapters of his proposed autobiography, covering his time at Repton and Cambridge, and was planning four more, which would take the narrative as far as 1929. In the event, the book would contain seven chapters, and the material would be far more integrated than the outlines in his notebooks suggested. Jimmy Stern, choosing a simile he knew Isherwood would find sympathetic, had compared writing to cancer. "You're right," Isherwood responded; "it *is* like a cancer. All books are. I hope to finish cutting mine out of myself by the end of January. But it will grow again. All of them do."

His one concern was that by the time he finished it, the autobiography would have been overtaken by history. He felt that, compared with the worsening political situation, his "reminiscences of the twenties seem like the chatter of a nursery governess over the tea-table," but added: "perhaps that's as well. It will prevent the book being pompous." Although he thought it might be the best thing he had written,

> the dangers are that the whole thing may become too genial, or merely a series of archly risky revelations, or so private as to be quite incomprehensible. I have to make it very objective—and yet not sneer. The things which were important to me *then* have to be treated with a kind of respect: and yet quite calmly taken to pieces and examined. Another problem is how to cut down the number of characters by three quarters without unnecessarily distorting the facts. I want to build the whole book round a small group of people: G. B. Smith, Edward, Hector, the Quartet (if possible hardly mentioning Olive—though this seems difficult!) Lichtenberg, Wystan, Maunder,[5] Moody. [. . .]
>
> I write all this, and pick up the paper, to read that Hitler seems to be intervening quite openly in Spain. The prospect of one's getting any literary work finished without interruption doesn't seem too brilliant—but I only ask to be given till the end of January!

Meanwhile, his financial situation was very bad indeed. In *Christopher and His Kind,* Isherwood wrote of the money that his mother had handed over for Salinger that "Whatever happened, [I] fully intended to pay it back to her." The chances of his doing so must have seemed remote at the time. His bank balance was "an awful shock," he confessed to Kathleen at the beginning of November. "It means that I have only thirty pounds actually saved. And the two hundred [capital] is down to one hundred and five![6] All these moves cost so much. And, to cap it all, I now hear there is no cash coming from USA for [the American publication of] Dogskin. We've had it al-

---

5. It is impossible to identify Maunder with certainty. The only other mentions of a Maunder in any of Isherwood's papers is in a pocket diary for 1937, which records a couple of meetings with someone of that name in October, and in a fragmentary diary for that year in which Isherwood lists "helping Maunder" among his current occupations. Kathleen, whose spelling of surnames was unreliable, mentions Isherwood visiting someone called "Mander," who was being treated for some sort of nervous illness, in her diary for the same period. It seems this person had checked himself into a hospital only to find that it was a lunatic asylum. Isherwood got him seen by John Layard, but it is not clear what happened after this. In the back of his pocket diary Isherwood lists a Maunder at an address in Freshwater, and it seems likely that he was the person Isherwood portrayed as "Lester," the unstable young war veteran, in *Lions and Shadows.*

6. This £200 was presumably capital in a deposit account. It may have been part of the £300 left to him by Agatha Trevor.

ready, they say. This is almost certainly a swindle, but what is one to do? Curtis B[rown] didn't even draw up the contract, so they aren't really responsible. I can't help feeling that they're not on our side. I wish I could find an honest efficient agent." In fact, if mistakes were made over *Dogskin,* then Auden was to blame, since Isherwood had signed a document on June 7, 1935, giving his co-writer the authority to sign any agreements on his behalf.

Financially, things were even worse by the end of the month. Joe Ackerley had a backlog of Isherwood's reviews and so could not commission any new ones. "November is the first month for years that I haven't earnt a penny!" Isherwood complained. A possible source of income was John Lehmann, who enjoyed another visit to Brussels at the beginning of the New Year. Isherwood gave him part of the manuscript of his autobiography to read. Lehmann was flattered to be the first of Isherwood's friends to be shown the book and felt that Isherwood genuinely valued his opinion. "All the tension gone," he had reported happily in his diary, "so that my idea that our friendship had come to a dead end drifted away like a bad fog showing a spring day." Having carefully buttered up his prospective editor, Isherwood showed him "Sally Bowles." "I hardly think it would suit the serious tone of *New Writing,*" he wrote. "It is an attempt to satirize the romance-of-prostitution racket. Good heter stuff." He was not altogether sure, however, that the story was quite right, and wanted to show it to Upward first. There was a further obstacle to publication: he would need Jean Ross's consent, and she was proving difficult to pin down. When Lehmann read the story (which had been "passed" by Upward), he did not find it insufficiently serious for his magazine, but he was worried about its length. He was also nervous of publishing a story in which an illegal abortion played so prominent a part—even though his sister Rosamond's novel, *The Weather in the Streets,* in which an abortion is not only featured but is described in harrowing detail, had been published by Collins earlier that year. Isherwood was unwilling to remove the scene: "It seems to me that Sally, without the abortion sequence, would be just a silly little capricious bitch. Besides, what would the whole thing lead up to? And down from? The whole idea of the study is to show that even the greatest disasters leave a person like Sally essentially unchanged." Had Ross read this correspondence, she might have had second thoughts about agreeing to publication, but after much understandable vacillation, she eventually wrote to Isherwood in February 1937 to give him the go-ahead. She did this chiefly because she knew Isherwood was hard up and didn't want to stand in the way of his earning some money, but even having received her consent, Lehmann remained reluctant to publish the story.

As a substitute, Isherwood offered him his (fictionalized) "Berlin Diary," describing it as "only mildly (heter) dirty and chiefly about my landlady, fellow-lodgers, pupils, etc." It was published in the third issue of *New Writing.* A little more money (£10) came in when Isherwood agreed to provide English versions of the lyrics in Brecht's *Dreigroschenroman,* which Desmond Vesey was translating for the publisher Robert Hale under the title *A Penny for the Poor.* Some of the lyrics were taken from Brecht and Weill's *Dreigroschenoper,* but Isherwood's translations (though rhyming) were fairly literal, demonstrating that when he gave up poetry it was no great loss to literature. His version of the famous *"Moritat von Mackie Messer,"* familiar in subsequent translations as "Mack the Knife," begins awkwardly:

For the shark, he has his teeth and
You can see them in his face,
And MacHeath, he has his knife but
Hides it in a different place.

Hackwork this may have been, but it was necessary hackwork, because Isherwood was about to incur considerable medical expenses for Heinz. Touching as Isherwood found his lover's squashed nose, Heinz had been experiencing increasing difficulties with his breathing. A doctor advised surgery, involving a tonsillectomy and the construction of a false bridge, which would free the nasal passages. Heinz was not unnaturally apprehensive about such a procedure, but on December 7 he went into a clinic in Brussels. "He certainly looks a nasty mess at present, poor thing," Isherwood reported to Kathleen immediately after the operation, "—just a mouth wide open groaning, surrounded with bandages. But the doctor seems satisfied." Indeed, the operation was a great success and Heinz was pleased to acquire a profile again.

A typescript of *The Ascent of F6* had reached John Maynard Keynes, who in 1935 had founded the Arts Theatre in Cambridge and was on the lookout for new plays. It came with a strong recommendation from the theater producer Maurice Browne. Keynes was not impressed:

> I believe the two authors have considerable talent, and I much looked forward to reading the ms. But almost the greater part of it strikes me as both puerile and perfunctory, equally in theme, sentiment and diction. Since both the authors are as clever as monkeys, this return on their part to a sort of infantilism must be presumed to be deliberate. Yet I cannot but think that the play might strike the audience, as it strikes me, as being in the nature of a charade composed by exceedingly gifted boys of about 15 or 16 years of age.
>
> The play appears to be of enormous length, and no doubt something could be done by cutting and rewriting. This was my first view. But by the time I got to the end I am afraid the whole thing seemed hopeless [. . .]
>
> I should like to meet the authors sometime and discover what they really think they are at. I suspect them of being grown-up, which makes it twice as difficult to play children's games. Send them a copy of this letter if you are inclined to.

It seems unlikely that Browne did forward the letter, and publication of the play went ahead in September. The text was reviewed both by Forster and Spender. "I hope you won't feel I've been unfair," Spender wrote to Isherwood, enclosing a copy of the *Left Review* in which his critical notice appeared. "Really my only objection is that at the end of the play instead of giving the *consequences* of Ransom being the kind of person he is, you give an acute piece of analysis. To my mind the most interesting thing about Ransom is that he is a prig: perhaps that is even more important than his fascism, which is after all a doctrinaire point. I am sure it is more important than that he is in love with his mother. I can't help taking it for granted that all Wystan's & your heroes are in love with their mothers." Isherwood took the criticisms in good part, assuring Spender that they were so constructive that he and Auden had already started revising the play. "We're neither of us very satisfied with the play as it's printed," he told Forster, "and have been trying to alter it [. . .] We are doing this partly by attempting to show more clearly how Ransom was, at the critical moment in the Monastery, forced into going up the mountain by his followers, like every dictator. And we're also making Mrs. Ransom more like a dictator's public; submitting to him and yet preying on him. I don't know quite how this will work out. In the last resort, of course, every play is a kind of mad rugby scrum, out of which the players fish balls of various colours and rush off with them in all directions." Rupert Doone was scheduled to act as referee when the play went into production in the new year.

I n October Spender wrote to tell Isherwood that he and Tony Hyndman had become "semi-independent." Hyndman acquired a small flat in South London and got a job on the *Left Review,* although he continued to perform secretarial duties for Spender, who had taken a lease on a cottage in Suffolk, retaining a pied-à-terre in Brook Green, West London. The separation was, Spender said, "an experiment," but shortly afterward he met a young woman named Inez Pearn at an Aid-to-Spain meeting. Within three weeks they were married. This may have come as a surprise to Isherwood but not a shock. Two years earlier Spender had written to him somewhat sheepishly to explain that he had been having a sexual relationship with a woman, and although he still found men more sexually attractive than women he had become sick of "the whole life of the lokals and of the people I see pursuing boys." Isherwood had replied:

> I am very interested to hear of your change of life. I hope you will have lots of fun. I approve of it very much myself, in theory. But I come to feel more and more (and I suppose Wells would agree) that these much-advertised normalities and abnormalities are, in nearly all cases, so entirely a question of place, time, opportunity, environment, temperature, income, class, latitude, longitude, altitude and gratitude and, as Wystan says, knowing that I am I, I just accept my present position until something comes along and jerks me out of it. All the same, I should be sorry if we either of us ever came to despise the old jokes and haunts; we had some fun there, didn't we, in our day?

Since at the time Spender was also in a stable relationship with Hyndman, Isherwood had clearly not taken this unexpected burst of heterosexual activity too seriously. Marriage was an altogether different matter, and explaining this "defection" to Isherwood caused Spender some trouble. "I am in love with [Inez], and, I think, she is with me," he wrote. "It is useless to say any more at present, because you will meet her either when you come to London or if we go over to Brussels next year." Useless or not, he went on to analyze his reasons for marrying, which seemed to have as much to do with his relationship with Tony (who was not unnaturally "very upset indeed") as with his relationship with Inez. After explaining that he couldn't merely have an affair with Inez because he "would all the time be having a much more dynamic one of scenes and reconciliations" with Hyndman, he hastened to add:

This is not why I am marrying; a whole lot of things go to make an absolutely final step necessary. I'm just not capable any more of having 'affairs' with people; they are simply a part of a general addiction to sexual adventures. She also wants to marry me, and I think we shall be able to build up a satisfactory life together. I am sure that you will understand this necessity for a permanent and established relationship, because I know that you have always felt it so strongly yourself.

Spender conceded that his letter was "rather a muddle," and he wrote again three days later to say that he and his bride intended to come to Brussels in January. "Should you think my marriage may embarrass you in any way, it needn't at all impinge on you. Still, it will be very pleasant to know that Heinz & you are there & that we can occasionally have meals together. Do let me know how you feel about it." What Isherwood felt at the time is unrecorded, except in a letter to his mother ("What on earth made him have such a stupid wedding?") and in his guarded reply to Spender himself: "Like you, I won't venture any comments—except that I hope you'll be happy. I am very fond of all my friends' wives (in fact, Mesdames Auden, Upward,[7] Stern and Burford are four of the nicest women I ever met) so I've every hope of liking and being liked by Inez, too. As you remark, I'm a warm supporter of domestic life, in all its forms." The form Spender had chosen was unlikely to please Isherwood, however, who arranged for a bottle of sherry to be delivered to the newlyweds, then immediately invited Hyndman and his new lover, the journalist T. C. Worsley, to come to Brussels for Christmas.

Instead of Worsley, Hyndman brought Giles Romilly, with whom he had decided to go to Spain to fight with the International Brigade. Romilly and his elder brother Esmond were the rebellious nephews of Winston Churchill and had caused a furor when as schoolboys at Wellington College they published a left-wing, anti-establishment magazine called *Out of Bounds*. Giles's most notorious contribution to the magazine, which was hastily banned at many schools, was "Morning Glory," a frank and favorable account of homosexual activity at Wellington. The brothers had published a precocious joint autobiography, also called *Out of Bounds,* in 1935, and Esmond—who had spent some time in a remand home after being arrested for drunk and disorderly behavior outside his parents' London house—had already run away to the Spanish Civil War (on a bicycle). Hyndman had met the Romilly brothers through Worsley, who had been a sympathetic teacher at Wellington. Esmond, who was unwaveringly heterosexual, had worked for John Grierson and been obliged to fend off the advances of Auden on one occasion. Giles, on the other hand, was at this period of his life homosexual, and it is quite possible that he and Hyndman were having an affair.

The Christmas gathering in Brussels was hosted by a wealthy young writer Isherwood had met there named Wentworth, who had a flat in the same block as Gerald Hamilton. The other guests were Hamilton, Humphrey Spender, William Robson-Scott and Rico Bixener, and everyone seems to have enjoyed themselves, although

---

7. Upward had recently married Hilda Percival, a teacher who had been a member of the Communist Party since 1930.

Romilly lost a ring given to him by his mother and regarded this as a bad omen. Stephen Spender had been very concerned that his treatment of Hyndman had contributed to his former lover's decision to join the International Brigade, but Isherwood was able to reassure him. "You can set your mind absolutely at rest about one thing: Tony is not going to Spain on account of your marriage. And he's not feeling badly about it any more. I am absolutely certain of this, because we had a conversation when we were very drunk, and the way he said it was really convincing." Spender was enormously grateful for Isherwood's reassurances. "I can tell you what you will understand," he replied, "that I love him more than I have ever loved anybody. Just now, I get moments of awful sickness when I am reminded of things that are associated with him." Where this left Inez is anybody's guess, but this letter must have allayed any fears Isherwood may have had about Spender's "defection."

On December 27 Isherwood accompanied Hyndman and Romilly to the railway station in order to see them off to Paris, where they would join other volunteers. Hamilton appeared, bringing with him a reporter from *Le Soir,* Belgian's leading liberal newspaper, and the two recruits were interviewed. "Both Giles and Tony were pleased, I think, to have this opportunity of striking another blow for intervention," Isherwood told Spender. "Whether the interview will be published depends, however, on what the editor says." He confessed that he "felt very drawn to Giles," who was a highly decorative twenty-year-old. "I shall always like him, now; even if he goes back to being posh after this is all over." The fact that Romilly was frank about his fear of fighting made him seem attractively vulnerable, and the parting from the two young warriors at the station was emotionally charged. "Luckily, the train went off rather quickly, without the least warning, while we were all talking and laughing about Gerald's fur-collar overcoat, so there were no tears and nothing upsetting. We had barely time to give the U[nited] F[ront] salute."

By this time Isherwood had received a dramatic letter from Auden, who wrote: "I'm going to Spain in early January either Ambulance driving or fighting. I hope the former." He asked whether Isherwood could possibly meet him in Paris and reminded him that "in case of accidents" he and Upward were to act as executors. He had already instructed Faber that £100 should be paid toward the further education of his schoolboy lover Michael Yates, who was now seventeen, but that "After that all cash is yours." "I so dislike everyday political activities that I won't do them," Auden had told his friend E. R. Dodds, "but here is something I can do as a citizen and not as a writer, and as I have no dependants, I feel I ought to go." Isherwood himself did have a dependent. "I can't help feeling the worst sort of swine to be staying safe here when Wystan is going," he told Spender. "And yet I can't leave H. in the middle of his passport business being arranged, and I do want to finish my book. Look here, let's see if we can't both arrange to get reporter jobs and go out together in the Spring? I suppose Inez would come too? In any case, you must both come to Brussels and then we can talk it over." A few days later he wrote again to tell Spender that he was "rather thinking of volunteering to go [to Spain] as an interpreter between the English and German forces," while back in England, Upward was writing to advise Isherwood not to "think for a moment of following Wystan without seeing Stephen or Olive or me, first."

Before any such consultation could take place, Isherwood received a letter from

Spender announcing that he and Worsley were on their way to Spain to do "rather an important job." This was a journalistic assignment for the *Daily Worker* to discover the fate of the crew of a Russian ship recently sunk by the Italians. Spender appears not to have told Isherwood that he had joined the Communist Party, which he had done largely because he believed that by doing so he could help the republican cause in Spain. The mission was in fact quite dangerous. "A correspondent who knows Spain said that, if he's really got behind the rebel lines and they discover who he is he may even be not merely expelled or imprisoned but shot," Isherwood told his mother. "That I doubt, but an accident is always possible."

Meanwhile, Auden had arrived in Paris, and he and Isherwood spent two days in each other's company. Auden got very drunk at dinner and they spent the night together at the Hôtel Quai Voltaire. Although Isherwood did not really imagine that Auden would be in any genuine danger in Spain, it was "a solemn parting, despite all their jokes. It made them aware how absolutely each relied on the other's continuing to exist." "I found [Wystan] with a very bad cold and a batch of letters of introduction to the authorities in Valencia, where he hopes to get a job with the ministry of propaganda," Isherwood told Kathleen. "Failing this, he will work with the Red Cross Unit or do auxiliary newspaper work, either at Valencia or in Madrid." By now Auden was a newsworthy figure, but he had begged journalists not to mention his departure for Spain and was displeased by such headlines as "AUDEN, On Eve of New Play, Goes to Madrid" in the *News Chronicle*. The paper went on to report, quite inaccurately, that Auden was on his way "to take part in the defence of Madrid." Auden's plan to drive an ambulance was vetoed by the Spanish government, who recruited him to make propaganda broadcasts instead.

Looking back at this period forty years later, Isherwood reflected: "Christopher could never have done alone what Wystan was doing. He was too timid to take the step independently. Would he have gone to Spain with Wystan, if it hadn't been for Heinz? I think he would, despite his timidity, because he could have found no other good enough excuse for staying behind. As things were, he didn't feel guilty about this, only regretful for what he was missing." He did, however, go so far as to consult Forster, who wrote: "Would Heinz go too if you did? Feel muddled too. I am sure you *oughtn't* to go, but then matters are seldom decided by one's sense of duty." Forster recalled a passage in *War and Peace* "to the effect that people when war approaches them sometimes take every precaution and sometimes are utterly reckless; they tend to the first course when they are alone and to the second when they are with their friends, and both courses are equally sound." When Forster visited Brussels with Bob Buckingham in mid-January, however, it is likely that he would have dissuaded Isherwood from going to Spain. As it was, Auden must have asked Isherwood to oversee the forthcoming production of *The Ascent of F6,* which meant a spell of several weeks in London in February 1937.

It seems there was some idea of Isherwood trying to bring Heinz to England with him, since Salinger had been looking into the file on the young German deposited at the Home Office. "The result was neither as bad nor as good as we had expected," Isherwood told Kathleen.

The official reason why H. was refused admission is definitely 'moral'. Salinger, who happened to be in London and saw the people personally, said, of course, what nonsense: Mr Neddermeyer was going to stay with Mrs Isherwood. Mr I. wouldn't even be present in England. And anyhow Mr Neddermeyer was the most respectable of persons, enjoying the friendship of such well-known Englishmen as Mr E. M. Forster, who would be prepared to vouch for him. (Morgan is actually writing a letter to this effect.) Forster's name made a great impression on the Home Office people, Salinger said. Indeed, he came back from London convinced the whole business would go off smoothly. But on Saturday [i.e. January 15, 1937], we heard that the application had been provisionally refused for the present. Unofficially, however, we have been advised to try again later in the year. The explanation is that the authorities are being very strict because of the coronation [of George VI] and not reversing any black marks, on principle, until that is over. In any case, it is encouraging to know that H. is not regarded in any way permanently stigmatized. Indeed, the officials admit that he was only excluded on suspicion in the first place and that they may well have been wrong.

Leaving Heinz in Brussels, Isherwood arrived in London late at night on February 3, 1937. The following day he went straight to the Mercury Theatre in Notting Hill Gate, where *The Ascent of F6* was in rehearsal. In 1934, the manager of the Mercury had offered his premises as a permanent home for the "new poetic drama," and *Dogskin* was to have been put on there. Although this plan foundered, the Mercury remained one of several venues used by the Group Theatre. Over the next few weeks, Isherwood spent almost every day at the theater, watching the actors rehearse under the direction of Rupert Doone. The twenty-three-year-old composer Benjamin Britten, who had worked with Auden in John Grierson's GPO Film Unit, had been recruited to write the music for the play and conduct the orchestra, and Isherwood once again experienced that sense of camaraderie he had enjoyed at Gaumont-British— though in this case it was a particularly homosexual one.

Isherwood was especially delighted to take Britten under his wing. Britten appeared to be unsure—or at any rate fearful—of his sexuality and Isherwood took it upon himself to help the young man out. Britten gratifyingly described Isherwood in his diary as "a grand person, unaffected, extremely amusing & devastatingly intelligent" and was soon in thrall to his new friend. Although he seems to have had no sexual interest in Britten, Isherwood took him to dinner, sat in parks talking to him, read aloud to him, and on one occasion, having got him drunk, dragged him off to the notorious Turkish baths in Jermyn Street, where they spent the entire night. "Very pleasant sensations—completely sensuous, but very healthy," Britten wrote in his diary. "It is extraordinary to find one's resistance to anything gradually weakening." This was exactly what Isherwood intended. "Well, have we convinced Ben he's queer, or haven't we?" Isherwood asked Basil Wright, a producer with the GPO Film Unit. Not everyone approved of Isherwood's influence. Marjorie Fass, a friend of Britten's mentor Frank Bridge and one of many women who attempted to mother the young man, refused to be impressed when he boasted of his new acquaintance. "I'm having a bit of fun with him by not being bowled over by everything that Auden &

Christopher Isherwood do," she told a friend. "I'm definitely *bored* with Christopher's adolescent 'smartness' & his unwise interest in prostitutes male & female." She nevertheless recognized that it would be difficult to bring Britten to his senses: "Dear Benjy," she lamented, "he *is* so young & *so* dazzled." This is just how Isherwood liked people, and Britten rapidly became a close friend who often stayed at Pembroke Gardens when in London.

I t soon became clear that the text of *F6* needed even more revision it if it was to work on stage, and Isherwood and Doone made a number of further alterations. "Rewrote last scene," Isherwood noted laconically in his pocket diary on February 9. The scene had to be rewritten once more three days later, and was further revised after it opened at the Mercury on February 26 and had been subjected to an extended critique by Forster, who had already reviewed the published version in *The Listener.* Robert Medley, whose recollections of working with Isherwood and Auden were not altogether happy, and who in any case had a low opinion of their collaborations, commented witheringly in his memoirs that the play was "flawed by a fatal uncertainty as to what it was really about. Moreover, once again, the climax as written was dramatically weak, and bound to fail theatrically. Neither Christopher nor Wystan could think of a satisfactory solution to the problem, and consultations with E. M. Forster, the sage of Abinger, proved not surprisingly of little avail, serving only to muddy already disturbed waters." In his view, it was only Britten's music "that redeemed the final scene." When Auden finally saw the play, having returned from Spain a week into its run, he turned to Isherwood in the darkened auditorium and demanded in a loud voice, heard by most of the audience: "My *dear,* what *have* you done to it?"

Medley's doubts about *F6* proved unfounded and the play was widely and, on the whole, very well reviewed. Most people agreed that it showed a considerable advance on *Dogskin.* "This time Auden and Isherwood have brought it off," the *New Statesman* announced, going on to praise "a poetical drama containing some brilliant comedy, deep psychology, and a central theme—the exploitation by imperialists of all that is best in the youth of the Empire, with the help of their love of adventure and the influence of their parents. This is profoundly moving. It is also an extremely well-constructed play, showing a true sense of the theatre and a knowledge of the limitations of a small cast and a small stage." Britten's music and Doone's production were both judged "worthy of the talent of the authors, and seeing the written word so handsomely given life will generate in the playgoer nothing but admiration, in the writer an envious respect." The *New English Weekly*'s critic thought there was "no show in London better worth seeing at the moment," and that "probably nobody today writes better contemporary dialogue than Mr Isherwood." After fifty performances at the Mercury, the play was staged for four nights at the Cambridge Arts Theatre (Keynes having apparently overcome his original objections, and presumably seen a later version), before returning to the Little Theatre in London at the end of April.

The *New English Weekly* had predicted that "this is the sort of play that we are going to see much more of in the near future," but this proved not to be the case. The Group Theatre was to stage only three more plays before the war put a stop to its activities. *The Ascent of F6* is undoubtedly the most successful of the three plays Isherwood wrote with Auden, but is not often revived. When Random House published it with *The Dog Beneath the Skin* in a single volume for its Modern Library series of paperbacks, the book was titled *Two Great Plays*. This is to overstate the case somewhat. Although the plays both contain marvelous scenes and some very fine writing, they remain curiosities, more interesting as period pieces than as enduring drama.

I n *Christopher and His Kind,* Isherwood mentions that during rehearsals he met a young dancer from the Ballet Rambert, which leased the basement of the Mercury as a studio. This incident provides an amusing anecdote, in which Isherwood had difficulty in making his intentions known, but the resulting relationship was far more serious than he was prepared to admit. The first mention of John Andrewes in Isherwood's pocket diary is on Thursday, February 11, when Isherwood took him to the Gargoyle and the 45, two well-known and distinctly louche night-clubs. He saw him again the next day, then the following week was out to lunch or dinner with him on Monday, Tuesday, Wednesday and Saturday. The two lovers spent at least one night at Pembroke Gardens, where, creeping in late, they surprised Richard emerging stark naked from the bathroom. By this time, Isherwood had decided to take Andrewes on a romantic weekend trip to Paris, flying for the first time in his life. The ostensible reason for the trip was to arrange for Heinz to learn silversmithing, a suggestion made by Tania Stern after abandoning an initial idea that she might teach him to become a masseur. "What I dread is that he might just slowly lose interest in everything, like Toni Altmann, and become an amiable toper," Isherwood told the Sterns. "Not that he shows signs of this at present: but idleness is fatal." Shortly before meeting Andrewes, Isherwood had written to the Sterns, who were now back in Paris, to ask whether they might be able to find Heinz a room there and "start him with the silversmith *without* my being present? It's a terrible lot to ask, I know; but it would save me an awful amount of time, money and nervous energy if I didn't have to rush over to Paris just now." Jimmy Stern agreed that this was an awful lot to ask. "Christopher never turned up, and at the moment we don't feel too amicably disposed towards him," he told Stella Burford. "With infinite trouble, even at some expense, Tania managed to find a place where Heinz could work when he comes. She wrote a long letter to C., telling him of what she had discovered—and we've not even had an acknowledgement of her letter. I wrote him a pretty sharp pc this morning." The conservation of time, money and nervous energy seemed less important to Isherwood now there was the chance of being accompanied by a personable young lover.

Just before setting off for the aerodrome, on the evening of February 20, Isherwood dined with the Woolfs at 52 Tavistock Square. It was the first time he had met Virginia Woolf, and he made a good impression on her:

> Isherwood & Sally[8] last night. I[sherwoo]d rather a find: very small, red cheeked nimble & vivacious. We chattered. He lives in a pension at Brussels; is heir to an E[lizabe]than house near Manchester; & likes my books. This last put some colour in my cheeks. He said Morgan & I were the only living novelists the young—

---

8. Sally Chilvers, who was writing *A History of Socialism* for the Hogarth Press under her given name, Elizabeth Graves.

he, Auden, Spender, I suppose—take seriously. Indeed he admires us both I gathered warmly. For M.'s books he has a passion. 'I'll come out with it then Mrs
Woolf—you see, I feel you're a poetess: he does the thing I want to do . . . a perfect contraption.' But I was satisfied with my share of the compliment wh. came
very pat in these days of depression [. . .] I[sherwoo]d. is a most appreciative
merry little bird. A real novelist, I suspect; not a poet; full of acute observations
on character & scenes. Odd how few 'novelists' I know: it wd. interest me to discuss fiction with him. Sally rather smudged & pale: but then I[sherwoo]d. & I
were such chatterboxes. Suddenly he said he must meet John Andrews [*sic*] at
Rules & motor to Croydon. Has to fly to Paris for one day today. Such is the life
of the young when theyre not preparing revolutions. One of the most vital & observant of the young: & a relief after the mute dismals of the others.

Isherwood and Andrewes spent the night at the Aerodrome Hotel in Croydon, then
flew to Paris the following morning, booking into the Hôtel Quai Voltaire. In a diary
entry made nine months later, Isherwood recalled the trip, listing it with memories of
traveling to Mohrin and wondering whether Heinz would be waiting for him on the
platform, and of loitering in the changing-rooms at Repton on the lookout for a boy,
as examples of the continuity of love, in which each episode is part of all those that
have gone before: "Waking up at night in the Hotel Voltaire with John in the neigh-
bouring bed and wondering: 'What on earth is the matter with me? Have I caught a
chill? Am I going to be sick? Am I hungry? Am I dying? I feel so strange—' and then
realizing: 'No. It's only that I'm happy.' " It might be thought that after the past three
or so years, Isherwood had earned some portion of happiness. The surprising thing
about this episode with Andrewes is that Isherwood should later look upon it as an
epiphany, rather than the brief romance it appears to have been at the time.

Isherwood saw the Sterns in what turned out to be the last meeting for some time.
They were clearly fed up with Isherwood's behavior toward them and the letters that
had been exchanged with some regularity now stopped. Isherwood also organized the
silversmithing lessons for Heinz and visited the Ballet Museum with Andrewes, flying
home the following afternoon. The affair continued after their return, and Isherwood
decided to take the young man with him when he went to spend five days with Auden
at Threlkeld in the Lake District, where the Auden family had a holiday cottage. This
was to be a working holiday, since Auden and Isherwood were still hoping to provide
yet another revised ending for *The Ascent of F6* by the time it opened at the Little Theatre. This trip earned Andrewes a place in Auden and Louis MacNeice's poem "Their
Last Will and Testament," published in *Letters from Iceland* that August. In what must
have seemed a rather tactless conjunction, Auden made the following legacies:

Item my passport to Heinz Nedermeyer [sic]
And to John Andrews [sic], to rub with after a dance,
As many L.M.S. towels as he may require.[9]

---

9. "L.M.S." were the initials of the London, Midland and Scottish Railway, on which Isherwood
and Andrewes had traveled to the Lakes.

While at the cottage, Isherwood developed a painful abscess under one of his wisdom teeth and had to have an emergency extraction in Keswick, during which the tooth broke and part of it was left still embedded in the gum. Despite undergoing "tortures" and enduring blizzards, Isherwood managed to work, and by the time they returned to London, he and Auden had not only written a new ending for *F6* but had mapped out a scenario for a new play, *On the Frontier,* and collaborated on "A letter to Christopher Isherwood, Esq." included in *Letters from Iceland,* in which Auden replies to a series of questions about the island.

Three days after returning from Threlkeld, Isherwood set off for Brussels, where he collected Heinz and took him to Paris. No accommodation seems to have been found for Heinz, so rooms were once again booked in the Hôtel Quai Voltaire. Heinz began his lessons almost at once, while Isherwood worked on his autobiographical volume, completing the fifth chapter, which dealt principally with his friendship with Auden and the Burfords.

Cyril Connolly and his wife, Jean, were in Paris, accompanied by a young American named Tony Bower. Described by Spender as "rich—and therefore a friend of Cyril," Bower was in fact not quite as wealthy as the Connollys imagined. He was merely generous. His principal friendship was with Jean, who was also American and had a penchant for homosexual men. Isherwood and Bower seem to have become friends at once, and saw a great deal of each other over the next week or so. When Isherwood returned to London on April 1, Bower came too. Isherwood does not mention this in *Christopher and His Kind,* giving the impression that Bower came over from Paris on his own.[10] He recalls that Bower was "somewhat in love with" him, adding that he was "well aware of this." He insisted that he did not respond to Bower's overtures, though he was evidently happy to spend time with the smitten young man, whose name appears frequently in his pocket diary at this period.

Shortly after Isherwood arrived in London, the remains of his tooth started to spread infection to his tonsils and his throat, and he was obliged to retire to bed with a volume of Firbank. He soon developed a high temperature and fever, and his mouth became ulcerated. In *Christopher and His Kind,* Isherwood claimed that his condition deteriorated "partly because Kathleen refused to take his illness seriously," adding that his fever was a manifestation of his "fury against her scepticism." This is pure invention. If anything, Kathleen was always over-protective of her children's health, even when they were adults. Both Christopher and Richard seem to have been particularly prone to dental problems, and Isherwood hardly needed, as he once claimed, to eat lots of sweets in order to ruin his "bourgeois" teeth. Far from ignoring Isherwood's condition, Kathleen moved out of her own bedroom the moment her son became ill, and rearranged the entire house around him. What Isherwood perhaps resented was the fact that she ascribed his ill-health (probably rightly) to the sort of life he was leading. He was constantly out to lunch or dinner, coming home late and drunk after visiting night-clubs. He was also working hard on both his book of memoirs and the collaborations with Auden, was making frequent and taxing journeys to

---

10. Bower is described as "just over from Paris" on p. 203.

and from the Continent, conducting wearying negotiations with lawyers and embassies, and living under the permanent strain of his fears for Heinz's future. He had in fact complained to the Sterns in February about the state of his health and his nerves, which he said were not being much improved by the long days he put in at the Mercury. Rather than taking a proper rest in solitude, however, Isherwood encouraged visitors. John Andrewes brought grapes and a friend, and read aloud to the invalid; Doone came with a huge bunch of daffodils; the Upwards dropped in for lunch, Britten and Humphrey Spender for tea; Stephen Spender brought Inez ("One wondered why he married her!" commented Kathleen); Bower was in and out with peaches, lilies, irises and a nosegay of violets, primroses and forget-me-nots; the phone rang more or less constantly. Isherwood's temperature continued to rise, peaking at 103°, his back ached, and he developed a new crop of mouth ulcers which were so bad that he was unable to talk. He declared Kathleen's GP useless and summoned another doctor, who came regularly to syringe his throat, administer mouth-washes and take away swabs for analysis.

"He is not an easy patient," Kathleen confessed, and her natural sympathy soon began to wear thin. "Christopher feeling very limp & worn out, with all the discharge & his mouth so sore & tender, & the ulcers seem no better," she wrote after he had been in bed a week. "He gets so tired, & yet if he sees people is quite exhausted after (though the alternative is boredom!)." William Coldstream, who came regularly to paint Isherwood's portrait, was at least doing something constructive and was, Kathleen thought, "so appreciative & nice." Other visitors, such as Auden and Olive Mangeot, were less welcome. Auden smoked incessantly, dropping ash all over the carpet, thumped out hymns on the piano and demanded a bed for the night (which meant that Richard had to sleep on a sofa)—"he is a most restless unpeaceful person for anyone not well!" Kathleen exclaimed. Olive overstayed her welcome: she "came at 5 & stayed till 7." "As usual C was very aggrieved and irritable after being with her," Kathleen complained, "though this time I daresay it was largely because he was thoroughly over-tired not being fit for much talking. She brought 'The Daily Worker' which always makes him feel how unsympathetic we are with his political views and he went to bed very offended & vexed as well as very tired . . . I think we are all tired & he does not realize we are trying to do our best!" The Daily Worker may have engaged Isherwood's sympathies on a theoretical level, but it did not prevent him from making use of such bourgeois amenities as an old Nanny, who at the age of sixty-three was kept trotting up and down the stairs, fetching and carrying for him.

Heinz's status in Paris remained precarious. In order to remain in France he had to renew his visa by April 19. Isherwood was convinced that if only he were strong enough to travel, he could go to Paris and sort this out. In the event, Auden (who was to have accompanied Isherwood) went alone, though he met up with Forster there. Salinger was also on hand, offering reassurances but not much else. By this time Kathleen had met "the dreaded Mr Salinger," and had not been greatly impressed. "He has been helpful to C," she wrote in her diary, "although the object for which he has been employed has not yet been accomplished. He is said to be very clever. I hope not too clever. About 34 and looking distinctly of Jewish origin. Not quite the type I would have chosen."

On April 17 Auden telephoned to say that Heinz had got into trouble with the

French police. He had been sitting in a café, rather drunk but minding his own business, when it was raided. An Englishwoman[11] had complained that her necklace had been stolen, and everyone was questioned. According to Isherwood, Heinz had become belligerent and so was detained for further questioning, in the course of which it was discovered that he had lost his identity card in a street fight. Making further inquiries at the hotel where Heinz was staying, the police were told that Heinz was a male prostitute and had seduced a chambermaid.

Heinz was informed that his *permis de séjour* would not be renewed when it ran out in two days' time. Furthermore, although he was not charged with any crime, his arrest was reported to the Belgian police, with the result that he was unable to renew his residency permit for that country either. Salinger advised Isherwood that Heinz should go to Luxembourg, the "last resort of the police-chivvied," and wait there until his new Mexican passport was issued in Brussels. Auden and Forster were on hand to lend Heinz money, and Tony Bower, out of a misguided sense of gallantry, offered to travel to Paris and escort the young German to Luxembourg. He carried out his task, Kathleen reported, "with surprising efficiency," getting Heinz safely across the border and then traveling to Brussels to make arrangements for a new permit. The idea was that as soon as Heinz "ceased to be a boche," as Isherwood put it, the Belgian authorities would look upon his case more leniently.

Increased anxiety over Heinz and a diet consisting of beef tea, calf's-foot jelly and bananas and cream were not doing much for Isherwood's temper. He was, Kathleen complained, "so very grand & lordly & exacting [. . .] N[urse] feeling very tired, & (rather naturally) aggrieved at the way C takes everything for granted & hardly answers, or says thank you, & we really all spend our time running up & down stairs!! While he poses as a sort of sultan! & very impatient & inconsiderate, expecting series of teas to be carried up for his friends, & finding fault with the cooking . . . !" After a fortnight in bed, however, Isherwood's condition improved and "looking pinched & white & thin," he set off for Luxembourg on April 25. "Began to feel rather less tired—!" Kathleen commented.

Although Heinz's position remained precarious, Salinger had told Isherwood that the Mexicans had agreed to issue a passport and that all the papers would soon arrive in Brussels. Isherwood settled down in the Hôtel Gaisser to do some more work on his autobiography, while Heinz went out dancing. Meanwhile, the French police had been in contact with their Luxembourg colleagues and on May 12 Heinz was given six hours to leave the country. Salinger told Isherwood that the only way for Heinz to get a new permit for Belgium was to travel to Germany. This carried enormous risks, since Heinz was registered as a *Fahnenflüchtig,* but Salinger assured Isherwood that there was no real danger involved. Salinger himself would travel to join Heinz at Trier, just over the border, and arrange a new visa at the Belgian consulate there before accompanying the young German back to Brussels. Neither Isherwood nor Heinz was at all happy with this plan, but there was not much else they could do. They set off for the station, where Heinz boarded a train for Germany and Isherwood one for Belgium.

---

11. A drug-addicted former wife of Peter Quennell, according to Richard Isherwood.

All went according to plan and Heinz was issued with a new visa, but as he was about to return to the hotel he was stopped by two Gestapo officers, who asked to see his papers and promptly arrested him. Salinger did what he could: he hired a German lawyer to defend Heinz, then traveled back to Brussels to give Isherwood the bad news. Isherwood met the lawyer and discussed tactics. Heinz was in serious trouble. Isherwood told Kathleen that draft-dodging carried a possible sentence of ten years. In addition to this, Heinz could be charged with attempting to change his nationality, with mixing with anti-Nazis, and with "moral offenses." Fortunately, Isherwood had urged Heinz that if he got into trouble he should pretend to be wholly naïve, a decent young man who had been led astray by a degenerate foreigner. He should pretend to be stupid and admit no knowledge of politics whatsoever. Presumably, if Heinz could be presented by the defense as someone who had been corrupted, any charges made against him on moral grounds—charges for which Germans were at that time being sent to concentration camps—could be dismissed. The only sexual act to which Heinz should admit was mutual masturbation.

Having done what he could in Germany and Belgium, Salinger came to London to tell Kathleen what had happened. Encouraged by Olive Mangeot and Stephen Spender, neither of whom trusted Gerald Hamilton in the least, Kathleen had become suspicious about the outcome of this affair. Going over the events of the past two years, since Hamilton had offered to help obtain Heinz a new nationality, Isherwood himself began to wonder whether his unreliable old friend had done anything at all other than pocket the money. Given that he wrote an entire novel about Hamilton and his untrustworthiness, it is surprising that it had taken so long for these suspicions to surface. He now posited an elaborate plot worthy of Mr. Norris himself whereby everyone, from the woman who claimed to have lost her necklace to the man who said he represented the Mexican legation, was involved in a vast conspiracy. However, while Hamilton was capable of any sort of treachery, for the smallest financial reward, Isherwood reasoned that Salinger was "too prudent, too conventional to join in [. . .] a hazardous conspiracy" for his share of the £1,000.

Salinger, meanwhile, assured Kathleen that the money had not been wasted and that even if Heinz were given a term of imprisonment, the Mexican passport would be waiting for him on his release—a remark that shows a curious optimism about what was likely to happen in Europe in the near future. In *Christopher and His Kind,* Isherwood writes that when he visited Kathleen, Salinger "began—according to Kathleen's diary—by deploring Heinz's indiscretion in bringing Christopher's name into the case. [Salinger], of course, knew perfectly well that Heinz had only done what Christopher had told him to do. He was lying to Kathleen because, I suppose, he thought it would please her to hear Heinz blamed. Kathleen might well have been pleased, if she hadn't known that he was lying; she had already been told the true facts by Christopher." There is, however, no mention at all in Kathleen's diary of Salinger deploring Heinz's behavior. Her comment that "H seems to have been incredibly stupid in saying much more than he should" may have been based on what Salinger had told her, but there is no suggestion that this relates to incriminating her son, nor that it was not what she genuinely felt or was at odds with anything she had already been told by Isherwood.

Isherwood himself arrived in London the following day, having come via Paris where he had made inquiries at the hotel where Heinz had been staying when he was arrested. The hôtelier told him that the chambermaid who had accused Heinz of assaulting her had been lying and had been summarily sacked. The purpose of Isherwood's brief visit was probably to see the final night of *F6,* which was due to finish at the Little Theatre on May 22. The run, however, was extended by another fortnight. Isherwood nevertheless went to see the play, having had dinner with Medley and Doone, before returning to Brussels.

While awaiting developments in Trier, Isherwood was offered a job polishing dialogue written by the novelist G. B. Stern for a film about the Ballets Russes, to be produced by Alexander Korda. This meant another trip to London to discuss the project with the German director, Ludwig Berger. On the advice of his cousin Graham Greene, Isherwood decided to ask for £120 a week, but he was warned by his agent that the studios were all cutting back and that he would be unlikely to get more than half that. A trip to the studios at Denham in order to discuss terms proved fruitless, and so he returned to Brussels with the matter unresolved.

In the middle of June, Heinz's trial finally took place. He was found guilty and sentenced to six months in prison, followed by a year's labor service for the German government and two years' military service. It could have been a great deal worse, but it meant that Isherwood and Heinz would be unable to meet again for at least three and a half years. For Isherwood the *Wanderjahre* were over. There was only one place left to go: home.

ELEVEN

I SHERWOOD ARRIVED BACK AT PEMBROKE GARDENS ON JUNE 21, 1937. He settled into his old room and set to work revising his autobiography, which now included an entire section devoted to his job with the International String Quartet. "The handling of the Mangeot question is perhaps the greatest tour-de-force of tact achieved by this generation," he told Kathleen. "André I've boosted to the skies." At this point he still intended to call the book *The North-West Passage,* which sounded impressive but had very little to do with the comparatively untroubled life he described in its pages. Unfortunately, this title had already been used for an American bestseller, described by Kathleen, who read it out of curiosity, as "a ponderous book of 700 pages [. . .] with a great deal of fighting & adventure & slaughter of Indians." Leonard Woolf firmly vetoed this title and so Isherwood fell back on *Lions and Shadows,* which was equally intriguing and no more relevant.

Isherwood was also still in negotiation with the film studio. Someone else must have ended up working on the Ballets Russes movie, since the film Isherwood did eventually work on, although produced by Korda and directed by Berger, was based on a story by Carl Zuckmayer and set in the Tyrol. "My life is ruled by fat pale imperious schoolmistressy old Berger, with his hanging jowl, his grey hair brushed across to conceal the bald patch, his old queen's arrogance and vanity," Isherwood complained. "It's like collaborating with Queen Elizabeth." The contract was for four weeks and earned him £200.

He made very few entries in his diary during the summer, and most of them were about Heinz. "I think all day of Heinz over there in prison," he wrote on July 26.

Beethoven reminds me of him, when I strum on the piano. This work [on the film adaptation of Zuckmayer's story] reminds me of him, because it is in his language. When I meet a cat or a dog in the street, and stop to stroke and talk to it, as I always do now, my eyes fill with tears. I am snivelling a little as I write this. There are other times—in publishers' offices, at cocktail parties—when the little patent-leather devil of success whispers in my ear: 'He travels furthest who travels alone!' I wish I could accept this or any other consolation, however base. I suppose it isn't so much H. himself that I miss—but that part of myself which only existed in his company. That aching, melting tenderness: 'Mein kleiner Bruder'. I want to watch over him, protect him, serve him—anyhow, anywhere, on any terms. This is the feeling the Schöffengericht [magistrate's court] at Trier describes as: eine ausgesprochene Sucht zur Wechselseitigen Onanie! [an out-and-out craving for mutual masturbation]

In *Christopher and His Kind,* Isherwood quotes (very selectively and with the dates altered) from his diary entries about Heinz, commenting: "In this mirror of a diary, Christopher reveals a few frank glimpses of himself. The rest is posing." The acknowledgment that it was not so much Heinz himself as what he stood for that Isherwood really missed evidently seemed rather too frank and revealing, and was omitted. It recalls his observation about the homesickness he experienced at prep school: "I suppose that this loss of identity is really much of the painfulness which lies at the bottom of what is miscalled Homesickness; it is not Home that one cries for but one's home-self." Isherwood's notion that he could not imagine what his characters were doing when they were, as it were, out of the room, also finds an echo here. There is a suggestion that, as with his fictional characters, Isherwood thought of his lovers principally in relation to himself, rather than autonomous beings. That he even thought of old friends in the same way is suggested by his remark that seeing Spender after a long interval made him feel that "part of me had been closed all this time, like the disused wing of a house." Over the next eighteen months, Isherwood started to question the whole idea of identity, of who he really was, and this would lead him to make decisions about his future.

Humphrey Spender's prediction that in losing Heinz Isherwood would also lose "the decisive factor in his life" had been fulfilled. It was not merely that Isherwood no longer had any reason to wander round Europe, or that his long and tiring struggle to defy those who wanted to part him from Heinz was over; he had also been left with a void at the center of his emotional life. However unsatisfactory in many ways life with Heinz had been, it had given Isherwood an emotional focus, and there is no doubting his sense of frustration and loss. "One can only laugh—for fear of becoming quite mad with futile, foaming rage and hate," he wrote in his diary. "At present, I don't hate much. I must be careful. I must work conscientiously. Work, as usual, is the only solution."

There were, nevertheless, other solutions and consolations. He later acknowledged that "widowerhood lent glamour to his image," and this was something he was quite prepared to exploit. Perhaps his most spectacular conquest took place at Humphrey Spender's wedding on July 13. Humphrey had fallen in love with a young woman called Margaret ("Lolly") Low. Lolly worked in an architectural practice, but her brother Oliver was, as his father put it, "sailing down the river of idleness to the sea of unemployment." Oliver was supposedly a confirmed heterosexual, but Isherwood managed to seduce him at the wedding reception. Alcohol may have played its part in lowering Oliver's resistance, but he appears not to have regretted the experience, and he and Isherwood spent a great deal of time in each other's company over the next couple of weeks.

Of this period, Isherwood said that he "preferred to have two or three affairs running concurrently; in that way, he felt less involved with any particular individual." Indeed, he would often have lunch with one lover and dinner with another, while going off for weekends with a third. This sounds more enjoyable than it evidently was, and Isherwood got into an increasingly desperate muddle over what he really felt about the various young men in his life. Having decided at last that he perhaps did want to sleep with Tony Bower after all, he was disappointed to find that his formerly ardent suitor had lost interest. Isherwood had, however, somewhat tardily embarked on a sexual relationship with Tony Hyndman. Stephen Spender had gone to Spain earlier in the year to become head of English-language broadcasting for the Socialist Party in Valencia, only to find that the job did not exist. He decided to visit Hyndman, who was still serving with the International Brigade but was desperate to return to England. Hyndman said he had joined the Brigade on an impulse, had become disillusioned and now believed himself to be a pacifist. He was suffering from stomach ulcers and evidently at the end of his psychological tether, but Spender declared that it would be bad for morale if Hyndman abandoned the Brigade. Perhaps he could get transferred to a non-combatant job? Hyndman seemed to accept this idea, but subsequently deserted, was caught and ended up in prison. Despite the reassurances Isherwood had given when Hyndman marched off to Spain, Spender still felt responsible for his former lover's plight and spent a considerable amount of time and energy securing his release. When Hyndman returned to England, he and Spender once again became involved, even though Spender now had a wife.

Isherwood claimed that he and Hyndman first had sex in the back seat of a car being driven back from the beach by the Spenders, who sat in the front apparently unaware of the gropings and fumblings going on behind them. Isherwood decided that having sex with Hyndman represented "a spontaneous counterdemonstration against Stephen's marriage," but it was largely a matter of sheer lust. The relationship was entirely unromantic, but Isherwood and Hyndman found themselves sexually compatible and continued to go to bed together frequently during the next year.

At the same time, Isherwood had become involved with two other men, Derek Neame and Richard Buzzard. Nothing is known of Buzzard, but Richard Isherwood remembered Neame as boyish and good-looking though rather "slovenly" in his dress, possibly hard up and receiving some sort of handout from Isherwood. Meanwhile, on July 26 John Andrewes "came to say goodbye." (He was presumably off on tour with the Rambert company.)

At the same time, Isherwood was writing in his diary: "Oh, Heinz, don't forget me! Or do forget me, if it makes things easier to forget. Now I am crying. How futile it all is. Sleep well tonight, my dear little brother. How am I to go on living and never see you again?" Isherwood's diaries at this period are littered with similarly self-dramatizing outbursts, many of them probably written late at night and after a fair amount to drink. Perhaps he felt that by having a lot of casual affairs that didn't really "count" he was in some way remaining emotionally faithful to Heinz. He did not make another entry in the diary until three months later:

Just five months today since that ghastly parting at Luxembourg. In another month, H. will be free. And then? A year in a labour camp: two in the army. I'd better face it. I shall never see him again. And perhaps that is the best, for us both. I had a talk with Erika [Spender] the other day, which cheered me up a lot. She really understands. Only a German can understand everything I feel.

This does indeed seem like posing, but he continues:

But not to see H—never again—can I face it? No, I must go on hoping. And, in the meanwhile, I must do something about my life. It's no use just living on one's will. The stiff upper lip gets so stiff that it turns into a kind of paralysis.

Never to forget H. Never to cease to be grateful to him for every moment of our five years together. Never to cease to hope that, somehow, some day, all will be well. And yet to find a real warm decent relationship—something not of the same kind, but really worthwhile. That's the hardest part.

A year later, he looked back on his relationship with Heinz and decided:

Heinz knew me better than anybody else. He stands in a different category. He knew my weaknesses, my fears, my meannesses, my self-cheatings—everything. So I loved him, utterly, helplessly, rather ignobly. I loved him, and still love him—as though he'd only gone away for a weekend—and yet, if I heard that he was coming back, I should face the prospect with mixed feelings. Perhaps I am softer and weaker than I was. To have to start that life again, hunted from pillar to post, always in debt, jealous, worried about the future—always nagging and fussing and having to impose my will. No. No. And yet, since he's gone, my life has seemed increasingly empty, meaningless and wretched.

The relationships he was pursuing now were certainly of a different order than the one he had experienced with Heinz. His partners were by and large his social and intellectual equals, and if he did not love them, he at least appears to have had a good time with them. Love, however, was waiting just around the corner, ready to ambush him.

Meanwhile, he was getting a great deal of work done. At the end of July he finished work on the film (which was never made) and he spent the August Bank Holiday weekend at a Group Theatre conference, hosted by the painter John Piper and his wife, Myfanwy, at Fawley Bottom Farm near Henley-on-Thames. According to Robert Medley, "It was planned to be a pleasurable get-together for the Group Theatre executive and its supporters, during which future plans could be discussed." A major part of that future was the new play Auden and Isherwood were supposed to be writing. "Wystan and Christopher arrived late in the afternoon, accompanied by Beatrix Lehmann and Bertold [sic] Viertel, like two black crows, an uninvited professional backing," Medley recalled in 1983 with a bitterness the intervening forty-six years had done nothing to soften.

The authors had come to announce, without any previous warning, that the next play was destined for West End production. They were out for commercial success. In the absence of a legal contract, which nobody had considered necessary (quite apart from the fact that there was no money to pay for it) they expected that this betrayal of trust would be accepted as a *fait accompli*. As the matter was not open to negotiation they would speak only with Rupert [Doone]; and this to everybody's acute discomfort was precisely what they did—in camera. The rest of the weekend party, who had arrived at Fawley Bottom in high spirits and with great expectations were left to get on with it in an atmosphere soured with disappointment and anxiety. The grisly scenario thus imposed came to a climax when Wystan teamed with an innocent and embarrassed Benjamin Britten to vamp hymns on the piano, and then to pick out with one finger, to Ben's brilliant two-handed accompaniment, an ironic 'Stormy Weather'.

Isherwood and Auden spent a whole day closeted with Doone, who emerged battered but triumphant to announce that *On the Frontier* would, after all, be produced by the Group Theatre. When asked by Medley years later what had taken place during the meeting, Isherwood replied: "It may surprise you but I simply cannot remember. Nature kindly removes unpleasant memories." Medley suggested correctly that there was a basic incompatibility of outlook between Auden and Doone: "Wystan's domineering attitude that theatrical artists were servants of the word was pitched against Rupert's unwavering assertion that he had equal rights as a creative artist." It is also likely that Auden's camp cry of dismay when he saw *F6* on his return from Spain concealed a genuine resentment at Doone's treatment of his play. Isherwood could be forgiven, but Auden's dislike of Doone would become positively homicidal by the time *On the Frontier* was ready for production.

Meanwhile, he and Isherwood had to write the play, and so went to spend a month together in Dover. Familiar chiefly as the point of departure for the Continent, Dover had recently become a popular resort for London's homosexual literati. William Plomer had set up house there during the summer of 1936, and more transient visitors included Forster and Ackerley—the latter attracted by pubs crowded with off-duty servicemen, since Dover was not only a port but also a garrison town. Forster observed that if a bomb fell on Dover it would wipe out almost all the country's undesirables. Isherwood and Auden rented a top-floor flat overlooking the sea at 9 East Cliff, where their indulgent landlady, a Mrs. Slaughter, described them as "a couple of scamps." ("Did she KNOW more than she SAID??!!" Isherwood later wondered.) The landlady's daughter, Joan, remembered some of the visitors' foibles: "They always had special coffee which they showed [my mother] how to make, very black, with demerara sugar, Turkish I think it was, and grapefruit and toast for breakfast. That's all they used to have. [. . .] Isherwood was quite nice. I used to go swimming with him—he could never find anyone to go with." She recalled the two writers working surrounded by piles of books, presumably review copies sent by Ackerley. "We threw reams of paper away!"

Isherwood may not have had anyone to go swimming with (Auden proving immovably unamphibious),[1] but there were plenty of visitors, including the Stephen Spenders, Ackerley, Forster and the Buckinghams. His concurrent lovers, Derek

---

1. "Auden loathed (and still rather dislikes) the sea—for the sea, besides being deplorably wet and sloppy, is formless," Isherwood noted immediately after the month in Dover.

Neame and Oliver Low, each came to spend a weekend. Isherwood's determination to immerse himself in work as a way of dealing with his unhappiness over Heinz was highly productive, and by mid-September he and Auden had not only completed a draft of the play, but he had also revised his autobiography and written numerous reviews for *The Listener.* In addition, working alongside Auden proved fruitful for a contribution that had been solicited from Isherwood for the special "Auden Double Number" of Geoffrey Grigson's periodical, *New Verse.* He wrote "Some Notes on Auden's Early Poetry" in two days flat as soon as he got back to London in mid-September.

Grigson was an energetic proselytizer for the new generation of 1930s poets, but the fact that he planned this special double issue of his magazine entirely devoted to Auden says much for Auden's growing celebrity. Isherwood, whose name had been linked with Auden's in the public imagination because of their collaborations, shared the limelight, and the activities of both writers were frequently reported in the press—not always accurately. Readers of the *News Chronicle,* for example, were told of the authors' brief excursion to the Lake District, and were informed that Mr. Isherwood, whose writing career was outlined, had once been "a medical student (for one term!)." Isherwood's return from his base in Brussels for the first night of *F6* and Auden's absence in Spain "acting as a stretcher-bearer" were reported in the *Birmingham Evening Despatch* and the *Daily Mail,* while the play itself was even reviewed (quite favorably) in the *Horse and Hound,* a magazine more usually concerned with equestrian sports. When, in May, the New York Theater Guild acquired the rights of the play for an American production, it was reported in the *Morning Post,* a famously Tory newspaper, whose readers would be unlikely to find Auden and Isherwood's leftist work the least bit sympathetic.

Isherwood recalled that at the time he wrote his article, Auden "was probably the most famous literary figure of his generation." The public may have been in awe of this prodigy, but Isherwood was not. "I was still his despotic, possessive, slightly envious mentor and elder brother," he wrote. "I wanted the world to know that I had first claim on him. I claimed the right to interpret him to the world. At the same time, my own admiration for him rather embarrassed me. This explains the somewhat aggressive, patronizing tone in which these *Notes* are written." These later reflections are to some extent just, but Isherwood's analysis of Auden's work and character was also highly acute. The "three things" which he suggests readers should bear in mind when encountering Auden's early poetry—that he was "essentially a scientist," that he was "a musician and ritualist" shaped by the Anglican faith of his childhood, and that he was of Scandinavian descent, profoundly influenced by the Icelandic sagas—may have been humorously expressed, but they remain cornerstones of later critical assessments of the poet. Isherwood also noted the influence of T. S. Eliot and of Homer Lane; Auden's "clinical" approach to poetry; his love of mountainous scenery, mines and caves, and the decaying industrial Midlands; his climatic preference for the cold north over the more usual desideratum of sunny southern lands. Having known Auden so well for so long, and having watched over the phases of his development, Isherwood was indeed in a unique position to "interpret him to the world." The tone is admiring, though far from deferential, taking advantage of the license usually granted to those (such as the best man at a wedding) called upon to sum up in public an old and close friend. It is a tone familiar from Auden's own public pronouncements on Isherwood in "August for the people," with its references to his friend's "squat spruce body and enormous head."

Isherwood's essay was certainly written in the knowledge of, and possibly in response to, another birthday poem, which Auden had recently inscribed on the blank pages of a copy of D. H. Lawrence's *Birds, Beasts and Flowers*. Annotated "Dover. Sept 3 1937," the poem is at once a highly skilled pastiche of Lawrence and a very funny and acute analysis of Isherwood's character. In its mixture of exasperation and affection, of mockery and appreciation, of gentle teasing and genuine tribute, it prefigures Isherwood's article, which was written just over a fortnight later.

> *Who is that funny-looking young man so squat with a top-heavy head*
> *A cross between a cavalry major and a rather prim landlady*
> *Sitting there sipping a cigarette?*
> *A brilliant young novelist?*
> *You don't say!*
>
> *Sitting in the corner of the room at a party, with his hair neatly brushed, quite clean*
> *Or lying on the beach in the sun*
> *Just like the rest of the crowd*
> *Just as brown, no, browner*
> *Anonymous, just like us.*
>
> *Wait a moment.*
>
> *Wait till there's an opening in the conversation, or a chance to show off*
> *And you strike like a lobster at a prawn*
> *A roar of laughter. Aha, listen to that*
> *Didn't you fool them beautifully,*
> *Didn't they think you were nobody in particular,*
> *That landlady*
> *That major*
> *Sold again.*
>
> *With your great grey eyes taking everything in,*
> *And your nicely creased trousers*
> *Pretending to be nobody, to be quite humdrum and harmless*
> *All the time perfectly aware of your powers*
> *You puff-adder*
> *You sham.*
>
> *And your will, my word!*
> *Don't you love to boss just everybody, everybody*
> *To make all of us dance to your tune*
> *Pied Piper*
> *At an awkward moment*
> *Turning on your wonderful diplomacy like a fire-hose*

Flattering, wheedling, threatening,
Drenching everybody.
Don't you love being ill,
Propped up on pillows, making us all dance attendance.
Do you think we don't see
Fussy old Major
Do you think we don't know what you're thinking

'I'm the cleverest man of the age
The genius behind the scenes, the anonymous dictator
Cardinal Mazarin
Mycroft Holmes
Lawrence of Arabia
Lady Asquith
Always right.'

And if anything goes wrong,
If absolutely the whole universe fails to bow to your command
If there's a mutiny in Neptune
A revolt in one of the farthest nebulae
How you stamp your bright little shoe
How you pout
House-proud old landlady
At times I could shake you
Il y a des complaisances que je déteste.

Yet how beautiful your books are
So observant, so witty, so profound
And how nice you are really
So affectionate, so understanding, so helpful, such wonderful company
A brilliant young novelist?
My greatest friend?
Si, Signor.

Standing here in Dover under the cliffs, with dotty England behind you
And challenging the provocative sea
With your enormous distinguished nose and your great grey eyes
Only 33 and a real diplomat already
Our great ambassador to the mad.

Use your will. We need it.

Although *On the Frontier* was to be the last play Isherwood and Auden wrote to-gether, they were already in negotiation with Faber in England and Random House in America to get a commission for another joint venture. In August they signed a contract with each publisher to write a book on "The Far East." A so far un-declared war between China and Japan decided them to choose China as their desti-nation. Planning the journey would take some time, and meanwhile they had to finish *On the Frontier,* which they did in September, sending it to Spender, who was conva-lescing after an appendectomy. Once again, the final scene had caused difficulties, but after Spender sent his comments, the authors revised it and delivered it to the pub-lishers and to the Group Theatre.

The quarrel with Doone had been patched up sufficiently for Medley to paint Isherwood's portrait in September, although the title of a lecture Isherwood gave in November—"The Mind in Chains *or* Drama Writing for Doone"—was hardly tact-ful. The Group Theatre was, however, a sort of family, subject to frequent rows and bickering, but remaining close-knit: even Richard Isherwood was to be found in their offices in Newport Street addressing envelopes for circulars. Isherwood himself spent the autumn promoting the Group Theatre at lectures and readings in London, Oxford and Cambridge. "OXFORD PLEA BY MR CHRISTOPHER ISHERWOOD FOR GROUP THEATRE'S DEVELOPMENT IN BRITAIN" ran a headline above a long report in the *Oxford Mail* of a talk Isherwood delivered to the English Club at Rhodes House in mid-November. "We want to build up something worthwhile, something which will really be an arts centre," he announced. He went on to talk about the nature of the theater "from an architectural point of view," explaining that "in the theatre one had the sen-sation of being trapped in a box, and that as a result of this there existed a direct re-lationship between actors and audience—a common demand for release." This made the theater a medium "extremely well suited to conveying ideas connected with the problems of society. The theatre was the only art in which the audience could take an active part in the drama. Every play depended on the collaboration of the audience." He went on to discuss the use of symbolism and realism in modern drama. "Ibsen's was an age in which all the social problems were domestic," he pronounced authori-tatively.

> But as soon as the problems tend—as they do to-day—to be of an international, an inter-class character, then I believe that drama must have a strong tendency towards expressionism. To create the looming atmosphere of horror which over-shadows events at present one is apt to resort to expressionist treatment [. . .] By and large the West End stage is clinging to realistic drama. But it is up against a difficulty because plays to-day must have a wider reference than formerly if they are to be significant, because the intrusion of the outside world into our lives is so forcible that it cannot be neglected.

Evidently thinking of the Nuremberg Rallies, he suggested that theater provided the Left with a way of turning fascism's chief weapon against itself. "This age was ruled by eloquence, as was proved by the presence of dictators. Such an age was favourable to the theatre, which thrived on eloquence." He told an audience at Cambridge that "As fascist dictators rule by effective eloquence, so must the most high-powered methods be used in the progressive drama, in fact, verse. But, in a contemporary drama, it is difficult to avoid anti-climax; for this reason comic relief, as in Eliza-bethan days, will be needed." The *Cambridge Review* reported that "Both during his address and in answering questions Mr Isherwood dealt with a great number of other dramatic problems, including the value of the technique of collaboration introduced by the film, the need for the apron stage, and the great value of costume as against elaborate scenery." Despite these pronouncements, Isherwood conceded that he and Auden still had a lot to learn about the theater and insisted that their plays should be regarded as experiments. Some two hundred enthusiastic and appreciative people nevertheless turned out at the City Literary Institute to hear him lecture on "The Craft of the Playwright."

These lectures refute persistent suggestions that Auden was the sole intellectual driving force behind the plays and that Isherwood was merely brought in to provide comic dialogue and basic plotting. That said, Isherwood chiefly enjoyed giving talks because they added to his "glamour," which had been considerably enhanced in October by the publication of *Sally Bowles* as a book. After Lehmann had rejected the story, Leonard Woolf stepped in, but then discovered that Spencer Curtis Brown was hoping to palm it off on him as a novel and thus fulfill Isherwood's contractual obligations to the Hogarth Press. This would free Curtis Brown to offer his client's next book to another publisher. When Woolf discovered what the agent was up to, he was furious. He had been waiting patiently for a full-length novel from Isherwood and at a mere twenty thousand words, *Sally Bowles* could scarcely even be called a novella. He told Curtis Brown that he would certainly lose money on the book, which was something he was not prepared to do unless this could be justified as an investment in the author's future. Under the circumstances he would have to reject it. He accused Curtis Brown of sharp practice, and forwarded the entire correspondence to Isherwood with an icily polite letter suggesting that there must have been some sort of misunderstanding. Like a schoolboy summoned to the headmaster's study, Isherwood was obliged to visit Woolf's office to assure his publisher that of course there was never any intention to cheat him, and that the Hogarth Press would retain its option on his next book. Mollified, Woolf agreed to publish *Sally Bowles* but did not pay an advance. He had hoped to eke the book out to 152 pages, but his printers told him that even by moving lines of type around they could not bring it in at more than 144 pages. This in itself was something of a typographical feat: when the book was reprinted as part of *Goodbye to Berlin,* it occupied a mere seventy-eight pages.

Short it may have been, but *Sally Bowles* remains one of Isherwood's most accomplished pieces of writing. "In England the ablest exponents of the colloquial style among the young writers are Christopher Isherwood and George Orwell," Cyril Connolly observed a year after *Sally Bowles* was published, "both left-wing and both, at the present level of English, superbly readable." Isherwood's story was certainly colloquial, much of it presented as dialogue. This is appropriate since both Sally and Chris are play-actors, giving very fine and lively performances. Their exchanges are exaggeratedly theatrical, as if each is feeding lines to the other, and the story is full of references to the stage. Sally enters the story with a flourish, arriving late at Fritz Wendel's flat, where she immediately telephones a lover. "Fritz and I sat watching her, like a performance at the theatre," Isherwood writes, and this is how she is seen throughout the book. One of her characteristics is "a silvery little stage-laugh"; she has pretensions to being *La Dame aux Camélias;* an unusually sober ensemble of a black dress with white collar and cuffs produces "a kind of theatrically chaste effect, like a nun in grand opera." Absurdly solemn conversations about Sally's personal and professional ambitions almost always end in laughter, because she can only keep up the pretense of taking herself seriously for a short time, as Chris very well knows. Their relationship is presented as a sort of comic parody of a love affair ("good heter stuff"), but although extremely funny, the story is also very touching. When they quarrel, the reader is as anxious that they should make up as if they were indeed lovers, and Isherwood ends the story on a deliberately poignant note. Not having heard from Sally for six years, he openly appeals to her to send him a postcard. Sally Bowles remains Isherwood's most endearing and enduring creation. Part of the reason for this was that the story was frequently adapted, but none of the various stage and screen Sally Bowleses were as vivid as Isherwood's original.

Isherwood recognized that success could easily go to his head. "I am getting ludicrously ambitious," he confessed in his journal. "I want to be known, flattered, talked about; to see my name in the papers. And, the worst of it is, I can. It's all so cheap and easy." After a hugely successful and well-attended Group Theatre event at the London Book Fair on November 20, where he and Auden read a scene from the new play, he wrote: "I am now mildly ashamed of myself for having so much enjoyed the publicity, the applause, the autographing of our books which followed. It was like Satan's view of the Kingdoms of the World—and didn't I play up to it: grinning, handshaking, theatrically putting my arm on Wystan's shoulder? This kind of thing really constitutes the greatest possible danger to my integrity. I am a born actor."

It was not merely his integrity as a writer that was threatened. He was in the happy position of discovering that fame could be as potent an aphrodisiac as "widowerhood." The previous day he had noted: "Stephen's affairs are in a fine old tangle. The triangle has turned into a quadrangle." His own affairs were no less complicated. Among the audience at the Book Fair were at least three of his lovers, including a young Frenchman named Jean Bühler. It is almost certain that Isherwood had in fact met and had an affair with Bühler in Brussels in the early summer, while making arrangements for Heinz's trial. On May 30 he had noted in his pocket diary: "To cinema with Jean." This cannot have been Jean Ross, who was not in Brussels at the time. The only other "Jean" who appears in the address book at the back of the diary is Jean Bühler. Over the following two weeks Jean's name had occurred almost daily in the diary, which recorded dinners, visits to the cinema and a long weekend in Ostende. Back in Brussels on June 15, Isherwood noted: "Jean returned"—presumably to England—after which Jean's name disappears from the diary. Six days later, Isherwood was back in London.

It is possible that in the wake of the disaster that had just overtaken Heinz, Isherwood regarded Bühler as someone with whom he could have a brief consolatory romance, assuaging some of the loneliness he complained of in his journal. Isherwood may have kept Heinz in his heart, but the probability of their being together again in the near future was remote in the extreme. Bühler may have seemed unimportant at the time, and perhaps Isherwood never really expected to see him again. On November 18, however, he records an "Evening with Bühler," and the following day he made what was only the third entry in his journal since May. It begins: "So I'm in love again. How curious." Having had some hours to reflect on this new state of affairs, he decided: "Love has its own continuity. This time is part of all the other times."

Isherwood fails to mention in his journal that a week earlier, on November 11, a telegram arrived at Pembroke Gardens announcing that Heinz had been released from prison and was now with his aunt back in Berlin. Heinz was not, of course, free, since he still had a year's labor and two years' military service ahead of him. He would be put to work on a building site at the Potsdamerplatz, and there was little Isherwood could do apart from send greetings, although he also bought Heinz a camera and sent that as well.

On November 19 Isherwood arranged to meet Bühler at a BBC concert at which Sophie Wyss gave the first performance of Britten's *On This Island,* which set five poems by Auden.

> I felt sick and queer. He was punctual—with his sister. I was rather theatrically polite: 'Je suis heureux, mademoiselle, d'avoir fait votre connaissance.' As always before, at these three-cornered meetings, the setting was grotesquely unsuitable—the Brasserie Universelle—and I actually felt impatient to leave them. In the Underground, Jean did a really charming thing: he brought his sister specially through to my platform in order that we could be together until my train arrived. Only the French can think of gestures like that. Of course, there was absolutely nothing to say.
>
> All this has nothing, as I've already written, to do with my ordinary life. Nothing to do with H[einz]. Or with Jean, even. It's just a condition, like being asleep. La condition inhumaine.

Having then looked back through the diary and recognized the unhappiness it recorded, he wrote:

> Nevertheless, I have to admit that, after reminding myself of all those bad moments with H, I feel consoled. Here alone, lonely as I am (for I *am* lonely—and neither Jean nor anybody else will be able to alter that) I am, at any rate, stronger. I want, above all, to be strong—to give protection, like a tree. This isn't mere conceit, it is part of my deepest nature.

It is not clear, however, who it is he hopes to protect.

> What should I feel, now, if by some miracle, H. was let out? [By which he presumably means released from his labor and military service.] Great joy, of course—joy I can't even imagine. But also (I must be absolutely frank), I should be a little bit doubtful: for what, really, have I to offer him? Only happiness, by fits and starts—nothing solid. Not even a proper home or a place in any kind of social scheme. I can be strong for others—not for myself.

This last observation seems to be a non sequitur, and indeed this whole conversation with himself is unusually muddled—perhaps because it was written late at night, perhaps because the sudden and apparently unforeseen access of emotion caused by Bühler had confused him. He feels that he has gained protective strength, but recognizes that it is of little use to Heinz, for whom he can do no more. Happiness seems too little a thing to offer, and yet he goes on to suggest that it is all there is.

> I must recognize the possibility (quite apart from any pleasing romanticism) that I may die in China. I must live these next two months as if I were certainly condemned to death, quietly, sensibly, working hard, making my preparations. And may I be allowed, for the last time—some minutes of happiness? I nearly had happiness last night, in Jean's dirty room, sitting before the fire. It isn't much one asks—just a fire, and two faces side by side, looking into it. Yes, I am sentimental in an essentially German, cosy way.

Although Isherwood initially wrote about being "in love," Bühler may simply have been the right person in the right place at the right time. In a letter written on the day of the Britten concert, Isherwood had told Lehmann that he was "mildly in love again, and it's not reciprocated, which is always so much more fun." Whatever the case, by the time Isherwood made his appearance at the London Book Fair, Bühler had certainly superseded the other suitors also present, Oliver Low and Derek Neame. After he had signed his books, Isherwood left with Bühler, "playing a little at being the great man escaping from the crowd—but really glad to be alone with him after all the fuss. His complete abandon is so attractive—practically embracing me in the Haymarket. He says he sat up half the night writing in his journal, as I did. I didn't altogether believe this (I'd told him first) but at any rate Jean is capable of making the right kind of flattering pretences. He knows how to *play* at love—and that's nearly all I want."

This sudden doubt cast upon the seriousness of his relationship with Bühler may have had something to do with the unexpected appearance of another young admirer at the Book Fair: "A strikingly handsome young man, whom I'd noticed almost as soon as I'd entered the hall, came up and introduced himself as Ian Scott-Kilvert." Attracted and intrigued, Isherwood suggested they go for a drink—presumably abandoning Bühler. Isherwood had not seen his former pupil, now an undergraduate at Cambridge, for ten years. He was suitably impressed. "He is really charming, wants to write for the stage, is so vivid and gay—just as I remember him: with the same awful stammer. He gurgles and rolls his eyes when he speaks. It was so extraordinary to be sitting there with him—already a grown-up man. I shall go down to Cambridge to stay with him, I think. I want to find out all about his mother and the psychological harm she has done the whole family."

Isherwood may have pretended to his journal that he was principally interested in Scott-Kilvert's mother, and that this was merely psychological, but his less than scientific interest in her charming and handsome son is quite apparent. The feeling was entirely mutual, and two days later he wrote in his journal:

> Out of the blue, this morning, comes this astounding letter from Ian. Now, after re-reading it for the tenth time, I still can't make out, or daren't make out, what it

really means. Perhaps nothing very much—perhaps more than I've ever hoped for in my most extravagant dreams. Is it the kind of thing Henry James writes about in 'The Pupil'—or is it just a kind of sublimated undergraduate literary snobbery? On Thursday, if I see him, I shall know.

"The Pupil," a short story first published in 1891, is an account of a young man hired as a tutor for a precocious but delicate eleven-year-old with a heart murmur. The boy's parents lead a peripatetic and indigent life in Europe, taking advantage of the tutor's growing affection for the boy by paying him only when he insists. Eventually the parents offer to commit the boy (now about fourteen) to the tutor's permanent care, but the pupil is so overcome with joy at the prospect that his heart fails and he dies. Isherwood was haunted by this story and had already admitted the influence of James on "The Summer at the House," his abandoned novel inspired by the Mangeots.

Scott-Kilvert had not only stepped out of Isherwood's past; he had also stepped out of his volume of *Lions and Shadows,* the proofs of which Isherwood had just finished correcting. In the book Scott-Kilvert was portrayed as "Graham," a precocious eight-year-old who often caught out his tutor "in the clumsiest self-contradictions and mistakes." "An exceptionally nervous little boy, with a pale, lively, charming face, fair hair standing up in a tuft, and big steel spectacles which were perpetually getting lost," "Graham" is clearly a pleasure to teach. Isherwood particularly admired, and claimed to have stolen, the subversive essays the boy had written for his governess on such topics as "Duty," "Make Hay While the Sun Shines" and "Playing the Game." His account of the Lang household was to have provided a whole chapter of the autobiography, but eventually occupied a few paragraphs which give the impression that Isherwood had no idea (or particular interest in) what happened to "Graham." Of course, he now knew very well, but he evidently decided that it made a better story if "Graham," like Sally Bowles, disappeared from the narrator's life.

Scott-Kilvert certainly had no intention of disappearing again and invited Isherwood to visit him at Caius College. The prospect of a new love affair filled Isherwood with equal amounts of excitement and trepidation. "Suppose, just for a moment, that it is the real thing," he wrote

> — how shall I ever rise to the occasion. It make me dizzy merely to think of [it]. I feel I want to take him away—thousands of miles—from the whole world. But no—I mustn't even dare, for an instant, to suppose . . . And yet, that ridiculous meeting, in a corner of the Langham [Hotel] lounge, was something quite unique in my life. It was like discovering a long-lost brother. But I mustn't dwell on it too much, or I'll spoil everything.
>
> I didn't imagine I could ever feel like this, again.

Far from being unique, the rediscovery of Scott-Kilvert, a "long-lost"—and much younger—"brother," fulfilled one of the recurring fantasies in Isherwood's life. Here, he felt, was another vulnerable young person he could adopt and protect from the world. The auguries, both in life (Heinz) and fiction ("The Pupil"), were not good, but Isherwood traveled to Cambridge in high expectation.

Scott-Kilvert was not at the station to meet him, so Isherwood went to Caius, where he spent a leisurely twenty minutes examining the young man's rooms and rifling his possessions. "A piano. Chopin. Beethoven. Lots of books—classics, mostly. In the writing desk a letter beginning 'Ian, dear . . .' Upstairs, an attic bedroom, very bare, with photos of Mrs Lang, Derek, Pam. The whole place uncomfortable, and badly lit." When Scott-Kilvert returned, they went out to lunch. It was only when they were walking back that they talked of anything other than social trivialities.

> Ian blurting out sentences angrily above the noise of the traffic. We hardly looked at each other at all.
> He is all angles and prickles and sharp corners—so young still, and so angular that it makes one want to shed tears. Underneath this, I think, he is soft and feline—yes, a bit catty: awfully like myself at the same age.

This, no doubt, was another attraction for Isherwood, particularly since he had just finished writing a book about that younger self. Other lovers would strike Isherwood as just like himself at an earlier age, and there was undoubtedly a strong element of narcissism in such relationships. Back at Caius, Scott-Kilvert played the piano for a while, then, stopping abruptly, exclaimed: "Hell. This is awful."

> On the sofa, after supper, it was better. 'What am I s-supposed to do now? Fall into your arms?' My answers seemed to amuse him. He said, in the morning: 'I'm still in a mist of admiration for the way you handled things last night.'

Scott-Kilvert was not as inexperienced as this report might suggest, and indeed had been conducting a relationship with a slightly older student named Nik Alderson, who had gone down from Cambridge in the summer. "I am rather jealous, of course," Isherwood admitted. "I want to see him." Meanwhile, he suggested that he and Ian spend a few days in Paris, although this had to be squared with Mrs. Lang, who still maintained "a stranglehold on all her children." "I am to meet her and try to put across the old tutor stuff—very hearty. It really is the most extraordinary situation."

Isherwood then had to travel to Brighton, where he had already arranged to spend the night with Jean Bühler. He had thought of trying to back out, but in the event decided "before we started" to tell Bühler what had happened with Scott-Kilvert.

> He was sad, of course. But things went off quite well, nevertheless [. . .] We stopped at the Old Ship Hotel—which is stodgy but comfortable. Faint disapproval.
> Jean is really very nice—but I think I was kidding myself from the start.

Back in London, Isherwood received a letter from Scott-Kilvert declaring: "I seem to be yours quite hopelessly." This was followed by an awkward telephone call.

> As usual, there was nothing to say. Had I got his letter? Yes. And I'd written a long one to him. 'Good—that'll get me through the rest of today.' He stopped talking, but didn't ring off. Neither did I. Then I said: 'Goodnight' again. 'Oh . . . G-good-

night . . .' Still he didn't ring off. I hung up my receiver, with a bang. It was like killing something—a small animal, with a stone.

The following morning, Isherwood awoke feeling jealous: "how do I know he doesn't write like this and say these things to Alderson and to others? Maybe he does. I can't help it. The truth is, one never really altogether likes anyone one is in love with." Nevertheless, Isherwood was determined to pursue the relationship, even to the point of spending £13 at Austin Reed on evening wear with which to curry favor with Mrs. Lang, who had had the "impudence" (a furious Kathleen noted) to say that she hoped her former employee would "look presentable" for the occasion. Kathleen told young Scott-Kilvert that he hoped his mother realized that it was a great compliment to her that Christopher had deigned to accept a dinner invitation at all—"a great concession" on the part of a rising young figure of the Left who usually preferred to flout bourgeois convention. Isherwood's sartorial efforts seem not to have impressed Mrs. Lang, who treated him "graciously but rather as though he were a former servant of hers who had since pulled himself up in the world by his bootstraps and almost become a gentleman." Isherwood had confided in Humphrey Spender that if one wanted to have an affair with a boy, it was important to get in with the parents and impress them with one's comparative maturity in order to dupe them into thinking one's interest was paternal rather than erotic. This ploy clearly worked with Mrs. Lang, who not only agreed to the Paris trip, but even contributed toward the couple's expenses, on the grounds that Ian's education was continuing under Isherwood's guidance. As, in a way, it was.

They set off on their five-day trip on December 9 in appalling weather, the airplane alarmingly buffeted by a snowstorm, but eventually they landed safely in Paris, where they booked into the Hôtel Quai Voltaire, which must have by now become accustomed to Isherwood and his various young companions. "Was it a success?" Isherwood asked himself after their return to London.

Yes. No. Yes. Anyhow it was terrific [. . .] I forget what we did. We wandered about the streets in a kind of daze. I was in a perpetual state of watching Ian's face—his long, severe, rather childish profile, with the water-colour hair and small blue eyes; waiting for his smile, which makes you think someone is tickling him under the chin with a feather, or the first twitchings which mean that he is going to speak. One afternoon, we lay together for hours reading Cocteau's Knights of the Round Table [. . .]

On the last morning—when I'd been waiting for the volcano to erupt—Ian exclaimed, after ten minutes' weighty pause: 'D-do you write m-m-much criticism?' This seemed so ridiculous that we both laughed ourselves quite hysterical, and I stabbed the bolster with a breakfast-knife, reciting a speech from 'Macbeth'.

As we were coming back from Croydon [Aerodrome] in the 'bus, he said that he didn't feel Paris was an episode. 'You've domesticated me already.' I said I hoped so—but that during the next nine months things might change. 'Why should they?' he said. 'They haven't changed in ten years.'

No wonder Isherwood was smitten.

The next nine months included a long period, between January and July, when Isherwood was traveling with Auden to China. There was also a plan for both of them to join a delegation of writers and artists on a visit to Spain where they would "declare the solidarity of left-wing artists and intellectuals with the Spanish government," which was still fighting the fascist rebels. In the event the travel documents did not arrive before it became necessary for Isherwood and Auden to confirm their tickets to China. Abandoning the Spanish mission came as something of a relief to Isherwood, who had written in his diary with less than revolutionary zeal: "[Wystan] wants to go to Spain—so, of course, I shall go too." Although Isherwood was later to accuse himself of posturing, putting on a hammy but effective performance as the departing hero, there is a sense in his 1937 journal that he was always glad when decisions were taken out of his hands. For much of the 1930s he had been exerting his will and plotting his life in a vain attempt to keep Heinz safe. Now that he was relieved of that responsibility, he was content to let life take him wherever it wanted. To some extent, the worst had already happened, and this, combined with his sense that a war he was unlikely to survive had become inevitable, made him fatalistic. Scott-Kilvert, he decided, would

> just have to take his place in my life—I can't alter it to suit him. I must stick to the things I know are right. I must be absolutely without fear. What must come must come.
>
> If any young man reads this book, I implore him: Don't be anxious. Don't worry. Half my life has been wasted, just worrying. And there's so little to be afraid of, really.

Meanwhile, in preparation for the Far East trip, he had to undergo a series of debilitating inoculations, which meant spending several days in bed, where he received frequent visitors. Scott-Kilvert came bearing a gift of socks and a tie from his mother, who (having learned nothing from her own experiences with her second husband) seems to have remained unaware of the exact relationship between her son and his old tutor. Kathleen later told Isherwood that Mrs. Lang had said to her: "After all, your Christopher was the first man in my Ian's life," a remark Kathleen—rather more alert to the situation—relayed to her son with a somewhat sour smile.

When not holding *levées* in Pembroke Gardens, Isherwood spent his time having his photograph taken for posterity by Howard Coster and visiting old friends—presumably still mindful of the fact that he might be killed in China. Amongst these friends was Rolf Katz, who had recently moved from Paris to settle in London, bringing with him all manner of "inside information" about the political situation. He also told Isherwood all about a recently arrested German serial killer named Eugen Weidmann, whose story inspired Isherwood to think about resurrecting *Paul Is Alone*.

> About 7 years old when the war broke out: the excitement of the posters—'5,000 Russians dead': struggle for food during the hunger-blockade developed self-preservation instinct. Very charming. Lots of affairs with women. Got to know some cooks during a prison-sentence in Germany for robbery with violence. The

people he ultimately murdered always got the impression that they were going to get something out of *him*—a film contract, a business deal: their greed destroyed them. He shot them in the back of the neck and buried them in cellars or woods. Shows no remorse in talking about his crimes. Quotes Heine and Goethe, with great feeling. He did all his murders partly for money—£30 or £40 a time.

Yes—that's the solution I've been waiting for—Paul must be a murderer.

Weidmann's career did indeed echo the fictional one Isherwood had plotted for Paul, and his story could stand as a parable of the chaos and criminality into which Germany had descended after the First World War. Isherwood's enthusiasm was not sustained, however, and no further work was done on the book. Instead, he concentrated on finishing the Berlin stories he was assembling for a volume still called *The Lost* but which would eventually be published as *Goodbye to Berlin:* "On Ruegen Island," "The Landauers" and "A Berlin Diary (Winter 1932–33)." As he later explained to Spender, he "hurried through" these stories "because I thought I might be killed in China and wanted to leave everything tidy." It was not, in the end, as tidy as all that, and John Lehmann was left to collate the typescripts. Lehmann and his sister Beatrix were to be the book's dedicatees.

The imminent departure of Isherwood and Auden for China was widely reported in the press during January 1938. Their public profiles had been further boosted by the announcement of Isherwood's forthcoming volume of autobiography and by Auden's appearance at Buckingham Palace to be presented with the King's Gold Medal for Poetry. Not everyone was impressed by the publicity the two authors were receiving. On the other side of the English Channel, James Stern, who had never really forgiven Isherwood for abandoning him and Tania in Portugal and then leaving them to cope with Heinz in Paris, looked on with some disdain. "Whenever I open the *News Chronicle* I see a picture of Mr. Isherwood," he complained to Roger Burford. "And now that Mr. Auden has received a Copper from the King, I suppose one must expect at least a visit from the Queen Mother to Madame Isherwood. Roger, if I scribble off half a play will you write the other? Then we can be photographed together, staring into each other's eyes, with underneath the caption: 'The Perfect Combination'. At worst, it would do famously to advertise Lady's Underwear, and surely we'd make a packet one way or another."

The date set for boarding the train at Victoria was January 19, and Pembroke Gardens was turned upside down as Isherwood packed and generally set his affairs in order in case he did not return. A farewell party had been arranged by the Directors of the Group Theatre "to meet W. H. Auden and Christopher Isherwood on the eve of their departure for the Far East," as the printed invitations put it. The party was to be held from 10 p.m. onward at the home and studio of the painter Julian Trevelyan at Durham Wharf on the river at Hammersmith. "Evening dress optional," the invitation stated. "Admission only on this card." Fully aware that some of the people invited might consider dress optional *tout court,* Trevelyan and his wife had insisted that their bedroom should remain off limits. The centerpiece of the party was to be a performance of some of Britten and Auden's cabaret songs by Louis MacNeice's wife, Hedli Anderson.

Before the party the Stephen Spenders gave a dinner for Isherwood attended by Benjamin Britten, John Lehmann, and Humphrey and Lolly Spender. Britten had as usual arranged to spend the night at Pembroke Gardens, and Ian Scott-Kilvert had been entrusted to his care during Isherwood's absence in China. "So glad you liked Ian," Isherwood had written; "the liking was mutual, I may say. Of course, I'd be only *too* delighted if you saw him occasionally, and, maybe, introduced him to some of the gang, as well? I've had no time to do that, alas." Kathleen had been invited to the party, but although she wanted to attend she felt she could not face going alone. Now that Isherwood was once more living under his mother's roof, his relationship with her had again become difficult. While he was abroad—and, it has to be said, in need of her financial and moral support—Isherwood seems to have been able to maintain good relations with her. The intimacy between mother and son displayed in letters rapidly evaporated once they were living together. " 'One must risk something or one gets nowhere,' " Kathleen wrote in her diary, perhaps quoting her son. "All my life I have avoided risks—for fear of rebuff's, and getting hurt . . . and so through fear the wall remains impenetrable—& it seems will never now be broken down." She would have been even more hurt had she known that her beloved son and Brian Howard had spent Christmas dressing up as their mothers to entertain guests at a Sussex house party hosted by Cyril Connolly. Kathleen desperately wanted to be part of Christopher's life. She loyally attended his lectures and most of the events organized by the Group Theatre; she proudly copied reviews of his books into her diaries; she automatically took his side against anyone who dared to criticize him. But his world was not her world, and whenever she gained admittance to it she knew that she was there only on sufferance.

Durham Wharf had been decked out with "some remarkable surrealist *objets*" for the farewell party, which was widely reported in the press. "The *avant-garde* was there in full force," according to the *Sunday Times* correspondent. "The party, on the whole, was a young one. But I noticed flitting through the crowd some of the ghosts of old Bloomsbury, still nursing the unconquerable hope, still clutching the inviolable shade." The *News Chronicle* ran a wicked piece in its "Present Company" column, comparing the junketings at Durham Wharf with a rather more austere leftist gathering in a smoky room above a pub in Holborn, where Harry Adams, "a grizzled, compact building-trade official," described to representatives of the Labour Research Department his recent visit to the Soviet Union.

It was estimated that between two hundred and three hundred people were crushed into Durham Wharf, and the event ended, Trevelyan recalled, "in a bit of a rough-house." According to Britten's elliptical diary, even before his party arrived at Durham Wharf there had been a "colossal row—on phone Christopher & me v. Rupert Doone." This presumably concerned the forthcoming production of *On the Frontier,* which was to have taken place at the Cambridge Arts Theatre during the authors' absence abroad, supervised by Britten and Spender, who were both now directors of the Group Theatre. Medley recalled that the two playwrights arrived at the Durham Wharf party

suitably late for a star entry, accompanied, as if on a state visit, by Prime Minister E. M. Forster; Secretary of State Cyril Connolly; and supported by the drunken halberdiers Brian Howard and Edward Gathorne-Hardy.[2] Predictably, these latter soon invaded the out-of-bounds bedroom and were discovered by Julian holding a private party on the bed. After a sharp exchange, during which Howard loudly proclaimed that he would not have his best friend, Eddie, insulted by the worst painter in London, Bob Wellington [the Group Theatre's business manager] was called in to attempt an eviction, and was immediately challenged to a fight in the small courtyard, in the centre of which was a newly planted magnolia. This ridiculous combat, which I witnessed less as a referee than as a kind of policeman on behalf of the management, lasted but a few moments, as Bob's spectacles were knocked off his nose, and Eddie was too drunk to press his advantage.

This version of events (one of many), is disputed by Trevelyan's second wife, Mary Fedden, who said that the principal fight (perhaps also one of many) was between Trevelyan and Connolly, who disliked each other. Unsatisfied by the drink on offer, Connolly ostentatiously produced a hip-flask, which was subsequently handed round. When it reached Trevelyan, Connolly bellowed: "I'm not having that man drink my bloody whisky." Trevelyan promptly knocked Connolly down, whereupon he was floored by one of Connolly's friends. At the end of this altercation, several distinguished members of what the *Sunday Times* described as "London's literary and artistic clans" were to be seen "bleeding in the flowerbeds." "Beastly crowd & unpleasant people," Britten noted in his diary. "Christopher leaves in temper." Unfortunately for Britten, Isherwood had also left without giving him a spare set of keys for Pembroke Gardens, and by the time he remembered his obligations as host and telephoned Durham Wharf, the young composer had left, having begged a sofa for the night from a friend.

Britten appeared on the doorstep of 19 Pembroke Gardens in time for breakfast the following morning, and shortly after ten he set out with Isherwood, Auden and (for some reason) William Coldstream's wife, Nancy, for Victoria. The press was out in force to record Auden and Isherwood's eleven o'clock departure on the *Golden Arrow* for Paris. "It seems that from now on they must accept themselves as news value," commented the *Bystander:* "with notable exceptions, there is nobody the Great British Public likes so well as the people who tell it how rotten are its institutions and society." While "the celebrated authors" were posing for the cameras, Medley recalled sourly, "at Durham Wharf we were completing the washing up." Auden had worn a smart suit for the occasion, a spotted bow-tie characteristically askew at his neck, while Isherwood was dressed more casually, one point of his shirt-collar poking out over a crew-neck pullover. In tweed overcoats, cigarettes burning in their hands, they posed obligingly in front of their railway carriage. Isherwood's type-

---

2. The Hon. Edward Gathorne-Hardy (1901–78) was the son, but fortunately not the heir, of the 3rd Earl of Cranbrooke. An Oxford contemporary and close friend of Brian Howard, he was almost equally notorious for his flamboyant homosexuality. The character of Miles Malpractice in Evelyn Waugh's *Decline and Fall* and *Vile Bodies* is a scarcely exaggerated portrait.

writer was stowed safely with his luggage, but Auden had a small pair of binoculars hanging from his shoulder in a neat leather case. Their whole appearance gave the impression that they were headed for a local point-to-point rather than a war zone on the other side of the world.

A uden and Isherwood joined the French ship *Aramis* at Marseilles on January 21, and began keeping a joint diary. This was not easy because, to their dismay, their cabin in second class was much smaller than they had anticipated and did not have a writing table. They decided it would be worth paying for first-class accommodation, but were dissuaded by a stout rubber merchant, who negotiated with the purser for two larger cabins in second class. They now had one cabin for sleeping in and another for work. Much of the joint diary is taken up with satirical observations of their fellow passengers. The opinions of an entirely conventional young planter provided Auden with pages of copy, and he horrified both writers by producing a photograph album depicting social life in Ceylon and Malaya:

> men in shorts, with pipes; girls in shorts, with nauseatingly plump knees—Tiny Tim, the best chef east of Suez, and Doc Wilson, the finest tennis player west of Penang. An appalling aroma of suburban Surrey exuded from the album. Wystan and I both agreed—better face a thousand deaths in China than a fortnight of planter's hospitality. Malaya, it seems, is the women's kingdom.

Although they frequently addressed "my readers" in these notes, Auden and Isherwood were doing little more than limbering up in preparation for the proper task of reportage ahead of them. As Port Said appeared on the horizon on January 25, Isherwood remembered that he was supposed to be a travel writer and began producing the goods:

> We woke to the immediate sense of a changed vibration, the ship was beating through shallow sandy water. Port Said came up on the horizon, in the oblique sunshine, a denture of brilliant new false teeth, ready to devour the traveller. Wystan and I watched it draw nearer, wondering how the name 'Port Said' appeared as a mental image in the minds of certain English clergymen and suburban spinsters—a great quaking swamp, we decided; or an exceedingly dirty washbasin in a station lavatory.

The notes Isherwood and Auden made of their onward journey to Hong Kong, via Cairo, Djibouti and Colombo, would form the basis of an article which, tidied up and shorn of its outrageously misogynistic remarks about British women and lascivious observations of Singhalese men, would be published in *Harper's Bazaar* under what Isherwood later described as the "repulsively modish title" of "Escales."[3]

The planter had offered to show them round Port Said, where, he promised them, "the 'vice' was amazing." Fortunately they had already arranged to be met by a guide

---

3. It is the French for "ports of call."

more attuned to their tastes: Francis Turville-Petre. Fronny was waiting on the dock, "shaky and a bit shrunk, but wonderfully little changed." He assured them that Port Said's exotic reputation was greatly exaggerated and whisked them straight off to Cairo in a hired car. Having visited the pyramids ("looking ugly and quite new, like the tin heaps of a prosperous quarry"), heard about "barely credible instances of Egyptian corruption" from a professor at the university, and bought some "indecent pho- tographs" from a street hawker ("miserably out of focus, ten years old, and French," Isherwood complained), they left Cairo at two a.m. in a car driven by two "pretty sin- ister" Arabs, procured for them by Fronny. "We were both drunk, and they knew it," Isherwood confessed. "They knew also that we had money. In the middle of the desert, the car stopped. The arabs got out and consulted. Wystan brandished our only weapon, his shoe; and we both determined that, if the worst came to the worst, neither of them should ever become a father." Without saying anything to their passengers, the Arabs got back in the car and drove to the outskirts of Suez, which was as far as they were now prepared to take them. After some halfhearted haggling, the two travelers agreed to pay extra to be taken to the quay, but when they arrived there was no sign of a boat. Informed that the *Aramis* was not due to dock until 8:00 a.m., they repaired to a hotel to continue haggling with the drivers, eventually paying them the equivalent of fifteen shillings more than the previously agreed price. It was with some relief that they boarded the *Aramis,* but Isherwood declared that "Nobody besides ourselves had made the Cairo trip, so we felt adventurous and very pleased with ourselves."

The next stop was Djibouti, where Auden was thwarted in his attempts to photo- graph a baby camel, and they were invited to witness some belly-dancing. "I don't know how Wystan felt," Isherwood wrote,

> but I admit that I was tremendously thrilled. The vision of something slippery, brutal, gross, inconceivably disgusting and pleasant: 'That time I saw the Danse du Ventre at Djibouti' I imagined telling my gaping grandchildren—for, of course, this would be the real thing, rank and hot from the bowels of Africa, and not to be confused with the miserable wrigglings I'd seen already in Brussels and Berlin.

It did not, of course, turn out to be the real thing. Their guide produced a dozen young women, who were paraded in a hut, so that Isherwood and Auden could make their choice. They selected three, who immediately started removing their clothes, then clapped, stamped on the floor and started chanting, all the while haggling over the price. "They were exactly like prep-school boys," Isherwood noted,

> alternately ragging and showing off before three indulgent members of staff. It was plain that none of them had the faintest notion how to do the Belly-dance, or, indeed, any kind of dance whatsoever. Getting tired of the stamping, they decided to try the effect of a little sex. 'Soixante!' one girl exclaimed, going round to catch each of us in turn and giving our private parts a sly pinch. She even tried to get Wystan to sit on an upturned bucket—quite with the air of inviting him to sink down upon a voluptuous couch. Anything less vicious and more amateurish could scarcely be imagined. We were so weak with laughing that we could hardly stand

upright. At length, the negresses scrambled into their clothes, took our fifty-franc note and let us out.

The next port of call was Colombo, which Isherwood thought looked like the White City, and they made an excursion to Kandy through countryside which Auden compared to Aldershot or Henley overtaken by Kew Gardens. On the way back they were held up when their incompetent driver knocked over and injured a pedestrian. While they went to look for a policeman, Auden's camera and cigarettes were stolen. They were terrified that they would miss the boat, but after an alarming journey at speed through the dark with ineffective headlamps, they arrived on the jetty at 8:30 p.m., half an hour before the boat was due to sail.

There were brief stopovers in Singapore and in Saigon, where the rickshaw boys overcharged them by a thousand percent and offered them a "marie Française" or a "wonderful boy." ("The difference in language is perhaps significant," Isherwood observed.) Eventually, on February 16, they docked at Hong Kong. Their period as tourists was over: they were now war correspondents.

Relations between China and Japan had been deteriorating since September 1931, when the Japanese invaded Manchuria and set up the puppet state of Manchoukuo at the beginning of 1932. Once they had gained a foothold in northeastern China, the Japanese made further incursions, largely unopposed by General Chiang Kai-shek, who recognized that their forces were superior to his own. In July 1937, however, came the so-called "Peking Incident" during which Chinese and Japanese troops exchanged fire at the Marco Polo Bridge to the north of the city. Negotiations for a settlement broke down almost immediately and so by August the two countries were officially at war, a war China appeared to be losing. By December, Peking, Shanghai and the capital, Nanking, had all fallen to the Japanese.

When Isherwood and Auden reported to the offices of the *China Morning Post,* they discovered that stories they had heard in England of Japanese troops landing on the coast round Hong Kong were untrue, and that Canton could still be reached either by river or by the Kowloon–Canton railway. The railway was being bombed occasionally and ineffectually by the Japanese air force, whose marksmanship was cheerfully derided, and any damage was very quickly repaired by gangs of coolies. People in Hong Kong were nevertheless pessimistic about the outcome of the war.

On the day of their arrival, Isherwood was worried to find there was no letter from Ian Scott-Kilvert awaiting him. He sent a cable, but after two days had not received a reply, and so wrote to Kathleen asking her to find out whether anything was wrong. His concern was such that he followed this with a cable: "Worried because Ian has never written can you find out if ill and cable me both send love—Christopher." Kathleen telephoned Hampstead, where Mrs. Lang told her than Ian was back at Cambridge, so she sent a reply-paid wire to Caius: "Cable from C arrived HK no letter from you hope all is well—Isherwood." Scott-Kilvert wired back: "Letter lost have wired and written C since—Ian." The cable had in fact arrived, but the *poste restante* in Hong Kong was staffed by Chinese, who proved "very vague about names and addresses." It eventually turned up, along with a letter, at the home of D. J. Sloss, the Vice-Chancellor of Hong Kong University, who had invited Isherwood and

Auden to stay with him. They attended various social functions, including dinner with the Governor, and met the British ambassador, Sir Archibald Clark Kerr, who turned out to know Auden's poetry and be a fan of *Sally Bowles*. This was not altogether surprising, for Archie Kerr was not quite the conventional career diplomat he appeared. His collection of pipes and his addiction to detective stories made him seem down to earth, but his first posting had been to Tangier, where he is supposed to have taken advantage of the local homosexual amenities. He had subsequently served as British ambassador to Chile, where he acquired a chic little wife described by Auden as a "beautiful Santiago whore," and Iraq. He liked nothing more than the company of young left-wing intellectuals, with whom he could discuss his sympathy for Chinese and Soviet communism. He invited Auden and Isherwood to stay with him in Shanghai at the end of their tour.

Their plan was to go to Canton by riverboat, then by car to Hankow, where they were to travel by boat again up the Yangtze river to Chungking and the Front. It would take a month or more and Isherwood warned Kathleen that she might not hear from him for some time. They left Hong Kong on February 28. "Here we were, steaming smoothly into the estuary of the broad, softly-swimming river," Isherwood wrote, by now well into his stride as a war reporter,

> steaming away from the dinner tables, the American movies, the statue of Queen Victoria on the guarded British island, steaming west into dangerous, unpredictable war-time China. Now *it*—whatever it was—was going to start. This wasn't a dream, or a boys' game of Indians. We were adult, if amateur, war-correspondents entering upon the scene of our duties. But, for the moment, I could experience only an irresponsible, schoolboyish feeling of excitement. We scanned the river-banks eagerly, half-expecting to see them bristle with enemy bayonets.

The style may be a parody of the *Boy's Own Paper,* but the dangers were real enough. They passed a Japanese gunboat in the estuary and had their first glimpse of the enemy. "Absorbed in their duties, they scarcely gave us a glance," Isherwood noted. "That is what War is, I thought: two ships pass each other, and nobody waves his hand."

In Canton, they experienced—in the distance—their first air raid. Having equipped themselves with camp beds and mosquito nets, and acquired visiting cards on which their names were phonetically rendered as Y Hsiao Wu and Au Dung, they boarded the train for Hankow, "the real capital of wartime China," on March 4. The British consul had informed them that the line had been badly bombed, that frail bridges had been imperfectly mended, and that the journey might take much longer than expected, but they arrived in Hankow after four days. Here they interviewed several VIPs, including Mme Chiang Kai-shek, the formidable wife of the Chinese Generalissimo. They also attended a press conference straight out of Lewis Carroll, at which a government official read out the latest news bulletin. "Every Japanese advance is a Chinese strategic withdrawal," Isherwood noted.

> Towns pass into Japanese hands in the most tactful manner possible—they simply cease to be mentioned. He reads very fast and keeps losing the place in his pa-

pers. 'Of seven planes brought down by Chinese ground forces, fifteen were destroyed by infantry.' Nobody bothered to question the arithmetic, or, indeed, to pretend any interest whatsoever. Any scraps of genuine news would be circulated later, when the journalists had dispersed to the bars for a pre-dinner drink.

The absurdity of these proceedings was highlighted three days later, when Isherwood and Auden learned that Germany had invaded Austria. "The bottom seemed to drop out of the world," Isherwood wrote. "What does China matter to us in comparison with this? Bad news such as this sort has a curious psychological effect: all the guns and bombs of the Japanese seem suddenly as harmless as gnats. If we are killed on the Yellow River front our deaths will be as provincial and meaningless as a motor-bus accident in Burton-on-Trent." The Japanese seemed less harmless, however, when viewed from the top of one of Hankow's tallest buildings, where Isherwood and Auden were taken in order to get a good view of an air raid. From this vantage point, the streets below seemed silent and empty.

> Then, far off, the hollow, approaching roar of the bombers, boring their way invisibly through the dark. The dull, punching thud of bombs falling, near the airfield, out in the suburbs. The searchlights criss-crossed, plotting points, like dividers; and suddenly there they were, six of them, flying close together and high up. It was as if a microscope had brought dramatically into focus the bacilli of a fatal disease. They passed, bright, tiny, and deadly, infecting the night. The searchlights followed them right across the sky; guns smashed out; tracer-bullets bounced up towards them, falling hopelessly short, like slow-motion rockets. The concussions made you catch your breath; the watchers around us on the roof exclaimed softly, breathlessly: 'Look! look! there!' [. . .] I don't know if I was frightened. Something inside me was flapping about like a fish.

The effects on the ground of such raids were brought home to them several days later, when, having traveled north to Cheng-chow, they were taken to see a squalid and poorly equipped military hospital at Shang-kui. Nothing in Isherwood's brief medical training had prepared him for these dark, crammed huts, in which patients lay on urine-soaked straw and the air was filled with the "sweet stench of gas-gangrene." Having replaced his stolen camera, Auden took a number of photographs.

From Cheng-chow they boarded a train for Sü-chow, and then, accompanied by their servant, Chiang, they set off in rickshaws in search of the Chinese front line. En route they saw deserted trench systems and a soldier riding a horse that had been painted green in order to camouflage it. The soldier told them that part of the village of Han Chwang, where they were heading, had fallen to the Japanese, and the canal that divided the village was now the Chinese front line. They met the general in command of the Chinese troops in the area, who arranged for them to visit the Front that evening on small ponies. They only got as far as the second line before night fell, but the following morning, Auden insisted that they must get to the front line, even if this meant forfeiting the protection of their military guides. The sight of a dog "gnawing what was, only too obviously, a human arm" on some waste ground in the village reminded them of the dangers ahead: the corpse was that of someone shot as a spy. "Out came Wystan's camera at once," Isherwood told Spender, "but the dog was shy and ran away, and Wystan, in trying to coax it back, practically had to pick up a bit of the corpse and say: 'Come here, Ponto. Lovely spy! Wuff wuff.' " Auden thought this episode gave them one over Hemingway, whom he thought unlikely to have seen anything so gruesome in all his experience of war zones.

Having managed to persuade two officers to accompany them back to the front line, they once more mounted their ponies and trotted off. "There were the same semi-farcical precautions," Isherwood recorded: "the advance in single file across the fields and some dramatic dodging along communication trenches, only to emerge from them right on the crest of the skyline as brilliantly illuminated targets." They did, however, reach the canal safely, largely because in the daylight the Japanese withdrew to the village. "Auden popped his head above the parapet and took two pictures without getting shot at," but a bombardment started almost at once, prompted by the firing of one of the Chinese troops' big guns some distance away. Here it was at last: The Test. Isherwood and Auden were in trenches, with large guns booming all around them, a scene straight out of the First World War. As a soldier escorted them back behind the lines,

> the Japanese fired back, shelling the trenches we had left. The Chinese guns were far out of their reach—they seemed to have a range of at least seven miles. We could hear the great slam of the explosion, then the express-train scream of the shell right over our heads, then the dull crash of the burst, and a black, escaped genie of smoke would tower, for a moment, above the roofs of Han Chwang, or the open countryside beyond.

Here, finally, was something to tell the boys back home.

Stumbling back toward safety, they heard the drone of approaching airplanes. "They circled the sky several times, passing quite low above us. Whenever they came, the soldier signalled to us to lie down. It was an unpleasant feeling lying there exposed in the naked field: one couldn't help remembering the many anecdotes of aviators' caprice—how a pilot will take a sudden dislike to some solitary figure moving beneath him, and waste round after round of ammunition until he has annihilated it, like an irritating fly." They were spared, however, and managed to cadge a lift on a troop train back to Sü-chow.

The following morning, they traveled west, back past Cheng-chow to Sian at the far end of the Lung-Hai railway. Part of this trip passed close to the Yellow River, where the Japanese had a gun emplacement, and this stretch of line could be traveled on only at night. A boisterous Canadian missionary-doctor they had befriended told them gleefully that the line was "nothing but a shooting-gallery," but they reached Sian unscathed after a long, fitful and alarming journey. While Isherwood took such precautions as opening windows so as not to be showered by glass in the event of an attack, Auden slept, assuring his companion that they were perfectly safe. "Wystan, of course, knows he won't be killed, because Nanny would never allow it, and It Can't Happen Here," Isherwood told Spender. "So whenever we do get into any danger (and so far it has been certainly of the very mildest description) he sulks and fusses: 'Why can't they SHOOT?' or 'It's not nearly LOUD enough.' One would think to hear him talk that the Japs were a fifth-rate orchestra, trying to play Beethoven."

They stayed in Sian for several days, sightseeing and conducting interviews about Russian support for the Chinese forces, before setting off back to Hankow on April 10. They photographed Agnes Smedley, the American activist, who had spent a decade in China allying herself to the communist cause, and the agitator Chou En-lai, who happened to be visiting her. They interviewed Du Yueh-seng, a politician and businessman who insisted on talking entirely about the Red Cross rather than his part in helping Chiang Kai-shek purge his former allies after coming to power, and visited the film studios, where propaganda films with such titles as *Fight to the Last* were being churned out. On their last day in the city, they donned dark glasses and lay on the lawn of the British Consulate in order to watch an air raid, mounted by the Japanese in honor of their Emperor's birthday. When it was over, they raced to the Arsenal, which although evacuated long before had been the target. A bomb had destroyed a row of cottages, killing five civilians.

> They were terribly mutilated and very dirty, for the force of the explosion had tat-tooed their flesh with gravel and sand. Beside one corpse was a brand-new, un-damaged straw hat. All the bodies looked very small, very poor, and very dead, but, as we stood beside one old woman, whose brains were soaking obscenely through a little towel, I saw the blood-caked mouth open and shut, and the hand beneath the sack-covering clench and unclench. Such were the emperor's birth-day presents.

Another reporter in Hangkow was the travel writer Peter Fleming, who had been sent to China by *The Times*. "In his khaki shirts and shorts, complete with golf-stockings, strong suede shoes, waterproof wrist-watch and Leica camera, he might have stepped straight from a London tailor's window, advertising 'Gent's Tropical Exploration Kit,' " Isherwood noted. It was rather alarming for amateur freelancers such as Auden and Isherwood to be confronted by a bona fide war correspondent, but they overcame their initial defensiveness ("a blend of anti-Etonianism and profes-sional jealousy"), and agreed to accompany Fleming on a grueling tour of the south-eastern Front in May. This was accomplished by car, on horseback, on pole-slung chairs carried by coolies, and on foot, and Isherwood and Auden entertained them-selves along the route by extemporizing passages from an imaginary book called *With Fleming to the Front*. Isherwood suffered from sore feet and mosquitoes, and the guides almost collapsed, but at the end of the journey, after they had waved good-bye to Fleming, Auden felt able to announce: "Now we're real travellers for ever and ever. We need never go farther than Brighton again."

On May 20 they took a bus to Wenchow on the coast, then caught a steamer to Shanghai, where they stayed in considerable and well-deserved luxury at Clark Kerr's private villa in the French Concession in the city. They had a slightly awkward lunch with four Japanese businessmen at the Shanghai Club, at which they assured their fellow diners, not altogether truthfully, that morale in Hankow was high and that the Chinese had no intention of negotiating a peace settlement. After the rigors of the

Front, they spent much of their time relaxing in the city's bathhouses, where attractive young attendants performed ablutions and other services.

Their trip was over, and on June 12 they boarded the *Empress of Asia,* arriving in Vancouver a fortnight later. They took advantage of a docking in Japan to cross the country by train, rejoining the boat at Yokohama. This stopover provided them with material for an article on "Meeting the Japanese," published later in the year in the left-wing American periodical *New Masses,* but Isherwood and Auden spent most of the sea voyage revising *On the Frontier,* the premiere of which had been delayed until their return on the instructions of Maynard Keynes. Isherwood had authorized his mother to act on his and Auden's behalf in negotiations over *On the Frontier.* "On *no* account sign any contract for our new play with Rupert until you hear from me," he had warned.

> The important thing is to see that there's no chance of giving him or the Group Theatre any share whatever of the film rights. He may have his share of the broadcasting and television, however. And, of course, no share whatever of the book rights. He agreed to all this while I was in England, but there's no knowing what he'll do behind our backs.

Kathleen must have been heartened that, in spite of their quarrels and her feeling of being left out of things, Christopher was still prepared to entrust important business matters to her. (One wonders, incidentally, what Curtis Brown was doing on his client's behalf in order to earn his commissions.) "I don't know what I would have done without you," Isherwood later acknowledged, "and I certainly refuse to allow the Group Theatre to have you; they aren't worthy of such a secretary!"

From Vancouver he and Auden took a train to New York, where they were greeted by the novelist George Davis, who was fiction editor of the magazine *Harper's Bazaar.* They had met Davis when he visited England the previous year, and he had volunteered to help them place articles in the American press. Extracts from a "Chinese Diary" they had sent to him had been published in the *New Republic* at the beginning of the month, and so Davis was able to present the two authors with ready cash on their arrival. He also suggested they stay in his apartment and offered to act as their guide. Davis was well connected and introduced them to several celebrities, including two famous figures from Berlin, Kurt Weill and Lotte Lenya.[4] More significantly, toward the end of their ten-day stay in the city, he also introduced them to a young man whom Isherwood always referred to as "Vernon."

Vernon, who had just celebrated his seventeenth birthday, had been born in New York. When he was eight, his parents divorced and he was sent to a strict Catholic boarding school run by Franciscans. It was not long, however, before his father's business was affected by the Depression. He was removed from the school and spent some time living with his grandparents. He had previously done well at school, but these disruptions affected him badly and by the age of fifteen he had attended seven

---

4. Although homosexual, Davis was to marry Lenya after Weill's death.

different schools. He abandoned his education altogether in the autumn of 1936 and spent a year traveling round America paying his way by casual labor. He returned to New York in 1937, went back to school part time, moved in "bohemian" circles, and supported himself by doing manual labor to supplement a small allowance from his mother. He attended evening classes in art history and painted as a hobby.

Isherwood recalled that he had specifically asked Davis to find him "a beautiful blond boy, about eighteen, intelligent, with very sexy legs." Vernon fitted the bill almost exactly, and Davis arranged a dinner for him to meet the two British authors. "Naturally, we all understood that it was a 'set-up,' " Vernon recalled, "an adventure in which I participated enthusiastically." Isherwood's and Auden's names were only just becoming widely known in America, and so Vernon was not overawed to meet them. He was entranced by their witty conversation and ended up by going to bed with Isherwood. Over the next few days he and Isherwood went for several long walks around the city, talking about their lives. Vernon's background, so quintessentially American, struck Isherwood as very romantic. He felt he had got to know and really understand Germany by having affairs with the boys of Berlin. Now, by embracing Vernon, he would be embracing the entire United States.

TWELVE

I SHERWOOD AND AUDEN SAILED FROM NEW YORK ON JULY 9, arriving in England eight days later. They had spent just under six months in each other's company, and Isherwood later felt that, "despite their occasional frictions," the trip had bound them together closer than ever. At the time, however, he confessed in his diary:

> In China I sometimes found myself really hating [Wystan]—hating his pedantic insistence on 'objectivity', which was merely a reaction from my own woolly-mindedness. I was meanly jealous of him, too. Jealous of his share of the lime-light; jealous because he'll no longer play the rôle of dependant, admiring younger brother. Indeed, I got such a *physical* dislike of him that I deliberately willed him to get ill; which he did. Then, in New York, and on the Atlantic cross-ing, we had those extraordinary scenes—Wystan in tears, telling me that no one wd ever love him, that he wd never have my sexual success. That flattered my vanity; but still my sadism wasn't appeased.

Isherwood does not elaborate on these "extraordinary scenes," but it seems possible that they were the result of a realization on Auden's part that his close sexual rela-tionship with Isherwood had finally run its course. Isherwood later stated that this re-lationship "went on intermittently between 1926 and 1938," without explaining why it stopped. One possibility is that Isherwood decided he could no longer go to bed with Auden "unromantically," knowing that Auden needed more. After enjoying the sexual favors of a seventeen-year-old who was his physical ideal, Isherwood may have found the prospect of sex with the thirty-one-year-old Auden less alluring than hitherto—hence the mention of his otherwise inexplicable sense of "*physical* dis-like." Becoming ill would have put Auden sexually *hors de combat,* thus saving Ish-erwood the embarrassment of refusing to go to bed with him. Auden had enjoyed other sexual relationships during the period he and Isherwood had been intermittent lovers, but apart from Michael Yates (the subject of his most famous love lyric, "Lay your sleeping head, my love"), none appears to have anything like the importance or significance of Isherwood. In the list of "emotional milestones" Auden drew up, no one is mentioned between 1926 and 1939 apart from Isherwood and Yates. Auden's feeling that no one would ever love him may have been a result of Isherwood's inability to return Auden's love in kind. A deeply committed friendship enlivened by bouts of recreational sex was not at all the same thing.

Whatever the immediate complications of their relationship, however, and whatever Isherwood might have written about his "mean jealousy," their friendship was one that would survive all such difficulties: a symbiosis that had its roots in their shared past, but was also the result of the intense periods of collaboration they had enjoyed since 1934. Their names had become firmly linked in the public imagination—and, indeed, in the joint telegrams they sent from their travels, which were invariably signed "Wystopher." It seemed inevitable that when the previous year Auden had announced his intention to attend the writers' conference in Spain, Isherwood should have commented: "so, of course, I shall go too." Regardless of their personal or professional relationships with other people, the one they had with each other had endured. Their future lay together.

Back in England, however, Isherwood was determined to play the role of "Returning Hero" alone, and even refused to allow Auden to spend the night at Pembroke Gardens. He subsequently acknowledged that his treatment of Auden had been disgraceful, but insisted that "these confessions sound far worse than they are. My essential feeling for Wystan is untouched by all this, and will remain so." Kathleen was delighted to have the Returning Hero all to herself. He had sent reassurances about the battle zones, and told her that he had slept through one major air raid on Hangkow ("which only shows you they aren't very terrible"), but she must have known that the China expedition was not without its dangers. Isherwood had warned her that when he and Auden were traveling they might be unable to send letters or cables, and had suggested that after the beginning of May all correspondence should be sent care of Curtis Brown in New York. Kathleen and Mrs. Auden, whose relationship was a great deal less warm than the one between their sons, had exchanged any news they received, and friends such as Forster and Britten had kindly passed on any information from their letters they thought suitable for a mother's ears. By early June, however, both Kathleen and the Audens had become concerned about their sons' whereabouts, and had considered trying to find out something from the Foreign Office.

On July 17, a Sunday, Kathleen had got up early, just in case Christopher arrived sooner than expected—"but the morning dragged on, & no sign." The boat train from Southampton was late, and Isherwood did not arrive until mid-afternoon. He regaled his mother with news of his travels while unpacking his cases. Spender came round for an early cold supper and then accompanied Kathleen and Christopher to the Westminster Theatre, where Beatrix Lehmann gave a remarkable solo performance in an English translation of Cocteau's *La Voix Humaine,* directed by Berthold Viertel. Kathleen had remained a familiar presence at Group Theatre performances and lectures. In Christopher's absence, this had been a way of keeping in touch with him vicariously. She had even started going to the Group's offices to lend a hand addressing circulars, as Richard still did occasionally. She was almost seventy, and although youthful must have been a somewhat incongruous figure among the Group's employees, most of whom were in their twenties or early thirties.

One of the first things Isherwood needed to sort out back in England was his relationship with Ian Scott-Kilvert. On board the ship going out to China, Auden had written a "Passenger Shanty," which included the lines:

> *Christopher sends off letters by air,*
> *He longs for Someone who isn't there,*
> *But Wystan says: 'Love is exceedingly rare.'*

Wystan, it turned out, was right. He may have intended a mild rebuke to Isherwood, a firm but gentle reminder that what Auden could offer was not easily found elsewhere. Or he may simply have been skeptical about the great romance that Isherwood had built up out of his affair with Scott-Kilvert. The longed-for reunion has not quite as rapturous as Isherwood had imagined it would be. He had enjoyed the idea of Scott-Kilvert devotedly waiting for him on the dock at Southampton when he got back from New York, but this did not in fact happen. He was also slightly piqued to discover that his young lover, rather than spending the summer moping about at home, had very sensibly taken a holiday in Greece. Their first meeting turned out to be "awkward, tongue-tied, meaningless."

> There is no electric current between us, at the moment: nothing but embarrassment. Next week, he goes away to his stammering-cure. On the 20th [August], it is planned, we start on a month's holiday together—which must surely make or break the whole relationship. But, at present, nothing. How can I tell him what I used to dream, staring at the sunset from the liner's rail: that our friendship was to be a challenge, an assertion of the right to live and be happy—a challenge to this whole death-struck era? In New York, soppy and exalted after an absurd film about Dr Barnardo's Homes, I mentally said to him: 'Yes, I know I am base, cowardly, deceitful, a sham: but why shouldn't there be one person for whom I'm heroic and decent and fine? Why shouldn't we believe in each other? And why shouldn't our relationship be better, more beautiful, more honest than either of us?'
>
> But no. There's something wrong. I must just wait and see if it comes right. If it doesn't, it doesn't—that's all.
>
> I understand Ian so well—too well, perhaps. Everything he feels now I felt, in 1926. He is dreaming of a kind of monastic life. He doesn't want to be touched. Actually, he wants it terribly—more than anything else. But by whom? Oh dear, oh dear—the English . . . And while he hesitates, time is going past, minute by minute—the last minutes allowed to us before war is upon us, the last minutes in which we could be happy—wasted.
>
> Maybe I'll write to him, at once.

Whether or not Isherwood did in fact write is not known: Scott-Kilvert destroyed all Isherwood's letters. But the planned holiday was abandoned when Mrs. Lang insisted that Ian should continue his speech therapy at the "stammering-school," and then go on holiday with her. It was, Isherwood reported, "all very tactfully put, but it told me plainly enough that I wasn't wanted. Ian very upset, writes pages. Do I care? Yes, in a way, of course." The very fact that Isherwood had to ask himself this question shows that the relationship was in serious difficulties. But he also felt that his whole life was in a state of flux. After conducting a seven-page analysis of himself and of his relationships with his friends, he concluded:

> And Ian? Honestly, I don't know. To be frank, my feelings have cooled off a lot. Physically, we are out of touch—and this high-powered emotional correspondence is beginning to bore me. The marriage of true minds has been repeatedly announced, but no date is fixed for the wedding. The whole thing might flare up again if we ever meet properly—but shall we? At present, I think far more about [Vernon]—who gave me the freedom of New York. It was so lovely, waking up in George's apartment that morning and seeing [Vernon] and thinking: 'this is the sane, the natural function of human beings. This is Life. My life has been merely death.' But all that hadn't very much to do with [Vernon] himself.

One senses that at this period Isherwood was casting around for something permanent and valuable to counteract his sense of the world's disintegration, the inevitable plunge towards another European war. Snatched moments of happiness with a teenager in New York acquired an almost symbolic substance and importance: he was right in stating that it didn't have very much to do with the actual person who was Vernon.

I sherwood's name had appeared frequently in the press during his absence in the Far East. *Lions and Shadows* had been published by the Hogarth Press on March 17 at the same time as "The Landauers" had appeared in John Lehmann's *New Writing 5*. In June and July three extracts from the "Chinese Diary" had been published under Isherwood's name alone in the *New Statesman* and *The Nation*. The character of "Christopher Isherwood" was becoming as well known as the author himself. Reviewing *Lions and Shadows* in *The Listener,* Edwin Muir had observed that Isherwood "cannot resist turning everyone he knows into a character." That everyone included Isherwood, as Stephen Spender complained in a long letter he wrote to Isherwood about "The Landauers." "I can't help protesting against the little comic-cuts Charlie Chaplin figure into which you are getting so adept at turning yourself," Spender wrote,

> especially as you are now called Isherwood in these stories. The self-portrait could scarcely—even in Lions & Shadows—be more evasive. By sneering at the more self-pitying & even tragic aspects of yourself, you are really showing a typically English brand of dishonesty, which consists in admitting the real and then making it seem unimportant by the exercise of a sense of humour. The fact is that at Cambridge you really were miserable; in Berlin, you really believed yourself to be poor, you really believed yourself to be deeply in love with Walter, you certainly really suffered; added to all this, you are despotic and passionate. You are

far more interesting, and rather more sinister in some ways, than you make out. You can't really go on indefinitely reducing your personality to a formula in terms which evoke delighted sniggers from Bloomsbury; always with the little saving piece of 'seriousness' up your sleeve which shows that in spite of the humour you are serious,—like them.

Isherwood was beginning to agree, partly because he was in danger of becoming Herr Issyvoo in real life as well as in fiction. "Of course you're right about 'Isherwood,' " he replied: "he is an evasion and altogether too harmless and too knowing— 'the sexless nitwit,' as somebody called him [. . .] I will drop 'Isherwood' altogether in future. I always meant to."

After also criticizing Isherwood's portrayal of Wilfrid Israel and Gisa Soleweitschick in "The Landauers," Spender concluded: "all I'm saying is that I prefer the side of you that wrote the Nowaks and the Memorial, to the side which writes fake autobiography. Perhaps your mistake—from my point of view—is to despise your own suffering. You ought to exploit it." Although this is a very subjective judgment—Spender was certainly adept at exploiting his own agonies in his work—it is also acute. Within a week of being back in London, Isherwood was sketching out the synopsis for a new novel based on his relationship with Heinz, but in which "Christopher Isherwood" played no part.

Standing in for Isherwood was a young Englishwoman called Karin, who has "revolted from a rich upper-middle-class family," but unlike Isherwood "refuses to take their money." She has joined the KPD and teaches English at the Marxist Workers' School, where one of her pupils is a young carpenter called Erich. She and Erich, who is some nine years her junior, embark on an affair, and she wonders whether she should marry him: "Why not? The real way of entering the proletariat: the thing she wants to do." When Hitler comes to power, Karin takes Erich out of Germany "after grave qualms: has she the right to do this to him? He isn't deeply involved." They travel to Las Palmas: "The dream-island, where they can forget everything and be happy. But not for long." Their money runs out and Karin realizes they must go to England and face her family, but the immigration officials note that Erich has "*Tischler*" (carpenter) on his passport and allow him only one month's visa. Karin introduces Erich to her family and this is so disastrous that she decides to leave England, traveling with Erich to France, Belgium and Holland. "Here the relationship is really studied [. . .] They depend more and more on each other. Sometimes they are happy. But always, always the shadow of Germany, of war—through the loudspeaker. Always the police. They keep moving on." They end up in Copenhagen, where Karin gets involved in communism again. A German comrade is sent to Berlin, and when he doesn't return, the Danish communists ask Erich to go to find out what has happened: "He goes. The tortures of waiting. No news. Erich has been arrested. Karin wants to go. Is dissuaded. Gradually, she realizes that she must simply carry on with her life. There is no consolation. There is only hope. One day, perhaps . . . She returns to England."

This was certainly more in line with Spender's suggestions about Isherwood's future as a writer, exploiting his suffering in the cause of art, but the attempt was doomed. Isherwood lacked the earnestness Spender displayed in his work, and his greatest strength was to treat somber topics with sardonic humor, but without diminishing the underlying seriousness of his subject matter. Not everyone understood this. The surface of his work was so beguiling, his narratives so amusing, that people seemed able to enjoy the books without really relating to what they described. This had been his complaint about the reception of *Mr Norris Changes Trains*. Spender thought that this was a problem Isherwood had brought upon himself by his insistence on remaining detached from the events and characters he wrote about. By treating everything as marvelous copy, he did not, Spender felt, face up to the realities of evil—it was one of the few things Spender and Lehmann agreed upon. Spender even went so far as to suggest many years later (and with more mischief, perhaps, than seriousness) that Isherwood's morally neutralized response to interesting people was such that he might rather have liked Hitler if he'd met him. What Spender was really talking about in his letter, however, is the difference between a politically and socially committed writer such as himself and a sympathetic but objective outsider such as Isherwood.

The principal problem with "Karin and Erich" was that Isherwood had merely tacked a sensational plot on to what was in effect a book about a relationship. He made further detailed notes for this novel, and several brief attempts at an opening chapter, including some in which, forgetting his promises to himself and Spender, he introduced himself into the narrative, as an observer of Karin and Erich. This was a ploy that had worked in "On Ruegen Island," but it seems halfhearted here. He soon abandoned the novel, and this is not altogether surprising. It was one thing to write about his relationship with Heinz in coded language, so that its nature remained ambiguous; it was quite another to attempt to recast the story as a heterosexual one. Isherwood describes Karin as having "a bony face, peculiar eyes—grey-green, and a kind of masculine quality which makes her relationship with Erich sometimes appear almost homosexual." In other words, she is a vaguely feminized Isherwood, and this sort of fudging and fumbling shows quite clearly that Isherwood had little confidence in his ability to portray a convincing heterosexual affair. Having got stuck after writing a draft of the first chapter, he was obliged to acknowledge this: "I don't believe in Karin's first seduction by Erich. Why not? Because the account of Erich at the beginning of this book makes him seem so boyish, so feminine, that the story is really the story of a homosexual seduction."

A t the end of July Isherwood took a nostalgic trip to the Isle of Wight, staying with John Lehmann and his mother, who had rented a house in Totland Bay. Isherwood's sense of encroaching doom was highlighted during the first night he spent there. "We walk up over the heather downs towards the sight of the Needles," Lehmann recorded. "And the swinging searchlights, the aeroplanes revealed, the mysterious coloured lamps on the water, the barbed wire and the notices up by the Napoleonic forts, all give a startling hint of war approaching, of secret preparations and spies." They spent the weekend talking about the future, about Lehmann's plans for the Hogarth Press, which he was thinking of taking over from the Woolfs, about *New Writing,* and about their own books.

C. revealed himself again as the supreme describer of his unfinished, unbegun, novels. I had not been so fascinated, listening to his description of the next novel founded on the exile-years with H[einz], since I heard him describe, in a Lokal in

Antwerp, the never-written novel 'Paul is Alone'. I think this is really his great talent: telling a *story*. Because the story is so vivid and luminous in all its details before he puts pen to paper, perhaps that's why all he's written up-to-date have [*sic*] been mere glimpses of what he could do, why the novels seem boring when he comes to the real effort of writing them. This, coupled with his cat-like laziness. I had another, even more startling view of this quality of his imagination, when he told me, on the way to Dover, the whole fantastic but coherent saga that fills his daydreams—like a serial in a magazine that never finishes. He never broke down at a single point, he never seems to have to improvise among all the subtle (and extravagantly sensual) details and turns of the story. To live with a thing like that in one's mind, seems to me definitely to set one apart from normal humanity.

Isherwood's ability to spin elaborate tales and create a whole world in his imagination has its roots in Mortmere, when invention was all that mattered and writing down or completing a story was of secondary importance. Now that he was a professional writer, he was only too aware of the need to transform the material he had been gathering over the past decade or so into solid fiction, and the numerous drafts he wrote and notes he made show that it was not simply laziness that prevented him from achieving his goals. It was the sheer difficulty of wrestling brute facts into fictional submission.

It is quite likely that the principal reason he embarked on "Karin and Erich" in the first place was merely in an attempt to fulfill part of the outstanding contract with Methuen, who had yet to see a single word in return for the £150 they had paid him almost three years earlier. He swiftly abandoned the novel, partly because he had more urgent projects on hand. He had several articles to write about China, as well as the book he and Auden had been contracted to write, and was still revising *On the Frontier*.

Although Isherwood's principal role was that of a writer, whose relationship was with readers he never met, he nevertheless liked a live audience, one to whom he could talk about his life and work, tell funny stories, and effortlessly entertain. Lehmann described him at Totland "endlessly lecturing my Mother—to her fascination and delight—in a gentle, bright persuasive way that is his own patent for young or old disciples, explaining China, discussing America, describing W.H.A. and the lives of his friends, blissfully ignorant of the enormous indiscretions that I see popping up like cowpats in his path."

Quite how much of a performance this was, and quite how dangerous that could be, Isherwood was beginning to realize. An extensive, analytical self-portrait Isherwood wrote in his diary immediately after returning from the Isle of Wight goes some way to explaining the decisions he would make about his future in 1938. He starts with a physical description, one which photographs confirm. It is not quite as succinct, nor as caricature-like, as Auden's in the Lawrence pastiche, but the overall image is the same.

In six days from now, I shall be 34 years old. You probably wouldn't think this, to look at me. Wystan says that the top half of my face is much younger than the lower half. But this isn't true because I have a lot of crow's feet wrinkles round the eyes. My mouth is lined, too, with two big brackets, grooved into my cheeks by perpetual nervous pursing of my lips, and my curious muscular trick of 'making faces', which I once described in another [i.e. the St. Nicholas] journal. Also, I have a good many white hairs. No, I only seem young because my face is lean and usually animated, and because I have very bright large grey-green eyes, and regular, if nicotine-stained, teeth. My nose is too big, of course, and it will become fleshy later; but even if it were small and straight, I certainly could never be called good-looking: my head is such an odd shape. The most I can hope for is to be described as 'interesting'. The majority of people would probably say that my face had a lot of 'character'.

Stripped, I am no Adonis. My body looks fairly young because it is soft and not heavily muscled. My shoulders are narrow, and my hips too big. Nevertheless, as long as I hold myself well and remain full-face to the audience, my figure looks passably good—or, at any rate, quite cosy to lie on. When I turn sideways, you see the plump, soft, impotent belly, the big rather feminine bottom, the disproportionate shortness of the thighs and calves. I am getting steadily fatter, and keep meaning to do something about it—diet, exercise, etc.

He then went on to analyze his character:

I once read the title of a German novel (I forget the author's name) Der Mann ohne Eigenshaft [sic].[1] That, I've come to feel more and more, just describes me. For the more I think about myself, the more persuaded I am that, as a *person,* I really don't exist. That is one of the reasons why—much as I'm tempted to try—I can't believe in any orthodox religion: I cannot believe in my own soul. No, I am a chemical compound, conditioned by environment and education. My 'character' is simply a repertoire of acquired tricks, my conversation a repertoire of adaptations and echoes, my 'feelings' are dictated by purely physical, external stimuli. And yet, of course, like everybody else, I make a certain average impression upon the outside world.

What impression? Most of my friends think of me, apparently, as a diplomatist, rather amusingly sly. Wystan finds me completely unscrupulous—capable of anything to further my own designs. There is a lot of talk about my 'will'. Very few people trust me, I think—and how right they are. Der Mann ohne Eigens[c]haft is never to be trusted.

On the way out to China, Wystan and I had many arguments on the 'personality' question. I maintained that Christopher in Saigon and Christopher in Ken-

---

1. The author was Robert Musil, who was in fact Austrian. The first two volumes of his novel were published in 1930 and 1932 and would have been widely noticed in the German press. The whole novel—or at any rate what Musil had finished of it—was not published until 1952, twelve years after his death. It is usually translated as *The Man Without Qualities,* although the first definition of "Eigenschaft" in Isherwood's own German-English dictionary was "character," and the word could also be translated as "attributes."

sington were two different people. This sounds self-evident, but Wystan disputed it. This feeling of being quite different in different places and with different people is very strong in me.

Auden may have disputed it at the time, but he clearly remembered it a couple of years later, when playing a parlor game called Self-Images in which people had to describe themselves as they thought others might see them. Auden commented: "Now Christopher—were he here playing this game—would pull a picture from his mind's purse, slap it onto the table, then as quickly snatch it back, saying, 'No! That's not quite right!' And fetch out another: 'Really, not this, either!' Then pull out others, but none satisfying, for dear Chris has an uncertain image of himself."

Isherwood went on in his diary to ask himself what his faults were. "That's always an easy game," he decided. "Too dangerously easy. I am a violent physical coward, a liar, selfish, vain."

But am I? If I was scared in China—far more often than Wystan—I, at least, didn't show it. And, maybe, as taking those little risks was more difficult for me, I even displayed a kind of mild courage. I am a liar. But I lie very often to save people's feelings, and quite frequently I'm justified. I'm selfish, but about very few things—not about food, or the vast bed, or my comfort in general. Perhaps I'm even less selfish than most other people. I'm vain—but isn't this vanity (seeing my name in print, being praised, having affairs with admittedly attractive people) really only the interest which Der Mann ohne Eigens[c]haft is bound to feel in his *outward* 'personality' just because he knows himself to have no inner life at all?

Isherwood's sense of himself was intimately bound up with his fictional alter ego. As Spender had pointed out, "Christopher Isherwood," the amusing, charmingly self-deprecating narrator of *Sally Bowles* and the other Berlin stories that had already appeared in magazines, had also danced upon the stage of *Lions and Shadows*. "Because this book is about the problems of a would-be writer," Isherwood had declared in a prefatory note "To the Reader" of *Lions and Shadows,*

it is also about conduct.[2] The style is the man. Because it is about conduct, I have had to dramatize it, or you would not get farther than the first page. Read it as a novel. I have used a novelist's license in describing my incidents and drawing my characters: 'Chalmers', 'Linley', 'Cheuret' and 'Weston' are all caricatures: that is why—quite apart from the fear of hurt feelings—I have given them, and nearly everybody else, fictitious names.

---

2. There is a curious echo here of Auden's poem "Journey to Iceland," in which the poet hopes that "the student of prose and fine conduct" should find "places to visit" on the island. One of the photographs of MacNeice in the book is captioned "The Student of Prose and Conduct," but Isherwood seems to have borrowed this idea. His note is dated September 1937, a month after Auden's poem was republished in *Letters from Iceland,* with the letter to Isherwood appended.

The one character who is not given a fictitious name is of course "Christopher Isherwood," the delightfully candid and confiding narrator. "Christopher Isherwood" is in fact quite as much a caricature as "Chalmers" and "Weston," perhaps even more of one than the "Christopher Isherwood" of the Berlin stories. This "character" was also being put through his paces in *Journey to a War,* the book he and Auden were writing about their China trip. In spite of the warnings, readers were unable to distinguish between the two Isherwoods. As sometimes happens in a long-running soap opera, the identities of the character and the actor playing him had become confused. Readers felt that they knew the author because they knew the character, and indeed the two were sufficiently alike for it to be hard to distinguish one from the other. Isherwood himself had begun to be confused, had begun to see himself simply as a "character" who performed in public—at lectures and readings, when meeting strangers—just as much as he performed on the page. He had always acknowledged that he liked play-acting, putting on a show, impressing people. He was always, as it were, "on." The style was the man: what else was there? *Der Mann ohne Eigenschaften* is a man without character, properties or attributes, with no recognizable soul, indeed "no inner life at all."

In Isherwood's case, he felt that this man was at his most hollow in his dealings with his mother. "I am on very good terms with Mummy nowadays," he admitted.

> We are exceedingly charming to each other—I simply use my friendship-technique on her, and it works. Underneath our delightful relationship yawns the old pit—but it is gradually filling up with rubbish; press-cuttings, photographs from the Bystander, telephone-calls from the powerful and distinguished. She is proud of me. Her ambition gluts itself on my praises. For she, too, is ambitious; and in much the same way as myself. Together, we admiringly regard Christopher Isherwood—our ventriloquist's dummy, our joint creation.

How far Kathleen really colluded with her son in this creation is open to doubt. She undoubtedly was proud of him, paying her own subscription to a cuttings library and copying the choicest quotes from reviews of his books into her diaries; but the pleasure she took in his success was quite as much for his sake as for her own. As those diaries show, she was a great deal shrewder than Isherwood liked to believe, and was perfectly capable of distinguishing between her complicated, antagonistic and exasperating Christopher and the smooth, delightful and accomplished public character he presented.

Isherwood felt that the only way to understand the "character" he had created was to look at how it reacted with other people. "I make friends easily—for several reasons," he admitted.

> My approach, I know, is sympathetic. I listen to people's troubles and problems with evident interest. I flatter them, subtly. I am capable of genuine, if temporary, enthusiasm for new acquaintances. My vanity urges me to make special efforts with those who might ordinarily dislike me. I frequently overcome their prejudices. Also, I am an amusing talker. Elderly people like me because my manners are good. Young people like me because I am a little older, the born 'elder

brother', and have a romantic air of having been places and seen things. With the young I am a little world-weary, romantically sad, flattering, bold and charmingly frank. With the old, I am young, enthusiastic, diffident, and flattering. Sometimes I lay on the flattery a little too grossly, however. Then I am seen through, mistrusted, disliked. But I learn from these failures and become increasingly careful.

Why do I bother to do all this? What keeps me going? Why don't I despair?

Well, there's my work. I am very ambitious, and becoming increasingly so. I want to be a damn good writer. And I like what I have written, on the whole, already. I know that I can only become a better writer through perpetual self-criticism, discipline and honesty—so my morals are part of the régime. I am ambitious in my friendships, too. I am proud of them, like a collection—and the affection of my friends is like a large sum of money invested in the Bank.

But have I any real friends at all?

This question, at first sight, seems staggering. For, surely, there are plenty—Morgan, Beatrix, Berthold, Hector, Benjamin, Edward, the Burfords, Olive, Robert Moody, Tony Hyndman, Tony Bower, etc., etc., etc.? But with all these, I remain, essentially, a façade. I value their company too much to risk going beyond a certain point. I don't want them to know me too well. Of all these people, and many more, there is not one whose good opinion would survive *any* shock, *any* revelation. Or I think not. So I keep what I have—which is a great deal—and am careful. I remember how I lost the Sterns.

That leaves two—Wystan and Stephen.

Auden, he wrote, remained "my 'best friend', knows me behind the façade; and the knowledge is creditable to neither of us." Whatever happened between him and Auden, however, he felt that their friendship was indissoluble, and that whatever they knew about each other merely strengthened it. The same thing did not apply to Spender: "Stephen I feel warmly about for the moment, because I haven't seen him much. But Stephen, too, knows more than he should about me, and I about him—so we are cautious with each other, and mistrustful." So, whatever it was that *did* exist behind the "Christopher Isherwood" everyone recognized, it was not something Isherwood wanted others to see.

He would make one last bid to free himself of "Christopher Isherwood." When he came to publish *Goodbye to Berlin,* he included another prefatory note, warning that

Because I have given my own name to the 'I' of this narrative, readers are certainly not entitled to assume that its pages are purely autobiographical, or that its characters are libellously exact portraits of living persons. 'Christopher Isherwood' is a convenient ventriloquist's dummy, nothing more.

But it was already too late.

During the unsettled period of the late 1930s, the one thing that kept Isherwood from despair, apart from work, was sex. Ian Scott-Kilvert may have become untouchable and "monastic," but there were plenty of other people with whom Isherwood could conduct sexual relationships. One was Hugh Chisolm, a young American who had been an undergraduate at King's College Cambridge, and with whom Isherwood had stayed when giving two lectures in the city in the summer of 1937. Chisolm had wanted to accompany Isherwood and Auden on their China trip, but they had decided he was too young. This had not prevented Isherwood from seeing quite a lot of him at that period, and Kathleen described him as "a dear little thing, very spruce as if he had come out of a band box." He had caused great amusement at Pembroke Gardens by politely declaring that one of Elizabeth's worst culinary efforts ("a <u>shocking lunch</u>" of "tasteless mince & badly made apple charlotte") was better than anything one could have at the Ritz. Chisolm was now living in a house on the Thames at Richmond. Toward the end of August, Isherwood went to spend the night there—with inevitable results. "We play the friendship game very brilliantly together," Isherwood recorded.

> Last night, we were quite emotional—and the pretty scene, which he'd no doubt planned, took place. He is warm and soft and gentle. Holding my cigarette, and giving it me occasionally to puff, he reminded me of the Chinese boys in the Shanghai bathhouse. This morning, it was tacitly understood that something beautiful and intimate had occurred. We were 'real' friends, now. Hughie put on a pair of shorts which unfortunately exposed his legs. They were a shade too thin.

So much for Hughie.

As this diary extract makes clear, Chisolm was never more than a minor diversion, and Isherwood was still seeing Derek Neame, despite being irritated by his "obstinate neuroticism, a priggish cult of failure." He was also still having sex with Tony Hyndman "whenever an opportunity offered itself." One evening he and Robert Moody

> got pretty tight and compared notes on our sexual adventures. Robert, like myself, has just discovered that he can have absolutely anybody he wants to. We boasted, and were very hearty and jolly. We both agreed that what really attracted us in sex was the ambivalence; the masculine beneath the feminine exterior, and vice versa. Robert is getting regular sex with a female colleague. He fairly beams with it. He looks years younger than the boy who, five years ago, complained that nobody loved him.

In order to improve on the somewhat disheartening figure he had glimpsed in the mirror during his self-analysis, Isherwood started doing exercises every morning. "I am in perfect health," he noted, "and feeling loaded with sex, like a gun."

Although he was able to have (and indeed having) anyone he wanted, Isherwood's principal amorous preoccupation remained Scott-Kilvert, who always seemed at his most desirable when he was not actually around. Isherwood could spin romantic fantasies around their relationship: letters and daydreaming rather than actual physical contact were the things that made him believe that he was in love with the boy. He now intended to do something about this. At the beginning of September, Scott-Kilvert returned from the holiday with his mother and he and Isherwood arranged to spend some time together. "At present this means nothing,"

Isherwood wrote in anticipation of this reunion. "I must avoid feeling anything about it. I mustn't try to force the pace. Our letter-relationship has been built up like an insecure sky-scraper. He and I must abandon it, and live in a hut."

This image of how to share his life with Scott-Kilvert was derived from a letter he had just received from E. M. Forster, who had outlined the discarded Arcadian epilogue to *Maurice,* which Isherwood had been rereading. Forster was still in search of a happy but convincing ending. The one in which Maurice and Alec Scudder part at Southampton avoided imprisonment or suicide, and could therefore be counted "happy," but it was also ambiguous and unsatisfactory: would the lovers ever see each other again, and if so, how? "The temptation's overwhelming to grant to one's creations a happiness actual life does not supply," Forster had explained to his friend Goldsworthy Lowes Dickinson.

'Why not?' I kept thinking. 'A little rearrangement, rather better luck'—but no doubt the rearrangement's fundamental. It's the yearning for permanence that leads a novelist into theories towards the end of each book. The only permanence that is not a theory but a fact is death. And perhaps I surfeited myself with that in *The Longest Journey.* At all events the disinclination to kill increases.

That disinclination may have been increased by the fact that when Forster wrote this letter, in December 1914, Britain had been at war for four months. Now, as another war approached, there was once again an increased yearning for permanence, one Isherwood himself was increasingly feeling. He wrote Forster a fulsome letter of praise about *Maurice,* adding:

I have nothing, really, to criticize about the ending—except that you shouldn't stop there. Or there should be a sequel. Alec and Maurice have all their troubles before them. Maybe, it'll be all right—but one wants to know. I suppose Maurice threw up the office? I suppose they both went out to the 1914 war? I should love to know what they're doing now.

Re-reading the novel made Isherwood realize that the trouble with his relationship with Scott-Kilvert was that it was more like the one between Maurice and Clive (high-minded and high-flown) than the one between Maurice and Alec (equally romantic, but more down-to-earth).

It was shortly after this exchange of letters that Scott-Kilvert came back from his holiday to spend time with Isherwood. They booked into a hotel near Abinger Hammer, and went to see Forster, who lived nearby and offered to lend the couple his London flat for two nights. On the second night in the capital, having come back from a performance by the Ballets Russes, Isherwood and Scott-Kilvert sat down for a long talk.

I said what I've been feeling, underneath, for some time now: It won't do. Let's just be friends. The truth is, my going to China did sink our relationship—though not in a way either of us could have foreseen. It was those letters: altogether too noble, too beautiful. We built a sham cathedral round our friendship, and then found it too chilly to live in. You can't cook sausages on the high altar or wash dishes in the font.

Ian agreed—but said he wasn't sure. After all, there *had* been that night in Gastzimmer B. We'd have to wait, that was all. Maybe it'd come right in the end.

But it won't. Even if Hitler—who is now the Bank manager to all friends, all lovers—allows us another six months' overdraft.

There is some suggestion here of sexual incompatibility, or at any rate an imbalance of sexual desire. That night in Gastzimmer B clearly wasn't enough for someone who was "loaded with sex, like a gun." Isherwood was all too aware that time was running out and, like many lovers since Andrew Marvell, felt that there was neither world enough nor time for sexual reticence. It seems likely that part of Isherwood's enthusiasm for sexual experience was caused by a sense of *carpe diem* as war became every day more inevitable.

There was, however, another reason for the failure of this relationship. Isherwood was always insistent in his diary that none of the relationships he was pursuing at this time had any bearing on his relationship with Heinz. Scott-Kilvert, partly because he had emerged so romantically and unexpectedly from Isherwood's past and was another "younger brother," was the one person who might have supplanted Heinz in Isherwood's life. It was his bad luck that at this crucial point in their relationship Isherwood received direct news of Heinz from John Lehmann, who had been in Vienna and had, at Isherwood's request, called in at Berlin on his way back to London. "What John told me about Heinz impressed me tremendously," Isherwood wrote.

H, it seems, has been actually hardened and strengthened by his time at Trier. He now lives only for the day when he can get out of Germany and meet me again. Also, he is fully politically conscious: he knows we may be in for a war. He and Werner Jahr have met again, and may set up house together.[3]

And all this makes me feel: I must remain free. I must be ready for H. if he needs me. I never really supposed, somehow, that he would. We must be able to trust each other absolutely, now.

Scott-Kilvert was not to be shaken off, however. The following day, Isherwood received a letter from him, "full of complicated feelings. Wants to see me on Monday. I don't, and won't." Scott-Kilvert nevertheless turned up at Pembroke Gardens, and Isherwood took him to see Rolf Katz, who was now living in Richmond. It was September 12, the day Hitler was due to make his closing speech at the Nuremberg Rally. This speech was widely anticipated as providing an indication of the Führer's intentions toward Czechoslovakia, from which he was demanding the return of the Sudetenland. The future, peace or war, depended on it.

The disintegration of Isherwood's affair with Scott-Kilvert ran parallel to, and was closely bound up with, the worsening international crisis. Isherwood was so con-

---

3. Unidentified, but probably the young man with whom Francis Turville-Petre was having an affair when he shared a house with Isherwood at Mohrin.

sumed by the ever-increasing threat of war that he would buy as many as twelve newspapers a day, merely to read the stop-press items before throwing them away. He would discuss the situation with everyone he met, but still regarded Katz as the most reliable source of news, and his mood tended to fluctuate with this man's daily pronouncements. When the Sudetenland ultimatum was announced in the evening papers on September 13, Isherwood recorded: "I felt, at once: this is the end. My whole body froze." The following morning, however, Katz seemed relatively cheerful. "Says he has just heard from a man who returned yesterday from Germany. The General Staff is violently opposed to war. Goering also. His 'illness' is really a form of arrest. The Czechs have complete control in the Sudeten areas, which are now full of Czech troops." This was good news, and Isherwood was able to concentrate sufficiently to work on a second article on China for *Cosmopolitan*. Then, at midnight, came the announcement of Chamberlain's proposed flight to Germany to meet Hitler. Isherwood believed that it "may well avert this crisis, which is something. One asks only for time—like a hopeless debtor. We owe History so much that bankruptcy can only be postponed." At the same time he felt that, much as he would like to see a war avoided, it would be at a high moral cost, and imagined Chamberlain returning with "some dirty deal to lay before the cabinet."

A visit to Marple Hall did little to improve his spirits. Ever since Uncle Henry had abandoned the vast, cheerless pile for his cozy flat in Knightsbridge, the house had been poorly looked after and seemed to Isherwood "no more than a ruin, with the roof still on." He detected a "horrible chilly breath of decay," but the caretakers were nevertheless offering "Dainty Teas" to intrepid visitors. "Ah, how I still hate the place!" he exclaimed. "How I revolt from everything it stands for—the sucking, romantic, maternal death-wish! Seeing it again, I felt a pang of hate for M[ummy] such as I haven't experienced since China. Immediately, the incipient cold, from which I'd been suffering, became much worse."

Meanwhile the papers played the crisis for all it was worth, "with evil hints about conscription, *if* we're spared this time." Isherwood noticed how "older ex-servicemen gloat a little over the young." His own view of the young—notably Scott-Kilvert and Richard Buzzard—was also becoming somewhat ruthless. This was almost certainly prompted by a conversation he had with Spender, who had been undergoing psychoanalysis. Spender said that because his mother had been an invalid, he had always felt obliged to side with the weak. An experience in Spain had changed this. He had been talking to members of the International Brigade about Hyndman's desertion, "and saw a kind of shadow pass over their faces. Nobody said a word of condemnation. But, said Stephen, 'I thought: I'd do absolutely anything rather than see that look on anybody's face because of myself.' " Spender now felt that his "real love went out to the strong, to the people who do things, who don't run away." Apparently forgetting his own long-standing zeal for protecting vulnerable "younger brothers," Isherwood now started turning against his two lovers:

Buzzard throws temperaments, and Ian isn't sure, but now thinks Yes. I compare them with H[einz], who sent me a charming letter yesterday—trying to console *me*. I thought I had felt everything possible towards H— but I hadn't; I had never before admired his extraordinary courage. It might be an example to me. The truth is, H is feminine. Buzzard and Ian are merely effeminate. Perhaps that's brutal and unjust—it's how I feel at the moment.[4]

He was still prepared to sleep with Buzzard ("quite pleasant, though I didn't altogether want it"), but meetings with Scott-Kilvert were fruitless: "Sat for a long time with Ian—but his helplessness bored me. I have nothing to do with him, any more." It is likely that Isherwood was repelled by the sort of passivity and feeling of hopelessness that he was himself feeling. The psychological anxieties of his lovers suddenly seemed trivial beside what was happening in the world.

> Nothing matters but this crisis—nothing. We are all mad, and drowned with madness. It is ridiculous even to think of running away—for one would carry the madness with one. Those far-off towns where life is still sane and happy might as well be on the moon. I hardly even think of H[einz] now. I daren't. And [Vernon] is just a dream. At a moment like this it seems utterly impossible to understand why one was 'unhappy' in the old days. The memory now seems almost impossibly sweet and lovely. I had better think about them a good deal, now—if I want to keep some last shreds of sanity.

He was finding it difficult to sleep, had lost his appetite, smoked and masturbated incessantly, and spent much of his time gloomily recording his state in his diary. Katz's prognoses continued to depress him: general pronouncements such as "Europe is lost. English fascism in two years" had become horribly specific, and more horribly immediate, by September 24: "War is inevitable"; "London will be bombed in 2 or 3 days." Katz was not alone in these dire predictions, and everywhere he went Isherwood saw evidence of pessimism. Trenches were being dug in Hyde Park, railway stations were thronged with servicemen, and a notice from the local council about the issuing of gas-masks arrived at Pembroke Gardens. People were beginning to hoard tinned food and petrol was running short. A woman who heard a rumor that the government would order the destruction of all pets had her dog put down, and a man who committed suicide after hearing Hitler's Nuremberg speech left a note reading simply: "I have never been a hero. Selfish to the last." Olive Mangeot's lodgers were disappearing into the forces or the country and she was considering closing up her house and leaving London. Berthold Viertel said he feared that the government would soon start imprisoning foreign refugees such as himself. "Everybody is enlisting or running away," Isherwood reported on September 28. "I have written to the Foreign Office, to offer my services in propaganda work. Nanny is wonderful. She trots up and down stairs, with cups of Ovaltine." Not even Nanny, however, could stop history in its courses.

Although films still provided a refuge ("All troubles forgotten: that's what the

---

4. It was certainly unjust to Scott-Kilvert, who was quite as courageous as Heinz. He registered as a conscientious objector in the war and served in Africa with a Quaker ambulance service. Having decided that he was not, after all, a pacifist, he subsequently parachuted behind enemy lines in Greece, where he acted as an army liaison officer with the guerrillas.

films can do for you," he commented after seeing Mickey Rooney in *Boys' Town*),
Isherwood no longer found fame quite the drug it had been earlier in the year. He
went to see *The Ascent of F6* being recorded for television at the Alexandra Palace
studios, but couldn't be bothered to write about this in any detail. Once again, the
only thing to do was to work, and writing up his and Auden's China diaries was just
the sort of solid job he needed. On September 28 Auden returned from Brussels,
where he had been writing a sequence of sonnets for the book and being entertained
by a boy known as "*le Petit Jacques.*" There was still a great deal of work to do on
the book, and on the last day of September Isherwood made his final entry in his
diary. Chamberlain had returned from Munich the previous day, holding aloft his
piece of paper and declaring that the agreement signed by Britain, Germany, France
and Italy would produce "Peace in our time." The immediate crisis, it seemed, was
over.

> What was the worst moment? There were two. September 13, when, walking with
> Buzzard, I saw the news of the Sudeten ultimatum; and Sept 23, when Rolf rang
> up to say that the Czechs had mobilized, and war was certain. Both these occa-
> sions were bad because I wasn't alone. On both I was with pathic types—Richard
> [Buzzard] and Ian—whom I couldn't help, and who were therefore millstones
> round the neck. On Wednesday last [i.e September 28], when war seemed pretty
> certain, I was quite cold and calm, just a flicker of excitement.

Isherwood could certainly have helped Scott-Kilvert, had he wanted to, and his treatment of the young man was considered heartless by a number of their friends. Many
years later Isherwood wondered what might have happened if he had found Scott-
Kilvert waiting for him on the dock at Southampton when he returned from China.

> Suppose he had been there [. . .] and had convinced C[hristopher] that he still
> loved him? Would C have been so dazzled that he would have silenced his own
> doubts? Would they have remained together through the Munich crisis and the
> next eleven months, right up to the outbreak of War? It's improbable but just pos-
> sible. In those days, C's plans were all provisional. If he had had someone to stay
> in England for, he might never have gone to America.

Isherwood's notion of approaching the Foreign Office for war work came about
through Lehmann. On his return from Berlin, Lehmann had undergone another
mauvais quart d'heure while considering his relationship with Isherwood, but this
swiftly evaporated when they met for tea at the Athenaeum. "The odd, morbid doubt
about [Isherwood's] closeness to me that occurred almost immediately after our happiest meeting on my return from Berlin and the letters we wrote to one another, vanished again.[5] I saw that he wanted above all to be with me if anything happened."
Lehmann's morbid doubts were in fact justified, since Isherwood's desire to be with
him if war broke out was a matter of expediency rather than affection. Lehmann evi-

---

5. Lehmann was careful to keep all Isherwood's letters, but these have disappeared.

dently had useful contacts, and as Isherwood told him, "If we've got to have war, I'm going to see to it that I have a good war anyway." Lehmann noted that Isherwood seemed "amazingly light-hearted: as he's been in a state of alarm about war for five years, now that it's right at our elbow, perhaps in a way it's almost a relief for him." After discussions with one of his Foreign Office contacts, Lehmann wrote in his diary: "As far as I am concerned, probably the die is cast, & perhaps for C. as well."

Lehmann exerted pressure by proposing that, since in the event of war Kathleen and Richard planned to move to Wales and close down Pembroke Gardens for the duration, Isherwood should come to live with him in his London flat. Isherwood seemed grateful, but he was biding his time. He and Auden had decided to go to America in January, and Lehmann had proposed, against his better judgment, that they should write a travel book for the Hogarth Press based on their experiences there. Like many other people, Lehmann had assumed that his authors would spend no more than a few months in America before returning to England. Isherwood's final diary entry for 1938 does not mention the fact that he and Auden had that day visited Lehmann's office in order to sign a contract. Lehmann recorded Isherwood "sitting with his schemer's gleam on his face, watchful for signs of pleasant treachery in a flabby world." Isherwood had been scheming far more than Lehmann guessed. On their way to Lehmann's flat to interview the builder, they bought the papers with the news of "the sell-out of the Czechs." "Well that's the end of Europe as we wanted it," Lehmann said. "That doesn't matter any more to me," Isherwood replied: "I shall be in America." Lehmann was so stunned by this announcement that he simply recorded it, without any further comment, in his diary. He did, nevertheless, subsequently report "fantasies of joining C. in America," largely prompted by his Austrian boyfriend Toni Sikyr, who saw Isherwood as a pioneer who would go ahead to America to prepare the way for him and Lehmann. The fantasies would remain just that, however, for Lehmann had a far stronger and more grandiose sense of duty and destiny than Isherwood, and he decided that his place was in England, defying Hitler and maintaining some sort of international cultural exchange through his assorted publishing ventures.

If Auden and Isherwood intended to stay in America, then "Address Not Known," as their travel book was provisionally titled, would lose much of its point. According to Lehmann's later (public) recollections, the idea for the book was abandoned "when both Christopher and Wystan realized they were making a mistake in committing themselves to a book that would be little more than a repetition of something of which they had already exhausted the possibilities [in *Journey to a War*], a collaboration that was only keeping them from the work that was more essentially their own." In the diary he kept at the time, however, Lehmann revealed that the principal reason the book had been commissioned in the first place was in order to finance something else to which Isherwood had rashly committed himself.

Sometime during the autumn, Isherwood had acquired yet another new lover, one who would cause him more guilt and anxiety than all his other recent lovers put together. The son of a riveter, Jack Hewit had been born in Gateshead on Tyneside in 1917. His family background was unhappy, and his mother committed suicide when Jack was twelve, probably driven to it by her husband. His father had insisted that Jack, having left school at the age of fourteen, should be apprenticed to a plumber, but Jack had ambitions to be a dancer. He ran away to London and got a job as a page-boy at a hotel in Bayswater, where he shed his Geordie accent and was encouraged by some of the theatrical residents to go on the stage. He found an agent and was soon appearing in the chorus of *No, No, Nanette* at the South London Palace, near the Elephant and Castle. Hewit became a regular patron of the numerous homosexual pubs, clubs and bars that now existed in London, and it was at The 45 in 1937 that he met a Hungarian diplomat who invited him to a party at the War Office. Among the guests were Rolf Katz, who tried to pick him up, and a man Hewit recognized from his days at the South London Palace. This was Guy Burgess, who had been having an affair with one of the chorus boys and had been a regular stage-door johnny. Burgess now came to Hewit's rescue, detaching him from Katz and whisking him off to his flat in Chester Square.

Hewit soon found himself falling deeply in love with Burgess. This proved a bruising experience. "When you're young, you expect everything to be in apple-pie order and a one-to-one relationship to be a one-to-one relationship," he recalled. "But it never worked with Guy. He invented promiscuity. His theory was that anything from the age of seventeen [to] seventy-five was have-able, and he never stopped trying to prove it." Sometime in the autumn of 1938, when Hewit and Burgess were having one of their regular fallings-out, they bumped into Isherwood in the foyer of a cinema in Leicester Square. Isherwood had known Burgess, who worked as an assistant in the Talks Department at the BBC, for about a year. Burgess had recently commissioned him to do a talk about China, which was due to be broadcast in November.

Unlike Ian Scott-Kilvert, Hewit was anything but untouchable. "I'd been passed around from hand to mouth since I was about fifteen," he recalled. Isherwood invited him out to dinner and they shortly embarked on an affair. Isherwood claimed that when Burgess realized what was going on, he asked Isherwood whether he was in love with Hewit. When Isherwood replied (untruthfully) that he was, Burgess was content. "He had other fish to fry," as Hewit put it—the chief fish being a very beautiful and rich young man named Peter Pollock, with whom Burgess had become besotted. It was therefore very convenient for him to offload Hewit onto Isherwood, having salved his conscience by first ascertaining that Isherwood's motives were honorable. Isherwood believed that Hewit fell seriously in love with him, though Hewit always denied this. "I *liked* him. All right, I *loved* him, but I wasn't *in love* with him, and there's a difference," he said toward the end of his life. "I've only ever been in love once in my life"—with Burgess—"I don't think it ever happens again. The only person that Christopher ever felt deeply about was Heinz."

Indeed, one of the reasons Isherwood was attracted to Hewit was that he bore a slight physical resemblance to Heinz, in his build and in the fullness of his mouth. Isherwood even got Hewit to part his hair on the other side so as to increase this resemblance. It was well known in Isherwood's circle that he was still obsessed by Heinz and that any lovers he took on would always be a substitute rather than a person in his own right. (Hewit remembered that there were jokes going around about the 57 varieties of Heinz.) It is hardly surprising, then, that Isherwood's affairs were so thwarted at this period.

Whatever Hewit may have claimed subsequently, he had evidently begun to see his future with Isherwood and was keen to accompany his new lover to America. Isherwood had weakly agreed to Hewit's proposal without properly reckoning the financial and emotional implications. Writing about "Address Not Known" in his diary, Lehmann revealed that the only reason Isherwood had grudgingly agreed to take on the book was so that he could pay for Hewit to accompany him across the Atlantic. When Isherwood visited Lehmann in early December in order to discuss the American trip and to admit his doubts about Hewit as a suitable companion, Lehmann leaped in to agree. He was in a strong position to do so, since he had only recently been subjected by Isherwood to a lecture about the unsuitability of one of his own lovers. Isherwood had told Lehmann that he should not string this young man along, which as Lehmann recognized was precisely what Isherwood had been doing to Hewit. At the time, Lehmann had been furious, fulminating against "the enormity of [Isherwood's] moral lecture" and the "masterly hypocrisy only the English are capable of, and a ruthlessness of illusionism only C. is capable of." According to Lehmann, Isherwood subsequently felt he had behaved badly, and his guilt made it all the easier for Lehmann to make the case against Hewit.

> The more I urged the fatal mistake of him & W[ystan] doing this book, [. . .] & added pleas for him to look at the J. business with a little hard-headedness (I recapitulated my view of all recent infatuations in their inevitable recurrent pattern) the more he weakened, the more I urged the necessity for him to be alone, with the dignity of an artist alone (except for Heinz) & write above all novels, the more he turned against all his plans, until suddenly he exclaimed: 'For God's sake someone get me out of this!' The rest of the evening was devoted to considering precisely the ways & means of getting him 'out of this'.

They talked so far into the night that Isherwood was obliged to sleep at Lehmann's flat. Lehmann feared that once alone his friend would change his mind—"I can't bear you being out there, thinking different thoughts," he shouted pathetically through the bedroom door—but in the morning Isherwood's resolve remained firm. He would try to break the news gently to Hewit that he was Not Wanted on Voyage. Lehmann characteristically referred to this incident as the "colossal victory in the battle for C."

On the Frontier was due to go into rehearsal for its premiere in November at the Arts Theatre in Cambridge, after which it was hoped to transfer it to London's West End. The least satisfactory of the Auden-Isherwood plays, it was highly topical, being concerned with a war between Ostnia, an exhausted monarchist democracy, and Westland, a fascist dictatorship. Auden had complained that when Doone got hold of the plays he covered them with his "spittle"—"God, why doesn't he DIE," he appealed to Spender. On the Frontier was nevertheless, as promised, a Group Theatre production, directed by Doone, designed by Medley and with music by Britten. Maynard Keynes may have revised his opinion of Auden and Isherwood as playwrights, but he nevertheless felt that he needed to keep a schoolmasterly eye on these two young men, and on October 5 wrote to Isherwood proposing a "general conference." In preparation for this he thought it would do no harm to concentrate their minds a little:

> I have no doubt that you have been giving thought to the plot of the play in the light of recent events. It is a bit unlucky that the development of history is so near

to the facts and yet so far from them! Do you still feel that you can go through with it in precisely its present form without feeling at all silly? If there were to be a new inspiration, which might be possible without any change whatever in the main fabric, I should not be sorry to hear of its occurrence.

The authors declined to make further alterations to a play that had been substantially revised several times, although the intervention of the Lord Chamberlain's office meant that references to Westland's "Leader," "Storm Troopers" and "Labour Camps" had to be altered so as not to offend Nazi Germany. This story was picked up by some of the newspapers, the *Star* informing its readers that

> Mr Auden is the young poet who was awarded the King's Gold Medal for Poetry, and Mr Isherwood almost as distinguished an Englishman. Their plays are therefore of national importance these days, and it seems, international importance as well. This is the only possible reason why the Censor, who had altered scarcely anything else in this new play about dictators, has cut out the word 'Leader'.
>
> English poets, as it happens, are ingenious.
>
> Their Westland dictator will be called Guidanto. That is Esperanto for 'Leader'.

Describing it as "A Play for the People," the reporter, who had attended rehearsals, informed readers that *On the Frontier* was "full of controversy, strongly topical and extraordinarily vital." This was just the sort of publicity the Arts Theatre wanted. They produced a flyer which stated:

> This lyrical melodrama of the psychology of contemporary war will have an appeal to all who have an interest in the reactions of human beings to the tension of the modern crisis, or in the literary, poetical and musical developments of drama in the hands of the most gifted representatives of the younger generation, or in the movement towards new theatrical forms as shown in the productions of the Group Theatre. This is the most exciting theatrical event seen in Cambridge for some time.

First-night invitations were sent to numerous political and pacifist organizations, including the Peace Pledge Union, the Labour League of Youth, the League of Nations Union and the Friends of the Soviet Union.

The play opened on November 14, with Maynard Keynes's wife, the former ballerina Lydia Lopokova, in the role of Anna, the play's Juliet. Keynes gave a dinner for the authors, which was also attended by T. S. Eliot and Ashley Dukes. "You certainly gave the boys a great send-off," Eliot wrote the following day. He thought the play worked well, but felt that "Hitler is not quite the simpleton that the authors made him out to be." Dukes congratulated Keynes for "giving these two undergraduates another chance to graduate." Although he felt the play showed no advance on *F6*, he nevertheless thought that Auden and Isherwood "at their best make all other young writers seem like tuppence halfpenny. Their instant contact with the intelligence of the audience, which was most marked in the first act, has something really valuable, and promises big things for the future." Not everyone agreed, and Auden and Isherwood were subjected to an extraordinary attack in the *Observer* by the notoriously reactionary playwright and critic St. John Ervine. He described them as "incorrigibly middle-class, suburban in the marrow of their bones," and wondered if they had "ever seen or spoken to a workman in their somewhat precious lives." He particularly objected to Mrs. Thorvald's line about her servant saying that war is inevitable and predicted in Revelation: "She tried to explain it to me, but she's so difficult to understand: her false teeth fit so badly." "What gales of girlish laughter that jest must have evoked from the Boy Bolshies of Cambridge." Other reviews were more measured, and on the whole favorable, and Isherwood himself later described *On the Frontier* as the "best-constructed, least successful" of the plays he wrote with Auden.

By December 2, Isherwood had finished his part of *Journey to a War,* and in the middle of the month he ducked out of his BBC contract to do another radio talk (causing Burgess's knuckles to be rapped), and went to Brussels with Auden in order to collate their material. They were accompanied by Hewit, who appears to have recovered from his disappointment about New York—probably because Isherwood fudged the issue and suggested that once settled he would send for him. Hewit was not the only person Isherwood had to deal with: Ian Scott-Kilvert now wrote to him to say that he wanted to give their relationship one more chance. Isherwood traveled to Cambridge, where Scott-Kilvert "came on very strong, rolling about with [me] on the sitting-room floor and urging [me] to come up with him to bed." But it was too late, and Isherwood refused. He returned to London and then took the boat train to Brussels with Hewit.

Isherwood rented a flat at Rue de Stassart 29, in a residential area slightly to the north of the center of Brussels. It consisted of a single room with a bed behind a partition, and a small kitchen which also contained a bath. While Isherwood corrected the proofs of *Goodbye to Berlin,* Hewit cooked, shopped and kept house. He also provided company, which Isherwood always craved, and they spent most evenings in the pubs and bars, often with Gerald Hamilton, who was currently living in the city. Auden, who was staying in a nearby square and turned up each morning to work on *Journey to a War,* thoroughly approved of Hewit, who he thought had a "feminine soul" and was an ideal partner for Isherwood. "My married life is being a great success," Isherwood informed Lehmann. This did not, however, prevent him from conducting other liaisons with "the trade of Old Brussels," as Auden characterized it. As a result, he contracted gonorrhea.

Auden made a sly reference to this infection in the final lines of "The Novelist," one of a series of sonnets he wrote in Brussels during December. Although this poem is a general statement about the novelist's art and duties, Auden clearly had Isherwood in mind. Unlike a poet such as Auden himself, given to grand statements and abstract generalizations, the novelist has to create characters by a process of empathy,

> *must*
> *Become the whole of boredom, subject to*
> *Vulgar complaints like love, among the Just*

Be just, among the Filthy filthy too,
And in his own weak person, if he can,
Must suffer dully all the wrongs of Man.

As in "August for the people" and (in a lighter mode) "Who is that funny-looking young man," Auden reminds Isherwood of the expectations he had of him back at Oxford when he envisaged him indeed as "the Novelist."

Journey to a War was completed in mid-December and the typescript was dispatched to Faber in London. Isherwood and Auden decided to remain in Brussels to await proofs of the text and Auden's photos, which would form an extensive "picture commentary" in the finished book. "We decided to cut out the dialogue between Hong Kong and Macao," Isherwood told his mother. "Wystan wrote two more sonnets, instead. I'm afraid readers are going to get very little for their money." The finished book consisted, as one reviewer put it, "of a sandwich; two layers of poetry with a meaty prose between." (Writing about the book in the *Spectator,* Evelyn Waugh affected to believe that Faber had "hit on a new dodge" for selling poetry by incorporating it in "a more solid and marketable work.") The prose "travel-diary," although presented as if it were Isherwood's, was in fact the work of both authors. They had each kept diaries, which Isherwood subsequently collated, edited and rewrote to make a consistent first-person narrative. The voice is certainly Isherwood's, familiar in its self-deprecation and mockery from *Lions and Shadows.* Indeed, although the authors diligently record facts and figures and attempt a serious overview of the war, the book turns out to be another absurdist Isherwood comedy, in which the narrator is "all too conscious of being Little Me in China," as he later put it.

Throughout the book, Isherwood self-mockingly contrasts his own nervousness in the face of any danger with Auden's "monumental calm." The description of their first air raid is characteristic. While taking tea with their missionary hosts, Isherwood becomes aware of a worrying noise:

> Somewhere, from far away across the river, came a succession of dull, heavy thuds; felt rather than heard. And then, thin and distinct, the whine which a mosquito makes, when it dives for your face in the dark. Only this wasn't a mosquito. More thuds. I looked round at the others. Was it possible that they hadn't noticed? Clearing my throat, I said as conversationally as I could manage: 'Isn't that an air-raid?'
>
> Our hostess glanced up, smiling, from the tea-tray: 'Yes, I expect it is. They come over about this time, most afternoons . . . Do you take milk and sugar?'

It is stressed throughout that for all their left-wing affiliations and journalistic accreditation, Isherwood and Auden are essentially amateurs. Driven in the Consul-General's car to see the mayor of Canton, Isherwood writes: "This was our first attempt at a professional interview, and we were anxious not to disgrace ourselves. Seated proud but nervous behind the consular chauffeur, and the fluttering Union Jack on the bonnet, we wondered what questions we should ask him." The interview is, of course, farcical, the mayor speaking the sort of English familiar from popular detective stories set in Limehouse: "We not wan' to fight Japanese. Japan wan' to fight *us*! Ha, ha, ha. Japan velly foolish. First she wan' to be number *tree* power. Then number *two*. Then number *one*. Japan industrial country, you see. Suppose we go Japan, dlop bomb—woo-er, boom! Velly bad for Japanese, I tink?" And so on.

A German aide-de-camp is similarly caricatured, but then so are the authors themselves. Isherwood affects a getup—beret, cavalry boots and turtleneck sweater—that "would not be out of place in Valencia or Madrid," a war zone he conspicuously failed to get to, of course, unlike Auden, as he pointedly reminds the reader. Just as in *Lions and Shadows* we know that when Isherwood buys a motorbike he will be unable to ride it properly, so in this book we know that the smart riding-boots which he has had specially hand-made for the trip will fail to impress anyone and turn out to be extremely uncomfortable. Auden's "immense, shapeless overcoat and woolen Jaeger cap" may look ridiculous but are at least practical. As they set off toward the Front in rickshaws, accompanied by their dapper servant, who looks as if he "might be about to wait at a Hankow consular dinner-party," Isherwood reflects that "Collectively, perhaps, we most resemble a group of characters in one of Jules Verne's stories about lunatic English explorers." Some of the reportage has a distinctly dutiful feel about it, and the book is at its best when Isherwood describes such episodes as their visit to The Longest Journey, a preposterous hotel in the Kuling hills run by an eccentric Englishman who could have given Mr. Norris a run for his money. Several pages are devoted to this louche establishment, with its fetching staff of boys and its enjoyable prep-school atmosphere. It is wholly characteristic of the book that of the many news releases put out by the China Information Committee on such topics as "Trade revival in Western China" and "Humanitarian services of the Chinese Red Cross," the one the authors chose to reprint is about hairdressing, and starts with the stirring declaration that "With the tide of war surging on many fronts, the 'permanent wave' is now at its very ebb in China."

This sort of larking did not please all readers. "There are only two good reasons for journeying to a country racked with war," wrote Randall Swingler sternly in the *Daily Worker* when the book was published the following March: "to find out what is really happening and to report it or to participate." Auden and Isherwood had fallen victim to bourgeois subjectivity: they were "too preoccupied with their own psychological plight to be anything but helplessly lost in the struggle of modern China." He concluded that "It is impossible to escape the impression that the authors are playing: playing at being war correspondents, at being Englishmen, at being poets."

While Auden and Isherwood were waiting for proofs of the book they had a row with Lehmann, who had been counting on including some of the China material in the next issue of *New Writing*. Isherwood told Lehmann that there was nothing left over apart from "shavings and scraps, and they are worse than useless." "At first it upset me badly," Lehmann wrote of this letter in his diary. "I felt: he always leaves you holding the baby. Then, after sleepless hours at night, I acquitted him, feeling I was being unjust, seeing how loyally he has supported me the last year." Evidently, acquittal did not mean that Isherwood would be getting off without a stern caution, and Lehmann fired off an aggrieved letter, to which Isherwood was obliged to reply that "only my best is good enough for N.W.—and if I can't give it, I can't." He told Lehmann, who was constantly at odds with Leonard Woolf at the Hogarth Press, that he should make more use of the advisory board, on which both Isherwood and Auden served. They would also be glad to read any submissions to the Press that Lehmann cared to send them. Although Lehmann confided to his diary that this was "the letter I have really been waiting for [. . .] to show that he was with me, would in the end always rally, could always be depended on in the last instance about our schemes," he was not about to admit that he was pacified. "And how, may I ask, are you to lighten my work of reading at the Press, if you use England rather as I use The Bath Club—to drop in very occasionally and watch a distasteful species at play?" he demanded. "A few weeks a year you seem to be available, and then off on the great trek again [. . .] The simple fact is, not merely that you're rarely to be found, but that people must (and most certainly should) be rewarded for reading work, and the H.P. just can't afford a heavy overhead on this item." He nevertheless sent Isherwood the manuscript of *Party Going,* the third in a series of dense, elliptical novels written by an eccentric businessman named Henry Yorke under the nom de plume of Henry Green. Dent had turned the book down, and although Lehmann was very keen to publish it, the Woolfs were undecided. Isherwood read the manuscript and his enthusiasm—one that extended to Green's subsequent books and led to a cordial friendship between the two writers—tipped the balance. This was the sort of long-distance support for which Lehmann was always grateful.

Isherwood also started sketching out a new novel. It is not clear from his correspondence what this was, but he told Lehmann that he would not be able to make any progress on it until he got to America. Although it is almost certain that Isherwood and Auden had decided to return to America when they were in New York in the summer of 1938, Isherwood had remained strategically vague as to his exact plans. Kathleen evidently believed, as Lehmann had until brutally disabused by Isherwood, that Christopher and Wystan were merely off on another "great trek." Isherwood had assured her that although the situation in Europe appeared no better, his own future looked bright. The wife of the first secretary at the British embassy in Brussels was a palm-reader and had told Isherwood that he would make a lot of money in 1940. She also told him: "I see a capital letter in your hand. It's the name of someone who has been of great importance in your life. The name begins with H." Naturally, Isherwood took this to refer to Heinz, although it might equally have referred to Hewit, to Uncle Henry, who had certainly been of financial importance, or indeed to Vernon, whose real name began with "H." Heinz, however, was most on Isherwood's mind at the time because he had failed to answer any letters. Isherwood had been sending money to Berlin and was worried that this might have got Heinz into trouble. In fact, Heinz had been receiving the letters and telephoned Pembroke Gardens and spoke to Kathleen. He had thought Isherwood was leaving for America before Christmas and wanted to speak to him before he went.

Isherwood and Auden spent Christmas and the New Year in Brussels, and on New Year's Eve Auden hosted a party at which he recited "Ode to the New Year," in which he addressed those present, as well as absent friends, and the complaisant boys with

which Brussels apparently teemed. He summed up their present lives and made predictions, or merely gave good wishes, for 1939. After apostrophizing the city of
Brussels, Auden next addressed Isherwood:

> *Dear Christopher, always a sort of*
> *Conscience to which I'd confess*
> *In the years before Hitler was thought of*
> *Or the guinea-pig had a success;*
> *Now reviewers are singing your praises,*
> *And lovers are scratching your back,*
> *But, O, how unhappy your face is,*
> *So I wish you the peace that you lack;*
> *May your life in the States become better,*
> *May the shadow of grief disappear,*
> *But—God!—if you ever turn heter,*
> *I won't wish you a Happy New Year.*

As Isherwood acknowledged in his long self-analysis, and as Auden had already
demonstrated in "Who is that funny-looking young man," his best friend knew him
"behind the façade." He knew, for example, that Isherwood, for all his boasts about
married life, did not treat Hewit all that well. His New Year's hope for Hewit in the
poem was that "You *will* find One worth your devotion." As Isherwood rightly observed, "I think Auden identified with Jack, a little."

On January 8, 1939, Isherwood returned to England. He and Auden were sailing
to America on the nineteenth, and the days before were spent packing and seeing old friends, although Isherwood also had time to give a lecture on social conditions in China at the Chelsea Polytechnic, as a favor to Olive Mangeot, who was now
a leading member of the local Labour Party. It was probably during this period that
Isherwood burned the diary he had kept in Berlin. He had mined it very thoroughly
for both *Mr Norris* and *Goodbye to Berlin* and it had now—or so he thought—served
its literary purpose. He was also concerned that the diary, which gave a detailed account of his sexual exploits and implicated numerous young men in Berlin, might
somehow fall into the hands of the authorities and cause all sorts of problems. He
preferred to tell people that he had "destroyed his real Past because he preferred the
simplified, more creditable, more exciting fictitious Past which he had created to take
its place," but admitted that this explanation was "unconvincing." It was another instance of play-acting, and although it is true that he was to some extent tidying up
that past and putting it behind him before heading for a new life in America, he was
careful to keep other diaries from this period, including ones covering his time with
Basil Fry in Bremen and with Fronny in Greece.

On January 15 he had lunch with Upward and tea with Forster, then went to the
Café Royal for a farewell dinner with Viertel and Beatrix Lehmann. Since Isherwood
recognized that the parting from Kathleen and Richard was likely to be painful and
prolonged, he and Auden arranged to spend their last night in England on board the
Champlain, which was docked at Southampton. On the evening of January 17, Ben-

jamin Britten and his new friend, the tenor Peter Pears, held a small farewell party for the two travelers in their recently acquired flat at 67 Hallam Street, just around the corner from Broadcasting House. They had invited a curious and rather uneasy mix of old friends and current lovers: Forster, Stephen and Inez Spender, Olive Mangeot, Robert Moody, Bill and Nancy Coldstream, Jack Hewit, a young German friend of Britten named Wulff Scherchen, and someone described by Coldstream as "a boy Wystan had met at Bryanston," probably Michael Yates, whom he in fact met at the Downs School. According to Coldstream,

> The evening was slightly sticky—probably because Benjamin does not like Stephen and Inez very much because he most likely knows that they don't like his music. Also the presence of two anti-boy women, Nancy and Inez, complicated the atmosphere because Benjamin likes to be with Wystan & Christopher, all boys together without disturbing foreign elements such as slightly hostile ladies or gentlemen hostile to the gay music. [. . .]
>
> Hedli Anderson came in very theatrical & self-assured. 'Queen of the boys tonight.' [. . .] She sat on the piano and sang Wystan's songs & Benjamin played with great gusto.

Pears subsequently sang Britten's setting of one of Spender's poems, during which Isherwood was observed looking "very bright & dry like a sardonic Robin." After the party, Isherwood stayed the night in Bloomsbury, probably at Forster's flat, returning to Pembroke Gardens at midday. "The horrid day," as Kathleen called it, was spent in writing letters and making the final arrangements for his departure. At 6:30 p.m. Hewit arrived in a taxi in order to take Isherwood to the boat train at Waterloo. "M[ummy] cried when I left," Isherwood recalled,

> I cried, Jackie cried in the taxi to the station and gave me a keepsake, his first champagne cork. Forster, who had come to see us off, asked me 'Shall I join the communist party?' I forget what I answered. I think it was 'No'. At any rate the question was oracular. The departing and dying are credited with a kind of psychic wisdom.
>
> As the train pulled out, there was a nasty sharp wrench, and then, as always when I am a traveller, a quick upsurge of guilty relief. Auden and I exchanged grins—grins which took us back, in an instant, to the earliest days of our friendship. Suddenly, we were twelve and nine years old. 'Well,' I said, 'we're off again.' 'Goody,' said Auden.

part two

BECOMING AN AMERICAN

THIRTEEN

T HE JOURNEY TO NEW YORK LASTED A WEEK. AS THE SHIP MADE
its slow way through the stormy Atlantic, Isherwood and Auden took stock.
They had left England at a time when their reputation, both individually and
as a team, was extremely high. Throughout 1938 they had been very much in the public eye, both in print and in person, and were regarded as "the 'heavenly twins' of the
avant-garde in English literature." Their trip to China had been widely reported; although *Journey to a War* had not yet been published, various articles about their experiences had already appeared, and they had both given lectures and made
broadcasts. Similarly, although *Goodbye to Berlin* had yet to go through the press,
several of the episodes had been published in advance to considerable acclaim, and
Lions and Shadows had attracted a great deal of favorable notice. Newspapers and
periodicals had recently reviewed both the production and the published text of *On
the Frontier*. In Cyril Connolly's *Enemies of Promise,* which (among other things)
provided a magisterial overview of the contemporary state of English letters in 1938,
Auden had been described as the country's "one poet of genius" and Isherwood had
been hailed as "the hope of English fiction."

The temptations and dangers of fame were apparent to them both and had been
fully rehearsed in *The Ascent of F6,* in which Ransom is cajoled and flattered into
leading the expedition against all his best instincts. "Your temptation, Mr Ransom, is
written in your face," he is told by an abbot just before he begins the disastrous ascent.
"You know your powers and your intelligence. You could ask the world to follow you
and it would serve you with blind obedience." People were more inclined to look to
Auden (who wrote this scene) than to Isherwood for this sort of leadership, but both
men felt they had spent far too much time pontificating in public, "running all over the
place chatting about China," as Auden put it dismissively. "When I look at the newspapers I wonder what the hell I'm doing," he confided to a friend. Isherwood too had
spent the last year wondering what the hell he was doing, and he knew that his es-
pousal of left-wing causes was even more suspect than Auden's. It was symptomatic

of their disenchantment, he later felt, that their most recent play, *On the Frontier,* was "dutifully leftist, but the only really sympathetic character is Valerian, the tycoon."

Now that they had cast off together into the unknown, Isherwood "was able, literally, to speak his mind—to say things which he hadn't known were in it, until the moment of speaking."

> One morning on deck, it seems to me, I turned to Auden and said: 'You know, I just don't believe in any of it any more—the united front, the party line, the antifascist struggle. I suppose they're okay, but something's wrong with me. I simply can't swallow another mouthful.' And Auden answered: 'Neither can I.'
> Those were not our words, but psychologically it was as simple as that.

It was not, of course, *quite* as simple as that. This account was written retrospectively and exists in at least two versions. Isherwood also claimed that he had realized, with equal suddenness and simplicity, that he was, and had always been, a pacifist—although elsewhere he suggested that disillusionment over the Spanish Civil War and the sight of the dead and injured in China had some bearing on his becoming one. It suited Isherwood's self-mythologizing to present his passage to America as a road to Damascus: in fact he was in no psychological state to make any rational decisions about his life. It would take several months, but eventually he would be able to acknowledge that he had got into a terrible muddle, both in his beliefs and in his personal relationships.

He later wrote that "Both Auden and I felt it was our duty to tell our friends what had happened. We wrote to most of them soon after our arrival in New York." The correspondents Isherwood specifically mentions are Kathleen, Lehmann, Upward, Forster, Spender and Olive Mangeot. In fact, although his letters to Kathleen frequently mention the worsening situation in Europe, he did not tell her "what had happened" until the end of March, two months after he had arrived in New York. Forster and Spender were told at the end of April, Lehmann at the beginning of May. He could not bring himself to write to Upward until August 6 and only then in reply to a letter he had received—which, perhaps significantly, has not survived. Upward had evidently heard Isherwood's news from Olive Mangeot, whose letter from Isherwood no longer exists, but must have been written sometime in the summer.

Isherwood's rejection of politics was connected with his leaving England for America and thus finally cutting himself off from everything against which he had rebelled—"separating himself from Mother and Motherland at one stroke." The real question, however, is not whether he suddenly stopped believing in the united front, the party line and the anti-fascist struggle, but whether he had ever really believed in any of it in the first place. Throughout the 1930s he frequently gave the impression that he was not so much a fellow traveler as someone who was simply coming along for the ride. The friends he made during his youth undoubtedly influenced his political opinions, such as they were, but his social outlook was intimately bound up with his own family background. He was always a great deal more interested in attacking the class he came from than in alleviating the lot of the people that class had supposedly oppressed and exploited. By removing himself from his mother's sphere of influence, he was in effect becoming apolitical.

His principal interest was always people rather than politics, effects rather than causes. He was in Berlin not as a political commentator but as someone observing the consequences of politics quite literally at street level. Although he had seen the rise of fascism at first hand in Germany and had every reason to oppose it, his opposition was personal rather than strictly political, and was chiefly motivated by Heinz. Judging by what he wrote at the time, Isherwood was even more enraged by the British customs authorities for not allowing Heinz into England than he was by the Nazis. They were all "the Enemy." "Edward [Upward] had always said, quite rightly, that my mind was unfitted for abstract ideas," Isherwood noted;

> it could only grasp concrete examples, special instances. Anti-Nazism had been possible for me as long as Nazism meant Hitler, Goering and Goebbels, the Gestapo, and the consuls and spies who potentially menaced Heinz on his travels. But now Heinz was caught. He had become, however unwillingly, a part of the Nazi war machine, at work in a Berlin factory. Now Werner [Jahr] was helping to build the Siegfried line, and dozens of boys I had known were in the German army.
>
> Suppose I have in my power an army of six million men. I can destroy it by pressing an electric button. The six millionth man is Heinz. Will I press the button? Of course not—even if the 5,999,999 others are hundred per cent Jew-baiting blood-mad fiends (which is absurd).

Almost any position Isherwood took was empirical, and he later wrote: "It is useless for the reader to ask me indignantly, 'Can you pretend that you would still be a pacifist if you belonged to a racial minority threatened with extermination?' I can't tell him. I haven't been in that situation. So I don't know." This is both logical and consistent with Isherwood's approach to life, but in its refusal to embrace imagination it seems evasive.

In fact, Isherwood had several very good reasons for being a pacifist, one of which was that he was the son of a professional soldier who had refused to take warfare seriously. Frank had nevertheless gone off to the First World War and died in it. Not only had Isherwood lost his father, and witnessed the effect of that loss upon his mother, but he had been brought up on the literature of protest that had gradually emerged from that conflict during the 1920s and 1930s. Isherwood's reluctance to take part in a war in which German "boys" would be slaughtered owes more than a little to the attitudes of Wilfred Owen, one of the guiding spirits of his and Upward's adolescence. Stephen Spender acknowledged the influence of writers such as Owen and Siegfried Sassoon, whose work is notable for its homoerotic concern of officers for their men, on the political ideology of his generation of writers. It is also possible that Isherwood had been influenced by Benjamin Britten, who was a pacifist of long standing and who also planned to go to America at about this time. Peter Pears recalled that he and Britten had "decided—as Auden had decided earlier—that the only thing to do was to go to America" if war broke out in Europe. This gives the impression that they were following Auden's lead, but Britten had in fact been considering an extended trip to America since October 1937, when Pears had gone there on a concert tour. It seems inconceivable that Isherwood, who had become a close friend of Britten during 1938, had not discussed with him both pacifism and the possibility of living in America.

None of this alters the fact that Isherwood knew that he was running away, and he would repeatedly have to justify both to himself and to other people his and Auden's decision to go to America at a time when a European war seemed inevitable. Auden did not really give a damn what other people thought of him, but Isherwood craved public approval, and continued, throughout his life, to provide numerous explanations for what others called his "desertion." It wasn't a question of cowardice or a fear of death or injury: he and Auden had exposed themselves to physical danger in China and discovered that they were not particularly frightened by air raids. It was more a dread of the regimented life of soldiering, the conformity and obedience it demanded. Isherwood did not want to be like Heinz, swallowed up by a military machine. "He didn't want to be caught, like his father was," Upward decided. Throughout 1939, Isherwood assured correspondents in England that he would come back if war broke out. It was almost as if he were trying to convince himself.

To Auden's disgust, the *Daily Express* had reported that in America he would "be reunited with his wife, Erika Mann, daughter of the Nobel prize-winner Thomas Mann, who is now a don at Princeton." It also reported the circumstances of the marriage, details of which the journalist could only have got from someone who knew Auden personally. (Gerald Hamilton seems the most likely source.) Although such a reunion had never been the purpose of Auden's trip, the first person to welcome the two travelers to New York was indeed Erika, who along with her brother Klaus came out to the *Champlain* on the quarantine launch. To ensure that Vernon would not make the same mistake as Ian Scott-Kilvert, Isherwood had radioed ahead to shore asking the young man to meet him on the quay. He had corresponded with Vernon while he was in England, but must have viewed this reunion with some trepidation. It was not just Vernon himself who gave him pause, but all that he represented: the New World Isherwood wanted to embrace. He was also, however, still attached to the Old World in the person of Jack Hewit. Although Isherwood had left Hewit "under the impression that he would soon be sent for," he later wondered whether this had been a ruse.

> It's impossible now [in 1971, over thirty years later] to be quite certain, but I would say that C[hristopher] never had any intention of sending for Jack. I think C had grown tired of him before leaving England and was merely afraid to tell Jack so because Jack was so much in love with him and so emotional and potentially desperate. At most he thought of Jack as a kind of understudy who might conceivably be called upon in the event of a highly improbable crisis—that is to say, if C was unable to find himself an American boyfriend. But C had [Vernon] already waiting for him in New York.[1]

---

1. Hewit disputed this version of events. He maintained that Isherwood had merely said to him: "If I sent for you, would you come?" He was, he said, still involved with Guy Burgess and was never in love with Isherwood, desperately or otherwise. There is, however, considerable evidence to suggest that while Isherwood may have exaggerated Hewit's devotion, Hewit *had* been hoping to join him in America.

As instructed, Vernon was waiting for Isherwood, and they immediately resumed their affair. Vernon's previous sexual experiences had been heterosexual, but his life at this point was rather rootless. He was unsure what he wanted to do, and was, he remembered, "desperately wanting to get a handle on all the new experience that came my way." "Chris spoke at some length on the positive aspects of male relationships," he recalled, "loyalty, devotion, commitment and of course Classical Greeks. It sounded very idealistic, feasible and appealing."

Hewit was not forgotten, however. "I miss Jacky terribly," Isherwood told Lehmann three weeks after arriving in New York, but his principal feeling about him was one of guilt.[2] As a parting gift, he had agreed to pay for Hewit to take a course in shorthand and typing at the Pitman School, in the hope that this would lead to some form of gainful employment, and Lehmann had been deputized to organize the payments. Isherwood sent Hewit noncommittal letters, but rarely received a reply. "I wrote to him only the other day," Isherwood assured Lehmann, "but goodness knows what happens to *his* letters. I suppose they are piling up somewhere, misdirected, against the Day of Judgement. . . ." As late as May, he was still telling Vernon that he "would have to bring [Hewit] to America sooner or later."

O n their arrival in New York, Isherwood and Auden booked into the George Washington Hotel at Twenty-third and Lexington, which despite its name was a little bit of England in Manhattan. The proprietor was an eccentric and flamboyant man with the happy name of Donald Neville-Willing, who ran the hotel, Isherwood recalled, "as though he were the Victorian housekeeper of an English ancestral mansion." An ancestral mansion Neville-Willing knew all about was Marple Hall, since he originally came from Manchester, and he was delighted to have a Bradshaw-Isherwood to stay. He charged his two guests low rates and invited them to tea in his private rooms, which were hung with framed photographs of the British royal family. Although highly "respectable," the hotel numbered a large number of actors from Broadway shows among its guests. The atmosphere struck Vernon, who shortly moved into the hotel from the room he had been renting a few blocks away, as "very theatrical." Vernon swiftly became "very much one of the family," Isherwood told Lehmann. "Indeed, he goes around so much with Wystan to parties that many people must think it's a Design for Living."[3]

Although Isherwood took great pleasure in Vernon's company, he found life in New York unsatisfactory. While Auden, fueled by daily intakes of Benzedrine, was working furiously and seemed to adapt to the city immediately, Isherwood was in a daze of indecision and inertia. Auden claimed that he disliked the attention and publicity they were receiving—it was indeed one of the reasons he had decided to leave England—but he appeared to be very good at dealing with journalists and making public appearances. Isherwood, who had always enjoyed attention and was a past master at playing

---

2. Isherwood was inconsistent when spelling Hewit's pet name: Jacky and Jackie seem to have been interchangeable.

3. Isherwood is referring to Noël Coward's bold 1933 play about a triangular relationship between two men and a woman.

to the gallery, lost all his enthusiasm for, and skill at, appearing on public platforms. "It is a little as if he and I had changed places," he noted ruefully in his diary.[4] At a dinner at the Algonquin Hotel, he misunderstood the nature of the evening and, called upon to speak first, disgraced himself by making a facetious speech to the assembled members of the PEN Club, who had gathered for an anti-fascist meeting. Auden, by contrast, read an impressive new poem in memory of W. B. Yeats, who had just died. Isherwood began to feel that New York was defeating him.

> It had been easy to find the city thrilling when I had visited it previously in 1938. The hugeness of the buildings, the crowds, the noise had stimulated me, as long as I was experiencing them as a foreign tourist. [Now] I had to face the fact that this was to be the scene of my life, my creative activity and my wage-earning in the foreseeable future. And, at once, I began to feel scared. I suspected that I couldn't cope. And, having suspected, I was sure that I couldn't.

Money was certainly a major difficulty, and after five weeks in the city, Isherwood had earned only $15. A production of *Dogskin* had been mooted, but although the two authors spent some time revising the play, no agreement could be reached between them and the theater company. As Isherwood explained to his mother, "They want very childish alterations, which would increase the topical value of the production for one week after writing them, and would be hopelessly out of date in a fortnight, since history moves so fast." They had clearly learned their lesson with *On the Frontier.* Isherwood was also trying unsuccessfully to start a new novel and write a story for the magazine *Redbook.* The story was guaranteed to bring in a very welcome $400, but he never managed to complete it. Although he and Auden were granted concessionary rates, the George Washington was still a hotel, and their living costs were high, particularly since the exchange rate was against them. "A dollar, which costs about four and threepence to buy, has the purchasing power of barely half a crown," Isherwood complained to Kathleen. Quite apart from his own expenses, he was paying Hewit's tutorial fees and an allowance to Heinz, whose enforced work on a building site in the Potsdamerplatz had been interrupted when he suffered a hernia. Bennett Cerf of Random House, who had published the Auden-Isherwood plays, was due to publish *Goodbye to Berlin* in the first week of March and *Journey to a War* in the autumn, but he turned down *Lions and Shadows.* He did, however, pay Isherwood a small advance of $500 (about one third of the amount he had received for the China book) for a new novel. Isherwood told Kathleen that he could not expect much income from the sales of *Goodbye to Berlin:* "The American

---

4. This, and subsequent quotations from the 1939–44 diaries, are necessarily taken from the revised and annotated version Isherwood made in 1946, since he subsequently destroyed the originals. (He had in fact already started revising the first volumes in 1942, so the 1946 version represents a second revision.) Unlike the fragmentary diaries of 1933–38, therefore, this material benefits— or, rather, suffers—from a degree of editorial hindsight. Quite how much Isherwood altered, and to what effect, is not known, but he could be extraordinarily vague about facts and dates in his annotations.

market is most unsatisfactory for novels. The *average* sale is far lower than in England—although best-sellers and film-scripts get paid fantastically."

Goodbye to Berlin remains the book with which Isherwood will be forever associated, and it was undoubtedly his most impressive achievement so far, the one in which his easy, laconic prose style is at its most ubobtrusively skillful. As Edmund Wilson noted in the *New Republic:* "Christopher Isherwood's prose is a perfect medium for his purpose. It has the 'transparency' which the Russians praise in Pushkin. The sentences all get you somewhere almost without your noticing that you are reading them; the similes always have a point without ever obtruding themselves before the object. You seem to look right through Isherwood and see what he sees." Wilson rightly noted that Isherwood's "real field is social observation, and in this field it would not be too much to say that he is already, on a small scale, a master."

Having encountered all sorts of difficulties with a storyline when attempting to write *The Lost,* in *Goodbye to Berlin* Isherwood dispensed with plot altogether. Sandwiched between two "diaries," which provided snapshots of the city in the comparatively carefree autumn of 1930 and the climatically and politically chillier winter of 1932–33, are four overlapping but contrasting character sketches. Isherwood used these scenes and characters to create a vivid, perceptive and enduring portrait of Berlin in the early 1930s. "Why have [these stories] moved me so strongly?" Klaus Mann asked in the *Nation.* "Because they describe the Berlin which I know; because they conjure up the people, streets, and landscapes which once filled me with love or exasperation; because they picture the *real* Berlin—not the Berlin of the guidebooks, or the conducted tours, or the diplomatic memoirs; not 'the wickedest city in Europe'; not the Berlin of splendor and parade which famous journalists have so brilliantly described." Such recommendations did not, however, help the book sell in America, where it was, Isherwood reported, "the most utter flop, final and irrecoverable."

The novel fared much better in Britain, gaining widespread coverage and good sales. Particularly gratifying was a very substantial piece in the Sunday *Times* by its chief critic, Desmond MacCarthy. Having admitted he read fewer and fewer novels as he grew older, MacCarthy (then in his late sixties) wrote: "Nevertheless, now and then a novelist does appear who has something to present even to those who think themselves thoroughly saturated in experience; and when his technique is lively and original, and when he writes with exhilarating precision, then the most blasé novel-reader may find himself just as entertained by fiction as he used to be." The opinion of MacCarthy's fellow Bloomsburyite David Garnett in the *New Statesman* that "The writing of *Goodbye to Berlin* could not, I think, be better" was echoed in many reviews. V. S. Pritchett in the *Bystander,* for example, declared that Isherwood was "one of the most individual and accomplished writers alive today." There was a general feeling that with his second book set in Berlin, Isherwood had made the city his own.

While in New York, Isherwood and Auden collaborated on two minor projects. One was a film scenario, which they conceived of as

a cheap four-reeler [. . .] in which the part of the central character was taken by the camera. The hero sees life through the lens of a camera, so that the audience identifies itself with him. To make this possible, the story must be as ordinary and universal as possible. We suggest the life of an average American.

All the other characters speak and act as in any other film, but the hero's voice is represented by a commentator speaking in the first person, as if telling the story. When necessary, he describes his feelings. e.g. 'I turned away because I didn't want her to see how much I cared.'

Much of the interest in the film would be the use of subjective camera angles, suggesting the central character's growth from infancy and any physical activity, including "a fight, visiting the oculist or the dentist, weeping, kissing." Isherwood typed up a brief outline and it seems likely that the original idea, clearly derived from the stated narrative methods of *Goodbye to Berlin,* was his. Nothing ever came of this project, although in 1946 Robert Montgomery directed an adaptation of Raymond Chandler's *The Lady in the Lake* using precisely this method.

Auden and Isherwood's other collaboration was on an article for American *Vogue* on "Young British Writers on the Way Up," published in August. Perhaps recalling their difficulties with *On the Frontier,* they declared: "The realistic novelist, trying to write about Europe today, is like a portrait-painter whose model refuses to sit still. He may hope to catch certain impressions, jot down a few suggestive notes—but the big, maturely considered masterpiece must wait for better times. Most of what passes for fiction is, of necessity, only a kind of high-grade news reporting. The writer is far too close to his violently moving, dangerous subject." The writers they were thinking of in particular were George Orwell, Arthur Calder-Marshall and Ralph Bates, but there is a sense here that Isherwood also had his own career in mind. As he later wrote of himself at this period: "I still intended to practice my craft as a writer, but I could no longer justify to myself my existence as a pure, self-sufficient artist." The other writers discussed in the article were mostly friends and family: Graham Greene, Rex Warner, Edward Upward, William Plomer, James Stern, Henry Green and Stephen Spender, whose *Burning Cactus* was loyally described as "so good that one can only suppose that it was unsuccessful because it was unfashionable."

Part of Isherwood's difficulty in New York was that he was in a state of suspended animation. Unlike Auden, who with his experience and his higher public profile would find it easy to get a job teaching, Isherwood had no obvious way of earning a living, except in the movies, which would mean going to California. Auden was always capable of cutting himself off from the past and, if necessary, his surroundings (often literally, by closing the curtains), but Isherwood, for all his talk of removing himself from both Mother and Motherland, found that he could not sever the umbilical to Europe. The escalating crisis there continued to fill him with dread and a feeling of hopelessness, exacerbated by the American newspapers, which seemed even more alarmist than the British ones, cheerfully predicting that in the event of a war Germany had the capacity to destroy the whole of London within twenty-four hours. "Auden was strong in a way which I was not," Isherwood recalled.

He didn't worry unnecessarily about things which he couldn't control. The European war-threat hung over us, throughout that spring, like a thunderstorm which won't burst. Auden could live with this, but I became subject to fits of almost insane depression, during which I refused even to answer the phone. When I went out to parties I drank far too much. When I had to speak in public, I felt like a fake and often made a fool of myself.

The threat of war made his life in America seem precarious. "Wystan is determined to go back to England if war breaks out—and I shall go with him, I suppose," he wrote in his diary. "If I were alone, I mightn't. Quite aside from being scared, I am entirely disillusioned about what kind of war this is going to be. Just another struggle for world trade. But they are all over there—all my friends—and the impulse to join them is very strong." This was written two days after Germany had invaded and annexed Czechoslovakia, and it is hard to credit that Isherwood, having followed so closely the progress of Hitler's ambitions and seen at first hand what had been going on in Berlin, could genuinely believe that the war would simply be about world trade.

On March 31, Isherwood, Auden and Vernon abandoned the Little England of the George Washington Hotel for the Little Germany of Yorkville and took a large furnished apartment at 237 East Eighty-first Street. One of several immigrant villages in New York, Yorkville had a large German population, one that had settled on the Upper East Side long before the current exodus of refugees from the Nazis. Indeed many of the residents were strongly pro-Nazi. Isherwood felt at home among the bookshops and *Bierkellers,* all of which increased his nostalgia for Berlin. The apartment was on the top floor and consisted of a hall, a living room, two bedrooms and a study, which Auden immediately commandeered. Vernon recalled that Auden established a disciplined working routine, sitting at his desk every day until lunchtime. Isherwood was "more relaxed in his habits, observing and exploring the life around him." Stuck with his novel and unable to fulfill the *Redbook* commission, he did most of his writing in his diary, squirreling away his observations for future use.

Auden and Isherwood had soon got to know a wide cross-section of New York society through such people as the Manns (who had taken them to visit their father at Princeton) and Bennett Cerf. Perhaps the most important new friend they made was Lincoln Kirstein, to whom they had been given an introduction by Spender. Isherwood had taken some of Auden's Benzedrine before meeting Kirstein for the first time, which may be why Kirstein was left with the impression that Isherwood "went into friendships at 200 miles per hour." "The afternoon passed with an effect of terrific, smooth effortless speed," Isherwood recalled. "Neither Lincoln nor I stopped talking for a single moment. We were intimates at once." Three years younger than Isherwood, Kirstein had been born into a wealthy Jewish family in Rochester, New York, and had been brought up in Boston in an atmosphere of highly cultured anglophilia. His school and university vacations had been spent traveling in Europe, visiting galleries and museums, and at Harvard he had organized exhibitions of leading modernist painters and founded and edited an influential avant-garde magazine, *Hound & Horn,* publishing contributions from major contemporary poets. Although he studied ballet with Fokine, he never danced professionally, instead putting his energies into several ballet projects, including the School of American Ballet (which he founded with George Balanchine in 1934), the American Ballet, and the touring Ballet Caravan. His other passion was photography, and in 1938 he wrote the catalogue copy for Walker Evans's first major exhibition at New York's Museum of Modern Art. A huge man, whose monumental head was emphasized by his closely cropped hair, Kirstein had attracted the attention of numerous artists. He had been photographed in Harlem by Carl Van Vechten, been sculpted nude by Gaston Lachaise, and was the subject of a startling triple portrait by Pavel Tchelichev, in which he stands, arms akimbo, in a scarlet-sleeved baseball jacket, flanked by two further images of him, one naked except for a pair of boxing gloves, the other fully clothed and bespectacled. He towered above Isherwood, who noted: "In his blue pea jacket, he looks like a mad clipper captain out of Melville."[5] Although he would shortly embark on a successful and enduring marriage to the sister of his friend the painter Paul Cadmus, Kirstein was predominantly homosexual, and was currently living with a Mexican dancer named José Martinez, whom he dubbed "Pete" after Walt Whitman's lover Peter Doyle. Kirstein's almost parodically masculine appearance disguised a broad streak of camp in his character that became apparent in conversation and, more particularly, in letters to close friends. When he wrote to Isherwood he addressed him as "Dearest Cwiss" and used a lot of capital letters and exclamation marks. One letter begins: "LISTEN MARY!"

Kirstein introduced Isherwood to the photographer George Platt Lynes, who made a series of portraits of Isherwood, including one in which he appears to be clinging rather anxiously to a stage pillar. Kirstein dubbed it "the rat with a nervous breakdown." Isherwood's expression shows all too clearly how discontented he was with his new life. "My time in New York has been a bad, sterile period for me," he decided. He described April 1, a day spent in Philadelphia with Kirstein and Martinez, ostensibly to see Orson Welles's *Five Kings* but mostly taken up with a drunken lunch and a visit to a bathhouse, as "the only really enjoyable day I've spent in America, so far."

Something of his dissatisfaction had communicated itself to Kathleen. "You are quite right in feeling that I am restless and ill at ease in New York," he had confessed at the end of March. He was evidently unnerved by the fact that *Goodbye to Berlin* had made so little impact in America, and he had begun to wonder about his future as a writer.

> I wish I could write novels, real ones, but perhaps I can't. Maybe I have come to the limit of my talent, and shall just go on being 'promising' until people are tired of me. Of course, I secretly feel there is something more inside me; but it won't come out. I could describe anybody, anything, in the world; but I can't make it all into a pattern. Perhaps that's the penalty you pay for not believing in anything positive. Perhaps it's a certain lack of vitality. Perhaps it's only New York. Wystan, on the other hand, flourishes exceedingly. Never has he written so much.

Kathleen was perhaps the only person to whom Isherwood could confess his fears. To do so to friends—particularly to Auden, who increasingly seemed a more suc-

---

5. It was perhaps for this reason that Kirstein was the dedicatee of Auden's poem about Melville, which was written at this time.

cessful rival—would be to lose face, and Kathleen could always be relied upon to make reassuring noises. "I don't wonder you can't settle down to work but maybe the knowledge of American Life & being able to look at things from a distance will help your work—I am <u>certain</u> you havent come to the limit of your talent, its just New York—I <u>wish</u> we were all together & yet its a sort of relief that you are out of possible happenings here."

An opportunity to discuss the pacifist position more fully came when Isherwood was introduced to the British playwright John van Druten. Three years older than Isherwood, the plump and prosperous van Druten had found popular success in both England and America, and for much of the 1930s had divided his time between the two countries, spending summers in France with a group of homosexual literary friends. He had now decided to settle in the States, and had become a pacifist. He and Isherwood sat down together in order to write a letter to three leading members of the pacifist movement: the M.P. George Lansbury, Runham Brown of War Resisters International and the wealthy journalist and landowner Rudolph Messel. They wanted the answers to three questions:

1. What is a pacifist to do in wartime (apart from merely refusing to fight) and what activities are permissible to him, by way of defence or otherwise, if he is (a) in England, or (b) in a non-combatant country?
2. What permissible alternative is there to war in opposing an aggressor whose pledge cannot be relied upon?
3. If none, does one open all doors to the aggressor and let him take everything he wants?

Messel advocated active resistance to war and no cooperation at all in defense work, even if this meant defeat by fascism. Lansbury and Brown were more pragmatic, suggesting that pacifists should carry on with their civilian jobs and "do relief work, but not under government auspices, and not as an alternative to military service." They should "practice civil disobedience to the aggressor, no matter what the consequences." Lansbury added encouragingly that "passive resistance has never yet been tried out, but war has been tried through all the centuries and has absolutely failed." Although these answers seemed satisfactory, Isherwood wanted to talk to an old acquaintance named Gerald Heard, who had settled in California and was apparently devoting himself to Eastern mysticism, yoga and pacifism.

Heard was an Irish polymath to whom Isherwood had been introduced by Auden in London in 1932. A writer on philosophical and scientific matters, he was enormously well read, and appeared to be qualified to talk—which he did at length—on almost any subject that presented itself. This made him a popular figure at the BBC, where he was frequently employed to broadcast on popular science programs. He was the author of several books with such imposing titles as *The Ascent of Humanity* and *The Emergence of Man,* and was a fluent conversationalist whose rapid and allusive speech flattered people into imagining that they were as erudite as he was. It was, on the whole, easier to nod appreciatively than to engage Heard in discourse—besides which, his monologues rarely gave anyone a conversational opening. Had he been less articulate, fewer people might have taken him seriously. Isherwood later parodied Heard's mode of conversation: "You've read Frump's great work on the filter-passing viruses, of course? No? Well, then you'll remember how he says there how this curious thing which La Touche, for some *extraordinary* reason, dismisses in a single footnote to his account of the Battle of Actium—you find the same process, of course, described in the Civitas Dei—and there's that queer little reference to it in Constable's last letter to his old aunt, just before he died—this curious thing *always* follows the three stages—as Mazarin seems to have seen very clearly, though he lacked the courage to follow it through—first you get selection, then suction, and then—much as we may hate to face the truth of that saying which Mirski attributes—I believe quite wrongly—to the last of the great Cistercian abbots—then, inevitably, the wheel comes full circle, and you have the solution. Did you see that curious little monograph which was published the other day in Brisbane—?"

Isherwood got on particularly well with Heard's partner, Chris Wood, with whom he shared a passion for films, books, boys, and nursery food. They had been to bed together, once, immediately after they first met. Although some ten years Wood's senior, Heard was officially employed by him as his "secretary." Since Wood didn't actually do anything, Heard's duties were negligible. Income from a family business which provided condiments for the grander London department stores allowed Wood to lead the life of a wealthy dilettante. He was an extremely gifted pianist, but declined to appear on the concert platform, preferring to play for his own enjoyment, and he wrote short stories which, ignoring Isherwood's enthusiasm for them, he refused to publish. When Isherwood first met them, Heard and Wood lived in a luxurious modernist flat behind Oxford Street, with a cat whose "colouring toned in perfectly with the furnishings," but in 1937 they had come to America with Aldous and Maria Huxley and settled in Hollywood. Wood spent most of his days bicycling, sunbathing or playing the piano, but Heard and Huxley had embraced pacifism, met a swami and taken up yoga.

Isherwood had a typically British attitude to Eastern mysticism, derived more from boys' adventure stories than from works of scholarship. Heard, however, was not only someone he had known and admired for some time, but was also a close friend of E. M. Forster, whose judgment of people Isherwood trusted implicitly. If Heard and Huxley (whose recently published *Ends and Means* was regarded as a seminal pacifist text) were taking yoga seriously, then Isherwood felt that there must be something in it. He decided first of all to write to Heard, and entered a correspondence chiefly about pacifism rather than about mysticism. Heard encouraged Isherwood to come to California, where he was trying to organize pacifist groups. Isherwood agreed at once. By traveling to California, he could escape the disappointments of New York, see more of the country and perhaps find work at the Hollywood studios. By studying Chris Wood in his new habitat, he could also "measure the effect of California on an Englishman and thereby find out what California might be expected to do for and to me."

He used the fact that he had not yet settled in America as another reason for putting off sending for Hewit. "I have told him that it would be fatal for him to come out here at present," he told Lehmann.

Partly because I couldn't possibly support him. Partly because I must go through this period alone—that is to say, alone among Americans. He knows me well enough to understand what I mean by this. It may be more neuroticism, but I value our relationship too much to endanger it, for whatever reason.

This, as Isherwood very well knew, was less than truthful. One of the undeclared reasons he couldn't support Hewit was that he was supporting Vernon, whom he had persuaded to accompany him to California—hence the shifty rider about being "alone among Americans."

Although the California trip was to be in the nature of a reconnaissance, Isherwood was only too glad to leave New York. "Oh God, what a city!" he complained to Lehmann. "The nervous breakdown expressed in terms of architecture. The skyscrapers are all Father-fixations. The police-cars are fitted with air-raid sirens, specially designed to promote paranoia. The elevated railway is the circular madness. The height of the buildings produces visions similar to those experienced by Ransom in F6." Furthermore, his relationship with Auden had undergone a significant change. On April 6 they had joined Louis MacNeice and the American poet and novelist Frederic Prokosch (who had contributed to the Auden number of *New Verse*) to present an evening of talks and readings to the League of American Writers at the Keynote Club on West Fifty-second Street. In the front row of the audience were a student and a recent graduate from Brooklyn College, whose chief interest in the event was to view two famous British homosexuals at close quarters. At the end of the evening, Chester Kallman and Harold Norse introduced themselves and asked whether they could interview Auden and Isherwood for a college magazine. Isherwood gave Norse his card, which Kallman "borrowed," nipping round to the Yorkville apartment two days later. Auden opened the door and came face to face with his future.

The son of a cultivated Jewish dentist, Kallman was eighteen, blond and full-lipped, with attractive shadows under his eyes. He had the sort of sensual beauty that ripens at eighteen, but quite quickly begins to look pouchy and debauched. He was clever, precocious and cultured, and he simply exuded sex. Kallman was officially Norse's lover, but he was insatiably promiscuous. Auden had been hoping for a visit from another member of the audience who had caught his eye, and his first judgment of Kallman—that he was "the wrong blond"—was one that history would endorse. Whereas Auden was almost instantly smitten with Kallman, Isherwood never really understood the attraction. Kallman was quick and witty and good company, but he could also be condescending and sarcastic. Vernon remembered that from the outset there was "a certain friction" whenever Isherwood and Kallman were together, and that this made things awkward with Auden. According to a friend, Kallman soon "had a clear image of himself as Christopher's successor to Wystan's love," and Isherwood may have resented this ambitious young usurper, who planned to become a writer and take over the role in Auden's life Isherwood had himself become accustomed to playing.

Both personally and professionally, Auden had been the one constant in Isherwood's life, and their trip to America had been undertaken as a joint enterprise. Now it seemed the relationship was being unraveled by circumstances. Auden had not only made a success of New York but had also secured a job teaching at a school in Massachusetts for a month. There was nothing in the city for Isherwood and, now that Auden was taken up with Kallman, no longer any reason to stay. Auden had not become a pacifist, had no interest in Eastern mysticism, and would have been temperamentally unsuited to sun-drenched California. The parting, even if it was to be only temporary, was inevitable. Vernon recalled Auden was "quite willing to see us go. Wystan and Christopher's personal preoccupations made the parting not only painless, but expedient. They both seemed to feel the need for a change."

Isherwood was still telling people back in England that he would return if war broke out, but he took measures before leaving for California to make this less likely. On May 1 he sent Bennett Cerf a legal document drawn up by an employee of Kirstein's Ballet Caravan. In this affidavit, Cerf undertook to act as a financial guarantor so that Isherwood could apply for "a visa to enter the United States for permanent residence [. . .] and become a citizen of the United States." Although residency could be granted quite quickly, citizenship could be obtained only if the applicant had lived in the States continuously for five years. The document stated that Isherwood was "under contract to write several works of prose for Random House, Inc." and that Cerf was "making this affidavit voluntarily and of his own free will, and for the sole purpose of convincing the Hon. American Consul that he is well able and most willing to assume full responsibility for his dear friend, Christopher Isherwood, and to insure against his becoming a public charge after his admission into the United States." Cerf might have been less eager to help his dear friend if he had known that in private letters Isherwood was referring to him as "a twister" who "makes big gestures of friendship followed by mangy offers," and that the advance he had paid Isherwood was already running out with nothing to show for it. There is no mention of this document in Isherwood's (self-edited) diaries.

Traveling across America by Greyhound bus would give Isherwood an opportunity to see more of the country he intended to adopt. He and Vernon left New York in the early morning of May 6, arriving in Washington, D.C., in the afternoon. Isherwood carried with him a letter of introduction to a senator, and met several prominent politicians. After three days in the capital, being wined and dined and seeing the sights, they set off for Memphis, Tennessee, where they were foiled in their romantic idea of going down the Mississippi by steamer and so took the bus to New Orleans. From there they traveled through Texas to El Paso, up the Rio Grande to Albuquerque, then on to Flagstaff, Arizona, where they visited the Grand Canyon and quarreled because Vernon wanted to be photographed clinging to a vertiginous pinnacle of rock. As they crossed the Colorado, a woman on the bus sang "California, Here I Come!"

The journey was far from comfortable—it was very hot and the buses were not air-conditioned—but Isherwood enjoyed himself more the farther he got away from New York. They arrived in Los Angeles on the evening of May 20. Isherwood's first impression of the city was not favorable. He complained that it was "featureless and grimy," and described it in his diary as "perhaps the ugliest city on earth." They booked into a downtown hotel in an area where drunks thronged the streets, and then telephoned Chris Wood, who exclaimed: "How wonderful to hear an effeminate British voice!"

The following morning they found rooms at the Rose Garden Apartments on Franklin Avenue in Hollywood, an area of the city much more to Isherwood's taste: "an enormous suburb of little white houses, wooden or stucco, wide open to a technicolor blue sky, with a background of brushy brown-green hills. A suburb of little gardens crowded with blossoms and flowering bushes; its architecture dominated by its vegetation. A suburb without privacy; the houses look into each other's bedrooms and share a street-long lawn which is seldom subdivided by fences. I recognized the look of these houses and this lawn instantly, from many scenes out of silent-screen kid-gang comedies." Not only was the apartment building a classic Los Angeles Spanish-style structure, built around a courtyard and filled with bit-part film actors, it was also, coincidentally, just around the corner from the headquarters of the Vedanta Society of Southern California on Ivar Avenue. It was here that Gerald Heard had found his swami.

Isherwood had arranged to meet Wood at a drugstore that first afternoon (a meeting he liked to compare to that of Stanley and Livingstone), and thereafter he and Vernon spent a lot of time with Wood and Heard, who lived at Arlene Terrace in the Hollywood Hills. In fact, Heard lived in an annex built on to the back of Wood's house consisting of a small bedroom, with a shower and lavatory. Whereas Wood had hardly changed at all, apart from acquiring a deep tan from spending every morning at the beach, Heard was almost unrecognizable. In London he had been something of a dandy (Joe Ackerley recalled him turning up for dinner in purple suede shoes and a leather jacket with a leopard-skin collar), but in California he had embraced asceticism with characteristic zeal. Gaunt and bearded, he reminded Vernon of an El Greco saint—but this was a saint whose robes were a painter's smock worn over blue jeans and sneakers. One thing that had not changed was his volubility, and at meals Isherwood and Vernon were treated to "lengthy learned monologues about almost everything."

The old Isherwood might have found this curious figure a suitable case for fictional treatment and started transforming him at once into a character. The new Isherwood, however, had come to learn, not to mock. Heard told him that "to become a true pacifist, you had to find peace within yourself; only then, he said, could you function pacifistically in the outside world." This would certainly prove a challenge to Isherwood, who had been a seething caldron of resentments, anxieties and discontents for almost as long as he could remember. Heard outlined an alarming spiritual regime, in which six hours a day were devoted to meditation, celibacy was embraced, stimulants were outlawed, and the principal sources of physical sustenance were raisins, raw carrots and innumerable cups of tea. A skeptical, sybaritic, chain-smoking, egotistical and morally confused homosexual atheist such as Isherwood can hardly have seemed the most likely convert to the rigorous self-discipline Heard was advocating. Heard, however, though he may have looked holy, was certainly no fool, and he cunningly appealed to Isherwood's vanity.

During the lengthy, searching conversations he had with Isherwood over the next few months, Heard explained that very few people were chosen to follow this particular path toward spiritual enlightenment. He was careful to avoid any mention of "God," knowing that this word would merely remind Isherwood of the Christian God he had long since rejected, the God of his childhood, the God of the classroom. This God, Isherwood had been told, "high in heaven, ruled with grim justice over us, his sinful and brutish subjects, here below. He was good. We were bad. We were so bad that we crucified Jesus his son, whom he had sent down to live amongst us. For this crime, committed nearly two thousand years ago, each new generation had to beg forgiveness. If we begged hard enough and were sincerely sorry, we might be sent to purgatory and even eventually led into heaven, instead of being thrown into hell where we by rights belonged." To see the damaging effects of such teaching, Isherwood had only to look at his brother, whose adolescence had been traumatized by fears of a vengeful God. Heard spoke instead of the need to explore one's own nature and discover what it really is, something Isherwood had been trying to do in his diaries during his final year in England.

The teachings of Vedanta are derived from the Vedas, the world's oldest sacred writings. Two of the basic tenets of Vedantan philosophy are that man's real nature is divine and that his aim in life should be to realize this divine nature. "To seek to realize my essential nature is to admit that I am dissatisfied with my nature as it is at present," Isherwood subsequently wrote in an essay explaining Vedanta to what he described as "intelligently sceptical" Westerners. "It is to admit that I am dissatisfied with the kind of life I am leading now." He was ostensibly talking in general terms, but he clearly had in mind his own predicament.

> Suppose I have actually attained some of the world's advertised objectives, and found beyond them an emptiness, a teasing question which I cannot answer. I am confronted with Life's subtlest riddle: the riddle of human boredom. In my desperation, I am ready to assume, provisionally, that this Atman, this essential nature, does exist within me, and does offer me lasting strength, wisdom, peace and happiness. How am I to realize this nature? How am I to enjoy it?

The answer given by Vedanta is "By ceasing to be yourself." This clearly presents problems for anyone, but more particularly, perhaps, for someone whose work was based so closely on his own life and personality. "How can I stop being myself?" Isherwood wondered. "I'm Christopher Isherwood, or I'm nothing." But what *was* "Christopher Isherwood?" This was the question he had attempted to answer in August 1938, when he subjected himself to that long and searching self-analysis in his diary. The conclusions he reached now were very similar:

> He is a constellation of desires and impulses. He reflects his environment. He repeats what he has been taught. He mimics the social behaviour of his community. He copies gestures like a monkey and intonations like a parrot. All his actions are conditioned by those around him, however eccentric and individual he may seem to be. He is subject to suggestion, climate, disease and the influence of drugs. He is changing all the time. He has no essential reality.

The first thing he had to do was to conquer what it was that made him believe in that entity called Christopher Isherwood: "an egotism which is asserted and reinforced by hundreds of your daily actions."

Every time you desire, or fear, or hate; every time you boast or indulge your vanity; every time you struggle to get something for yourself, you are really asserting: 'I am a separate, unique individual. I stand apart from everything else in this universe.' [. . .] Try to overcome this possessive attitude towards your actions. Stop taking credit for your successes. Stop bemoaning your failures, and making excuses for them. Stop worrying so much about results. Just do the best you can. Work for work's sake.

In order to achieve this spiritual rebirth it was necessary to practice yoga. Although to most people "yoga" suggested some form of beneficial contortionism (of the sort once practiced by Isherwood's Uncle Jack), Heard explained that it was in fact a Sanskrit word for "yoking" or "joining." Through meditation it was possible to achieve union with "this thing," which was Heard's slyly evasive term for what other people would have termed "God." Heard was also careful to avoid the word "soul," although Yoga taught that people had two selves, a notion which would seem familiar to anyone brought up in the Judaeo-Christian belief of body and soul. According to Yoga philosophy, the two selves are the "outer" or "apparent" self, which makes people think of themselves as individuals, subject to emotions and external stimuli; and the "inner" or "real" self, which is part of a larger consciousness shared by everyone, and everything, alike. Isherwood came up with a useful image to explain the "real self:" "there is a part of myself which, being infinite, has access to the infinite— as the sea water in a bay has access to the sea because it *is* the sea." The "apparent self," for all its power to shape people's everyday lives, is in fact an illusion; it is the "real self" that matters, and meditation assists in the process of discovering and holding on to that "reality." The relevance of all this to pacifism soon became clear: by concentrating on what makes us individual, we are really emphasizing our separateness and difference from other people, and this can lead to hatred, and thence to war; concentrating instead on what connects us to everyone else induces feelings of unity. The equation works both ways: hatred increases one's sense of apartness, love increases one's sense of belonging. A further lesson was that "all positive feeling and action towards other people is in one's deepest interests, and all negative feeling and action finally harm oneself."

It is clear why this would appeal to Isherwood at this stage in his life. He had become increasingly disillusioned with his "outer self," the Christopher Isherwood who traded upon his reputation as one of the leading young stars of Britain's left-wing intelligentsia. It might bring some money, and the sort of fame that made young men fall at his feet, but what was the lasting value of any of this? Ever since Heinz had been arrested, Isherwood had pursued the sort of life that suggested its principal motive had indeed been the staving off of boredom and despair. Humphrey Spender had been right when, back in 1936, he had prophesied that in losing Heinz, Isherwood "would lose the decisive factor in his life." Without Heinz, there was no cause or pattern; actions became meaningless. Work, cigarettes, drink and sex got him through each day, but his discontent was palpable. Coming to America had been a way of breaking with the role he had been expected to play, but New York had shown him very quickly that he could not get by in this country by reputation alone. He was unable to work, he was short of money, he was worried about the war, he was guilty about abandoning his mother, his brother and Jack Hewit—not to mention various other friends such as Forster—to face whatever Hitler had in store for them. He had just parted from his closest friend, the person with whom he had intended to establish himself in a new country. He admitted to Lehmann that he was "often very homesick for London." He was in "the most Goddamawful mess." He was ripe for conversion.

"The driving-forces, which separate people, are so dull, really," he explained to Lehmann.

> Just their needs and greeds; sex and money and ambition. Oh dear, why do we have to have bodies? By the time they've been satisfied, there is only half an hour a day left over for Talk. And talk is all that finally matters.
>
> John, I am so utterly sick of being a person—Christopher Isherwood, or Isherwood, or even Chris. Aren't you, too? Don't you feel, more and more, that all your achievements, all your sexual triumphs, are just like cheques, which represent money, but have no real value? Aren't you sick to death of your face in the glass, and your business voice, and your love-voice, and your signature on documents? I know I am.
>
> Don't be alarmed. This isn't a prelude to suicide. Nor am I suffering from a hangover. I am perfectly well, and this is a beautiful morning [. . .] I am just trying to tell you, quite sanely, how I feel. And maybe why I'm not writing, just now. I'm just tired of strumming on that old harp, the Ego, darling Me.

Vedanta offered a way out of this cul-de-sac. *Der Mann ohne Eigenschaften,* Isherwood had recognized during his last year in England, has "no inner life at all." It was an increasingly desperate search for an inner life that had led him to California. He would have to abandon his "apparent" self and try to find the "real" one; but this would take time.

Meanwhile, although Chris Wood had lent him $2,000, Isherwood needed to earn some money. He had promised Lehmann something for the autumn number of *New Writing,* perhaps an article about his impressions of New York. Then he started writing a memoir of Ernst Toller, the exiled German playwright who had committed suicide in May. Eventually, he was obliged to confess to Lehmann that neither piece would do. "New York needs endless polishing. The Toller piece just sounds stupid and patronizing and rather offensive. It has a certain smart-alecky value, but I was fond of Toller, and can't publish it as it stands. I doubt if you'd want to print it, either. So once again, I am the criminal, the oath-breaker. And, once again, I can only say I'm sorry." Lehmann had every reason to feel let down, but when rumors reached him that Isherwood was running short of money, he generously offered to send £50 against expected royalties on the sales of *Goodbye to Berlin,* which was having a much greater success in Europe than in America, with foreign rights selling to several countries.

It was clear that Isherwood could not rely on handouts and occasional bits of journalism to keep him solvent. He needed to find proper employment and this meant getting a proper visa. He had come to America on a visitor's visa, but to enter the country on a more long-term basis, he had to leave it, obtain an immigrant's visa, then be readmitted. The easiest place to do this was from Ensenada in Mexico, and he was put in touch with a lawyer who specialized in immigration and could arrange the papers in advance. Given all the difficulties he had endured over the years with consulates and at borders, he was astonished at how easy it was. The lawyer herself drove Isherwood to Mexico, and on June 9, 1939, he reentered America as a permanent resident.

A few days earlier, Isherwood had gone to have dinner with Berthold Viertel's wife, Salka, at the family home in Santa Monica. Viertel was expected back in Hollywood shortly, but meanwhile Salka said she would try to get Isherwood some work on a film about Madame Curie, a somewhat unlikely vehicle for her friend Greta Garbo. Salka herself had been commissioned by a producer at MGM named Bernie Hyman to write a treatment, and then Aldous Huxley was brought in. Huxley was the sort of "name" Hollywood moguls liked to have on the payroll—not so much to produce viable scripts as to give their studios intellectual clout. Huxley had produced a treatment by August 1938, but Hyman had not found time to read it and so gave it to his secretary who reported back "it stinks." For all Salka's efforts, Isherwood never did get to work on the film, which eventually appeared in 1943, with Greer Garson in the title role.

Isherwood found Salka almost as fascinating as he had found her husband. He thought her personality

> every bit as dramatic as Berthold's, though her style was different. She referred frequently and challengingly to her Jewish ancestry, but I always thought of her as being Slav. She had a face of great power, handsome and leonine, carried on a strong but graceful neck. She had played leading roles on the German and Austrian stage. One could easily picture her as a royal personage, making absolute, but not necessarily unjust decisions, sometimes subject to caprice; then, when everybody was listening, she would smilingly, coquettishly reply 'Yes! *Absolutely!*' or '*No! Absolutely not!*' She had much more poise than Berthold; she didn't flare up. But she could make up her mind to approve or disapprove extremely of some particular person. These decisions were always subject to reversal, however.

Salka became one of Isherwood's closest friends in Hollywood, and his entrée into the close-knit community of European émigrés who would congregate at her house, 165 Mabery Road.

In mid-June, Isherwood and Vernon found a new home at 7136 Sycamore Trail, a rough road which wound up among the woods in the Hollywood Hills. The house was built into the hillside and stood at the top of a flight of steps, where a terrace shaded by a large pepper tree looked out over the San Fernando Valley. Vernon was delighted with the house, which they furnished from second-hand stores, and he started creating a garden. They bought an old Model T Ford, and Isherwood managed to pass a California driving test on the third attempt, although he was never a particularly reliable driver. Vernon enrolled in an art school, and appeared to be enjoying

HUXLEY

life, but Isherwood found it hard to share in his optimism. He had a dispiriting interview with a Hollywood agent, who evidently had no idea who he was and no interest in finding out. He managed to write a review of Steinbeck's *The Grapes of Wrath* for the *Kenyon Review* and knock out a story with a title appropriate to his circumstances, "I Am Waiting," which the *New Yorker* published, but he seemed no more able to settle to work in California than he had in New York. "I Am Waiting" is an insubstantial tale about an elderly man who shares Isherwood's fears about the coming war and who has a series of glimpses into the future, all of which are frustratingly banal and unrevealing. The narrative is flat and unstylish and one senses that Isherwood is merely treading water.

When Vernon drove off to art school, Isherwood was left without transportation and felt trapped. It was as if the house absorbed his own dark moods.

> The more time I spent in the house, the less I liked it. It wasn't exactly sinister. But there was the psychic equivalent of a bad smell in it—the smell of small-scale undramatic failure, not of big tragedy or crime. What I inhaled from its atmosphere was worry, the frustration of waiting for phone-calls which didn't come through. I sniffed extravagance, debts, lies—amateurs coming up against professionals. Bluffs brutally called. Attempts to convince film-studio secretaries of one's importance, naming influential names in vain, getting a brush-off. And, finally, after obstinate self-deception, the facing of Fact. Followed by the retreat from an untenable position (Hollywood and houses like this one) to where you came from, back East. The sour smell of failure should not be sniffed. It is infectious. It clogs the veins with laziness, inviting surrender.

Fortunately, before Isherwood succumbed entirely to this spiritual miasma, Berthold Viertel arrived back in Santa Monica and at the beginning of July recruited his former collaborator to work on a film provisionally titled *The Mad Dog of Europe*. It was the story of a young German who serves as an army officer during the First World War and is subsequently won over to the Nazis, in the process abandoning his wife, who is the daughter of an eminent Jewish gynecologist. It was to end on an optimistic note, however, with the protagonist rejecting the Nazis and working against them in the underground resistance. Every morning Vernon dropped Isherwood off at Mabery Road on his way to art classes, and picked him up again in the afternoon. Isherwood and Viertel almost immediately fell back into their old working relationship, progress on the film interrupted by gloomy discussions of the approaching war.

Mabery Road and Arlene Terrace soon became the two fixed points in Isherwood's Hollywood life, and they represented different aspects of his existence. Mabery Road was distinctly European in atmosphere, almost like being back in Berlin, and it was here that Isherwood could discuss the vanished past with other exiles, and listen anxiously to radio reports of the coming war. His spiritual future, however, lay at Arlene Terrace, where he continued his long conversations with Heard. Mabery Road was grounded in the everyday world of the film industry and contemporary politics, whereas at Arlene Terrace what most people regarded as the "real" world was dismissed as an illusion. The real world, however, had a nasty way of asserting itself. Isherwood found himself becoming jealous because Heard had seized upon Vernon as someone who was capable of "mutating"—"a favorite Heard term, meaning that you had managed to turn yourself from a directionless, erring worldling into a conscious being who lived in a constant state of awareness of life's spiritual goal." Heard and Vernon would go off for long walks together, and Isherwood felt neglected. He began to wonder whether Heard thought him a lost cause. "I was probably too old, too corrupt, too set in my ways. The underworld of Berlin had coarsened and deadened my better nature. Whereas Vernon was still young; he had the whole future before him [. . .] The truth is, I had fancied myself in the role which was now being offered to Vernon."

Worldly concerns were still occupying much of Isherwood's time. In particular, there was the unresolved matter of Jack Hewit, stuck in London awaiting his summons. Isherwood had been sending him the occasional friendly but evasive letter and had not yet told him about Vernon. He was eventually forced to make a decision by a letter he received from Lehmann. "I have seen a lot of Jacky and been rather worried for him," Lehmann wrote. "He has been under a terrible strain, and I sometimes wonder Christopher whether you realize over there how neurotic he is and how great the strain of being separated from you and not knowing for how long is for him. Please forgive me for saying that; I know I may be absolutely wrong and not in a position to judge accurately. He's a volcano underneath." Isherwood summoned up courage and wrote what he described as "a bloody letter" telling Hewit that he must give up his plans to come to America. At the same time he wrote to Lehmann, informing him of what he had done. It was not just because of Vernon, he tried to explain.

I simply know, in my deepest bones, that it wouldn't work. Having to break things off, and not being able to, was part of the mess I was and am in. Damn, my hand is shaking so much I can hardly write this. Hope you can read it. Of course everybody will say I behaved like a skunk. I can't help that. But it is vital that Jacky gets over it, and that he finishes school [at the Pitman College]. Keep an eye on him, will you? How is he off for money?

I am not writing to Guy [Burgess], or anybody else—because I despair of being understood, and anyway it's Jacky's happiness, not my reputation that matters. But I want you to believe that I am doing the only honest thing. It's so horrible to have to write it, not say it.

Here, the sun shines, and it's beautiful. I am recovering from New York—that's why I feel strong enough to take this step. I should have done it a month ago. But I wanted to be absolutely sure.

Isherwood later admitted to Forster: "I wasn't quite exact in what I wrote about my reasons for not wanting [Hewit] to join me out here. I had to express things in Jacky's terms. What I couldn't explain to him—perhaps not entirely to anybody—was a feeling of utter spiritual impotence. I just suddenly knew that I couldn't cope. I knew that, however much I dread loneliness, there is something inside me which has to be alone, and which wasn't alone when J. was around. Heinz was different. So is [Vernon]. Perhaps because they are foreigners. I don't know. Anyhow, this all sounds rather tiresome when I write it down, like the sensations of a character in D. H. Lawrence."

When Hewit received Isherwood's letter, he was living in the Hallam Street flat owned by Britten and Pears, who had crossed the Atlantic at the end of April and were now in New York. He telephoned Isherwood and begged him to change his mind. Hewit was "in tears, sobbing that he was frightened, there was going to be a war, that [Isherwood] had promised to help him come over," Isherwood recalled. He had taken Hewit's call at Sycamore Trail, and remembered lying on the bare floor-boards and writhing around in guilt and embarrassment; but he remained firm.[6]

Hewit's cause was taken up by Guy Burgess and his friend Anthony Blunt, who accosted E. M. Forster at a commemoration dinner at Cambridge. They "came fussing me," Forster told Isherwood,

> because you had behaved so badly to Jacky. As I dare say you have, and then they wanted me to read a letter from you to him which they had brought to the banquet. This I declined to do, to their umbrage. I could not see why I had to, when neither you nor J had requested me to do so. G.B. was insistent I should write to you, which I should have done in any case. He is a most cerebral gangster.
>
> I wrote not long ago to J, suggesting a meeting, but had no answer, and now understand why, and am glad he did not answer. I guess the situation, and feel sorry for the boy. This much I will say, that now you know you can miscalculate you will be more careful another time. Have you to provide for him at all?

Isherwood recognized a rebuke, even one as gently delivered as this, and he replied to Forster shamefacedly:

> Yes, of course I have behaved badly. Very badly indeed, but, I hope, quite straight-forwardly—if breaking promises can ever be called straightforward. [. . .] Why didn't I tell you about it? Because I felt ashamed of myself. I am still ashamed; but don't see that I could have acted differently, having got things into such a mess. The whole business was a problem of distance and money. I couldn't afford to fly to England and speak to J. personally, which would have straightened everything out, and left no hard feelings. So I wrote. And all letters of that sort, however well expressed, sound brutal.
>
> You are right to warn me to be careful in future; but don't worry, I shall be. This time, I really have learnt my lesson.

After an appeal from Guy Burgess, Isherwood offered to pay £50 so that Hewit could take a five-year apprenticeship at a hotel. Of this, half was a bond, returnable if Hewit

---

6. Hewit firmly denied that this telephone call ever took place. He maintained that nothing would have induced him to leave Guy Burgess and go to America. Isherwood's account, however, is substantiated by a letter Britten wrote to his friend Wulff Scherchen, in which he complained that Hewit left the flat in a terrible state with several bills outstanding, among them a "telephone bill with a trans-atlantic call of £3 odd!."

finished the apprenticeship; the other £25 was to pay for clothes. This time, Kathleen was co-opted as a go-between. "I don't know how much money I have in the Bank," Isherwood wrote to her, "but I would like him to have it. The rest I can pay later. The point is I don't want Jacky to know that the money comes from me." Having consulted Forster, Kathleen felt that some sort of legal contract should be drawn up, but was then phoned by Blunt, who told her that Hewit had discovered that instead of a bond, he could pay the hôtelier five shillings a week out of his wages and that this money would be paid back to him in full at the end of his apprenticeship. He would still need about £20 to pay for his uniform. Kathleen liked the idea of the scheme, but asked Hewit to come to see her. "He is a funny little person with untidy hair a common nose and voice & bright brown eyes—but interested in things," she noted in her diary. (Perhaps only Kathleen could describe someone's *nose* as "common.") The following day she sent him a cheque for £20.

At this period of his life, Isherwood compared himself to "the ground under this part of California [. . .] there is a 'fault' inside me which may produce earthquakes." It was in an attempt to overcome this fault that Isherwood continued his studies with Heard, who finally felt that his pupil was sufficiently prepared to be introduced to Swami Prabhavananda. The swami immediately appealed to Isherwood. "Outwardly, he was a Bengali in his middle forties who looked at least fifteen years younger, charming and boyish in manner, with bold straight eyebrows and dark wide-set eyes." Unless he was lecturing in the temple or attending Hindu rites, he wore casual Western clothing—"a white shirt with or without a tie, a woollen pullover, gray flannel slacks, and leather slippers"—and so did not seem off-puttingly Eastern and exotic. He was physically small, something that always appealed to Isherwood, and was a chain-smoker, a habit which suggested both worldliness and an encouraging dash of human frailty.

Prabhavananda had been born Abanindra Nath Ghosh into a Hindu family in Bengal in 1893. He had become interested in the teachings of Ramakrishna (1836–86), the avatar who was responsible for the nineteenth-century revival of Vedanta. One day Ghosh met Ramakrishna's widow, Sarada Devi, and when he paid her homage, she asked: "Son, haven't I seen you before?" Some years later, when he was an eighteen-year-old student of philosophy, Ghosh visited Belur Math, the Ramakrishna Order's monastery near Calcutta, where he was greeted by one of Ramakrishna's principal disciples, Brahmananda, with the words: "Haven't I seen you before?" Ghosh was so impressed by this apparent coincidence that he decided to become a disciple of Brahmananda, but Brahmananda insisted the young man should finish his university studies first. At college Ghosh became involved in a revolutionary organization opposed to British rule in India: he believed that political action was more important than religion, although he continued to receive instruction at Belur Math. One morning he was doing obeisance before Brahmananda when an old man who was also present asked: "When is this boy going to become a monk?" "When the Lord wills," Brahmananda replied, and Ghosh decided at once to remain in the monastery. In 1921 he took his final vows and assumed the name of Prabhavananda, which means "one who finds bliss within the Source of all creation."

Two years later, Prabhavananda was sent to the Vedanta Center in San Francisco as an assistant swami, and in 1925 set up a new center in Portland, Oregon. While lecturing in Los Angeles he met an elderly American follower of Ramakrishna named Carrie Mead Wyckoff. Mrs. Wyckoff had become a disciple of another of Ramakrishna's followers, taking the name of Sister Lalita, and in 1929 she offered her home at 1946 Ivar Avenue in Hollywood as a center for what would become the Vedanta Society of Southern California. The Society started off small, but by the mid-1930s had raised enough funds to build a small temple in the garden. Even in the architecturally eclectic streets of Hollywood, the white temple with its onion domes and gilded pinnacles looked exotic, but inside it was as simple and unadorned as a Quaker meeting house. Prabhavananda lived in an adjacent bungalow along with those whom Heard disparagingly referred to as "the holy women." Although in good health, and a very keen and active gardener, Sister was in her eighties and so she and Prabhavananda had hired an Englishwoman named Ella Corbin as a housekeeper. Corbin, who had come to Hollywood as a dialogue coach after the failure of her marriage, studied with Prabhavananda, became a "nun" and took the Sanskrit name of Amiya. The third holy woman was a former music and dance student in her early twenties who had become Prabhavananda's prize pupil and been given the name of Sarada. The household was completed by Sister's ancient dog, who also had a Sanskrit name: Dhruva.

Isherwood's first meeting with Swami (as Prabhavananda was usually addressed) took place in July. "I felt terribly awkward," he recalled. "Everything I said sounded artificial. I started acting a little scene, trying to make myself appear sympathetic to him." Isherwood was concerned that he wouldn't be able to combine meditation with his proposed career in the distinctly worldly atmosphere of the Hollywood studios. Swami replied: "You must be like the lotus on the pond. The lotus-leaf is never wet." Since, as he confessed to Swami, Isherwood had been inclined to regard yoga as mere mumbo jumbo, it is surprising he did not abandon the whole idea there and then. Prabhavananda, however, did not always talk like this, and he tried to reassure his prospective pupil by telling him that he should not be afraid of failure. "There is no failure in the search for God," he insisted. "Every step you take is a positive advance." In his present state, this was just what Isherwood needed to hear. He nevertheless flinched at the word "God," whereupon Swami, whose undoubted spirituality was always tempered by pragmatism, followed Heard's line and said that "God" was just another word for "The Self." He explained the three tenets of Vedantan philosophy: "First, that Man's real nature is divine. Second, that the aim of human life is to realize this divine nature. Third, that all religions are essentially in agreement." After some further discussion, Isherwood left feeling that "As soon as I had taken at least one tiny step by myself, we would be able to talk practice instead of theory."

That tiny step led Isherwood back to Ivar Avenue on August 4, when at a second meeting with Swami he received his first lesson in meditation. There were four basic instructions:

1. Try to feel, all around you, the presence of an all-pervading Existence.
2. Send thoughts of peace and good will towards all beings—transmitting these thoughts consciously towards four points of the compass in turn: north, south, east and west.

3. Think of your own body as a temple which contains the Real Self, the Reality, which is infinite existence, infinite knowledge and infinite peace.

4. The Reality in yourself is the Reality within all other beings.

To sum up: this plan of meditation was a three-stage process. You sent your thoughts outward to the surrounding world, drew them inward upon yourself, then sent them outward again—but with a difference; for now you were no longer thinking of your fellow creatures as mere individuals but as temples containing the Reality. As mortal beings, you had offered them your good will; as the Eternal, you now offered them your reverence.

It had been some considerable time since Isherwood had practiced beaming good will upon mankind, but he set about following Swami's instructions, meditating for periods of half an hour each morning and evening.

He explained to Kathleen that "the *immediate* object of yoga is to overcome greed, fear, the tyranny of possessions, vanity, etc. etc. And to give you a permanent sense of calm and acceptance of whatever may come. This acceptance is so difficult, because it isn't mere fatalism or passive resignation. It is an inner ring of defence, which cannot be broken down." The fact that there were no special exercises to perform and no Sanskrit terms to learn lessened his resistance to the actual process of meditation. The only physical demand was that one should sit with one's spine erect, but there was no need to assume the cross-legged lotus position. Isherwood found sitting on the floor useful because it changed his perspective of the world, but Heard always meditated while sitting on a chair. As explained by Swami, meditation seemed not unlike practices familiar to any artist. "You go through it when you are planning a novel," Isherwood told his mother, "and have to put yourself into each of the characters, and accept and understand them for what they are. A painter puts himself into a landscape in the same way, and becomes, for a moment, part of the landscape, and feels that the landscape is part of himself."

Explaining Vedanta and pacifism to Kathleen was one thing: explaining it to Edward Upward quite another. Isherwood had funked writing to Upward directly, presumably banking on the fact that the contents of a letter he had written to Olive Mangeot would be passed on. It is small wonder that in response Upward had written Isherwood what he remembered as a "bitter letter" (which has not survived). The only thing Isherwood could do was to throw himself on his old friend's mercy, and the letter he wrote is the clearest contemporary account of what he was feeling in the late summer of 1939. "What I wrote to Olive was no doubt very muddled and hasty, and full of clap-trap words and capital letters which you find only too easy to explode," he began.

Instead of trying to defend myself, I will tell you as well as I can what has been happening to me since we met. I have never yet appealed to you in vain to interpret any of my experiences, and I hope that, if I stick to autobiography and don't try to generalize, you will feel less disgusted. Only hold your hat on, because there's a bit of a shock coming.

You can imagine our time in New York: press interviews, photographs, dinners for Spain, lunches for China, lectures, crooked publishers, long-haired Trotters and stern Reds. You can imagine how unsavoury and smelly the whole hate-Hitler racket becomes when it operates in first-class restaurants, with the whole Atlantic between it and the bombing-planes. We met some very unappetizing creatures, screaming for the English to go in and do their fighting for them, and naturally we got disgusted. That was the first step.

I began to feel myself, increasingly, in a false position. From the very beginning, I now realize, I have made a mess of my leftism. Laziness, dilettantism and cowardice have prevented me from doing the only possible thing: becoming a humble rank-and-file worker, as you did. Then this stupid little phase of notoriety as a writer pitchforked me into the limelight as Wystan's second fiddle. We went to China, and I produced this travel-diary which so annoyed the Left, because it was messy, personal, sentimental and confused, like myself. That is the way I will always be: personal. So I don't belong in any movement; and I cannot really take sides in any struggle. My only integrity can be to see the members of both sides as people, only as people, and to deplore their sufferings and crimes as personal sufferings and personal crimes.

So what remains to me but pacifism, of some kind? And what revolution can I attempt to promote but a revolution inside myself? This brings me to the next stage. I came to California to see Gerald Heard. Heard believes that mankind can only escape from its present revolutionary-counterrevolutionary cycle (excuse this jargon) by attempting a new phase of evolution: psychic evolution. Certainly, he says, a socialist world-order would be a step forward, but it will bog down in materialism, unless men themselves are really and radically changed. He sees the only hope for the future in building up a nucleus of psychically-trained leaders who will gradually spread their influence over the world, and become the directors of the new socialism. These leaders will be trained in the principles of Yoga—not pure eastern Yoga, but Yoga adapted for the needs of the west.

(Are you still reading, or have you fallen under the table in a dead faint?)

Yes, believe it or not, your unlucky Starn [Isherwood's Mortmere *alter ego*] has set his feet on the bottom of this crazy goat-track which is to lead over the peaks of the never-never mountains. What else can I do? I can only believe in what I experience myself. I have got to try it. I feel scared and unspeakably silly. I wish to God you were doing this, not me. But our wisest and bravest are occupied elsewhere, and there's nobody to send except the village idiot. All I can tell you is, I can see no other way out of my little personal valley of despair. I hear behind me the cries of Forster, frankly lost in the desert, I hear the yells of the scalping head-hunters, and I feel: No. I am not going back. I can't help what people will think of me. I can't worry about my writing. This is more important. It is also the only way in which I can even remotely hope to be of use to anybody, now.

But this is enough confession for one letter. If you're interested, even disgustedly interested, I will tell you more. If you say: 'poor Christopher has become an escapist. He has betrayed us all.' well, I shan't blame you. I only know that, for myself, I am doing the only possible thing. If I fail, it will be through my own weakness. All this sounds dreadfully F6, I daresay. I am quite well aware that I am making myself ridiculous. Wystan is very much amused. If only I could see you, I could make you accept my position, at any rate on a Mortmere basis.

Thank you for writing so frankly.

However you feel, do please write again at once.

Isherwood recalled that Upward sent a reply to this letter that was "a model of charity towards an attitude one can't understand." The letter has not survived, and there followed a long gap of over six and a half years in the correspondence between the two old friends.

FOURTEEN

B Y THE SUMMER OF 1939 IT BECAME CLEAR TO EVEN THE MOST optimistic observers that a world war had become not only inevitable but imminent. As crisis followed crisis throughout August, Isherwood and Viertel found their film project being overtaken by events, and they spent more and more of their time listening to the radio. For some months Isherwood had been urging Kathleen and Richard to leave London as soon as war became a certainty. On August 30, at the prompting of E. M. Forster, who told them they should leave London while they could, they had closed up the house in Pembroke Gardens and gone to stay with friends at Brabyns Hall, near Marple. (Nanny was with her sister in Bury St Edmunds, and Elizabeth was staying put in London.) It was at Brabyns, on September 3, the day England declared war on Germany, that they received a telegram from Christopher: "Love and thoughts with you writing." In the letter that followed, Isherwood wrote: "All through this crisis, I've postponed writing to you—hoping that I could do so after it was all over. And now there seems nothing to say. You know how I feel about this war." He decided that the only thing he could do was to get on with the film. "That seems the most practical work I can do, right now. Later, unless I see some other way of being useful here, I shall come to Europe—perhaps with an American red cross unit: I'd like that best, I think."

He wondered what Richard would do, as did Kathleen, whose diary is full of repeated news about the probability of universal conscription. It ought to have been clear that Richard, who was three months short of his twenty-eighth birthday, was totally unfit for any sort of military service, but both he and Kathleen still feared that he might be called up. During the summer they had taken first-aid courses, practicing their bandaging techniques on Nanny, but Richard had failed his test after answering the wrong questions in the written section. He now made inquiries about serving with the Air Raid Patrol, but the obvious solution would be for him to do some sort of agricultural work. About the only experience of work he had was on the farm at Wyberslegh Hall, spending the odd week helping the Coopers with the milk round and other odd jobs. This had also allowed him to attend to repairs to the other half of the Hall, which was currently let to Isherwood's former admirer, the heavily pregnant Rachel Monkhouse, and her husband, and to spend time at Marple Hall, where he was pursuing a characteristically obsessive and one-sided friendship with the caretaker's teenage son. Agriculture was considered work of national importance and farmers and laborers were often exempted from conscription. The Coopers, however, were worried that if they took on Richard, the government might consider that they no longer needed their two full-time workers. They suggested that Richard could stay at the farm as a paying guest, helping out as he had before. The only problem with this was that in order to avoid being called up, Richard would have to register as a farm laborer. In the event, something was sorted out, and at the end of September Richard began his work on the farm. Whether or not Richard was fit for agricultural service is a moot point. While cleaning out the cowsheds he tended to get muck on his hands, which then got transferred onto his face, because he was always rubbing his cheeks with his palms in a nervous gesture. At the end of the working day, he would go to the local pub without bothering to wash. "Let them all see that I'm doing a job," he said. Kathleen, meanwhile, had left Brabyns Hall and gone to sit out the war with her cousin Maude Brunton at Penmaenmawr, where she was shortly joined by Nanny.

The outbreak of war prompted John Lehmann to write what he called, with his usual self-importance, "a kind of testament" in the form of a letter to Isherwood. He described the blackout, the air raid sirens and the deserted London streets and gave news of Isherwood's British friends. He concluded: "I miss you terribly, nearly all my best friends seem to be so far away. And I don't think I would have let you down. I could have found you that job you wanted [in the Foreign office], most likely. But don't come back now—across those barbarous seas. I want someone to survive. I want you to survive." Isherwood replied: "How much simpler things would have been if [the war] had come in September [1938], and we'd shared that flat," but it is unlikely that they could have lived together very long without some sort of quarrel breaking out.

Lehmann, though careful not to say so in his letters to Isherwood, was horrified by the whole direction of his friend's life in America. He complained in his diary about Isherwood's unreliability as a correspondent and noted that Isherwood seemed "to be sinking deeper and deeper into the Yoga bog." Another person who had good reason to feel let down by Isherwood was Jack Hewit, who still received letters from his erstwhile friend and protector, but was upset by their remote tone. He still felt that Isherwood was "the only person who could do anything for him." He told Lehmann that "the Yoga business is in line with C's general refusal to think." "The more I consider this," Lehmann commented, "the more true it seems: as C. never wanted to use a reasoning mind about literature—or his friends—but preferred intelligent prejudice—and in fact gloried in his prejudices, so now he's grown tired suddenly of a reasoning *general* attitude, and retires into a faith, particularly as it is associated with a plausible and delightful character (G[erald]. H[eard].) This seems to be the only way to square the extraordinary new C. with the old cynical, sensual, absurd C. And even so it's hard." A letter from Isherwood a few days later caused him to change his mind again: it made Lehmann "feel all the warmth of his personality and all the happiness we have had together, this time without any intervening walls. It made me suddenly feel certain again of the bond between us."

In mid-September Isherwood and Vernon moved from the house on Sycamore Trail and took rooms at 303 South Amalfi Drive in Santa Monica Canyon. By way of farewell to a house he had always disliked and to a period of his life which now seemed over, Isherwood buried Jack Hewit's champagne cork under a tree in the garden before leaving. Isherwood described the Canyon, as it was always known to its residents, as "a shallow flat-bottomed little valley, crowded with cottages of self-consciously rustic design, where cranky, kindly people live and tolerate each other's mild and often charming eccentricities." It was, he thought, a "western Greenwich Village, overrun now by various types of outsider, but still maintaining an atmosphere of Bohemianism and unpretentious artiness." It was the place Isherwood would eventually regard as "home."

South Amalfi Drive was not only cheaper than Sycamore Trail, but was also just around the corner from Mabery Road. The Viertels' house was full of "armchair generals," Isherwood told Kathleen, émigrés who "have taken complete possession of the war, and are ready to wage it to the last drop of the last English boy's blood." Unfortunately, Isherwood also wrote to Gerald Hamilton about the émigrés' behavior and Hamilton gave the letter to Tom Driberg, who published part of it in the William Hickey gossip column he wrote for the *Daily Express*. Isherwood had written: "The refugees here are very militant and already squabbling over the future German government. God help Germany if some of them ever get into power! Others are interested, apparently, in reconquering the Romanisches Café, and would gladly sacrifice the whole British army to make Berlin safe for night life." One of Viertel's refugee friends in London sent a clipping of this report to Santa Monica, where it caused great offense. Viertel tried to make Isherwood write an apology, but he refused.

He did, however, make a far more important apology in October, perhaps as a result of his meditation exercises. Kathleen was the first recipient of Isherwood's new feelings of good will to all mankind, and he wrote to her:

> I wish we were together and could talk—because now I don't feel that you are any particular age, or that I am any particular age. Or even, especially, that you're my Mother. There's so much I want to ask—so much I should have asked, instead of lecturing you from the sitting-room fireplace—simply as a fellow-traveller. I have often made you very unhappy; but, believe me, I have been punished for it—so severely punished that I don't even need to apologize. My punishment has been that I have always, in one way or another, made the people I loved behave to me as I behaved to you. Goodness, how long it takes to learn.

It is not clear who Isherwood had in mind: none of those who loved him treated him with anything like the hostility he was capable of turning on Kathleen. Not that this mattered: the important thing was that this gesture was appreciated. "A great joy," Kathleen commented in her diary, "another letter from Christopher a very kind one & now we are so far apart." It was, of course, precisely because they were so far apart that Isherwood could afford to treat his seventy-one-year-old mother with the consideration she deserved.

By November Isherwood realized that the film he was working on with Viertel was never going to be made. Fortunately, the collaborators got taken on by Samuel Goldwyn to write "a spy film." The original treatment they were handed seemed to them "melodramatic and old-fashioned," quite beyond salvage, and Viertel suggested that they should write a new story around the character of Mr. Norris. This new scheme was suggested to Eddie Knopf of the Goldwyn Studio's script department, who seemed very enthusiastic, particularly since he would in effect be securing the film rights to Isherwood's novel without having to pay the author over and above the wages he would receive as a scriptwriter. Isherwood then went to see Goldwyn himself, and told him how he saw the basic plot. Goldwyn seemed equally enthusiastic.

It soon became clear, however, that Goldwyn's idea of what made a commercial spy story was entirely different from Isherwood's. The first treatment Isherwood and Viertel produced is very much in the style of Isherwood's novel, with Mr. Norris taking center stage and the whole story treated as a black farce. Goldwyn, who was unlikely actually to have read Isherwood's original novel, was expecting something rather more hard-boiled. Several characters from *Mr Norris Changes Trains*—including Frl. Schroeder, Baron von Pregnitz and Schmidt—reappear in slightly different roles, and the plot is concerned with passing a vital document about the Siegfried Line to the British. There is a great deal of exciting action, but rather more comedy, and the story ends in absurdity with Mr. Norris revealing that he has smuggled out the crucial information by writing it in invisible ink on his bald pate beneath his wig. The William Bradshaw character (topographically rechristened Bill Disley, a relation of Lord Marple) acts out of love for Mary Hill, a young English girl employed by the British as a spy, but although Isherwood makes him clearly heterosexual, Goldwyn felt that he "lacked initiative and virility" and was "too innocent and too naive." He also wanted the story to be told through these two characters, not through Mr. Norris.

Isherwood was not unnaturally irritated by these criticisms and although he immediately wrote another outline, in which much of the action was transferred from Norris to Bill and Mary, he sent it to the script department with an aggrieved letter. He complained that when he first discussed the original conception with Goldwyn, the mogul had seemed very satisfied. Isherwood had wanted to show spying as mundane rather than glamorous, and intended Mary to be "quiet, efficient, brave and charming rather than exotic, sensational, alluring and rash." "I was thinking in terms of Edith Cavell and not of Mata Hari," he explained unenticingly. He had conceived of Bill as "a kind of British Mr Smith," the decent, ordinary hero of Frank Capra's recent hit, *Mr. Smith Goes to Washington.* He wanted him to be an innocent civilian accidentally caught up in dangerous events; he would have plenty of opportunity to display his "virility" in the chase sequences toward the end of the film. Isherwood's biggest complaint was about the character of Mr. Norris, whom the simple-minded Goldwyn regarded as a criminal deserving punishment rather than glory. "I never thought of Mr Norris as a complete crook," Isherwood complained, and I should protest very strongly against any attempt to make him so. (Mr Norris, as you know, is a character out of one of my own novels; and his status as such is expressly recognised in my contract with Mr Goldwyn.) Mr Norris is foolish and dishonest, but he is not *evil* at all [. . .] The fact that it is he who eventually brings the document to England is the whole essence of my comedy. Just as in those fairy stories in which the hero is kind to an ugly and seemingly unpleasant dwarf who afterwards helps him to win the treasure. It was very important to me that Norris should be an amateur in this spying business [. . .] In fact the whole theme and fun of the story was to have been: amateurs versus professionals. I cannot speak, of course, for the taste of American audiences—but I am quite certain that if a British audience in wartime is to be shown a spy picture, this is the type of picture it will want to see.

This was a courageous letter, since before getting the job at the studio, Isherwood had been down to his last $15. Samuel Goldwyn, however, was not about to be lectured on movie audiences by some limey novelist. He summoned Isherwood to his office and dressed him down in front of several executives. It was perhaps fortunate that Isherwood, having made his protest, had ended his letter on a conciliatory, not to say fawning, note: "However much I may believe that an excellent picture could have been made out of the materials I offered, it is still my duty to do my utmost to please Mr Goldwyn and I have therefore started thinking along quite different lines."

These lines—"a serious drama with a modern angle, the possibility of very strong situations, and two central figures of the kind which I think Mr Goldwyn has in mind"—proved singularly unfruitful. The subsequent treatments Isherwood submitted are less subversive, less amusing and altogether more conventional than his original outline. Mary acquires a title and becomes a sort of Mitford, "a beautiful, high spirited, aristocratic girl—the daughter of an English peer." She mixes in Berlin's high society, pretending to be a passionate admirer of the Nazis, all the while preparing to pass information she gleans from such circles to the British. Bill is transformed into a seasoned Canadian war journalist, "a vigorous, plain-spoken young man" who has been in Abyssinia, Spain and China. He has a rival in his love for Mary in a German officer, who poses as a Nazi but really wants to overthrow Hitler and is appalled when Mary declares she "longs for the day when England, like Germany, will be dotted with concentration camps." War breaks out and there is an attempted coup. Isherwood remained rather vague as to how the plot was to resolve itself but decided that "Mr Norris, as I see him, has no place in this kind of story." Meanwhile, he had been offered a job at Metro-Goldwyn-Mayer, starting in January, writing dialogue for a film adaptation of James Hilton's novel *Rage in Heaven*.

By the end of 1939, Isherwood had started to take his place in the California film colony, and had met several of the stars whose careers he had followed during his youth—though not his current teenage pin-up, Mickey Rooney ("as remote from my life as the planet Uranus," he reported disappointedly to Lehmann). The social mix in Hollywood, both nationally and intellectually, was a rich one, and at a picnic he attended at the end of November, organized by Aldous and Maria Huxley, the other guests included the Viertels, Anita Loos, Bertrand Russell, Krishnamurti and

Garbo—"an all-star cast which you would hardly find the equal of in any other place, I should think," as Isherwood boasted to his mother. Much as he wanted to befriend Garbo, whom he had already met at the Viertels', he found it impossible to breach her famous reserve. She struck him as "very silly and gay and sympathetic," he told his mother, adding: "If she weren't Garbo, I could be great friends with her—but she is so terribly isolated: always having to cover her face with her hand or her hat when we pass anyone, for fear of being recognized. It is like going around with someone who is wanted for murder." It says something for Isherwood's confused state that he seems to have been more interested in talking to Garbo than to Russell, a leading pacifist of long standing. It may have been that he hesitated to interrupt the conversation Russell was having with Krishnamurti and Huxley. Although he found Maria Huxley enormously sympathetic, he was still rather in awe of her husband, and had not entirely changed his first impression of the older novelist as "nice, but oh so bookish and inclined to be pontifical." He was, in fact, just the sort of donnish figure Kathleen had originally wanted Isherwood to be.

Isherwood's attitude softened when he was introduced to Huxley's brother Julian, who had come to America on a lecture tour. Isherwood had expected Julian Huxley "to be more human than Aldous, warmer, less pedantic. Actually, he seemed prim, severe and schoolmasterish, and Aldous, by contrast, appeared much more sympathetic." Isherwood subsequently became a close friend of Aldous Huxley, and at the Huxleys' parties he met other British exiles, notably Iris Tree. An actress, poet and pacifist with youthfully bobbed blond hair, whose bohemian dress combined "a suggestion of cultism with the gypsy artiness of her Augustus John girlhood," Tree was eight years older than Isherwood, who found her "very gay and sympathetic." She had originally come to the States with her father, Herbert Beerbohm Tree, and married a society photographer, Curtis Moffatt, with whom she had a son, Ivan, who became a successful screenwriter and something of a playboy. Long since divorced and remarried, she was now running a theater group in the Ojai Valley founded with the intention of performing her plays, and was a friend of Krishnamurti, who lived there.

Isherwood decided that Julian Huxley had arrived in America "very much the official representative of England at war": "Behind his sternness, I thought I could detect a certain puritanical sadism—a satisfaction that the lax peace-days were over, and that we'd all got to suffer." Isherwood asked whether he should return to England, but Huxley told him he should remain in America and represent "the British point of view." He also suggested that Isherwood might like occasionally to get in touch with the British authorities to report on Hollywood's attitude to the war. Isherwood later reflected that

> if I had really been willing to become some sort of half-assed British Agent, then I should have had to face up to the decision either to do something really useful for Britain here in the States or else go back there. I couldn't pretend to the kind of patriotism that would make me ready to support 'Britain' in Julian's sense, while staying on here. I wasn't on Britain's side—except in the sense that I wasn't a pro-Nazi [. . .]
>
> Another factor in this [indecision] was Auden. He was still in New York, and it seemed that he would stay there because of Chester. I couldn't feel this way

about Vernon, fond as I was of him, because Vernon was so completely independent. He discouraged any moves towards founding a more domestic life between us. Still, the fact that Auden and I had come to this country together was still very powerful in motivating my actions. I felt a sort of responsibility towards him—we must co-ordinate our attitudes towards each other. I didn't exactly expect him to stay in America because of me, and yet I never quite forgot that America had been our joint project.

Vernon's independence was partly the result of the way Isherwood treated him. He encouraged him to read widely, to have friends his own age, and to pursue his studies as a painter. There were, however, tensions developing in the relationship. Although Vernon had always considered himself primarily heterosexual, he had believed it possible to change his sexual orientation through choice. He now began having serious doubts about his ability to "adjust to, commit to and continue the homosexual lifestyle and involvement" with Isherwood, and their relationship had become "essentially platonic." Various people had begun to notice that something was awry, and when Vernon told Heard about his dilemma, Heard (who, though homosexual, was himself a celibate) warned him of "the psychological danger inherent in this conflict." Vernon, he declared, "was really an alien in the gay world," and he suggested that if the relationship continued it would result in "severe emotional damage" to both parties. Vernon thinks it likely that Heard made his views known to Isherwood, but if he did Isherwood did not record them. "Needless to say," Vernon adds, "we didn't take his advice for a long time."

After spending most of his time in Hollywood "in a coma of nicotine poisoning," Isherwood had made an early New Year's resolution to give up smoking. This was certainly not a requirement of his chain-smoking swami, but after the painful first days of withdrawal, Isherwood hoped that he might become less jittery without the stimulus of nicotine.

The prospect of a full-time job at MGM also improved his nerves. A salary of $500 a week was not particularly high for Hollywood at this period, but it seemed a great deal to Isherwood, whose finances had remained in a poor way ever since he came to America. The job had been arranged for him by Salka Viertel. She had recently been fired from MGM for having the temerity to acquire an agent who asked for an increase in her salary, but she used her contacts among the film community's émigrés. Gottfried Reinhardt had come to Hollywood with his father Max, the great Austrian theater producer. Reinhardt senior's sole contribution to the cinema was a film of his spectacular stage version of *A Midsummer Night's Dream,* featuring Isherwood's beloved Mickey Rooney, a very young-looking fifteen-year-old in a fur loincloth, as Puck. Gottfried, however, had become a producer with MGM and wanted Isherwood to work with the screenwriter Robert Thoeren on *Rage in Heaven.* He was on a trip to New York when Isherwood started work at the studio on January 8, 1940, and was not expected to return for several weeks. Isherwood had his own air-conditioned office, but nothing to do, so he sat there catching up on his personal correspondence.

Although Isherwood had swiftly adapted to life in California, and enjoyed the climate, letters from cold, damp England still made him homesick. There were signs, however, that he missed England more than England missed him. In mid-January he received a letter from Tom Driberg asking permission to publish in his column a verse that was apparently doing the rounds in London.

> *The literary erstwhile Left-wellwisher would*
> *Seek vainly now for Auden or for Isherwood:*
> *The dog beneath the skin has had the brains*
> *To save it, Norris-like, by changing trains.*

The poem was eventually published in the *New Statesman* in February under the appropriate pseudonym "Viper." The author was identified by Kathleen, who copied the verse into her diary, as the novelist Anthony Powell, a representative of another school of 1930s writers: right-wing, militarist and scornful of what it described as "the pansy Left." Isherwood also copied the verse into his diary. "Why does this sting me so?" he asked himself. "Simply because it is really clever. It succeeds in making me look ridiculous—in a way that mere abuse can't. My vanity is hurt. Yes, I had better admit it. I am not in the least ashamed of myself, but I feel foolish." He was, however, sufficiently disturbed by Powell's undeniably witty malice to embark once again upon an assessment of his position and his motives for being in America. "I'll try to be absolutely honest about this," he wrote.

> Am I a coward, a deserter? Not according to my standards. If I were told that somebody else had 'run away from England', I should ask, 'What did "England" mean to him?' 'England' to me meant a place that I stayed away from as much as possible during the past ten years. From a strictly patriotic standpoint, you can be 'disloyal' in peace as well as in war. Yet no one blamed me then. And I certainly didn't blame myself.

There is a certain amount of casuistry about this argument. Although Isherwood certainly went to Berlin partly in order to escape England, he does not acknowledge that he would have been quite content to have returned to live in London after 1933 had Heinz not been prevented from entering the country. It might equally be said that England was a place he returned to as much as possible, in order to see his friends, sort out his business affairs, find work and experience some home comforts. Furthermore, wandering around Europe in peacetime—even a precarious peacetime—cannot really be compared to going to America and taking out naturalization papers in advance of a war which would inevitably involve England.

Isherwood may not have felt any particular loyalty to his country but, mindful of Forster, he wondered whether he was betraying his friends.

> Maybe my place is with them, over there. Maybe my attitude would only pain them. Maybe I should become their enemy?
> Oh, it's not the smallest use trying to work this out, logically. And it's certainly no use running home to protect my vanity. If I really have to go, I shall know when the time comes. Life will give me some signal. I must just wait for it.

At the same time, however, he was writing to Jimmy Stern, who had settled in New York: "If one has decided, like ourselves, to survive this war, we must make a world fit for shirkers to live in."

There had been a hiatus of several months in Isherwood's correspondence with Stephen Spender, who was much preoccupied with the unexpected and total collapse of his marriage: Inez had run off with the poet Charles Madge, and Spender was now living in Lavenham with Humphrey and Lolly. The latter had developed incurable Hodgkin's disease, and so there was another crisis to face. Isherwood now received a copy of a new magazine Spender was editing with Cyril Connolly. *Horizon,* which described itself as "A Review of Literature & Art," was launched at an unpropitious time, and to some extent stepped into the breach left by the closure of such influential magazines as *Criterion* and *New Verse.* It had the financial backing of Peter Watson, a wealthy and highly cultivated *flâneur,* whom Connolly had got to know through his wife, Jean.

Spender had asked Isherwood if there was any possibility of his writing something for the new magazine, but had got the same dusty answer that Lehmann received. Lehmann himself was incensed at the whole idea of *Horizon* since he had been negotiating with Watson about producing a paperback edition of his own *New Writing.* He particularly resented the fact that Spender, who was on his editorial board, had become (in effect, though not on the masthead) co-editor of this rival magazine. This "defection" caused a major falling-out of the sort that characterized Lehmann's personal and professional life. He wrote furiously in his diary that it was "impossible to have a direct and natural relationship with [Spender] as a friend or even close collaborator, pathologically eaten up as he is with jealousy, vanity, egotism, and utterly corrupted by years of extravagant self-deception." Although Lehmann seems to have been unaware of the fact, the defects he complained of in Spender's character are precisely the defects that ruined his own life. He may have been angry, but he was careful not to attempt to involve Isherwood in this feud. Instead he made a bid for sympathy in a more general way. "I feel very alone now, sometimes, and get moods of almost suicidal gloom," he wrote. "This is of course chiefly because of Toni and Vienna [visits to his Austrian lover were no longer possible], but it's also because you're so far away. It's got worse since that stupid and destructive row with Stephen. That really was the last straw that seemed to break something in me, and I am oppressed by a lethargy from which I still can't rouse myself to organize a new NEW WRITING or write any of the things I've got in my head." Isherwood replied that he was very sorry about the argument and hoped it would sort itself out. "It makes me very sad to think that The Gang is splitting up. But I'm sure it can't and won't, in the long run."

This was unduly optimistic, as became clear when the second issue of *Horizon* appeared in February 1940. Unable to produce any material for the magazine, Isherwood had instead taken out ten four-month subscriptions which he hoped to sell in America. He must have wondered whether this had been wise when he opened the February issue of the magazine and read Connolly's "Comment." Snide and inaccurate remarks about Auden and Isherwood's life in America had been appearing in the newspapers for some time. The *Evening Standard* had reported the previous June that "the young pair are not wholly impressed with the New World."

> For a time they sampled the pleasures of New York intellectual society. But they came to find it unintelligent, told it so, and donning their shabbiest clothes, shut themselves up in a flat in one of the city's less fashionable slum districts. Here, in conclave, they proceeded to evolve a new philosophy of life. Its main principle, I gather, is a negation of Auden's previous thesis that art is inseparable from politics. Meanwhile the pair have separated. Mr Isherwood has gone off to visit the film stars in Hollywood. Mr Auden is teaching in a boys' school in New England.

Isherwood crossly described this article as "certainly very ill-natured and quite untrue," but thought it a waste of time to write a correction. In his "Comment," Connolly referred to a "homily" in *Reynolds* magazine, "in which the editors of *Horizon* are identified with the émigré writers Huxley, Heard and Isherwood, who have gone to California to 'contemplate their navels.'" He then went on to suggest that *Reynolds* was "quite right to link up *Horizon* with a sneer at the English émigrés in California, for the departure of Auden and Isherwood to America a year ago is the most important literary event since the outbreak of the Spanish War." Connolly then delivered his own verdict on the action of his erstwhile friends.

> It is extremely unfortunate that they began to settle in their new surroundings and send word home, just as we went to war with Germany, for it puts too easy a construction on their departure, and turns Isherwood's professions of faith in Yogi [*sic*] into a weapon that reactionary papers such as *Action* have used against him. But the fact remains that at the moment (and not because of the war) two of our best writers, who were also two of our most militant left-wing writers, have abandoned England and are taking out naturalisation papers in America—a country which artists up to a few years ago had fled in horror, and which only one English author, Richard le Gallienne, had made his home. [. . .]
> Auden is our best poet, Isherwood our most promising novelist. They did not suffer from a lack of recognition in England where they received a publicity which they did everything to encourage, nor have they gone to America to animate the masses, for Auden has been teaching in a New England school and Isherwood writing dialogue in a Hollywood studio. They are far-sighted and ambitious young men, with a strong sense of self-preservation, and an eye on the main chance, who have abandoned what they consider to be the sinking ship of European democracy, and by implication the aesthetic doctrine of social realism that has been prevailing there. Are they right? It would certainly seem so. Whatever happens in the war, America will be the gainer. It will gain enormously in wealth, and enormously (through the refugees) in culture. England will be poverty-stricken, even in victory [. . .]
> The flight of Auden and Isherwood to a land richer in incident and opportunity is also a symptom of the failure of social realism as an aesthetic doctrine, and this brings us back to the policy of *Horizon* . . .

It was one thing to be sniped at by *Reynolds* and *Action,* but this "Comment" from someone Isherwood considered an ally, published in a magazine co-edited by one of his closest friends, wounded Isherwood deeply. It would be hard to imagine a more calculatedly offensive assault, with its references to Isherwood's "*professions* of faith" in yoga, and its suggestion that he and Auden had been hungry but ungrateful publicity-seekers, who had had the foresight, and been sufficiently unworried by moral scruples, to abandon a doomed Europe for a safe, culturally dead but financially remunerative neutral country. Connolly makes strategic use of such words as "flight" and "abandon," while the reference to le Gallienne, a relic of the 1890s who was generally considered to have long outlived what literary fame he had enjoyed, was gratuitously bitchy.

As the magazine rolled off the presses, Spender received a letter from Isherwood complaining about Hamilton and the William Hickey column and asking him to ensure that nothing in his letters was repeated to any journalist. It ended: "And now, Stephen dear, I must tell you again in conclusion how constantly I think of you, and how more than happy and proud I am to know that you are my friend, at this time when one needs the best friends one can lay hands on." Spender was aghast, and hastily wrote a letter to "Dearest Xtopher" (later adding, clearly as a tactical afterthought, "and Wystan") in which he attempted both to apologize for and justify Connolly's editorial. He began, typically, by reminding Isherwood of another occasion on which extracts from one of his letters appeared in the *Express.* Spender claimed that Giles Romilly had stolen one of Isherwood's letters to him and shown it to Driberg in order to further his journalistic career, but nevertheless blamed himself for his carelessness. "The only thing is that I am the only one who has gone on feeling upset about it, because the letter was to me," he wrote. Having established that his own distress over this incident was greater than Isherwood's, he went on to claim emotional rights in the coming débâcle over the *Horizon* article.

> In the same way, I feel upset about the remark in *Horizon* which you & Wystan may find offensive, because I feel that I ought to have told Cyril that it might be considered so, and the fact that I've been tremendously preoccupied with my own worries isn't really an excuse, though I offer it to all of you, Cyril included, for what it's worth.

Rather than let well enough alone, he continued:

> But really these things work both ways, because although I hate to feel that there is any acrimony between us, my first reaction on reading a thing like this is to think, well Horizon can't be a clique, and I can't enter into an understanding not to criticise people who are my friends, nor am I a censor. Also all Cyril's comments amounted to saying was that you are ambitious, and if someone said that Spender had 'an eye on the main chance', I would merely think 'that is true, in a way, certainly'. Anyhow, I blame myself for thoughtlessness now, just as I do in a lot of cases, and I apologize once more for my recurrent thoughtlessness, but I shall try not to regard it as too serious a crime. You might forward this letter to Wystan.

Before this unsatisfactory letter reached California, Isherwood had already sent Spender his reactions to the article. "I must say I was a little staggered when I read the 'Comment'—especially as I know it must have been written by you, or by Cyril with your approval," he wrote.

I am well aware we are being attacked in the English Press, and I have no intention of answering these attacks. There is really nothing to say except: Mind your own business. But when you, or Cyril, writes something, it is different. When a close friend criticizes you, it is only fair to him to reply—not so much in self-defence as in explanation. The alternative is sulking and feeling hurt—which is silly.

I appreciate that, in the second paragraph of the 'Comment', you are trying, though rather half-heartedly, to deprecate the charges made by *Reynolds* and *Action* (I haven't read either). But, when you get to the third paragraph, you adopt a tone which I can only describe as coldly hostile.

'They did not suffer from lack of recognition in England where they received a publicity which they did everything to encourage' . . . Stephen, what the hell do you mean by that? In what way have either Wystan or I 'encouraged' publicity? It is utterly unfair and untrue.

. . . 'nor have they gone to America to animate the masses'. If by 'animate' you mean 'make propaganda among', you seem to suggest that this has always been our mission and duty in life. You know perfectly well it hasn't. When did we ever 'animate masses' anywhere? Who ever expected us to? Certainly, we both spoke about Spain and China, and we have done the same thing here, repeatedly, both on the platform and over the air.

Why shouldn't Wystan teach in a school? He has his living to earn and he happens to be a schoolmaster by profession. Why shouldn't I work in a Hollywood studio? I have to eat, don't I? But I expect you have no idea how anonymous and humble my position at MGM is. It's just like working in an office. I am one among many. Hardly anybody even knows I ever had a reputation as a writer in the outside world. I only got the job because I am a friend of the Viertels. I am certainly not surrounded by 'publicity' and fans.

'with a strong instinct of self-preservation, and an eye on the main chance'. I don't want to bring myself into this—I am certainly no hero, and am popularly supposed to be ambitious—but, applied to Wystan, I consider that sentence a really disgusting libel. Wystan—wandering vaguely off to Spain with his pockets full of toilet-paper; sitting on the top of the front-line parapet to photograph the Japanese trenches; Wystan, who loses important business letters, fails to turn up at lunches on which his social career depends—no I can hardly believe that anybody who knew him well, and liked him, could write such nonsense.

But now I'm starting to get angry and that wasn't what I intended at all. All that really concerns me is that *you* have written or, at any rate, approved this article. Because it can only mean that, consciously or unconsciously, you are turning against us both. And I want to know why.

I am quite aware, of course, that it seems unpardonable, nowadays, that anybody should be living in safety, in a beautiful climate, earning money. And I often feel guilty about this. But consider the circumstances. This emigration wasn't a last-moment flight. It was a deliberate act, planned a long time ago—indeed, it had been in my mind for several years. You cannot seriously think that my interest in Yoga (not 'Yogi'!) is a pose, or that my change of feeling about violence is not sincere. As for being here, everybody, even the British authorities, agree that those who are in the US should stay. And what could I do at home? Protest? Sulk? Sit around silently disagreeing? As a matter of fact, if the war goes on, Wystan and I most probably *will* come over, in an ambulance unit. But this will be an act of pure self-crucifixion. I can't imagine that either of us would be very useful.

Why have I decided to become an American citizen? Because I believe that the future of English culture is in America, and that the building of this future will be assisted by the largest possible cultural emigration. The two elements have got to mix. I know, when I say it, this sounds nauseatingly pompous—but that's only because I'm trying to formulate what I feel, instead of giving you the whole thought-stream. Anyhow, I gather, from the 'Comment', that you do understand this—although you disapprove.

Well, having shot off all this talk, I feel exhausted, and mild, and increasingly aware that I can't possibly be angry with you, whatever you do or say. I accept you completely—and woe betide the skunk who calls *you* any nasty names! So please accept this letter in the spirit which dictates it.

Replying, Spender insisted that he was "not in any way responsible for the editorial, which is always written by Cyril." Directly contradicting what he had written in his earlier letter, he said "the question for me is simply how far I should censor" the editorial. He tried to argue once again that the editorial was "fair comment," and although he regretted Connolly's use of the phrase "an eye on the main chance," he repeated that he did not think this so terrible a thing to write about someone. Himself apart, he added, Auden and Isherwood were the most ambitious people he knew. "What surprises me is that you should think there is anything shameful in this attitude which, I should have thought, is one of the first things that one has to reckon with in oneself." Isherwood, of course, had been acutely aware of his own ambition during his last year in England, and had indeed regarded it as rather shameful, particularly when he was obliged to admit that his professional life had been made a lot easier when he and Heinz were forcibly parted. But Spender must have realized that Connolly's suggestion that America represented an opportunity for Auden and Isherwood was far less damaging than the suggestion that it represented a safe haven.

"You go on to say that the Commentary [*sic*] disapproves of you going to America," Spender continued. "Here I think you are quite wrong because on the contrary Cyril says that you are quite right to have done so." It is unlikely that anyone else reading Connolly's article would gain this impression. Isherwood's argument that the cultural future lay in America rather than Europe—an assertion not altogether easy to justify from an office at a Hollywood studio where one spent one's day being paid large sums of money to write dialogue for a screen adaptation of a distinctly middlebrow novel—failed to impress Spender, who rightly described it as "just a meaningless noise."

As long as England exists and is having a history, it is absurd to talk of culture emigrating. Culture isn't something which is quite separate from the lives of people. No doubt writers may decide to emigrate, and that may have the effect of silencing literature as it is silenced in Germany and Italy. But this is really an artificial state of affairs caused by the intellectuals themselves, and it is natural that people wanting to have their lives expressed for them in art may regard it as a betrayal.

Whenever people discuss with me your going to America, I always defend you.[1] That is to say, as far as going to America is concerned, to me it seems that you had no reasons whatever for doing so except the most casual ones, but I believe in you and therefore I think that what you do is comparatively unimportant because I have confidence that in some way you will be able to assimilate it. If anything were to upset me it would not be your going to America but your writing a scenario for 'Goodbye Mr Chips'.[2] However, I have long since stopped feeling censorious about anything of this kind and my attitude about the Commentary is an example of my uncensoriousness, not of my hostility. If you read my Journal, it must be obvious to you that I cannot be having any feelings of hostility about Wystan and you as you say.

Spender was clearly doing his best in an impossible situation, but the more he wrote the worse he made things. If Isherwood replied, the letter has not survived, and there was no more contact between the two friends for the next nine months.

Isherwood evidently complained to Forster about the article and about Spender's attitude to the episode. Forster had never much cared for Connolly, and, though fond of Spender, thought him muddled and occasionally silly, referring to him out of his hearing as "the Goose." "I have thought a good deal about the comments on you in Horizon which you mention," he wrote,

and with indignation, as you may surmise. I think Connolly is just an opportunist, who saw good material for journalism—I have no opinion of him, although many of his attitudes are acceptable and cleverly put. Stephen (whom I have gently ticked off) is another case, of course. I think he gets hypnotised by the notion of being sincere. Once when I was a child eating rice and sweet sauce alone in a room with my great-aunt Monie's picture, I got up and smeared some of the sweet sauce upon the gilt picture-frame. I did this not because I wanted to but because I had the *idea* of doing it and felt that I should be more straightforward if I put the idea into practice. This is the explanation of much of Stephen's conduct, I think. Afterwards, as I did, he tries to rub the sweet sauce out, and, as I did not, he probably succeeds.

---

1. As well he might. "Why don't you go to America?" he had asked Isherwood back in 1935. "I somehow feel that you would be able to write there even better than in England."
2. Spender has confused two of James Hilton's novels.

As well as providing a characteristically acute analysis of Spender's behavior, Forster also reassured Isherwood about his self-imposed exile.

> If you could save us, even at the cost of your own life, I might beckon you back, but such a notion is utter balls. You could do nothing. Where you are you can do something: manipulate the civilization of the USA. You will smile thinking that I know nothing of the hardness the hurry the shoddiness and the salary in which your public life is spent. I think I do know. And I think they constitute *something* to get hold of, whereas Europe, having missed its boat at the moment of the Spanish war, provides nothing. We may—having reached exhaustion point—start again, and have enough good books unburnt and good buildings standing to make the start a successful one. But that is mere speculation. Your immediate job is to stop and work where you are.

This was a generous letter—particularly if, as his friend May Buckingham recalled, Forster really did disapprove of Isherwood going to America at such a time—and it must have been gratefully read.

Lehmann was, as usual, less tactful. He continued to wring his hands over the prospect of "The Gang" splitting up, adding: "But how could it be otherwise with you and Wystan settled for good on the other side of the Atlantic?" Perhaps realizing that the last thing Isherwood needed was further sniping from his friends, he continued: "You mustn't think from what I've just said that I criticize you for going. You know I don't: but it makes me sad all the same, because I'd be much happier if it were possible to see you constantly." Of those who did criticize Isherwood and Auden publicly, he wrote: "I have a feeling that these people fall chiefly into two categories: those who were jealous all along (like [J.B.] Priestley), and those who can't forgive themselves for not having got across in time (like Cyril?). Last week I had a letter from leftist New Zealand writer Frank Sargeson, who said, without irony, that he thought your departure was the most courageous thing imaginable. I only wish there wasn't going to be a gulf between us here and you there after the war, made by all we're going through." In fact, so far Lehmann and his fellow countrymen were not going through very much at all, since this was the period of the so-called "Phoney War," before the Germans started bombing London and other British cities. But the implication was clear: those in Britain would be experiencing something unimaginable to those in the Lotus Land of Southern California.

Gottfried Reinhardt had meanwhile returned from New York and Isherwood had to concentrate upon *Rage in Heaven* rather than worry about what England thought of him. Now that the real work had started, Isherwood began to enjoy himself, finding both Reinhardt and Thoeren pleasant and easy colleagues. Heard, however, did not share Swami's beliefs about the lotus leaf and had begun to warn Isherwood about the spiritual dangers of working for MGM. "Theoretically, it *is* possible to live in both worlds, and recognize that one of them is unreal," he told Isherwood, adding: "I shouldn't dare to try it myself." He pointed to the sad example of Huxley, who was writing a screen adaptation of *Pride and Prejudice* and, thought Heard, becoming far too involved in his job. He now made an attempt to wean Isherwood from Metro in order to work instead on uplifting documentaries with the Polish-born filmmaker Henwar Rodakiewicz.

Heard had got to know Rodakiewicz through the latter's wife, Peggy, a Philadelphian he had first met in England. At that time she was married to the lawyer and author W. Curtis Bok, who had won a Pulitzer Prize in 1921 for his autobiography, *The Americanization of Curtis Bok*. The Boks had three children and were divorced in 1933, after which Peggy married Rodakiewicz. The Rodakiewiczes were among the first of Heard's friends to whom Isherwood had been introduced, and Peggy became one of his closest women friends, to some extent filling a role similar to that previously played by that other Peggy, Beatrix Lehmann. "It is very hard for me to write about Peggy," Isherwood noted of Rodakiewicz in the mid-1940s, "because I know her so intimately—*so* intimately that I think of her with the kind of love-hate I'd feel for a sister. In some ways we are deeply alike. I think the most dominant of her characteristics is her bad conscience." Peggy had a bad conscience because as the wealthy, attractive wife of Bok she found herself elevated to an exalted position in Philadelphia society. Feeling guilty about her good fortune, she determined to cancel what she thought of as a debt to fate. One way of doing this, she supposed, was to manage other people's lives, but although this often produced creditable results, she had little patience when people failed to perform to the high standards she expected of them. She drove herself equally hard, and was even more critical of herself than of others. One of the attractive things about her was that, although she had a sharp tongue, she was always ready to apologize. She was at her best when people actually needed help, rather than having advice and encouragement thrust upon them whether they liked it or not. Once she had helped people, however, she was like a hospital matron, expecting them to undergo a speedy recovery and bullying them mercilessly until they did so. Isherwood detected an element of hysteria in her character, a frantic uncertainty about herself even though she thought she could sort out the lives of others. Much as Isherwood liked Peggy, he had a low opinion of her husband's skills, and had no intention of leaving a lucrative job with a major studio to work on worthy but badly made documentaries.

If Heard could do nothing to prevent Isherwood's mind from being polluted by the demands of commerce, he could at least do something about his friend's body. Isherwood had been suffering from what he thought was a recurrence of the gonorrhea he had contracted in Brussels. Heard introduced him to Dr. Kolisch, a Viennese émigré who had studied with Prabhavananda and become house doctor to the yoga set. Kolisch assured Isherwood that his symptoms had nothing to do with venereal disease—that, moreover, he had probably never even had gonorrhea in Belgium. The discharge and burning sensation Isherwood experienced when he urinated were attributable to some disturbance of the nervous system. Isherwood underwent a course of treatment and appeared to recover. Now Heard recommended that Isherwood should go on one of Kolisch's fruit and vegetable diets, supplemented by herbal teas, cod-liver oil, mysterious red and green capsules, injections and "quartz-lamp baths." Three times a week, he would report to Kolisch's surgery for a check-up, which involved blood tests, being weighed and having his pulse taken. This regime cost $100 a month, and at the end of the first four weeks Isherwood reported that he was "still feeling much the same. Gas, fits of depression, nervous headaches." He was by now on six different kinds of medicine. "The Huxley, Isherwood, Heard circle was very susceptible to all kinds of fads, during this period," recalled Vernon, who remembered one diet consisting entirely of coconut milk and fresh pineapple: this was "designed to cure everything, but in the end changed nothing." After a further month of Kolisch's regime, however, Isherwood thought there were signs of improvement.

There is no doubt that most of Isherwood's health problems were psychological in origin. Having done his best, legally, to make a return to England unlikely, he was still unsure of what he *ought* to do, and this uncertainty was made worse by the criticism, veiled or otherwise, of people in England. Although he had European friends in California—Heard, Wood and Viertel—there was no one there with whom he had such strong and long-standing links as Spender or Forster. He was also separated geographically and psychologically from his closest ally, Auden. "It is strange to live among these psychically virgin Californians, with their sound teeth and intact nerves," he told Lehmann. "Partly it is very stimulating; partly it makes you feel lonely. Sometimes I think that I must return to Europe, anyhow, at any price—just to merge my individual aches in the big general ache. But I'm afraid I would feel myself just as much of an outcast there. There are few people I could honestly agree with, about this war."

It was at this point that another attack was launched in England on Isherwood and Auden by another person they might once have regarded as an ally. Harold Nicolson, who had been strongly opposed to Chamberlain's policy of appeasement, wrote an article in the *Spectator* complaining that

> It is not so much that the absence of [Isherwood, Auden, Huxley and Heard] from Europe will cause us to lose the Second German War. It is that their presence in the United States may lead American opinion, which is all too prone to doubt the righteousness of our cause, to find comfort in their company. For if indeed four of our most acute and sensitive writers demonstrate by their exile that they wish to have no part in the blood-stained anarchy of Europe, then surely the ordinary American is ten times more justified in remaining aloof from so inhuman a business and in proclaiming that isolationism is not only comfortable and convenient, but righteous and intelligent as well? How can we proclaim over there that we are fighting for the liberated mind, when four of our most liberated intellectuals refuse to identify themselves either with those who fight or with those who oppose the battle. For in truth the Americans well know that this is no ordinary case of petty shirking. It should matter little were a handful of interior decorators or dress designers to remain in, or to escape to, the United States and thereby to evade the anxieties and deprivations of their friends. The only feeling which that type of *embusqué* could rouse among the Americans would be a feeling of contempt. But these four exiles are striking figures; they are men of high intelligence, honour and courage; and if they, at such a moment, deny Europe, then the Americans will feel, with a relief of uneasy conscience, that Europe is in fact something which a man of integrity, strength and education has the right to deny.

Nicolson went on to write that he did not for one moment doubt the sincerity of Huxley's pacifism at any rate, but felt that a pacifist should be "militant" and should not "in times of stress and danger [. . .] remain outside the conflict."

Here, essentially, is my quarrel with these Four Horsemen of the Apocalypse, who have now dismounted and led their horses back into the distant Hollywood stable. I have small criticism to make of the ivory tower so long as one remains in it. My criticism is against those who leave their tower when the sun of June is upon the meadows and then retreat to it when the winds of autumn begin to howl [. . .] It is easier, when Western civilization is bursting into flames and thunder, to retreat into the gentler solitudes of the Wisdom of the East. Mr Huxley strives, by practising 'detachment', by refusing to concern himself with what is terrible or wicked, to find 'illumination'. I do not imagine for one moment that so fine a soul as his can find detachment easy or illumination rapid. There must be moments for him, even in Hollywood, of doubt whether the Higher Wisdom can best be defended at a distance of three thousand miles. There must be moments when he must ask himself whether or not it is conceivable that he is being guilty of spiritual arrogance.

It was not, of course, the accusation of spiritual arrogance that stung so much as the scarcely veiled implication that these men, even as self-proclaimed pacifists, were shirking their duty, which was at home rather than in Hollywood. Auden was not, of course, in Hollywood, and Heard had no connections with the film world, but "Hollywood" was a convenient and damning shorthand. It suggested a place of illusions and escapism where for vast amounts of money writers frittered away their talents on crowd-pleasing projects wholly unworthy of them. As with Connolly's remarks, it is the tone as much as what was being said that was so offensive. In particular, there was a nasty hint about the sexuality of these shirkers in Nicolson's reference to "interior decorators" and "dress designers," two occupations not usually associated in the public mind with heterosexuals. This, coming from a homosexual married to a lesbian, was certainly a bit rich; no wonder Kathleen referred to him furiously in her diary as "that flabby *worm*."

Nicolson's article in effect declared open season on the English exiles, and soon there were comments in several newspapers. The reactionary *Daily Mail* wondered "why Americans should be invited to risk a single drop of blood when young Englishmen remain in America instead of coming here to help our war effort." Although both of military age, at thirty-five and thirty-three respectively, Isherwood and Auden were not in fact considered prime military material by the British authorities. When in early July British actors working in Hollywood were summoned back to England, the upper age limit was thirty-one. The attacks continued regardless. The left-wing *Daily Mirror* ineptly parodied Auden's epigraph for *The Orators* by declaring that

Poetical faces in distant places
Are safer and sounder
Than poetical faces in homeland places.[3]

---

3. Auden's verse had read:

   Private faces in public places
   Are wiser and nicer
   Than public faces in private places.

The Dean of St. Paul's, cowering behind his private initials ("W.R.M."), was also moved to verse, declaring in lines which combined the vocabulary of the hymnal and the prep-school dormitory, and showed no evidence whatsoever of Christian charity,

> *'This Europe stinks,' you cried—swift to desert*
>   *Your stricken country in her sore distress.*
> *You may not care, but still I will assert*
>   *Since you have left us, here the stench is less.*

The *Spectator,* where the Dean's ill-tempered address "To Certain Intellectuals Safe in America" was published, remained the chief debating ground for this controversy. Spender, who was a friend of Nicolson, was once again in a difficult position, but managed not so much to sit on the fence as to skip nimbly along it. He wrote a letter to the magazine, in which he stated that much of the criticism of the voluntary exiles had been misguided and that what really mattered was their writing: "And if they succeed in writing better in America than they have done here they will be justified, in spite of the very sensible objections raised by Mr Nicolson." F. Desborough wrote to the magazine quoting a letter from "a Professor of one of the leading American Universities," who declared that the "absent authors" were not welcome in America:

> When they announce that they won't read war news, that they are attempting to evade their contracts and stay on in America until they can go back and '*help make the peace*', '*That Europe stinks*', &c., &c., *we* want to say 'we don't want *such* in America. *Get out.*'

"I will make no comment on these remarks," Desborough added, "except to say that everyone worthy of the name of Briton will say: 'We, also, don't want such in Great Britain. *Get out.*' " This correspondent evidently wasn't the sort of person the poet Frances Bellerby had in mind when she wrote to the magazine to observe: "Some intellectuals are extremely excited because other intellectuals have seen fit to go to America. They say so, in well-managed words strongly scented with self-righteousness and rationalized malice. In my village women say much the same things, with different concepts, of a butcher whose meat and manners please them not." She asked the magazine's editor to stop giving space to such malicious comments and "to silly, nasty little verse such as that of W.R.M."

E. M. Forster, who had felt that Spender's letter was "not what was wanted," agreed with Bellerby and wrote to ask "whether there should now be a close time for snarling at absent intellectuals."

> About half a dozen of them—not more—are away in America, and week after week their fellow-authors go for them in the newspapers. The attacks are highly moral and patriotic in tone, but their continuance raises the uneasy feeling that there must be something else behind them, namely unconscious envy; they are like the snarl of an unfortunate schoolboy who has been 'kept in' and is aggrieved because the whole of his class has not been kept in too, and therefore complains

and complains about those stinkers out in the playground instead of concentrating on his own inescapable task.

Forster went on to say that people should be directing their attentions instead to "denounce our resident Quislings," a group of people he declined to identify but who, he maintained, had far more power and influence than emigrant writers. "The consequences may be unpleasant for [the commentators], for Quislings sometimes hit back," he continued in his best feline manner. "But they will have had the satisfaction of exposing a genuine menace instead of a faked one, and this should be sufficient reward." The editor added a note to say: "We are glad to publish Mr Forster's letter, but so far as the *Spectator* is concerned the controversy would not have been continued in any case." Someone else who was glad to see Forster's letter was Kathleen. Forster had sent her a postcard alerting her to his letter, which she carefully copied into the back of her diary. He also wrote to Isherwood telling him to take no notice of "all this stupid chatter." As he complained to Britten later in the war: "scarcely any of his former friends over here seem able to think of Christopher as a human being whom one has loved and therefore loves. They turn all niggling and pedantic [. . .] I remember all this prim ungenerosity in the other war too, and am depressed at the ignorance and feebleness of the heart."

By the time Forster's riposte was delivered, Isherwood and Auden's case had been taken up in Parliament. On June 13 the Conservative M.P. Major Sir Jocelyn Lucas, relying upon inaccurate press reports of the two writers' views, asked the Parliamentary Secretary to the Minister of Labour about "British citizens of military age, such as Mr W. H. Auden and Mr Christopher Isherwood, who have gone to the United States and expressed their determination not to return to this country until the war is over." The minister, evidently not a reader, confused W. H. Auden with H. W. ("Bunny") Austin, a famous tennis player, and assured Sir Jocelyn that this eminent sportsman had given an undertaking to return to Britain if summoned. Sir Jocelyn pointed out the minister's confusion and suggested that the miscreant authors should have their British citizenship revoked unless they registered as conscientious objectors. The minister, presumably still in a daze, gave no answer to this request, and there the matter seemed to end.

"One would think Parliament had more useful things to consider," Kathleen complained. She detected spite as a motivating force in the whole saga, and she was undoubtedly right. It is interesting, for example, that no one seems to have been very interested in the plans of two other newsworthy left-wingers who had gone to America. Giles Romilly's younger brother, Esmond, and his wife, Jessica Mitford, had frequently attracted the attention of the papers, but no one seemed to question their decision to go to New York in February 1939 so that Romilly could get a job in an advertising agency. They, too, had taken out citizenship papers, and had declared to friends when the war broke out that they had no immediate plans to return to England. They subsequently traveled round America, writing frivolous journalism which appeared between January and March 1940 in the *Washington Post* under the headline "Baby Blue Bloods in Hobohemia." The first installment was advertised romantically but unequivocally: "Introducing Two Youthful Escapists Who Fled to

Jessica Mitford

America With a Song in Their Hearts," and yet no one asked whether Romilly ought not to have fled at such a time, or whether he should have returned to England by now and joined up, rather than travel to Miami and run a bar there. He was showing no inclination to return, even when questions were being asked in Parliament about Isherwood and Auden. It was only the advances made by Hitler during the summer of 1940, culminating in the fall of France in June, that persuaded Romilly that he should take part in the war: he applied to join the Canadian air force at the beginning of July, while declining to write a propaganda piece about his decision for the American press.

Stung by the attacks in the press, and worried by the questions in Parliament, Isherwood took Auden's advice and wrote to the British Embassy in Washington to ask whether he should return to England to perform non-combatant duties. He received a courteous reply from the First Secretary who wrote that "your position in the United States, like Mr Auden's, is understood and that the offer of your services is much appreciated." The Secretary went on to suggest that Isherwood might like to keep in touch with the Consul in Los Angeles, who would be able to advise him in the future.

All this fuss was very unsettling for Isherwood, who recalled that he hardly referred to it in his diary, "because, at the time, it made me feel so guilty—guilty, and, at the same time, defiant." His life in America was becoming more settled, since he had just signed a year's contract with MGM at $600 a week, and was about to embark on a film version of Chopin's life, to be produced by a British émigré of longer standing, Victor Saville. He set to work reading the composer's correspondence with George Sand, but after three months the film was abandoned and he was laid off by the studio.

This sort of money allowed Isherwood to perform one significant act of charity, one that he modestly omitted to record in his diary. The Canadian writer Elizabeth Smart, then living in America, had fallen in love with the British poet George Barker after reading his work. She had yet to meet him, but had begun a correspondence with him. Barker was living in Japan with his wife, having secured the post of Professor of English Literature at the Sendai Imperial University. Although relieved to have a salaried job, Barker greatly disliked living under Japanese military rule and had appealed to Smart to rescue him. She set about trying to raise funds to pay for the Barkers' passage to America, approaching anyone she thought was interested in literature and therefore might be prepared to help. Of the hundred or so letters she wrote, most were returned or ignored, and so she was delighted to receive a letter from Isherwood, who declared himself "a great admirer" of Barker's work and promised $200, representing about two thirds of the total she needed. Unfortunately, this money never arrived, and Smart was obliged to visit Isherwood to make inquiries. Isherwood told her that the money must have been stolen or gone astray in the mail. "Well, that's too bad, isn't it?" he commented, and promptly gave her another $200. Throughout the war he also sent regular food parcels to Kathleen and Richard and to other friends in England containing such increasingly scarce items as cocoa, fruit cakes, chocolate and soup cubes.

When not working at the studio, Isherwood had time to brood, and to have rows with people like Klaus Mann, who urged him to make his position on the war clear.

Once again, he was torn between two sets of loyalties: to Viertel and the bellicose émigrés and to Heard and the pacifist Vedantans. "I came away from him so calm and happy, as I usually do," he wrote after a visit to Heard. "I wish I could live in a temple where he was a monk, and just sweep the floor and listen." This calm tended not to last long, and later the same day he endured a furious row with Vernon, who complained that Isherwood did not treat him as an adult. This was hardly surprising, since it was not in Isherwood's nature to treat his partners as adults: a large part of their attraction was that they were considerably younger than he was, and they were expected to undertake the role—albeit incestuously—of kid brother, or even son. Just as many parents want to create children in their own image, so Isherwood looked for similarities that would suggest this "familial" bond. Vernon's resentment at Isherwood's failure to "treat him as a grown-up person, an artist," seemed oddly familiar. "I am simply being confronted by myself at nineteen," Isherwood acknowledged—just as he had written of Ian Scott-Kilvert. "There is so much in Vernon to admire and respect, and he is struggling so hard. How often I forget this! What if he is priggish and humorless sometimes? Can't I supply enough humor and understanding for both of us? If I can't, what is the use of having been through all those quarrels with M[ummie]?"

Isherwood's real family obligations were about to assert themselves. On July 9, four days after his seventy-second birthday, Uncle Henry died. In April he had undergone an operation to deal with a septic bladder. He came though the operation, but a month later suffered a relapse and began speaking of himself as "poor old Uncle Henry who is going to die." His estranged wife, Muriel, hurried to London for a deathbed reconciliation. ("I expect she had been longing for some word from Henry & it is most thrilling & pathetic," Kathleen commented, rather as if this episode belonged in a novel or film.) Although Henry was given the last rites on May 9—the fateful date, according to Kathleen, of both his father's and his brother Frank's deaths—he subsequently left the nursing home and, under the devoted care of his housekeeper, Mrs. Leach, survived two more months. When news of his death reached Kathleen, she commented: "I am surprised to find how <u>really sorry I am</u> & the blank it makes to have him no longer there—it is not <u>only himself</u> but the Epoch for which he stood & there <u>was</u> something lovable about him, though I <u>never</u> admired him for his virtues! (though no doubt he had some)—but he had been spoilt all his life." Indeed, although Kathleen never really got on with Henry, she couldn't help, in her amused way, admiring his style, which was so reminiscent of Marple Hall in what she described as "its happy palmy days." "He stood for <u>so much connected with the past</u> & still carried on in the grand style in his little house at 29 South Eaton Place in the lavish & expensive ways of his former days (with the aid of the invaluable Mrs Leach & poor Guiseppe[4]) [. . .] It was <u>nice to think of him</u> still carrying on, & the

---

4. Henry's valet had Kathleen's sympathy because he had been interned. Although many foreign nationals were rounded up and imprisoned by the authorities for no reason whatsoever, Giuseppe was not one of them. An ardent devotee of Mussolini, he invariably greeted visitors to his employer's flat with a fascist salute. Henry, who always wintered in Italy and admired il Duce, did not entirely disapprove.

expensive little luncheon parties!" She would even have been prepared to overcome her anti-Roman prejudices and attend his requiem mass at St. Mary's, Cadogan Street in London, but the telegram arrived too late for her to travel from Wales. Henry evidently valued his link with Marple less than Kathleen did and had deleted from his will a request that if he died in England he should be interred in the family vault: he ended up, rather more prosaically, in a cemetery in the North London suburb of Mill Hill.

Another alteration in Henry's will seems to have been ignored. He left legacies to his brother Jack and his wife, his sister Esther, Kathleen and Mrs. Leach, but left "all my personal effects and the residue of my estate to my *Nephew Christopher William Bradshaw Isherwood*."[5] At some point the words in italics were crossed out and re-placed with the words "brother John," but this cannot have been legal, since the en-tire estate was settled on Christopher, with Jack acting as Henry's executor. Although the estate, already considerably run down by Henry's father, had continued to de-cline, it was still worth £44,000, while Henry's personal property was valued at £31,787. Isherwood had already decided to hand over the entire legacy to Richard. "I always half knew that [. . .] when Marple and all the money became mine, it would be too late," he noted. "It is too late now—not merely because of the war, but because the absurd boyhood dream of riches is over forever. It is too late to invite my friends to a banquet, to burn the Flemish tapestry and the Elizabethan beds, to turn the house into a brothel. I no longer want to be revenged on the past."

By passing on this unwanted legacy to Richard, Isherwood was also doing what was morally proper. "It's his, not mine, by right, because he loves the place and is prepared to live there." But there were other motives. By giving Richard what he had always wanted, Isherwood assuaged some of the guilt he had felt at abandoning his brother not only to whatever the war had in store for England, but also to Kathleen. Somewhat melodramatically, Isherwood came to see in Richard what he himself might have become had he not been able to escape his mother. This is not altogether absurd. It was always said that as boys Christopher was a Machell-Smith, while Richard was a Bradshaw-Isherwood, but these differences merged over the years. Al-though it does not show in photographs (Richard's nervous twitches making such portraiture something of an ordeal for both the photographer and the sitter), the two brothers were strikingly similar in appearance, particularly when Richard had al-lowed his unruly hair to be combed and slicked into some sort of order. Although their lives were very different, they had a great deal in common psychologically. When asked to describe Richard, Spender said: "a sort of mad version of Christo-pher—or, a very clear, pure, undiluted form of Christopher." Tom Bradshaw-Isherwood recalled that in the family, Kathleen was always referred to as "poor Aunt Kathleen with those two abnormal sons." Richard certainly thought he and his brother were alike, and to some extent even did things which were intended to em-phasize their similarities. He too was homosexual, with a penchant for those much younger than himself. He too was subject to rages and resentments. He too kept an extensive diary that Isherwood thought very good and interesting, and wrote fiction,

---

5. Henry's other sister, Moey, had died in 1935.

which may not have appeared in print but was at least considered by publishers. And in later life, he too followed an exotic religion, becoming a Rosicrucian and rising to the status of "neophyte in the Second Degree." For his part, Isherwood tended to regard Richard subjectively. For example, his claim that there was nothing really the matter with Richard—that his odd mannerisms and behavior were willful, not the result of genuine psychological disturbance but adopted as a sort of revenge upon Kathleen, to whom he had become inextricably bound—says perhaps more about Isherwood than it does about Richard.

Even if Isherwood's analysis was unconvincing, there is no doubt that Kathleen and Richard's claustrophobic, symbiotic relationship was unusual. It was also easy enough to explain. Christopher had enjoyed the benefit, briefly, of a father in his life. Although not a conventional military man, the athletic Frank, with his uniform and Indian-clubs exercise regime, was a distinctly masculine presence. During the crucial years of his development, until the age of nine, Isherwood had two parents. Richard, on the other hand, never knew his father and retained only one, vague physical memory of him. Indeed, his principal feeling about his absent father was one of fear.

In the wake of his father's death, Richard temporarily lost the attention of his mother, whose overwhelming grief meant that her entire identity became that of a widow rather than that of a mother. Richard later suggested that it was only in the early 1930s that she emerged from her extended period of mourning—by which time he was an adult. Kathleen was acutely aware that her devotion to Frank's memory, and the demands made upon her by her own mother, denied Richard the sort of maternal attention he needed during his childhood, as the guilty computation in her diaries of the days she spent with him each year show. To complicate matters further, Richard was a "difficult" child, who gradually developed into a disturbed one. Kathleen's principal feeling about him was one of anxiety: Was he developing quickly enough? Would he always be fractious and a prey to unfathomable fears? Would he ever manage to find a school he enjoyed and from which he would not run away? Any decision she had to make about Richard, she had to make alone: relatives and friends could proffer advice, but there was no husband with whom she could discuss things. Kathleen wanted to act in Richard's best interests, but was torn between the need to discipline him and to protect him; and the professional advice she received from doctors and psychiatrists, less widely available then than now, seems to have been unhelpful.

When Frank died, Kathleen had pinned her hopes on Christopher, but when Isherwood began to move away from her both psychologically and geographically, she concentrated her attentions upon Richard. She never stopped loving and being both protective and proud of Christopher, even when she disagreed with him or disapproved of his actions, but from 1929 onward he had removed himself from her sphere of influence. The literal loss of Frank and the metaphorical one of Christopher left Kathleen with Richard. In some ways, history was repeating itself: as Kathleen had been enslaved by her mother, so Richard was enslaved by Kathleen. When they were together, they would address each other as "Darling" the whole time, saying it every time they passed each other in the house. When apart, they wrote to each other almost every day, long chatty letters full of family and local gossip and exaggerated mutual concern. Kathleen's writing covered the entire page: when she filled the available space, she sometimes turned the page and wrote across, so that one gets the odd sense of Richard trapped in the web of her handwriting. The more protective Kathleen was of Richard, the more dependent he became on her; the more dependent he became, the more Kathleen protected him. It was nobody's fault, but there was no escape—for either of them.

By passing the Marple estate and the financial wherewithal to keep it going to Richard, Isherwood was giving his brother some measure of control, some sense of independence. He was also cutting one of his last ties to England, as Kathleen recognized. "The idea of his coming in for Marple seemed a sort of link to this country & if he gives up that there is nothing binding," she predicted. Although she appreciated what Christopher was doing for Richard, she acknowledged that "from his babyhood I alway's thought of C living there some day . . . and it makes me v sad to think of him an exile & no settled home—he has such a domestic side, & yet the little villa at Cintra was the nearest approach to a <u>home</u> of his own—But maybe it is my old fault of wanting people to enjoy themselves in my way rather than theirs—& maybe it will all come right for them both in the end."

The responsibility of managing the Marple Hall estate, which included not only the Hall and its home farm and Wyberslegh but several other rented farms and parcels of agricultural land, was indeed considerable, and it is possible that Isherwood had a further motive in handing it over to Richard. It may not have been a conscious one, but Isherwood would have realized, had he stopped to think about his grand gesture, that one way of destroying Marple without actually setting fire to it would be to hand over its care to someone who, whatever his good intentions and best efforts may have been, would be unlikely to halt its serious decline. Uncle Jack certainly believed that Richard would prove quite incapable of handling the estate and he thought Christopher utterly irresponsible in making this gift. Jack wrote Kathleen a "not very friendly" letter in which he made it plain that as far as helping out went "he would do his duty, nothing more!" Like the rest of the family, he was of the opinion that Christopher could not be forgiven for "ducking the war," while Richard "didn't know whether it was Christmas or Easter."

In the event, Jack was impressed by the efficiency with which Richard entered upon his duties as new squire of Marple. Under the slipshod stewardship of the caretakers, much of the Hall itself had become uninhabitable and its fabric was in need of urgent attention. Had Christopher held on to his inheritance, the Hall would most likely have been sold. Now there seemed a real possibility that Isherwoods might once again live in it. The principal outcome of Christopher's gesture, however, was that Kathleen would be able to return to Wyberslegh, assuming that Rachel Monkhouse could be persuaded to give up the tenancy. In fact, Rachel was no longer actually living at Wyberslegh. While her husband was serving overseas with the RAF, she had decided to move back in with her mother, and she had sublet the house to an elderly woman who had been bombed out of her house in London. Kathleen was extremely annoyed that Rachel seemed to be determined to exercise her option of renewing the lease purely so that she could get some income from the tenant, and sought legal advice. It would take more than a year of wrangling before Kathleen was able to take possession of her old home.

H aving relinquished the responsibilities of squirearchy, Isherwood turned his attention once more to scriptwriting. While laid off from MGM, he became involved in several other film projects. His old Gaumont-British associate Robert
Stevenson was now at RKO and asked him to contribute a film in aid of the British
War Relief Fund. Isherwood and van Druten worked on an episode that took the form
of a murder mystery. Isherwood felt useless and envied the ease with which van
Druten, the consummate professional, worked on the project. There was also a somewhat unlikely plan for Isherwood and Huxley to work on a film adaptation of *Lady
Chatterley's Lover,* and Thoeren suggested a film set in the Sino-Japanese War. Nothing came of either idea, and at the beginning of August Isherwood was summoned
back to MGM to polish Lesser Samuel's dialogue for a Joan Crawford melodrama
called *A Woman's Face.* Isherwood thought the film "ridiculous." "It is about a girl
who has a horrible scar on her face, due to a childhood burn, and this scar makes her
bitter, so she becomes a blackmailer," he told John Lehmann.

> Her professional duties cause her to visit the wife of a plastic surgeon (who is
> two-timing her husband) and the plastic surgeon takes pity on her and operates,
> turning her into the most beautiful woman of her epoch. So she immediately be-
> comes good, as well—only to remember that she has (while still bad) arranged to
> go up to a house in the north of Sweden and murder a small boy, for the very mod-
> erate sum of sixty thousand crowns. Being a girl of her word, she goes up there,
> falls in love with a man, protects the small boy from the villain (who falls over a
> cliff in a sleigh) and ends up happily. If you know anyone, living or dead, who
> could write satisfactory dialogue for this masterpiece, I should be glad to hear it.

This work unfortunately coincided with a week's visit to California by Auden,
who was staying with the Mann family—the "wife and in-laws," as he put it—in Pacific Palisades. "It has been an unsatisfactory visit," Isherwood reported after Auden
had left; "we've hardly had any time for a proper talk." What talk they did have was
mostly arguments about religion. Auden was in the process of returning to the Angli-
canism of his childhood, but doing so with typical intellectual rigor, reading and absorbing a large number of theological texts. This was in stark contrast to Isherwood's
intuitive approach to Vedanta. Partly as a result of reading Reinhold Niebuhr's *Christianity and Power Politics,* Auden had abandoned his pacifist position, which had
never in fact been very well fortified. Unlike Harold Nicolson, Auden felt that the
true pacifist had to withdraw entirely from the world into a life of contemplation. Although suspicious of Heard's ideas, he told Isherwood that "No one can be a pacifist
who isn't trying to live Gerald's life." Auden was well aware when he said this that
Isherwood was indeed trying—but as far as Auden was concerned he wasn't trying
hard enough. As Heard had recognized, Isherwood had one foot planted very firmly
in the world. He may have expressed a momentary wish to live in a temple, sweeping floors, but he was not yet ready for such a step.

Auden's views had changed so much that he declared that he *wanted* to kill people and intended to allow himself to be drafted if America entered the war. Isherwood

felt that he and Auden had been "both too much disturbed to be able to talk properly," which may have been just as well. Setting their differences aside, they agreed on parting that neither of them would return to England without consulting the other.

Two days after Auden left, Isherwood went to the temple and received new instructions from Swami.

> First, I am to think of people all over the world—all kinds of people, at all kinds of occupation. In each one of them, and in all matter, is this Reality, this Atman, which is also inside myself. And what is 'myself'? Am I my body? Am I my mind? Am I my thoughts? What can I find inside myself which is eternal? Let me examine my thoughts and see how they reflect this Reality—for I can only know it by its reflection. And now let me think of this Reality as seated in the top of my head, throned in a white lotus. I am infinite existence, infinite knowledge, infinite happiness. Finally, I approach the red lotus, in my heart. I look into this chamber, in which the light is burning. I say: 'Reveal yourself to me.'

What Auden, currently steeped in complex works of Christian theology, would have made of this is anyone's guess.

Whether as a result of Auden's unsettling visit, or merely because the need to withdraw from the world was made stronger by the news from England, where an invasion was widely predicted, Isherwood started dedicating more and more time to meditation. Part of the object of these exercises was to stop feeling hatred and to conquer the ego. This was an enormous challenge to someone for whom worked-up fury against other people had been a source of creative energy and whose principal subject as a writer was himself. Now, as he had acknowledged to Forster, he had to "stop hating." He also had to suppress his ego. "I think he was deeply and sincerely in love with himself, and that he had a guilty conscience about that," Lincoln Kirstein observed. This is a little harsh, but Isherwood had never been short of admirers who flattered his ego and fanned his vanity. He had come to acknowledge this in New York, when he said he had become sick of "Christopher Isherwood," the marionette who had capered upon the public stage, making all the right noises and supporting all the right causes. Unfortunately for him, "Christopher Isherwood" was not that easy to discard, partly because he was the character through whom Isherwood narrated his fiction. Kirstein felt that Isherwood had come to believe in this projection of himself and made an instructive comparison: "As someone said of Hugo: 'He's a madman who thinks he's Victor Hugo.' "

One of the most penetrating things Isherwood ever said about himself was that he was "a play-actor," and a habit of self-consciousness, exacerbated by his lifelong habit of keeping a self-analytical diary, meant that he was forever in the spotlight in his own private theater. With that spotlight permanently focused upon him, how could he ever act spontaneously—even in his personal relations? One of the temptations of fame, he acknowledged, was that it gave one sexual power. Were his many suitors attracted to the real Isherwood, or to "Christopher Isherwood?" If he was always putting on some kind of performance, how could anyone tell?

He had hoped that by coming to America, he could escape "Christopher Isherwood." He could forge a new identity, become an American both literally, by taking out naturalization papers, and metaphorically, by absorbing the language and customs of his adopted country. It is not surprising that Isherwood should gradually come to use American idiom, pronunciations and intonations in his speech. What is more striking is that by 1944, after almost half a lifetime of using British spelling, this person who wrote every single day and whose job consisted of putting down words on a page, had switched to American orthography. This must have been a conscious decision, an act of his famous will. It is also significant that the majority of his American friends addressed him as "Chris," and this was how he customarily signed himself when corresponding with them.

It was possible, of course, to shed all this baggage while still being a prey to the ego. "My chief effort is to stand outside the Ego, to try to catch a glimpse of the world with a non-attached eye," he wrote now, in a curious echo of his Berlin notion of being a camera. "But the Ego, with its gross body and great swollen, sullen pumpkin head, is like a man who *will* stand right in front of you at a horse race: you can only catch a glimpse of the race by peeping under his arms or between his legs. It is terribly difficult, but the mere discipline of trying brings its own rewards—cheerfulness, long periods of calm, freedom from self-pity." While Vernon was delighted with the move he and Isherwood made in August to a new house at 8826 Harratt Street in West Hollywood, Isherwood found it hard to meditate because the neighbors' children were noisy. "Once again, I feel the dreadful guilt of ownership," he complained—though the little wooden house was hardly comparable with Marple Hall. "If I could join Gerald's future monastery,[6] I think I'd regret the world less than at any time in my life. But I have my problems right here, and it's no good running away from them."

A new problem for Isherwood occurred at around this time when his former admirer Tony Bower, who was now living back in the States, reintroduced him to Peter Watson's lover, Denham Fouts, who had just arrived in Los Angeles with Jean Connolly.[7] Like several of the people who served as models for Isherwood's books—like Jean Ross, like Gerald Hamilton—Denny Fouts has become so entangled in his fictional counterpart, the "Paul" of *Down There on a Visit,* that it is hard to decide where one leaves off and the other begins. To complicate matters further, Fouts often made up stories about his life and has been memorialized by Truman Capote and Gore Vidal, two writers whose recollections—by accident or design—are notoriously unreliable. "Paul" is described in *Down There on a Visit* as "the most expensive male prostitute in Europe." This was undoubtedly Fouts's reputation when he and Isherwood met, but whether it was verifiable by audit or had merely been deduced from the identity of some of his clients is unclear. There is even some disagreement as to where he was born: the writer Glenway Wescott, who met him in 1934, understood that he came from Georgia, but his Southern drawl and grandeur were in fact acquired in Jacksonville, Florida. It was here that his first sexual experience took place—out of doors, with a younger brother. He never lost a taste for young boys, but

---

6. Heard had been given $100,000 by an anonymous benefactor to set up a retreat outside Los Angeles. It would not materialize for another two years.

7. Isherwood had apparently first met Fouts in London in 1938, but only in passing.

for substantial remuneration was prepared to have sex with wealthy older men. One version of events is that Fouts worked in his father's bakery until whisked away at the age of sixteen by either a cosmetics tycoon or a German baron, depending upon who is telling the story. What had in fact happened was that by the age of eighteen or nineteen his behavior had become so unacceptable that his family sent him to Washington in the hope he would be given a job by an uncle who was president of the Safeway chain of grocery stores. He shortly moved to Manhattan, where his exceptional looks attracted so much attention that he decided he should capitalize on them. Wescott recalled how Fouts "used to come to me, in the Spring of 1934, and enquire (as of a like but elder Rubumpré or Rastignac) how to pursue his future, how to manoeuvre his youth in the great world." It was then that he met the German baron and moved to Europe. Subsequent lovers reputedly included a Greek shipping magnate; Lord Tredegar, who as the Hon. Evan Morgan had been the unresponsive object of Ronald Firbank's passion; Prince Paul of Greece, before he married and became king; and, finally, Peter Watson. One story has it that he was briefly incarcerated in a concentration camp, but somehow managed to escape.

Although some people have described Fouts as stunningly beautiful, this is not strictly true. He had "the torso of an athlete," with "beautiful shoulders and golden forearms," but his face was asymmetrical, the eyes appearing to be on slightly different levels. This does not show in photographs, which contrive merely to make him look unexceptional, though neatly groomed. He affected—possibly for professional reasons—the appearance and wardrobe of a clean-cut, well-brought-up college boy. This look, like much else about him, was deceptive. Lincoln Kirstein described Fouts as "Pure, unadulterated poison. *Poison!*" Borrowing from James Joyce, the rather more susceptible Wescott designated Fouts "Foible-minded and fable-bodied," though according to Isherwood, who felt that it explained a great deal, "the last of the professional *tapettes*" suffered from a "sense of disendowment in the particular of virility"—as Wescott put it with characteristic circumlocution. He clearly had other talents and charms, however.

Fouts surprised Isherwood by taking an interest in Vedanta. They had long talks about religion, during which Isherwood gradually became convinced that Fouts was absolutely sincere in his wish to change his life altogether, to study with Prabhavananda and pursue a simple, chaste, solitary and sober existence in a shack. His approach was somewhat similar to that of another famous sinner, St. Augustine, and while he talked of his resolve to lead a better life, he still spent much of his time getting drunk at parties. Isherwood, meanwhile, was setting a good example, working hard at his meditation. By the end of October he was able to announce: "There is no longer any question, now, that 'this thing' works, as far as I'm concerned. Whatever happens, I don't think I shall ever quite lose this knowledge." He decided to risk taking Fouts to the temple, but he did not find the presence of his companion conducive to concentration. "I was thinking all the time of Denny," he confessed "—trying to 'introduce' him to Ramakrishna, and hoping he wouldn't be put off by the photographs on the shrine, and the flowers, and the ivory and brass figures of Krishna, Buddha and Shiva. It *does* look rather like the mantelpiece in an old-fashioned boudoir. Actually Denny liked it all very much, but was dismayed because he had thought what a wonderful place it would be to have sex in." Almost anywhere would have struck Fouts as a good place to have sex in, so this was not quite as sacrilegious as it sounds. Isherwood continued to believe in his new friend's spiritual aspirations, but his motives were not entirely altruistic. He later admitted that it would have been a great personal coup had he been able to convert this notorious figure.

Unfortunately, Prabhavananda was not at all impressed by Isherwood's acolyte and told Fouts firmly that what he needed was not meditation but a proper occupation. Deeply, or at any rate theatrically wounded, Fouts burst into tears when he told Isherwood about his interview with Swami. Like many a stage courtesan before him, he declared himself despicable, worthless and friendless. "I protested, of course—as anybody would," Isherwood recalled. "In fact, I said far more than I meant. I told him that *I* didn't despise him, that I admired him and liked him and wanted to be his friend." Indeed, it is quite possible that Isherwood wanted to be rather more than a friend. His relationship with Fouts was turbulent and complicated, and Lincoln Kirstein, who knew both men well, maintained that Isherwood had in fact been in love with Fouts. If so, Isherwood never admitted as much in his diaries or to anyone else.

Fouts soon recovered from his disappointment and went to see Gerald Heard, who was rather more impressed with the young man than Swami had been, and immediately offered to instruct him. Isherwood suspected that Heard was pleased to have an opportunity to prove himself more charitable than Prabhavananda, and the growing rivalry between the two spiritual teachers was fueled by their disagreement over Fouts's vocation. Fouts was shortly removed from Isherwood's sphere of influence when Heard sent him off for five months to work on a "biodynamic" farm in Pennsylvania. Heard wanted his proposed community to be self-supporting and Fouts's unlikely mission was to learn all about the organic production of vegetables.

I sherwood himself was by now considered sufficiently advanced to undergo his initiation at the temple. Just as he said he would have understood Marxism if he had met Marx, he attributed his new faith in Vedanta to the fact that he had met Prabhavananda. "I would never, never have taken even an interest in it, let alone been able to understand it, if it hadn't been that I met this very remarkable man who is a Hindu monk here," he explained many years later. "After I got to know Prabhavananda, I gradually ceased to be an atheist; because I found myself unable to disbelieve in his belief in God." He subsequently came up with a tentative credo: "I believe that there is something called (for convenience) God, and that this something can be experienced (don't ask me how), and that a man I know (Swami) has had this experience, partially, at any rate. All this I believe because my instinct, as a novelist and a connoisseur of people, assures me, after long observation, that this is true in Swami's case."

Conscious that many people were criticizing him for his actions—for leaving England as war loomed, for retreating from the world at a time of crisis, for apparently abandoning his promising career as a novelist—Isherwood gladly embraced a father figure who did not judge him and a religion which did not talk, as the orthodox Christianity of his childhood had, of sin and punishment. And indeed the relationship between a guru and his disciple, like that of a parent and a wayward child, was central to Vedanta.

> According to Hindu belief, the tie between the guru and his initiated disciple cannot be broken, either in this world or on any future plane of existence, until the disciple realises the Atman within himself and is set free. Meanwhile, the disciple may neglect, reject, or even betray the guru, but the guru cannot disown him. In such cases, the guru must continue to guide the disciple mentally, from a distance, and protect him through prayer.

This was hugely reassuring. Vedanta provided Isherwood with "a sort of ultimate resource—some kind of thing you can turn to when what one calls one's own resources are exhausted: a reassurance that you won't just go screaming mad or flip under pressure."

The date chosen for his initiation was November 8, the birthday of Ramakrishna's wife, Sarada Devi, who was worshipped as the "Holy Mother." The ceremony started at seven in the morning and involved rituals that a year earlier would have made Isherwood recoil. He had to offer up flowers to Ramakrishna, Holy Mother, Christ and Swami. He was given a rosary and his own personal and secret Sanskrit mantra to recite while telling his beads, a form of prayer known as "making *japam.*" He then had to offer up all his past actions, the good and the bad, to be purified in a fire, the ash of which was used to make a sign on his forehead symbolizing the third eye, that of the spirit. He also attended his first full-scale *puja,* a communal ritual worship in celebration of Holy Mother's birthday. On the way home, Isherwood and Heard "agreed that this sort of thing could never be transplanted to the West," and the fact that Isherwood was prepared to undergo this initiation, and all its attendant rituals, shows how far he had come from his original suspicion of all things "eastern." He was now, officially, a disciple of Swami Prabhavananda.

later, with Isherwood now initiated into the order, Prabhavananda could afford to be rather more direct.

M editation, lectures and other meetings associated with discipleship left Isherwood little time to write his diary. During the last quarter of 1940, he made only one entry in September, none in October, five in November, and one in December. He opened his 1941 diary on the first day of the year to admonish himself: "I really must try to keep this journal more regularly. It will be invaluable to me if I do. Because this year is going to be one of the most decisive periods of the twentieth century—and even the doings and thoughts of the most remote and obscure people will reflect the image of its events." As so often when he recognized that he was in danger of sounding self-important, he immediately qualified this, commenting: "That's a hell of a paragraph to start off with. Why are we all so pompous on New Year's Day? Come off it—you're not Hitler or Churchill. Nobody called on you to make a statement." Isherwood may not have been a world leader, but he was still a long way from subduing the ego to the point where he genuinely regarded himself as remote or obscure. Even so, his diary-keeping did not much persist beyond mid-January, and apart from a few entries in July appears to have remained blank.[2]

The previous October, legislation had been passed requiring men between the ages of twenty-one and thirty-six to register for the draft. Isherwood was just outside this age range, but realized that if America joined the war he might well be called up. He wanted to preempt this and declare his pacifism by registering as a conscientious objector. If he did so, one option would be to volunteer for work at a forestry camp run by the Civilian Public Service at San Dimas to the northeast of Los Angeles. This would involve a separation between himself and Vernon. The relationship had run its course, and both men knew it, but neither was willing to make the final break. Before the decision was forced by events, the rows and sulks and simmering resentments came to a head, and on February 17 they moved out of Harratt Street and went their separate ways—"quite amicably, though," Isherwood told Forster. Isherwood moved into a small hotel for a while, then in mid-March took up residence in an apartment at 2407 Green Valley Road, which was on the corner of Heard's street, Arlene Terrace.

By this time, Heard had decided to disassociate himself from Prabhavananda. The swami's relatively comfortable life at the temple, where he was looked after by "the holy women" and indulged in the worldly addiction of chain-smoking, offended Heard's asceticism. His letter of resignation deeply irked Prabhavananda, and Isherwood was obliged to listen to recriminations on both sides. He found Swami's addiction to nicotine sympathetic, but shared Heard's misogynistic view of the female household at Ivar Avenue. He nevertheless continued to attend meetings at the temple, and during the spring he got to know and like the women there, making a particular friend of Amiya. Garrulous, enthusiastic, generous, well-meaning, but also

---

2. "Appears" because all that exists is the revised version, most of which is taken up with a later narrative recounting the major events of Isherwood's life during 1941. It is possible that he did make further diary entries for the year, which he subsequently destroyed.

markedly self-centered and unself-aware, Amiya was the sort of blundering figure whom people either found endearing or took against at sight. If you hadn't seen her for a while, you genuinely looked forward to an encounter, a niece recalled—but within half an hour you were exhausted and longing for another six months' respite. "I must never forget this about her," Isherwood admonished himself after a row: "her longing for affection, her loyalty, her struggle to create a family and a home." It was indeed largely thanks to Amiya, who was also an excellent cook, that Ivar Avenue was comparatively cozy.

Heard's austere existence, in which personal relationships were granted little importance, may have been good for the soul, but Isherwood also required sympathy and distraction, since he was finding life without Vernon lonely and depressing. The "religious bohemianism" and "oriental laissez-faire" of Ivar Avenue answered that need. As Isherwood put it, "Gerald offered me discipline, method, intellectual conviction. But the Swami offered me love."

Perhaps in an attempt to show Heard that in spite of Swami's poor example he could renounce worldly pleasures, Isherwood once again gave up smoking. Now that Vernon was out of the picture, he had given up sex, and all that was left to him was meditation and work. One of his jobs at MGM was to provide a prologue for the British film *The Stars Look Down,* the story of a miner's son who wants to become an MP. The film had been adapted from the novel by A. J. Cronin, a middlebrow writer whose books dealing with social issues Isherwood admired. The studio felt that the film was too political, and so the former darling of the Left was paid $600 a week to come up with eight hundred words to explain that humanity rather than socialism was the film's message. As Auden commented of Isherwood's work in Hollywood, "Well at least you sell dear what is most dear." In the event, Isherwood failed to produce anything the studio could use, and the film was released uncompromised by any palliative gloss. Isherwood was then given the job of polishing the script of *Free and Easy,* a piece of high-society froth adapted from Ivor Novello's *The Truth Game,* which had already been filmed by MGM in 1930. The producer, Bernie Hyman, was one of the few people who admired the first version (an early talkie starring a hapless Buster Keaton); indeed, he was so fond of it that he scarcely allowed Isherwood to change a word. Isherwood was relieved that his work was uncredited on a film on which *Variety* commented: "This one must have slipped through the Metro wringer while the brains department was out to lunch." Isherwood's inglorious year at MGM drew to a close with *Crossroads,* an adaptation of a French film about the blackmailing of an amnesiac diplomat, his contribution to which went uncredited—rightly, he thought. His contract expired in May, and he told the studio he intended to join the forestry camp.

Meanwhile, Denny Fouts returned from his spell of organic farming and accepted Isherwood's invitation to share the apartment on Green Valley Road. Fouts had already registered as a conscientious objector with the draft board and been classified 4-E: someone who refused to serve in the forces in any capacity, but was fit enough to do "civilian work of national importance." He expected to be sent to San Dimas, but while waiting lived with Isherwood in a would-be monastic brotherhood. They established a routine, which involved getting up at six every morning to do an hour's meditation in different rooms of the apartment, not even speaking to each other until they had breakfast. The rest of the morning was spent reading aloud from improving feel the same. That is why I so distrust public statements of one's position, or criticism of other people's.

Back in Los Angeles, Isherwood and Vernon, who had kept in touch after they had parted company, went on one last, idyllic trip in the mountains together, during which Isherwood realized two things. The first was that he had fallen in love with California, and that it would remain his home. The second was that, although he and Vernon found living together impossible, their relationship would endure: "No matter what either of us did, or where we went, we should be, in some way, responsible to each other for the rest of our lives." He had said much the same thing about Heinz.

While Isherwood had been at La Verne, Kathleen and Richard were moving back in to Wyberslegh Hall, which had survived an alarming shower of incendiary bombs in January 1941. (Some of the farm buildings had been damaged, but the bombs bounced off the roof of the main house to land harmlessly in the garden.) With the help of lawyers the issue of Rachel Monkhouse's tenancy had been resolved, and the house was now empty and ready to receive the furniture from 19 Pembroke Gardens. Richard had continued doing agricultural work during the war, but in March 1941 had transferred from the Wyberslegh farm to one at Dan Bank on the edge of the Marple estate. He lived with the caretaker at Marple Hall as a paying guest. His friendship with the caretaker's son appears to have been extremely fraught, causing him a great deal of unhappiness, and Kathleen believed that some form of extortion had been taking place. Kathleen saw no harm in the boy: "it is [the boy's mother] not him whom I *profoundly* dislike and mistrust," she confided in her diary, when Richard had been on the farm for just over a fortnight. "She seems in some mysterious way to have Richard under her thumb & fleeces him unmercifully—he has spent over £6 since he has been up here & cigarettes cannot account for much of it—he pays fantastic sums for each night he goes there, & gets practically nothing to eat & a maximum of discomfort." It is possible, though cannot be proven, that the caretakers had recognized the nature of Richard's interest in their son and were in fact blackmailing him. "I was afraid of the wife because of my affection for her son," Richard recalled, and he had got into such a state that at one point he wanted to give up any idea of coming to live at Wyberslegh. Matters seem to have been sorted out, however, and he and Kathleen finally moved into the old family home in July, bringing with them their daily help from London, who stayed with them for a month while they settled in. "It all seems so homely and peaceful and we both love it," Kathleen wrote.

The peace did not last long, for they were shortly joined by Nanny, who did nothing but complain about her new accommodation. "She was in a most unreasonable mood," Kathleen wrote:

> I hadnt got her a <u>wardrobe</u>. She <u>couldn't sleep</u>—the room was so stuffy [and] small she couldnt breathe & yet she was so cold & I had taken no trouble about the room, & she hadn't got the looking glass she wanted, & the whole house was a muddle & if she had come to help it would have been quite different & it was dirty, & so unlike it was when she first came here 36 years ago etc. etc.—till I re-

ally wished she would take herself off—which if she is going to grumble would be the happiest for her & everyone.

Things were not much improved by the arrival of Elizabeth the cook. Kathleen had hoped she had seen the last of this particular employee, and had unfortunately said as much in a letter intended for a friend which she mistakenly put in an envelope addressed to Elizabeth. "I had most unluckily said in it that I hoped to get a cook who was cheerful after putting up with 15 years of grumbling from Elizabeth. I meant it as a joke but fear poor E must have been hurt." Hurt or not, Elizabeth wrote a few days later to offer her services once more. "I am afraid her coming is a venture," Kathleen commented, "but on the whole and since she had so nicely offered—I wrote & thanked her & said we should be very glad if she would come for a month or two." This venture proved no more successful than it had when Elizabeth visited Penmaenmawr and she seemed "much more peculiar" even than she had been in London. Within days of her arrival at Wyberslegh, it became clear that her presence wasn't "going to make for peace," and shortly afterwards Nanny took to her bed, even though the doctor said that she was quite capable of working. Nanny thought differently and thereafter allowed Kathleen and Richard to fetch and carry for her. "Poor Elizabeth's grumblings and her atrocious cooking quite marred any advantages of having her," Richard recalled. Becoming steadily older and odder, she would stay on for another three and a half years before finally retiring.

While moving into Wyberslegh, Richard had taken the opportunity to stop working at Dan Bank, and seemed disinclined to return. Kathleen worried that "people may well criticize, & pass remarks for every young man is or should be doing war work . . . Though much of it cant be congenial—and I fear comment is all the more likely to be made on the lines of 'one law for the rich & one for the poor.' " He did eventually return to work, hated it and started drinking heavily. He felt—probably rightly—that he was no good at the work and was only employed on sufferance. Although farming was a reserved occupation, Richard still received inquiries from the authorities, one asking why he had not joined the Home Guard. Fortunately, his doctor was able to write a letter saying that Richard was entirely unsuited to bear arms and he eventually got an exemption.

While working, Richard frequently spent the night at Marple Hall to avoid the long journey to the farm from Wyberslegh on dark mornings. Kathleen was not pleased by the renewal of this arrangement with the caretakers. "They take advantage of him in every way—it makes my blood boil—but R does not wish for any interference." Matters finally came to a head, however, Richard returning one day "very upset over the scandalous & disgraceful behaviour at M.H. . . . so utterly outrageous that one would not have been surprised if Grannie Isherwood had risen from her grave." What precisely happened is not known, but Kathleen recorded that Richard "felt he would never forget the horror of it." There appears to have been some sort of confrontation which eventually led to Richard giving the caretakers notice. The house was left in an appalling condition: a friend of Kathleen "said she had never seen in the worst slum tenements in Hull rooms left so dirty & untidy or in such an uncared for state." Roofs had been left to leak and other damage had gone unreported. Fortunately, a local couple called Crosby were quickly installed and immediately set about tidying up some of the mess.

Richard was also being tidied up, thanks to Alan Bradley, a young man who worked on the farm at Wyberslegh. One morning, Kathleen had approached him and asked if he would mind giving Richard a shave. Richard had never quite mastered the art of wet shaving, his attempts tending to be harrowingly bloody. "I simply cannot do it myself," he told his brother, "never could, if I try to, even with a so-called safety razor the result is disastrous"—and on one letter russet blots are speckled amidst the blue ones from his leaky fountain pen. His nervous twitches, with his head jerking suddenly to one side like a horse shying, must have made it difficult to perform smooth strokes with a razor. He had presumably made use of a professional barber in London, but such luxuries were not easy to come by in Cheshire, and so Bradley became used to helping out, not only with shaving but also with other jobs. Although Kathleen was not in the least embarrassed by Richard's behavior and would sit with him in smart restaurants apparently oblivious of the attention his twitches and mutterings drew from other diners, she found it increasingly difficult to cope with his violent outbursts, which usually occurred when he had drunk too much beer. Bradley was able to manage Richard and Kathleen regarded him as a savior, trusting him implicitly. For his part, Richard was delighted to have found a new "pal," particularly since Alan was extremely handsome, though entirely heterosexual.

I sherwood started work at the AFSC hostel in October 1941. Vernon and the Huxleys came to the railroad station to see Isherwood off on the four-day journey to Haverford. There was no fellow voyager to whom he could say cheerfully: "Well, we're off again"; no Auden to reply "Goody." For the first time in many years, Isherwood was setting off into the future alone. The Friends had rented a large house belonging to a proprietor of the *Saturday Evening Post*. Like the newspaper, 824 Buck Lane was long past its best, but it had a sort of faded grandeur and the presence of many of the owner's objects made it seem still a home rather than an institution. At any one time some twenty or thirty refugees were living at the hostel or in nearby houses belonging to other Quakers. Isherwood himself lived with an elderly couple called Yarnall around the corner at 605 Railroad Avenue. The aim of the hostel was to prepare the refugees, many of whom had enjoyed distinguished professional careers in Germany, for finding work in America. A process of acclimation was inaugurated, whereby the refugees would be introduced to the "American Way of Life" at lectures and social gatherings. Isherwood's principal job was to give English lessons to those who needed them, using that bible of the American Way of Life, the *Reader's Digest,* as a teaching aid. The refugees, many of whom hoped to become teachers, also attended lectures at the nearby Haverford College.

Isherwood intended to continue with his meditation at Haverford, leading the life of "a sort of invisible monk: my spiritual life was to be neither seen nor heard." He would also, however, have to live as a Quaker—and he even began using their old-fashioned locutions, addressing Caroline Norment as "thee." La Verne had been a good preparation, since living at the hostel was communal, and although there was a full-time cook, everyone, including Isherwood, was expected to help with washing up and cleaning. The day started with breakfast at 8:15 a.m., after which there would be a meeting of about twenty minutes during which everyone sat in silence. The rest of the day was taken up with classes and lectures until at 5:00 p.m. everyone assembled at the Meeting House for lessons in phonetics. On Sundays there would be a Bible class, followed by a Quaker meeting, at which people could speak. While adjusting to America, the refugees also liked talking of the old days in Germany. In some ways, it was like being back in Berlin, but the atmosphere was very different and the work was a great deal harder: Isherwood was giving up to six individual lessons a day.

Uprooted from their homes and cast adrift in a new country, the refugees not unnaturally had difficulty in adjusting. Not all of them were cooperative or even grateful, but Isherwood decided that the only thing to do would be to remind himself that they were all part of God and God was part of them. "Let me recognize Him beneath these preposterous disguises," he would pray when confronted with some particularly irritating or recalcitrant refugee. As soon as jobs and homes had been found for the refugees, they would move on and their places would be taken by a new influx. Isherwood may have been turning his thoughts inwards, but he also maintained a beady eye for the physical and psychological oddities of both the refugees and the hostel's staff, and made copious notes in his diary, suspecting that they would one day prove useful for fiction. Of Norment, whom he genuinely liked and admired, he observed: "Like all hysterics, she was everlastingly appealing to the norm." He contrasted her well-intentioned but inefficient ways with those of one of her colleagues, who "could have run the United States—as a dictatorship." This woman he described as "a great big whale of a girl, with breasts like an Alpine meadow, and a great pouchy purple face surrounded by nondescript hair like sofa stuffing, worn in a sawed-off bob."

Although he found life with "the Quakes" demanding and frequently boring, Isherwood had determined not to stray outside the fold, where worldly temptations lurked. This resolve did not last long, and when he received a call from Teddy le Boutilliere, who ran a bookstore at Bryn Mawr and was an ardent fan of the Mortmere saga, his vanity was sufficiently tickled for him to pay a visit. Like many of Isherwood's friends, le Boutilliere and his wife thought that he ought to be back in the world, getting drunk and enjoying himself. As the months passed, this was indeed what Isherwood started doing. He was the only male member of the staff at Haverford and he found the atmosphere there oppressively female. To complicate matters further, one of the married refugees declared that she was in love with him. Isherwood turned this awkward situation to his advantage by developing an intimate but sisterly relationship with the woman, who proved to be an extremely good source of Haverford gossip.

By the beginning of 1942, however, Isherwood was longing for breaks from the hostel. He made trips to New York to see Viertel, Kirstein and a friend of Tony Bower named Johnny Dickinson. Bower himself was now in the army and stationed at a camp on Long Island, which Isherwood visited. He described it as "colder than Greenland," and was horrified by the conditions that Bower was enduring there, "the raw misery of the army, the awful crowded loneliness." Having got drunk on cheap red wine, he wandered off into the woods to throw up and was nearly shot by a sentry. Kirstein introduced him to his brother-in-law Paul Cadmus, who made a drawing of him. "Although we've only met three or four times, I feel he's an intimate friend," Isherwood wrote of Cadmus; "we have so much in common—chiefly our love for Forster, whom Paul has never met. Perhaps Paul should have been a writer; he's far more sensitive and intelligent than his pictures." Isherwood may not have greatly admired Cadmus's paintings, but he reveled in "the sensual pleasure" of being drawn, claiming "this isn't a question of ordinary vanity: you command, as at no other time, someone's total attention: every touch of his pencil on the paper is like an exquisite kind of massage. It is intensely intimate and yet impersonal: there are really three people present—the artist, yourself, and yourself as the model. And you find you can talk to the artist in a particularly frank, natural way. The ego doesn't interfere. It is far too busy posing." They met infrequently, but Isherwood and Cadmus would maintain their intimacy through letters.

Although Isherwood had no ear for music, he went to Philadelphia to hear Paul Wittgenstein give the first performance of Benjamin Britten's *Diversions* op. 21. Britten and Pears were also at the concert and afterwards sat with Isherwood getting "sadder and sadder and drunker and drunker." Britten told Isherwood that he and Pears were returning to England, where they would register as conscientious objectors. One of the reasons for their return was that the previous summer Britten had come across a copy of the poems of George Crabbe in a second-hand bookstore, and at almost the same time read in *The Listener* the transcript of a talk given on radio by Forster about the poet. "To talk about Crabbe is to talk about England," Forster had declared. Crabbe's England was the East Anglian coast where he—and Britten—had been born. Forster particularly mentioned a section of the long narrative poem *The Borough* telling the story of Peter Grimes, a brutalized Suffolk fisherman who murders his apprentice boys and is eventually ostracized by the community in which he had lived. Britten later recalled: "in a flash I realized two things: that I must write an opera, and where I belonged."

Britten now asked Isherwood whether he would consider writing the libretto. When Britten got back to Amityville, where he and Pears were staying with friends, he wrote to Isherwood repeating his suggestion and enclosing a copy of Crabbe's poems. Isherwood can hardly have seemed the most likely opera librettist, even given his theatrical collaborations with Auden, but it is possible that Britten thought his friend might be swayed by the veiled pederastic element of the story. Isherwood appears to have been fully aware of this theme, but he raised several practical objections to the proposed collaboration. "I have thought it over carefully," he wrote:

> it surely is good melodramatic material, and maybe something more than that: the setting is perfect for an opera, I should think. But the real point is that I am quite sure I shan't have the time for such work for months or maybe years ahead; and frankly, the subject doesn't excite me so much that I want to *make* time for it; I mean to use every available spare moment out of a life like the one I lead at present, or in a work camp, or somewhere even more strenuous. Also, I doubt very much if collaborators can work so far apart as we seem likely to be. So let's drop it, regretfully but finally.

"I can't pretend that I wasn't disappointed that you can't do Grimes with me," Britten replied. "But I understand of course. I know that as it stands, P.G. is no more than a rather bloodthirsty melodrama; but it has elements of what I want in an opera, and we are slowly but surely getting nearer to a serious plot. Incidentally a lot of your hints dropped that Saturday afternoon have proved useful—thank you!"

Perhaps recognizing that Isherwood was finding the atmosphere at Haverford somewhat ungay, Kirstein proposed that Pete Martinez, who was filling in time while waiting to be drafted, should come to the hostel as a volunteer worker. Isherwood was slightly anxious about what sort of impression this lively dancer would make, but Martinez was on his best behavior and charmed everyone over supper on his first day there. "Later, we ran most of the way to Ardmore—to see Garbo in *Two-Faced Woman*—screaming hysterically with laughter and release from tension," Isherwood wrote. "It's wonderful having him here."

Toward the end of March, Isherwood and Martinez moved into the same bedroom at Railroad Avenue, ostensibly in order to make room for a new arrival, although this was highly convenient since they were enjoying a sexual relationship. Unfortunately, Isherwood immediately came down with a cold, but for once did not merely lie about groaning and complaining. "I've never enjoyed being sick so much in my life," he confessed. "Pete spends practically the entire day with me. He dresses up in blankets and clowns around, or he sings Mexican songs, or we tell each other stories. Caroline came up to see me, yesterday. She didn't know what to make of us—particularly of me, because my workshop personality had entirely disappeared. I was another person, whom she'd never met. I couldn't switch off the giggles." Once he had recovered, Isherwood fell into a routine of going into Philadelphia with Martinez to eat lobster, get drunk and visit the baths. Just as bereaved boys at St. Edmund's removed their black armbands so as to be able to join in games, so Isherwood took to removing his AFSC lapel-badge on these forays. After addressing another Quaker group on the topic of La Verne and prayer the day after one of these outings, Isherwood acknowledged:

> They would have fits if they could have seen me last night, and yet I'm not being exactly hypocritical: as far as I am able, I try to tell the truth about myself and impart information without suggesting that I'm holy. The worst of it is, you can say you're lazy, vain, sensual, full of resentment and hate, and your audience doesn't turn a hair. But if you illustrated these statements by describing your actions, they'd die of horror.

Isherwood had in fact begun to feel guilty about his little sensual indulgences. He even began to blame Martinez for leading him astray. The more Martinez chafed against the sober life of the hostel, the more Isherwood became "greyer and more Calvinistic." He reported that "all our spontaneous gaiety is disappearing." When, a couple of weeks later, Martinez decided to leave Haverford, Isherwood missed him terribly, but was also relieved. "Now I can get back into the thick Quaker gloom which I hate, but in which I feel strangely at home. I often detest the Quakes and the Jews for being so stuffy and cautious and safe; but I understand them because, at bottom, I'm stuffy and cautious, too. I'm a cautious old auntie who, in her heart of

25. "From my window, the deep solemn massive street": Herr Issyvoo in Berlin (in fact at Stephen Spender's window), photographed by Humphrey Spender.

26. Jean Ross represented "the whole idea of militant bohemia," and provided Isherwood with a model for the character of Sally Bowles.

27. Auden, Spender, and Isherwood on Rügen Island, 1931: three young men who "ganged up and captured the decade."

28. Heinz tucked up in the sand by Isherwood, Rügen Island, 1932.

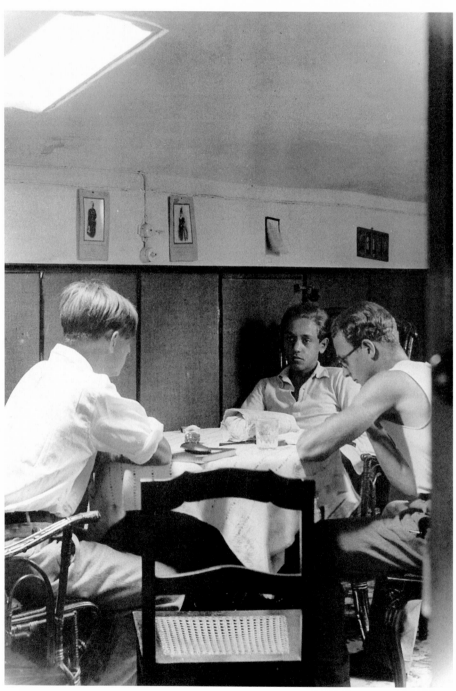

29. All the Conspirators: Isherwood, Heinz, and Humphrey Spender in a carefully staged photograph at Pension Seeadler on Rügen Island, July 1932.

Their ostensible reason for going to America in January 1939 was "travel," but they were in fact crossing the Atlantic to avoid the war. The decision was Beesley's, since Smith disliked travel and would have preferred to stay in England for the duration because she thought it would provide her with good copy. She also felt that they were running away, and this gave them something else in common with Isherwood. "I did not realise what good company he would be in," she wrote of Beesley's decision to leave England in the face of criticism from their friends and colleagues.

Isherwood took to the Beesleys at once, paying Dodie the ultimate compliment by saying she reminded him of E. M. Forster. "She has his nervous, touching eagerness to communicate with you, to be friendly, to understand what you mean." He thought her a little crazy—particularly over Buzz and Folly, the Dalmatians she acquired after Pongo died—but found her craziness harmless and rather engaging. Alec conformed to Isherwood's notions of heroism: "It seems quite natural that he's a C.O. He has that peculiarly British kind of individualism which takes the unpopular side as a matter of course." The Beesleys were equally drawn to Isherwood. "He is the nicest person imaginable, simply radiating goodness, but with a good sense of humour," Smith recorded in her diary. "He obviously has a brilliant mind but there is a very charming simple quality about him—almost humble. He frequently says 'as you, of course, know' when imparting information—and usually I don't. He is, of course, a CO . . ." This may not be the impression everyone had of Isherwood, but Smith was no fool and if she felt that he was radiating goodness and humility rather than resentment and vanity, then it may be because his meditation was at last paying dividends. Smith herself would not necessarily subscribe to this diagnosis. "I have a—probably unjustified—suspicion of Eastern religion for Westerners," she confessed, "and am never quite at ease with such *very* good people—Alec is just about as good as I can stand—but I do like Christopher enormously and think I *should* feel at ease with him if I got to know him better."

There would be many opportunities to do so since Isherwood got into the habit of visiting the Beesleys at their house in Beverly Hills every week. Another thing Isherwood had in common with Smith was that neither of them was doing much writing apart from the occasional film job, but both were filling diaries with very thorough records of their lives in America. In Smith, Isherwood found a confidante who was sympathetic without being sentimental, someone who would listen but argue, someone above all who was a fellow writer and who understood the creative processes. For her part, Smith provides in her diaries a frank, funny, deeply affectionate but unillusioned portrait of Isherwood at a crucial juncture in his life.

Smith was horrified when, shortly after they met, Isherwood announced that he would be moving to Ivar Avenue in February and embarking on a monastic life. Oddly enough, this course of action had been prefigured in *The Ascent of F6*. During his lecture about the perils of fame and leadership, the Abbot suggests that Ransom abandon his expedition and instead remain at the monastery. Isherwood was still attracted by the idea of altruistic but glorious public service. "Sometimes I daydream myself into a Florence Nightingale role in a typhus camp," he confessed to Lincoln Kirstein, who was now serving with the U.S. Army as a private, first class. "Then Master says gently: "You silly little thing—why, you couldn't even take it at Haverford. We had to keep you half doped with fucking and rum. Don't worry. We're train-

ing you as fast as you'll let us." One way of getting that training was to find somewhere where fucking and rum would be in short supply. It is probable he chose the
Vedanta monastery rather than Trabuco because his first loyalty was to Prabhavananda rather than Heard. It may also have been that Trabuco would not have provided him with the discipline he felt he needed. At the same time, the monastery was
not totally isolated amongst the southern Californian uplands, but sat in the middle of
Hollywood, making it easier for Isherwood to keep one foot in the real world. He had
never heard from the draft board about his application for a 4-D classification, but in
any case the age limit had been lowered again and so Isherwood was automatically
exempt from service. "It's very odd to glimpse—or fancy one glimpses—the workings of the karma mechanism," Isherwood reflected in his diary. "If the question of
going to CPS camp had never arisen, I would probably never have actually signed on
with the Swami at all."[3] Smith was baffled.

> It seems so strange to me that a man of over 38, brilliant and with a great sense of
> humour, can want to live in a house largely because there is a shrine there (pre-
> sumably a Hindoo Shrine) and three services a day. Apparently he longs for dis-
> cipline—he cannot just practise his religion alone. He doesn't appear to like the
> Hindoo side of it at all but is willing to swallow that because he likes the other
> things about it. I simply cannot understand the craving for *discipline* . . . He
> seems to want to force himself beyond his own inclinations. He has given up
> smoking and longs for it; he will give up drink when he enters the order. He will
> entertain friends there and even visit them; but not go to parties or restaurants. I
> fancy the truth is that he has had a muddled and rather dissipated life and feels he
> might slip back. It is hard to imagine such a thing for he is genuinely good but
> now that I have read his book 'Goodbye to Berlin' I can understand a little better.
> He has lived with such extraordinary people and one fancies many of his friends
> may be like that and might move him to a lower life if he does not shut himself
> off from it. But I cannot like the whole business—it seems faintly hysterical for a
> man of his age.

Isherwood might have agreed with some of this, but insisted that he didn't "want to
kid myself that going to live at the Swami's, or anywhere else, will do more than fifty
percent towards keeping me on the tracks. But it *will* help." Smith consoled herself
with the thought that "some pretty devastating studies of life in that household may
get written in—say—ten years' time or so."

---

3. "The Sanskrit word karma has a primary and a secondary meaning," Isherwood explained. "A
   karma is a mental or physical act. It is also the consequences of that act; good, bad or mixed
   [. . .] The Law of Karma is the natural law by which our present condition is simply the product
   of our past thoughts and actions, and by which we are always currently engaged in creating our
   own future."

who left the bathroom he shared with Isherwood in a less than pristine state. Isherwood admitted to Sudhira, who was also finding life at the Center difficult: "I don't really like Indians as a race; Swami is an exception. Swami Vishwananda is sympathetic, but he's a murderee like nearly all of them, and I don't respect him." Isherwood had made similar complaints about the Jews, whom he tended to regard as self-elected victims, people who virtually collaborated with the Nazis during the early stages of their persecution in Germany. Indeed, in *Christopher and His Kind,* Isherwood acknowledges this link when discussing his treatment of Wilfrid Israel in the character of *Goodbye to Berlin*'s Bernhard Landauer. The book's references to the "oriental" aspects of Bernhard's character were derived from the author's prejudice against Hindus. Placing this prejudice firmly in the past, Isherwood writes of his former self:

> He found something repellent—that is to say, personally disturbing—in Hindu humility and passivity and the arrogance he felt that it concealed. As a matter of principle, he sided with the Hindus against the British Raj and agreed that they had every right to treat their English conquerors with arrogance. Still, he identified instinctively with the English. And so he found deeply disturbing the picture of himself confronted by one of these humble-arrogant figures, a Hindu, or a Wilfrid—someone who 'knew' about life and whose knowledge might be superior to his. 'He is not going to tell me what he is really thinking or feeling, and he despises me because I do not know.' This prejudice of Christopher's, I now realize, sprang from fear—fear of the unknown something which the Hindus knew; the something he might one day have to accept and which might change his life.

This was written with hindsight, of course, and presents Isherwood as a misguided young man who had a very satisfactory comeuppance when he became the disciple of a Hindu and found himself bowing down before "superior" spiritual knowledge. There is no suggestion here that Isherwood's prejudice persisted and caused him difficulties while he was living in a Hindu community.

After being made by Vishwananda to chant "*Ram, Ram, Ram, Jaya, Ram,*" which unfortunately reminded him of the fake-Tibetan chants he and Auden had invented for *The Ascent of F6,* Isherwood was ready to tell Prabhavananda (who had returned from the East Coast) that "India is getting between me and God"; but he eventually decided against it.

> If I am too dainty-stomached to swallow a little Sanskrit, how can I possibly prove to my friends that there is something more to Ivar Avenue than mere quaintness? I think how they would all laugh at Vishwananda, and at moments I really hate them all—everybody outside this place—savagely: there they all sit sneering and doing nothing to find out what it's all about. But I'm really hating myself for not being strong enough to convince them.

Squeamishness about the oriental aspects of his calling was a minor problem, however, compared with celibacy. Every time Isherwood thought he had his libido under control something would come along and disturb his precarious equilibrium.

Paul Cadmus often sent him photographs of his drawings and paintings, many of which were of young men. One of Pete Martinez stirred happy but distracting memories of Haverford. "You caught that brilliant long-lashed alertness, like a bird, or a cat watching a bird," he wrote to the artist. "And the compactness of the head with those neat little ears. What a bird! What a cat! What a little Aztec aristocrat! And the long eyelashes stroking your hand with their flattery, then whisking away, flicking you off, like a fly-whisk . . ." Isherwood decided to destroy another picture because he found it too erotic. A rather pale substitute was copies of Kirstein's *Dance Index,* the magazine sent to him by the young writer Donald Windham who had been left in editorial charge while Kirstein was serving in the army. Isherwood may not have cared for ballet—he'd been delighted to be told of the actor Nigel Bruce's remark "Why should I pay five dollars to see buggers jump?"—but he appreciated pictures of male dancers. "I shall look at them many, many times," he told Windham. Shortly after boasting to Prabhavananda how free he had been recently "from sexual thoughts and fantasies," he was obliged to confess:

> I'm at what seems a new all-time low ebb. We are in the midst of a heat wave. I haven't said a real prayer in weeks, or meditated in months. I spend all the meditation hours rattling through my japam, so as not to be bothered with it at any other time. At present I have no feeling for the sacredness of the shrine and not the least reverence for Ramakrishna or anybody else. If you ask me what I want, I reply: Sex, followed by a long long sleep. If offered a painless drug which would kill me in my sleep, I would seriously consider taking it: and I've never played much with thoughts of suicide before.
>
> I inhabit a world in which people are scarcely real. Real are my sex fantasies and memories. Real are the devices I think up for not being woken by Asit's alarm clock. Utterly, utterly unreal are Ramakrishna, religion, the war with all its casualties and suffering, and the problems of other people. I *long* to get away from this place. And yet, if I do manage to wriggle out somehow, I know that, in two or three months, I'll pine to get back in again.

Had he felt happier he might have celebrated August 6, 1943, which marked "six months at Ivar Avenue, six months of technical celibacy." Quite what "technical celibacy" was supposed to mean is unclear, but he may have decided that masturbation didn't really count. Whatever he meant, he regarded this period of abstinence and communal living as a genuine achievement, one that "would have seemed positively supernatural" a year ago. "Now I see it as the very first step, merely: less than the first. It has no value except as a reassurance that nothing is impossible." Quite how small that step was became clear a couple of weeks later.

In mid-August Isherwood took "a few days' rest" from the monastery and found temporary accommodations in a house opposite the Viertels' in Santa Monica in a room recently vacated by one of the director's mistresses. Piqued that the Viertels were too busy to spend much time with him, Isherwood called up Tennessee Williams, whom he had met earlier in the year through Donald Windham. "We got together yesterday, and had to laugh a lot," Isherwood told Windham, "as I'd been expecting, from his voice, an enormous fat man with a walk like a schooner under full sail." Williams had told Isherwood he thought the *Berlin Stories* as good as Chekhov. Normally, this was just the sort of thing Isherwood liked to hear, particularly from young men, but as he explained to Lincoln Kirstein, "I feel more and more that I do *not* want any acquaintances: and taking on a new friend is a very serious business. If you say you like someone that much you have got to show it, and showing it involves a great deal of time and emotional energy—or else 'friend' is just another misused word." Having heard no more from Isherwood after this initial meeting, Williams had decided to call unannounced at Ivar Avenue, where he made his boredom apparent and talked of Krishnamurti under the assumption the former Theosophist was somehow involved with Vedanta. Isherwood was not amused, and matters were not helped when he subsequently received a letter from Williams which criticized his behavior in the same breath as asking a favor. James Laughlin, editor of the literary periodical *New Directions,* had commissioned Williams to write a profile of Isherwood, "encountered under strange and exotic circumstances in a Hollywood seraglio." Whatever else Ivar Avenue may have been, it certainly wasn't a harem, but this may simply have been ignorance of terminology on Williams's part. "Somehow or other I anticipate a refusal," Williams had blunderingly continued.

> I don't think you like me particularly, or perhaps you distrust me, or you would not be so cagey. Ordinarily I only like people who like me (vanity, you know) but the attachment and sympathy I felt for Herr Issyvoo in Berlin has even withstood the intensely Anglican cold-shoulder which he has given me in Hollywood.
>
> It seems Laughlin would like to run an account of you and your new way of living along with an article by Henri [sic] Miller on Dali. You may not regard this as a flattering juxtaposition, nor do I think it a very congruous one, but I would be pleased to undertake the job if being in the New Directions Gallery would amuse you.

"Amuse" was no more tactful than "seraglio" and Williams had received a distinctly stiff reply.

> British [i.e. 'Anglican'] is, of course, the most savage word of abuse you could possibly have thrown at me, and it must mean you are feeling really hurt about something. I am sorry. Maybe the life I am trying very feebly to lead makes you uncomfortable, chilly down the spine? You think I have murdered Mr Issyvoo? Many others do. Perhaps I have. You see, I suspect that the truth is that you don't really want to see *me:* you want to see Mr Issyvoo, and I can't produce him.

Isherwood had gone on to say that if Williams wanted to write an article about Ivar Avenue he was welcome to do so but he could not count on Isherwood's personal cooperation. "However 'fair' and 'respectful' the account might be, it would still have the fatal distortion of self-advertisement: ISHERWOOD and Vedanta—instead of VEDANTA and Isherwood." The letter was signed: "Yours (really) sincerely, Christopher."

Williams had written back to say that he came from a very religious background and that as the grandson of an Episcopalian clergyman he would of course treat

Vedanta with respect, but Isherwood was having none of it and the article was never written. "Tho I 'like' Tennessee, or could get to like him, we have very little in common," Isherwood told Kirstein, "and that being so I simply cannot waste my not very extensive free time keeping up a fiction which neither of us believe in—it simply isn't fair to the several people in this town I really am fond of, and the others all around the globe I want to be free to write to. Does that sound impossibly snooty? If it does, I'm sorry: it's a confession of limitation and weakness, but snooty I must be."

Now, however, that the Viertels seemed to be too busy to see him, Isherwood decided to be rather less snooty and tracked Williams down to "a very squalid rooming house," where he was working on a film story. (Isherwood subsequently told Laughlin that he had seen nothing like Williams's apartment "since he visited a cheap abortionist in the slums of Berlin.") In his rebuffing letter to Williams, Isherwood had said he was happy to meet up, but asked: "What are we going to talk about?" Sex, of course, was what they talked about "the entire evening." Writing from the monastery, Isherwood had piously told Williams: "I'm not really interested in anything except this place and this kind of life and what they imply," but a couple of beers soon put an end to this pretense.

A probable result of this talk was that a week later Isherwood's celibacy ceased even to be technical. Wading into the virtually deserted ocean, he removed his trunks and slung them around his neck to enjoy the sensual pleasure of swimming naked, an action he likened to "a flirtation with Sex." It became rather more than a flirtation when another swimmer, who turned out to be a deaf-mute, approached him in the water and they began having sex. Isherwood broke away before reaching orgasm, thinking that in some way this might mean the liaison wouldn't "count." Back in his room, however, he realized he was fooling himself and so finished the job himself. "I did so with difficulty," he recalled. "The act gave me no pleasure. It seemed idiotic."

The act with the swimmer, however, had given him a great deal of pleasure and in order to resist further temptation he decided to return to Ivar Avenue two days earlier than planned. When he confessed to Swami, without being specific, that he was having "trouble with sex," Prabhavananda patted his head and replied: "It's a hard life. Just pray for strength. Pray to become pure." It was not as easy as that, and the encounter with the swimmer, insignificant in itself, was the first serious breach in the wall Isherwood had built to surround and protect his spiritual intentions. It reminded him of the world he had given up to follow the paths of Vedanta. Desperate to make the best of this lapse, he attempted to persuade himself that "within this defeat lies the possibility of an enormous victory. If I can resume my life here and carry on as if nothing has happened, then that'll be much more reassuring than if I'd never slipped. Morale is the only thing that matters."

Isherwood felt that Denny Fouts might be able to help him, "because he's the only person who can view my life as a whole, and therefore the only one who can give me any valuable advice. He isn't shocked by the squalid bits of it, and he isn't repelled or mystified by Vedanta." The only problem was that Isherwood felt that "Denny's company is very disturbing to me, a lot of the time. Because his life is free, bohemian, agreeable and full of affairs." Worse still, Fouts was often surrounded by attractive men, including one named Bill Harris, whom Isherwood met on August 21. One of the great beauties of the age, Harris was often compared with Marlene Dietrich. A male Blonde Venus, he had fair hair which fell in a wave over his right eye, where it contrasted alluringly with his dark eyebrows. His features were clean-cut and rather boyish, giving him an innocent look faintly compromised by full, sensual lips. He was well built and had—the ultimate Isherwood desideratum—good legs. In a doomed attempt to prove himself rather more masculine than his appearance, Harris had enlisted in the army, where he lasted all of two weeks. After being shouted at during a kit inspection, he had burst into tears and was immediately packed off to a psychiatrist, who declared him unfit for service and gave him an honorable discharge. He was now at college. Isherwood was instantly attracted to Harris and accused Fouts of deliberately putting temptation in his way. Although he did not see Harris again for over six months, he found that this "young man's image had been stamped on my mind and would reappear at inconvenient moments, in the shrine room and elsewhere. It would be all the more disturbing because I realized already that he himself wasn't unattainable." The battle was already lost.

In late September Isherwood had another sexual encounter on the beach at Santa Monica, and two days later Pete Martinez arrived to visit his parents in Long Beach. "He suddenly exploded into my world, and disturbed everything," he told Cadmus, "but beautifully and sweetly. I was more than glad to see him." And, indeed, did rather more than just see him. "I'm just back from spending the entire night downtown," Isherwood reported in his diary, without mentioning that he and Martinez had slept together. It was Martinez's final leave before being posted overseas and as Isherwood later put it, "I realized that he expected our goodbyes to be said in bed. Was I going to refuse him—knowing that we might never see each other again? Of course not." It turned out to be a long goodbye, and a few days later Isherwood skipped a class at Ivar Avenue for another assignation with Martinez. He asked Cadmus to send more photographs of Martinez to replace those he had previously burned.

Isherwood was now smoking again, drinking and having sex: he was himself once more. Or, as he put it: "I felt like quite a different version of myself—Pete's Christopher—who hadn't been taken out of the closet in a long while, but had been there all the time, waiting to be called forth." He added that "The whole legend, the whole cult of Pete, which Lincoln has established, made the room into a sort of shrine, with Pete himself cross-legged in the middle of the floor, a minor but authentic deity." Isherwood knew Martinez far too well to make a cult of him: the dancer was a highly amusing friend with whom Isherwood could relax and with whom he could also have sex with genuine affection but without complications. In his present state of mind, however, this distinctly corporeal deity seemed to represent something far more tangible and attractive than anything in the shrine at Ivar Avenue.

Perhaps recognizing the nature of his disciple's present difficulties, Prabhavananda took a characteristically pragmatic line. When giving Isherwood permission to miss his lesson, he had said, "You know, Chris—even if one gives up the spiritual life altogether for a while, he will come back to Ramakrishna before he dies. We know that for a fact. We have witnessed it." He nevertheless arranged for Isherwood to spend a month visiting other Vedanta centers in San Francisco and Portland. It can hardly have been coincidental that one of the people Isherwood met at the San Francisco Center was an Englishman who had left the order so that he could get married, but who had returned in his old age. This was a message from Prabhavananda. Somewhat surprisingly, Isherwood found the all-male atmosphere of the center oppressive and even wrote to Sudhira to announce that he had "never realized before how absolutely *necessary* women are"—not a sentiment he voiced very often during his life. Although he was unable to find "adventure" in the city, San Francisco provided other temptations. "It is pre-eminently the city of departure," he wrote. "The ships steal out into the fog and the shadowy Pacific, where the war is, across the cold water-hemisphere. And in the bars, the young soldiers sit waiting for their orders to leave and go into battle. You long to take wing from the tall terraces and fly, fly away to the uttermost islands. From the roof of the center, you can see the spider-slung bridges, and Alcatraz, that other kind of monastery." Such contrasting images of confinement and escape show just how much he was straining at the leash.

Isherwood may have been having problems with his monastic vocation, but he had no intention of relinquishing his guru-disciple relationship with Prabhavananda. Whenever he found life at Ivar Avenue lonely, whenever he found his fellow disciples tiresome, when he couldn't meditate and merely clacked mechanically through his *japam,* when he found thoughts of sex distracting him in the shrine room and the burden of celibacy unbearable, when he rebelled against chanting or the prospect of being made to adopt a Sanskrit name and lose his identity altogether—he clung to his role as a *chela,* or disciple. Having completed his tour of the other centers, and met numerous other swamis, he decided: "Prabhavananda is the only one of them who's really civilized, really tolerant; the only one who really understands the West." His unspoken commitment to Prabhavananda was: "I am your disciple, not a member of the Ramakrishna Order."

None of this, of course, made life back at Ivar Avenue much easier. There were further lapses from celibacy (including, at some point, sex with Tennessee Williams), but most of Isherwood's energies were devoted to the translation of the *Gita,* and he made only five entries in his diary between his return in mid-October and the end of the year. Peggy Kiskadden (as she now was, having married Bill Kiskadden in July) had been helping Isherwood and Prabhavananda revise the completed text, and towards the end of November reluctantly admitted that she didn't think their translation much better than those already in print, adding that Huxley agreed. Isherwood recognized the truth of this, and after giving in to a momentary depression, went away and came up with a new idea. Instead of the rather creaky prose he had been producing, he started putting passages into heavily stressed, alliterative verse, a style borrowed from Old English epic poems. Having discovered a style for the *Gita,* Isherwood raced through the text and had completed the revision by the beginning of February 1944.

The following month he spent a week at the Huxleys' house at Llano in the Mojave Desert working with Aldous on "Jacob's Hands," a film treatment supposedly based on a true story. This project would occupy the two novelists, on and off, until June. It is not altogether clear how this collaborative process worked, but it seems they roughed out the story together, then wrote several drafts, passing them back and forth between them and meeting to discuss their progress. By April 21 Huxley had finished a draft, telling his son Matthew: "Let's hope that when Chris has added his quota, we shall be able to sell the thing and live in cultured ease for a bit." This was unduly optimistic. Isherwood's "quota" took three months, and the final draft of the treatment was not completed until July 18.

This ludicrous story, largely told in flashback, concerns a ranch hand named Jacob, who manages to cure a calf of a disease called Black Quarter. He then graduates to humans, first curing his employer's crippled daughter, then joining a church in Los Angeles mostly attended by blacks, Chinese and poor immigrants. He is blackmailed into working for the Psycho-Magnetic Medical Center, from which he is summoned to heal a mother-dominated millionaire who subsequently runs off with Jacob's girlfriend before suffering a well-deserved and fatal relapse. Thoroughly disillusioned, Jacob decides that he should cure only animals, and retires to live modestly with the millionaire's black chauffeur, George. Asked by a bickering couple whose dog he heals why he no longer practices on humans, Jacob replies: "It is easy enough to cure the body. But how many can cure the soul?" The film ends with the couple driving away:

> They are no longer tense and petulant, as in the earlier scene. Both are thoughtful. Their faces are relaxed and happy.
>
> 'You know,' says the husband at length, 'there's something about that guy. Something wonderful. Just being with him—it did something to me.'
>
> 'To me, too,' the woman agrees. She glances quickly at her husband. 'Allan—'
>
> 'Yes, Mary?'
>
> 'I think—maybe—it wasn't only Topsy he cured.'
>
> 'Darling—couldn't we maybe start all over? The way we used to be? It isn't too late, is it?'
>
> The man gives her a tender smile. Then he puts his arm around her and draws her closer to him.
>
> 'No,' he says, 'it isn't too late.'
>
> The car moves slowly down the valley.
>
> Jacob and George stand looking after it, side by side. Both of them are smiling.

"There is no reason whatever why a novelist or playwright, however talented, should be able to do good work on the films," Huxley had informed readers of the *Daily Mail* in 1927. Nevertheless, both he and Isherwood appear to have been pleased with this hackneyed, sentimental, sub-Steinbeck farrago and were optimistic about selling it. In the event, even James Geller, the story editor at Warner Bros., who had been "practically prepared to buy it sight unseen," balked when actually shown the treatment. The authors took comfort in the suggestion by an agent at William Morris that the reason for the "universal rejection" of their treatment was that the studios were afraid of the reactions of the powerful medical establishment. The sad truth is that even by the standards of Hollywood "Jacob's Hands" was sorry stuff, displaying none of the distinction one might reasonably have expected of such a collaboration.

Isherwood was employing his talents rather more productively by finally starting to write his novel. It was to be based on his time at Gaumont-British. The principal characters would be "Christopher Isherwood" and a film director based on Viertel.

Reflecting on Swami's determination to keep him busy with Vedanta projects, Isherwood concluded: "The fiction writer was thus being forced to go underground. But he was determined to survive, and maybe these restrictions were just what he needed to provoke him into becoming active again." Toward the end of March he spent ten days with John van Druten and his friend Carter Lodge at the AJC Ranch at Thermal. The ranch was run by Lodge, who had been van Druten's lover and now managed his financial affairs. Isherwood spent his ten days at the ranch roughing out the first draft of his novel, which he had named *Prater Violet* after the fictitious film "Isherwood" and the Viertel character were working on in the story. It was van Druten who supplied Isherwood with the film's scenario, a sentimental tale of old Vienna.[4] Progress was slow, and the hugely productive playwright was astonished to discover that Isherwood sometimes put in no more than twenty minutes' work each day. Isherwood was, however, trying to ease himself slowly back into a fiction writer's regime. "Gradually, gradually, the muscles of the invention become more flexible," he noted in his diary. "I just have to keep on at it. It's my karma yoga."

Back at Ivar Avenue, Prabhavananda wanted to concentrate his disciple's mind on a different sort of yoga, instructing him that he should spend three hours every day in the shrine room and perform a whole day's vigil every month. Evidently alarmed that Isherwood should be devoting his creative talents to fiction rather than Vedanta, Prabhavananda had pointedly asked another disciple in Isherwood's presence: "Why do you read novels? All books that do not give the word of God are trash." Four days later, while spending an enforced day of silence in the shrine room, Isherwood felt that he should tell Prabhavananda that he no longer intended to become a monk.

It was not merely Swami's professed antipathy toward Isherwood's nonreligious writing that caused this reaction. A month earlier, Bill Harris had reappeared in Isherwood's life, a more solid obstacle to the novitiate's vocation than the image that had disturbed his attempts at meditation during the last six months. Far from being a disappointment, Harris more than lived up to Isherwood's memory of him. The attraction, however, was no longer merely sexual. Isherwood had fallen in love. In his (edited) diaries, Isherwood calls Harris "X." and refers to his infatuation as "the X. situation." He later explained that "as far as I was concerned, X. wasn't a human being at all but simply a state of mind [. . .] my 'love' for X. was, in fact, nothing but sentimental obstinacy—quite cruel and calculating under the sugar coating." How this cruelty and calculation manifested itself, or even what Isherwood meant by the terms, is not clear. Looking back, he decided that he had used Harris as a way of testing his vocation. The young man was, as he put it, a temptation "to be overcome by temporarily yielding to it." At the time, however, he was more involved than that. The situation, he recalled, "was particularly idiotic, because I never had any real intention of doing anything about it: even if X. had returned my feelings, I would never have left Ivar Avenue on that account." Isherwood may have been able to assert as much in retrospect, but there is no doubt that at the time Harris posed the biggest threat to his

---

4. The *Prater* was an area of Vienna where people promenaded, often on the lookout for sex of all kinds. Ludwig Wittgenstein was one of those who is rumored to have sought out rough trade there.

merit." He went on to comment yet again on Auden and Isherwood's departure for America: "as artists they were perfectly free to go and live where they liked when they emigrated, though as leaders of a literary-political movement they have done untold harm to their cause by remaining there."

Connolly now commissioned Isherwood's erstwhile admirer Tony Bower, who was working as an assistant on *Horizon,* to contribute to a series of letters from foreign parts, titled "Where Shall John Go?" Bower's apparent interest in Vedanta when he visited the temple with Fouts three years earlier had aroused Isherwood's suspicions. "He sniffs all around the subject with jealous curiosity," Isherwood had complained. "He's hoping it's all true, and yet he's also hoping like hell that it's a fake, and that I shall come to my senses finally and have to admit this." At the time, Isherwood had thought that Bower was worried at the prospect of losing his fellow *âme damnée* to the opposition. Bower was in fact storing up copy for future use, and in the January 1944 issue of *Horizon,* writing as "Antony Bourne," he had a great deal of satirical fun describing life in New York and California. The article was amusing but wildly inaccurate, mentioning for example the staunchly Anglican Auden's "long flirtation with the Catholic Church." Prabhavananda was depicted as "an emissary from an Indian Yogi training college whose command of the English language left something to be desired, and who did little, to my mind, to clear up the confusion between Eastern and Western thought processes." When Isherwood spoke in the Temple, Bower continued, "the place became quite a major Hollywood attraction." Isherwood was now "living with the Swami in a little house near the Temple, translating the Upanishads via the Swami's somewhat basic English into readable prose. This is as far as I know his only literary activity."

His life is largely spent in religious pursuits and exercises, he spends long hours at contemplation, is a vegetarian, doesn't smoke and doesn't drink; his social life is slightly limited as a result, and he sees very few people indeed. Since going to live with the Swami he seems to have committed himself entirely to the contemplative life, and it seems safe to say that the 'Mr Norris' Isherwood has gone for good. While admiring the intellectual honesty which compelled him to commit himself so wholeheartedly to his experiment, it is impossible not to regret the disappearance of such a talented novelist, for it is very doubtful if anything in his new life will afford an opportunity for his malicious gift, unless of course he completely abandons it, in which case he and the reading public should have a field-day.

Having seen both pieces, Isherwood wrote Connolly a long letter, which was remarkably temperate in the circumstances, but which in the event he never sent. In it he once again rehearsed his reasons for coming to America and staying there, shifting his position a little from the defiant one he had adopted four years earlier. Coming to America, he now admitted, "was an altogether irresponsible act, prompted by circumstances."

When the war broke out in 1939, it was a fifty-fifty chance what I'd do. I was a bit bewildered, a bit guilty, pulled by personal relationships to stay, and pulled by other relationships to return. I delayed, because that is always easiest. Then came the press attacks, and cowardice and defiance hardened. Yes, I quite admit that there was cowardice—not of the Blitz (which I think, from my limited experience of air raids, would have bothered me no more and no less than it did all of you) but chiefly because I knew that, if I returned to England, I would have to take the pacifist position and strike out on my own line—not yours. That decision was made some time before the war started, and I have never changed it. I needn't go into the whys and wherefores of that now. I think I have always been a pacifist, and that the whole Hitler episode confused me into thinking that I wasn't, because it affected me personally. I had never properly thought the whole thing through.

He did not want to discuss his beliefs in detail but wrote that meeting Prabhavananda "offered me personally a solution and a way of life which I desperately needed, and which seems to work, and within which I can imagine living the rest of my life with a feeling of purpose and lack of despair."

Tony says, and you report, that I may not write again. I think if I hadn't found something like this I never would have written again: now I think I shall, I'm pretty sure I shall. [. . .] I am trying to hatch out into something different, and if you object that I have chosen the darnedest time to do it, I can only answer that chickens can't choose. This is not in any way to defend my conduct in leaving England in the first place—that, I repeat, was irresponsible. Whatever good or bad motives are found for it, I can't honestly accept them. I can't think of myself either as a traitor or as a disgusted prophet. From my personal point of view, it has all turned out for the best—through no merit or foresight of mine. And I suppose, if the result of what I am doing has literary fruit, people will one day say it was for the best all round.

Isherwood also came in for criticism in *Penguin New Writing*. For what he whimsically called "the twenty-first birthday of the Penguin," by which he meant issue No. 21 of his magazine, Lehmann wrote a piece titled "Without My Files" in which he looked back over its history. The reason he was without his files was that they were stored away for the duration, "inviolable:" "A fatherly care no doubt increases the interest for myself, but it has a wider interest, for in it can be traced something of the history of the mind of our times," he announced. Lehmann was incapable of taking himself anything but seriously, but this was just the sort of statement that made friends such as Isherwood think him a pompous ass. Lehmann went on to recall discussing his original idea for *New Writing* with Isherwood, somewhat exaggerating Isherwood's subsequent contribution to the project: "Christopher Isherwood and I were a strange pair of collaborators, because while he was in Holland, or Belgium, or Portugal, I was in Austria or France or England, and our letters took a long time to reach one another. The delay of distance was no doubt enhanced by the inquisitive eyes of various European brands of police-snoopers. But it worked, and though he had necessarily to leave most of the job to me, his ideas and his advice were as valuable as his own stories."

The degree of collaboration was largely a fantasy on Lehmann's part. It was all too typical of him to claim his well-known friend virtually as a co-editor and then to administer a sharp little rap about being in the end left to do most of the work. There was worse to come, however. After praising Isherwood's contributions to the magazine, and congratulating himself for providing a showcase for sections of *Goodbye to Berlin,* Lehmann went on to analyze "what nine years have done to a generation of poets and novelists."

> *The Nowaks* stands at one end of the nine years. At the other end stands *Vedanta and the West* [. . .] It is certainly a gap of some size and has bewildered many of Isherwood's former admirers. Communal meditation at La Verne seems a far cry from Frl. Schroeder, Sally Bowles and the evenings at the Alexander Casino. The conjunction of the Nowaks and the Landauers, observed with such a witty and compassionate eye and set down in prose so subtle and so simple in appearance, seemed to promise a row of novels at once intensely English in spirit and European in sympathy, a creative achievement that would bridge more than one gulf in our culture. A mystical parable called *The Wishing Tree* and a couple of slick and unimportant *New Yorker* stories have been a poor recompense for the hopes of those years, a stone indeed for those who hungered in wartime for bread. Many who did not know him well, and some whose motives have not been altogether free from suspicion, have rebuked him in public for not returning from America to be with his countrymen when war broke out. Others who knew a little more of the complex issues involved, and who respected his motives as they would respect the motives of a Quaker or a serious Conscientious Objector among themselves, have felt not only the lack of stories that might have meant so much to them, but also an anxiety that so great a difference of experience would sever him irretrievably from his roots and his generation. *Vedanta and the West* has not allayed their anxiety, but judgement should be suspended until the pattern can be seen more clearly.

While Lehmann was undoubtedly right about the deeply disappointing quality of Isherwood's recent output compared with his prewar writing, his tone is insufferable. He dresses up his remarks as the objective views of a cultural commentator, but is in fact airing his own very personal grievances about what he saw as Isherwood's defection. He mounts a defense of Isherwood clearly intended to redound to his own credit, and in doing so draws attention once again to the widespread criticism of his friend that many people felt was entirely justifiable. The pity of it is that Lehmann probably didn't even realize how clumsy and transparent he was being.

Isherwood was surprisingly unruffled by this article. "*Of course* I don't think it is monstrous," he assured Lehmann. "You know I have always appreciated the way you went to bat for W. and myself, at a time when everybody else was, shall we say, jumping to conclusions." Isherwood would only have known of Lehmann's support from what Lehmann himself had told him by letter. In fact, Lehmann was much more equivocal than he pretended. Quite apart from his own personal sense of loss, Lehmann genuinely believed that America was ruining Isherwood's and Auden's talent, as his article made clear. (Auden likened Lehmann's frequent pronouncements about him to "crossing the name of an erring daughter out of the family Bible.") Rather than defend himself, Isherwood told Lehmann that he was "a bit bothered by the references to Wystan's 'New Year's Letter'—quite an old work of his, by now, and not, I think, indicative of his general development. Since then he has published what I consider his masterpiece—the Christmas Oratorio called 'For the Time Being.' " There was, however, a veiled rebuke in his reaction to Lehmann's comments about Isherwood's own recent short stories: "Damn you, why do you have to read the *New Yorker*? Wystan, whose heart is even greater than his genius, has an awful time, apparently, trying to prove to people that they are really most significant and interesting! There's friendship for you."

To Kirstein, who had written in protest at the article, Lehmann sent a self-exculpatory reply, which Kirstein copied out for Isherwood complete with his own waspish annotations. Lehmann had gone on, as usual, about his deep regret, for personal reasons as well as literary ones, that Auden and Isherwood had gone to America and therefore been unable to share "certain profound and changing experiences." He added: "Guilt, I also fancy, will permanently corrupt their subconscious about it all" and ended piously: "Incidentally you ought to know that the backwash of the row over their departure slopped over the rest of us in a not too pleasant way: some of us might have reason to be a good deal more hostile than we are." "This is revolting," Kirstein commented. "He is a disgusting man. I am glad he is and want to stick his head in his filth, with all the others, all monsters, all awful [. . .] The English don't deserve good writers. No wonder they came to the US." Isherwood defended Lehmann wearily: "I think he was honestly trying to cover up for me; but the effect was that of an unnecessary apology. Oh, what does it matter, anyway? One tiny mess more within the general swamp."

Vernon eventually arrived at Ivar Avenue in August, staying in the monastery for a week before moving into a nearby apartment Isherwood had found with the original intention of sharing it. "It's difficult to tell if Vernon has really changed," Isherwood wrote after a couple of weeks; "only time will show that. But he certainly has a different attitude towards me, and he has certainly learnt a great deal. He is wonderful to talk to—really intelligent, not just repeating things out of books; and he speaks my language. He has exactly the right attitude towards Ivar Avenue; sees the funny side of it, and yet realizes the necessity of the funny side, and the significance behind it. I think he may be on the way to becoming a good painter. That I can't judge. I only know his being here seems to lighten up the whole place and every minute of the time. I no longer want to rush away to Santa Monica. And the X. situation has practically ceased to exist." Prabhavananda, however, may have regarded Vernon as a threat, and almost immediately persuaded him to move to Montecito, near Santa Barbara, where the Society had just been given a house and some land on which to establish a new center. The donor was a painter, and Vernon would be able to have his own studio there.

On August 26, 1944, Isherwood turned forty, an event that proved surprisingly untraumatic. He faced the future with some optimism:

He then added a substantial postscript, praising the presentation of "Isherwood" and the *"new dimension"* the novel brought to Isherwood's work. It was, therefore, for all the forcefulness of its principal objection, a very friendly letter, signed "With all my love." It nevertheless worried Isherwood, who replied by pointing out that the whole point of the film Bergmann was making was that it seemed "heartless" when held up against "the hard horror of the political situation in Vienna." He also explained that Bergmann's remark about his wife and daughter is "meant in an entirely rhetorical way." Viertel still felt "sacrifice" was rather too strong in the context, and held out for something to crystallize the father-son relationship, but he urged Isherwood to use his own judgment. "There is no reason for you to worry," he wrote. "Don't hesitate to publish my imaginary passport photo. And don't work too much on it, or you'll destroy the lightness and the charm of it!"

The failure of his relationship with Vernon forced Isherwood once more to ask himself where and how he should live. "With or without him, I have to go on trying to live this life," he told himself. Any plan to become semidetached from the monastery seemed impractical and he could no longer stay at Montecito with Vernon there. Nor did he want to return to Ivar Avenue, because he found Sudhira suffocating. He spent a week with Peggy Kiskadden, but it was not a success. Their friendship was under strain because Prabhavananda disapproved of it. "I don't know why," Isherwood wrote, "—but maybe he's right. I really shouldn't run to these elder sisters, nannies and mummies." Kiskadden herself suspected that Prabhavananda had been piqued by her criticism of the *Gita* translation, a theory Isherwood dismissed as "fantastic." Whatever the cause, the friction between her and Prabhavananda made things very difficult for Isherwood. He also felt that Peggy was putting all her energies into her new marriage: "She's got Bill. Artificial uncles are no longer needed." He could not possibly stay with Denny Fouts, whose life was too far out of control. Fouts was once again pursuing what Dodie Smith referred to as "little boys" (in fact adolescents), something that finally put him beyond the pale as far as she was concerned. Even such stalwarts as Chris Wood, the Huxleys and the Beesleys no longer seemed people Isherwood could confide in and lean upon. He nevertheless spent a week at Wood's house doing some final polishing of *Prater Violet*. While there he decided that he needed to get another film job, and that, like it or not, he would have to return to Ivar Avenue. "I've got to learn to live with the family without becoming involved in it," he vowed. "Avoid gossip. Avoid participation in their feuds. Concentrate on what is essential—contact with Swami and prayer."

By the end of 1944, nothing had been resolved, but Isherwood felt he had reached a sort of equilibrium. This required some moral juggling, since he had started seeing Bill Harris again. "Sure, I ought to stop seeing X., or leave Ivar Avenue, or both," he wrote on the last day of the year.

I ought either to get a movie job or start a new story. But the whole problem—just because it seems insoluble at present—has to be accepted for what it is, and simply offered up. I'll let it develop and try to stop worrying. Sooner or later—probably much sooner—X. will go away. Sooner or later, I shall write another story, or get work, or money, or go East or to England. Nothing that is happening or may happen really prevents me from doing the one thing which ultimately matters. Make japam, watch and wait. Put all your emphasis on that. Everything else—even your scruples about your conduct—is vanity, in the last analysis. Never mind what other people think of you. Never mind what you think of yourself. Go ahead with the only valid activity, the one which never fails. Stop trying to tidy up your life. Stop making vows—you'll only break them. Less fussing and more faith. You've been an awful nuisance lately, but I forgive you. No, don't thank me. No more tears, I beg. Blow your nose, and pull up your socks, and shut up. You don't have to be a grim old stoic, either. Your life could be such fun. Now run along and enjoy yourself. And let's try to make this a *happy* new year.

Nanny couldn't have put it better.

SEVENTEEN

PRABHAVANANDA WAS DELIGHTED WHEN IN JANUARY 1945 A RE-porter from *Time* magazine came to interview him and Isherwood. What he innocently imagined would be some friendly free publicity for the *Gita* translation (which was reviewed favorably in the same issue of the magazine) turned out to be inaccurate and sensational, treating Isherwood just as he feared Tennessee Williams would have treated him in the proposed article for James Laughlin—as a celebrity convert. "Ten years ago," the journalist wrote, "Christopher Isherwood was one of the most promising of younger English novelists, and a member of the radical pacifist literary set sometimes known as 'the Auden circle.' Now, thinking seriously of becoming a swami (religious teacher), he is studying in a Hindu temple in Hollywood, California." This, Isherwood felt, put him in a false position because he was by now seriously thinking of leaving Ivar Avenue. The article was littered with errors and Isherwood found its tone offensively patronizing. He cringed when he read the caption beneath a photograph of him and Prabhavananda grinning inanely on the steps leading to the temple: "In their world, tranquillity."

Isherwood felt anything but tranquil and was especially annoyed to read that he was supposed to be the model for "the dissatisfied hero of Somerset Maugham's current best-selling novel, *The Razor's Edge*." In the course of his researches for the novel, which features a young man whose quest for spiritual enlightenment leads him to a guru in India, Maugham had in fact consulted Isherwood, and had taken out a subscription to *Vedanta and the West*. He had specifically asked Isherwood about the lines from the *Katha Upanishad* in which the path to salvation is likened to "the sharp edge of a razor." Isherwood had explained that a proper translation would make it clear that the difficulty lay not in passing *over* the razor's edge, as Maugham had it, but in treading *along* it, but Maugham disregarded this advice and used a nonsensical translation for his novel's epigraph. Prabhavananda was nevertheless keen that he and Isherwood should give Maugham further advice when the novelist came to Hollywood in June in order to work on a film adaptation of the novel. In the event,

Maugham's screenplay was jettisoned and the replacement writer failed to respond to offers of help from Ivar Avenue.

In February Isherwood himself returned to the studios, signing a contract with Warner Bros. at $600 a week to work on several films, starting with an adaptation of Wilkie Collins's *The Woman in White*. He spent much of his time with the British writer John Collier, who possibly recommended him for the job. The author of macabre short stories and engagingly fanciful novels such as *His Monkey Wife*, about a man who marries a chimpanzee, Collier was a couple of years Isherwood's senior and an old studio hand, having spent several periods in Hollywood. He preferred working at night and so during the day distracted Isherwood with conversation and literary games.

Further distraction was provided by an attractive messenger boy at the studio with whom Isherwood embarked on an affair in May. After a farewell bout of *al fresco* sex with Isherwood beside the Beesleys' swimming pool, Bill Harris had left Los Angeles for New York in February to join his other lover, a wealthy Argentinian named Pancho Moraturi. It was clear that Harris's relationship with Isherwood had run its course, although Isherwood himself was unwilling to admit this. "At the moment, I am not very glad that I am in love with Bill Harris; because he doesn't even write," he told Cadmus two months after Harris's departure. "He is one of the sweetest creatures on this earth, but you have to take him the way you find him, and not get rattled." The problem was that a great many other people were inclined to take Harris as they found him, and Isherwood continued to suffer sharp pangs of jealousy at the thought of what Harris might be doing in New York. "Every so often, I feel I want him all to myself, and then it's torture," he told Cadmus.

> Not having the agent's mentality, I find it hard to be content with ten percent. But ten percent is all anyone is going to get, until he meets an entirely mythical Prince Charming, who is a blend of Laurence Olivier, his brother, Heathcliff, you and me. Please let me have some news of him, excluding the list of his affairs, which I prefer not to hear [. . .]
>
> My own life is very uncertain [. . .] I have got to leave Ivar Avenue and look at it from the outside. I'll probably go back. I don't know. Needless to say Bill keeps appearing in my plans; but that's probably just daydreaming. I might come East in the summer, but that seems doubtful. Again, much depends on Bill, if he wants it to.

When Isherwood met the messenger boy, he was looking not so much for someone to replace Bill Harris as for diversion—and the studio, which had a large homosexual presence, certainly supplied that. Monitored by a fascinated Collier, Isherwood's affair with the messenger (who went under several names, none of them his own) weathered a dose of clap and continued for about three months. A slight, and slightly effeminate, figure (brutally categorized by Denny Fouts as "a department-store queen"), the messenger might have fitted the role of *"kleiner Bruder"* had he been less obviously self-reliant. Unfortunately for him, Isherwood was still stuck on Harris. What finally put paid to the relationship with the messenger, however, was a twenty-fourth birthday party held on June 2 for a man named Bill Caskey.

Isherwood was told by Fouts that Caskey had just emerged from a relationship with a rich old man and had vowed he would never again sleep with anyone older than himself. This, as Fouts very well knew, was a direct challenge. Isherwood made a play for Caskey on his birthday, buying him a shirt as a present and then persuading him to sneak away from the party and come to Fouts's apartment. Caskey did so and joined Isherwood in bed.

Although almost seventeen years Isherwood's junior, William Caskey was a very different prospect from the *tabula rasa* youths Isherwood normally chose as his long-term partners. Born into a Kentucky horse-racing family, he was part Irish and part Cherokee, a Roman Catholic and—like his father—a heavy drinker. Caskey insisted that it was his mother who had driven his father to drink, but this may simply have reflected his view of American women, whom he characterized as maenads intent upon destroying their menfolk. He had served in the U.S. Navy but had been caught during an anti-homosexual purge and been released from service. He had subsequently come to California with his close friend Hayden Lewis. Isherwood disliked Lewis instinctively but—apart from the occasional explosive row—decided to get on with him for Caskey's sake. (Lewis had an equally low opinion of Isherwood and behaved with equal diplomacy.) Caskey was currently working at a restaurant in Santa Monica, a small and discreet place where movie stars could safely dine out with the sort of escorts the studios would have vetoed.

Caskey was short—even shorter than Isherwood—stocky and hirsute, his body, like his head, covered with close-curling hair, which earned him the affectionate nickname of "Fuzzpig." He had only one testicle, but this does not appear to have stood in the way of an extremely active sex life. He was particularly proud of his ability to pick up heterosexual men. Although Isherwood continued to see the messenger boy, it soon became clear that in the unlikely person of the ebullient Caskey he had found someone with whom he could share his life. He later felt that there was an element of snobbery in this decision, that Caskey was in some way more "presentable" than the messenger, someone who could be introduced to his friends without embarrassment. Indeed, when the occasion demanded, Caskey could dress and behave with the utmost decorum, every inch the Kentucky gentleman. Dodie Smith's first impression was of "a nice, gentle boy with very little to say for himself." Caskey's more usual manner, however, particularly after a few drinks with homosexual friends, was raucous and foul-mouthed. He could be astonishingly and gratuitously rude, but at his best he was very funny and very good company.

For the first couple of months, however, Isherwood was mooning over Harris, whom he still dreamed of having all to himself. Isherwood later wrote of himself: "He cannot have wanted to carry Bill off from Pancho permanently. He must have known then what became obvious to him when he was rewriting his journals a year later, that his intentions towards Bill were not and had never been really serious."[1]

---

1. Isherwood wrote this in his "reconstructed" diary, eventually published as *Lost Years*. From 1945 until he began making notes about a journey to South America in September 1947, Isherwood kept no diary at all. Thereafter he wrote a journal only sporadically, and it was not until March 1955 that he began to make regular entries again. In 1971, however, he began an attempt to "reconstruct" this lost period. He never explained why he gave up writing his diary at this critical juncture in his life. It was his usual custom, when wondering what to do with his life, to rehearse the alternatives in a journal, but the decisions he made during the year were not analyzed on paper.

This was not the impression he gave at the time. "I simply cannot face the prospect of seeing Bill again, if I must see him under the same competitive circumstances as in Hollywood," he told Cadmus two months after meeting Caskey, who was clearly not yet considered a tie.

> If Bill was to say 'Come,' I would leave as soon as my job at Warner's was over— that is, in a few weeks. But he doesn't say it. And, after all, why should he? No doubt he would like to have me around, but only as part of the scenery. If I can't live with him, it is really better for us not to meet.

When Harris failed to send a birthday letter, Isherwood finally decided: "There is really nothing left for me to do but wish him well, from the bottom of my heart." The affair was finally over, although the two men remained friends.

Whatever his feelings about the two Bills, Isherwood's position as a "demi-monk" had become increasingly untenable. On August 23, 1945, he left the monastery and went to live with Caskey in the chauffeur's apartment at 19130 Roosevelt Highway, a house overlooking the Pacific that the Beesleys had recently moved into on a temporary basis. "I don't remember any farewell scene with Swami," Isherwood wrote in the early 1970s, "and I have no doubt that C[hristopher] did everything to make their parting seem temporary and without any particular significance." Indeed, there is no account of Isherwood's departure from Ivar Avenue in *My Guru and His Disciple*. Isherwood simply writes: "When I did finally move out of the Center, at the end of August 1945, it was for a reason which had nothing to do with the Vedanta Society." That reason, he says, was Caskey. In the "reconstructed" diary, however, he recalls being angry with Peggy Kiskadden for "bitchily pretending to think Caskey was the reason why C. had left the Vedanta Center. (She knew perfectly well that this wasn't true, for C had told her repeatedly that he was going to leave, long before Caskey had even arrived in California.)"

There may have been further, unacknowledged reasons for Isherwood's finally leaving the monastery, after threatening (in his diary and elsewhere) to do so for some considerable time. In May the Germans had surrendered to the Allies, and on August 14 the Japanese surrendered to the Americans. The war was over, and just over a week later Isherwood returned to the outside world. It was the war that had propelled Isherwood into the monastery in the first place, as he had acknowledged in 1942: "If the question of going to CPS camp had never arisen, I would probably never have actually signed on with the Swami at all." As a pacifist, he felt that by submitting himself to some form of discipline he was doing something equivalent to those who had chosen to fight.

Isherwood had also returned to the world as a fiction writer. In July the American publisher New Directions had reissued *Mr Norris Changes Trains* and *Goodbye to Berlin* in a single volume as *The Berlin Stories*. More importantly, Isherwood now had an entirely new work, *Prater Violet,* ready for publication. He had finished the novella in defiance of Prabhavananda, who had thwarted its progress at every turn by lumbering his disciple with more "spiritual," and immensely time-consuming, literary projects. To have finished the book at all showed some measure of hard-won independence from the swami.

Not that leaving Ivar Avenue meant that Isherwood was severing links with Prabhavananda—or indeed being relieved of Vedanta tasks. He continued to visit the monastery, and almost as soon as he had settled into the Beesleys' apartment he began collaborating with Prabhavananda on a new project, a translation of the *Vivekachudamani* written by the early Indian exponent of Vedanta, Shankara. Prabhavananda had already made a reasonably coherent English translation of the work under the title *Shankara's Crest-Jewel of Discrimination.* Isherwood's job was to transform this draft into "a clear and suitable prose style," a task that would occupy him for well over a year.

To celebrate his freedom—not only from the Center but also from Warner Bros., where he finished work on an adaptation of Somerset Maugham's *Up at the Villa* for Wolfgang Reinhardt in September[2]—Isherwood bought himself a Lincoln Zephyr convertible for $1,500. The car may have been second-hand, but it was extremely showy. It would be hard to imagine a vehicle that more clearly announced Isherwood's return to the world, and no one seeing it zooming around Los Angeles, with Caskey and Fouts shrieking from the back seat, would imagine that the driver had until recently been a monk.

Isherwood's residence with the Beesleys was, fortunately, a temporary one, since Fouts was due to move to New York and had offered Isherwood the sublet of his apartment at 137 Entrada Drive in Santa Monica Canyon. Dodie Smith had greatly looked forward to having Isherwood as a guest, but almost at once got into an argument with him when she offered to have a spare set of keys cut in case he lost his. Isherwood claimed that he had never in his life lost a set of keys or locked himself out of a house. The problem, which had not arisen when Isherwood merely visited the Beesleys, was that Smith tended to see Isherwood as a much loved but rather wayward son, and found herself worrying when she heard his car go out after he had left her dinner-table supposedly to go to bed. Furthermore, the apartment was very small, consisting only of a bedroom and a bathroom. It was a relief for everyone concerned when Isherwood moved out at the end of September.

Fouts's apartment was not much larger than the Beesleys', consisting of two rooms and a bathroom. The living room had been dominated by *Girl Reading,* a huge painting by Picasso which Fouts had been given by his former lover Peter Watson. Isherwood believed that sleeping beneath it one night had given him terrifying nightmares about Nazi Germany, which he subsequently used in *Prater Violet.* Stephen Spender used to claim that Isherwood, in one of his anti-culture outbursts, had once used the painting as a dartboard, but it is unlikely that Fouts, who was very well aware of the painting's value, would have allowed such barbarism. Indeed, before leaving for New York he sent the picture on ahead and made a memorandum, witnessed by Caskey and dated September 20, 1945, in which he stated that the picture "is to be the property of Christopher Isherwood in the event of my dying or disappearing before it is sold in consideration of debts I owe him & because he is my best friend." In the event, he sold the picture in New York, supposedly to someone he met at a cocktail party. Dodie Smith reported that at Entrada Drive Isherwood had "put up

---

2. The film was never made.

anatomical charts to replace it," adding dryly: "he would. He says he never looks at them—I doubt if he has any need to, he knows too much about the human body without their aid." According to Isherwood, these "charts" were in fact army posters concerned with venereal disease, and had been put up by Fouts. One depicted a prostitute, warning, "She may be a bag of trouble"; the other was "a diagram of a penis, with dotted red lines to show the spreading of gonorrhoeal infection up the urethra and into the bladder."

By the time Isherwood left Ivar Avenue he had managed to save $7,000. Even with the expense of the new car, he still had enough money to live on without worrying unduly. He was also expecting some income from *Prater Violet,* which Random House published in November. The illustration on the dust-jacket was of a movie camera standing at an angle in front of a cityscape (London? Vienna? Berlin?) across which searchlights were playing. On the back, under a highly unflattering photograph of an open-mouthed Isherwood looking adenoidal if not actually moronic,[3] "A Note on the Author" informed readers that after being hailed as "one of the most gifted of the younger English novelists" for his Berlin books, Isherwood had gone "into virtual literary retirement [and] devoted himself to mystical studies while living monastically in Hollywood." Readers were assured, however, that in this new novel "there is no trace of mysticism; his satirical gifts are at their sharpest and he is, above all, the engrossing story-teller whose tale has hard dramatic impact and many subtle overtones of meaning."

It is not in fact true that *Prater Violet* is untouched by mysticism, and the circumstances in which it was written had a considerable bearing upon it. Ostensibly another chapter in the life of "Christopher Isherwood"—written in a similar manner to, and sharing many of the concerns of, the Berlin stories—*Prater Violet* is an altogether more complex work. Isherwood uses an account of his work at Gaumont-British as the basis for a profound meditation on friendship, collaboration and betrayal, and provides a nervy evocation of the slow but inevitable approach of a world war. The most memorable and brilliantly drawn character in the book is Dr. Friedrich Bergmann, who is not merely an exasperated, irascible artist forced by circumstances to work on a trivial and unworthy film: he is an emblem, "a tragic Punch." "The name, the voice, the features were inessential," the Isherwood character remarks on being introduced to Bergmann; "I knew that face. It was the face of a political situation, an epoch. The face of Central Europe."

Isherwood had taken note of Viertel's reservations and altered the book accordingly. In order to point up the contrast between the film's triviality and world events, Bergmann is given a comically over-the-top but entirely characteristic aria:

The picture! I s—up the picture! This heartless filth! This wretched, lying charade! To make such a picture at such a moment is definitely heartless. It is a crime. It definitely aids Dolfuss, and Starhemberg, and Fey and all their gangsters. It

---

3. "Many of my friends objected to the photograph," Isherwood complained to Bennett Cerf. He sent the publisher a new set of photographs, taken by Caskey, for future use.

covers up the dirty syphilitic sore with rose leaves, with the petals of this hypocritical reactionary violet. It lies and declares that the pretty Danube is blue, when
the water is red with blood. . . . I am punished for assisting at this lie. We shall all
be punished. . . .

At which point he is interrupted by the telephone. At the same time, we see that making the picture is genuinely important because Bergmann brings real passion to it
and takes pride in his craftsmanship. On the other hand, Isherwood toned down
Bergmann's melodramatically self-pitying reference to his family. Instead of claiming that he had sacrificed his wife and children to the film, Bergmann now says: "For
this picture, I have given everything—all my time, all my thought, all my care, all my
strength, since months."

Isherwood's recent appearances in print—the *New Yorker* short stories and "The
Day at La Verne"—had failed largely because he had been unable to find an appropriate narrative "voice." In *Prater Violet,* he returns to the old "Christopher Isherwood" of the prewar books, but this character is guyed more than ever before. The
book's opening not only reassures readers from the very first words that "Christopher
Isherwood" is back, but also slyly hints at the real Isherwood's recent absence from
the literary scene:

> 'Mr Isherwood?'
> 'Speaking.'
> 'Mr Christopher Isherwood?'
> 'That's me.'
> 'You know, we've been trying to contact you ever since yesterday afternoon.'
> The voice at the other end of the wire was a bit reproachful.
> 'I was out.'
> 'You were out?' (Not altogether convinced.)
> 'Yes.'
> 'Oh . . . I see . . .' (A pause to consider this. Then, suddenly suspicious.)
> 'That's funny, though . . . Your number was always engaged. All the time.'

We then see the Isherwood puppet, as usual, putting on a performance, pretending to appear nonchalant to his mother and brother about a summons from a film studio. We also get a satirical glimpse of the Isherwood who toed the party line and gave
Group Theatre lectures. When his mother mentions the views of her cousin Edith's
dentist on the possible invasion of Austria, Isherwood proceeds to "set up and knock
down every argument the dentist could possibly have been expected to produce, and
many that he couldn't."

> I used a lot of my favourite words: Gauleiter, solidarity, démarche, dialectic,
> Gleichschaltung, infiltration, Anschluss, realism, tranche, cadre. Then, after paus-
> ing to light another cigarette and get my breath, I started to sketch, none too
> briefly, the history of National Socialism since the Munich Putsch.
> The telephone rang . . .

... as indeed it often does in this novel when people are in full flow about the current political crisis. And it is always the film people on the other end of the line, the crass, commercial, unflustered creators of make-believe, reminding us that the world, however trivial its concerns may be, carries on regardless. Throughout the book, the Isherwood character parrots Bergmann, expressing opinions that for him are largely a matter of dogma, whereas for Bergmann they are very real indeed because the worsening crisis in Europe touches him personally (his family is still in Austria) as well as politically. At the time, of course, Isherwood had an equally urgent and personal interest in what was happening in Europe, since it materially affected Heinz, but this is deliberately suppressed in order to point up the contrast between the fictional characters of Isherwood and Bergmann. The director tells Isherwood that despite its apparent frothiness, the film they are making is a "symbolic fable," and it is one that concerns him directly:

> The declassed intellectual has two choices. If [...] he is loyal to his artistic traditions, the great liberal-revolutionary traditions of the nineteenth century, then he will know where he belongs. He will know how to align himself. He will know who are his real friends and his real enemies [...] Unfortunately, however, he does not always make this choice. Indeed, he seldom makes it. He is unable to cut himself free, sternly, from the bourgeois dream of the Mother, that fatal and comforting dream. He wants to crawl back into the economic safety of the womb. He hates the paternal, revolutionary tradition, which reminds him of his duty as a son. His pretended love for the masses was only a flirtation, after all. He now prefers to join the ranks of the dilettante nihilists, the bohemian outlaws, who believe in nothing but their own ego, who exist only to kill, to torture, destroy, to make everyone as miserable as themselves—

This, like many of Bergmann's pronouncements, is grossly exaggerated ("In other words, I'm a Nazi and you're my father," Isherwood responds, and they both laugh), but this is not unlike Isherwood's own feelings about himself in the late 1930s. He also acknowledges that for all his political posturing he cannot come up with lines for his proletariat characters in the film to speak: "Shakespeare would have known how [such characters] spoke. Tolstoy would have known. I didn't know because, for all my parlour socialism, I was a snob. I didn't know how anybody spoke, except public-school boys and neurotic bohemians."

Isherwood's own feelings about abandoning Viertel in 1934 and England in 1939 also feed into the book. Bergmann treats his script-writer as an ally against the studio executives, but we learn early on that the story editor, who is the producer's right-hand man, was at Cambridge with Isherwood. Isherwood's stock immediately rises with the producer, and Bergmann, the foreigner, recognizes that such ties are important in English society. The producers treat Isherwood as one of them, frequently trying to involve him in their intrigues. When Isherwood discovers that the studio wants to remove Bergmann from the picture, he fails to warn the director. When Bergmann is finally told of the studio's plot, he is astonished: "You knew this all the time?" he says to Isherwood. "You were in this conspiracy against me?" Isherwood wasn't, of course, but "My one cowardly idea was: Bergmann has got to hear this from somebody else, and not when I'm around." Isherwood unwillingly colludes with the executives to keep Bergmann from being distracted by events in Austria and to finish the film.

In the earlier books, we rarely have much insight into the inner life of the Isherwood character, but here it is acknowledged in the final scene with Bergmann, when, after the shoot is finished, they walk home through the dark streets in the small hours, each wrapped in his own thoughts. "It is that hour of the night at which man's ego almost sleeps. The sense of identity, of possession, of name and address and telephone number grows very faint. It was the hour at which man shivers, pulls up his coat collar, and thinks, 'I am a traveller. I have no home.' " Isherwood asks himself what it is that makes us go on living, what makes it bearable? The answer sometimes seems to be love, and Isherwood outlines a current affair with someone called J., whose gender is not revealed. (Isherwood clearly had Ian Scott-Kilvert in mind.) But such affairs do not last: there will be successors, "K. and L. and M., right down the alphabet." Whatever you do, the fear remains. There is, however, an alternative, one that Isherwood had attempted to explain to Upward in August 1939, and the image he uses for the way out of the valley of despair in *Prater Violet* is taken directly from that letter. Isherwood considers the inescapable fear of being afraid, the most terrible fear of all:

> And, at this moment, but how infinitely faint, how distant, like the high far glimpse of a goat track through the mountains between clouds, I see something else: the way that leads to safety. To where there is no fear, no loneliness, no need of J., K., L., or M. For a second, I glimpse it. For an instant, it is even quite clear. Then the clouds shut down, and a breath off the glacier, icy with the inhuman coldness of the peaks, touches my cheek. 'No,' I think, 'I could never do it. Rather the fear I know, the loneliness I know . . . For to take that other way would mean that I should lose myself. I should no longer be a person. I should no longer be Christopher Isherwood. No, no. That's more terrible than the bombs. More terrible than having no lover. That I can never face.'

But of course it is precisely what Isherwood had faced since the publication, six years before, of *Goodbye to Berlin*. *Prater Violet* may seem a light, amusing account in the old style of Isherwood's involvement with one of his great monster-characters. In fact, it is really an apologia, an explanation of what went wrong with the old Isherwood, and a glimpse of what he had been doing since last we heard from him.

Even if reviewers did not always understand this, they were nevertheless impressed, as were readers. "Dearest Christopher," Viertel wrote after receiving an inscribed copy of the novel,

> Thanks for your beautiful dedication of the by now famous book of yours—and congratulations to the stupendous success! Everybody reads the book and everybody loves it. There is a lively chance that it will become the book of the year. I am so happy, dear Chris, that Bergmann did not fail you!
>
> What makes the tragic Punch especially happy is that people tell me it is the one book in which one can feel your heart best (closest). And that is, I believe, the

secret of the spreading success: your humaneness which singles you out in your generation of writers.

The letter was signed: "Love from 'your father' Berthold."

John van Druten rather ungraciously remarked that he was "staggered" by the excellent notices the book received in the United States. While writing the book, Isherwood had told Kirstein: "I'd like to get it finished, just as a reassurance for the future." The American critics seemed to agree that *Prater Violet* demonstrated that Isherwood's future as a writer was definitely assured. *Time* magazine described it as "a fresh, firm peach in a dish of waxed fruits," an opinion echoed by Diana Trilling, who wrote in the *Nation* that it was

> a book written in the author's own person, yet utterly without ego; it is a novel about movie writers which is yet about the life of every serious artist; it is a book without a political moral, but a profound moral-political statement; it is gay, witty, sophisticated, but wholly responsible [. . .] Small as it is, 'Prater Violet' suggests, better than any book of the last three years, the charms and satisfactions which some few of us ask for from current fiction but which current fiction so persistently refuses us.

The book even went into an Armed Services Edition (No. 1115), specially designed to be carried in the pockets of uniformed American forces serving overseas, where it joined such titles as *Joe Louis: American, My Greatest Day in Baseball, The Case of the Black-Eyed Blonde* and *Selected Poems of Carl Sandburg.*

This reception was in marked contrast to the one the novella received in Britain, where it was published by Methuen in the spring of 1946. Isherwood had very publicly rejected the country of his birth and upbringing and had, like Lord Byron before him, shaken the dust of England from his feet. Whereas Byron had gone off into a romantic exile, dying in a foreign war, however, Isherwood had apparently abandoned England for the Lotus Land of California, where he had been content to spend his time contemplating his navel while London was bombed. This was the first opportunity for his critics to comment on his work, and they did a very English thing. The reviews were small and snubbing. Whereas notices of Isherwood's previous books had taken up many column inches, the reviews of his first "American" book—albeit one set among Europeans in London—were tiny. "I think Christopher has been more hurt than he will admit by the English critics," Dodie Smith observed, "—not only by the content but by their size and the fact that they don't treat the book as important one way or another." She added that he was particularly upset by a review of the novel by Julia Strachey in *Horizon.* The book was reviewed alongside Elias Canetti's *Auto Da Fé,* which (Strachey informed readers) was considered by "leading Viennese critics" as "one of the great novels of the century." Strachey devoted over two thirds of her notice to this 464-page novel, which had clearly exasperated and exhausted her, before turning to *Prater Violet.* "Up to the surface again we bob," she begins, "and there we stay." While she praised Isherwood's portrait of Bergmann, she claimed that when dealing with other characters Isherwood "merely makes cracks." There was no suggestion here that the novel had any serious themes, and she dismissed the book as "Altogether a most elegant piece of journalism."

> We don't get the mark of the artist—significant architecture. But we do get a most stylish little prefabricated house—with a printed notice, hung rather unexpectedly, in the very last section that we walk through, which tells us all about the builder of it, and in what part of the country he is to be found. As a matter of fact (since we are admittedly on personal ground) we had rather been given to understand that he had lately taken a long journey . . . far away from home. But can this be so? There is certainly no trace here of any pilgrimage having been taken since the production of his last work.

Thus *Horizon* had taken the opportunity once again to take a little swipe at Isherwood's "desertion." Strachey—though never, apparently, an admirer of Isherwood[4]—was an intelligent and perceptive person, and it says much for the still-prevailing attitude toward the "absent intellectuals" that she could have been so blinded by prejudice that she failed to notice how good the novel is. Isherwood was quite justified in being hurt by "the coldness and contempt" with which this subtle and complex book was received in England.

I sherwood had told an interviewer from the *Los Angeles Times* that *Prater Violet* was the first in a projected trilogy of novellas about refugees, covering "the whole period of immigration between Hitler and the war." Rereading this article many years later, he was unable to remember what the other books would have been—if indeed he ever really planned them. He certainly told his American publisher in January 1946 that he was "at work on another long-short story [. . .] about the Emigration Period." This was a book based upon his time at the Haverford Co-operative College Workshop, and his attempt to create fiction from that experience would occupy him for almost a decade. The novel, he told Kathleen, was to be "funny and yet serious—satirical and yet admiring." In consultation with Dodie Smith, he worked out "a rather tricky plot about [a] pathological liar and [a] fire." The liar is yet another version of Paul, the character who had caused Isherwood so much trouble over the years, but whom he seems to have been reluctant to abandon altogether. The fire was probably based on one that had occurred during Isherwood's time at Haverford, the cause of which was never satisfactorily explained. Isherwood had been intrigued to discover that this was the fifth fire in which Caroline Norment had been involved, two of which (both unexplained) had destroyed all her possessions. "One can't help wondering—does she, in some extraordinary way, *attract* them," Isherwood had written at the time. "Is she even perhaps a kind of schizophrenic pyromaniac?" It is unlikely Isherwood really believed this, but it gave him an idea for the novel, which did not, however, progress much beyond a draft of the plot.

---

4. On November 13, 1937, she had attended a Group Theatre evening where, she told her friend Frances Partridge, she sat amongst "Day Lewis, Spender, Auden and all their admirers. [Isherwood] gave a stupid talk and said many tiresome things, but it was all quite a slice of life."

Although Isherwood was able to do the occasional bit of film work, which did not require extended periods of concentration, any attempts at more sustained work were thwarted by the sort of life he was now leading with Caskey, which was extremely rackety. In the "reconstructed" diary Isherwood analyzed his relationship with Caskey at great length and at a distance of some twenty-five years. Since one purpose of the reconstruction was to investigate what he called his "sexual mythology" and identify his "sexual archetypes," Isherwood was led to conclude that his relationship with Caskey "lacked a myth": "I doubt if he realized this at the time," he continues, writing of himself in the third person. "Or, if he did, he regarded the lack of one as an advantage. He used to think the relationship between himself and Caskey as being more down-to-earth and therefore more mature than any other he had previously experienced." At their most rowdy, which they frequently were, their inhibitions suppressed by large amounts of alcohol, jokes and fists flying, Isherwood and Caskey would have struck few people as "mature," but there is no doubt that their relationship was different from any other Isherwood had been involved in.

Had Isherwood wanted, Caskey could have provided him with excellent credentials as a mythical figure. There was his gentlemanly background in the horse-breeding and racing world of Kentucky—curiously at odds with his distinctly less respectable life of drunken, promiscuous carousing in California. His naval service and its dramatic end had a certain mythical quality too, as did his later spell in the merchant marine, romantically shipping out of San Francisco. Then there was an element of the outlaw in Caskey, and during his life he was often in trouble with the authorities—something which Isherwood had always found attractive. It was not so much that Isherwood was unable to cast Caskey in a mythical role, but that, unlike his usual lovers, Caskey was very much his own man. In previous relationships, Isherwood had always been the instigator, the leader, the decision-maker, the protector. With Caskey this was impossible. Caskey was quite capable of taking the lead himself and was certainly in no need of protection. His will was quite as strong as Isherwood's and he was not looking for an older brother who would love him, look after him and always maintain the upper hand. Isherwood later decided that "to some extent" Caskey had been "subconsciously on the lookout for a substitute father and was now casting C. in this role." He decided that "the father-figure wasn't merely to be a stand-in for Mr. Caskey Senior; it was also a father-confessor [. . .] Once, Caskey came near to asking C right out to be his father-confessor—when he muttered (drunk but nevertheless still embarrassed) that he wished C would tell him whenever he did anything wrong." This may be the role of a father, but not of a confessor, to whom one goes when one *knows* one has done something wrong. Caskey had given up going to confession at the age of sixteen, after an old Jesuit, to whom he had admitted some homosexual act, had merely told him "not to make a habit of it" and given him "5 'Our Fathers' and 5 'Hail Marys' for a penance." Thereafter Caskey ceased to regard sex as a sin and never again went to confession. "I simply don't like organized religion," he recalled, "and became what's known as a Renegade Catholic." Caskey's request to Isherwood was more likely to have been of the kind one drunken partner makes to another and had nothing to do with fathers, cassocked or otherwise.

It was precisely because these two men were more evenly matched than was customary in Isherwood's emotional history—because neither was the father, neither the son—that the relationship was so difficult. Isherwood is much nearer the mark when he writes about the "conflict of wills" in their relationship. Right from the outset, neither wanted to declare his feelings until absolutely sure what the other felt. Even when it became clear—as it soon did—that they were in love, the battle of wills continued. There was never any intention that the relationship should be monogamous, but their habit of having sex with other people was a way of asserting their independence from—or denying their dependence upon—each other. This, however, could only be done within certain limits. Casual, promiscuous sex was accepted by them both, but Isherwood in particular would find it difficult not to become jealous when anything more regular or sustained appeared to be developing between Caskey and one of his sexual partners.

Fueled by large amounts of alcohol, their struggle to find a balance within the relationship occasionally erupted into physical violence, alarming for witnesses but—apart from the occasional bruise or bloodied nose—not very serious for the participants. According to Isherwood, alcohol also led to their moments of greatest intimacy, when they could relax without either of them worrying about spoiling his image of himself as the dominant partner. One result of this was that Isherwood now routinely began to spend a great deal of time drunk.

Caskey had enrolled on a course to become a professional photographer. There was talk of putting together a book of his photographs of Los Angeles, for which Isherwood would provide a text, but this project never materialized. (Never one to waste material, Isherwood later revised his text and sent it to Cyril Connolly, who published it in a special American double number of *Horizon* in October 1947.) Although Caskey took his new career seriously—and indeed became a highly accomplished photographer—he still spent a great deal of his time holding impromptu and very rowdy parties at the apartment. The resulting tiredness from lack of sleep and illness from too much drink undoubtedly contributed to the difficulties Isherwood experienced in trying to resume his own career as a writer.

In January 1946 Isherwood decided to consult a Dr. Gorfain about pains he had been experiencing in his penis for several months. He had at first thought these were a legacy of a bout of gonorrhoea he had weathered the previous year, but Gorfain told him that he had an obstruction—a median bar—at the top of the urethra inside his bladder. This was not very serious but it needed to be removed by surgery. Presumably Isherwood did not at this stage know his maternal grandfather's medical history or he might have been more concerned about submitting himself to an operation similar to the one which led to Frederick's decline into permanent ill-health and death. Instead, he rather looked forward to the procedure on January 12 and recruited Sudhira to be his private nurse. (This was the sort of suffocating Isherwood could endure very happily.) The doctor's nonchalant manner may have reassured him, but it was not until he was actually in the hospital, woozy from tranquilizers, that it became clear just how casual the medical profession could be. Gorfain informed him that in order to prevent infection he intended to tie up Isherwood's spermatic cords. This would leave the patient sterile, so he hoped Isherwood (whom he knew to be homosexual) was not planning on having any children.

Isherwood was pleased to regard the operation, and the subsequent uncomfortable treatment during which his urethra had to be syringed, as a "ritual penalty" for his failure to become a monk. When he went to see Dr. Kolisch, however, he discovered that the penalty might be greater than he had expected. Kolisch told him that after a while he would be left completely impotent. Fortunately, this alarming prognosis turned out to be wrong. Isherwood could achieve an erection and experience orgasm. The only thing he could no longer do was ejaculate, a deprivation he characteristically used to his advantage: when bored by sex he could fake an orgasm without his partner being able to tell. Some years later, however, Isherwood did begin to suffer from bouts of impotence, and it is possible that this was a long-term effect of the operation.

In the short term Isherwood found himself highly potent and discharged his sexual energy in the Pits, an area of dunes on Santa Monica's State Beach which had become a notorious playground for gay men. At a safe distance from the tide-line and further protected by the boundary wall of Marion Davies's beach house, the Pits were somewhere men congregated in the off-season months to sunbathe naked, with inevitable results. Ever the performer, Isherwood enjoyed the extra thrill of having sex there in front of other people. This is something he also did in bathhouses, or simply at other people's houses with fellow guests looking on. Isherwood enjoyed a great deal of casual sex during the period he lived with Caskey, and he wrote about it in graphic detail some twenty or so years later in his "reconstructed" diaries. Predictably, he appears to remember every single sexual compliment he was paid during this period and emerges from his diaries as "a Triton amongst the minnows," as one person put it, having seen him in action at a party. When these diaries were published, a close friend of Isherwood commented that the only two men he knew who had slept with Isherwood "laughed out loud" when they read this preening self-portrait. There is no doubt, however, that by any standards Isherwood enjoyed a successful and extremely busy sex life during the late 1940s and early 1950s, taking full advantage of Los Angeles' thriving if covert homosexual life.

During the spring Denny Fouts paid a visit to California, staying at his apartment, where he had a serious quarrel with Caskey. Isherwood, with some justification, saw himself as the cause of the argument. Having been responsible for bringing them together in the first place, Fouts now resented the fact that Isherwood and Caskey had entered what seemed to be a permanent relationship. It was clear that he no longer had the claim on Isherwood he had once enjoyed and his attempt to reassert it was doomed. Isherwood was forced to choose between the two men and in the process lost not only his present home but also Fouts's friendship.

Fortunately, the chauffeur's apartment at Salka Viertel's house at 165 Mabery Road had just fallen vacant. The apartment had been built over the garage alongside the main house and consisted of a spacious bed-sitting-room, a bathroom and a long private balcony overlooking the garden, with the Pacific beyond. There was also an additional downstairs bathroom, which Caskey used as a darkroom. The apartment was smaller than Fouts's, but much lighter. It was inexpensive and came with a friendly but discreet landlady. Unlike Dodie Smith, Salka Viertel was not the sort of person to lie awake worrying about what her tenants were up to. Her house was still a meeting place for refugees and other intellectuals and Isherwood was always welcome, but never pressured, to drop in. This meant that he could keep a foot in both worlds: the nostalgic, heavyweight European one of the Viertel "salon," and the uninhibited, sexually charged Californian one of Caskey and his friends.

Isherwood nevertheless continued to miss the sort of life he had led in literary London, particularly now that he was no longer in his monastic fastness but out in the social world once more. This was something he would admit only when his guard was down. One evening, after four whiskies, he told Dodie Smith that he had attempted to introduce himself to John O'Hara and been given a cold reception. "American authors should stand together," Isherwood complained to Smith, evidently now counting himself as one. "I asked if he wanted to provide himself with an American clique as a substitute for his lost English one," wrote Smith,

> and he admitted that this was exactly what he did want. 'I shall talk to them,' he said with a very little St Christopher look and tone of voice. 'Hemingway, Faulkner, Dos Passos, Steinbeck—I shall talk to them all.' The vision of Christopher approaching Hemingway with a sweet 'Let's be Friends' would appal me— if I believed it possible. I fear my picture of American authors is that they are mostly drunken egotists. But Christopher longs for playmates to make up for lost ones.

Smith's view of American writers may have been a little harsh, but it is hard to imagine Isherwood finding real friends amongst such a group, all of whom (unlike his literary circle in London) were heterosexual.

Isherwood's apparent nostalgia for the days of "the Gang" may have been prompted by his awareness that now the war was over he would have to visit England to see his mother and brother. He rather dreaded the trip, not least because he was unsure of the reception he would get from his fellow writers, particularly in the wake of the critical response to *Prater Violet*. "They will all think I'm creeping back, repentant," he had complained to Kirstein. "Not that I really care. Only I so hate having to work up anger and defiance." He assured Kathleen that he would be spending most of his time with her as there was no one in London, apart from Forster, that he really wanted to see. "He insists that he doesn't intend to spend more than a few days in London and will see as few of his old friends as possible," Dodie Smith reported. "Of course, it largely depends on how they receive him—if they make the first efforts." He may have missed literary London, but he was still unsure how much it really missed him.

Isherwood told Smith that "he had come to think that his leaving England was a completely spur-of-the-moment irrational act." Smith concluded from this that, although he was unable to admit this to himself, when the war came and people suggested he should return to England "his obstinacy kept him here. And his whole life has had to be made to fit."

Meanwhile, he tinkers with his journal and I don't think he is ever planning any story. I think a great deal is going on in his mind—perhaps working on the journals is showing him things about himself he doesn't know. He recently said that one reason he was glad he came to America was that he 'wished to identify himself with Auden'—which, frankly, seems to me nonsense as he is pretty well out of touch with Auden.[5] I see Christopher's mind again and again throwing up justifications in a way it never used to. Something is going on below the surface that he has no intention of fully admitting.

Smith was certainly correct when she added that she did not believe that Isherwood was working on the proposed book, or books, about refugees. He felt that since the garage apartment was too small for Caskey to hold parties in, he might get down to some sustained writing. In the event, however, he spent most of his time revising his 1939–44 diaries. Since these described both the exiled writers, musicians and artists that gathered at the Viertel house as well as the refugees who passed through Haverford, this work might originally have been intended as a preparation for the planned novels, but if this was the case Isherwood nowhere says so. In the event, he became so absorbed in his task—reliving these crucial years, adding passages to explain or expand upon what he had written at the time—that the work became an end in itself. "It was always [my] intention that they should be read by at least a few other people," Isherwood recalled. One of those people was Smith, to whom he showed the revised 1939 volume. She was not altogether impressed:

> The work is as interesting as everything Christopher writes is but is very incomplete as a picture of (a) his life (b) his mind. The most interesting part is about his gradual turning towards religion—but it is so sketchy. I doubt if, to anyone who did not know him (and know him during these last years), it would ever appear to be convincing or sincere.

She felt that he would do better to rewrite it as fiction, as he had done with *Prater Violet*. "Handled as truth, the gaps imposed by discretion are very damaging. I fancy he funks creative work at present and soothes his conscience by assuring himself that he will one day make use of the revised journals." This is characteristically acute. Although he wrote the occasional book review, the only other work Isherwood was doing was at the studio: a collaboration with Lesser Samuels on a treatment entitled *Judgement Day in Pittsburgh* and a rather less profitable attempt to adapt Ibsen's *Rosmersholm,* which proved so unmemorable that Isherwood failed to record it in his "reconstructed journals." Reading on, Smith conceded that the diaries contained "admirable things" but when she came to Isherwood's depiction of herself and her husband, she questioned his methods of editing. "I found that he had not done a retrospective passage but actually faked several journal entries." She copied some ex-

---

5. For his part, Auden had confessed to John Lehmann in 1945 that he was "a little baffled and uncertain about [Isherwood's] recent developments [. . .] but stressed how far away from him he was."

amples into her own diary, "because they are completely phoney and I want the record of them *as* phoney." Having done so, she commented: "Now practically all this is the most obvious fake." Isherwood had silently added in later information and impressions, which she recognized were flattering of her but which she nevertheless felt were bogus.

A t one point, when it looked as if Isherwood would never be granted U.S. citizenship because of his refusal to agree to bear arms for his adopted country, Dodie Smith commented: "He wants to become an American so much that I sometimes think he will rationalize his pacifism to fit the occasion." In the event, this proved unnecessary. Toward the end of the summer he attended another hearing and still insisted that he would not even help to load ships during a war if the cargo included a single rifle. Fortunately, it had been recorded that at some point during the recent war he had volunteered for noncombatant service in the Medical Corps, and this went in his favor. (Isherwood later commented sardonically that he had volunteered when he was over military age and at a time when it had become fairly certain that the age limit would not be raised again.) On November 8, 1946—the sixth anniversary, he noted with his mother's attention to significant dates, of his initiation as a disciple of Prabhavananda—Isherwood officially became an American citizen. As was his right, he took the opportunity to shed legally both "William" and "Bradshaw," his significant but superfluous middle names, along with that doubtful hyphen. It was the final, symbolic severing of those ties that bound him to the Past—to family, home and country—and he became, legally, what he had always wanted to be, plain Christopher Isherwood.

Secure in his new persona, he felt ready to face England. He was not altogether pleased when he realized that if he wanted to travel to the country he had so firmly rejected he now needed to obtain a visa. "In order to convince the British Consulate I'm a suitable person to be admitted to England at this time of shortages, I have to prove that I have important business there," he told Kathleen. "Therefore I would like, as soon as possible, a letter written to myself, urging me to come over as soon as possible, and saying that I should come over without delay as there is family business to attend to, and adding that you are an old lady, etc. etc. I know this sounds ghoulish and is absurd, under the circumstances, but it will help a lot, the Consul told me, and there is no need to go *too* far or suggest that you are on your deathbed!" A past mistress at penning persuasive letters for the scrutiny of immigration officials, Kathleen wrote one which, Isherwood said, "would have melted the heart of Himmler." The visa was granted.

He finished the *Judgement Day in Pittsburgh* treatment and attended a *puja* at Ivar Avenue and a farewell dinner at Salka Viertel's house, thus fortifying himself with three important strands of his American life: the studios, the temple and the émigrés. He was also saying goodbye to them, since he and Caskey had decided that when he came back from England they would try living in New York. Further "last rites" performed the day before he departed included breakfast with Prabhavananda, lunch with the Beesleys and dining out with Caskey at Romanoff's. The following day, January 19, 1947, Isherwood enacted one of the recurring scenes from his life, being seen off on a long journey by friends and lovers: Caskey, Hayden Lewis and the latter's new partner, Rod Owens. Isherwood noted that January 19 was the same date as two previous important departures: the one for China in 1938 and the one for America in 1939. Memories of these trips—and of how in one significant respect this journey was different—were stirred when he got to New York and was put up for the night by Auden, no longer a fellow adventurer, but living in an apartment in Greenwich Village with Chester Kallman.

England seemed to Isherwood even more of a caricature of itself than the Hollywood versions of it he had derided at the cinema. A village he passed on his way from the airport to London struck him as "so absurdly authentic that it might have been lifted bodily off a movie-lot at MGM." He had arranged to stay with John Lehmann at his house in Egerton Crescent, South Kensington, where a welcoming party of Forster, Plomer, Joe Ackerley and Bob Buckingham awaited him. His host apart, it would have been difficult to find people more likely to greet Isherwood with unequivocal warmth and no suggestion of regarding the visit as a prodigal's return. Further parties were held at which Isherwood met up with old friends and colleagues who appear to have been genuinely pleased to see him again. "Looking around me at the faces of my old friends, I discovered a happy paradox," Isherwood recalled: "namely that, while England seemed fascinatingly strange, my friends and our friendship seemed to be essentially what they had always been, despite the long separation."

Although people in California thought Isherwood's accent absolutely typical of the English ruling classes, people in London insisted that he now sounded American. He did not, however, make the mistake Auden did, visiting England in 1945 in the uniform of a U.S. major, delivering impromptu lectures about the superiority of American culture and telling everyone that Britain was no longer considered a world power and should think itself extremely fortunate to have survived the war at all.[6] Isherwood had rather more tact—although, in retrospect, he suspected he may have exaggerated the Americanisms he had picked up in order to impress upon everyone the extent to which he had been assimilated by his adopted country. This sounds plausible, given his determination not to apologize for his "desertion," and the willpower it must have taken for him to suppress any twinges of nostalgia for the old country. He later insisted that on his arrival in England he felt genuinely homesick for America—just as he had felt homesick for Berlin when "exiled" from Germany in 1933. However, the stark contrast between the balmy Pacific coast and a northern European country in the midst of a winter that would turn out to be one of the most savage on record, between the land of plenty and an England where wartime rationing still prevailed, may also have contributed to this burst of feeling.

Just how ground down, uncomfortable and bleak post-war Britain really was became abundantly—even parodically—clear when on January 25 Isherwood traveled in an unheated train to Cheshire to be reunited with his mother and brother. He took

---

6. Auden had been en route for Germany, where he had a job with the United States Strategic Bombing Survey, interviewing people about how civilian morale had been affected by the Allied air raids during the war.

a taxi from Stockport station through ominously thickening snow to the house where his birth, more than forty-two years earlier, was regarded as having secured the future of the Bradshaw-Isherwoods. Greeted at Wyberslegh Hall by the present head of the family, he was appalled. Although he had corresponded regularly with Kathleen and Richard and thought about them a great deal since he last saw them, they had, like his fictional characters, been out of the room too long for him to imagine exactly what they had been doing, how they had fared. "I don't picture you or M. as being any different," he had told Richard in 1942. Nothing prepared him for what he found.

While, at first glance, Kathleen, who was now seventy-eight, seemed little altered, Richard appeared to have very thoroughly fulfilled all Isherwood's fantasies about the degeneration of a once noble line: "idiots and maniacs, in their solemn dwellings, all victims of terrible passions." The undeniably eccentric young man of twenty-seven Isherwood had last seen in Kensington had undergone an almost lycanthropic transformation, his hair wild, his clothes filthy, his nose running, his teeth ruined, "staring and grimacing and muttering and breaking into screaming laughter." Isherwood nevertheless decided that his brother was not in fact mad, nor (contrary to rumors that had reached him) was he a drunk: "he was a sensitive, intelligent soul in torment."

A major change brought about by the war in the lives of women of Kathleen's class was that many of them could no longer afford domestic staff. Kathleen could easily have done so, but apparently felt that managing without help in the home was a contribution to the national post-war effort. It was quite an achievement for a woman of her advanced age to learn to cook, especially with food and fuel strictly rationed—though almost anything produced by a novice would probably have been an improvement on the pre-war efforts of Elizabeth. One member of staff had in fact remained with the family, and Isherwood discovered her sitting in front of the kitchen fire, more than ever resembling a character from one of Beatrix Potter's books. Five years younger than Kathleen, Nanny had "turned into an aged crone who laughs toothlessly at mysterious private jokes" and was plagued by bunions. After all the years they had lived together, the two women still got on each other's nerves, and Kathleen still complained in her diary of Nurse's tiresomeness and obstinacy.

Kathleen had got a local woman in to do some cleaning and tidying in preparation for the visit, but the house seemed to Isherwood, used as he was to American standards of modernity and cleanliness, almost as filthy as Richard. Dust from the now-rationed coal appeared to have crept into every corner and crevice, blown about by drafts which rushed in through ancient doors and window frames. The gas pressure was so unreliable that it was hardly worth lighting the new gas fire that had been specially installed in his bedroom. Outside the snow fell steadily.

Isherwood felt that in her puritanical English way his mother rather enjoyed the discomfort, much of which could have been alleviated if she had been prepared to spend some money. She did in fact believe that for once, in spite of the weather, she had managed to get the house comparatively warm. It was not, however, warm enough for someone who only the week before had been swimming in the Pacific. "Oh God—the north!" Isherwood exclaimed in a letter to John Lehmann. "I was never meant for these latitudes, and I huddle miserably in front of a blue gas-fire." Kathleen had the satisfaction of being able to blame all the shortages on the Labour government, which had enjoyed a landslide victory in 1945. Although Isherwood remained, in principle, a Labour supporter, he was careful not to let political differences spoil Kathleen's pleasure at this reunion. "There is so much to say & hear one could only touch on the fringe of things," Kathleen wrote in her diary, "but it is wonderful to have him with us . . . so supporting & kind." Isherwood certainly owed his mother a little kindness and they got on well, their past battles largely forgotten. "She was as good a listener as ever. At 78 her mind was clear, her memory excellent and her hearing perfect. She was even prepared to be interested in Vedanta."

He spent the time sorting his books, many of which he sold, and his papers, a steady supply of which he fed on to the fire in the Stone Parlour. He was pleased to rediscover the diary he had kept while in Greece, which he thought "full of possibilities." He read parts of it aloud to Kathleen and Richard, and told Dodie Smith that he intended to write a "Greek Island novelette." A book based on his time with Fronny on St. Nicholas would have fitted the project he had mentioned to the *Los Angeles Times* of a trilogy of novellas about refugees. Nothing came of this idea immediately, and he worked instead on an article about visiting England after being away for so long. This was intended for an American publication but appears to have been rejected. It was eventually published ten years later, in a revised version, in a series of essays called "Coming to London," edited by John Lehmann.

Meanwhile, the weather continued to get worse, with strong, bitter winds causing the incessant snow to drift. Transport was being brought to a halt and industry was beginning to suffer, with factories having to close. National fuel supplies were running low and, even with the introduction of emergency restrictions, longer and longer power cuts followed. The BBC was forced to reduce its output, broadcasting only on the Home Service. The gas fire in Kathleen's bedroom flickered fitfully as the supply came and went, and the temperature fell to only two degrees above freezing. She was forced to move into the smaller spare room, where it was four degrees warmer. The taps were still working in some of the rooms, but water left in the hand-basins quickly iced over. When Isherwood took a bath one evening the water would not drain away because the waste pipe had frozen solid. The gas supply became so poor that it took ages to boil a kettle, while cooking was almost impossible. Nanny took to her bed with a bad back. The snow drifted right up to the house and, armed with a shovel, Isherwood could do no more than clear the front and back doorsteps. It must have seemed at times as if he would be trapped at Wyberslegh forever.

The only thing was to make a joke of it. "Thought maybe you'd like a word from Capt. Isherwood's arctic expedition," he wrote to Kirstein. "The north-west passage was found to end in our own front yard, where it's blocked by eight feet of snow. My mother cooks, my brother goes back and forth to the cellar with buckets of noninflammable coal-dust, wuthering away to himself. I just shiver." On the last day of February, however, he returned to London, sped on his way by the very welcome news that *Judgement Day in Pittsburgh* had been sold to RKO for $50,000. He instructed his agent to pay his share (which, minus commission and typing costs, came to $22,461.58) to Caskey, presumably hoping there would be some of this left by the time he returned to California. Meanwhile, he told Kirstein that he proposed "to get stinking," adding: "This is possible if you have about a hundred pounds." He had rather more than this, as he discovered when he went to visit his bank. The money left

is what really interests me: to show a relationship between a man and a woman which is sexual, but *neither* a mere affair *nor* a romance leading to marriage or tragedy." This may have interested Isherwood in theory, but for someone whose entire literary output was based upon a distillation of his own experience, it clearly presented some problems.

On April 14 Isherwood returned to London to stay once again with Lehmann, before boarding the *Queen Elizabeth* for New York. During the six-day voyage, Isherwood whiled away the time with a fellow passenger, with whom he enjoyed some thrilling, because clandestine, sex. When he saw Caskey waiting for him on the dock, however, he "felt himself falling in love, all over again." Caskey had driven their car all the way from California and he and Isherwood were due to move into James and Tania Stern's apartment at 207 East Fifty-second Street, which they had agreed to take for the summer while the owners were in Europe. Isherwood's quarrel with the Sterns seems to have been patched up, perhaps due to the influence of Auden, who had become an intimate friend of the couple when they came to live in New York in the spring of 1939. Stern had subsequently spent several months with Auden in the United States Strategic Bombing Survey.

"Jimmy's apartment is a dream (I even have my own room to work in) and Caskey is sweeter than ever, and I'm very happy," Isherwood told Lehmann. The apartment was certainly more spacious than anything Isherwood and Caskey were used to in California, with a sitting room, study, bedroom, kitchen and bathroom—the last particularly welcome, Isherwood thought, after several months of "filthy" English plumbing. "Inspired by your workroom, I've started a novel," he informed Stern, although inspiration had in fact struck him at Wyberslegh. Being Isherwood, he quite possibly felt that the coincidence of names—those of the man who had provided him with his title and the couple who had provided him with accommodation—was a good omen. If so, he was wrong, and his initial optimism about really getting on with the novel quickly evaporated. He sketched out a rough synopsis and made a list of the characters, borrowing names from the past (Miss Altmann and Miss Szczesny) and the present (Mr. Pilates, named after the man—later to become famous—who ran the gym he had begun to attend). Some of the characters would be based on the Haverford refugees, and he noted the real names in brackets beside several of them. Much of this was mere fiddling, however, so he bought "an enormous flat notebook with pages the size of music-sheets (152 of them: about three go to 1000 words)" and on May 8, using a ballpoint pen he had recently been given by Dodie Smith, he embarked on the task of actually writing the book.

By May 14 he had managed to cover four pages. "Just bulldozer work, of course," he told Smith. "I have to break up the ground. Then comes the rewrite, and the real toil, sweat and tears." Eight pages later, he came to a halt. The following month, two days after going to a Quaker meeting, he began a new draft. Caroline Norment had been at the meeting, and they lunched together shortly afterwards, but this refresher course amongst the Friends failed to kick-start the book. He managed to produce just under three pages, in which Charles conducts a dialogue with himself about his desire to leave the hostel, much as Isherwood did in his own diaries when faced with a problem. "My novel won't start," he was obliged to confess to Upward in early July.

I really don't know why. Partly it's New York, which is noisy and jittery and hot. Partly it's a kind of stage-fright. I just gasp and stammer whenever I try to speak the opening lines. As never since our earliest days, I feel that you are my only pattern and exemplar. Journey to the Border has shown me how this kind of book must be written, and I don't believe there is anything else in literature which attempts that particular tone of voice.

Quite how Isherwood intended to apply Upward's narrative technique to his own floundering project is unclear, and it may be that he was simply giving his old friend a much-needed boost of confidence. "My real trouble with the novel is the creation of the leading character," he told Upward.

I am determined to write in the third person and abolish 'Christopher Isherwood,' but this other character has to be such a lot of things which I am and also am not. He has to be: my age, an orphan, rather rich, born in America of a wealthy Quaker Philadelphia family but educated in England and having spent most of his life in Europe. In youth he was a bit of a Cote d'Azur playboy, was married and divorced: he has a bad conscience about the kind of life he led and has reverted to Quakerism, largely because of the social service involved. He doesn't really get along with the Quakers, however, because they are such awful puritans, and he can't just write off art and sex and pleasure as being wicked in themselves. At the same time he is 'religious'—i.e. he believes in the validity of mystical experience, to a degree which makes him a bit impatient with the super-intellectual liberal materialism of the Central European refugees.

In other words, Charles is indeed to all intents and purposes Isherwood himself—but with the vital and ultimately disabling difference that he is both American and heterosexual.

It was true that New York was noisy, jittery and hot, but it was also, preeminently, Caskey's city, and the round of parties and drinking began again in earnest. There was also the distraction of Isherwood's own friends in New York: Auden, with whom he spent several weekends at the poet's summer residence, a tar-paper shack on Fire Island, Kirstein, Viertel, and Forster and Spender, both of whom visited the States during this period. There were numerous social functions, which he claimed to dislike "unless they were sexy," but nevertheless attended. At these gatherings, "drinking was his social anaesthetic but hangovers were the destruction of his precious private mornings." Most unsettling of all was the knowledge that he would shortly be setting off on a trip to South America in order to write a travel book commissioned by Random House. One of the attractions of this project was that it would be a collaboration with Caskey, who was to accompany him and take photographs with which to illustrate the book, which would be based on his diary of the trip. To some extent, then, he was recreating his last collaboration with Auden, *Journey to a War,* which had been conceived along similar lines (Auden providing the photographs). A contract was drawn up, with an advance of $2,500, and a sailing date was arranged for September.

Throughout July and August Isherwood and Caskey traveled around out of New

York. One of the people they visited was "the boy genius" Truman Capote, who was spending the summer on Nantucket. Capote had been introduced to Isherwood at the offices of Random House, which was shortly to publish his first novel, *Other Voices, Other Rooms*. Isherwood was informed by the publishers that Capote's book could be compared to Proust, but of rather more interest to him was that it described the journey (to presumed homosexuality) of a thirteen-year-old boy. The author looked not much older, particularly in the carefully posed photograph taken for the book's dust-jacket, although Capote was in fact going on twenty-three. "This extraordinary little figure came into the room with his hand raised rather high, possibly indicating that one should kiss it," Isherwood recalled. "My first reaction was 'My God! He's not kidding!' But then I realized that though he was putting on an act, it was an act that represented something very deliberate and quite genuine. Something happened which one wishes occurred far more often in life: I loved him immediately." Capote was equally taken and invited Isherwood and Caskey to Nantucket, where he was staying with his partner and mentor, Newton Arvin, an academic and literary biographer twenty-four years his senior. Intrigued, Isherwood accepted the invitation, but the arrival of these two lively guests did not entirely please Arvin, who was trying to write a biography of Melville.

From Nantucket they traveled to see Paul Cadmus in Provincetown, where they were photographed naked and not altogether flatteringly by Jared French. Isherwood told Cadmus that the photographs "should win prizes in any natural history magazine if you send them in entitled Sea-lions Courting." They also made several visits to Fire Island to stay with Auden and Kallman. It was on one of his visits to the island that Isherwood had to share a bed with Lincoln Kirstein, who made a "half-joking, tentative" pass at him. Isherwood "jokingly" declined on the grounds that "he hated mixing sex with giggles," by which he presumably meant that one didn't have sex with one's "sisters." Such distractions meant that Isherwood did not, as he had hoped, send Upward the first fifty pages of his new novel before he left for South America, but he did write and send a detailed synopsis. It was important to fix the story in his mind before he took time off to write his contracted travel book.

In mid-August Isherwood reencountered someone who connected his distant past and his immediate future. Berthold Szczesny, last seen in London in 1933, had settled in Argentina in the early years of the war, and had been set up as part owner of a factory by two of his female lovers. He had prospered and now presented a very suave figure, but underneath the beautifully cut suit and carefully knotted tie, the old Bubi—the adventurer and free spirit, who had roamed the world and come back with fantastic stories—was still very much there. He now had a substantial house in Buenos Aires and invited Isherwood and Caskey to stay with him during their trip. Szczesny accompanied Isherwood and Caskey to Fire Island for another reunion. It was the first time since January 1939 that Auden, Isherwood and Spender, whose names were still and would always be linked, had been together. The occasion was celebrated in a photo taken by Caskey of the three writers standing together on a beach, just as they had for Stephen Spender's "masturbatory camera" on Rügen Island in 1931. Spender once more stood between Auden and Isherwood, his arms around their shoulders. They all smiled. The shutter clicked.

EIGHTEEN

AT MIDDAY ON SEPTEMBER 19, 1947, THE *SANTA PAULA* STEAMED out of the harbor at New Jersey, bound for Venezuela. It was not until the ship approached La Guiara that Isherwood began making notes in an American school exercise book he had somehow acquired. By this time, the boat had already stopped off at the island of Curaçao, and for the opening few pages of his travel book he would have to rely on his memory. The diary starts with a few sensory impressions of their arrival in Venezuela, very much in the style of Isherwood's Portugal and China diaries.

> Coming into La Guiara, around 6.00AM. The foothills of the Andes, rising steeply from the shore, wooded to the summits, their folds streaked with red and yellow in the sunrise. The houses, straggling high up the mountain, blue and crimson and orange, very poor. The smell of garlic, quite far out to sea. The modern docks, the big rafts and the runways for unloading. The negroes seated, pushing crates. Every color of skin, from Germanic blond to velvet soot-black and plum-purple.

Little of it found its way into the final book, but it was already a great deal livelier than Isherwood's last attempt at reportage "The Day at La Verne." Much of the diary takes the form of notes rather than a cohesive narrative. As in Berlin, he was taking snapshots which would one day be developed, carefully printed, fixed.

The trip, which lasted over six months, took Isherwood and Caskey down the western side of South America, through Colombia, Ecuador and Peru, then curving inland to Bolivia and down through Argentina, ending up on February 16, 1948, in Buenos Aires. "S. America fills me with an increasing and quite serious uncampy horror," Isherwood told Kirstein from Quito.

> It is *rotten* somehow. Like Ibsen's Ghosts. [. . .] Just a few who care and are trying to do something. The rest look on with their hopelessly sneering syphilitic eyes, and hate and envy and admire and curse the bustling gringos. [. . .]

The Homintern as such I find gruesomely dreary and corrupt. They spend three quarters of their time and all of their money pretending not to be, and are mean and vile in their personal relationships. It's a real *vice,* here.

Porky [i.e. Caskey] bears up boldly, and is very sweet. One or other of us is usually sick. At present we both have festering insect-bites, from that mean old jungle. I cannot say I entirely enjoyed flying over all those trees, laden with gasoline, and nowhere to land, but there was the sweetest little head-hunter who had just killed three men to avenge his father's murder.

By the time they reached "llama-land," as they dubbed Peru, they were homesick and weary. "I ask and ask and ask myself while I'm so bored here," Isherwood told Kirstein. "Perhaps it's largely me going through the change of life or something, but it is also partly the local citizenry." Although many of the people he met were individually charming, he felt that on the whole the Peruvians were

> boring because they lack philosophy—I mean that they aren't seriously disquieted about life—and because they confuse sex with vice. There is a gruszly [*sic*] lawyer here who has a special little hideout in town where he conducts his vie privy [i.e. private life]. It is entirely lined with nude photos: 90% women and a discreet smattering of boys from Strength and Health. Boys sit around in the back room as if waiting for a train, and the gents glance at them and whisper together and giggle. This guy imagines he's terribly discreet and unsuspected, but another queen from the British Embassy warned us not to be seen around with him because he was 'known.' Faugh . . .

Unfortunately, this was not the sort of local color Isherwood would be able to include in his book about their journey.

They were greatly relieved to reach Buenos Aires, where they were among friends. They spent four weeks there, mostly with Berthold Szczesny in his house on the Calle Rivadavia. Another figure from Isherwood's Berlin days was also living in the Argentine capital. Rolf Katz had left England in 1939, apparently in the wake of a homosexual scandal involving naval personnel, although he may also have wished to escape the possibility of internment. He had settled in Buenos Aires and was now running a weekly financial magazine called *Economic Survey,* which was published in both Spanish and English. He proved, as he had in Berlin and London, to be a useful source of inside political information, describing U.S. policy in South America as "catastrophic," and predicting that Colonel Peron's ambition was to build a South American empire, ruling over the entire continent. These observations found their way into Isherwood's book, but were tactfully ascribed to a "foreign observer." Other insights, such as Katz's comparison of the Nazi and Peronist regimes, Isherwood would pass off as his own.

For the greater part of the journey Isherwood wrote his diary almost daily, but after a few days in the Argentine capital, the entries stopped. "How time has slipped by," he exclaimed toward the end of March, having made no entries for over a month. "The people we've seen." But that was it. Consequently he failed to record his visit to South America's only Ramakrishna Mission, where he joined in the celebrations for the avatar's birthday. The ceremonies were conducted in Spanish, but the visit seemed to Isherwood "like coming home."

Szczesny was an indefatigable guide, taking his guests to visit vast *estancias,* a seaside resort and a casino, and introducing him to prominent figures in Argentinian society. Not even Bubi, however, could effect an introduction to the President's glamorous and powerful wife, Eva, whom Caskey had hoped to photograph. None of this was recorded at the time. Worse still, at the end of this long journey Isherwood noted:

> Glancing through the pages of this diary I ask myself: why do I feel so dissatisfied with what I have written? And I don't mean this in the merely literary sense. The narrative is disconnected, certainly, and information is dealt out in small doses, the impressions are superficial, the judgements are hasty. This doesn't matter—or it wouldn't matter if something else were present.

It had been a long time since Isherwood had kept a diary of this sort. The one covering his first years in the United States had become increasingly introspective, but in South America he needed to look outside himself and record what he saw. He had to deal with the culture, customs and politics of six different countries, many of them undergoing crisis and change. To that extent these countries were not unlike Germany in the early 1930s, but in Berlin he did not have to take in and process a great many, often very dry, facts and figures. And rather than writing from his own interest, he was writing to commission. To create a lively and properly informative travel book out of these notes would take him a great deal of time and cause him a great deal of frustration.

On March 27 Isherwood and Caskey boarded the French ship *Groix,* having decided to extend their travels by going to England. It would take them almost four weeks to make their way via Rio de Janeiro and Dakar to Le Havre, and Isherwood managed to complete two chapters of his travel book by the time they got to Africa, where even more passengers joined the already crowded boat. It was frustrating to hear the news of a violent revolution in Colombia, sparked by the assassination of the country's popular Liberal president on April 9. The second chapter would need rewriting in the light of these events, which Isherwood was in fact lucky to have missed, since there was a great deal of bloodshed.

He started another diary, something he was inclined to do on sea voyages, largely to record his impressions of his fellow passengers, people rather than places being his principal interest. He also read Conrad's *Nostromo,* set in a fictional South American republic and published in the year of Isherwood's birth and therefore seeming a suitable spur for his own literary endeavors. As the journey continued, the diary became a repository of Isherwood's growing detestation of all things French, which had the result, as he predicted, of preventing him from "working or even thinking about anything important." They were very relieved when the ship finally docked on April 22.

The voyage had taken Isherwood past the Canary Islands and Portugal and, in nostalgic mood, he tried to book a room in the Hôtel Quai Voltaire when he and Caskey got to Paris. Unfortunately, the hotel was full, and so they went to stay in the rue Jacob. There was a reunion with Denny Fouts, who was living in an opium daze on the rue de Bac with his dog, Trotsky. Isherwood had been warned by Bill Harris that Fouts's mind had been addled by drugs, but apart from a deathlike pallor he seemed relatively unchanged. Indeed, he managed to provoke an argument by trying to get Caskey to collect a package of opium from a dealer. Isherwood had intervened, worried that Caskey might be arrested. It was the last time Isherwood saw Fouts. Having undergone an unsuccessful "cure," he decamped with the now blind Trotsky to Rome in the wake of some sort of criminal proceedings against him, and in December died there on the lavatory of a heart attack. Since no one was able to trace any of his family, the U.S. consulate paid for him to join Keats and Shelley in the English Cemetery.

In Paris Isherwood also met one of Fouts's new acquaintances, a young man who came up to him in Aux Deux Magots and introduced himself as Gore Vidal. Still in his early twenties, Vidal was already the author of three novels, and had been published in England by John Lehmann on Isherwood's recommendation. His most recent book was *The City and the Pillar,* which caused a considerable stir when it appeared in January 1948 because of its homosexual theme. Vidal had sent Isherwood an advance copy of the novel, which tells the story of "a completely ordinary boy of the middle class" called Jim Willard. During a camping trip he has sex with a recently graduated school-friend called Bob Ford, who subsequently goes to New York. Obsessed by the memory of this event, Jim is unable to form any other relationship and gradually descends into "the homosexual underworld," earning his living as a tennis pro and male prostitute. Years later, during the war, he meets Bob again—now married with a baby and serving in the merchant marine. After a drunken evening they end up in a hotel bed together, but when Jim tries to rekindle their sexual relationship and is angrily rejected, he kills Bob.

Isherwood received his copy of the book while in South America and had not much liked it on first reading, describing it to Kirstein as "better than many, but the usual defeatist trash about poor little me, I'm so queer and horrid and should be put away somewhere quietly, or maybe have a bit of my brain cut out, so I won't know a marine from a monkey." On reflection, he had decided to write a puff for it, because the book was at least "a welcome change after Jackson and all those wistful books about folded leaves and primrose men[1] that I feel it ought to be encouraged, though the style is Satevepost [i.e. the *Saturday Evening Post*]." He had told Vidal that *The City and the Pillar* was "certainly one of the best novels of its kind yet published in English. It isn't sentimental, and it is extremely frank without trying to be sensational and shocking. These are enormous virtues. I believe it will be widely discussed and

---

1. Repressed homosexuality was one of the things that drove the protagonist of Charles Jackson's bestselling *The Long Weekend* to drink, a theme reprised in more detail in the same author's *Fall of Valor* (1946), in which a married man unwisely tells a serviceman friend of his feelings for him and is half beaten to death with a poker. "Folded leaves" refers to William Maxwell's celebrated 1945 novel, *The Folded Leaf,* in which the relationship between two adolescent boys is never sexually expressed but has distinct homosexual undertones.

have a big success, well-deserved." The book had certainly been widely discussed, and was widely condemned by the press, the general feeling of revulsion delighting the author and boosting sales. There was outrage that Vidal should depict a clean-cut all-American athlete indulging in the sort of practices people liked to believe were mostly confined to easily identifiable effeminates. Isherwood nevertheless went on to explain that he was disappointed that the book resembled earlier novels with a homosexual theme. "There are certain subjects—including Jewish, Negro and homosexual questions—which involve social and political issues," he told Vidal.

There are laws which could be changed. There are public prejudices which could be removed. Anything an author writes on these subjects is bound, therefore, to have certain propaganda value, whether he likes it or not. I am sure that you, personally, would wish to see the homosexuality laws repealed or at any rate revised? Very well, now the question arises: how will your novel affect public opinion on this matter?

This brings me to your tragic ending: Jim's murder of Bob. Dramatically and psychologically, I find it entirely plausible. It could have happened, and it gives the story a climax. (I wasn't absolutely convinced that Jim cared for Bob that much—but let that pass.) What I do question is the moral the reader will draw. This is what homosexuality brings you to, he will say: tragedy, defeat and death. Maybe we're too hard on these people—maybe we shouldn't lock them up in prison; but oughtn't they to be put away in clinics? Such misery is a menace to society . . . Now, as a matter of fact, it is quite true that many homosexuals are unhappy; and not merely because of the social pressures under which they live. It is quite true that they are often unfaithful, unstable, unreliable. They are vain and predatory, and they chatter. But there is another side to the picture, which you (and Proust) don't show. Homosexual relationships can be and frequently are happy. Many men live together for years and make homes and share their lives and their work, just as heterosexuals do. This truth is peculiarly disturbing and shocking even to 'liberal' people, because it cuts across the romantic, tragic notion of a homosexual's fate. Certainly, under the present social setup, a homosexual relationship is more difficult to maintain than a heterosexual one (by the same token, a free-love relationship is more difficult to maintain than a marriage), but doesn't that merely make it more of a challenge and therefore, in a sense, more humanly worthwhile? The success of such a relationship is revolutionary in the best sense of the word. And, because it demonstrates the power of human affection over fear and prejudice and taboo, it is usually beneficial to society as a whole—as all demonstrations of faith and courage must be: they raise our collective morale.

This was the beneficial revolution Forster wanted to promote with the (unpublished) *Maurice,* but Isherwood was particularly concerned with public perceptions of homosexuality because he was planning to present a "normal" picture of such a relationship in *The School of Tragedy.* When he went on to tell Vidal that "I am really lecturing myself, because I, too, have been guilty of subscribing to the Tragic Homosexual myth in the past, and I am ashamed of it," he may have been thinking of

Edward in *The Memorial* or von Pregnitz in *Mr Norris Changes Trains,* but it also likely he had in mind the way he planned to kill off the doctor's boyfriend in the new novel.

The unexpected appearance of this bold young author in the flesh was a pleasant surprise: "Paris . . . youth . . . springtime . . . the chestnuts on the Bois . . . The Eiffel Tower . . . The Mona Lisa . . . Gore Vidal—but I can't go on. My cup is just too full!" he told Kirstein. He nevertheless recognized Vidal as "a pretty shrewd operator" who wanted the older writer's advice on how to "manage" his career. Isherwood was always happy to provide guidance for handsome young men, and Vidal seemed to him "a big wide-open prep-school boy." He later observed that the diary he wrote at the time didn't "betray the fact that he found Gore Vidal sexually attractive, and that Gore was flirting with him." Vidal's flirtation seems to have been professional rather than sincere. He ungallantly commented in his own memoirs that Isherwood was far too old to interest him sexually.

Isherwood and Caskey saw a good deal of Vidal during the remainder of their stay in Paris. They also bumped into Chester Kallman, who was in Paris for the night with Auden, en route for Italy, where they were going on an opera-crawl as reward for having just completed a libretto for *The Rake's Progress,* which they were writing for Stravinsky. Isherwood found Kallman much improved, "very funny, and so anxious to be friendly that it is quite touching." Isherwood and Auden spent a morning together, sunning themselves and chatting—"and suddenly it was like a scene from Chekhov. I thought: 'Here we are, just two old bags—and only a moment ago, it seems, we were boys, talking about our careers. Like Truman and Gore. How sad.' "

On April 30 Isherwood and Caskey boarded the *Golden Arrow* for England, where they intended to remain until the end of August. They stayed in John Lehmann's flat while he was visiting America, then moved to a hotel when he returned. There was the usual round of parties, including one at *Horizon*'s new offices in Bedford Square. Now that the war was long over and Isherwood was properly settled in America, he could drink champagne with the magazine's editor and contributors without any lingering feelings of resentment at their various comments about him. He renewed his acquaintance with Henry Green, whose books he had continued to admire and recommend to his friends, and began to cultivate several young artists in Lehmann's *Penguin New Writing* circle, including John Minton, Lucian Freud and Keith Vaughan. Isherwood had a very good eye, but it was the candidly homoerotic nature of Vaughan's paintings that particularly appealed to him. On his last trip to London he had bought one of Vaughan's paintings and borrowed several other pictures to take back to America in the hope of promoting the artist's career. He also found Vaughan attractive, but these feelings were not reciprocated: Vaughan later described Isherwood, with the deadly precision characteristic of his diaries, as "looking like a dehydrated school-boy."

Leaving Caskey in London, on May 13 Isherwood set off for Wyberslegh, which in early summer seemed a great deal more inviting than it had during the 1947 blizzards. Nanny had died after a stroke since Isherwood's last visit. Kathleen may have grumbled frequently about "Nurse," but was much grieved by the loss of someone who "had been as one of us for 44 years . . . alway's there faithful & true, considering our interests, ready to speed us on our way, & there to welcome us back, a prop in the background—our interests hers too, so fond & proud of Christopher & Richard, so full of pride in our possessions, so careful of them." She and Richard "just broke down & wept helplessly" on hearing the news, and Kathleen unreasonably but predictably "felt filled with remorse to think I had not been and done all that I might." Now she and Richard were alone in the house.

They had been much preoccupied by plans to requisition twenty-two acres of the Marple Hall estate in order to build a grammar school for five hundred pupils. "The site they insist on for the School could not be worse from our point of view—on the left hand side of the Private Drive immediately in front of the HOUSE!" Kathleen complained. "It is unthinkable that Marple Hall so beautiful so full of dignity & Romance should be desecrated by this wretched Government, & its immediate surroundings ruined for all time—curses on them, they are out to destroy all Freedom—& I don't wonder hundreds of the younger generations are determined to emigrate." Worse still, the wretched government had decreed that all those not gainfully employed or occupied must register at their local labor exchange by a certain date, an indignity to which Richard submitted himself on the very last day. He had explained that he was fully and gainfully occupied in looking after his elderly mother and overseeing the Marple Hall estate, and that he had been exempted from work during the war because of his health. He was firmly told to go away and produce a doctor's certificate. Kathleen commented that they might as well be living in Soviet Russia.

Richard was staying with friends in Marple when his brother arrived at Wyberslegh, and Kathleen told Isherwood that he had "worked himself up into a fit of jealousy" over the "favoured" son. Increasingly, Richard wanted Kathleen all to himself and appeared to think Christopher was encroaching on his territory. Relations between the two brothers remained perfectly affectionate when Isherwood was safely in America, but whenever they were together in England Richard's behavior became even more disturbing than usual. Richard was now forty-six, but had never really lived. "I know what it is to love and that it's stronger than any emotion," Richard had told his brother; but he was referring to his disastrous passion for the son of the former caretakers at Marple Hall. Richard's life had no goals, he was merely drifting, although all too securely anchored to his mother.

Having spent a couple of days in Cambridge with E. M. Forster, Caskey arrived at Wyberslegh. Kathleen's first impression of him was that he was "quiet & very interested in things and intelligent with a particularly pleasant smile"—evidence that he was on his best behavior. He even lent a hand with the cooking and Kathleen repaid this kindness by making him a cake for his twenty-seventh birthday. By this time Richard had returned to Wyberslegh and been subjected to Caskey's Southern charm, but he remained wary of this new interloper.

Each day Isherwood worked on his travel book, and Caskey went around taking photographs of local sites. While searching for the best angle from which to photograph the Stockport viaduct, Caskey aroused the suspicions of the local police. He was not carrying his identity card, but the police immediately sent him on his way with their apologies when told he was a guest of Mrs. Bradshaw-Isherwood at Wyberslegh. His efforts were not much helped by the weather, which turned dull and rainy. On June 6 "the Boys," as Kathleen now referred to them, returned to London.

"I wished so I could have made it a nicer visit for them instead of so dull and quiet," she lamented. Her customary feeling that a light went out whenever her son departed was made real by a power cut that evening. She thought Christopher seemed depressed: "I feel he has many more problems than he would have one think." Isherwood's principal problems were writing the travel book and getting on with his intransigent novel, but during the remainder of his stay in England he put these behind him. His final weeks were much cheered by a call from Gottfried Reinhardt, who rang to ask if he could cut short his visit and come to Hollywood to work on a film about Dostoyevsky. The script had already been written by Reinhardt and Ladislas Fodor, but needed substantial revision. Isherwood was offered a salary of $1,250 a week, as well as the cost of first-class airfare from London to Los Angeles. He accepted, but only on the condition that he could travel back to New York first class on the *Queen Elizabeth*, then on to Los Angeles by train. Isherwood recalled receiving Reinhardt's call during a party held at Cuthbert Worsley's house, where he and Caskey were staying. He returned to the party and "casually told Cuthbert and his guests: 'That was Hollywood. They've offered me a film job.' " If so, this was a case of life imitating art, since a similar scene occurs at the beginning of *Prater Violet*.

The protagonist of that book was also in London, and Isherwood had what turned out to be his last meeting with Berthold Viertel. "He was no longer an important figure in C's world," Isherwood recalled, with all the weariness of someone obliged to reencounter old copy.

As C became increasingly detached from his own German-refugee persona (which belonged to the post-Berlin years of travel around Europe with Heinz) Viertel had lost his power to make C feel guilty and responsible for him. On C's side, strong affection remained. But Viertel's huge old-fashioned ego, his demand to be respected as a German Poet and Thinker, his masochistic Jewishness— 'I wanted only to keep the wound open', he had declared in one of his poems— had made it hard for C to go on being intimate with him; it was just too much trouble. If this sounds brutal, here's what Beatrix Lehmann wrote to C many years earlier (1938?) while she was having a sort of love-affair with Viertel: 'Absence of poor old B.V. for a few days—really like coming out of a mad-house into a green field.'

Isherwood seems to have forgotten that he'd been able to put up with Viertel's ego and masochistic Jewishness when he had first arrived in Los Angeles, in need of friends and work. Viertel was undoubtedly overbearing, but he was also endlessly kind and forgiving. There is in this summing up more than a whiff of Henry V dismissing Falstaff. Five years later, Viertel was dead.

Isherwood visited the Aldeburgh Festival, newly set up by Britten and Pears, and enjoyed a sexual reunion with Tony Hyndman while Caskey was away for a night. Gore Vidal was also in London, and John Lehmann gave a party in his honor. Years later, Vidal published an account of this party which included an embarrassing incident in which Isherwood attempted to get Forster to tell him what he thought of *Prater Violet*. According to Vidal, Isherwood asked Forster whether he had received the copy of the book he had sent him. Forster, who was talking to William Plomer, ignored this question. Isherwood repeated his request, at which point a hush fell over the room. Forster turned and mischievously replied that he had indeed received the novel—without venturing an opinion as to its merits. Isherwood was so upset by this very public snub from an old and highly valued friend that he subsequently got drunk and beat up Caskey. The following morning he told Caskey that it was Vidal who had punched him. This disobliging little anecdote is highly implausible on several counts. It would be wholly out of character for Forster to behave in this manner toward Isherwood, particularly in public. Furthermore, *Prater Violet* had been published back in November 1945, and Isherwood would have had ample opportunity to ask Forster his opinion during his earlier visit to England in 1947. Isherwood's own memory of the party was that "Caskey got drunk and told Gore that he was a lousy writer—which was unfortunate, because Gore naturally suspected that this must be C's private opinion which Caskey was merely echoing. I'm not sure what happened next. Caskey certainly said many other things. I think Gore hit him." He added: "It may seem odd that I can't remember such simple visual facts more clearly, but no doubt [I] was stupid-drunk on this as on so many similar occasions." Stupid-drunk he may have been, but it is unlikely he would still be stupid enough the following morning to attempt to persuade Caskey that Vidal had assaulted him if this was not the case.

The burgeoning friendship between Isherwood and Vidal survived this domestic scuffle. Vidal sent his "Uncle Chris" manuscripts of plays and books for his opinion, and Isherwood took delightedly to his role as wise old adviser. "Last night we had the pleasure of your protegee [*sic*] M. Gore Vidal, the well known novelist," Kirstein reported from England the following year. "He is a spoiled, ambitious little industrious boy, too dainty for this old crab, and stuffed with envy. He has a nice complexion, and, as far as I'm concerned is good for one thing. He speaks lovingly of you; he thinks he is Balzac, who turned one novel out after another, like breathing, like an elemental force, like the life-force itself, like Glenway Wescott." Isherwood and Vidal chose nicknames for each other from *The Wind in the Willows,* Mole and Rat respectively. These were supposed to reflect their working methods as writers: Isherwood "silently and patiently burrowing underground," Vidal "doing it more with his teeth."

On July 2 Isherwood and Caskey returned to Wyberslegh to say goodbye to Kathleen and Richard.[2] The weather was slightly better and a visit to Marple Hall was arranged, so that Caskey could take some photographs. The light was still poor, but this worked to Caskey's advantage and he took a series of extremely atmospheric photographs of Isherwood standing in front of the Hall. On the day of their departure, he took a group portrait of the family standing outside the front door of Wyberslegh. Neatly dressed in a suit and tie, Isherwood places his arm around his mother, while to one side a distinctly unkempt Richard stands awkwardly, his eyes cast heavenwards in the sort of pose adopted by martyrs in early Renaissance paintings. Kathleen's smile seems genuine, but she had been very disappointed that Christopher's visit had been cut short by almost two months, and she dreaded his de-

---

2. Isherwood's conjecture in the "reconstructed" diary that Caskey had "probably" stayed behind in London is incorrect.

parture. "It always gives one such a flat feeling to see someone starting off on fresh adventures & to return to the deserted rooms lately so full of their personality & individuality, & we felt very sad and lonely," she wrote. "I covered C's bed in a dust sheet, everything was tidied up & put away & the room became just an ordinary room again."

Isherwood arrived back in Los Angeles on July 18, having left Caskey to follow more slowly, visiting his mother in Kentucky en route. He settled into Santa Monica's El Kanan Hotel (popularly known as "El KY") and reported to the studio for a happy reunion with Reinhardt, the producer he most enjoyed working with. He was handed Fodor and Reinhardt's script and told he could remodel it in any way he chose. *The Great Sinner* was based on Dostoyevsky's story "The Gambler" and elements borrowed from *Crime and Punishment,* with the novel twist that the protagonist was based on the author himself. Isherwood thought the script professional in its superficial way but felt more could be done with the story, particularly with the Dostoyevskyan character. His attempts to darken it were doomed, however. Every time he made changes they were immediately discarded by Fodor, who fought—very politely—to maintain as much of his original scenario as possible. Isherwood saw himself as "a model employee. He despised amateurs like Brecht who, when they condescended to work at a film studio, whined and sneered and called themselves whores or slaves. C prided himself on his adaptability." Adaptability is, of course, a requirement of prostitution, and Isherwood rarely fought very hard for artistic integrity in his film work. The only real difference between him and people like Brecht was that he was, on the whole, a happy hooker.

It was certainly pleasant to work in the *gemütlich* company of Reinhardt and Fodor, two European Jews who, unlike Viertel, had no pretensions to being great Poets or Thinkers. The money was good, the work relatively undemanding—and Isherwood could put off writing his travel book and his novel with a clear conscience. He renewed old friendships, enjoyed a fair amount of casual sex, and spent weekends at the beach, soaking up the California sun. His feeling of well-being was significantly enhanced when he was introduced to a young man named Jim Charlton. Born in Reading, Pennsylvania, in 1919, Charlton was the son of an airmail pilot who flew into a mountain during a storm when Jim was just six months old. He was brought up by his nervously possessive mother, who had already lost one child in infancy. A rather solitary boy, he enjoyed playing with his toy train set and was clever at modeling scenery, a skill that proved useful when he started training as an architect with Frank Lloyd Wright at Taliesin West, Arizona. "He may be a genius," Wright remarked, observing a table at which Charlton was working on a model of the Lewis House, "but he sure makes a mess." Charlton had been obliged to be rather more tidy when, arriving early one semester, he had had sex with a fellow student in Mrs. Wright's bed.

Undaunted by his father's fatal accident, Charlton was attracted to the romance of flying and left Taliesin to become an officer cadet in the air force when America entered the war. He emerged unscathed to practice architecture in California, spending his leisure hours in pursuit of sex, mostly among servicemen. "I had only Caskey as a rival," he observed of his relationship with Isherwood, "whereas Chris had the entire military establishment." When he met Isherwood he was having sessions with "a pipe-smoking psychiatrist," in fact an analyst, who thought Charlton's tales of promiscuity sounded "lugubrious." Charlton had been recommended to see an analyst after consulting a plastic surgeon about his nose, the tip of which swerved slightly to the right. This was a minor flaw which in fact added to Charlton's unassuming attractiveness, and the surgeon suggested his would-be patient should try to discover *why* he disliked his nose. Wright had observed that Charlton had "a cowboy's slim buttocks," and his face would not have looked out of place in a Western, where he could have played the slightly dopey and probably doomed sidekick of the movie's real star. His outdoors looks, army-surplus clothes, and the stories he told about his life made him, even more than Vernon, the very image of the All-American Boy. With scant regard for geography, Isherwood decided that he was a "Tan-Faced-Prairie-Boy" of the kind apostrophized by Walt Whitman. He was the sort of person who could knock together a cabin in which two men could live a simple life. He also, fatally for Isherwood, spent some of their first evening together "talking romantically about a long ago love for a teenage boy."

Unlike most of Isherwood's conquests (then reckoned at around four hundred), Charlton had an appeal that was not primarily sexual. Indeed, Isherwood later described him as "too wholesome to be really exciting." Charlton stirred something deeper in Isherwood, who very quickly fell "violently in love with him." More accustomed to giving blow jobs to Marines on the boardwalk at the Santa Monica pier, Charlton was slightly bemused to find himself being very definitely courted. The relationship was sexual from the very start, but it was accompanied by dinners in restaurants, during which long, intimate conversations took place. Isherwood was naturally very disapproving of Charlton's analyst, whose principal aim seems to have been to persuade his patient to "grow out of" his homosexuality, marry and have children. The only children that really interested Charlton, however, were teenage boys, and he filled sketchbooks with drawings of them in various stages of intimacy and arousal.

When Charlton told his analyst about Isherwood, the analyst replied: "You must be on Mount Olympus." He wasn't, because although he had read and enjoyed some of Isherwood's books, he was no more impressed by literary fame than Caskey. (When told that Isherwood had been listed in the American edition of *Who's Who,* Caskey commented: "Who's *She?*") Charlton's passion was for architecture, about which he was very knowledgeable, and this—along with his gravelly voice—added to his appeal for Isherwood as a "real man," involved in the distinctly masculine world of construction. Although Charlton loved his job—he was currently working on a housing project in Brentwood—he found the architectural world almost oppressively heterosexual, later claiming that Philip Johnson was the only gay architect he ever met. Through Isherwood he was introduced into the more homosexual milieu of writers and actors—not to mention the campy world of Caskey and his friends.

It seems to have been understood by all parties that Isherwood and Charlton could enjoy a terrific romance, but that this would not interfere with Isherwood's relationship with Caskey. They did, however, make the most of their time before Caskey's return, driving off for weekends together. Isherwood described Sunday, September 5, when they had driven from Laguna Beach up into the mountains, as "one of the happiest days of my life." A fortnight later, Caskey arrived back in town in a station wagon he had bought in the East and driven across America. He had kept in touch with Isherwood by letter and warned him that he had picked up a driving companion along the way. In spite of his own far more serious involvement with Charlton, Isherwood felt very jealous. Worse still, on the night of their reunion at the El Kanan, Isherwood found himself unable to perform sexually. Whatever Caskey might have felt about this privately, he made light of it, perhaps because he did not quite realize the seriousness of Isherwood's feelings for Charlton.

Charlton would in fact have been a far more suitable partner for Isherwood than Caskey. He was hard-working, had a job which required him to put in a full day's work either in his office or on site, and would have brought some much needed calm into Isherwood's life. He was not, however, prepared to take on a supporting role in anyone else's life and had no intention of becoming known among Isherwood's circle as "Chris's boyfriend, who's an architect." In the event, he was introduced to Caskey and they got on very well.

On September 28 Isherwood and Caskey moved into 333 East Rustic Road, which they had rented from Lee Strasberg, who was in New York setting up his Actors' Studio. It was a neat little two-story house in the Santa Monica Canyon, tucked into a hillside, overhung by sycamores, and reached by a wooden bridge spanning a deep concrete drainage channel. On the ground floor were a living room, a kitchen and a room they converted for Caskey to use as a darkroom. Upstairs were a bedroom, a bathroom and a second living room, which doubled as another bedroom and had a glassed-in porch, which Isherwood used as a study. It was a short walk from the beach and from Mabery Road, so Isherwood was back on home territory.

He was still working on *The Great Sinner,* which had now been cast with Gregory Peck and Ava Gardner in the lead roles. Even in a scrubby beard, Peck was not everyone's idea of a tortured Dostoyevskyan soul, but Isherwood and Reinhardt had faith in the director, Robert Siodmak. When Isherwood went to watch the filming, which started in early October, he soon realized that his optimism was misplaced. He nevertheless made one further contribution to the film when one of the actors failed to turn up in order to do a voice-over. In one of the film's more ludicrous scenes, the gambler is tempted to steal money from a collection plate in a church. As his hand hovers over the coins, Isherwood's own curiously high-pitched mid-Atlantic voice is heard bleating: "They divided my garments among them and they cast dice for my robe." It is possibly the least convincing impersonation of the deity in Hollywood's history.

Isherwood now had no more excuses to put off his book about South America. He needed to finish it not only to fulfill his contract but also to give Caskey's career as a photographer a boost. While traveling he had written several articles, which he had sold to magazines such as *Holiday, Vogue,* the *Geographical Magazine* and *Horizon,* but he now had to work these into a flowing narrative, combining them with additional material. "The truth is, I am bored by the very mention of the place, and feel ashamed that I'm bored," he admitted in November. He was once again drinking too much and doing *japam* only occasionally. He hadn't made any entries in his diary since May.

At this period Isherwood felt that happiness was merely "the breaking of contact with pain," arguing that "it is in our nature to be happy whenever the reasons for being unhappy cease to exist." Charlton had been a positive cause of happiness, but the holiday mood that had characterized the early days of their affair soon evaporated. Since Caskey seemed not to object to Charlton's presence in their lives, Isherwood should have been content; but he wasn't, and he felt guilty that he wasn't. It is possible that the arrangement between the three men was not working as well as Isherwood imagined. If Isherwood was as much in love with Charlton as he claimed, his relationship with Caskey would inevitably suffer some degree of erosion. It is possible that this too was a cause of guilt. While Isherwood struggled with his travel book, Caskey set about smartening up their new house. "Sometimes I ask myself uneasily, what will happen when the home is built?" Isherwood wrote in his diary. "But I don't think I really need worry. It's just that I'm being confronted, at last, with the problem of the householder—and who ever dares to say that they are less than the problems of the monk?"

As a matter of fact, Isherwood had been confronted with the problems of the householder a few years earlier and, although he seems not to have recognized it, he was undergoing the same doubts as at Sycamore Trail. While Vernon happily furnished that house and planted its garden, Isherwood had fallen into a gloom he blamed partly on the house itself. Curiously, the new house was similarly located, tucked into a hillside and overshadowed by trees. Some people thought the house looked cozy, but for Isherwood it had an "unpleasant psychic atmosphere," particularly on the upper floor. Like his mother, Isherwood appears to have been particularly susceptible to such atmospheres. During his last visit to England, he and Caskey had been taken on a guided tour of Lyme Hall, near Marple. Having gone ahead of the guide, they found themselves in a room which for no good reason gave Isherwood the creeps. The guide then arrived and announced that this was the Haunted Room. He had also had an unpleasant experience while driving through a sequoia forest with Vernon a few years earlier. They had come across an isolated store and Isherwood had gone in to buy some cigarettes. When the proprietor emerged from the back room, Isherwood was so frightened that he fled back to the car and told Vernon to drive away as fast as possible. The store and the man were perfectly ordinary, but Isherwood felt that he had interrupted something "unspeakably evil" that had been going on in the back room.

Marple Hall was not the only place Isherwood had lived in which apparitions actually manifested themselves. The apartment he, Auden and Vernon had rented in Yorkville in 1939 had also been haunted. Footsteps, rustling and moaning had been heard by all three tenants in daylight and at night, even when they were alone in the apartment. There seemed no plausible explanation for these noises and Auden's chief concern had been to prevent their cook from being frightened away. They discovered, however, that she was perfectly aware of ghostly presences, and even claimed to have felt someone walk through the kitchen when she had her back turned. At East Rustic Road the figure of a man was seen by at least two visitors. Chris Wood, calling unexpectedly, saw someone he assumed was Isherwood walking about the glassed-in porch. When he rang the bell and got no answer, he went into the house and found it empty. Had there been an intruder, he could not have escaped from the upper story except by passing Wood on the stairs. Later on, Bill Harris was staying in the house and awoke one night to see someone coming out of Isherwood's bedroom. The figure turned to Harris and said, "You son of a bitch!" before descending the staircase. Harris wondered what on earth he had done to offend his host, then wondered whether the figure was indeed Isherwood—it was dark and he hadn't seen the face clearly. He got up, went to look in Isherwood's bedroom and saw Isherwood sound asleep in bed. Isherwood himself sometimes had the distinct impression when working alone in the house that there was someone standing at his shoulder, and he would occasionally wake up, frightened, in the night, but he never actually saw anything. Caskey and some of his friends spent one evening trying to discover the house's secrets using a Ouija board and received a message from a woman which said she had killed herself in the house, but no one seems to have followed this up by pursuing investigations by a more orthodox method. The longer Isherwood stayed in the house, and the worse his life became, the more he felt that the atmosphere of the house was "*both* something which had belonged to the place before he came there *and* something which was a projection of his own disturbed, miserable, hate-filled state of mind."

On February 20, 1949, Isherwood made another attempt to start his diary, but managed only fifteen entries during the entire year. The work he was doing was almost wholly unrewarding: he struggled to meet a deadline of April 15 for his South American book, and was recruited by Prabhavananda to collaborate on the translation of yet another ancient Hindu text, the *Yoga Sutras* of Patanjali. The work with Swami involved providing a commentary as well as an English translation of these mystic aphorisms, and represented another means by which Prabhavananda reined in his increasingly wayward disciple. Word of the sort of life Isherwood was leading had reached Ivar Avenue, and although Prabhavananda was too subtle to confront Isherwood directly, it was evident that he thought Caskey a bad influence. This was true, up to a point, but it set up another conflict of loyalties for Isherwood to grapple with. It was the old battle between the spirit and the flesh, but now involved personalities. Had Isherwood not been with Caskey, he would most probably not have been arrested in the small hours on suspicion of smoking marijuana, nor fined for jaywalking. On the other hand, Caskey provided Isherwood with some sort of emotional stability, and life with him was undoubtedly a great deal more fun than it had ever been at the monastery. Prabhavananda was content to bide his time, and Isherwood was startled to discover that, like Kathleen, Swami kept a room ready for the prodigal's return. "It rather scares me—the way he waits," Isherwood admitted. "Shall I ever find myself back there? It seems impossible—and yet—"

Caskey's behavior was sometimes enough to drive Isherwood out of the house in search of peace and quiet. When not cooking Isherwood his favorite fishcakes, Caskey would head off for the Tropic Village, "a bar such as pre-blitz Sodom never dreamed of," and often brought back "a few of the girls" for an all-night party. Even when not entertaining guests, Caskey would sit alone playing records very loudly, keeping Isherwood awake and so ruining his concentration the following day. "He absolutely cannot understand why I mind being kept awake," Isherwood complained. "And I absolutely cannot understand how he can keep me awake, even if he doesn't understand why. However, I freely admit that I am kept awake by a kind of obstinacy—just as it is obstinacy that makes him play the records." On one occasion, Isherwood stormed into the room where Caskey was entertaining and tore the arm off the record player.

Although he spent many sleepless nights, Isherwood managed to finish his travel book on April 2. He decided to call it *The Condor and the Cows,* these creatures representing the Andean mountain states and the flat Argentine respectively. As well as providing ninety-six photographic illustrations, Caskey also did a pen-and-ink sketch of Cuzco for the end papers and a photomontage, "meticulously designed under the influence of marijuana," for the dust-jacket. Isherwood was on very cordial terms with both his English and his American editors, Alan White at Methuen and Robert Linscott at Random House. Their reactions to the book must have come as a relief. "I read it at home and was continually obliged to read bits to my wife and to laugh aloud," wrote White. "You make your readers smell South America; one can't give a travel book higher praise than that." He admitted that he preferred the parts of the book where Isherwood was at his most subjective and noticed that when called upon to generalize Isherwood did it reluctantly.

While Isherwood's public collaboration with Caskey was going through the press, his personal relationship with him was in steep decline. He turned once more to his diary to ask himself whether they should part. "Leaving Caskey—quite aside from being terribly painful—wouldn't really solve anything," he felt. "Unless there were somewhere else to go to—which there isn't. Or unless I was prepared to return to Ivar Avenue—which I'm not. Therefore we have to stay together." Whenever Isherwood considered separating from one of his lovers, he always reached this sticking point: however bad the relationship had become, it was better to continue in it than face the prospect of being alone. The fear of being alone was even more acute now that Isherwood was approaching his forty-fifth birthday. He may still have looked young, but he was beginning to feel distinctly middle-aged and was now suffering regularly from bouts of sexual impotence. *The Condor and the Cows* had been praised by his publishers and received good reviews when it came out, but he regarded the book as hackwork, and his career as a novelist appeared once more to have ground to a halt. The days when he considered himself a catch, a bright young writer who could "have anyone," were behind him. It is perhaps surprising that he did not consider leaving Caskey and putting his relationship with Jim Charlton on a more solid footing, but he had decided that Charlton was "one of the Dog People." "The Dog People share this quality with real dogs—you mustn't kid yourself that their devotion is personal," he explained. "If you go away and someone else feeds them for a month—well—that's all the same." Charlton, though genuinely affectionate, was indeed happy to sleep with almost anyone: it was part of his good nature. And although his love-making was enthusiastic and involved, out of bed he had a certain quality of detachment. He was almost too self-sufficient. This, of course, was part of his attraction, part of the romantic myth which Isherwood had spun around him. Charlton was the sort of person with whom you had an affair rather than settled down.

A recent incident in which Caskey and a "sailor buddy" had crashed the car while drunk had set Isherwood back $250. "What can you do with him?" he appealed to

Kirstein. "I know all too well that if I ever did manage to ditch him somewhere I'd be miserable, and dash out before a week was over, and get me another, ten times worse." He vowed that he must not try to change Caskey, but learn to live with him as he was. This proved increasingly difficult. The general rowdyism that Caskey seemed to attract undoubtedly contributed to the problems Isherwood was having re-starting *The School of Tragedy,* but there were other factors. He could not decide how to approach his main character: at one moment he felt that he should be a partial self-portrait with the action of the novel seen from his perspective, "written out of the middle of *my* consciousness"; the next he thought the book should be narrated from the perspective of several different characters. Another problem was with dialogue, as he evidently complained to Henry Green, who paid a great deal of attention to the technical aspects of writing. "Surely your difficulty with dialogue is the change in the idiom you hear around you," Green observed wisely.

> Sentences are entirely differently constructed in your country & when you went there you were as a writer attuned to the British idiom which you haven't lost yet. I remarked to Bill Caskey that although you spoke with an American accent, & more power to your elbow, you were still talking in the British idiom & he agreed. Till you forget it entirely, & after all the British idiom is only one means of com-munication out of many, you must be in agonies over dialogue because you are unconsciously hearing constructions you still don't fully use.

This was a difficulty Isherwood never quite solved when writing this, his first truly "American" novel. "I'll be working on that problem for the next ten years—to evolve an individual Anglo-American idiom—and that means starting by writing 100% American," he had predicted a couple of years back. Among the many false starts he made is an undated effort in which the protagonist goes to his job at a studio, where he has just been complimented on the "swell job" he'd done on a script called *Babes in the Blitz.* To his dismay, he sees he has an appointment with an Elizabeth MacEl-wee at the Brown Derby.

> I've got the hell of a hangover, Charles thought. But the hangover was only one part brandy, three parts Kay. Kay was the pain in his joints, the sourness in his stomach, the dryness of his eyeballs. She never called last night. Swore she would. Didn't. Wonder where she was? Don't want to know. Do know. That guy she met at Ciro's. The bitch. Oh, Kay, Kay, Kay. Bitch. My darling. Swell job. Hangover. Blitz. Warmth. Elizabeth MacElwee. Derby. Temporary. Kay. Kay. Kay. Kay. Kay . . . For Christ's sake, stop it. Come on, now. That's enough. We've got to work.

Raymond Chandler clearly didn't have much to worry about.

A further attempt to start the novel faltered before he had written a thousand words. He told Upward that the book was "nosing out of the fog, hooting loudly to reassure itself," and he had found a new name for his protagonist: Stephen Monk. Two more false starts each consisted of less than half a page, but at the end of June Isherwood noted in his pocket diary that he had finished the first chapter. If so, he did not write it in his large manuscript book, and it has since been lost. The more difficulty he had with the novel, the more life with Caskey seemed intolerable.

On the usually propitious November 8 (the anniversary of his becoming Prabhavananda's disciple and acquiring American citizenship), Isherwood reported: "The novel is barely at page eighteen, creeping along against frightful resistance. My life with Bill has reached such a point of emotional bankruptcy that he is leaving, by mutual consent, in a day or two, to hitchhike to Florida to see his sister. Will this solve anything? It didn't with [Vernon]. Well, anyhow, we have to try it." His regret at the impasse he and Caskey had reached may be inferred from the fact that he refers to his lover as "Bill" rather than the more usual "Caskey."

The novel was not, as Isherwood might have hoped, kick-started into some sort of life by Caskey's departure on November 11. It remained, he reported a month later, "undented, unformed—like some rubbery bit of material which pops back into shapelessness the minute you take your hands from it." A week later he was "Stuck. I can't get the right technique for writing this book. Stephen can't narrate, and yet, if he doesn't, I can't say half the things I want to." Another problem, he confessed to Plomer, was that "most of the characters are Americans, and what do I *really* know about Americans?" This may seem a surprising question for this famously observant writer to ask after living among Americans for over a decade: he had, after all, managed to portray Berliners after living in the city, on and off, for only a couple of years. It was one thing to observe a nation from the outside, but quite another to write convincingly out of the consciousness of someone born and raised in another country. In his manuscript book he was reduced to mere doodling: drawing up a new list of characters, making a seating plan for the hostel's dining room, and assigning the refugees room numbers. By now several new elements had been introduced into the plot. Stephen had been married twice: the first time to an older novelist called Elizabeth Rydal, who had died; the second time to "a Riviera girl" called Jane, whom he has recently divorced. It was the failure of his second marriage and a chance meeting with Sarah that led Stephen to the refugee hostel and his work there. The basic plot remained, but its balance was gradually shifting, with increasing emphasis on Stephen's story.

A "sixth draft" was started, but once again got no further than a few paragraphs. "I put it off and put it off, and I do nothing about getting a job," he complained, "and I drift toward complete pauperism, with nothing in sight." This was something of an exaggeration. Visiting him earlier in the year, Glenway Wescott (himself no pauper) remarked of Isherwood in his diary: "Noteworthy how well off he is: thirty-five grand last year, twenty this year."

Life at home without Caskey may have been quieter, but it was also lonely. Isherwood spent much of his time at parties, where he drank a great deal and looked for new sexual partners, usually with some success. Several of these he met at an Italianate house called the Palazzo in Benton Way, which runs between Wilshire Boulevard and Silverlake. The house was inhabited by a group of friends, mostly homosexual, including a pair of twins called Sam and Isadore ("Eddie") From. Sam, who was Isherwood's particular friend, was a successful businessman, Eddie a psychiatrist. As well as hosting numerous parties, the Froms took a serious interest in the psychological and sociological aspects of homosexuality. One of their friends was

Evelyn Caldwell, a psychologist based at UCLA who was to become a leading expert on homosexuality and carried out a good deal of field research among the Froms' friends and acquaintances. She was one of the first psychologists to argue—and to demonstrate, using the Rorschach test and other methods—that homosexuality was a "normal" condition rather than a mental or physical aberration. She further proved that, even given the difficulties homosexual men encountered in a society that branded them "perverts," a majority of them were psychologically quite as well adjusted as heterosexuals. Her first marriage was brief and, it was rumored, the cause of her professional interest in homosexuality. She subsequently married one of her colleagues at UCLA, Edward Hooker, who was a professor of English, and as Evelyn Hooker she became a well-known researcher and therapist, her work honored late in her life by the founding of the Evelyn Hooker Center for Gay and Lesbian Mental Health at the University of Chicago's Department of Psychiatry. In order to increase her understanding of the homosexual world, Isherwood offered to smuggle her into the Crystal Baths on Ocean Park, a notorious center of gay activity, but jokingly added that once she had learned the secrets of this world she would have to be put to death. He nevertheless took a genuine interest in her research, which led to a far greater understanding and acceptance of homosexuality.

It was also during this period that Isherwood met Igor Stravinsky. The Huxleys introduced him to the composer, his second wife, Vera, and his young and (thought Isherwood) "cute" amanuensis, Robert Craft, over lunch at the Farmer's Market, a predominantly vegetarian haunt in Santa Monica. Craft made a detailed entry in his diary about this first encounter, providing a lively portrait of Isherwood as he approached his forty-fifth birthday. Having agreed with and baroquely amplified Virginia Woolf's comparison of Isherwood with a jockey, Craft observed:

> Isherwood's manner is casual, vagabondish, lovelorn. One does not imagine him in a fit of anger, or behaving precipitately, or enduring extended states of great commotion. At moments he might be thinking of things beyond and above, from which the conversation brusquely summons him back to earth. He is a listener and an observer, with the observer's habit of staring, rather than an initiator, a propounder and expatiator, of new subjects; his trancelike eyes will see more deeply through us and record more essential matter about us than this verbosity of mine is doing about him. At the same time, his sense of humour is very ready, and he maintains a chronic or semi-permanent smile (a network of small creases about the mouth), supplementing it with chuckles and an occasional fullthrottle laugh, during which the tongue lolls. But he is not at ease in spite of the drollery. Underneath—for he is as multi-layered as a *mille* (in practice rarely more than a *six* or a *huit*) *feuille*—are fears, the uppermost of which might well be of a musical conversation or high general conversation about The Arts. But I could be miles off.

In fact Craft was spot-on, and one of the reasons why Stravinsky liked Isherwood was that he did not treat the great man with awe and address him, as so many other people did, as *"Maestro."* Indeed, he was one of only about five people who called Stravinsky "Igor," and he always greeted him by kissing him on both cheeks. Isherwood knew almost nothing about music and didn't even much like it. Nor did he pretend to. According to Stravinsky, when Isherwood first came to supper, he fell asleep while listening to a recording of the composer's music: "My affection for him began with that incident." Isherwood denied this, but remembered that Stravinsky had greeted him by saying, "Shall we listen to my Mass before we get drunk?" Isherwood would have been too polite to decline the first half of this invitation, and would have been fortified by the promised reward. Indeed, drink—and a great deal of it—was one of the things that cemented the friendship between the two men, and Stravinsky would later say that he and Isherwood got drunk together "as often as once a week"—a calculation Isherwood thought "a wild exaggeration." Isherwood nevertheless recalled many occasions on which he got paralytically drunk (he blamed "a fatal, beautiful liquid called Marc"), and this was something he did without embarrassment because he felt "completely at home" with Stravinsky. "I remember once I'd actually passed out on the floor, and, looking up, I saw at an immense altitude above me, Aldous Huxley, who was very tall, standing up and talking French to Stravinsky, who never seemed to get overcome, however much he drank. And Aldous, who I think was very fond of me, was looking at me rather curiously, as much as to say, 'Aren't you going a little far?' " As far as Stravinsky was concerned, Isherwood never did.

Unlike Huxley, Stravinsky was physically small, and this was another thing that drew Isherwood to him: he even claimed to find the arachnid composer "cuddly." Isherwood was soon describing him as "the most fun person" in Los Angeles and "the wildest camp." By the end of that first evening at Stravinsky's house, Isherwood had also fallen under the spell of Vera, a highly gifted painter, whose generous bulk emphasized her husband's spindliness. Isherwood became a regular visitor to the Stravinskys' home in West Hollywood. It was as if the roles between the musician and the writer were reversed, for it was Isherwood who put on the performance while Stravinsky settled on a sofa with a tumbler of scotch "as if he were at a play." In spite of what Isherwood claimed, Stravinsky was sometimes overcome by alcohol. He once fell asleep on the sofa and Isherwood, who had no doubt drunk just as much, remained behind while the other guests were taken by Vera to look at the garden. When they returned they discovered that Isherwood had tucked himself up on the other end of the sofa and was also asleep. The composer and the writer reminded one observer of Ariel and Puck.

Bob Craft appealed to Isherwood as "an outstanding specimen of the American disciple type," particularly when he discovered that this discipleship extended toward himself, for Craft turned out to be a knowledgeable admirer of the Isherwood *œuvre*. Although Isherwood became closest to Stravinsky, he recognized that Vera and Craft formed an apparently indissoluble triumvirate with the composer, and almost all the postcards he received from the Stravinskys while they were on their travels were signed by all three.

Isherwood later questioned Craft's use of the word "lovelorn" to describe him, but he was undoubtedly on the lookout for young men to substitute for Caskey during the latter's absences. Some of these encounters developed into casual relationships, others into more solid affairs. The most important of Isherwood's sexual partners during this period was a young man of eighteen named Michael Leopold, later described by a distinctly un-nostalgic Isherwood as "a Jewboy with thinning hair, a high forehead, spectacles (his sight was very poor), a cute cheerful face (resembling Anne Francis, a starlet of the period), a hideously ugly Texan accent (which C tried to persuade him to modify) and a pair of long sturdy legs (of which C thoroughly approved)." At the time Isherwood told Kirstein that Leopold looked "awfully as I imagine you at 18" and that the hideous accent was "Greenwich Village," which suggests he had some way to go before mastering American voices and idiom. Leopold was amusing, well read and sexually inexhaustible. He wanted to be a writer and looked up to Isherwood as a literary mentor. Having reached a creative impasse, Isherwood needed all the literary admiration he could get, and in a mood of optimism started the New Year by sketching out "Some ideas for stories," one of which would be about the

> relationship between a middle-aged 'established' writer and a very young writer, still unpublished. The middle-aged writer is going through a period of complete impotence, but the young one doesn't know this. He is tremendously impressed by the older man and quite overwhelmed when the latter asks him to stay. Every morning, the young man sits down joyfully in the living room, thinking, 'We are working under the same roof,' and writes as never before, in a fever of inspiration. Meanwhile, the older man goes up to his study and stays there all day, pretending to work. Does the young man unconsciously 'cure' him? Perhaps.

Unfortunately, although Leopold did spend time at East Rustic Road, working on his own writing and proving a far more restful cohabitant than Caskey, he did not "cure" Isherwood. A New Year's resolution to find out what was wrong with *The School of Tragedy* and to fix it came to nothing. Isherwood was still unable to decide how the book should be narrated: in the first person? in the third person? from one perspective? from several?

Meanwhile, he needed to earn a living. During the winter he and Huxley had worked on an idea for a film set during a revolution in South America, possibly at the suggestion of the director John Huston. Huxley was to spend much of 1950 in Europe, and so it was left to Isherwood to write the treatment, which he eventually finished on July 5, but they had no more luck selling it than they had with *Jacob's Hands*. Isherwood was also working with Lesser Samuels on a modern ghost story called *The Vacant Room,* drawing upon his experiences at East Rustic Road.

Caskey returned in mid-April. The separation, which had always been thought of as temporary, had been prolonged by Caskey's need to sort out family matters in the wake of his father's death. ("No money left to his mother, & his sisters acting like in King Lear," Isherwood reported.) It may have been the prospect of sharing the house with Caskey once again that made Isherwood consult a hypnotist and therapist named Leslie LeCron, whom he had met through the Huxleys. Isherwood had boasted that he was immune to hypnotism, characteristically regarding the process as a battle of wills between himself and the practitioner. When LeCron told Isherwood that hypnotism required cooperation, Isherwood allowed himself to be lulled into a semi-trance, saving face by assuring LeCron that he could still assert his will if he chose to. After emerging from the trance, Isherwood drove home in a state of eupho-ria, "moving in perfect harmony with all the other cars"—which was certainly dif-ferent from his usual nervous-aggressive method of driving. He realized that the hypnotism had relaxed him very thoroughly, and when he got home he slept ex-tremely well. He wondered whether LeCron could help him to get rid of tension and insomnia by teaching him auto-hypnotism, but unfortunately this failed. The round of drinking and squabbling started once more, and the outbreak of the Korean War gave Isherwood a new dose of "war jitters." He saw the escalating international cri-sis, with American troops being sent in, as something he ought to record in his diary, as he had done during the Munich period, but he managed only three entries before being overwhelmed by *accidie*.

He was stirred from his torpor in June by an invitation to write extended reviews for a magazine called *Tomorrow*. Since he would be paid $400 an article, Isherwood saw this as a possible "way out of this whole movie mess into a more serious literary life." He chose an omnibus edition of Ford Madox Ford's tetralogy, *Parade's End*, for his first essay, and over the next year or so wrote six more pieces on H. G. Wells, Robert Louis Stevenson, Stephen Spender, Katherine Mansfield, Ray Bradbury and George Santayana. He had also begun work again on *The School of Tragedy*, picking over the plot and the characters in his notebook rather than actually attempting to write the novel. The stumbling-block remained his inability to decide how to narrate the story. By now he realized that the novel had two plots: "(1) The external story of a group of people going through 'The School of Tragedy' (2) The internal story of Stephen's gradual change of heart towards Jane. In 'forgiving' Jane (but *not* going back to live with her) he forgives himself." It is evident that to some extent the story of Stephen and Jane was being modeled on that of Isherwood and Caskey. The open-ing scene, for example, in which Stephen discovers Jane having sex with another man at a Hollywood party, was closely based on an incident when Caskey was sur-prised *in flagrante* at Norma Shearer's beach house. The novel was also being influ-enced by Isherwood's reading of *Parade's End*, a reading which in turn was influenced by Isherwood's relationship with Caskey. An initially puzzling entry in Isherwood's diary notes that Ford's book

> has somehow shown me, once again, that I must not make any conditions, any plans as to my relations with Billy. Billy is a human being in trouble, and so am I. We are not Truman and Stalin, or a pair of businessmen. We cannot settle any-thing by bargaining. We have to live this through, with great patience, but without any of that 'neither-do-I-condemn-thee' stuff. Oh, I shall never, never get out of this rut until I do that, once. The funny thing is it's exactly the subject of my novel.

This makes a little more sense if one considers Isherwood's relationship with Caskey alongside his notebook for *The School of Tragedy* and his essay on *Parade's End*. Ford's novel tells the story of an unhappy marriage between an English squire called Christopher Tietjens and his wife Sylvia, set against the backdrop of the First

World War. In detailing the plot in his essay, Isherwood refers to Tietjens not by his surname, which would be normal (and indeed Ford's) practice, but by his first name, which suggests a certain, perhaps unconscious, degree of identification. He characterizes Sylvia as "a bad Catholic and an hysterical bitch," which clearly suggests Caskey at his worst. Tietjens returns from the trenches suffering from some sort of war trauma. "He is fighting to keep his sanity," Isherwood explains with evident fellow-feeling, "and Sylvia is doing everything in her power to make him lose it. Tortured by her love-hatred of Christopher and baffled by her failure to break his self-control, she slanders him grotesquely to his friends, involves him in humiliating money troubles, bombards him with accusations of infidelity [. . .] Christopher can do little more than endure all these blows with passive stoicism, for he is bound hand and foot by his own principles and by the pride which Sylvia hates." Isherwood then goes on to consider Ford's attitude toward his protagonist, which he finds ambiguous. "Christopher is constantly being presented to us as charitable, gentle, generous, just, loyal and courageous, a near-saint; and yet one has the impression that Ford does not really like him—that he agrees, in fact, with Sylvia, in finding Christopher a maddeningly inhuman, arrogant prig, who, beneath his mask of Job-like patience, can be obstinately and coldly cruel." Isherwood points out that in his introduction to the volume, Robie Macaulay "suggests that Ford wanted to show the Age of Reason, in the person of Christopher Tietjens, giving way to our modern era of chaos, madness and squalor." Isherwood suggests that "Ford's conscious design underwent a radical—but possibly subconscious—change during the process of its execution. What he has actually shown us is not the sane Past confronting the insane Present, but a contrast between two kinds of insanity. The cold madness of self-righteous Reason opposes the hot madness of uncontrolled Instinct; and the result of their collision is War." Whether or not this is a just analysis of Ford's book may be open to question (the summary Isherwood provides is, he acknowledges, "as unfair and misleading as all such summaries must be"). It is undoubtedly, however, an interesting—but possibly subconscious—gloss upon Isherwood's relationship with Caskey.

Isherwood was now working on a substantial draft of *The School of Tragedy,* keeping a record of his progress and the difficulties thrown up along the way in his notebook. By early July he had decided that the draft was "utter nonsense," but that he must nevertheless persist with it. The one piece of advice from the first professional writer Isherwood ever met, Allan Monkhouse, was that you should always finish a book once you had started it. It must, therefore, have been with a wan smile that Isherwood noted a passage in Cyril Connolly's *The Unquiet Grave,* which he read around this time, a passage he said he kept quoting to himself:

> . . . the true function of a writer is to produce a masterpiece . . . no other task is of
> any consequence. Obvious though this should be, how few writers will admit it,
> or having made the admission, will be prepared to lay aside the piece of iridescent
> mediocrity on which they have embarked! Writers always hope that their next
> book is going to be their best, for they will not acknowledge that it is their present
> way of life which prevents them from ever creating anything different or better.

A trip Isherwood and Caskey made to Sequoia with the Stravinskys and Robert Craft provided what seemed like a breakthrough. Stravinsky was using the car journey to think hard about *The Rake's Progress,* and the composer's evident concentration encouraged Isherwood to consider his own work as they crossed the San Fernando Valley. More and more the novel was becoming focused on Stephen, but as yet this character lacked dynamism. Isherwood suddenly decided to make him bisexual, noting: "The degree to which this scares me only proves I'm on the right track." He also decided that Stephen's Quaker upbringing had made him "an inverted Puritan," who revolts against his background and indulges in lots of homosexual affairs, without ever allowing himself to fall in love. This is because he still believes that homosexuality is wrong. His first wife, Elizabeth, "understood" and offered him a refuge, but after her death he had become very promiscuous, and then met Jane, "who turned out to be the only girl who could really satisfy him sexually. She was glad to marry him, for his money and because she found him attractive too—but she was promiscuous by nature and of course she started to cheat on him. This upset him violently—because it made him feel so insecure." When he catches her with another man, he runs away to Dolgelly. Stephen would still have the relationship with Gerda, but he would also fall in love with the doctor, now called Charles Kennedy. This would mean that the plot about the doctor's doomed boyfriend would have to be jettisoned, because Isherwood wanted Stephen's relationship with Kennedy to be serious and uncomplicated by notions of infidelity.

> If this story is to mean anything, it will show Stephen functioning on all levels[:] bisexuality—i.e. flirting because one can't make up one's mind—has to be exposed spiritually, economically, politically, socially, as well as sexually. Stephen has to find adjustments on all levels before the book ends. It is necessary to get this clear by degrees. But already I see possibilities of introducing the pacifist problem—for example. And the conquest of Stephen's Puritanism. If Stephen's 'conversion' means anything, it means that he can accept an apparent paradox— he still believes in God—or more than ever believes in God—while doing something the God-mongers condemn—that is, loving another man. This is the essence of what I want to say. This is what makes the story really significant.

It would also make the story reflect Isherwood's own experience of finding a religion that he could practice while still pursuing an active sex life.

This, clearly, altered the entire conception of the novel. Isherwood may have been led to re-imagine his protagonist as bisexual because he had given him the same forename as Spender. Although he would always regard Spender as one of his closest friends, Isherwood also thought of him as a "prime example" of the bisexual man. He frequently complained that bisexuality involved all manner of compromise and deceit, that it inevitably led to betrayal since by their very nature bisexuals could not be faithful to one person—not that sexual fidelity was anything Isherwood himself ever practiced. Indeed, his disapproval of married bisexuals in particular was a great deal less moral than he pretended. Whenever he spoke of "betrayal" there was a strong suggestion that the betrayal that most concerned him was not that of the wife but that of the bisexual's homosexual friends. By marrying, people like Spender had unforgivably "gone over to the other side." Making Stephen Monk bisexual may have seemed like a breakthrough, but it also made him a character that Isherwood found basically unsympathetic, with disastrous consequences for the novel.

The character of Kennedy was now based on Kirstein. "I hope you won't mind about this," he wrote. "It is not really recognizable, except to those who love you; and the character is handled with warmth, the way Degas handled the ballet girls, and with pity." The tone of this remark, and indeed of much of Isherwood's correspondence with Kirstein, explains why in the novel it is left to Kennedy to give Stephen a lecture on the meaning of camp. "The Ballet is camp about love," Kennedy explains, choosing Kirstein's own discipline, which he took very seriously but nevertheless sent up in letters. Furthermore, anyone who had seen a picture of Kirstein would recognize him immediately from Stephen's description of Kennedy:

> He was a huge man, powerfully built. He wore rimless glasses, which slightly magnified his dark lively eyes. His clothes were so severely plain that they looked like a uniform: a dark blue suit, a white shirt, black tie, shoes and socks. Though he was probably a few years younger than me, he was nearly bald; and the remains of his black hair were shaved so close that they gave the appearance of a mere shadow over the top of his skull. His baldness emphasized the tense, firmly modelled muscularity of his head; compact with nervous energy, it reminded you of a clenched fist. He was handsome, in a brooding archaic way, like a face from early Asiatic temple sculpture. I supposed he might be Jewish.

Kirstein told Isherwood that he felt "flattered that my poor warped character was in any way a jet-propulsion to your gift."

I n order to escape from "the misery of the mess at Rustic Road," in August Isherwood took an extended trip to New Mexico with Peggy Kiskadden and her three-year-old son, Little Bill, usually known as "Bull." En route they stayed with a couple who were employing Jim Charlton to design and help them build a house in Arizona. Isherwood hadn't seen Charlton for some time and in this perfect Whitmanesque setting found himself falling in love all over again. Charlton, however, was going through "a monastic stage" and enjoying his new, comparatively sober and celibate life away from the bars and beaches of Santa Monica. Isherwood, Kiskadden and Bull next traveled to the house of the painter Georgia O'Keeffe at Abiquiu, where they stayed for several days. O'Keeffe was a former admirer of Peggy but had very little time for Isherwood. She nevertheless organized a trip to Taos, where the spirit of D. H. Lawrence was very much alive. This was an important pilgrimage for Isherwood, who had acknowledged before coming to California, "The real America, for me, was the Far West. All my daydreams were based on D. H. Lawrence's *St Mawr*." Isherwood, whose own literary style was distinctly laconic, also had an enormous and rather surprising reverence for Lawrence as a writer. "Not his philosophical point of view," Isherwood explained, "but I admire tremendously his approach to writing." What he liked about Lawrence was his "brute subjectivity": "For so many of us he gave the wonderful feeling that your subjective impressions were the best you could offer the reader." He visited Lawrence's grave, and picked two red flowers to press in his wallet as souvenirs.

Isherwood returned to Los Angeles after eleven days to find the house in an appalling state. Caskey had evidently been partying and had left filthy glasses, crockery and moldering food everywhere. Peggy reacted with horror, clearly believing that the psychological "mess" of Isherwood and Caskey's relationship had somehow manifested itself physically. She urged Isherwood to come to stay with her—for as long as he liked. The implication was clear. Isherwood knew that Peggy disapproved of Caskey, and of what she perceived as the squalor of homosexual life. She did not let this show in any obvious way, but—as she had with Vedanta—made sharp little jokes that needled Isherwood. He was becoming increasingly fed up with her big-sister act, and there had been some awkward moments on the New Mexico trip, notably when, intending a compliment, she told him that no one would guess that he was homosexual. Whether Isherwood was as offended by this at the time as he was when recalling it in the 1970s is open to question. He admitted that he had been "amused and pleased" when during the trip a waitress assumed he and Peggy were husband and wife. His militant sense of homosexual identity had certainly not been much in evidence the previous December when he and Jim Charlton had been arrested during a raid on the Variety gay bar on the Pacific Coast Highway. They were both taken to the Santa Monica police station for questioning. After ascertaining that neither of them had a criminal record, the police insisted upon interrogating them separately. They were asked if they were homosexual and both said "No." They were not entirely believed and they endured a fair amount of ill-natured but unthreatening joshing before being released with a caution. "The utter brutality of those cops, the night before last," Isherwood wrote in his diary two days later, "and my guilt that I didn't handle them properly—wasn't wonderful and poised and mature. I ought to have called their bluff, insisted on being locked up, hired a lawyer, taken the case to the Supreme Court, started a nationwide stink. Why didn't I? Because I'm cowardly, slack, weak, compromised." The fact that Caskey, who didn't give a damn and would have stood up to the cops, was away may have had something to do with Isherwood's sense of guilt. And now Peggy Kiskadden was putting Isherwood in a position where he had to choose between Caskey and her. As in the case of Denny Fouts, Isherwood chose Caskey, and immediately called Ben and Jo Masselink to help him clear up the mess.

"The Masselinks" were only that by courtesy, since they were not in fact married. Their situation was similar to that of Isherwood's other close heterosexual friends, the Beesleys, in that Jo was the older partner (in her case by about nineteen years) and the one with a well-established career. A former dancer, she had set herself up as a designer of sportswear for women, including several Hollywood stars. She had met Ben during the war, when he was serving with the Marines and while on leave had wandered into the Friendship Bar in Santa Monica. The Friendship catered for a "mixed" clientele. Heterosexual and homosexual men and women drank there together in an atmosphere that earned the bar its name. Ben had been drunk and Jo, who lived nearby, took him home. After the war they continued to frequent the bar and it was almost certainly here sometime in 1949 that they met Isherwood and

Caskey, and struck up a close and enduring friendship. Ben had studied architecture and was probably responsible for introducing Isherwood to Jim Charlton.

Unlike Peggy Kiskadden, the Masselinks were genuinely fond of Caskey, and accepted the fact, as Isherwood was constantly struggling to, that his "bad behaviour" was as much a part of him as his sharp wit and his Southern charm. They were just the right people to be enlisted to clean up the results of that behavior, and did so uncensoriously and with good humor. It turned out, however, that Caskey's antics had finally caught up with him, since he was not, as Isherwood had thought, basking in Baja California, but languishing in the Santa Ana jail, serving a three-month sentence for drunken driving. He had been given the option of paying a fine, but had refused—largely, Isherwood thought, because a spell in jail would seem to this "black Catholic" a more appropriate penance for his sin. He told Kirstein that Caskey was enduring his incarceration "with a kind of incredible sweet gracious majesty somewhat like Mary Queen of Scots right along towards the end. His eyes have a distant shine of boyhood due to the fact that you can get nothing to drink there but methylated spirits." Caskey refused all offers to attempt to get him an early release through bribery, and Isherwood suspected that he preferred being in jail rather than back in Rustic Road, where Isherwood's "martyred forebearance would make him feel more guilty, as well as hostile." Since it was Caskey who was being martyred, albeit quite enjoyably, Isherwood felt very affectionate toward him rather than angry, and visited him every Saturday. He was nevertheless quite relieved that he could put off facing up to the problem of their living together for a couple of months.

Caskey was released from jail at the end of October, whereupon Isherwood took to his bed with what he later acknowledged was some kind of psychosomatic illness. Dr. Kolisch told him that he had "the kind of constitution which is capable of simulating every species of pathological condition," something he shared with his maternal grandmother. "In the past two years, I've also been a martyr to pseudo-heart-ailments, hysterical blindness, sham infantile paralysis (very impressive, this) and hardening of the arteries," he boasted to Upward, who had complained of "pseudo-consumption." Kolisch went on to advise Isherwood never to consult a doctor again, adding cheerfully: "It will only be necessary once—and then it will be too late."

NINETEEN

THE LEASE ON EAST RUSTIC ROAD WAS DUE TO EXPIRE AT THE end of 1950 and so Isherwood and Caskey started looking for a new home, hoping that this would represent a genuine fresh start to their relationship. Toward the end of November they found a house at 31152 Monterey Street, South Laguna, a coastal resort to the southwest of Los Angeles. The house, up in the hills but with a clear view of the beach and the ocean, struck Isherwood as romantic, a left-over from the days of the early settlers, whom he made sound exactly like the English colony at Sintra: "third-rate water colorists, mild eccentrics, British expatriate ladies who ran 'Scottish' teashops, astrologers, breeders of poodles. . . ." The surrounding terrain, with lanes leading down from the hillside on to the beach, reminded him of childhood holidays at Penmaenmawr and Ventnor.

"I know that [Caskey] *means* to make this 'a new start,' though we don't discuss it much," Isherwood wrote in his diary the day after they moved in, "and I'm eager to meet him three quarters of the way. Sometimes I begin to venture to say to myself that maybe we *have* passed some kind of danger point and are now on our way to better times. But that's still wishful thinking, I do know that *if* it were true, and *if* the political situation improves, and *if* we can get enough money to live on, this might be the start of one of the happiest periods of my life." By "the political situation" he meant the Korean crisis, which had escalated at the end of November with a Chinese deployment to North Korea in support of the communist troops, who had been driven back out of South Korea. Isherwood worried not only that the shadow of "total war" was once again falling across the land, but that Caskey might be drafted into the United Nations army, which was under American command.

As usual, Isherwood made a set of resolutions: "Calm, meditation, work, regular habits, study, discipline, proper exercise; the absolute necessary regime for middle age." Unfortunately, Isherwood was sharing his middle age with a man in his late twenties, to whom such a regime was inconceivable. For a while, however, Caskey was occupied with various home-improvement projects, while Isherwood wrote reviews for *Tomorrow* and roughed out four chapters of his troublesome novel. "I am feeling my way towards an Anglo-American style," Isherwood told Upward, "and this in itself is very hard. It *ought* theoretically to be wonderful and funny to be a detached mongrel, talking a bastard jargon, but I fear this will only come with much more practice."

I n March 1951, Isherwood sent the four chapters of what he now referred to as "this horrible bitch of a book" to Dodie Smith, complaining that it was

awful and false and bogus. This wretched rat of a Stephen, and all these boring people, and the lack of movement, and the slowness, and the sort of grim-lipped Americanoid wry humor. What am I to do? I feel there is something integrally wrong. Stephen is neither objective nor subjective enough. I long for a *plot*. I wish to God I didn't have so much happening before the book opens. I wish . . . I wish . . .

This is the real dark night of the soul, and I can only appeal to your insight. Don't just wince at this rubbish, try to see *why* it's so bad, and tell me. When you and Alec have read it, I'll come up, if I may, and talk. It is no use discussing this on the basis of what I would *like* to have done; you have to know the worst.

Would it be better if it were all objective, with me looking down on them?
Or different parts told by different people?
Or Stephen somehow made more real, but still the subjective experience?
Fewer characters?
A very tight short action-period, and the rest flashbacks?
The whole thing told years later—by whom to whom?
Is there something fundamentally wrong with the anecdote?
Is there an anecdote?
HELP!!!!

Frequent discussions seemed constructive but produced very few results: the Beesleys were no more capable of getting this novel properly under way than Isherwood was. They did, however, feel that they might be able to do something about Isherwood's finances. The previous spring Isherwood had met an engaging young writer from Louisiana named Speed Lamkin. At the age of twenty-two, Lamkin had already found a publisher for his first novel, and had, in the words of one observer, arrived in Los Angeles with his beautiful sister, Marguerite, "like characters in Balzac, come to storm Paris." Speed also wanted to carry out some research for his second novel, which was to be based on the character of William Randolph Hearst, who was conveniently dying at his grandiose California castle, San Simeon. Although Isherwood found it hard at first to take this flirtatious and amusing young man altogether seriously, he became increasingly friendly with him, and authorized him to adapt *Sally Bowles* for the stage. Lamkin called in a screenwriter named Gus Field as a collaborator, and Isherwood gave the two men a good deal of help. When he showed the Beesleys a draft of this adaptation, they were unimpressed—but it gave them an idea.

What Isherwood and his novella needed was someone with long experience in stagecraft and a good commercial track record. Knowing that John van Druten always accepted a challenge, they decided to issue one, as if spontaneously. While swimming in the reservoir on van Druten's ranch, Alec popped his head out of the water and said to his host, who was sitting on the bank with Dodie, "Why don't you turn *Sally Bowles* into a play?" Before van Druten could reply, Alec dived under the water again, leaving his wife to further their plan. "It couldn't be done," she said. Van Druten said he disagreed, but the idea didn't interest him. Smith continued to outline the difficulties of such an adaptation, then suggested ideas for overcoming them, ideas which van Druten, drawn inexorably on, started improving upon. The topic continued to dominate the conversation over dinner, with van Druten still claiming that his interest was entirely academic. Ten days later, however, he produced a version he felt confident enough to read aloud to Isherwood. Trying to recall his first impressions of the play thirty years later, Isherwood merely remembered that he had disliked some of van Druten's jokes, the concept of the "Christopher Isherwood" character, and the insertion of speeches about the Nazi persecution of the Jews. Dodie Smith remembered Isherwood thought the play "cold and dirty—a combination he particularly disliked." She claimed that van Druten's agent and a producer to whom he sent the play also disliked it. It did not, however, take the author long to iron out any difficulties and find backing for the play, which van Druten titled *I Am a Camera*.

The question of royalties then arose, van Druten suggesting a 75–25 percent split in his favor. Dodie Smith was outraged by what she regarded as van Druten's rapacity and told him firmly that a 50–50 split would be customary in such cases. Van Druten refused to discuss the matter and got his agent, Monica McCall, to write to Isherwood with a list of examples of plays adapted from other works where the original author agreed to 25 percent or less. Isherwood felt that by writing to him directly rather than to his agent, McCall was attempting to browbeat him. He forwarded the letter to James Geller, who was now acting as his literary agent and who disputed the accuracy of each and every one of the examples given. Van Druten, meanwhile, emerged from his fastness and wrote an aggrieved letter addressed jointly to Smith and Isherwood. "I think that this is something we have got to have out now on paper, or it can grow into something quite unpleasant and dangerous to a friendship," he wrote.

> Dodie has made me feel quite strongly that she thinks I have been behaving unfairly and greedily and maybe dishonestly over the sharing terms of S[ally] B[owles]. I think that Chris thinks so too, though he did not so express himself. I have to tell you that it has shocked me a good deal that you can think of me like that, and that is where I think friendship comes in. It is dodging issues to leave it to agents to settle: agents ultimately do only what is told them by their principals [i.e. clients]. So we must come to the issue now.

He said that he would never normally agree to a 50–50 split and to do so now would make him feel that he had been morally blackmailed. He felt that they were overestimating the box-office potential of Isherwood's book, which was merely a "minor classic." He rejected as unfair Smith's tactless suggestion that ten days' work would be unjustly remunerated by the proposed split since she knew that he was constitutionally a quick worker. The fact that he had more money than Isherwood was irrelevant. "I did not embark on this as a gesture of charity," he complained. "This must necessarily be a business arrangement, and the real trouble is that I did not make a business deal before I started work. There I do blame myself, and my own kind of enthusiasm when I start on something." He added that his last offer had been for Isherwood to receive 40 percent and it had now been made "impossible" for him to alter this. Isherwood accepted this "with grace and humour," Smith recalled. "Amicable relations were resumed between us all—but were they ever quite so amicable?" They certainly underwent further strain when van Druten attempted to bag the entire royalties on the published text of the play.

While van Druten set about finding backers, Isherwood had taken a step which had been inevitable for some time: he split up with Caskey. The first half of 1951 had been particularly difficult, and he had achieved very little. He even became nostalgic for the privileged but fettered life he had led with his mother in Kensington, a life of "solitude in the midst of snugness."

> I want to be looked after. I want the background of a home. I see now how well the arrangement at Pembroke Gardens suited me, during the last year or so in England (much as I complained about it). I could go out as much as I wanted to, but I had the snugness of a bedroom and breakfast. Now, I suppose this arrangement is really almost impossible to set up again. One needs an undemanding aunt. A wife would be no good, because she'd demand all kinds of things.

Caskey's ideas were rather different. Although a competent homemaker, he wanted action and parties and fun, and he wanted Isherwood to join in rather than sit about brooding over his inability to write a novel. Although in urgent need of some discipline, Isherwood had become too accustomed to the pleasures of the world to return to the monastery. He therefore did the next best thing and on May 21 checked in to the Huntington Hartford Foundation. Set up in Pacific Palisades in 1949 by the wealthy heir to the A&P grocery stores empire, the Foundation was a comfortable retreat which offered three-month fellowships to writers, painters and musicians. Speed Lamkin had introduced Isherwood to Huntington Hartford himself, and got him a position on the Foundation's board. Benefiting from his position, Isherwood now took up temporary residence in one of the studios.

The period at the Foundation was reasonably peaceful, but not very productive. Isherwood knew what was really wrong with his novel: it bored him. The difficulty was to find out *why* it bored him and then proceed accordingly. He had formulated "a working rule": "*whenever* I'm stuck, to ask myself who I would like to hear about." Lamkin, who had professed admiration for the first chapter, was nevertheless in no doubt whatsoever about who he did *not* want to hear about: refugees. "Nobody had condemned the refugees before," Isherwood recalled. "The Beesleys were probably dubious about them but hadn't wanted to upset C by upsetting the applecart. Speed with his ruthlessness had disregarded C's feelings and expressed his own. C could never be grateful enough to him. And how quickly everything now fell into place." By June 1, after further discussions with Lamkin and the Beesleys, "the main outline of the novel in its final form had already been decided on."

This did not of course mean that Isherwood could just sit down and write the wretched thing, and after two months at the Foundation he was once again castigating himself. "It is such ages—more than 4 years—since I started messing with this project. And even if you subtract two years for S. America, movie work and the writing of 'Condor & Cows,' it is disgraceful. Now I'm stuck again—why? There is somehow a subtle lack of interest. Shit. What's the matter with me?"

A further distraction, one which Isherwood seems not to have mentioned either in his diaries or in letters to friends, was provided by the Federal Bureau of Investigation. In May, Isherwood's old associate Guy Burgess, who had long since left the BBC and was now working in the Foreign Office (largely for the Russians), defected to the Soviet Union. He had recently returned to England in disgrace after a characteristically accident-prone stint as second secretary at the British Embassy in Washington, and was about to be sacked. His fellow spy Donald Maclean had recently been made head of the FO's American department. Maclean had for some time been under surveillance by MI5, the British government's counter-intelligence agency, and was about to be questioned. It was vital that he should escape. Burgess's persistent drunkenness and fantastic lack of discretion, both about his homosexual exploits and his anti-American sympathies, had somehow prevented his coming under suspicion. The original intention seems to have been that Burgess would therefore accompany Maclean just as far as Prague. All that was known publicly was that the two men had "disappeared," and when this news broke in the papers they became known as "the Missing Diplomats."

Meanwhile the FBI began its own investigations into Burgess and Maclean, starting at the British Embassy in Washington. There, under questioning, a secretary recalled that while in America Burgess had been in touch with a writer named Christopher Isherwood. The two men, their differences over Jack Hewit resolved, had met for a drunken supper during Isherwood's first postwar visit to England in March 1947, and it seemed possible that they had kept in touch thereafter. Robert J. Lamphere, the FBI's chief of counter-intelligence, immediately ordered two agents from the Los Angeles bureau to find Isherwood and question him. "It was Christopher Isherwood who really opened up the whole can of worms," Lamphere recalled. If he did so, he did it unwillingly and was, to say the least of it, economical with the truth.

Interviewed on June 15, Isherwood admitted that, like "all the writers and literary people of London," he had known Burgess in the later 1930s, when the missing diplomat had been working for the BBC. He was "not at all clear" about Burgess's political interests at this time, although like most of his circle, Burgess was "warmly in favor of the Spanish Loyalist Government." Apart from this "(which Isherwood does not consider to be pro-Communist in the light of the thinking of that period)," he had "no knowledge of any Communist sympathies on the part of Burgess." He described Burgess as "a person who was given to excess in drink and who was trying very desperately to be 'one of the group,' meaning the literary circle in which Isherwood et al traveled."

Isherwood went on to tell the agents that when he saw him in 1947, Burgess was working for the Foreign Office and "always wanted to be 'on the inside' insofar as significant political events and activities were concerned." Burgess was "known to be a homosexual," but Isherwood "did not consider this unusual, adding that even if his condition were generally known to Burgess's friends and employers of that period it would not have made much difference." Consequently, he did "not feel that Burgess' homosexuality would be a weakness which could be used to advantage by the Soviets." He thought it "inconceivable" Burgess would be recruited as a spy, since he was well known for his "drunkenness and emotional instability."

Perhaps worried that he was giving the impression that he knew rather too much about the missing diplomat, Isherwood hastily added that "actually he did not know Burgess as well as some people thought; that in reality he did not have very much in common with Burgess and did not know or care enough about him to learn anything about his family or background." He had not seen Burgess at all, or corresponded with him, between 1939 and 1947. Isherwood did of course have a great deal more in common with Burgess than he was admitting—not least a homosexual partner, Jack Hewit.

What particularly interested the agents were the links Isherwood provided between Burgess and a number of friends and associates from the 1930s who were known to be left-wing and almost certainly suspected of being homosexual. While the names of Auden, Spender and Isherwood himself probably caused little alarm or interest, those of Lord Inverchapel and Rolf Katz must have come as a nasty surprise. When Isherwood had met him in China in 1938, Inverchapel was plain Sir Archibald Clark Kerr. In 1942 Clark Kerr had been posted to Moscow. Elevated to the peerage, he subsequently became British Ambassador to the United States. He arrived in Washington in 1946 accompanied by a Russian valet—a personal farewell present from Stalin, with whom he had been on friendly terms. The presence of this servant, along with Inverchapel's often expressed enthusiasm for the Soviet Union, alarmed the State Department. The valet, it insisted, had to go, but Inverchapel remained at his post until 1949, when he was retired on the grounds of "ill-health," probably at the request of J. Edgar Hoover. Maclean had been First Secretary at the Embassy during Inverchapel's incumbency, and the information that the wayward ambassador had mixed in the same social circles as Burgess naturally roused further suspicions at the FBI.

The fact that Katz, too, knew Inverchapel and Burgess was even more disturbing. Isherwood had told the FBI that Katz not only knew Burgess socially, but had worked with him sometime between 1936 and 1938 on "a magazine which devoted itself to surveys of economic and political matters." It is unclear exactly what the FBI knew about Katz, but Isherwood was overcome with uncharacteristic vagueness when asked about his old friend's political connections. He "stated that he knew of no Communist Party activity or activity on behalf of Soviet Russia on the part of RUDOLPH KATZ, stating that as far as he knew KATZ's field lay more in the line of economics and matters of finance although he did indulge a bit in 'political analysis.' " Isherwood added that he had written about Katz "in his book entitled 'The Condors and the Crows' [sic] and said that as far as he was concerned KATZ was in no way identified with Communist Party activity but was an independent thinker whom ISHERWOOD very much admired." This was somewhat disingenuous. While it was true that Katz seemed not to be currently involved with any communist organization—indeed, he had told Isherwood in Argentina that he had converted to capitalism on the grounds that "power is always evil"—his past links were very strong indeed.

Isherwood's flannel had not convinced the FBI, which almost immediately uncovered Katz's links with the German Communist Party. Consequently Isherwood received a second visit from FBI agents and was obliged to reconsider his earlier statement. "Upon reflection," he stated that in Berlin Katz was "undoubtedly leftist in some of his political thinking," and that he "did remember hearing something about Katz's publishing a Communist Party newspaper in Berlin," but this would have been before Isherwood knew him and he had "never heard Katz discuss it." This is extremely unlikely, and Isherwood's further assertion that "he never could conceive of [Katz] being a true follower of Communism" was clearly untrue, as was his statement that "he had no knowledge of Katz's ever having been a member of the Community Party."

Isherwood concluded by pointing out that "it was quite impossible to analyze activities of the period 1936 and 1937 in which he and [Auden, whose name has been censored] and others were engaged, in the light of the political thinking of today [. . .] it was not until the news of the Moscow purge trials in the late 1930s began to leak out and other events came to light that Russia had undermined the Spanish Loyalists that people began to realize that perhaps they had been duped in some of their so-called United Front activities [. . .] He re-emphasized that he had no knowledge of any espionage activities on the part of Burgess or Rudolph Katz. He stated that he had no reason to withhold information of such a nature were he to possess it and his present feeling is that he recognizes the evil of Soviet Communism and would do anything in his power to combat it." With this declaration ringing in their ears, the agents departed and that was the last Isherwood heard from the Bureau.

Given the anti-communist hysteria which prevailed in the United States in 1951, it was hardly surprising that Isherwood, as a comparatively recent American citizen, should have been circumspect in his answers. What is odd, however, is that he seems never to have referred to this episode, suppressing it from accounts of his life, as he did his friendship with Rolf Katz, who subsequently disappeared, possibly murdered by agents.

By the time of his second FBI interview in July, Isherwood had returned to Monterey Street where Caskey was installed once more, although Isherwood had no intention of living with him again. Prabhavananda was once again urging Isherwood to take up the monastic life, but at Trabuco rather than Ivar Avenue. Isherwood still felt the need of God in his life, but he could not really countenance this suggestion. The alternatives, however, were no more appealing. The idea of living with Jim Charlton was attractive, but they both decided that it would not work out, largely because Charlton did not like the feeling of being tied down. Isherwood even contemplated living with Speed Lamkin, though not very seriously. Other friends already had partners and any attempt to live with them, even if they agreed to such a proposition, would only lead to an increased sense of isolation.

Meanwhile, *I Am a Camera* had gone into rehearsal under van Druten's direction, with Julie Harris playing Sally and William Prince in the Isherwood role. Whatever Isherwood might have thought of the play privately, he had a vested interest in its commercial success and was prepared to do publicity for it. This also allowed him to escape his troubles and responsibilities for a while, and he traveled to Hartford, Connecticut, where the play was having its out-of-town opening on the always propitious November 8. Caskey packed up the house in Laguna before going to San Francisco to get a job with the merchant marine. "The house seems very empty now," he wrote to Isherwood, and I refuse to go out and round up a lot of Marines just from loneliness."

> Your understanding of our separation at this time makes me very happy, and gives me courage to go ahead with what I'm trying to do; tho even that I'm not sure of. But I feel I must try something completely on my own with no influence of any kind and it would have been much harder if I felt I was hurting you in carrying out such a plan. I have never meant to hurt you, Sweetie, though it must have seemed that way at times. Already I miss you very much and always will as long as we are apart. But neither your staying in Laguna nor my going to New York would have worked out. That might only have made things worse and we might have lost everything that we've had together. But there has to be some progress in a relationship and my just hanging around wouldn't have brought it about. I only ask that you keep in close touch with me for when I need you I do want you to be there, always. And wherever I am it won't really be so far away if you think of all we've known together. And I can come back from the end of the earth if you really physically need me.

The letter was signed: "All my love always, Bill."

According to Robert Craft, who celebrated Thanksgiving with Isherwood, Auden and the Stravinksys a few days before *I Am a Camera* opened on Broadway, Isherwood still had distinct reservations about the play and had even threatened to boycott its gala première. In the event, he was photographed with Julie Harris by Richard Avedon, and wrote an article boosting the production: "Author Meets Himself in 'I Am a Camera.' " Isherwood recalled his first meeting with Harris:

> Now, out of the dressing room, came a slim sparkling-eyed girl in an absurdly tartlike black dress, with a jaunty little cap stuck sideways on her pale flame-colored hair and a gay, silly, naughty giggle. This certainly wasn't Miss Harris (who is a married lady of serious tastes and a spotless moral reputation); it was Sally Bowles in person—my unserious, somewhat shop-soiled but always endearing heroine. Miss Harris was more essentially Sally Bowles than the Sally of my book, and much, much more like Sally than the real girl who, long ago, gave me the idea for my character.
>
> I felt half hypnotized by the strangeness of the situation. 'This is terribly sad,' I said to her, 'you've stayed the same age while I've gotten twenty years older.' We exchanged scraps of dialogue from the play, we laughed wildly, hammed and hugged each other while Mr Avedon's camera clicked.

It was in Isherwood's interest to boost the play now that he had managed to get a reasonable percentage out of van Druten, but his praise for the playwright and cast was echoed in the press, and *I Am a Camera* proved a great success when it opened at the Empire Theatre in New York at the end of November. "Far from boycotting the event," Craft recalled, "Christopher was at the door greeting the celebrities, and, during intermissions, in the foyer revelling in the success."

Isherwood ascribed much of the play's success to Harris, but the London production, which opened in March 1954, also made a star of Dorothy Tutin in the role of Sally. William Plomer, who had seen a preview in Brighton, described Tutin to Isherwood as "a *tour de* (if I may put it like this) *farce*." He rightly predicted that the play would have a long run, having overheard two stockbrokers on a tram discussing the play, which they had heard was "very sexy."

I sherwood had looked forward to going to New York for the première and seeing Auden, Kirstein and other East Coast friends, including the Beesleys, who were now living in Connecticut. After the play opened he had no particular plans, except to spend Christmas in England with Kathleen and Richard, who had escaped the discomforts of Wyberslegh for a hotel in Kensington. Life at Wyberslegh during the past couple of years had become very dispiriting, and Kathleen's diaries are a record of mounting desolation. The pleasure of returning to her beloved house had worn off relatively quickly. She had known all along that it could not be the same as it was when Frank was alive, but she found it hard to make many friends and she missed those she had in London. She was "always longing for someone who would turn out to be 'real people,' as she put it, someone she could drop in on informally and who would drop in on her," Richard recalled. Neither she nor Richard had ever learned to drive and they had become very isolated. To go any distance they had to make use of the local taxi service, which ferried them to and from the shops or Marple Hall, where children had smashed windows while the caretakers were away, instigating an eventually fatal reign of vandalism. The caretakers had become depressed by the sheer discomfort of the Hall and by their inability to stop the rot into which it was gradually subsiding. Richard spent most of his time worrying about the house but had neither the will nor the funds needed to haul it back from the brink of ruin. He and Kathleen went for walks, had lunch in the local café, and distributed the parish magazine, but their life seemed increasingly aimless. Kathleen had always found it difficult to cram her account of the passing days onto the small pages of her diaries, and would often have to use the margins to get everything in. Her 1950 diary was much smaller than usual, but even so she found it impossible to fill the pages, obliged to note the cost of lunches for want of anything else to record. She had no regular help in the house apart from an eccentric housekeeper inherited from a recently deceased London cousin. Although this woman helped with the chores, having her to live at Wyberslegh was largely a misguided act of charity. They were relieved when they finally got rid of her, but Kathleen wrote in her diary: "Feels so lonely now at nights— Wondered who we could ask to sleep in, to keep us company." Their principal companions were a succession of much-loved cats, who tended to produce unmanageable litters of kittens and succumbed to various illnesses.

The need to escape from this dismal atmosphere had led Kathleen and Richard to take short breaks in London. "Drizzly but what did it matter?" Kathleen wrote during one of these trips. "We were here! away from washing up & the feeling that we just couldnt manage to keep the house tidy and clean!" They would visit the cinema and theater and galleries, but it was the company they most enjoyed: "there feels more stability & friendliness here," Kathleen noted of the United Services Hotel, "it is most pleasant in the Lounge having little talks to the different people we know." She felt that there was no one left in Cheshire, apart from Mrs. Monkhouse and a couple of spinster sisters named Wilson, that she would want to invite to tea.

Back at Wyberslegh they did their best to find someone to live in as a cook-housekeeper, but many prospective employees were so horrified by the state of the house that they declined the offer of employment. They had taken to getting a school-boy Richard had befriended to spend the night to keep them company. The boy's father, who had been absent for some time, suddenly re-appeared in his life and sent the police over to Wyberslegh to fetch him home. Kathleen sent the police away, but the boy was obliged to return to his family, after which Richard went into a decline. Some months later the boy started visiting once more. Kathleen suspected he might be pilfering things and he was subsequently arrested for breaking into another house.

It seems likely that in the regular letters Kathleen wrote to Isherwood she kept her troubles to herself.[1] She was a stoic and she certainly didn't want to spoil the precious time she spent with her beloved Christopher when he came to England by dwelling on her woes. As far as she was concerned, he had made over the estate and this act of generosity had absolved him from any further duties. Isherwood was, however, worried enough to encourage Amiya to introduce herself to Kathleen and Richard and to keep an eye on them for him. Amiya was now living in England, and in some splendor, at The Cottage, in fact a large mock-Tudor dower house at Hinchingbrooke, the Huntingdon estate of the Earls of Sandwich. After the death of his first wife, an American devotee of Vedantism, George Montagu, 9th Earl of Sandwich, had traveled to California to find out more about this religion. While visiting Ivar Avenue, he fell in love with Amiya, who was some twenty years his junior, and proposed to her. Amiya had been very concerned about abandoning Prabhavananda, but he gave his blessing (with suspicious alacrity, according to her family) and she accompanied Montagu back to England, where they married. Although she had exchanged the comparative austerity of a monastery in Los Angeles for a substantial country house in England, plentifully supplied with servants, she continued to follow Vedanta and kept her Sanskrit name, styling herself somewhat exotically Amiya, Countess of Sandwich.

As a close friend of Christopher, and one who could talk about his religious interests from the inside, Amiya was welcomed by Kathleen, who also had an abiding enthusiasm for the aristocracy. It was Richard, however, who was supposed to be the chief beneficiary of Amiya's visits to Wyberslegh. "I am more happy than I can tell you that your meeting with Richard had such impact," Isherwood wrote to Amiya after hearing of her first visit. "I really feel it was heaven-fated. You are so exactly the person who could help him; and he just loved you, and so did my Mother." He had deliberately not said anything much about Richard because he wanted Amiya's "unbiased impression."

I do indeed know why it was so startling. It was for me, too, when I came back to England in 1947. I don't think I have ever come into contact with a case quite like

---

1. Not a single letter has survived.

his, and perhaps these borderline personalities are really more tragic than the ones that go over the edge into breakdown and a mental hospital. I think they suffer more.

You ask how all this happened. Twenty years ago, I would have answered partly with a lot of Freudian stuff. The dominating mother, the dead Father and Husband and (though I might not have included him) the selfish successful brother. Other people suffer much more severe handicaps and traumas and nevertheless build lives for themselves. You know many such instances. So do I. So we're back at dear old Karma, which explains everything and nothing.

By "Karma," Isherwood meant the accumulated consequences of this and previous lives. As the Vedanta Press's own *Ramakrishna-Vedanta Wordbook* (on which Prabhavananda worked as consultant) put it: "Although each person imposes upon himself the limitation of his own character as determined by his past thoughts and actions, at the same time he can choose to follow the tendency he has formed or to struggle against it." Isherwood's view of both Kathleen and Richard was that they had chosen not to struggle.

It seems that Richard was never diagnosed as having any specific mental illness, but among his and Kathleen's papers was a British Medical Association pamphlet written for the general public titled *Schizophrenia—the divided mind.* The undated pamphlet refers to a study of several pairs of twins, which concluded that the one who became schizophrenic "lagged behind his twin in development during his early years, and was less independent, less competent, and less secure [. . .] He did less well at school and made fewer friendships. During adolescence the stronger twin developed more skills and took more responsibility. His successes increased the feelings of inadequacy in the weaker twin. It was found that from birth the parents tended to over-protect the weaker child and to dwell on his deficiencies and failures." While Christopher and Richard were not, of course, twins, much of this seems startlingly familiar from their own history. The pamphlet also mentions several characteristics of schizophrenia that certainly applied to Richard, including "fatuous grimacing and laughter" and a "refusal to wash." There has never been any suggestion that Richard was schizophrenic, but someone may have thought it a possibility. The most likely person to have done so and provided Kathleen or Richard with a copy of the booklet was the well-intentioned Amiya.

The truth is that no one seems to have known what was "wrong" with Richard— a not uncommon occurrence in England at the time, where any amount of bizarre behavior could be attributed to "eccentricity" of a kind widely believed to characterize the upper classes. Letters written to him by local people who did odd jobs for him or helped around the house were very far from deferential, but the certain amount of teasing they contain is affectionate. One suspects that he was considered something of a joke, but that people also felt genuinely kindly toward him. He was clearly intelligent, and if he lived largely in a world of his own, it was a harmless and relatively safe one.

Richard provided an insight into his own view of his circumstances in a poignant letter he wrote to Isherwood during the war: "I am like the ship which has stuck at the mouth of a river, other ships that came into being in the dockyard long after me are constantly passing me, but unless someone gives me a push I shall stick where I am." He complained that he was full of "furious resentments and dislikes against people," just as he remembered Isherwood being before the war. He felt he had ruined a chance of happiness with the caretakers' son, but acknowledged that if he met him again, "I would only find that he had long passed me in 'the river' and was far out at sea [. . .] I'm not dramatizing myself but it's a relief to put it on paper and you often tell us *your* feelings in your letters and we are really very alike in many ways." As Isherwood said of Richard to Amiya: "There isn't much that escapes him."

Amiya clearly regarded Richard as a new project and began devoting her considerable energies to taking him in hand, urging him to shop for new clothes and writing him frequent letters of sympathetic exhortation. She had a theory that one of the reasons he neglected his appearance was that he identified so strongly with Marple Hall and its "gradual disintegration and ultimate ruin." She reminded him that buildings were the works of man, whereas the human body should be respected as "a temple of the Living God." "I know my dear that you do not wish to assist in the demolition of Marple Hall, and I understand & sympathize profoundly with your sentiments, but at the same time *I* do not want it to *destroy you*! It *must* not! It belongs to the past—*You* belong to the present and the future, and as a living & thinking human being, you are superior to bricks & mortar!" She suggested that he should work off his feelings about Marple Hall by writing a history of the house. "Remembering your many stories of those childhood days which have long since passed I have the sad and very strong impression that you are still living there in your heart! And by your identification with the past you are letting the present slip by you, while the future is filled with a deep sense of insecurity & uncertainty."

I t was during Isherwood's trip to England, where he remained until the end of February, that E. M. Forster took the opportunity to have another discussion about *Maurice.* Isherwood pointed out a major logistical flaw in its optimistic ending. Forster had left Alec, the gamekeeper with whom Maurice has fallen in love, departing by boat for Argentina. Alec promised Maurice that they would meet again, but how this would be achieved was not explained, and Isherwood felt another chapter was needed. Forster agreed and started writing one, "humility my guide." Within a few days he had roughed out the new chapter and showed it to Isherwood. "I'm afraid it isn't right in itself," he confessed, "and couldn't be after so many years, but my wanting to do it is important, and I am sure it is wanted, and may—despite the jar in tone—strengthen the stuff on each side of it [. . .] I do feel so grateful to you. I have had the story much in my mind these weeks, wondering whether A's entry up the ladder could be heated up without becoming hot stuff. But your query is infinitely more important."[2]

As a mark of gratitude for Isherwood's help, Forster assigned him the American rights in the novel and asked that he should oversee its eventual publication there. Isherwood would not benefit from this gift financially. "What I would like," Forster had explained rather vaguely, "is for the money to be kept in America for people from

2. Alec Scudder first enters Maurice's bedroom by climbing up a ladder and in through the window.

here who want to visit America, and can't. Bob specially in my mind. Alternately [*sic*], to help any one who is in trouble." A charity of which Bob Buckingham was to be the principal beneficiary was clearly not going to work and the terms were subsequently refined so that the money could be used to set up a travel scholarship for British writers.

Isherwood was also collared by Lehmann to appear on his recently launched radio program, *New Soundings,* giving a talk about six up-and-coming young American writers. Isherwood chose Ray Bradbury, Truman Capote, William Styron, Speed Lamkin, Norman Mailer and Calder Willingham. The program was to have been broadcast live, but was canceled when King George VI died on February 6, 1952. Isherwood nevertheless recorded his talk for future broadcast, giving "a highly characteristic performance," Lehmann recalled. "He was very confidential in manner, serious and yet managing to give the impression that some of the information he was giving his audience was peculiarly funny, so that he could hardly refrain from chuckling."

On February 10 Isherwood flew to Berlin, under contract to write two articles about the city for the *Observer* newspaper. It was a sentimental as well as a professional journey and one he did not undertake without some misgivings. Conversations with Auden and James Stern would have left him with no illusions about the state of Germany and its people in the aftermath of the war. "It is one thing to feel sympathetic and send food parcels," he confessed; "it is quite another thing to be actually confronted by people who are much less fortunate than yourself and face the fact that there is really very little you can do to help them. I dreaded meeting the people I had known. I dreaded seeing familiar places in ruins." This dread manifested itself in the form of a suspected duodenal ulcer, and Isherwood even claimed that he nearly broke a leg while negotiating some stairs, an accident he naturally ascribed to an attempt at sabotage by his subconscious. Since his expenses were being paid, he stayed in a smart hotel on the Kurfürstendamm, which was populated by people "who might have stepped straight out of the cartoons in which George Grosz satirizes the plutocracy of the inflation period." Although the Kurfürstendamm had retained its *chic,* much of the rest of the city was unrecognizable. The Tauentzienstrasse, where he had stayed briefly at the Pension Kosmann during the winter of 1929, was "like an avenue of broken monuments. Through wide gaps between its houses, across formless mounds of rubble, you get views of the great central desert of destruction and see the Sieges Saeule, the 1870 Victory Column, rising forlornly from the treeless plain of the Tiergarten, which is dotted here and there with exposed remains of statuary." He likened the experience to standing in Chelsea and being able to see right across a flattened Kensington to the Albert Memorial.

His first call was Nollendorfstrasse. The street was even more down-at-heel than it had been in the 1930s. "The fronts of the buildings were pitted with shrapnel and eaten by rot and weather so that they had that curiously blurred, sightless look you see on the face of the Sphinx." Bombs had left gaps in the street, but No. 17 was still standing and Frl. Thurau, now in her seventies, was still living there—and still taking in lodgers, even though poverty had forced her to move into a smaller flat. She had managed to cram in most of her heavy old furniture and Isherwood was able to identify the bed he (and many others) had slept in and the table at which Isherwood the Artist had written every day. Among many familiar objects was the stylized bronze figure of a dolphin, which had a clock hanging from its upturned tail. It had been damaged during an air raid, but had been repaired and Frl. Thurau now presented it to Isherwood as a souvenir. He took it back to California, where it stood on his desk for the rest of his life, "a symbol of that indestructible something in a place and an environment that resists all change."

A more daunting reunion was the one Isherwood had with Heinz, now married and the father of a son. Heinz had written to Isherwood immediately after the war ended from an American prisoner-of-war camp in France. The standard-issue post-card had been sent care of the Hogarth Press and took some time to reach California. "Dear Mr Isherwood! You'll be astonished to hear from somebody whom you think will be already dead," Heinz wrote. "After I had a bad time in Germany as you may know, I had to become a soldier and was caught then at the Reihu-River. Who knows what my life will look like after I get discharged. Yours, effectionately [sic] H. Ned-dermeyer." Other cards followed, as well as several to Kathleen, detailing his release from the camp and his movement between the various national zones of Berlin. "It is wonderful to be in touch with him—although I suppose it might be years before we meet," Isherwood had written to Kathleen in 1946. "But now, at any rate, he won't vanish into post-war Germany without giving us an address." When he heard from Kathleen that Heinz was married, he declared: "it was just what I'd hoped for him [. . .] the girl sounds just the right sort of person for him, doesn't she?"

Isherwood left no record of his Berlin reunion with Heinz, but *Down There on a Visit* contains a fictionalized version of this meeting in which "Waldemar" asks "Isherwood" whether he would sponsor his family's emigration to the United States. He suggests that they could look after him in California, and be a family to him, but "Isherwood" proves evasive.

> 'I don't know,' I muttered, 'I'd have to think it over. My plans are so uncertain. We'll see. We'll write to each other—' It wasn't that I grudged the money. But I utterly refused to have a family. I was determined not to be anybody's Uncle. And yet, I felt guilty because I refused.

This is, of course, fiction, and may be based on a later request Heinz made, by letter in 1956, that Isherwood should sponsor his emigration to the States. On the other hand, if Heinz had asked this favor in 1952, or hinted at it, and Isherwood had felt guiltily obliged to refuse, it may explain why he made no record of their meeting and why, shortly after his return to London, he appeared to fall into a fit of despair. He burned a lot of letters, refused to re-record another radio program and got out of doing the second article for the *Observer*. Any number of things may have caused this depression. It was probably during the Berlin trip that Isherwood learned that the Nazis eventually caught up with his other companion on his 1933 journey to Greece, Erwin Hansen, who had died in a concentration camp. The reunion with Heinz re-minded him of a past that was now irrecoverable, a time when he was writing the books which made his reputation rather than struggling with a novel he was begin-ning to fear would never be any good even if he managed to finish it.

On board the *Queen Elizabeth,* shortly before docking in New York, Isherwood gave himself a pep talk, telling himself that he now had yet another opportunity to make a new start. He had to persist with his novel, finish the Patanjali translation, and write a piece on California for *Harper's Bazaar.* His relationships with Caskey and Charlton would sort themselves out; meanwhile he felt he needed to re-establish a proper contact with Prabhavananda and sort out the mess his life had become ever since his return from South America. He was still prey to "dullness and jitters" and to "really horrible vanity," but decided that "there is still some love and joy somewhere in this old pincushion of a heart." He told himself he should be thankful for his friends, though, significantly, those he named—Auden, Kirstein, Forster, Spender, Upward and Eric Falk—were either in New York or England. He also told himself that in spite of a long period of sterility, there was "something I still want to say in my writing—oh, I haven't even started." This, however, was somewhat undermined by his admonishing himself to "Fear not. Cling to what you know is real." A principal reason why he found writing *The School of Tragedy* so difficult was precisely because it was *not* real, did not reflect his own experiences, was about totally invented and insufficiently realized characters.

Still, he reasoned, reminding himself of the pioneering spirit that was so much a part of his adopted country: "One can only live here by being strong and standing alone. And how does one get to be strong and stand alone? By opening the heart to the source of all strength and all love and not-aloneness." Just how much of a muddle Isherwood was still in may be judged by the language he uses: an uneasy mix of the Hollywood Western and the revivalist meeting. "I shall expect you to keep this journal regularly—to revive the faculty of observation," he warned himself. "And to remind you of your job. And I *mean* observation. No personal moanings." This was good advice, since (as the Berlin trip perhaps reminded him) observation had indeed been the hallmark of his books, but it was advice he was unable to heed. He managed three brief paragraphs on one of his fellow passengers, then put aside the journal for over a fortnight.

No sooner had Isherwood arrived in New York than the old pincushion of his heart was pricked once more. On March 9 he was introduced to a twenty-four-year-old, who is called Sam Costidy in the published diaries, and Costidy's lover, the American poet Gerritt Lansing. Attractive without being conventionally handsome, Costidy was tall and stooped, had crooked teeth and bore the scars of childhood acne. A mutual friend described him as "emotionally appealing in a waif-like way," which is precisely why Isherwood was attracted to him. After a few days in New York, Isherwood persuaded Costidy to accompany him back to California. Lansing was due to follow shortly. The five days they spent in Bermuda en route provided Isherwood with another of those epiphanic moments that occasionally surprised him. "Today we cycled about eighteen miles and swam from a cove," he wrote on March 20. "What shall I say about it? There is nothing to say—directly. Except to state that this has certainly been the happiest day of my life since 1948, when I went to Ensenada with Jim."

Such moments were almost always connected with romance (rather than sex), and Costidy appealed to all Isherwood's older-brotherly instincts. "I will really truly and sincerely try to give him an experience of happiness—however he wants it—without intrusion of my dreary old show-off ego," Isherwood told himself. "I'm beginning to respect and like him so much. And I feel a certain identification with his problems, which helps." These problems were shyness and "a disgustingly weak will," but the young man also had qualities which Isherwood admired, including "a tremendous capacity for affection." This transformed Costidy's appearance for Isherwood. "Quite often, he looks touchingly and innocently beautiful, with his small sensitive rabbit nose and clear brilliant blue eyes," he wrote. "His voice is rather deep, and the general impression he makes is extremely masculine, though boyish [. . .] Standing alone [. . .] he looks like the last lone Irish immigrant, utterly abandoned by life, the predestined victim of all the wickedness of the world. Yesterday, we were out in the pouring rain in New York; and Sam wore my elegant raglan. By the time he was through with it, it looked like a garment which might be worn by a modern Oliver Twist." The appeal of Dickens's (or, more specifically, Jackie Coogan's) posh urchin, that innocent victim of the wickedness of the Victorian underworld, was an enduring one, and Costidy was already being transformed into an archetype. It was hardly his fault that he would be unable to live up to the demands of the role. More importantly, Costidy was also providing Isherwood with a "partial model" for Bob Wood, the doctor's young lover in his novel. Isherwood even managed to restart the book.

"I move blindly into the future," he declared at the end of the holiday. That future did not, however, really include Costidy, or any permanent partner. He spent some time at Trabuco, where he managed to finish the Patanjali translation and do substantial work on his novel, but he realized that in order to maintain this volume of production, he needed to live alone, with no dependents. He still found Costidy "sometimes so sweet he moves me to tears," but he was also "an expensive nuisance and a burden." "I am absolutely infatuated and at the same time quite cold, if you know what I mean," he told Kirstein. He was alarmed to learn that Gerritt Lansing, having found a job in New York, had decided not to come to California. Costidy was perfectly happy about this and would gladly have lived with Isherwood, who had been offered the garden house at Evelyn and Edward Hooker's home on Saltair Avenue in Brentwood. Jim Charlton had been commissioned to redesign the house, which he did at considerable expense, with custom-made teak shutters and furniture, and shelving with a row of glass globe lights under it. Everything was hand-crafted— and therefore took a long time to build and install. While waiting, Isherwood took up residence in a "tacky but clean apartment house" on Second Street in Santa Monica.

A visit from Caskey went so well that Isherwood felt "our relationship is permanently established," something that seemed possible now they were no longer living together or even in the same city. This also left him free to pursue other men, including Thomas E. Wright, a boyhood friend of Speed Lamkin who had come to the Hartford Foundation. According to Wright, Isherwood had been shown some of his work, but did not feel he could recommend the young man for a place at the Foundation. When he was shown a photograph of the applicant, however, he wondered whether he had made a mistake. Fortunately, Wright then had another piece of work published in the *Johns Hopkins Review,* and when Isherwood read this he felt he could put forward Wright's name with a clear conscience. Shortly after Wright's arrival at the Foundation, Isherwood dropped by to introduce himself and soon added Wright to the retinue of young men with whom he had sex without any fuss about commitment. This suited Wright, who also took the opportunity to hop into bed with Costidy—

with Isherwood's "tacit approval." He felt that no one really stood a chance with Isherwood while Caskey continued to "loom in the background," and Isherwood may well have been hoping that Wright would take Costidy off his hands. Wright did in fact perform this office after Isherwood and Costidy had a violent quarrel, which probably had to do with money. Isherwood's resources were certainly dwindling rapidly as Charlton continued his program of improvements to the garden house. Wright, whose spell at the Foundation had come to an end, wanted to visit his parents in Louisiana and took Costidy with him. He returned some time later without the troublesome young man, who never saw Isherwood again and subsequently married.

Although Isherwood reported in early June that he had become "wonderfully indifferent to alcohol" and that he planned to reduce his smoking by cutting each cigarette in half, a month later he was confessing that drinking and smoking were stalling progress on the novel. Charlton's own lack of progress on the house and the ballooning expenditure caused Isherwood further anxiety, particularly since *I Am a Camera* was finishing its Broadway run. In the autumn, however, he finally moved in. "It's the witch's cottage out of Hansel and Gretel, if the witch had had a nephew who'd studied under Frank Lloyd Wright," he told Spender. "The door is cocktail cherry red; the rest is the color of poisoned toffee." Caskey, who had returned from a trip to Japan where he had managed to catch clap from a geisha, immediately condemned Isherwood's new quarters as "chi-chi," but what he really objected to was that by making a home just for himself, Isherwood was establishing his independence. In a drunken rage one evening Caskey smashed all the globe lights. He nevertheless retained a certain romance for Isherwood, who dubbed him "Billy Budd-Caskey" and told Spender: "He has become the most famous seaman west of the Rockies, and there's nothing left for me to do but record his exploits."

Caskey's exploits certainly seemed more interesting than the novel Isherwood was still struggling to write. "It deals with all the subjects about which I know absolutely nothing, like marriage, the Austrian tirol [*sic*], heart disease and the American middle class," he confessed, "and I fear it is wishy-washy and dirty-sentimental." By the end of January 1953, however, he was able to report from Trabuco that he had finished a rough draft. Even with the assistance of Ramakrishna, to whom he had prayed for help, "it was a hard push all the way through." He sent a dispatch from the battlefield to Upward:

> After an examen de minuit scene in which reason really tottered on her throne, I said to myself Enough, and gave orders for a frontal attack on the material with everything we had. Throwing all sinuous approaches to the winds, we advanced straight to the end of the novel and arrived there the day before yesterday. True, it's rather like General Patton's rush into Germany. We'll probably have to withdraw and look at the map to find out what we've captured. Probably the position has no military value whatsoever.

Although what he had written seemed "the crudest nonsense," to have produced it at all was "a genuine victory": "I feel as if my whole future as a writer—and my sanity, almost—had been at stake."

Isherwood may have secured his future, but he nearly lost his whole past when he was woken up a few days later in his garden house by the smell of burning. A wire had short-circuited in his recently acquired Sunbeam-Talbot coupé and, fanned by a high wind, had started a fire in the garage, which was separated from the house by a plaster wall. "I left quite briskly in my pyjamas, and spent the next fifteen minutes under the impression that my house had surely caught too and that all my manuscripts, letters, books, clothes had gone," he told Kirstein. "It was a strangely exhilarating feeling: okay—here we go, a new start. But as soon as I discovered that the firemen were winning I was wild with anxiety about water coming through the ceiling and spoiling the Mexican rug." Fortunately, the fire had been caught in time and although his car was a complete write-off the house and its contents were unharmed.

Isherwood was, however, about to make a new start of a different sort. In his diary he had jotted down a list of names that seemed to express the diversity of America and its tradition of European immigration. Among the names was "Ted Baccardi." This was a phonetic rendering of the name "Bachardy," which was itself an immigration official's approximation of the family's original Hungarian name, which has now been forgotten. Isherwood had first noticed Ted on the beach at Santa Monica, and been particularly struck by his beautiful legs. In October 1952, Ted and his younger brother, Don, who had just enrolled at UCLA, received an invitation to after-dinner drinks with some friends who were entertaining Isherwood. "Ted and I were obviously being brought in for sex and entertainment," Don Bachardy recalled. They had several drinks and the next thing he knew, Don was standing up in the dining room being kissed by Isherwood. "We'd both had quite a lot to drink and lost our balance. We fell against the window and broke a small pane in it. I was horrified and scandalized at myself and immediately insisted that Ted and I should leave. Ted was warming up to have sex with one of the hosts, but as a dutiful older brother he escorted me home."

The following February, the brothers were on their way to the Will Rogers State Beach in Santa Monica, where homosexual men congregated to swim, sunbathe and size each other up, when Ted suggested they drop in on Isherwood for breakfast. Isherwood seemed pleased to see them and—always glad of an excuse to get away from his desk—decided to spend the day with them. They enjoyed themselves so much that they arranged to meet the following weekend. After a day at the beach they went to a party given by the playwright Jerome Lawrence. "Whether by plan or by accident, Ted found someone he wanted to spend the night with," Bachardy recalled. "I was going to be driven home first, but I thought that since Ted had his evening laid out nicely there was no reason I shouldn't go home with Chris—and he seemed willing." It was February 14, 1953, St. Valentine's Day.

TWENTY

LITTLE DID ISHERWOOD REALIZE, WHEN HE LED THE EAGER YOUNG freshman back to Saltair Avenue, that he had his future in tow. Bachardy was a slight figure, with neat, fair hair and a wide grin that displayed an appealing Huck Finn gap between his two front teeth. Although eighteen, he looked a great deal younger. Even in his late twenties, he would still shop for boys' formal suits, which fitted him perfectly and cost half the price of adult ones. At forty-eight, Isherwood was slightly older than his new lover's father. Standing beside Bachardy in a photograph taken that year, sporting his "faux-brutal" crewcut and a houndstooth-check sports jacket, he looks alarmingly like a scoutmaster with his favorite cub.

Bachardy's grandmother had left Hungary for America in the early years of the century. She was of peasant stock, pregnant, recently widowed, and spoke not a word of English. Several of her children had already immigrated to America and she decided to join them after her husband accidentally drowned. Water continued to feature significantly in her life, since her youngest child, Jess, grew up to become a cargo man on the Great Lakes. It was here that he met his future wife, Glade, whose father was a boat captain. Although old Mrs. Bachardy never learned much English, Jess had been born in America and had a horror of being thought "foreign." By marrying Glade, he felt that he would become fully assimilated. It was probably Jess's comparatively lowly job, rather than his origins, that opposed Glade's father to the match, but Glade was a very determined young woman. The newlyweds started their married life in California, but it was the Depression and work was scarce. After two months they were forced to return to Glade's family home in Cleveland, Ohio. Jess eventually found work with the Lockheed Corporation, working his way up to become a tool-planner, someone who looked at a proposed job and decided what equipment would be needed. Their first child, Ted, was born in 1930, their second, Don, in 1934, by which time the family had settled back in Los Angeles.

The two boys shared their mother's love of the movies and by the age of five Don was a regular cinema-goer. Like Isherwood, he was a born film fan. What interested

—or not in the way we used to think it did. What matters is the experience and understanding of life. Sometimes the writing is an end-product of the understanding. Sometimes you get the understanding by actually going through the process of writing. Art is just another kind of yoga, and I think one might become very wise even in the process of writing something quite bad. I mean, the wisdom doesn't always seem to get into the writing.

Isherwood does not say what he learned in the process of writing *The World in the Evening*—which was certainly very bad indeed—except that he could still construct a book and complete it.

Isherwood may have dodged Upward's verdict, but he sent the novel to the Beesleys. They were duly appalled. "It is the only work of Chris's we have really disliked," Smith confided in her diary.

It is written in the first person, but the narrator is not, as in the past, Chris himself. And, as far as I am concerned (and Alec) he is not anyone. None of the characters really lives for me. In one thing, they seem to have no physique. And the overpowering amount of sex in the book is not so much shocking as embarrassing. The narrator has one affair after the other, both normal and homosexual. And the homosexual love scenes are as bad as such scenes usually are. And the normal sex scenes don't, to me, ring true. There is little humour—and what there is is weak. In some parts, the book is actually boring—an unbelievable fault for an Isherwood book.

Of course, there is much to praise—some admirable pieces of description. And some vitality. And we praised like mad . . .

They did indeed. "We both think you have done a brilliant job of work," Smith told the author.

The form of the book is so clever that it conceals its cleverness. One scarcely realizes the transitions of time and place. The whole thing just flows along as if it were straightforward narrative. One is never held up to think, 'Let's see—are we in the present or the past.' You have brought the whole idea off marvellously [. . .]

All the characters are absolutely vivid. And there is no sign anywhere that the book has been an agony to write [. . .]

I cannot find anything to criticize as regards construction, dialogue, characterization. I haven't even been able to dig up my usual finicky suggestions as regards punctuation or tiny unclearnesses—

though she did, characteristically, note that a dog previously described as having one eye apparently has two a few pages further on.

Having reiterated her opinion that she considered the book "a tremendous success and a very fine achievement," Smith ventured "one or two reservations" in response to Isherwood's request that she should be "really frank." In her diary she described herself and Alec "wrapping our criticisms up by saying we were probably fuddy-duddies as regards sex scenes (quite untrue, really)." The Beesleys had of course been around the theater long enough not to be shocked by homosexuality *per se,* and they counted numerous homosexual men and women among their close friends, but like many British people of their generation they preferred such matters to be understood rather than described. "The truth of the matter is that the sex is a mite too wild for me," Smith told Isherwood. "I found it all wildly interesting, but it made me a bit lose sympathy with Stephen. This wouldn't be the case in real life, I'm sure. There is nothing you could tell me about yourself, for instance, that would ever make me like you less. But in a book, things get crystallized." She went on to say that *she* could just about believe that Gerda would go to bed with Stephen, but doubted whether the reading public would, and that furthermore she found the scene unsympathetic. Acting on this vote of no confidence, Isherwood altered the passage so that Stephen and Gerda almost go to bed but in the end decide not to.

It was left to Alec to tell Isherwood—quite rightly—that the scenes between Stephen, Charles and Bob were embarrassing. Both Beesleys said that they regretted that Isherwood had deleted the refugees from the narrative, but both ended on further notes of congratulation, and assurances that they were proud to be the novel's dedicatees. The truth was they hated the book. Smith blamed its failure on the company Isherwood kept in California. "It is destroying his sense of values and even his taste," she complained. "He needs the company of his peers—as almost every writer does. I believe America has almost ruined his talent."

Isherwood no doubt saw through the Beesleys' protestations about the book's *overall* excellence, particularly since a few years earlier he had himself been "forced to say something complimentary" to Smith in a fulsome letter about her novel, *I Capture the Castle,* which he unjustly dismissed in his diary as "mere magazine writing." After receiving their verdict, he wrote to Upward:

> Last night, I dreamt I showed you my novel, saying 'always, before, when I finished something, I've felt it was pretty good. This time, I'm sure it isn't'. And then you made some kind of problème de style noise or gesture, briefly designating the anfractuous rocks, and I instantly saw how the whole thing could be rewritten from beginning to end. It had something, I remember, to do with a cliff-plant which had small flowers which were, or resembled, tiny hard-boiled eggs.

This Mortmerish solution to the problem had come too late, since Isherwood had already sent typescripts, "for better or for worse," to his American and British publishers. "I'm curious to know what you'll think," he told Bob Linscott. "At least, it's a new departure." Linscott didn't know quite what to think when this extraordinary novel landed on his desk.

"Forgive my tardiness in writing you," he eventually replied.

> A first reading of THE WORLD IN THE EVENING left me in a mood of such ambivalence that I put it aside for a second and more objective reading. For I love the writing and everything about Elizabeth, but I'm troubled by the character of Stephen, the double underlining of the inversion [i.e. homosexual] motif, and the ending.

To me Stephen somehow rings hollow in the extent of his obtuseness and lack of empathy. (How could Elizabeth have loved him?) Mightn't he be made a little more perceptive; a little more understanding of people and situations?

The second criticism is also partly of character. To have two inversion episodes strikes me as bearing down a little heavily on this note, but it's the false (to me) heartiness of Bob Wood that makes me most uneasy. Also I wish you would consider toning down the crucial paragraph on page 202 [in which Stephen is seduced by a young man called Michael during a mountaineering expedition in the Canary Islands].

My criticism of Part III seems to boil down to its patness; the problems solved, the chords resolved, and everybody happy.

Linscott cited several other scenes that troubled him, echoing many of the Beesleys' concerns, and concluded: "It's a melancholy business to criticize a favorite author, but, God help him, the editor must tell the truth as he sees it. Anyway, and in spite of these criticisms, I want you to know that we will be glad to publish the novel exactly as is if you so desire."

Isherwood replied that he was glad that Linscott liked "most of the book" and would certainly consider his comments very carefully. He also asked the editor to be more specific about the passages he found "offensive." Linscott replied that this put him on the spot: "it's the tone rather than the words themselves that makes me uneasy." He did, however, supply some examples of Bob's linguistic "boisterousness": " 'Stop talking crap.' 'You're pretty God darn broadminded.' 'Why do you think I stick around this dump?' 'It does something for the old curves.' 'Lap up the joy juice.' 'Jesus, how unworthy of me can you get?' 'He'll drag your holiest secrets down in the gutter and mash them with his hooves.' " He also remained worried by the scene in which Stephen and Michael go to bed and suggested "omitting the whole paragraph beginning 'In the dark . . .' or at least the word 'cuddling,' " and the scene in which Stephen and Gerda almost end up in bed, which he found unconvincing. Finally, he thought Stephen and Jane's reconciliation at the novel's close had "too much heartiness and joviality."

By the time Isherwood wrote back, he had received what he called "quite a number of reactions to the novel," many of them he said "unreservedly favorable." Apart from asking that the Stephen-Michael episode be toned down, Alan White at Methuen seemed very pleased. "I have never in all my experience had such an enthusiastic prepublication letter from any publisher. 'Much your best book,' etc. etc." Whether or not Isherwood believed this, he evidently felt that White's letter could be used to argue against too many changes. He did, however, promise Linscott that he would rewrite the scenes to which he had objected, but added: "I am not going to do anything whatsoever about Stephen, as such, except make him a little less priggishly noble at the end; and I'm not going to eliminate either of the homosexual episodes. If I were to do so, the entire balance of the book would be upset. You see, its working-title is really 'Ghosts,' and everything has to happen twice or be somehow echoed or repeated in another key." He completed the revisions by the end of November, deciding eventually that Stephen should go to North Africa alone to serve with an ambulance unit (a detail borrowed from Ian Scott-Kilvert) rather than with Charles

Kennedy, as he originally planned. He sent these off to Linscott with a rather pompous page of notes explaining what he had—and hadn't—done.

I sherwood spent Christmas 1953 in New York, which "was a huge success: that is to say, Donny really loved it." This, increasingly, was how Isherwood would judge things. What he did not know was that one of the reasons Donny really loved it was that he had met George Platt Lynes, who fell in love with him at first sight. Platt Lynes took a series of photographs of Bachardy and started sending him passionate letters. "I want you. I want you here," he wrote from New York in February. "But what the hell am I to do about this?" He felt that he could not "in good conscience" attempt to detach Bachardy from Isherwood, but added: "probably conscience has nothing to do with the case—in circumstances like these it has a wonderful way of not asserting itself." Bachardy's own conscience proved equally unassertive and he spent some time secretly corresponding with Platt Lynes. "He was infatuated," Bachardy recalled, "really just because of my youth, and he would, if he could, have taken me away from Chris, maybe for six months or a year, and would then find somebody a little bit younger than I was. I think I knew that then. I was nineteen and I was flattered. He seemed to me a glamorous creature, but I knew that he was no-body to rely on. I wanted to encourage Lynes, but I could only have seen him when I went to New York with Chris, and what would have been the point?"

As was customary, Isherwood greeted the New Year with a list of goals and projects, the chief of which was "a more intentional life." Among the projects under consideration was an anthology of English short stories commissioned for Dell by Frank Taylor, a bisexual movie producer and book editor whom Isherwood had got to know in Hollywood. Isherwood had also been persuaded by Prabhavananda to undertake a biography of Ramakrishna, and had promised an article for Lehmann's new venture, *London Magazine*. Keen not to waste discarded material from *The World in the Evening,* he was also planning to write a short story about the refugees, perhaps somehow putting this together with stories based on the diaries he had kept while visiting Basil Fry in Bremen and Fronny on St. Nicholas. The other thing he wanted to do was to turn the edited version of the diaries he had kept during his first five years in the United States into a book.

None of these was likely to generate much in the way of income, and since he was now also supporting Bachardy, Isherwood was greatly relieved when MGM offered him the job of writing a script for a film based on the life of Diane de Poitiers. Before getting the job, however, he was obliged to answer some questions about his past. A Republican senator from Wisconsin named Joseph McCarthy had managed to persuade America that the entire infrastructure of the country was riddled with communists. His investigations were about to result in a series of "hearings" before the preposterously named House Un-American Activities Committee. Various public figures were interrogated in public and the whole circus was shown on television. Isherwood had already signed a petition demanding a review of the case of the so-called "Hollywood Ten," a group of writers, producers and directors who had been jailed and subsequently blacklisted for refusing to answer when asked whether they were or had ever been members of the Communist Party. Isherwood's own record as a leading figure in the distinctly left-wing literary culture of the 1930s Britain, not to mention his association with the Soviet spy Guy Burgess, meant that the studio thought it advisable to give him a grilling before employing him. He was called in to an office and presented with a list of reports from left-wing publications that suggested he may have had links with communist organizations. It had been noted, for example, that in February 1936 the *New International* reported that "one Christopher Isherwood collaborated with W. H. Auden on play 'The Dog Beneath the Skin,' a story condemning a decaying capitalist world." Isherwood was also reported as having contributed an article on the Sino-Japanese War to *New Masses,* "cited as a Communist periodical by US Attorney General, 9–24–42," and the *Socialist New Leader* had apparently noted his authorship of "the play 'Lions and Shadows' " in 1948. (These reports were compiled by agents of the FBI, whose knowledge of literary and indeed many other matters was severely limited.) Isherwood was also presented with "evidence" of the communist sympathies of Salka Viertel and her former daughter-in-law Virginia (who had previously been married to the left-wing writer Budd Schulberg) and was asked for his comments.

On January 21 Isherwood wrote a letter to Loews Incorporated, the owners of MGM, to assure them of his innocence. "As I explained to Mr [Marvin] Schenck, the chief political emotion of the thirties was anti-fascism, and none of us are to be blamed if we welcomed as allies any political party which promised cooperation against Hitler. That we were deceived by the communist party in this connection is a matter of history." He claimed to "know nothing" about Salka Viertel's "alleged political activities" and said he had never heard Virginia discuss politics. He was less inclined now to show solidarity with the Hollywood Ten.

> I did not, as is stated, 'protest' the case against the Hollywood Ten. I merely signed a petition requesting a review of their case, without saying that I necessarily believed in their innocence. I did this with entirely non-political motives—simply as a civil liberties issue. I acted in good faith at the time, but I think that I should have informed myself much more fully before taking this step, and I don't think I would do the same thing now—I mean, in relation to this particular case.
>
> I am not, and never have been, a member of the communist party. I have never knowingly contributed money to the party funds, even indirectly. As a naturalized citizen, I have been thoroughly investigated by the FBI and the Immigration Department, and I have never been accused of the smallest disloyalty towards the USA. If I may say so, I think that the communist party has no more determined enemies than liberals such as myself. The tendency to confuse liberals and communists in not only completely unfair; it is actually playing into the hands of the communists themselves. I am sure that you, gentlemen, are well aware of this; and I make this personal explanation to you with confidence that you will receive it as friends, not judges.

MGM was entirely satisfied with this fulsome self-exculpation, and four days later Isherwood signed a contract to work on the new film at a salary of $1,000 a week. Some years later Isherwood admitted that one of the things he was most ashamed of in his life was "having consented to answer the loyalty questions which Marvin Schenck put to me." He added: "This always rankles, but, on the other hand, it gave me a chance to put in a good word for Salka and for Virginia, and I said nothing that wasn't true." He recognized, however, that his principal concern at the time was that he might have lost out on the job, or even have been put on "an 'unco-operative' list." One of the attractions of working on the film, apart from the financial stability it brought, was that it absolved Isherwood from having to do any of his own work. "Everything is conveniently shelved until the film is finished," he admitted.

In February he took a lease on a modest house at 364 Mesa Road in Santa Monica and moved in with Bachardy, who had left UCLA to enroll at Los Angeles City College. One good reason for Bachardy to continue his education was that students were exempt from the draft. The prospect of Bachardy's having to serve in the forces, particularly during the politically volatile mid-1950s, became one more thing for Isherwood to worry about obsessively. He had begun to feel that his relationship with Bachardy might endure for some time, and had even given up his "harem" of young men, devoting himself exclusively to his young partner. This did not please Caskey, who still felt that he could drop in without notice, treating Isherwood's new house more or less as his own. He remained as proprietorial as any reluctant divorcée and made it clear that he regarded Bachardy as a gold-digging interloper. For his part, Bachardy had by now become disengaged from Platt Lynes, who died of lung cancer the following year.

Bachardy was still very young and uncertain. "I had really no identity," he recalled. "I was still going to college and I knew that wasn't leading me anywhere I wanted to go." As far as Isherwood's friends were concerned, he felt, his identity was simply that of Chris's latest boy, and none of them took him at all seriously. He was intelligent, but no one seemed very interested in what he might have to say, and they were inclined to ignore him at social occasions. He felt that even Isherwood sometimes treated him like a child and complained, for instance, that on one occasion Isherwood discussed *On the Waterfront* with Caskey in a way he never would with him. He was quick to take offense, and if he felt he had been slighted or overlooked he would fly into a rage or sulk.

Bachardy's character was reflected in the nickname Isherwood had given him: "Kitty." Like any domestic cat, his mood could change in an instant: at one minute he would be docile and affectionate, the next he would unsheathe his claws, lash out and wound. He gave every appearance of being reliant upon Isherwood, yet retained a fierce independence and would often prove entirely unbiddable. Isherwood characterized himself as "Dobbin" (sometimes "Dub" or "Drub"), a plodding old workhorse, carrying his burdens through life with a certain stoicism. They referred to themselves as "the Animals," and any representation of cats or horses acquired a sentimental significance for them. Like all such play-acting between lovers, this was a mythology that remained essentially private. These persona were related to the "nursery atmosphere" in which Isherwood always felt most comfortable domestically, and "the Animals in their basket"—that is, the bed they shared—conjured up a domestic ideal of physical coziness and companionship, a private refuge from other humans. It was also a refuge from their own more complicated and antagonistic relationship. John Osborne's *Look Back in Anger* would provide Isherwood with another example of this idea, of "how a myth can keep a marriage going":

When Jimmy and Alison find it intolerable to go on being themselves and still relate to each other, they change focus and become The Bear and The Squirrel in
their private myth world. And instantly they are happy and safe, because, in the
world of animals, hatred is impossible; The Bear and The Squirrel can only love
each other. They focus their aggression on mythical external enemies.

Isherwood had spent his life focusing his aggression upon representatives of the
Enemy, the Others, those he elevated to mythic status as a way of dealing with them.
One of the strongest bonds that would develop between Isherwood and Bachardy
would be their sense of standing together against those who disapproved of them.

At one point, at Bachardy's urging, Isherwood even started keeping a separate
diary to record this parallel animal life. "I'll try to write it rather like a study in natural history," he decided; "their behavior, methods of communication, feeding habits,
etc." He did not get very far, perhaps because, as he acknowledged right from the
start, he felt that writing such an account would constitute "an invasion of privacy."
He reasoned with himself that "The privacy of the unconscious is the only store-
house," but in the end he may have felt that to study and record this imaginary world
would destroy it.

Although he was sometimes less than tactful when out with Bachardy in company, Isherwood could also be fiercely protective. In July he drunkenly punched the
filmmaker Curtis Harrington in the face after a friend of Harrington's made a pass at
Bachardy during a party. Isherwood's aggression was normally vented verbally and
in his diaries, and this unexpected loss of control was a costly mistake. Harrington issued a writ for assault, demanding $600 in damages. The case was eventually settled
out of court, with Harrington accepting $350, but it was a worrying and humiliating
episode.

Isherwood was beginning to agree with Gerald Heard, who regarded the relationship with Bachardy "as a most significant biological (or should I say evolutionary?)
experiment." Heard urged him to make a record of this experiment, but Isherwood
had lost the habit of keeping a diary, and could always use the demands of his work
at MGM as a reason for not writing anything else. "Slowly, slowly," he told himself
in November, after he had finished the revisions of the script and run out of excuses.
"Make no plans for writing. Don't say: I *ought* to write. Just wait until inspiration orders. Be content with daily jottings. Put down anything that occurs to you, however
seemingly silly. *All* that matters is to cultivate the habit of recording. I've been saying that for the last thirty years—and yet I don't do it." It was not until March the following year that he began recording his life again with any regularity.

On August 26, 1954 Isherwood celebrated his fiftieth birthday. Work on *Diane*
would keep him occupied for some time yet, but the long-term problem he faced was
"what to do with the next twenty years." The publication of *The World in the Evening*
in June had done little to boost any confidence he might have had in his future as a
novelist. Although there were occasional words of praise, most critics were gravely
disappointed by the book. Before revising the novel, Isherwood had confessed to Upward: "It is terribly slipshod, and vulgar and sentimental at times in a Hollywoodish
way, and there is a great deal of sex, including some homosexual scenes which will

shock many people, I dare say, worse than anything I've written—though they're not in the least pornographic."

There is no doubt that for some people, the mere mention of homosexuality was enough to damn the book. A Miss Edith Shackleton, writing about the novel in *The Lady* (of all places), described Michael as "a perverted youth" and went on: "I deplore Mr Isherwood's lapse into a fashion of today's writers of detailed dwelling on homosexuality. Abnormality cannot inspire any great work of fiction. There are passages in *The World in the Evening* which almost make one wish for a return of the savage old restrictions—not so much from disgust as from boredom." Even those less inclined to condemn homosexuality out of hand were worried by Isherwood's handling of this controversial theme—"with more social courage than literary discretion," as Peter Quennell aptly put it in the *Daily Mail*. Angus Wilson, writing in *Encounter,* found the characters of Bob and Charles particularly egregious examples of "embarrassing facetious 'goodness.' " The author of a recent novel, *Hemlock and After,* in which homosexual characters were treated with a refreshing lack of condescension or special pleading, Wilson rightly complained: "From their first appearance, the tone of their relationship is set in this awful, selfconsciously humorous key [. . .] The reason, I think, for this extraordinary lapse of judgement is a curious confusion between 'goodness' and 'cosiness.' " Some homosexual readers, grateful for any positive depiction of homosexuality in fiction, reacted more favorably. "I have lots and lots of fan-mail of the type you can guess," Isherwood told Spender. "I believe if I gave the word, right now, I could start a queer revolution; they are just longing for a Hitler, poor dears. I don't mean that nastily, and I don't really mean a Hitler. Actually, it's heart breaking, the sense you get of all these island existences, dotted about like stars and nebulae, all over the great black middle west." The poet Thom Gunn recalls that he found the book "empowering," placing the word in heavy quotation marks and adding: "Still, I was young then." Gunn, who had recently come to live in California, wrote a long, considered and generous review of the book for *London Magazine.*

It was not merely the subject matter that struck some people as unworthy of the author, however; it was the prose style. Isherwood described the novel as his "cleverest and worst book," but later came to believe that it was "not nearly as bad" as the critics claimed. It was. Although it is well constructed and boasts some fine passages, it also contains some startlingly dud writing, particularly in the dialogue. "If his name was not on the title page no one would guess that this book is by Christopher Isherwood," wrote Edwin Muir in the *Observer,* a sentiment echoed by the reviewer in *Punch,* who felt obliged to assure readers that "The author's name at the head of this notice is not a misprint."

Not everyone thought the book a disaster, and several friends, including Salka Viertel and Glenway Wescott, wrote encouraging letters. Upward, as was customary, was more frank. Isherwood had not arranged for him to be sent a copy of the novel, perhaps hoping to escape judgment, but Upward managed to obtain a review copy. He praised the book's construction and successful use of flashback, but complained that the characters "just don't seem to matter much." Spender perhaps put his finger on what was fundamentally wrong with the book. Having heroically read it three times, he told Isherwood: "Its defect, I think, is that you are of the devil's party, but you wrote about it during a period when you were trying to have a love affair with virtue. The result is that it lacks the moral certainty and diabolical charity of a book like Mr Norris. You don't love your characters enough because you don't let yourself hate them enough. Therefore the reader is inclined to hate them a bit for you." Isherwood acknowledged the justice of this. "I believe I have learned my lesson about this," he replied. "I think I forgot because I was so engrossed in getting the technical part of it right." He later acknowledged the fatal mistake he had made with the novel, one that undermined it right from the start. "I can't write an 'I' who isn't me. I tried to call Stephen 'I' and just hope for the best. In real life [I] wd have hated him."

No author enjoys a bad press, but Isherwood was more vulnerable than most. He had been wounded out of all proportion by a comic strip in *Punch* earlier in the year. Presumably inspired by Stravinsky's recent opera, Ronald Searle had drawn a series titled "The Rake's Progress," in which various types were seen stumbling through life. In "The Poet," a composite Thirties figure with curly hair is depicted following that well-worn path: discovering *The Waste Land* at university, settling in Berlin, joining the International Brigade, appearing in *Horizon,* and ending up in Los Angeles in a mescaline haze with Aldous Huxley. Searle introduced most of the notable figures of the period in the captions to each cartoon, and the second picture showed the foppish Rake, cigarette holder drooping, sitting in the Romanisches Café and gazing raptly out of the window at a passing group of *Lederhosen*-clad, pert-bottomed *Wandervögels.* "Captivated by German Youth Movement," ran the caption. "Settles in Berlin. Shakes hands with W. H. Aud*n and Christopher Ish*rwood. Deported." It was mild enough, but Isherwood was hurt by it. "My besetting fault is the same as it has always been," he commented at the time "—a vanity which is hypersensitive to criticism. I just can't bear to see one member of the audience yawning—even if it's someone I'd ordinarily despise as a dolt." This, of course, is precisely the criticism Connolly leveled at him when he said that Isherwood's "greatest defect is ingratiation—he charms the reader because he doesn't really trust him."

What mattered, though, was that in spite of everything, Isherwood had managed to produce a book at all. He presented the Beesleys with a bound typescript of the novel, inscribed:

> That this is no masterpiece is really beside the point. At least it is a symbol of the great pains taken and not for one moment regretted. And I can't ever be grateful enough to you both for helping me win a moral and psychological victory—what a big one it was, I'm only just beginning to discover!

"I had to break the spell and write that full-length contraption novel," he told Upward. "Now I'm allowed to do as I please." What that was he still had to decide.

By October, Isherwood had finished revising the script of *Diane.* In search of youth and vigor, he was undergoing a course of vitamin and hormone injections, even though he had been warned by Bill Kiskadden that the latter might cause prostate cancer. His financial future seemed reasonably secure since there was a promise of further work on *Diane* as it went into production, and he had been asked by the film's producer, Eddie Knopf, if he'd be interested in writing a screenplay about the life of the Buddha.

In December Isherwood and Bachardy went with the Masselinks on an extended trip to Mexico. The threat of the draft had finally lifted. Bachardy had gone before the board clutching a letter from Evelyn Hooker which stated that he was homosexual. The army was in a difficult but self-inflicted position when it came to the sexuality of its draftees. On the one hand, it did not want to recruit homosexual men, and on the other it resented the fact that men could avoid the draft by claiming to be homosexual. Not wishing to let this young degenerate off lightly, the army psychiatrist insisted Bachardy should appear before another board, which he did the day before he left for Mexico. He was classified 4-F, unfit for military service.

Traveling once again spurred Isherwood to start keeping a diary, but the trip also triggered something more important. While attending a fiesta in Álamos, he

> glimpsed an idea for a novel. Something quite unlike me—Kafkaesque—about a journey. A journey which is meticulously described and yet unreal: the reality being the relationships between the characters. Maybe they are all dead—as, in a sense, the characters are in Hemingway's *The Sun Also Rises.* Also I see elements in it of *The Day's Journey,* my projected film.[1]

A month later, back in Santa Monica, he noted that "The novel seems attractive, though still very vague"—and it would remain so for some considerable time.

Now that Isherwood was living with a film fan as ardent as himself, much of his social life revolved around Hollywood. He was still a little in awe of some of the stars—an unimpressed Natasha Spender was taken to the commissary in order to enjoy the thrill of having lunch at a table next to Clark Gable's—but was now well enough known around the studios to invite almost anyone to dinner or drinks. Thom Gunn, who had come to California with a letter of introduction from John Lehmann, remembers that he and his boyfriend, Mike Steen, met all sorts of famous people with Isherwood and Bachardy. He once attended a dinner at which the other guests were Aldous and Maria Huxley and Janet Gaynor and Adrian, the costume designer. "It was quite a dinner party for two young men in their twenties to be asked to," Gunn recalled. "They were all of them terribly old, of course." And indeed terribly queer, Huxley being the only fully paid-up heterosexual present. (Forgetful of his "lavender" marriage to Gaynor, Adrian spent most of the evening eyeing Steen.) Isherwood complained that he didn't really enjoy parties, and always drank too much, but people still came round regularly. A characteristic diary entry from this period reads: "Last night were Salka, Peter Viertel [her son], the [Robert] Parrishes and Lauren Bacall, who later took us to her house where we watched *To Have and Have Not.* Judy Garland came in, very fat, with her husband. I like Betty Bogart, who's a very lively

---

1. This film, which was never made, would depict a single day in someone's life which would represent the whole of that life.

do-it-yourself kind of girl. Don loved every minute." Not that you could rely on such people. A preposterously starry birthday party Isherwood planned for Bachardy, hosted by Marguerite and Harry Brown, ended in disaster. The guest list included Garland, Bacall, Lana Turner, Joan Crawford, Burt Lancaster, Dorothy McGuire, Shelley Winters and Marlon Brando, almost none of whom bothered to turn up.

There were, however, people in Hollywood who became real friends, among them Cecil Beaton, Leslie Caron, Charles Brackett, George Cukor, Doris Dowling, Jack Larson and James Bridges, and Don Murray and Hope Lange. What these people had in common was that they were Bachardy's friends as much as they were Isherwood's. It was important not merely to acknowledge Bachardy as Isherwood's partner, but to value him in his own right—something old friends such as Ben and Jo Masselink did right from the start. This was perhaps easiest with other couples such as the Murrays and Larson and Bridges, who were in any case closer to Bachardy than Isherwood in age. Part of the attraction of Marguerite Brown for Isherwood was that she would be a "playmate" for Bachardy, and she took to this role with enthusiasm, organizing dinners and parties and spending a lot of time with him—so much so that at times Isherwood began to feel rather jealous.

On January 31, 1955, Isherwood signed another contract with MGM at an increased salary of $1,250 a week. He spent much of his time sitting in his office at the studio while his secretary read books about the Buddha on his behalf, but he eventually got down to writing the screenplay. He was also on hand for the casting and filming of *Diane,* ready to rewrite lines that the actors found difficult. For all his joking to Lincoln Kirstein about working on "a nistorical opus about Catherine de Medici, Henri Doo of France, and Diane de Poitiers, who kept beautiful by taking an ice-cold bathe every morning," Isherwood had conceived the film as a serious work with a European cast headed by Ingrid Bergman. "MetroGoldwynMire," as he dubbed his employers, had other ideas. When informed that Lana Turner would be taking the title role, Isherwood insisted to a skeptical Gore Vidal: "Lana can do it." She couldn't, and wasn't much helped by having Roger Moore as her love interest, nor by an international supporting cast including the Italian Marisa Pavan as Catherine de Medici and the Mexican Pedro Armendariz as Henri. Isherwood had seen Armendariz in the 1948 adaptation of John Steinbeck's *The Pearl,* a film in which he thought the Mexican cast's delivery of English lines "made the dialogue sound ridiculously clumsy." He'd heard that Armendariz in fact spoke fluent English, but commented: "If so, he deliberately faked a thick Mexican accent to fit in with the others." Whether or not the actor could speak clearly was hardly the point by the time they came to shoot *Diane:* "I'm afraid Armendariz just isn't much good," Isherwood was obliged to concede. Nor, indeed, was anyone else. Turner was too old for the part and both she and Pavan struck Isherwood as essentially "amateurs." As for the men, Torin Thatcher (playing Henri) behaved like Hollywood rather than French royalty, treating Isherwood's script with "disgusted condescension," while Roger Moore's legs, exposed by the period costume, were not up to Isherwood's exacting standards.

One might have thought that writing such a film (which at one point was going to be retitled *The Gilded Cage*) would hardly be very rewarding work, but Isherwood claimed to have enjoyed it. "I steal bits from Balzac, Dumas and history, and have lots of poignards, poison and purple velvet," he told Plomer delightedly. He even believed, in the face of all the evidence and the dreadful reviews, that his script was not to blame for the film's failure. When he finally saw the movie after its release, he rightly described it as "a hideous mess—so badly cut and directed and (for the most part) acted." He nevertheless added: "But now I quite clearly know that I'm not in the least ashamed of the script. Many of the scenes are still excellent. But of course no one else has noticed or will ever notice this." With lines such as "There is more than beauty on those shoulders, Madame," "Does duty bid me swear a lie before the holy altar?" and "I would be loved as a woman, not as a goddess," this is not altogether surprising. Dodie Smith reported that Isherwood subsequently consulted her about writing drama:

> He wanted to know what I meant by dramatic construction, technique, etc. And, my God, judging by the two film scripts he brought for me to read, he needs to know [. . .] Chris's dialogue in [*Diane*] is utterly flat, and bad even as modern dialogue, let alone period dialogue. There is no characterization. And the story-line is slack and dreary. It is heartbreaking to think of Chris wasting his time doing a job not worth doing extremely badly, while the years slide by and his brilliant promise as a novelist is never fulfilled. He seems quite oblivious that the work is bad and gave a happy description of how he dictated it to a secretary with the greatest enjoyment.

The reviewers agreed, both *Variety* and the *Hollywood Reporter* complaining that Isherwood's script was "wordy and slow." The film also got bad notices in England, which was particularly depressing for Isherwood since he was in London when it opened. Indeed, the trip he and Bachardy made to England in the winter of 1955 was altogether dispiriting. The idea had been to have a break from Isherwood's long spell in MGM's gilded cage and to give Bachardy a European tour. Isherwood had finished and revised his script for the Buddha film, *The Wayfarer,* by September (it was never made), and in October he and Bachardy flew to New York, where they spent a couple of days with Julie Harris and her husband and seeing their East Coast friends before boarding a liner for Gibraltar. "When the great ship thundered goodbye to the echoing towers of Manhattan, I could hardly hold back my tears—it was so beautiful," Isherwood wrote in his diary "—the Hudson full of fussing tugboats and brimming with silver light—the thought that it was Don's first voyage, never to be quite duplicated for him."

The trip would take in several places to which Isherwood had traveled with Heinz in the 1930s, and their first port of call was Lisbon. They had a couple of hours in the city before traveling to Tangier, where they visited Isherwood's old Berlin acquaintance Paul Bowles and smoked *kif*. Heard and Huxley had been investigating the uses of drugs to induce different states of consciousness, and Isherwood had been very displeased to discover that the two sages had decided he should not be allowed to take mescaline because "it would undoubtedly prove fatally habit-forming." Isherwood was determined to procure some mescaline himself in New York. A friend of Denny Fouts had provided seven tablets, but Isherwood was waiting for the right moment to take them.

Isherwood now found Bowles's offer to try both *kif* and *majoon* irresistible, particularly without Heard and Huxley there to monitor his reactions. It was as well that they weren't, since once Isherwood had allowed the drug to take hold ("I was aware that part of me was fighting the action of the drug," he recalled), the experience was highly unpleasant. "I'm fairly certain that, if I had taken this stuff among real friends, the effect would have been quite different," he noted in the long account he wrote up in his diary. "As it was, I saw myself now as a pretty wretched creature, scared, claustrophobic, utterly insecure. I was afraid [Bowles and his other guests] would leave me alone. I was aware that I was terrified of being on my own." He felt tired and time seemed to pass very slowly. Bachardy appeared to be having no reaction to the drugs, but then suddenly became paranoid, believing that the others were plotting against them and insisting that he and Isherwood leave. They did so and started making their way back to their hotel. Isherwood felt an additional responsibility for Bachardy while trying to deal with his own fears: at one point he imagined that their taxi driver might be an "agent" of Bowles, but instead of returning them to his "master," the driver delivered them to their hotel. They spent the next two and a half hours in terror. Bachardy, who had his own reasons to fear mental disturbance,[2] began to believe that he was caught in a world of illusion and was in reality still in California but had become insane. Isherwood himself, though still too frightened to switch off the light, gradually remembered that what he was experiencing was the result of the hashish. When the effects of the drug finally wore off, they slept soundly and the following day suffered no serious after-effects.

Oddly enough, although Isherwood recorded this episode in great detail, he did not analyze it at all. The drug appears to have enhanced traits already present: Isherwood's fear of not being in command, Bachardy's insecurity. The other thing Isherwood got from taking the drug, apart from a nasty fright, was a new sense of his relationship with Bachardy. "I saw that the relationship between two people can be a rock to which they cling in the midst of chaos," he wrote. "I feel that a new and very strong bond exists between Don and myself." This bond would be further strengthened in adversity when the pair finally reached London, but before that they spent six weeks traveling round Europe, dropping in on Somerset Maugham at Cap Ferrat.

They arrived in London on January 7, 1956. Isherwood's apprehension about this visit, exacerbated by Maugham's report that he had been shocked by the envy and spitefulness of the English when last there, manifested itself in an atavistic fear that he and Bachardy would be prevented from entering the country by immigration officials. "Actually, it couldn't have been easier," he reported, "but I can never forget that traumatic experience with Heinz." Indeed, the customs officials proved altogether more welcoming than many of Isherwood's friends. "Our stay here has opened disastrously," Isherwood confessed. "After two days at John Lehmann's, Don announced that he just couldn't take it any more—he even thought we'd have to stop living together—because my friends all treated him like dirt, or worse." What had in fact happened was that old friends, keen to catch up with Isherwood and talk about old times,

---

2. His brother had suffered further episodes of mental instability over the past two years and was a constant anxiety.

tended to exclude Bachardy from conversations. Many of them found him attractive, but the fact that he looked like a schoolboy, particularly when dressed in a suit and tie, meant that he was often treated like one. Lehmann "couldn't have been stuffier if he'd been John van Druten," while his partner, the dancer Alexis Rassine, was "pissy and grand." Things improved slightly when Isherwood and Bachardy moved to the Cavendish Hotel, which Isherwood found reassuringly "snug," but old friends continued to cause difficulties. "Stephen, even, was very off-hand in his manner. Even William Plomer, the affable, took very little trouble to make Don feel at home." When Bachardy refused to accompany Isherwood to lunch with the Spenders and then stormed out of a party given by John Gielgud, Isherwood complained: "He is too tiresome with his neurosis and I'm weary of being tied to all this fuss, when there is so much fun to be had." After a fortnight of this sort of behavior, Isherwood really began to wonder whether Bachardy was in need of professional help. "I'm alarmed, because I see, in back of it all, an ugly dangerous psychotic will-to-unhappiness."

A brief respite was provided by a visit to the Beesleys, who had returned to England and now lived in a cottage in Essex. Bachardy felt they were the only friends of Isherwood who made any effort to notice him. What struck Dodie Smith at once was the disparity in Isherwood's and Bachardy's ages. "Don looks so young that I do not quite know how Chris has the nerve to go about with him," she commented in her diary. "He is actually 21—Chris says, but looks about 15." She thought him "certainly an improvement on Billy [Caskey]—which is not saying much," but added: "Don deserves much, much good to be spoken of him. He really is a nice, really intelligent, very unusual boy." Bachardy's mood lightened considerably in this friendly atmosphere. "It was truly touching how he responded to their kindness," Isherwood wrote, but he had been soured by his whole experience of England and added that the Beesleys' behavior "wasn't so kind after all, because why in the hell shouldn't they like him—he is (and was particularly on this occasion) charming."

In fact his relationship with the Beesleys was no longer as warm as it had been. When they had first returned to England, Isherwood had told Spender that he missed them very badly: "I seem to have everything I could wish for in my life here but someone I can talk to about writing problems. This is the only way I feel lonely." After the débâcle of *The World in the Evening,* with its consequent loss of frankness, productive discussion about writing had become more tricky, and a second visit got off to a bad start when Isherwood telephoned to say that he and Bachardy would have to take a later train than arranged because he had to have a cap replaced on his tooth. The Beesleys suspected—quite wrongly—that this was an excuse and that Isherwood and Bachardy had merely been too idle to get up in time to catch the early train. Isherwood told Smith that he planned to write a play based on *The World in the Evening* and was undeterred by her tactful warning against reworking old material. She reported that she now found this sort of discussion more exhausting than rewarding, but this may have been partly due to the fact that she was grieving for one of her beloved dogs, which she had had to have put down since Isherwood's last visit. She recovered herself, however, for what Isherwood described as "a very happy evening," during which Bachardy, who had started trying to draw from life, made sketches of his hosts. "How he expands and warms, as soon as he dares to believe he is amongst friends!" Isherwood noted.

As the time approached for Isherwood to visit Wyberslegh, a duty he had been dreading, he developed a mysterious pain in his right leg, which he thought might be varicose veins. It seems not to have occurred to him that his body might have been playing an elaborate psychosomatic joke and that he was now literally as well as metaphorically dragging his feet. He consulted Patrick Woodcock, a genial general practitioner very popular among writers and actors, who gave him some vitamin pills. Ever since his experiences at Ivar Avenue, Isherwood was inclined to regard vitamin shots as miraculous cure-alls, and these pills seemed to do the trick.

Leaving Bachardy "alone to his hysteria and self-pity," he set off for Wyberslegh on January 30. He would be away for a week and hoped that his absence might make Don "feel more independent and freer and perhaps [. . .] find out something useful about himself, and us." He had long been dreading this part of the trip, fearful of "reopening the whole dismal tragedy." His fears were confirmed when he was met by Richard at Stockport station.

Stooped over, with head bowed, he came toward me, looking down and away. Then he threw his head back, and his eyes closed as if he were blind as he turned his face to the sky. His cheeks are rough red and his nose quite purple—probably because of bad circulation. Several of his front teeth were missing. His thick curling dark hair shows no sign of grey. His hands are nicotine stained, chapped and usually covered with coal dust, since he is constantly building fires.

His face would also get daubed with coal dust because of his nervous tic, and any attempts made by Alan Bradley to tidy him up were doomed. Although he could rarely be persuaded to wash, Richard would submit to having his hair neatly combed before going out, but as soon as he was out of sight down the road he would ruffle it up again into its usual tangle.

Although the weather was not as bad as it had been during Isherwood's first postwar visit to Cheshire, it was still a contrast to California. "I arrived in mild damp weather, and this little old stone house, standing amidst its sodden fields, was sponge wet. The books in the shelves smelled of corpse, the bedclothes were like shrouds, you smelt stale smells everywhere of old fat in unscoured skillets. The two white, black-patched cats eat food all over the kitchen floor. The rugs are dark with grime. In buckets you find very old, frighteningly foul black rags, reminiscent of the labor conditions of the nineteenth century and *Oliver Twist*." The sheets were not only damp but also smeared with coal dust where Richard had solicitously put a hot water bottle between them. "His blue eyes are still innocent and charming, and he is constantly eager to serve my wishes. He apologizes for the cold, begs me to accept extra blankets and overcoats. During the day, he wears a sports jacket so dark and stiff with grease that it might belong to a garage mechanic. But only a real hobo would accept his shirt. He laughs loudly and explosively, startling and annoying M., as always."

Isherwood escaped to the pub with Alan Bradley, whom he met for the first time on this trip and took to immediately. He regaled Bradley, who now worked in the building trade and was married with a daughter, with stories about Berlin. The first time they went to the pub, he ordered a gin. "Small or large?" Bradley asked, and was startled when Isherwood demanded a tumbler filled to the brim. Shortly after Isherwood arrived in Cheshire, there was a fall of snow and a severe frost, with water freezing in the basins and the usual reduction in the gas supply. Although rather stiff in her joints, Kathleen still looked twenty years younger than her true age of eighty-seven, and her faculties were scarcely impaired. Isherwood was nevertheless appalled at the conditions in which she and Richard were living and annoyed by Kathleen's disdain for modern conveniences such as paper towels, which she pretended were "some weird newfangled and somehow degenerate US invention." His attempts to remonstrate with his family caused a terrible scene when Richard arrived home drunk just after Isherwood and Kathleen had been having their supper, prepared for them by the daily woman, Mrs. Barber. Richard upturned the dining table, shouting: "This is the end! I'm at the end of my tether! I haven't a friend in the world! You're all prigs—all of you!" Raising his arm as if about to strike his brother, he yelled: "I hate you! You come up here so smug and tell me my Mother's overworked. I hate you! I hate you!" "After the first moment of being startled, I felt more amused than anything," Isherwood reflected.

> I ought to have felt sorry for Richard, I know, and I do, theoretically—but the fact is, there have been too many such scenes in my life during the past few years—Billy, Harry Brown,[3] Don, etc. etc. Well, anyhow, I tried to get him to talk but I couldn't, properly, because the women were there. M. left the room when I asked her to, but Mrs Barber—as she mopped up the mess—everything on the table had been smashed—kept reproving Richard like a nanny; telling him he'd be ashamed in the morning, that he knew we were all his friends, that he loved his kind brother, etc. Worse, Richard fell in with this mood and clasped my hand and told me he loved me very much, which only embarrassed me, because I don't love *him*—most certainly not as a brother. I have a hundred brothers already and a thousand sons—and all this talk about blood relationships just nauseates me. It's the evil old sentimental lie I've been fighting for the past thirty-five years.

Isherwood was inclined to work himself up in his diaries, sometimes, as here, with unintentionally comic effect: his remark about his hundred brothers and thousand sons, with its unfortunate echo of *Goodbye, Mr. Chips,* is quite as much of a sentimental lie as any notions about blood relationships.[4] It was also quite untrue that Isherwood was devoid of brotherly feelings, in which genuine affection was overlaid but not eradicated by guilt. Every time he saw Richard, it was like looking into a distorted mirror, like seeing himself unfettered by social constraints, the id unmodified by the ego or the superego. There was uncomfortably little difference between Richard's drunken rages, in which tables were overturned and crockery sent flying, and Isherwood's, in which people were punched in the face at parties. It was simply

---

3. Brown's marriage to Marguerite Lamkin had disintegrated spectacularly amid drunken scenes involving firearms.

4. As Hilton's eponymous long-serving schoolmaster lies on his deathbed he overhears someone remark what a pity it was that he never had children and replies: "Yes—umph—I have . . . Thousands of 'em . . . thousands of 'em . . . and all boys . . ."

a matter of degree. In a subsequent argument with Kathleen about families, Isherwood was alarmed to hear in his own voice "a faint echo of Richard's hysteria." He felt that he "wanted to denounce [Kathleen], and the society she represents, and its sanction of motherhood and the marriage bed. It is shocking how insane and immature I must still be—that I can harbor such feelings against a poor old woman." Watching Richard having vomit sponged off him by Mrs. Barber "as though he were a dog" was distressing partly because it could have been Isherwood himself, he felt, had he, rather than his brother, remained with Kathleen.

The following morning Isherwood attempted to have a serious talk with Richard, whose clothes still reeked of beer and vomit. Isherwood reminded his brother that he had enough money of his own to leave Cheshire and live in London. As Isherwood well knew, Richard felt he could have no such freedom until their mother was dead. Furthermore, the dependence of mother and son was mutual: the last time Richard had ventured to London unaccompanied he was arrested for being drunk in the street. How would a man who was incapable even of shaving himself without substantial bloodshed be able to survive alone in the metropolis? It was all very well for Isherwood to declare "I'm glad that my life is what it is—wandering, insecure, imprudent," but he had psychological resources which had somehow failed to develop in Richard.

Part of the reason for this lack of development, Isherwood felt, was Richard's self-immersion in the past, in family history and all the things that he himself had jettisoned by going to America. The dead weight of the past was aptly symbolized by Marple Hall, which had been virtually abandoned since Isherwood's last visit to Cheshire. In order to keep the house habitable, it would have been necessary to install a new water supply, and the cost of this proved prohibitive. The caretakers had left in the summer of 1953 and although attempts were made to secure the building it gradually fell victim to vandalism. Numerous suggestions about salvaging the fixtures and fittings had been made, but came to nothing. A plan to remove the main staircase to the safety of a museum was foiled when an engineer pointed out that this would be impossible without threatening the entire structure of the house. As it was, the ominously bulging east side of the building had been shored up with wooden props. Shortly after the caretakers left, a chimney fell down, crashing through the roof and covering the staircase in debris. The following year the *Manchester Guardian* reported on the state of the house, which it judged "one of the finest in Cheshire," urging that it should be saved from further dereliction. "Thieves, vandals, and destructive children have wrought more havoc to Marple Hall in months than time achieved in centuries," ran the report.

> Viewed from the enclosing court, the gate into which has been torn from its hinges, the rich sandstone front still has a desolate grandeur; and so has the terraced rear, commanding a dizzying drop to the meadows, the wood, and the River Goyt below. But broken finials and pinnacles from the roof litter the weed-smothered ground, and every one of the scores of mullioned windows has been smashed. Lead looters have stripped the roof, and a magnificent sundial which stood outside the main entrance on a tier of steps was recently pushed over for no other reason than a test of strength.

The sundial was subsequently rescued and installed in the village, and several other important items, including paintings and furniture, had gone to Wyberslegh. Other features, including the portrait of Moll of Brabyns, had been abandoned to their fate. Richard confessed that he "felt strongly disinclined" to have Moll at Wyberslegh and so she was left at Marple, "hanging in her usual place high up on the stairs looking proud and arrogant and defiant as ever," until thieves carted her off. The *Guardian* reported that "wreckers are said to have come on cycling expeditions armed with saws and axes": oak paneling had been smashed or looted, doors wrenched off their hinges and carried away, wooden coats of arms chiseled from their settings. Although some late Renaissance glass had been saved and taken to a local church, the stained-glass panel commemorating Bradshaw the regicide had been stolen. "What is the future, if it has a future, of this beautiful, stricken house?" the paper asked. "If its days as a habitable building are over, could it be preserved as a shell in the grounds, which at least are reclaimable?"

This would prove impractical, as Isherwood realized when he accompanied Richard to look over the building.

> We went up the back stairs—the front staircase looks unsafe and there is a great hole in the roof above where the chimney-stack fell through—and had to climb over the bathtub which had been dragged down the steps and left stuck between the banisters. The only intact thing left in the house is the pink marble fireplace which Uncle Henry brought back from Venice and had fixed up in the drawing room.
>
> A double row of red brick villas runs along the edge of the park bordering on the main road. Before long the council is going to force Richard to sell land opposite the house in order to put up a school and lay out the sports fields. But before this happens, a good deal more of the Hall will most probably collapse. It is a perfect death trap for children. Richard and I left like two ghosts—the kind that other people see and never suspect of being ghosts until much later, when someone exclaims in horror: 'You say you saw Mr Richard and Mr Christopher? But, man, *they've* been dead for *years!* [. . .]
>
> Got home and urged M. to have the Venetian fireplace removed. She probably won't, till it's too late. I realize now that all kinds of things in the house could have been rescued from theft and vandalism if M. and Richard hadn't absolutely refused to admit to themselves months ago that it was a doomed ruin. Even now, M. doesn't admit it. She kept asking if certain parts were still standing, as if it matters.

It was no wonder that Isherwood felt like a ghost when he visited Marple. He had left that old life behind him. Walking through the snowy Cheshire landscape of his childhood, he was "deeply moved," but reflected: "This is my native country. Thank God for it—and thank God, *on my knees,* that I got out of it!"

I sherwood's railing against emotional ties may have had something to do with the insecurity he was feeling about the state of his relationship with Bachardy. "There's only one thing I really fear and that's dependence," he wrote, while at the same time recording how far away Bachardy seemed and how he longed to get back to London to be with him.

The reunion was a happy one and Isherwood was able to report that relations between them were "as harmonious as it is possible to imagine." This mood did not last, however. While E. M. Forster, whom they visited at King's College Cambridge, gained favor by paying Bachardy proper attention, Spender was still in disgrace, and Bachardy once again refused to attend a dinner at his house. "Another explosion" followed a meeting with Peter Watson and the painter Francis Bacon when Bachardy felt he was being ignored. "I'm seriously worried by this, because it was so neurotic," Isherwood wrote. "He is getting an obsession about being rejected, and I don't seem able to help him." The weather did little to improve Bachardy's mood, and Isherwood eventually arranged for them to cut their trip short by a week with the intention of booking an early appointment with a psychiatrist back in America.

They managed to avoid seeing too much of Lehmann. "I'm still sorry for John—perhaps it would be friendlier not to be—but God he is such a square! So stupid," Isherwood complained. "I suppose his stupidity really consists of this: he has no curiosity. Lehmann, meanwhile, had been jotting down his thoughts about Isherwood:

> Though there are still constant touches of the old, inimitable humour & wit [. . .] it struck me that he is getting alarmingly self-engrossed (A[lexis] shrewdly but cruelly suggests it's come about because by Hollywood standards he's a failure), & I noted that the continual switching on and off of the famous smile was almost becoming a kind of confidence trick to put across plausibly original but really slightly phony opinions. There was much talk of Gerald Heard, whom he still so profoundly (& oddly) believes in, & various novels (as usual) he had not written . . . I had a sudden, and rather horrible feeling: in a few years—and far more quickly than I would have imagined possible last time I saw him—he will have become an eccentric little old gentleman rather set in his ways.

Lehmann was certainly set in *his* ways, but lacked eccentricity or any real spark of originality. He was appallingly stuffy about almost everything except sex. Isherwood was quite correct in accusing him of lacking curiosity. It is hard to imagine Lehmann, for instance, taking mescaline, which Isherwood did while staying in London, making extensive notes about the intensity of perception he experienced. Lehmann does, however, provide a glimpse of the sort of impression Isherwood was making when he attended the literary gatherings he criticized so much.

It was Lehmann who offered to host a farewell party for Isherwood, but he received no reply to this suggestion. Kathleen and Richard had traveled down to London to say goodbye and attended an evening with the Spenders and Peter Watson and his boyfriend. During the course of this evening, they phoned Lehmann several times, inviting him to join them with increasingly drunken enthusiasm. Constitutionally incapable of spontaneity, Lehmann declined the repeated invitations and went to bed. Isherwood subsequently felt he had "mortally offended" Lehmann, and sent a contrite but insincere letter when he reached New York:

> I feel I must write to you at once to thank you for all your kindness to us while we were in England. I only wish that we had met more often. The last evening was

particularly unfortunate. It developed quite differently from the way in which I'd planned it, because of my Mother's redoubtable powers of sitting up and drinking! To my astonishment, she showed not the least inclination to go to bed and so there we sat until the small hours, with her sober and me & the rest of the company utterly pie-eyed! I fear I annoyed you with late phone-calls of a drunken nature! Please forgive me. I feel badly about the whole business. I *will* try to write you something for the magazine, if that will make any small amends.

Tiresome as Lehmann could be, Isherwood did not want to alienate someone who might publish him in England. Lehmann was not entirely taken in by this, but he in his turn valued Isherwood as a potential contributor whose name would bring some luster to his new enterprise. "Chris. has been a great disappointment this trip, remote & vague, but he's conscious of it at least, only of course he'll never be any different now," Lehmann wrote. "I fear it's the beginning of the end—for *us*." It wasn't, and the two men continued to send each other fulsome letters signed with "much love as always."

30. Mr. Norris lends a hand: Isherwood and Heinz
with a distinctly shifty-looking Gerald Hamilton.

31. Berthold Viertel on the set of *Little Friend,* sitting between two of the film's leads, Matheson Lang and Nova Pilbeam, 1935.

32. Isherwood's publisher and sometime confidant John Lehmann.

33. Lehmann's sisters, Rosamond and Beatrix. The latter represented for Isherwood "woman in an acceptable form."

34. Stephen Spender and Tony Hyndman, taken by Humphrey Spender at Lake Garda, 1935.

35. A windblown Isherwood in Amsterdam,
photographed by Humphrey Spender during his visit there in 1935.

36. E. M. Forster, Bob Buckingham, Heinz and Stephen Spender in Holland, 1935: a photograph probably taken as a souvenir of Isherwood's thirty-first birthday party.

37. Self-sufficiency: Heinz building accommodation for the doomed livestock at Sintra, 1936.

38. The household and visitors at the Villa Alecrim do Norte: James Stern, Isherwood and Teddy, William Robson-Scott, Tania Stern, Heinz.

39. "A grand person, unaffected, extremely amusing & devastatingly intelligent": Isherwood snapped by an impressionable Benjamin Britten.

40. War Reporters: Isherwood and Auden at Victoria Station,
about to embark on their Journey to a War, January 1938.

41. New Found Land: Isherwood and Auden on their
first visit to New York, July 1938.

42. Jack Hewit, the lover Isherwood
shared with Guy Burgess.

43. My Guru and His Disciple: Swami Prabhavananda and Isherwood
outside the Hollywood Temple, Ivar Avenue, Los Angeles.

44. Amiya, garbed for life
at "The Swamitage."

45. Prema (né John Yale), Isherwood's
Ivar Avenue informant.

46. Isherwood contemplates his future as a citizen of the United States of America.

47. The Great Seducer: Isherwood photographed by Caskey.

TWENTY-ONE

D URING HIS TRIP TO ENGLAND, ISHERWOOD DEVELOPED SOME new ideas for his proposed Mexican novel, about which he had been jotting down notes throughout 1955. "In the first place," he had decided, "I want a central character who avoids the weakness of Stephen in 'The World in the Evening.' Someone who is more relaxed, less ashamed, more amusing, more outrageous, more despotic [. . .] So no more apologies. No more repentances and regenerations."

> The journey to Mexico is somewhat of a modern Dante's visit to Purgatory. It is a *warning* to the visitor. But—unlike Stephen—I don't think one should feel that he will heed the warning. Probably not.
> It is very important not to suggest that the story is a fantasy right from the start. So I think maybe he and his friends get terribly drunk at a party and, the next thing he knows, they have crossed the border and are driving down through Mexico. And perhaps the story will maintain a surface realism clear through.

He subsequently decided to make his central character "a religious fraud," based on two of John van Druten's associates, Walter Starcke and Joel Goldsmith. Starcke was an actor and theater producer who had replaced Carter Lodge as van Druten's lover. Goldsmith had worked as a healer and preacher within the framework of the Church of Christ, Scientist, and subsequently founded an independent movement called "The Infinite Way," funded by subscription. Isherwood thought Goldsmith a charlatan, but both van Druten and Starcke had become devotees, the former contributing an introduction to Goldsmith's book *The Infinite Way* (1952), the latter setting himself up as a healer. As well as preaching, meditating and even working miracles, this character would also be a heavy drinker and perhaps be involved in "some kind of squalid sex messup." Isherwood imagined the book being partly about "the 'New Era' of American prosperity. Everything booming. We never had it so good. Tragedy is unmodern." The healer would be "a prophet of the boom—think positive thoughts, goodness is more real than evil—all the familiar Christian Science stuff. He is not stupid, certainly. And he isn't entirely a fiend. But he has gotten in very deep. That's why he is warned."

Isherwood was unsure how he was going to write what sounds like a Christian Science *Elmer Gantry*. The only way to proceed, he felt, was to start writing. "I want to see if this 'freehand' technique of composition gives anything. I believe it will. I believe I have always, in the past, delayed too long before starting my books." This echoes Lehmann's observation that Isherwood had talked about his novels brilliantly, but far too much, and that by the time he got down to writing them the original spark had gone. Isherwood needed to start writing in order to discover what this book was—or was not—about. "I'm trying to poke my way down to the underground river of subconscious creation, instead of making plans—laying out a city on the surface, as it were, and then hoping the water will bubble up to bring it life. And it almost seems I'm succeeding. Because, as I continue to write this nonsense, some impatient voice is beginning to tell me how I *ought* to write. The only thing is, I know I must go on with the instinctive nonsense-work until the rational brain has been blackmailed into giving up its secrets."

He had put together a rough outline to send to Edward Upward, who had written back in great detail. Upward wanted to know whether a proper appreciation of the novel relied upon readers' being aware that it was based on Dante and having some knowledge of *The Divine Comedy*. What precisely did Isherwood mean by Hell or Purgatory? Was he writing an allegory, and if so, about what? Perhaps he should write an "inverted allegory," "a story that doesn't so much show Purgatory in the likeness of Mexico but Mexico in the likeness of Hell."

Encouraged by Upward's general interest in the idea, Isherwood continued to make notes and began several drafts of the novel during 1955. He must have had doubts about the outline, since he gradually began to introduce familiar faces: among those encountered in the Inferno would be "the refugees," Francis Turville-Petre, Basil Fry, Denham Fouts, Paul from the abandoned "Paul Is Alone" and Isherwood's old Berlin acquaintance Aleister Crowley. He even gave the novel the much-used working title "The Lost."[1] Other characters he considered including were "someone who is impossibly rich," based on Edward James and Huntington Hartford, and an "unco-operative witness" borrowed from the McCarthy hearings.

Having made little progress, he had put the novel on one side, but while in London, he had been struck by a new inspiration. "It came to me in a flash—while Don and I were sitting at Simpson's yesterday, awaiting the special steak and kidney pudding advertised for Thursdays, only to find that it was all gone," he wrote in his diary on February 10, 1956.

'Imagine,' I told Don, 'that John van Druten gets a call, long distance, from the editor of the London *Times*. He comes from the phone into the living room, sits down dramatically: "Well—! They want me to leave for hell on Thursday. I'm to

---

1. It was subsequently retitled *The Forgotten*, so to avoid confusion it is referred to here as "the Mexican novel."

do a series of ten articles—" Shall he accept? He phones Dodie in England, Joel Goldsmith in Honolulu. He studies Dante, tries an article to see if he can do it, decides that he can. Carter and Starcke encourage him. He says yes. Then hasty reading up on Virgil, who is to come by to fetch him and will lunch at the ranch first. Virgil arrives. Johnny is terribly thrilled. Virgil reminisces about the Roman theatre. Johnny is enchanted. Finally they drive away together—'

Isherwood did not intend writing "a hard-boiled modern version of the *Inferno*," but felt the idea could be "a dream which gives my principal character the idea of *pretending* he is visiting hell, as a sort of sophisticated game. He goes to Mexico, keeping up the pretence. Then, right at the end, during a hashish experience in Mexico City, he gets a horrible scare: maybe he really *is* in hell?" He had discussed this idea—which at least had the merit of coherence—with the Beesleys and developed it further, casting Denny Fouts as the Virgil figure. He nowhere says so, but it is possible Isherwood was recalling Auden's epic poem "In the year of my youth when yoyos came in," begun in September 1932 but subsequently abandoned. This too had drawn on Dante and featured a Virgil figure (based on Gerald Heard) guiding a poet down through the circles of a twentieth-century urban hell. It seems likely that Isherwood would have read this poem at the time, particularly since parts of it were later incorporated into *Dogskin*.

I sherwood intended to start work on the novel as soon as he got back to Los Angeles, where he and Bachardy temporarily rented a house at 322 East Rustic Road, almost opposite the house Isherwood and Caskey had lived in between 1948 and 1950. "So, after six years and about 60,000 miles of travel, I've only succeeded in moving a hundred yards," he told Spender. "It makes me wonder. . . ." Isherwood had known his new landlord for some time. Michael Barrie had trained to be a monk and lived at Trabuco, but had recently left the monastery and become Heard's secretary, a job he continued to hold until Heard's death some sixteen years later. Heard provided accommodations, so Barrie's house was now free.

Surrounded by packing cases, Isherwood took out his diary on March 25, 1956, and wrote: "Well, this is quite a solemn moment. A new start [. . .] It's a grey Pacific morning, and my sinus is giving me perpetual sniffles. But I feel well and quite energetic. There is nothing to stop me from getting on with the novel except my own neurotic laziness and anxieties." There were in fact several other things to stop progress on the novel: drink ("Another hangover"), "Dangerous idling weather," worries about Bachardy's behavior and future, and Prabhavananda, who almost immediately "brought up the question of the Ramakrishna book again." Isherwood had agreed to write the biography almost as an unadmitted penance for his failings as a disciple and approached the project dutifully rather than with any real enthusiasm. "My resolve is to do something on the novel at least twice a week, and some reading on Ramakrishna at least four times a week," he wrote. "That's a good minimum." Good or not, it was a minimum he was unable to meet.

A visit to the convent at Santa Barbara in mid-April provided some much-needed discipline, but back in the world there were too many distractions. Some of these, such as finding a house to buy and then moving into it, were unavoidable. He and

Bachardy discovered a small house at 434 Sycamore Road, which runs parallel to East Rustic Road. It was set back from the road behind a patio garden filled with roses, wisteria and subtropical plants, and was reached by a small flight of steps. By the time they came to move, at the beginning of May, Bachardy was hospitalized with hepatitis, looking (a doting Isherwood thought) "like some beautiful Asiatic image of pure gold; a Krishna." No sooner was Bachardy back in their new home than Isherwood came down with the same illness and had to endure a week in the Cedars of Lebanon hospital. He had imagined that he was merely suffering from the exhaustion of completing the move, getting on with the novel, making his slow way through *Sri Ramakrishna the Great Master* (the standard biography, written by a disciple, Swami Saradananda), and writing his "accursed" article for Lehmann's "Coming to London" ("a sheer loveless grind"). The recuperation period for hepatitis, a thoroughly debilitating illness of which depression is a side effect, is long, but it had one decidedly beneficial aspect: Isherwood was not allowed to drink alcohol for six months. This undoubtedly helped his writing and by the end of June, although still feeling below par, he had written sixty pages of the Mexican novel, roughed out introductions to the stories he had selected for the long-delayed Dell anthology, and written a foreword for Gerald Hamilton's latest volume of memoirs, *Mr Norris and I*. Buying a house and paying medical bills had made him worry again about his finances, but not enough to accept film projects—such as an adaptation of T. H. White's *Mistress Masham's Repose*—which did not attract him. "But really I should never be seriously depressed as long as all goes well with Don," he admonished himself. "That's chiefly what matters to me."

Considering the upheavals of moving and illness, all was indeed going reasonably well. Bachardy had been to see Evelyn Hooker, who had pronounced that there was nothing wrong with him and that his volatile behavior was only to be expected in the circumstances. "In other words, she thinks that our life together constitutes a genuinely big problem," Isherwood noted.

> Now of course I quite see this. And yet I can't in my weakness, help feeling hurt when I'm treated as a sort of classic monster—a standard monster, almost—out of a textbook, like a dragon in a fairy tale. Don, on his side, cannot understand that I mind. I ought to accept my monsterhood humbly, he thinks.
>
> But isn't all this the purest justice of karma? Go back twenty years. For Don substitute Richard. For Evelyn, John Layard. For me, my mother.

Isherwood always saw the difficulties he had with his lovers as fitting into some sort of pattern from the past, but while Bachardy could undoubtedly be impossible, he was at least connected to the world in a way Richard never was. Isherwood may have been accepting responsibility for the part his own character played in Bachardy's problems—just as his mother had been asked by the psychiatrist back in 1926 to accept her contribution to her children's problems—but at the same time he resented this interpretation, just as Kathleen had.

Isherwood was drawing up blacklists in his diary of (other) people who he felt had treated Bachardy badly, but a positive step had been taken when, after considerable indecision, Bachardy enrolled at the Chouinard Art Institute at the beginning of

July. Bachardy's childhood hobby of making drawings from photographs of actors and actresses out of film magazines, though giving him little scope for his own creativity, had resulted in an ability to get a good likeness. It had also made him principally interested in drawing people, and he had started practicing drawing from life with Isherwood as a model. He remained insecure about his talent and it needed all Isherwood's powers of encouragement to get him to art school. As well as direction in his life, art would also provide Bachardy with a sense of identity: he would be doing something entirely independently of Isherwood, something for which Isherwood himself had no talent.

By his fifty-fourth birthday on August 26, Isherwood had written 150 pages of his novel, completed the Dell anthology and finished reading Saradananda's biography. The anthology would be published as a small paperback in May 1957 under the title *Great English Short Stories*. This appears to have been the publisher's choice, since Isherwood's original intention was less canonical. "I want to make an anthology of things I like best in English prose," he wrote in a proposal. "These are not necessarily the things I would recommend to an English literature class as the greatest and most admirable; they are what I personally love and often re-read, because they move and stimulate me as an individual and a writer." The aim of the anthology was "to encourage other readers to ask themselves frankly 'what do *I* like?' and '*why* do I like it?' without worrying about the goodness or badness of their taste."

His provisional list included not only short stories, but extracts from novels, and would be international, with room for friends such as Upward and Spender and literary heroes such as Katherine Mansfield and E. M. Forster alongside Chekhov, Turgenev, Maupassant, Tolstoy, Dostoyevsky, Hans Christian Andersen and something from *The Arabian Nights*. He eventually chose only complete short stories by British and Irish writers: Conrad, Chesterton, Wells, Forster, Kipling, Lawrence, Mansfield, Graves, Maugham, Pritchett, Plomer, Conan Doyle, George Moore and E. C. Mayne. Reading the anthology, he hoped, would be like being with him at home, where he would take down books from the shelf, read from them and explain what they meant to him.

Sometimes it is because I love the author as a literary personality. If you love an author in this way, it is like loving a close friend: you like everything about him, even his silliness, weaknesses and prejudices. I would not love Tolstoy so much if he had never been silly, nor D. H. Lawrence, nor Hemingway. Then, again, there are authors for whom I have no particular personal feeling, but who move me enormously by the particular accent of their style and the rhythm of their dialogue. There are authors like stern but truthful uncles, who are always at your side, warning you of life's real nature. And there are authors who create private worlds of such magical happiness that you return to them again and again with ever-growing nostalgia.

He battled on with the Mexican novel, "bored but dogged," determined as was his habit to get something down on paper, however silly or inept it might seem. He needed to make some real progress because he was negotiating to work on a film adaptation of Romain Rolland's ten-volume *roman-fleuve, Jean-Christophe,* for the producer Jerry Wald at Twentieth Century–Fox. Isherwood had been offered $5,000 to write a treatment, but told his agent that he needed $6,000, which he got. This would help pay for planned renovations of the new house. Pocketing the $2,000 signature advance, he was obliged to admit: "So far I haven't the least clue how I'm going to handle this gush of French wah-wah." Published between 1904 and 1912, Rolland's vast satirical novel about a musical genius traveling through Europe while anatomizing the value and purpose of art was calculated to arouse and confirm all Isherwood's francophobia, but he nevertheless managed to produce a "rough first treatment" within eight days. Once this was complete, he felt that he would be able to get on with the novel: "I should be able to find the time at Fox easily," he decided. In this he would be assisted by his "dream secretary," Eleanor Breese, who had worked with the great American editor Maxwell Perkins and had herself published a novel. She had been married to a pilot named Vance Breese, and remained on close terms with him after their divorce, and they both became good friends of Isherwood and Bachardy. Isherwood was particularly pleased when, after hosting a dinner party, Vance "proved himself a very great gentleman by walking Don out to his car (the first time any host anywhere has done this)." Isherwood was beginning to attach as much importance to social protocol as did that other British exile with a frequently snubbed partner, the Duke of Windsor.

At Thanksgiving he was able to report that he had completed a draft of the Mexican novel. "It certainly doesn't amount to much at present," he admitted. "Yet I still feel that this procedure—of writing recklessly through to the end—was well worth while and creative of a better and freer rhythm." This had not, however, solved the problems he was experiencing with the book's narrative voice. An idea to rewrite it "in the third person with 'William Bradshaw' as its chief character" suggests a fatal vagueness about what sort of book he was writing. The introduction of his *Mr Norris* alter ego may have been a step toward using the character of "Christopher Isherwood" once more, but it did not help a great deal and the novel stalled for two months. Uncertainty about the identity and function of the narrator was what had caused Isherwood so many of the problems he encountered while writing *The World in the Evening,* and this should have rung alarm bells. More worryingly, he appeared to be ignoring the warnings sounded by reviewers of that novel—notably *The Times,* which felt with some justice that "on the whole he is better as a camera than the conscience of mankind"—and was once again attempting a novel with spiritual dimensions.

The despair Isherwood was beginning to feel about the book may be gauged by the fact that in February 1957 he wrote in his working notebook: "For some reason, I find it helpful to think of the novel as being in French." He was not, however, thinking of *le style* "wah-wah," but of something "concise, epigrammatic, even a bit obscure," perhaps a little like Baudelaire's *Journaux intimes:* "Entries in a notebook. Abrupt. More gaps. *Not* a narrative." This was not altogether helpful since a strong narrative was precisely what the book really needed. Three months later, he had produced a mere twenty-eight pages of the new version and was no clearer as to what he was writing.

Part of his slowness was due to other projects that he needed to work on during 1957. There were some last-minute hitches over the Dell anthology when the Dylan Thomas Estate asked for too high a fee and the Conan Doyle Estate would allow Isherwood to reprint "The Speckled Band" only under certain stipulations. Isherwood took great pleasure in outlining these stipulations in his revised foreword to the volume: "The Trustee of the Conan Doyle Estate made it a condition of his agreement that my comments on the story should be submitted to him and subjected to his editing. This condition I rejected on principle, believing it to be an unallowable kind of censorship." Isherwood had to substitute Joseph Conrad's "The Secret Sharer," which meant providing a new introduction to this story. He had also been given yet more "homework" by the Vedanta Society: the English in a long and detailed history of the Ramakrishna Math and Mission in India needed tidying up.

In addition, Isherwood was plagued by other problems, mostly related to a general feeling of getting old. One that directly affected work was a painful right thumb, which made it increasingly uncomfortable to write longhand. He thought that he had somehow strained the joint while kneading modeling wax, a habit he had developed as "a tension-release substitute for smoking," but when both thumbs became affected decided that it was arthritis. The pain prevented him from writing as much as he wanted in his diary and he eventually switched to typing. He had also been suffering once again from bouts of impotence, which he thought might be a side effect of hepatitis or be related to his median bar operation. His sense of encroaching age was highlighted because he had a much younger partner, and he felt that however tactfully and patiently Bachardy responded to sexual failure, it jeopardized their relationship. He was once again attending a gym to keep himself in trim, and this became part of his routine.

Increasingly, his own happiness was dependent on that of Bachardy, whose moods continued to fluctuate. One day Isherwood would be asking: "*Why* are Don and I so happy right now?"; the next he'd be complaining that he felt "lousy and worried" about himself and wondering why he could not "snap out of this state." He was also going through another period of escalating resentment: against those who failed to take enough notice of Bachardy; against Bachardy himself, whose highly emotional periods of discontent induced feelings of guilt; against the noisy children next door; against old friends such as Peggy Kiskadden, reports of whose marital difficulties pleased him out of all proportion. "My resentments are becoming chronic," he admitted. "I detect a growing rejection-hate against women which is truly disconcerting in its proportions." Although Isherwood had numbered several women among his close friends, he increasingly reacted to the female sex with hostility. His own experience had led him to regard mothers with suspicion, and he tended to view wives and girlfriends in much the same way: they whined, nagged, bullied and generally curtailed the freedom of men; they used their fiendish wiles to seduce perfectly nice boys into heterosexuality; their principal aim in life was to trick men into marriage and saddle them with such tiresomely adult duties as pursuing safe and solid careers, paying exorbitant mortgages, and raising hellish broods of children.

Jews also got under his skin. An offhand anti-semitism, closely linked to social snobbery, was characteristic of his upper-middle-class background in Britain. Back in 1938, when Spender had objected to "a scarcely concealed note of anti-semitism" in "The Landauers," Isherwood had replied: "As for my being anti-semitic: I suppose the very idea is so absurd to me that I feel privileged to say almost anything I like about individual jews [*sic*], which is wrong, I know. None of this is meant to excuse;

only to explain myself." Without entirely rewriting the story, there was little he could do to meet Spender's objections to the portraits of Bernhard and Natalia, but he removed two sentences from the description of Bernhard's party when he republished the story in *Goodbye to Berlin:* "Nearly everyone except myself was a Jew. They were of all kinds—the city Jew, the hairy athletic Jew, the thin cultured Jew, the dark exotic Jewess and the pretty blonde." He had also been obliged to alter an unfortunate sentence in *Mr Norris Changes Trains.* Describing Arthur Norris's young manhood, and the way he got through his inheritance, the narrator comments: "Well-groomed and witty, with money to burn, he must have been one of the most eligible young bachelors of his large circle; but it was the Jews, not the ladies, who got him in the end." "Money lenders" was substituted for "Jews" in 1954, when the novel was republished in the American omnibus volume, *The Berlin Stories,* but the text remained unaltered in British editions of the book into the 1970s. "Even I can't explain psychologically just why I wrote 'Jews,' since I was every bit as conscious of the implications of doing so as I am now," Isherwood wrote to his British publisher in 1975. "I think I was writing that paragraph in a sort of nineteenth-century jargon." He added that none of his "very many Jewish friends" had ever commented on this passage, but asked for it to be altered in future editions. Isherwood did indeed have many Jewish friends, just as he had many women friends, but his distaste for what he saw as certain aspects of the Jewish character was reinforced rather than dissipated by his years in Hollywood, working in an industry rich in Jewish émigrés. In his diaries the words "Jew" or "Jewish" tended to be used in denigration—even when writing of friends. Recalling that the Sterns had made a tidy profit when they sublet their New York apartment to him for a rent much higher than the one they were paying, he commented that Jimmy was "just being Jewish, of course."

It must almost have seemed as if the tamped-down rage he was currently feeling manifested itself physically when he found a small lump on his belly. He naturally assumed it must be cancer, particularly since he discovered it on the second anniversary of Maria Huxley's death from this disease. It was in fact a benign tumor, which he had removed under local anesthetic, but he had been badly frightened. "Let this be a lesson," he told himself. "Let me not forget what I felt—and let it make a difference. Let me think of myself as a reprieved person—with the obligations of the reprieved."

These obligations were difficult to meet. "The novel is at a standstill—and why? Because I have gotten into this hair-splitting perfectionistic mood in which I piddle for a few weeks over a few pages." This, of course, is what writers do when they find real progress on a book difficult to achieve. Progress on *Jean-Christophe* had also slowed down and he was finding it difficult to write a foreword to *All the Conspirators,* which he had been commissioned to provide for a new British edition.

He ascribed his inability to work to the after-effects of his operation, and felt he had not yet regained his full vitality. Disregarding the assurances of his surgeon, he insisted that his scar was taking too long to heal. He was experiencing pyloric spasms and rectal bleeding and had indigestion and sick feelings in the pit of his stomach (which cannot have been helped by his habit of gorging on marshmallows when Bachardy was at art school during the evenings). He was still convinced that somewhere inside him a cancerous tumor was stealthily growing. While recognizing that such symptoms were partly psychosomatic, related to anxiety, he was unable to conquer them, relying instead upon further vitamin shots—now supplemented with some sort of sexual stimulant, which proved reasonably effective. With characteristic exaggeration, he described himself as "literally dying of tension," and urged himself to stop neglecting his *japam*.

The "long siege of melancholic tamas" (a Hindu term for laziness and resistance to any sort of progress) persisted for some time. An article by the critic Francis Wyndham in Lehmann's *The Craft of Letters in England* announced that Isherwood's best work lay behind him, and that since the 1930s all he had produced was the "inconsiderable" *Prater Violet* and the "unsatisfactory and uncharacteristic" *The World in the Evening*. "This depressed me," Isherwood admitted. "And yet I don't know why it should, because I don't really care what they think." He did, of course, and went on to suggest the effect of such criticism by asking himself: "What am I fit for, nowadays? What am I accomplishing?" He was in such a poor way that he began to pin his hopes for his literary future not on his novel, but on the Ramakrishna biography: "*That* will sum up what my life has been about since the thirties." His gloom deepened during June when Bachardy went on a fortnight's trip to New York. He was fatalistically convinced that Bachardy would find another lover or decide he preferred being on his own. He completed the *Jean-Christophe* screenplay, but continued to waste his energies on "aggressive resentment" against "lady drivers, children, cops, Jews, journalists, etc. etc." Part of the problem was that he was "utterly bored" by his novel, and he welcomed any diversion. The most recent was to collaborate with the British writer Gavin Lambert on a television drama series for Hermione Gingold about a female detective called Emily Ermingarde.

Twenty years younger than Isherwood, Lambert had worked around film ever since leaving Oxford prematurely, and for five years had edited Britain's leading serious film journal, *Sight and Sound,* as well as writing reviews for assorted newspapers and magazines. His short stories had been published in *New Writing* and elsewhere and he had arrived in Hollywood in 1956 to work as the personal assistant of the movie director Nicholas Ray, with whom he was having an affair. He got a job at Twentieth Century–Fox and had been introduced to Isherwood by Ivan Moffatt, whom Isherwood had got to know through Moffatt's mother, Iris Tree. Lambert had written a collection of interconnected "Scenes from Hollywood Life," rather like *Goodbye to Berlin,* called *The Slide Area,* which Isherwood read in manuscript. "It's not bad and I envied him for having seized the opportunity to write about Lost Angeles," Isherwood noted, "—but it's mostly just journalism." It was in fact rather more than that, and a great deal better than anything Isherwood himself was writing at this period. It is likely that Isherwood was dismissive precisely because he realized that he really *had* missed an opportunity. When the book was published two years later, he provided a more just endorsement: "Having lived twenty years in the 'Slide Area,' I can say with some authority that these are the most truthful stories about the film world and its suburbia that I have ever read [. . .] How I wish I had written this book."

It had taken a while, but by this time Lambert had become a close friend of both Isherwood and Bachardy. Lambert had been warned that Isherwood was quixotic, appearing to be friendly, but then suddenly turning on people. This was ascribed to drink, although it is equally likely that at this period many people fell quickly out of favor when they failed to pay proper attention to Bachardy. Lambert shared Bachardy's passion for, and encyclopedic knowledge of, the movies and this was undoubtedly a help. He felt that at first Isherwood remained quite cool, often failing to engage with people in the early stages of knowing them in case he would later have to extricate himself from a friendship he did not wish to cultivate. Collaboration, however, was a bond, reminding Isherwood of the days when he and Auden worked together, and he and Lambert soon fell into a friendly partnership.

Emily Ermingarde was the first of several unfruitful projects they undertook, chiefly to make money. It evolved through long discussions, after which Lambert went away and produced a pilot script, which James Geller tried to sell. Had he been successful, the series would have been lucrative, but it would also have involved an enormous amount of work. The prospect of producing thirty-nine teleplays within the first year did not fill Isherwood with a great deal of enthusiasm. Everything relied upon Gingold's willingness to take the title role, but she was currently filming *Gigi* and seemed unable to make up her mind. Although the money would have been useful, particularly since *Jean-Christophe* had been shelved, Isherwood was partly relieved when Gingold finally turned them down. Even so, the project did not entirely die and for some time they entertained hopes that other eccentric British actresses of a certain age (including Beatrice Lillie and Elsa Lanchester) might be interested in the idea.

I sherwood always liked to set a date to work toward, however badly his writing was going, and the Mexican novel was going very badly indeed. An extended Far Eastern trip with Bachardy had been planned for the winter, taking in Japan, Hong Kong, Singapore, Bali, Bangkok and Angkor Wat. They would then travel on to India in order to do some research for the Ramakrishna biography, and would spend time in England on their way back to the States. In all, this would take about four months, and Isherwood was determined to make a new start on his novel before their departure. He had come to the conclusion that the book should concentrate on the relationship between William, a successful Hollywood writer, and his friend Paul, with whom he travels to Mexico. Paul is the tempter, even the Devil, but at the same time a reflection of William, Mr. Hyde to his Dr. Jekyll. Perhaps the two characters were indeed "two halves of one person" or represented "two ways of life that this one person could have taken." He still hoped to make use of some ancient material, but one senses that this would have been a case of shoehorning it in when he wrote, for example, that in one episode "William visits the British Consul in some horrible little seaport and the Consul treats him exactly as if he were a boy of nineteen—until he feels as if he *were* and goes through, relives, all the ghastly humiliations of the young."

One of the reasons Isherwood was floundering was that he was making exactly the same mistake that he had made in *The World in the Evening:* he was trying to use a central character who both was and wasn't Christopher Isherwood. The ostensible model for William was Ivan Moffatt, whom Isherwood regarded as a heterosexual version of himself. In his notebook he wrote that William "is attractive, still boyish, romantic, sly with the girls—he has lots—successful. The only thing is: he has bad

Rather than turning his mind to something useful, Isherwood concentrated upon an even less fruitful project. Bachardy was still experiencing bouts of depression, feeling that he would never amount to anything. Although he had done well at art school, he continued to lack self-confidence. The first portrait he had done of someone other than Isherwood had been of Gerald Heard, and Stravinsky had subsequently bought it. Even this propitious start proved insufficient encouragement, and Bachardy had offered to give up any idea of an independent career as a painter and to become Isherwood's "secretary and collaborator." Isherwood thought this would be a very bad idea, but since Bachardy had asked whether Isherwood thought him "intelligent enough" for the proposed job, a tactful reply had been required. "I, of course, said what I had to say: don't put all your eggs in one basket." He did, however, feel that an attempt at some sort of literary collaboration would shore up his lover's confidence. They hit upon the idea of salvaging something from the disaster of *The World in the Evening,* and the play they began writing together used some of the novel's characters and ideas. It was, Isherwood explained, "an effort to restate what was misstated in *The World in the Evening,*" but it was "quite a different story with different problems, not in any sense an adaptation." They seem also to have tried to incorporate some of the ideas Isherwood had been tossing around for the Mexican novel, but the play's title, "The Monsters," refers to Stephen and Elizabeth. They wasted a great deal of time and energy on this doomed idea—and even sought professional advice from beyond the grave by listening to a recording of John van Druten (who had died in December 1957) explaining "how to write a play."

By the time they had finished the second act, Isherwood noted, much as he had with the Mexican novel: "Heaven only knows what it's *really* about. It *seems* to be making sense." He was no clearer by the time they were well into the second draft. "It seems entirely uninteresting," he confessed. "There is only one thing to do: finish it as quickly as possible." The collaboration did, however, have beneficial side effects. "Don and I have a curiously snug relationship right now, thanks to the play," Isherwood felt in December. "We're like winter animals storing nuts." These particular nuts, however, would not prove very sustaining. When they finished the play they very sensibly decided to ask Cecil Beaton and the Beesleys, both of whom had experience in the theater, what they thought of it, before showing it to anyone else. What Dodie Smith thought was that it was "bad; old-fashioned, conventional and unconvincing," though she expressed herself rather more tactfully when she wrote to the authors about it. Beaton was equally unimpressed, and "couldn't find one good word to say about it." The play was put away, and when Isherwood and Bachardy took another look at it several years later they recognized just how hopeless it was.

Another collaboration that came to nothing was a travel piece based on their Far East trip, which would be written by Isherwood and illustrated by Bachardy. Beyond justifying the travel expenses he would be submitting to the tax authorities, and giving Bachardy something positive to do, Isherwood had no real inclination to produce an article. He asked to read Bachardy's own diary of the trip and was both impressed by the deft character sketches it contained and dismayed by the portrait of himself that emerged. "The disagreeable things he writes about me are no more than he has often said. And of course the claustrophobia of a relationship is much more strongly felt while travelling." In order to combat the claustrophobia, Isherwood encouraged

Bachardy to do things on his own, to go on trips, cultivate friendships, even have sexual encounters. His well-intentioned attempt to give Bachardy a sense of independence came at some cost, for whenever Bachardy went away or stayed out at night, Isherwood missed him and worried that he might find someone else and leave him: "it would be the end of everything. It's true, I depend on him too much. And I criticize his selfishness, instead of restraining my own."

As well as battling with his own projects, Isherwood was also trying to help Edward Upward. One of Isherwood's most admirable qualities was his willingness to advise and encourage other writers, and he seems rarely to have suffered from professional jealousy. He was forever recommending writers to John Lehmann, hoping to secure them British publication, and spent a great deal of time nurturing the talents of such people as Ben Masselink and Peter Viertel, both of whom benefited greatly from his interest and enthusiasm. With Upward, this was a lifetime's work, and one that was always repaid in kind. Upward had at last finished his novel, most of which had to be written during the school holidays, and—with retirement in view—had embarked on the second volume of what he had planned as a semi-autobiographical trilogy. The first volume had already been rejected by several publishers, however, and Upward was becoming despondent. He feared that the book might seem "old-fashioned and too red"—Leonard Woolf had blithely suggested the book might be publishable if the communist element was removed—but Isherwood disagreed. "I read IN THE THIRTIES yesterday," he wrote after persuading Upward to send him a typescript. "It is an altogether extraordinary book, I think; extraordinary in itself and extraordinary that you should have written it." He followed this with a closely typed page of commentary, concluding: "Well—anyhow, it is *all* I hoped for, and more than I expected, even, and it is an extraordinary surprise. What more can one say?"

He had in fact said exactly what Upward wanted to hear. "Your letter cheered me more than I can say," Upward wrote back. "I shan't break my heart now even if the book is never published. Your approval is what I most want, and I had been afraid that I might not get it this time." When *In the Thirties* was finally accepted for publication, Isherwood offered to write a puff. "You have always done me more than proud," Upward replied gratefully. "Without you I don't think I should ever have got anything published at all." Isherwood and Upward's voluminous correspondence is concerned above all with their writing, forming a sustained dialogue about the processes and problems of their craft. They had been intimately involved in each other's work for almost forty years, and each knew he could rely on the other to be both sympathetic and frank. "I hope you know what your criticism and encouragement always means to me," Isherwood told Upward. "It is so easy, in the dull toxic half-light of middle-age, to get depressed about one's work and to imagine one's powers are failing."

It was all the easier to imagine this at the end of 1958 because Isherwood had very little to show for his considerable efforts during the year. He never wrote the travel article, attempts to write a film script and a play had come to nothing, and he had been forced to scrap both his novel and most of the work he had done on the Ramakrishna biography. As with the novel, Isherwood seemed unable to find a way into the biography. He had therefore gone back to what he knew best: his own experience.

I decided that I would have to begin with a few chapters of autobiography, explaining how I personally came to hear about Ramakrishna and was drawn to become his devotee. This was how I reasoned: I had first made contact with Ramakrishna through a person, not through a book. My approach to him had been that of getting to know the friend of a friend, as it were; an emotional rather than an intellectual experience. Therefore, I could only describe this experience to others in the form of a personal statement.

He hammered out seventy pages and then realized that this had no place in an official biography and so reluctantly put it to one side. In fact, all was not lost because this personal statement was the best and most clear writing Isherwood ever produced about religion, and five years later he published it as a slim book, *An Approach to Vedanta.*

The failure of these various projects meant that Isherwood was once again needlessly but genuinely worried about money. There seemed little prospect of earning much in 1959, apart from the two scripts he and Gavin Lambert were still hoping might be taken up: the detective serial, *Emily Ermingarde,* and *The Vacant Room,* the ghost story he had started writing with Lesser Samuels. In January, while on a not altogether successful holiday in New York ("This utter hell of so-called pleasure," as he described it), Isherwood learned that a writer named Victor Chapin was keen to turn the Berlin stories into a musical. A composer and lyricist were lined up, a producer was interested in the project, and Chapin had already produced a script, which he asked Isherwood to read. "I know you want me to be frank," Isherwood wrote to Chapin. "I must say, therefore, that I'm afraid I don't think this succeeds, even as a rough draft. Indeed, I don't feel this is the script of a musical at all, or of a play. You have just taken scenes from my novel and reproduced them exactly." Furthermore, Isherwood thought that the character of Sally Bowles had been badly handled, the minor characters were too prominent rather than acting as a chorus, and the political background was insufficiently emphasized. He then heard the songs and felt they did not have enough "*sting.*" When he was asked by Frank Tayler, in the role of producer, whether he might be interested in working on the project himself, he had the sudden inspiration of inviting Auden and Kallman to write the lyrics. "I need hardly explain why, to me at least, Auden is the most desirable lyricist obtainable anywhere for this book," he told Claire Degner, who handled theater projects at Curtis Brown's New York office. "I hadn't thought of him before simply because I hadn't, so to speak, looked high enough. And frankly I didn't think he'd agree." In fact, Auden had agreed with alacrity, immediately bombarding Isherwood with ideas: he hoped they might be able to introduce both Mr. Norris and Fronny into the narrative and that Lotte Lenya might be persuaded to play the landlady.[2] "It must be at least as brutal as *Pal Joey,*" he wrote, referring to Rodgers and Hart's night-club musical which had shocked audiences by its cynicism and sexual frankness.

Meanwhile, Isherwood had also heard from the screenwriter Arthur Laurents, who had become a friend, that the Broadway producer Hal Prince was very interested

---

2. As indeed she would in the Broadway production of *Cabaret.*

in the project. Since Isherwood's permission would be needed for any adaptation of the stories, brushing off Chapin and his collaborators would be easy enough. Nevertheless, Isherwood appreciated the work they had done—not least because without it he might never have thought of the idea—and wanted this to be done tactfully. This was also pragmatic:

> I am most anxious not to offend anyone unnecessarily. But the truth is as follows, and I may as well say it right away. If I have to choose between a 'sure-fire' commercial presentation of the material, and an exciting off-beat more speculative presentation, such as Auden would give, then I choose Auden every time. But, on the other hand, if it is *absolutely* impossible to get such an off-beat presentation produced, well, then let's try to make the venture as commercially fool-proof as we can!

The initial enthusiasm waned a little after discussions had taken place in New York. Degner suspected that whatever Taylor may have thought of Auden and Kallman as opera librettists, he did not consider their talents suited to Broadway. A further difficulty would be geography. Taylor felt that it was "practically hopeless to co-ordinate the writing of a musical at great distance by mail," although this was in fact the way Auden and Isherwood had always worked, usually in different countries, meeting only for short, intensive periods of collation and revision. Having discussed the matter with Degner, Auden started to worry that they would not be able to produce a script as quickly as the producers would like. "Given that none of us are professionals in this field," he wrote to Isherwood,

> I do not think it worth the while of any of us to work unless we can have the time to do something quite fresh and to our satisfaction. If we cannot have that time, then I would advise you very strongly to hand the whole thing over to the professionals. Above all, *please* don't think for a second, that you having asked me & Chester if we would be interested, commits you to the slightest degree. As you know, we would love to work together, but on condition that the time needed is available. And if it ain't, it ain't.

To Auden's delight—"It is what we both prayed but did not dare hope for"—Isherwood replied that he would far prefer to keep Auden and Kallman on board. Auden suggested that all three could meet any time between June and October at Kirchstetten in Austria, where he had bought a house in which to spend his summers. Knowing of Isherwood's reluctance to leave California, he added: "If the only obstacle is financial, I would be delighted to lend you the needful, for as long as you like." He thought they would need to re-read all the relevant work from the period, including *The Memorial, Lions and Shadows* and *Dogskin.*

> It seems clear that we should regard all the material not as literature but as historical documents which we inspect from the standpoint of 1960, and then ask ourselves—what have we here (and in our memories) that are suitable raw materials for conversion into a musical that is definitely American yet as unsentimental and

get to the nerve." Isherwood found that, unlike "Ambrose," what he called "this strange story of mine" was "writing itself—almost against my will." He evidently found it stimulating to write with the sort of sexual explicitness that would prevent the story from being published at that time—certainly more stimulating than writing "Ambrose" or the Ramakrishna biography. He knew perfectly well that having too many irons in the fire was bad for him, having earlier told Stephen Spender: "My own projects are so numerous that I'm in danger of not really getting ahead with anything." He nevertheless finished a draft of the story in under eight weeks. He gave it the title "Afterwards" and would spend further time revising and typing it later in the year, eventually sending it under plain cover to John Lehmann—and then worrying that the packet would be opened and he would be prosecuted for obscenity.

"Afterwards" takes the form of a diary kept over a couple of years by a nameless middle-aged writer living in California. He is grieving for his younger lover, who has been killed in an accident, and gets through his days by indulging in casual sex and raging against heterosexuals, who he thinks cannot fully understand his loss. At the gym he meets an attractive couple, Leonard and Forrest, with whom he falls into a close friendship. Forrest is very much the narrator's type and seems rather flirtatious, so much so that the narrator decides he ought to follow up the offer of a job in New York to get away from him. Before he can do so, Forrest seduces him and the two men embark on a highly charged sexual affair. One evening, the narrator goes to a secret assignation in a bar to find Leonard instead of Forrest waiting for him. Leonard has found out about the affair and wants to confront his rival. After several drinks they go back to the narrator's apartment where a mock fight ends up with them having sex. The following day, the narrator heads for New York. A year later he returns to California and learns that Forrest has left Leonard for someone else. He goes to see Leonard and the story ends with them setting up house together.

The descriptions of sex, which are frequent and extended, are extremely graphic and faintly ludicrous. The tone is evidently meant to be tough, but the writing is merely slapdash, and few readers handed this typescript blind would find it easy to identify the author. Literary merit is not of course a prerequisite of pornography, but it is evident that Isherwood was trying to do something more than merely arouse his readers. One suspects that he was aiming for some sort of homosexual authenticity, but the mixture of hard-core sex and soft-boiled sentiment is not successful. "Afterwards" is, however, interesting as a forerunner of both the novel Isherwood was trying to write at the same time, *Down There on a Visit,* and the one he would write next, *A Single Man.* It opens with the narrator being sent a novel for review:

> The blurb of this one says: 'This story has been written with maturity and restraint by an astonishingly youthful author. His striking gift for portraying the poignancy and heartbreak of young love, in the persons of Dirk, the Dutch schoolboy in Semarang, and Marie, the lovely French-Javanese girl, make this a truly memorable experience.'
> Fuck them.
> I loathe all heterosexuals of all ages everywhere. I loathe the poignant restrained heartbreaking books that are written about their nasty amours. Let them

all rot. No—let them live. But I don't want to hear about them or read about them. I find them a bore. Worse than that. Disgusting. I find their love as disgusting as they find mine.

And so on.

A little bit of maturity and restraint from Isherwood would not have gone amiss here, and he found them by the time he came to write Ambrose's wearily elegant dismissal of heterosexuality in *Down There on a Visit* and George's savage but beautifully turned tirade on the subject in *A Single Man*. The latter novel borrows some of the plot of this story, along with the well-meaning but inadequate response of "liberal" heterosexuals to bereavement. The story was never published, but circulated in typescript, drawing admiring comments from various of Isherwood's homosexual friends. Stephen Spender recalled being telephoned by John Lehmann, who said "darkly": "I want to see you, Stephen. It's about Christopher. No, I'm sorry it's something I can't tell you about over the phone. I think you'd better see me as soon as possible." Spender went round for lunch the following day and was told about the story, which couldn't possibly be allowed out of Lehmann's flat. "I warn you, Stephen," Lehmann had said, "it may give you the feeling that in this strange and fascinating world which Christopher describes, you'll find yourself, among those people, pretty inadequate. It is a world where if you were too long or too short or too quick or too slow, no one would have the slightest spark of affection for you." After lunch, sustained by "an enormous tumbler of brandy," Spender dutifully sat down to read the story. Lehmann, he said, "sat with a glass opposite, watching my pants." Spender judged the story "marvellous" and "really terribly true to life."

Forster was also summoned to Lehmann's flat, where in front of a roaring fire he read the story "in comfort and with great interest, but too hastily as time was short." As a former practitioner in this genre, he felt that "the opening and the closing exercises [i.e. sex acts] vary too little, and there is scarcely anything extra left for Leonard. I would have been sketchier and more restrained earlier." He felt that the ending was sad because he sensed "an absence of progress" in the story. "I think this is because it isn't developed into a sufficiently important event," Isherwood explained to Spender, who had also found the story melancholy, "and so one gets a saddening sense of repetition and futility. Just another fuck. One day I'll try to write something really more substantial in this genre. It is fun to try. The sense of freedom is exciting."

In February 1959 Isherwood embarked on what became a close friendship with another British expatriate, Charles Laughton, who had for some years been based in Los Angeles with his wife, Elsa Lanchester. Laughton had been invited to play King Lear in the autumn season at Stratford-upon-Avon and was for some reason keen to discuss his interpretation of the role with Isherwood, whom he knew socially but not well. The Laughtons had been married for almost thirty years, and frequently worked together, but they were a distinctly odd couple. Isherwood's senior by five years, Laughton looked much older, a great lumbering potato-faced hulk of a man who was morbidly convinced of his own ugliness. Lanchester was equally bizarre-looking, a gamine figure with unruly red hair and protuberant eyes. Both had made good professional use of their unusual appearance, Laughton famously playing Quasimodo in the 1939 film of *The Hunchback of Notre Dame* and Lanchester cast as the eponymous *Bride of Frankenstein* in James Whale's classic 1935 movie. Lanchester felt that it was not only on screen that she was married to a monster. She and Laughton were known as one of Hollywood's most famous couples, but their private life was rather less happy than the frequent publicity shots suggested, chiefly because Laughton was homosexual. Although Laughton told his wife that "he only felt really comfortable with his 'own kind,' " by the time they met Isherwood, some sort of uneasy accommodation had been reached.

Laughton was now a grand old man of the stage and screen, while Lanchester was achieving a cult reputation in cabaret, something she did with more panache than musicality. Some idea of her popular but deranged show at Los Angeles' Turnabout Theatre—in which she adopted all manner of costume in order to sing mock-Victorian ballads, "bawdy Cockney songs" and the infamous "Yashmak Song"—was given by a critic in the *New Yorker,* who wrote: "Her songs take one out of a close, tidy world into a disquieting place filled with sharp winds of unsteady laughter. . . ." Laughton was privately satirical about Lanchester's abilities, claiming that when she went on tour she had to rehearse for several days in order to change her opening greeting from "Hello, L.A.!" to "Hello, Miami!," but he encouraged her career—partly because Lanchester was having an affair with her accompanist, which let him off the hook.

Laughton evidently recognized Isherwood as one of his "own kind," and possibly realized that one way of securing Isherwood's friendship was by flattering him. It was indeed an enormous compliment to be consulted by one of the great actors of the age about one of the great classical roles. Eager to see the result of these discussions, Isherwood decided to make a lightning trip to England that summer, combining a visit to Stratford with one to Wyberslegh. Laughton's Lear, much heralded in the British press, was not universally acclaimed, and Isherwood agreed that it did not quite live up to expectations, although the scene on the heath, which they had discussed in some detail, was "wonderful."

Kathleen had survived a stroke the previous year but at over ninety was clearly not going to live a great deal longer. When Isherwood saw her, he was pleasantly surprised by how well she seemed, though appalled by Richard, who was dirtier than ever and had lost yet more teeth. He was also horrified by the increasing squalor in which they were both living: "Black sooty cobwebs everywhere. The walls cracked. The wallpaper hanging in tatters. The carpets stiff with greasy grime."

On his fifty-fifth birthday, in perfect weather, he and Bachardy went for a drive through the Peak District: "It was like that sinister summer passage in *Wuthering Heights,* when they go up to Penistone Crag and it is so lovely, but the shadow of the oncoming winter and death is over everything." When he left Wyberslegh, he knew that he was saying goodbye to Kathleen for the last time, but could not really accept this fact. Kathleen, unusually, made no comment about Christopher's departure in her diary (dictated since her stroke to Richard), perhaps refusing like him to acknowledge that they would not see each other again.

Back in Santa Monica, Isherwood started another draft of "Ambrose," encouraged by the fact that Lehmann had accepted "Mr Lancaster" for the *London Magazine,* where it appeared in the October 1959 issue. "We consider it so important that we are devoting almost the whole of this number to it," Lehmann announced in his editorial, in which with his usual blundering tactlessness he also took the opportunity to revive the controversy about Auden and Isherwood's emigration. Lehmann attacked those who had criticized the two writers, but then added:

> An original creative artist, under the compulsion to question convention at every point and realize his own moral vision, must be allowed to make his own mistakes as well as his own positive discoveries. He stands at a certain distance from himself, able to accept what might, with the pseudo-artist, harden into inhibition, as grist for his mill. If he eventually feels sorry to have changed his country, or guilt at having missed a battle in which his friends were involved, the regret and the guilt become part of the experience on which he builds his art. If they have enlarged his vision, the rest of us should only feel glad.

In the course of a long and fulsome letter to Lehmann about the latter's latest installment of autobiography, *I Am My Brother,* which also dealt with "the Auden-Isherwood question," Isherwood wrote: "I can't tell you how I *ought* to have chosen, because now it seems that the choice was made for me. And the I who looks back is anyhow foreign to the I who would be looking back if I had stayed in England. *All experience is wonderful, and, if properly digested, formative*—as you say so well in your editorial." It is doubtful whether this is any more sincere than his general praise of Lehmann's book, which in his diary (on the same day he wrote this letter), he described as "worthy and well documented and liberal and almost noble and a big fat bore." He added: "John is a bore because he's so fucking grand. Rather like van Druten, he watches himself with the greatest respect, to see what he'll do next—but alas no humor."

Unlike Lehmann, when Isherwood looked in a mirror, as he did on the day he wrote that diary entry, he did so with no respect whatsoever. Looking back at him was a "funny old thing [. . .] with a neck turning scraggy unless pulled tight, and eye bags." This apparition was, however, "still potentially useful and capable of being used, if only the old silly doesn't waste its few precious years in resentments, tantrums, cantankerousness." The mirror would prove a useful device in *Down There on a Visit,* in which each of the principal characters acts as a looking-glass held up to the author at various stages in his life. Isherwood was also very much preoccupied with the notion of the different stages of "I" in an autobiography. The "I" who narrates the novel is the present-day author, but within each section there is another "I," the person the narrator was at that time. This is an objectifying device that Isherwood was to develop later in his less fictionalized autobiographies.

Isherwood started his new career as a lecturer at the Los Angeles State College on September 22, a week before he moved into Adelaide Drive. He gave two lectures a week, and students were expected to think about not only the writers under discus-

cut it. These fears proved justified when Isherwood received a long letter, typed but with numerous qualifying handwritten additions and alterations. Spender felt that his initial reaction to the story had been colored by his own recollections of the people and the period (he had himself stayed with Turville-Petre on St. Nicholas shortly after Isherwood did), and that he needed to canvass the opinion of others, specifically his co-editor, Melvyn J. Lasky. The story had aroused "a great deal of controversy" in the office, he wrote, and on re-reading it he began to have his own reservations. His two principal criticisms were that it was "too long and rather too loosely constructed" and that Isherwood had not yet resolved the relationship between the present-day narrator and his 1933 self.

> If you consider the matter, there are really a series of three Isherwoods, Isher-wood I—yourself now writing, Isherwood II—at the age of 25, Isherwood III—the person in the story. The possibility of a false tone being introduced is dangerously heightened. For instance, in the *London Magazine* story [i.e. "Mr Lancaster"], you seem a bit too contemptuous of yourself when young, and in this story your feelings about Waldemar are complicated by being those of an older man remembering his own youthful feelings about him.

Isherwood knew that the handling of his various selves was crucial to the entire book, and both Upward and Dodie Smith had expressed similar concerns. The fact that Spender felt that "the story has a masterpiece submerged in it and that with rewriting, you will bring this out" did little to mollify Isherwood, who was particularly annoyed that Spender had dictated the letter to a secretary and appeared to be putting forward the opinions of others rather than saying what he really thought. Isherwood sent what must have been an aggrieved reply (it has not survived), and asked Spender to for-ward the typescript to Upward. Spender wrote again, apologizing for appearing to change his mind about the story, but reiterating his criticisms, adding characteristi-cally: "We have just had our house burgled, so I am a bit confused." He then sent an-other letter to "confess" that he had shown the story to Auden, who thought it "*extremely* good" but had similar reservations. This may not have been the most tact-ful thing to have done in the circumstances, but Spender's criticisms were largely jus-tified and Isherwood took note of them when revising the story.

Meanwhile, Upward sent a favorable report on "Ambrose." "When the verdict ar-rived from the Supreme Court, we danced for joy," Isherwood told him. "Of course I still realize there is a lot wrong with AMBROSE, but the point is, you *like* it. I don't feel that the ENCOUNTER people did. And I shan't worry about it any more for the present but get ahead with the next section." This was the one set during the Munich crisis, and Isherwood was delighted to find it easier to write than the previous two episodes, completing a "*very* rough" draft in under five weeks.

"Waldemar" was, like "Ambrose," based on Isherwood's diaries. He realized that September 1938 had been a sort of limbo between war and peace, neither one thing nor the other. "I do think [the diary] conveys the misery of the crisis," he wrote in his workbook. "In a whole variety of ways. I like the bits about Morgan [Forster]. And the sense of things going on as usual. And the almost *snugness* of the approaching war. It is the Agony in the Garden—after which the crucifixion will be positively a relief." Forster, "the great liberal," was to be one of the significant characters in this episode, as was Rolf Katz, "the Cassandra," and Ian Scott-Kilvert, "the lost generation boy."

Having completed two drafts, he started on the final section, "Paul," based on his relationship with Denny Fouts. Since he had already depicted "The Damned" in three episodes, Isherwood intended to hold out the possibility of salvation in this final one:

> Paul is 'converted'—partly by me, partly by another character (Gerald? Swami?). We start an 'intentional' life. It gradually goes wrong. Paul relapses.
>
> And the question is posed: is 'good' really good—is 'bad' really bad? In other words, isn't enlightenment what matters? Paul has learned something from his life. Won't his next one, therefore, be better? Some of my 'good' characters haven't learnt anything. So what'll happen to them?

This general idea seemed fine, but somehow Isherwood could not really make any progress with writing the story. He may have found it helpful—or merely a displacement activity—to keep a record of his struggles to write various books, but by doing so (and preserving them) he gave them a significance they did not perhaps deserve. He seems not to have realized that all novelists undergo similar difficulties, suffer blocks, get into muddles and occasionally wonder what on earth it is they are supposed to be writing.

He blamed his current impasse on the fact that "I simply haven't bothered to plan it all properly," although this was in fact something he rarely did in the latter part of his career. He now attempted to construct an outline, into which he crammed a great deal of autobiographical material, starting with meeting Fouts in 1940 and ending with an imaginary final confrontation in Berlin after the war. He realized that this was perhaps over-ambitious, but saw that what really mattered was "to keep to the fore the whole relationship between Paul & me. I see it as a sort of dialogue, a love-affair on the metaphysical plane. Something that goes deeper than surface-personality." One aspect of this biographical material which had to be altered was Fouts's pursuit of young boys. In the novel, Paul's relapse would take the form of seducing an underage girl, the twelve-year-old Dee-Ann Swendson. This was shocking enough, but at least had a respectable literary precedent in Nabokov's *Lolita*, a novel Isherwood greatly admired.[3] He finished a draft of "Paul" quite quickly. "I don't yet quite know what it's about," he confessed to Upward, "but I think it is psychologically daring. I mean, it attempts to describe mystical experience (among other things) in a tone of serious farce."

This burst of creativity may have been helped by the fact that Isherwood was regularly taking Dexamyl, a mixture of the amphetamine Dexedrine and the tranquilizer Miltown. Bachardy had been taking this drug, easily available by prescription, for some time, having found it gave him both "extra pep" and a boost to his self-

---

3. Isherwood himself remained susceptible to the under-aged. At about this time he wrote enthusiastically to Spender about the writer Henry Miller's "very beautiful blond thirteen-year-old son Tony, who surfs and scorns writing."

confidence when he was doing sittings with people of whom he was nervous. Isherwood found that the drug alleviated hangovers and helped when he was obliged to carry out "heavy-duty writing chores." He had in fact given up drinking for a month in May, but as soon as he started again had got "utterly plastered" at a supper party, fallen down some steps and slipped a disc. He was in considerable pain, unable to walk or drive, but this did not prevent him from getting drunk again four days later, and frequently thereafter. "This fucking back doesn't get any better," he complained. "I'm weary of it, and ill-tempered because of a hangover."

On June 15, 1960, at the age of ninety-one, Kathleen Isherwood died peacefully in her sleep after suffering a further series of minor strokes and developing bronchitis and pneumonia. Isherwood had been told a week before she died that she was sinking fast, and when the telegram arrived, he wrote in his diary: "There is nothing to be said about this at present. I am sad, yes, but I don't really feel M.'s loss. Perhaps I never shall; perhaps I've been through it already. My feelings aren't important, anyway." His immediate concern was that he might have to go to England for the funeral, a journey he was unwilling to undertake and which he convinced himself he could not afford. He argued that Richard had always been very possessive of Kathleen and might resent any "interference" on his brother's part, preferring to handle these final arrangements himself. This reasoning may have been plausible, but the simple truth was that he didn't want to go. Fortunately, Amiya Sandwich, although she had only just emerged from hospital after a kidney operation, traveled to Wyberslegh to help out.

During Kathleen's final illness, Richard had taken to sharing her bed, and according to Amiya, he had woken up to find his mother's corpse beside him. The lives of mother and son had become so entwined that Kathleen's death, though expected, came as a terrible shock to Richard. "It is the early mornings and the nights when I miss her almost unbearably and cry myself to sleep on the latter occasions," he told his brother; "this is only for myself and we grieving ones who are left, not for her, she is *far* happier now than she has been for a long time." On the evening before the funeral, he consumed an entire bottle of whisky and passed out. While waiting for him to wake up, a large *famille rose* bowl at the ready in case he was sick, Amiya wrote to Isherwood about Richard's plans to sell many of his mother's possessions, which he felt he could no longer bear to see. She rightly worried that he might sell them at well below the market value to anyone who asked, and she suggested that some of the pieces should be sent to Sotheby's or Christie's.

She was even more worried when her attempts to rouse Richard from his stupor entirely failed. Fortunately, after her first stroke, Kathleen had managed to find a couple named Mr. and Mrs. Vince who lived in and took care of her and Richard. They had been out for the evening, but now returned and took charge, administering an effective emetic, the results of which revealed that Richard had, like his brother, been taking a large number of "pep pills." Mr. Vince hoisted Richard onto his shoulder and carried him upstairs to his bed.

The following morning, Richard was suffering "the father & mother of all hangovers," but started drinking once more. As he later confessed to his brother: "I made the rather *inexcusably* cowardly mistake before we left home [for the funeral] of having *too much to drink,* to deaden my nervousness." Consequently he sat through the service in something of a daze. The funeral was followed by a cremation, after which Kathleen's ashes were brought back to Wyberslegh and buried in the garden alongside the remains of her beloved cats. Amiya stayed on to help Richard through the difficult days. "I must say that, except for an occasional weepy spell, R. is holding up *very* well," she reported. "I've made him laugh loudly & long several times! And shall be with him here until Sunday, by which time I think he will be feeling not only much better, but also the itching of the sprouting wings of Freedom from Bondage. Already he is talking of a little holiday. . . ."

Richard was now forty-eight and had never really lived alone. "Whatever is going to become of him?" Isherwood wondered. "Of course we none of us can guess that, because the decision is really entirely up to him. What I fear is—does he have any kind of interest in life, any vocation, which will keep him going? Or will he relapse into being sorry for himself and drinking and being victimized, more or less, by hangers-on? How little I know him, really. That is, how little I know him apart from our Mother." It was indeed difficult to imagine how Richard would function without Kathleen. Although Amiya warned that "the leeches are crawling round him thick & fast," she thought Richard was wise to them. He was also surrounded by people who had his interests at heart, not only the Vinces, but also Alan Bradley and his wife. Other supposed friends were less altruistic, and Amiya had already seen off a man with whom Richard had been involved, almost certainly asexually, for many years. Toward the end of her stay, she and Richard had a long conversation, during which he told her what she already knew: that he was homosexual. "I realize that his need is far greater than his prepossessiveness [*sic*] or attraction to another!" she told Isherwood. "And that is where he *could* get into trouble—But we won't meet that trouble half-way. It may not arise." One of the reasons Richard was not very prepossessing was that he was obsessively worried about constipation and not only used large numbers of suppositories but also drank quantities of liquid paraffin. "I wish you would write him that <u>liquid paraffin can</u> be <u>poisonous</u>!!" Amiya begged Isherwood. "He ruins his clothes, <u>everything</u> he sits on etc! Small [the Hinchingbrooke butler] is now trying to get the oil out of my car seat cover! It is the major problem at W.H. at the moment! [. . .] What unpleasant details I have had to write you—But you should know—& perhaps help."

Isherwood had long ago adopted a policy of not helping Richard, for fear of being accused of meddling. Not everyone understood this, and Amiya, worried about the state in which Richard and Kathleen had been living, had written to him "reproachfully" earlier in the year after Richard had told her he was concerned about the future of Wyberslegh when Kathleen died. Isherwood replied that he was under the impression that Richard rather than Kathleen owned Wyberslegh and that even if this was not the case he would immediately make over anything that Kathleen left him to his brother, just as he had when Uncle Henry died. "I am the first to realize that Richard has ruined his life for my Mother's sake," he told Amiya. "I always told you so—and years ago, I told *her.*"

Since Isherwood was clearly not going to adopt the role of protective elder brother at this late stage, Amiya risked writing a letter to Richard when she got home, taking advantage of their newfound intimacy. "My *one* concern is, darling Richard,

weight. He was sent home on a strict diet and throughout the period of his collaboration with Isherwood was morose and unwell, although the two men appeared to enjoy their work together. Laughton finally had the operation in August and became considerably debilitated, looking, Isherwood thought, "terribly shaky, and so old." Convinced that his health would never fully recover, Laughton subsequently suffered a breakdown.

By this time, Isherwood had taken up his post as Regents' Professor of English at Santa Barbara, a post previously held by Aldous Huxley. He spent two days of each week at the university, taking seminars and delivering eight lectures, and this involved him in a long and tiring commute of some two hundred miles there and back from Santa Monica. Huxley had spoken on "The Human Situation," and a similarly daunting title had been chosen for Isherwood's lectures: "The Writer and His World." In the first of his lectures, Isherwood made an immediate disclaimer: "This is a title I should never dare to choose for a series of talks, because it makes assumptions of some sort of over-all knowledge of writers and their worlds in general," he told his students. He preferred to talk about "A Writer and His World": "that means one individual writer and one individual aspect of the world, and, as I daresay most of you have guessed by this time, the writer is me."

His first lecture was on "Influences," followed by talks on "the whole question of 'why write at all,' " "the nerve of the interest in a novel," the writer and the theater, the writer and films, the writer and politics, and the writer and religion. In the event, he delivered two lectures on "the nerve of the interest" and dropped the lecture on politics, perhaps having felt they could be dealt with in his lecture on writing for the Group Theatre. He assured his audience that he was not going to hold forth in his first lecture like one of those "great men" of the nineteenth century who "used to say that life was never the same after they had read the sixth book of Plato's *Republic* or whatever it might be." His notion of influences was "something much less pretentious, much less clearly defined and operating at a deeper level probably of consciousness." It was, in fact, going to be much more personal. Consequently he talked a great deal about his family background, Judge Bradshawe, Marple Hall, his anti-heroic soldier father, Brontë country, Beatrix Potter and "animal totemism," the Outsider, Dickens and Little Jo, Tolstoy and capital punishment, and E. M. Forster's essay "What I Believe." He ended this eclectic talk with an anecdote about Tallulah Bankhead and found himself "a truly smashing success." This particularly pleased him because UCSB's chancellor had originally vetoed his appointment. "It was very funny to see how sincerely relieved and somewhat surprised Chancellor Gould was that my lecture was such a hit," he noted with satisfaction. He celebrated his triumph by getting drunk at a barbecue, falling over and damaging his shin so severely that his doctor thought he might have cracked the bone.

Isherwood was evidently hoping to be seen by his students as a "no shit" lecturer: he was candid, funny, self-deprecating. A natural speaker—and showoff—he lectured from brief notes, allowing himself numerous ad libs, digressions and asides, sometimes running out of time, and on one occasion entirely mislaying an extract from a book that he had intended to read by way of illustration. The lectures reached a wider audience than the one at the university since they were broadcast on the radio, resulting in some fan mail. Spender was keen to publish some of them in *Encounter.* Isherwood agreed in principle, but was furious when, having heard nothing more, he was sent a galley proof of the first lecture. He wrote a fierce letter to Spender, reminding him that any decisions about publication were supposed to have been agreed in advance. He had already refused UCSB permission to print the lectures "because they were 'all done with mirrors'—i.e. they depended on my personal performance for any effect that the audience got from them." The broadcasts may have been a success: "But, written down, [the lectures] are just nothing at all. I can even recognize lines which, delivered with suitable pauses, in my nasal twang, brought the house down. Here they are just silly, or worse, coy."

While Isherwood's professional life seemed to be going well, life at home was less satisfactory. "Relations with Don are perfect," he had reported at the beginning on the new decade. By the end of January, however, he was complaining that Bachardy had been "carrying on at breakfast about how he ought not to be living in Santa Monica—*his* studio, *his* school, *his* gym are all in town. I try to let this go over me, but the whine of neurotic selfishness is irritating. Oh well—moods. What *does* it matter?" Shortly afterward, Bachardy suggested that he should get an apartment near his art school and spend four nights a week there. Isherwood told himself that "this was largely a sort of test of my reactions," but he was nevertheless worried. They had now been together for seven years, and reviewing this period Isherwood wrote that Bachardy "has mattered and does matter more than any of the others. Because he imposes himself more, demands more, cares more—about everything he does and encounters. He is so desperately alive [. . .] How he ventures further and further, deeper and deeper, into the jungle of his life. It is terribly moving, and exciting, to watch him." It was also unsettling. By now Isherwood felt that he could not imagine a future without Bachardy. "I do believe he still imagines I might willingly leave him," Isherwood wrote in his diary after one drunken and violent scene during which Bachardy appeared to be venting his frustrations by attacking the car and smashing a piggy bank. This notion struck Isherwood as "ridiculous and unthinkable." Almost as unthinkable, but a real possibility, was that Bachardy might leave Isherwood.

In October Bachardy went away for three weeks, the longest time he and Isherwood had ever spent apart. He traveled to Delaware to do drawings of the cast for Tennessee Williams's new play, *Period of Adjustment,* which was opening there, then went on to New York to oversee the framing of portraits he had done of the Broadway cast of Shelagh Delaney's *A Taste of Honey.* These would be hung in the foyer of the theater and had been commissioned by the British stage and screen director Tony Richardson. The flamboyantly bisexual Richardson, who was currently married to Vanessa Redgrave, had become a friend of Isherwood in Los Angeles, and through him Isherwood was to meet the playwright John Osborne, and his wife, the actress Mary Ure. Osborne's complicated personal life, which at this period involved him with several women at the same time, fascinated Isherwood, who wrote about it at length in his diary. Bachardy's trip was a success, but the experience of being the center of attention, rather than viewed merely as Isherwood's partner, made him restless. Shortly after his return, Isherwood reported a major row in a restaurant. "Told me he wanted to be independent. Wanted to go to New York for several months. That all I ever did was to find ways of making him dependent on me. That he didn't see why he should be grateful to me, because after all he had given me so much of his life, and it was time that counted." Bachardy admitted that he felt guilty over being financially dependent on Isherwood, who wrote:

> I believe more firmly than ever in Don. I believe in his talent *and* his character, and I believe he will evolve into the kind of person we both want him to be. I believe, furthermore, that he has taken giant steps in this direction already; and that therefore these outbursts mean much less than they meant three or four years ago. He is becoming more and more independent in the only way that matters—inside himself.

It was largely in order to make Bachardy truly independent that Isherwood continued to encourage him as an artist. Past experience had shown Isherwood the consequences of having a partner with no proper occupation, and whenever Bachardy felt insecure about his talent and his vocation or felt that his longed-for career was never going to materialize, Isherwood was there to encourage him. There was always the risk, as Isherwood very well knew, that once he was independent of Isherwood, Bachardy might develop a taste for freedom, but it was a risk Isherwood knew he had to take. That risk was considerably increased when in December Bachardy found a sponsor who offered to fund an extended trip to Europe to study art. The plan was for Bachardy to spend six months at the Slade School of Fine Art in London, where generations of leading British painters had been trained. Competition for places at this prestigious establishment was fierce, but Isherwood thought he might be able to pull strings via his former 1930s associate William Coldstream, who taught there. Having had no contact with Coldstream since 1939, he did not feel that he could approach him directly and so asked Spender to act as an intermediary. Spender cabled a couple of days later to say that the Slade would accept Bachardy as soon as he liked. "I feel hideously sad whenever I think about it," Isherwood wrote, "especially when I wake in the mornings. I dread it and yet I know it may be the best, the only possible way for us to go on together."

Bachardy left for London in January 1961, within days of learning he had a place at the Slade. Isherwood made plans to get through the six months: exercise, meditation, work. "Must be prepared for a psychosomatic coup," he warned himself; "getting sick in order to be able to call Don home [. . .] There are moments when I think, *can* I bear it? But I must—not only that, but make something out of the experience; discipline and train myself. Not run around to parties getting drunk and looking for 'consolation.' " Consolation materialized almost at once, however: "Considerable excitement because Tom Deeley is to come and stay with me. Well—" Deeley was an attractive young teacher, specializing in literature, and was in a stable relationship with a naval man named Brad Kelsey, who was frequently absent. Isherwood was of the opinion that Kelsey did not sufficiently appreciate his good fortune in having Deeley as a lover, though this may have been a way of justifying his own involvement with the young man.

Having given Bachardy his sexual freedom, albeit reluctantly, Isherwood had also enjoyed several "extramarital" affairs during the past seven years. Perhaps the most important of these was with a young man named Paul Kennedy, and as soon as Deeley had left after his weekend visit, Isherwood went to see him. Compared with Deeley, whom Isherwood judged "a very sweet boy—intelligent, though on the prissy, academic side, and capable of serious love," Kennedy seemed to have lost his charm and was now described as "hopelessly sloppy and tacky and passive." This did not, however, prevent Isherwood from continuing a sexual relationship with him.

The weekend with Deeley had not been an unqualified success, although Isherwood was obliged to write about it somewhat guardedly in his journal, since he suspected that Bachardy occasionally sneaked a look at it. They had spent some time discussing Deeley's future life with Kelsey, and at the end of their time together Deeley "left feeling frustrated." This frustration may have been sexual, since it seems that although Deeley and Isherwood often spent the night together, they were not in fact having sex. This did not make the relationship any less intense or less significant. When they were not together Isherwood was left feeling "doubly lonely. Lonely for Don, as always. Lonely also a little bit for Tommy Deeley. This is silly, but harmless and nice. I do feel he's a wonderful person—anyone who can love, properly, is wonderful. People like that always get me romantic over them."

The fact that Isherwood was a little bit in love with Deeley did not mean that he was any less in love with Bachardy. It was Bachardy who remained at the center of his life. People such as Deeley were enjoyable and relatively safe diversions: although Isherwood disliked Kelsey, thinking him "a self-centred ass," he also knew that Deeley was committed to this partnership. Indeed, while visiting Deeley, he was obliged to listen to him yelling down the telephone on a bad line to the West Indies: "Brad—*I love you* more than anything else in the *world*!" He tried to analyze his own infatuation with Deeley by telling himself "Some of my loneliness has spilled off on to him, that's all; don't let's call it anything more. It only *feels* like love." He could never quite work out how serious Deeley was about their relationship. He was of course charmed when the young man telephoned just to say "I've been thinking about you all day," but nevertheless decided that "teasing is still teasing, however tastefully conducted." He tried to convince himself that time spent with Deeley "didn't really add up to very much in terms of emotion," and that the persistent "stupidest nagging little ache of wishing Tom was around" when they were apart didn't "really mean anything" and was "just nervousness." It was in fact rather more than that. "We reached a sort of climax in our relationship, and got by it rather successfully, I think," he wrote in his diary when Deeley accompanied him home after a party to spend the night at Adelaide Drive. "I don't really quite know how I feel about this yet, however. So I'll go into it later. Or maybe I won't. Anyhow, it's very good that he's going to Mexico in two days. I suspect some playacting on both sides. And yet he is a sweet boy and fun to be with."

Isherwood's behavior during this period is curiously reminiscent of his behavior in 1937, when, parted from Heinz, he pursued a number of affairs, some of which were serious. Whether or not he realized it, his account of this relationship with Deeley is very similar to the account of his affair with Ian Scott-Kilvert in his 1937–38 diary. Once again, he was being pleasurably pursued by a younger man who was already involved elsewhere, and although increasingly caught up emotionally, he was aware of an element of "playacting." It may simply have been a coincidence that Isherwood had been thinking a great deal about the Munich crisis, re-reading his diary of the period and transforming it into fiction for "Waldemar," in which Scott-Kilvert was originally going to be featured. His workbook shows that he had been subjecting his behavior during the Munich period to intense scrutiny, analyzing his feelings, his motives, his fears. Even if Isherwood was not consciously aware of the similarities between his current situation and that of 1938, the pattern seems to be there in his writing. In later life he would analyze his sexual life in terms of archetypes, but he never dealt with either Scott-Kilvert or Deeley—possibly because both of them were still alive.

Isherwood's account of the climactic encounter with Deeley is infuriatingly oblique, and although he did write about it later, the record is no clearer:

> He claimed—on the night we got drunk and had the big showdown, and he said he left it to me if we should or not; as far as *he* was concerned, he wanted to; and I said No—that he has a violent temper and is capable of physical violence. Yes, I suppose that is possible. Of course, fundamentally, we were on our best party manners throughout. I guess, if there had never been a Don, I would have had a try at living with him; and I think that it could have worked out. But then, so it could have with a lot of people. That doesn't make him a Don, or even a substi-tute-Don, by a million miles.

This suggests that Isherwood had turned down the offer of sex with Deeley. The reasons are complicated. Since he was evidently spending time with other men, it was not a case of wishing to remain faithful to Bachardy. On the other hand, his involvement with Deeley was far more serious than a mere sexual encounter, and therefore more of a threat to his relationship with Bachardy. It is also possible that because this involvement *was* serious, because Isherwood was *romantically* involved, then it was important that if he and Deeley did have sex it should be a success. Isherwood reported that he had been "eating celery like crazy because someone said Kinsey discovered it was the only thing for potency." He also gave up drinking, but found that although he was in better shape physically than he had been for a long time, he was "absolutely impotent." "Is it old age," he asked himself, "or just that all the gism [*sic*] has gone into novel writing, as it's supposed to?" This may be the reason that Isherwood reports that both he and Deeley experienced frustration. Interesting as such speculation is, the real significance of Isherwood's relationship with Deeley is that he would draw upon it when writing *A Single Man*.

With Deeley headed for Mexico, Isherwood decided to go to England. He had been asked whether he would be interested in writing a screenplay based on his cousin Graham Greene's novel *England Made Me,* and he needed to visit London to discuss the project with the British producer John Sutro. He suspected that he would not be paid well enough, but now that the idea had been put into his head, he thought he could travel to London anyway and perhaps find other work there. Before he left, he was committed to delivering three lectures at UCLA, as part of the University Extension program. He had been outraged when the university attempted to persuade him to accept a fee of $200 per lecture. Isherwood insisted on $300, but suspected that the negotiators might have agreed to an even higher fee had he pushed them.

"Whatever anyone says, this kind of thing nauseates me," he wrote in his diary; "it is Jewy and vile and utterly shameful, coming from the representatives of a serious institution of learning instead of an old clothes dealer."

The lectures, held over three consecutive Sunday evenings, were titled "The Voices of the Novel." A flyer, designed by Bachardy and incorporating one of his drawings of Isherwood, announced Isherwood's manifesto, printed over a facsimile of his signature: "One of the most essential things about a writer is his tone of voice. Just as you may form a tremendously strong impression of a stranger to whom you talk for the first time over the phone, so, even a quite brief excerpt from an author—provided it is truly characteristic—can tell you a great deal about his work. I try to identify the magic of each individual personality." Although Isherwood had taught at L.A. State and been Regents' Professor at UCSB, he was promoted by UCLA not as an academic but as a literary personality, giving his audience "the opportunity to enter the private world of *belles lettres* in which [he] has moved so freely." The first lecture dealt with "The Forefathers": "Dickens, Forster, James, Conrad, Melville, Emily Brontë and others who influenced his youthful development." Then came "Our Group and Its Older Brothers" (a characteristic Isherwood concept) dealing with the Moderns, including Auden, Spender, Upward and Henry Green. For the final lecture, Isherwood acted the literary uncle, talking about "The Young": "Williams, Welsh,[4] Capote, Beckett, Osborne, Thomas, Kerouac, Willingham, Mailer, [Ray] Bradbury, and those many to whom he listens for a new, unique voice." The lectures proved very successful, largely because Isherwood evidently enjoyed being back on the public stage, playing up to his audience as he had done during his public performances in the late 1930s.

The preparation he had to do for these lectures and the pleasurable hours he was spending with Deeley did not entirely distract him from the task of revising "Paul," which he finished on March 15—the thirty-first anniversary of his first visit to Berlin, he duly noted. He was anxious to have Gerald Heard's reaction to the story, particularly since his old friend and guru appeared in the book in the character of Augustus Parr. He had hoped to carry off the difficult feat of showing Parr "to be an actor and superficially phony, and yet *not* a fake." Heard seemed disinclined to deliver his verdict until Isherwood pressed him. He apparently had no opinion of his own portrait, but compared the episode unfavorably with "Waldemar," the section of the book set during the Munich period, remarking that it seemed "a narrow, limited, trivial story, and one lost all sense of the world-crisis in it." He appeared to be more interested in the current world-crisis, in which the threat of nuclear war was increasingly present. "Gerald still feels we have a chance," Isherwood reported. "He believes that the Demiurge who has been governing life on this planet may not wish to see the extermination of his experimental farm. The Demiurge very seldom intervenes in human history, but he may now do so; perhaps by direct telepathic action upon various world leaders." There was no doubt that Heard's pronouncements and preoccupations were becoming more and more eccentric—he had for some years been obsessed by UFOs—and it is unclear whether Isherwood took this sort of guff seriously, or

---

4. This is almost certainly a misprint for (Denton) Welch.

it's all *exactly* like 1938." It must sometimes have seemed to Isherwood that he had slipped back in time: here he was in London again, seeing the old familiar faces— Spender, Lehmann, Forster, Ackerley, the Buckinghams, the Mangeots, the Upwards, Robert Moody, Eric Falk, Gerald Hamilton, Jean Ross—during "a time of loud late parties and unsteady fumbling comings-home in the small hours," as he wrote of 1938 in *Down There on a Visit*. His diary is full of complaints about the large number of social events he was attending, the amount he was eating and drinking, the general sense of dread. He was indeed just in the same psychological frame of mind as he had been twenty-three years before.

Although Bachardy was still suffering from self-doubt, worried in particular that he could only draw and would never learn to paint in oils, he was by now an accomplished portraitist. He received an enormous boost to his confidence when he was offered a small solo exhibition by the Redfern, a leading gallery of contemporary art in London's Cork Street. Isherwood's immediate reaction was to consider "how best to exploit the victory and turn it into a rejoicing for our friends and a rebuke to our enemies." Here was proof that Bachardy was someone to be reckoned with in his own right, someone who had started to make a real career for himself.

Since the show was not until October, they had to decide whether to stay in England throughout the rest of the summer or whether to return home for a couple of months and come back in the autumn. Whatever happened, Isherwood realized that he would have to change his mind about returning to L.A. State to take up the offer of another semester's teaching, a job he had all but agreed to accept. Although he missed Santa Monica, he dreaded returning there alone, particularly because an international crisis was escalating in Berlin. Relations between East and West deteriorated steadily during the summer, and Isherwood was not alone in fearing that this could result in a third world war. He felt that if war came, he wanted to be with Bachardy wherever that might be, but was aware that in some ways Bachardy was keen for him to return to America. "It's the old story," Isherwood noted: "he can't have any friends of his own as long as I'm around, because, even if he finds them, they take more interest in me as soon as we meet." This was compounded by the fact that in London they were back amongst Isherwood's old friends, and almost any encounter with them would be followed by a row in which Bachardy complained that he was left out of the conversation, ignored, condescended to, or otherwise insulted. The Spenders were once again in bad odor, despite the fact that it was Stephen's intervention that had secured Bachardy his place at the Slade. Bachardy refused all invitations to the Spenders' house and raged and sulked when Isherwood went alone. Spender himself was designated "private enemy number one." Dodie Smith also put herself in the wrong by making some mild remark about Isherwood and Caskey, Mary Ure was "rude," and even Joe Ackerley caused offense because he didn't pay Bachardy "the right sort of attention." Isherwood found Bachardy's reaction to these slights irritating and wearying, and told himself that it arose because of his partner's continuing insecurity: "Just because I in fact won't leave him, I have taken it for granted that he somehow knows this. He doesn't."

There was also the recurring problem of how to deal with sexual infidelity. Bachardy wanted his freedom, but would be furious if Isherwood appeared to have other interests. Isherwood's particular interest in London was a young man called

Jonathan, whom he had originally met in California. "Oh, I used Jonathan against Chris for *years* as an example of flagrant infidelity," Bachardy later admitted cheerfully, but at the time he was very jealous. "As soon as I found out about this 'special relationship,' I didn't see Jonathan any more—or he was kept from me." Isherwood did his best to be discreet, but then got into difficulties when he refused to show Bachardy his pocket diary because it contained several references to meetings with Jonathan. "It is too idiotic for words," Isherwood wrote. "If only [Don] could realize how utterly unimportant all that kind of thing is. But no one can be expected to, of course—no one." By "no one," Isherwood clearly meant himself. Unimportant or not, Isherwood knew when to retreat, and he did so from Jonathan in August, when he felt that "the whole thing is getting too sticky."

Bachardy was preoccupied with preparations for his exhibition, making drawings and black-and-white paintings of actors and writers, including Auden, who was in England with Kallman in order to attend the British premiere of Hans Werner Henze's *Elegy for Young Lovers,* for which they had written the libretto. Although Isherwood was pleased to see Auden, he knew that it would mean coming to a decision about the Berlin musical, which Tony Richardson had now offered to produce. An idea of how to proceed had come to Kallman in a dream, but remained rather vague, with the emphasis more on music than on plot. This, along with Auden's discovery of "the right composer," a completely unknown young German, increased Isherwood's concern that his collaborators' approach might prove "too cerebral," tending toward the operatic. Kallman infuriated Isherwood by doing the crossword at the same time as they discussed their ideas for the play. Furthermore, Isherwood was unhappy with the proposed three-way split of any proceeds, feeling that he ought to receive a larger share of the money as the author of the books on which the play would be based.

Relations between the collaborators deteriorated further when Isherwood felt obliged to attend the British premiere of *Elegy for Young Lovers* at Glyndebourne. He was not an admirer of opera, particularly not of contemporary opera, and resented the fact that he and Bachardy would have to wear (and therefore hire at some expense) evening dress. Glyndebourne, with its elaborate picnics, its atmosphere of pleasures taken solemnly and a self-conscious reverence for art, was just the sort of stuffy English event Isherwood had hoped to escape by immigrating to California. It was a bore for them to travel down to Sussex, they ended up with bad seats, and Bachardy was once again "insulted" by the Spenders, who had been friendly toward him "without realizing how he feels about them." The only thing Isherwood really liked was the sets; he compared Henze's music to "pangs of arthritis, sudden and sharp and unpredictable."

Auden and Kallman left for Kirchstetten two days later, without any decision being reached about the future of the musical. Auden seemed reluctant to relinquish the idea altogether, even though he acknowledged that "the essential donné at which the imagination catches fire, has not yet been granted us." He suggested that they should just wait until one of them had "a flash of vision." When, later that summer, Isherwood learned that Sandy Wilson was interested in a similar project, he saw a chance to bow out. Since Wilson had enjoyed a great success in London and on Broadway with his pastiche 1920s musical, *The Boy Friend,* he seemed an ideal choice to adapt *Goodbye to Berlin*. He eventually got a commission and wrote a musical, but it never reached the stage.

I n September, Isherwood and Bachardy traveled to France to stay with Tony Richardson, who had bought a cluster of small houses not far from St. Tropez and renovated them in order to accommodate the numerous friends with whom he liked to surround himself. Richardson had indicated that he was keen to collaborate with Isherwood on a film—perhaps an adaptation of Alain-Fournier's *Le Grand Meaulnes*—but this idea seemed to have evaporated, and they spent most of their time in France lying in the sun and witnessing the latest episodes in the long-running saga of John Osborne's personal affairs. One day they drove to see Somerset Maugham and his companion Alan Searle at Cap Ferrat. They found the writer older, deafer and unsteadier, but apparently pleased to see them. Isherwood's fondness for Maugham may be judged by the fact that he refused to take offense when, having consumed "staggering martinis," the older writer suddenly said: "L-let's face it, Christopher, if it hadn't been for Berlin, where would you be now?" Maugham had once said that Isherwood held "the future of the English novel in his hands," but in the wake of *The World in the Evening* he was inclined to cry "Butterfingers!" He declared that Isherwood had " 'thrown it all away' for happiness and Vedanta," but added: "I envy you." Other guests were rather shocked by this outburst, and Isherwood would not have taken it from many people, but he felt that

> The whole thing sounded like a literary over-simplification. [Maugham] was really composing a short story. The Great Old Novelist who has sacrificed happiness and love for his art confesses that he envies the younger brilliantly promising writer who sacrificed his art for happiness and love. The only thing that embarrassed *me* was that Willie implied that *he* was without love, and this reflected on Alan . . . But, really, we were all too drunk to be taken seriously.

Maugham was, in fact, perfectly serious. After being sent *The World in the Evening* by Methuen, and disliking it, he wrote to L.A.G. Strong: "Perhaps I shouldn't have felt so let down if I had not greatly admired and cherished the Christopher of twenty years ago. What damage Gerald Heard did to our English literature when he induced these talented writers to desert their native country for America!"

Isherwood was at this time more concerned about Bachardy's future than his own. He fretted that the international crisis might interfere with the forthcoming exhibition, and was as anxious as any parent that Bachardy's work should be properly appreciated. The show was heralded by the reproduction of some portraits in the fashion and society magazine *Queen,* and by a small exhibition of his *A Taste of Honey* portraits in the foyer of the Leicester Square Theatre for the film's premiere. It opened on October 2, with a well-attended party at which Bachardy took center stage, being interviewed by various journalists, while Isherwood remained firmly in the background "nearly splitting with pride." There were almost as many famous people at the party as there were on the walls, which were hung with portraits of the numerous actors, writers, dancers and composers Bachardy had drawn. Several pictures were sold and a number of commissions were secured, but Isherwood and

Bachardy were disappointed that there was not more coverage of the event in the press.

When Isherwood returned to Santa Monica in mid-October, Bachardy stayed on in London, preparing for an exhibition at the Sagittarius Gallery in New York. Isherwood had felt that Bachardy was "quite eager" for him to leave, but was not too worried about this: "we both need a holiday from each other," he decided. His anxiety was refocused on his health, since he had been suffering some stiffness in his jaw. It was unfortunate that Marion Davies chose this moment to die of cancer of the jaw, since it put the idea into Isherwood's head that he would shortly follow her. "Heart-attacks, sclerosis, T.B. or strokes" did not worry him, he claimed, even though "strokes run in our family and I shall very probably end up with some, and they can be unspeakably terrible. No—all my fears are centred on cancer." Back in California, the usual cycle of visits to the doctor and the demand for assorted tests was put in motion and, as usual, nothing untoward was found. Isherwood recognized that he always needed something upon which to exercise his neurotic anxiety: if it wasn't his health, or money, then it was the threat of war, exacerbated by reports that fallout shelters were being constructed in Los Angeles. "I *must* lay off the newspapers," he told himself. "The newspaper-reader dies many times before his death, the non-reader not nearly so often."

He had the Ramakrishna book to occupy him and had promised Spender that he would write an article on Virginia Woolf for *Encounter.* He was now regretting this commitment, since he felt he did not have enough to say about her. He was reluctant to admit this to Spender, partly because he was "only too aware that part of this decision comes from laziness and part from a desire to get back at him for accepting and then rejecting Ambrose!" Having heard nothing from London, he began to worry again about his relationship with Bachardy. He would have preferred to sit around waiting for the mail but was committed to spend two days at Trabuco. While there he said to Prabhavananda: "You're really *certain* that God exists?" The swami laughed and replied: "*Of course!* If he doesn't exist, then *I* don't exist." "And do you feel He gives you strength to bear your misfortunes?" Isherwood asked. "I don't think of it like that," Prabhavananda replied. "I just know he will take care of me . . . It's rather hard to explain . . . Whatever happens, it will be all right." Isherwood may have been reassured by this, but was unnerved when Prabhavananda, no doubt taking advantage of the apparent rift in his disciple's relationship with Bachardy, asked him to stay on at Trabuco, adding that he would initate him as a monk. Isherwood, always inclined to see his wily old swami in the best, most innocent light, wasn't altogether sure whether or not Prabhavananda was being serious.

Isherwood returned to Adelaide Drive to find a long and loving letter from Bachardy, which had been held up by customs, and on December 14 he flew to New York for a reunion and the opening of the exhibition at the Sagittarius Gallery. Isherwood immediately came down with a "toxic condition," which resulted in his consulting a doctor, underoging tests, being given penicillin and staying in bed for two days. Having emerged from the sickroom, he found himself in what he described as "curiously good health," and professed himself astonished that the doctor had been unable to find anything "significant" the matter with him. As always, he found the

which he claimed made him "a bit more aware of the messiness of alcohol," he had been involved in another traffic accident, sideswiping a parked car on his woozy way home from a friend's house, and damaging the black Volkswagen Beetle he now drove. "I was too drunk to go out and look to see what I'd done to the other car," he admitted. He had in fact caused considerable damage, but once again got off comparatively lightly after the police were persuaded to drop the case against him. Although he escaped prosecution by the LAPD, he was handed with a bill for almost $900. More than half this sum went to an attorney, who arranged for an anonymous payment to be made to the owner of the other car, who innocently imagined that the culprit was "a fine upstanding boy" who had confessed his youthful misdemeanor, rather than a drunken middle-aged neighbor trying to get off the hook.

In spite of the continuing disarray of his life, Isherwood completed the second draft of the novel by the end of July, and Bachardy came up with a title for it: *A Single Man*. Given the precarious state of their relationship, with Isherwood's prediction about them parting during the summer apparently about to be fulfilled, this title had a certain grim irony, but Isherwood realized at once that it was perfect for the novel. Both Gavin Lambert and Edward Upward delivered highly favorable reports on the book, while making suggestions for further improvements. Upward's judgment that Isherwood had "even outdone your best," Isherwood felt, "made up for much misfortune, and I feel really eager to rewrite it, now." Before doing so, however, he had to battle on with the final two chapters of the Ramakrishna biography. Predictably, writing about the avatar's death from cancer of the esophagus led to an alarmingly persistent sore throat, which his doctor insisted to the skeptical patient was merely an infection. Isherwood nevertheless completed the biography—"the longest and cruellest of all my Vedanta chores"—on September 19. He was not altogether joking when he declared: "It's marvellous that writing it didn't make me lose my faith altogether."

TWENTY-THREE

CELEBRATIONS HAD BEEN HELD THROUGHOUT 1963 MARKING THE centenary of Vivekananda's birth, which had taken place in January. These were to reach a climax at Belur, the Ramakrishna mission near Calcutta, at the end of the year, when a "Parliament of Religions" was taking place. This was in effect a celebratory conference at which devotees of Vivekananda from all over the world had been invited to give talks. At the same time a number of monks would take *sannyas,* including two of Prabhavananda's disciples, Prema and Arup Chaitanya (née Kenneth Critchfield). Prabhavananda decided that with the Ramakrishna biography at last completed Isherwood was free to accompany him on the long trip to Bengal. "I guess you can imagine how I feel about coming to India," Isherwood wrote to Prema, who was already at Belur Math; "almost unmixed horror." He nevertheless had one faint hope of escape. He wondered whether Prema would really welcome him, "this disturbing reminder of the beefeating outside world, a visitor from The City of Night,"[1] when he was preparing to take the final step of becoming a swami?

The trip would at least give Isherwood some respite from his domestic troubles. He was finding Bachardy's continuing relationship with George intolerable. "Jealousy: Not what they do together sexually. But the thought of their waking in the morning, little pats and squeezes, jokes, talk through the open doorway of the bathroom. For that one could kill." Particularly when the bathroom was one's own. Bachardy had decided that the best thing for all concerned would be for George to be brought into their life at Adelaide Drive rather than being hidden away. Unsurprisingly, Isherwood did not like this at all. "I have been very low," he reported at the beginning of November, "largely because of drinking too much. Terribly violent

---

1. A reference not to James Thompson, but to John Rechy's recently published semiautobiographical novel about homosexual prostitution in various American cities.

resentment of George, whom I'm nevertheless committed by Don to seeing quite often. I suffer in a way that is utterly grotesque. That must stop, of course. But how can it be stopped?" When asked if he knew how much Isherwood minded these affairs, Bachardy replied: "I *wanted* him to mind. I knew that he would not leave me unless I made it intolerable for him. I certainly made him suffer, but I never made it intolerable." This sounds harsh, but it was a way of ensuring that he retained Isherwood's love. Isherwood's tolerance was certainly tested by George, and he eventually told Bachardy that he did not want to see the man any more, under any circumstances, and he certainly didn't want his photograph displayed in the house. "God, how I hate lowering the boom like this! And yet it is, ultimately, the only decent and truthful and friendly way to act. The alternative is sulks and silent reproach."

Although a break from each other would seem to be called for, Isherwood was not sanguine about the prospect of India. The only thing to be said for the trip was that it would at least provide him with a deadline for preparing both the Ramakrishna biography and the novel for publication. He completed the final draft of *A Single Man* in October, then, after a week's break, he started the unrewarding job of revising the biography, which he had decided to call *Ramakrishna and His Disciples*. It was largely a matter of "taking out words expressing vehement overemphasis," and he had finished the work by the end of November.

Both his British and American publishers accepted *A Single Man* and decided that although J. P. Donleavy had recently published a novel called *A Singular Man,* the title could stand. This was a great relief to Isherwood, who recognized that Bachardy's apparently simple title summed up much of what he was attempting to do in the book. George is a single man in the legal sense that he is unmarried, in the euphemistic sense that he is homosexual, and in perhaps the most important sense of all: that he is an outsider. Isherwood felt that no one could be more single, more isolated, than a homosexual man whose partner had died, because society did not acknowledge the partnership, and so did not recognize this particular bereavement. He had also taken a single man, just one individual, to illustrate a whole culture and way of life, and he had done this by taking a single day in this man's life, which begins with an assertion of individuality:

> Waking up begins with saying *am* and *now.* That which has awoken then lies for a while staring up at the ceiling and down into itself until it has recognized *I,* and therefrom deduced *I am, I am now. Here* comes next, and is at least negatively reassuring; because *here,* this morning, is where it had expected to find itself; what's called *at home.*

This aging body, this consciousness, gradually reveals itself as George, a fifty-eight-year-old professor, who is physically vain, gleefully misogynistic, and homosexually militant, and has a love-hate relationship with England, the country of his birth. He is witty, irascible, combative and not altogether likable, but his ferocious engagement with life is wholly admirable. We see him get up, use the bathroom, have breakfast, and prepare himself for the day ahead. He drives to the college where he gives a lecture on Aldous Huxley, has a workout at the gym, visits a woman dying in the hospital, endures a bibulous dinner with his friend Charlotte, and skinny-dips in the ocean with one of his students, Kenny. Kenny invites himself back to George's house, where George passes out and is put to bed. He awakes to find that Kenny has gone, leaving a note. He masturbates, then falls asleep. The novel ends by imagining what would happen if George died in the night. With some relish, one imagines, Isherwood read up on coronary occlusion, lifting his detailed anatomical description of this event from a book called *Man's Presumptuous Brain*. Moving seamlessly from the scientific to the mystical, Isherwood describes George's individuality dissolving and merging itself with a universal consciousness. After death, George's body would be a mere shell, of no more importance than the trash can. In the novel's final words: "Both will have to be carted away and disposed of, before too long."

Shortly before Isherwood left for India, he received a letter from Roger Angell of *The New Yorker,* who he had hoped might publish the book in whole or in part. "While I can believe this novel," Angell wrote, "I don't find it particularly interesting." This is the worst sort of criticism someone could make of a book, particularly one as potentially controversial as this one, and it did nothing to cheer Isherwood on his way to the subcontinent. In preparation for the journey, Isherwood had undergone a "*passionate* psychosomatic revolt," deciding that he was "almost capable of dying at Belur Math, out of sheer spite." "I have all the shots, visas and other necessaries for the journey, and now it seems inevitable," he told Prema, "so I try to accept it and dwell on its pleasant aspects; seeing you and seeing you turned into a swami." He nevertheless warned that, even though his travel and expenses were being paid, his timetable must be respected, and he would not be coerced into doing anything more than the minimum that had been agreed. "If there are any plots to make me stay longer, it is far better that I don't come at all," he wrote; "because if I come, and then refuse, as I shall inevitably, then they will feel I have cheated them and not given them what they paid for. *Please* make this clear; and, please, if there is any doubt in your mind about their real intentions, tell me *at once*!"

This last-ditch attempt to get out of the trip failed, and on December 18, stuffed full of Librium, he accompanied Prabhavananda and Krishna (who had taken *sann-yas* in 1958 and become Swami Krishnananda) to the airport, where they were seen off by a large crowd of devotees. The journey took three days, and they arrived at Calcutta in the middle of the night. "As we drove through the empty lanes and streets to the Math, I felt a magic begin to work. You both smell and feel the strange perfumed softness of India." The monastery itself proved "far more delightful" than Isherwood had remembered from his previous visit, and he seemed all set to put aside his fears and prejudices and enjoy the visit. When he bolted the door of his room in the guesthouse, he experienced "a sense of snug individuality in the midst of all these surrounding millions of people."

For the first few days Isherwood had no particular duties, but on Christmas Day he was obliged to attend the opening of a Women's Congress: "A stunning bore." Isherwood felt that "the only gleam of joy" was the presence of Swami Amartyananda, who was "really one of the handsomest boys I have seen in this part of the world. He comes from Trivandrum, at the Southern tip of India. His magnificent, nearly black eyes, very dark skin and fierce white teeth. His smile is fierce, tigerish, and challenging; but his eyes regard you with a languishing intimate sweetness. You can imagine him using phrases of classic oriental endearment like "soul of my soul" without the least embarrassment." Equally, at a seminar held at the Ramakrishna Mission College, Isherwood was more interested in the audience of "thin, pliant-waisted youths with dark mocking eyes and smiling teeth," who sat there with their arms around each other, than he was in any of the speakers, although he was pleased with his own talk. He was less pleased when the swami who organized the seminar told him that his lecture had not been recorded, and asked if Isherwood could provide a copy of it. "Told him with sadistic relish that there was no copy; I never write my speeches. But then he produced a short version of the speech taken down in longhand by one of the students—quite inaccurate, but earning a big B for emotional blackmail. Now I'm obliged to go back to the college and redictate the whole thing to a tape-recorder. Fuck them."

In preparation for the Parliament of Religions, Isherwood moved to the International House of the Ramakrishna Mission Institute of Culture in Calcutta, where he was pleased to find Swami Amartyananda installed, "looking older today and unshaven, but still beautiful." Isherwood had already made a habit of "playing it very broad with pranams," the gesture of taking the dust from the feet of a spiritual superior. "As an elderly man, I'm not expected to show such respect to the young swamis, but I do it anyway. (*My* kind of aggression)," he noted. But there wasn't much aggression in the gesture when he was confronted by Amartyananda. "I took the dust off his feet, and he tried to do the same to me. When I jumped backwards, protesting, he said, 'we regard you as more than a swami.' " It is not clear why Isherwood had gained such a reputation, particularly since he had signally failed even to live as a monk. His translations of Vedanta works and editing of *Vedanta and the West* undoubtedly made him an important figure amongst anglophone devotees, but this cannot have meant much in India. It seems most likely that, having just completed a new biography of Ramakrishna, Isherwood had gained the status of Evangelist. He now offered to help Amartyananda produce biographical notes in English on the foreign delegates, a task made to seem "even lighter" by the presence of the young swami's roommate, "an adorable Brahmachari named Shashi Kanto," which translates as "Moon Beauty." "He is from near Bombay, a big boy of about eighteen, bulky and yet graceful in his cocoon of white muslin. The cropped hair and little topknot suit the charm of his long sensitive affectionate nose and dark soft velvet eyes. He seems utterly incapable of anything but love. He finds all manner of excuses to be around us." And vice versa.

Not even the presence of lovely young swamis could mitigate the inaugural session of the Parliament of Religions, however. "It began at 3.30 pm and went on for three hours," Isherwood complained.

Next to the hashish experience in Tangier, this was the least endurable time-stretch I have ever known. Not one of the speakers bothered to project; they droned out their written speeches as if they were saying mass. There was an audience of about eight thousand people, and I doubt if eighty of them really understood English. They sat there with—no, one can't call it patience—with the inertia of cows [. . .] When it came to my turn, I spoke too loud and too urgently—rather like a communist speaker in the thirties.

Playing to the gallery, as usual, Isherwood delivered a rather more successful speech the following day. "I pretended to myself that the audience could understand me, and indeed they seemed to—probably because I talked a lot of political stuff about Vivekananda and the English, the oppressors in their bondage to the oppressed, etc."

This lecture may have been a success, but Isherwood had begun to feel just as he had in the late 1930s in England, when he appeared on various public platforms spouting politics. Lying in bed with the onset of a violent stomach upset, he was

> swept by gusts of furious resentment—against India, against being pushed around, even against Swami himself. I resolved to tell him that I refuse ever again to appear in the temple or anywhere else and talk about God. Part of this resolve is quite valid; I *do* think that when I give these God-lectures it is Sunday religion in the worst sense. As long as I quite unashamedly get drunk, have sex and write books like A Single Man, I simply cannot appear before people as a sort of lay minister. The inevitable result must be that my ordinary life becomes divided and untruthful. Or rather, in the end, the only truth left is in my drunkenness, my sex and my art, not in my religion. For me, religion must be quite private as far as I'm publicly concerned. I can still write about it *informatively,* but I must not appear before people on a platform as a living witness and example.

There is no doubt that, although he had great personal affection for Isherwood, Prabhavananda valued his unruly disciple precisely because he *could* be held up as an example of a worldly and famous Westerner who nevertheless followed Vedanta. Whatever Isherwood may have told himself about Prabhavananda's tolerant view of sexuality—at any rate, Isherwood's own sexuality—he knew that abstinence was the ideal, and that there would always be for him a fundamental conflict between the flesh and the spirit. If this conflict remained private, then he could deal with it, but he recognized that if it was unresolved he had no business to be promoting in public a way of life to which he was constitutionally unable to adhere. At every turn, he was confronted with a reminder of the world he would never abandon, as when he visited a school being set up by the Mission and found among the teachers "a handsome and sexy nineteen year old boy from Cheshire."

Isherwood awoke on New Year's Day 1964 still determined to stick to his resolution, which was no doubt strengthened by "a flirty tea-party with Amartyananda and Shashi Kanto. Such languishing looks, delicate hand-touches and flashing glances are perhaps only possible for the absolutely innocent. Though I'm not sure Amartyananda is quite as innocent as all that. I feel he has been around." That evening, Isherwood had a three-hour talk with Amartyananda, who told him all about his background and his decision to join the Order, which came about not through a person but through reading the works of Vivekananda. "Behind all A's stories there is a certain suggestion of 'see what a tiger I am—yet I'm as gentle as a dove if you treat me right,' " Isherwood noted. "Also, there's a good deal of name-and-fame awareness. In what other situation in life, he asks, would you find famous men and women actually taking the dust off your feet? He frankly delights in this. And he told me, encouragingly, that I should become far better known by my book on Ramakrishna than by any of my novels." Isherwood began to feel rather less warmly about the young swami.

In the afternoon Isherwood presided over one of the sessions of the Parliament and delivered his Presidential Address. "I am drawn very strongly to other devotees of Sri Ramakrishna who have been, as it were, a little outside the group, who have been, as it were, individualists," he told the assembled delegates, "and of all these devotees the one who was peculiarly sympathetic to me, the one whom I liked since I first read about him, and the one who gave great reassurance and inspiration was Girish Chandra Ghosh." Ghosh was a playwright, songwriter and actor who founded the Star Theatre in Calcutta in 1883 and became a pioneer of modern Bengali drama. He was also a drunkard and was often to be found patronizing the city's brothels. He was, Isherwood, decided, "a bohemian artist." Like Isherwood himself, Ghosh was "not respectable in the ordinary sense of that word. He caused considerable scandal to those who held strict views of conduct. He shocked them, and it is not surprising that he did so." He was nevertheless brought to God by Ramakrishna and became a great devotee. One of the things that drew Isherwood to Ramakrishna was his willingness to accept Girish Ghosh as a disciple. If someone as dissolute as Ghosh could come to God, then Isherwood himself stood a chance. "I would not dare to pretend to have one part of Girish's devotion, his extraordinary devotion which saved his spiritual life. I would not even claim to have half as much talent as Girish had, nor half the capacity for drinking." (This last remark did not, as Isherwood had hoped, raise a laugh.) "Nevertheless," he continued, "we are kindred spirits in certain respects and it is to Girish rather than some of the other more austere devotees that I turn for inspiration." As he reached his peroration, someone handed him a slip of paper asking him to speak for a further fifteen minutes because the next person to address the Parliament had not shown up. Irritated by this request, Isherwood ignored it.

A trip had been organized for Isherwood, Krishna and Prabhavananda to Brahmananda's birthplace, a remote village in the Ganges delta.

> Throughout the drive, I felt awful. Partly upset stomach and headache, but chiefly rage against the Parliament of Religions, the Ramakrishna Math, India, everything. This is a very deep aversion which I have been aware of from time to time ever since I first got involved with Vedanta. It has—as far as I can figure out—nothing directly to do with Ramakrishna, Vivekananda or Swami. (Did Roman converts to Christianity loathe the Jews all that much the more?) Anyhow, it all expressed itself in the old cry of the ego, *I'm being pushed around!*

His original plan was not to tell Prabhavananda about his resolution to retire from the Vedanta stage until after he had delivered another talk at Belur on January 6, but he had now worked himself up into such a state that he determined to have it out with the swami. He asked for a car to take him back to Belur at once. Prabhavananda was puzzled, but agreed.

> On such occasions, he seldom asks leading questions. If you want to make a scene you have to make it all by yourself, under your own steam. So now I did. I

said, approximately, 'Swami—it isn't just that I'm sick—I feel awful about everything. I've made up my mind: I can't ever talk about God and religion in public again. It's impossible. I've felt this for a long time.' (Already I had withdrawn the concession I had previously planned—to agree to talk in Hollywood [about the trip to India] after I get home. Some instinct told me that this ultimatum must be drastic or it would make no impression at all.) 'I suppose I've wanted to spare your feelings, but that's not right, either. After all, you *are* my Guru—you have to be responsible for me anyway—and you're probably a saint. Anyhow, you're the nearest thing to a saint I have ever met. So why shouldn't you be told how I really feel? It's the same thing, really, that I told you years ago when I was living at the Center: the Ramakrishna Math is coming between me and God. I can't belong to any kind of institution. Because I'm not respectable—'

Prabhavananda laughed at this Mary Magdalene impersonation, and replied: "But, Chris, how can you say such things? You're almost *too* good. You are so frank, so good. You never tell any lie—" Isherwood persisted:

I can't stand up on Sundays in nice clothes and talk about God. I feel like a prostitute. I've felt like this at all of these meetings of the Parliament, when I've spoken . . . I knew this was going to happen. I should never have agreed to come to India. After I promised you I'd come, I used to wake up every morning, feeling awful—

Prabhavananda interrupted to apologize for asking Isherwood to accompany him, but Isherwood was not to be deterred:

You know the first time I prostrated before you, that was a great moment in my life. It really meant something tremendous to me, to want to bow down before another human being. And here I've been making pranams to everybody—even to people I've quite a low opinion of. And it's just taking all the significance out of doing it—

Prabhavananda reminded Isherwood that no one expected him to make *pranams,* and Isherwood felt that the swami hadn't understood a word he was saying. He told Isherwood he didn't want to lose him.

I told him there was absolutely no question of that. That I loved him just as much as ever. That this had nothing to do with him. But still he didn't understand. He looked at me with hurt brown eyes. I felt rather awful and cruel—but not very. However dishonest all this may have been in one sense (for, after all, by taking this stand, I am saving myself one hell of a lot of work and annoyance) at least its expression was honest and frank. It was far better to have spoken than not to have spoken. The boil was lanced and I felt better immediately.

As he was driven back to Calcutta "in a cloud of red dust," he noted that "Through the eyes of my relief, India suddenly seemed charming. The long fruit-market alongside the street of De Ganga village, where we were stalled behind produce-trucks. I almost loved the dark-skinned country people, so completely absorbed in the business of their world, and shouting at each other in angry voices without anger and with campy fun. And I was so happy to get back to my quiet room at the Guesthouse."

Prabhavananda returned the following day and retired to his bed with a cough. "The country dust is blamed," Isherwood reported; "but I got a strong impression (later confirmed by Prema) that the sickness has a lot to do with me. This is perhaps the only respect in which Swami can be described as sly; he is absolutely capable of getting sick to make you feel guilty, though I doubt if he realizes this—it is purely instinctive." Isherwood nevertheless remained firm in his decision, even when Prabhavananda developed an alarming swelling on his face.

Dawn broke on the morning of January 6 with drumming and wailing to announce that the *sannyas* ceremonies would be reaching their climax that day. Upon being woken up by this din, Isherwood "jacked off as a protest and went back to sleep." Prabhavananda's condition had not improved: he talked of wanting his *mahasamdhi* (i.e. death) in India, and when Isherwood seemed reluctant to massage his hands, he demanded: "Why can't you do something for Swami you never did before?" Isherwood knew perfectly well what it was the swami really wanted him to do, but told himself that Prabhavananda was indulging in "a kind of inspired playacting."

> Wasn't he perhaps in a high spiritual mood and giving us the privilege of serving the 'It' which had taken him over? I hate this explanation because it sort of embarrasses me; but I don't discount it. In that building, with Vivekananda right next door, it made perfect sense. In that atmosphere, the edges of personality get blurred, and Swami becomes a little bit Brahmananda-Vivekananda-Ramakrishna.
>
> Swami said to me this evening, 'I can't believe you're going, Chris.'

Isherwood did not attend the final *sannyas* ceremony, which took place during the night, but the following morning, he got up early in order to greet the new swamis, Vidyatmananda (Prema) and Anamananda (Arup), and take the dust from their feet. "The onlookers were much edified, I felt, to see us westerners playing the game according to their rules." As the two swamis set off to beg alms, the first of their obligations in their new roles, Isherwood bade farewell to Amartyananda and Shashi Kanto: "I gave Shashi a great big hug, which surprised and delighted him. I prostrated before Amartyananda and then hugged him. But he was a couple of degrees cooler. He really is quite a cool-blooded creature."

Isherwood himself was leaving in the evening. Before he left, he visited Vivekananda's room and offered prayers for himself and Bachardy.

His prayers were partly answered, and he felt that his homecoming was a happy one. Bachardy's affair with George had fizzled out, and Bachardy subsequently came to feel that these relationships, which had caused so much unhappiness, were less of a danger than Isherwood imagined. He said that he tended to get involved with people who would turn out to be totally unsuitable for him. "I think I was expressing my need for sexual freedom while unconsciously choosing only people who could never pose a serious threat to my life with Chris." Their reunion at Adelaide Drive after a separation of some eight weeks made Isherwood look at their life together philosophically:

> When Don isn't here, my life simply isn't very interesting. He creates distur-
> bance, anxiety, tension, and sometimes jealousy and rage; but never for one mo-
> ment do I feel that our relationship is unimportant. Let me just recognize this fact,
> and not bother about making good resolutions. He will behave badly; I shall be-
> have badly. That's par for the course.

The Indian trip had given Isherwood the idea for a new short novel, the final title of which, unusually, he already had in his head: *A Meeting by the River*. The river would be the Ganges, and the meeting would involve a confrontation between two world views, and a struggle between two men to win the other over to his own way of thinking. This was a revival of the theme of the abandoned Mexican version of *Down There on a Visit*. It would, however, be a year before Isherwood started writing the new book. He had several more urgent commitments, the first of which was to write a piece for a memorial volume about Aldous Huxley, who had died the previous November. The book was being put together by Huxley's brother Julian and was built around the four addresses—by Julian Huxley himself, Kenneth Clark, Stephen Spender and David Cecil—delivered at a "Memorial Gathering" held at Friends' House in London in December. Other contributors included T. S. Eliot, Steven Runciman, Osbert Sitwell, Leonard Woolf, André Maurois, Naomi Mitchison, Isaiah Berlin, Raymond Mortimer, Stravinsky, Gerald Heard and Anita Loos. Isherwood read through his diaries to find references to Huxley, and there is a quirky immediacy to his affectionate contribution. As in all Isherwood's work, a certain amount of veiled autobiography is evident in this essay. Isherwood clearly had his own career in mind as well as Huxley's when he wrote defiantly: "I am one of those who maintain that nearly all of Huxley's best work was done in the latter, American half of his life." Of "the far-reaching effects" of Huxley's involvement with Prabhavananda, he observed: "it was widely represented as the selling-out of a once brilliant intellect. As a matter of fact, it actually enlarged Huxley's already vast intellectual horizons by introducing him to mystical experience as a fact, a phenomenon of existence."

While leafing through his diaries, Isherwood also had in mind his projected "Autobiography of My Books," but in February he was approached by Methuen to compile "a book of bits and pieces" consisting of uncollected stories, articles and verses. The result was "fragments of an autobiography which tells itself indirectly, by means of exhibits—exhibit A, exhibit B, and so forth; dug up for display in a museum (if you wish to study the past) or a courtroom (if you hope to convict the author of hitherto unpunished crimes)." He decided to call the volume, which he dedicated to Richard, *Exhumations*.

Isherwood also had to make final revisions of *Ramakrishna and His Disciples*, adding in material gathered from his Calcutta trip. "I want to go through it and suck out some of the sweetness and switch off some of the light," he told Upward. Dedicated to Prabhavananda, the book was published the following April, with all royalties paid to the Vedanta Society of Southern California. Methuen appear to have published the book out of loyalty to the author rather than with any real interest or hope of sales. Isherwood had been disconcerted at a very late stage to receive a letter from one of the directors of the firm, who declared that the company was looking forward to his biography of Krishnamurti. The book, however, looked handsome, with a jacket decorated with Ramakrishna's elegant Bengali signature. This must have pleased Prabhavananda, who had wanted the signature used as an illustration to scotch the myth that Ramakrishna was illiterate. Isherwood's British editor cheerfully suggested that the book "should fox the critics," but the reviews were, on the whole, respectful, in both Britain and America, many of them praising Isherwood's lucidity.

Unusually, Isherwood did not send a copy of the book to Upward. "And when I saw the frontispiece, with that photograph of Ramakrishna surrounded by a halo, I knew why," Upward commented. There does indeed appear to be a circle of light surrounding the avatar's head, but the photograph was taken in 1879 and the "halo" is a result of technical limitation. Even so, some commentators felt that Isherwood had in every sense written a hagiography and had failed to put sufficient critical distance between himself and his subject. The British Labour paper, *Tribune,* dismissed the book as a "second-rate fairy story," and in the *Sunday Times* Raymond Mortimer was equally skeptical. Isherwood himself shared some of the critics' doubts about the book, and wrote to friends to warn them that they would find it "too 'party line.' " "That the reaction [of the critics] should be hostile certainly doesn't surprise me," he told Dodie Smith. "I hardly take it personally, even. At the same time I have to admit that this kind of writing—an 'official' life—is bound to ring wooden, if not hollow." Smith replied frankly: "To be honest . . . This is the only book by you that I've not wanted to go on and on with. I find I keep starting out fresh and hopeful; and then I bog down." Overcoming his objections to the frontispiece, Upward commented briefly but favorably: "It is very well written. And though it's all very esoteric to me I feel the same sort of closeness to it as I think you would to a life of Mao Tse Tung written by me."

Isherwood's attempt to remove the sweetness and light from the book was not entirely successful. Like all his books, the biography is highly readable, but his habit of making direct appeals to the reader makes him sound on occasion like a Sunday school teacher faced with an inattentive and not very bright group of children. No one reading the book could doubt Isherwood's sincerity or his belief, but virtue never brought out the best in him as a writer. He told Vidyatmananda that it was not the book he would have written had he been left to his own devices: "I might get drunk in a bar and recount more vividly in a few sentences the greatness of Ramakrishna than I did in that whole volume."

Offers of movie work continued to come in: an adaptation of R. L. Stevenson's *The Beach at Falesa* for Richard Burton, which had originally been mooted back in 1960, and an adaptation of Evelyn Waugh's *The Loved One* for Tony Richardson. The Burton film never materialized, but although Isherwood disliked Waugh's scathing satire on Hollywood, Forest Lawn and California values, he got the job of adapting it and enjoyed being once again on the MGM payroll and preparing an outline. He finished a screenplay toward the end of May, but Richardson, who had decided to update the novel to the 1960s, brought in Terry Southern as a collaborator. Southern had enjoyed some success and notoriety with *Candy,* a lubricious contemporary reworking of Voltaire's *Candide,* which he had written in collaboration with Mason Hoffenberg and published under a pseudonym for Maurice Girodias's underground Olympia Press. It had been banned, but subsequently reappeared under another title. He had also published two other satirical novels: *Flash and Filigree,* about the medical profession, and *The Magic Christian,* a would-be Swiftian attack on materialism. Although *Flash and Filigree* was much admired by Henry Green, Southern's other books tended to be fairly broad and knockabout. In fact, it would be hard to imagine a less likely collaborator for Isherwood, or indeed an adapter of Waugh. Southern had, however, enjoyed a recent success as the writer of Stanley Kubrick's *Dr. Strangelove,* and Richardson appeared to know what he was doing.

By the time the film went into production, there was very little left of either Isherwood's original script or Waugh's original novel. Isherwood calculated that 99 percent of the dialogue was Southern's, and that all that was left of his script was "some of the skeleton." "Tony just used Chris's script as a kind of Christmas tree to hang ornaments on, and Terry Southern was in charge of the ornaments," Bachardy recalled. "Southern's forte was to be on set and think of lines on the spur of the moment. Chris was amazed by his wit and spontaneity and didn't feel the least ownership of the film. He'd been paid for the work he'd done." Richardson assembled a distinguished cast of leading British and American actors, including John Gielgud, Robert Morley, Margaret Leighton, Rod Steiger, James Coburn and Milton Berle, but unfortunately gave the principal role of a young British poet to Robert Morse, an American comedy actor whose background was in musical theater. Morse had recently won a Tony for his performance in the musical *How to Succeed in Business Without Really Trying* and was therefore considered "hot." On stage he may have been, but in the film he was unconvincing both as an Englishman and as a writer, leaving a catastrophic void at the film's center. Southern subsequently published a "journal" of the making of the film. On the book's psychedelic jacket the question was posed: "What happens when the co-author of CANDY and DR. STRANGELOVE is hired by the director of TOM JONES to collaborate on the script of a motion picture 'based on' a famous novel by EVELYN WAUGH?" The answer was: a shambles. When the film was released in 1965, it was universally panned. *Variety* complained that "Poor taste is prominent in the Terry Southern–Christopher Isherwood script," but then the original novel was hardly in good taste. The real problem, apart from Richardson's unwise decision to update the 1948 story to include assorted 1960s fads, was that, as *Variety* put it: "Most of the subtlety of Waugh's approach is lost in an episodic screenplay bearing only a wavering story line and given often to sight gags." One of those gags was the appearance of Isherwood himself, who can be glimpsed in the film as a mourner at the funeral of the character played by Gielgud. He looks distinctly ill at ease, as well he might.

Undaunted by this fiasco, Isherwood agreed to write another screen adaptation for "Tip Top Tone," as Southern had optimistically dubbed, Richardson. *Reflections in a Golden Eye* was one of Carson McCullers's less satisfactory novels, a lurid melodrama about sexual repression set in an army camp in Georgia. Isherwood and Richardson may have been attracted by the strong homosexual element in McCullers's tale (a reviewer had noted of the book that "not even the horse is normal"), and Richardson was very pleased with Isherwood's script, a first draft of which was finished by the end of July. Isherwood produced a further draft, but the film was never made, largely because Richardson was unable to put together the cast he wanted. John Huston subsequently acquired the rights and hired another writer to adapt the book.

A *Single Man* was now going through the press. Alan Collins at Curtis Brown was concerned that the last quarter of the novel, from the point at which George spends an evening with Kenny, seemed to be like the start of a new book altogether. He also thought that the ending should be more explicit: does George die or not? Isherwood's new editor at Simon and Schuster, Peter Schwed, had no such qualms, and had telephoned his acceptance. He did, however, suggest one excision. In a fairly graphic scene in which George masturbates while fantasizing about two young men, the sentence "His hand feels for a handkerchief from under the pillow, wipes his belly dry" was felt to be too much for an American readership. In Britain, however, that supposedly stuffy and repressive country Isherwood had fled, this sentence was allowed to stand.[2] Friends continued to be enthusiastic about the book, Heard exclaiming "Now, obviously, you can write anything" (and advising him, therefore, to "deal with awe"), and Auden telegraphing to tell Isherwood it was the best thing he had ever written.[3]

Dedicated to Gore Vidal (who repaid the compliment by dedicating *Myra Breckenridge* to Isherwood), the novel was published in the United States and Britain, in August and September respectively, to what can only be called mixed reviews. "A lot of the critics over here were just plain shocked," Isherwood was obliged to acknowledge. "England has been much more understanding." Not all of England, however. Few critics could see beyond their own prejudices—against homosexuality, against California, against Isherwood himself. The difficulty that many of them had with the book was frankly admitted in the *Newcastle Journal:* "If you don't happen to like reading books about queers, it's hard to review them with any fairness without sounding unconvincing." Evidently unequal to the task, the reviewer confessed that reading Isherwood's book had left her in a "depressed state" which "took about three days to clear properly." This sort of thing might have been expected by Isherwood from a provincial British newspaper, but the very worst review appeared on his home territory in the *Los Angeles Times.* It appeared under the headline "Disjointed Limp Wrist Saga." It was written by someone named Richard G. Hubler, whose remarks suggest that he had not bothered to read the book with any attention. For example, he stated that George "gets drunk and tries to seduce one of his male students," which is untrue, and that he "blacks out to end another day with another dullard," whereas George ends the day alone. Hubler described the book as if it were a tract, "an

---

2. It has now been restored in the U.S. edition of the book.

3. Auden neverthess complained that George "stays far too long in the bathroom," a circumstance that inspired him to write a poem titled "The Geography of the House," dedicated to Isherwood and collected in *About the House* (1965).

unlovely exhibit" which "advances the superiority of the slapwrist, here-comes-Charley cult and their rights of social intercourse." Rising nicely to Isherwood's bait, he expressed outrage at George's lack of "feeling for family life," and complained of George's rants:

> All this defense mechanism built up for the homosexual is, of course, both feeble and disgusting. But the tasteless fatuity of the book is not its most unfortunate aspect. It is simply a poor work.
>
> Far from being 'one of the great writers of our time,' as the publisher's blurb insists, Isherwood is far enough down the list as to be virtually invisible. He is little more than competent. He has the off-ear for words and the irresolution about situations that betray the veteran novice. His 'George' lives in a gamy half-world of student titterings, resentment against growing old, anger at a world which refuses him a perverted lebensraum—rattling the tin cup of his despair against the bars of his peculiar practices.

As this last garbled and nonsensical paragraph amply demonstrates, Hubler was unwise to criticize anyone else's prose style.

It was perhaps to be expected that the *Catholic Herald,* which grudgingly admitted that the novel was "well-written," should nevertheless describe it as a "horrible little book," which "would be less nauseous if the homosexuality of [George] were less taken for granted as part of a completely normal pattern—and 'normality' not so obviously regarded as something slightly devious." There were also predictable cries of outrage from Washington's *Catholic Standard* and newspapers in Ireland, but Isherwood might reasonably have hoped for better from Britain's communist *Daily Worker,* which complained: "To flaunt a human abnormality is not the best way to gain the true sympathy of understanding. Prejudice against homosexuality and ignorance of its causes, problems and treatment, are sufficiently widespread to doubt the wisdom of writing a novel in which the principal character pines for his dead boy friend, has a flirtation with a male student, drinks heavily, and dies after a masturbatory orgasm."

Things had, however, moved on a little since the publication of *Down There on a Visit* and even in Nashville, Tennessee, a critic felt able to write that "by making his leading character a sex deviate, [Isherwood] has provided a sharp contrast with the normal man and yet he has been able to show that all people experience the same emotions and face similar crises, no matter how they may differ in normality and perspective." A reviewer in the *Coventry Evening Telegraph,* Bob and May Buckingham's local paper, commented: "I have a feeling that this novel is not trivial, that it is both true and important so unobtrusively that one is in danger of missing the fact." Many critics did, but elsewhere people recognized what Isherwood was trying to do. In England, the novelist Francis King, who later wrote the booklet on Isherwood for the British Council's "Writers and their Work" series,[4] chose the novel as his book of the year in the *Sunday Telegraph:* "a marvellously tough, sinewy and spare work of

---

4. This series, by happy chance, was edited by Ian Scott-Kilvert.

art, as cruel in its all-pervasive irony as it is consoling in its mastery of style and technique." Several people nominated *A Single Man* as one of the year's highlights, including Graham Greene, somewhat provocatively, in the *Catholic Herald,* thus offsetting the appalled review the paper had run earlier, and Alan Pryce-Jones in the *New York Herald Tribune.* Pryce-Jones recognized the book as "a small masterpiece" which fulfilled "the blazing promise" of Isherwood's early career.

A Single Man is certainly Isherwood's most profound and most skillfully written book, one that seems to be all surface, but is properly engaged with that most important of subjects: what it is to be alive. In particular it is about what it is to be alive now, in the present, in Southern California. George's determination to let go of the past—memories of Jim, the possibility of returning to England—and to live in and for the present is emphasized by the book's present-tense narrative. It is not just about George, but about the individual person in society, unattached people in a world of married couples and families, those who may be fully assimilated but still feel outsiders in a predominantly WASP America. Other minorities than the homosexual one are represented in the book: Myron Hirsch, the Jewish student who sees anti-semitism everywhere; Estelle Oxford, the touchy, race-conscious black student; Lois Yamaguchi, the Nisei whose family was treated so badly during the war that she feels she can only marry a Japanese. But all of these, whether other people like it or not, are part of that one unifying majority: the human race.

Even some sympathetic critics thought the book sad, somehow failing to register its essential optimism and its ferocious comic energy. The book harnesses to great effect the flailing rage Isherwood expressed in his diaries against heterosexuals, women and children. George's life may not seem very edifying, and in many ways it is not particularly happy, but George is tough, he is a survivor who is glad to be alive, and that gives cause for hope. When he goes to visit Jim's former lover, who is dying of cancer, he realizes that "the very last traces of the Doris who tried to take Jim from him have vanished from this shrivelled mannikin; and, with them, the last of his hate." Instead there is a sense of fellow-feeling: *"we are on the same road, I shall follow you soon."* This may seem a cheerless prospect, but as George drives away from the hospital past shops decorated for Christmas and packed with shoppers, he is

> very far, right now, from sneering at any of these fellow-creatures. They may be crude and mercenary and dull and low, but he is proud, is glad, is almost indecently gleeful to be able to stand up and be counted in their ranks—the ranks of that marvellous minority, The Living. They don't know their luck, these people on the sidewalk; but George knows his—for a little while at least—because he is freshly returned from the icy presence of The Majority, which Doris is about to join.

Although Isherwood was dismayed that his novel had been given a "sour reception" in America, he declared: "I still feel very good about it. Not so much as a work of art but as a deed. I feel: I spoke the truth, and now let them swallow it or not as they see fit. That's a very good feeling, and this is the first time that I have really felt it." A few months later, he would write: "I now feel that, *according to my rules,* A Single Man is a masterpiece; that is to say, it achieves exactly what I wanted it to achieve. I keep dipping into it and always I feel yes, that is exactly the effect I was trying for."

In September 1964 Tony Richardson asked Isherwood to work on another screen adaptation. The principal reason he wanted to film Marguerite Duras's *Le Marin de Gibraltar* (*The Sailor from Gibraltar*), which he admitted would be difficult to adapt since it was "full of highfalutin French metaphysics," was that it was the favorite book of the French actress Jeanne Moreau, with whom he was having an affair. He had already hired the British playwright David Mercer to work on a script with him, but somewhere along the line Mercer dropped out. Richardson was already scheduled to make another film with Moreau, from a script by Jean Genet, and he had the idea of having *The Sailor from Gibraltar* ready to shoot immediately after he had finished filming *Mademoiselle*. Richardson admitted in his memoirs that "In the rush to finalize production facilities, the one thing forgotten was the script." Although he fails to mention it in his account of making the film, Richardson eventually asked Isherwood to amend this oversight. Setting aside his francophobia and his genuine doubts as to whether this "pretentious frog stuff" was suitable material for a film, Isherwood got to work and produced a finished script within two months.

This left him free to concentrate on his own work. He finished assembling *Exhumations* by the beginning of February 1965, and on his and Bachardy's twelfth anniversary he started writing *A Meeting by the River*. He had decided that the two protagonists should be brothers, one very worldly, the other about to take *sannyas*. "I know almost nothing about this," he confessed, "but I may just as well make a stab at it. Something will emerge—something quite different, probably." He wrote twenty-five pages and then got stuck. Looking at this draft in mid-March, he realized: "It is all wrong. Not just every word of it is wrong, which is to be expected at this early stage. The method is wrong." He had attempted to write the confrontation between the two brothers as a series of dramatic scenes, but felt that everything important in the book "is below the surface of this encounter, except on a very few occasions." He decided that the novel should be written entirely as a series of letters and diary entries. It made sense that the letters should be from the more outgoing brother (at this stage called Martin), who was visiting India, and that the diary should be kept by the monk (Leonard), who was already there preparing to take *sannyas*. The diary would be straightforward enough, but Isherwood needed to invent a number of other characters with whom Martin might be corresponding.

He initially thought that Martin and Leonard should be half-brothers, with a shared mother. The mother would be one of the people Martin wrote to, along with his wife and a mistress. They would have been born in England, but Martin would have immigrated to the States where he was enjoying a successful career, perhaps in business or the movies. Leonard might have done "some sort of social service, maybe with the Quakers and then met a swami of this Order, not in India but somewhere in Europe and lived with him there a while." In other words, the two brothers would not only share between them Isherwood's background but would represent the two warring sides of Isherwood's own character, the worldly and the spiritual—although at this point Isherwood intended to base Martin on Ivan Moffatt.

I n February, Isherwood became a Regents' Professor in the philosophy department at UCLA, a post he had accepted because the campus was nearby, he thought the job would be easy, and it would net him $10,000. The idea of a Regents' Professorship was that "a man distinguished for his other than academic attainments" should spend one semester on campus, taking classes, giving lectures and otherwise "freshening the academic environment." He kept regular office hours two days a week, encouraging students of creative writing to bring him their manuscripts. Having discovered to his cost at LASC that students who read their work aloud in class were shown no mercy by their fellows and that the entire process became destructive, Isherwood read manuscripts in private, then discussed them with their authors in a relaxed, informal way, often while walking around the campus.

At his inaugural public lecture on "Writing as a Way of Life" in February, Isherwood was introduced to a packed audience as "a man who may be recorded as the finest novelist of our language and period." Since he had been made a professor of philosophy, Isherwood addressed rather more abstract issues than usual in his talks. He spoke of writing in terms of exploration, in particular the exploration of the writer's own personal myth. This concept was taken from Jung, who had written in *Memories, Dreams, Reflections:*

> My life is the story of an act of self-realization by the unconscious. Everything contained within the unconscious seeks outward manifestation, and the personality also desires to evolve out of its unconscious conditioning factors and experience itself as a whole [. . .] What we are to our inner vision [. . .] can only be expressed by way of a myth. Myth is more individual and expresses life more precisely than does science. Science works with concepts of averages which are far too much generalizations to do justice to the subjective variety of an individual life. So it is that I have now undertaken [. . .] to tell my personal myth. I can only tell stories. Whether or not the stories are true is not the problem. The only question is whether what I tell is *my* fable, *my* truth.

Isherwood spoke of his own experience of life, his feeling that "some kind of intention is behind the whole thing, and that this intention has gradually fulfilled itself." He believed that: "Writing is the exploration of one's myth, rather than one's experience. One's myth becomes evident in one's choice of subject-matter; the kind of things one chooses to invent and write about [. . .] All writing is about your personal version of experience." The talk was judged a great success; he later learned that there was standing room only in the hall and two hundred people had to be turned away.

Isherwood was by now becoming a seasoned public speaker. He may no longer have wanted to stand on a platform for Vedanta, but he was increasingly in demand to talk about homosexuality and, as a long-standing member of the ACLU, on other civil liberties issues. A few days before taking up his post at UCLA, he had delivered a talk on "A writer and a minority" at a meeting organized by *One* magazine. This journal had been started by the Mattachine Society, one of America's first homosexual-rights organizations, founded in California in 1950 largely as a response to the promised purge of "sexual deviants" from government announced by Senator McCarthy. At first, the society was run along secret lines, with "cells" meeting in people's homes to discuss both male and female homosexuality. The reason for this secrecy was partly to reassure nervous members, who may not have wanted family and friends to know about their sexual orientation, but also because the Society's founder, Harry Hay, was a member of the Communist Party, and it was thought that this association, if known, might put people off. The organization fought and won a case in the courts when one of its members was prosecuted for soliciting a plainclothes policeman, and in 1953 founded *One,* a magazine boldly subtitled "The Homosexual Viewpoint." Although the magazine's contents were highly respectable, mainly consisting of articles on literary, scientific and sociological topics, the U.S. Postal Service refused to distribute it until, in a landmark legal case, it was ordered by the Supreme Court to do so. At its peak, the magazine achieved a circulation of some five thousand, and it had hailed *A Single Man* as "The most honest book ever written about a homosexual," an endorsement that would be blazoned on the paperback edition. Isherwood himself would gradually become a figurehead of the emerging gay liberation movement.

This reputation led people to seek Isherwood out. The young British artist David Hockney had arrived in Los Angeles in January 1964, carrying with him a letter of introduction from Stephen Spender, whom he had got to know in London. Hockney was an admirer of Isherwood's books and after graduating from the Royal College of Art in London in 1962, he had traveled to Berlin and gone looking for the bars mentioned in the Berlin stories. Now he had come to Los Angeles, with John Rechy's *City of Night* as his literary guidebook. He summoned up courage to telephone Isherwood and was invited to tea. Isherwood, Hockney recalled, "was the first author I'd met that I really admired," and he liked the portfolio of drawings the young artist had brought with him. The two men became friends at once, Isherwood exclaiming: "Oh David, we've so much in common; we love California, we love American boys, and we're from the north of England." As Hockney observed, the north of England he knew as a working-class boy brought up in Bradford was rather different from the one at Marple Hall: Isherwood had never even visited Blackpool.

Fame also brought Isherwood letters from fans and other people who felt the need to communicate. Astonishingly, even given the content of his books, not everyone understood what Isherwood meant when he stated in the author biography he wrote for their dust-jackets that he was "unmarried." On one occasion he received a proposal of marriage from a thirty-two-year-old woman in Texas. Having consulted her astrology charts, she thought she and Isherwood were well matched. She described herself as a "refined domestic type, quite serious, attractive, healthy but nervous" and imagined that Isherwood must be "sober and kind." She added that she had three small children who "need a loving Father to raise and educate them." If this litter was not sufficient, she would be prepared to have further children with Isherwood. She concluded her letter by saying: "If you don't want us under any circumstances would you give my picture to some other big Artist or Musician."

I n October 1964 Bachardy went to New York, where he was having a show of his
work, and he remained there until December, fulfilling a commission from Lin-
coln Kirstein to produce a portfolio of drawings of the twelve principal dancers of the
New York City Ballet. This would bring in a substantial fee and would result in
Bachardy's work being shown while the company was on tour and back in New York.
When Isherwood heard about this commission he wrote:

> Just at first, I felt a slight pleasurable excitement, because I shall have another five
> weeks alone, and being alone is always a challenge. But already there is the
> aching realization that I won't see Don for another five weeks; and that is a most
> awful long time. Without him, I'm not complete.

This Platonic notion was undoubtedly true, but there was also a sense that for the
present the relationship worked better when they were apart, particularly while
Bachardy was still engaged in the struggle to find a style of painting he believed in.
When he returned to Santa Monica, he and Isherwood took a trip to New Mexico and
enjoyed a brief but trouble-free period together—"the best I've ever had with him,"
Isherwood felt. Bachardy returned to New York in January 1965 for an indefinite period, and at the end of the month, Isherwood went to join him for a fortnight. "New
York was as dirty, cold and brutish as usual; but the visit was a success, as far as relations with Don were concerned," Isherwood reported. "Not that we didn't quarrel a
bit—if we hadn't it would only have meant that we were on our party behavior. There
is still the old problem of our seeing other people together. But I do feel the whole
thing between us has strengthened and changed out of all recognition, since this time
two years ago." One of the things they quarreled about was the ballet. Bachardy was
a genuine aficionado, but Isherwood persisted in finding dance theater boring. "Don't
be so *pleased* that you don't like it," Bachardy snapped, after dragging Isherwood to
a performance of *Harlequinade*.

Bachardy returned to Santa Monica for most of April and May, suffering from a
liver complaint and consequently depressed about his painting, but he was still working on his ballet drawings and spending much of his time in New York. "He is literally everything I have in this world," Isherwood wrote. "He is what keeps me alive.
When he isn't with me, I am in a partial coma, most of the time. Which is okay. Because the alternative would be pangs of misery because of our separation. I eat ab-
normally and am fat, but not as fat as I would be if I drank." (He had once again given
up drinking after getting plastered with the Masselinks, falling over in the bathroom
and hitting his head against the tub.) The pattern of long separation persisted to the
degree that Isherwood described Bachardy's returns to Santa Monica as "visits." Isherwood was still mulling over the idea of an autobiographical book, but without
much enthusiasm. He realized that this was partly because he disliked planning
books, preferring to plunge in and see what happened. This might work as a method
for fiction, but could prove less successful for an analytical work based on history
and facts. He told Dodie Smith that the book would "deal with characters and subjects mentioned in my books, not the books themselves. For example, the Father-

figure, the Mother-figure, the Home-image, the romance of distant places, loneliness, homosexuality, the cult being an Outsider, the anti-Hero, Vedanta as anti-religion, High Camp, etc., etc." Smith replied discouragingly that she preferred autobiography to be straightforward and urged him to write an account of his life in America before embarking on his quest for personal myths.

Isherwood concentrated instead on *A Meeting by the River,* worrying that the second draft seemed "awfully thin" and even telling Spender that it would "probably end up in the morgue, like the first draft of *Down There on a Visit.*" It was hard to concentrate on another draft because Isherwood was expecting any moment to be summoned to Italy, where Richardson had started shooting *The Sailor from Gibraltar.* In the event he was never called upon, which was a lucky escape since the shoot was a disaster, partly because the male lead, Ian Bannen, was in a bad psychological way, and partly because Richardson had cast his unhappily estranged wife in the film alongside his mistress. Isherwood may have avoided the rigors of filming, but there was no dodging the verdict of the critics. *Variety* spoke for many when it noted that Duras's books were not strong on narrative and that "with such interpreters as Christopher Isherwood and Tony Richardson (neither famous for clarity of intent) [. . .] the ensuing screenplay is replete with repetitive sequences."

By October 10 the second draft of the novel was finished to Isherwood's satisfaction, although it was, he warned Upward when sending him this draft, "very late Isherwood": "I have the gravest doubts about it, but I know I can't attempt another draft until I have left it alone for a while, and I badly need your advice. Maybe it will just set your teeth on edge." Upward's principal reaction was that the confrontation between the brothers, now called Patrick and Oliver, lacked drama. "I mustn't dismiss this suggestion as being merely square, which is what at present it seems to me to be," Isherwood told himself.

> As I have been seeing it, Patrick's opposition to Oliver's vocation is quite largely a kind of teasing, and not fundamentally serious. My feeling is that Patrick is really incapable of being serious enough and passionate enough to take any drastic steps to get Oliver out of the monastery—*and that that is his tragedy.* I am quite ready to agree that many of the moves and countermoves in the present draft of the novel are wrong, and perhaps Patrick's fundamental indifference ought in itself to be dramatized more strongly. Perhaps Oliver should even reproach him for it.

Isherwood had set himself an almost insoluble problem: how to depict a "confrontation" in which one party suffered from fundamental indifference. If the conflict between the two brothers was largely a tease, then it would be hard to provide much tension in this important encounter.

Part of Isherwood's difficulty was that the confrontation he was attempting to dramatize was based on an internal, psychological one. The book had to present a struggle of wills between two people, but was in fact drawn from his own experience. Isherwood said in a radio interview that *A Meeting by the River* was "less autobiographical than anything I've ever written." This was not true, and it is puzzling that he should make such a claim. Oliver has worked with the Quakers, and his reasons for converting to Vedanta are very similar to Isherwood's as outlined in his diaries and in letters—and indeed publicly in *An Approach to Vedanta*. Oliver shares Isherwood's prejudice against anything "oriental" and is led to Vedanta by meeting a swami who is "small" and has an "extraordinary calm assurance," just like Prabhavananda. The "three things" that Oliver tries to "hold on to" when he fears that Patrick has come to India to undermine his faith are exactly the things Isherwood clung to when he had religious doubts:

> I have known a man who said *he knew* God exists.
>
> After living with him for five years and watching him closely, watching the way he lived, I'm able to say that I believe (nearly all of the time) that he really did know. I also believe the possibility of my having the kind of experience which gave him that knowledge.
>
> That man chose me for his disciple. I may be poisoned with hatred and half mad, but nevertheless I'm his disciple. *And he can never desert me.*

Like Isherwood, Oliver realizes that he is something of a "catch" for Vedanta and is aware that people may feel that there is something faintly ridiculous about a middle-class Englishman becoming a Hindu monk.

Isherwood is also very much present in Patrick, whom he had decided to make bi-sexual. Patrick shares his creator's vanity and sexual rapacity, and his connoisseurship of boys' legs. His letters to his lover, Tom, telling him that he is missing him so much that he is literally feeling sick, recall Isherwood's entries in his diaries about his feelings for Bachardy. Patrick's reassuring, faintly patronizing and yet curiously frank letters to his mother are very like the ones Isherwood wrote to Kathleen, and his horror of India is Isherwood's. To some extent, the novel can be read as Isherwood's attempt to explain, even to convince himself about, Vedanta.

He was gradually coming to agree with Upward's criticism that the book seemed satisfactory up to the moment at which Patrick arrives at the monastery: "After that, it gets confused and loses direction." He spent much of the spring of 1966 working on the novel. Stravinsky had recently asked him how many hours he wrote each day and how much he produced in that time. Isherwood had replied that these days, on average, he wrote three hours a day, which resulted in a page of writing. Progress on this novel was even slower. One of the obstacles to writing the book was the prospect of showing it to Prabhavananda before he published it. He had become accustomed to the swami's lack of interest in, if not downright disapproval of, his fiction, but knew that a novel which dealt directly with the faith would need his guru's blessing. "I hate the thought of him reading the parts about Tom—but *why* should I, actually? I'm not ashamed of them, I would never apologize for them artistically or morally, they are absolutely right for the book, I know. Furthermore, Swami has praised me for being myself, making no pretences about the way I live my life. Just the same, I squirm." In fact, the parts of the book dealing with Patrick's relationship with Tom are among the least satisfactory, a regrettable throwback to the arch manner of *The World in the Evening*. Patrick's first letter to Tom is particularly shymaking, and it is not altogether clear how far Isherwood intended this:

That coverless and obviously much thumbed-through paperback novel you suddenly pulled out of your pocket and gave me at the airport—*Wow* (as you would say)!! You know, you might at least have warned me what it was about! I suppose I should have guessed, from your wicked grin. Anyhow, I didn't. After we'd taken off, I opened it in all innocence at the first chapter and almost immediately found myself involved in that sizzling love-scene between the character called Lance and that younger boy. Did you think a hard-boiled publisher couldn't be shocked? I began blushing, yes actually!

And Patrick would not be the only one.

Prabhavananda nevertheless approved the final draft, claiming: "As I finished reading the last scene there were two tears running down my cheeks." He even went so far as to suggest the novel should be sold in the Vedanta Center's bookshop. Although he assured Isherwood that nothing in the book would offend Belur Math, there was a slight problem that the monastery in the novel would be recognized. Isherwood had been sending drafts of the novel to Vidyatmananda, who was now in France running the Centre Védantique Ramakrichna at Gretz. Appointed "technical adviser," he had supplied Isherwood with valuable notes as well as an extract from his own diary describing taking *sannyas*. Reading the final draft, he too was moved to tears, and was much relieved that some of the sexual explicitness had been toned down. He sent a detailed list of comments, and by way of thanks Isherwood decided to dedicate the book to him. His original idea was to dedicate it "to John Yale," but he subsequently felt it ought to read "to Swami Vidyatmananda." "I have always regarded a dedication as a public tribute to the dedicatee," he explained, "and I feel that any reader who is interested should be able to identify him." Prabhavananda, having approved the dedication to "John Yale," was uneasy about a book being dedicated to a swami by his monastic name. Swami Pavitrananda from the New York Society, who was a trustee of Belur Math, was strongly against the idea. Made aware of the opposition of his seniors, and concerned about what sort of publicity might attend the publication of the book, Vidyatmananda regretfully declined the honor and so the published book was dedicated instead to Gerald Heard, who had suffered the first of an increasingly debilitating series of strokes.

I sherwood had completed the book while acting as a visiting professor at the University of California at Riverside, just outside Los Angeles. He spent two days a week there, staying overnight in a motel, and found his students "both bright and beautiful." Although he told Upward that the work was "clowning" rather than teaching, he took it seriously, and when his appointment terminated at the end of May, and the novel was finished, he found himself drifting aimlessly. Bachardy had returned from New York at the end of April and as usual Isherwood anticipated their reunion with "a lot of joy and some apprehension." They were united, however, when the ballet project Bachardy had been working on for Kirstein foundered. Bachardy had spent a year and a half making drawings of all the principal dancers, choreographers, and costume and set designers, and these had been expensively printed to make up a glossy souvenir portfolio. Unfortunately, Kirstein had gone ahead with this project without authorization from George Balanchine, who was still running the New York

City Ballet. Balanchine told Kirstein that he disliked the portfolio, partly because Bachardy's portrait of the ballerina the choreographer was currently in love with was "truthful" (as Bachardy put it) rather than flattering. Kirstein, who had always been in awe of Balanchine, decided that without the Master's wholehearted approval the portfolio could not be put on sale. Hideously embarrassed by the tangle he had got himself into, Kirstein "went crazy" and had the boxes of the portfolios, unaccompanied by any explanatory note, delivered to the apartment where Bachardy was staying. Bachardy wrote a letter of protest and Kirstein broke off all relations with him and Isherwood. Isherwood made an attempt to mend the breach, but to no avail. There were no further communications and they never saw Kirstein again.

N ow that Bachardy was back in Santa Monica, his relations with Isherwood were reasonably good, but there were still occasional tensions, largely caused by Bachardy's continuing struggle with his art. ("Don said of his work, the day before yesterday, 'my drawings are studies made under stress.' The operative word is *stress!*" Isherwood noted in his diary.) Isherwood himself was once again drinking too much, bored with writing his diary, and unable to meditate. Visiting Vedanta Place (as Ivar Avenue had been renamed) for the annual Father's Day lunch, he endured a theatrical show which made use of "Vedantically-revamped" numbers from popular musicals. One of the songs, delivered in the approximate Cockney made infamous by Dick Van Dyke in the 1964 film *Mary Poppins,* was a tribute of sorts to Isherwood himself:

> *Aow, Mistafah Christafah Ishtafa,*
> *Blimey, he's a blinking limey and a real fine bloke . . .*

And so, excruciatingly, on.

> I squirmed, but I was touched of course and pleased. It *is* a Family, even though I know so few of my relatives and can't honestly take much interest in them. Some woman came up to me afterwards and well-meaningly cooed, 'now you know how much we all love you!' Well, perhaps I am mildly liked—as an institution rather than a person—and that's quite sufficient.
>
> I have always been and am now more than ever alien from the Society as such. Only Swami's loyalty has forced them to accept me—for of course there must be all manner of lurid (and fairly accurate) rumors about my life. And then there are those dreadful novels of mine for the faithful to gag on. The fact that I've written a life of Ramakrishna and translated the Gita must only make my novels the less excusable in their eyes.

Several film jobs—including proposed adaptations of Anthony Burgess's bleakly futuristic *A Clockwork Orange* and Morris West's papal epic, *The Shoes of the Fisherman*—fell through, but in July Isherwood heard that he had got a job writing a "Christmas Spectacular" for the ABC television company about the origins of the popular carol "Silent Night." This project appealed to Isherwood's *Song of Bernadette* side and he liked the producer, Daniel Mann. It would also involve his visiting Austria, where the carol was composed in 1818, and he hoped to combine this with a trip to England to visit Wyberslegh to consult family papers for the auto-biographical project he had discussed with Dodie Smith. Some idea of his approach to family history can be gathered from the working title he gave the book: "Hero-Father, Demon-Mother."

Isherwood set off for Salzburg on September 21, his regrets at leaving Bachardy and a particularly warm California autumn manifesting themselves physically in bad back pain. Although suspicious of its sheer tidiness and the "Disneylike unconvincing charm" of its inhabitants, Isherwood rated Salzburg one of his favorite towns, on a par with San Francisco and London. He particularly appreciated the shortness of Austrian shorts, when worn by the right (male, young) sort of Austrian, and the numerous "dobbins," both live and sculpted, that thronged the town. Isherwood stayed there for ten days working on the script before traveling to England, where he visited the Spenders in London, went to Cambridge to see Forster, but spent most of the trip in Cheshire with Richard.

Since Kathleen's death, Wyberslegh Hall had fallen into further disrepair and was now "ghastly with damp and mould and black deathly dirt." Richard had given up living there and had moved in with Alan Bradley's brother Dan and his wife, who lived in a modern house in Disley. When she was dying, Kathleen had asked Alan to look after Richard, which he had gladly agreed to do, but Richard's drinking made matters very difficult. Alan tried to ban him from drinking in their house, where he frequently stayed, but Richard would return from binges the worse for wear, whereupon Alan would send him to his room. Richard never forgot his behavior and would always apologize the next morning, but when drunk would scream and shout and claim he was being held captive. The Bradleys didn't mind too much what the neighbors must have thought, but began to worry about the effect all this was having on their young daughter. Eventually, Alan asked his brother to take over. Having been injured at work, Dan Bradley was on permanent sick leave and so was always at home to deal with Richard if he became difficult.

Richard grew to be very fond of "the Dans," as he called them, and although he saw them more as friends than employees, they always addressed him as "Mr. Richard." The couple, who were in their fifties, had taken Richard in hand and tidied him up considerably, insisting he wear a clean suit and tie (though he was still inclined to leave his flies gaping) and ensuring that he ate properly. He visited Wyberslegh regularly, ostensibly to keep an eye on it, but more often than not to drink there alone. Crates of beer would be delivered by taxi from the local off-license and Richard would slowly but steadily work his way through bottle after bottle. Unlike his brother, he had a reasonably strong head, and when drinking like this—rather than going on a concentrated binge—rarely appeared drunk, however much he consumed. If he drank enough to make himself sick, he would simply clean himself up and carry on. In spite of this heavy intake he remained alert and easily able to answer all the questions Isherwood asked him about family history without apparent effort and in considerable detail. "He seems to have the Past at his fingertips," Isherwood noted, "and maybe this is partly because he can scarcely be said to live in the Present at all. He does nothing in particular, except go over to Wyberslegh in the car, putter around and leave again." He was a familiar local sight, going down to the shops, a basket on his arm, stopping every now and then to consult his shopping list or count the change in his purse. As he passed houses, he always made a point of closing any garden gates that had been left open.

Apart from the occasional complicated, fantasy-driven friendship with young men, most of Richard's remaining relationships were with incredibly old ladies, either distant relatives or acquaintances of his mother, and were largely conducted by letter. His principal interests were his diary, which he kept as assiduously as Isherwood kept his, and Rosicrucianism. He had told Isherwood about becoming a neophyte of the Ancient Mystical Order of the Rosy Cross the previous year in the course of a letter thanking him for a copy of *Ramakrishna and His Disciples*. Supposedly founded in the fifteenth century, the AMORC was a form of mystical Christianity centered on the symbols of resurrection (the rose) and redemption (the cross), and its followers laid claim to occult powers. In its way, it was far more exotic than Vedantism—which may have been part of the point.

In preparation for his new book, Isherwood read the letters his father had sent home from the trenches and his mother's diaries of the First World War period. He also felt that he needed to visit Marple Hall one more time. There was not, by now, much of the Hall to visit, since it had been compulsorily purchased by the local council and demolished. Isherwood took a taxi to the site, driving down what used to be the main drive, now a suburban road called Marina Drive, past the brash new buildings of the Marple Hall Grammar School, which included an Isherwood Building. (An outraged Richard had refused the authorities permission to emblazon the Isherwood coat of arms on the school uniform.) On previous visits, Isherwood had hated the atmosphere of decay that permeated the Hall, that smashed and gutted symbol of his childhood and family background. "But now the whole feeling was different," he wrote in his diary.

> You could barely trace the foundations of the house, they were thickly grassed over. Only the stone over one of the doorways to the terrace lies there in the grass, engraved with the date 1658. And the two great beech-trees are still standing—the one near the front gate and the one at the end of the terrace, in which I shot the wood-pigeon with my air rifle (my most painfully remembered youthful 'war crime'). It was a beautiful morning, and in the classrooms they were sitting at lessons, and over on what used to be the Barn Meadow a football game was going on. A new life had taken over. The Hall and its curse were forgotten, or remembered only as something romantic and mildly benevolent. And I felt as the narrator feels at the end of Wuthering Heights, when he sees that the graves are becoming overgrown by the vegetation of the moor and thinks you could not imagine unquiet slumbers for the sleepers in that quiet earth.

With this potent image in his mind, and with a great sheaf of notes taken from family papers, Isherwood flew back to California.

TWENTY-FOUR

T HERE WAS STILL WORK TO BE DONE ON *SILENT NIGHT* WHEN Isherwood got back to Santa Monica, but most of what he had written was cut from the finished film, which was broadcast on Christmas Day 1968. It ended in front of the United Nations building with Kirk Douglas and a group of international moppets warbling the much-loved carol. Given Isherwood's equivocal feelings about children, it is hardly surprising that this injection of schmaltz infuriated him: having seen a preview, both he and Mann attempted unsuccessfully to get their names removed from the credits.

While Isherwood settled into the long period of research needed to write his book about his parents, he was looking around for other projects to bring in money. Among the more promising options were stage adaptations of Bernard Shaw's fable *The Adventures of the Black Girl in Her Search for God* for a theater in Los Angeles and Wedekind's "Lulu" plays for London. He also toyed briefly with the idea of writing a film script based on the Mexican version of *Down There on a Visit* and performed various Vedanta chores for the ailing but still persuasive Prabhavananda. Isherwood had begun to have doubts about *Hero-Father, Demon-Mother* as a title for his autobiography, since both Bachardy and Truman Capote disliked it. He was also, as usual, having difficulty finding a way into the book. He had started a draft but quickly given up because it seemed too slick and had begun to bore him. Reading André Gide's *So Be It* gave him the idea of writing the book as an exploration, in which that exploration became part of the story, rather like A.J.A. Symons's classic *The Quest for Corvo* (1934). He then decided, as he had so often before when looking for a narrative strategy for his fiction, that "this book is not about my Father and my Mother, it's about me." It seems remarkable, and faintly absurd, that Isherwood had not realized, even at this late stage, that *all* his books were to a greater or lesser extent about himself. This one, he thought, would take the form of "an archaeological excavation": "I dig into myself and I find my Father and my Mother in me. I find all the figures of the past *inside* me, not outside."

He decided that the book should be written as *A Single Man* was, in the present tense and narrated by "a disembodied observer." The principals, including Isherwood himself, would all be referred to by their first names: Kathleen, Frank, Christopher, Richard. He felt that by not insisting on their family relationships to each other— omitting such words as "mother," "father" and "son"—it would "involve them all much more closely and organically with each other, as part of a process." Once again, Virginia Woolf provided a model: "I have always wanted to write my own version of Virginia Woolf's *The Waves,*" he wrote; "this book will be it, I think. I see it as a collection of scenes, jumping back and forward in time." In this, the book would also resemble Isherwood's fictional family saga, *The Memorial.* He spent most of the spring of 1967 trying out different approaches to the material, but eventually realized that he would need to use Kathleen's diaries extensively. This would mean a prolonged stay in England since he feared that Richard would not allow him to take the diaries back to California.

Meanwhile, an important part of Isherwood's past was being served up with music on Broadway. A writer called Joe Masteroff had collaborated with the lyricist Fred Ebb and composer John Kander to produce a musical based on *I Am a Camera* and, more distantly, *Goodbye to Berlin.* Setting the *Weimardämmerung* to music did not seem like everyone's idea of good taste, nor something likely to result in a hit show, but *Cabaret* confounded expectations when it opened on November 1966, running for 1,165 performances and winning a total of eight Tony awards. Isherwood's interest in the show was entirely financial. After considerable wrangling, he received a cut, but this was nothing like as large as people imagined. The original 40–60 split between Isherwood and what was now the van Druten estate persisted, but others also got a cut of the proceeds, including Masteroff, Kander and Ebb. Because Gertrude Macy, co-producer of the stage version of *I Am a Camera,* was also entitled to some money, it was some months before Isherwood saw a cent of his share. He disliked everything he heard about the show—"It sounds Jewish beyond all belief"—and decided not to see it. Bachardy did go and dutifully reported back that it was "awful." "I try to keep as far away from it as possible," Isherwood told Upward after the play had been running on Broadway for over a year and had just opened in London. "It's an ill bird that fouls the nest where the golden eggs are laid. Especially when the nest is anyhow made entirely of sawdust and shit." Although the show brought in a useful trickle of royalties, it reinforced an impression that already had some currency among the critics that Isherwood would always remain famous for his Berlin books and that nothing he wrote afterward would be as good.

In May 1967 Isherwood flew to England, where he hoped to wrest his mother's diaries from Richard, discuss the Wedekind adaptation with the director Anthony Page, persuade the trustees of G. B. Shaw's estate to give him permission to adapt *Black Girl,* and get a firm decision from the Mercury Gallery as to whether they were prepared to give Bachardy a show. His trip would also coincide with the British publication of *A Meeting by the River* and Methuen set up a number of press interviews for him. He achieved most of his objectives, spending a perfect summer's day at Cambridge. Forster was still very much alive, and Isherwood spent a weekend with him and Ackerley at the Buckinghams' in Coventry. It was here that he met a gloomy young man who had trained to be a Catholic monk but was now writing a book about Isherwood's work ("His interest in my work must come from a suppressed area of his psyche," Isherwood decided). It was to be a final meeting with Ackerley, who died suddenly from a coronary thrombosis shortly before Isherwood returned to California.

A *Meeting by the River* might have been seen as a timely book since it was published during a period when young people were becoming increasingly interested in Indian mysticism. The Maharishi Mahesh Yogi, for example, had gained a very high media profile thanks to such followers as the Beatles, who had traveled with their colorful entourage to India to sit at his feet and gain wisdom. Isherwood himself went to hear the Maharishi talk after the novel was published and was "quite favorably impressed—I mean, I don't think he's an out-and-out fake." This was hardly an endorsement, but Isherwood was naturally skeptical when it came to anyone who might be seen as some sort of rival guru to Prabhavananda. The Maharishi, who certainly courted publicity and usually appeared on a flower-bedecked stage brandishing a gerbera, had plugged into "Flower Power." This current youth movement, dedicated to peace, "free love" and communing with nature, came out of San Francisco, and Isherwood knew a number of people he described as hippies. His novel could well have found an audience amongst these young seekers after enlightenment, but naturally enough fell into the hands of less youthful and more conservative literary critics.

The novel divided them to the extent that it is difficult to imagine that they were all reading the same book. While some described the book as "a remarkable *tour de force*" and "a triumph of craftsmanship," others thought it "clumsy" and "embarrassing." Elizabeth Hardwick sympathetically referred to Isherwood's recent books as "the product of a fatigued but admirable courage," but criticized his technique, complaining that the novel was written "with spectacular casualness." Isherwood had indeed set himself a puzzle: he had decided that the letters and diaries that made up the narrative needed to be "written loosely, in a seemingly non-literary manner," but had worried that the way he had done this was "merely sloppy." An example of this sloppiness was the unfortunate tendency he had developed to overuse the exclamation mark in his writing, occasionally giving it a wide-eyed, "gee-whiz" tone. This is particularly noticeable in *A Meeting by the River,* where, as the reviewer of *The Times* noted, "exclamation-marks have to prop up commonplace sentences like emotive crutches."

Isherwood himself did not write about the book's critical reception in his diary, but his final comment on it, when correcting the proofs of the American edition, was less than confident. "I still don't know what I think of the book," he wrote. "It seems thin and unconvincing at the beginning; later I think the fun and the psychological interplay start to be felt. I am pleased with the final moves leading to the climax. But it's clever rather than emotionally powerful (whatever *that* means!)." He would subsequently attempt to rewrite the story for both the stage and the cinema, which suggests that he was not altogether happy with the novel and felt that it was unresolved. The book is undoubtedly one of Isherwood's least successful, and it fails on several counts. The first is a failure of technique. By keeping certain crucial characters offstage, Isherwood fatally underwrites them. Tom remains little more than a gay fantasy figure, young, handsome and bursting with sexual energy, and the reader gets absolutely no notion of Penny's character, or what it was about her that made both Patrick and Oliver fall in love with her. Indeed, it is hard to conceive of Oliver even being heterosexual. The only moment in the novel when he shows any sexual awareness at all is when he sees his brother exercising naked: "I couldn't help being aware of his rather big penis slapping against his bare thigh as he jumped," Oliver confides in his diary. "Patrick always had a beautiful body and it's still in perfect shape, he must exercise all the time. You can tell that he's been lying in the sun completely nude. He's dark brown all over, with only the faintest trace to show the part the swimming-trunks have covered." Patrick is deliberately showing off in order to test Oliver in some way, as Oliver recognizes, but it might have been possible for so worldly a character to have tempted his supposedly heterosexual brother in a more orthodox manner—with, say, a copy of *Playboy.*

There is also a problem of balance between the two brothers. It would be too crude to say that Oliver represents the spirit and Patrick the flesh, and that their battle is one between the sacred and the profane. Isherwood acknowledged that to some extent the two brothers were opposing sides of the same person—an idea emphasized by the common gene pool that brothers would have but that two friends (such as Peter and Paul of Isherwood's original concept) would not: "Heredity has made us part of a single circuit," Oliver writes; "our wires are all connected." Neither represented goodness or badness, but they had "the occupational vices or bad tendencies which monks and worldly people respectively have." If the reader is supposed to have equal sympathy for both brothers, then a careful balance must be maintained: it would be disastrous if Patrick seemed merely sensual and Oliver merely priggish. When the novel starts, Patrick does to some extent seduce the reader, and some reviewers felt that he was in danger of running away with the novel. It comes as a shock, therefore, when Isherwood presents the first extracts from Oliver's diary in which Patrick's motives are questioned. Patrick's hold on the reader gradually slips because his letters to Tom in particular are so off-putting.

A "puzzled" Julian Jebb, reviewing the book in the *Financial Times,* suspected that "the reader sees Patrick in a light far worse than the author intended," with the result that "Oliver becomes wholly the more sympathetic and interesting of the protagonists and the delicate balance on which the story is built lies in ruins." It is not altogether clear how far Isherwood intends the reader to find Patrick's letters excruciating—and this is the novel's second failing: a failure of tone. It seems possible that Isherwood's distaste for bisexuality had undermined his own good intentions toward Patrick. In a discussion of the book on the BBC radio program *The Critics,* Edward Lucie-Smith declared that Patrick renounces Tom "in terms which seem to me so odious that I can't believe in the conversion at all." Patrick even goes so far as to suggest that Tom might like to consider sleeping with girls—something which Isherwood himself would have considered all too characteristic of the patronizing and dishonest behavior of bisexuals. It is perhaps significant that Oliver calls his brother Paddy, suggesting that the name—consciously or not—was borrowed from Patrick Monkhouse, the sexual confidant of Isherwood's youth who played along with Isherwood's homosexual interests, but then discovered women, settled down and married. Paddy Monkhouse was the first of Isherwood's friends to "change sides," and their friendship did not survive. By the end of the novel, Patrick has become so unsympathetic that one doubts the sincerity of his taking the dust from Oliver's feet, a doubt reinforced by the novel's final sentence: "And everybody was smiling and murmuring, as much as to say how charming it was of Patrick to play the scene according to our local Hindu rules, and how very right and proper it was that we two brothers should love each other." Since this is in fact written in Oliver's diary, we must take it on trust, but the tone will strike many readers as ironic. Does Oliver really believe in his brother's gesture, or is Patrick's *pranam* one final bit of heartless camp? As the critic of *The Times* complained, Patrick remains "a slightly droll puppet pulled by strings you never see nor are helped to understand." Isherwood admitted the book could "be criticized, and has been, because it's like a court and all the evidence for the prosecution and for the defense is presented and you suddenly realize there isn't going to be a verdict. There isn't any jury or judge." This led one critic to declare: "Isherwood, the believer, has written an honest and sparkling small novel about the ultimate futility of all beliefs"—which was hardly Isherwood's aim.

By this time Isherwood was concentrating on his next book, now titled *Kathleen and Frank,* and he spent much of the next twelve months going through the mass of material that Richard had allowed him to bring back from Wyberslegh. He read his mother's diaries from 1891, when she began keeping one regularly, to the end of the First World War, and other family letters: those from Frank to Kathleen during their courtship and from the trenches, letters from Emily to Kathleen, from Frederick to the Isherwoods, and numerous other documents. He eventually read thirty-two volumes of Kathleen's diaries and seventeen bundles of letters, copying out passages that he thought he might need. This resulted in some four hundred single-spaced typed pages of extracts. Although he was finding the material interesting, he began to wonder whether he could ever make a book out of it. Part of this interest was getting to know Kathleen and Frank as individuals rather than as parents, learning about their lives as young people before he was even thought of. Even so, he still found himself to some extent in conflict with Kathleen:

> Reading M's Diary gives a very strange sense of the inner nature of a life—just because it is written from day to day. Or perhaps it would be truer to say that it gives you a sense of the utter mystery of a life when it is viewed from very close to the surface. The mystery is in the lack of meaning. Everything Kathleen does seems compulsive. Does she really give a damn about all those art galleries and churches she visits? Does she give a damn about horse racing? And how about the dancing and the flirtations? She obviously finds some meaning in nursing Emily, partly because she loves her and perhaps even more because this represents self-control, self-sacrifice, etc., which is her compulsive religion. But how much of the Christian ethic did she really believe in? And how squeamish she is about sex! Everything has to be *just so* between the sexes, otherwise Kathleen starts to get outraged or shocked. And yet at the same time she was an extremely perceptive person in many ways. Sometimes in later life she used to talk as if she viewed the whole of human activity as a sort of masquerade. Then, dismissing it all, she protested with genuine indignation that it would be 'unfair' if there wasn't an af-

terlife in which she could be with Frank! At such moments she seemed to regard God as a hotel manager.

He found the drafts Kathleen had kept of letters she had written to Frank much more revealing and less "cagey," and by the time he had read through all the diaries he felt that he had come to know his father "for the first time."

In tandem with this time-consuming project, Isherwood began work on his adaptation of *The Adventures of the Black Girl in Her Search for God,* which had to be submitted to the Shaw estate before it could be mounted at the Mark Taper Forum, an experimental theater in downtown Los Angeles. Isherwood appears to have made a first draft by dictating to a machine, then handing the tape over to someone to type it up for him. This was a method he used when writing film scripts. He would get a draft absolutely clear in his head—as Lehmann had once observed—and then dictate it to someone. After that, of course, he would make numerous revisions until a final version emerged.

Isherwood also worked on an adaptation of Dickens's *A Christmas Carol* for television, with Rex Harrison cast as Scrooge. He finished the script by the middle of January 1968 and the producer, Hunt Stromberg, Jr., whom Isherwood and Bachardy knew socially, was very pleased with it. Stromberg even proposed flying Isherwood to England for the filming, and so Isherwood arranged to borrow David Hockney's flat in Notting Hill. The film fell through because Stromberg was unable to assemble the cast he wanted, but since Hockney's flat was there for the taking, Bachardy went to London instead.

Isherwood and Bachardy's relationship, though still disrupted by the occasional storm, had gradually settled into longer periods of contentment. They had, it seemed, achieved the difficult balance between freedom and commitment, having their own separate lives as well as a shared one. This relationship was celebrated by Hockney, who spent six months in 1968 painting a double portrait of the couple, the first of several such compositions. He had started by taking photographs and making sketches of them at Adelaide Drive, and noticed that whenever they posed, Isherwood always looked at Bachardy. This helped him decide on a composition for this very large painting, which measured seven feet by ten feet. Side by side, Isherwood and Bachardy sit in armchairs behind a coffee table, on which are carefully arranged a bowl of fruit, a corncob and two neat stacks of books (in fact volumes of the *Encyclopaedia Britannica* selected by Hockney from the bookshelves). Bachardy sits in the chair on the left of the picture and looks straight out of the canvas; Isherwood sits on the right, his head turned to look at his lover. The picture is cool and uncluttered and yet intimate.

Part of Hockney's aim was to portray Isherwood and Bachardy not simply as two friends, but as a couple, and in that sense the picture was intended as a record of a successful, domestic and long-lived homosexual relationship. Ironically, it was painted at a time when that relationship was once again put under considerable strain. Bachardy seemed reluctant to return from London and Isherwood had started to wonder what precisely he was up to there. Hockney was unaware of this, but while he was working on the painting, Isherwood regularly visited round at his studio, which was not far from Adelaide Drive, and talked in general terms about the peculiar difficulties of homosexual partnerships. Hockney himself was involved in a relationship that had its own problems. Two years earlier, while teaching art at a summer school run by UCLA, he had fallen in love with one of his students, Peter Schlesinger. The attractive eighteen-year-old Californian, with his mop of unruly fair hair, had become Hockney's lover and his principal subject, appearing in many drawings and paintings. Schlesinger was completing a course in history at UCLA and although the couple spent much of their time together, Hockney was still based in London, and so there were long periods of separation.

Some of Isherwood's complicated feelings about his relationship with Bachardy appear to have found their way into the finished painting, which subsequently achieved an almost iconic status in the gay world. In an earlier period it might have found its place in Magnus Hirschfeld's gallery of homosexual couples, hanging alongside equally famous but rather less reassuring images of Oscar Wilde and Lord Alfred Douglas. The painting is, however, more subtle and ambiguous than this would suggest. While Bachardy (who, because of his trip to London, was painted largely from photographs) looks straight ahead, almost as if he is unaware of his partner, Isherwood's expression is enigmatic. The downturn of his mouth and his beetling eyebrows give him a somewhat baleful look, but he might be expressing anxiety, or even simple concentration, the focused gaze of the camera, recording, not thinking.

When Bachardy was away for extended periods, Isherwood tended to lapse into idleness, eating and drinking too much and lazing about reading pornographic novels and the personal ads in the *Los Angeles Free Press*. Bachardy was somewhat at a loss when he got to London and talked about coming home, but he found work in England and postponed his return several times. Isherwood's reaction to this was to suffer "gas and stomach pains and the shits." The usual battery of tests were run by his patient M.D., all proving negative, but the longer Bachardy postponed his return, the worse Isherwood's ailments became: backache, sore throat, painful left knee and "nerve pains" in the groin and belly, which he began to worry were "the beginnings of cancer." Bachardy assured Isherwood that he would return just as soon as he had finished doing some drawings for the programs and posters for three of John Osborne's plays, which were being directed by Anthony Page at the Royal Court Theatre. When Bachardy finally returned on June 10, after an absence of ten weeks, most of the symptoms cleared up.

It was not only work that had kept Bachardy so long in London: he had also embarked on an affair with a young Englishman he had met there. This man knew Isherwood and considered him a friend, and was not unnaturally concerned that if he discovered what was going on he would be very upset. Bachardy assured him that Isherwood approved of his having "extramarital" relationships. When Isherwood learned of this affair, however, he was not at all happy. He rightly suspected that it was more serious than a mere holiday romance. Partly in order to shore up his relationship with Bachardy, he decided that they should collaborate on a stage adaptation of *A Meeting by the River*. He had been discussing this idea for some time with his young friend James Bridges, who seemed interested in adapting and directing the play himself, but had numerous other stage and film commitments and was making no real progress on a script. It gradually became clear that Bridges would be happier merely to direct the play, and so Isherwood and Bachardy roughed out a draft. Although Isherwood, when he had been asked to write a brief foreword to a new edition of *Journey to a War,* claimed that he did not share with Auden "this urge to revise things," he found recasting his novel for the stage of absorbing interest. "I love taking things apart and putting them together differently," he admitted, but the chief pleasure, as it had been with Auden, was the intimate act of collaboration. They completed a draft within seven weeks. Bachardy typed it up and took it to New York, where Bridges was directing a play written by his partner, Jack Larson. Bridges seemed enthusiastic, but both Isherwood and Bachardy realized the play needed a great deal more work done on it and immediately began revising it.

This work was interrupted when Bachardy returned to London to be with his English lover. Although Isherwood cautioned himself not to end up like Jo Masselink, who had sunk into a mire of self-pity after Ben left her for a younger woman, he was unable to live up to his own admonitions. His fears about the threat this man posed manifested themselves in a vivid dream in which it seemed that he and Bachardy were in the process of parting forever. Waking up, Isherwood felt that Bachardy's presence in the dream "had all the atmosphere of an appearance before or at the moment of or just after death." He was so unsettled that he recorded the exact time of the dream and almost broke his promise not to telephone Bachardy to check that he was all right. Bachardy was, and returned to Santa Monica after four weeks. Isherwood was increasingly concerned about Bachardy's affair, trying to keep it in perspective, while at the same time wondering just how serious it was. People in London certainly thought it serious, and there was even talk of Bachardy leaving Isherwood. It was difficult and painful to discuss the situation, but as Isherwood reluctantly acknowledged: "The really important thing is that we do talk about [Bachardy's lover] and similar problems. It's when we don't talk that the tension builds up." The play proved a welcome distraction, and by Christmas, Isherwood and Bachardy had completed their revision and began sending it out to producers.

One of Isherwood's last sights of 1968, encountered while jogging along the ocean's edge, was "An old seagull dying on the sand with wings flopped open and legs crumpled under it. It kept opening its beak in terrible fierce gasps." Isherwood was only sixty-four, but he regarded the bird with a certain amount of fellow-feeling. His own sense of encroaching time was exacerbated by living with a man still in his mid-thirties, who ran faster and farther along the beach when they took exercise together. Much of the happiness Isherwood felt about his relationship with Bachardy was undermined by the idea that it would end all too soon. He was, as usual, in perfectly good general health—taking regular exercise at the gym or the beach, religiously checking his weight on the bathroom scale—but he began dwelling on the approach of death as if this were just around the next corner. Watching home movies proved disillusioning:

> I marvelled to see how fat, grotesque, anxious-eyed, nervously grinning, stiff-jointed and joyless-laughing I already was—at that time [in the mid-1950s] when

I still preened myself and imagined I was quite attractive! What phantoms such film-figures are; the bright flicker of activity and compulsive fun, gone in an instant and forever. And behind it, the mystery. What *is* Life really about?

He was becoming increasingly concerned with this last question, morbidly telling himself that whatever life was, he had somehow failed to live it satisfactorily. "In six months I shall be sixty-five," he wrote in February 1969.

> I seem to understand less and less about life. I try to think about it, or indeed about anything, but it all blurs. Why aren't I wise, like it tells you you will be towards the end? One is [. . .] dull-witted, gluttonous, timid, ill-natured [. . .] I do *not* write this in humility or even dismay, however. I know I have made a mess of my life but so do most of us. With the advantages I have had, the friends I have known and indeed all the happiness which still surrounds me—greater in some respects than ever before—I ought to have become a living wonder. And I, to put it mildly, haven't. So? Krishnamurti would tell me that self-improvement is a delusion and Vivekananda would tell me that duty is a snare. Perhaps I know this, deep down.

He felt somewhat rejuvenated, however, by a visit from John Lehmann, who was giving a lecture on writers of the 1930s at the University of Texas at Austin, and who seemed to have settled very solidly into dreary late middle age. Lehmann thoroughly enjoyed his five-day visit, finding it "marvellously easy to pick up the old relationship . . . perhaps better than ever before, because in this last lap of our lives I can allow no tension to come between us, and we seem to have even more to say to each other." To Isherwood and Bachardy, however, the five days dragged as if they had been a fortnight. "He didn't really want to see us," Isherwood reported.

> It was all symbolic. Now he can say that we have entertained him and introduced our friends to him. But it is the symbolic aspect of anything which really impresses him—for instance, that Don has had a drawing [of Auden] bought by the National Portrait Gallery and that he is going to draw the Harewoods.[1] And John himself thinks of his life in terms of his CBE and meetings with The Queen Mum. I sound venomous but I am not; I ended up, as always, feeling simply sorry for him. He is quite stupid and thickskinned and he expects to be waited on hand and foot, and he was scared lest he should somehow be manoeuvred into having to buy us a meal.

In fact, Isherwood himself had been crowing in his diary about Bachardy's sale to the National Portrait Gallery—his first work to be bought by a public institution—and his commission to draw the Earl and Countess of Harewood, but there is no doubt that Lehmann had become more impressed by the Establishment, of which he was

---

1. The Earl of Harewood was a cousin of the Queen and a patron of music. The commission had been arranged by the ballet critic Richard Buckle.

now a member, than by writers and artists. Whatever he might have believed, his friendship with Isherwood had finally worn absolutely threadbare. Isherwood was later to describe Lehmann's visit as the most boring thing to have happened all year.

I sherwood had been keeping an eye on *The Adventures of the Black Girl in Her Search for God,* which had received the approval of the Shaw estate and had gone into rehearsal in February. He reckoned that at least 90 percent of the dialogue in the play remained Shaw's own, but was intrigued to find that under Lamont Johnson's direction, "The whole thing has practically turned into a spade musical with African singing and dancing, directed by native experts." In Shaw's fable the Black Girl casts off the Christian teachings of a missionary and sets off in search of the real God. Along the way she encounters, challenges and rejects various versions of God, brandishing a knobkerrie at them. Shaw's story, written during a visit to South Africa in 1932, may have been somewhat patronizing in its attitude to the Black Girl, but it was revolutionary for its time, suggesting that God might be female, the next important civilization might be a black one, and racial hostility could be ended by intermarriage. As such, it spoke to a new generation of African Americans fighting for their civil rights in the late 1960s. There was a considerable amount of racial conflict in America at this period, much of it centered on the Watts ghetto in Los Angeles, and this spilled over into rehearsals of the Isherwood-Shaw play. Johnson, who had made television documentaries about the ghettos, thought the tension amongst the actors, if contained, might benefit the play, but one of the black actors complained that Isherwood had not written "a proper protest play." Isherwood was called in to devise with the actors a scene where they stepped out of character to discuss the play, but this idea simply didn't work and was subsequently dropped. By the time the play was ready to open in March, Isherwood judged it "as all right as it will ever be in this production," but it received poor reviews in *Variety,* the *Los Angeles Times* and the *Herald-Examiner.* Audiences appeared to get a great deal more out of the play than the critics did, although Isherwood finally abandoned his attempt to produce a definitive text of the play, which he hoped the Shaw estate would approve so that it could be published and then, he optimistically imagined, "performed all over the world in all possible languages."

While *The Black Girl* was still running, Isherwood was approached to write a screenplay of *Cabaret.* Much as he disliked the idea of the play, he saw this as an opportunity to collaborate once more with Bachardy, to reclaim the story for himself, and to make a great deal of money. A treatment would bring in $10,000, a screenplay a further $90,000, plus a bonus of $25,000 if the film was made and Isherwood and Bachardy were credited as sole authors, or $10,000 if they shared the credit. The British director Anthony Harvey had been appointed to direct the film, and Bachardy cut short his trip to England, where he was drawing the Harewoods and seeing his lover, in order to begin work. They settled into a routine of working in the morning on the treatment, then going their separate ways after lunch: Bachardy to the studio to paint, Isherwood to his study to work on *Kathleen and Frank.* They finished a treatment within a month and sent it to Harvey in England, only to receive a note in which the director said that it confirmed his doubts about the whole project. In fact, Harvey simply didn't like the treatment and was not prepared to give Isherwood and

Bachardy another chance. Worse still, the producer tried to get out of paying the agreed fee on the grounds that they had not provided what Harvey had told them in advance that he wanted.

Isherwood nevertheless felt that he now had a proper working partnership with Bachardy, and he expected other people—such as Tony Richardson, who had asked him to rewrite a script for a film of Robert Graves's *I, Claudius*—to recognize it. They were hoping to get a free trip to Australia out of the Graves project, which they needed to discuss with Richardson who was out there filming *Ned Kelly* with Mick Jagger. They made the mistake of telling Richardson that they wanted to visit Australia anyway and so forfeited their free plane tickets. The only thing to do was to look upon the trip as a holiday and regard any work that arose from it as a bonus. Having received a blessing from Prabhavananda, they flew to Tahiti in July, paid homage at Robert Louis Stevenson's grave (partly on behalf of Frank, who was a great admirer), then after a few days flew on to Auckland, then to Australia, where they began work on the *I, Claudius* screenplay, providing Richardson with a new outline. They were away for just over three weeks, and Isherwood described the holiday as "one of the best trips of my whole wandering life."

As soon as they got back, however, Bachardy went off to London, partly to discuss the idea of mounting a production of *A Meeting by the River* at the Royal Court Theatre, but also to spend time with his lover. Bachardy asked Anthony Page to read the play, and was furious when Page passed it on to an associate who ran the smaller (and far more suitable) Theatre Upstairs. Isherwood, meanwhile, felt he needed to get on with the *I, Claudius* script and was dismayed when Bachardy wrote to tell him that he thought the original book a bore. Bachardy also announced that he was going to stay on in England for a further week, which increased Isherwood's anxiety about his rival. He was once again testing Isherwood to the limit. "I was absolutely secure because I knew that he loved me," he recalled. "What I didn't know was how much I loved *him*. I *played* with the idea of leaving him without ever facing the fact that I never would. And I never did." Bachardy did finally return and they set to work on the script, missing the original deadline, but producing a script far better than Isherwood had originally predicted. Richardson's initial reaction, after reading the script quickly, seemed positive, but then they heard nothing for more than two weeks. Isherwood telephoned the embarrassed director, who had to admit that the script was not what he wanted and that he had already written another one himself.

By the beginning of 1970 it looked as if *A Meeting by the River* was at last going to get a production in London, and so in early February Isherwood and Bachardy flew there to discuss the play with the director Clifford Williams. If the play went ahead, they would remain in England while it was cast and rehearsed, flying back to Los Angeles after it opened in March or April. They stayed at a house belonging to a friend of Bill Harris in Moore Street, just north of the King's Road in Chelsea. Negotiations with Clifford proved protracted and by March 2, when Bachardy had to fly to New York to prepare for the opening of his one-man show at the Irving Blum Gallery, the play had been given a reading but had not been cast. Isherwood and Bachardy had spent part of February rewriting scenes after discussions with the director, who was also involved in—and, Isherwood worried, distracted by—mounting a London production of the "erotic revue" *Oh! Calcutta!*

Once Bachardy had gone to New York, Isherwood renewed old acquaintances and settled back into the London life he had abandoned more than thirty years earlier. So much was familiar that Isherwood was sometimes taken aback to find that his friends had not also remained as he first knew them. "Like so many of my contemporaries, Robert looked like a little old man," Isherwood noted after having supper with Robert Moody. "But then the boy reappeared from behind the wrinkles." Sometimes the boys he had known failed to re-appear in this manner: Sylvain Mangeot, he complained, "seemed quite middle-aged"—which was hardly surprising, since he was now fifty-eight. Olive had died the previous November, while André was now in steep decline, being looked after by Sylvain, who never married. Although Isherwood visited the house, he did not look in on his old adversary, who was to die in September at the age of eighty-seven. Jean Ross was the same age as Sylvain, looking "old but still rather beautiful," and still very much the left-wing political activist—rather too much so for Isherwood, who felt that if he lived in London he would want to see a great deal of her if he could do so "without being involved in her communism." Amiya Sandwich "seemed much fatter, quite piggy, and drunk of course, but with her skin still white and smooth." Alec Beesley was "much fatter, quite bulging in both face & figure, but still tanned brick red & very healthy looking." Dodie Smith, however, had "aged greatly; she's now almost a freak with her little white waving arms and her head sunk into her tiny trunk." Although he had greatly disliked Smith's latest novel, describing it in an extended aria of misogynistic ill temper as "so pleased with itself, so fucking smug, so smugly cunty," Isherwood felt that the moment he was with the Beesleys he experienced "a marvellous sense of continuity. Nothing had to be rediscovered or reassessed—we simply picked up the threads."

Someone with whom Isherwood was not prepared to pick up the threads was the friend with whom Bachardy had been having an affair. The affair had now ended, and while Isherwood was very relieved, he was not in a forgiving mood. He blamed the man for becoming involved with Bachardy and rejected his conciliatory overtures. He refused to meet him, and if both men turned up at the same party, Isherwood would leave. He also failed to visit Edward Upward, who was now living at Sandown on the Isle of Wight. Back in 1961 Upward had written to Isherwood: "One day— perhaps at eighty instead of the forty that we imagined when we were twenty—we'll meet somewhere for a whole week and sauntering along the shore will learn from each other in electric language everything that's ever happened to us both during the past sixty years." Now that Isherwood was in England for an extended period, Upward hoped to realize this dream, issuing several invitations and even offering to come to London if that proved more convenient. Isherwood did not seem able to find the time.

He did, however, make two trips to Cheshire to stay with Richard and the Dans. This was partly a matter of family duty, but he also felt that he needed to breathe the northern atmosphere once more in order to complete *Kathleen and Frank*. Part of that atmosphere was a literary one. Leaning out of his bedroom window on his first morning there, gazing out over a new fall of snow and breathing what he considered (with some geographical exaggeration) "the beautiful pure Brontë air," he suddenly noticed blood on the sill. It was merely the result of a nosebleed, but the image of the snow splashed with scarlet struck him as pure *Wuthering Heights:* "Cathy bleeding into the snow!" Although he complained as much as ever about the British climate, he was also stirred by it when in Cheshire. There was

> such a feeling of the hills all around in the heavy snow. They are so powerfully present, so aloof and yet so suburban, and really so small; but I have never experienced any hills like them. And there comes a sense of how Kathleen saw them, from the Wyberslegh windows, and how her wish was granted, to end her long life amongst them and die amongst them, grumbling but finally contented.

It was here that he truly connected with his family, a geography and climate steeped in personal history and mythology, and this would help him to write about a place he had at one time loathed and rejected and had left far behind him. He went through papers looking for additional details of Kathleen's life, and spent some time walking around the locality. "I feel the spirit of the place very powerfully here," he wrote.

> And it *is* a spirit or it's nothing. Physically, Disley is just a rather smug little suburb. When I looked at postcards, down in the village [. . .], the hills seemed flattened and utterly undistinguished, the Ram just another little pub, Lyme Cage a tiny dump and Lyme itself quite lacking in grandeur. And yet, despite the cheerless ugliness of the stucco and brick villas which are steadily crowding in, the spirit of the place is powerful indeed; the rooks caw fatly around the church with its big gold ball below the weathercock, the little sweet & cigarette shops seem stoically North Country, the Ring O'Bells is so sturdily ancient, Lyme Cage is sinister and numinous, and the air of the hills is still poignantly refreshing and stirs longings—even if they are longings for escape!

The most tangible connection with the story he was trying to tell remained Richard, who was "looking a bit heavier but somehow much more distinguished and indeed, if one can use such an expression, more like other people—though he still twists his head about and blinks." Richard was also still drinking, but not nearly as much as he used to, and mostly "offstage" during afternoon visits to Wyberslegh, where he would spend hours "sort of communing with" the house. Richard was still in mourning for Marple Hall and could not bring himself to visit the site of the old place. "I still feel that a part of me has died with the cessation of it—although perhaps not a healthy part," he told his brother. He castigated himself for not somehow keeping the house from falling down, but Wyberslegh was rapidly going the same way. Richard seemed unaware of the condition it had got into: he still showed interested people around the house, but stubbornly refused to have any repairs carried out.

As with the landscape, Isherwood carried with him various versions of his brother and his mother. "Richard really does seem much less bizarre," he wrote; "perhaps I am comparing him with a fright-Richard of my imagination, but I don't think so." He found that by reading Kathleen's diaries for 1936 and 1937, at the height of the Heinz crisis, he was conjuring back into existence that Mother-figure he had rebelled against and at times hated, and this interfered with his current attempts to write about the young Kathleen who was courted by Frank and the older woman with whom he became reconciled. "I want to forget her," he wrote of the Kathleen who mistrusted Upward, disapproved of Heinz because he was "socially unsuitable" and hated Olive Mangeot "as a domestic subversive influence." "I have no use for her, whatsoever; she doesn't come into the scope of my book."

Back in London, Isherwood was racketing around with a younger crowd of gay men, led by David Hockney and Peter Schlesinger. He liked, as he acknowledged, to be surrounded by "bright eyes & bushy tails" and he found plenty of these at parties hosted by Tony Richardson and Robert Medley. The latter could be relied upon to produce "astonishing impressive amounts of edible food and delicious boys." Among these was Wayne Sleep, the diminutive rising star of the Royal Ballet, whose presence on stage helped Isherwood overcome his aversion to dance theater. An outing to Sadler's Wells to see a Polish company perform a piece called *Gilgamesh* excited Isherwood so much that the page of the diary on which he recorded it is uncharacteristically dotted with crossings out and additions. The plot of this ballet may explain why: "The hero-brothers wrestling naked, falling in love, sleeping with hands clasped, becoming involved in and escaping from the snares of women, dying with desperate spasms, wandering into terrible underworlds or dreams where a huge bird flutters its wings with a most intense menacing vibration." *Coppélia* it wasn't.

Isherwood was astonished at the way homosexual men kissed one another in greeting and parting quite openly in public, which did not square at all with his vision of England as a country characterized by convention, puritanism and emotional frigidity. He realized that in Hockney's case, this sort of thing was part of the defiance he displayed in his painting. Such attitudes, along with Hockney's critical popularity, carried risks. After attending the opening of a major retrospective of Hockney's work at the Whitechapel Gallery in the East End, Isherwood noted in his diary:

> David's overwhelming success must make anyone who loves him (as I do) afraid. Surely the world will make him pay for it, cruelly. For David is not only a 'golden boy', as the Press calls him, but a crusader for his way of life, for our minority. (He kissed me on the mouth, without the least affectation, when I came into the Gallery.) Many people must be gunning for him.

Attitudes in England were changing, however. "How relaxed the English are!" Isherwood was forced to exclaim when he witnessed a demonstration against the Vietnam War marching up Whitehall while the police held up the traffic. Like any tourist, he marveled at the theatrical clothes young people wore—though he was horrified by the women's fashion of "very long maxi coats which open to show madly indecent glimpses of mini skirts and endless leg beneath." Far more to his taste were the tanned and well-knit bodies of young men, and he found himself surrounded by these when he went with Hockney and Schlesinger to stay with Richardson in the South of France toward the end of March. There was, as usual, a large house party, and although Isherwood found most of his fellow guests attractive or interesting, describing it as "quite a sexy gathering," it was with Hockney and Schlesinger that he spent most of his time, sightseeing and relaxing. His friendship with them deepened, "despite the frictions of travelling" and despite the fact that their own relationship was under strain. He saw distinct parallels between their situation and his own. Like Bachardy, Schlesinger (who was now studying at the Slade) found his older partner too possessive and was longing to have his own place to live and a degree of freedom. Isherwood liked both men individually as well as as a pair and was able to act evenhandedly as a confidant, advising them with a wisdom born of experience.

Back in London, plans for the play remained very uncertain. Clifford Williams dropped out as the director and various other people were considered. Numerous actors—including Alec Guinness, Dirk Bogarde, Tom Courtenay, and Horst Buchholz (whom Isherwood had run into at the Jermyn Street Baths)—were sent the script, but no principals had yet been found. The opening of Bachardy's show in New York had been a success, but the pictures had failed to sell and the exhibition had not resulted in any commissions. Bachardy nevertheless seemed unwilling to return to London unless there was a firm prospect of their play getting a production. Isherwood realized that it would be a waste of time and money if Bachardy flew to London for no good reason but had begun to miss him badly. He was tempted to return to Santa Monica but felt he ought to see the project through to some sort of conclusion. He had plenty of other things to occupy him, including a brief and inconclusive romance with a young geneticist he had met at Cambridge while visiting Forster.

At ninety-one, Forster had become rather frail, although he was still mentally alert. He loved receiving visitors, particularly if they hugged or kissed him, but worried that he no longer had any news or anything to show them now that he lived such a quiet life. He announced that he was ready to die and had authorized P. N. Furbank, whom he had known since the late 1940s, to write a biography of him. Although happy to cooperate with Furbank, who assured him that the biography would be absolutely frank in describing Forster's sexual life, Isherwood at first refused to allow him to read his letters from Forster. "I said they are too personal and much more about me than Morgan, but of course what I mean is that I would like to turn them into a book, myself," he confessed. He subsequently relented. Furbank had shown him two of Forster's "unpublishable" (because homosexual) stories, and they discussed the posthumous publication of *Maurice*. Forster had once again revised the novel and in 1960 had written an afterword explaining its genesis, with brief notes on homosexuality and the three principal characters. Forster agreed with George in *A Single Man* that public attitudes toward homosexuality had changed, but not necessarily for the better: "from ignorance and terror to familiarity and contempt." He had once hoped that his book would increase the general understanding of homosexuality, but had come to realize that "what the public really loathes in homosexuality is not the thing itself but having to think about it." This may be why he was unwilling to see his novel published during his lifetime.

Apart from keeping a diary, Isherwood was doing almost no work, and was feeling guilty about this. Prabhavananda had given a twitch upon the thread by sending him a translation of Shankara's *Garland of Questions and Answers* to tidy up. He had numerous meetings with Robert Chetwyn, who had agreed to direct *A Meeting by the River,* and their discussions led to some rewriting, but Isherwood began to realize that this was no more than mere fiddling with no secure end in view. It was beginning to look as if a West End production would no longer be feasible, and Isherwood consoled himself with the thought that the play might be better suited to a small theater. Leaving casting in the hands of Chetwyn, he decided that he would head back to California at the end of April, partly to escape the dismal British weather. He had begun to lapse into old British habits, recording his weight in stones rather than pounds and referring to the British in his diary as "we," which he then corrected to "they." It was time to go home.

I sherwood's principal task, once he had returned to Santa Monica, was to finish *Kathleen and Frank,* but although he found the commentary interesting, he found the task of selecting and typing passages from letters and diaries into the text to be tiring and tedious. He chose his birthday as a date to work toward and managed to finish a rough draft by late August. This was just as well, since shortly afterward he was offered the job of adapting Mary Shelley's *Frankenstein* for a television "special." Universal Studios had been looking at some of their old properties with a view to exploiting them, and Hunt Stromberg had been investigating horror films. James Whale's 1931 film had long been regarded as a classic, but its narrative departed considerably from Shelley's original novel. The idea was that Isherwood and Bachardy would write a "definitive" adaptation of the book, which Isherwood had not in fact read. When he did so, he found it would need substantial reworking in order to make it into a film, largely because in Shelley's telling of the story the doctor and his creature are soon parted and much of the narrative follows their individual stories. As usual with Hollywood, it took a long time between Isherwood being approached and any decision being taken by the studio, and this gave him time to start on the revisions of *Kathleen and Frank,* which he finished in mid-November.

While he was awaiting the reactions of his agents to the family memoir, and a decision from Universal, Isherwood began to plan another book. Some time earlier, he had wondered whether it might be possible to write a novel based on his relationship with Prabhavananda. He soon recognized that this would involve too much faking and he would do much better to write a straightforward memoir. The death of Forster shortly after Isherwood's return to California reminded him of his idea of using their letters to write a memoir. He now considered writing a double memoir, "a Tale of Two Gurus, as it were." It would be difficult, however, to write about Prabhavananda while he was still alive. Instead, Isherwood embarked on a long-term project to "reconstruct" the missing parts of the diary he had kept since coming to America. The main gap was the decade 1945–55, the principal events of which he could establish from his pocket appointment diaries. He intended to use these as a basis for what would, in effect, be a memoir.

Having, in *Kathleen and Frank,* explored his family "myths," Isherwood now wanted to explore his sexual ones: the sort of people he found attractive and the reasons he did so. He told Upward that in this he was once again influenced by Jung, but it seems likely that he was also influenced by J. R. Ackerley's *My Father and Myself,* an extraordinarily frank and detached exploration of the author's relationships with his family and his lovers. Ackerley's book had been published in 1968 to great acclaim in spite of its unblinking account of homosexual practices, and had been reviewed at length by Auden in *The New York Review of Books* the following year. Auden had taken the opportunity to introduce the *Review*'s readers to such esoteric terms as "Plain-Sewing" (mutual masturbation) and "Princeton-First-Year" (fucking between the thighs), partly in the hope of being subsequently cited in dictionaries based on historical principles. In the course of the review he complained that "Frank as he is, Mr. Ackerley is never quite explicit about what he really preferred to do in bed. The omission is important because all 'abnormal' sex-acts are rites of symbolic magic, and one can only properly understand the actual personal relation [between sex partners] if one knows the symbolic role each expects the other to play." It is inconceivable that Isherwood did not read this article (particularly since Auden told him that it was appearing) and, consciously or not, it must have influenced him to be absolutely specific when recalling his immediate post-war experiences. He described the work to Upward as "embarrassing but wildly funny."

Although Isherwood was sure such a book could not be published during his lifetime, he was encouraged to write it by a sense that homosexuality was beginning to be discussed more openly and rationally than ever before in America. As in London, homosexual men were beginning to emerge from an era of furtiveness and shame into one of openness and defiance. What became known as the gay liberation movement was sparked by a raid on a New York bar, the Stonewall Inn on Christopher Street, in the early hours of June 18, 1969. Now sanctified as the birthplace of gay liberation, the Stonewall was in fact a fairly squalid dive, owned by the Mafia and catering to a mixed clientele of homosexual men and women, drag queens and prostitutes. That evening, many people were mourning a gay icon, Judy Garland, whose funeral had taken place in the city earlier in the day. Evidently inspired by Garland's career, with its nothing-to-lose resilience, those released by the police without charge emerged triumphantly from the bar and joined the quickly gathering crowd outside. As the police loaded the less fortunate into a waiting van, the crowd began booing, then started throwing beer cans and bottles. The startled police were obliged to take refuge in the bar they had been attempting to clear and to call in reinforcements. After thirteen arrests had been made, order had been restored, but not the status quo.

Following decades of being pushed around and persecuted, homosexual men and women started to fight back. This was not about tolerance or even acceptance: this was a demand for civil rights. Rather than hiding in bars or behind pseudonyms, men and women were taking to the streets and declaring their homosexuality with a newfound pride. The new term that everyone was using was "coming out of the closet," and even after the efforts of Kinsey and other researchers into the sexual life of the nation, America had no idea just how big those closets had been and just how many people they had contained.

Isherwood had for many years viewed his homosexuality as defining his own place in society. He liked to characterize himself as someone who didn't *want* to fit in with everyone else, preferring to maintain his privileged position on the outside looking in. He believed that the outsider ought to be seen as "one of the most socially valuable people in the whole community." In his calmer moments he felt that the outsider "must not harden into defiance in his disagreement" with the majority. "He must always go along with the other people as far as he can possibly manage to go, and only when the choice is quite flatly between that and the betrayal of what he thinks right must he very regretfully say I'm sorry, and now there has to be a show-down between us." This sweet reasonableness had gradually been eroded by his feel-ing that unless you *were* defiant, you were simply ignored. The mutinous tone adopted by those now fighting for gay rights was one he had embraced long ago, not only in private but also in his books. Ambrose's fantasy of a homosexual dictatorship in *Down There on a Visit* may have been no more than that, an enjoyable joke at the expense of the unthinking heterosexual majority, but George's eloquent tirade in *A Single Man* was almost a blueprint for homosexual dissent. Tolerance, of the sort practiced by George's neighbor Mrs. Strunk, is not enough:

> She is trained in the new tolerance, the technique of annihilation by blandness. Out comes the psychology book—bell and candle are no longer necessary. Read-ing from it in sweet singsong she proceeds to exorcise the unspeakable out of George. No reason for disgust, she intones, no cause for condemnation. Nothing here that is wilfully vicious. All is due to heredity, early environment (shame on those possessive mothers, those sex-segregated British schools!), arrested devel-opment at puberty, and/or glands. Here we have a misfit, debarred forever from the best things of life, to be pitied, not blamed. Some cases, caught young enough, *may* respond to therapy. As for the rest—ah, it's so sad; especially when it hap-pens, as let's face it it does, to truly worthwhile people, people who might have had so much to offer. (Even when they are geniuses in spite of it, their master-pieces are invariably *warped*.) So let us be understanding, shall we, and remem-ber that, after all, there *were* the Greeks (although that was a bit different, because they were pagans rather than neurotics). Let us even go so far as to say that this kind of relationship can sometimes be beautiful—particularly if one of the parties is already dead; or, better yet, both.

George's final address to the heterosexual majority—"Your exorcism has failed, dear Mrs. Strunk [. . .] The unspeakable is still here; right in your very midst"—looks forward to a much later but equally forceful and unapologetic slogan of the gay rights movement: "We're here. We're queer. Get used to it."

Isherwood had never forgotten his failure to act as the queens at the Stonewall Inn did when he and Jim Charlton had been caught up in a raid on the Variety bar on the Pacific Coast Highway in 1949 and told the police that they were not homosexual. Over twenty years later, Isherwood still felt "bitterly ashamed" about his behavior that night. "And yet, I'm well aware of the counterargument: why in the hell should you give yourself away to the Enemy, knowing that he can make use of everything you tell him?"

The Enemy was now rather less powerful and Isherwood began to address all sorts of gay meetings. The few qualms he had about these public appearances were largely to do with an unwillingness to rock the boat at Vedanta Place. Prabha-vananda's attitude toward homosexuality was always less liberal than Isherwood liked to believe, and many of his followers thoroughly disapproved of his famous dis-ciple. Although tempted to accept an invitation to address, and "rap with," the Na-tional Students Gay Liberation Conference in San Francisco, Isherwood eventually decided against it.

I highly enjoy the role of 'the rebels' only Uncle' (not that I would be, this time—
for there are scores of others—and [Allen] Ginsberg their chief) and, all vanity
aside, I do feel unreservedly *with* them, which is more than I can say for ninety
per cent of the movements I support. But something prevents me from accepting.
Oddly enough, it all boils down to not embarrassing Swami by making a spectacle of myself which would shock the women of Vedanta Place! I can admit this
because I am perfectly certain there's no other motive. I am far too sly and
worldly-wise to suppose that I'd be injuring my own 'reputation' by doing this.
Quite the reverse; this is probably the last opportunity I'll ever have of becoming,
with very little effort, a national celebrity. And I hope I'm not such a crawling
hypocrite as to pretend I wouldn't enjoy that, even at my age.

If he was worried about marching shoulder to shoulder with the gay rights movement, he nevertheless made it a policy from now on to mention his homosexuality in
any interview he gave. There can have been very few people left who did not realize
that Isherwood was homosexual, but *Kathleen and Frank* would provide the first opportunity for him to say so, unequivocally, in print.

I sherwood's British and American agents both responded enthusiastically to the
book, but suggested that it was too long. Isherwood wanted it sent to Methuen and
Simon and Schuster to see what cuts editors might suggest. He began rereading it
himself with a view to making excisions, but found it difficult to find anything substantial to remove, and he did little more than take out a few of the letters detailing
Frank's negotiations with his future father-in-law. The most significant change he
made was the result of a visit from a Gay Liberation activist, which inspired him to
beef up his remarks about his own homosexuality, making them "much more aggressive." In the original version, Isherwood had written:

> Without even trying to decide between the relative disadvantages of alimony and
> police persecution, [Christopher] is now quite certain that heterosexuality
> wouldn't have suited him. And he has always felt content and well-adjusted being
> as he is . . .

In the finished book this was emended to:

> Despite the humiliations of living under a heterosexual dictatorship and the fury
> he has often felt against it, Christopher has never regretted being as he is. He is
> now quite certain that heterosexuality wouldn't have suited him; it would have fa-
> tally cramped his style.

Shortly after making this alteration, he discovered that he had been "outed," "quite
flatly, without further explanation," in the course of a profile published in Britain in
the ultra-conservative *Daily Telegraph.* "I think this is the first time anyone has said
this right out, in print," he reflected. "I'm glad he did. It sort of prepares readers for
my remarks in Kathleen and Frank."

really can't imagine myself working with Evelyn on this sort of thing; it would be like having to write a book in a foreign language.

He eventually summoned up courage to tell Hooker this, pleased to be able to draw an analogy with *Kathleen and Frank*. Like the case histories, he explained, Kathleen's diaries, "can be commented on, they can be elucidated and conclusions can be drawn from them; but they can't be rewritten because nothing can be as good as the source-material itself." He still felt guilty, however, partly because back in the 1950s, when he was living in her garage apartment, he had agreed to write a "popular" book on homosexuality with her—one day. "Of course I was always saying things like this, quite irresponsibly, subconsciously relying on the probability that I wouldn't ever be taken up on them. To Evelyn yesterday I said, 'Well, you know, in those days I was nearly always drunk'; which, the more I think of it, was a silly tactless altogether second-rate remark."

Hooker's material seemed particularly rebarbative compared with Isherwood's own recollections of his days of sexual glory, which were much on his mind as he continued to think about writing up from memory the period not covered by his diaries. The reconstruction, although covering the years 1945 to 1951, and dealing extensively in the commentary with the 1930s, was psychologically rooted in the period in which it was written. Hooker's book was intended principally for a heterosexual readership, for academics and other disinterested parties; Isherwood's book was addressed squarely to those he increasingly referred to as "our minority" or "my 'people,' the queers." That minority was not only becoming increasingly visible and vocal, but was beginning to exercise its financial muscle. Just before the Halloween weekend in 1970, Isherwood received a letter from the homosexual rights organization One Incorporated urging homosexuals to buy Hamm's beer because the company had taken advertising space in the *Advocate*.[2] Isherwood and Bachardy demonstrated "Gay Purchasing Power" by going out to buy a six-pack. Businesses were gradually coming to realize that homosexual men in good employment, with no dependents and therefore plenty of disposable income, were valuable consumers. It would be some time before people started talking enthusiastically about "the pink dollar," but it was already becoming apparent that wily businesses were less and less interested in the color of a person's money. The success of such publications as the *Advocate, Gay Sunshine* and *Christopher Street* demonstrated that there was a literate homosexual readership that wanted more from a magazine than soft porn and ill-written erotica. This increasingly became Isherwood's literary constituency.

I sherwood was not only maneuvering himself into position as the homosexual movement's favorite uncle: he was about to provide it with a grandfather in the untidy shape of E. M. Forster. Having received confirmation of Forster's gift of *Maurice* from the executors, Isherwood contacted Glenway Wescott, who was now a leading figure at the American Academy and National Institute of the Arts, having

---

2. Founded on the West Coast in 1967, the *Advocate* rapidly became one of America's leading homosexual periodicals.

served as its president between 1957 and 1961. Wescott and his partner, Monroe Wheeler, who had been director of publications and exhibitions at New York's Museum of Modern Art, had known Forster and been involved in his plans for *Maurice* at an early stage. It seemed sensible to hand over the rights to the Institute, of which Forster had been an honorary member since 1949, and an E. M. Forster Award was founded, given to writers for a body of work rather than any individual book. Isherwood joined the judging panel for the first award of five thousand dollars, which was presented to the British novelist Paul Bailey in 1974 at a very grand literary lunch in New York.

Isherwood did not attend the ceremony but had overseen the publication of *Maurice* himself. He felt that Forster's "Terminal Note" would prove inadequate for the American market and was therefore keen to commission an introduction. In the event, P. N. Furbank wrote one for the British edition and this was used when the novel was published in October 1971. While some reviewers were rather sniffy about Forster's story, which in the light of 1970s gay rights activism certainly seemed somewhat quaint, the publication of *Maurice* allowed Forster to take his place at last in the history of homosexual literature. Here was a figurehead of real substance, one of the major novelists of the twentieth century.

Isherwood was also keen to welcome Gerald Heard to the fold. After suffering thirty-one strokes, Heard finally died on August 14, 1971. He had become increasingly wayward in his beliefs and interests over the years, declaring for instance that "all children from the age of seven should have their sphincters penetrated and loosened to dispel anxiety and nervous tension," but Isherwood had remained a loyal disciple and kept a series of photographs of the etiolated sage in his kitchen for the rest of his life. "My chief feeling," he wrote in his diary the day Heard died, "is that I would like to get on the air and tell the great stodgy thickskinned world that it has lost one of its most tremendous men, one of the great magic mythmakers and revealers of life's wonder." Evelyn Hooker told Isherwood that the *Advocate* was keen to run an obituary, but Michael Barrie objected on the grounds that Heard had never declared his homosexuality in print, and had always used a pseudonym when writing on the subject.

Isherwood's obsession with his age was exacerbated by the deaths of other friends: Gerald Hamilton the previous year, Stravinsky in April. In September, Isherwood himself prepared to approach "the frontier-post of death," as he put it. For some time he had been bothered by what appeared to be a cyst on the joint of the little finger of his left hand. This made typing uncomfortable and Isherwood's fears that the cyst was malignant were increased when a painful lump appeared on his palm. This was diagnosed not as a cancer but as the beginnings of a Depuytren's Contracture, a rare condition in which the tendons of the hand gradually tighten, pulling the fingers down into a claw. The condition sometimes abates long before this stage, but if it becomes serious it can be cured by surgery. Isherwood dreaded the prospect of an operation, partly because it meant having to relax his will and relinquish control, but also because being anesthetized and made unconscious seemed a sort of forerunner to the long sleep of death, the final parting from Bachardy.

Although he boasted that he was (for once) "in the pink of health," Isherwood noticed a characteristic bit of psychosomatic acting-up: "Just before the operation, my right hand became violently 'jealous,' because the lazy left hand, which it supports by earning their living, was getting all the attention. So it started an acute attack of arthritis in its thumb." After a tranquilizing shot of scopolamine, however, Isherwood felt "relaxed enough for execution." "I laid my left hand on the chopping block, thinking, with dopey humor, of Cranmer and feeling that I was behaving with remarkable grace and style." In fact, he was put under for the operation (a fasciectomy, he noted, always keen to record medical detail), which lasted just over an hour, and he was sent home the same day with his hand in a cast and his arm in a sling. This meant that he was unable to type his diary and so, as in London earlier in the year, he wrote it longhand, typing his words up later when his hand had recovered and the metal splint was removed from his little finger. His handwriting was as small and neat as it had been at twenty.

One unforeseen advantage of having the operation was that it gave Isherwood an excuse to cancel a trip to England to publicize *Kathleen and Frank*. He had been prepared to undertake the trip until he got a letter from Bill Caskey, who was now living in Greece. Because of the mutual loathing that characterized Caskey's relations with Bachardy, Isherwood had kept his old lover at a distance. Caskey now wrote to say that he was going to be spending some time in London trying to organize an exhibition of his photographs and get them published as a book. Wouldn't it be nice if they coincided in London? "Don at once said that he didn't want to see Billy, if we were all in England together," Isherwood reported. "As for me I know that, if he were there, I would have to introduce him around to people who could help him, and that this would establish all sorts of embarrassing links." What these embarrassing links might be Isherwood did not reveal.

I n March 1972 Isherwood received news that the Mark Taper Forum in Los Angeles wanted to mount a production of *A Meeting by the River* with Jim Bridges as director. Isherwood and Bachardy were involved in the casting and attended rehearsals, enjoying the experience of seeing these characters brought to life at last. "All in all, we got a cast far and away beyond what we might have expected," Isherwood reported as rehearsals started, "and we feel that the play will get as good a presentation as it could have, anywhere in America." Laurence Luckinbill and Sam Waterston led the cast as Patrick and Oliver, with Florida Freibus as their mother, Susan Brown as Penny, and Gordon Hoban (on whom Isherwood developed a crush) as Tom. The play opened to packed houses on April 26 for a run of one week, and Isherwood was very pleased with it. The reviews, however, were disappointingly lukewarm, suggesting the play was too wordy and static and needed considerable work done on it. Isherwood and Bachardy already knew this and had started doing rewrites as soon as the play opened, but their hope that it might be taken up for a longer run was unfulfilled.

The poisonous opinion of one of the play's reviewers on KPFK radio, who described Isherwood as a "has-been novelist" who was now only fit to write "a gay series for TV," was confounded on May 16 when Isherwood received a Hollywood Authors' Club award for "a lifetime of distinguished contribution to literature." The honor was somewhat diminished by the fact that the Authors' Club had been founded by Rupert Hughes, a "nasty old horror" who in 1940 had complained, "we send a gangster to the electric chair but we do not treat these pacifists as traitors." Further-more, the award itself—a statuette of "The Book" depicting "a nude woman appar-ently overcome with disgust after reading what looks more like a filmscript open in front of her"—was not the sort of object Isherwood cared to have on display amongst the Keith Vaughans and David Hockneys at Adelaide Drive.

Isherwood's own Hollywood career appeared to be stalled. He and Bachardy had worked on the Frankenstein screenplay without a great deal of enthusiasm. They were not altogether sure what Stromberg wanted—and neither, it seemed, was he. As usual on such projects, there were flurries of excitement which proved to be as evanescent as snow. At various times it was thought that the whole thing could be made into a musical with Leonard Bernstein as composer; that Elizabeth Taylor would play the Bride; that Richard Burton would play Praetorius; or maybe Rex Har-rison; or Albert Finney; or that it might, after all, end up as a feature film rather than a television special. Sometimes Isherwood asked himself "why, at the age of nearly 67, do I have to be involved in projects like this?" The answer, he conceded, was that he didn't. "Actually it pleases my vanity that I am still employable and that my wits are still quick enough to play these nursery-games." Even though he had savings to-taling $74,000 and had made investments in property, he remained insecure about money and did not want to start living off capital. Working on the script remained, however, "a ghastly chore" and not even collaboration with Bachardy cheered him much. "Don is upset because he feels he is a drag on me. Actually he is and he isn't. He is a drag when he's typing because he simply cannot sit quiet and work something out, it drives him up the wall. And yet without him I wouldn't work on the fucking thing at all. And he does very often have good and even brilliant ideas. Oh I wish to Christ we had never started it." When they finished the screenplay, however, Univer-sal were so pleased that they immediately offered them the job of writing a new ver-sion of The Mummy.

This did not mean that their work on Frankenstein was over. Stromberg had once again decided that the Frankenstein project would be a movie rather than a television "spectacular" and this meant that the screenplay had to be cut. John Boorman was being touted as director, with Jon Voight in the title role. Meanwhile, without a great deal of enthusiasm, Isherwood and Bachardy embarked on their version of The Mummy, which they called The Lady from the Land of the Dead. "Mummy-talk has become a terrible time-waste," Isherwood acknowledged, and whereas he and Bachardy played some interesting variations on the Frankenstein theme, their lack of real interest in the Mummy is only too apparent in the finished script. They were paid for their efforts, but the film was never made.

Isherwood did, however, remain an excellent source for films he did not write. He and Bachardy had been to see a preview of Bob Fosse's beautifully mounted and hugely acclaimed movie version of Cabaret, which was much more sophisticated and far truer to the Berlin stories than the stage show. Isherwood did not record his immediate reaction to the film, but wrote when he saw it for a second time that he "liked it much better." "I still don't think it adds up to anything much," he reported, and he felt that as Sally Bowles Liza Minnelli was "clumsy and utterly wrong for the part, though touching sometimes, in a boyish good-sport way." Sally had not only been transformed into an American, but into one who sang extremely well. Isherwood commented that if Sally had been that good and the cabarets she sang in as stylish as the movie's Kit-Kat Klub, then people would have been queuing to get in. He objected strongly to the way the Isherwood character—English once again, renamed Brian Roberts, and played by Michael York—was depicted in the film. "He has an affair with Sally and, later, with one of Sally's lovers, a German baron," Isherwood wrote. "At the end of the film, he is eager to marry Sally. But Sally reminds him of his lapse and hints that there may be others in the future. Brian's homosexual tendency is treated as an indecent but comic weakness to be snickered at, like bedwetting." This is a willful misrepresentation of the film's approach to the subject, written several years after Isherwood saw the film in the course of a book which was attempting to tell the "truth" behind the Berlin stories. Far from having a "homosexual tendency," Brian is depicted frankly as homosexual, as he explains early in the film when rebuffing Sally's peremptory sexual advances. He and Sally do eventually fall in love and have an affair, but Brian's relationship with Maximilian, the German baron, is treated romantically and, in one memorable scene, made explicit. During an argument with Sally, Brian loses his temper and shouts: "Fuck Maximilian!" "*I* do," Sally replies. "So do *I,*" says Brian, laughing. Many homosexual members of the audience recall this exchange with gratitude and affection because it was funny and very direct—although in America it had to be toned down, with "screw" replacing "fuck." Sally's suggestion that marriage to Brian would be a disaster because he was bound to stray is no more than an admission that having an affair with a woman—as the young Isherwood had with Mrs. Lanigan—does not make a homosexual man heterosexual. In life Isherwood frequently berated those people whom he considered basically homosexual who had nevertheless married. In the film, it could be argued, Sally brings Brian to his senses by pointing out his true nature, thus saving him from what Isherwood judged the most compromised and dishonest of fates, life as a bisexual.

Isherwood may not have liked the way the role had been written, but he was delighted to have Michael York playing it. Isherwood had already met York and his American wife, Pat, a photographer, and been smitten by the actor's very English public-school good looks. The couple had become regular visitors to Adelaide Drive, and when, some time before *Cabaret* was made, York had heard that the studio had been looking for a "Michael York type" to play the Isherwood role, he determined to pursue it. For Isherwood, to have his much-altered but still recognizable alter ego played onscreen by someone he thought had "perhaps the most beautiful broken nose of his generation" was some compensation for the liberties he felt had been taken with his stories. Seeing the film for a second time, he thought York "seemed not only adorable and beautiful but a really sensitive and subtle actor." This provided him with something enthusiastic to say about the film when asked his opinion of it in public, going so far as to complain that York was "very underestimated by the critics." He realized, as with earlier adaptations of the story, that he had a small vested interest in the film and that he would be foolish to damn it publicly.

When *Cabaret* went on to become an enormous popular and critical success, that interest increased in value: after some wrangling over his share of royalties, he received a handy cheque for $25,000 at the beginning of 1973. He even went so far as to celebrate the "triumph" of the film at the Academy Awards that year, where it trounced *The Godfather.* "They got only three awards, we got eight," Isherwood crowed proprietorially. The film went on to become the subject of a television documentary in a BBC series titled *Success Story.* When this was broadcast in 1974, Isherwood gamely posed for a photograph for the cover of the listings magazine *Radio Times,* with Liza Minnelli draped over him. He also wrote a new introduction to a Hogarth Press single-volume reissue of *Mr Norris Changes Trains* and *Goodbye to Berlin,* which was published under the by now highly commercial title *The Berlin of Sally Bowles* and featured a photograph of Minnelli in character superimposed against a swastika-draped Brandenburger Tor. A banner across the jacket assured readers who may have been unfamiliar with Sally's origins that the book contained "*Goodbye to Berlin* with *Sally Bowles.*" Isherwood started his introduction in the character of Frl. Schroeder, complaining at the cheek of Frl. Bowles for laying claim to Berlin as her own property. "If the Berlin which is here described can be said to belong to any of my characters," Isherwood wrote, "then surely it belongs to [Frl. Schroeder], the most genuine Berliner of them all." Sounding rather like the Dr. Frankenstein he had recently been writing about, Isherwood described how his original character had taken on a life of its own, quite independent of its creator. "Today, it's doing us the honor of a visit—looking in on the book, that quaint old homestead where everything began. We don't even think it rude when it pushes Frl. Schroeder and others to one side. This Berlin is now its own, by right. I have to agree with our new title. After all, it is supporting me in my old age."

Quite apart from the royalties Isherwood continued to receive for *Cabaret,* the film brought him a new readership, particularly among the rising generation of gay men. He was very amused when someone sent him a clipping from the personal columns of an Australian newspaper: "Single Man, Isherwood fan, seeks another, 28 plus, to share snug Sydney northside flat." Some members of this rising generation would themselves become writers. Armistead Maupin admitted he did not know of Isherwood's work until he saw *Cabaret,* a film which had a profound effect on him as someone just coming to terms with his homosexuality. He started reading all Isherwood's books and became captivated by them. He then saw Isherwood on television: "He absolutely hypnotized me with those blue eyes and I instantly wanted to know more about him." Isherwood also showed Maupin, Edmund White and other writers of that generation that writing openly about homosexuality was no longer "some sort of career suicide," and his literary prestige encouraged them to write the sort of books they wanted to write. White recalled that along with Gide's journals, Isherwood's novels were the only non-pornographic accounts of homosexual experience he had ever come across. Maupin remembered trawling through various so-called gay "bookshops" in the Earls Court area of London. "These shops sold only porn, lubricants and dildos, but there in a very neat little row would be the Isherwood *œuvre.* Maybe the idea was to make the bookshops seem legitimate, but I found it terribly impressive and never had any sense that Chris would be anything other than thrilled at the thought." Young writers came to sit at Isherwood's feet just as he had sat at Forster's. "He always had a sweet gift for making the young feel comfortable," Maupin recalled. "He would never tell long, involved stories and assume you knew anything about him or everyone he knew. He'd explain who everyone was and about his relationship to them. You didn't have to adjust for him in any way. He was

reader who doesn't know the correspondents can get absorbed in their relationship. If the correspondents don't have an interesting relationship, then at least their letters to each other must combine to create a picture of the times they are living in, full of detail and insight. Don't you agree with me about this, in general? Surely you must. Then, John, how can you possibly claim that our letters satisfy any of these requirements?

This was brutal, and bound to wound Lehmann deeply. Isherwood knew perfectly well that Lehmann regarded his relationship with Isherwood not only as "interesting," but one of both personal and historical importance. Isherwood went on to say that he was a bad correspondent who only wrote letters under duress and that what he wrote was always "cagey."

> I have made a few big mistakes in my life—expressing feelings I should have kept to myself and then being quoted—but most of the time I am careful and it shows. Letters are not my natural way of communication. I don't feel free when I am writing them. I instinctively save my best phrases and ideas for my literary work.

Lehmann had considered himself, with some justification, one of Isherwood's closest confidants, and had received numerous letters from him, particularly when Isherwood first went to America, that were in fact very revealing indeed. Isherwood's suggestion that he took no trouble over the letters he wrote and was careful not to waste his "best phrases and ideas" on communicating with Lehmann, whether true or not, was extremely cruel. Worse, however, was to come: "These letters of mine are dull, dead, insincere. Their falseness shames me. And the prospect of seeing them dished up to the Public as 'literature' makes me squirm." He was convinced that they would both be pilloried if such a book was published and concluded by saying that, although Lehmann might be "shocked, saddened, puzzled, or even terribly offended" by his decision, in years to come he would thank Isherwood for preventing "an awful humiliating mistake." He offered in a postscript to pay for his share of the photocopying.

Lehmann was indeed offended and replied in what Isherwood heartlessly but accurately described as "a tone of restrained pathos":

> My dear Christopher,
>
> Very well.
>
> You owe me nothing for the Xeroxing. I enjoyed having it done and that's that.
>
> As you remind me, I like and continue to like your letters very much, indeed I treasure them, and I hate to be told that the writer of them thinks they are false. That is painful, and I mind it a lot.
>
> Also—though by the way now—I think they do tell a story, the story of our literary relationship (as well as our personal relationship), though I agree with Billy [Abrahams, Lehmann's U.S. editor] that they need more letters of mine to complete the exchange, or dialogue.

The real problem I have to deal with is disengaging from Methuen and my agent. They both put a lot of work into their side of the scheme. Luckily, no money passed.

We shall just have to wait until someone makes a fuck-up of it after our deaths. 'We'!—our ghosts.

Of course I shan't be coming to Texas/California this Autumn. No point now. Mid-March, however, I shall be on my way to Berkeley, and look forward very much to seeing you, and Don.

> Love
> John

If Lehmann was hoping to shame Isherwood, he had misjudged his man. Isherwood was merely irritated by this performance and drafted "quite a stinker" in reply, which he said Bachardy "wisely restrained" him from mailing. Instead he sent a brief note:

It pains *me,* and *I* mind it a lot that you have decided to take this personally and make up your mind that my friendship is false because I tell you my letters are. We'll talk it over before long. I won't write any more on the subject—it's too silly. Treasure the letters, by all means—but one day try to read them through objectively. If you can, you'll see what I've saved us from.

It is hard to see how Lehmann could have interpreted Isherwood's remarks any other way, and Isherwood himself was obliged to concede that this letter was "weak and evasive." He realized that if he continued to discuss the matter, he would find himself

telling John *why* my letters to him during the war are so false—namely because I knew he wasn't on my side, I knew he didn't believe I was serious about Vedanta or pacifism and I knew he would disapprove, on principle, of any book I wrote while I was living in America. I was false because I didn't want to admit how deeply I resented his fatherly tone of forgiveness for my betrayal of him and England—'England' being, in fact, his magazine . . . Well, I probably shall tell him one day if he provokes me enough, but I'll do it face to face, not in writing. The stupid thing is that I'm fond of him in a way, and that I've often defended him, even though I think, as everyone in London thinks, that he's an ass and that he has almost no talent. But I am fond of him, which is more than most people are.

The real embarrassment for Isherwood was that Lehmann was about the only British friend who had continued to correspond with him on a regular basis during the war. Lehmann may sometimes have been pompous and tactless, but there is no doubt that at the time Isherwood really did appreciate someone who took trouble to keep in touch. At the same time, the friendship between the two men had grown increasingly one-sided, and it would indeed have been deeply shaming to see their volatile and uneasy relationship paraded in public as some sort of historically significant exchange between senior men of letters.

Any further bouts of recrimination were forestalled by the sudden and unexpected death of Auden on September 29. ("I would like our last exchange of letters to be forgotten altogether," Lehmann wrote solemnly at the end of his letter of condolence.) Auden had returned to his hotel in Vienna after giving a poetry reading to the Austrian Society of Literature and was found dead in bed the following morning. "Needless to say, the news reached me from the media—Reuters & the BBC," Isherwood told Upward. "The latter, after a respectful pause of 10 seconds so I could indulge my private grief, asked me for a 'comment'—'how would you place him as a writer?' They really are grotesque." Isherwood's grief was made public when this interview was broadcast on the radio news program *The World at One* and his voice was heard breaking as he recalled his lifelong friendship with Auden.

Isherwood's first reaction to the news was incredulity. "It was one of those shocks which one had neglected to prepare oneself for," he told Upward. "I'd always taken it for granted that he'd survive to write all our epitaphs." He wept to think that the one thing he believed Auden really craved, the Nobel Prize for Literature, was denied him. But there were other things Auden had wanted. One of them had been to see Isherwood more often.

Auden may have been stern about some of Isherwood's later work, dismissive of his religion and disapproving of many of his pronouncements, but he continued to love the man. From the moment they parted in 1939, Auden made it clear how much he missed Isherwood, and his letters frequently give notice of his movements and express the hope that the two friends will meet up. He remained throughout their relationship "the more loving one," as he had put it in one of his most touching poems. Auden had Kallman in mind when he wrote these lines about the inequalities of affection, but the poem also represented a pattern in his life. While it would be unfair to suggest that as far as Isherwood was concerned the friendship had worn out, it is certainly true that Auden *minded* far more than Isherwood that they had drifted apart and no longer shared the intimacy they had once enjoyed. Part of the problem was geographical: by choosing to live on the opposite coasts of their adopted country in a period when crossing the vast space between was less easy than it is now, they had cut themselves off from each other. There was also a considerable cultural gap between self-consciously bookish New York and movie-dominated Los Angeles, and Auden felt no more at home in Isherwood's city than Isherwood did in his. The one serious quarrel Auden and Isherwood had had was about religion, but they had long since learned to avoid this subject, and the largest obstacle between them remained Chester Kallman.

"I suspect that Chester would have said that Chris made it impossible and that Chris would have said Chester made it impossible," Bachardy observed. "I think they were both right." On the surface, Isherwood and Kallman appeared to get on, dutifully sending greetings to each other and behaving civilly when they met, but there was always a strong underlying current of mistrust between them. Auden was perfectly well aware of this friction, but appeared to be incapable of easing it, and occasionally made matters worse. On one occasion, Kallman published a hugely expensive limited-edition volume of his poetry. Isherwood had absolutely no interest at all in Kallman's verse, but it became clear that he was expected to buy a copy. "Wystan did it in a kind of pre-emptive way that said you cannot get out of this," Bachardy recalled. "He even took a certain relish in making Chris fork out the money."

Isherwood was also obliged to acknowledge the importance of Kallman to Auden. "I know that Chris was glad that Wystan had found *somebody*," said Bachardy. "I think that *relieved* Chris. But it just so happened that that somebody was Chester, with whom I don't think he ever felt comfortable." Quite how relieved Isherwood was that Kallman had, as Bachardy put it, "taken Wystan off his shoulders" is unclear. Kallman not only took on Isherwood's role in Auden's life, however: he also took Auden into another world, and it was a world in which Isherwood felt out of place. Auden and Kallman's principal interests—such as opera—had no real meaning for Isherwood, and he felt unable to countenance many of Auden's opinions or his more eccentric enthusiasms, such as for the works of J.R.R. Tolkien. Perhaps more importantly, although Isherwood continued to admire Auden's poetry, and always wrote to say so, he did not feel as personally connected to it as he had in the 1930s. Auden tried to maintain the connection by occasionally sending Isherwood poems in typescript—as a gift rather than for criticism. As late as 1964 he dedicated "The Geography of the House" (the poem inspired by George's sessions on the lavatory in *A Single Man*) to Isherwood.

There was also the difficulty of Auden's social manner as he grew older. He was not the easiest of hosts or guests, and he refused to alter his own strict timetable to fit in with anyone else. "When they were together it was always a matter of Chris's indulging Wystan in whatever terms he set," Bachardy said. "But he also had a genuine affection for Wystan that went beyond considerations of how, from his point of view, Wystan had changed and how he was no longer interested in the things that interested Chris." Auden valued his old friendships enormously, and people such as Isherwood continued to figure in his world far more than they might imagine from his behavior toward them. As Spender put it, "He thought about his friends so much that it was a bit disconcerting how little notice he appeared to take when you were in the room with him." Now that Auden was dead, Isherwood acknowledged: "Whatever he may have said, he was awfully lonely—isolated is what I mean—he made a wall around himself, for most people, by his behaviour and prejudices and demands." Isherwood was one of the people who might have been able to breach that wall, but he never did.

Some time after Auden's death, while Bachardy went on a trip to New York to make plans for a new show there, Isherwood spent two days looking at all the letters and manuscripts of Auden he had kept. Alone in the house, he found himself once more very close to Auden.

> I seem to see the whole of his life, and it is so honest, so full of love and so dedicated, all of a piece. What surprises me is the unhesitating way he declared, to the BBC interviewers, that he came to the US not intending to return to England. Unless my memory deceives me altogether, he was very doubtful what he should do when the war broke out. He loved me very much and I behaved rather badly to him, a lot of the time. Again and again, in later letters, he begs me to come and spend some time alone with him. Why didn't I? Because I was involved with some lover or film-job or whatnot. Maybe this is why he said—perhaps with more bitterness than I realized—that he couldn't understand my capacity for making friends with my inferiors!

of his generation." Isherwood had allowed himself to be interviewed for Wilde's book, and been rewarded with a second study that took his work seriously. "There is probably no living writer less justly valued at the present time than Christopher Isherwood," Wilde wrote in his preface,

> none, therefore, more in need of a revaluation. The lack of any book-length study and the relative scarcity of articles devoted to his work testify to the state of general neglect. What has been accepted is Isherwood's importance to the literary history of the 1930s; what has still to be recognized is that, both before and since the war, he has been one of the period's most original ironists and one of its most subtle moral thinkers as well.

This is the sort of thing any writer might like to see in print, and the book had also earned the approval of Upward. A biography, however, was a rather different matter. Although Finney would subtitle his book "A Critical Biography" and publish it with an academic press, he wanted to provide a detailed biographical framework; Fryer was hoping to write a full life for the general reader. Isherwood had considerable qualms about this, but agreed to cooperate with both writers, while at the same time imposing certain restrictions. The principal one was that they were not to attempt to contact either Vernon or Richard. Vernon had managed to retain his anonymity, but Richard had already been ferreted out back in 1968 by journalists keen to discover the identity of "the real Sally Bowles," and had not at all cared for the experience. Isherwood wanted to protect Richard, but also perhaps wanted to protect himself. Neither of them would have welcomed embarrassing news stories about a famous author's "odd" brother in his Cheshire seclusion, and there was no knowing what Richard might say if plied with drink by an investigative reporter. Isherwood had told the makers of a television documentary about him for the BBC's *Omnibus* series that if they wanted to film Wyberslegh, they would have to get Richard's permission. He was pretty certain that Richard would refuse, unless overcome by the need to please his brother, and wrote to him: "*Please,* Richard, don't feel it is the least important that you should give them permission—even if they ask for it, which they may well not do; I mean they may decide they have enough material without any of these past scenes. They knew about the existence of Wyberslegh somehow, or I wouldn't have told them! I know how infuriating it is to be bothered." "I don't mind them filming the outside," Richard replied, "but I don't much fancy them coming inside and 'rooting round.' " Isherwood's letter warning Richard about Finney and Fryer has not survived, but Richard's reply was reassuring: "there doesn't seem the least point in them contacting me as I couldn't really give them any extra information, I mean other than what you have already told them: And also I would feel apprehensive lest I might give them, quite unmeaningly on my part, 'unauthorized' information. So if I should hear from either of them I will take your advice and ignore it."

Another danger area was Caskey, who was very happy to cooperate with both Finney and Fryer, pleased to be the center of attention and to be given the opportunity to make mischief. Isherwood was appalled to receive a letter from Finney saying that Caskey had made a couple of suggestions for additions to his book:

To mention Jo Lathwood's name as 'a G.I. bride', to say that Lincoln Kirstein was my model for Charles in *The World in the Evening,* and to describe 'Vernon' as 'a typical hustler from a male brothel'.

This last really amazes me, it's so viciously untrue. *Any* mention of Lincoln will offend him. And the statement about Jo [Masselink] is false. All this Caskey knows perfectly well.

He would have been even more appalled had he seen the long and increasingly scurrilous correspondence Caskey was enjoying with Fryer. Prompted by the inquiries he had received from several people writing about literary life in the 1940s ("the price one pays for sleeping around in the good old days"), Caskey subsequently decided to embark on his own volume of reminiscences. He told friends that *Inside Isherwood* might make a good title.

Isherwood had assured both Fryer and Finney that they could see his new book before it was published, and both of them had promised not to publish before he did. This sort of pressure did not help when it came to writing the book, however. "I begin, almost for the first time, to seriously doubt that my life is interesting," he told Upward in the summer of 1975. "And I also feel that anything I write about myself is oh so subtly a lie. But I will force myself to finish the first part, and you shall see it." He was still having trouble marshaling the facts, and six months later appealed for help: "As I now get into the last chapter of my book (1937–38) I seem to lose touch with you. Didn't we see each other? Of course I remember a few times, like you & Hilda coming to see Virginia Woolf when I was there. But communication seems to have been less?" After consulting his diaries, Upward was able to provide a list of dates and places to show that the two friends had indeed seen quite a lot of each other at this period—"in spite of what you call your 'pursuit of boys and notoriety' and in spite of the endless meetings, demonstrations etc. I was involved in."

It was not until June 1976 that Isherwood had a fully revised typescript of the autobiography, which stopped in January 1939 and was titled, at Bachardy's suggestion, *Christopher and His Kind.* The book—his first for six years—was gratefully accepted both by Methuen and his new American publisher, Farrar, Straus and Giroux, and was swiftly set up in type. Having corrected the proofs, and celebrated his seventy-second birthday, Isherwood tried to decide what he should do next. *Christopher and His Kind* ends with the *Champlain* docking in New York: "This is where I leave Christopher, at the rail, looking eagerly, nervously, hopefully towards the land where he will spend more than half his life." This, indeed, was where Isherwood decided to leave himself for the time being, abandoning the idea of continuing the story as he had originally planned. He considered the possibility of simply publishing the diaries he had kept between 1939 and 1944, which he had already edited substantially back in 1946. Having read them straight through, however, he decided

There is a great deal of good material in them but I still feel it would be a mistake to publish them in their present form. Not only because so many of those written about are still living. Because the material itself is too *dense*. There are so many minor characters whose portraits follow each other boringly, I fear. For example, the people at the Vedanta Center, and the people at the Haverford refugee Hostel.

48. Dodie Smith, Isherwood and a clutch of Dalmatians, Malibu Beach, Christmas Day 1945.

49. Alec Beesley, with Vernon and Bill Caskey, posed and photographed by Isherwood in imitation of Millais's *The Boyhood of Raleigh*, summer 1946.

50. Gerald Heard and Isherwood at Prabhavananda's feet.

51. Former brothers in Vedanta: Vernon and Isherwood.

52. "The X. situation": Bill Harris.

53. Bill Caskey, with his pictures of Isherwood and Bill Harris behind.

54. Isherwood's "tan-faced prairie boy": Jim Charlton, in uniform.

55. Isherwood and Don Bachardy, July 1953: "Don looks so young that I do not quite know how Chris has the nerve to go about with him," Dodie Smith commented.

56. Isherwood, Marguerite Brown and Tennessee Williams in Philadelphia for the out-of-town opening of *Cat on a Hot Tin Roof*, March 1955.

57. Isherwood revisiting Wyberslegh in the late 1950s: "This is my native country. Thank God for it—and thank God, *on my knees,* that I got out of it!"

58. Kathleen in old age with one of her beloved cats.

59. Isherwood and Richard in Cheshire, 1960s.

60. Isherwood and Bachardy
in the 1970s.

61. Isherwood and Bachardy in the pool of a house in Beverly Hills
rented by Marguerite Littman (Lamkin).

62. Isherwood, age eighty, on the deck at Adelaide Drive.

One virtue of the material used in *Christopher and His Kind* is that it composed much more easily into the form of a non-fictitious novel. Its major characters are most of them extremely active and there is a sense, all through the narrative, of outside menace—from The Others in general and the Nazis in particular. The major characters in the 1939–44 material are both contemplatives rather than actives—Swami and Gerald Heard—and there is little sense of outside menace, even though the war is on during nearly all of the period.

He therefore returned to an earlier idea to write about his relationship with Prabhavananda. The swami had died on July 4, 1976, while Isherwood and Bachardy were staying with Gavin Lambert in Tangier, and so the story, in narrative terms, was now complete. It is also possible that Isherwood wanted to write the book partly in order to keep in touch with his guru, particularly since he had been finding it hard to concentrate while making *japam*. This book would be both narrower and wider in scope than the planned continuation of *Christopher and His Kind*. It would deal exclusively with Isherwood's relationship with Prabhavananda, but would cover a far longer period, coming right up to the present day. Now that he knew what he wanted to write, Isherwood had to find a method of doing it.

> The difficulty is that this kind of portrait lends itself to posing; the author is tempted at every point to present himself as the disciple the Guru loved, the disciple who betrayed him, the disciple who helped him most, the disciple who was the lowest, morally, of them all and therefore avoided being a hypocrite, like all the others . . . Still and all, even as I wrote the above sentences, I began to feel a stirring excitement: Yes, yes, this *is* something. Why shouldn't I at least try it? What can I lose? At worst, it'll be an unusual document. I am bound to say a few interesting things on the subject.

The only way Isherwood could write the book was as a personal account: he had no interest in writing a biography as such.

> What I should try for is a highly subjective memoir—always stressing the idea that what I am describing is a personal impression, a strictly limited glimpse of a character very different from myself and therefore often quite mysterious to me. Without being fake-humble, I should also—even for purely artistic reasons— stress the materialistic, gross, lustful, worldly side of myself—but without making Swami appear merely "better" than me. The real artistic problem is to find a way to do that.

Dedicated to Bachardy, *Christopher and His Kind* was published in America in November 1976, and in Britain at the beginning of the following year. Its most ardent admirer was Richard Isherwood, who bombarded his brother with letters at the rate of three a week for a whole month after receiving an advance copy. He told Isherwood that he and the Dans had been reading it aloud to each other, a chapter at a time, and that the Dans "got so interested and absorbed that they *quite* lost interest in watching their favourite afternoon programmes on television." Richard complained that airmail forms were a great nuisance because they limited the available space for correspondence, though he continued his heartfelt but increasingly rambling and woozy compliments from letter to letter: "But my dear, I find it most terribly moving and full of pathos—I mean the parts about Heinz and about Wystan, and your personal feelings toward them—it is rather beautifully told, on a par with hearing parts of the 'Unfinished Symphony,' or 'The Cuckoo Song in Spring'." When the book was published in Britain, he let off another fusillade of letters, equally wild and many of them merely repeating his earlier ones. Part of the excitement for Richard was the book's homosexual content and he told Isherwood that he thought it was "going to 'do the trick' as regards putting across homosexuality to the majority." The book was certainly Isherwood's most confrontational to date. As the dust-jacket blurb of the Methuen edition warned, "Christopher is a born minority member. He rages against The Others in all their manifestations, including the heterosexual dictatorship." At the very opening of the book, he scotches the idea, put forward in *Lions and Shadows,* that he wanted to travel to Berlin solely to meet John Layard: "He did look forward to meeting Layard, but that wasn't why he was in such a hurry to make this journey. It was Berlin itself he was hungry to meet; the Berlin Wystan had promised him. To Christopher, Berlin meant Boys." This challenging and simplistic announcement was calculated to upset those as yet untouched by the gay rights movement and who still thought that homosexuality was better left undiscussed. Early reviews suggested that Isherwood was on target. *Publishers Weekly,* the U.S. book trade magazine, complained that "always his ultimate measure of the world seems to be sexual," while the *Chicago Tribune Book World* concluded: "The big, bold book of fact has become a fairy tale." Isherwood consoled himself that this last opinion, offered by Penelope Mesic, might well backfire because "its viciousness has a tone which will probably sell a lot of copies and inspire loyal indignation in the hearts of Chicago queers."

Christopher and His Kind was very much a book of its time: not so much the 1930s as the 1970s. Although the basic material was the same as that used in the Berlin stories and *Down There on a Visit,* Isherwood's vantage point was different. It was not merely that he was writing about his experiences from a greater distance in time (forty years on from most of the events described); he was writing from a different perspective. As Isherwood had predicted, not everyone felt comfortable with his device of writing about himself in the third person: it could be seen as both arch and evasive, and there are passages in the book when the "I" narrator treats young "Christopher" with the same sort of indulgence that Nanny did. John Lehmann told Edward Upward that he enjoyed the book, "But I have to say that I quite strongly dislike the new habit of calling the thirties (or twenties) self 'Christopher': 'Christopher did this, but I now think, etc.' It seems uncomfortably affected. He is, after all, a very continuous person, in spite of the USA & yoga & all." Lehmann had, as usual, missed the point. Isherwood understood all too well the technical difficulties he had set himself by using this method of narration, but his purpose was precisely to view his younger self through the prism of later experience. He had done something similar in *Lions and Shadows,* but by separating himself as subject and commentator in *Christopher and His Kind,* he was making manifest the sort of objectivity he wanted to achieve.

He was also addressing a different sort of reader. Bachardy's title for the book defined not only its theme, but also to some extent its audience. As Heilbrun and Wilde had suggested, Isherwood's literary stock was not particularly high, but Christopher did have a growing readership amongst his Kind, a generation hungry for books which showed that homosexuality had a historical and literary lineage. Those acquaintances who disparagingly referred to the book in private as a "Gay Lib manifesto" were not altogether wrong. While correcting the proofs, Isherwood had come across a scrap of paper that had been lying on his desk for several months. On it he had written: "For the homosexual, as long as he lives under the heterosexual dictatorship, the act of love must be, to some extent, an act of defiance, a political act." *Christopher and His Kind* was much concerned with acts of love and was both explicitly defiant and, in the broadest sense, political. Isherwood had always enjoyed playing the rebel, but there was a sense now that he was rallying the troops. The rhetoric he employed in interviews he gave to the gay press when publicizing the book was distinctly bellicose in tone and sounded not unlike the battle-cries of the Left in the 1930s. "Everything has to be considered from one standpoint alone—tactics," he told *Out* magazine.

> There may be strong arguments against some forms of demonstration, but you can't make moral arguments against it, as a principle. When you get down to specific cases you argue what should be done on this occasion, just like a military operation; should we attack from there or here or not attack at all? The trouble is we're such a disarrayed army, and the fronts have very little contact with each other. Someone's going screaming ahead on the left, while the people on the right are digging ditches and defending the position.

This sort of militancy may have pleased the readers of gay journals, but it made some heterosexual readers of *Christopher and His Kind* distinctly uncomfortable. "Quite aside from what anyone may feel towards me personally, I must say that my rather mild little book seems to have caused waves in some places I would have least expected," he told *Q International*.

> There's obviously still a great deal of prejudice against us, and it shows in various ways. The conformists are saying: 'Of course we've nothing against gays, but if only they'd be a bit quieter. Why all this Gay Lib? Horrible—it makes me shudder. And why are they so very noisy? Are they trying to convert everybody or something?' They of course blissfully forget the struggle of the blacks, the Jews, and so forth. Everybody you can name had to be pushy in order to get listened to. It's the paradox of there being a dictatorship of the majority in certain areas of life, and if you're an Uncle Tom–type, if you're a good gay, then you're all right. But you are also still a serf of the establishment and as soon as you start being other than that people are first shocked, then resentful and maybe even finally openly hostile. But perhaps in a way that's what our life will always be like, give or take a bit.

Indeed, a characteristic review, in the *Sydney Morning Herald,* adopted exactly this tone. John Douglas Pringle declared that he had "great sympathy with homosexuals who suffered grievously from the legal and social persecution which forced them to keep silence in the past"; he was "glad, too, that they are now able to speak openly about their homosexuality and defend it without fear of prosecution and ostracism." That said, he felt that Isherwood's book "protests too much and, in consequence, becomes slightly boring." He far preferred the "sad, funny, bittersweet and always absorbing" city of the Berlin stories to the "merely sordid" one of the new book, "with a rather muddled young man frantically pursuing working-class boys" and enjoying affairs that were generally "brief, promiscuous and commercial."

The British *Sunday Times* evidently disagreed that the book was dull and serialized it in advance of publication. This resulted in a letter of protest from Auden's brother Bernard. "Wystan has been dead for less than four years, so that relatives who bear his surname may feel sensitive about or even damaged by the adverse publicity that can result from these articles [*sic*] in such a widely-read newspaper," he complained. What he meant by this, of course, was the revelation that Auden and Isherwood had been lovers. "Had Wystan been alive he would have been able to present his own account of his relationship with Isherwood. At this time no one can directly confirm or deny some of the more sensation-seeking details." The portraits of Auden, Forster and other writers were described in the *Guardian* as "so brilliant that one wonders if Isherwood could have published them in their lifetimes." Isherwood replied: "Only they could answer that. I would have submitted it to them first. But I never write about people I don't like." While this may not be entirely true, there is no doubt that these portraits were as affectionate as they were frank.

Not everyone, however, was interested in the literary characters and aspects of the book. The formidable *grande dame* of British letters, Dame Rebecca West, wrote a review that was so savage that it achieved a certain notoriety. It was headlined "A Symphony of Squalor," and explained that the book dealt with

> two groups of insanitary people. The first consists of male prostitutes, children and adolescents who are dirty, drunken, often afflicted with unpleasant diseases, and treacherous.
>
> The second group consists of their patrons, grown men of all ages, possessing the same characteristics.

This is, to say the least of it, a somewhat reductive account of the book. West concentrated in her review almost entirely upon Isherwood's descriptions of Fronny's island, but seems not to have read even this part of the book with any attention. She stated that Isherwood left Berlin "with two German adolescent friends," although it is quite clear from the text that Erwin Hansen, described by Isherwood as a former "gymnastics instructor in the Army" now "running to fat," was a mature man. She later claimed that reviewing "makes you really open your mind to a book," but this is not the impression anyone would take away from reading her attack on Isherwood. When questioned about it, West replied: "I was so horrified by the way he treated the little German pansy. Also I thought it must have been so disgusting for the people in the village on the Greek island. I know Greeks love money, but I think a lot of money would have to pass before you'd be reconciled to Isherwood making such a noise." Since there was no village on St. Nicholas, there were no villagers to be disgusted, of course, and the dismissive reference to Heinz as a "little German pansy" says much about West's supposedly liberal credentials. Isherwood apparently told a bookseller who asked him what he thought of West's review: "I shall think of some way of turning it to my advantage"—and it certainly gained him some sympathy.

Not, however, in the even more right-wing *Sunday Express,* where in his famously intemperate column John Junor worked himself up into his customary lather over Isherwood and his book:

> Mr Christopher Isherwood, of *I Am a Camera* fame, will no doubt make a mint of money out of his new book in which he relates with relish his experience as a homosexual.
>
> Maybe enough to allow him in his old age to seduce more simple-minded 16-year-old working class boys with the same ease as he did in Berlin.
>
> What I find extraordinary is that a literary lunch is to be given in London in Mr Isherwood's honour and that in attendance will be people like Lord Clark of Civilization fame, Lady Diana Cooper, Sir Alec Guinness—all lining up to shake Mr Isherwood by the hand.
>
> Don't they give a damn about Isherwood's proclivity for getting into bed with little boys? Or do they work on the principle that they will go anywhere for a free meal?

Elsewhere, *Christopher and His Kind* was treated with more respect by people who had bothered to read it properly. In a very long review in the *TLS,* Gabriele Annan dealt with the homosexual content of the book at length and without distaste or kid gloves, declaring that: "If Proust is the great master of the homosexual novel, Isherwood is its *petit maître.*" She concluded that "His prose is as impeccable and irresistible as ever. Just once or twice Christopher seems in danger of turning into Christopher Robin. But since the death of Waugh, Isherwood is the funniest living English writer—funny-dry, that is, not funny-fantastic." Peter Conrad in the *Spectator* wrote that Isherwood had "managed the small miracle of writing about himself with a narcissism which is graceful, pitiless and detached," and even Isherwood's old adversary Anthony Powell, in the *Daily Telegraph,* while doubtful about Isherwood's mission to tell the "truth" that was omitted from the Berlin stories, praised the book's narrative clarity and enjoyed hearing familiar stories once more. "One feels like a child at bedtime: 'Tell me again about Mr Norris in the brothel, Uncle Christopher'; or 'Let's hear the one about the nice film director when you were in pictures.' "

Boosted by KH3 capsules, a Swiss antiaging product brought back from trips to Europe and Mexico (it was not licensed in the United States), Isherwood did publicity tours for the book in both America and England. He enjoyed making personal contact with his new fan base, and was particularly touched by the long line of people, "mostly quite young," waiting outside New York's famous gay bookstore, the Oscar Wilde Memorial Bookshop on Christopher Street. "I had such a feeling that this is my tribe and I loved them," he wrote. Gore Vidal commented: "They're beginning to believe that Christopher Street was named after you"—and indeed some time later a gay bookshop called Christopher's Kind opened in Atlanta.

Isherwood had begun to receive large amounts of fan mail from young people, and frequently complained in his diary about the chore of answering letters.

The least aggressive image I have in mind is of slamming tennis balls back across a net—this is a crazy singlehanded game I am playing against dozens of opponents. The balls they have served me lie around the court and I have to return them. Meanwhile, every day, more balls keep coming over, and some of these are balls I've already hit back once—in other words, some of my letters get answered. The real demon players are those who want to start a rally—a pen-pal correspondence which could continue for years.

It was difficult, however, to feel too curmudgeonly when among his birthday greetings were such messages as: "Our gay pride is built upon the dignity of your life and work. Our love finds honesty in your words." Although Isherwood threw away most of the letters he received from his fans, he kept those that intrigued him. Several sent photographs of themselves (sometimes naked), and one correspondent sent snapshots, annotated on the reverse, of a succession of heterosexual men he was courting—with occasional success. A pair of impertinent British schoolboys, addressing him as "Dear Queen Chris," sent a series of flirtatious, stream-of-consciousness letters in envelopes decorated with pink triangles, the badge worn by homosexuals in concentration camps which had recently been adopted by Gay Liberationists. These boys clearly knew Isherwood's work well, even his writings on Vedanta, and complained that what they considered his best book, *A Single Man,* had been banned from their school library. Having suggested that if Isherwood ever got fed up with Bachardy they would be more than happy to fill his place, they realized that they had perhaps overstepped the mark, and the next letter was contrite, as well it might have been. Isherwood made the mistake of replying to this letter, which only encouraged them further. One of the boys sent a photograph of himself captioned: "My tits are on fire." He looked about fifteen.

Another correspondent, signing himself "just another 'Silly Boy,' " wrote to say:

Dear Mr Isherwood,
    I love you. Period.
    I should like to write a much longer exposition, but frankly I do not feel up to meeting the degree of effort or caution needed to properly justify my 'worthiness'.
    Be it sufficient to note I shall always have a deep and intense personal rapport with your work, your life and, above all, you.
    I should like to think one day I might have a chance to meet you.

Touched as Isherwood was by such declarations, he did not allow them to turn his wise old head:

the kind of love which young people feel for old figurehead people like me is perfectly healthy, beautiful indeed, not in the least silly and woe unto young people who are incapable of feeling it; they are emotionally lame. *But* it is so important for the old figureheads *not* to take this love personally; to understand that it is simply an effect of the interaction between age-groups—to understand this makes it more beautiful, not less.

as if the act of recreating their relationship and thus consigning it to a historical period had become a substitute for the real thing which until then had persisted beyond Prabhavananda's death. When asked by a young visitor to explain to him what Prabhavananda had done for him, Isherwood found himself "stumbling and faking defensively. I couldn't say anything really clearly and I knew he was deciding that the whole thing was a self-delusion." It was always difficult to write about contentment, but Isherwood felt "an obligation to declare that Don and I are somehow "saved," that we have been given "the pearl beyond price" and that we'll never lose it and that death has lost its terrors in consequence. Obviously, I mustn't end on a note of vulgar uplift, like an ordinary self-satisfied 'religious writer.' But surely I can make *some* statement?" He knew that he had somehow to silence what he called "the mocking agnostics" amongst his readers. He was not looking for converts, but he wanted to convince a wide range of people "from asses like Lehmann to intelligent bigots like Edward [Upward]" that Vedanta had real meaning for *him* and had made all the difference in his life. "Everything I write is written with a consciousness of the opposition and in answer to its prejudices," he reminded himself.

Isherwood found the process of revising the book painfully slow. It took, he calculated, fifty-two days to revise the sixteen pages of the first chapter, which meant that revising the whole book could take as long as three years. The winter brought its share of troubles. After a long illness, Bachardy's father, Jess, died in early December. "It would be hypocritical to say that I personally am unhappy," Isherwood wrote, "because the situation produces an extra closeness between Don and me, and closeness between us is my life." Jess's death did, however, put Bachardy under an enormous strain, since his mother, who was entering the first stages of premature senility, really needed someone to visit her daily. Don's brother Ted, whose mental stability remained fragile, seemed unwilling to share this task. "Sometimes I think he is the toughest person I have ever met in my life," Isherwood wrote of Bachardy; "then suddenly he shows the strain by blowing up about some trifle." Isherwood bore the brunt of these explosions, but realized: "There is really nothing I can do to help him. Except love him and make *japam*."

Isherwood was also worried by the prospect of surgery on his knee to repair a ligament torn while jogging. The previous year, he had signed papers leaving his body to the UCLA Department of Anatomy, and thereafter carried a card in his wallet stating his intentions in the event of his dropping dead in the street. "I am very glad I have done it," he wrote at the time, "although there are occasional absurd qualms at the thought of Dobbin's old pickled carcase hanging on a hook ready to be carved." He had equal qualms about old Dobbin being carved up on the operating table, and became so depressed that Bachardy persuaded him not to undergo surgery but to try physiotherapy. Isherwood had a new doctor, Elsie Giorgi, whom he trusted implicitly, and she agreed with this course of action, but when he went to see a specialist he was told that the ligament would not repair itself. Determined to put off the dreadful decision, Isherwood consulted someone who was reputed to have worked nonsurgical miracles on damaged Hollywood stuntmen. Isherwood rather fell for this man, finding him "sweet and faded-cute," but failed to respond to treatment. He decided to live with his painful knee, just as he was learning to live with the dimming of sight in his left eye.

The prospect of a large tax bill started him worrying about money again, and he considered several unlikely projects, including a collaboration with the rock star David Bowie and another adaptation of *Lady Chatterley's Lover,* this time for television. Unsurprisingly, these came to nothing and he was reluctantly thrown back onto his book about Prabhavananda. He had provisionally bestowed the excruciatingly arch title "Another Kind of Friend" on the memoir, which he was revising by sheer willpower and regular doses of Dexamyl to make his brain seem clearer. The block he was experiencing made him wonder if there was "something wrong with the whole project," or with himself. "Some days I feel really a bit nuts, I cannot concentrate, and I cannot write one line which I don't begin to pick to pieces as soon as it's written, a truly fiendish and sick sort of perfectionism. I ask myself, have I had some very slight strokes." He hadn't, but Dr. Giorgi thought he might be suffering from pernicious anemia and recommended a course of vitamin B_{12} shots.

His days had a fixed routine: "I have to do my various specimen tasks each day— my midday beads, my isometric stretchings, my bit of the Swami book, and this diary. Perhaps it is the only way I can function now. Well, at least I am functioning." He also spent time each day, when the weather was good, at the beach, which had lost none of its romance in all the forty years he had been living beside it. He imagined that each warm weekend "there must be at least two or three couples of boys who will meet for the first time and plunge into a real love-affair, maybe *the* affair of their lives." In order that such romances should flourish, Isherwood vigorously lent his opposition to retrograde legislation such as the so-called Briggs Initiative, named after a California senator, John Briggs, who organized a referendum to support a ban on homosexual teachers in state schools. Briggs gave speeches suggesting that if his Proposition Six was not accepted and steps were not taken to bar such teachers by law, homosexuality would spread like an infection through the public teaching system. "The evil breath of the Briggs Proposition Six begins to be smelt terribly strong," Isherwood noted in his diary in October. "The polls say it will win. And it's certain to be followed by worse." He felt it necessary to do something about this, but at the same time get on with work, otherwise rage against the Proposition would merely become one more distraction from finishing his book.

Other worries preoccupied him. A German publisher had secured the rights of *Christopher and His Kind* and a translation had been prepared. Isherwood realized that he would have to obtain Heinz's permission before allowing publication to go ahead. "Although I don't expect any trouble—at least, not from him personally—and although I don't *really* care even if he says it mustn't be published in Germany at all—I feel a bit tense about the whole thing, as I always do before a showdown of any kind." Writing a letter to Heinz about the book proved a "psychologically gigantic feat," not least because Isherwood's German was fairly rusty. He explained that although Heinz naturally played a large part in the book, he was only ever referred to by his first name and there was no chance of anyone identifying him. Even so, he wrote, "if you find something you don't like it will be changed or struck out. If you tell me you object to the book being published in German, it won't be published. Your friendship is worth a great deal to me. I don't actually think you will feel insulted because everything I have written is written with love. But it's possible that your relations might feel differently." Heinz replied immediately that he was delighted to hear from Isherwood and that he would let him know what he thought of the book as soon as he received the translation. A fortnight later he wrote to say that he was horrified by Isherwood's frankness and that reading the book had brought him to the edge of despair. He was appalled by the idea that his wife, son or grandchildren might read it. If they did, he might end up being divorced and he would have to blow his own head off. Isherwood wrote back to reassure his old lover that the book would not be published in Germany under any circumstances and pleading with Heinz not to be angry with him. Heinz replied in a friendly enough manner, but the two old friends never communicated again.

Isherwood was also anxious about his relationship with his current lover. Isherwood did not mind spending nights alone in front of the television when Bachardy went out "mousing," as he termed it. Indeed, he recorded his lover's exploits with some amusement in his diaries, drawing heavily upon Beatrix Potter: "Kitty and his mouse smoked till the mouse fell asleep, so there was no gobbling; and then, this morning, the mouse's mousefriend appeared without warning and so Kitty had to pit-pat away pronto." When the mice looked as if they might stay on and start nesting at Adelaide Drive, however, Isherwood found it impossible to master his jealousy. During the summer of 1978, Bachardy became involved with a man named Bill Franklin, whom Isherwood actively disliked. Isherwood nicknamed him "The Downer," and even Bachardy admitted that his new lover was "ugly, undersexed, Jewishly competitive, sorry for himself, always worried about his health." Bachardy did, however, feel that he could "connect" with Franklin. Isherwood tolerated Franklin's visits, but not always with very good grace. On one occasion, when Franklin unwisely stated his opinion that Los Angeles "would be a dull dreary place if it wasn't for the big Jewish population," Isherwood lost his temper. "I'll have to watch myself when he's around," he wrote in his diary, "because I really don't like him and I shall show it if I'm not careful, which'll be upsetting and inconvenient for my Darling." Since this was the sort of thing Isherwood often wrote in his diary, he was very angry a couple of weeks later when he found Bachardy looking at an old volume left open on the desk in the study. Bachardy accused Isherwood of dressing him down "as if he were 'a chambermaid' caught snooping." Isherwood explained that Bachardy might read something about himself in the diaries that he would find upsetting and would find himself unable to forget it. He was always aware that however strong and enduring his relationship was with Bachardy, the day-to-day living of it was a delicate balance.

Isherwood was not altogether reassured when Bachardy announced that he was planning a trip to Yucatán with Franklin. Isherwood recorded "the ominous feel of pre-departure, sadness, tenderness" in his diary. It would be the first time Bachardy had been on a trip without Isherwood in four years—"and why the hell shouldn't he?" Isherwood asked himself. The reason was that Isherwood felt threatened. He found watching Franklin in the kitchen at Adelaide Drive cooking pasta "particularly depressing": "I had such a vision of his doing this after I'm dead." Intellectually, Isherwood knew that such feelings were silly, but his body was telling him something different: "Am indulging in some interesting physical symptoms; I begin to feel a certain weakness in my right knee, the first twinges in many months. Also, today, I peed blood twice. But I won't say anything about this to Don unless it gets really bad before he leaves." It didn't, but then the last time Isherwood was concerned by the appearance of blood in the lavatory bowl, his "rectal bleeding" turned out to be nothing more than discoloration caused by eating beets.

While Bachardy was away, Isherwood fretted over reports of earthquakes in Mexico, ogled the young men who were repainting the house, drank too much, and got a ticket for running a red light. His principal preoccupation was with the forthcoming stage production of *A Meeting by the River*. The producer Harry Rigby had found someone he considered the perfect director: Albert Marre. Isherwood and Bachardy disagreed, having heard that Marre was keen to cut out the play's homosexual theme on the by now familiar quasi-liberal grounds that the subject was "boring." In the event they were pleasantly surprised by the intelligence of Marre's comments and suggestions. The prospect of Michael Moriarty's being involved had long since evaporated, and the British actor Keith Baxter had been cast in the role of Patrick. The hunt was now on for another British actor to play Oliver. A happy fantasy of getting Michael York failed to materialize, but Simon Ward agreed to take the part.

As soon as Bachardy returned, he and Isherwood started work on yet another draft of the play, finishing it in ten days and sending it to New York, where rehearsals were due to start in January. Unfortunately, Marre was not satisfied by the rewrite. Isherwood told Rigby that the director must "write out exactly what he does want and send it to us, because we obviously don't understand." Although he felt that this was probably "not so serious as it sounds," it was a bad omen. Things looked as if they were going to get a lot worse when he learned that Elsa Lanchester had been sent the play to see if she wanted to play Oliver and Patrick's mother. Isherwood knew that any attempt on his and Bachardy's part to work with Lanchester would be disastrous, but in the event Siobhan McKenna was cast in the role.

At the beginning of 1979 Isherwood and Bachardy set off for New York to attend rehearsals. Harry Rigby had enjoyed great success with his revival of the 1920s musical *No, No, Nanette,* and he now wanted to earn critical kudos by putting on what he regarded as a highbrow, literary play. His first big mistake was to attempt to stage a chamber piece like *A Meeting by the River* in the vast, cavernous Palace Theater on Broadway. Given the venue, and Marre's background as a director of musicals, it was decided that the play should have a "big number," and so the *sannyas* ceremony was developed into a theatrical spectacle. Isherwood and Bachardy were very unhappy about Keith Baxter's interpretation of the role of Patrick, which they felt was far too sympathetic. They intended Patrick to have charm, but to be sly and manipulative as well. Isherwood made a scene and demanded that Baxter should play the role as it had been written. Baxter did so for one run-through, which the authors thought a vast improvement. Baxter disagreed and, with Marre's approval, went back to play the part as he always had. Marre had also insisted on cutting as much of the homosexual material as possible, including a scene with Tom that the authors thought absolutely crucial.

These disagreements became increasingly ill-tempered and it soon became clear that the cast and director had turned against Isherwood and Bachardy. "We were just as green and silly as we could be," Bachardy recalled. "There was no excuse. Of course, that's always easy to say in retrospect, but novices are always wide-eyed, thinking that all the theatre needs is 'quality.' " By the time the play began to preview, the authors knew that they had a disaster on their hands. This was swiftly confirmed on the first night, March 28, 1979. Although there was a general sense of foreboding, the first-night party was quite enjoyable, since Isherwood and Bachardy were by now beyond caring. This was just as well because when the notices arrived they carried such headlines as "Stagnant 'River' " and were unanimous in panning the play. Richard Eder in *The New York Times* was particularly vitriolic, laying the entire blame on the authors. Describing the play as "an exercise in High Twaddle," he wrote that it "fails because its central action—conversion—is invisible; it becomes a tedious failure because its personages have no believable character but only a series of ascribed emotions and beliefs, conveyed in speeches that can hardly get through an actor's mouth." These "almost literally unspeakable" lines "play havoc with a cast that includes some accomplished actors," he concluded, and "Albert Marre has directed in what seems to be a state of desperation." Clive Barnes, whose notices in the *New York Post* were famously reputed to make or break a play, was a little more respectful, but described the adaptation as "the rape of a rather important novel." "The acting is impeccable and exemplary," he concluded. "How well the British behave under fire." Unlike Eder, he deemed that the play was at least an honourable failure, but elsewhere it was described as "stately, discursive nonsense" and simply "not up to snuff as theatre."

Harry Rigby accompanied Isherwood and Bachardy back to their hotel in a cab and was astonished at how lightly they were taking this disaster. "He'd expected all kind of theatrical sobbings and regrets," Bachardy recalled. "We were just so relieved by that time. We hated being in New York, we hated the whole experience. It meant nothing to us now. We'd just stayed to see it out, like soldiers, and now we couldn't wait to get out." Rigby told them before they reached the hotel that he was going to close the show. They knew that he could afford a failure and began to wonder whether the whole production had in fact been mounted to lose money, as in Mel Brooks's movie satire, *The Producers*. Since they had never taken Rigby very seriously, and liked him, they did not blame him for this fiasco, but it put an end to their theatrical ambitions.

Bachardy's recollections may have become rather more cheerful at a distance of fifteen years. Isherwood failed to keep his diary while in New York. Resuming it as soon as they got back to Santa Monica at the beginning of April, he reported that various bits of unwelcome news in his previous entry had "NOT been the end of the bad karma." He added: "Am not sure if I care to relate all the bumpy and grindy times between then and now." And he never did. Clive Barnes had suggested: "Whether Isherwood or his co-author, Bachardy, is the more to blame is a question safely to be left to the energies of biographers and future writers of graduate theses." The principal and perhaps unspoken reason they persisted with the idea of the play after a long catalogue of problems and rebuffs was because it was a collaboration. It would be difficult to imagine a novel less suited to theatrical presentation than *A Meeting by the River*. Quite apart from the subject matter, which Isherwood always acknowledged was "difficult," there was the question of how to dramatize a book that consisted largely of letters and diary entries. This had never been resolved, and most of the reviews commented on the fatally undramatic notion of having actors stand about on stage, their heads bowed over bits of paper as they "read" letters and diaries. In the cinema, this dilemma might have been solved by the use of voice-over, and both Isherwood and Bachardy acknowledged that their screenplay of the book was vastly superior to their stage version. However, their names had been briefly up in lights, linked and equal, and that was what they had wanted. Had the play worked, the credit might have redounded to them jointly. As it was, Barnes wrote of Bachardy that he "seems to be best known as a portrait artist": he was still considered, as Eber nastily put it, merely an "associate" rather than a true co-author. This was not forgiven, nor were the director or Baxter, both of whom were cast as Judases.

Back in Santa Monica Isherwood finished revising the Prabhavananda book, for which Bachardy had once again provided a title: *My Guru and His Disciple.* At the end of May he sent off a typescript to his editor in New York, Michael di Capua, but realized that whatever the publishers thought of the book, he would also have to take into account the reactions of people more intimately concerned with the story. He required, if not the approval, then at least the sanction of the Vedanta Society, and had to ensure that Vernon did not find his account of their relationship "too intimate." In the event, Pravrajika Anandaprana, the senior woman swami who now virtually ran the Center, "raised no shattering objections," although Isherwood guessed that "she rather hated the whole tone of the book and was embarrassed to death at the prospect of having to excuse it to the congregation at Belur Math." Vernon, far from raising any objections, declared the book "beautiful" and wrote Isherwood "a sweet but embarrassing letter saying that I am one of the few people one meets in a lifetime that one can really trust and signing himself my disciple." Isherwood had also sent a typescript to Swami Vidyatmananda (Prema), who thought the book "a complete success." He made only one minor correction and suggested that the year should be stated more often in diary entries so that the reader could keep track of time. "You have done in an interesting way what you set out to do—present Swami Prabhavananda in terms of your relationship with him, warts and all," Vidyatmananda wrote. "More a case study than hagiography. I would call it a lively biography of a mystic done in the modern way and bound to appeal to anyone interested in you and/or contemporary movements in religion. You have touched on subtleties in the guru-disciple relationship never so clearly stated (as far as I know) before." Isherwood was very pleased: as he told Vidyatmananda, whose own relationship with Prabhavananda had been far from unclouded: "Nobody else is in a position to be able to judge [the book] as you can."

The only person Isherwood needed to hear from now was Caskey, to whom he had sent the pages dealing with their relationship. He was anxious about this, since he had failed to respond to a number of letters Caskey had been sending him during the past year. Amongst other things, Caskey had wanted Isherwood's blessing for the memoir he still hoped to write, which would describe his life in three parts: Kentucky, New York and California. His relationship with Isherwood would be the subject of the final section, and Isherwood was worried about what Caskey might write. Caskey had also asked permission to show some of his letters from Isherwood to Humphrey Carpenter, who was writing a biography of Auden. The year before, Isherwood had refused to cooperate with Carpenter unless the project had the support of Auden's executor, Edward Mendelson. He had himself sought Mendelson's permission before writing about Auden in *Christopher and His Kind.* When Mendelson decided to help Carpenter, Isherwood followed suit. Isherwood nevertheless thought that any dealings, literary or otherwise, with Caskey were likely to cause trouble and so had continued simply to ignore Caskey's letters. At first Caskey was puzzled by Isherwood's attitude, then became hurt and angry. "I may never hear from him again, except in court," Caskey told Jonathan Fryer. "He refuses to recognize that I have a right to do a book about my life, with or without him."

Caskey's most recent letter had been very aggrieved, demanding that Isherwood "return" a pre-Columbian figure they had bought in South America and threatening that if Isherwood did not cooperate he would find himself portrayed in Caskey's memoirs as "a freak." Isherwood had received reports that Caskey was to be seen in Athens "drunk and belligerent and beatup with legs caked with dirt because his water in the apartment had been cut off," so this outburst had not altogether surprised him. He hoped, however, that Caskey might be mollified by an offer to cut him out of *My Guru and His Disciple* altogether if he objected to the way he had been portrayed— while at the same time, of course, he hoped that this offer would not be taken up. Caskey was surprised that no apology had been offered by Isherwood for his failure to answer letters but, nevertheless, replied with "a few corrections for accuracy" and challenged Isherwood's account of his religious feelings and beliefs. Isherwood was grateful for this response, but managed to upset Caskey all over again. "I quote from his last letter," Caskey wrote to Fryer: " 'when you write (I hope) your autobiography." Why the parenthesis? Doesn't he know that's a put down? You're damn right he does." He suggested that *My Guru and His Disciple,* which he thought "rambling and not concise Isherwood at all," should be retitled *Way Down the Swami River.*

On May 15, 1979, at the age of sixty-seven, Richard died suddenly after suffering a heart attack. Isherwood had long since freed himself from any sense of responsibility for his brother, but Richard had been a final link with the past and the family he had spent so much time trying to escape. Under the terms of Richard's will, Wyberslegh Hall was left to his cousin Thomas, Uncle Jack's only son and the last of the Bradshaw-Isherwoods. What remained of the family portraits, salvaged from Marple Hall, were left to Thomas and Christopher jointly. Richard's bungalow was left to the Dans' daughter and her husband, its contents to the Dans themselves. There were small bequests to various friends and relatives, including £300 for the Dans, £350 for Alan Bradley, £400 for Thomas and £650 for Christopher. The residue of the estate was divided equally between Thomas and Christopher.

Considering how long the Dans had taken care of Richard, and that his estate was valued at an astonishing £105,665 (more than four times the value of Kathleen's), they had been left surprisingly little. It was evident that they were in some financial difficulties, and Isherwood suggested that he and Thomas should give them some extra money. Thomas had never trusted the Dans and refused to cooperate, and so Isherwood made over to them his entire share of the money that had come to Richard through the Trevor Will Trust, set up by his godmother, Agatha Trevor.

Apart from testily noting these financial complications, Isherwood made no comment about his brother's death in his diary at the time. He recorded that he had received "a very touching letter" from Evelyn Bradley, extracts from which he intended to copy into the diary, but he did not do this until October 1, which would have been

Richard's sixty-eighth birthday. The letter gives a snapshot of Richard's relationship with the Dans:

> He could tell me all his little fears and secrets, knowing they would be kept forever . . . While he was with us he knew he was safe in our own little world . . . On Sundays he liked the services on television and he sang the hymn they played, "Eternal Father," he had a very strong voice and a very hearty laugh and we used to laugh at the silliest things . . . He came with us everywhere. He liked the motion of the car, he said it soothed him to sleep, which it did. We never both went out [*sic*] the car together as he always wanted one of us to be with him . . . This last week he said to me, Mrs Dan, do you think I'm going to die, as all the happenings of my past keep coming before me, and I told him that we were all going to die, the three of us . . . And as Dan was helping him out of the car he crumpled up and died in the arms of Dan whom he loved.

As Isherwood observed, despite the obvious difference in the brothers' two lives, there was a distinct similarity between Richard snug in his bungalow with the Dans and "the Animals in their basket." Compared with the travels, adventures and packed days that characterized his brother's life, all the happenings of Richard's past could not have amounted to very much, and yet, like his brother, he had recorded them meticulously in an extensive diary. Isherwood hoped to read the diaries when he next visited England, noting: "There is a special fascination in exhaustive accounts of seemingly eventless lives." Mrs. Dan disagreed and, when questioned about Richard's effects, remembered tossing a number of moldy books into the flames of a large bonfire she had made after his death. The record of his unlived life that Richard had kept in his unformed hand was gone.

It was in October that Isherwood and Bachardy finally started the long-mooted "Drawings and Dialogue" book. They had been unwilling to undertake the project unless someone could be found to reproduce Bachardy's drawings to a high standard. Weidenfeld had long since dropped out, but Nick Wilder had suggested Jack Woody, whose Twelvetrees Press in Pasadena had a growing reputation for impeccably produced art and photography books. Rather than supplying their memories of sitters, it was decided that Isherwood and Bachardy should record a single month of their lives in tandem. Each day Bachardy would draw a different person and Isherwood would make an entry in his diary and the results would be published together. "It's a crazy project because it will surely be almost impossible to relate the text to the drawings," Isherwood felt. "Don has a sort of mystic faith that their drawings and text will do this of themselves—and who shall say he's wrong?"

During October Bachardy in fact made forty-six portraits, including one of Isherwood, which meant that he need only publish those he thought successful. Isherwood's contribution was not quite the spontaneous diary it pretended to be. He wrote every day throughout the month, but then set about revising and polishing it substantially. Bachardy read it and made notes and suggestions. By Valentine's Day 1980, Isherwood was still complaining as usual that he had not really made much progress on the text:

his sophisticated, Westernized tastes. This was, he kept emphasizing, a personal story, the story of a relationship between two people, one of whom happened to be some sort of saint. "The very last thing I wanted to write was yet another book in which the author meets somebody, gets saved, now is saved, and is telling people to come and do likewise," he insisted in a radio interview. "I didn't want to write a book which would end in gleams of otherworldly light and say in fact to the reader: You can't hope to understand what happened to me then, and this kind of thing. I was trying very hard to present the experience in such a way that it would at least seem credible to the skeptical reader."

Perhaps because he wanted to avoid anything too "Indian" or evangelical, Isherwood wrote the book in a very plain, not to say flat, style. Indeed, it is not until about two thirds of the way through the book that he provides a truly striking image, that of Huxley dying: "a great noble vessel sinking quietly into the deep; many of its delicate marvellous mechanisms still in perfect order, all its lights still shining." Unlike much of the book, this was newly minted rather than mined from Isherwood's diaries. Isherwood's original concern that quoting freely from his early American diaries would leave "large holes" in the version of them he intended publishing soon evaporated. Great chunks of *My Guru and His Disciple* consist entirely of extracts from the diaries, and while the intention may have been to give immediacy to the story, the impression it leaves is that Isherwood simply couldn't be bothered to write new prose when there was all this old stuff at hand. In several extracts, his tone slips alarmingly into that more usually found in the sort of pamphlets handed out on street corners by beaming evangelicals, and his weakness for the exclamation mark is particularly damaging in this book, resulting in some passages that are distinctly happy-clappy. Isherwood's prose had always gained much of its energy and effectiveness from rage and comedy, both of which are largely absent from the book. Instead there is a sweet reasonableness that simply cloys.

The most dismaying thing about *My Guru and His Disciple,* however, is its lack of candor. Considerable and important discrepancies are to be found between the diaries Isherwood purportedly "quotes" in *My Guru and His Disciple* and what he actually wrote at the time. Sometimes, and quite justifiably, it is simply a matter of tidying up the original for purely literary reasons or clarity. Elsewhere, he fakes diary entries or censors them. He does this sometimes for effect, as when he asked Gerald Heard in 1951 about whether he should go to live at Trabuco. Heard said that Isherwood should do this, because he was in danger of losing his faith altogether. This is reported in *My Guru and His Disciple* in the form of a diary entry for August 22, which continues:

> He then became very mysterious, saying that he feared I was being followed by "something" which was trying to possess me, and even hinting that he had had a glimpse of it. I asked him to describe what it looked like. He gazed at me solemnly for a moment and then answered sternly, "No."

This may indeed be what happened, but what Isherwood in fact wrote on August 22 was a great deal less dramatic:

He also told me that he thought I was being followed by something that was trying to possess me. I answered that I felt that Ramakrishna would surely protect me from anything of that kind. He agreed.

So far, so innocent. Elsewhere, Isherwood tones down his original diaries. At the end of Chapter 15, for example, he "reproduces" an entry from his diary describing his attendance at the Kali *puja* at the Hollywood center in November 1961, something he did

> just to please Swami. I never feel I have any part in it. It belongs, quite naturally, to the women, and how they dress up for it, in their saris! One of them had let her hair down, falling loose over her shoulders, but, oh, so elegantly arranged. Well, it's their party . . .

while what Isherwood had actually written in his diary was a good deal sharper. He attended the *puja,* he wrote,

> for no reason in the world but to please Swami. I hate the puja itself as much as ever—no, not hate, but it is quite meaningless to me, with all those posturing women fixed up in their saris. Even Sarada, with her hair loose on her shoulder but oh so elegantly arranged, seemed theatrical.

There is no sense here that Isherwood felt in the slightest bit indulgent toward the women, whose party this was. Indeed, the distaste for the nuns and women members of the congregation, most of whom he regarded as troublemakers, is largely absent from *My Guru and His Disciple,* as is any sense that the monasteries were not quite the centers of peace and tranquility that they should have been. Clearly, Isherwood needed to be discreet when writing about the Vedanta Society, but this led to a quite extraordinarily sanitized account of life at both Ivar Avenue and Trabuco. As Isherwood's diaries make clear, the Society was frequently riven by factions and not everyone had been as devoted to Prabhavananda as Isherwood himself was.

The most serious charge against *My Guru and His Disciple* concerns the central question of Prabhavananda's attitude toward homosexuality. Isherwood recalls the occasion when he asked Prabhavananda whether it would be possible to lead a spiritual life while at the same time having a sexual relationship with another man, and the Swami answered somewhat equivocally: "You must try to see him as the young Lord Krishna." "I wasn't at all discouraged by the Swami's reply," Isherwood writes: "indeed, it was far more permissive than I had expected. What reassured me—what convinced me that I could become his pupil—was that he hadn't shown the least shadow of distaste on hearing me admit to my homosexuality." He goes on to suggest that Prabhavananda "did not think in terms of sins, as most Christians do. Certainly, he regarded my lust for Vernon as an obstacle to my spiritual progress—but no more and no less of an obstacle than lust for a woman, even for a lawfully wedded wife, would have been." This is less than candid. In attempting to persuade his readers— and perhaps himself—of Prabhavananda's winning combination of saintliness and worldliness, Isherwood is capable of withholding facts and fudging the evidence.

mance." He felt much the same when doing publicity or appearing at gay rallies. He kept seeing himself as he imagined others must see him: "the spry little old man who is 'wonderful,' merely because he hops around, is still quick with his answers and jokes, and looks perhaps ten years younger than his age." (He would have been alarmed by the writer Gilbert Adair's impression that coming toward you across a room, Isherwood appeared to age incrementally with every step closer he took.) By becoming a figurehead of the gay movement, Isherwood was doing what he had always said he had escaped by coming to America. After years of comparative anonymity, he was becoming once again a recognizable public figure, a spokesman for a cause. This was, however, a cause he genuinely and passionately believed in; it was no longer merely a matter of self-promotion. He nevertheless remained painfully aware that he was to some extent acting a role, becoming once again "Christopher Isherwood." He kept telling himself to get on with his work, but he was still inclined to take life quietly, devoting most of his time to documenting the passing days in his diary. Life was centered almost entirely upon "Angel" and "Darling," as he now referred to Bachardy, and their life together. What mattered to him was Bachardy's career and the domestic life they had created, and this is what he liked to record.

He always felt that his year ran differently from the calendar, beginning at the summer's end, shortly after his birthday. September traditionally marked the start of a new "workseason," and he now began to make notes from his 1939–42 diary in preparation for the autobiography. He had also been approached by a producer who wanted to film the "Paul" section of *Down There on a Visit,* and agreed to write a screenplay, more because he wanted to show he could still do it than for any other motive. Bachardy was heavily involved in his own work, preparing for a one-man show in New York, and this meant that a lot of the groundwork on the screenplay was left to Isherwood himself. He dictated scenes to a tape recorder, but he found it hard to work on his own and did not complete a draft until the following April.

An unexpectedly large tax demand of $26,548 made Isherwood glad of the work, but bouts of ill-health, mostly the aches and pains of getting older, brought an awareness that he should sort out his priorities, and what he should really be doing was working on his autobiography, which had the working title *California.* He had also had a forceful and unpleasant reminder of how precious and fragile life could be when in October 1980, shortly after returning from the opening of Bachardy's show in New York, he was the victim of an aggravated burglary. While working on the screenplay in his study, he went to investigate a noise in the passage and discovered two youths, one of whom had a knife and demanded money. Isherwood called out to Bachardy, who was out of earshot in the studio, in the hope of scaring them off. One of the youths punched Isherwood in the face, causing his lip to bleed, and then the two intruders bound and gagged him with the cord of his bathrobe and a sock. They also wrapped his Japanese robe round his head and made him lie on the floor. "My situation seemed to me corny in the extreme," Isherwood recalled, "something which only belongs in a book. Instinctively I began playing up to it, fretting like a baby and groaning like an old man. I even tried to worry them by crying 'O mi corazon!' in the hopes I'd seem to be having a heart attack." Although the youths were Hispanic, they spoke perfect English and told him that if he was quiet he would not get hurt. They took his watch and his rings and between $100 and $200 from his wallet before going into Bachardy's room, where they rifled a chest of drawers. Finding nothing more to steal, they climbed through an open window and made their escape.

A farcical scene ensued when Isherwood hobbled to the studio and banged on the door. Bachardy had been entertaining a lover and greeted the battered Isherwood stark naked, followed by his partner, who was struggling into his pants. The police were called and interviewed Isherwood, who noted that Bachardy's sexual partner was "impressed by Dobbin's sang-froid, not having seen the old ham perform before." The only real physical damage was some sore ribs, and Isherwood felt that the episode had given Bachardy a much greater shock than it had him. His health, however, continued to trouble him. "Work, work—that's the cure, even if temporary, for so many ills," he declared, but he had also begun to feel that he "might die quite suddenly—the vital supports are beginning to give way." He was worried about his deteriorating eyesight, caused by cataracts, and by the occasional loss of his sense of taste. He was also losing weight, normally a cause for celebration but now an additional anxiety. What principally concerned him, however, was that he had a hernia, which was causing him a great deal of pain, the worst and most persistent he had endured since he suffered from rheumatic fever at the age of ten. Dr. Giorgi sent Isherwood to see a surgeon, who advised an operation as a matter of urgency. Anxious to avoid surgery if at all possible, Isherwood tried wearing a truss and taking some gentle walks, this being the only exercise he could manage. "But walks are such a bore," he complained. "I realize, now I'm old, that the greatest part of my physical exercise used to be fucking, which was largely wrestling and which kept me in very good shape." He had not altogether given up sex and while in New York had been happily seduced by the man in whose apartment they were staying. "Drub gave satisfaction, I think, by the vigor of his response," he reported. He was delighted when his partner commented: "Don's very lucky."

Bachardy did not always feel very lucky, however. Although their relationship, as Isherwood kept noting in his diary, was closer and more loving than it had ever been, Bachardy was still subject to the occasional outburst, his annoyance sometimes manifesting itself in scenes disproportionate to the offense. Isherwood was once asked whether his long-term relationships had been "satisfactory and fulfilling." "Fulfilling, yes," he replied.

> I'm a bit shy about the word 'satisfactory'. It suggests that something has been delivered as ordered, according to specifications. It suggests the phrase 'fit and forget', as applied to something absolutely reliable and predictable; you install it and it functions from then on, no need to worry. With love there *ought* to be a need to worry, every moment. Love isn't an insurance policy. Love is tension. What I value in a relationship is constant tension, in the sense of never being under the illusion that one understands the other person [. . .] He's eternally unpredictable—and so are you to him, if he loves you, And that's the tension.

Tension of one sort or another had certainly characterized Isherwood's relationship with Bachardy. By experiencing this, Isherwood—who once could have had "absolutely anybody"—came to recognize the complex nature of love, and what it was he really needed from it. But he also recognized that he was "becoming increasingly senile, slipshod, self-indulgently invalid, unwilling to leave the house or see people," and what, with characteristically gloomy relish, he called "the pre-terminal stage" of his life, emphasized the physical differences between a man of seventy-six and one of forty-six. He worried that it was asking a lot of Bachardy to "face up to this, at best, grim experience of watching me fade away while his own most valuable years are squandered."

Determined now not to squander what remained of his own years, Isherwood decided to abandon the screenplay of "Paul," and in May 1981 he began writing the new autobiography—"nothing very inspired but quite okay, I think." He had eventually decided to tell the story in a straightforward manner, beginning with him setting out from New York on a Greyhound bus on May 2, 1939. He returned to his usual practice and typed it, making corrections by hand and producing a page a day. "I can feel how powerfully it's a pro-life force, countering my body-aches," he wrote of this process of starting a new book.

His body-aches had become worse, however, with pains at the tops of his legs, backache and cramp, and he decided that he ought to undergo surgery for his hernia in the hope of gaining some relief. He would also undergo various tests because Dr. Giorgi was worried by his continuing weight loss. The operation was carried out at the end of June and appeared to have been a success, but it took him a long time to recover from the effects of the anesthetic. He was still groggy the day after the operation, annoying the doctors, who suspected him of being "self-indulgent." It was general policy at that time to give all patients massive doses of anesthesia without checking their individual tolerance, and as Bachardy observed, by this stage of Isherwood's life, "one glass of wine would have a noticeable effect on him, and three or four could probably have got him through the surgery without a murmur."

Isherwood's immediate reaction once he got home was that he had "the curiously strong feeling of assurance that I am at last about to get better—that's to say, stop feeling so miserable." His back hurt less and he felt that he had more energy; but a week or so later he was still feeling unwell, unable to face food without feeling nauseated. It did not help matters that the weather was very hot and enervating. He underwent massage, acupuncture and ultrasound therapy, and he was at last able to walk again without a stick. He felt in better shape, but he wasn't. Tests taken while he was in the hospital revealed that he had prostate cancer.

When he and Bachardy returned home after receiving the news, Bachardy made Isherwood sit for a portrait. The picture shows a face racked by fear and despair. In an attempt to confront his illness, Isherwood turned to his diary. "Well," he wrote on October 16,

> the moment has come when I must recognize and discuss the situation with myself, which means, as usual, writing it down and looking at it in black and white. I have got some sort of malignancy, a tumor, and that's what's behind all this pain. They will treat it, of course, and so we shall enter the cancer-recognition phase and its gradual retreat to the terminal. I shall get used to the idea, subject to fits of blind panic. The pain may actually be lessened, but there will be the constant awareness of it. Before all, there will be the need to accept what is going to happen. My goodness—at my age, should that be so difficult? No, it shouldn't be. Yes, but it will be.

Just how difficult it would be is clear from the diary, which stops after this entry. He did not resume it until the beginning of the new year, when he confessed that he had given way to "the dreariest, most cowardly depression and thus stopped writing in this book." After all the false alarms, Isherwood had finally received the news he feared almost every time he went to see a doctor, and he found it impossible to "settle down sensibly and matter-of-factly to having cancer." The doctors assured him that the cancer could be "kept at bay" by the drugs they prescribed, and a biopsy in December appeared to be negative, giving Isherwood a moment of false hope. The only thing to do was work, but he was finding this increasingly difficult. His concentration had deteriorated markedly ever since his hernia operation, and Bachardy was convinced that the anesthetic had done permanent damage: "His mind was never quite as sharp and clear as it had been, though probably I was the only one who could have detected this. The change in him was subtle, but to me unmistakable." He spent less and less time writing his diary, making only thirteen entries in 1982 and four in 1983. His final entry, appropriately for someone who had embraced America so wholeheartedly, was made on July 4, 1983.

K nowing Isherwood's propensity to take any pill that was offered, Bachardy did his best to keep him off painkillers in order to prove to him that he could manage without them. Isherwood realized, however, that the problem that confronted him was not pain: "What I have to face is dying." He had to conquer panic and fear, live as if he were immortal, and turn to his religion. "I pray hard to Swami, asking him to make me feel his presence, 'now and in the hour of death,' " he wrote on Easter Day 1982.

> The response I get from this is surprisingly strong. I'm moved to tears of joy and love. I pray for Darling also, seeing the two of us kneeling together in his presence. Religion is about nothing but Love—I know this more and more. And who's to say exactly what I mean by 'his presence'? As long as I feel Love at the hour of death, then I pray it will save me from fear—and save Darling too.

He had for some time felt "Don's love and Swami's love as two combined forces, not always distinct from each other." They were what kept him going.

Although the prospect of being parted from Bachardy was still painful, Isherwood was reassured by the new confidence his lover had gained in his work. Bachardy's career had received an enormous boost when a Swedish dealer had offered to buy twenty-five paintings. Isherwood saw this, as he often saw his own achievements while writing, in military terms: "a first European beach-head." He also believed that the dealer would "be obliged to make propaganda in the art world to secure his investment." In the event, the dealer bought thirty paintings. Isherwood felt that Bachardy was now working at the height of his powers: "Oh the pride of feeling that Kitty is airborne! He doesn't need Dobbin any longer. He can fly." While Bachardy's long-term future and independence seemed secured, Isherwood knew that in the short term the burden of any debilitating illness he might suffer as he approached death would fall on his partner. For the present, although he experienced bouts of backache and of nausea caused by the smell of certain sorts of food, he remained reasonably well.

tough with themselves and really decide which side they're on. You know, fuck God's will. God's will must be circumvented, if that's what it is."

Isherwood's memory and concentration continued to deteriorate, and he would appear to drift off, or switch off, in the middle of a conversation. He was sometimes aware of this and on one occasion, clearly thinking of Marple Hall and making a macabre joke of it, acknowledged: "Yes, the whole of the East Wing has gone dark, I'm afraid." Before he was diagnosed with cancer, Isherwood defined the "pre-terminal stage" of a life as the period when "the event of death is *more or less* recognized and accepted although health remains still pretty good, with regular bowel-movements, full nights of untroubled sleep, adequate amounts of energy available." He had now entered what he called "the terminal phase," in which, he had predicted, "one's principal occupation is dying—that is to say, a phase in which death becomes a constant threat and, to some degree, a desired release." He had concluded the diary entry he made about being diagnosed with cancer with an image of frail mortality: "The love between me and Don has never been stronger, and is heart-breakingly intimate. Every night he goes to sleep holding the old dying creature in his arms." At the time, this was something of an exaggeration. By 1985, however, in spite of the assorted medications he received, including hormone shots which made him develop small breasts, Isherwood was indeed dying, and he gradually entered what doctors would also call the terminal phase.

Isherwood had been promised that he would die at home, not in the hospital, but it was evident that Bachardy would need some help beyond regular visits from Dr. Giorgi. He did not want professional caregivers or other strangers in the house, but persuaded a young friend, Dan Gerischer, to help. Gerischer, who was himself an artist, had frequently sat for Bachardy: he was big, blond and strong, and was able to lift Isherwood when necessary and help him to bathe and shower. During the latter stages of Isherwood's illness, he slept in the storeroom below Isherwood's study.

Bachardy continued to draw Isherwood, as he always had, not only as a record but also as a way of maintaining the connection between them. He had always insisted that his portraits were collaborations between the artist and the sitter, but the drawings he did during the last months of Isherwood's life were a more than usually intense collaborative project. It was, as Stephen Spender observed, a way for Bachardy to participate in Isherwood's dying. "I love to sit close," Bachardy once said of his method of portraiture, "because I have more contact with the sitter." His daily sessions with the increasingly withdrawn Isherwood would become his only real contact. The process Bachardy was recording at his easel was also being observed in his diary. By late August 1985 Isherwood was having difficulty managing the fly of the jumpsuit he liked wearing, "unable to figure out how to undo the line of snaps down the front and unzip the long zipper." Long accustomed to Isherwood's ability to hold a pose and concentrate, Bachardy now found it difficult to keep his attention:

> Chris, sometimes very sweet, agreeable and co-operative, is sometimes tiresome, full of complaints and startlingly dense. In the middle of drawing he will suddenly ask if he can put on his robe. Just getting him on to the bed and positioned

against the pillows is a real chore. He grimaces with pain as he inches his rump towards the pillows, often letting our piercing cries. 'If you *knew* what it's like, this pain!' he often says to me, as though reprimanding me. Yesterday, when he said it again, I defended myself. 'Don't blame *me*,' I said. 'It's not my fault. It's bad enough having to listen to you and your complaints. Don't make me responsible for the pain.' My outburst surprised us both. Chris was noticeably subdued for the rest of the afternoon. He realized he'd been provoking me.

Spender described Bachardy's drawings as "both merciless and loving," a judgment with which Bachardy agreed, adding: "But then, all my work is merciless and loving. And since *real* love *is* merciless, one might just say my work is loving—merciless is redundant." Bachardy's last drawings of Isherwood are in this way very similar to Isherwood's early portraits of Bachardy in his diaries.

By late September, Isherwood seemed unable to understand Bachardy's instructions and was having a great deal of difficulty signing and dating the drawings, although his hand remained reasonably clear. The last picture he signed was dated October 20, 1985. Bachardy worked on, drawing Isherwood clothed and naked, in daylight and at night, awake and, increasingly, asleep. He sometimes worked for hours at a stretch, producing as many as seven drawings in a session. At the end of October, there was a three-week respite when Isherwood went into the hospital to be given chemotherapy and radiation treatment, and then the sessions started again. Bachardy acknowledged that he must have seemed ruthless. "My only defence is that Chris brought it upon himself by making me into an artist. And, it is the most intense way I know to be with Chris. It is the only situation now in which we are both truly engaged. If I am tormenting him, I suppose it is an extension of something basic in our interaction."

The most difficult thing for Bachardy was Isherwood's indifference: he was, for the first time in all the years Bachardy had been painting, showing no interest in what had been achieved. Isherwood said little, but occasionally surprised Bachardy by a stray remark. Having for once taken a look at a selection of drawings, he said: "I like the ones of him dying." A couple of days later, hearing Bachardy return from the studio, where he had gone to get some paint, Isherwood muttered to Gerischer: "Here comes the torturer again." "It was said in a wry playful tone of voice which he *meant* to be loud enough for me to hear," Bachardy noted. "We all three laughed. It was such a pleasure to have a taste again of Chris's sly wit. The torturer then took up his instruments and he and his victim performed for another two hours, until the light went."

By December, Bachardy judged that Isherwood no longer understood the purpose of the sittings. All he knew was that he had to sit where he was put and that if he did not Bachardy would scold him. Even Bachardy began to wonder whether he was any longer achieving anything during these sessions, but he still felt that he was somehow, at some subliminal level, keeping the lines of communication open. Isherwood was due to go to the hospital to be hooked up to a morphine drip on January 2, 1986, but Bachardy decided against this, fearful that once Isherwood had been admitted to hospital he would never get out again. There was a further consideration: Bachardy wanted to complete the series by drawing Isherwood when he was dead more than once, *Down There on a Visit* represents a return to form, skillfully reprising themes from earlier books and introducing the perspective from which Isherwood would view his younger self in *Kathleen and Frank* and *Christopher and His Kind*. Almost everything Isherwood wrote bears the clear stamp of his personality, and taken together, both the good and the bad, his books constitute a sort of *Bildungsroman*, describing the long journey of a man who was always learning about himself and the world in which he moved. "My defence at any Last Judgment would be 'I was trying to connect up and use all the fragments I was born with,' " his friend E. M. Forster once said. It is, perhaps, all that any writer can do.

BIBLIOGRAPHY

BOOKS BY CHRISTOPHER ISHERWOOD

Both UK and US editions are noted, in order of publication, even when published almost simultaneously. The edition used is marked with an asterisk or added in square brackets. Abbreviations of titles are those used in the source notes.

All the Conspirators / *AtC* Jonathan Cape, 1928; US: New Directions, 1958 [Penguin, 1976*]
The Memorial / *TM* Hogarth Press, 1932*; US: New Directions, 1946
Mr Norris Changes Trains / *MNCT* Hogarth Press, 1935; US [as *The Last of Mr. Norris*]: William Morrow, 1935 [Penguin, 1942*]
Sally Bowles / *SB* Hogarth Press, 1937*
Lions and Shadows / *L&S* Hogarth Press, 1938*; US: New Directions, 1947
Goodbye to Berlin / *GtB* Hogarth Press, 1939*
Journey to a War / *JtaW* [with W. H. Auden] Faber, 1939*; Random House, 1939 [revised edition Faber, 1973*]
The Berlin Stories / *TBS* [US only, comprising *The Last of Mr. Norris* and *Goodbye to Berlin*] New Directions, 1945*
Prater Violet / *PV* Random House, 1945*; Methuen, 1946
The Condor and the Cows / *TC&tC* Random House, 1945; Methuen, 1945*
What Vedanta Means to Me [pamphlet] Vedanta Press, 1951*
The World in the Evening / *TWitE* Random House, 1954; Methuen, 1954*
Down There on a Visit / *DToaV* Simon & Schuster, 1962; Methuen, 1962*
An Approach to Vedanta / *AtV* Vedanta Press, 1963*
A Single Man / *ASM* Simon & Schuster, 1964; Methuen, 1964*
Ramakrishna and His Disciples / *R&HD* Methuen, 1965*; Simon & Schuster, 1965
Exhumations / *E* Methuen, 1966*; Simon & Schuster, 1966
A Meeting by the River / *AMbtR* Simon & Schuster, 1967; Methuen, 1967*
Essentials of Vedanta / *EV* Vedanta Press, 1969*
Kathleen and Frank / *K&F* Methuen, 1971; Simon & Schuster, 1972*
Frankenstein: The True Story / *FtTS* [with Don Bachardy] Avon Books, 1973*
The Berlin of Sally Bowles [UK only, comprising *Mr Norris Changes Trains* and *Goodbye to Berlin*] Hogarth Press, 1975*

Christopher and His Kind / *C&HK* Farrar, Straus and Giroux, 1976; Methuen, 1977*
My Guru and His Disciple / *MG&HD* Farrar, Straus and Giroux, 1980; Methuen, 1980*
October / *O* [with Don Bachardy] Twelvetrees Press, 1980 [trade edition, 1981*]
People One Ought to Know / *POOtK* [with Sylvain Mangeot] Doubleday, 1982; Macmillan, 1982*
The Wishing Tree / *TWT* [ed. Robert Adjemian] Harper & Row, 1986*
Where Joy Resides: An Isherwood Reader / *WJR* [ed. Don Bachardy and James P. White] Farrar, Straus and Giroux, 1989; Methuen, 1990*
The Mortmere Stories / *TMS* [with Edward Upward] Enitharmon Press, 1994*
The Repton Letters / *TRL* [ed. George Ramsden] Stone Trough Books, 1997*
Diaries, Volume One: 1939–1960 / *DI* [ed. Katherine Bucknell] Methuen, 1996*; HarperCollins, 1996
Jacob's Hands / *JH* [with Aldous Huxley] St. Martin's Press, 1998; Bloomsbury, 1998*
Lost Years: A Memoir 1945–1951 / *LY* [ed. Katherine Bucknell] Chatto & Windus, 2000*; HarperCollins, 2000

Plays [with W. H. Auden]

The Dog Beneath the Skin Faber, 1935; Random House, 1935
The Ascent of F6 Faber, 1936; Random House, 1937
On the Frontier Faber, 1938; Random House, 1939
Plays and Other Dramatic Writings, 1928–1938 by W. H. Auden and Christopher Isherwood [ed. E. Mendelson] Princeton University Press, 1988*

Translations

Intimate Journals / *IJ* (Charles Baudelaire) Blackamore Press, 1930 [Picador, 1990*]
A Penny for the Poor (Bertolt Brecht) [prose trans. Desmond Vesey; poems trans. Isherwood] Robert Hale, 1937; Hillman-Curly, 1938 [as *Threepenny Novel,* Grove, 1956*]
The Song of God: Bhagavad-Gita [with Swami Prabhavananda] Marcel Rodd, 1944 [Phoenix House, 1947*]
Shankara's Crest-Jewel of Discrimination [with Swami Prabhavananda] Vedanta Press, 1947*
How to Know God: The Yoga Aphorisms of Patanjali [with Swami Prabhavananda] Harper, 1953; George Allen & Unwin, 1953*

Editor

Vedanta for the Western World / *VftWW* Marcel Rodd, 1945; George Allen & Unwin, 1948*
Vedanta for Modern Man Harper, 1951; George Allen & Unwin, 1952*
Great English Short Stories / *GESS* Dell, 1957*

SECONDARY SOURCES

ALEXANDER, PETER *William Plomer* Oxford University Press, 1989
ANSEN, ALAN [ed. N. Jenkins] *The Table Talk of W.H. Auden* Ontario Review Press, 1990
APPIGNANESI, LISA *Cabaret: The First Hundred Years* Studio Vista, 1975
ASHBEE, H. S. [as "Pisanus Fraxi"] *Index Librorum Prohibitorum* privately printed, 1877
―――― *Bibliography of Prohibited Books* [3 vols] Jack Brussel, 1962
AUDEN, W. H. *Thank You, Fog* Faber, 1974
―――― *The Dance of Death* Faber, 1933
―――― *For the Time Being* Faber, 1945
―――― *Poems* Faber, 1930
―――― *A Certain World* Faber, 1970
―――― *Forewords and Afterwords* Random House, 1973
―――― *Collected Poems* [ed. E. Mendelson] Faber, 1976 [revised edition 1991*]

WESCOTT, GLENWAY [eds. R. Phelps and J. Rosco] *Continual Lessons* Farrar, Straus and Giroux, 1990

WHITE, JAMES P. AND WHITE, WILLIAM H. *Christopher Isherwood: A Bibliography of His Personal Papers* Texas Center for Writers Press, 1987

WILDE, ALAN *Christopher Isherwood* Twayne Publishers, 1971

WILSON, ANGUS [ed. K. McSweeney] *Diversity and Depth in Fiction* Viking, 1983

WINDHAM, DONALD *Lost Friendships* William Morrow, 1987

——— [ed.] *Tennessee Williams' Letters to Donald Windham 1940–1965* Holt, Rinehart & Winston, 1977

WISHART, MICHAEL *High Diver* Blond & Briggs, 1977

WOLFF, CHARLOTTE *Magnus Hirschfeld* Quartet, 1986

WORSLEY, T. C. *Fellow Travellers* London Magazine Editions, 1971

WRIGHT, ADRIAN *John Lehmann: A Pagan Adventure* Duckworth, 1998

WRIGHT, THOMAS E. *Growing Up with Legends* Praeger, 1998

YORK, MICHAEL *Travelling Player* Headline, 1991

SOURCES

References to quoted material are listed by page number and in order, identified by a brief phrase or the subject matter. Locations are listed at the end of these source notes. Published sources are referred to by the author's name. Abbreviations used for Isherwood's and other books are listed in the Bibliography.

The bulk of Isherwood's papers, formerly the property of Don Bachardy, are now housed in the Huntington Library, and manuscripts, notebooks, lectures, articles, etc. are identified by a call number beginning "CI." Both page numbers and dates are provided for quotations from Isherwood's published diaries; unpublished diaries are referred to simply as "diary," with a date.

Other abbreviations:

n.d. – not dated   pm – postmarked   fn – footnote

Leading figures and frequent correspondents in Isherwood's life are referred to here by initials:

CI – Christopher Isherwood
KI – Kathleen Isherwood
RI – Richard Isherwood
FI – Frank Isherwood
EU – Edward Upward
WHA – W. H. Auden
SS – Stephen Spender
HS – Humphrey Spender
JL – John Lehmann
EMF – E. M. Forster
EF – Eric Falk

RB – Roger Burford
FT-P – Francis Turville-Petre
GBS – Graham Burrell Smith
BL – Beatrix Lehmann
WP – William Plomer
LK – Lincoln Kirstein
DS – Dodie Smith
BC – Bill Caskey
DB – Don Bachardy

I refer to myself as PP.

Chapter 1

3 "separating himself": *K&F*, p. 508.
4 "the author says": diary, 11/30/1966.
4 "a book called": *C&HK*, p. 9.
9 "a great psychosomatic": *K&F*, p. 19.
9 "Miss Machell-Smith": *Bury and Norwich Post*, n.d.

11 "He sat": Jack Reid to CI, 12/9/1968.
11 "Your father": Reid to CI, 5/17/1969.
12 "Mr. Isherwood": KI diary, 2/26/1896.
12 "Mr. Isherwood as Sarah": *ibid.*, 2/18/1897.
12 "a good deal . . . ": *ibid.*, 2/20/1897.
12 "It is . . . ": *K&F*, p. 48.

13 "utterly unexpected": *ibid.*, p. 69.

13 "Mama very unhappy": *ibid.*, p. 80.

15 "A pretty state . . . ": *ibid.*, p. 122.

16 "a wilderness": "A Writer and His World," CI 1169.

16 "England's green": *ibid.*

Chapter 2

17 "only a quarter": KI diary, 8/27/1905.

17 "later welcomed": "Hero-Father, Demon-Mother" ts [CI 1082], p. 11.

17 "COLOUR OF HAIR" *et seq.:* "Babys Progress" [CI 519].

18 "I hear": *K&F,* p. 276.

19 "Nurse went off": KI diary, 7/24/1906.

19 "Poor C": *ibid.*, 8/7/1906.

20 "She also suggests": *ibid.*, 7/18/1905.

20 "C. W. taking": *ibid.*, 6/22/1905.

20 "They are evidently": *ibid.*, 1/5/1906.

20 "a great interest" *et seq.:* "Babys Progress."

21 Potter was: *Beatrix Potter's Letters,* p. 96.

21 "a bit feudal": Elizabeth Monkhouse to PP, 6/21/1996.

22 "Mrs. Singleton's": KI diary, 12/27/1906.

22 "Miss Monkhouse": *ibid.*, 6/25/1905.

22 "because Christopher": *ibid.*, 6/11/1908.

22 "Considering father": CI 1082, p. 21.

22 "an obsolete," *ibid.*, p. 23.

22 "Marple was": RI to CI, n.d. but Nov. 1970.

22 *Cheshire Herald:* 3/20/1915.

23 "up to the Technical": KI diary, 6/11/1918.

24 "muzzy old woman": *ibid.*, 8/10/1907.

24 "is now inclined": *K&F,* p. 316.

24 "an imaginative": *ibid.*

24 "a sort of": *ibid.*, p. 313.

25 "whatever it was": *ibid.*, p. 314.

25 "opposite the barracks": KI diary, 3/6/1906.

26 "Eight weeks": *ibid.*, 4/27/1908.

26 "a most deadly": *K&F,* p. 334.

26 "so nice": KI diary, 11/13/1908.

26 "make it up": *K&F,* p. 338.

27 "Lilah McCarthy," KI diary, 5/23/1911.

27 "You can never": *K&F,* p. 347.

27 "the astounding": KI diary, 2/7/1910.

27 KI on Woking: *ibid.*, 2/17/1910.

27 "very seedy": *ibid.*, 2/28/1911.

27 "From various": *ibid.*, 6/15/1911.

27 "the gloom": *ibid.*, 6/26/1911.

27 "Rather": *ibid.*, 10/1/1911.

27 "innocent": *ibid.*

27 "I begin": *ibid.*, 10/6/1911.

28 "Poor C": *ibid.*, 10/25/1911.

28 "as far as": *ibid.*, 12/8/1911.

28 Penrose: "Babys Progress."

29 "a tiny": CI 1082, p. 71.

29 "When we went": *ibid.*, pp. 71–2.

29 "There was": *K&F,* p. 367.

29 Reid: to CI, 5/17/1969.

30 Mercer: to KI, 10/12/1912.

30 "Thought the arrangements": KI diary, 6/10/1909.

30 "Horrified": *K&F,* p. 388.

30 "powerfully built": "Memoirs of Pine House" [CI 1098].

31 "was weatherbeaten": CI 1082, p. 82.

31 "a little London": "Babys Progress."

31 "The combination": CI 1082, pp. 76–7.

31 "Granny Emmy": *ibid.*, p. 77.

31 "To Christopher": *ibid.*, p. 79.

32 "very incapable": KI diary, 5/1/1914.

32 "Nurse felt": *K&F,* p. 392.

32 "If only": KI diary, 3/5/1913.

32 "It was all": *ibid.*, 5/1/1914.

32 "a rather pathetic": KI diary, 5/4/1914.

32 Mona Morgan Brown: *K&F,* p. 395.

32 "I think": *ibid.*, p. 396.

32 telegram: 5/1/1914.

33 FI to CI: n.d. [May 1914], [CI 564].

33 "Facing Page One" *et seq.:* "Memoirs of Pine House."

34 "a tireless": *K&F,* p. 398.

34 "A photograph": "Memoirs of Pine House."

35 "I haven't": CI 1082, p. 83.

35 "The images": *ibid.*, p. 81.

35 "becoming, in": "Influences" 1963 [CI 1072].

35 "looked very well": KI diary, 7/29/1914.

35 "It seems": *ibid.*, 7/31/1914.

35 "It presents": CI 1082, p. 86.

36 "It makes": *K&F,* p. 410.

36 "He might": FI to KI, 11/21/1914.

36 "I am so glad": FI to CI, n.d., [?8/25/1914].

36 "I am afraid": FI to KI, 11/10/1914.

36 "Mama seems": FI to KI, 1/5/1915.

36 "I don't think": FI to KI, 1/10/1915.

36 "You will hardly": FI to KI, 4/12/1915.

36 "I am very sorry": FI to KI, 1/28/1915.

37 "violent temperament": FI to KI, 4/5/1915, *K&F*, p. 449.

37 "I am sorry": FI to KI, 11/9/1914.

37 "I asked him": *K&F*, p. 318.

37 "She probably": RI to CI, 10/24/1970.

37 "Purden says": FI to KI, 3/8/1915.

38 "the general": KI diary, 3/16/1915.

38 "found C": *ibid.*, 3/20/1915.

38 "I don't much": *K&F*, p. 450.

38 "You mustn't": *ibid.*, p. 454.

38 "La Bonne": KI diary, 4/28/1915.

39 "Meanwhile, Marple": unidentified clipping, n.d.

39 "could not": *K&F*, p. 463.

39 "a fact": *ibid.*, p. 468.

39 Red Cross letter: *ibid.*, pp. 470–1.

39 "—and so": *ibid.*, p. 471.

39 "heaps": *ibid.*, p. 472.

39 "against": *ibid.*

39 "prepared": *ibid.*, p. 473.

39 Julia Fry: to KI, 6/27/1915.

Chapter 3

40 "Eric was" *et seq.*: *TM*, p. 15.

41 "the Frank": *K&F*, p. 503.

41 "I don't think": FI to KI, 4/9/1915.

41 "I did so hate": CI 1082, p. 7.

42 Kathleen's letter: n.d. but 1915 [private collection].

42 "Not I thought": KI diary, 12/8/1916.

42 "in communication": *ibid.*, 12/17/1916.

43 "The misery": *ibid.*, 8/17/1915.

43 "Did you blub": *E*, p. 170.

43 "a plague" *et seq.*: KI diary, 7/2/1917.

44 "Unwell": CI diary, 1/31/1917.

44 "I never much": "Memoirs of Pine House."

45 "mouse-faced": CI 1082, p. 70.

45 CI on WHA: *L&S*, pp. 181–2.

46 "not that Cyril": KI diary, 6/5/1918.

46 "a very kind": *ibid.*, 6/28/1918.

46 "quite unilluminating": *ibid.*, 6/19/1918.

46 poem: private collection.

48 "had much liked": "Babys Progress."

48 "The end": KI diary, 11/12/1918.

48 "Cyril's comment": *ibid.*, 12/7/1918.

48 "I assume": *ibid.*, 8/24/1918.

48 "I had arrived": *L&S*, pp. 12–13.

48 "Has worked very well" *et seq.*: "Babys Progress."

49 "The idea of": "A Writer and His World," lecture 1 [CI 1169].

49 "He looks": KI diary, 2/24/1918.

49 "advised above all": *ibid.*, 2/25/1918.

49 "there is a good": *ibid.*, 8/7/1917.

50 "like the little": *ibid.*, 4/3/1915.

50 "tears & laughter": *ibid.*, 10/26/1919.

50 "R talked": *ibid.*, 5/23/1920.

50 "I was always": RI to CI, 12/27/1971.

50 "It used": *ibid.*

51 "I remember dimly": RI to CI, 11/7/1977.

51 "the prospect": RI to CI, n.d. [pm 8/28/1973].

51 "sedative": KI diary, 10/26/1919.

51 "very excited": *ibid.*, 10/10/1919.

51 "The Lives": RI to CI, n.d. [?June/July 1971].

52 "R had": KI diary, 11/20/1919.

52 "seemed to think": *ibid.*, 10/21/1919.

52 "he . . . now": *ibid.*, 12/5/1919.

52 "doing well": "Babys Progress."

52 "a boon": CI to KI, 2/1/21.

52 "a short": *L&S*, p. 9.

53 Smith's lecture: CI to KI, 2/6/1921.

53 Gallie: Gallie, pp. 76–7.

53 "Never in my": *L&S*, p. 18.

53 "perhaps the most": "Influences" lecture notes, 1963 [CI 1072].

54 "Then how can": quoted Finney, p. 32.

54 poem: *St. Edmund's School Chronicle,* June 1917.

54 "the kind": "A Writer and His World" notes, 1960 [CI 1168].

55 "Eton behaved" *et seq.*: EU to PP, 8/10/1993.

55 "under an obligation": *K&F*, p. 502.

56 "everyone was": EU to PP, 8/10/1993.

56 "certain practices": *ibid.*

56 "Knights was": CI to KI, 2/6/1921.

56 "as they seem": CI to KI, 5/15/1921.

56 "a wretched": CI to KI, 3/16/1921.

56 "You will be": CI to KI, 5/15/1921.

56 "My relations": CI to KI, 7/3/1921.

57 "That evening": CI to KI, 3/24/1921.

57 "fatal facility": *L&S*, p. 79.

57 "The stars": *Phoenix*, July 1921, p. 19.

58 "the spelling": *L&S*, p. 16.

58 "very creditable": *ibid.*, p. 17.

58 school novel: [CI 1143].

58 "most awful": CI to KI, 12/16/1921 ["Babys Progress"].

58 "Is the telephone": CI to KI, 11/2/1921.

59 "He gives": CI to KI, 9/24/1921.

59 "I quite feel": CI to KI, 9/28/1921.

59 "After some": CI to KI, 10/24/1921.

59 "Even though": CI to KI, 11/28/1921.

60 "like the departure": KI diary, 1/17/1922.

60 "thought his case": *ibid.*, 3/22/1922.

60 "Poor R": *ibid.*, 8/22/1922.

60 "had a vision": RI to CI, n.d. [pm 10/5/1977].

60 "Do hope": KI diary, 10/9/1922.

61 "damned good": EU to CI, 2/15/22.

61 "If I ever": CI to KI, 1/29/1922.

61 "Although I could": EU to CI, 2/15/1922.

61 "I have been": CI to KI, 7/13/1922.

61 "& Mr. G.B. Smith" *et seq.:* CI to KI, "Friday Evening" [6/16/1922].

62 "cold and friendly": *D1*, p. 525.

62 "I enclose": CI to KI, 5/10/1922.

62 "Fisher said": CI to KI, 6/28/1922.

62 "I don't believe": CI to KI, 7/2/1922.

62 "a very determined": KI diary, 8/2/1922.

63 "consigning mountains": *L&S*, pp. 31–2.

63 "used a novelist's": *ibid.*, p. 7.

63 "Next morning": *ibid.*, p. 33.

63 "It was misty": CI to KI, 8/7/1922.

63 "hopelessly seraphic": *Benson*, p. 166.

63 "There are": CI to KI, 9/24/1922.

64 "The fags": CI to KI, 10/1/1922.

64 "I don't suppose": *L&S*, p. 43.

64 "The Winter Term": CI 1152.

65 "The other day": CI to KI, 11/12/1922.

65 "Yes, Cambridge": EU to CI, 11/23/1922.

65 Fisher's report: "Babys Progress."

Chapter 4

66 "his grown-up" *et seq.:* "Babys Progress."

66 "as that is": CI to KI, 5/10/1922.

66 "I was a born": *L&S*, pp. 85–6.

67 "a delightful": KI diary, 2/10/23.

67 "Adequate Coogan": film notebook.

67 "Richard in very": KI diary, 1/29/1923.

67 "going to pieces": *ibid.*, 3/19/1923.

67 "It is most": *ibid.*, 3/13/1923.

68 "after long": *ibid.*, 3/14/1923.

68 "grotesque": CI to RI, 2/9/1967.

68 "The Professor": CI to EF, 4/17/1923.

68 "You can imagine" *et seq.:* CI to EF, 5/30/1923.

69 "The flame": CI to EF, n.d. [June 1923].

69 "Apropos" *et seq.:* CI to EU, "Saturday Night" [June 1923].

69 "I am keen" *et seq.:* CI to EF, 5/8/1923.

69 "Abandoning all" *et seq.:* CI to EF, 5/30/1923.

70 "I appreciate" *et seq.:* "Saturday Night" [June 1923].

70 poem: Patrick Monkhouse to CI, 8/28/1923 [CI 1835].

71 "in a despairing": KI diary, 5/7/1923.

71 "miserable & hysterical": *ibid.*, 5/8/1923.

72 "very tearful": *ibid.*, 5/9/1923.

72 "quite worn out": *ibid.*, 5/13/1923.

72 "storms of tears" *et seq.: ibid.*, 5/14/1923.

72 "one of the": *ibid.*, 5/26/1923.

72 "was generally": *ibid.*, 5/29/1923.

72 "The Brute": *ibid.*, 5/28/1923.

72 "of a semi-facietious": *ibid.*, 5/29/1923.

72 "not at all": *ibid.*, 6/27/1923.

73 "She wasn't": RI to CI, n.d. [?June/July 1971], 1/17/1972.

73 "The jerking": KI diary, 7/30/1923.

73 "a bevy": CI to EF, "Saturday Night" [June 1923].

73 Tynan: quoted KI diary, 11/27/1923.

73 "simply an": *L&S*, p. 75.

74 GBS letters to CI: 2/3/1923, 5/2/1923, 5/12/1923.

74 "in Literal English": Henry Bradshaw-Isherwood's notebooks [private collection].

74 "the best edition" *et seq.:* Ashbee, pp. 82, 413.

75 "in a scientific": Upward, *Christopher Isherwood*, p. 16.

75 "Perhaps Jackie": film notebook.

75 "Pickthorn is": EU to CI, 3/23/1923.

75 "I wouldn't have": GBS to CI, 2/3/1923.

75 "Pale": *L&S*, p. 61.

76 "In France": CI 1022.

77 CI on Burford: *L&S*, p. 85.

77 "in exceedingly" *et seq.: CAM* magazine, Lent 1966.

78 "At that time": *ibid.*

78 "In desperation": EU to CI, 3/23/1923.

78 "a hot-bed": *ibid.*

78 "Get out": A. D. Francis to CI, 7/6/1924.

78 "Thank you": Francis to CI, 12/10/1924.

79 "the rare luxury": Francis to CI, 12/15/1924.

79 "It is always": Francis to CI, 7/6/1924.

79 "Here they are": CI to EU, n.d. [pm 5/24/1929].

79 "a strange-looking": *L&S*, p. 68.

79 "a feeling that": CI 1169, p. 10.

79 "psychic tourists": *TMS*, p. 41.
79 "the special brand": *L&S*, p. 70.
80 "I remember": *TMS*, p. 34.
80 "seemed in some way": *L&S*, p. 72.
80 "We capped": *ibid.*, p. 68.
80 "Most of": *TMS*, pp. 45–6.
81 "an ideal" *et seq.: L&S*, pp. 66–7.
81 "moral offences" *et seq.: TMS*, pp. 34, 40, 39.
82 "The Old Game": CI 1125.
83 "a Westminster boy": CI to EU, 4/7/1924.
83 "The Hero": CI 1067.
84 "Two Brothers": *ibid.*
84 "immortal," "tosh": CI to EU, 4/7/1924.
84 "The teenage": CI 1082, p. 9.
84 "rubbing his hands": *L&S*, p. 55.
84 "Just think": EU to PP, 8/8/1997.
84 "In approaching": *TMS*, p. 172.
85 "Nothing had": *K&F*, pp. 503–4.
86 "Like most": *L&S*, pp. 75–6.
86 "How I loathed" *et seq.: ibid.*, pp. 84–5.
87 "I could talk": *ibid.*, p. 57.
87 "Why hadn't he": Upward, *No Home*, pp. 195–6.
87 "Don't let": *L&S*, p. 83.
88 "A Letter": *TMS*, pp. 168–9.
88 "Upward educated": "Influences": CI 1072.
88 "We educated": Upward, *Christopher Isherwood*, p. 8.
88 "an intensely": Barbellion, *Journal*, p. viii.
88 "Miserable," "Self-disgust": *ibid.*, p. 305.
88 "almost without": *The Listener*, 3/28/1946, p. 404.
89 "My chief": *L&S*, pp. 96–7.
89 Cummings: Barbellion, *A Last Diary*, p. xxxix; *The Listener, loc. cit.*
89 "Felt very": KI diary, 5/10/1942.
89 "Very affable": *ibid.*, 5/27/1924.
89 "The sense of loss": *ibid.*, 11/11/1924.
90 "I said": RI to CI, 1/17/1972.
90 "the possibility" *et seq.:* KI diary, 7/6/1924.
90 "I worshipped": RI to CI, 1/30/1967.
90 "You laid": RI to CI, n.d. [pm 10/5/1967].
91 "I forget": RI to CI, 1/30/1967.
91 "The relations": *K&F*, p. 320.
91 "does not seem": KI diary, 1/4/1924.
91 "A truly remarkable": *ibid.*, 10/21/1924.
91 "four thick": *L&S*, p. 80.
91 "I churned": *ibid.*, p. 79.

95 "the only girl": CI to EF, "Saturday Night."
96 "very depressed": KI diary, 2/2/1925.
96 "A young man's": *L&S*, p. 123.
96 "What mattered": Upward, *Christopher Isherwood*, p. 8.
96 "Edward Upward": CI 1072.
97 "wise and understanding": *GESS*, p. 250.
97 "At least": *K&F*, p. 79.
97 "I longed": KI diary, 3/31/1925.
97 "very bored": *ibid.*, 4/2/1925.
97 "rather unfortunately": *L&S*, p. 132.
97 "It was a blow": KI diary, 6/2/1925.
98 "After a good": *ibid.*, 6/16/1925.
98 "Years afterwards": *L&S*, p. 135.
98 "sent to me": GBS to CI, 3/25/1938.
98 "I am never": GBS to CI, 7/29/1925.
98 "How could I": *L&S*, pp. 134–5.
98 poem: *TMS*, p. 167.

Chapter 5

100 "real but unofficial": KI diary, 8/26/1925.
100 car: *L&S*, p. 136.
101 "How anyone": KI diary, 9/15/1925.
102 "Dark and elegant": *L&S*, p. 139.
103 "She was very": F. Mangeot to PP, 7/8/1993.
103 "This is how": *L&S*, p. 139.
103 fn: *TM*, p. 12.
104 "I thought they": KI diary, 10/5/1925.
104 "It must be": *ibid.*, 10/29/1925.
105 "attitude to sex": *L&S*, p. 195.
105 "no literary": *E*, p. 30.
105 "A thousand": WHA to CI n.d. [autumn 1925].
105 "I still": *ibid.*, p. 24.
106 Spender: *Journals*, pp. 368–9.
106 "Don't you love": quoted Finney, p. 288.
106 Spender: *World Within World*, p. 123.
106 "When Auden": *E*, p. 32.
107 "brilliant teenager": *ibid.*
107 Title page: [CI 1128].
108 "At first": *L&S*, p. 141.
108 "I had long": *ibid.*, p. 153.
108 "one of the most": *ibid.*, p. 151.
109 "yes, they": *TM*, p. 250.
109 "livelier": *L&S*, p. 139.
109 "riper": *ibid.*, p. 150.
109 "a real star": John Ridley to PP, 6/11/1996.

109 "I had better": CI to RB, 5/15/1926.

109 "inspired vaguely": *L&S*, p. 17.

110 "Rain was" *et seq.:* "The Summer at the House" [CI 1138].

112 "I doubt": EU to CI, 1/22/1926.

112 "Yes, he got": EU to CI, 9/25/1926.

112 EU on EMF: *L&S*, pp. 173–4.

113 "My latest novel": CI to RB, 4/23/1926.

113 Monkhouse: *LY*, p. 90.

114 "as almost": *L&S*, p. 175.

114 "But *of course" : ibid.*, p. 179.

114 "tremendous": *ibid.*, p. 177.

114 "some mystical": *ibid.*, p. 180.

114 "on special reserve": KI diary, 5/20/1926.

114 "a jolly sham": *L&S*, p. 180.

115 "Parents": *ibid.*, p. 199.

115 "Laughter": *ibid.*, p. 189.

115 "fumbling begins": "Souvenir de Vacances."

115 "had been going": *C&HK*, p. 197.

115 dates: *LY*, p. 58.

115 "They couldn't": *C&HK*, p. 197.

115 CI to Carpenter: 9/23/1979.

115 "I think Auden": *LY*, p. 93.

116 Mendelson: *Later Auden*, p. 266.

116 "was rooted": *C&HK*, p. 197.

116 CI to Carpenter: 9/23/1979.

116 "who find": WHA to O. Mangeot, n.d. [Feb/Mar. 1935].

116 "And there was": RI to CI, 11/1/1977.

116 poem: Auden, *Juvenilia*, p. 124.

117 "The earliest": *E*, p. 19.

118 "He thought": KI diary, 7/31/1926.

118 CI to O. Mangeot: 8/11/1926.

119 *"frivole" et seq.*, F. Mangeot: to PP, 7/8/1993.

120 "I shall miss": KI diary, 9/5/1926.

120 "created fresh": *ibid.*, 9/29/1926.

120 "suffering from": *ibid.*, 1/24/1926.

120 "must have": *ibid.*, 6/30/1926.

120 "absolutely like": *ibid.*, 10/12/1926.

121 "To see Crichton": *ibid.*, 10/15/1926.

121 "I don't like": *ibid.*, 11/16/1926.

121 "The Truly Strong": *L&S*, pp. 207–8.

122 "Owing to": KI diary, 11/19/1926.

122 "seemed more stupid": *ibid.*, 12/3/1926.

122 critique: CI to RB, 12/30/1925.

122 "Your romantic": CI to RB, 5/15/1926.

123 "the one who can": KI diary, 12/13/1926.

123 "With a sinking" *et seq.: ibid.*, 12/14/1926.

123 "very fond": *AtC*, p. 110.

123 "as if everything": KI diary, 1/27/1927.

123 "another little": *ibid.*, 1/10/1927.

124 "Ah, *there" :* CI 1145.

124 "vulgar as shit": *LY*, p. 103.

124 "Oh, Mr Isherwood": *ibid.*

125 "Can a prep": EU to CI, n.d. [spring 1928].

125 "charming" *et seq.: E*, p. 172.

125 "exhibits": *ibid.*, author's note.

125 "end up": *ibid.*, p. 172.

126 "very period": KI diary, 6/3/1927.

126 "The wall": *ibid.*, 7/13/1927.

126 "Very well written": *ibid.*, 9/20/1927.

126 "story of": *AtC*, p. 9.

127 " 'So what' ": *ibid.*, pp. 43–4.

127 "easily" *et seq.: ibid.*, p. 44.

127 "Philip's got": *ibid.*, p. 150.

127 "pretentious": *ibid.*, p. 78.

127 "delicately pencilled": *ibid.*, p. 29.

128 "The Mother": KI diary, 10/11/1927.

128 "the life": *L&S*, p. 262.

129 "the most chilly": KI diary, 1/19/1928.

129 "striding about": EU, *Christopher Isherwood*, p. 12.

129 "preliminary ideas" *et seq.:* CI 1099.

131 "How extraordinary": M. Tristram to KI, n.d. [1904].

131 "very overwrought": KI diary, 9/22/1904.

131 "Letter from": *ibid.*, 1/30/1906.

131 "all in black": *ibid.*, 2/5/1906.

131 "a sublimated": CI 1109.

132 "sooner or later": *L&S*, p. 269.

132 "The rain": diary [CI 1147] 5/8/1928.

133 "a small": *ibid.*, 5/19/1928.

133 "strong as brass" *et seq.: ibid.*, 5/20/1928.

133 "My cousin": CI to EU, "Wednesday."

133 "Very tall" *et seq.:* diary, 5/21/1928.

134 "a spotty" *et seq.: ibid.*, 5/24/1928.

135 "It will be" *et seq.: ibid.*, 5/26/1928.

135 "Basil, messing": *ibid.*, 5/28/1928.

135 "Keats was" *et seq.: ibid.*, 5/29/1928.

135 "I'm really": *ibid.*, 5/26/1928.

135 "I dreamt" *et seq.: ibid.*, 5/31/1928.

136 "grumbled": KI diary, 6/16/1928.

136 "How strange": *ibid.*, 6/17/1928.

136 "terrific": diary, 6/19/1928.

136 "bad or mediocre": *L&S*, p. 275.

136 "badly troubled": *ibid.*, p. 274.

136 *Guardian:* 5/25/1928.

137 "It is curious": *World Within World*, p. 102.

137 "I was incapable": *ibid.*, p. 33.

138 "A group": *ibid.*, pp. 51–2.
138 "He burst": *L&S*, p. 281.
138 "The hero": *ibid.*, p. 280.
138 "In an instant": *ibid.*, p. 281.
138 "a quite formal": *World Within World*, p. 102.
139 "grammar": *L&S*, p. 280.
139 "a long talk": KI diary, 6/24/1928.
139 "as extraordinary": EU to PP, 9/9/1992.
139 "I do think": KI diary, 9/13/1928.
140 "very horrified": *ibid.*, 8/5/1928.
140 "He might": *ibid.*, 8/6/1928.
140 "thoroughly worn": *ibid.*, 5/23/1928.
140 "I must say": RI to CI, n.d. [pm 2/2/1978].
140 "She spoke": KI diary, 3/18/1929.
140 "It was like": *L&S*, p. 284.
141 "at the tail-end" *et seq.:* "Homer Lane" ts by J. Layard, p. 4.
141 "His face": Layard ts autobiography [ed. James Greene], p. 1.
142 "You never": Layard, "Homer Lane" ts, p. 6.
142 "He thinks": KI diary, 12/28/1928.
142 "I visited": *L&S*, p. 310.

Chapter 6
144 "To Christopher": *C&HK*, p. 10.
144 "after an interesting": KI diary, 3/22/1929.
145 "I was ashamed": "Berlin Journal," p. 5.
145 "No cold": Wolff, p. 177.
146 "pornography": "Berlin Journal," p. 3.
147 "every variety": Lewis, pp. 24, 14.
147 "dens": *C&HK*, p. 29.
147 "the dirtiest": Howard to James Stern, n.d. [Oct. 1927].
148 "the most obliging": *C&HK*, p. 12.
148 "*Du bist"* : "Berlin Journal," p. 7.
148 "This Loved One": *English Auden*, p. 31.
149 "*Du weisst"* : "Berlin Journal," p. 9.
149 "Pimping" *et seq.: ibid.*, pp. 3, 7, 9.
150 "one of the decisive": *C&HK*, p. 10.
150 "only vaguely": *ibid.*, p. 13.
150 "the man-thirsty" *et seq.:* RI to CI, n.d. [Oct. 1973].
150 "Till he was 16": "Berlin Journal," p. 89.
151 "elements of truth": F. Mangeot to PP, 7/8/93.
151 "explaining to me": KI diary, 5/3/1929.
151 "It seems like": *ibid.*, 5/15/1929.
151 "Idiotic": *ibid.*, 5/23/1929.
151 "Christopher used": *K&F*, p. 507.

152 *Brothers and Sisters:* KI diary, 6/11/1929.
152 Ehrenburg: *C&HK*, p. 16.
153 "Preliminary Statment": *Plays*, p. 460.
153 "A Play": *ibid.*, p. 530.
153 "my play": *ibid.*
153 "That is what": "Berlin Journal," p. 3.
153 "The marriage": 10/25/1964.
154 "We'll 'ave": *Plays*, p. 46.
154 "very tired": KI diary, 7/19/1929.
154 "It seems": *ibid.*, 7/28/1929.
154 "The wind": CI to RB, 8/9/1929.
155 "first—and last" *et seq.: C&HK*, pp. 16–17.
155 "heterosexual dictatorship": *K&F*, p. 380.
156 "if C.": KI diary, 8/28/1929.
156 "he is amazingly": *ibid.*, 3/8/1929.
156 "Technically": CI 1109.
157 "Totally rewrite": EU to CI, 6/20 [1929].
157 "I discovered": CI to RB, 12/20/1929.
157 *Intimate Journals:* pp. x, vii, ix.
158 "[He] may": KI diary, 11/20/1929; 11/29/1919.
158 "a clinic": *ibid.*, 12/12/1929.
159 "Do forgive": *C&HK*, p. 18.
159 Keith: *The Times*, 9/2/1925.
159 Garstang: *The Times*, 8/15/1925.
160 "cosy little nest" *et seq.: C&HK*, p. 26.
160 Maeder: Wolff, p. 431.
161 fn: *English Auden*, p. 42; *The Hustler*, pp. 29–30.
162 "I would get": *CwCI*, p. 108.
163 "failed": KI diary, 12/16/1929.
163 "want of": *ibid.*, 2/1/1929.
163 "sketchy way": *ibid.*, 2/3/1930.
163 "Amazed": *ibid.*, 2/11/1930.
163 "If your father" *et seq.: C&HK*, pp. 35–7.
164 "got into" *et seq.:* KI diary, 3/22/1930.
164 "and then": *ibid.*, 3/24/1930.
164 "Everything was": "Influences" 1963 [CI 1072].
164 "to inspire": KI diary, 3/24/1930.
165 "& without": *ibid.*, 3/28/1930.
165 "arose indirectly": RI to CI, n.d. [?June/July 1971].
165 "a great deal": KI diary, 3/29/1930.
165 "How could" *et seq.: C&HK*, p. 36.
165 "We talked": KI diary, 4/1/1930.
165 "He accused": *C&HK*, p. 36.
165 "must have been": RI to CI, n.d.
166 "It seems": KI diary, 4/28/1930.
166 "with his usual": *C&HK*, p. 36.
166 "for a few": KI diary, 4/27/1930.

166 "after years": RI to CI, n.d. [?June/July 1971].

166 Upward to PP: 7/3/1992.

166 "Richard was": C&HK, p. 37.

166 "C. very": KI diary, 4/29/1930. ·

166 fn: RI to CI, n.d. [?June/July 1971].

167 "did the heavy": KI diary, 3/12/1930.

167 "She must" et seq.: ibid., 5/8/1930.

167 "so that all": ibid., 5/12/1930.

167 "rather like Star": CI to RB, n.d. [1931].

168 "Although [Walter's]": C&HK, pp. 39–40.

168 Spender: World Within World, pp. 104, 103.

168 "Christopher spoke": "World Within World," draft 2.

169 "After my work": World Within World, p. 105.

169 CI letter: n.d. [spring 1929].

171 "I went": EU to CI, 9/3/1930.

171 "Sunday": The Railway Accident, p. 84.

172 "We weren't political": CAM, Lent 1966.

172 "My father": EU to PP, 8/10/1993.

172 "the best hope": CAM, Lent 1966.

172 "Here was the seething": C&HK, p. 43.

173 "I am a camera": GtB, p. 13.

173 fn: Century Magazine, Nov. 1924, p. 38.

173 "political mentor": C&HK, p. 42.

173 Upward: to CI, n.d. [1931].

173 "He began": C&HK, p. 43.

174 "Slumming": ibid., p. 45.

174 "A family": KI diary, 10/4/1930.

174 "most heroic": SS to CI, 11/27/1973.

174 "In the early": World Within World, p. 126.

174 "to see a girl": SS to CI, 2/6/1930.

174 "The truth is": CI to SS, 2/6/1930.

174 "I corresponded": World Within World, p. 126.

176 "gorgeously coloured": GtB, p. 14.

Chapter 7

177 "an attractive": KI diary, 1/6/1931.

177 "Richard darling": RI to CI, 5/2/1977.

177 "I have read": EU to CI, n.d. [1931].

178 "looking particularly": HS to PP, 11/13/2000.

178 "He was liable": HS to PP, 4/3/1997.

178 "a charming": C&HK, p. 75.

178 "the experience" et seq.: CwCI, p. 42.

178 "surrounded by": World Within World, pp. 122–3.

179 Spender on Ullmann: to JL, 10/4/1936.

179 "such a bottle": CI to SS, n.d. [?Nov 1932].

179 "grossly underrated": Billee Hughes to PP.

179 Lady Windemere: GtB, p. 48.

179 SS on Ross: to PP, 7/22/1993.

179 Ross's background: Sarah Cockburn to PP, 11/25/1993.

180 "the whole idea": CwCI, p. 78.

180 "is not an obvious": I Am a Camera, p. 6.

181 P. Bowles: Bowles, pp. 110–11.

182 "brother of": Symonds, p. 28.

182 "suckled": ibid., p. 180.

182 "I remember": The Way It Was with Me, p. 116.

182 Rugby Register: Symonds, p. x.

182 "this interval": Mr. Norris and I, p. 106.

182 "a sister": ibid., p. 28.

182 "set off": ibid., p. 34.

183 "not inconsiderable": ibid., p. 43.

183 "I propose": Symonds, p. 121.

183 "opening his watch": ibid., p. 54.

183 "claiming as an Irishman" et seq.: Mr. Norris and I, pp. 65–79.

184 "The reason": The Way It Was with Me, p. 96.

184 "the mantle": Mr. Norris and I, chapter title.

184 Skrzydlewski: Symonds, p. 66.

184 "from the cracking": CI to SS, 10/28/1935.

185 "Whatever the reasons": Mr. Norris and I, p. 121.

185 "her entire fortune": ibid., p. 120.

185 "This serves" et seq.: ibid., p. 122.

185 "my long hair": ibid., p. 15.

185 "a friendly chemist": ibid., p. 106.

186 "without showing" et seq.: C&HK, pp. 61–3.

186 "with Gisa": World Within World, p. 128.

186 Soleweitschick: to PP, 1/15/1993.

187 "was an altogether": CwCI, p. 173.

188 "culture-worshippers": C&HK, p. 55.

188 CI on Israel: ibid., p. 59; GtB, p. 240, CI to SS, 11/3/1932.

189 "should close": World Within World, p. 131.

189 "Christopher had": C&HK, p. 65.

190 "very sad": KI diary, 12/10/1930.

190 "It was almost": ibid., 3/10/1931.

190 "the state": ibid., 3/12/1931.

190 "I dream": CI to SS, 3/14/1931.

190 "Nothing but": CI to SS, 3/17/1931.
190 "All well": KI diary, 3/19/1931.
190 Cape letter: *C&HK*, p. 66.
190 F. Mangeot: to PP, 7/8/1993.
191 Smith: diary, 9/21/1954.
191 "with a revolver": CI to SS, n.d. [Aug. 1931].
191 Campbell and Blomshield: SS to PP, 7/22/1993.
192 Williams: Windham *Letters*, pp. 95, 89, 94.
192 lodgers: CI to WP, n.d. [2/10/91].
193 CI on Katz: *TC&tC*, p. 170.
193 "Christopher always": SS to PP, 7/22/1993.
193 "But the situation": *GtB*, p. 313.
194 "the most famous": SS to CI, 11/27/1973.
194 "Stephen, in": *C&HK*, p. 67.
194 Waugh: *The Tablet*, 5/5/1951.
194 "I have": CI to SS, 7/18/1931.
194 "This is the first": *C&HK*, p. 67.
195 CI to SS: 7/12/1931.
195 SS on JL: ms Journal, 6/6/1982.
196 "There are": SS to JL, 7/12/1931.
196 "an extremely important": *The Whispering Gallery*, pp. 179–81.
196 "I'm afraid": CI to SS, n.d. [?Aug. 1931].
197 "rather smart": SS to JL, 7/12/1931.
197 "Phew": CI to EU, n.d.
197 "spent the last": CI to RI, 9/30/31, quoted *Serendipity Books Catalogue 45*.
197 "So deep" *et seq.*: *Mr. Norris and I*, pp. 123–4.
197 "the notorious": quoted Costello, p. 168.
198 "central emotional": quoted Hayman, p. 69.
198 "Strong impression": *ibid.*, p. 323.
199 "children of": *ibid.*, p. 358.
199 CI on Mann: *E*, p. 136.
199 "How is": CI to SS, "Thursday night" [Oct. 1931].
199 "I'm frightfully": "Friday Evening" [Oct. 1931].
200 "couldn't relax": *C&HK*, p. 10.
200 "whenever": *ibid.*, p. 197.
200 SS to JL: 2/11/1932.
200 Georg: SS to JL, 3/9/1932.
200 "up at the": *GtB*, pp. 13–14.
200 "something more": SS to JL, 2/11/1932.
200 ten marks: SS in *Independent on Sunday*, 12/5/1993.
201 "All boys": CI to SS, "Saturday" [April 1932].
201 "You can": CI to SS, n.d. [May 1931].
201 "a tout": CI to EU, n.d. [summer 1932].
201 "For God's": CI to SS, "Sunday" [Oct. 1931].
201 "They're the dirtiest": EU to CI, n.d. [autumn 1931].
202 "Communism to us": *World Within World*, pp. 132–3.
202 "a heartless fairy-story": *Mr. Norris and I*, p. 11.
202 "At present": CI to JL, 1/13/1932.
202 "in letter form": Spotts, p. 304.
202 "The 'Enemy'": CI to JL, 1/13/1932.
202 "The moods": *The Whispering Gallery*, p. 192.
203 "I don't feel": CI to JL, 2/6/1932.
203 "I'm afraid": CI to JL, 3/10/1932.
203 EMF: CI to EU, n.d. [?July 1932].
203 CI on sales: to JL, "Tuesday" [July 1932].
204 "offensively dull": *K&F*, p. 261.
204 "fond of": *ibid.*, p. 39.
204 "they would have curtsied": *TM*, pp. 83–4.
204 "had placed": *ibid.*, p. 45.
204 EU on *TM* to CI, 2/19/1932.
205 "contained": *C&HK*, p. 72.
205 WHA on *TM*: to Naomi Mitchison, 3/4/1932.
205 CI on Heinz: *C&HK*, pp. 73–4.
206 "Männer Haus": CI to SS, "Friday" [?May 1932].
206 "denouncing": CI to SS, n.d. [?June 1932].
206 "soon got": *C&HK*, p. 74.
206 "I persuaded": CI to SS, "Saturday" [1932].
206 "I was so unpleasant": CI to SS, 6/7/1932.
206 "No lover": *C&HK*, p. 74.
206 "tried hard to discourage": *ibid.*, p. 75.
207 "For some reason": SS to JL, 3/9/1932.
207 "I have thoroughly": SS to JL, 3/24/1932.
207 "rather hard": RI to CI, n.d. [pm 11/15/1976].
207 "Clicking": *C&HK*, p. 75.
207 "God knows": CI to SS, 1/20/1933.
207 "*Two* great": CI to SS, 5/13/1932.
207 SS to JL: 5/8/1932.
207 "in spite of": CI to JL, n.d. [July 1932].
207 "We have Bibel": SS to JL, 7/20/1932.
208 "short and vigorous": *C&HK*, p. 185.
208 "a very *precise*": Elaine Robson-Scott to PP, 10/12/1990.
208 "There was something": *C&HK*, p. 185.

208 "From my window": *GtB*, p. 13.

209 EU on KI: to CI, 1/29/1933.

210 "awfully good": CI to SS, n.d. [1931].

210 "very small": Plomer, p. 101.

210 "The latest": CI to WP, 10/17/1932.

210 "In the early": Plomer, p. 101.

211 JRA on CI: 4/24/1933, quoted Parker, *Ackerley*, p. 179.

211 "Compactly" *et seq.*: Plomer, p. 101.

211 "My literary": *C&HK*, p. 84.

211 "I shall spend": CI to SS, 9/14/1934.

211 "Christopher made": *C&HK*, pp. 84–5.

211 "a anti-heroic": *DToaV*, p. 177.

211 "Dear Isherwood": EMF to CI, 10/12/1932.

212 "I didn't send": CI to EMF, "Tuesday" [Oct. 1932].

212 "the self-exiled": *C&HK*, p. 87.

212 "Christopher showed": *World Within World*, p. 174.

213 "very 'erschuttert' " *et seq.*: SS to CI, 2/26/1933.

213 "He needed": *C&HK*, p. 86.

213 "It made me": *World Within World*, p. 174.

213 "It is immeasurably": *C&HK*, p. 86.

214 WP to CI: "Sunday" [1932].

214 IAH: CI to SS, 11/14/1932.

215 "bright pillar-box": CI to WP, "Thursday" [Nov. 1932].

215 "horrified" *et seq.*: CI to EU, 8/6/1939.

215 "Katz gave": CI to SS, 11/14/1932.

215 "Suddenly about": CI to SS, "Tuesday" [?11/3/1932].

215 *GtB*: pp. 307–8.

216 "They keep arriving" *et seq.*: CI to SS, n.d. [Jan. 1933].

216 "It is lighter": CI to SS, n.d. [Jan. 1933].

216 "I get uglier": CI to SS, 11/14/1932.

216 "Walter called": CI to SS, "Saturday" [summer 1932].

216 "a rich cosmopolitan": CI to SS, "Tuesday" [June 1932].

216 "a number of": CI to SS, n.d. [Jan. 1933].

217 Georg: CI to SS, 11/14/1932.

217 "Of course": CI to SS, 11/14/1932.

217 CI on *Poems*: 1/20/1933.

217 "In the old": CI to SS, n.d. [1933].

218 "went to": BL to R. Lehmann, 12/16/1932.

218 SS on BL: to PP, 7/22/1993.

218 "much alike": *C&HK*, p. 91.

218 "I see" *et seq.*: BL to R. Lehmann, n.d.

218 "On Christmas" *et seq.*: CI to SS, n.d. [Jan. 1933].

219 "I fuss": CI to SS, "Monday" [1933].

219 JL on CI: diary, 2/26/33; 3/1/1933.

219 "very dull" *et seq.*: CI to SS, 1/23/1933.

219 *New Country*: CI to WP, n.d. [Nov. 1932].

220 "He'll get a bit": *E*, p. 207.

220 Roberts: *New Signatures*, p. 13.

220 "All words": CI to SS, n.d. [Mar. 1933].

220 "Adolf, with": CI to WP, "Sunday" [Feb. 1933].

221 KI on Hamilton: KI diary, 4/18/1933.

222 "his face": *Maurice*, p. 10.

222 CI on *Maurice*: *C&HK*, p. 99.

223 "Shame!": *ibid.*, p. 101.

223 "It is a quarter" *et seq.*: *ibid.*, p. 104.

224 "The real": "Influences," 1963 [CI 1072].

Chapter 8

225 "We are all": diary [CI 2749], 5/13/1933.

225 "I should like": *ibid.*, 5/14/1933.

225 "They talked": *ibid.*, 5/15/1933.

226 "Soldiers": *ibid.*, 5/19/1933.

226 "Hullo, lovey" *et seq.*: *ibid.*, 5/20/1933.

226 "a succession" *et seq.*: *ibid.*, 5/21/1933.

226 "tastes accordingly": CI to WP, 7/3/1933.

226 "Every arrangement" *et seq.*: diary, 5/22/1933.

227 Tasso: *ibid.*, 5/23/1933.

227 "probably first": CI to WP, 7/3/1933.

227 "Erwin lectured": diary, 5/24/1933.

227 "At the moment": *ibid.*

227 "with suspicious ease": CI to EU, n.d. [July 1932].

227 *"Wir haben"*: CI to SS, 8/7/1934.

228 CI on FT-P: diary, 5/25/1933.

228 "with a hum": *ibid.*, 5/26/1933.

228 "Never let": *ibid.*, 5/28/1933.

228 "The rings": *ibid.*, 5/31/1933.

228 MacGregor: *ibid.*, 6/7/1933.

229 MacGregor conversation: *ibid.*, 6/9/1933.

229 "He only seems": *ibid.*, 6/7/1933.

229 "I can't": *ibid.*, 6/23/1933.

229 "Looking at": *ibid.*, 6/22/1933.

229 "Everything was": *ibid.*, 6/29/1933.

230 "It is no use": *ibid.*, 6/30/1933.

230 "Today I have" *et seq.*: *ibid.*, 7/1/1933; 7/4/1933.

230 "I have pains": *ibid.*, 7/6/1933.

230 "potentially jealous" *et seq.*: *ibid.*, 7/8/1933.

231 "Our extraordinary": *ibid.*, 7/10/1933.

231 "F. demurred": *ibid.*, 7/18/1933.

232 "as a servant": *C&HK*, p. 111.

232 "burst out": diary, 7/24/1933.

232 "I have conquered": *ibid.*, 8/11/1933.

232 "They're a bit" *et seq.:* Lassalle, pp. 21–2.

232 "probably got": diary, 8/15/1933.

232 "After lunch": *ibid.*, 8/16/1933.

233 "be patient" *et seq.: ibid.*, 8/17/1933.

233 "I'm in a dead": *ibid.*, 8/23/1933.

233 "very pleasantly": *ibid.*, 8/28/1933.

233 "It was so simple": *ibid.*, 9/6/1933.

234 "After lunch": *ibid.*, 9/7/1933.

234 "Well, we've got": *ibid.*, 9/8/1933.

234 Costi's lunch: Lassalle, p. 23.

235 "Slowly": diary, 9/10/1933.

235 "He understands": KI diary, 9/30/1933.

235 WHA poems: CI to SS, 3/29/1936.

235 "very depressed": KI diary, 10/15/1933.

236 "with a carelessness": *C&HK*, p. 113.

237 "Mr Isherwood" *et seq.:* draft Viertel article [CI 1021].

238 "strong, attractive": Viertel, p. 73.

238 "brilliant Jewish": "Scenes from life at the Studio" 1934 diary [CI 2750].

238 "The animals": *ibid.*

238 "necessary for him": diary, 12/29/1933.

238 "black fuzzy" *et seq.: ibid.*, 12/27/1933.

239 "What a year": *ibid.*, 12/31/1933.

239 "It meant": *C&HK*, p. 134.

239 "Reconsideration": diary, 12/17/1933.

240 "Well, well": *MNCT*, p. 22.

240 "relationship between": diary, 12/25/1933.

240 "picks up": *ibid.*, 12/19/1933.

241 "He belongs": *ibid.*, 12/25/1933.

241 "It ticks": [CI 2750].

241 "a mere translator": diary, 1/4/1934.

241 "This wasn't" *et seq.: C&HK*, p. 124.

242 "thick-skinned": *ibid.*, p. 125.

242 "returned late": KI diary, 1/6/1934.

242 "very vexed": *ibid.*, 1/8/1934.

243 "During the whole": [CI 2750].

243 "Hot up": [CI 2750].

244 Viertel quotes: [CI 2750]; *C&HK*, p. 128.

244 "thrown even more": *C&HK*, p. 126.

244 "smiling young": *D1*, p. 111.

244 "They have given": [CI 2750].

244 The Balcons: *C&HK*, p. 127.

245 "dissatisfied": KI diary, 3/6/1934.

245 Viertel letter: to CI, n.d. [1934].

245 "the most complicated" *et seq.:* CI to EMF, 4/5/1934.

245 "someone of another": EMF to Florence Barger, 5/25/1922.

245 "Character": EMF to CI, 5/15/1934.

245 "the coming smash": EMF to CI, 3/15/1934.

245 "I don't think": EMF to CI, 2/17/1934.

245 "I feel": CI to EMF, 4/5/1934.

246 "an African town": CI to EMF, 4/30/1934.

246 "Olive showed": EU to CI, 5/1/1934.

246 "The original scheme" *et seq.:* diary, 5/23/1934.

246 "little tea-house": CI to JL, 6/29/1934.

246 "It is a": CI to JL, 7/22/1934.

247 "less a blow": CI to EMF, 8/26/1934.

247 "If it gets": CI to JL, 8/26/1934.

247 "connoisseur": *MNCT*, p. 39.

247 "the crimes": *ibid.*, p. 53.

247 "Tell me": *ibid.*, p. 192.

247 "As you get": *ibid.*, p. 170.

248 "I didn't write": CI to JL, 4/1/1935.

248 Hamilton quotes: *MNCT*, pp. 22, 105.

248 "and he did": KI diary, 10/15/1935.

248 EMF: to CI, 5/11/1934.

248 Woolf: quoted KI diary, 9/11/1934.

Chapter 9

249 "fearfully thrilled": KI diary, 8/27/1934.

249 *New York Times:* clipping, n.d.

249 Viertel: to CI, n.d. [1934].

250 "Heinz wheedled": CI to JL, 6/29/1934.

250 "Children with" *et seq.: E*, pp. 217–18.

251 "It is remarkable": diary, 5/23/1934.

251 "Did Villon": CI to EMF, 8/26/1934.

251 "Thirty years old": CI to JL, 8/26/1934.

251 "whose relations": CI to EMF, 8/26/1934.

251 "except when": CI to JL, 8/26/1934.

251 "As long": CI to JL, 6/22/1934.

251 "They ought": CI to EMF, 8/26/1934.

251 "I admire": CI to JL, 7/22/1934.

251 "most vexing": KI diary, 9/12/1934.

252 "compromise": CI to EMF, 8/26/1934.

252 Copenhagen: CI to WP, 10/2/1934.

252 "But one day": Spender, *World Within World*, pp. 45–6.

252 "He took": HS to PP, 4/8/1998.

252 "suffered from": *World Within World*, p. 46.

252 "He was very": HS to PP, 4/8/1998.

252 flat; "nothing to do": CI to SS, 10/12/1934.

253 manifesto: quoted Sidnell, p. 50.

253 Medley: Medley, p. 134.
254 "a realist writer": WHA to SS, 6/28/1935.
254 CI on *Dogskin:* UCSB lecture [CI 1177].
254 "Always, in the background": diary, 5/23/1934.
255 "I can't stand": *ibid.,* 11/24/1934.
255 police: CI to KI, 1/2/1935.
256 "Wystan floated": CI to WP, 1/13/1935.
256 "I think about it": CI to KI, 2/11/1935.
256 "might gradually": CI to KI, 2/26/1935.
256 "As soon as": quoted *C&HK,* p. 152.
257 "arty": SS to CI, n.d.
257 "should be followed": *TBS,* p. vi.
257 "He tells me": CI to JL, 4/1/1935.
257 "C. simply": JL to J. Stern, 3/27/1962.
257 "held no opinions": *World Within World,* p. 101.
258 "So stupid": CI to KI, 2/26/1935.
258 "I can't say" *et seq.:* CI to KI, 3/12/1935.
258 *Telegraph: MNCT* dust-jacket.
259 *Mercury* and *Observer:* dust-jacket of 1966 reprint of *GtB.*
259 "I quite understand": CI to JL, 4/1/1935.
259 "About H.": CI to SS, 4/19/1935.
259 "in the pink": *ibid.*
259 "Gerald was": *C&HK,* p. 156.
260 Ackerley on CI: Parker, p. 179.
260 "who still obstinately": *C&HK,* p. 157.
261 "a big novel": CI to KI, 3/12/1935.
261 *Paul Is Alone:* diary, 1935–8 [CI 2751].
261 "pack a section": *C&HK,* p. 160.
261 "In 1": diary, 6/21/1935.
262 Greene: to E. V. Rieu, 5/24/35.
262 "£150 down": CI to KI, 6/16/1935.
262 "Heinemann would": CI to KI, 7/30/1935.
262 Higham: CI to KI, 7/1/1935.
262 Ackerley and Bles: CI to KI, 7/6/1935.
262 "working with": CI to KI, 7/20/1935.
262 "If nobody": CI to KI, 6/8/1935.
262 "You might": CI to KI, 8/12/1935.
263 "Kathleen behaved": *C&HK,* p. 162.
263 "Humphrey arrived": CI to SS, 6/16/1935.
263 Lehmann diary: July 1935.
264 Howard: quoted Lancaster, p. 5.
265 Altmann: *ibid.,* pp. 353, 332.
265 CI on Altmann: CI to KI, 8/6/1935.
265 "August for the people": *English Auden,* pp. 155–7.
266 Hyndman on SS: *C&HK,* p. 168.
266 SS poem: "For T.A.R.H.," *Poems,* p. 36.
266 "It was so": CI to SS, 9/2/1935.
266 "When I see": *C&HK,* p. 147.

267 "a holy cause": SS to PP, 7/22/1993.
267 "Now that all" *et seq.:* diary, 9/1/1935.
267 CI to SS: 9/10/1935.
268 "Toni began": diary, 9/2/1935.
268 "Although I like": CI to SS, 9/27/1935.
269 "any sudden moves": CI to KI, 9/21/1935.
269 "very nice little manager": KI diary, 9/25/1935.
269 "The Nowaks": *GtB,* p. 215.
270 "We are in": diary, 10/19/1935.
270 Ypres: diary, 11/11/1935.
270 EMF: to CI, 2/23/1936.

Chapter 10

272 diary: Portugal Diary, 1935–6 [CI 1130], 12/12/1935.
272 bedrooms: *ibid.,* 12/20/1935.
272 "nasty washy": CI to KI, 12/21/1935.
272 "a Syrian lad": CI to EMF, 1/15/1936.
272 "I'm not sure": CI 1130, 12/20/1935.
272 CI to EMF: 1/15/1936.
272 Ikerrin: CI to KI, 6/7/1936.
272 "universal rage": CI to SS, 7/13/1935.
273 "quite a fair success": UCSB lecture [CI 1177].
273 reviews: *Aberdeen Press,* 3/31/1936; *News of the World,* 2/2/1936; *Daily Worker,* 2/7/1936. *Evening News,* 2/7/1936; *New Statesman,* 2/8/1936.
273 "The virtue": CI 1177.
274 "Stephen had": HS diary, 1/20/1936.
274 "all this RSPCA" *et seq.:* diary, 3/2/1936.
274 "Heinz has" *et seq.:* HS diary, 1/20/1936.
275 "I suppose": HS to PP, n.d. [2002].
276 "infantile": CI to EU, 12/29/1973.
276 "At school": *C&HK,* pp. 30–1.
276 HS: diary, 1/20/1936.
276 SS: to PP, 7/22/1993.
276 Auden: CI diary, 4/17/1936.
277 "will be lord": *Plays,* p. 302.
277 "truly strong": *ibid.,* p. 313.
277 "the complete abnegation": *ibid.,* p. 328.
277 "a cross between": *ibid.,* p. 598.
277 "cribbed": quoted Fuller, p. 137.
278 "short and": *Plays,* p. 315.
278 "and his end": *L&S,* pp. 207–8.
278 "People's attitudes": *ibid.,* p. 206.
278 "Refused it?": *Plays,* p. 312.
278 *Paul Is Alone:* diary, 5.5.1936.
279 "the experience": *CwCI,* p. 42.
279 Spender: to PP, 11/18/1992.

279 "How does": diary, 8/13/1935.
279 "on the way": *ibid.*, 5/29/1936.
280 "compose into": *ibid.*, 6/23/1936.
280 "We live": CI to WP, 5/12/1936.
280 "sometime": diary, 6/26/1936.
280 "one of the worst" *et seq.: ibid.*, 7/2/1936.
281 "hadn't been used": KI to RI, 6/29/1936.
281 "an atmosphere of": KI diary, 7/9/1936.
281 "fairly encouraging": *ibid.*, 7/5/1936.
281 "Every time": diary, 7/9/1936.
281 "for reasons": *ibid.*, 7/31/1936.
281 "stay on": *ibid.*, 7/9/1936.
282 Stern: Huddleston, pp. 56, 57.
282 Stern on CI: quoted *ibid.*, p. 60.
282 "He hates noise": diary, 8/9/1936.
282 "really does less": Stern diary, 8/9/1936.
282 "was violently sick": quoted Huddleston, p. 60.
283 "the first news": Stern, *The Hidden Damage*, pp. 70–1.
283 "most emphatically": KI diary, 6/30/1936.
284 "a good deal": *ibid.*, 7/31/1936.
284 "He begs": *ibid.*, 8/10/1936.
285 "The news": CI to Sterns, 8/15/1936.
285 "like a schoolboy": Stern diary, 8/2/1936.
285 "*Could* you": CI to Sterns, 8/25/1936.
286 Teddy: Stern diary, 9/9/1936.
286 *C&HK:* pp. 191–2.
286 "developed interesting": CI to KI, 8/28/1936; 9/3/1936.
286 "Salinger now": CI to KI, 10/24/1936.
287 JL diary: No. 7, "End September" 1936.
288 CI to Stern, 11/17/1936.
288 "reminiscences": CI to KI, 11/8/1936; 12/2/1936.
288 *C&HK:* p. 192.
288 "an awful shock": CI to KI, 11/8/1936.
289 "November is": CI to KI, 12/2/1936 [CI 1247].
289 JL diary: No. 7.
289 "Sally Bowles" negotiations: JL, *Christopher Isherwood*, pp. 27–9.
290 "*For the shark*": *Threepenny Novel*, p. 124.
290 Heinz's nose: CI to KI, 12/7/1936.
290 Keynes: to Maurice Browne, 9/15/1936.
290 SS to CI: 10/30/1936.
291 CI to EMF: 10/25/1936.
291 "semi-independent": SS to CI, 10/5/1936.
291 "the whole life": SS to CI, 9/14/1934.
291 CI reply: CI to SS, 10/19/1934.
291 SS on Inez: to CI, 11/22/1936.

292 "Should you think": SS to CI, 11/25/1936.
292 "What on earth": CI to KI, 12/22/1936.
292 "Like you": CI to SS, 11/25/1936.
293 "You can set": CI to SS, 12/7/1936.
293 "I can tell you": SS to CI, n.d. [c. 12/30/1936].
293 "Both Giles" *et seq.:* CI to SS, 12/7/1936.
293 WHA to CI: n.d.
293 WHA to Dodds: quoted Davenport-Hines, p. 163.
293 CI to SS: 12/23/1936.
293 "rather thinking": CI to SS, 12/27/1936.
293 EU to CI: 12/28/1936.
294 "rather an important": SS to CI, 1/5/1937.
294 "A correspondent": CI to KI, 1/18/1937.
294 "a solemn parting": *C&HK*, p. 197.
294 "I found": CI to KI, 1/18/1937 [CI 1252].
294 *News Chronicle:* 1/21/1937.
294 "Christopher could never": *C&HK*, p. 197.
294 EMF to CI: 12/29/36; 1/5/1937.
294 "The result": CI to KI, 1/18/1937.
295 Britten on CI: quoted Carpenter, *Benjamin Britten*, p. 107.
295 "Very pleasant": Britten, p. 19.
295 "Well, have we": quoted Carpenter, *loc. cit.*
295 Fass: Britten, p. 19.
296 Medley: Medley, p. 139.
296 "My *dear*" *:* *C&HK*, p. 201.
296 *New Statesman,* 3/6/1937; *New English Weekly,* 3/11/1937; quoted KI diary, 3/14/1937.
297 "What I dread": CI to J. Stern, 1/22/1937.
297 "start him": CI to J. Stern, 2/6/1937.
297 J. Stern to S. Burford: 2/19/1937.
297 Woolf: Bell, p. 59.
298 "Waking up": diary, 11/19/1937.
298 "*Item*" *:* Auden, *Prose 1926–1938*, p. 369.
299 "tortures": KI diary, 3/4/1937.
299 SS on Bower: to PP, 7/22/1993.
299 "somewhat in love": *C&HK*, p. 204.
299 "partly because": *ibid.*, p. 203.
300 "One wondered" *et seq.:* KI diary, 4/18/1937.
300 "Christopher feeling": *ibid.*, 4/15/1937.
300 Coldstream: *ibid.*, 3/22/1937.
300 Auden: *ibid.*, 4/21/1937.
300 O. Mangeot: *ibid.*, 4/15/1937.
300 Salinger: *ibid.*, 2/5/1937.
301 "last resort": CI to EMF, 4/27/1937.
301 Bower: KI diary, 4/20/1937.

301 "ceased to be": CI to JL, 4/30/1937.
301 KI complaints: KI diary, 4/19/1937; 4/20/1937.
301 CI's departure: *ibid.*, 4/25/1937; 4/26/1937.
302 "too prudent" *et seq.: C&HK*, pp. 211–12.
302 "H seems": KI diary, 5/20/1937.

Chapter 11
304 Mangeots: CI to KI, 12/22/1936.
304 "a ponderous": KI diary, 1/23/1938.
304 Berger: diary, 7/26/1937.
305 *C&HK:* p. 216.
305 "I suppose": CI 1082, p. 81.
305 "part of me": diary, 9/2/1935.
305 "One can only": *ibid.*, 7/26/1937.
305 "widowerhood": *C&HK*, p. 216.
305 Oliver Low: HS to PP, 11/26/1998.
306 "preferred to": *C&HK*, pp. 216–17.
306 "a spontaneous": *LY*, pp. 114–15.
306 "Oh, Heinz": diary, 7/26/1937.
306 "Just five": *ibid.*, 10/13/1937.
307 "Heinz knew": *ibid.*, 8/20/1938.
307 Medley: Medley, pp. 140–1.
308 "Did she KNOW": CI to WP, 10/11/1949.
308 Joan: J. Czarnowski to Margaret Crick, 6/6/1994.
308 fn: *E*, p. 20.
309 Press: *News Chronicle*, 3/19/1937; *Birmingham Evening Despatch*, 2/27/1937; *Horse and Hound*, 3/7/1937.
309 "was probably": *E*, pp. 11–12.
310 poem: quoted Finney, pp. 287–9.
312 *Oxford Mail:* 11/16/1937.
312 "As fascist": *Cambridge Review*, 11/12/1937.
313 Connolly: Connolly, p. 82.
313 "Fritz and I" *et seq.: GtB*, pp. 45, 46, 51–2.
314 "I am getting": diary, 10/13/1937.
314 "I am now": *ibid.*, 11/20/1937.
314 "Stephen's affairs": *ibid.*, 11/19/1937.
316 "playing a little *et seq.: ibid.*, 11/20/1937.
316 "Out of the blue": *ibid.*, 11/22/1937.
317 "Graham": *L&S*, p. 224.
317 "Suppose": diary, 11/22/1937.
317 Caius visit: *ibid.*, 11/27/1937.
318 Bühler: *ibid.*
318 "I seem to be" *et seq.: ibid.*, 11/28/1937.

319 "how do I know": *ibid.*, 11/29/1937.
319 "impudence": KI diary, 12/3/1937.
319 "graciously": *LY*, p. 104.
319 "Was it": diary, 12/15/1937.
320 "declare the solidarity": *C&HK*, p. 217.
320 "[Wystan] wants" *et seq.:* diary, 11/29/1937.
320 Mrs. Lang: *LY*, p. 104.
320 "About 7": diary, 12/30/1937.
321 "hurried through": CI to SS, 7/5/1938.
321 Stern to Burford: n.d. [1937].
321 invitation: KI diary, 1/13/1938.
322 "So glad": CI to B. Britten, 12/22/1937.
322 " 'One must risk:' " KI diary, 1/17/1938.
322 *Sunday Times*, 1/23/1938; *News Chronicle*, 1/20/1938.
322 Trevelyan: Britten, p. 545.
322 Britten diary: Mitchell, p. 128.
322 Medley: Medley, p. 141.
323 M. Fedden: to PP, 6/8/1998.
323 *Sunday Times*, 1/23/1938.
323 Britten: Mitchell, p. 128.
323 *Bystander*, 1/26/1938.
323 Medley: Medley, pp. 141–2.
324 "men in shorts" *et seq.: JtaW* ms, p. 8 [CI 1036].
324 "repulsively modish": *E*, p. 141.
324 "the 'vice' " *et seq.: JtaW* ms, pp. 8–14.
326 CI cable: rcd. 2/22/1938.
326 "very vague": CI to KI, 2/25/1938.
327 "beautiful Santiago whore": WHA to John Auden, 4/21/1938.
327 "Here we were": *JtaW*, 1939 ed., pp. 28–9.
327 Hankow: *ibid.*, p. 50.
327 press conferences: *ibid.*, p. 54.
328 "The bottom": *ibid.*, pp. 58–9.
328 air raid: *ibid.*, p. 71.
328 "sweet stench": *ibid.*, p. 93.
328 dog: *ibid.*, p. 112; CI to SS, 4/27/1938.
328 front line: *JtaW*, pp. 114–15.
329 missionary-doctor: *ibid.*, p. 119.
329 "Wystan, of course": CI to SS, 4/27/1938.
330 casualties: *JtaW*, p. 175.
330 Fleming: *ibid.*, pp. 207, 214.
330 "Now we're real": *ibid.*, p. 232.
331 "On *no* account": CI to KI, 2/8/1938.
331 "I don't know": CI to KI, 4/21/1938.
332 "a beautiful blond": *C&HK*, p. 234.
332 "Naturally, we all": Vernon to PP, 1/10/1994.

Chapter 12

333 "despite their": *C&HK*, p. 235.

333 "In China": diary, 8/20/1938.

333 "went on intermittently": *LY*, p. 58.

334 "these confessions": diary, 8/20/1938.

334 "which only shows": CI to KI, 4/21/1938.

334 "but the morning": KI diary, 7/17/1938.

334 "Passenger Shanty": *The English Auden*, p. 234.

335 "awkward, tongue-tied": diary, 7/30/1938.

336 "all very tactfully" *et seq.: ibid.*, 8/20/1938.

336 Muir: *The Listener*, 3/16/1938.

336 Spender: to WHA and CI, 5/18/1938.

337 CI reply: to SS, 7/5/1938.

337 "all I'm saying": SS to WHA and CI, 5/18/1938.

338 notes on novel: diary, 7/24/1938.

338 SS on CI and Hitler: to PP, 7/22/1993.

338 notes on novel: "The novel as I see it at present" [CI 1079].

339 Lehmann: diary, 8/20/1938.

340 self-analysis: diary, 8/20/1938.

341 "Now Christopher": Miller, pp. 82–3.

341 fn: "Journey to Iceland" and photo: Auden, *Prose 1926–1938*, pp. 185, 193.

342 CI on KI: diary, 8/21/1938.

342 "I make friends" *et seq.: ibid.*, 8/20/1938.

343 Chisolm: *ibid.*, 11/19/38, 10/3/1938.

344 "We play": diary, 8/21/1938.

344 Neame: *ibid.*, 8/29/1938.

344 Hyndman: *LY*, p. 115.

344 Moody: diary, 8/23/1938.

344 "I am in perfect": *ibid.*, 8/27/1938.

344 "At present": *ibid.*, 9/2/1938.

345 EMF to Dickinson: 12/13/14, quoted *Maurice*, p. 8.

345 "I have nothing": CI to EMF, n.d. [Aug. 1938].

345 "I said what": diary, 9/8/1938.

346 Heinz: *ibid.*

346 "full of": *ibid.*, 9/10/1938.

347 "Says he has just" *et seq.: ibid.*, 9/14/1938.

347 Marple: *ibid.*, 9/16/1938.

347 "with evil": *ibid.*, 9/18/1938.

347 "older ex-servicemen": *ibid.*, 9/14/1938.

347 Spender: *ibid.*, 9/8/1938.

347 "Buzzard throws": *ibid.*, 9/18/1938.

348 "quite pleasant" *et seq.: ibid.*, 9/24/1938.

348 "Nothing matters": *ibid.*, 9/26/1938.

348 Katz: *ibid.*, 9/22/1938.

348 "I have never": *ibid.*, 9/30/1938.

348 "All troubles": *ibid.*, 9/24/1938.

349 "What was": *ibid.*, 9/30/1938.

349 "Suppose he": *LY*, p. 106.

349 "The odd morbid" *et seq.:* JL diary, 9/25/1938.

350 "As far as": *ibid.*, 9/26/1938.

350 "sitting with his" *et seq.: ibid.*, 10/2/1938.

350 "when both Christopher": *I Am My Brother*, pp. 14–15.

350 Hewit: to PP, 7/30/1991.

352 "the enormity": JL diary, 11/24/1938.

352 "The more I" *et seq.: ibid.*, 12/2/1938.

352 WHA on Doone: to SS, n.d. [July 1938].

353 *Star.* 11/9/1938.

353 Dukes: to Keynes, 11/15/1938.

353 Eliot: to Keynes, 11/15/1938.

354 Ervine: *Observer*, 12/4/1938.

354 "best-constructed": UCSB lecture [CI 1177].

354 "came on": *LY*, p. 106.

354 "feminine soul": WHA, "Ode to the New Year" (ms poem).

354 "My married life": CI to JL, 12/13/1938.

354 "The Novelist": *The English Auden*, p. 238.

355 "We decided": CI to KI, 12/21/1938.

355 "of a sandwich": *John O'London's Weekly*, 4/7/1939.

355 Waugh: *Spectator*, 3/24/1939.

355 "all too conscious": *JtaW*, 1973 rev. ed., p. 8.

355 "monumental calm": *JtaW*, 1939 ed., p. 120.

355 "Somewhere": *ibid.*, p. 32.

355 "This was our": *ibid.*, p. 34.

356 "We no wan": *ibid.*, p. 35.

356 CI and WHA get-up: *ibid.*, p. 104.

356 "With the tide": *ibid.*, p. 156.

356 *Daily Worker*, 3/29/1939.

356 "shavings": CI to JL, 12/19/1938.

356 JL diary: 1/1/1939.

357 "only my best": CI to JL, 1/2/1939.

357 JL diary: 1/4–5/1939

357 "And how": JL to CI, 1/6/1939.

357 palm-reader: CI to KI, 12/21/1938.

358 "I think Auden": *LY*, p. 93.

358 "destroyed his": *C&HK*, p. 37.

359 Coldstream: quoted Britten, p. 1337.

359 "very bright": *ibid.*

359 "The horrid day": KI diary, 1/18/1939.
359 "M[ummy]": *D1*, p. 4.

Chapter 13
363 "the 'heavenly twins:' " *Evening Standard*, 6/5/1939.
363 Connolly: pp. 143, 86.
363 "Your temptation": *Plays*, p. 327.
363 Auden: quoted Davenport-Hines, p. 177.
364 "dutifully leftist": UCSB lecture [CI 1177].
364 "was able": *C&HK*, p. 247.
364 "One morning": *D1*, p. 6.
364 pacifism: *What Vedanta Means to Me*, p. 6; Plimpton, *Writers at Work*, pp. 217–18.
364 "Both Auden": *D1*, p. 7.
364 "separating himself": *K&F*, p. 508.
365 "Edward [Upward]": *D1*, p. 7.
365 "It is useless": *AtV*, p. 10.
365 Spender: Parker, *The Old Lie*, p. 274.
365 Pears: quoted Carpenter, *Benjamin Britten*, p. 128.
366 "He didn't want": Upward to PP, 7/3/1992.
366 *Daily Express:* 1/19/1939.
366 Hewit: *LY*, p. 92.
366 fn J. Hewit to PP, 7/30/1991.
367 "desperately wanting" *et seq.:* Vernon to PP, 1/10/1994.
367 "I miss": CI to JL, 2/13/1939.
367 "I wrote to": CI to JL, 5/2/1939.
367 "would have to": Vernon to PP, 5/1/1994.
367 Neville-Willing: *D1*, p. 8.
367 "very theatrical": Vernon to PP, 5/1/1994.
367 "very much": CI to JL, 3/8/1939.
368 "It is a little": *D1*, p. 10.
368 "It had": "Scenes from an Emigration" ts, p. 1.
368 "They want": CI to KI, 2/7/1939.
368 "A dollar": *ibid.*
368 "The American market": CI to KI, 2/28/1939.
369 *New Republic*, 5/17/1939.
369 *Nation*, 4/22/1939.
369 "the most utter": CI to JL, 5/2/1939.
369 *Sunday Times*, 3/5/1939; *New Statesman*, 3/11/1939; *Bystander*, 3/8/1939.
369 "a cheap": Auden, *Libretti*, pp. 419–20.
370 "The realistic": Auden, *Prose, 1939–1948*, p. 21.
370 "I still": *What Vedanta Means to Me*, p. 6.

370 "so good": Auden, *Prose, 1939–1948*, p. 23.
370 "Auden was": "Scenes from an Emigration" ts, p. 2.
371 "Wystan is": *D1*, p. 10, 3/18/1939.
371 "more relaxed": Vernon to PP, 2/22/1994.
371 "went into": LK to PP, 11/18/1991.
371 "The afternoon": *D1*, p. 11, 3/18/1939.
372 "In his blue": *ibid.*
372 "LISTEN": LK to CI, 4/18/1949.
372 "the rat" *et seq.: D1*, p. 11, 3/18/1939.
372 "You are quite": CI to KI, 3/26/1939.
373 "I don't wonder": KI to CI, n.d. [Apr. 1939].
373 questions and answers: *D1*, pp. 15–16.
373 Heard parody: CI to LK, 10/15/1949.
374 cat: RI to CI, n.d.
374 "measure the effect": "Scenes from an Emigration," p. 11.
374 "I have told": CI to JL, 5/2/1939.
375 New York: *ibid.*
375 "a certain friction": Vernon to PP, 2/22/1994.
375 "had a clear": Miller, p. 83.
376 "quite willing": Vernon to PP, 6/27/1995.
376 affidavit: Random House Archive.
376 "a twister": CI to JL, 2/13/1939.
376 Los Angeles: Vernon to PP, 2/22/1994; *D1*, p. 20.
377 Wood: *ibid.*, p. 20.
377 "an enormous": "Scenes from an Emigration," p. 10.
377 "lengthy": Vernon to PP, 4/25/1994.
377 "to become a": *MG&HD*, p. 11.
378 "high in heaven": *AtV*, p. 13.
378 "To seek": *VftWW*, p. 1.
378 "intelligently sceptical": *ibid.*, p. 11.
378 "It is to admit" *et seq.: ibid.*, p. 4.
378 "an egotism" *et seq.: ibid.*, p. 5.
379 "this thing": *D1*, p. 26.
379 real and apparent selves: *AtV*, p. 19.
380 "often very homesick": CI to JL, 7/7/1939.
380 "the most Goddamawful": CI to JL, 5/2/1939.
380 "The driving-forces" *et seq.:* CI to JL, 7/7/1939.
381 "it stinks": Viertel, p. 223.
381 "every bit": "Scenes from an Emigration," pp. 42–3.
382 "The more time": *ibid.*, p. 27.
383 "mutating" *et seq.: ibid.*, p. 29.

383 "I have seen": JL to CI, 5/12/1939.
383 "a bloody letter" *et seq.:* CI to JL, 5/28/1939.
383 CI to EMF: 7/3/1939.
384 "in tears": "Scenes from an Emigration," p. 31.
384 "came fussing": EMF to CI, 6/17/1939.
384 CI to EMF: 7/3/1939.
384 fn: J. Hewit to PP, 7/30/91; Britten, p. 742.
385 "I don't know": CI to KI, 7/17/1939.
385 KI on Hewit: KI diary, 7/27/1939.
385 "the ground": CI to JL, 7/7/1939.
385 "Outwardly": *AtV*, p. 25.
385 Prabhavananda: *MG&HD*, pp. 30–3.
386 "I felt terribly" *et seq.:* *AtV*, p. 26.
386 tenets: *VftWW*, p. 1.
386 instructions: *AtV*, pp. 26–7.
387 "the *immediate"* : CI to KI, 8/8/1939.
387 "You go": *ibid.*
387 "bitter letter": *Spectator*, 1/18/86, p. 17.
387 "What I wrote": CI to EU, 8/6/1939.
389 "a model": *D1*, p. 7.

Chapter 14

390 "All through": CI to KI, 9/5/1939.
391 "a kind of testament": JL diary, 9/6/1939.
391 CI's reply: 9/27/1939.
391 "to be sinking": JL diary, 10/20/1939.
391 "the only person": *ibid.*, 12/12/1939.
391 "the Yoga" *et seq.:* *ibid.*, 10/20/1939.
391 "feel all": *ibid.*, 10/27/1939.
392 The Canyon: *E*, p. 163.
392 "armchair generals": CI to KI, 10/15/1939.
392 "The refugees": *D1*, p. 55.
392 "I wish we were": CI to KI, 10/15/1939.
392 "A great joy": KI diary, 11/11/1939.
393 "melodramatic" *et seq.:* CI to Guy Trosper, 12/11/1939 [CI 133].
394 Rooney: CI to JL, 7/7/1939.
394 picnic and Garbo: CI to KI, 11/27/1939.
395 A. Huxley: CI to JL, 7/7/1939.
395 J. Huxley: *D1*, pp. 57–8.
395 Tree: *ibid.*, p. 345.
395 J. Huxley: *ibid.*, p. 58.
395 "if I had really": "Scenes from an Emigration," p. 52.
396 Vernon on relationship: to PP, 4/25/1994.
396 "in a coma": *D1*, p. 46.
397 verse: *New Statesman*, 2/17/1940.

397 "Why does this" *et seq.: D1*, p. 83.
398 CI to J. Stern: 11/13/1939.
398 "impossible to have": JL diary, 10/13/1939, quoted A. Wright, p. 101.
398 "I feel very alone": *ibid.*, 12/27/1939.
398 "It makes me": CI to JL, 1/11/1940.
399 *Evening Standard*, 6/5/1939.
399 "certainly very": CI to KI, 7/8/1939.
399 Connolly: *Horizon*, Vol. 1, No. 2, pp. 68–70.
400 CI to SS: 1/10/1940.
400 SS to CI: 1/30/1940.
401 CI to SS: 2/17/1940.
402 "not in any way" *et seq.:* SS to CI, 3/6/1940.
403 fn 1: SS to CI, 3/7/1935.
404 EMF to CI: 4/21/1940 [CI 825].
404 "But how could" *et seq.:* JL to CI, 2/12/1940.
404 "Theoretically": *D1*, p. 72.
405 CI on P. Rodakiewicz: *D1*, p. 33.
405 "still feeling": *ibid.*, pp. 92–3.
406 Vernon: to PP, 4/25/1994.
406 "It is strange": CI to JL, 4/16/1940.
406 Nicolson: *Spectator*, 4/19/1940.
407 "that flabby": KI diary, 4/22/1940.
407 *Daily Mail*, 4/27/1940.
407 *Daily Mirror*, 8/15/1940.
407 fn: *The English Auden*, p. 59.
408 W.R.M.: *Spectator*, 6/21/1940.
408 Spender: *Spectator*, 4/26/1930.
408 Desborough: *Spectator*, 5/31/1940.
408 Bellerby: *Spectator*, 6/28/1940.
408 "not what was wanted": JL diary, 5/1/1940.
408 EMF letter: *Spectator*, 7/5/1940.
409 "all this stupid": JL diary, 5/1/1940.
409 "scarcely any": Forster, *Selected Letters*, p. 209.
409 "One would think": KI diary, 6/9/1940.
410 "your position": *D1*, p. 56.
410 "because, at the time": *ibid.*, p. 55.
410 CI and Barkers: Sullivan, p. 149.
411 "I came away": *D1*, p. 102.
411 "treat him": *ibid.*
411 "poor old": KI diary, 5/7/1940.
411 "I expect": *ibid.*, 5/9/1940.
411 "I am surprised": *ibid.*, 5/11/1940.
412 "I always half": *D1*, p. 103, 7/12/1940.
412 "It's his": *ibid.*
412 Spender: to PP, 7/22/1993.
412 T. Bradshaw-Isherwood: to PP, 10/29/1993.

413 "neophyte": RI to CI, 4/23/1965.
414 "The idea of": KI diary, 7/13/1940.
414 "not very friendly": KI diary, 7/25/1940.
414 Jack on CI and RI: T. Bradshaw-
Isherwood to PP, 10/29/1993.
415 *A Woman's Face:* CI to JL, 9/16/1940.
415 "wife and": WHA to Minna Curtis, n.d.
415 "It has been": *DI*, p. 116.
415 "No one can be": *ibid.*, p. 115.
416 "both too much": *ibid.*, p. 116.
416 instructions: *ibid.*, pp. 116–17.
416 "stop hating": CI to EMF, 4/29/1939.
416 Kirstein: to PP, 11/18/1991.
417 "My chief effort": *DI*, p. 119, 8/18/1939.
417 "Once again": *ibid.*, p. 120, 8/4/1940.
417 "the most expensive": *DToaV*, p. 210.
418 Wescott: to CI, 12/25/1948.
418 Fouts's physique: Wishart, p. 50.
418 Kirstein: to PP, 11./18/1991.
418 Wescott and CI: Wescott, p. 211; *DToaV*,
p. 210; Wescott to CI: 12/25/1948.
418 "There is no longer": *DI*, p. 122,
10/26/1940.
418 "I was thinking" *et seq.*: *ibid.*, p. 123.
419 Kirstein: to PP, 11/18/1991.
419 "I would never": *CwCI*, p. 56.
419 "After I got": *E*, p. 97.
419 "I believe": *DI*, p. 729, 9/29/1957.
420 "According to": *MG&HD*, pp. 66–7.
420 "a sort of": *CwCI*, p. 56.
420 "agreed that": *DI*, p. 126, 11/8/1940.

Chapter 15
421 "The more you": *DI*, p. 127, 11/13/1940.
421 "a small": *ibid.*, p. 126, 11/12/1940.
421 "symbolic visions": *ibid.*, p. 127,
11/13/1940.
421 "Oh, my goodness": CI to JL,
12/26/1940.
422 "At first": *DI*, p. 134.
422 "all sex": *ibid.*, p. 127, 11/13/1940.
422 *MG&HD:* p. 25.
423 "I really must": *DI*, p. 132.
423 "quite amicably": CI to EMF, 2/14/1941.
423 Amiya: *DI*, p. 302, 7/7/1943.
424 "religious bohemianism" *et seq.*: *DI*,
p. 151.
424 Auden: "Writing As a Way of Life"
(UCLA lecture) [CI 1186].
425 "And all day" *et seq.*: *DI*, p. 156.

426 "It's no use": CI to JL, 10/31/1940.
426 "I couldn't count": CI to JL, 6/24/1941.
426 "half-a-dozen": *E*, p. 134.
426 "One writes": CI to JL, 5/9/1942.
426 Spender: JL diary, 3/19/1941.
426 "the yawning": *ibid.*, 2/15/1941.
427 "I was very": CI to JL, 5/9/1942.
427 "Denny was": *DI*, p. 171.
427 "have Denny": *ibid.*, p. 155.
427 "In all these": *Penguin New Writing 14*,
p. 13.
428 "The atmosphere" *et seq.*: *DI*, p. 181.
428 "In every other": *ibid.*, p. 181.
428 "I feel quite happy": WHA to SS,
1/16/1942.
429 "No matter": *DI*, p. 182.
429 caretakers: KI diary, 9/18/1939.
429 "I was afraid": RI to CI, n.d. [Nov. 1970].
429 "It all seems": KI diary, 8/2/1941.
429 Nanny: *ibid.*, 9/15/1941.
430 Elizabeth: *ibid.*, 10/3/41; 10/8/1941.
430 "going to make": *ibid.*, 10/18/1941.
430 "Poor Elizabeth's": RI to CI, 8/10/1970.
430 "people may": KI diary, 10/29/1941.
430 "They take": *ibid.*, 11/6/1941.
430 "very upset": *ibid.*, 3/22/1941.
430 "said she had never": *ibid.*, 6/22/1942.
431 "I simply cannot": RI to CI, 8/7/1960.
431 "a sort of invisible": *DI*, p. 185.
432 "Let me recognize": *ibid.*, p. 186.
432 "Like all hysterics": *ibid.*, p. 194.
432 "could have run": *ibid.*, p. 195.
432 "colder than": to LK, 1/19/1942.
432 "the raw misery": *DI*, p. 209, 2/8/1942.
433 Cadmus: *ibid.*, pp. 209–10, 2/4/1942.
433 "sadder and sadder": *ibid.*, p. 206,
1/16/1942.
433 Crabbe: *The Listener*, 5/29/1941.
433 "in a flash": Britten, p. 962.
433 "I have thought": CI to Britten, 2/18/1942.
434 "I can't pretend": Britten to CI,
3/10/1942.
434 "Later we": *DI*, p. 209, 2/13/1942.
434 "I've never": *ibid.*, p. 216, 3/21/1942.
434 "They would": *ibid.*, pp. 216–17,
4/5/1942.
434 "greyer" *et seq.*: *ibid.*, p. 216, 4/4/1942.
434 "Now I can": *ibid.*, p. 217, 4/22/1942.
435 "doesn't make": *ibid.*, p. 218, 4/22/1942.
435 "a potboiler": *ibid.*, p. 230, 7/30/1942.
435 "I have an idea": *E*, p. 230.

435 "You notice": *ibid.*, p. 231.
435 "practically my best": CI to SS, 4/12/1942.
435 "fair curly": *DI*, p. 224, 5/15/1942.
436 "no draft board": *ibid.*, p. 228, 6/17/1942.
436 medical: *ibid.*, p. 230, 6/30/1942.
436 Trabuco: "Trabuco" article [CI 1140].
436 "When Steere": *DI*, p. 217, 4/7/1942.
437 "had better be" *et seq.:* CI 1140.
437 "I wanted": *DI*, p. 238.
438 "Woman's play": Grove, p. 79.
439 "I did not realise": *ibid.*, p. 114.
439 CI on Beesleys: *DI*, pp. 258–9, 11/29/1942.
439 Smith on CI: DS diary, 12/21/1942.
439 "Sometimes": CI to LK: 1/19/1942.
440 "It's very odd": *DI*, p. 261, 12/30/1942.
440 Smith: DS diary, 12/21/1942.
440 "want to kid": *DI*, p. 261. 12/30/1942.
440 Smith: DS diary, 1/24/1943.
440 fn: *AtV*, p. 55.

Chapter 16
441 "glamorous final": *DI*, p. 263, 1/29/1943.
441 "I am not going": *ibid.*, p. 266, 2/3/1943.
442 Sudhira: *ibid.*, p. 269.
442 "quite skittishly": DS diary, 2/14/1943.
443 "I'm still" *et seq.: DI*, p. 272, 2/26/1943.
443 "Tried to": *ibid.*, p. 276, 3/26/1943.
443 *Bhagavad-Gita: AtV*, pp. 51, 58.
443 "the meaning of": *E*, p. 98.
444 *dharma: R&HD*, p. 7.
444 "All mankind": *ibid.*, p. 8.
444 "I observe": lecture notes for U.C. Riverside, 1961 [CI 1070].
444 "the way that leads" *et seq.: PV*, p. 126.
444 "He'd write": Thomas Bradshaw-Isherwood to PP, 10/29/1993.
444 "He is the most": CI to LK, 3/29/1943.
444 "If you want": *ibid.*
445 "Harold [Nicolson]": LK to CI, 9/18/1944.
445 "square, plump": *DI*, p. 268.
445 "the usual": *ibid.*, p. 276, 3/26/1943.
445 poem: *E*, p. 8.
445 fn: Waugh, p. 39.
446 "For those": *ibid.*, p. 5.
446 "eminent writers": advertising circular, November 1960.
446 "the most famous" *et seq.: VftWW*, p. 268.

447 "You can picture": *ibid.*, p. 270.
447 "The blackness": *ibid.*, p. 272.
447 "Swami didn't": *MG&HD*, p. 125.
447 "Right now": *DI*, p. 293, 5/22/1943.
448 "much better": *ibid.*, p. 298, 6/21/1943.
448 "sailors on leave": *ibid.*
448 "We had": *ibid.*, p. 305, 7/19/1943.
448 "Suppose Swami's": *ibid.*
448 Vishwananda: *ibid.*, p. 308, 7/27/1943.
449 "He found something": *C&HK*, p. 58.
449 "India is": *DI*, p. 309, 8/10/1943.
449 "If I am": *ibid.*, p. 308, 8/6/1943.
450 "You caught": CI to Cadmus, 4/13/1943.
450 Bruce: quoted A. Beesley to CI, 3/15/1947.
450 CI to Windham: 3/17/1943.
450 "from sexual": *DI*, p. 303, 7/16/1943.
450 "I'm at": *ibid.*, p. 306, 7/23/1943.
450 "six months" *et seq.: ibid.*, p. 308.
450 "a few days": *ibid.*, p. 311, 8/17/1943.
450 CI to Windham: 5/13/1943.
451 CI to LK: 7/15/1943.
451 "encountered under": Williams to CI, n.d. [June 1943].
451 "Somehow or other": *ibid.*
451 "British": CI to Williams, 6/10/1943.
452 "Tho I 'like:' " CI to LK, 7/15/1943.
452 "a very squalid": *DI*, p. 311, 8/18/1943.
452 "since he visited": Windham, *Tennessee Williams' Letters*, p. 121.
452 "What are we going": CI to Williams, 6/10/1943.
452 "a flirtation": *MG&HD*, p. 138.
452 "I did so": *ibid.*
452 confession to Swami: *DI*, p. 313, 8/31/1943.
452 "within this": *ibid.*, p. 314, 9/1/1943.
452 Fouts: *ibid.*, p. 316, 9/15/1943.
453 "young man's": *MG&HD*, p. 137.
453 CI to Cadmus: 9/29/1943.
453 "I'm just": *DI*, p. 320, 9/22/1943.
453 "I realized": *MG&HD*, p. 143.
453 "I felt like": *DI*, pp. 321–2, 9/24/1943.
453 Prabhavananda: *ibid.*, p. 321, 9/24/1943.
454 "never realized": *ibid.*, p. 323, 10/1/1943.
454 San Francisco: *ibid.*, pp. 323–4, 10/2/1943.
454 "Prabhavananda": *ibid.*, pp. 327–8, 10/15/1943; p. 325, 10/9/1943.
454 "Let's hope": Dunaway, p. 190.
455 "It's easy enough" *et seq.: JH*, pp. 121–2.

455 Huxley: quoted *ibid.*, p. ix.
455 "universal rejection": Huxley to CI, 7/28/1944.
456 "The fiction writer": *MG&HD*, p. 125.
456 "Gradually, gradually": *D1*, p. 337, 3/27/1944.
456 "Why do you": *ibid.*, p. 343, 4/13/1944.
456 "as far as": *ibid.*, p. 336.
456 "to be overcome": *LY*, p. 6.
456 "was particularly" *et seq.*: *D1*, p. 336.
457 "I need": CI to Cadmus, 6/10/1944.
457 "To have to": *D1*, p. 345, 5/14/1944.
457 "deliberately played": *ibid.*, p. 362, 8/31/1943.
457 "I need him": *ibid.*, p. 347, 6/7/1943.
458 "This worked": *ibid.*, p. 350, 7/15/1943.
458 "Sometimes I almost": *ibid.*, p. 358, 8/6/1943.
458 "would mean": *PV*, p. 126.
458 "to relax": *C&HK*, p. 10.
458 "sexual colonialism": *CwCI*, p. 144.
458 "I want you" *et seq.*: *D1*, p. 352, 6/30/1944.
459 "there weren't any" *et seq.*: *ibid.*, p. 353, 7/8/1944.
459 "ephemeral": Styan, p. 99.
460 "an essentially": *JH*, p. xvii.
460 "had a jolly": *D1*, p. 331, 1/3/1944.
460 *The Miracle*: *JH*, pp. xviii–xxiv.
460 Connolly: Orwell, p. 135; Spender *The Thirties and After*, p. 89; Orwell, p. 131; *D1*, p. 365.
461 "He sniffs": *D1*, p. 140, 1/10/1944.
461 "Where Shall John Go": *Horizon* Vol. 9, No. 49, pp. 19, 20, 21.
461 CI to Connolly: *D1*, pp. 365–7.
462 "inviolable," "A fatherly": *Penguin New Writing 21*, p. 137.
462 "Christopher Isherwood": *ibid.*, p. 138.
463 "what nine years": *ibid.*, pp. 139–40.
463 *"Of course"*: CI to JL, 11/15/1944.
464 "crossing the name": WHA to CI, "Friday morning" [Apr. 1945].
464 "a bit bothered" *et seq.*: CI to JL, 11/15/1944.
464 "certain profound" *et seq.*: LK to CI, n.d. [?Dec. 1944].
464 "I think he was": CI to LK, 12/18/1944.
464 "It's difficult": *D1*, pp. 359–60, 8/28/1944.
465 "So now": *ibid.*, p. 360.
465 *Prater Violet*: *ibid.*, p. 356, 7/27/1944.

465 Smith: *ibid.*, 7/30/1944.
465 "The other": *ibid.*, p. 374, 10/10/1944.
465 "The Vernon": *ibid.*, p. 375, 11/11/1944.
466 Viertel letter: to CI, 26.10.1944. [CI 2638].
467 "heartless" *et seq.*: quoted Viertel to CI, 11/8/1944.
467 "There is no": *ibid.*
467 "With or without": *D1*, p. 375, 10/19/1944.
467 "I don't know": *ibid.*, pp. 352–3, 7/4/1944.
467 "fantastic": *ibid.*
467 "She's got": *ibid.*, p. 375, 11/7/1944.
467 "little boys": DS to CI, 12/27/1948.
467 "I've got": *D1*, p. 376, 11/25/1944.
467 "Sure, I ought": *ibid.*, p. 379.

Chapter 17
469 *Time*: *MG&HD*, p. 182.
470 "At the moment": CI to Cadmus, 3/30/1945.
470 "a department-store": *LY*, p. 32.
471 "a nice, gentle": DS diary, 9/22/1945.
471 "He cannot": *LY*, p. 13.
472 "I simply" *et seq.*: CI to Cadmus, 8/2/1945; 8/28/1945.
472 "demi-monk": *MG&HD*, p. 187.
472 "I don't remember": *LY*, p. 45.
472 "When I did": *MG&HD*, p. 189.
472 "bitchily": *LY*, pp. 45–6.
472 "If the question": *D1*, p. 261, 12/30/1942.
473 memorandum: CI 877.
474 charts: DS diary, 1/3/1946; *LY*, p. 51.
474 fn: CI to Cerf, 4/4/1946.
474 "a tragic Punch": *PV*, p. 16.
474 "I knew that": *ibid.*, p. 17.
474 "The picture!": *ibid.*, p. 96.
475 "For this picture": *ibid.*, p. 118.
475 opening: *ibid.*, p. 3.
475 "set up": *ibid.*, p. 8.
476 "symbolic fable" *et seq.*: *ibid.*, pp. 50–1.
476 "Shakespeare would": *ibid.*, p. 35.
476 "You knew": *ibid.*, p. 111.
476 "My one": *ibid.*, p. 109.
477 "It is that hour": *ibid.*, p. 122.
477 "K. and L.": *ibid.*, p. 125.
477 "And, at this moment": *ibid.*, p. 126.
477 "Dearest Christopher": Viertel to CI, 11/23/1945.
478 "staggered": DS diary, 1/13/1946.

478 "I'd like": CI to LK, "Monday 26th"
[?1943].

478 *Time:* LY, p. 48; *Nation,* 11/17/1945.

478 Smith: DS diary, 7/13/1946.

478 Strachey: *Horizon,* Vol. 14, No. 79,
pp. 60–4.

479 "the coldness": CI to EU, 5/20/1955.

479 "the whole period": *LY,* p. 49.

479 "at work": CI to B. Cerf, 1/7/1946.

479 "funny and yet": CI to KI, 2/21/1946.

479 "a rather tricky": CI to DS, 4/7/1947.

479 "One can't help": *DI,* p. 214, 3/1/1942.

479 fn: Partridge, p. 152.

480 "lacked a myth": *LY,* p. 60.

480 "I doubt": *LY,* p. 61.

480 "to some extent" *et seq.: ibid.,* p. 55.

480 Caskey on religion: BC to J. Fryer,
10/3/1979.

481 "conflict of wills": *LY,* p. 50.

482 "ritual penalty": *ibid.,* p. 61.

482 "a Triton": *LY,* p. 280.

482 "laughed out loud": Anon to PP, 9/5/2002.

483 "American authors" *et seq.:* DS diary,
9/21/1946.

483 "They will all": CI to LK, 3/29/1945.

484 "He insists" *et seq.:* DS diary, 12/30/1946.

484 "It was always": *LY,* p. 73.

484 Smith: DS diary, 7/13/46; 9/19/1946.

484 fn: JL diary, 5/6/1945.

485 "He wants": *ibid.,* 3/16/1946.

485 "In order": CI to KI, 11/13/1946.

485 "would have melted": CI to KI, 11/28/1946.

486 "so absurdly": *E,* p. 154.

486 "Looking around me": *ibid.*

487 "I don't picture": CI to RI, 12/5/1942.

487 "idiots and maniacs": *IJ,* p. 16.

487 "staring and grimacing" *et seq.: LY,* p. 87.

487 Nanny: CI to WP, 1/27/1947.

487 "Oh God": CI to JL, 1/27/1947.

488 "There is so much": KI diary, 1/26/1947.

488 Kathleen: *LY,* p. 69.

488 "full of": KI diary, 2/3/1947.

488 "Thought maybe" *et seq.:* CI to LK,
2/23/1947.

489 "those great neutrals": JL diary,
3/19/1941.

489 "showed the least": *LY,* p. 84.

489 "lost awareness": *ibid.,* p. 101.

490 "Writing has begun": EU to CI,
3/23/1947.

490 "personal relations": Scott-Kilvert to CI,
4/22/1942.

490 Scott-Kilvert reunion: *LY,* pp. 106–7.

490 Hewit: *ibid.,* pp. 94, 99.

490 "a wasp-waist": *ibid.,* p. 101.

491 "Symonds": *ibid.,* p. 111.

491 "R had been": KI diary, 3/24/1947.

491 "Sad that": *ibid.,* 1/28/1947.

492 "start thinking": notebook [CI 1158].

492 "Such people": *DI,* p. 229, 6/24/1942.

492 "too funny" *et seq.:* CI 1158, 4/4/1947.

492 "Too Queer": CI to LK, 4/19/1946.

492 "that boring": CI 1158.

493 "felt himself": *LY,* p. 117.

493 "Jimmy's apartment": CI to JL,
4/28/1947.

493 "filthy" *et seq.:* CI to J. Stern, 4/2/1947.

493 "an enormous": CI to D, 5/14/1947.

493 "Just bulldozer": *ibid.*

493 "My novel": CI to EU, 7/8/1947.

494 "My real trouble": CI to EU, 7/30/1947.

494 New York parties: *LY,* p. 123.

495 "the boy genius": CI to J. Stern, 7/9/1947.

495 Capote: quoted Clarke, p. 146.

495 photos: CI to Cadmus, 7/27/1947.

495 Kirstein: *LY,* pp. 129–30.

Chapter 18

496 "Coming into": Diary of a Trip to South
America, 1947–48 [CI 2752], 9/24/1947.

496 "S. America": CI to LK, 11/20/1947.

497 "llama-land" *et seq.:* CI to LK, 1/8/1948.

497 "foreign observer": *TC&tC,* p. 188.

497 "How time": CI 2752, 3/23/1948.

498 "like coming": *TC&tC,* p. 182.

498 "Glancing through": CI 2752.

498 "working or even": *DI,* p. 396, 4/11/1948.

499 "a completely ordinary": Vidal, *The City
and the Pillar,* p. 158.

499 "better than many": CI to LK, 12/17/1947.

499 "a welcome change": CI to LK, 1/8/1948.

499 CI to Vidal: 12/19/1947 [*TLS,*
12/20/1996].

501 "Paris . . .": CI to LK, 4/29/1948.

501 "a pretty shrewd": *DI,* p. 401, 4/27/1948.

501 "a big wide-open": CI to LK, 6/2/1948.

501 "betray the fact": *LY,* p. 142.

501 "very funny": *DI,* p. 402, 4/28/1948.

501 "and suddenly": *ibid.*

501 Vaughan: Vaughan, p. 97.

501 Nanny: KI diary, 11/12/1948.

502 "The site": *ibid.,* 1/7/1948.

502 "worked himself": *LY,* p. 144.

502 "I know": RI to CI, 7/4/1943.

502 "quiet &": KI diary, 5/18/1948.

503 "I wished" et seq.: ibid., 6/6/1948.

503 "casually told": LY, p. 146.

503 Viertel: ibid., p. 148.

503 Vidal: see Palimpsest, p. 190.

504 "Caskey got" et seq.: LY, p. 146.

504 "Last night": LK to CI, 11/28/1949.

504 working methods: DB to PP, 12/16/2001.

504 fn: LY, p. 148.

505 "It always gives": KI diary, 7/5/1948.

505 "a model employee": LY, p. 152.

505 Wright on Charlton: "A Life" ts by Charlton.

505 "I had only": Charlton to PP, 2/12/1993.

506 analyst: Charlton to PP, 3/12/1993.

506 "a cowboy's": "A Life."

506 "Tan-Faced": LY, p. 159.

506 "talking romantically": ibid., p. 157.

506 "too wholesome": ibid., p. 159.

506 "violently in love": ibid.

506 "You must be": "A Life."

506 "Who's She?": Charlton to PP, 2/17/1993.

507 "one of the happiest": D1, p. 406.

507 "Chris's boyfriend": Charlton to PP, 2/17/1993.

507 "The truth is": D1, p. 407, 11/6/1948.

507 "the breaking": LY, p. 163.

508 "Sometimes I ask": D1, p. 407, 11/6/1948.

508 "unpleasant psychic": LY, p. 183.

508 "unspeakably evil": ibid., p. 186.

509 "You son": ibid., p. 185.

509 "both something": ibid., p. 187.

509 "It rather scares": D1, p. 409, 3/1/1949.

509 Tropic Village: CI to LK, 4/14/1949; BC to LK, n.d. [?May 1949].

509 "He absolutely": D1, p. 411, 3/3/1949.

510 White: to CI, 2/26/1949.

510 "Leaving Caskey": D1, p. 411, 5/22/1949.

510 Dog people: ibid., p. 416, 11/18/1949.

511 CI to LK: 10/15/1949.

511 "written out": D1, p. 414, 8/17/1949.

511 Green: to CI, 2/8/1949.

511 "I'll be working": CI to JL, 5/1/1943.

511 "I've got": CI 1157.

511 "nosing": CI to EU, 6/14/1949.

512 "The novel": D1, p. 415.

512 "undented": ibid., p. 418, 12/6/1949.

512 "Stuck": ibid., 12/13/1949.

512 "most of": CI to WP, 10/11/1949.

512 "a Riviera girl": CI to EU, 8/20/1947.

512 "I put it off": D1, p. 419, 12/14/1949.

512 Wescott: Wescott, p. 228.

513 "cute": LY, p. 203.

513 Craft: Craft, p. 26.

514 "My affection" et seq.: LY, p. 201.

514 "a fatal" et seq.: Plimpton, Writers at Work 4, pp. 231–2.

514 "cuddly": LY, p. 201.

514 "the most fun" et seq.: CI to SS, 3/27/1951.

514 "as if he were": Libman, p. 291.

514 "an outstanding specimen": LY, p. 202.

515 Leopold: ibid., p. 220.

515 CI to LK: 3/28/1950.

515 "Some ideas": D1, p. 420, 1/2/1950.

515 "No money": CI to LK, 3/28/1950.

516 "moving in perfect": LY, p. 231.

516 "way out": D1, p. 425, 6/30/1950.

516 plots: ibid.

516 "has somehow shown": ibid., p. 429, 8/19/1950.

516 Sylvia: E, pp. 32–3.

517 "Christopher is" et seq.: ibid., pp. 35–6.

517 "utter nonsense": CI 1158, 7/9/1950.

517 Connolly: quoted LY, p. 275.

518 "The degree" et seq.: CI 1158, 7/9/1950.

518 "prime example": DB to PP, 11/1/1994.

519 "I hope": CI to LK, 3/25/1952.

519 "The Ballet": TWitE, p. 125.

519 Kennedy: ibid., p. 65.

519 "flattered that": LK to CI, n.d. [May 1952].

519 "the misery": D1, p. 428, 8/13/1950.

519 "The real": ibid., p. 14.

519 "Not his": CwCI, p. 147.

519 "brute subjectivity" et seq.: ibid., p. 93.

520 "amused and pleased": LY, p. 249.

520 "The utter": D1, p. 418, 12/6/1949.

520 CI to LK: 10/19/1950.

521 "martyred forbearance": LY, p. 257.

521 Kolisch: ibid., p. 272.

521 "In the past": CI to EU, 12/5/1950.

521 "pseudo-consumption": EU to CI, 11/20/1950.

521 Kolisch: LY, p. 272.

Chapter 19

522 "third-rate": D1, p. 433, 12/11/1950.

522 "I know that" et seq.: ibid.

523 "I am feeling": CI to EU, 12/5/1950.

523 "this horrible": CI 1158, 3/28/1951.

523 CI to DS: 3/28/1951.

523 "like characters": Gavin Lambert to PP, 5/17/1996.

524 "Why don't" *et seq.:* Smith, p. 158.

524 van Druten: to CI and DS, 6/6/1951.

525 "with grace": Smith, p. 159.

525 "solitude" *et seq.: D1,* p. 435, 5/6/1951.

525 "a working rule": CI 1158, 3/28/1951.

525 "Nobody had" *et seq.: LY,* p. 284.

526 "It is such": CI 1158, 7/17/1951.

526 Lamphere: Costello, p. 288.

526 FBI interview: FBI file NY105–3246.

527 "ill-health": Costello, pp. 292–3.

527 Second FBI interview: FBI file WFO 65–4648CI.

529 "The house": BC to CI, 10/24/1951 [CI 668].

529 "Author Meets": unidentified clipping, n.d.

529 Craft: *TLS,* 8/18/2000, p. 13.

530 Plomer: to CI, 3/10/1954.

530 "always longing": RI to CI, n.d. [Nov. 1970].

530 "Feels so lonely": KI diary, 2/25/1950.

530 "Drizzly" *et seq.: ibid.,* 4/18/1950.

531 "I am more": CI to Amiya, 9/5/1953.

532 karma: *A Brief Dictionary,* p. 41.

532 "I am like": RI to CI, 7/4/1943.

533 "There isn't much": CI to Amiya, 9/5/1953.

533 "gradual disintegration" *et seq.:* Amiya to RI, 9/4/1953.

533 "humility my guide": EMF to CI, 1/14/1952.

533 "I'm afraid": EMF to CI, 1/18/1952.

533 "What I would like": EMF to CI, 11/15/1952.

534 "a highly characteristic": Lehmann, *Christopher Isherwood,* p. 82.

534 "It is one thing" *et seq.: Observer,* 3/23/1952.

535 HN card: CI 1870.

535 "It is wonderful": CI to KI, 7/11/1946.

535 "it was just": CI to KI, 9/1/1946.

535 " 'I don't know' ": *DToaV,* p. 244.

536 "dullness and jitters" *et seq.:* CI to LK, 3/31/1952.

536 "something I still" *et seq.: D1,* pp. 442–3, 3/4/1952.

536 "emotionally appealing": T. Wright to PP, 7/16/1994.

536 "Today we cycled" *et seq.: D1,* pp. 443–4, 3/20/1952.

537 "I move blindly": *ibid.,* p. 445, 3/24/1952.

537 "sometimes so sweet": *ibid.,* p. 449, 5/25/1952.

537 "I am absolutely": CI to LK, 5/25/1952.

537 "tacky but clean": *D1,* p. 448, 5/25/1952.

538 "tacit approval" *et seq.:* T. Wright to PP, 7/15/1994.

538 "wonderfully indifferent": *D1,* p. 450, 6/8/1952.

538 "It's the witch's" *et seq.:* CI to SS, 11/11/1952.

538 "It deals": CI to SS, 2/13/1953.

538 "it was a hard": *D1,* p. 453, 1/27/1953.

538 "After an examen": CI to EU, 1/29/1953.

538 "the crudest *et seq.: D1,* p. 453, 1/27/1953.

539 "I left": CI to LK, 2/11/1953.

539 "Ted Baccardi": *D1,* p. 417, 11/18/1949.

539 "Ted and I" *et seq.:* DB to PP, 2/19/1995.

Chapter 20

540 "faux-brutal": CI to SS, 2/13/1953.

541 "In her innocent": DB to PP, 2/19/1995.

541 "And his little": *D1,* p. 454, 3/6/1953.

541 "sinking-sick": *ibid.,* p. 455, 4/20/1953.

541 "rare experiences": *ibid.,* p. 454, 3/6/1953.

541 "I'd never met": DB to PP, 2/19/1995.

541 "the *va et vient" :* Evelyn Hooker to PP, 2/21/1993.

542 "No ill will": CI to SS, 7/22/1954.

542 "twins": CI to EU, 12/5/1950.

542 "I had staked": EU to CI, 2/4/1953.

542 "The strain": CI to H. Upward, 3/12/1953.

542 "still the judge": *AtC,* p. 9.

542 "My novel": CI to EU, 1/29/1953.

543 "—or not": CI to EU, 8/31/1953.

543 Smith: DS diary, 10/5/1953.

543 "We both think": DS to CI, 8/14/1953.

544 Beesley on *TWitE:* to CI, 8/16/1953.

544 "It is destroying": DS diary, 10/5/1953.

544 "forced to say": *LY,* p. 176.

544 "Last night": CI to EU, 8/31/1953.

544 "I'm curious": CI to R. Linscott, 8/23/1953.

544 "Forgive my tardiness": Linscott to CI, 9/17/1953 [CI 1665].

545 "most of the book": CI to Linscott, 9/21/1953.

545 "it's the tone": Linscott to CI, 9/24/1953.

545 "quite a number" *et seq.:* CI to Linscott, 10/6/1953.

546 "was a huge": *D1*, p. 464, 1/12/1954.
546 "I want you": Leddick, p. 257.
546 "He was infatuated": DB to PP, 11/16/2002.
546 "a more intentional": *D1*, p. 464, 1/12/1954.
547 list of reports: CI 1316.
547 "As I explained": *ibid.*
547 "having consented": CI diary, 9/7/1969.
548 "Everything is": *D1*, p. 467, 9/9/1954.
548 "I had really": DB to PP, 2/19/1995.
548 "how a myth": *LY*, p. 60.
549 "I'll try": CI diary, 3/19/71.
549 Heard: *D1*, p. 469, 10/23/1954.
549 "Slowly, slowly": *ibid.*, 11/2/1954.
549 "It is terribly": CI to EU, 8/31/1953.
550 reviews: *Lady*, 6/24/1954; *Daily Mail*, 6/18/1954; *Encounter*, Aug. 1954.
550 "I have lots": CI to SS, 7/22/1954.
550 Gunn: to PP, 4/29/1994.
550 "cleverest and worst": notes for "The Autobiography of My Books" [CI 1018].
550 "not nearly": UCLA lecture, 5/18/1965 [CI 1089].
550 *Observer*, 6/20/1954.
550 *Punch*, 6/23/1954.
550 "just don't seem": EU to CI, 7/31/1954.
551 "Its defect": SS to CI, 6/9/1954.
551 "I believe": CI to SS, 7/22/1954.
551 "I can't write": notes for "Autobiography of My Books" [CI 1019].
551 Searle: *Punch*, 3/24/1954.
551 "My besetting": *D1*, p. 467, 9/9/1954.
551 Connolly: Orwell, p. 135.
551 "I had to break": CI to EU, 9/16/1954.
552 "glimpsed an idea": *D1*, p. 475, 12/16/1954.
552 "The novel": *ibid.*, p. 476, 1/13/1955.
552 Gunn: to PP, 4/29/1994.
552 "Last night": *D1*, p. 495, 5/6/1955.
553 "a nistorical": CI to LK, 1/26/1954.
553 "MetroGoldwynMire": *ibid.*
553 "Lana can": *WJR*, p. ix.
553 "made the dialogue": *D1*, p. 408, 11/7/1948.
553 "I'm afraid": *ibid.*, p. 499, 5/18/1955.
553 "amateurs": *ibid.*, p. 535, 10/1/1955.
553 "disgusted": *ibid.*, p. 494, 5/2/1955.
553 "I steal": CI to WP, 4/24/1954.
554 "a hideous": *D1*, p. 586, 2/25/1956.
554 Smith: DS diary, 2/18/1956.
554 "wordy": *D1*, p. 562, 12/30/1955.

554 "When the great": *ibid.*, p. 537, 10/20/1955.
554 "it would undoubtedly": *ibid.*, p. 519, 8/6/1955.
555 "I was aware": *ibid.*, p. 542, 10/30/1955.
555 "I saw that": *ibid.*, p. 544.
555 "Actually, it couldn't" *et seq.*: *ibid.*, p. 564, 1/10/1956.
556 "He is too": *ibid.*, p. 566, 1/16/1956.
556 "I'm alarmed": *ibid.*, p. 567, 1/20/1956.
556 "Don looks": DS diary, 1/31/1956.
556 "It was truly": *D1*, p. 567, 1/25/1956.
556 "I seem to have": CI to SS, 2/13/1953.
556 "a very happy" *et seq.*: *D1*, p. 581, 2/12/1956.
557 "alone to his": *ibid.*, p. 567, 1/20/1956.
557 "feel more": *ibid.*, p. 570, 2/1/1956.
557 "reopening": *ibid.*, p. 562, 1/5/1956.
557 "Stooped over": *ibid.*, p. 570, 2/1/1956.
557 "I arrived" *et seq.*: *ibid.*, pp. 570–1.
557 "Small or large?": A. Bradley to PP, 9/30/1995.
558 "some weird" *et seq.*: *D1*, p. 571, 2/2/1956.
559 "faint echo": *ibid.*, p. 576, 2/5/1956.
559 "as though": *ibid.*, p. 572, 2/3/1956.
559 "I'm glad": *ibid.*, p. 576, 2/5/1956.
559 *Manchester Guardian*, 4/7/1954.
560 "felt strongly": RI to CI, 10/24/70; 6/23/1954.
560 "We went": *D1*, pp. 576–7, 2/5/1956.
560 "deeply moved": *ibid.*, p. 573, 2/3/1956.
560 "There's only" *et seq.*: *ibid.*, p. 576, 2/5/1956.
561 "as harmonious": *ibid.*, p. 578, 2/9/1956.
561 "Another explosion": *ibid.*, p. 584, 2/18/1956.
561 "I'm still sorry": *ibid.*, p. 565, 2/10/1956.
561 Lehmann: JL diary, 1/10/1956.
561 "mortally offended": *D1*, p. 595, 3/11/1956.
561 "I feel": CI to JL, 3/12/1956.
562 "Chris has": JL diary, 3/16/1956.

Chapter 21
563 "In the first": CI 1158, 4/3/1955.
563 "a religious fraud" *et seq.*: *ibid.*, 4/29/1955.
563 "the 'New Era:' " *ibid.*, 5/22/1955.
564 "I want to see": *ibid.*, 6/3/1955.
564 "inverted allegory": EU to CI, 8/27/1955.

564 characters: CI 1158, 7/11/1955.
564 "It came": *D1*, pp. 579–80.
565 "So, after six": CI to SS, 3/29/1956.
565 "Well, this": *D1*, p. 597.
565 several other things: *ibid.*, pp. 599, 601.
565 "My resolve": *ibid.*, p. 600, 4/1/1956.
566 "like some beautiful": CI to SS, 7/26/1956.
566 "accursed": *D1*, p. 615, 5/15/1956.
566 "But really": *ibid.*, p. 624, 6/27/1956.
566 "In other words": *ibid.*, p. 609, 4/19/1956.
567 "I want to make" *et seq.:* CI 1119.
568 "So far": *D1*, p. 647, 9/20/1956.
568 "I should": *ibid.*, p. 649, 9/30/1956.
568 "dream secretary": *ibid.*, p. 648, 9/24/1956.
568 "proved himself": *ibid.*, p. 662, 11/13/1956.
568 "It certainly": CI 1158, 11/28/1956.
568 "in the third": *D1*, p. 672, 1/1/1957.
568 *The Times*, 6/24/1954.
568 "For some reason": CI 1158, 2/10/1957.
569 "The Trustee": *GESS*, p. 12.
569 "homework": *ibid.*, p. 668, 12/4/1956.
569 "*Why* are Don": *ibid.*, p. 686, 3/11/1957.
569 "lousy": *ibid.*, p. 687, 3/18/1957.
569 "My resentments": *ibid.*, p. 679, 2/7/1957.
569 "a scarcely concealed": SS to CI, 5/28/1938.
569 "As for my": CI to SS, 7/5/1938.
570 "Nearly everyone": *New Writing 5*, p. 32.
570 "Well-groomed": *MNCT*, p. 44.
570 "Even I": undated letter quoted in letter from Peter Grose to Christopher Maclehose, 1/14/1975.
570 Stern: *LY*, p. 117.
570 "Let this": *D1*, p. 681, 2/15/1957.
570 "The novel": *ibid.*, p. 689, 4/3/1957.
571 "literally dying": *ibid.*, p. 696, 5/6/1957.
571 "long siege": *ibid.*, p. 697, 5/9/1957.
571 "inconsiderable" *et seq.: ibid.*, pp. 702–3, 6/10/1957.
571 "aggressive resentment": *ibid.*, p. 709, 7/10/1957.
571 *The Slide Area: ibid.*, p. 708, 6/27/1957; jacket copy, Penguin ed., 1963.
572 "two halves" *et seq.:* CI to EU, 8/12/1957.
572 "is attractive": CI 1158, 8/16/1957.
573 Lehmann: CI to JL, 4/6/1951.
573 "Something is alive": *D1*, p. 721, 9/4/1957.
573 "I shan't": CI 1158, 10/6/1957.

573 "high fever" *et seq.:* CI to Prabhavananda, 12/5/1957 [CI 1035].
574 "great pilgrimage" *et seq.:* CI to Prabhavananda, 12/27/1957 [CI 1035].
574 "in preparation": KI diary, 12/13/1957.
574 "so well": *ibid.*, 12/26/1957.
574 "We did not": *ibid.*, 12/27/1957.
574 "practically adopted": *ibid.*, 12/26/1957.
574 "It is so nice": *ibid.*, 12/27/1957.
574 "No sensation": *ibid.*, 1/1/1958.
574 Smith: quoted Grove, p. 245.
575 Hinchingbrooke visit: DS diary, Vol. 5, pp. 795–803.
576 "pages always": *D1*, p. 739, 2/28/1958.
576 "flash of insight": CI 1158, 3/4–5/1958.
576 Selznick: *D1*, p. 741, 3/13/1958.
576 "exclusive right": contract, 3/24/1958.
576 "So now": *D1*, p. 759, 6/23/1958.
576 "There is no clear": CI 1158, 9/26/1958.
576 "Yesterday": CI 1158.
577 "secretary": *D1*, p. 779, 9/26/1958.
577 "intelligent enough" *et seq.: ibid.*, p. 780, 9/26/1958.
577 "an effort" *et seq.:* CI to DS, 2/10/59; 1/19/1959.
577 "how to write": *D1*, p. 786, 10/28/1958.
577 "Heaven only": *ibid.*, p. 789, 11/19/1958.
577 "It seem entirely": *ibid.*, p. 794, 12/28/1958.
577 "Don and I": *ibid.*, p. 790, 12/2/1958.
577 Smith: DS diary, 3/23/1959.
577 Beaton: *D1*, p. 800, 2/7/1959.
577 "The disagreeable": *ibid.*, p. 752, 5/25/1958.
578 "it would be": *ibid.*, p. 751, 5/15/1958.
578 "old-fashioned": EU to CI, 9/28/1958.
578 "I read": CI to EU, 10/11/1958.
578 "Your letter": EU to CI, 10/16/1958.
578 "You have always": EU to CI, 11/4/1961.
578 "I hope you know": CI to EU, 6/17/1959.
579 "I decided": *AtV*, p. 5.
579 "This utter": *D1*, p. 800, 2/7/1959.
579 CI to Chapin: 2/21/1959 [Curtis Brown Archive].
579 "*sting*" *et seq.:* CI to Claire Degner, 2/28/1959.
579 "It must be": WHA to CI, 2/26/1959.
580 "I am most anxious": CI to Degner, 2/28/1959.
580 "practically hopeless": Degner to CI, 3/4/1959.
580 "Given that": WHA to CI, 3/4 [1959].

580 "It is what" *et seq.:* WHA to CI, 3/10 [1959].

581 "the customer" *et seq.:* Outline [CI 1064], with CI to Kallman, 4/25/1959.

582 "juiceless": *D1,* p. 811, 4/24/1959.

582 "At last!": CI 1158, 3/17/1959.

583 "I do try": *CwCI,* p. 42.

583 "When I write": J. Kingston diary, 6/9/1961.

583 "It will be": CI to Edith Haggard at Curtis Brown, 5/23/1959.

584 new house: *D1,* p. 829, 10/2/1959.

584 new story: *ibid.,* p. 816, 6/13/1959; 6/16/1959.

585 "My own projects": CI to SS, 12/11/1958.

585 "The blurb": CI 1015, p. 1.

585 Lehmann: SS to CI, 12/15/1959.

585 Forster: EMF to CI, n.d. [pm 1/14/1960].

586 "I think this is": CI to SS, 1/19/1960.

587 "he only felt": Lanchester, p. 200.

587 *New Yorker,* quoted on CD insert of *Elsa Lanchester (The Bride of Frankenstein) Sings Bawdy Cockney Songs.*

587 "wonderful": *D1,* p. 824, 9/2/1959.

587 Wyberslegh: *ibid.,* p. 823.

587 Peak District: *ibid.,* p. 824.

588 Lehmann: *London Magazine* Vol. 6, No. 10, pp. 8–9.

588 "I can't tell you": CI to JL, 11/9/1959.

588 "worthy": *D1,* p. 833, 11/9/1959.

589 "Watching a living": Michael Harper in Berg & Freeman, *The Isherwood Century,* p. 54.

589 "I can make": CI to SS, 9/28/1959.

589 "treading water": *D1,* p. 832, 10/31/1959.

589 health troubles: *ibid.,* p. 817, 6/24/1959; p. 819, 7/8/1959; p. 825, 9/3/1959; p. 825, 9/11/1959.

589 visiting doctor: *ibid.,* p. 830, 10/9/1959.

590 "Pains": *ibid.,* p. 828, 9/28/1959.

590 "like a bad": P. Woodcock to PP, 3/17/1997.

590 "huge assigned": *D1,* p. 804, 3/11/1959.

590 "somewhat": *ibid.,* p. 789, 11/27/1958.

590 "ten miles": CI to SS, 12/11/1958.

590 "Got very": *D1,* p. 836, 12/4/1959.

590 "Two days": *ibid.,* p. 841, 1/3/1960.

Chapter 22

591 "I think": CI to SS, 1/19/1960.

592 Prema: *D1,* pp. 717–18, 8/23/1957.

592 "You will be": CI to Prema, 10/22/1963.

592 "psychologically queer": DB to PP, 12/16/2001.

592 "sum up": *D1,* p. 703, 6/10/1957.

592 "Oh God": CI to DS, 2/8/1960.

592 "far the best": CI to SS, 2/17/1958.

592 Spender on "Ambrose": CI to SS, 4/11/1958.

593 "We have just": SS to CI, 4/22/1960.

593 "confess": SS to CI, 4/28/1960.

593 "When the verdict": CI to EU, 5/9/1960.

593 "*very* rough": D1 p. 857, 5/30/1960.

593 "I do think": CI 1158, 3/26–27/1960.

594 characters: *ibid.,* 3/25/1960.

594 "Paul is": *ibid.,* 6/9/1960.

594 "I simply haven't" *et seq.: ibid.,* 6/15/1960.

594 "I don't quite": CI to EU, 8/12/1960.

594 Dexamyl: DB to PP, 8/8/2001.

594 fn: CI to SS, 10/29/1961.

595 "utterly plastered": *D1,* p. 869, 6/23/1960.

595 "This fucking": *ibid.,* p. 873, 7/1/1960.

595 KI's death: *ibid.,* p. 863, 6/16/1960.

595 "It is the early": RI to CI, n.d. [June 1960].

595 "the father & mother": Amiya to CI, 6/30/1960.

595 "I made": RI to CI, 7/31/1960.

596 "I must say": Amiya to CI, 6/22/1960.

596 "Whatever is going": CI to Amiya, 6/24/1960.

596 "the leeches" *et seq.:* Amiya to CI, "Sunday night" [6/19/1960].

596 "I wish you would": Amiya to CI, n.d.

596 "reproachfully" *et seq.:* CI to Amiya, 1/27/1960.

596 "My *one* concern": Amiya to RI, 7/1/1960.

598 "as a manifestation": DB to PP, 2/21/1993.

598 "no equals": *D1,* p. 812, 5/2/1959.

598 "to get away": *ibid.,* p. 857, 5/30/1960.

598 "so domineering" *et seq.: ibid.,* p. 811, 5/2/1959.

598 Bachardy on Lanchester: to PP, 2/19/1995.

599 "terribly shaky": diary, 9/14/1960.

599 lecture: CI 1169.

599 "a truly smashing": *et seq.:* diary, 10/2/1961.

600 publishing lectures: CI to SS, 5/23/1962.

600 "Relations with Don": *D1,* p. 841, 1/3/1960.

600 "carrying on": *ibid.* pp. 843–4, 1/29/1960.

600 "this was largely": *ibid.*, p. 845, 2/10/1960.

600 "has mattered": *ibid.*, 14.2.60; p. 847, 3/3/1960.

600 "I do believe": *ibid.*, p. 899, 8/23/1960.

600 "Told me" *et seq.*: diary, 11/15/1960.

601 "I feel hideously": diary, 12/23/1960.

601 "Must be prepared": diary, 1/20/1961.

601 "Considerable excitement": diary, 2/6/1961.

602 "a very sweet": diary, 2/13/1961.

602 "left feeling": *ibid.*

602 "doubly lonely" *et seq.*: diary, 2/23/1961.

602 "Some of my": diary, 2/24/1961.

602 "I've been thinking": diary, 3/19/1961.

602 "teasing" *et seq.*: diary, 3/7/1961.

602 "We reached": diary, 3/27/1961.

603 "He claimed": diary, 4/2/1961.

603 "eating celery": diary, 2/23/1961.

603 "absolutely impotent" *et seq.*: diary, 2/28/1961.

604 "Whatever anyone says": diary, 1/17/1961.

604 UCLA flyer: "Voices of the Novel," 1961.

604 "to be an actor": CI 1158, 6/15/1960.

604 Heard: diary, 3/23/1961.

605 "I love you": diary, 4/6/1961.

605 "about 15,605": diary, 4/19/1961.

606 "what does Christopher" *et seq.*: diary, 5/15/1961.

606 "confident": diary, 6/6/1961.

606 "cold and bitchy": diary, 7/9/1961.

606 "much richer": diary, 7/4/1961.

606 Auden: WHA to CI, 1/9 [1962].

606 *Manchester Guardian*, 3/15/1962.

606 *Esquire,* May 1962.

607 "just a conditioned": diary, 3/18/1962.

607 *Herald Tribune,* 3/11/1962; *Baltimore American,* 4/22/1962.

607 "I was counting": diary, 4/7/1962.

607 "It is a measure": *Oxford Times,* 3/23/1962.

607 *Miami News,* 2/11/1962.

607 *Detroit Free Press,* 3/11/1962.

607 reviews: Rev. Charles E. Davis, *Omaha World Herald,* 4/15/1962; Lady Margaret Sackville, *Gloucester Echo,* 5/11/1962; Herbert Mitang, *New York Times,* 3/23/1962.

607 *Hackensack (NJ) Record,* 4/14/1962.

607 fn: EU to CI, 8/17/1962.

608 Ambrose: *DToaV,* pp. 109–10.

608 "loathes women": *DToaV,* p. 111.

608 "really depressed": diary, 4/7/1962.

608 "shocked to find": diary, 4/19/1962.

608 "suddenly came": diary, 7/14/1961.

608 "in the grip" *et seq.*: diary, 9/2/1961.

609 "a time of": *DToaV,* p. 202.

609 "how best": diary, 6/9/1961.

609 "It's the old story": diary, 6/20/1961.

609 "private enemy": diary, 6/7/1961.

609 Ure and Ackerley: diary, 6/14/1961; 6/20/1961.

609 "Just because": diary, 6/8/1961.

610 "Oh, I used": DB to PP, 2/21/1993.

610 "It is too idiotic": diary, 7/28/1961.

610 "the whole thing": diary, 8/12/1961.

610 "the right composer": WHA to CI, 2/24 [1961].

610 "too cerebral": *D1,* p. 811, 4/24/1959.

610 Glyndebourne: diary, 7/14/1961.

610 "the essential donné": WHA to CI, 8/8 [1961].

611 Maugham visit: diary, 9/18/1961.

611 "the future": Bell, p. 185.

611 Maugham to Strong: quoted Fryer, p. 248.

611 "nearly splitting": diary, 10/6/1961.

612 "quite eager": diary, 9/27/1961.

612 "Heart-attacks": diary, 6/23/1962.

612 "I *must*" : diary, 10/29/1961.

612 "only too aware": diary, 10/28/1961.

612 Prabhavananda conversation: diary, 11/8/1961.

612 "toxic condition": diary, 12/16/1961.

612 "curiously good health": diary, 12/16/1961.

612 "significant": diary, 12/22/1961.

613 "As far as": diary, 12/31/1961.

613 "My face": diary, 1/12/1962.

613 "Goodbye to": diary, 1/23/1962.

613 "most of the students": diary, 2/5/1962.

613 "the most talented": CI to SS, 12/3/1963.

613 "rambling": diary, 9/28/1960.

614 novelette details: diary, 2/12/1962.

614 "a Study in Exile": CI 1158, 3/25/1962.

614 "The Outsider": second UCSB lecture [CI 1171].

614 "I am a foreigner": eighth UCSB lecture [CI 1183].

614 "Loneliness": CI 1158, 3/25/1962.

615 "And in the way": fourth UCLA lecture, 5/18/1965 [CI 1089].

615 "My idea" *et seq.:* CI 1158, 3/26/1962.

615 "I know already": CI 1158, 3/26/1962; diary, 3/28/1962.

616 "The opening": diary, 4/22/1962.

616 "still acute": diary, 8/11/1962.

616 "unless it's something": diary, 8/15/1962.

616 "until things": diary, 8/22/1962.

616 "very little": diary, 9/14/1962.

616 discussion with Bachardy *et seq.:* CI 1158, 9/19/1962.

617 health worries: diary 9/10/1962.

617 "to show all kinds": CI 1158, 9/19/1962.

617 "Was [the Past]": *ibid.,* 9/24/1962.

617 *Mrs. Dalloway:* diary, 8/22/1962; 8/26/1962.

617 "everything in": fourth UCLA lecture, 5/18/1965 [CI 1089].

617 "symbolic status": diary, 5/9/1962.

617 "a youngish man": CI 1158, 11/27/1962.

618 dying Laughton: diary, 11/30/1962.

618 funeral: diary, 12/20/1962.

618 "written by": CI 1158, 11/27/1962.

618 "still not absolutely": CI 1158.

619 Bachardy: to PP, 11/16/2002.

619 "I don't even want": diary, 12/26/1962.

619 "A bad year": diary, 12/31/1962.

619 "I am wildly": diary, 2/9/1963.

619 "probably the best": diary, 2/16/1963.

619 "This is one": diary, 3/6/1963.

619 "This is a strange": diary, 3/20/1963.

620 "a discussion": *K&F,* p. 509.

620 "psychological convalescence": diary, 4/14/1963.

620 "Oh I did so need": diary, 4/26/1963.

620 "face the idea": diary, 5/18/1963.

620 "I have proved" *et seq.:* diary, 4/26/1963.

620 "the calm": diary, 6/2/1963.

621 "a bit more aware" *et seq.:* diary, 6/23/1963.

621 "a fine upstanding boy": diary, 8/9/1963.

621 Upward: quoted diary, 8/16/1963.

621 Ramakrishna book: diary, 9/19/1963.

Chapter 23

622 "I guess": CI to Prema, 10/22/1963.

622 "Jealousy": diary, 11/1/1963.

622 "I have been": diary, 11/5/1963.

623 "I *wanted":* DB to PP, 11/16/2002.

623 "God, how I hate": diary, 11/11/1963.

623 "taking out words": CI to EU, 11/15/1963.

623 "Waking up": *ASM,* p. 7.

624 "Both will have": *ASM,* p. 158.

624 Angell: quoted, diary 12/11/1963.

624 *"passionate* psychosomatic": diary, 10/31/1963.

624 "I have all the shots": CI to Prema, 11/25/1963.

624 "As we drove": diary, 12/21/1963.

624 "far more delightful" *et seq.:* diary, 12/22/1963.

624 "A stunning bore": diary, 12/25/1963.

624 Amartyananda: *ibid.*

625 "thin pliant-waisted": diary, 12/27/1963.

625 "Told him": diary, 12/28/1963.

625 "looking older": diary, 12/29/1963.

625 "As an elderly": diary, 12/22/1963.

625 "I took the dust" *et seq.:* diary, 12/29/1963.

625 Shashi Kanto: diary, 12/30/1963.

625 "It began": diary, 12/29/1963.

626 "I pretended": diary, 12/30/1963.

626 "swept by": diary, 12/31/1963.

626 teacher: *ibid.*

626 "a flirty" *et seq.:* diary, 1/1/1964.

627 "I am drawn": "Presidential Address," 1/1/1964.

627 "a bohemian artist" *et seq.: R&HD,* p. 247.

627 "I would not dare": "Presidential Address," 1/1/1964.

627 "Throughout the drive" *et seq.:* diary, 1/2/1964.

629 "The country dust": diary, 1/3/1964.

629 "jacked off" *et seq.:* diary, 1/6/1964.

629 "The onlookers" *et seq.:* diary, 1/7/1964.

629 Bachardy: to PP, 8/8/2001.

630 "When Don": diary, 2/11/1964.

630 Huxley: Huxley pp. 154, 158.

630 "a book of" *et seq.: E,* author's note.

630 "I want to": CI to EU, 6/11/1964.

631 "should fox": CI to DS, 10/11/1964.

631 "And when I saw": EU to PP, 5/12/2003.

631 *Tribune,* 7/16/65; *Sunday Times,* 4/18/1965.

631 "too 'party line': Lehmann, *Christopher Isherwood,* p. 105.

631 "That the reaction": CI to DS, 5/2/1965.

631 Smith: to CI, 5/8/1965.

631 Upward: EU to CI, 5/31/1965.

631 "I might get drunk": Vidyatmananda memoir, p. 36.

632 "some of the skeleton": diary, 9/7/1964.

632 "Tony just": DB to PP, 2/19/1995.

632 *Variety:* Elley, p. 503.

633 "His hand": *ASM*, p. 153.

633 Heard: diary, 3/15/1964.

633 "A lot of the critics": CI to the Beesleys, 10/11/1964.

633 *Newcastle Journal,* 9/26/1964.

633 *LA Times,* 8/2/1964.

634 *Catholic Herald,* 11/27/1964.

634 *Daily Worker,* 10/24/1964.

634 "by making": *Nashville Tennessean,* quoted in Lancer, pbk ed.

634 *Coventry Evening Telegraph,* 10/15/1964.

634 *Sunday Telegraph,* 1/3/1965.

635 *New York Herald Tribune,* 8/30/1964.

635 "the very last": *ASM*, p. 86.

635 *"we are on"* : *ibid.,* p. 82.

635 "very far, right now": *ibid.,* p. 87.

635 "sour reception": diary, 9/7/1964.

635 "I now feel": diary, 11/23/1964.

636 "full of highfalutin" *et seq.:* Richardson, p. 175.

636 "pretentious frog stuff": CI to EU, 10/5/1964.

636 "I know almost nothing": diary, 2/14/1965.

636 "It is all wrong": diary, 3/20/1965.

636 "is below": "How I Began A Meeting by the River" [CI 1096].

636 "some sort of": diary, 3/20/1965.

637 "a man distinguished": "Writing As a Way of Life" [CI 1186].

637 "a man who may be": *ibid.*

637 Jung: quoted in notes for "Writing As a Way of Life" [CI 1187].

637 "some kind of intention" *et seq.:* CI 1186.

638 "The most honest": quoted in Lancer, pbk ed., 1965.

638 Hockney: Hockney, p. 98.

638 Texan suitor: [anon] to CI, 5/21/1956.

639 "Just at first": diary, 11/15/1964.

639 "the best": diary, 1/7/1965.

639 "New York was": diary, 2/7/1965.

639 "Don't be so *pleased"* : *ibid.*

639 "He is literally": diary, 4/2/1965.

639 "visits": diary, 7/4/1965.

639 "deal with characters": CI to DS, 7/22/1965.

640 "awfully thin": diary, 8/27/1965.

640 "probably end up": CI to SS, 6/16/1965.

640 *Variety:* Elley, p. 725.

640 "very late Isherwood" *et seq.:* CI to EU, 6/12/1965; 10/11/1965.

640 "I mustn't dismiss": diary, 10/22/1965.

640 "less autobiographical": *The World of Books,* BBC radio [n.d.].

641 swami: *AMbtR,* p. 13.

641 "As I finished": *ibid.,* p. 43.

641 "After that": diary, 12/1/1965.

641 Stravinsky: diary, 11/13/1965.

641 "I hate": diary, 3/31/1966.

642 "That coverless": *AMbtR,* p. 39.

642 "I have always regarded": CI to Vidyatmananda, 7/9/1966.

642 "both bright": diary, 3/7/1966.

642 "clowning": CI to EU, 3/28/1966.

642 "a lot of": diary, 4/23/1966.

643 Kirstein row: DB to PP, 11/16/2002.

643 "Don said": diary, 9/2/1966.

643 "Vedantically-revamped" *et seq.:* diary, 6/26/1966.

644 "Disneylike": diary, 10/8/1966.

644 Wyberslegh visit: diary, 10/29/1966.

Chapter 24

646 "this book" *et seq.:* diary, 11/30/1966.

647 "a disembodied observer" *et seq.:* diary, 1/2/1967.

647 *Cabaret:* diary, 11/30/1966; CI to EU, 3/11/1968.

648 "His interest": diary, 6/15/1967.

648 Maharishi: diary, 9/25/1967.

648 reviews: *Telegraph* 6/1/1967; *Standard,* 6/6/1967; *The Times,* 6/1/1967, *TLS,* 6/15/1967.

648 Hardwick: *Vogue,* June 1967.

648 "written loosely": diary, 5/31/1966.

648 *The Times,* 6/1/1967.

648 "I still don't know": diary, 11/23/1966.

649 "I couldn't help": *AMbtR,* p. 58.

649 "Heredity has": *ibid.,* p. 95.

649 "the occupational vices": *The World of Books,* BBC Radio [n.d.].

649 *Financial Times,* 6/1/1967.

649 Lucie-Smith: *The Critics* (BBC radio), 6/11/1967.

650 "And everybody": *AMbtR,* p. 160.

650 *The Times,* 6/1/1967.

650 "be criticized": *CwCI,* p. 82.

650 "Isherwood, the believer": *New Republic,* 4/15/1967.

650 "Reading M's diary": diary, 11/23/1966.

651 "cagey": diary, 9/25/1967.

651 "for the first time": diary, 8/9/1968.

652 "gas and stomach pains": diary, 4/24/1968.

652 other ailments: diary, 5/15/1968; 5/18/1968.

653 "this urge": diary, 8/13/1968.

653 "I love taking": diary, 8/9/1968.

653 "had all the atmosphere": diary, 10/16/1968.

653 "The really important": diary, 1/9/1969.

653 "An old seagull": diary, 12/25/1968.

653 "I marvelled": diary, 2/28/1969.

654 "In six months": diary, 2/26/1969.

654 "marvellously easy": quoted A. Wright, p. 232.

654 "He didn't really": diary, 3/19/1969.

654 boring visit: diary, 1/3/1970.

655 "The whole thing": diary, 2/17/1969.

655 "a proper protest play": diary, 2/26/1969.

655 "as all right": diary, 3/19/1969.

655 "performed all over": diary, 11/28/1970.

656 "one of the best": diary, 9/7/1969.

656 "I was absolutely secure": DB to PP, 11/16/2002.

657 Moody and Mangeot: diary, 3/23/1970.

657 Ross: diary, 4/24/1970.

657 Amiya: diary, 4/11/1970.

657 Beesleys: diary, 4/5/1970.

657 "so pleased": diary, 4/3/1970.

657 "a marvellous sense": diary, 4/5/1970.

657 "One day": EU to CI, 11/4/1961.

658 "the beautiful pure": diary, 3/7/1970.

658 "such a feeling": diary, 3/8/1970.

658 "I feel the spirit": diary, 4/15/1970.

658 Richard: diary, 3/7/1970, 3/8/1970, 4/15/1970.

658 "I still feel that": RI to CI, 10/24/1970.

658 "Richard really does": diary, 3/8/1970.

659 "I want to forget": diary, 4/16/1970.

659 party boys: diary, 4/28/1970, 3/22/1970.

659 ballet: diary, 4/29/1970.

659 Hockney: diary, 4/1/1970.

659 "How relaxed" et seq.: diary, 3/2/1970.

660 "quite a sexy": diary, 3/29/1970.

660 "despite the frictions": diary, 3/25/1970.

660 Forster letters: diary, 3/16/1970.

660 "from ignorance" et seq.: Forster, Maurice, pp. 221–2.

661 "we"/"they": diary, 4/26/1970.

661 "a Tale": diary, 11/26/1970.

662 Auden review: Forewords and Afterwords, p. 453.

662 "embarrassing but": CI to EU, 3/11/1973.

662 "one of the most socially": "A Writer and His World" [CI 1169].

663 "She is trained": ASM, pp. 21–3.

663 "bitterly ashamed" et seq.: LY, p. 217.

663 "rap with" et seq.: diary, 7/30/1970.

664 "much more aggressive" et seq.: diary, 12/30/1970.

664 "Despite the humiliations": K&F, p. 380.

664 "quite flatly": diary, 1/13/1971.

665 Spender review: diary, 10/27/1971.

665 "the time for": CI to SS, 3/7/1972.

665 "I have to admit": diary, 10/27/1971.

665 Wescott: diary, 10/7/1971.

665 Vogue, 3/1/1972.

666 Spender: Sunday Telegraph, 10/24/1971.

666 "Even her mourning": K&F, p. 507.

666 "the funny ward": diary, 3/20/1970.

666 "What a plodding": diary, 2/22/1971.

667 "can be commented" et seq.: diary, 3/2/1971.

667 "our minority": diary, 8/8/1971.

667 "Gay Purchasing Power": diary, 11/1/1970.

668 Heard: diary, 8/14/1971.

668 "the frontier-post": diary, 9/23/1971.

668 "in the pink": diary, 9/23/1971.

669 operation: diary, 10/1/1971.

669 "Don at once": ibid.

669 "All in all": diary, 4/7/1972.

669 KPFK and Award: diary, 5/23/1972.

670 "why, at the age": diary, 2/10/1971.

670 "a ghastly chore" et seq.: diary, 6/3/1971.

670 "Mummy-talk": diary, 7/2/1972.

670 Cabaret: diary, 11/5/1972.

671 Brian: C&HK, p. 53.

671 "Michael York type": York, p. 202.

671 York's nose: diary, 7/25/1972.

671 York's performance: diary, 11/5/1972.

671 "very underestimated": Success Story (BBC TV) 4/22/1974.

671 Oscars: diary, 3/29/1973.

672 "If the Berlin" et seq.: The Berlin of Sally Bowles, pp. 1, 5.

672 clipping: diary, 6/24/1972.

672 Maupin: to PP, 5/2/1994.

673 Frankenstein: "retrospective diary," n.d. [?Feb. 1973], p. 27.

673 Upstairs, Downstairs: RI to CI, n.d. [pm 9/27/1976].

673 "I feel goaded": RI to CI n.d. [Nov. 1970].

673 "He showed this" *et seq.*: "retrospective diary," p. 38.

674 "The Hall": *ibid.*, pp. 38–9.

674 "No need": EU to CI, 2/26/1973.

674 H. Spender: to PP, 11/13/2000.

675 "Our poor Frankenstein": CI to DS, 10/5/1973.

675 Frankenstein verdict: diary, 8/14/1973.

675 "chore" *et seq.*: diary, 4/22/1973.

675 "I fear": "retrospective diary," p. 36.

675 "relevant": JL to CI, 6/15/1973.

675 "I am happy": CI to JL, 6/24/1973.

677 "railroad": diary, 8/3/1973.

677 "John, I had thought": CI to JL, 8/1/1973.

677 "I'm terribly sorry": JL to CI, 8/7/1973.

677 "It is exciting": CI to JL, 5/15/1973.

677 "marvellous" *et seq.*: JL to CI, 8/7/1973.

677 "dull, mechanical": diary, 9/14/1973.

677 "having finally" *et seq.*: CI to JL, 9/6/1973.

677 "a tone of": diary, 9/25/1953.

677 Lehmann's letter: 9/18/1973 [CI 1653].

678 "quite a stinker" *et seq.*: diary, 9/25/1973.

678 "I would like our": JL to CI, 10/2/1973.

679 "Needless to say": CI to EU, 10/9/1973.

679 "It was one": CI to EU, 10/9/1973.

679 "the more loving one": *Collected Poems,* p. 584.

679 Bachardy on WHA and CI: DB to PP, 11/1/1994.

680 Spender: SS to CI, 11/7/1973.

680 "Whatever he may": diary, 9/30/1973.

680 "I seem to see": diary, 11/6/1973.

681 "I was also fascinated": WHA to CI, 1/9/1962.

681 "I, too": WHA to CI, 2/21 [?1962].

681 "The night he died": diary, 9/30/1973.

681 "I should have hated": CI to SS, 10/16/1973.

681 "I long to": CI to SS, 10/16/1973.

681 "I am in the absurd": CI to SS, 11/2/1973.

682 "His death": diary, 9/30/1973.

682 "I thought": SS to CI, 10/21/1973.

682 "would have preferred": *ibid.*

682 "a page or two": SS to CI, 11/27/1973.

682 "first-person" *et seq.*: diary, 10/29/1973.

683 "Should I simply": diary, 12/6/1973.

683 "When I reread": diary, 11/2/1973.

683 "I don't think": diary, 12/6/1973.

683 "It's really all about": CI to EU, 12/29/1973.

Chapter 25

684 "For a long time": CI to P. Knowlton, 11/20/1973.

684 "get really nasty": diary, 12/6/1973.

684 postcard: CI to Knowlton, 1/20/1974.

684 Lazar: diary, 6/16/1974.

685 Donadio: CI to EU, 10/28/1975, 12/17/1975.

685 Wilder: diary, 12/8/1973.

685 "slobbish and incompetent": diary, 2/23/1974.

685 "Don and I": diary, 2/25/1974.

685 *LA Times,* quoted diary, 11/15/1974.

686 "My relations": diary, 12/14/1974.

686 "not marvellous": diary, 12/27/1972.

686 "Enough": DB to PP, 2/19/1995.

686 "hit upon": diary, 4/10/1975.

687 "suddenly the bottom": DB to PP, 2/19/1995.

687 "It seems to contain": diary, 11/2/1973.

687 "I could easily": diary, 2/11/1974.

687 "I keep feeling": diary, 5/27/1974.

687 "I feel so": diary, 7/30/1974.

687 Spender: to CI, 3/8/1974.

687 "If only": CI to EU, 12/29/1973.

688 Richard: to CI, n.d. [?Oct. 1973].

688 "It seems that" *et seq.*: diary, 8/31/1974.

688 Spender: diary, 4/8/1974.

688 "We had better": York, p. 273.

688 Heilbrun: CI, p. 72.

689 "There is" *et seq.*: Wilde, p. 5.

689 *"Please,* Richard": CI to RI, 11/13/1978.

689 "I don't mind" *et seq.*: RI to CI, 11/18/1968.

689 "there doesn't seem": RI to CI, n.d. [1974].

690 "To mention Jo": diary, 1/25/1975.

690 "the price one pays": BC to J. Fryer, 2/23/1979.

690 "I begin": CI to EU, 5/22/1975.

690 "As I now get": CI to EU, 11/12/1975.

690 "in spite of what you call": EU to CI, 11/20/1975.

690 "This is where": *C&HK,* p. 252.

690 "There is a great deal": diary, 10/14/1976.

691 "The difficulty is": diary, 9/7/1976.

691 "What I should": diary, 9/14/1976.

691 "got so interested": RI to CI, n.d. [pm 11/15/1976].

692 "But my dear": RI to CI, n.d. [?11/14/1976].

692 "going to 'do the trick:' " RI to CI, 5/2/1977.

692 "He did look": *C&HK,* p. 10.

692 *Publisher's Weekly* and *Chicago Tribune:* diary, 11/21/1976.

692 Lehmann: JL to EU, 7/23/1976.

693 "For the homosexual": diary, 8/8/1976.

693 *Out,* June/July 1977.

693 *Q International,* issue 10 [1977].

693 *Sydney Morning Herald,* 6/11/1977.

694 B. Auden: *Sunday Times,* 4/10/1977.

694 *Guardian,* 4/10/1977.

694 "Only they": *ibid.*

694 West: *Sunday Telegraph,* 4/3/1977.

694 Hansen: *C&HK,* p. 27.

694 "makes you really open" *et seq.:* Plimpton, *Women Writers at Work,* p. 101.

695 "I shall think": quoted *ibid.,* p. 102.

695 *Sunday Express,* 4/3/1977.

695 *TLS:* 4/1/1977.

695 Conrad and Powell: quoted *Bookseller,* 4/9/1977.

695 bookshop line and Vidal: diary, 12/23/1976.

696 "The least aggressive": *O,* p. 17.

696 "Our gay pride": diary, 8/27/1978.

696 "just another": [anon] to CI, 12/10/1976.

696 "the kind of love": diary, 2/18/1977.

697 deranged letters: diary, 12/29/1976.

697 nomenclature: Higgins, jacket copy.

697 Vidal: Vidal, *United States,* p. 598.

697 Murphy: A Maupin to PP, 5/2/1994.

697 Cukor: D. Hockney to PP, 6/26/2002.

698 Lahr: diary, 9/2/1978.

698 "seemed to give": diary, 2/18/1977.

698 "Perhaps the best": *ibid.*

698 "all higgledy-piggledy": CI to Prema, 5/1/1977.

698 "I still haven't": diary, 8/7/1977.

699 "We'll probably regret": diary, 7/4/1977.

699 Bachardy show: diary, 7/25/1977.

699 *Time and Tide:* 8/16–23/1962.

699 "I suspect": EU to CI, 11/5/1976.

699 "It filled me": EU to CI, 7/31/1977.

699 "As I finished": EU to CI, 10/22/1971.

700 "when I look": EU to CI, 11/13/1971.

700 "to make Christopher" *et seq.:* White and White, pp. 79, 80.

700 Gunn: *The Threepenny Review,* Summer 1990, p. 5.

700 "cut off from": diary, 7/4/1977.

701 "stumbling" *et seq.:* diary, 10/23/1977.

701 "It would be hypocritical": diary, 12/17/1977.

701 "Sometimes I think": diary, 1/20/1978.

701 "I am very glad": diary, 3/16/1977.

701 "sweet and faded-cute": diary, 2/26/1978.

702 "something wrong": diary, 4/16/1978.

702 "Some days I feel": diary, 5/12/1978.

702 routine: diary, 10/4/1978.

702 beach: diary, 9/24/1978.

702 Briggs: diary, 10/6/1978.

702 "Although I don't": diary, 10/13/1978.

702 "psychologically gigantic;" diary, 10/18/1978.

702 "if you find": CI to Heinz, 10/19/1978.

703 "mousing": diary, 10/5/1978.

703 "ugly, undersexed": diary, 9/19/1978.

703 Franklin on LA: diary, 10/26/1978.

703 dressing down: diary, 11/8/1978.

703 "the ominous": diary, 11/26/1978.

703 "particularly depressing": diary, 11/20/1978.

703 "Am indulging": diary, 11/26/1978.

704 "write out exactly": diary, 12/22/1978.

704 "We were just": DB to PP, 2/20/1995.

705 *New York Times,* 3/29/1979.

705 *New York Post,* 3/29/1979.

705 other reviews: unidentified clipping [NY paper]; *Stage,* n.d.

705 Rigby: DB to PP, 2/20/1995.

705 "NOT been": diary, 4/1/1979.

705 Barnes: *New York Post,* 3/29/1979.

706 Eber: *New York Times,* 3/29/1979.

706 "too intimate": diary, 5/26/1979.

706 Anandaprana: diary, 7/4/1979.

706 Vernon: *ibid.*

706 Vidyatmananda: to CI, 8/20/1979.

706 "Nobody else": CI to Vidyatmananda, 8/30/1979.

706 Caskey: to J. Fryer, 8/27/1979.

707 "a freak": diary, 7/28/1979.

707 "drunk and belligerent": diary, 9/10/1979.

707 "a few corrections" *et seq.:* BC to J. Fryer, 10/3/1979, 11/15/1979.

708 Bradley letter: diary, 5/30/1979; *O,* p. 7.

708 "There is a special": *O,* p. 11.

708 "It's a crazy": diary, 9/17/1979.

709 "This is the kind": diary, 2/14/1980.

709 "dreary empty chore" *et seq.:* diary, 4/17/1980.

710 "I keep wondering": diary, 5/27/1979.

710 "I still don't know": diary, 2/17/1980.

710 Bachardy: diary, 4/17/1980.

710 "a losing battle" *et seq.:* diary, 6/8/1980.

710 reviews: diary, 6/9/1980.

710 *Economist,* 7/12/1980.

710 *Punch,* 7/16/1980.

711 radio interview: *Kaleidoscope* (BBC radio), 7/9/1980.

711 Huxley: *MG&HD,* p. 259.

711 "large holes": diary, 2/17/1977.

711 August 22 entries: *MG&HD,* pp. 200–1; *D1,* p. 438.

712 Kali *puja: MG&HD,* p. 241; diary, 11/8/1961.

712 "You must try" *et seq.: MG&HD,* pp. 25–6.

713 "During November": *ibid.,* pp. 221–2.

713 diary: *D1,* p. 663, 11/16/1956.

713 "in great distress": *ibid.,* p. 661, 11/8/1956.

713 "Swami has taken": *ibid.,* p. 665, 11/22/1956.

713 "It is absolutely necessary": diary, 11/26/1970.

713 "I know that Swami": *D1,* p. 665, 11/22/1956.

713 "He says he only": *ibid.,* p. 667, 12/2/1956.

714 "Should I have": diary, 7/7/1979.

715 "The house": diary, 7/17/1979.

715 "Well, as usual": diary, 7/22/1979.

715 "too formalistic": diary, 7/28/1979.

715 Carpenter: diary, 7/16/1980.

715 "Well, what *do* I feel": diary, 7/17/1980.

716 "ruthless" *et seq.:* BC to J. Fryer, 11/15/1979.

716 "I really do": diary, 7/20/1980.

716 "I am always": diary, 9/26/1978.

717 "the spry": diary, 10/19/1980.

717 burglary: *ibid.*

718 "Work, work": diary, 4/17/1981; 4/19/1981.

718 "But walks": diary, 4/28/1981.

718 "Drub gave": diary, 10/8/1980.

718 long-term relationships: *CwCI,* p. 106.

718 "becoming increasingly senile": diary, 4/17/1981.

719 "the pre-terminal": diary, 4/12/1981.

719 "face up to": diary, 3/12/1981.

719 "nothing very inspired": diary, 5/16/1981.

719 "I can feel": *ibid.*

719 "self-indulgent": DB to PP, 12/16/2001.

719 "one glass": *ibid.*

719 "the curiously strong": diary, 7/17/1981.

720 "the dreariest" *et seq.:* diary, 1/1/1982.

720 "His mind": DB to PP, 12/16/2001.

720 "What I have to face": diary, 10/16/1981.

720 "I pray hard": diary, 4/11/1982.

720 "Don's love": diary, 8/2/1981.

720 "a first European": diary, 1/24/1981.

720 "Oh the pride": diary, 12/6/1980.

721 *Sunday Times,* 8/26/1984.

721 *Observer,* 8/12/1984.

721 Spender: *Journals 1939–1983,* p. 466.

722 "He didn't seem to know": *Last Drawings,* p. 116.

722 *Village Voice,* 7/2/1985.

723 "Yes, the whole": *Threepenny Review,* Summer 1990.

723 stages: diary, 4/12/1981.

723 "The love between": diary, 10/16/1981.

723 "I love to sit close": *Daily Telegraph,* 10/25/1996.

723 "unable to figure out": DB diary, 8/8/1985, *Last Drawings,* p. xi.

723 "Chris, sometimes": DB diary, 9/12/1985, *ibid.,* p. xii.

724 Spender and Bachardy: DB diary, 9/18/1985, *ibid.*

724 "My only defence": DB diary, 12/1/1985, *ibid.,* p. xiv.

724 "I like the ones": DB diary, 12/2/1985, *ibid.*

724 "Here comes": DB diary, 12/9/1985, *ibid.,* p. xv.

725 "coughing, moaning and": DB diary, 1/3/1986, *ibid.,* p. xvii.

725 "on his way": DB diary, 1/4/1986, *ibid.*

725 "that consciousness": *ASM,* pp. 155–6.

725 "a real horror": *Last Drawings,* p. xviii.

Afterword

726 Barbellion: *The Listener,* 3/28/1946.

726 "You try to describe": *CwCI,* p. 137.

726 "I have no idea": *ibid.,* p. 138.

726 "experience is": *ibid.*

726 California: *Women's Wear Daily,* 3/22/1979.

727 "the process of exploring": *AtV,* p. 19.

727 "As soon as": DB to PP, 10/10/1996.

727 "There are all kinds": *ibid.*

727 "the boiling rage": *CwCI,* p. 121.

728 "Diaries record": DB to PP, 10/10/1996.

727 Caron: *D1,* p. 533, 9/23/1955.

728 "development tasks": Schwerdt, p. 10.

729 "My defence": quoted Forster, *Maurice,* p. 9.

LOCATIONS

Bancroft Library, University of California at Berkeley: letters from CI to Stephen Spender, "Portugal Diary," and Spender's journal [BANC MSS 76/184]; drafts of *World Within World* and letters from Spender to John Lehmann [BANC MSS 70/177].

Beinecke Rare Books and Manuscripts Library, Yale University: letters from CI to Richard Isherwood and Kathleen Isherwood, 1942–74.

Berg Collection, New York Public Library: W. H. Auden's 1929 Berlin Journal, 1964–65 notebook; letters from W. H. Auden to Stephen Spender, Naomi Mitchison, Olive Mangeot, John Auden and Mina Curtiss: CI's letters to Kathleen Isherwood, 1921–22 (published in *The Repton Letters*). CI's letters to Olive Mangeot.

The Dodie Smith Collection in the Special Collections at Boston University: Diaries of Dodie Smith; letters from CI to Dodie Smith and Alec Beesley.

The British Library (Manuscripts Department): letters from CI to Edward Upward and James Stern; James Stern diaries; letters from John Lehmann to Edward Upward; manuscripts of the Mortmere stories of A. D. Francis (in Upward papers).

Rare Book and Manuscript Library, Columbia University: letter from Claire Degner to CI and letters from CI to Perry Knowlton and Victor Chapin (Curtis Brown Archives); letters from Robert Linscott to CI, Bennett Cerf affadavit (Random House Archives); letters from CI to Humphrey Carpenter.

University of Durham Library: Letters from CI to William Plomer.

Harry Ransom Humanities Research Center, University of Texas at Austin: letters from CI to Eric Falk, Tennessee Williams, Swami Vidyatmananda (Prema); Kathleen Isherwood's diaries, 1911–59; contract between CI and David Selznick; Swami Vidyatmananda ts autobiography.

The Huntington Library: all letters to Christopher Isherwood (except those from A. D. Francis); Kathleen Isherwood's diaries, 1904–10 and her correspondence with Frank Isherwood; CI's letters to Kathleen Isherwood, 1935–39; Richard Isherwood's transcripts of Mamie Tristam's letters to Kathleen Isherwood.

Modern Archive, King's College Library, Cambridge: letters from CI to E. M. Forster, in E. M. Forster Papers [GBR/0272/EMF]; letters of J. M. Keynes, Ashley Dukes and T. S. Eliot, in J. M. Keynes Papers [GBR/0272/JMK].

McFarlin Library, University of Tulsa: letters to Richard Isherwood from Kathleen Isherwood and Amiya Sandwich; letter to Kathleen Isherwood from Julia Fry; ms of "Lions and Shadows" (novel).

Methuen Archive: letter from Graham Greene to E. V. Rieu.

Princeton University Library: Journals of John Lehmann in the Lehmann Family Papers, Manuscripts Division, Department of Rare Books and Special Collections.

Reading University Library: Jonathan Cape, Chatto & Windus and Hogarth Press archives.

PERMISSION ACKNOWLEDGMENTS AND CREDITS

Permission acknowledgments

Quotations from the unpublished writings of Isherwood are © the Estate of Christopher Isherwood, 2004.

Quotations from "Photograph of a Boy in Costume" (© 1994 by W. H. Auden), "Which of you waking early" (© 1930 by W. H. Auden), "Their Last Will and Testament" (© 1937 by W. H. Auden), "Journey to Iceland" (© 1936 by W. H. Auden), "Passenger Shanty" (© 1938 by W. H. Auden) and the epigraph from *The Orators* (© 1937 by W. H. Auden) reprinted by permission of Curtis Brown Ltd.; acknowledgment is also made to Faber and Faber and Random House Inc. for permission to reprint quotations from Auden's published work.

Picture credits

INDEX

on Indians as race, 449
influence on younger homosexual writers,
    672–73
insecurity and depression, 370–71, 372–73,
    382
interest in cigarette cards, 44, 125
interest in family history, 5
as invalid, 301
jealousy, 645
on Julie Harris as Sally Bowles, 529
on karma, 440
on Kathleen's diaries, 650–51, 667
on Katz, 192–93
on Klaus Mann, 199
lack of candor in *My Guru and His Disciple,*
    711–13
on laziness, 717
as lecturer, 599–600, 642
on Lehmann, 588, 678
Lehmann on, 219, 287, 289, 338–39
on licensing laws, 76
and life in New York, 367–68, 416, 705
literary collaboration, 153, 253, 254, 277,
    298–99, 313, 653
on love, 718, 720
love of roller-skating, 60–61
on Mangeot home, 103
on marriage of convenience, 260–61
on *A Meeting by the River,* 648, 669–70
on *The Memorial,* 156
and monastic life, 442–43, 460
Mortmere saga, 79–81, 98–99, 112, 117,
    131, 133, 142, 154, 171, 174, 199, 201,
    254, 266, 339, 388, 421, 432, 490, 544
on *My Guru and His Disciple,* 709
on mysticism, 437
narcissism, 277, 458
on New York, 372–73, 374–75, 383, 387–88,
    494
on "The Outsider," 599, 614
pacifism, 85–86, 364, 365, 388, 443, 472,
    485
on political situation in Germany, 199,
    210–11, 219, 251, 608
political views, 114–15, 151–52, 172,
    364–66, 388, 522
on prayer, 720
and presentation of homosexuality in litera-
    ture, 500, 549–50, 614, 661–65
private language with Upward, 133*n*
problems with American novel, 511, 515,
    523, 525

problems with celibacy, 445, 449–54, 626
problems with South American diary, 496,
    498
prose style in dialogue, 545, 550, 554
as public speaker on homosexuality and civil
    liberties issues, 637–38, 663–64
on Quakers, 434–35
questions of identity (in life and work), 305,
    378–80, 416–17, 458, 477, 568, 572–73,
    593, 616–18
as radio broadcaster, 534
reaction to accusations of disloyalty and de-
    sertion, 397–98, 410, 463–64, 489
reaction to criticism, 571
receives fan mail and hate mail, 695–97, 726
references to Jews, 123, 124, 189, 225–26,
    280, 434, 449, 503, 515, 569–70, 571,
    604, 647, 703
refuses to meet Bachardy's lover in London,
    657
rejection of Christianity, 84
resentment of and alienation from Kathleen,
    84–85, 108, 114–15, 121, 126–28, 129,
    151–52, 163–64, 280–81, 347, 559, 617,
    682
on reviewing friends' books, 665
on Richard, 488
Robert Craft on, 513
self-criticism, 217
self-description, 340–43, 726
self-presentation, 4–5, 336–37, 338, 340–43,
    416–17, 572, 583, 692, 717
sense of northern atmosphere in Cheshire,
    658
separation from Auden in USA, 406, 484
and sexual infidelity, 619
sexual orientation and activities, 55–56, 62,
    68–71, 78–79, 105, 155, 173–74,
    199–200, 276, 305–6, 343–44, 345–46,
    422–23, 427, 446, 447, 448, 452–54, 458,
    482
smoking, 396, 423, 538
on Spender, 138–39, 267
Stern on, 282
as storyteller, 338–39
and The supernatural, 23–25, 508
on terms used for homosexuals, 697
and "The Test," 122, 128, 329
on theater, 312–13
and theories of Homer Lane, 145
third-person references to self (as "Christo-
    pher"), 336–37, 692

ABOUT THE AUTHOR

PETER PARKER is the author of *The Old Lie: The Great War and the Public-School Ethos* and a biography of J. R. Ackerley. He is the editor of *A Reader's Guide to the Twentieth-Century Novel* and *A Reader's Guide to Twentieth-Century Writers*. He is an associate editor of the *Oxford Dictionary of National Biography* and writes about books and gardening for a wide variety of publications. He was elected a Fellow of the Royal Society of Literature in 1997 and lives in London's East End.

ABOUT THE TYPE

This book was set in Times Roman, designed by Stanley Morrison specifically for *The Times* of London. The typeface was introduced in the newspaper in 1932. Times Roman had its greatest success in the United States as a book and commercial typeface, rather than one used in newspapers.